FOLKLORE, MYTHS AND LEGENDS OF BRITAIN

Folklore, Myths and Legends of Britain

PUBLISHED BY THE READER'S DIGEST ASSOCIATION LIMITED

FOLKLORE, MYTHS AND LEGENDS OF BRITAIN
was edited and designed by
The Reader's Digest Association Limited, London

Second Edition Copyright © 1977
The Reader's Digest Association Limited

Paper, printing and binding by
F. A. Churchill and Partners Ltd, Southampton
Commercial Process & Co. Ltd, London
Litra Machine Plates Ltd, Edenbridge
Danish Repro Group, Copenhagen
City Engraving Co. (Hull) Ltd, Hull
Bowater Sales Co. Ltd, London
Koninklijke Nederlandsche Papierfabriek NV, Maastricht
Redbridge Book Cloth Co. Ltd, Bolton
Sir Joseph Causton & Sons Ltd, Eastleigh
Hazell Watson & Viney Ltd, Aylesbury and Cymmer
Winter & Co. Ltd, London

Printed in Great Britain

CONTENTS

PART ONE

Lore of Britain

MYTHS AND LEGENDS THAT HAVE ENDURED FOR 2000 YEARS

THE MYSTERIOUS WORLD OF NATURE

LIFE, LOVE AND WORK

CONTENTS

PART TWO

Romance of Britain

A REGIONAL GUIDE TO BRITAIN'S FOLKLORE

CONTENTS

PART THREE

People of Myth

A GALLERY OF HEROES, SAINTS AND SCOUNDRELS

CONTRIBUTORS

The Publishers wish to express their gratitude for major contributions
by the following people:

Authors

Russell Ash BA, FRAI

Geoffrey Ashe BA, FRSL *Co-founder and Secretary, Camelot Research Committee*

Katherine Briggs MA, D PHIL, D LITT *Vice-President of the Folklore Society*

Theo Brown *Honorary Research Fellow in British Folklore, Exeter University*

Alan Bruford BA, PH D *Archivist, School of Scottish Studies, University of Edinburgh*

T. A. Bushell *Vice-President of the Association of the Men of Kent and Kentish Men*

L. C. Candlin *President of the Brighton and Hove Archaeological Society*

Mark Child · H. R. Ellis Davidson MA, PH D, FSA · T. D. Davidson · Tony Deane

J. M. Eltenton · The late Gerald Findler · R. P. Goddard

A. E. Green BA *Lecturer in Folk Life Studies, University of Leeds*

L. V. Grinsell OBE, MA, FSA, FMA

Hamish Henderson · Christina Hole *Honorary Editor of 'Folklore'* · Lavender M. Jones

Robin Gwyndaf Jones
Assistant Keeper, Department of Oral Traditions and Dialects, Welsh Folk Museum

Doris W. Jones-Baker MA, BA · E. F. Ladds BA, ALA · Eric Maple

Harry Martin · Hugh D. Martineau BA · Barbara Matthews

Venetia Newall MA, FRGS
Honorary Secretary, The Folklore Society, Honorary Research Fellow in Folklore, London University

Roy Palmer MA · Crichton Porteous

Enid Porter MA, BA *Curator and Secretary, Cambridge and County Folk Museum*

Jon Raven FRGS · Neil Rhind · Colin Robinson · Anne Ross MA, PH D

Stewart Sanderson MA
Director of the Institute of Dialect and Folk Life Studies, University of Leeds

Tony Shaw · Jacqueline Simpson MA · Alan Smith BA

Gregory Stevens-Cox MA · James Stevens-Cox FSA · Eric Swift BA · C. F. Tebbutt OBE, FSA

Ruth L. Tongue · Royston Wells · Ralph Whitlock FZS

John D. A. Widdowson MA, BA
Director of the Survey of Language and Folklore, The University, Sheffield

Artists

Derek Crowe · Eric Fraser FSIA · Robin Jacques · Jeffery Matthews

Charles Keeping · Peter Reddick ARE · George Tute ARE

Photographers

Julien Calder · C. M. Dixon · Paul Hill

Christine Pearcy · Julian Plowright · Tom Scott · Michael St Maur Sheil

Patrick Thurston · Michael Wells

Story without End

AN INTRODUCTION TO THE FOLKLORE, MYTHS AND LEGENDS OF BRITAIN

MYSTERIES are as irksome to the human mind as a grain of sand to an oyster. Just as an oyster will form a pearl around its centre of irritation, so men, baffled by the wonders of the universe, will create marvels of the imagination out of their need to understand. From this need springs the richness of folklore, myth and legend. All the same, though we now dismiss many of our forefathers' notions as mere superstitions, there is no reason for thinking that the men and women who held them were more credulous than ourselves. Like us, they were sensitive to the fears and uncertainties of their time, and like us too they depended on their powers of imagination to explain what lay beyond the limits of their knowledge.

One definition of folklore is that it is the study of beliefs which were once firmly held, but which have long ago lost their adherents. No one now believes in giants, but throughout Britain there are hundreds of curious rock formations and prehistoric monuments that were once thought to be their work. Few people now imagine that they will ever encounter a fairy, though as recently as a century ago, belief in the Little People was almost a religion in the lonelier parts of Celtic Britain. Many people are convinced that Loch Ness harbours an unidentified monster; but who now recalls the many other beasts that were once said to lurk behind the northern mists – Cailleach Bheur, for instance, the fearsome blue-faced hag, who wandered around the Highlands freezing the ground with every tap of her staff? Yet not so long ago they were accorded much greater respect than has ever been lavished on 'Nessie'.

There are some beliefs, however, which have stood the test of time, though they may fail the test of reason. Even today, many of us are guilty of an odd kind of double-thinking about ghosts. We deny their existence, yet would hesitate to spend the night alone in a 'haunted' house; we do not believe in them, yet might trust the word of a close friend who said he had seen one.

Many of the hundreds of ghost stories in this book are traditional; they are echoes of tragedies of long ago. But others are not so easily explained; these are the personal accounts of frightening experiences which happened to people who are still alive, and whose truthfulness is beyond question.

A tale of two heads

There is, for instance, the story of Dr Anne Ross, the eminent Celtic scholar and archaeologist and a major contributor to this book. Dr Ross does research work for a number of museums, and late in 1971 she was asked to examine two carved stone heads which had been discovered near Hadrian's Wall. What happened next is best told in her own words:

'Though there was nothing unpleasant about the appearance of the heads, I took an immediate, instinctive dislike to them. I left them in the box they had been sent in, and put it in my study. I planned to have them geologically analysed, and then to return them as soon as possible to the North.

'A night or two after they arrived – I didn't connect this experience with the heads until later – I woke up suddenly at about 2 a.m., deeply frightened and very cold. I looked towards the door,

11

and by the corridor light glimpsed a tall figure slipping out of the room. My impression was that the figure was dark like a shadow, and that it was part animal and part man. I felt compelled to follow it, as if by some irresistible force.

'I heard it, whatever it was, going downstairs, and then I saw it again, moving along the corridor that leads to the kitchen; but now I was too terrified to go on. I went back upstairs to the bedroom and woke Dick, my husband. He searched the house, but found nothing – no sign at all of any disturbance. We thought that I must have had a nightmare (though I could hardly believe that a nightmare could seem so real), and decided to say nothing about it.

'A few days later, when the house was empty, my teenage daughter Berenice came home from school at about 4 p.m., two hours before Dick and I returned from London. When we arrived home, she was deathly pale and clearly in a state of shock. She said that something horrible had happened, but at first would not tell us what. But eventually the story came out.

'When she had come in from school, the first thing she had seen was something huge, dark and inhuman on the stairs. It had rushed down towards her, vaulted over the banisters, and landed in the corridor with a soft thud that made her think its feet were padded like those of an animal. It had run towards her room, and though terrified, she had felt that she had to follow it. At the door, it had vanished, leaving her in the state in which we found her.

'We calmed her down as best we could, and feeling puzzled and disturbed ourselves, searched the house. Again, there was no sign of any intruder – nor, in fact, did we expect to find any.

'A cold presence'

'Since then, I have often felt a cold presence in the house, and more than once have heard the same soft thud of an animal's pads near the staircase. Several times my study door has burst open, and there has been no one there and no wind to account for it. And on one other occasion, when Berenice and I were coming downstairs together, we both thought that we saw a dark figure ahead of us – and heard it land in the corridor after vaulting over the banisters.

'The reason why I associate the heads with this haunting, if that's what it is, is this. Later, I learnt that on the night when the heads had first been discovered, the North-country woman who lived next door to the garden where they had been unearthed was putting her child to bed when a horrifying creature – she described it as half-man and half-animal – came into the room. She began screaming, and only stopped when her neighbours arrived. She was convinced that the creature had touched her, but what happened to it, she did not know. There was no sign that anyone had broken into the house, and the incident, like the incidents which have taken place in our house, is quite without any rational explanation. The strange thing is, the heads have gone now, back to the museum. But this thing doesn't seem to have gone with them.'

Like all real ghost stories, this is tauntingly inconclusive, and almost too extraordinary and frightening to believe. But Dr Ross believes it, and so do the others who were personally involved. All that remains is a chilling question mark.

Examination of the heads showed that they were carved from local Northumbrian stone, perhaps during the Romano-British period about 1800 years ago. Possibly they had come from a military shrine or temple of the Celtic legionaries who made up a large part of the Roman garrison on Hadrian's Wall. If this were the case, they would have been placed as guardians outside the shrine of a local god, such as Maponus – the 'Divine Son' – a hunting god who is known to have been worshipped in North Britain. Similar carvings have been found all over Europe; the Celts were head-hunters who believed that the severed human head had magical or divine properties. The heads of enemies were buried beneath altars, nailed to the gateposts of hill-forts or thrown into wells, where they were thought to convey fertility and ward off evil spirits. Similar powers were vested in the stylised stone heads; once, those sent to Dr Ross may have stood guard over a god who has long departed. Or has he?

The nation's unwritten history

In spite of its frequent excursions into a twilight world where nothing is known for certain, folklore supplies answers as readily as it poses questions. When the myths and legends of Britain are gathered together with surviving customs and superstitions, they provide a unique insight into the long story of the British people –

a memory-bank which reveals the hopes and fears, ideas and experiences of the numberless generations of our ancestors.

Behind the one word 'luck' lie the shadows of forgotten religions and of social systems which have long since been abandoned. The man who touches wood for luck is brother to the men of long ago who revered the spirits of the trees. If he throws a coin into a wishing well, his reasons are remarkably close to those of the pagan Celts who used to drop human heads into the water as a plea for good fortune. When you avoid walking under a ladder, you go back through time to the days when a condemned man had to climb a ladder to the gallows – the ladder was then twisted so that he fell to the rope's end beneath it.

According to a centuries-old tradition, fairies feel that they alone have the right to wear green, and are apt to deal harshly with any mortal foolish enough to infringe this right. This accounts for the widespread superstition that green is an unlucky colour – a superstition which is shared by many motorists, who are convinced that green cars are more likely to be involved in accidents.

But for every terror, tradition usually supplies an antidote. One of the most potent is the horseshoe, curved symbol of the moon-goddess. More important, fairies and most other inhabitants of the spirit world will flee at the sight of cold iron. Rather than being lucky in itself, a horseshoe over a door is a guardian that prevents the entry of evil forces.

Some authorities have claimed that the idea that fairies fear cold iron is in its turn part of a memory of an unnamed race who once inhabited these islands. When the Celts, armed and armoured with iron, landed on these shores during the 500 years or so before Christ, they displaced an earlier, simpler people whose weapons were made of bronze or flint. Though the Celts, with their superior organisation and weapons, easily overcame them, the vanquished were still a people to be feared. They lived closer to the earth, they had a greater understanding of wild creatures, and with their superior knowledge of fieldcraft, it seemed as though they could be visible or invisible at will. They buried their dead in stone-lined chambers beneath grassy hillocks that were also the home of the fairies. In the fairies' world, as in that of the dead, time has no meaning; out of this confusion of ideas, it is thought, came the many stories of people who spent years in Fairyland, and re-emerged believing that only an hour or two had passed.

The terrible horseman

Britain's folklore is in a constant state of change, and owing to the island's turbulent history, it is drawn from a wide variety of sources. Every invader, refugee or settler has left his beliefs to us, just as he has left his blood in our veins. Such beliefs would overlap, or dovetail into those which had gone before. The successful invader would enslave the natives, but the slave would tell his master's children of the gods and past glories of his own race; and they would never forget. In time, one set of gods would be confused with another, and newer legends would be superimposed upon the old. Out of this complexity there emerged the diverse pattern of British folklore, a pattern which not even Christianity could erase. In times of stress, the old gods stood at the back of men's minds (though perhaps their names were now dignified by the title of 'saint'), and they would remember the holy places where their forefathers made blood sacrifices. Whatever the Church taught, the old gods were a force to be reckoned with.

One of the most persistent of British legends – though it appears in many guises – is that of the Wild Hunt. Similar legends occur all over northern Europe; they tell of a giant horseman who rides through the skies on stormy nights accompanied by a pack of baying hounds. To look on his face or to speak to him is death; or at the very least, you will be whirled up into the sky and carried off to some distant country.

Once, the giant huntsman was Odin, the Norse god of the dead, who rode through the night skies seeking the souls of the dying. Though his name changed with the coming of Christianity, his role did not. Often he was thought of as the Devil himself; but in different parts of France he was identified as the ghost of King Herod, or of Charlemagne. In northern England he was sometimes called Woden, while other counties saw him as Wild Edric, who defied William the Conqueror, or even as Arthur. The phantom hounds were the spirits of unbaptised children, or of unrepentant sinners. In the West Country they are called Wish Hounds and, in the north, Gabriel Ratchets. Some critics have pointed out, however, that their cries, as they seek the souls of the damned, closely resemble those of migrating geese.

In some areas, the demon horseman has taken advantage of more recent inventions. On Dartmoor, the leader of the Wild Hunt has been confused with Sir Francis Drake, who tears across the countryside in a black coach drawn by headless horses, followed by a pack of baying Wish Hounds. But it is equally fatal to meet this terrible equipage; those who hear it coming must throw themselves face downwards and let it pass without a glance. Curiously, similar warnings are given about one or two ghostly lorries on our roads, while the tradition of the Wild Hunt has even reached the United States. There, the ghost riders are a band of cowboys, condemned, for the evil they did in life, to pursue a herd of hellish cattle across the night skies for ever.

The splendid heritage

Now, as we approach the last quarter of the 20th century, most of us would dismiss legends such as that of the Wild Hunt as being fanciful stories, but nothing more. All the same, we are often closer to the ideas of our forefathers than we know. Few of the people who have lived in Britain passed without leaving some heritage to the generations that followed. Our country roads – and some of the city ones too – twist and turn, apparently aimlessly, but in fact, their bends avoid some long-forgotten freeholding, or perhaps a spring, a wayside grave or a gallows site.

Many of the memories our ancestors left us are equally tenacious. Their bravery is recalled in folk-songs and ballads; even nursery rhymes record the tragedies and trivialities of history. 'Ring o' Roses', for example, lists the symptoms of bubonic plague, while 'Goosey Gander' is said to refer to Cromwell's troopers, who marched in goose-step. Not even television serials can obliterate the pageantry of children's games, whose origins go back to time out of mind. Hopscotch, marbles and tops follow each other through the seasons as they did in the days of Homer; children's truce words, such as 'Fains', were those used by medieval knights.

Nor have adults cut completely adrift from the old formulas. At the main staging-posts of our lives – marriage, the birth of children, the death of friends – we turn to ancient magic for luck or reassurance. This may not be entirely misguided. Astrology, in which many people still believe, showed the way to astronomy. Some of the cures prescribed by folk-medicine must have had startling results, but at least they provided firm roots from which modern pharmacy could grow.

The stories collected together in this book have been gathered from many sources. County archives supplied the background to tales of witches, saints and villains. Fishermen and fenmen, gipsies and churchmen, craftsmen, farmers and tinkers recounted their traditions. There are legends which are part of our national heritage, and village customs whose origins, obscured by time, are hotly argued by scholars. The one quality the stories have in common is that some or all of the British people have told them from generation to generation. Sometimes the customs and stories altered as populations shifted and social conditions changed but, taken together, they amount to a vivid picture of ourselves.

In the greatest shift of all, the mass migration of the British from the countryside to the cities, some of the older beliefs became submerged. People struggling to exist in the squalor of the Industrial Revolution were too exhausted to tell stories; and where traditional stories did survive, they were usually tales of the village transformed to an urban setting. Only the older trades, such as mining and shoemaking, retained a lore of their own.

Much of Britain's urban folklore remains to be told, for it is largely a folklore in the making. Now that many of us are generations removed from the countryside, new patterns are emerging. There are signs that our native lore – the product of many invasions and migrations – is to be enriched still further by that of more recent immigrants.

The upheavals of modern times, too, have produced their own legends. On a long-deserted Lincolnshire airfield, the scream of rending metal is said to be that of a wartime bomber that crash-landed there with a dying crew. The sounds of the Blitz are reputedly etched on the south London air, and train disasters are re-enacted on their anniversaries. Phantom hitch-hikers stand at cross-roads and ghostly lorries speed silently along the motorways. The more traditional Roundheads and Cavaliers, misty coaches and headless horsemen, no longer ride alone.

Lore of Britain

MYTHS AND LEGENDS THAT HAVE ENDURED
FOR 2000 YEARS

THE MYSTERIOUS WORLD OF NATURE

When man confronts nature and tries to tame it, he is setting himself up as the controller of the most mysterious of forces; for nature is the power that makes plants grow and animals breed, that keeps the sun in the sky and draws water from the earth, that makes one season follow another in an endless cycle. In his search for the key to nature's mystery, man has often turned to a power that he believes transcends it – the power of the supernatural

LANDSCAPE OF THE SUMMER SOLSTICE *In this detail from a landscape by Paul Nash, the midsummer sun stands high over a fertile earth. The sun was one of the first gods worshipped by man*

THE SUN GOD IN HIS GLORY

Once upon a time the sun god was lord of heaven and earth, and men worked by the light they worshipped. But today, little remains of his power and glory. Some people say that it is unlucky to point at the sun, and others claim that a mourner on whom the sun shines at a funeral will soon be buried himself. At a wedding, the sun god is benevolent, hence the saying: 'Happy the bride the sun shines on.' This illustration of the sun god comes from Splendor Solis, a 16th-century alchemical work kept in the British Museum

18

The sovereign sky

*The sun was a god, the moon was a magical source of energy,
and in the stars man's destiny was written*

For some 7000 years, ever since men learnt to grow and harvest grain, and were therefore dependent for survival on the round of the seasons, the life-giving properties of the sun have made it the supreme deity of primitive peoples. Even today, many Britons cling to superstitions and customs which had their beginnings in the awe every farmer must have felt as the sun god made his miraculous daily march across the sky.

Sun worshippers lit fires to back up their prayers, for fire kindled on earth was thought to increase the sun god's strength. Many relics survive of pagan fire festivals held in honour of the sun. These include the bonfires which burn all over England every Guy Fawkes' Day, which hold memories of the rites associated with Celtic Samain (November 1) when fires were lit to strengthen the winter sun; the fiery ceremony of Up-Helly-Aa held in Shetland every January; and the chain of bonfires which blaze every midsummer across Cornwall.

December 25 was a holy day long before the 4th century, when Pope Julius I gave the Church's sanction to the dubious belief that the date marked the birthday of Christ. From time immemorial, the winter solstice had been the moment when bonfires were lit all over the northern pagan world to welcome back the sun after the unease of the shortening days. To the Romans, December 25 was *Dies Natalis Invicti Solis* – the Birthday of the Unconquered Sun. Today, fire and light remain basic ingredients of a happy Christmas, though few people now recognise how the prayers of their forefathers are recalled in the brandy-fed flames on a Christmas pudding.

About 4000 years ago, disciples of the sun god built a 'cathedral' at Stonehenge. Though the exact origins of this ancient temple remain obscure – some authorities suggest that it was the first attempt to chart the solar system – there is little doubt that men gathered there some 1500 years before Christ was born, to worship the sun.

Their spiritual descendants gather there still. Every June 21, after an all-night vigil, members of the Most Ancient Order of Druids pay ritual homage to the midsummer sun. The Order was inaugurated in 1717, and claims to be carrying on ancient Druidic traditions which the Romans tried to stamp out but succeeded only in driving underground. It was one of the few native cults with which the invaders would make no compromise.

The sun gave more to man than light and life. It was also a divine source of order, a heavenly timepiece. To someone in the northern hemisphere, the sun appears to move clockwise around the earth, and sun worshippers were always careful to perform their ritual dances and processions in a clockwise, or 'sun-wise', direction.

The feeling that turning 'widdershins', or anticlockwise, is somehow 'wrong', is a hangover from the time when turning 'against the sun' was believed to be evil and an open invitation to disaster. Witches at their sabbats danced widdershins to please the Devil, and an army attacking a castle in the early Middle Ages could invoke supernatural aid by marching anti-clockwise round the castle walls. Again, a Christmas tradition harks back to pagan belief, for it is said that a wish made while mixing the Christmas pudding will come true only if the ingredients are stirred clockwise.

Magic and moonlight

The moon has not lost its magic, even after the scientific onslaught which has been made on it in the last few years. Many people believe that it is unlucky to see the new moon through glass, for this obstructs the good luck which a new moon naturally brings. Some even insist that it is bad luck to see it through a tree's branches. There are still people who show their money to the new moon, so that it may grow as the moon grows, or who turn over any silver coins in their pockets (by tradition, silver is the metal of the moon) and make a wish. Others, before wishing on a new moon, bow to it and turn round three or nine times.

The waxing and waning of the moon was once believed to affect all living things. A waxing moon was thought to radiate energy which stimulated growth; as it waned, the energy diminished. Superstitious gardeners and farmers planned their sowing so that the young plants could grow with the moon, and the plants were best picked, or trees felled, when a moon on the wane was weakening their resistance. The flesh of animals killed under a waning moon was likely to shrink in the pot, and business deals and marriages had the best chance of

CORNFIELD BY MOONLIGHT

Even today some people believe that moonlight makes plants grow, and that the best time for sowing is just before a new moon. Traditionally, seed sown when the moon is waning will not prosper. This illustration is a detail from the painting by Samuel Palmer (1805–81)

success if they were timed to take effect as the moon began to wax.

The moon was also widely thought to influence human beings, and until about 100 years ago it was officially recognised as a prime cause of madness. A lunatic, as the word suggests and as the Lunacy Act of 1842 clearly stated, was a person 'afflicted with a period of fatuity in the period following after the full moon'.

It was not just the risk of madness that made sleeping in moonlight dangerous. Fairies, witches and other evil creatures were thought to be particularly fond of moonlit nights; and moonbeams, it was said, could cause blindness or disfigurement of the face. Some women even believed that the moon could make them pregnant, an idea which has a modern counterpart in the theory that the moon controls a woman's menstrual cycle.

The notion of a 'Man in the Moon' is as much a part of modern moonlore as the idea that the moon is made of green cheese. But in many mythologies, the moon was essentially female, and a goddess ruled over it.

In classical tradition, the moon was sister to a male sun, and it became the domain of the Greek goddess Artemis and her Roman counterpart, the huntress Diana. Diana lives on to the present time as the patroness of some latter-day witch covens, a role which her traditional mastery of night-flying makes her especially well-suited to play.

Stars of destiny

Not since the Middle Ages has the 5000-year-old art of astrology been as popular as it is today. Some 7 million Britons now regularly read their horoscopes, and the popular press has become a tireless supplier of supposedly heaven-sent predictions. The turning point in this revival came in 1930, when an astrologer working for the *Sunday Express* forecast danger to British aircraft on the day 48 people died in the R101 airship disaster.

The first principles of astrology were laid down by Babylonian priests somewhere around 3000 BC. The priests observed that seven 'wanderers' – the sun, moon and five planets – seemed to move round the earth along a track which passed through 12 constellations, or fixed groups of stars. They divided the track into 12 equal segments, and named them after the constellations. Today, the segments are known as the signs of the Zodiac.

Each month, as the earth moved in its annual circle round the sun, the sun appeared to rise in a different segment. At first, the priests used this knowledge to devise a calendar. Later, it occurred to them that the shifting pattern of sun, planets and signs might govern the apparently random course of events on earth and decide the characters and destinies of individual human beings.

Astrology still rests on much the same principles as those the Babylonians worked out, though over the centuries, Greeks, Romans, Arabs and Renaissance scholars have gradually refined the astrologer's art. Today, adjectives such as martial, jovial, saturnine and mercurial sum up in a word thousands of years of astrological tradition. The planet Mars has come to be a symbol of action, energy and aggression; Jupiter denotes health and humour; Saturn limits and inhibits; and Mercury is the planet of intelligence and communication.

To cast a horoscope, an astrologer must know the date, time and place of a person's birth. This tells him in which sign the sun was then rising, and where all the planets lay. By complicated calculations, he can then determine how far the signs and planets, and the traditional qualities ascribed to them, are likely to affect the person's life.

THE ASTROLOGICAL DOCTOR

Until as late as the 17th century, many doctors studied their patients' stars as carefully as their symptoms, and some declared flatly that there was no need to examine patients at all, for diagnosis could be made simply from a urine sample and interpretation of the sky at the time when the urine had been passed. Sick people who could not afford to see a doctor could always consult one of the many popular pocket almanacs to find out which days were astrologically favourable for purging, blood-letting and other forms of medical treatment.

Astrological doctors were purveyors of more than just medicine. They were also prophets, marriage counsellors and the first psychiatrists. Almost everyone with a problem turned to an astrologer for advice, from women wanting to know whether they were pregnant or whether they would outlive their husbands, to men suspicious of their wives' fidelity, or people wanting guidance in their love affairs.

Aries the ram rules the head

Taurus the bull rules the neck

Cancer the crab rules the breasts

Gemini the twins rules the arms

Leo the lion rules the heart

Virgo the virgin rules the intestines

Libra the scales rules the kidneys

Scorpio the scorpion rules the genitals

Sagittarius the archer rules the hips and thighs

Capricorn the goat rules the bones and knees

Aquarius the water-bearer rules the ankles

Pisces the fish rules the feet

ASTROLOGICAL MAN *The signs of the Zodiac were once widely believed to rule different parts of the body and to be linked with different diseases. Someone born under Aries, for example, was prone to headaches, while a Taurean was vulnerable to colds, a Leo to heart attacks and a Libran to kidney troubles*

THE SIGNS OF THE ZODIAC

The most important clue to a person's character is his birth sign – the sign of the Zodiac in which the sun was rising when he was born. But for an in-depth character analysis, the exact positions of the moon and planets must also be taken into account. By tradition, each planet rules over at least one birth sign, and exerts a specially powerful influence over people born under that sign.

ARIES (MAR. 22–APR. 20)
Ruler: Mars. Good traits: energetic, brave, direct. Bad traits: impatient, selfish, unsubtle. Ideal partner: Gemini or Libra

TAURUS (APR. 21–MAY 21)
Ruler: Venus. Good traits: warm, determined. Bad traits: stubborn, possessive. Ideal partner: Taurus, Pisces or Capricorn

GEMINI (MAY 22–JUNE 22)
Ruler: Mercury. Good traits: lively, versatile. Bad traits: superficial, inconsistent. Ideal partner: Gemini, Aries or Libra

CANCER (JUNE 23–JULY 23)
Ruler: Moon. Good traits: kind, imaginative, sensitive. Bad traits: over-emotional, unforgiving, moody. Ideal partner: Capricorn or Taurus

LEO (JULY 24–AUG. 23)
Ruler: Sun. Good traits: strong, generous, creative. Bad traits: intolerant, pompous, conceited. Ideal partner: Aries or Libra

VIRGO (AUG. 24–SEPT. 23)
Ruler: Mercury. Good traits: modest, practical. Bad traits: aloof, fussy, over-critical. Ideal partner: Virgo, Capricorn or Taurus

LIBRA (SEPT. 24–OCT. 23)
Ruler: Venus. Good traits: idealistic, charming, romantic. Bad traits: indecisive, lazy, frivolous. Ideal partner: Libra or Taurus

SCORPIO (OCT. 24–NOV. 22)
Rulers: Mars and Pluto. Good traits: passionate, purposeful, subtle. Bad traits: jealous, secretive. Ideal partner: Capricorn or Taurus

SAGITTARIUS (NOV. 23–DEC. 22)
Ruler: Jupiter. Good traits: optimistic, active. Bad traits: tactless, restless, irresponsible. Ideal partner: Gemini or Aquarius

CAPRICORN (DEC. 23–JAN. 19)
Ruler: Saturn. Good traits: careful, ambitious, witty. Bad traits: mean, pessimistic, rigid. Ideal partner: Capricorn or Cancer

AQUARIUS (JAN. 20–FEB. 19)
Rulers: Saturn and Uranus. Good traits: independent, original. Bad traits: perverse, obstinate. Ideal partner: Aquarius or Gemini

PISCES (FEB. 20–MAR. 21)
Rulers: Jupiter and Neptune. Good traits: intuitive, kind. Bad traits: vague, weak-willed. Ideal partner: Pisces or Taurus

Seasons and festivals

Beneath the beliefs and customs associated with our Christian festivals lies a forgotten world of pagan rites and symbolism

Whatever names we give them now, many of our most hallowed festivals are far older than Christianity. Long ago, they marked the key dates of the Celtic rural year – for example, the days when planting began or when harvesting was completed.

The early Christian Church, fully aware of the hold that these festivals had on the community, wisely adopted them into its own calendar. Thus, we still celebrate Easter with the same awareness of sacrifice and rebirth that our pagan ancestors brought to the apparent yearly miracle of returning spring and the wonder of new green life.

The calendar reformed

The Imperial Roman calendar was based on an average year of $365\frac{1}{4}$ days, which gave a cumulative error of eight days added in 1000 years. In 1582, Pope Gregory XIII annulled the ten extra days that had accumulated and inserted the Leap Year day as the nearer approximation to the solar year. Britain did not adopt the change until 1752, by which time

---

THE BLEAK SEASON: NOVEMBER–FEBRUARY

November 5: Guy Fawkes' Day

Bonfires are lit to commemorate the failure of the Gunpowder Plot in 1605. The bonfires, however, also perpetuate Celtic Samain, when they were lit to ensure the sun's return after winter. Samain became All Saints' Day and among both pagans and Christians November was associated with the cult of the dead.

November 23: St Clement's Day

Because he was tied to an anchor and drowned, St Clement was nominated as the patron of ironworkers. The trade celebrated his feast-day until fairly recent times. Until 1880, for example, blacksmiths gathered at Twyford, near Winchester, to perform the ceremony of 'firing the anvil' – ramming gunpowder into a small hole in an anvil and igniting it. Afterwards, St Clement's effigy was carried round the village and money was collected for a feast at the Bugle Inn.

In view of the importance of smiths in primitive society and the numerous legends concerning the Saxon smith and wizard, Wayland, who forged mail for the gods, a much older festival of smiths may once have been celebrated on this day.

ST CLEMENT'S DEATH *The saint was drowned tied to the anchor which became the symbol of his martyrdom*

November 30: St Andrew's Day

There are indications that the Samain slaughtering of livestock was moved to this date, particularly in Scotland, where cool summers meant a late harvest. The number of beasts to be kept through winter depended on the harvest fodder available. This could not be assessed until all crops had been cut, dried and threshed.

THE CHILDREN'S SAINT *St Nicholas, patron of children, miraculously revived three schoolboys murdered by an innkeeper. His generosity was legendary, and people often found his gifts in their homes at times when they needed them most. His counterpart is Father Christmas, who is associated with December 25*

The Christmas Festival

The Nativity – the Birth of Christ, the Light of the World – is celebrated on the traditional early Christian date for his birth, since the real one is unknown. The occasion also absorbed several pagan festivals, many of which were held in honour of the sun's rebirth after the winter solstice.

One of the earlier rites celebrated at this time was the Norse Yule sun-worship festival. Yule logs and Yule candles became a traditional part of Christmas, symbolising fire and light; so too did the northern European custom of the candlelit Christmas tree, which was believed to shelter the woodland spirits when other trees lost their leaves. There is a 15th-century account of a Christmas tree set up in a London street, though Prince Albert is usually credited with having introduced the custom into the English home in 1841.

The licentious Roman Saturnalia, when masters and servants changed roles, ended on December 25. Though disapproved of by the Church, many of its traditions were observed well into the Middle Ages in this country. A servant was crowned as Lord of Misrule, and held a wild court over Christmas. In the British armed forces still, officers and NCOs wait on the men and serve them Christmas dinner.

The custom of singing Christmas carols is very old – the earliest English collection was published as long ago as 1521. Mumming plays were also part of the Christmas celebrations. Their traditional central theme symbolised the season's eternal conflict between darkness and light.

The Old English word 'wassail' was a greeting meaning 'be of good cheer'. At the Christmas feast, friends toasted each other by drinking from an elaborate wassail cup. Often, parties of poor people went to the houses of the rich, singing traditional wassail songs and begging drinks or money.

SACRED PAGAN PLANT *Mistletoe, a traditional Christmas symbol, was once revered by our ancestors. It was so sacred that it had to be cut with a golden sickle. Holly and other evergreens were also respected, in the belief that they provided refuge for woodland spirits until other trees regained their leaves*

we were 11 days behind the rest of Europe. The date was simply moved forward – September 3 became September 14.

This amendment explains why some inappropriate traditions are still attached to certain festivals. Snow, for example, is associated with Christmas, though it is rare before January. It would be appropriate on Old Christmas Day (January 6).

Timeless festivals remembered

The Celtic calendar, based on the agricultural and pastoral year, began on November 1, which our ancestors celebrated with the great festival of Samain. Surplus livestock was slaughtered for winter food, and sheep were mated to provide the following year's stock.

Samain was believed to be a time when natural laws were suspended, and ghosts and demons roamed abroad. It was a time, too, when great fires were lit to ensure the renewal of life in the earth after its long winter sleep. This all-important day could

not be ignored by the early Church, who rededicated the occasion to the saints in Heaven. It was instituted in AD 835 and called All Saints' Day. Traces of Samain still linger in Hallowe'en (All Saints' Eve – October 31), and its traditional associations with ghosts and witches.

Imbolc (February 1) marked the beginning of the lambing season. Perhaps there is a parallel in Candlemas (February 2), the Feast of the Purification of the Virgin Mary. For centuries, the Church observed this day in veneration of child bearing.

The Celts celebrated the return of summer at Beltane (May 1). Bonfires were lit, houses bedecked with greenery and flowers, while people greeted the awakening earth with songs and dancing.

Lugnasad (August 1) was the beginning of harvest. To Christians, it was the Festival of the First Fruits, the time when the first corn was ground and made into loaves which were dedicated to God. The day was called by the Saxons 'hlaf-maesse' (loaf-mass), now known to us as 'Lammas'.

CHRISTMAS REVELS AND FEASTING *The holiday provided an opportunity for vast family gatherings – especially in Victorian times – to eat traditional fare, and to dance, sing and play games in rooms decorated with evergreens and candles. Traditional food included the flaming Christmas pudding which, as a stiffened form of the earlier plum porridge, was introduced about 1670. Mince pies were enjoyed by our 16th-century ancestors; even today, to eat a mince pie on each of the Twelve Days will bring 12 happy months in the following year. About this same time the turkey appeared on Christmas tables, though it did not immediately replace goose and beef. Once, in wealthy homes, boar's head was the main dish – a tradition dating from Norse Yule celebrations, where the boar was considered sacred.*

In medieval England, the Christmas season concluded with Twelfth Night (January 6). Up to Victorian times, this was a night for parties and games, when a Twelfth Night King and Queen were chosen. Until well into the 19th century, every family had its Twelfth Cake, containing a dried bean and pea. The man who found the bean was king, and the girl who found the pea was queen. Decorations are normally removed after Twelfth Night – to keep them up longer is believed to bring bad luck. In earlier centuries, however, it was safe to leave them until Candlemas (February 2)

January 25: St Paul's Day

A day that figured in rural prophecy – if fine, there would be good harvests; if rain or snow, scarcity and famine. Clouds and mist signified pestilence, and high winds, war.

February 2: Candlemas Day

The Church observed this day as the Feast of the Purification of the Virgin Mary. Mothers who had borne children during the previous year attended church, bearing lighted candles. This ceremony was established in the 5th century, and took the place of the Roman festival of Februa – when candles were carried through the streets, and purification rites were observed by women.

February 14: St Valentine's Day

This was the eve of Roman Lupercalia – a festival of youth – when young people chose their sweethearts by lottery. St Valentine, martyred on this day, was renowned for his chastity, and appears unconnected with the day's customs. The element of chance still appears in the tradition that the first member of the opposite sex seen on the morning is one's Valentine. Young girls placed bay leaves under their pillows before they went to bed on this day, hoping to dream of their future husbands.

MESSAGE OF LOVE *Lace-edged, heart-adorned Valentine cards, Victorian in origin, are still sent by lovers to the sweetheart of their choice*

23

SEASON OF REBIRTH: MARCH–MAY DAY

The Lenten Fast

Lent is the 40-day annual fast in which Christians recall Christ's sufferings in the wilderness. The name is derived from *lenct*, the Saxon word for spring, and in earlier times spring may well have been a period of enforced fasting in agricultural communities, as the winter stores ran low.

Shrove Tuesday, the day before the Lent fast begins, was once celebrated with merrymaking and feasting – anything that would not last or could not be eaten over Lent was consumed.

TOSSING THE PANCAKE *Westminster School's Pancake Greeze is one of many traditional pancake ceremonies held on Shrove Tuesday. The boy who secures the largest part is rewarded by the Dean*

Rebirth at Easter

SYMBOL OF REBIRTH *'Pace' (Easter) eggs, hard-boiled and painted, were once common in the North and many places still hold egg-rolling ceremonies. Symbolically, eggs represent rebirth – the return of spring in pagan times, or the Resurrection for Christians*

The English name for the festival is said to be derived from Eostre, a northern goddess of spring. The rebirth of growing things in spring after the long winter was a time of rejoicing in the pagan world. Christ's Crucifixion and Resurrection took place at this time, and inevitably many primitive rites and symbols associated with ancient regeneration myths were carried into the Christian festival.

On Good Friday, the day of the Crucifixion, many people would not use nails or iron tools, in remembrance of their use on Calvary. The day was considered unlucky – until recently, miners refused to work, and many fishermen would not put to sea.

Easter Monday is a day of traditional games, many of them with a strong local flavour – the Hare-Pie Scramble and Bottle-Kicking, for example, at Hallaton in Leicestershire.

April 1 – April Fools' Day

LICENCE FOR JOKERS *The origins of this festival, when practical jokes can be played with impunity, are unknown. There may be a link with Lud, a Celtic god of humour, whose festival occurred during spring*

May 1: May Day

The May Day festival was superimposed on Beltane, when the Celts marked the beginning of summer with great bonfires in honour of the sun. On May Day in the past, young people collected greenery and flowers from the woods and fields and decorated their homes. This was a method of ritually conveying the fertilising powers of nature into the community. May Day rites, which have their origins in ancient fertility ceremonies, included the crowning of a May Queen, Morris dancing, traditional plays, and dancing round the maypole.

THE MAYPOLE'S SIGNIFICANCE *May Day celebrations centred round the white hawthorn, which was later replaced by the garlanded maypole. Both symbolised the fertile transition into summer*

MAY DAY REVELS *By the late 18th century, the traditional pageant, which included the Morris dance greenwood characters Maid Marian and Robin Hood, and the leaf-clad Jack-in-the-Green, who once represented the spirit of the green woodlands, had been appropriated by the chimney sweeps. Robin and Marian were replaced by a 'lord' and 'lady' in court dress. By 1825 a Grimaldi-type clown had been included, mainly to attract passers-by*

THE RIPENING SEASON: MAY–OCTOBER

Rogation, Whitsun and Ascension

Rogationtide, when the priest led the people through the parish, blessing the crops, sprang from the Roman feast of Terminus, god of fields and landmarks.

At Whitsuntide, the village Club, a primitive form of insurance society, spent any surplus funds on a feast and sports.

Ascensiontide well-dressing in the Midlands provides a link with pagan well-worship.

BEATING THE BOUNDS *Children still beat boundary marks in some parishes on Rogation Day. The children were once beaten to impress them with the importance of the marks*

May 29: Oak Apple Day

Commemorating the Restoration of Charles II, who hid in an oak to avoid capture, the rites may stem from tree-worship.

June 23: Midsummer Eve

In Celtic times, great sacrificial bonfires were lit in honour of the sun. Even in recent centuries, rural folk lit bonfires, and men and beasts passed through the embers to ward off disease and bad luck. It was also a night when girls practised simple magic to discover the identity of their future husbands.

July 15: St Swithin's Day

A wet July 15 is supposed to prophesy 40 days of rain. St Swithin, who disliked pomp, brought this retribution when his remains were moved from a common graveyard to within Winchester Cathedral.

August 1: Lammas-tide

This day marked the start of harvesting in the rural calendar – a period of hard work which culminated in the harvest-home festival. Rural people believed the Harvest Spirit dwelt in the fields, and that as the reapers cut the corn the spirit was forced to retreat into the ever-dwindling remainder. No man wished to be the one who destroyed her refuge, so the reapers took turns to throw their sickles at the last stand of corn. It was then plaited into a woman's form – known as the Corn-dolly or Kern-baby – which represented the Harvest Spirit. This was set in a place of honour at the harvest supper.

MEDIEVAL CORN-DOLLY *Symbolic of the Harvest Spirit, the straw image was preserved over winter and ploughed-in the following spring*

September 29: Michaelmas

This date coincides approximately with the end of harvesting. The amount of fodder available for feeding livestock in winter could be calculated and the number of animals to be kept could be assessed. It was, therefore, the time of great fairs and animal sales.

October 28: St Simon and St Jude

In medieval times, this day had a reputation similar to that of St Swithin's Day – and with reason, for towards the end of October the fine weather finally breaks up and winter gales begin.

WEATHER LORE

Many popular weather sayings have resulted from inherited lore and shrewd observations of seasonal events by rural folk. There is sense in the saying:

Long foretold, long past;
Short notice, soon past.

A storm may brew for a few hours or more before it breaks, whereas a sudden shower can fall from a passing cloud.

Animal lore which is considered generally reliable and which relates to imminent rain or storms includes: rooks feeding in village streets or not leaving their nests in the morning; unusually shrill blackbirds, woodpeckers or screech owls; fowls huddling outside their hen-houses; and spiders spinning very short webs, breaking their webs or not spinning at all. Fair weather is indicated by cattle remaining on the hilltops; spiders spinning long webs; geese flying out to sea; swallows and larks flying high and rooks flying far from their rookeries.

Several proverbs relate to winter weather.

Ice in November to bear a
duck,
Nothing afterwards but
slush and muck,

is sometimes accurate but less so than the old adage:

Black frost, long frost;
White frost, three days and
then rain.

RAINING CATS AND DOGS *The old saying dates from at least 1653, but there is no clue to its derivation. It may have been that everything imaginable falls in a downpour, since variations of the saying add pitchforks and shovels*

The sea's edge

*Mermaids and monsters, sea witches and drowned cities are
some of the lesser-known features of Britain's holiday beaches*

SEDUCTIVE SIREN OF THE SEA

Mermaid legends are very old, and are remarkably similar, whatever their country of origin. The mermaid is traditionally a seductive siren, personifying the beauty and deceitfulness of the sea, and her presence often foreshadows a calamity, either a storm, shipwreck or drowning. Sometimes she sits alone at the water's edge and longs for the soul which she can attain only by marrying a mortal; at other times, she lulls sailors to sleep with her sweet singing and carries them away beneath the waves. Many stories tell of weddings between humans and mermaids, or mermen. If a mermaid is injured or her amorous advances are rejected, she will call down curses on the offending human. On the other hand, kindnesses are rewarded with life-long service and good luck.

SEA TEMPTRESS *Like the centaur with its horse's body, the mermaid is a mythological composite of human and animal. Sailor's tales resulted in the 16th-century sketch (above), in which the mermaid is depicted with a lion's head. The 17th-century woodcut (left) shows the more traditional idea of the beautiful sea-creature who, with comb, looking-glass and song, lures sailors to their doom*

GIRL ON A DOLPHIN *In Arthur Rackham's 1908 decoration for* A Midsummer Night's Dream, *the mermaid rides a dolphin and sings so sweetly that 'certain stars' shoot 'madly from their spheres'. Despite these traditional props, it seems that by the 20th century the one-time terror of seamen had become a fairy-tale heroine*

The coasts of Britain, lashed by fierce storms and shrouded by frequent mists, form the setting for many old and curious legends. These tales are part of the heritage of everyone who lives by the shore, seamen and landsmen alike. They vary from the imaginary to the semi-historical; from tales of mermaids, phantom ships and ghosts of the drowned dead, to traditions which almost certainly have some foundation in fact.

Tales of mermaids abound, and there are some about mermen too; but the stories of mermaids are more common, perhaps because their long hair and alluring features make them more attractive than their ugly and uncouth male counterparts.

Encounter with a mermaid

Belief in the existence of the near-human race of merfolk was widespread among seamen and coastal dwellers until the late 19th century, and in some places it may persist still. As recently as 1947, an 80-year-old fisherman from the Isle of Muck, Highlands, declared he had seen a mermaid near the shore combing her hair. At Sandwood near Cape Wrath, traditionally called the 'land of mermaids', the appearance of a mermaid was reported on several occasions early in the present century.

Mermaid's Rock, near Lamorna, in east Cornwall, derived its name from a legendary mermaid who once haunted the spot, and whose singing foretold shipwrecks. Many fishermen, it seems, were lured to the rock by the sweetness of her singing, but none was ever seen again.

Also in Cornwall, there is a sandbank known as Doom Bar, which choked Padstow harbour and caused many shipwrecks. The sandbank is reputed to be the result of a curse laid by a mermaid after a local resident fired a shot at her while she was bathing. On the Isle of Man, the thick mists which often cover the island are also said to originate from a mermaid's curse. She punished the entire island when her amorous advances were rejected by a local youth.

In some accounts, merfolk lack the traditional fishy tail, while in others the creatures seem to be able to shed them at will. In the 12th century, some fishermen from Orford, in Suffolk, caught a creature in their nets which they described as having 'the appearance of a man in all his parts'. The fishermen's prize proved unable to speak, even though prompted by torture, and when taken to church, it showed no sign of Christian reverence. On being returned to the water to bathe, the creature quickly, and understandably, escaped by swimming out to sea.

A fisherman's choice

Beliefs that certain families or persons are of mixed human and merfolk descent have survived to within living memory among people who live near the sea. In north-west Scotland, where old traditions die hard, the Clan McVeagh in the Sutherland district are said to be the descendants of a union between a mermaid and a fisherman.

Sometimes the marine ancestor was a merman, but usually it was a mermaid who formed a liaison with a human, either through love or because she had been captured and could not escape. A mermaid was helpless without her cap or belt, and possession of one of these items by a human compelled her to remain on land.

Until quite recently, similar legends stated that seals were able to cast aside their skins and assume human form. In the Orkneys, Shetlands, the Western Isles and Ireland, seals were said to come ashore at night to sing and dance, though they had to resume their animal form by sunrise. However, if a man could steal a seal-maiden's discarded skin she would stay with him until it was regained.

The Clan MacCodum of North Uist are known in the Outer Hebrides as Sliochd nan Ron, the Offspring of the Seals, because a far-off ancestor married a seal-maiden. He stole her skin while she danced and kept it hidden for many years, during which time she bore him several children.

Water bulls and water horses

On the Isle of Man, the fearsome Tarroo-Ushtey, or water bull, would leave the sea to feed, and even mate with domestic cattle. Sometimes it fed placidly and at other times it would rage and bellow furiously. It is told that one island farmer was forced to board up his windows against the monster but, finally, it so terrified his family that he had to abandon the farm.

Water horses, with their creamy-white coats and manes, flashing eyes and fiery spirits, were among the more dangerous legendary creatures of Britain's shores. They usually grazed in pastures by the sea, ready saddled and bridled; should a person mount one, the horse would gallop into the water and drag the rider beneath the waves.

In 1910, a duck-shooter in Shapinsay Sound, Orkney, claimed to have sighted a creature whose 18-ft neck was surmounted by a horse's head. Most modern monsters, however, like the 28-ft creature washed ashore on an island in the vicinity of Scapa Flow in 1942, have been identified by experts as huge basking sharks.

The guardian of the cove

Many of the smaller fishing harbours about the coasts of Britain possessed their own local spirits or guardian angels. The Whooper of Sennen Cove, Cornwall, was different in that it made whooping sounds from within a thick blanket of mist that sometimes formed in perfectly clear weather over the cove. Apart from foretelling severe storms, the Whooper had the uncanny ability to prevent any fishermen from passing through to the open sea when a storm threatened.

Sadly, the guardian Whooper quit the cove for ever when two men, determined to reach the fishing grounds, beat their way through the mist with a flail. Neither of the two men was ever seen again.

Sea witches and sea phantoms

Superstitious sailors voyaged in fear of the witches of the sea. Most dreaded of all was the storm witch, who not only had power over the winds but had the

THE MONSTROUS KRAKEN

The Kraken, a fabulous sea monster reputed to be big enough to resemble an island when half-submerged, and able to swallow a large boat, has been known to seafarers since the days of the Vikings. A kraken was said to have entered the bay at Scalloway in Shetland early in the 19th century, but it seems that nobody present was bold enough to investigate the report

ability to drive a vessel on to a dangerous shore to please a powerful patron.

The enemies – and some of the admirers – of Sir Francis Drake used to say that he had sold his soul to the Devil in exchange for supremacy as a seaman and an admiral. The spirits of the witches he consulted are still said to haunt the headland called Devil's Point overlooking the entrance to Devonport. It was there in 1588 that Drake and the witches raised the storms that destroyed the Armada.

Witches have long been a hazard on British coasts. When a Shetland witch wanted to wreck a ship, she stood on her head and said: 'Sweery, sweery, linkum-loo! Do to them as I now do.'

Phantom ships are still occasionally reported, particularly on our Atlantic shores. One of these, a big three-masted sailing ship, which finally dissolved like a mist on the water, was seen off Deerness, Orkney, in the 1880's. Another, a large white ship that sailed into Scapa Flow during the Second World War, disappeared before several witnesses.

According to local legend, a mystery sailing ship once appeared off the coast between Land's End and Penzance. On a clear moonlit night, with only a gentle breeze, several villagers watched the vessel sail towards the shore, and certain disaster. Just when catastrophe seemed inevitable, the ship left the water and sailed over the land to finally vanish near the village of Porthcurno.

During the 18th century, the Norfolk village of Happisburgh was notorious as a base for smugglers, and it is thought that the particularly gruesome village spectre dates from those times. It appears as a legless body whose almost completely severed head hangs back between the shoulder blades. This ghastly apparition glides out of the sea on moonlit nights with a bundle in its arms. Legend claims that it is the ghost of a smuggler who was attacked and killed by rivals while landing from a boat. To make a more compact parcel, the murderers cut his legs off and threw the body into a well.

Smuggling was a lucrative part-time occupation on many coasts. During the 18th century, many gangs would invent stories, or elaborate upon existing legends, in order to frighten local people away from the centre of their activities. No doubt many of the tales of phantom ships, spectral horses and luminous dogs could be traced back to imaginative smugglers.

But smugglers' legends cannot explain the ghostly Roman legionaries of Richborough, in Kent. During the Second World War, soldiers in coastal defence reported watching whole cohorts march into the sea. Richborough was a Roman port and it may be that its defenders of long ago have not yet quit their posts. There are persistent reports of two figures seen fighting on the shore on misty nights. One is a Saxon warrior, while the other wears the armour of a Roman soldier.

Phantom lights have been widely reported in Welsh coastal regions. Naturalists prosaically suggest that they are due to phosphorescence emitted by the decomposing carcases of seabirds or seals, but local inhabitants call them *canwll corfe*, the corpse

SHIPWRECKS AND WRECKERS

This painting, The Shipwreck, *by the 18th-century artist Philip de Loutherbourg was possibly inspired by the wreck of the* Chantiloupe, *off Bantham, South Devon, in 1772. There, wreckers stripped and murdered a wealthy woman survivor who had worn her richest clothes and jewellery, hoping that her appearance would ensure assistance. Many coastal communities benefited from wrecking. On stormy nights, people watched eagerly for the lights of a stricken vessel, and ghoulishly swooped on wreckage and survivors, whose chances of life were considerably lessened by an ancient law. Since it was illegal to claim salvage if anyone from a wrecked*

candles. They are regarded as death omens and consist of small blobs of yellowish light which move over the ground until they stop at houses where death is imminent.

Stories of spectral dogs which are said to haunt the north and east coasts of England may owe their existence to a far-off memory of the Vikings. When the Norsemen invaded, they brought with them their own legends of the Hounds of Odin, the ghostly war-dogs of their chief god.

The creeks and mud-flats of East Anglia have been haunted for centuries by a hell-hound known as Black Shuck, a name which is derived from the Saxon word for the Devil. Sometimes he is said to have only a single eye set in the centre of his head; or he may be headless, yet have yellow eyes suspended by some means in front of him. At other times his eyes are crimson and glow fiercely in the dark.

Lost lands and cities

Though geologists affirm that the western coasts of Britain have changed little since men first inhabited these islands, it is in this part of the country that tales of sunken cities and drowned lands persist most strongly. Perhaps it was the blackened stumps of primeval trees, still visible at low tide, which gave rise to such legends as those of Cardigan Bay.

The story relates that the bay covers a land called Maes Gwyddno, a once-fertile country containing 16 splendid cities. At some time in the 5th century, it became submerged when a maiden failed to prevent water escaping from a well. By the 16th century,

however, the story changed. The submerged land was known as Cantref Gwaelod, 'the Lowland Hundred', which had been defended from the rising sea by a series of banks and sluices. A man named Seithennin was the keeper of the embankment, and one night, in a drunken stupor, he neglected to shut the sluices. The sea overwhelmed the land and only a few of the inhabitants escaped.

Another Welsh story is that of Tyno Helig, a once-prosperous land submerged beneath Conway Bay. In about AD 600 it was ruled over by Prince Helig ap Glannawg, and a natural formation of rocks some 2 miles out to sea from Penmaenmawr is still pointed out as the remains of Helig's palace.

The drowning of Tyno Helig was brought about by Prince Helig's daughter when she persuaded her penniless lover to murder a rich nobleman. The proceeds of the crime enabled the couple to marry, though at the wedding feast a ghostly voice promised to avenge the murder upon the fourth generation of their descendants. The couple lived to see their great-great-grandchildren, and the prophecy was fulfilled when the four generations were gathered together at Llys Helig. The sea burst over the land in a great flood and Tyno Helig was lost for ever; only two people lived to tell the tale.

This story is typical of legends of lands lost beneath the sea because of divine revenge upon the evil or foolish inhabitants. Such lands are always described as being rich and fertile, containing many cities and churches, whose bells are heard tolling beneath the sea for centuries afterwards.

ship was still alive, the law virtually condemned survivors to death. It was unlikely, however, that wreckers deliberately lured ships to destruction. Though there are many legends of lights being tied to horses' tails in order to lure ships on to the rocks, this type of wrecking, if it did occur, was rare. The reverse did occur – beacons were not lit in the hope that vessels would founder

LEGENDS OF THE LIGHTHOUSES

Lighthouses have stood sentinel for centuries on the 7000-mile coastline of the British Isles. Their development from the early, dimly seen beacons has not been uneventful. In Cornwall, local legend claims that the real motive of Sir John Killigrew in building the first lighthouse at the Lizard in 1619 was to lure ships nearer the shore, where they fell easy prey to a band of cut-throat pirates led by the enterprising Sir John himself.

Wreckers who once kidnapped the lightkeeper of the 18th-century Longships Lighthouse at Land's End, left his tiny daughter alone in the lighthouse facing a choice between her duty to warn ships of danger and Christian reverence. It was with commendable reluctance that the little girl was said to have stood on the thick family Bible in order to reach up and light the lamps.

The eerie reputation of the lonely Flannan Isles, west of the Outer Hebrides, was enhanced in 1900 when passing ships reported that no light was to be seen from the lighthouse. Investigators eventually found the living quarters in order, and the lamp filled and ready to light. But no trace has ever been found of the three keepers.

The second Eddystone Lighthouse built off Plymouth was a wooden structure which stood until 1755, when fire destroyed the tower. In trying to extinguish the blaze, the keeper, aged 94, involuntarily swallowed a stream of molten lead from the roof. He lived a further 12 days, and the 7½-oz. ingot afterwards taken from his stomach is now in the Edinburgh Museum.

The water-guardians

*Fascinating and frightening, rivers, springs and wells
had supernatural powers that might heal – or kill*

If you look for a time at a swiftly flowing river,
or peer into the ominous black depths of a well,
you can sense the awe-inspiring effect that
water had upon our ancestors. As far back as the
Bronze Age, and even earlier, people regarded
water as one of the prime sources of life, and rivers,
springs and wells were frequently believed to be the
dwelling places of the gods. They became places of
pilgrimage and worship, and the stories told about
many of them linger still.

Some of the oldest place names in Britain and
Europe are those which were given to rivers; such
was the sanctity of these names that they were
seldom if ever changed by later immigrants. It is

particularly significant that many British rivers
bear the names of Celtic goddesses who were
symbols of fertility. The Clyde was named after the
goddess Clōta, the 'Divine Washer' or the 'Divine
Cleanser'; existing Scottish legends about 'The
Washer at the Ford' – a sinister hag who may be
encountered beside lonely streams washing the
blood-stained garments of those about to die – are
probably far-off memories of this deity. The name
of the River Dee is derived from *Dēvā*, meaning
goddess.

The patroness of arts and crafts, called Brigantia in
Britain and Brigit in Ireland, also left her mark
upon our place names. The name of the River

TRADITIONS THAT HAVE SURVIVED THE YEARS

The Church found well worship the most difficult feature of paganism to
eradicate. Vestiges remain to this day, and wishing wells are still common.
In most places, coins, buttons or pins are thrown into the water, but in
remote parts of the Highlands offerings of broken pottery are placed beside
wells and springs. Another custom that has survived is for sick people, or
their relatives or friends, to leave offerings of rags near waters reputed to
have the power of healing. In many parts of Britain, wells are still decorated
with flowers and greenery on ceremonial occasions.

CAIN AND ABEL *Biblical scenes like
this stem from pagan well-garlanding
rites and were once banned by the
Church which imposed a three-year
fast upon offenders*

FLOWER PAINTINGS *In Derbyshire and Staffordshire, well-dressing has developed
into an art form. Biblical scenes are delineated with petals set in moist clay. The
ceremonies are usually held on Ascension Day. Examples of well-dressings are to be
seen at Tissington, Buxton or, as shown here, at Wirksworth, where this flowered
panel depicts the story of the three wise kings*

TEXT FROM ISAIAH *An illustration in
petals of 'how a little child shall lead
them'. The Buxton springs were
once worshipped under the aegis of
the Celtic goddess Arnemetia*

Braint in Anglesey is derived from Brigantia, as is that of the Brent, Greater London. A remarkable number of wells are dedicated to Brigit, and also to Bride, yet another form of her name. Her influence was so great that, with the coming of Christianity, she was renamed St Brigit; in the Hebrides local legend even placed her as midwife to the Virgin.

Many holy wells were also dedicated to St Anne, who was previously known in Ireland as Anu, the mother of the pagan gods. In Britain, her reputation was more sinister; there she was called Black Annis, the storm hag who devoured children. Much of the water-lore of England, Scotland and Wales is equally confused. Ancient legends of avenging gods became overlaid by those of gentle saints who blessed holy wells or who brought about the miraculous flow of their waters.

A cure for sterility

For both men and women, the inability to reproduce has always carried a deep sense of failure. Because of this, cures for barrenness have figured largely in every religious belief, whether pagan or Christian. Since water is essential to all living things, it is not surprising that it came to be associated with fertility, nor that certain rivers, pools, springs and wells should have been credited with the power of promoting life.

There is a well on the Isle of Skye that is still known as Tobar an Torraidh – the Well of Fertility, whose waters at one time were reputed to cure sterility in cattle. Pathetically, barren women also went secretly to the well, though the practice was frowned on by the community.

As head-hunters, the pagan Celts believed that the severed human head was also a fertility symbol. When a head was thrown into a well its influence was added to that of the water which was then thought to have acquired life-giving properties. There are many stories associating wells with heads, especially in Scotland and Wales. A tale from Dumfries tells how a young man, one of the MacMilligans of Dalgarnock, went courting, but on being challenged by the girl's brother, rode off. In the darkness, his horse galloped over the edge of a crag and, as he fell, his head was struck off by a sharp rock. It then rolled down the hill and into St Brigit's Well, which gained considerably in curative fame. MacMilligan's headless phantom, riding on his horse, has been frequently reported in the vicinity of the well, or galloping round the local church.

There is also a widespread Highland belief that epilepsy can be cured by drinking water from a holy well; the cure is particularly efficacious when the skull of an ancestor or a suicide is used as a drinking vessel. The ceremony is highly ritualised and is resorted to only in extreme cases, because it is believed that the power of a well is limited and will be weakened if the waters are drawn upon too frequently.

Welsh stories about severed heads and wells are usually connected with saints, who gave powers of healing, fertility or wish-fulfilment to the wells named after them. In north Wales, in the 7th century, a beautiful virgin named Winifred was decapitated by her rejected suitor. Her head rolled down the hill and, from the spot where it came to rest, a spring gushed forth. The murderer was immediately despatched by a heaven-sent thunderbolt. St Winifred's Well is at Holywell, Flint, and its healing powers have been famous for centuries. Its waters, it is said, are 'equally propitious to Protestants and Catholics'.

In a similar way, the head of St Llud caused a healing spring to gush from the earth after she had been beheaded in southern Powys. But the head of St Cynog, a saint from Brecknock, created the reverse effect when he was murdered while praying beside a holy well: his head fell into the well, which then dried up.

Many waters have been credited with the ability to change their levels suddenly, usually in a spirit of prophecy. Barton Mere, near Bury St Edmunds, Suffolk, was said to rise and fall with the price of corn; a spring in Langley Park, Kent, dried up if war threatened; and Marvelsike Spring, near Brampton, in Northamptonshire, flowed only before a death or calamity in the locality.

The vengeful gods

Norse legend says that when Christianity triumphed over paganism, the old gods retreated to the rivers. Originally, Aegir was a kindly god who stilled storms and calmed rough seas, but in Lincolnshire, where he was believed to have taken refuge in the Trent, he became cantankerous and was said to demand three lives a year. People in Gainsborough still respect the old pagan god and warn their children to be careful when playing on the river bank, particularly when the spring tide rushes past the steps of the warehouses.

It is understandable that such legends arose along dangerous rivers where there was always the chance of accidental drowning. However, many of the tales may have originated from ancient ceremonies in which human sacrifices were made to the river gods. Most rivers were believed to demand a quota of victims. The Dart in Devonshire and the Ure in N. Yorkshire took one life a year; the Ribble in Lancashire was content with a sacrifice every seventh year, but it could be appeased by offering a bird or an animal.

Wherever possible, great efforts were made to recover the bodies of the drowned so that they could be given a Christian burial. Various methods of recovery, all used within the last 100 years, were adhered to in different districts. In Derbyshire, the centre was scooped out of a loaf of bread which was then filled with quicksilver. The loaf was launched upon the waters in the belief that it would locate the body by hovering on the surface above it. Another method was to row a drummer about the river; when the boat was over the body the beaten drum would make no sound. Another approach, even if the chances of success were still slight, was to fire a gun over the water; the concussion was intended to burst the gall bladder and this would cause the body to float to the surface.

A cure for toothache

Well lore is perhaps richest in areas where a strong Celtic influence has survived, but every part of Britain has been influenced by the cult. Dozens of place names provide clues. Sadler's Wells in London, renamed after the theatre's founder, was originally called Holy Well and was famous for its curative powers. Many wells were believed to have special characteristics, and different kinds of ritual were necessary to persuade them to exercise their powers. Some wells were said to be able to cure toothache but they had to be given offerings of hazel twigs or nuts. Others, like the Silver Well near Otterburn in Northumberland, were credited with the ability to convert all things to precious metal, but they demanded offerings of pine cones. Wishing wells, such as that on St Anne's Hill in Surrey, were given coins or bent pins; wells that could influence the weather and cause storms were offered white stones.

The smashing of pottery in wells and the offering of broken crocks was ancient and widespread. Pottery is found in Bronze Age ritual wells and shafts, and smashed vessels and severed human

heads are commonly found in Iron Age and
Romano-British wells. In Roman times, the well at
Carrawborough, Northumberland, dedicated to the
Celtic goddess Coventina, was enclosed by a 40-ft
square temple. When the well was excavated a few
years ago, it was found to contain a vast number of
offerings including altars to the goddess, shrine
bells, more than 13,000 coins, quantities of whole
and smashed vessels, and a human skull.

All wells had to be treated courteously and
addressed in the correct manner or they could
react in an unfavourable, even dangerous, way.
They might become enraged and drown the
sacrilegious; they might dry up; or they might
move to another site. Certain wells, like that
dedicated to St Barrule on the Isle of Man, were
alleged to become invisible when people sought
them a second time.

Northumberland is especially rich in well traditions. To invoke the powers of the famous Pin
Well in Alnwick Park, the devotee must walk
three times around the well, jump across it, throw
in a pin and then wish. The three wells in Long-
witton Hall gardens are renowned for their curative
powers. Within living memory, crowds gathered on
Mid-Summer Sunday to drink the iron-rich water.
Similarly, at Wark, three wells were visited by
villagers early on New Year's morning. The aim
was to be the first to drink the waters and thus 'take
the flower' of each well. The one who achieved this
was said to be granted miraculous powers for the
ensuing year, even being able to pass through
keyholes and fly. The person who did manage to
obtain the first sacred drink cast an offering of
flowers, grass or straw into the water.

The wise old trout

Many wells were believed to have a guardian which
could be a serpent, a nymph, a toad or even a fly.
Snakes were closely linked with water cults, in
Europe as well as in Britain. A Christian warning
against avarice is told about a man who dreamt on
three successive nights that if he put his hand under a
stone which hung over the spring of a neighbouring
well, he would find a golden necklace. Finally, he
yielded to his curiosity, walked to the spring, and
felt under the stone. He was bitten by a viper, the
guardian of the well, and died.

It was also commonplace to keep one or two
trout in a sacred well. These were fed by the
community and no one dared disturb or harm them.
The fish were believed to live for many years. The
tradition of keeping trout in wells probably had its
roots in the pagan belief that divine trout lived in
sacred pools and fed on the nuts which fell from the
overhanging branches of sacred hazel trees. The
diet of hazel nuts was supposed to give the fish
supernatural wisdom.

Mermaids, usually associated with the sea, were
also believed to be guardian spirits of inland waters,
from where they would keep an eye upon the
affairs of men. When Aqualate Mere, in Staffordshire, was being dredged in the 19th century, workmen said that a mermaid appeared and warned them
that she would destroy two nearby towns if the lake
was harmed. A mermaid was believed to live in
Black Mere, near Leek, in the same county and,
because of this, animals refused to drink the water
and birds never flew over it.

Superstitions related to water still lie within us;
wishing wells are even incorporated in plans for new
buildings. But few people realise when they toss a
coin into a well or pool and make a wish that the
practice is thousands of years old, and they are
making an offering to a spirit in much the same way
as their far-off ancestors.

DANGER IN DEEP WATERS

*Fear of demoniac creatures which were believed to
inhabit deep pools in rivers, lonely lakes and tarns was
widespread. Fierce water-beasts and supernatural bulls
and horses were said to lie in wait for the traveller who
came to drink or bathe. The legend of the Loch Ness
monster is not unique; many Highland lochs are accredited*

with similar strange and mysterious guardians or
inhabitants. Running water, as portrayed in this 19th-
century painting by Samuel Palmer of waterfalls at
Pistil Mawddach, in North Wales, was regarded as a
powerful barrier against evil; anyone who feared that he
was being pursued by some supernatural being endeav-
oured to cross running water, confident in the belief that

the spirit would be forced to relinquish the pursuit.
Another common superstition was that it was unlucky to
part company with someone near a stream. There were
four main elements in the symbolism of water which has
had great influence throughout the ages: water gave life,
it could create chaos, it had the power to destroy, and it
embodied cleansing and purifying properties

THE ROCKS REMAIN . . .

Though he exaggerated the scale, J. M. W. Turner has given a soaring, ethereal quality to St Michael's Mount that well befits the former home of Cornish giants and Celtic saints.

Legend says that the Mount was built by the giant Cormoran, who forced his wife Cormelian to carry white granite boulders through the dark forest that once covered what is now Mount's Bay. While Cormoran slept, his wife tried to substitute the more easily collected local greenstone. The giant was furious, and kicked his wife so hard that her apron string broke, and the greenstone boulder dropped on the causeway where it still lies.

A later story says that St Keyne conferred on any husband or wife, who sat on the rocky chair within the castle first, the ability to dominate the marriage.

The 70 million year old echinite or sea urchin fossils (left) have been known as 'fairy loaves' to generations of country folk

Hollow lands and hilly lands

Long before the birth of geology, storytellers had an explanation for every strange feature of the landscape

In 1893 a Suffolk farmer explained that there was no point in picking stones off his land, for the earth would only grow more. Many of his contemporaries were prepared to go even further: stones grew and reproduced in much the same way as plants and animals. In Martlesham, Suffolk, a man kept a piece of rock on his window-sill which he called a 'mother stone', for he believed that pebbles were its offspring; in Hertfordshire the same kind of stone was known as a 'breeding stone'. The only recorded exception to the rule that stones grew was around Hereford, where they were supposed to have stopped growing when the rocks were rent at the Crucifixion.

It is easy to see how such beliefs might come about. A farmer clears the stones from his land, but within days it is as stony as it was before. This makes him curious, mainly because he would like to prevent it happening again. He knows nothing of geology, so he falls back on the simple explanation, based on his experience as a farmer, that all things grow that are not man made.

This need to understand the world underlies many of man's most ancient beliefs about mountains, hills and stones. All over Britain there are fantastic legends which explain the existence of natural curiosities, from towering hills to the tiniest fossils, or which try to make sense of the mysterious relics of forgotten cultures, such as standing stones and grave mounds.

The litter of fairies, the labour of giants
Everywhere, it seems, the small, round fossil known as an echinite is a fairy's loaf, and flint arrowheads are fairy-darts or elf-shots. In north Yorkshire, if cattle suddenly became excited it was because the elves were shooting at them; to cure an 'awf-shotten' beast it was necessary to give it water in which an elf-shot had been dipped. From the coast around Whitby comes the belief that the fossilised teeth of prehistoric animals are giants' teeth, and that their fossil bones are the remains of angels who fell from Heaven with Lucifer.

Extraordinary features of the landscape, whether natural or man made, are often described as the work of supernatural beings. St Michael's Mount in Cornwall was built as a dwelling place by the giant Cormoran and his wife; Wayland's Smithy, a passage grave on the Berkshire Downs, was built by a mythical, godlike blacksmith, who still lives there and will shoe any traveller's horse if sixpence is left on the capstone of his chamber; and Pudding Pie Hill near Thirsk in N. Yorkshire was raised by the fairies who live inside it.

Even more numerous are the stories which put such features down to accident rather than to design. Again, giants and the Devil, though apparently not fairies, are frequently held respons-ible; so too are Robin Hood, Little John, King Arthur and many local heroes, such as Merlin in the West Country and Jack o' Kent who, despite his name, has left his mark near the Welsh border. Frequently, a giant, the Devil or even Robin Hood attempts to destroy something, or somebody, by piling earth on top of it or by bombarding it with rocks; but only rarely do these ventures succeed. One success story with a brutal end con-cerns the Colwall Stone near Ledbury.

A terrible giant lived with his beautiful wife in a cave in the Malvern Hills. One day he looked down on the village of Colwall and saw his wife on the green, talking with a man whom he took to be her lover. In a rage, he flung a huge boulder at her, killing her outright. To this day, the stone is said to cover her broken body.

One of the Devil's few successes was at Graveley in Hertfordshire, where he managed to knock down the church steeple; but even this was more by luck than judgment. He had already taken six shovel-fuls of earth from Whomerly Wood, where the holes can still be seen, and had thrown them at Stevenage; all had fallen short, to form what are now the Six Hills (in reality Bronze Age barrows). Furious and frustrated, he tried one last throw, missed Stevenage by about 2 miles, and hit Graveley church.

Usually, the record of these missile-throwing tyrants is one of total incompetence and failure. While sitting on the Needles in the Isle of Wight, the Devil felt offended by the sight of Corfe Castle, and hurled his nightcap at it. He missed the castle and lost the cap, and the Agglestone, or Devil's Night-cap, still stands just outside Studland as a monument to his lack of precision.

Trials of strength
Many boulders and standing stones are seen as evidence of titanic but ineffectual struggles between two great antagonists. Two stones on the edge of Semer Water in North Yorkshire are said to have fallen there when the Devil and a giant were hurling rocks at one another from opposite hillsides; one stone still bears Satan's finger-prints.

Two giants, Herman and Saxie, lived on opposite sides of Burrafiord in the Shetland Islands, quarrel-ling incessantly. One day Saxie refused to lend Herman his 'kettle' – a rock basin into which the sea flows – to boil an ox, and they began throwing rocks at one another. Saxie's rock, now known as Saxie's Baa, dropped into the water just short of Herman's home on Hermaness, while Herman's, now called Herman's Hellyac, embedded itself in the cliffs at Saxafiord.

Often, the supernatural bully is outwitted by a quick-thinking man. This happened at Robin Hood's Butts, two small wooded hills near Canon Pyon and King's Pyon north-west of Hereford. Robin Hood and Little John, bent on destroying the monks at Womersley, set out each carrying a spadeful of earth. When they arrived at King's Pyon, they asked a travelling cobbler, who was laden down with shoes, how much further it was to Womersley. The cobbler replied that they would not get there even if they were to wear out all the shoes he was carrying and as many pairs again. In disgust, Robin and Little John dropped the earth on the two spots now known as the Butts.

Even when these brawny giants are not being malicious, their efforts are unimpressive. Almost always, they are hopelessly clumsy. Jack o' Kent and the Devil, while trying to dam the weir at Orcop Hill south of Hereford in order to make a fishpond, accidentally dropped their stones on Garway Hill; they are now known as the White Rocks. The giant of Cloud Hill in Cheshire was so frightened by a small creature which sprang up from the ground that he dashed off, leaving his shoe behind; it is still there – a rugged boulder on the summit.

One of the saddest stories is about the giant Sigger who gave his name to Sigger-hill in Orkney. Sigger loved fishing, and put a rock in the sea to fish from. But a stretch of deep water lay between the land and his rock, so he decided to have a stepping stone as well.

He found a suitable boulder on the hill, and began to stagger down to the sea with it. His wife saw him and cried in sympathy: 'Oh Siggie, Siggie! Mony an evil stane has lain on dy riggie (back)!' Startled, Sigger tripped and the boulder fell on top of him. He lies on the hillside still, for no one has ever been able to remove the stone.

Turned to stone

Many legends about standing stones and stone circles warn of the perils of misbehaving on the Sabbath. Three stone circles near Cleer in Cornwall, known as the Hurlers, are supposed to be the last remains of a group of men who were turned to stone for playing games on a Sunday. An even grimmer story is told of the stone circles near Stanton Drew in Avon, called 'The Wedding'.

Years ago, a couple held their wedding reception in a meadow outside Stanton Drew. It was a Saturday, and the drinking and dancing went on until midnight, when the piper, who was a devout man, refused to play any more. The bride was so furious that she swore she would find another piper, even if she had to go to Hell to fetch him.

At that moment, an old man appeared and offered to play. He started with a slow, solemn tune, but the guests complained, so he switched to something faster. The dancers were exhilarated by his music, but soon they needed to rest.

But their piper turned out to be the Devil, and the faster he played, the faster they danced, and no one could break the spell. By dawn, when he returned to Hell, the entire party had been reduced to a troop of grinning skeletons. And when the villagers of Stanton Drew came to the field in the morning, they found that even these remains had been turned into the stones that stand there today. Only the village piper had survived; the villagers found him cowering beneath a hedge, almost dead with fright.

Saints and other holy men have also left their mark on the landscape. A large flat stone in the churchyard of South Ronaldsay in the Orkney Islands bears the footprints of St Magnus, who sailed across from Scotland on it. At Epworth in Lincolnshire, two hollows in the tombstone of John Wesley's father are said to be Wesley's footprints; apparently, he delivered a sermon from there when the church pulpit was barred to him.

Not surprisingly, many natural hills and man-made barrows are thought, sometimes rightly, to be burial sites. Long barrows are frequently referred to as 'Giants' Graves', and have been so called since the Dark Ages. King Arthur, Merlin and many other kings, wizards and heroes are said to lie sleeping inside hollow hills and mounds in many parts of Britain. Occasionally, whole cities and their inhabitants are said to be buried beneath hills, as at Mellor Moor near Blackburn.

Legend or history?

Other hills and stones traditionally mark the sites of historical events. St Brandon's Stones, near Banff in Grampian, stand where the Scots fought a fierce hand-to-hand battle against Danish invaders,

THE ENIGMA OF STONEHENGE

Blue distances, changeable weather and the timeless mystery of Stonehenge are as characteristic of Salisbury Plain today as when Constable painted this watercolour a century and a half ago. Despite advances in archaeology

although the name of the stones suggest that here, historical tradition replaced a lost legend about St Brandon. The outcrop known as Drummer's Knob, on Cloud Hill in Cheshire, is said to be named after a young drummer boy with Bonnie Prince Charlie's army, who was killed by an English sniper while singing 'Hie thee, Jamie, hame again'.

A tumulus near Hay-on-Wye, called Twyn-y-Beddau or Mound of the Graves, is said to cover a battlefield where the Welsh made a desperate stand against Edward I. The battle was so fierce that the nearby stream of Dulas ran with blood for three days; the bones of the dead are supposed to lie inside the hill. In fact, Twyn-y-Beddau was probably already thousands of years old by the time Edward marched his invading army into Wales.

Creatures of the wilderness

By tradition, almost every wilderness has its supernatural inhabitants, from the Devil, giants, ghosts and fairies to horrible animals such as the Barguest, Padfoot or Black Dog. These wild creatures are infinitely adaptable; in East Anglia, where hills are rare, they inhabit the fens; in Northamptonshire, they ride through the remains

since that time, still no one has solved who built the great monument, or why. Possibly it was a temple to the sun; certainly only religious fervour could have motivated its builders to drag the huge bluestones from the Prescelly Mountains in Dyfed 4000 years ago. But where science is

vague about the origins of Stonehenge, legend is more definite. One story says that the stones were originally transported from Africa to Ireland by a race of giants, and were later brought to the Plain by Merlin and the Devil, who flew with them across the Irish Sea

---

of the once-vast Rockingham Forest. Even in built-up areas, they prowl through local cemeteries.

In their heyday, legends such as these helped to reinforce established values, or to sanction new ones. Early Christian priests probably encouraged the legends about men being turned to stone on a Sunday, partly to keep their churches full, and partly to discourage people from visiting sites linked with older, pagan beliefs.

The legends also had a practical function. Families living in wild and remote parts of Britain needed to discourage their children from wandering alone on to the moors or into the mountains. So they filled these lonely places with fearful creatures such as Black Annis, who roams the Dane Hills of Leicestershire, scratches children to death with her long fingernails, eats their flesh and drinks their blood, and when her foul feast is over, hangs their skins to dry in her cave.

The magic of stones
Though the Christian Church did all it could to discourage the worship of ancient stones, the fear and superstitious awe that these rocks could evoke lingered on for centuries, and is not entirely dead

today. Many stones are traditionally said to have strange magical properties. Near Glenavon, in north-east Scotland, a huge granite rock called Clachna-Bhan, the 'Stone of the Women', crowns a hill named Meall-Ghaineaih. Women nearing the end of pregnancy used to climb up and sit on it, believing that this ensured a quick and easy delivery.

The countryside of Britain is also littered with wishing stones, such as the one at Matlock in Derbyshire, which have the power to grant the wish of someone standing on them; and with holed stones and rocking or 'logan' stones which can cure various diseases. The 12 o'Clock Stone near Nancledra in Cornwall can cure children of rickets – so long as they are not illegitimate or the offspring of dissolute parents.

Some stones are not as inanimate as they appear. The Rollright Stones in Oxfordshire defy attempts to count them, and the Hoston Stone in Leicestershire will visit a succession of disasters on anyone who tries to move it. The Cock-Crow Stone at Looe in Cornwall turns round three times whenever it hears a cock crowing, and the Whetstone at Kingstone, south of Hereford, is said to walk slowly down to the River Wye to drink.

Green magic

The plants and trees witches used in their spells still grow in English woods and gardens

Until the Norman Conquest, a squirrel could cross England from the Severn to the Wash without putting foot to the ground. Much of the population lived in clearings, surrounded by the menacing forest, a place of wild beasts and wilder men. The trees themselves whispered together, or roared angrily during the autumn gales: their longevity made a mockery of the life-span of puny men. Small wonder, then, that primitive peoples should identify trees with gods, or even see in them their own far-off ancestors.

In Britain, the Druids worshipped such trees as the oak and the rowan and attributed great powers to them. When people touch wood to ward off misfortune, this is a relic of the days when guardian spirits were supposed to live in trees. Touching the tree was a mark of respect to the spirit, as well as a plea for good fortune.

Some plants and flowers had medicinal qualities, while the distillations of others could kill. All had magical powers or miraculous origins, and were consequently regarded with awe and respect.

THE SYMBOLIC TREE

From the dawn of civilisation, trees have influenced man's thinking and even his architecture. It is thought that the upright tree trunk inspired the erection of the standing stones in Britain and led to the development of the stone pillar and the obelisk in Mediterranean countries. Ancient Indian and Mexican sculpture depicted stylised sacred trees, and symbolised trees were often used in Greek paintings and on vases. The maypole is believed to date back to ancient fertility rites, and in May Day ceremonies the King or Queen of the May are still symbolically sacrificed. Even the Christmas tree and the Yule log are tokens of the rebirth of spring. To man, the tree has embodied all things in creation. An example of this may still be seen in Eastern jewellery in which the branches of a tree support a universe of diamond stars.

THE JESSE TREE *The family tree stemmed from manuscripts and stained glass portraying the genealogy of Christ. A vine issued from Jesse, father of David, leading to kings, prophets and Mary. Christ was above, among the terminal branches*

TREE OF KNOWLEDGE *Tree lore asserted its influence in the Old Testament. The tree of knowledge, depicted in a 13th-century manuscript, and the tree of life were said to grow in Eden*

THE CO-EXISTENCE TREE *English primitive artist Eden Box draws on an ancient theme in this contemporary painting which illustrates the interdependence of all things. The branches grow from a single trunk symbolising unity; the roots embrace and draw life from the earth, from which sap flows like blood through its veins; and the peaceful cats and birds illustrate the harmony of the system. Trees were seen by early man as being representative of the world and of all nature*

THE MAGIC OF THE TREES

Apple
The apple has long been a symbol of fruitfulness. The rhyme, 'An apple a day keeps the doctor away' probably comes from a Norse myth in which apples were given to the gods to stave off old age. Apples were used to discover who a girl would marry; the apple was peeled and the complete peel thrown over the shoulder. If it formed a letter, this was the initial of her future husband. 'Wassailing' – a ceremony to ensure a good apple crop – is still performed in the West Country, usually on Twelfth Night. The felling of an apple tree was unlucky, and to leave the last apple on a tree meant a family death.

Ash
An old Christmas custom is to burn an ash faggot bound with green twigs on the hearth, making a wish as each bond snaps. Unmarried girls can also choose a bond; the one whose bond parts first will be the first to marry. The ash tree was credited with magical properties that would cure a child of hernia or rickets. Before sunrise, the naked child was passed through a cleft tree trunk that was then bound and sealed with clay. As the trunk healed so did the child. To cure a lame animal, a hole was bored in an ash and a live shrew sealed inside. As the shrew died and the tree healed, the animal recovered.

Birch
Around Hereford, a birch tree decorated with red and white rags was propped against a stable door on May Day to protect the horses from being hag-ridden by witches or having their manes knotted by fairies. Nineteenth-century navvies and their brides considered themselves legally married if they jumped across a birch-broom held over the threshold.

Elder
It was considered to be unlucky to bring elderwood into a house. Perhaps this was because it was said that the Cross was made of elder and Judas Iscariot hanged himself from an elder tree. Elder was a witches' tree; whoever approached it after dark was at their mercy. The scent of the flowers was believed to poison anyone who slept under them.

Hawthorn
Maypoles were frequently made of hawthorn, a tree which symbolised joy at the return of summer. Hawthorn was often used for the wreath of summer's Green Man, who represented the spirit of the woods. Hung outside a cowshed, hawthorn assured a plentiful milk supply and, when laid on rafters by someone not in the family, guarded a house against storms, spirits and witches.

Hazel
Forked hazel wands, which must be cut on St John's Eve or Night, were used in searches for buried treasure and, up to the 16th century, to point out thieves. Hazel twigs are still used by diviners when looking for sources of water or metal buried underground.

Holly
A holly hedge around a house or field was believed to keep out evil influences. It was protection against poison, the evil eye, storms and fire. Cows thrived if a sprig of Christmas holly was left in the cowshed. The custom of using holly as a Christmas decoration seems to stem from the Roman Saturnalia, celebrated in December. Some hedgers still believe it is unlucky to cut holly and will leave a wild bush in the midst of a neatly trimmed hedge.

APPLE

HAWTHORN

HAZEL

Juniper
Fires of juniper wood were kept burning during outbreaks of plague in the belief that the smoke drove away demons. To dream about the tree's berries indicated the birth of an heir, or some other successful achievement, but to dream of the tree itself was considered unlucky.

Oak
Much of European mythology is based on the worship of this tree, whose human qualities include the shrieks and groans which it emits when felled. Particular reverence was paid to individual oaks and groves. The oak had a wide range of magical powers; it gave protection from lightning; a nail driven into a trunk cured toothache; and merely to carry an acorn preserved youth. In more recent times, legends have gathered about the escape of Charles II after the battle of Worcester, when he hid in an oak at Boscobel in Salop. The incident is still celebrated on May 29, the date of his Restoration.

Poplar
The Cross was also said to have been made from the trembling poplar or aspen, which still shivers in horror. Anyone suffering from an illness which had trembling as a symptom could be cured by pinning a lock of hair to the tree and chanting a spell.

Rowan
Most common in northern England, Scotland and Wales, the rowan or mountain ash was believed to give protection from witchcraft and evil. Many people wore crosses of rowan wood; milkmaids tied rowan twigs to buckets to prevent milk from going sour; loops of rowan twigs tied with red thread were hung outside houses and stables. Garlands of rowan were hung about the necks of pigs to make them fatten quickly, and rowan berries were fed to cows in calf and mares in foal to ensure uncomplicated births.

Willow
Sawn willow was very unlucky and the poorest man hesitated to use it for firewood. But a gift of willow on a May morning was lucky. The tree is the emblem of grief and lost love.

Yew
The yew was a sacred tree in most of the old European mythologies: many Christian churches stand on the site of a pagan yew grove. Because the tree may live for over 1000 years, it was a symbol of everlasting life, and its branches were used to line newly dug graves. Yews were planted in churchyards to protect them from storms raised by witches.

THE POWER OF PLANTS

Beans
The souls of the dead were believed to dwell in bean-fields, and beans were associated with ghosts and death, as were many other plants with sweet-smelling flowers. In Leicestershire, anyone sleeping in a bean-field overnight risked insanity. In witch areas a bean was kept in the mouth, to be spat at the first witch met.

Clover
The triple leaf of the clover has been associated with the Holy Trinity since St Patrick used it to illustrate the doctrine of the Three in One – although some say he used a sprig of wood sorrel. Apart from bringing good luck, a four-leaf clover gave second sight and the power to detect witches and to see fairies.

Fennel
An old belief was that snakes ate fennel to help them slough their skins and to improve their short sight. It was said that an unwilling horse could be caught if it were offered fennel-flavoured gingerbread.

Foxglove
The name of this flower derives from 'folk's-glove', because foxgloves were believed to have been worn by fairies.

Garlic
The juice of garlic is an antiseptic. In the 17th century, a drink made from garlic called 'vinegar of the four thieves' was taken by robbers of plague victims as protection against infection. In the First World War, the French Army used garlic to clean wounds. It was also considered to be a powerful aphrodisiac.

TANSY

MANDRAKE

Hemp
Though young women were not permitted to work in hemp-fields in case they became barren, they still used hemp seed in marriage divination. In Devon, if a girl walked from the church porch to her home half an hour after midnight on St Valentine's Day, scattering hemp seed as she went and reciting a spell, she would see the wraith of her future husband following behind, raking the seed into a winding sheet.

Honeysuckle
A wedding was sure to occur shortly after bringing honeysuckle into a house. The presence of the flower was said to encourage erotic dreams if placed in a girl's bedroom.

Ivy
It was said that an alcoholic would be cured if he drank from a cup made of ivy wood. In Salop, drinking from an ivy cup was believed to cure children of whooping cough.

DEVIL'S-BIT SCABIOUS   ST JOHN'S WORT   PURPLE FOXGLOVE

Mandrake
The subject of innumerable legends, mandrake was thought to cure sterility and promote passion. It was used as an anaesthetic and as an aphrodisiac. Mandrake was held to be more than just a plant: its long, forked root was said to embody a demon, and pulling it from the ground made the demon shriek so horribly that any man hearing it would die. Because of this, dogs were used to uproot the plant. A hungry dog was tied to the mandrake and some meat was placed near by. Theoretically, the dog would rush at the meat but would die as the shrieking plant was torn out. Mandrake is rare in Britain, but similar legends surround the white bryony.

Caraway
Credited with the power of preventing theft, caraway seeds were placed among valued possessions – the very presence of the plant could hold a thief in custody. To insure against the advances of other women, wives put caraway seeds in their husbands' pockets; and pigeons stayed in their lofts if caraway seeds were mixed with their feed.

Chicory
The leaf was believed to give the bearer the power of invisibility. The plant also had the ability to open locked chests, though this could only be done on St James's Day (July 25). It was essential to use a golden knife while holding a chicory leaf against the lock. The lockpicker had to work in silence, however; if he spoke, he would surely die.

Daisy
It was lucky to step on the first daisy of the year, but unlucky for a very young child to touch it. Should the plant be uprooted, the children of the family would grow up stunted. This flower was also thought to be injurious to any young animal which ate it. To determine when she would marry, a girl picked a bunch of daisies with her eyes shut. The number of flowers represented the number of years she had to wait. The flowers were an essential part of Midsummer floral decorations.

Devil's-bit scabious
The root of this plant was used to cure all manner of ailments. It was said that the Devil was so concerned that it might banish illness altogether that he bit the end off the root, leaving only its present truncated stump.

Marsh mallow
The sap of the marsh mallow was the main ingredient in a preparation used by medieval clergy to help accused but favoured persons to endure ordeal by fire. Smeared thickly over the accused's hands, the concoction was said to enable him to hold a red-hot iron without burning himself.

Mistletoe

A sacred plant of pre-Christian religions, the parasitic mistletoe was believed to hold the life of the host tree when the tree appeared to be dead in winter. It had an even greater significance when it grew on the oak which the Druids worshipped. Apparently the viscous, pearly berries were regarded as the seminal fluid of the oak and therefore of the oak-tree god or spirit. For this reason, it was held to be a charm to induce fertility, and the present-day custom of kissing under a sprig of mistletoe probably derives from this. White-robed Druids ceremoniously cut mistletoe with a golden sickle on the sixth day of the moon. The mistletoe was then divided among the people who fastened it above their doorways to protect their houses from thunder, lightning and all evil. The sprigs were regarded as a symbol of hospitality, and the plant was the base of so many remedies that for centuries it was known by the alternative name of all-heal.

Nightshade

One of the most poisonous of European wild plants, nightshade or its derivative, belladonna, was used mainly as a hallucinatory drug. It was also taken by clairvoyants to induce second sight. Nightshade was a principal ingredient in the ointment witches rubbed on their bodies when they wished to fly.

Onion

The onion was one of the many plants held to be portenders of weather. A rhyme stated that a mild winter could be expected if the skins of onions were thin, but that it would be 'cold and rough' if the skins were 'thick and tough'. Onions were widely used medicinally for complaints as varied as chilblains and baldness. They also were credited with protective qualities. Many old beliefs are still accepted: a Cheshire farmer's wife attributes their farm's remarkable escape from the 1968 foot-and-mouth disease outbreak to rows of onions placed along the windowsills and doorways of the cowsheds.

Parsley

A mass of superstitions were associated with parsley, most of them concerned with death and disaster. It should never be transplanted, or given away, or cut by a person in love.

Peony

Peonies in a garden were reputed to protect a house from evil spirits. Necklaces of seeds were worn to counter lunacy, epilepsy and nightmare, and the roots were also worn by children to help them cut their teeth. As with the mandrake, the plant had to be uprooted by a dog.

Potato

If warts are rubbed with a potato, which is then thrown away, it is said the warts will wither as the tuber decays. In the 16th century, potatoes were sought as aphrodisiacs. In this guise they were sold to gullible buyers at over £250 per lb.

Primrose

A primrose blooming in winter augured death; so did a single primrose brought into a house. If fewer than 13 were gathered in the first spring posy, the number picked would equal the chickens each hen would hatch that year.

Rosemary

It was believed the plant grew only where the woman ruled the house.

St John's wort

Midsummer was celebrated as a festival of the sun by our pagan ancestors, and this golden flower was an emblem of the sun god. Later, Christians dedicated Midsummer Day to St John the Baptist, and the sun-god's flower became St John's wort. Bunches of the flower were hung over doors to ward off evil spirits. The plant was believed to be able to move about to avoid having its flowers picked.

Tansy

Some women ate tansy leaves as a salad to encourage conception; others ate the salad to bring about a miscarriage. The juice of the tansy was used to flavour puddings and cakes given as prizes in Easter games. Sussex people put the leaves in their shoes to prevent ague.

Thyme

The herb's long folklore association with death is perpetuated in the Order of Oddfellows, whose members still throw thyme into a grave.

Valerian

In one account, the Pied Piper lured the rats from Hamelin with a pocketful of valerian. Rats and cats are attracted to the plant, which is also thought to arouse love in humans.

PEONY

Vervain

In the Fens, vervain oil was used to locate drowned bodies. It was believed to attract eels to the spot in the stream where the body lay. Vervain was supposed to have been used to staunch Christ's wounds on Calvary, and it was never gathered without first making the sign of the Cross.

Violet

Violets worn around the neck were said to prevent drunkenness. In some areas the flowers were believed to bring fleas into a house. Autumn-blooming violets were supposed to warn of a death or an epidemic.

Yarrow

Witches used yarrow in spells. In the Western Isles it was believed that yarrow leaves held over the eyes would give the wearer second sight.

The fantastic ark

Birds and beasts have been worshipped as gods, exalted as prophets, and feared as companions of the supernatural

Our far-off ancestors saw little difference between themselves and the animal world. They told each other 'true' stories about talking animals and about birds which performed heroic tasks. It was even possible, they thought, for human beings to take on non-human forms and to marry animals. As recently as 1895, a Shetland woman called Baubi Urquhart claimed in all sincerity that her great-great-grandfather had married a seal, and that she was their descendant.

Many animal legends grew out of the belief that the dead lived on as birds or beasts. Seabirds were often said to be the spirits of drowned sailors, while seals were the armies of Pharaoh, drowned in the Red Sea as they rode in pursuit of the Children of Israel. Coleridge's poem 'The Ancient Mariner', published in 1798, records the belief that an albatross embodies a human soul, and that to kill one brings misfortune. But this belief cannot have been universal, for sailors often used the webbed feet of albatrosses as tobacco pouches.

Birds and beasts have been used as oracles at least since the Celts were lords of Britain, and beliefs about 'lucky' and 'unlucky' animals are modern versions of this ancient custom. A traditional verse translated from Scottish Gaelic records some of the situations in which the sight or sound of certain birds was once said to be unlucky: 'I heard the cuckoo with no food in my stomach, I heard the stock-dove on top of the tree, I heard the sweet singer in the copse beyond, And I heard the screech of the owl in the night. I saw the wheatear on the

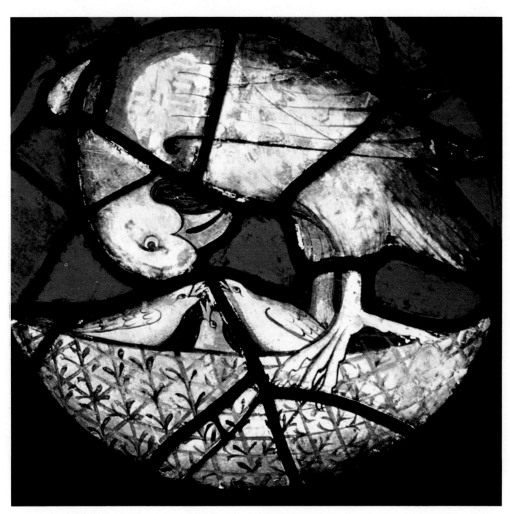

SYMBOL OF SELF-SACRIFICE

In the Middle Ages the pelican was believed to love its chicks so deeply that it pecked open its breast and fed them on its blood. It became a symbol of Christ's death on the Cross, as in this fragment of 14th-century stained glass now in the Victoria and Albert Museum in London.

Another legend explained that pelican chicks attack their parents, who eventually strike back and kill them. Driven by remorse, the mother mutilates herself, and her blood restores the murdered chicks to life. In heraldry, the pelican represents the noble virtue of self-sacrifice

dyke of holes, I saw the snipe while sitting bent, And I foresaw the year would not go well with me.'

Magpies are among the most ominous of British birds, and most people still know a version of the rhyme which begins:

One for sorrow, two for mirth,
Three for a wedding, four for a birth.

There are traditional methods of protection against the sorrow which the sight of a single magpie may bring. In England, people used to cross themselves, raise their hats to the bird, or spit three times over the right shoulder and once towards the bird, saying: 'Devil, Devil, I defy thee.' In Somerset the customary safeguard was to carry an onion with you wherever you went.

Evil omens and warnings of death

Night-flying birds, or birds with dark feathers or an eerie cry, are mostly thought to be ill omens. In Wales, if an owl hooted in a village, snow was on its way or a local girl was about to lose her virginity. Owls were regarded as birds of death as long ago as Roman times, and the belief may still survive in places that an owl hooting near a house means that someone inside is about to die. In AD 77, the historian Pliny said that the screech-owl was always the bearer of bad news, and for that reason was 'most execrable and accursed'.

On the credit side, the skin of an owl nailed to a barn door will protect the building from evil. Owl eggs will reputedly restore drunks to their senses, prevent epilepsy and improve bad sight. Owl broth was used to treat whooping cough, presumably because owls could 'whoop' without becoming ill, and an ointment made of pulverised owl mixed with boar's grease was said to ease the pains of gout.

The mournful cries of a flock of birds called the Seven Whistlers – they may have been curlews, whimbrels or plovers – were also believed to warn of impending death or disaster. In the Shrewsbury countryside, there were said to be six Whistlers searching for a seventh: if they found it, the world would end. Elsewhere, the Seven Whistlers were the grief-stricken souls of unbaptised babies condemned to roam the skies forever, or drowned sailors warning their former shipmates of danger.

Other signs which were sometimes said to be death omens included: an adder on a doorstep; a bat flying three times round a house; a cow breaking into a garden; a butterfly seen by night; a cricket leaving a house; a crow in a churchyard; a dog howling in the night; the appearance of a white hare; molehills encircling a house; a sudden plague of mice; clothing gnawed by rats; or a toad hopping over someone's foot.

The Devil and the Holy Ghost

In many parts of the country ravens were once said to be the Devil's birds, and in Yorkshire children were threatened with a Great Black Bird which would carry them off if they misbehaved. But in the West Country and Wales they were held to be royal birds – there was a legend that King Arthur had turned into one – while in London the ravens kept at the Tower traditionally protect Britain against invasion. In Somerset, where people tipped their hats to ravens, a baby was thought to die whenever eggs were stolen from a raven's nest. If the bird perched on the roof of any Welsh house, prosperity was assured for the family within.

Many birds are traditionally sacred, and killing them can have dreadful consequences. Swallows nesting beneath the eaves of a house protect it from lightning, fire and storms, and if a swallow flies into a house, it brings joy with it. But kill a swallow or destroy its nest, and one of the family may die or the

KINGFISHER
According to legend, Noah sent a kingfisher as well as a dove to search for dry land after the Flood. The kingfisher flew so high that its feathers were stained orange and blue by the sun and the sky

CUCKOO
Before bird migration was properly understood, many people believed that the cuckoo turned into a hawk during the winter, or hibernated in a fairy hill

COCK
As recently as the 19th century, a Midland builder buried a cock in the foundations of a church to protect the building from evil. Within living memory, similar rituals were observed in the Scottish Highlands, where cocks were buried at the junction of three streams to avert evil or to cure disease

WREN
Traditionally king of the birds, the wren was once cruelly persecuted every December 26. Boys hunted and killed wrens, then carried the corpses from house to house collecting money

SWALLOW
Inside their bodies swallows are said to carry two precious stones – a red one, which can cure insanity, and a black one, which brings good luck

MAGPIE
Tradition accuses the magpie of not wearing full mourning at the Crucifixion. In Scotland it was considered such an evil bird that it was said to carry a drop of the Devil's blood hidden under its tongue

WHEATEAR
In Scotland and northern England wheatears were ·he bringers of bad luck. They were also deeply feared in Orkney, where toads were thought to incubate their eggs

43

ROBIN
Many legends explain how the robin got its red breast: in one account it tried to ease Christ's pain on the Cross, and was splashed with a drop of his blood

OWL
For centuries, the cry of an owl has been taken as an omen of disaster. It warns of death or bad luck, especially if it is heard near a house, and it promises a cruelly unfortunate life to any child born within sound of it

CURLEW
Sailors dreaded the melancholy cry of a curlew, for they believed that it was a warning from a drowned friend. In parts of Scotland the bird is called a whaup, and there it is associated with a long-beaked goblin that carries off evil-doers at night

SWAN
Richard the Lionheart is said to have brought the first swans to Britain from Cyprus after the Third Crusade, and for centuries swans have been royal property. A person's 'swan song' – his final work – derives from the belief that swans sing only once – just before they die

SHEEP
At midnight on Christmas Eve, sheep are said to face east, in remembrance of the birth of Christ. They also possess healing attributes; children were once placed where sheep had lain to cure them of whooping cough

PIG
The bite of a pig was once thought to cause cancer, and a meal of pig's brains was reputed to make people speak as though they had taken a truth drug

CAT
Witches were once said to disguise themselves as cats, and many people refused to talk near a cat, for fear that a witch would learn their secrets

house will be destroyed by fire. In Scottish tradition, however, the Devil's blood runs in its veins.

Swallows and wrens are both said to have brought fire to mankind, and to have burnt themselves in the process. This accounts for the swallow's red breast, and for the robin's too, for legend claims that a robin threw itself on to the burning wren to stifle the flames.

The robin's red breast has given rise to many legends through the centuries. One says that the bird was singed while taking water to sinners burning in Hell; another, that it wounded itself while trying to lessen the agony of Christ's crown of thorns. It may also have been splashed with Christ's own blood on the same occasion. Holding a dying robin may cause trembling and palsy in the hands for the rest of one's life.

The most sacred of all birds is the dove, which has become the international symbol of peace and purity, as well as being the Christian symbol for the Holy Spirit. Witches, who claimed the ability to turn themselves into almost any creature, were incapable of changing into doves; sick people would not die so long as they were lying on a pillow or mattress stuffed with dove feathers. However, doves could also be death omens, especially if they were seen circling over someone's head, or settling on a roof.

Storms and halcyon days

Birds could be weather-forecasters as well as fortune-tellers. At sea, storm petrels were once thought to bring bad weather with them, a belief which had some foundation in fact, for petrels often feed when the sea is rough. Their curious method of flight – they skim over the waves as if walking on them – also linked petrels with St Peter, who walked on the Sea of Galilee. The name petrel was probably derived from this episode.

When the sea is calm, kingfishers are said to be sitting on their nests. Halcyon is another name for the bird, which in Greek means 'conceiving on the sea', and before it was known that the birds nest in burrows, the belief was widespread that they laid eggs at sea in floating nests of fishbone.

According to a Greek legend, Halcyone, daughter of the God of the Winds, married Ceyx, son of the Day Star. Ceyx drowned in a storm at sea, and the gods, taking pity on his wife, restored him to life, but turned both of them into kingfishers. For 14 days each year, while Halcyone is on her nest, her father holds back the wind – hence the expression, 'halcyon days'. This legend may also explain the old country belief that dead kingfishers make good weather-vanes – their bodies are said to turn in the direction of the wind.

Cuckoos were thought to bring fine weather, although in Yorkshire it was considered to be a sign of rain if they called repeatedly. They also brought good or bad luck, depending on what the hearer was doing when he heard the first call of the season. In Wales, it was lucky to hear a cuckoo call while standing on grass, but bad luck if you were on barren ground. Some people believed that if they turned the money in their pockets when a cuckoo called, and then spat on it, the money would last for the rest of the year. Others said that the hearer would continue to do whatever he was doing when he heard the call until the year was out. So if he was in bed, he was probably fated to become ill.

The power to see ghosts

Ancient British mythology contained an impressive list of sacred animals, including cats, dogs, cows, horses, snakes, hares and pigs. Traces of these legends have survived into the 20th century in the importance some people attach to animal mascots, in the superstitious fears animals can sometimes evoke, and in the widespread belief that certain animals possess peculiar psychic powers.

Dogs and horses are both commonly credited with the power to see ghosts: dogs are said to snarl, and horses to shy and sweat, when troubled by spirits invisible to humans. Until quite recently, horses were also thought to be particularly vulnerable to the Evil Eye, and their owners protected them with brasses. These are still fashioned in the traditional spirit-repelling shapes, such as symbols of the sun or the crescent moon.

Many traditional beliefs about dogs stemmed from the fear of rabies. Insanity and a hideously painful death are almost certain consequences of being bitten by a rabid dog, and it was not until strict quarantine laws were introduced in 1901 that the disease was controlled in Britain.

Even if a dog was healthy, it would probably have been killed if it bit anyone, for it was feared that if the dog ever became mad, then its victim would go mad too. Another precaution was to take some hair from the dog, fry it, and place it on the wound with a sprig of rosemary. This is the origin of the saying: 'The hair of the dog that bit you.'

Animal lore explains another saying, that children can be 'licked into shape'. It was once believed that bear cubs were born completely formless, and that their mothers then literally licked them into shape. Shakespeare knew of the belief, for in *Henry VI* the crippled Duke of Gloucester is described as an 'unlick'd bear-whelp'.

Witches' familiars

A peculiarly English feature of the witch-cult was the belief that witches possessed familiar imps or devils, which usually took the form of a cat or dog, but might also appear as a toad, a rat or a mouse, or even occasionally as a fly. The familiar advised the witch, and ran malicious errands for her, and so closely were their lives intertwined that if the familiar was ever wounded, the witch would suffer a similar injury.

Cats were probably the most common familiars, and many people still associate them with the supernatural and uncanny. Unlike dogs and horses, they are said to be fond of ghosts, and purr whenever they encounter them. They may also have the ability to forecast the weather: they predict the wind (or according to some accounts, raise it) by clawing at carpets and curtains; rain is certain to come when a cat busily washes its ears or sneezes. If a cat sneezes near a bride on her wedding morning, it is said to forecast a happy marriage for her.

Black cats are most often believed to be lucky, although in Yorkshire, where it is lucky to own one, it is very unlucky to come across one by accident.

White cats, unlike white horses, are usually said to bring bad luck.

Witches were also believed to turn themselves into hares, and in that guise, would steal milk from cows. In 1662, the Scottish witch Isabel Gowdie confessed that she had transformed herself into a hare by reciting the spell: 'I shall go intill a hare, With sorrow and sych and meikle care; And I shall go in the Devil's name, Ay while I come home again.' To change back she repeated: 'Hare, hare, God send thee care. I am in a hare's likeness now, But I shall be in a woman's likeness even now.' The only way to kill a witch hare was to shoot it with a silver bullet.

By popular tradition, rats and mice were soul animals, and stories used to be told about people whose souls, shaped like mice, came out of their mouths while they slept, and who died when someone chased the mice away.

DOG
Popular tradition credits dogs with the ability to see ghosts. Canine phantoms also abound, and spectral black dogs with huge, flaming eyes haunt lanes and lonely places in many remote areas

FOX
In the Middle Ages, foxes were associated with the Devil, and in Lincolnshire, a fox's bite was thought to be fatal. On days when rain and sunshine co-incided, foxes were said to be getting married

HARE
To the ancient British, hares were sacred, but in the Middle Ages they were associated with witchcraft. Witches were said to transform themselves into hares

HEDGEHOG
Farmers once killed hedgehogs as vermin, for they believed that 'pricky back otchuns' sucked milk from cows

POWER AND PERIL OF THE HORSE

The Celts believed that their souls travelled on horseback to the land of the dead, and popular tradition still claims that horses are clairvoyant. This power made them vulnerable to enchantment and the forces of evil and, in the Middle Ages, witches were said to 'hag-ride' them to their coven meetings, bringing them back to their owners just before dawn, exhausted and drenched in sweat

LIFE, LOVE AND WORK

The dangers and uncertainties of his existence often impel man to seek refuge in beliefs that reach far beyond the horizons of reason. Even today, hardly anyone can claim to be entirely free of superstitions, and strange, protective rituals still surround birth, childhood and marriage, work and leisure, sickness and death. Many of them defy interpretation, for they date from an age when most people believed in magic without question

THE DIGNITY OF LABOUR *In paintings such as 'Work', of which a detail is shown here, the Victorian artist Ford Madox Brown extolled the dignity and diversity of everyday activities*

THE VULNERABLE MOTHER AND CHILD

Our superstitious ancestors believed that a mother and newborn child, like this early 17th-century pair shown in detail from the Tate Gallery picture of the Cholmondeley sisters, were surrounded by many hazards. The baby in particular was exposed to evil supernatural forces until it had been baptised and cleansed of inherited sin. The child's mother also underwent ritual purification known as 'churching'. This religious service is still common in some areas; until it has taken place, the mother is not supposed to leave her house

The brink of life

Constant vigilance and spiritual safeguards were needed against the dark forces surrounding pregnancy and childhood

Birth is no longer the hazardous affair it once was, an event which in earlier times was fraught with danger to mother and child. As recently as 150 years ago a child had only an even chance of living to the age of five. Hence the joy of creation was inextricably bound up with the fear of death. Protection was necessary to combat the hazards, and the whole episode of birth became encompassed by magical ritual and charms, while omens pointing to the future well-being of the child were eagerly sought after by the parents.

Preparations during pregnancy

A pregnant woman is still regarded as a very special person in society; in earlier centuries she was set apart before the birth to protect her from supernatural influences, and afterwards to prevent her supposed uncleanliness from contaminating other persons and objects before she had been purified by a special Church ceremony. In Wales during the last century, a pregnant woman did not spin, nor could she work in the dairy. Until quite recently in some parts of northern England, it was considered the worst of bad taste for a heavily pregnant woman to appear in public.

Another reason for isolating the expectant mother was the belief that pre-natal events and contacts could influence the unborn child's future. One superstition, still current, holds that birthmarks are caused and shaped by something which has frightened the mother during pregnancy – a mouse, for example. In Hertfordshire, recently, a mother laid the blame for her child's throat ailment upon a snake. While pregnant, she had been startled by an adder, whose supposedly narrow gullet was transposed to her child. Many a modern mother is convinced that her child's aversion to a particular food is entirely due to her own dislikes during pregnancy.

Superstition played a large part in the preparation of the articles that were to be used by the newborn baby. In North Yorkshire, a family's first cradle was always paid for before it was brought into the home, otherwise a child that slept in it would eventually be 'too poor to pay for its own coffin' and would die a pauper.

Many modern parents choose the pram before the child is born – but it must not be delivered until the birth lest the child should be still-born. Many superstitions are based upon the idea that if one presumes upon future events, opposite consequences will result. Occasionally it is possible to cheat fate, as in the old Suffolk belief, where if a woman did not want another child, she kept the cradle, or some of the previous baby's clothes.

As the pregnancy advances, relatives and friends often try to forecast the sex of the infant. Many people think that boys are 'carried high' while girls are 'carried low', though this has little basis in fact. On the other hand, there does seem to be some statistical support for the belief that if a pregnancy runs more than the usual nine months, then a boy can be expected – though not because 'they need more effort in the making'.

A more complex form of divination was employed in N. Wales in the 19th century. A sheep's shoulder blade was scraped clean, scorched, then holed and threaded through its thinnest part. After this, it was suspended above the door of the house overnight. The first person to enter the following morning, apart from members of the household, would be of the same sex as the future child.

Confinement customs

Until recently, delivering the child was widely regarded as 'women's work', especially in rural areas where the event revolved round the local midwife – a character who was both respected and feared. Not only was she the encyclopaedia of all local birthlore, but she was an expert in folk medicine and other skills, many of which were believed to be magical by country folk. These attributes led to her being regarded as a local 'wise woman' or 'white witch'. As late as the last century a lingering East Anglian tradition suggested that midwives had supernatural powers which enabled them to arrive in time for a confinement, whether ordinary transport was available or not.

The arrival of the midwife was a sign for relatives and neighbours to gather in celebration of the happy event, and offer their congratulations to the parents. In Cheshire and some other areas a 'merry meal' was offered, at which cake, cheese and ale were dispensed. Whatever its local name, the traditional 'groaning cake' was always served, and in many northern areas a large 'groaning cheese' was also provided – 'groaning' being the Old English for lying-in or confinement. In Dorset, a barrel of beer,

PROTECTING THE CHILD

It was once common practice for the baptism to take place as soon as possible after the child was born. It was believed that an infant that died unbaptised could not go to Heaven, and its soul would wander through the skies as an avenging fury

called 'groaning drink', was also supplied and in Yorkshire gingerbread was served.

Many centuries ago, primitive rural communities used to observe a custom known as 'couvade' – from the French, meaning 'to hatch'. At the time of his wife's confinement, the husband took to his bed and behaved as if he was having the child. Even in recent times, if the husband suffered any aches, it was said that he was suffering for the mother so that her labour would be easier. In the Middle Ages it was believed that the mother's birth pangs might be transferred to her husband by the symbolic transfer of clothing or by the midwife's spells. 'Couvade' existed within living memory in Hereford and Worcester; in Yorkshire, too, particularly in the north, it gave rise to a curious tradition. If the mother of an illegitimate child would not reveal the father's name, her relatives would search the village for any man ill in bed – the first they found was supposed to be the father.

'Monday's child . . .'

The precise time and date of a child's birth is believed by astrologers to have a significant bearing on the infant's future life and character. In earlier centuries, it was customary for wealthy families to have an astrologer in attendance at the birth, so that an accurate prediction could be obtained immediately. For those who could not afford an astrologer, a less sophisticated method of divination relied on rhymes such as 'Monday's child is fair of face . . .' though there are many contradictory versions. Even the child's physical appearance at birth was significant:

'A dimple on the chin brings a fortune in;
A dimple on the cheek leaves a fortune to seek.'

In Lincolnshire, large ears are said to be a sign of future success. More widespread is the belief that if a child's eyebrows meet, it will have a jealous disposition or it will be bad-tempered. If a baby has a mole on its chin, it indicates that it will be successful in adult life.

If a child was born with a caul – part of the foetal membrane which occasionally clings to the new-born infant's head at the time of birth – then he possessed a powerful talisman, that should be retained throughout life. The caul was supposed to give its owner protection from drowning and many sailors paid high prices for them. Witches considered them valuable aids in working magic, so great care was taken not to lose them.

Children born as the clock strikes at particular hours are believed to possess supernatural powers. Those born at midnight have the doubtful privilege of seeing ghosts and hearing the supernatural Wild Hunt – the 'Gabriel' or 'Wish Hounds'. 'Chime Children' also have special powers. These are children who were born as the clock chimed the magical hours of 3, 6, 9 and 12, though in Somerset Chime Children are defined as those born between midnight on Friday and cock-crow on Saturday. Not only can they see spirits but they can also talk to fairies without being harmed. Furthermore, they are immune to ill-wishing; they have power over animals; and they are gifted with a knowledge of herbal lore and healing crafts.

It is also lucky to be the seventh child of a seventh child for they are gifted with wisdom and the power of healing. Many present-day healers who practise folk-medicine claim these unusual antecedents.

Unbaptised and vulnerable

Until a child was christened, our ancestors believed that its soul was in deadly danger from the evil forces which had sought to possess it since birth. Protective measures were essential during the days before the baptism. In some households, a piece of iron or a little salt was placed in the cot, while a Bible concealed beneath the baby was considered a powerful weapon against demons. If a bowl of primroses was set underneath the bed, it would act as a talisman against witches.

When babies died before baptism it was thought that they turned into butterflies, except in Devon where a more sinister belief held sway. There, they joined the phantom Yeth Hounds that hunt forever across Dartmoor. In northern England, people avoided the graves of stillborn or unbaptised children since to step over them might cause 'grave-merels', a feverish disease whose symptoms included uncontrolled trembling and difficulty in breathing. In the Welsh Marches and the south, however, such graves were considered lucky. To be interred in the same plot was a passport to paradise.

In many parts of Britain, friends and relatives of the parents still present newborn children with gifts of salt, eggs, bread, matches or silver coins – the combination of these items vary from county to county. In some parts of North Yorkshire, a packet containing an egg, a silver coin and a pinch of salt was pinned to the child's clothes, while in Somerset only a coin was given, though the child's lips might be touched with salt. It is supposed that the salt signifies health in mind and body, the egg signifies fertility and immortality, bread ensures all the necessities of life and matches symbolise the path of light leading to Heaven. However, both salt and fire have a much older significance as protective charms against the supernatural.

Purified and protected

Baptism was an old custom long before it symbolised initiation into the Christian Church. The ancient Egyptians, the Hebrews and the Greeks all employed ritual immersion as a means of spiritual purification. The Church, however, extended the idea to one of spiritual rebirth when the child was given the name by which it would be known. Pagan notions lingered on into the Middle Ages, when baptism was regarded as a form of magical protection for the infant's soul against the Devil's forces.

The water, blessed by the priest, was sacred, and shielded the child from evil. Sometimes a plate of salt was taken into the church for added protection. Even in the last decade, in the Roman Catholic ceremony, which included exorcism of the child and anointing with oil and spittle, salt was placed on the infant's lips in order to drive out Satan. Spittle symbolised the essential life fluids while oil was traditionally used in libation and propitiation.

A child is often baptised with the name of a well-loved or admired person, perhaps in the hope that he will take on some of that person's qualities. In some areas, however, particularly in Hertfordshire, it was considered unlucky to name a child after a deceased brother or sister, or even after a favourite animal. The child would certainly die, called away by the spirit of the dead.

Hazards of infancy

The first year of a child's life, particularly in previous ages when the rate of infant mortality was much higher, was fraught with anxiety for the parents. Seeking reassurance, they found hope or despair in superstitious beliefs as simple as that of a child crying on its first birthday, indicating that the infant would always be unhappy. Even to weigh a child before it was a year old was 'presuming the consequences'. It would grow up stunted or would die prematurely.

A child would become a thief if his fingernails were cut in the first 12 months – they should instead be bitten or broken off. The nails, like the milk teeth and locks of hair, had to be carefully destroyed, for fear that they should fall into the hands of witches and be used against the child.

Apart from herbal remedies, magical charms and spells to combat children's ailments were highly popular until well into the 18th century. In some parts of Yorkshire it was believed that teething troubles would be eased if the mother rubbed the inflamed gum with her gold wedding ring, while Suffolk children wore bead necklaces to relieve teething pains. Nowadays well-tried folk remedies such as these have largely vanished; they appear only as a second line of defence after the State Registered Nurse, the child psychologist and Dr Spock have all had their say.

SEEN BUT NOT HEARD

Custom and tradition played much stronger roles in the strict upbringing of children in earlier centuries than they do today. Adult standards were applied to children of all ages by parents who demanded that their offspring dressed and behaved in the manner of grown-ups, however constricting this might have been.

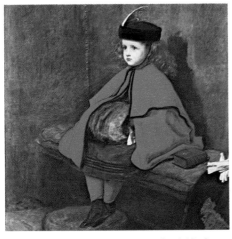 

THE TWO SERMONS *Millais' painting of a child's first and second sermons reflects the traditional Victorian attitude that children had to attend church on Sunday. Any play or jollity was threatened with a visitation by the Devil*

IN THEIR PARENTS' IMAGE *Hogarth's painting shows how the dress and manners of 18th-century children mirrored those of their parents. Obedience was a virtue and disobedience was controlled by the threat of a visit from a variety of supernatural figures. These included the Devil; Rawhead and Bloody Bones – a character who dined off young children; the barguest – a goblin dog; while Lancashire children were terrified by the evil Jenny Greenteeth*

Come out to play

Children are natural sticklers for tradition; when they play they enter a private world that has hardly changed for centuries

From the moment when a mother first sings a lullaby to her child, she gives oral tradition a new lease of life: for the words of her song have probably been sung to children for hundreds of years.

The best-known lullaby in England and America, 'Hush-a-bye baby, on the tree top', was first recorded in print *c.* 1765, and may have been popular long before. It is typical of many nursery rhymes in that while children have had no difficulty in accepting and repeating words which seem to have little point, adults have probed behind the words for a 'meaning'.

According to one theory, the author of 'Hush-a-bye baby' was a boy who sailed with the Pilgrim Fathers to America in 1620, and it can claim the distinction of having been the first English poem written on American soil. The words are said to have been inspired by a Red Indian custom of propping babies' cradles in the branches of trees. But a footnote to the 1765 version gave it an allegorical meaning. The lullaby, it said, 'may serve as a Warning to the Proud and Ambitious, who climb so high that they generally fall at last'.

The young traditionalists

More than 2000 years ago, the Athenian philosopher Plato warned that a child who was allowed to change the rules of a game might be tempted, later in life, to defy the rules of the State. He need hardly have worried. Children are such die-hard traditionalists that streets and playgrounds all over the world still echo to games of Whackem, Hide and Seek, Frog in the Middle, Blind Man's Buff and Tug o' War – games very similar to those played in the streets of ancient Athens.

Though a child nurtures tradition more carefully than any adult, children's games and customs do change gradually from generation to generation and from place to place. Kingy, for instance, is an immensely popular chasing game throughout Britain, in which one player throws a ball at the others, who join forces with him when they are hit. The first player with the ball is called He, Him, It, King, Man, On, Tag, Ticker or one of a host of other names, depending on where you live. In Scotland the game is known as King Ball; in parts of the Midlands as Hot Rice; in Lincolnshire, where the players are allowed to defend themselves with dustbin lids, as Dustbin. And there are many other local names, such as Buzz in Enfield and Croydon; Cheesy in Exmouth; Peasy in Cleethorpes; and Fisty in Orkney.

Games also change for practical reasons. Few of the games traditionally played with caps survive, because few schoolboys now wear caps. The game of Conkers (also known as Cheggies, Hongkongs, Obbley-onkers and Cobs), played with horse chestnuts, has preoccupied schoolboy minds every autumn since the 19th century, when it replaced a similar game played with cobnuts. The horse chestnut tree was introduced into England in the 17th century, and by the 19th century conkers were much easier to find than cobnuts, though sadly for children not so palatable.

Games with hidden meanings

Without knowing it, children preserve in their games many ancient and now largely forgotten folk-beliefs and customs. Since the 16th century, if not before, children have played a chasing game called Touch Iron, in which any player holding on to something made of iron is invulnerable and cannot be caught.

This is almost certainly a relic of the belief that cold iron terrifies fairies and malevolent spirits. According to one theory, this belief in turn relates to a dim folk memory of the Celtic invasions of Britain. Armed and armoured with iron, the Celts overcame the stone-wielding inhabitants with such ease that the metal itself was credited with magical properties.

Many folklorists have suggested that chasing games grew out of fear of the supernatural. In parts of Britain, the chaser is known as Horney, and it may be that he was once thought of as an evil spirit, or even the Devil himself. In some games, the chaser is actually called the Devil.

Even the seemingly innocuous name 'He', used mainly in London and the south of England, may have a hidden meaning. A century ago, in Sussex and probably elsewhere, the Devil was never referred to by his proper name, but was known instead as 'He'.

Though these theories may be true of a few games, there is little reason to suppose that they are true of chasing games in general; and certainly, the children's pleasure lies in nothing more than the excitement of the chase. The feeling that there is something supernaturally sinister or contagious about the chaser's touch survives only in games such as The Dreaded Lurgi, whose roots go no deeper than an edition of the BBC radio comedy, The Goon Show, broadcast in 1954.

Sacrificial victims and scapegoats

The nursery rhyme 'London Bridge is falling down', and the game that goes with it, are almost certainly survivals of pagan ritual sacrifice. The game occurs all over the world, and though the name by which it is known differs from place to place, the form it takes hardly varies.

Two children lift their arms and link them to form a bridge. The rest of the players hang on to one another to make a line, then rush under the arch chanting the song, terrified that at any moment the bridge will fall on them. Eventually it does fall, and the captured child becomes the 'watchman' who will protect the bridge against all the forces which may destroy it.

All over the world, there are legends about children being sacrificed so that their spirits may guard bridges – apparently, river spirits hate bridges, and can sabotage attempts to build them. As recently as 1843, a rumour ran through Halle in Germany that a child would have to be sacrificed to guarantee the safety of a new bridge being built over the River Saale. Again, according to tradition, children were sacrificed on the stones of the first London Bridge to protect it from the angry spirit of the Thames.

An intriguing theory, based more on guesswork than evidence, links the games children play with tops and whips to the pagan notion of a scapegoat. It was an old English custom that each parish should keep a top, and when the villagers whipped it they may have been re-enacting an ancient ritual which was meant originally to expel hardship and evil from the community. Parish tops have long since disappeared – they had gone by the late 18th century, if not before – but here again children may be the last custodians of beliefs more significant than they know.

Theories about the thunderspell are less speculative. There can be little doubt that this toy is a relic of the magical and religious ideas of primitive man. The thunderspell (also known as a hummer, buzzer, roarer, bummer and, in Scotland, as a thunderbolt) consists of a wooden device on a string, which buzzes as you swing it. Among primitive tribes in many parts of the world, it is still believed to be a powerful agent of magic: it is used to bring rain, to summon spirits or to frighten them away, to conjure up thunder and lightning and to control fertility in cattle.

Starting a game

To an adult, many children's games may seem boringly repetitive; to a child, repetition may be their most magical ingredient. Children love ritual as much as competition, and the more popular any game becomes, the more ritual is likely to become attached to it.

Often, just starting a game involves so much ritual that it becomes a game in itself. To start a chasing game, for instance, children have built up

RING-A-RING O' ROSES

The innocent game of 'Ring-a-ring o' roses', shown in this Kate Greenaway illustration, is said to be a macabre parody on the horrors of the plague. A ring of rose-coloured spots was one of the first symptoms of plague; *popular belief prescribed posies of herbs as protection against the disease; sneezing was a sure sign that you were about to die of it; and the last line, 'We all fall down', omits only one word . . . 'dead'*

elaborate 'counting out' systems to decide who should be He. Simple methods are generally shunned, though occasionally children just shout special words or phrases (such as, 'I bags not on it!' or 'Me fains first!') and the last to shout becomes the first to chase.

Counting out is fair, to a child's mind at least, because it brings in the element of blind chance. One child recites a rhyme or chant, pointing at the others one by one to the rhythm of the words. When the rhyme ends, the child being pointed at drops out (or, very occasionally, becomes the chaser), and the count begins again. The last player left is He.

The most popular counting rhyme in England and America is 'Eenie, meenie, miney, mo . . .', and in its present form it has been part of every child's repertoire of rhyme for at least the last 80 years. But the apparently nonsensical words at the beginning

and end of it, and strange words in other children's rhymes (such as 'Hickory-dickory, dock . . .'), may be of much greater antiquity than the reign of Queen Victoria.

Like the shepherds' tallies which they so closely resemble, these words may preserve a memory of Celtic counting systems in use long before the Romans invaded these islands. Victorian antiquarians even suggested that some children's counting-out rhymes were the last remnants of counting systems used by the Druids for selecting human sacrifices.

The laws of the playground
Ritual, superstition and a private language have been part of the schoolchild's world for centuries. In the playground, language has acquired all the sanctity of law, and the words children use to seal

---

THE BEST KNOWN VERSES IN THE WORLD

Many of the oldest nursery rhymes were never intended for the nursery. Some of them are fragments of ancient ballads or folk songs, others are remnants of forgotten rituals and customs. They may hark back to the street cries of medieval salesmen, to the marching songs of soldiers and rebels, or to drinking songs and barrack-room jokes. Many are thinly disguised political lampoons. They found their way into the nursery largely because in the 17th and 18th centuries children were treated as miniature adults, and their parents had no objection to letting them hear and repeat adult jokes and songs, though these were probably not understood.

Hark! hark! the dogs bark,
The beggars are coming to town;
Some in rags and some in tags,
And some in silken gowns.
Some gave them white bread,
And some gave them brown,
And some gave them a good horse-whip,
And sent them out of the town.

Elsie Marley has grown so fine,
She won't get up to serve the swine;
But lies in bed till eight or nine,
And surely she does take her time.

Jack and Jill
Went up the hill,
To fetch a pail of water;
Jack fell down
And broke his crown,
And Jill came tumbling after.

Hark, hark, the dogs do bark
Perhaps this rhyme is a last memory of the bands of wandering beggars who roamed Tudor England, terrifying lonely country-dwellers on their way. Or it may be, as another tradition suggests, that 'beggar' was slang for a Dutchman, and that the beggars in the rhyme were the followers of William of Orange, who flocked to England in the late 17th century after the Bloodless Revolution.

Little Miss Muffet
One theory suggests that the original Miss Muffet was Patience, daughter of a 16th-century entomologist, Dr Thomas Muffet. He described himself as a man 'whose admiration for spiders has never been surpassed', and he was the author of a book of verse called *The Silkwormes and Their Flies*. But the earliest mention of the rhyme dates only from 1805.

Elsie Marley
A much-loved 18th-century ale-wife called Alice Marley, proprietress of The Swan at Picktree in Durham, was the original lethargic Elsie. But according to her grandson, Alice was not lazy at all. The nursery rhyme is only the first verse of a song written while Alice was still alive, which attested to her considerable energy as a publican and drinker.

Little Jack Horner
Legend claims that the original Jack Horner was steward to the last abbot of Glastonbury, Richard Whiting. To save his abbey from being dissolved, Abbot Whiting is said to have sent Henry VIII a Christmas pie containing the title deeds to 12 manors. Jack Horner had the job of delivering it, and on the way he pulled out and stole his 'plum' – the deeds to Mells Manor in Somerset.

Jack and Jill
The 19th-century folklorist Sabine Baring-Gould traced this rhyme back to an ancient Scandinavian myth. Long ago, two children called Hjuki and Bil were drawing water from a well, when Mani, the moon, kidnapped them and carried them off to heaven. To this day, they can be seen on the face of a full moon, carrying their bucket on a pole between them. As they climb the hill, the moon waxes; as they descend, it wanes.

Goosey, goosey, gander
Cromwell's soldiers marched in a goose-step, and this rhyme may describe their long and intensive hunt for Royalist fugitives after the Civil War. Any suspect 'who would not say his prayers' was thrown into prison or, as the rhyme would have it, was 'taken by the left leg and thrown down the stairs'.

their agreements are just as binding to them as written contracts are to adults.

No word is more valuable to a child than his truce word, for by shouting it and making a sign with his hands he can gain instant respite from being chased. Some of these words are very ancient.

The term 'barley', widely used in Wales, north-west England, the Border country and east Scotland, dates from the 14th century at least, and was originally used by knights when offering their jousting partners a moment's rest. 'Fains' or 'fain-ites', the usual truce words in southern England, are survivals of the medieval English expression 'fain I', meaning 'I decline'.

Children exploit their gift for ritual, and draw on a rich supply of superstitions, to add authority to what they say. They usually back up their truce words with ritual gestures, such as crossing their fingers, raising their right hands, holding up three fingers or licking and holding up their thumbs. And if they want to prove that what they are saying is true, they have a wide variety of oaths and pledges to choose from.

'God's honour!' is the most common playground oath, and as soon as the child has taken it, he licks his forefinger and makes a sign of the cross on his throat. But there are many others, including oaths on the Bible, on the child's mother and on his own heart or honour.

The penalty for perjury, as every child knows, is violent death. This is not just make-believe. To a child, the words 'Cross my heart and hope to die, Drop down dead if I tell a lie' may be as awful as they sound. For 'true' stories about people who have died violently after defying an oath have coloured the folklore of children for centuries.

The old woman who lived in a shoe

Many women with large families have been identified as the old woman 'who had so many children she didn't know what to do', including George II's wife Caroline, who had eight children, and Elizabeth Vergoose of Boston, who had 16. In addition, the shoe has long been a symbol of female sexuality, and throwing a shoe after a bride leaving for her honeymoon is an ancient means of wishing fertility upon the marriage.

Mary, Mary quite contrary

The beautiful and tragic Mary, Queen of Scots is claimed as the heroine of this rhyme. The cockleshells are supposed to have been ornaments on a dress given to her by her first husband, the Dauphin of France; and the pretty maids mentioned in some versions of the rhyme were her ladies-in-waiting, the famous Four Marys.

Another interpretation says that it is 'a word-picture of Our Lady's convent' – an allegorical representation of a religious and devout community of women dedicated to the service of the Church. The bells are holy bells, the cockleshells are badges worn by pilgrims, and the pretty maids are nuns.

Little Boy Blue

Cardinal Wolsey, Lord Chancellor under Henry VIII, is sometimes linked with Little Boy Blue. He was the son of a prosperous Ipswich butcher and grazier, and would certainly have spent part of his childhood tending his father's livestock.

Tom, Tom, the piper's son

The pig Tom steals and eats was not, as many modern illustrations suggest, a real pig, but a pig-shaped sweetmeat sold by street hawkers called pig pye men.

Such hawkers were common in the 18th century, and some children are still taught their street cry, which began: 'A long tail'd Pig, or a short tail'd Pig, or a Pig without any tail; a Boar Pig, or a Sow Pig, or a Pig with a curly tail.'

Georgie Porgie

Tradition claims that Charles II was the model for Georgie Porgie, though there is no evidence that the rhyme was known before the 19th century. Other theories suggest George I, who lived openly with his mistress after divorcing his wife in 1694; and George Villiers, 2nd Duke of Buckingham, who was one of Charles II's most debauched courtiers.

Mary, Mary, quite contrary,
How does your garden grow?
With silver bells, and cockle shells,
And cowslips all of a row.

Georgie Peorgie, pudding and pie,
Kissed the girls and made them cry;
When the girls begin to play,
Georgie Peorgie runs away.

RIDDLE ME, RIDDLE ME REE

The art of riddling has survived only in the nursery and the playground, although it was a very popular amusement for adults until about the 17th century. One of the first books printed in England was a collection of riddles called *Demandes Joyous*: it was printed in 1511 by Caxton's apprentice Wynkyn de Worde. Some of the riddles it contained are still asked by schoolchildren today, such as:
How deep is the ocean?
Answer: A stone's throw.

In Elizabethan England, rhyming riddles were very popular; they usually described some everyday object in a deliberately obscure way, as in:
Little Nancy Etticoat,
With a white petticoat,
And a red nose;
She has no feet or hands,
The longer she stands,
The shorter she grows.
Answer: A lighted candle.

The skilful playground riddler switches quickly from one type of riddle to another. He may begin with a complicated rhyming riddle:
Four stiff standers,
Four dilly-danders,
Two lookers, two crookers and a long wig-wag.
Answer: A cow. And then he changes to a pun:
What is black and white, but re(a)d all over.
Answer: A newspaper.
At any moment he may switch to a true riddle:
A house full, a hole full
You cannot gather a bowl-ful.
Answer: Mist or smoke.

'He loves me, he loves me not . . .'

Superstitious lovers once hopefully used magic and ritual to guide Cupid's arrows to their target

Love and marriage, more than any other aspects of our lives, are still governed by a wealth of superstitions. Though few people these days seriously try to solve by divination the problem of who they will marry, many lovers still seek lucky omens and observe ancient rituals. The wedding ceremony itself has many old traditions which are still kept up, even when those taking part are unaware of their ancient significance.

The rituals and charms used in love have traditionally been the domain of young women whose concern was motivated by the seclusion in which they were forced to live. In many cases, a young girl had little choice in the selection of her future husband. Divination provided a way in which she could dream that things were different. Furthermore, in years gone by, marriage was the only future open to most girls. The fear of being 'left on

How shall I pass the lagging time untill
That day, when wedlock shall our vows fulfil?
How but in dwelling upon all you've said
Each kind attention, and each promise made?

How but in chiding every hour's delay
Between the present and that wished for day?
No otherwise . . . my chosen and my friend
In pledge of which this Valentine I send.

LUCKY DAY FOR LOVERS

As well as sending cards on St Valentine's Day, young lovers also played divination games. Young people, for instance, wrote the names of their favourites on slips of paper, sealed them in moist clay, and dropped the clay balls into a bowl of water. The named paper slip that floated to the surface first would be their future sweetheart. Once a Valentine was selected by a girl, it was his duty to give her a lover's gift

the shelf' hung over rich and poor girls alike, and spinsters searched assiduously for hopeful omens.

Who will I marry?

A number of superstitions apply to Hallowe'en (October 31), a particularly magical time, when a young girl hoped to see the candlelit reflection of her future husband in the mirror. It was also possible then to discover his initial by throwing a complete apple peel over her shoulder – the letter formed would be the initial of her true love.

A popular Hallowe'en game was to line a hot grate with hazel nuts, giving each the name of a prospective husband, and reciting 'If you love me pop and fly; if you hate me, burn and die'. In another variation, the nuts which cracked denoted the fickle suitors.

To guarantee a dream of her future love on Hallowe'en, a young girl could place her shoes in the form of a 'T', a potent talisman representing the hammer of the Scandinavian god Thor. She then said, 'Hoping this night my true love to see, I place my shoes in the form of a T'.

St Agnes's Eve (January 20) was also a significant night for dreams and visions. St Agnes is the patron saint of virgins – she herself refused to marry a man not of her choice and was put to death for her refusal. One practice on this night was to make a Dumb Cake. The cake was prepared by the girl in silence and in fasting, and then placed on the coals to bake; it was believed that at midnight the apparition of her future husband would turn the cake for her.

Hoping for a similar vision on St Thomas's Eve (December 20), an unmarried girl would peel a large onion at bedtime, stick nine pins in it, and then chant, 'Good St Thomas, do me right; Send me my true love this night'.

It is doubtful if traditions like these would have lasted so long had it not been for daring young men who used to creep into the house and substitute themselves for the expected vision.

Despite female emancipation, many young girls remain obstinately attached to the romantic old rites. Ancient chants, for example, accompany the counting of fruit stones around one's plate. 'Tinker, tailor, soldier, sailor, rich man, poor man, beggar-man, thief' is a popular means of divining the profession of a future husband, while 'This year, next year, sometime, never' determines the wedding date, when the girl will be dressed in 'Silk, satin, muslin, rags'.

Counting-out games play a large part in determining the odds of romantic chance. One method still used by schoolgirls is to write down their own names and those of their sweethearts, crossing out the letters they have in common and ticking off the remainder to the spell, 'Love, marry, hate, adore'.

Sentimental girls were tireless in their search for omens. In Devon, it was the custom for a girl to tap on the henhouse door at night. If the hens cackled, she would never marry; but if the cock crowed she would marry before the end of the year. A widespread Christmas tradition was for the would-be bride to visit the wood-pile after dark, bringing back an armful of logs to the fireside. They could not be counted until the next morning, when an even number of logs revealed that she would marry in the following year; an odd number meant she would have a longer wait.

Belief in the potency of the even number was common in West Country tradition. A girl who found an ash leaf with an even number of segments would chant, 'This even-ash I hold in my hand – the first I meet is my true man'. She would then ask the name of the first man she met; this would be the same as her future husband's. A two or four leaf clover in the right shoe worked similar magic. The first man encountered would be her future husband, or would bear the same name.

Helping love along

In medieval Britain, love philtres were in great demand; some were for self-dosing, while others had to be surreptitiously administered to the potential lover. Love philtres often had a so-called 'aphrodisiac' base. As well as herbs and exotic items like powdered rhinoceros horn, few new foods could be introduced without being credited with lustful properties. Elizabethan rarities like potatoes and tomatoes were not immune – nor was hot chocolate in the 17th century. In our own day, oysters, watercress and curry are all said to provoke deep passions. In fact, they are no more efficacious than the potato.

In rural districts, particularly in winter, privacy was rare. This gave rise to the custom of 'bundling' – in which the courting couple went to bed together wrapped in blankets, or with a bolster between them. These precautions, however, were not always effective, and shot-gun marriages were frequent. In some parts of Wales, 'bundling' continued until well into the 1940's.

The charmed circle

The unbroken circle of the ring has influenced spells, legends and rituals since the days of the Pharaohs. The ring has no beginning and no end, and symbolises perfect unity for lovers.

At one time, the wearing of rings had more significance than it has now. Unwillingness to marry could be indicated by putting a ring on the little finger of the left hand, while wearing one on the index finger showed that one was searching for a partner. The third finger on a woman's left hand has always been reserved for an engagement or wedding ring – any other is considered unlucky. This tradition arose out of the erroneous belief that an artery runs directly to this finger from the heart.

Most women still believe that to wear a wedding ring before marriage brings such bad luck that they will never be married themselves. A wedding ring should never be removed or lent to anyone, because if it should be lost the marriage will experience a similar fate. A wedding ring should also be new: 'A twice-used ring is a fatal ring.'

Wedding rings are usually made of gold which has supposed magical and curative powers. Even today in some country districts, wedding rings are rubbed on warts and styes to charm them away. They can also be used in divination by those bold enough to take them off. For instance, a ring suspended by a hair will at once begin to spin. If it spins slowly, then you may have a second marriage; if it rotates quickly, then you will marry only once.

Engagement rings are not so sacred and therefore possess less magic than wedding rings. Long ago, betrothal rings were also made of gold or silver, and fashioned in the shape of a true-lovers' knot. Most modern engagement rings, however, contain gems – often the birthstone associated with the wearer's sign of the Zodiac. Some gems are associated with bad luck – especially opals and emeralds – though this does not apply when they are the birthstones of the girls concerned.

Wedding fantasia

For most people, weddings are a magical time when even the least superstitious will watch for portents of future happiness. As a result, the wedding preparations, ceremony and feast have all become loaded with ritual practices to ward off evil and bless the marriage with fortune and fertility.

The choice of date is important – May is traditionally unlucky for weddings because in ancient Rome, this was a month for remembering the dead, and an ill-omened time for lovers. In contrast to this, there exists the Christian belief that you should not marry in Lent. Defying augury, many modern couples marry between Easter and late May, a practice much encouraged by tax rebates. The tradition that the brides' parents should pay for the wedding dates from two or three centuries ago, when wealthy families would pay an eligible bachelor to take an unmarried daughter off their hands in exchange for a large dowry. Sometimes, the groom would not wait to be asked, and would take the girl from her parents by force. His abettor in this act is represented at modern weddings by the best man, while the bridesmaids play symbolic roles as protectors of the bride.

Every bride regards her wedding dress as the most hallowed garment she will ever possess. At most formal weddings brides still get married in virginal white – many other colours are considered unlucky. Green, for example, is the fairies' colour and the wearer may fall into the power of the little people. Yellow, purple and orange are also to be avoided, though blue and red are safe.

The bride's veil is of great importance; it once had the double function of protecting the bride from the evil eye, and at the same time served to keep her in seclusion, in case her psychic powers at this time bewitched other people.

A bride will also ensure that her wedding outfit

THE LANGUAGE OF FLOWERS

Meanings have been invested in particular flowers since ancient times, though by the 18th century, their simple code had become a well-developed language for lovers. Flowered Victorian Valentine cards spoke volumes to initiates of 'the language of flowers'.

Almond blossom Symbol of sweetness and delicacy; its message is hope

Anemone Like earth's pleasures, the flower swiftly fades in the first chill wind; it means withered hopes

Lily Often regarded as an unlucky flower; (white) purity; (yellow) falsehood or gaiety

Periwinkle Flower of sorrow, that crowned criminals on their way to execution; (blue) early friendship; (white) pleasures of memory

Poppy A petal in the palm hit with the fist should make a snapping sound if your love is faithful; (red) consolation; (scarlet) fantastic extravagance

Rose Dedicated to love; the normal meaning is love; (red rosebud) pure and lovely; (yellow) jealousy

Snowdrop Transformed from a snowflake by an angel to comfort Adam and Eve after their expulsion from Eden; indicates hope or consolation

Sunflower Emblem of the sun; it means haughtiness

Tulip Symbolises the heart burning like a flame; (red) declaration of love; (yellow) hopeless love

Aster (michaelmas daisy). It symbolises afterthought; was once laid on the graves of war dead in France

Bachelor's button (cornflower). While its colour remained fresh, then so would love: if it faded so would romance; its message is delicacy or celibacy

Buttercup The flower of childhood; memories of childhood is one meaning, another is ingratitude

Carnation Ancient tradition suggests the flower sprang from the graves of lovers, and once it meant 'alas, for my poor heart'. More recently, however, it has become a Christian symbol of betrothal, marriage and eternal love

Columbine The symbol of deserted lovers; it also signifies folly

Chrysanthemum (red) I love; (yellow) slighted love; (white) truth

Daffodil Associated with death in Greek legend; regard or deceitful hopes

Forget-me-not Its small blue flower indicated true love

Hyacinth Used for bridal wreaths in ancient Greece; sport, game or play

includes 'something old, something new; something borrowed, something blue'. 'Old' maintains her link with the past; 'new' symbolises the future; 'borrowed' gives her a link with the present; and 'blue' symbolises her purity.

The 'true-lovers' knot' is a favourite motif for wedding cakes and dresses. These colourful bunches of ribbons representing the bonds of marriage, and the ties of love and affection, have been a part of weddings since Saxon times. In the 17th century, brides wore the knots lightly stitched to their dresses, so that young men at the wedding could snatch them off as 'bride favours'. The flower buttonholes that men still wear at weddings are a relic of these knots.

Even a modern bride will observe the taboos about wearing her dress before the ceremony. The groom must not see her in it until she enters the church. Nor must she wear the complete outfit before the wedding day. Certainly the veil should not be tried on at the same time as the dress; many brides put it on for the first time as they leave for church. Some brides even believe that the sewing of the dress should not be finished until the day itself, and leave a few stitches to be completed on the wedding morning.

It is a lucky omen if the bride should see a chimney sweep on her way to church. Sometimes a sweep is paid to attend the ceremony and kiss the bride – a relic of the old idea that soot and ashes are symbols of fertility.

After the ceremony, the couple are showered with confetti or rice as they leave the church. Traditionally, the guests threw corn to bless the marriage with fertility.

One old custom which has not entirely died out was for the bride and sometimes the groom to negotiate some obstacle as they left the church – guests would impede them with ropes of flowers, for example, or with sticks that had to be jumped over. Sometimes a stone was used – known in the North as a 'petting' stone – over which the bride had to jump or be lifted. The belief was that she left all her bad moods behind her, and that the jump symbolised her leap into a new life.

After negotiating these hazards, the bride is faced with the wedding feast. The most important item is the wedding cake, whose richness symbolises fertility, just as it has done since Roman times. Today, the first slice is cut by the bride to ensure a fruitful marriage, though once the cake was literally broken over the bride's head; guests then scrambled for fragments, which would bring good luck. Now the blessings are spread by posting slices of the cake to absent friends. If they are unmarried, they can follow the old custom of sleeping with the slice under their pillows; this brings dreams of future marriage partners.

The bride is still carried over the threshold of the new home by her husband – a custom that dates from pagan times when it was believed necessary to do this in order to avoid the evil spirits that gathered outside every threshold.

Until Victorian times, it was common practice for the bride and groom to be publicly assisted to bed, the bride by her bridesmaids and the groom by the groomsmen. The occasion developed into a huge frolic with much hilarity and ribaldry. Bridesmaids and groomsmen sat on either side of the bed and threw the newlyweds' stockings over their shoulders; if a girl hit the groom with a stocking or a man the bride, this was a sign that he or she would soon be married. From this derives the modern custom of the bride throwing her bouquet – the bridesmaid who catches it is soon to be married.

Man and wife

Judging by sayings which have come down the ages such as 'Wedlock's a padlock', the traditional view of marriage is a gloomy one. The hen is a symbol long associated with maternal care but the cock is supposed to rule the roost. To be henpecked, therefore, is to reverse these traditional roles; men, however, had several cruel methods of defence against sharp and gossiping tongues. A scold or shrew in the 17th and 18th centuries might find herself tied to the ducking stool and dipped in the local pond. A worse fate was the brank – an iron muzzle, sometimes with a spiked tongue-piece, which was locked over the woman's head until she promised to reform.

A custom which survived into this century in some rural areas was the making of 'Rough Music', which was designed to punish wife-beaters as well as shrewish or adulterous wives. The men of the district would go to the offender's home and beat on gongs, pans and tin sheets for several nights in succession. This public disgrace frequently forced the offender to leave the village.

A man who became completely disenchanted with his marriage sometimes sold his wife – a rare practice that dated from Saxon times when a husband bought his wife from her father. If the goods did not come up to his expectations, the husband felt he had a perfect right to sell them even though there was no legal justification. This practice flourished in some country districts – the last recorded sale took place as late as 1928.

If a wife was unfaithful, her husband was ridiculed for it. A favourite gibe directed at a wronged husband was 'cuckold' – derived from cuckoo, the bird that lays its eggs in another's nest.

House and home

From doorstep to chimney, strange defences were required to ensure that an Englishman's home really was his castle

To barge into a house without invitation is one of the most alarming discourtesies that can be offered to its occupants. Knocking before entering seems no more than an elementary politeness, yet, like so many of our basic courtesies, the practice is deeply rooted in human needs and fears. In most societies the privacy of the house has always been sacrosanct and, having entered, the visitor is expected to conform to the customs and taboos of the home, many of which have little application in the world outside.

In this sense, the threshold is the dividing line between two worlds, a frontier to be protected against the entry of evil influences. Horseshoes can still be seen nailed to the lintels and doors of older houses all over Britain; cold iron was regarded as a powerful defence against fairies, witches and demons, while the crescent shape of the horseshoe, symbol of the moon-goddess and of fertility, bestowed good fortune on the household. Usually, the horseshoe is fixed with its points uppermost so that its 'luck will not run out'; in earlier times, however, it was attached open end downwards as a charm against witchcraft. For this purpose, horseshoes are particularly effective if they are discovered by accident, or if they come from the near hind leg of a grey mare.

Throwing an old shoe – an ancient symbol of good luck – across the threshold when a member of the household leaves home is to wish them success; but if they should forget something and return immediately, disaster will follow unless they sit down before setting out on their journey again.

Spirits by the hearth

Despite the onslaught of television, the hearth is still the focal point of family life, the area of the house which, according to the Romans, was the dwelling place of the domestic gods. In Britain, the fireplace or the inglenook was thought to be the home of the brownies and other fairies who brought good luck to the household; they were even known to help with the chores. It was wise to avoid offending them, however, and in Derbyshire, housewives used to clean the hearth before going to bed. In the Western Isles, part of the fire would be left burning to keep the fairies warm after the household had retired for the night.

When the family moves to a new home, it is still traditional in some parts of Britain to take embers from the old fireplace and burn them in the new one. This is intended to signify that family ties will remain unbroken; the familiar housewarming party is a development of this old custom.

When chimneys smoked or the fire refused to catch, many housewives blamed the occurrence on witches or demons. Cold iron and a cross were the usual antidotes and, even today, many people are convinced that an iron poker laid across the grate will cure a troublesome fire. Traditionally minded families in the West Country will still use the poker to draw a cross on the hearth stone of a new house before lighting the first fire.

Another means of preventing witches from entering the house was to stud a sheep's or bullock's heart with pins and nails and place it up the chimney. The heart was a powerful charm against the forces of evil, and the practice may have stemmed from far-off memories of ritual sacrifice.

Portents in the fire

Firegazing was one of the simplest and most popular methods of foretelling the future. Tired people, gathered about the hearth, would peer into the glowing caverns of the fire and conjure omens from haphazard movements of coals and burning soot.

A flake of soot hanging on the grate is still said to foretell the arrival of a stranger; while coals burning in a heap with a hollow in the centre, or divided into two parts, signifies a parting. Escaping gas spluttering from a piece of coal means a quarrel in the offing,

---

NATURAL PROTECTION

People have always believed that it is lucky to have certain animals, birds and plants about the house, while others are considered malevolent, and must be carefully watched for omens of impending disaster. In the Midlands it used to be thought that if a house was suddenly overrun by mice, then the head of the house would not have long to live, while to have a mouse scurry over one's foot is a sure sign of death. If cats claw at cushions or chairs, they are thought to be raising a storm, and if a dog whines for no reason, it is a warning of misfortune.

INSURANCE AGAINST FIRE *Swallows have nested under eaves for a very long time, as this 13th-century manuscript confirms. The birds are said to protect houses from fire, lightning and storms*

PLANTS WITH POWER *Hawthorn (left) belonged to the woodland god, and it was unlucky to bring it into the house before May Day. Rowan (right) in the garden protected the house from witches, fairies and ill-wishing*

but this can be prevented by vigorously poking the coals in the fire.

In Dorset, a stranger is expected if a smouldering fire bursts suddenly into flame, while in Lincolnshire people believe that a death is imminent if a neglected fire burns for a long time. A live coal falling from the grate is the sign of a wedding in many parts of the country; a tall smoking flame indicates bad news; while to spit on the hearth stone brings seven years' bad luck.

Cinders jumping from the fire can carry many meanings. Generally, an oval-shaped cinder is regarded as the sign of a birth; an oblong cinder spells good luck and prosperity. East Anglian people sometimes spit on cinders. If they crackle, it means a full purse in the near future – if not, it means a shroud.

Poking the fire when visiting a new house in Yorkshire will bring good luck to the family; a more usual superstition, however, is that a visitor should not be allowed to poke the fire unless he has been known for more than seven years. To permit him to do so brings misfortune.

Kitchen magic

Food and its preparation were surrounded by so many taboos that it seems remarkable that some of our rural forbears ever got a hot meal at all.

Many housewives still believe that food will spoil if it is stirred 'widdershins' – that is, in the opposite direction to that followed by the sun. Perhaps this arose from the belief that 'widdershins' was the direction of the witches' circular dance.

Everyone knows that a watched pot never boils, and in Dorset it is common knowledge that a slow-boiling kettle is bewitched and may contain a toad.

Throwing egg-shells into the fire may stop hens from laying, or raise a storm at sea; while anyone who burns bread is said to be feeding the Devil. To sharpen a knife after sunset or supper incurs misfortune; even worse, it may bring thieves or murderers to the house.

The usual method of ensuring that bread would rise was to cut a cross in the top to 'let the Devil out'. Yorkshire housewives used to believe that bread would not rise if there was a corpse in the vicinity; and if both ends were cut off the loaf, the Devil would fly over the house.

Since salt had the seemingly miraculous power of preserving food through winter, many superstitions governed its use. Most of these were thinly disguised warnings against waste; to spill salt was to anger Providence. This may also have stemmed from a legend about Judas who was said to have overturned a salt-cellar at the Last Supper.

Spilling salt is still an omen of bad luck, though the evil may be countered by throwing a pinch over the left shoulder. To do so is to throw dust into the eyes of the Devil who always sits on the left shoulder; it must never be thrown over the right for this is where the guardian angel sits.

Table manners

Even if the taboos of preparing the meal were safely circumvented, there remained an equal number of hazards in eating it. Crossed knives

THE DILEMMA OF THE THIRTEENTH GUEST

Consternation is evident in the faces of these diners of 1851 as they realise that the party consists of 13 people. This, the worst of omens, is said to foretell the impending death of one of the group, a superstition that is generally associated with the Last Supper, at which 13 were also present. In fact, the superstition is older than Christianity, *and was shared by many peoples. In Norse mythology, 12 gods were feasting when Loki, the spirit of strife, appeared and provoked a quarrel which ended in the death of Baldur, the favourite of the gods. Another reason why the number was feared was that a witches' coven traditionally had 13 members*

signify a quarrel unless a second person uncrosses them, while to leave a white tablecloth on the table overnight means that the household will shortly have need of a shroud. Dropped cutlery announces the arrival of unexpected visitors; a knife for a man, a fork for a woman and a spoon for a fool. East Anglian people say that a pleasant surprise is expected if a spoon falls with the bowl uppermost, and a disappointment if the bowl is down.

There were many curious warnings about food. While intestinal worms might be contracted from raw bacon, especially if it had not been properly cured, madness from eating the marrow of pork bone seems unlikely. Nor is it known how many deaths have resulted from dining off mushrooms and almond icing, though according to legend, they are a fatal combination. Double-yolked eggs are considered ominous in Somerset; they foretell a hurried wedding due to pregnancy.

When beer was brewed at home, a cross would be made on the fermenting mash to ensure that it would be kept free from witches; and iron bars were laid across beer barrels to prevent demons from souring the contents. Even the innocent ritual of afternoon tea carried its own lore. Women hoped, or feared, they would become pregnant if they poured tea after someone else had already poured from the pot, while if milk were added before the sugar, a broken romance was imminent. Two teaspoons accidentally placed in the same cup, however, betokened a wedding in the near future.

The daily round
Though labour-saving devices have swept away many of the ancient customs and superstitions connected with housework, they have not yet been entirely obliterated from the memories of older countrywomen. Yorkshire wives firmly held that 'a sloppy washer will have a drunken husband', and thought, too, that if their apron strings became untied, someone they loved was thinking of them.

It was believed that two women could not wash in the same bowl without arguing, but if one remembers to spit in the water, the quarrel will not develop. Neither could they dry their hands on the same towel, for fear they should 'go begging together'. Leicestershire girls who fold linen or carpets will be married within the year, but to do so in most other parts of the country means that the wedding will be put off for a year at least.

Particular care had to be taken during spring-cleaning because 'good luck and money were swept away' if dust was brushed straight out of the house through the door, instead of being collected inside.

Apart from a vague belief that electricity leaks from an empty lamp socket, modern lighting has produced few fables to rival those about candles and lamps. Almost every important event could be foretold by a candle's flame: if it guttered, or if a spot of soot appeared on the wick, there would be a death in the household. A piece of tallow curling away from the flame was called a 'winding sheet' and betokened the same thing, while if anyone so far forgot themselves as to light a candle from the fire, they would be very poor.

A household accident which still makes most people uneasy is the breaking of a mirror. Said to herald seven years' bad luck, or even death, the superstition is thought to stem from an ancient belief that the image in the mirror was actually a person's soul: to break the mirror was to lose one's soul. This may have something to do with the reason why some people object to being photographed; subconsciously, perhaps, they feel that the camera is stealing their personality.

THE LORE OF LIVING

This dolls' house, now in the Bethnal Green Museum, London, reflects a late-Victorian middle-class home in miniature. By the 1890's, the harsh glare of gaslight would have lessened the force of many of the old domestic superstitions and, certainly, the head of the household would have been robustly sceptical about them. Nevertheless, the servants would have been very careful about spilling salt or breaking mirrors; and when the candles were lit for dinner, even the family might have felt uneasy if they noticed a diamond-shaped crease in the tablecloth, if the molten wax had run down any of the candles in the pattern called a shroud, or if two knives on the table had been crossed

THE THRESHOLD *Cold iron, holed stones and hoops of rowan once protected the door against evil spirits. The grotesque masks seen on some old door-knockers were intended to serve the same purpose*

THE KITCHEN *When cutting bread, never turn the loaf upside-down, or the bread-winner will be ill. If a girl finds nine perfect peas in a pod, she should place them above the door. The first man to enter will be her future husband*

THE STAIRS *To pass another person on the stairs is unlucky; but to stumble when ascending foretells a wedding*

DINING-ROOM *Sneezing before breakfast is said to predict the arrival of a gift; bad luck is caused by drinking from a jug; and it is an omen of death to eat from a plate which rests on another plate. Three candles burning on the table foretell a wedding; and a visitor who pushes his chair under the table after a meal will never return to the house*

LIVING-ROOM *The fire will go out if wood from the cursed elder tree is put on the fire, or a clock faced towards the fire-place. A picture or mirror falling from the wall portends a death. Finding a pin on the floor brings good luck*

BATHROOM *Two women using the same towel will either quarrel or go begging together. If you look in the mirror for too long the Devil's face might appear*

NURSERY *Carrying a newborn baby three times around the house will protect it from colic. But the baby will never be wise unless it falls from the cot three times before it is one year old*

BEDROOM *Using a mattress or pillow filled with wild birds' feathers causes a restless night. A dream of scissors means a quarrel and getting out of bed on the unaccustomed side induces bad humour*

CHRISTIAN AND PAGAN SYMBOLS COMBINE

In order to preserve continuity of worship, the Church allowed pagan symbols and legends to become grafted on to the stories of the saints. In this 14th-century window, St Catherine is shown with the spiked wheel to which she was bound and torn to pieces. Other stories give the saint a different end, but her wheel conveniently resembled the one which symbolised the sun in pagan fire festivals all over Europe. After the Anglo-Saxons were converted to Christianity, they continued to roll wheels wrapped with blazing straw and twigs across the fields, though now it was done in commemoration of the martyrdom of St Catherine. In this way, Christian blessing was given to an ancient pagan festival of purification and fertility

Angels and images

Some of the Church's most hallowed traditions were ancient practice when Christianity was new

One of the most striking features of the history of religion is the way in which people have clung to the holy places of their far-off ancestors. It seems that once a site was sanctified through worship, an incoming people – whether aggressive invaders, or the peaceful missionaries of a new religion – gained prestige by occupying the site. When this was done, the old religion could be overthrown and the area purified with new ritual and religious observance.

When Pope Gregory the Great sent St Augustine to convert the heathen Anglo-Saxons in the 6th century, he told him: 'Do not pull down the fanes (temples). Destroy the idols, purify the temples with holy water, set relics there and let them become temples of the true God. So the people will have no need to change their place of concourse, and where of old they were wont to sacrifice cattle to demons, thither let them continue to resort on the day of the saint to whom the Church is dedicated, and slay their beasts, no longer as a sacrifice but for a social meal in honour of Him whom they now worship.'

The ancient holy places
Hilltops, and the man-made burial mounds of the Neolithic and Bronze Ages, were favoured places of worship for the pagan Celts and Anglo-Saxons. Others were situated by holy rivers and wells. One of the most striking examples of Christian occupation of a pagan holy place is at Knowleton in Dorset. There a medieval church was built right inside a Neolithic stone circle. In Humberside, Fimber church stands on a Bronze Age barrow which was later used as an Anglo-Saxon burial place.

Sacred trees and stones worshipped by the local people were often incorporated into the construction of churches and churchyards. Sometimes the stones were sanctified by placing a cross on top: the huge free-standing crosses of the early Christian period may have derived from the pagan fertility cult in which great stone pillars were set up and worshipped. At St Martin's in Guernsey, the impressive stone figure of a pre-Christian mother-goddess, known locally as 'Gran'mere', used to stand in the church porch until her pagan nature so offended one of the incumbents that she was banished from holy ground. She now stands outside the church gate where offerings of money and flowers are still laid on her head, and omens are drawn from the way in which she appears to blink her eyes under certain conditions of the light.

Many of our older churches share the legend that the site of the building was pointed out to its saintly founder by some helpful animal, and the occasion is often recalled in carvings within the church, or in its stained glass. At Winwick, in Cheshire, the figure of a pig has been carved on the west front of the church; local tradition has it that the animal carried stones for the construction of the sacred building in its mouth. Similar stories are told of Welsh saints and churches, which may have their origin in the fact that the Celts worshipped the pig; pork was considered the finest of all meats and a direct gift of the gods.

Pagan and Christian symbols undoubtedly mingled in the early Church. Sometimes a legend associated a Christian saint with an episode involving a severed head, a wheel, a sacred animal or a holy well. Since similar attributes were credited to pagan gods and heroes, confusion was inevitable. It is likely that many of the saints, such as St Catherine, owe their fame to legends which pre-date Christianity.

Although the early Church would not accept the divinity of the pagan gods, it had a lively fear of their malevolent powers, and sought constantly to defend itself against them.

Gargoyles were given their horrific forms in order to frighten away the evil spirits that were constantly besieging churches and seeking entry into the buildings. This too may be the explanation for the erotic female 'fertility' figures found in or close to churches in Ireland and in Britain. These extraordinary carvings date from very different periods; some of them, like the one in St Michael's Church,

NYMPH IN THE CHURCH

In Ilkley church, W. Yorkshire, a stone relief portrays Verbeia, Romano-British goddess of the River Wharfe. Her draperies suggest drifting river weeds, while her hands hold what appear to be writhing serpents. Snakes were a part of water cults in both the Continent and Britain: their sinuous movements may have symbolised the twisting course of rivers

TERROR TEMPERED WITH WIT

In the remote corners of cathedrals, medieval masons often included their own interpretations of the architect's designs. The terrifying aspect of these imps of Ely Cathedral is somewhat offset by the fact that they are playing leapfrog

CULT OF THE GREEN MAN

Of all the pagan deities, the woodland spirit was longest lived. Variously called The Green Man or Jack-in-the-Green, he is still commemorated in pub signs and is depicted in medieval churches as a demonic composite of man and tree. This carving is also in Ely Cathedral

Oxford, probably belong to the time of the Roman occupation; others, such as those at Romsey Abbey, in Hampshire, were carved in relief as part of the basic decorative structure of the building. An alternative possibility is that the figures represent a pagan goddess in the guise of a hideous crone. The Celtic earth-goddess was believed to mate with the future king of the tribe, and so confer on him her blessings and ensure the success of his reign. She was believed to appear before him in the guise of a fearsome but lascivious hag and would invite him to sleep with her. If he agreed, she would then turn into a beautiful woman.

The cult of the severed heads

Another powerful pagan symbol adopted by the Church was the device of the severed head. The Celts were head-hunters, and used to set up skulls of their enemies to defend their sacred places. Today, severed heads in stone can be seen in countless churches all over Britain and are quite distinguishable by their severed necks from the benign heads of saints on the upper walls.

Many pagan altars and carvings of pagan deities have been incorporated in the walls of churches, and have even been used as fonts. An altar dedicated to the Celtic god Ocellus, 'The High One', is in the porch of the church at Caerwent, in Gwent. A Romano-British altar decorated with bulls stands within the church at Stone in Oxney, Kent, while a relief of the horned war-god of the Celts can be seen on the inner wall of the church at Kirby Underdale, Humberside.

Lore of the Church

Despite doubts and changes, the Christian Church has been a major influence in people's lives for the best part of 2000 years, and during that time many customs have arisen which have little authority in scripture. One of the most widespread beliefs was that the north side of the church belonged to the Devil, and many people still have an aversion to burial in the northern part of a churchyard. At one time, this section was unhallowed ground and was reserved for the burial of unbaptised infants and suicides. In the north wall of some medieval churches there is a small door, which was known as the Devil's door. This was opened only during baptisms and communion to permit the escape of evil spirits which had been driven out by the holy sacraments.

Until the Industrial Revolution at least, the church was the focal point of most communities. For rich and poor alike, it was a place to meet one's friends and a place to discuss important matters of the day. The church porch was the usual rendezvous. Whether large or small it was usually well lit and offered both warmth and shelter. Often, it contained a small altar, and there was usually a small room above the porch. It was from the porch that bread and alms were distributed to the poor.

Church bells were widely revered. They were given individual names and baptised, and it was firmly believed that they became attached to particular places and, if stolen, would return of their own accord. In Strathfillan parish, Tayside, St Fillan's bell was kept on a gravestone in the churchyard and was used to cure insanity. The sufferer was bound and left all night in the chapel; in the morning he was immersed in St Fillan's pool, after which the bell was placed on his head. Whether or not the treatment worked is speculative.

Holywell's ancient church stands on the sacred well of St Winifred, and when the bell was placed in position, it too was named after the saint in a christening ceremony in which it was sprinkled with holy water and dressed in a christening robe. Afterwards, the bell had the ability to keep all forces of evil at bay and, when rung, could prevent thunderstorms and thunderbolts. Many churches employed Passing or Soul Bells which were rung during prayers for the dying or the newly dead. There was a belief that the peals held back the powers of evil lying in wait for the departing soul.

Many of the minor Church customs also reveal links with the distant past. Fonts are still covered to keep out evil spirits, while the practice of bowing towards the altar at the east end of a church may have its origin in worship of the rising sun. The celebration of St John's Eve coincides with the old festival of the summer solstice; and the corn-dolly displayed at Harvest Thanksgiving symbolises the Corn Spirit.

It is a moving experience to enter a country church on Plough Monday – the Monday following the Feast of Epiphany – when ploughs are blessed before the altar. This is a real link with the past and shows man's dependence on the earth and its yield.

HAVEN AND RETRIBUTION

Though the Church has always been compassionate towards repentant sinners, it has never failed to point out the dreadful fate that awaits those who reject its teaching. The fires of Hell and the torments of the damned preoccupied religious painters and sculptors for centuries. However, in AD 633, Pope Boniface V determined to show that it is never too late to turn to a forgiving God. He authorised churches to give sanctuary to all who sought it. The practice quickly spread throughout the Christian world where the law offered complete protection to those pursued by enemies, and to criminals fleeing from justice.

SHELTER FOR THE FUGITIVE *The sanctuary knocker, called a hagoday, was a large bronze escutcheon adorned with the head of some monstrous beast, often with a human head in its jaws. When a fugitive grasped the ring of the knocker he could not be pulled from it without his pursuers breaking the laws of sanctuary. This was a serious offence punishable by excommunication from the Church.*

Originally, sanctuary applied only to that area of the church surrounding the bishop's throne. Later, the area was extended to include the whole of the interior of the church, the porch, the churchyard, and in some instances the approaches to the churchyard.

In the Middle Ages, the period of sanctuary was 40 days; if the hunted man wished, he could be escorted to a port during this time, so that he could leave the kingdom. James I abolished sanctuary for criminals in 1623, and the practice fell into abeyance entirely in the 18th century. The sanctuary knocker shown here is on the south door of Durham Cathedral

SOULS IN TORMENT *The medieval mind was greatly concerned with the hereafter, though the majority of people were more concerned with the fear of Hell than with the hope of Heaven. It was acknowledged that the latter goal was difficult to attain, even through the transitionary state of Purgatory where souls reconciled to God suffered for an indeterminate period. The Church capitalised on this fear: a speedy passage through Purgatory could be guaranteed by indulgences – by making a pilgrimage, building a church,* joining a crusade, or simply by making a cash donation. Only Italian artists showed much interest in Purgatory; most artists considered there was more dramatic material in Hell. Much medieval art is concerned with the Last Judgment and fearsome conceptions are found in many churches. This 12th-century 'Doom Painting' at Oddington, Gloucestershire, shows the torments of Hell. Sinners are driven into the jaws of Hades, depicted by a monster with a flaming mouth, while angels lead the righteous to the Heavenly Abode*

The seed and the harvest

The old beliefs and practices of a rural community are almost all concerned with the fertility of animals and soil

From earliest times, the farmer has been conscious that he dealt in mysteries. A man might plough his land, sow his seed and keep it free from weeds, but in doing so he knew he contributed only half the ingredients of a successful harvest. The remainder – the timely succession of soil-pulverising frosts, of rain and sunshine and, above all, the quickening of life in the seed – were matters over which he had little control.

Even today, this cycle is awe-inspiring. But to our primitive ancestors it seemed that the continuance of the pattern from year to year could be ensured only by placating jealous and capricious gods. These gods, it was believed, looked after crops and animals, sky and water, and almost every other aspect of rural life.

Why should spring come at all unless a sacrifice was made? And what offering could be more appropriate than the life of a king or prince? For the sake of better husbandry, royal victims once went willingly to their deaths, and their blood was spread on the winter fields. Only a hundred years ago, a farmer might still be advised to kill his best calf to save his herd from disease.

The wisdom of the countryman

Tied as it is to the recurring cycle of the seasons, farm lore contains many relics of ancient mystery beliefs. Besides superstition, there is much hard-won wisdom, gathered over centuries and passed from father to son in easily remembered rhymes and proverbs. Even in the era of the combine harvester, many of them are believed still.

Between farmers and their land there is often a bond which is enshrined in the proverb: 'A farmer should live as though he were going to die tomorrow, but farm as though he were going to live for ever.' To our ancestors, the soil was something to nurse, and venerate; it was the mother of all things and the home of the goddess of fertility. Even today, these old beliefs linger on in such phrases as 'Mother Nature' and 'Mother Earth'.

When drink is taken into the fields, particularly at harvest time, it is often the custom to pour a little on the ground for good luck. The origins of this ritual extend far back into pre-history, when it was a gesture of sacrifice to the gods. In Ireland and Wales, a draught will sometimes be poured on to the earth as a compliment to the 'Good People' or fairies.

It is well known that 'prevention is often better than cure'. In farming terms this is translated as: 'One year's seeding, seven years' weeding.' Seeds which have lain dormant in a field that has been neglected for one year can produce weeds up to seven years later. Another rural proverb that is still used frequently is the expression 'to buy a pig in a poke'. This applied to a farmer buying stock which he had not examined beforehand.

Nowadays farmers usually buy extra winter feed for their livestock to supplement their own produce, but in former times few could afford such luxuries. To feed their stock throughout the winter, farmers were entirely dependent on what they themselves had grown during the previous summer. Provident farmers tried to keep adequate fodder through the colder months, and found a sensible summary of their needs in the proverb:

> On a farm on Candlemas Day (February 2)
> There should be half the straw and two-thirds the hay.

It would be a poor farmer today who let pests and fungus disease rob him of three-quarters of the seed he sowed. Yet the handicaps our ancestors suffered were described in a pessimistic rhyme:

> Sow four grains in a row;
> One for the pigeons; one for the crow;
> One to rot; and one to grow.

Sound advice to a farmer inspecting his crops for damage at the tail-end of winter is: 'Plant a stride,

---

THE LABOURS OF THE MONTHS

Medieval calendars of saints' days, church festivals and other religious events were usually illustrated, sometimes crudely, sometimes exquisitely, with contemporary scenes of everyday life. The illustrations followed traditional themes concerning man's activities during the course of the seasons. In time, the subjects illustrated became known as the Labours of the Months, and the more familiar scenes were often beautifully reproduced in stained glass to decorate the parish church windows in country districts throughout Britain.

JANUARY TASK *Ploughing with oxen, from a medieval manuscript. Oxen performed most heavy haulage tasks in earlier times, until the faster-moving horses began gradually to displace them in the 17th century*

APRIL SOWING *One of the Labours of the Months reproduced in stained glass, now in the Victoria and Albert Museum. Such illustrations give an insight into medieval farming methods and implements*

let un bide.' It means that if one living plant can be seen for every stride he takes, the crop will be worth while. Sunshine and April showers can quickly revive plant growth.

Much farming lore concerns the belief that the moon governs the time to sow seed. Our ancestors were fond of the expression 'seed will grow with the moon'. According to primitive reasoning, as the moon waxes and grows bigger, it has the same effect on growing things, and as it wanes so growth similarly declines and plants lose their energy. This belief still flourishes among both primitive and more sophisticated peoples throughout the world, and the fact that experiments do not appear to support the belief in no way lessens faith in it.

The shepherd's calendar
Sheep were once far more important than cattle to the British economy, and are still the subject of a wealth of rural lore. Some of this may date from prehistory, for many of the 40-odd surviving breeds of British sheep are of very ancient stock. Soay sheep from the Outer Hebrides, for example, are almost identical with a type which grazed on the Wiltshire Downs 3000 years ago.

Much of the lore concerning sheep is based on the seasonal tasks of the shepherd's calendar. Lowland sheep begin lambing in early February, and the shepherd must then drive them to sheltered lambing pens or buildings to protect them from the cold weather. Hill sheep are hardier and lamb slightly later in the open. Both types are shorn in June and July, about three weeks after they have been washed

to clean their fleeces. Hill flocks graze the moors in summer, and then at the autumn sales the lambs are dispersed to lowland farms for fattening.

This calendar explains the proverb: 'Shear sheep in May, you'll shear them all away' – May is too early for shearing. The saying: 'You may shear your sheep when elder blossoms peep,' is sound advice. Elder flowers do not appear until the warmer weeks of June. 'Every move a sheep makes should be a move for the better' refers to the practice of moving lambs to progressively better grazing as they grow, finishing in rich, lowland pastures.

The shepherd's language
Every district once had its own strange words for counting sheep, some of which were probably derived from ancient Celtic. Shepherds still used these words until about 30 years ago, but nowadays they survive only in variants used by children in counting games. The words were chanted in groups of five, with the fifth word strongly stressed. On reaching 20 the shepherd raised a finger and began again from one. The counting continued like this until all ten fingers were raised, making a total of 200. A tally mark was then made on a piece of wood and the counting by words and fingers was recommenced by the shepherd.

In parts of Cumbria the count proceeded in single units: yan, tan, tethera, methera, pimp, sethera, lethera, hothera, dothera, dick, gave the count from one to ten. In Sussex, however, it was usual to count in pairs. Only ten words were used: wuntherum, twotherum, cockerum, cutherum, shetherum,

FAMILY TRADITION AT HARVEST

In his painting 'The Reapers', George Stubbs depicts the way in which an 18th-century country family tackled the most important task of the rural year. At harvest time, before mechanisation, all but the oldest and youngest members of labouring families would hire themselves out to farmers in gangs. The men cut the corn with long,

sweeping strokes of their scythes, while behind them their wives or older children would gather the fallen stalks into sheaves. These were tied with a plait of twisted corn made by the younger children. Farmers, anxious to complete the harvest while fine weather lasted, encouraged rivalry between gangs of reapers

shatherum, wineberry, wigtail, tarry-diddle, den; with each word indicating two sheep, the tally, indicated by one finger, was 20.

Beliefs about cattle

Cattle-breeders of long ago used to say 'Half the pedigree goes in at the mouth', which meant that feeding was as important as breeding. Modern ideas, however, favour the opinion that 'the bull is half the herd'.

Some strange applications of the notion of sympathetic magic can be found in animal breeding. In Britain it was once a common belief that the main colour seen by a cow while mating would be reproduced in her offspring. Farmers near Carmarthen, for instance, who favoured white cattle, tried to ensure that a cow mated with a bull in front of a whitewashed wall.

Many old beliefs relating to the health of cattle were sound; a good example concerned the presence of swallows in cattle byres. It was said that if a farmer destroyed the swallows' nest in his cowshed the cows would give milk with blood in it; and this belief had some scientific basis. Milk tinted with blood is evidence of mastitis, a disease spread by the flies on which swallows feed.

Power over horses

In many parts of the country there is an ancient belief that a bone taken from a toad would give its owner power over horses. The bone was obtained by pinning the toad over an ant-hill until the ants had stripped all the flesh from the bones. These were then thrown into a swiftly flowing stream and watched until, it was said, one bone detached itself and floated away upstream, screaming as it went. Possession of this bone made the owner a toadman, and horses would always obey him.

Other stories claim that before the owner finally became a toadman he had to take the bone on three successive nights to a stable or graveyard. On the third night the Devil was alleged to appear and try to gain possession of the bone. These rituals suggest that the origin of the story may lie in ancient warrior ceremonies connected with horses, when certain initiation tests were performed.

Even into the present century, many horse-handlers were believed to have hypnotic powers, almost of witchcraft, over their charges. It was believed that the most high-spirited horse could be tamed or its movements paralysed by whispering in its ear. Most probably, the power came from a shrewd understanding of a horse's delicate sense of smell, and the use of a scented substance which could hypnotise the beast.

Pigs, birds and bees

Pigs are intelligent animals. They seem to like music and respond to being fussed over. Therefore an old Hampshire tale of a piglet that was held on a wall to watch a band go past is perhaps not altogether ridiculous. But the widespread belief that a pig trying to swim will cut its own throat with its front trotters is untrue. Pigs are strong swimmers, with no

---

COUNTRY LORE AND TRADITIONS

HORSE WHISPERERS *Carters were thought to use a secret language to control horses. A whispered word immobilised the horse, and another broke the spell*

FARMYARD WEATHER LORE *A common country belief holds that pigs can see the wind, and that they forecast the arrival of high winds by becoming restless and tossing straw about with their snouts*

BIRDS FOR A FEAST *Until it was supplanted by turkey, roast goose was the traditional dish at many festivals. At Michaelmas, goose-herds would drive flocks of up to 20,000 geese to be sold at long-established goose fairs*

PASTORAL FAIRS AND MARKETS

This engraving shows Woburn sheep fair in about 1811, presided over by the 6th Duke of Bedford, seen on horseback in the centre. Fairs and markets have been held in Britain for centuries, and many of our market towns evolved from convenient sites such as crossroads where people met to buy or sell animals and produce. In the

fear of water. A sensible saying is 'unless your bacon you would mar, kill not your pig without the R'. Pigs should not be killed during any month which lacks the letter R in its name, for these are all hot months when pork soon spoils.

Of all domestic birds the farmyard cock has been credited with more magical powers than any other. In the Hebrides, cocks had the ability to banish ghosts, avert the evil eye and foretell fate. Just as the dog was the sentinel over earthly things, so was the cock for the unearthly; when it crowed at dawn the spirits of darkness fled and the farmer could then rise and work in safety. In Somerset it was said: 'A cock will frighten away the Devil himself,' which probably explains why its effigy was widely used on church towers as a weather-vane.

Bees once played a useful role in village life. Before the 17th century, when sugar was first imported from the West Indies, honey was used to sweeten foods and in the fermentation of drinks, such as ale, cider and mead.

Since those times much bee-lore has doubtless been lost, but one saying is still remembered: 'A swarm of bees in May is worth a load of hay, and a swarm of bees in July is hardly worth a fly.' Early swarms have all summer to collect and store nectar, whereas late swarms can barely collect enough to keep themselves through the winter.

There is an old, widespread but unproved belief that bee-stings are beneficial in curing rheumatism and arthritis. It is also claimed that bees are intelligent, peaceable creatures, and should be treated as

such. This possibly explains the belief that bees respond to different tones of the human voice and will not stay with a bad-tempered owner. From this stems the injunction that 'you must never swear in the hearing of your bees'.

SMALL MESSENGERS OF THE GODS

Since ancient times, when bees were regarded as messengers of the gods, people have whispered family news to the hive. If this is not done, the bees will fly away

Middle Ages, fairs provided town and country folk with a brief respite from the harsh conditions of daily life. The fairs began to decline in importance as established market-places grew in size and efficiency, but those which remained catered for all rural interests. Horse fairs were regular events everywhere; so were cattle, sheep, cheese and other fairs. 'Mop' – or hiring – fairs, once widespread, were still held in north Cumbria in the 1950's. At these

fairs, labourers were hired for the year. Men and women stood in groups wearing the badge of their trades: a whip for carters, straw for cowmen, a tuft of wool for shepherds. If hired, they were given a hiring penny or 'fastpenny' to seal the bargain, and used it to drink their new master's health. A farm labourer's lot was one of underpaid, back-breaking toil from childhood to old age. The fairs offered him a chance to buy and sell, while meeting his old friends

To the sea in ships

Many fishermen still use magic and ritual to protect themselves against the treacherous forces of the sea

Scattered along the coastline of Britain there are hundreds of villages huddled around small harbours, whose cottages face the sea and turn their backs on the fields and hills. Like the homes they live in, the villagers too once turned away from the rest of Britain, for until the social upheaval brought about by the Second World War, fishing villages were closed communities. Fishermen and their wives and children lived and died among their own kind, turned in on themselves by the dangers and uncertainties of trying to win a living from the sea.

Today, though the villages remain, the traditional pattern of a fisherman's life has changed. Harbours which once sheltered 30 to 40 inshore boats now often serve only three or four; where the fishing fleets once lay, there are now fleets of pleasure craft. Fishing has become industrialised, and from their homes in small villages fishermen commute to large ports, to work on modern, radar-equipped trawlers.

But the dangers of the sea are changeless. Like the line and drift-net fishermen before them, today's trawlermen have to contend with the treacherous forces of wind, tide, currents and waves; and their wives and children suffer the same ageless anxieties when the barometer begins to fall and dark clouds bank up on the horizon. In spite of the revolution which technology has worked in their lives, many fishermen still use magic to protect themselves and their boats, and they are still subject to the same powerful superstitions as their ancestors.

Boatyard luck

From the moment the keel of a new fishing boat is laid, tradition and superstition guide the boatbuilder's hand. Certain types of wood are traditionally lucky and, once, no boat would have been considered seaworthy unless some part of it was made of rowan, ash or some other lucky wood. In the 19th century, Scottish fishermen also believed that some woods were male and others female, and that a boat made of female wood sailed faster at night than during the day. She-oak, or chestnut, was thought to have this quality.

Gold and silver were also lucky. A gold coin was often built into some hidden recess of the boat's framework, and it is still customary for a silver coin to be placed underneath the mast. Seamen also seem to share the landsman's belief in the magical

BOATYARD SUPERSTITIONS

For fishermen, no moment in a boat's life was more fateful than when the boatbuilder began to lay its keel. In this 19th-century boatyard, it would have been disastrous to begin the work on a Friday. Sometimes the shipwright tied a red ribbon round the first nail he used, to protect the boat against accidents. Later stages in the boat's construction were also loaded with superstition; often, lucky pieces of gold and silver were hidden in the framework, and parts of the boat were built of traditionally protective kinds of wood such as rowan or ash

properties of cold iron; to bring good luck, many skippers nail up a horseshoe in the deckhouse or on the mast.

Ritual and superstition surround the launching of a boat. A sacrifice has to be made to the sea gods, so when a large ship is christened, a bottle of champagne is sacrificially smashed against its bows. Scottish fishermen use whisky for the same purpose, and sometimes sprinkle barley over a new boat. They also believe that a boat should be launched only when the tide is flowing, and that she should not be named until she is afloat.

Within living memory, the luck of fishing boats was regularly renewed, usually at Christmas or in the New Year, by carrying fire round them in the harbour; this purified them and protected them against ill-wishing by hags and witches. In the north-east Scottish port of Burghead, the custom was called 'burning the clavie'; tar barrels were sawn in half, mounted on poles and carried blazing round the harbour. In other ports, barrels were set on fire and rolled along the quay.

In many places, fishermen now call on the parish priest to help protect their boats. At Norham in Northumberland, for example, the vicar blesses both the boats and the nets at the beginning of the Tweed salmon-fishing season, and he is always offered the first fish to be caught.

But the intertwining of pagan and Christian beliefs is often uneasy, as is shown by the experience of a group of Welsh river fishermen who in 1965 revived the custom of having their nets blessed. When drought and disease led to a run of poor catches, they blamed their bad luck on the clergyman, whose blessing must have annoyed the river spirits.

Before putting to sea, many fishermen observe a strange assortment of protective rituals. One may touch the bows of his boat first thing in the morning; another may spit over the port side, or spit on a coin and throw it overboard. To the casual observer, such actions may appear to be prompted by private superstitions; but in fact, they are part of a nationwide pattern of custom and belief, like the landsman's habit of touching wood for luck.

Ritual and prohibition

Once at sea, there are many things which a fisherman will never do. He never points at another boat, or at any object, such as a knife or a box, which he needs. He avoids mentioning how many boats are fishing together. It is as if he believes that he can mislead the malign forces which he fears.

No fisherman mentions directly that he has fish on the line, or that the nets are full. Instead, he uses a private, oblique language, saying, for example, 'There's a white lug' to indicate that there are fish in the corner of the net. In north-east Scotland, long-line fishermen used to say 'She's cyarled' when the first fish was on the line. The expression derived from an old custom of throwing the first fish back into the sea in order to propitiate the carline, or old hag of the sea.

Many words are forbidden because they are unlucky. Salt, salmon, knives and eggs must never be named, nor must cats, pigs, hares, foxes and certain other animals. The salmon is usually called 'the red fish', 'the gentleman', 'the fish with scales' or 'the beastie'; and there are stories about fishermen who have run out of salt hailing other boats at sea with a request for 'some of that white stuff... not the stuff you put in your tea'.

The word 'gentleman' is also used to name other unlucky animals. The fishermen of Buckie in north Grampian, when working along the north coast of Highland, always refer to Rabbit Island, at the entrance to the Kyle of Tongue, as 'Gentleman's Island'. In many places, crabs are never mentioned by name. On the Buchan coast in east Grampian, where green crabs were often used for bait, the fishermen used to get round this problem by calling them 'sniffltie fits' – fit is the local pronunciation for foot, and sniffltie means dawdling.

Of all the animals which fishermen fear, pigs are reputedly the most dangerous. Perhaps this is because of their association with the wind, which by tradition they can see; or because they are said to bear the Devil's mark on their forefeet. Among the by-words fishermen use for pig are 'grumphie', 'curlie-tail', 'guffey', 'the Grecian' and 'the article'. And if they ever hear the forbidden word, many of them feel that they are in danger until they have touched a ringbolt, said 'cold iron', or held up their thumbs and crossed their forefingers.

Unwelcome passengers

Whatever church they belong to when on shore, many fishermen still fear pagan gods while they are at sea. For this reason, clergymen and the Church are often forbidden topics of conversation, and it is very unlucky for a fisherman to see 'the gentleman in black' as he makes his way down to the harbour. If he is particularly superstitious, he may call off the trip and go home.

This prejudice against the Church is also found among merchant seamen; the crews of ships carrying parties of priests and nuns have been known to blame bad weather upon these passengers.

Women, too, can be unlucky. Many fishermen are reluctant to go to sea with a woman on board, and to see a woman with a squint before sailing is as ominous as a glimpse of a clergyman. In the days of long-line fishing, women helped their husbands by gathering limpets and mussels for bait, and by baiting some of the lines. But once the lines were ready, it was very unlucky if a woman stepped over them. Today, the same superstition applies to fishing nets; if a woman steps over them, they will catch no fish that day.

Taboos applied to days as well as to people and animals. Friday was unlucky; it was sometimes called 'Tip Tod's day', meaning the Devil's day and it was said that work started on a Friday would never be finished. Once, sailors would never willingly put to sea on a Friday, nor would those already at sea change from one method of fishing to another on that day.

But however carefully fishermen observe these traditions, accidents still happen, ships are still wrecked and men drowned. Many fishermen fear becoming involved in the aftermath of a disaster at sea, as if by some mysterious contagion disaster will strike them too. They generally dread bringing ashore a corpse found floating in the sea, and they are more than usually reluctant to touch a body washed up on the beach.

Such fears are a relic of the old belief that, if a sailor rescued a drowning man, he would probably be drowned himself, for he had cheated the sea of its due. It was this belief that gave earlier generations of seamen their fatalistic acceptance of drowning; they often withheld aid from drowning men, and very few ever learnt to swim. It also explains why the corpses of drowned men were sometimes buried below the tidemark.

One protection against drowning was to carry a caul – the membrane which sometimes covers a baby's head at birth. The baby who was born with a caul was thought to be particularly lucky; so long as the caul was never lost, the child would not drown. The magic could also be transferred. Until well into the 20th century sailors still bought cauls, sometimes paying as much as £20 for one.

Many sailors and fishermen believe in death omens, though they are reluctant to talk about them to outsiders. A few years ago, a group of Humberside fishermen said that if they found a particular kind of fish in the crab pots they knew that they would soon be in mourning; it had happened twice within their memory. They claimed to have forgotten what the fish was called, but it is more likely that it belonged to a species whose name was a forbidden word.

Wind and waves
In the days of sail, becalmed sailors sometimes tried to raise the wind by sympathetic magic; they believed that if they whistled gently, a wind might begin to blow. Similarly today, whistling at sea is regarded as unlucky, for it may call up a gale. An exception is sometimes made for cooks in the Royal Navy, for as long as they are whistling, they cannot be surreptitiously eating the mess rations.

There is one situation in which fishermen are prepared to risk whistling up a wind. The rockling is sometimes known as the 'whistle-fish', and Cornish tradition in particular holds that whistling can charm it into the net.

Many of the beliefs that fishermen hold about the wind and weather are purely local, as when men from Seahouses in Northumberland say that bad weather is coming when they can hear seals barking on the Farne Islands. But others seem to be part of a common fund of superstition, and they are often enshrined in traditional verses or proverbs. One widely known fisherman's verse runs:

When the wind is in the east
It's good for neither man nor beast.
When the wind is in the north
The skilful fisher goes not forth.
When the wind is in the south
It blows the bait in the fish's mouth.
When the wind is in the west
Then 'tis at its very best.

Few fishermen would go along with the popular myth that every seventh wave is a big one. But Shetland fishermen used to steer their boats by the 'moder dy' or mother wave, which though it came irregularly always indicated the set of the sea. And Norfolk crab fishermen, who have to launch their boats from very exposed beaches, still wait when the sea is rough for what they call a 'level'. They count the waves in threes, and after three big waves in succession they expect a level, or stretch of calm sea, to follow on which to launch their boats.

THE TRADITIONAL ARTS OF THE SAILOR

To while away the days when their ships were becalmed, seamen tied fancy knots, tattooed themselves or their crewmates, or made ornaments out of wood or bone. Some of these had more than just a decorative function. A sailor with Christ's Crucifixion tattooed on his back believed that he would feel less pain if he was ever flogged; and, similarly, pictures of snakes, anchors and naked women were probably thought to be protective.

Ropework was one of the most popular pastimes. Sailors became very competitive about it, and would often demand a pledge of secrecy before explaining how a particular knot was tied. They also used a private language: two ropes were 'bent together', never 'knotted', and a knot was always 'opened', not 'untied'.

SAILOR'S TATTOOS *Some tattoos were protective symbols; naked women, for example, brought good luck*

TURK'S HEAD *In decorative ropework this knot was probably used more often than any other; hundreds of variations were developed from the basic, three-part version shown here. The name probably derived from the knot's resemblance to the type of turban worn by the Saracens*

THE ART OF THE IMPOSSIBLE *To put a ship into a bottle, a sailor first hinged the masts to the deck. With the masts flat along the deck he slipped the model into the bottle; then he pulled the masts up with a thread*

THE SPIRIT OF THE SHIP

The destiny of a ship was once thought to be so closely bound up with that of her figurehead that one could not sink without the other; to sail in a ship without a figurehead was highly dangerous, for the figurehead embodied the ship's soul.

The prevalence of figureheads carved to resemble naked women probably resulted from the pre-Christian practice of dedicating ships to goddesses; this is also said to explain why ships are always regarded as feminine. There may also be a link with the belief recorded by Pliny almost 2000 years ago that 'a storm may be lulled by a woman uncovering her body out to sea'. Surprisingly, sailors also believed that it was unlucky to go to sea with a woman on board.

The figurehead of the famous tea-clipper Cutty Sark (above), which is moored at Greenwich, represents the fleet-footed witch whom Robert Burns described in his poem 'Tam o' Shanter'. Dressed in a short petticoat or 'cutty sark', she chased Tom one night, and was prevented from catching him only when he crossed the River Doon

LALLA ROOKE *An Indian princess figurehead from a tea-clipper*

THE GREEK WARRIOR AJAX *Figurehead from a 74-gun warship*

The day's work

The traditions and superstitions of craftsmen of the Middle Ages are still adhered to in workshops and on factory floors

The skilled craftsman has always encouraged others to believe that there are mysterious aspects to his work. Only a century ago the blacksmith was held in awe as a man whose trade gave him strange powers; today, the computer technician invests his highly skilled profession with an aura of mystery.

This wish for mystery can perhaps be attributed to pride in being able to do something that others cannot do, and the instinct to close ranks against outside competition. These factors have always knitted tradesmen – and professional men – into tight groups in which the spinning of tales comparing the old days with the new, the use of a common jargon which emphasises the gulf between the insider and outsider, and the adoption of good and bad luck rituals, has bred its own brand of folklore. Even in relatively new professions, this folklore establishes itself remarkably quickly. Airline crews are said to have the sailors' prejudice against carrying clergymen and nuns as passengers; oil men ban women from their platform rigs at sea because they bring bad luck; and some shop-girls will not open their receipt books until the first sale of the day has been completed. The motor industry is still quite young, but already 'Tiny' Newman, who was on the production line at the Cowley works in the 1930's, has become a folklore figure.

BLACKSMITHS AS HEALERS *Some smiths acquired reputations for curing the sick. In Essex, water from a smithy's cooling trough was valued for its curative powers. J. M. W. Turner's painting shows a blacksmith disputing the price of iron*

THE ERA OF STEAM *New customs which were to grow into traditions were soon established in the infant railway industry. Here, Robert Stephenson drives in the last rivet in the Britannia tubular bridge over the Menai Straits, Wales, in 1850, a ceremony which is now traditional in railway construction. Passengers crossing the Forth Bridge for the first time toss a coin into the sea below, a pagan tribute in a modern setting*

BUILDERS IN STONE *Towards the end of the Middle Ages men such as the masons depicted in this 15th-century manuscript concerned themselves with charities and developing a system of moral teaching. The tools and terms of their trade are still used symbolically in Freemasonry*

'Tiny' was reputed to have great strength but a gentle disposition. He is said to have fitted car tyres by hand and to have once settled a dispute by holding his antagonist at arm's length over the side of an open-topped bus until the point at issue was conceded.

The blacksmith and the king

Of all trades, the blacksmith's is richest in tradition. The smith's magical status was early established because he worked with iron and fire – many primitive people still believe that iron is charged with mysterious powers. In addition, all other craftsmen depended on the smith for their tools. This aspect is reflected in the tale in which King Alfred called together representatives of all the trades which then existed to determine which of them was paramount. Swayed by the gift of a magnificent coat, the king nominated the tailor. Angrily, the blacksmith declared that he would not work again until the king acknowledged that the smith was the prince of all craftsmen. As time passed, the tools of the other craftsmen fell into disrepair; then the king's horse cast a shoe. In desperation the

tradesmen broke into the smithy to do the work themselves. In the confusion that followed, the anvil was knocked over and, as it hit the ground, it exploded. St Clement, the patron saint of blacksmiths, then entered with the smith, and the harassed king revised his judgment. The tailor was furious; he crept under the table and slashed the blacksmith's apron. Smiths wear ragged aprons to this day.

This story was retold by blacksmiths every November 23 when they celebrated the Feast of St Clement until the late 19th century. One blacksmith always impersonated the saint, and 'Old Clem' was paraded through the town while his thirsty henchmen collected beer money from bystanders. As part of their re-enactment celebrations, the smiths filled the anvil's hole with gunpowder and exploded it with a spark from a hammer blow.

Bricks and mortar

Since time immemorial, builders have believed that a new structure needed a sacrifice to ensure that their work would survive. When the Tower of London

SUPERSTITION BELOW GROUND *The Davy Safety Lamp of 1816 marginally improved the condition of coal miners, but the pits still fostered superstition. Miners did not like the form of a cross underground, even when made by the handles of tools on the floor*

BARREL MAKERS *The indoctrination of apprentices has helped keep the customs of industry alive. At the end of his apprenticeship the young cooper undergoes the trussing ceremony. He is put in the barrel he is making and the truss hoops are banged on. Oil and shavings are poured over him, he is rolled around, then offered beer which is also poured over him. He is then declared to be a cooper*

THE IRON FORGE *Joseph Wright of Derby is said to have been the first painter to express the spirit of the Industrial Revolution. He had a particular interest in the visual effects created by artificial light, and* The Iron Forge, *painted in 1772, is his best-known work. The blinding glare emitted by the white-hot piece of iron contrasts dramatically with the shadows, creating an aura of mystery which is in keeping with the reputation of the metal being shaped.*

The first iron known to man was in the form of meteors which plunged to earth from the heavens, a mode of arrival which made them seem like gifts from the gods. When man learnt to dig for iron and forge it into tools and weapons of great strength its reputation was further enhanced. In folklore, iron has always been a powerful talisman against evil spirits, particularly when shaped into horseshoes. St Dunstan, who was a blacksmith, is said to have once shod the Devil who cried for mercy and fled, vowing never to go near a horseshoe again

was built in 1078, the mortar used was mixed with the blood of bulls, symbolising strength; and in 1897, when a Methodist chapel was being built in Cambridge, the head of a slaughtered horse was placed in the first foundation trench. Beer was poured over the head, and more was drunk by the workmen. Today, beer is still drunk on a new building site and some is poured into the first trench; sometimes a few coins are thrown in as well. Traditionally, alcohol is a substitute for blood. Even the custom of laying foundation stones may have its origin in the pagan practice of burying an animal or child beneath a new building. Sometimes, the skeletons of dogs are discovered during alterations to medieval churches.

The completion of a building is still marked by the custom of 'topping out', which dates back to Roman times. A fir tree is fixed to the topmost part of the building to ward off evil spirits, and beer is provided for the workers. Occasionally, topping out is as significant as the laying of the foundation stone; in 1971 the Recorder of London, Sir Carl Aarvold, climbed to the top of the new South Block of the Central Criminal Court to fix the last slate. Custom decrees that if beer is not provided for topping out, workmen will fly a black flag and solemnly curse the building so that it will never prosper.

Taboos of the miners

Men who work in dangerous jobs tend to be superstitious, and mining has a mythology all of its own. For centuries, miners have ceased work immediately after a fatal accident and have refused to begin again until their mate was buried. In the 19th century around Worcester, 'dead money' was collected for a farewell drink. When work recommenced, men who had not been near the accident were put to work on the site; it is a widespread belief that ill luck clings to people and places. A woman met on the way to work, especially a squinting woman, was such a bad omen that a miner might go back home again. The same superstition is common among fishermen. It was equally bad luck for the miner to return home for some forgotten article – at a pinch he could go to the house door and ask for it, but to re-cross the threshold was fraught with danger. A variant of the belief permitted entry, but it was essential to sit down in a chair, however briefly, before setting off again. Precautions against bad luck were essential when lots were being drawn for positions at the coal face: each miner's wife hung the fire tongs from the mantelpiece and put the family cat in the unlit oven. It was bad luck to exchange shifts with someone in midweek: a lot once accepted should be adhered to.

The power of tradition in industry is nowhere more apparent than in a shipyard. At least one boat-builder in Appledore, Devon, still refuses to launch a boat on the same day of the week as that on which building began and will never launch on a Friday, a day associated with all kinds of bad luck. Grimsby men say that boats with names ending in the letter 'a' never do well.

When a ship was being rigged, a golden sovereign was placed under each mast. In 1965, the Sail Training Association's new schooner, *Sir Winston Churchill*, had its masts stepped on Churchill crowns instead. Eight days before the official launching, however, the ship launched herself and fell off the slipway. The masts were badly damaged, but despite this incident, they were once more firmly stepped on Churchill crowns.

Printing, introduced to Britain by William Caxton in 1477, was soon invested with an air of mystery. The printer's inky assistants were nicknamed 'devils', and there were puns about 'the black art'. To this day printers and journalists are organised for trade union purposes into groups known as 'chapels'. The traditional explanation of the term is that Caxton set up the first British press in the precincts of Westminster Abbey. This cannot be the correct explanation, however, because the term is also used in France where Caxton's name carried little weight.

Servicemen's superstitions

All recruits in the armed forces are taught the traditions of their service, but there is a mass of popular belief and custom which is the real folklore of the fighting man. Few soldiers will light three cigarettes off one match. This fetish can be traced back to the Boer War: the flame gave enemy snipers time to sight their rifles, and repeatedly the third man to light his cigarette was shot. Inevitably, Nelson is the focus of much naval tradition. Ratings commonly believe that the three stripes on their collars commemorate Nelson's victories at the Nile, Copenhagen and Trafalgar, but they are, in fact, only decorative.

Even the youngest service, the RAF, has its gremlins, the little green men responsible for the

TYNESIDE SHIPYARDS *It is said that if a shipwright uses wood from a tree near which an unbaptised infant has been buried, the ghost of the child will inhabit the ship and protect it*

JOINING THE CAKE *The Cockney rhyming slang for the army, 'Kate Carney', or simply 'the Kate' or 'the cake' has been absorbed in service folklore. This satirical 18th-century drawing shows yokels 'taking the King's shilling' on enlistment*

malfunctioning of planes when nothing should have gone wrong. Gremlins probably originated among desert-flying squadrons during the 1930's.

The services also have their ghosts. The roar of Lawrence of Arabia's motor cycle is heard in the lane near his Dorset house where he was killed; a kilted figure strides across the rifle range at Tidworth, and a Nazi officer called 'Herman the German' haunts a Tiger tank in the tank museum at Bovington Camp, Dorset.

Probably due to the uncertainties of their insecure profession, theatre people cling to their superstitions as determinedly as miners and sailors. It is in the worst possible taste to wish a fellow actor – or a trapeze artist – good luck. Neither real flowers nor real mirrors should be used on the stage. People should not whistle in the theatre, nor should anyone knit backstage. An actor should tear up all his first-night telegrams on the last night and he must remember to remove his soap from the dressing-room at the end of a run or he will not get another engagement.

Quoting from *Macbeth* is unlucky, and the taboo on saying the last line of a play until the first night is particularly observed when rehearsing this tragedy.

Though surrounded by the realities of life and death, doctors and nurses have their own folklore. Bunches of mixed red and white flowers are considered ominous, because in Roman times they were placed on the graves of lovers. The removal of flowers from wards at night was once an established ritual because they were thought to remove oxygen from the air. This has long ceased to have any scientific support, but the custom survives.

Folklore does not belong to any one period or group of people. Today's construction worker firmly believes tales of corpses being walled into the bastions of motorway flyovers, and factory girls about to be married are dressed by their fellow workers in good luck symbols of streamers, rosettes and tall, conical paper hats. In 1971, an American publication, called *Wall Street and Witchcraft*, reported cases of investors selecting their stocks and shares by horoscopes and magic charms. The claim was that these methods had shown better results than those of orthodox advisory services. Few occupations that involve an element of chance are entirely free of superstition.

FEEBLE TAILORS *In folk tales, tailors were regarded as effeminate. The saying 'Nine tailors makes a man' was a common saying amongst more robust trades*

PRINTERS' DEVILS *Apprentice printers or 'devils' still end their apprenticeship with the 'banging out' ceremony, when they are covered in oil, ink, tea leaves, sawdust and paper clippings*

Mr ANDERSON AS MACBETH.
London.Published by J.REDINGTON,73.Hoxton Street.Formerly called 208.Hoxton Old Town.

THE HAUNTED PLAY *To actors, who have strong superstitions about specific plays, Macbeth is notoriously unlucky, perhaps because of the witches in it, though the belief may have arisen because actors have been killed during the fight scenes. Actors are reluctant to quote from the play; the taboo on saying the last line of a play until the actual performance is particularly observed in Macbeth*

SPINNERS AND WEAVERS *Folklore of the textile trade survived the Industrial Revolution but, today, the influence of tradition is largely at the mundane level of apprenticeship initiation ceremonies. In at least one Huddersfield mill, black cat mascots are still attached to machines as an insurance against breakdown*

A song of Britain

Music is the language of emotion; it expresses man's deepest yearnings and sings his greatest triumphs

A STUART MASQUE – LAVISH PRIVATE ENTERTAINMENT

The masque, one of the earliest forms of theatre, developed from the mumming and dance revels with which medieval monarchs and their courts wiled away the dark and tedious days of winter.

The ancient masque grew in splendour in early Stuart times when nobles and rich commoners staged their own performances. Costumes and scenery became more ornate, but the sets were still scattered through the hall so that actors and audience were almost one – an essential ingredient of the earlier mumming plays. Great excitement and merriment were created when the masquers, who were all amateur performers of the same social standing as the audience, made their entrances into a palace hall. Suitably disguised as mythological figures, 'wild men' and other characters, the company would play their parts; sometimes the producer would explain the costumes and allegorical devices of the play. Finally the audience joined in and danced with the masquers

DANCING MUMMERS OF THE MIDDLE AGES

Intricate dance steps, each of which had some symbolic meaning, played a large part in medieval mumming plays; the strangely wistful music of the period provided an accompaniment. Mumming plays, whose origins are believed to be rooted in the oldest of pagan ceremonies, were a traditional part of Christmas at the court of Edward III. This 14th-century manuscript, now in the Bodleian Library, Oxford, illustrates some of the animal masks and costumes used by the court mummers

The uplifting effect of music on the human spirit is an important feature of many religions. It has always been so; song and dance were the vehicles which brought our ancestors closer to their gods and still do so for many religious people today. Though the old gods have been long forgotten, it seems likely that the themes of the dance and the rhythm of the music are still remembered in folk-drama and songs.

In remote pre-history, magical dances were performed to honour and pacify the spirits that men believed controlled the weather, the fertility of their crops and beasts, and the wild creatures that they hunted in the forests. The dancers dressed themselves in animal skins or greenery and, in their dancing, imitated the actions of the chase and the mating of animals.

The most gifted man in the community often headed the ceremonies as the representative of the god. Among many of the earliest agricultural societies, he was killed before his powers faded, his blood being sprinkled on the earth to nourish the soil, and a younger man took his place. Eventually, this form of sacrifice died out and changed to a symbolic spectacle of death and resurrection – the oldest and most dominant theme seen in folk dramas, such as the Padstow Obby Oss ceremony in Cornwall. Each May Day, the Oss is ritually killed and then miraculously revived again the next year.

PADSTOW OBBY OSS, CORNWALL

Christian miracle plays

Though such pagan practices were anathema to the early Church, its missionaries understood the place that ritual occupied in men's hearts. Rather than banning the old folk plays associated with seasonal ceremonies, the Church gave them new life by introducing saints and Old Testament prophets into the drama.

By the early Middle Ages, the Church was staging its own dramatic presentations in the form of miracle plays. Performed in the streets by members of the clergy or tradesmen from the Guilds, the style of the plays owed much to the old pagan traditions, though their content was firmly based upon biblical episodes. In dramatic form, they were closer to pageantry than the theatre, and the plays themselves were grouped together in repertoires or cycles. The York cycle, for instance, consisted of 48 plays. The only other cycles whose texts still survive are at Chester, Wakefield and Coventry. These plays are still occasionally performed at Whitsun and during the week following.

Drama of life and death

Despite the efforts of the clergy and the popularity of the miracle plays, they never quite succeeded in ousting the old pagan ritual. Mumming, or masking, plays were equally successful. In these, the players disguised themselves by blacking their faces or by wearing masks and garments made from ribbons or strips of parchment, a custom that is still followed by the mummers of Marshfield, in Avon. The

practice is based on an ancient belief that if the dancers were recognised, the magical power of their dance would be broken.

MARSHFIELD CHRISTMAS MUMMERS, GLOUCESTERSHIRE

Although there are many regional variations, the main plot of the traditional mumming play revolves around a battle between St George and an enemy who is variously called the Turkish Knight, Bold Slasher or the Black Prince of Paradise. The climax comes when one or other of the protagonists is killed; the Doctor then intervenes and miraculously restores him to life. This simple story symbolises the eternal struggle of good and evil, light and darkness, fertile spring and sterile winter – an expression of man's preoccupation with the cycle of the seasons.

Many mumming-play texts have been passed down from father to son through the centuries, and are still played during Christmas at Andover and Crookham, Hampshire; at Marshfield, Gloucestershire; and in Oxfordshire at Headington.

Easter mumming plays are presented at Midgley, W. Yorkshire and Rochdale, Greater Manchester; the players are known as Pace Eggers (from *Pascha*, the Latin name for Easter). Echoes of Celtic Samain, the night on which the dead were said to leave their graves, still reverberate in Cheshire on All Souls' Eve and All Souls' Day (November 1 and November 2). The mummers here are called Soul Cakers, and in their song they beg cakes or money for their dead ancestors, supposedly abroad that night.

Mumming plays in which the actors masquerade as animals were once common, but few of them survived the Second World War. Among those which are still performed, the best known is the Horn Dance at Abbot's Bromley, Staffordshire, in early September.

ABBOT'S BROMLEY HORN DANCERS, STAFFORDSHIRE

The dance has been described as a hunting dance, a fertility rite and a contest between good and evil; it appears to contain something of all these elements. Six dancers carry reindeer skulls and antlers, three painted white and three black. They are accompanied by a Fool, Maid Marian, the Hobby Horse and a boy carrying a bow and arrows. At the climax of the dance, the deer-men are chased by the other players, while the bowman pretends to fire his arrows at them.

Another type of folk play, also connected with

fertility, was performed in villages throughout the country on Plough Monday, the first Monday after January 6. Traditionally, this was the day when equipment was overhauled in preparation for the spring ploughing. The Plough Play, which is still occasionally revived in some villages, was performed by a group of ploughmen known as Plough Jacks or Plough Stots. They dragged a decorated plough around the village, stopping at houses to beg for gifts or money. If these were not forthcoming, they would plough up the villager's front garden. The plough was eventually dragged to the church to be blessed.

Often the local mummers would accompany the Plough Jacks, while in some villages, including Grenoside, near Sheffield, and Long Skelton near Stockton-on-Tees, Cleveland, the plough ritual often included six or eight long-sword dancers. The dancers, who still perform in these districts, hold the tips of their neighbours swords, weaving intricate patterns and never breaking the chain. Finally, the swords are plaited around the neck of one dancer in a star-shaped 'lock' or 'nut' and suddenly drawn away, simulating decapitation.

GRENOSIDE LONG-SWORD DANCERS, YORKSHIRE

The Rapper Dance of the Tyneside area has a similar theme, but in this, the swords or 'rappers' are shorter and more flexible, and have handles at each end.

The rites of spring

The Morris dance, whose present form dates back to the 15th century at least, is believed to be named after the Spanish *morisca*, meaning a Moorish play or dance. But it probably derives from a much older ceremony, and may be a survival of the sacrificial spring dances that took place throughout pre-Christian Europe.

The Britannia Coconut Dancers of Bacup, Lancashire, who perform at Easter, give support to the theory of Moorish origin. With blackened faces, white barrel skirts and black breeches, they are led by the Whiffler, who whips away winter and ill fortune. Each of the eight dancers wears small discs of wood fastened to his hands, knees and belt. These are clapped together, taking the place of the bells worn by most other Morris men.

BRITANNIA COCONUT DANCERS, BACUP, LANCASHIRE

HEADINGTON MORRIS, OXFORDSHIRE

Two forms of Morris are predominant – Cotswold and North-west. The Cotswold Morris, with handkerchief, stick and hand-clapping movements for six men, and jigs for a single man or a pair, can be seen during festivals and fairs at Headington and Bampton in Oxfordshire, Longborough and Bledington in Gloucestershire, and the town of Abingdon in Oxfordshire.

In Lancashire, the North-west style of Morris, revived in recent years by teams like the Colne Royal Morris group, once predominated at the Rushcart Processions held during Wakes Weeks – the annual holiday that originally commemorated the dedication of the local church. Although the towering rushcarts have long since gone, the Long Morris that once led the processions is still danced by wooden-clogged teams in towns and villages throughout the area.

COLNE ROYAL MORRIS, LANCASHIRE

Songs of work and play

The richness of Britain's folksong tradition has been the basis of inspiration for many composers. Though few folksongs had been 'collected' before the 19th century, they had survived in oral tradition for hundreds of years. During the Middle Ages, minstrels, troubadours and bards carried the songs from place to place, adding to them and enriching them. In later times, broadsheet sellers helped to preserve them for posterity.

Among the oldest of British folksongs are narrative ballads of the Scottish Borders such as 'Lord Randall' and 'The Cruel Mother'. The tunes have a stark simplicity designed to assist the lyrics, which can be historical or mythical, brutal or brave, but always mirror the harsh life of the Border people with astonishing clarity.

Traditional British love songs, such as 'Greensleeves' or 'A Sheiling Song', tend to be wistful, and their music is often of great melodic beauty. In contrast are the songs of seduction, like 'Blow the Candle Out'. Some of these are full of double meanings, and most were considered unfit for publication until only a few years ago.

Songs about work were a favourite theme of the balladeer, though different environments produced different emotions. Rural trade songs are generally optimistic about a prosperous future, while those of

RUSTIC PLEASURES AMONG THE GENTRY

Traditional country dances became fashionable among the upper classes in the 17th and 18th centuries. Steps and tunes were published in books known as 'Dancing Masters'. Some of the dances performed today, like the 'Sir Roger de Coverley' in Hogarth's painting above, are taken from these collections. Many of the earliest-known country dances are performed in a circle, and are possibly of ancient ritual significance

the towns more often tell of evil working conditions. Mining districts produced their own folk poetry. From County Durham, for instance, comes 'The Blackleg Miners', recalling the days when cheap non-union labour was imported from Cornwall and Ireland to defeat the striking colliers.

Work songs, as opposed to songs about work, are those whose rhythms are designed to help the job along. The most effective of these are the sea shanties, of which there are hundreds, each with many variations in both words and music. The beat of the songs matched particular shipboard tasks; for example, a long haul on a rope might be accompanied by 'Blow the Man Down', while for short-haul work, or heaving on the capstan, there were brisker songs such as 'A-rovin' or 'Rio Grande'.

Another type of sea song was the forebitter, sung by sailors when they were off-watch. These songs told of press-gangs, piracy and battles, and in nearly all of them, virtue triumphed in the end.

Sporting songs, like 'The Cockfight' and 'The White Hare', are numerous, and fox-hunting is celebrated in many country songs. Sometimes, the fox is allowed to speak in his own defence. Sentiments in praise of the underdog occur frequently in these sporting songs. As one cockfighting song says, 'We'll lay our money on the bonny grey' because he is smaller than his opponent but has more pluck. The grey cock downs his opponent and, once more, good qualities have won through in the end.

Present-day folksingers have given new life to old ballads, while the 20th century has added its own quota, inspired by the same causes that produced songs in the past – heroism and disaster, love and social injustice. Folk festivals too, have undergone a dramatic revival – a sign, perhaps, that our roots in the past are deeper than we believe.

WORK SONGS OF THE SEA

Sea shanties were work songs whose beat matched the rhythm of tasks on board sailing ships, all of which were accomplished by concerted human muscle-power. Pulling on the oars of a boat, short or long hauls on ropes, all required different work rhythms. In the case of capstan shanties, such as 'Rio Grande', the shantyman would sit on the capstan and softly sing or play the usually unprintable verse; then, heaving on the bars, the seamen roared out the chorus

Health, sickness and medicine

Many traditional cures for disease seem highly optimistic today; but not all can be written off as old wives' tales

There is hardly a substance known to man which has not at one time or another been taken as medicine; nor is there any disease for which folk-healers have failed to prescribe. As a cure for cancer, Saxon physicians recommended an ointment made of goat's gall and honey or, if that failed, they suggested incinerating a dog's skull and powdering the patient's skin with the ashes. For strokes, which they called the 'half-dead disease', they recommended inhaling the smoke of a burning pine tree. Many people still believe that the smell of burning pine cones improves their health.

Before the mid-19th-century revolution in medicine, saying the right words was as important in the treatment of many ailments as taking the right medicine. Herb women used to treat scalds with bramble leaves dipped in spring water, chanting as they dressed the wounds:

> There came three ladies out of the East,
> One with fire and two with frost.
> Out with fire, in with frost.

To cure a nosebleed, Orkney islanders repeated:

> Three virgins came over Jordan's land
> Each with a bloody knife in her hand.
> Stem blood, stem, letherly stand.
> Bloody nose in God's name mend.

Some people still repeat the old rhyme when rubbing nettle stings with a dock leaf:

> Nettle out, dock in.
> Dock remove the nettle sting.

Healing with herbs

The herbalist's craft has a recorded history dating back more than 4000 years. Even primitive man may have practised an instinctive form of herbalism – a suggestion that is borne out by the ability of many animals to seek out and eat healing plants when they are sick.

Recent medical research has often confirmed the healing properties of traditional 'simples' originally prescribed by village herb women. The juice of willow leaves, for example, was once used to treat fevers; in the form of drugs based on salicylic acid it is used for the same purpose today. An extract of the herb witch hazel is still used to soothe sprains and bruises. And penicillin recalls the mould poultices which white witches once made from bread, yeast, carrots and other vegetables.

But for each herbal remedy whose healing powers have been proved, there are many others whose reputations are based on their supposed magical powers, or simply on the curious appearance of the plants of which they are composed.

In the ancient herbal theory called 'the doctrine of signatures', the physical appearance of a plant determines which part of the body it is supposed to treat. So trefoil, a plant with heart-shaped leaves, was used to treat heart disorders and birthwort, because of its womb-shaped flowers, was used to help women in childbirth.

Among the best-known medicinal plants were angelica, which was used to treat coughs and other chest ailments; broom for kidney and heart troubles; coltsfoot for asthma and bronchial disorders; foxglove for palpitations; poppy for toothache and nerve pains; and violet for sore throats. Some may have worked, but others may have done the patient severe damage, or even killed him. The heart stimulant digitalis comes from foxgloves, but the plants themselves are highly poisonous.

Quake doctors and charmers

Like some present-day doctors, some folk-healers specialised in the treatment of particular diseases. In East Anglia, for example, people suffering from ague – a form of malaria characterised by fits of shivering – used to visit specialists known as 'Quake

---

THE KING'S EVIL

For hundreds of years the kings and queens of England were credited with being able to cure by touch the King's Evil, or scrofula, a very painful and often fatal inflammation of the lymph glands of the neck. At a special religious service, the monarch lightly touched each patient in a long queue of sufferers. Charles II administered the royal touch to almost 9000 sufferers during his reign.

GOD'S GIFT TO KINGS *The ability to cure the Evil was said to have been a personal gift from God to Edward the Confessor. The last monarch to use it was Queen Anne, though William III before her had abandoned the rite, and reputedly said to someone seeking his touch: 'God give you better health and more sense'*

ROYAL TOUCH-PIECE *After administering his touch, the monarch hung a special coin round the sufferer's neck. His healing power was said to reside in it*

doctors'. The doctor would first try to charm away the fever with a magic wand; if that failed he might recommend a traditional remedy such as wearing shoes lined with tansy leaves, burying salt in the earth or taking pills made of compressed spiders' webs before breakfast.

A locally famous 19th-century Essex Quake doctor was Thomas Bedloe of Rawreth, who was also known as 'the Dropsy Doctor' and 'the Cancer Quack'. A sign outside his cottage carried the advertisement: 'Thomas Bedloe, hog, dog, and cattle doctor. Immediate relief and perfect cure for persons in the dropsy, also eating cancer.'

Many people still know some of the strange cures recommended by wart charmers; among the best-tried methods are these:

Place in a bag as many pebbles as you have warts and leave the bag at a crossroads; the warts will be transferred to anyone who picks up the bag.

Take a lump of meat, rub the warts with it and then bury it; as the meat decays the warts will gradually disappear.

Prick the warts with a pin and stick the pin into an ash tree, reciting the rhyme:

Ashen tree, ashen tree,
Pray buy these warts from me.

The warts will be transferred to the tree.

Touch each wart with chalk and inscribe a cross for each on the back of a fireplace. As the crosses are obscured by soot, the warts will vanish.

In parts of the West Country, blood charmers were fairly common until about 70 years ago. The charmers of Zennor in Cornwall were credited with the power to staunch heavy bleeding without even seeing the patient. A bloodstained bandage from the injured person was delivered to the charmer's house, where it received his blessing. It was then returned to the patient, and from that moment his wounds were expected to heal.

A spell used for blood charming until well into the 19th century went as follows:

Christ was born in Bethlehem,
Baptised in the River Jordan.
The River stood,
So shall thy blood
(here the patient's name was spoken)
In the name of the Father, the Son and the
Holy Ghost. Amen.

This rhyme, and others like it, probably dates from before the Reformation, and reflects the belief in magic and miracles which the early Catholic Church encouraged among its followers.

The church and the gallows

The copper bracelets which people still wear to cure themselves of rheumatism have a long history; more than 1500 years ago copper rings were prescribed as a suitable treatment for colic, bilious complaints and 'the stone' (gallstones).

In the history of medicine, many other objects have been credited with healing powers that ortho-dox practitioners would never have guessed at; church furnishings were considered particularly efficacious. In the late 19th century a villager asked a Norfolk clergyman if she could borrow a church plate; she wanted to lay it on the stomach of a sick

THE MAGIC OF PEONIES

A 14th-century herbalist attempts to cure his patient of leprosy, holding a peony poised like a magic wand. Peonies were among the earliest known medicinal plants, and they were named after Paeon, legendary physician to the gods of ancient Greece. People once believed that apart from their remarkable curative properties, peonies had the power to keep away evil spirits and storms; they could also bestow long life and cure, among other diseases, lunacy, epilepsy and chronic nightmares. But digging them up was a highly dangerous undertaking, like digging up mandrakes. Peonies were said to shriek so horribly as they were uprooted that anyone near by would die. The safest method was to tie a dog to the plant and let the dog pull it up

child. Holding the key of a church door was once claimed to be a remedy against the bite of a mad dog, while a friar's coat, it was said, would protect whoever was wearing it from pestilence and the ague, both of which were usually fatal.

At the other extreme, the touch of a hanged man's hand could cure goitre and tumours – a macabre superstition which was only laid to rest by the abolition of public hanging in 1868. The swelling was said to disappear as the dead man's hand rotted away. Similarly in Hertfordshire, headaches could be charmed away by touching a rope that had been used for a hanging, while in Lincolnshire the same treatment cured fits.

Such dramatic forms of treatment could only have worked through the power of suggestion, if they worked at all. But even if they did not work, they at least brought hope to the suffering at a period when most physicians were unable to diagnose, let alone cure, most illnesses. In any event, few people could afford a doctor. Many of the more extraordinary folk remedies only make sense against a background of unrelieved poverty and misery. As late as 1714 a physician estimated that half the people who died each year did so from causes that could be ascribed directly or indirectly to poverty.

If all else fails

There were many bizarre, do-it-yourself treatments for minor complaints. During the early years of the last century, Cornishmen sometimes slept on stones in an attempt to cure themselves of baldness, and a standard treatment for colic was to stand on your head for a quarter of an hour. Boils were supposed to disappear if the sufferer crept on his hands and knees beneath a bramble that had grown to form an arch.

In 18th-century Sussex, someone suffering from rheumatism might try placing a pair of bellows between his back and the back of his chair; the idea was that each time he leaned backwards a little of the rheumatism would be blown away. Even today, there are people who try to cure or prevent rheumatism by placing a basin of water beneath their beds or by keeping a nutmeg in their pockets.

According to legend, the breath of cows is always sweet because a cow warmed the infant Christ by breathing on him in the manger. So in country districts, people suffering from lung complaints once inhaled the breath of cows or made up their beds in the loft above cow byres.

A popular 17th-century cure for knife wounds was to anoint and bandage the weapon which had inflicted the wound; this treatment was still practised in Essex and probably elsewhere until the 19th century, and East Anglian fishermen also used it to treat injuries caused by fish hooks. The theory on which it was based claimed that treating the blood which had congealed on the weapon was as effective as treating the patient himself; and in a book written to explain the cure, the 17th-century diplomat Sir Kenelm Digby made it clear that it could be accomplished 'naturally and without any magic'.

Oculists and dentists

Superstition also dominated the treatment of eye diseases, and there were many quacks in this field. One of the most flamboyant was the self-styled 'Chevalier' Dr John Taylor, who in the 18th-century was reputed to have blinded several horses in his search for the secrets of the oculist's art.

His lotions and secret remedies were so successful that Dr Taylor was appointed oculist to George II, and his fame even extended to the Continent, where he toured from town to town in a magnificent coach painted all over with eyes. But in the end, he himself became incurably blind, and died forgotten and unlamented in Prague. He was, according to his contemporary Dr Johnson, 'an instance of how far impudence will carry ignorance'; Johnson considered him the most ignorant man he had ever met.

For most people there was no hope of being treated by anyone as eminent as Dr Taylor, and they had to rely instead on traditional folk remedies. Rainwater, if collected and bottled in June, was supposed to heal most eye disorders; and dew, especially if it had been collected on May Day morning, made a soothing lotion for sore eyes. Even today, some people maintain that a stye can be cured by passing a gold wedding ring over it; and it is only within the last 50 years that the superstition has finally been refuted that a dog can lick away a stye. In fact, the creature would be more likely to spread the infection.

At Penmynydd in Wales, sufferers with eye disorders made an ointment with scrapings from a 14th-century tomb in the church. So great was the demand that by the 17th century, the tomb had become badly damaged.

Treating a toothache in the 18th century, the heyday of folk medicine, could be a gruesome business, for the village blacksmith or a fairground quack would probably do the job. Extreme pain could be

NEW TEETH FOR OLD *A dentist displays his patient's false teeth to a prospective client. Rowlandson's drawing caricatured the Frenchman Dubois de Chémant, who introduced porcelain false teeth to Britain in the late 18th century*

ROWLAND'S OIL *In the early 19th century Alexander Rowland made a fortune selling Macassar oil as a hair restorative. In this cartoon Rowlandson mocked Rowland's claims, and the conceit of those who made him rich*

relieved, it was said, by driving a nail into the tooth until the tooth bled, and then hammering the nail into a tree; the pain would be transferred to the tree. Alternatively, the patient could try inhaling the fumes of burning henbane; this might drive away the worms which were said to make teeth rot. To prevent toothache, a dead mole could be worn around the neck, presumably because moles were thought to have very strong teeth, and the strength would be transferred by sympathetic magic.

Magic and medicine

Before the nature of disease was properly understood, most people believed that sickness was caused by fairies or other evil spirits 'taking over' their bodies; and many cures were little more than attempts to exorcise these invisible trespassers. But, remarkably, much of this magic appears to have worked. Even the 17th-century scholar Robert Burton was able to remark: 'We see commonly the toothache, gout, falling sickness, biting of a mad dog and many such maladies cured by spells, words, characters and charms.'

There are many possible explanations for this. Probably, most people 'cured' by wizards and cunning men in fact recovered naturally – those suffering from fevers, wounds and warts, for example.

Others may have owed their recovery to the genuine healing powers of the herbs which herb women and white witches prescribed along with the traditional spells and charms.

But there may be another more fundamental reason for some of the wizards' miracle cures – the healing power of faith and the imagination. It is now generally accepted that fear, tension or any other mental disorder can have painful physical symptoms, and that the best treatment in such cases is directed at the mind, not the body. The wizards' spells and charms may have been hopelessly inadequate for bodily ills; but they were powerful medicine for the mind. There can be little doubt of the profound psychological effect of a consulting room festooned with drying herbs, skulls and musty parchments, over which presided a miracle-working seventh son of a seventh son.

In a deeply superstitious age, when most people believed unreservedly in magic and the supernatural, and lived in constant fear of witches and the forces of evil, a wizard's medicine, whatever it was composed of, could have effected many remarkable cures. That, at any rate, was Robert Burton's conclusion: 'As some are molested by fantasy,' he wrote, 'so some again by fancy alone and a good conceit are as easily recovered.'

THE GREAT AGE OF QUACKERY

KILL OR CURE *Every century, not least the 20th, has its quack doctors, though they were never more brazen than in the 18th century, when the caricaturist Thomas Rowlandson was alive. Rowlandson ridiculed these fortune-hunting opportunists, expressing his contempt in scathing cartoons such as this study of a quack chemist serving his clients while Death mixes poisons behind a curtain.*

One of the most notorious 18th-century quacks was the conjurer Gustavus Katterfelto. At the peak of his success, he toured England dispensing valueless flu cures at five shillings a bottle, entering each town in an antique, horse-

drawn carriage while two negro servants in coloured livery paraded through the streets blowing trumpets. Two black cats were his constant companions; they were known as 'the Doctor's devils', though Gustavus himself publicly denied that they were of diabolical origin.

One London quack used the Lisbon earthquake of 1755, in which 60,000 people died, as an excuse for selling protective 'earthquake pills'. Another sold pills which restored the memory. And Martin van Butchell, who practised in England in the 1770's, made a cult figure of himself by displaying in his home the embalmed body of his wife

Death and burial

The rituals that surrounded death and burial eased the soul's passage to the next world and prevented its return

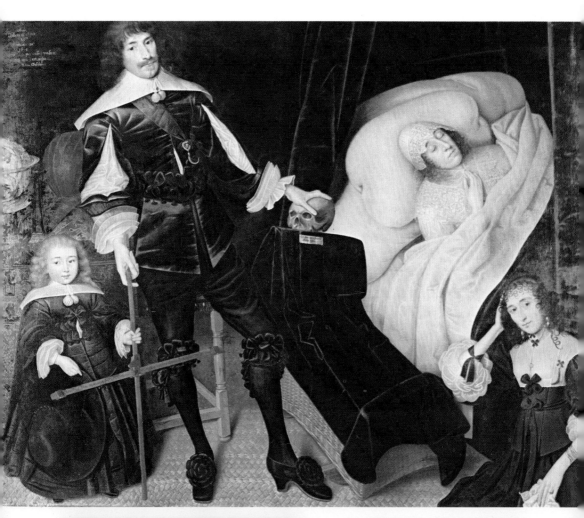

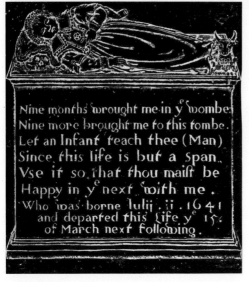

Nine months wrought me in y[e] wombe:
Nine more brought me to this tombe.
Let an Infant teach thee (Man)
Since, this life is but a Span,
Vse it so, that thou maist be
Happy in y[e] next with me.
Who was borne Iulij , ii .1641
and departed this Life y[e] 15.
of March next following .

SYMBOLS OF IMMORTALITY

For thousands of years, people have reached after immortality by ordering paintings or statues of themselves to be placed in or near their tombs. Memorial pictures, such as this death-bed composition, came into vogue in the early 17th century. The subject is Sir Thomas Aston and his wife, who died in childbirth in 1635, and includes a black-draped wicker cradle bearing a skull. The label below the skull bears a Latin inscription, which translated means 'He who sows hope in the flesh reaps bones' – a reflection on the futility of earthly ambitions. His wife is shown twice – lying dead in bed and seated at its foot. Thomas, their young son, helps his father to hold a cross-staff, a navigational instrument. A celestial globe and an unstrung lute lie together on an embroidered Indian cloth. They can name the stars and chart the seas, but they cannot measure their grief. Lady Aston, a beautiful and thoughtful woman in life, now lies as still and silent as the unstrung lute. (City Galleries, Manchester.)

The memorial (left) at Woburn, Buckinghamshire shows the nine-month-old son of Philip, Lord Wharton, lying on his tomb holding a rose – a symbol of purity. The child died in 1642

People have always tried to relieve their fear of death by channelling it into an elaborate series of rituals designed to help and protect not only the living, but also the newly dead. Relatives and friends always tried to make the passage of a dying man easier, and when he was dead they strove to aid his soul along the difficult road to the next world, and to lay his body to rest with respect and honour.

This was done from motives of affection, or duty, or from the belief that the dying man urgently needed their help in this moment of supreme crisis. At one time, there was a darker belief that the angry ghost might return to haunt them if the necessary help was not given. Many funeral customs have their origin in that ancient need to be sure that the departed spirit would never return.

Some of the rites which were common 80 or 90 years ago have vanished now, especially those that were observed within the home. But there are others which are still performed, at least in some households, even when the ideas from which they sprang are only half-believed by the performers. When the dead man has been truly loved, there is often an uneasy feeling that nothing should be omitted that might conceivably help him on his unknown journey.

Signs and portents
Death's approach is still believed to be heralded by small but noticeable interruptions in the pattern of everyday life. The cries and movements of certain birds, flowers blooming out of season, clocks striking thirteen times, pictures falling from the wall, the persistent appearance in ironed linen of the diamond-shaped crease known as a 'coffin', have all been cited as death omens. So has the sudden appearance of mice in a house. The abrupt departure of long-established crickets from a house, or an owl screeching near by, are also ominous. A dog howling continually outside a house where someone lies ill means that the sick person will certainly die, since dogs have the power of seeing death as it approaches.

Corpse Lights (or Corpse Candles) were formerly held to be infallible warnings. These were small lambent flames, possibly the result of ignited marsh gas. It was said that they floated over the ground between the churchyard and the home of the doomed person, and indicated the route that the funeral procession would take. If a child's death was foretold, the flame was blue; in the case of an adult, yellow.

If rigor mortis was unusually slow in setting in, or the eyes of a corpse remained open, another death could be expected in the same household before long. Keeping a corpse in the house over Sunday, or leaving the grave open on that day, was a sure sign of another death in the parish.

In the days when horses drew the hearse, it was a fatal sign if they refused to start with the coffin; they would soon be needed again by the same family. It was also said that if, during the journey, one of the horses turned its head and neighed outside a dwelling, someone in that house would soon die.

Helping the departing spirit
Death was believed to be a hard and difficult process which ought not to be prolonged by attempts to delay the end, once that end was certain. Tears in the death chamber had to be restrained, for they hindered the soul's departure by strengthening its earthly ties. An excessive display of sorrow at such times was known as 'crying back the dying' – a selfish and unkind act.

In coastal areas, it was thought that no one could die unless the tide was running out; if the sick man lived through one ebb tide, he would linger on until the next.

If a sick man's bed lay across the lines of the floor-boards, it had to be turned so as to line up with them, for death would not come while the bed stood 'athwart the planshuns'. Pigeon, dove or game-bird feathers accidentally included in the pillow or mattress stuffing would also keep death away; as a precaution pillows and mattresses were often re-moved. However, if some relative or friend was known to be coming and might be too late, a small bunch of feathers was placed between the sheets to preserve life for a few hours longer. This belief was current in rural areas until the beginning of this century.

Sometimes the dying man was lifted out of his bed and laid on the cold floor to hasten his end. The practice was effective, though not for the reasons supposed by his kindly relatives; many people believed that it was easier to die in contact with the earth from which all men sprang. The practice may have originated in the days when most cottages had floors of beaten earth.

There was also a widespread custom known as Drawing the Pillow. A pillow was placed behind the dying man's head and then drawn away, suddenly and sharply, so that he fell backwards. This was intended to ease his soul's departure.

Departure of the soul
As soon as death had occurred, certain things had to be done to allow the departing soul free passage. Many of these were common practice even in the last century and some linger now. Doors and windows were opened and knots loosened, and animals put out of doors until after the funeral to prevent the passing spirit entering them. Sometimes the fire was put out, because it represented the life of the house; and clocks were stopped because the dead have nothing to do with time.

If there was any perishable food in the room, it was immediately thrown away, or a piece of iron would be thrust into it to prevent the spirit from entering and corrupting it. Mirrors were veiled, or turned to the wall, for fear that the soul might become entangled in the reflection.

Candles were kept burning beside the corpse, as they still are in many households. A green turf wrapped in paper, or salt heaped upon a plate, was often laid on the dead man's breast. A common explanation for this last custom was that it prevented the body from swelling, but originally, like the burning candles, it had another meaning. Fire, salt and earth have always been regarded as antidotes to evil, and consequently they protected the soul from any demons which might try to capture it.

The news of death
Where bees were kept, it was customary to inform them of any death in the family. If this was not done, the bees would die or fly away. The owner's heir, or sometimes his widow, went to the hives, knocked three times upon each one with an iron door-key, and told the bees within that their master had gone. If any other member of the household had died, the news was conveyed by the head of the family. Black crepe was tied on the hives to show that their inmates were in mourning. Even today, bees are still notified of deaths in some widely spread

country districts, and for the same reason as of old – that they will be lost to their owners if the rite is not observed.

Rooks were also told of a landowner's death. The new owner would stand under the trees and give the news, usually with an added promise that only he and his friends would be allowed to shoot the birds in future. If he neglected this ceremony, the birds would desert the rookery, an evil omen in itself. If rooks flew away, it was believed to forecast the loss of the land and the downfall of the family through poverty.

This traditional sympathy between men and other living creatures that were part of their lives also extended to cage-birds and favourite plants. They too had to be made aware of their owner's death, and put into mourning with black bows tied about the cages, or flower-pots draped with crepe. Occasionally, little black flags were thrust into the earth beside a particular plant.

The long farewell

A deeply rooted notion, which still survives, is that a corpse should never be left alone between the death and the funeral. Nor should the corpse be locked in any room. Even now, to leave a corpse in an empty house, especially at night, is commonly

regarded as a shocking neglect of an essential duty. If it happens that only one mourner is at home and is compelled to go out, then the absence must be as brief as possible, and the house door, as well as the door of the death-chamber, must be left unlocked.

A visitor calling to pay his last respects in the 17th century might have been asked to take part in 'sin-eating'. By accepting food and drink together with a gift of money, the sin-eater took responsibility for the sins of the dead person. The food usually consisted of bread, and a glass of wine or beer which were handed to the visitor over the dead person's body, together with a small coin.

Formerly, an unbroken vigil used to be kept beside the coffin. Friends and neighbours joined in, partly to allow the family members some rest, and also to show their regard for the dead person. This traditional Wake or Lykewake survived in Scotland, Wales and the northern and western English counties until the end of the 19th century. The Wake became a sober ritual in its later years, with prayers, readings from the Scriptures, and conversation in hushed voices. But in earlier times, as in modern Irish Wakes, it was often a cheerful and merry occasion. A large company gathered about the corpse, ate and drank, sang and danced, told stories, played cards and occasionally indulged in practical

---

BLACK AND WHITE FOR MOURNING

AN INNOCENT'S DEATH *It was customary in 19th-century children's funerals for a white-sashed bearer to precede the coffin, carrying a white standard*

SIGN OF PURITY *A girl with a spotless reputation who died unmarried was sometimes commemorated with a Maiden's Garland, which was hung in the church after the funeral*

FUNERAL DRESS OF THE VICTORIANS *During the 19th century, families would advertise their grief for at least a year after the death of a relative, during which time it was almost compulsory to wear black. In the Western world, black has been the colour of mourning since Roman times, when it was associated with the underworld. Long ago, sombre clothes were thought to prevent recognition by angry ghosts – the widow's veil of full mourning may be a relic of this. White was sometimes used at funerals to indicate the purity of the dead person – white gloves were often pinned to Maidens' Garlands, and young children were buried in white coffins*

jokes. Although this may appear irreverent by some standards, a farewell party was considered an essential gesture of affection and respect for the dead man. There was also the feeling that a revel would, in some way, help to protect the departing soul from the dangers of its long journey, as well as providing some comfort to the bereaved.

Touching the Dead

The custom of Touching the Dead still lingers on in some rural areas, particularly in the North. A chance visitor who calls at a house in which a dead body lies may be asked to enter and view the corpse, and usually to touch it. For those strangers who did not know the dead person, the request is sometimes startling and embarrassing. However, it must not be refused, since this may give lasting offence.

One explanation given for this practice is that to touch the brow or the hand of the corpse, gently and reverently, is a final act of courtesy which no one ought to withhold. Another is that touching protects the person involved from being haunted by the dead man's ghost. Sometimes it is done to show that goodwill exists between the toucher and the dead man, and this idea gives a clue to the probable origin of the custom. It was once believed that a murdered man's body would bleed at the touch of his murderer. Long after this crude form of ordeal had been abandoned in the courts, it was sometimes resorted to in secret. Refusal to face the test, though it could prove nothing, often left a man under a permanent cloud of suspicion.

Burial preparations

Burial clothes were once prepared long before they were likely to be needed. In north-east England, girls included them in their wedding trousseaux as a matter of custom.

The usual burial garment was the shroud, normally made of linen, except between 1666 and 1814, when the use of anything other than wool was forbidden by law, in order to benefit the wool trade. Sometimes the dead person was dressed in his own clothes. Monks and nuns are still buried in their habits, and members of the armed forces in uniform. Gipsies are dressed in their best clothes as a rule, and sometimes a bride who has died soon after her wedding is buried in her bridal dress.

Until about 100 years ago, a small coin was placed in the dead man's mouth or in his hand, so that he might pay his way on the journey to the next world. Other things were sometimes placed in his coffin – a candle to give him light, or food to sustain him, and occasionally a hammer with which he could knock when he reached his destination. A Christian variant of these pagan customs was the inclusion of a Bible, or a Sunday-school certificate, to show that the dead person had been devout during his lifetime. A tuft of wool was put into shepherds' hands so that at the Last Judgment they could prove that their irregular churchgoing was due to the demands of their work.

It is not unusual for toys to be buried with children, or some cherished possession with adults, a custom now dictated by affection or sentiment, but springing originally from the pagan belief that the dead needed the same things beyond the grave as they did in this world.

Funeral customs and superstitions

On the day of the funeral, the corpse was carried from the house feet foremost, and always through the front door. Another custom was that the door should be left open while the funeral party was absent, either because another death might follow if this was not done, or because the soul might be imprisoned and therefore haunt the house.

Before the procession set out, sprigs of rosemary or evergreen were given to the mourners; these were thrown into the grave, as a promise to the dead man that he would not be forgotten. If rain fell during the procession or the service, it was a good portent for the happiness of the departed soul.

On the way to the churchyard, the coffin was always carried in front of the mourners until the lychgate was reached, where the clergyman came to receive it. Anyone attempting to precede the coffin was likely to die suddenly himself, or to suffer serious misfortune. The same was true of any person who entered the house before the next-of-kin when the mourners returned home.

To meet a funeral on the road was considered ominous unless the person who met it turned and followed it a little way. If it was a walking funeral the person should take his turn as a bearer for a short distance.

There was formerly a belief, inherited from pagan practices, that the dead must travel the way of the sun for part of the journey to the grave, or the soul's welfare would be imperilled. Bearers sometimes halted by some traditional mark – a wayside stone or the church cross – and carried the coffin round it clockwise, the direction of the sun, once or thrice times.

In most parishes, there was a traditional route for funerals – the Church Road or the Corpse Way. Usually, this was an ordinary road, but in some remote areas, it was a narrow path along which the dead from outlying farms and hamlets were brought to the local church. To use any other route was unlucky, and was never done unless bad weather made the Corpse Way impassable.

If private land was involved, then a permanent right of way was supposed to be created, though there was no basis for this in law. In 1948, permission was refused to the police to carry a drowned man over the toll-bridge at Iffley Lock near Oxford. The owners claimed that the passage of the corpse would automatically destroy the toll rights. It was sometimes said that the undertaker could overcome the difficulty by sticking pins into every gate or stile on the way, or by persuading the landowner to accept a small fee. Nevertheless, fights sometimes broke out between funeral parties and landowners' servants, the former struggling to reach the church by the shortest route and the latter striving to protect their masters' property.

The gap in the curtain

Whether moments or years away, the future is concealed by time's curtain; yet people still strive to open it

The main reason why people attempt to seek the unknown through divination is that it is only with a presumed knowledge of the future that they can feel emotionally secure in the present. Many future events can be planned with a reasonable degree of accuracy, but others are beyond our control. Tomorrow is a huge question mark – which is why we are so fascinated by books and films on time travel. We journey into the future with trepidation, and are grateful for even a tiny glimpse into that unknown land. Despite the gross inaccuracy of most fortune-tellers, they do offer us that glimpse; otherwise, we travel with no bearings at all.

In primitive societies especially, people were constantly placed in jeopardy by the forces of nature – crops failed, disease went unchecked, and sometimes the tensions that arose produced accusations of witchcraft. Divination was important because it provided a simple and impersonal solution to misfortune. The diviner himself was rarely accused of being wrong – it was his customers who were out of harmony with the supernatural.

In the 20th century, we still look for the same reassurance about the future. Though the spread of education has now brought many old ideas into discredit, astrologers, palmists and other types of fortune-tellers are still as popular as ever.

As well as employing the older type of diviner, we seek the advice of meteorologists, stockbrokers and marriage-guidance counsellors. Though they use knowledge and equipment of greater sophistication than the witch doctor, they can only predict the likely outcome of given sets of circumstances, and are still unable to supply a definitive picture of the future. Today, Macbeth would consult military strategists and diplomats rather than three witches before making his bid for the throne. But the tragic outcome might well be the same.

Where highly trained experts often fail, it seems unlikely that less orthodox methods can succeed. Yet, despite a fairly unconvincing record, fortune-tellers are as popular today as they have been for thousands of years. Some of the methods of divination, such as astrology and geomancy (divining through examination of the patterns made by thrown earth), are the realm of professional practitioners and are extremely complex. Some, like crystal gazing, are not so elaborate, but require instead particular states of consciousness or 'clairvoyance' which are believed to be possessed by only a few people. Other methods, such as tea-leaf

IN A GLASS, DARKLY

Forthcoming events are said to have been revealed in the surfaces of polished metal and pools of ink and water, but modern clairvoyants prefer the translucent crystal ball. After gazing into the ball for a few minutes, the seer goes into a trance and 'sees' the future in both abstract patterns and film-like images. Crystal-gazing episodes were a favourite melodramatic device of hack Victorian writers, as this 19th-century woodcut shows

reading, are so simple that they are little more than party games. But from occult science to childlike diversion, all divination techniques share a common aim – to reveal the future which, according to laws of science, cannot be revealed.

Lines and bumps

One range of divinatory arts includes some of the oldest techniques of all. Together, they are called 'somatomancy', and involve the reading of tell-tale signs upon the human body. Just as no two individuals share the same destiny, so none of the detailed features of their bodies is exactly the same. Since the last century, detectives have made use of the discovery that fingerprints are unique to each individual; diviners have been applying similar methods of differentiation for thousands of years.

Palmistry (or chiromancy) is perhaps the oldest of the several forms of somatomancy. It began in China about 5000 years ago, and probably reached England during the early Middle Ages. It is believed that various personality traits, past events and future happenings are printed in a sort of code upon the palms of the hands. The palmist attempts to decipher the code and interpret its meaning.

The code consists of more than just the depth of lines of the palm, their direction, length and breaks. The markings on the fingers and wrist, the positioning and size of the 'mounds' of the hand, its overall shape, and even the texture of the skin are equally important.

Generally, it is believed that the left hand shows

FATE'S LUMPS AND BUMPS

VICIOUSNESS

CHRONIC SICKNESS

INTELLIGENCE

Physiognomy, the art of divining character by lines and features of the human face, and phrenology, in which the inner self is reflected in bumps on the skull, were both extremely popular during the first half of the 19th century. So much so, that Queen Victoria had the bumps of several of her children 'read' in order to divine their characters.

Both 'sciences' evolved from a Greek concept that man in his physical make-up reflects the workings of the universe, and from a faulty understanding of the workings of different areas of the brain. Thus, in phrenology, an unevenness in one part of the skull might indicate Pride; in another, Destructiveness.

In physiognomy, similar deductions were made from the number and positioning of lines on the face. The lines on the woman (above left) were said to indicate viciousness; on the bearded man, chronic illness; and on the moustach-ioed man, intelligence.

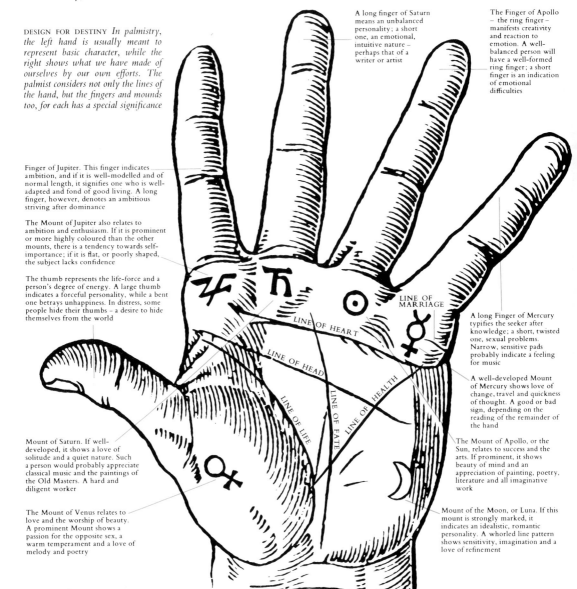

DESIGN FOR DESTINY *In palmistry, the left hand is usually meant to represent basic character, while the right shows what we have made of ourselves by our own efforts. The palmist considers not only the lines of the hand, but the fingers and mounds too, for each has a special significance*

A long finger of Saturn means an unbalanced personality; a short one, an emotional, intuitive nature – perhaps that of a writer or artist

The Finger of Apollo – the ring finger – manifests creativity and reaction to emotion. A well-balanced person will have a well-formed ring finger; a short finger is an indication of emotional difficulties

Finger of Jupiter. This finger indicates ambition, and if it is well-modelled and of normal length, it signifies one who is well-adapted and fond of good living. A long finger, however, denotes an ambitious striving after dominance

The Mount of Jupiter also relates to ambition and enthusiasm. If it is prominent or more highly coloured than the other mounts, there is a tendency towards self-importance; if it is flat, or poorly shaped, the subject lacks confidence

The thumb represents the life-force and a person's degree of energy. A large thumb indicates a forceful personality, while a bent one betrays unhappiness. In distress, some people hide their thumbs – a desire to hide themselves from the world

Mount of Saturn. If well-developed, it shows a love of solitude and a quiet nature. Such a person would probably appreciate classical music and the paintings of the Old Masters. A hard and diligent worker

The Mount of Venus relates to love and the worship of beauty. A prominent Mount shows a passion for the opposite sex, a warm temperament and a love of melody and poetry

LINE OF MARRIAGE

LINE OF HEART

LINE OF HEAD

LINE OF LIFE

LINE OF FATE

LINE OF HEALTH

A long Finger of Mercury typifies the seeker after knowledge; a short, twisted one, sexual problems. Narrow, sensitive pads probably indicate a feeling for music

A well-developed Mount of Mercury shows love of change, travel and quickness of thought. A good or bad sign, depending on the reading of the remainder of the hand

The Mount of Apollo, or the Sun, relates to success and the arts. If prominent, it shows beauty of mind and an appreciation of painting, poetry, literature and all imaginative work

Mount of the Moon, or Luna. If this mount is strongly marked, it indicates an idealistic, romantic personality. A whorled line pattern shows sensitivity, imagination and a love of refinement

the things that make up the person's character, while the right demonstrates what he will make of his life. By way of confirmation, doctors have found in the last ten years that much useful medical information can be gleaned from the patient's hands and nails concerning his general state of health or proneness to disease. For example, people with a tendency towards mongol characteristics have a unique fingerprint pattern.

Among the many other forms of somatomancy is phrenology, which relates bumps on the head to a person's character and abilities. Neomancy is a way of telling somebody's future by examining the moles on his body. Metoscopy causes less embarrassment to the subject than neomancy, since it holds that the moles are 'reflected' in the lines of the face. Similarly, in ophthalmoscopy, the person's eyes are studied to reveal hidden personality traits.

One of the most highly developed methods is physiognomy, in which the subject's head shape and features are compared with those of various animals. A 'lion-headed' man is courageous, an 'ass-head' stupid, and so on. This is akin to the idea that a dimpled cheek is evidence of a sweet nature, a square jaw shows strength of character, while a criminal type is essentially a man with close-set eyes.

Nowadays, psychologists have developed certain techniques of somatomancy for use in personnel selection – handwriting and colour-preference tests are employed by some British management consultancy firms to 'divine' an applicant's suitability for a particular job.

'The Devil's Books'

The 18th-century writer Jonathan Swift called playing-cards 'The Devil's Books', though he was referring to their use in gambling rather than in divination. Some authorities have pointed out that since both practices involve a large element of chance, it is not surprising that both should employ the same instruments. Fortune-tellers counter this by saying that the apparently random fall of the cards is not random at all; rather, it is dictated by a supernatural force whose messages are interpreted by the diviner.

Card-reading, or cartomancy, includes divination by both Tarot and ordinary playing-cards. Tarot cards are the elaborately decorated ancestors of present-day cards; their origins have been traced to both Egypt and Bohemia. They were probably introduced to this country by gipsies about 500 years ago. There are 78 cards in the pack, of which 56 are divided into four suits – Cups, Coins, Swords and Wands. These may represent the four classes of medieval society – cups or chalices for the clergy; coins for the merchants; swords for the nobility; wands or staffs for the peasantry. There are ten numbered cards in each suit, and a King, Queen, Knight and Knave. The remaining cards form the Major Arcana of 22 trump cards whose rich designs contain a wealth of occult lore, and whose symbolism is of the greatest significance when the pack is used in fortune-telling. There are many designs of Tarot packs, and several methods of laying out the cards and interpreting them. In one widely used

STARS OF THE BODY

Though it is now out of fashion, neomancy – foretelling a person's destiny by the positioning of moles on the face and body – enjoyed a considerable vogue, especially during the 17th and 18th centuries. The practice is related to metoscopy, in which the positioning of moles on the body is believed to be reflected in lines on the face. Like many of the divinatory arts, both are related to astrology, for it was once thought that man mirrored the universe in himself.

In neomancy, moles were usually referred to as 'Stars of the Body', and their positioning provided a key to both character and fate. For example, a mole on the right shoulder foretells happiness in both sexes, but one on the left means a quarrelsome man, or denotes that a woman will have many husbands. A mole on the right breast shows that a woman will be loved by great men, but if it occurs in a man, he will be a slave to passion.

Riches and honour are foretold by moles on the back and the right side of the stomach, and fruitfulness in either sex is denoted by a mole on the left cheek.

Good fortune in marriage is practically certain if you have a mole on the right hip, and the union will be blessed with many children if one of the partners has a mole near the navel.

If a child has one under the right thigh, he will grow up to be hard working, and if he should possess a similar blemish on his bottom, his industries will be rewarded by fame and riches

THE STUFF OF DREAMS

This woodcut is taken from an 18th-century pamphlet entitled 'The Old Egyptian Fortune-Tellers's Last Legacy'. Its author interpreted palms, lines on the face and dreams.

About dreams, he said: 'To dream of music signifies speedy marriage; to dream of falling denotes constancy; of having teeth drawn means loss of friends; to dream a ring falls off your finger, signifies the loss of a friend.'

'To dream of vermin, and have much trouble in killing them, signifies much riches', but the reader is warned that if he dreams of losing blood from the nose, it is 'of ill consequence'.

Trouble in crossing a dream river means that you have hard labour in store; to fly, signifies praise, and if you should fall a great distance without being hurt, then good fortune is around the corner.

Apparently, dreams can be influenced, because if you put rosemary under your pillow on Easter eve, 'you will dream of the party you shall enjoy'

method, the diviner and the questioner both shuffle the cards, and lay them out in the pattern of the ancient Hebrew 'Tree of Life'.

```
            1
    3           2
    5       4
        6
    8           7
        9
       10
```

As each card is upturned, its symbolism is interpreted in relation to its location. For example, Pack 9 refers to Health, and cards turned up from this position are said to foretell the health of the questioner. Each individual card has a special meaning, which includes such symbol-laden representations as 'The Hanged Man' 'The Juggler' and 'The Tower Struck by Lightning'. The numbers and suits of the minor cards are also significant; the Nine of Swords is the death card, and Swords are generally unlucky. The Knave of Coins is a card of ill-omen, though other Coin cards are associated with financial success. Cups are usually lucky cards, while Wands are connected with enterprise.

Names and numbers

In divination by numbers, or numerology, the diviner seeks to analyse the character of his subject by assigning certain numerical values to the letters of his name. There are several ways of arriving at these values, but the usual modern system is:

```
1  2  3  4  5  6  7  8  9

A  B  C  D  E  F  G  H  I

J  K  L  M  N  O  P  Q  R

S  T  U  V  W  X  Y  Z
```

The number of the subject's name is obtained by writing down his first names (or nickname) followed by his surname, and writing the appropriate numbers beneath:

```
J  O  H  N    S  M  I  T  H
1  6  8  5    1  4  9  2  8
```

The numbers are added together until a single figure remains:

$$1+6+8+5+1+4+9+2+8=44; 4+4=8$$

This number shows the subject's general character. Similarly, the digits of his birth date may be added to give a 'birth number', representing his destiny:
26 June 1932

$$2+6+6+1+9+3+2=29; 2+9=11; 1+1=2$$

The attributes and defects assigned to each number vary in different systems, but the following is a useful summary:
1. Singleminded; independent; unsympathetic; active.
2. Feminine; gentle; modest; sympathetic.
3. Brilliant; artistic; successful; ambitious.
4. Steady; hard working; unsuccessful.
5. Nervous; adventurous; versatile; eccentric.
6. Simple; domestic; loyal.
7. Scholarly; austere; mysterious.
8. Powerful; rich; worldly.
9. Idealistic; romantic; determined.

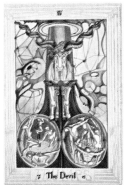

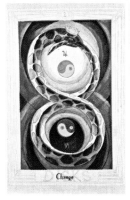

KEYS TO THE OCCULT

Fortune-telling is only a minor branch of Tarot; in its higher form it purports to provide a link between God, man and the infinite. According to its practitioners, careful study and interpretation of its symbols can unlock memories of our previous lives and free our thoughts from the bonds of words. There is no standard design for Tarot symbols, and there is an infinite number of interpretations depending on their places in the pack. Those above were designed by Aleister Crowley (1875–1947), self-styled 'Great Beast' and Master Magician. The Devil often symbolises power misused, while the Fool is sometimes taken to mean childlike innocence and goodness. The Discs signify change, and Death links the material and spiritual worlds

TOOLS OF THE FORTUNE-TELLER

Divination by playing-cards is much more clear-cut than by Tarot because each card has a more precise interpretation. The key to reading the cards is provided when the fortune-teller selects the court card which most closely resembles the subject's character. For example, the Knave of Diamonds and the Queen of Spades (above) might represent a successful young man and a dark, seductive woman. This card is removed, and the remainder of the pack is divided into nine piles, each reflecting an aspect of the subject's fortune

A nice cup of tea

When tea was first imported from China about 300
years ago, the art of reading tea leaves came with it.
The early methods may have derived from readings
of the cracks found inside bells, and there may be a
further connection between the shape of the inside
of the cup and early ideas about the shape of the
universe. Many people still read teacups, though
some devotees claim that they can predict events
only 24 hours ahead. The diviner can read his own
fortune or somebody else's. But the person whose
fortune is to be told must also drink the tea. The cup
should be broad and shallow, and the tea preferably
coarse-leaved. The subject drinks all but the last
few drops; then the diviner swirls the cup three
times in his left hand before draining off the
remaining liquid.

When the patterns made by the leaves are
examined, those near the handle represent the near
future, those in the upper part less close events,
those around the sides more distant still, while the
patterns at the bottom indicate the happenings
which will occur last. There are a great many
symbols and interpretations. Patterns shaped like
crosses, spades, knives, guns, snakes, cats or toads
foretell bad luck. Good omens include crescent
moons, clover leaves, flowers, trees, crows and the
number 7. Signs with particular meanings include
the anchor for hope and stability, circles for money,
an eagle for success, boots, ships and aeroplanes for
impending journeys. Patterns depicting large letters
are said to be places, while small letters represent
people; thus 'P' might be 'Paris' but 'p' might be
'Peter'. Numbers usually mean dates; whether days,
months or years away is determined by their
location in relation to the handle of the cup. Whole
dictionaries listing tea-leaf symbols have been
published in recent years and, as in other forms of
divination, it is important for the diviner to
memorise as many of them as possible so that he can
interpret them to his audience in a fast-moving
narrative.

Prodigies and portents

Many random, curious, often minor occurrences
have been viewed as predictions of major events.
During the trial of Charles I, for example, it was
noted that the head of his staff fell off; this was held
to predict the king's own fate. The death of his arch-
enemy, Cromwell, was foretold by the unusual
sight of a great whale that swam up the Thames to
Greenwich, and the Protector's final passing was
announced by a terrible storm. The appearance of
Halley's Comet in 1066 was taken as a warning of
the Norman invasion, while in recent times there
were those who saw the burning of the Crystal
Palace in 1936 as an anticipation of the ravages of the
Blitz. A falling cross at the funeral of George V
was said to be an omen of the abdication of Edward
VIII though it seems likely, as in many other cases,
that the occurrence was remembered after the
major event had taken place.

On a smaller scale, chance events of all kinds are
seen as omens. In bibliomancy, the random opening
of a book, usually the Bible, is believed to provide a
guide to the future. So may ceromancy, in which the
diviner studies the shapes assumed by molten wax in
cold water. Crystalomancy includes gazing into
crystal balls and other reflecting surfaces in search
of portents; and even the shape of clouds and the
length of shadows have been used in divination.
Though these methods seem absurd, few of us can
resist making our own interpretations of chance
events. When children 'count-out' in a game, when
we toss a coin, we are trying to find the gap in the
curtain of the future.

PROPHETS OR CHARLATANS?

As far back as written records go, prophets have
claimed the ability to 'see' great events or tragedies
before they actually occur. In the majority of cases, their
dreams or visions were not recorded, or their portents
were not understood, until after the event had taken
place. Several people, for example, 'foresaw' the sink-
ing of the *Titanic* and the death of Lord Kitchener, but
were presumably unable to convince the authorities in
time. Nevertheless, among the more extraordinary
forecasts which were made, several were uncannily
reflected in British history.

MOTHER SHIPTON This
15th-century Yorkshire
seer was said to have predicted both the Civil War
and the 1666 Fire of Lon-
don. Though they were
probably forged, the influence of the 'Shipton Pro-
phecies' was considerable.
When Prince Rupert
heard of the Great Fire, he
said 'Now Shipton's pro-
phecy is out!' She also
foretold the coming of the
railways and the invention
of the telegraph

MOTHER SHIPTON

WILLIAM LILLY (1602–81) A
yeoman's son, who spent
his wife's fortune in making himself an astrologer.
He enjoyed great fame
until 1666 when his pre-
diction of the Great Fire of
London came true; he was
accused of lighting the fire
himself but was found
guiltless. The hieroglyph
(above), which he drew in
1651, shows citizens fighting a conflagration. Gem-
ini – The Twins – above
the blaze, is London's
astrological sign

NOSTRADAMUS Born in France in 1503, Nostradamus correctly forecast the circumstances of the death of the French king, Henry II, at the hands of the Scottish Lord Montgomery in 1559. His prophecies are couched in obscure verse, but he may have foreseen the French and Russian Revolutions and Britain's part in the Second World War. Ominously, he also wrote of a world catastrophe due in July, 1999

JOANNA SOUTHCOTT (1750–1814) In middle age, this Devon woman declared herself to be the saviour of mankind, and gathered a number of disciples whom she assured would be preserved for the Second Coming. All the world's ills will allegedly be cured when her box of prophecies, kept in Bedford, is opened. This can only be done in the presence of a group of bishops, who have so far declined to co-operate

RICHARD BROTHERS (1757–1824) An ex-sailor who claimed to be a 'nephew of the Almighty' and a direct descendant of King David. He made remarkably accurate predictions of the deaths of Louis XVI and Gustavus III of Sweden, but was declared insane when he prophesied the death of George III and his own ascendancy to the throne. Like Joanna Southcott, he is buried in St John's Wood churchyard, London

NOSTRADAMUS

JOANNA SOUTHCOTT

RICHARD BROTHERS

JOHN DEE (1527–1608) Inventor, astrologer and secret agent, Dr Dee held minor posts at the courts of three Tudor monarchs. Although he failed to predict the death of the young King Edward VI, the new queen, Mary, employed him to cast the horoscopes of her husband, Philip of Spain, and herself. He showed the horoscopes to the future Queen Elizabeth, and was consequently imprisoned for treason.

On Mary's death, Elizabeth asked Dee to predict an auspicious date for her coronation; this gave so much satisfaction that he enjoyed the queen's friendship for many years, and was employed by her on secret missions abroad.

Apart from his interests in ciphers and navigational instruments, Dee began exploring the possibilities of turning base metals into gold. He also dabbled in crystal-gazing, and a form of spiritualism.

In these, he was aided by a confidence trickster named Edward Kelley, who claimed to see spirits in a crystal and to hold conversations with them. One of the spirits, called Madimi, apparently advised Dee that he should share his wife with Kelley. Dee's 'Spirit Warnings' became famous, and his advice was sought by the Polish king and the Holy Roman Emperor. Possibly he used his 'powers' to extract information for the English intelligence service. His scientific abilities led many to name him as a magician

RAISING THE DEAD *Aided by a man named Waring, Edward Kelley was said to have dug up a corpse at Walton-le-Dale, Lancashire, and magically forced it to speak*

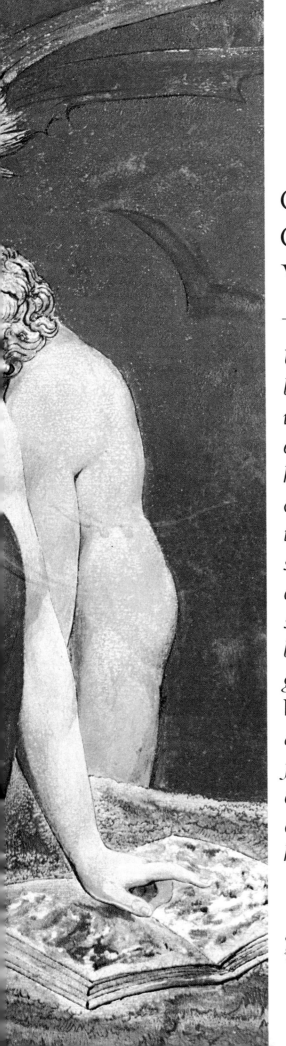

GODS,
GHOSTS AND
WITCHES

*Unable to accept the
boundaries of the visible
world, man has peopled the
edge of darkness with a
host of creatures of his
own imagining. Ghosts walk
the night because heroes
should not be bound by
death, and great evil
seemed to demand vengeance
beyond the grave. The
gods of Celt, Roman and
Viking are remembered
as goblins and monsters;
fairies may be our last
dim recollection of a
defeated race whose name
has been long forgotten*

QUEEN OF THE GHOSTS *The Greek goddess Hecate ruled over
ghosts and, as in this detail from William Blake's portrait of her,
was usually thought to have three separate identities*

HORNED GODS AND DIVINE ANIMALS

The horned god was one of the most important Celtic deities. He had two forms. In one he had antlers, wore a torc or necklace, and was accompanied by a ram-headed serpent. As such, he was symbolic of fertility and otherworld powers. In the other form, most common in northern Britain, the god was represented as a bull, a ram or a goat. The figure was usually naked; it carried weapons and wore a fierce expression. This horned deity symbolised fertility in man and beast but was also a warrior god bearing arms against the enemies of his people. The god illustrated above is carved in sandstone and comes from Maryport on the Solway Firth. Many animals and birds were also venerated by the Celts, and it may well have been that animal worship was the earliest form of the Celtic religion. They then evolved until a humanised god stood clear of the animal from which he had originated, independent of it but having its characteristics as his main attributes. In some instances, a divine being with human form was believed to be turned into, or had turned himself into, a beast

The old gods

*On cloud-shrouded hillsides and wild moorlands,
the aura of ancient gods lingers still*

A broken circle of stones, the outline of a giant cut in chalk upon a hill, names of cities and villages, the half-obliterated stone figure that has nothing to do with Christianity built into a church wall . . . all are vivid reminders of the many forms of pagan worship in early Britain.

Long before man conceived the gods in his own likeness, he worshipped still pools, rushing rivers, curiously shaped rocks, and lonely gnarled trees. Even when his religious ideas became more complex and he created images and idols in human and animal form, he retained his awe of natural things for thousands of years.

The religious significance of the great stone monuments such as Stonehenge and Avebury in Wiltshire and Callernish on the island of Lewis in the Outer Hebrides remains a mystery. No one can say with authority what gods or powers were associated with them, and the theory that the stone circles were built by the Druids has long been discounted. The Druids were the priests of the Celts who first came to Britain about 500 BC; Stonehenge was then more than 1000 years old. It is doubtful that the Druids ever exercised their own form of worship among the stones: they preferred shaded forest groves.

Traceable history of the forms of pagan worship in Britain really begins with the Celts who, in the 500 years or so before the Roman invasion, made themselves masters of the country. The Celts had hundreds of gods and goddesses; each tribe had its own deities which probably had different local names, though they were universal in type. Unlike the Roman gods the majority were not rigidly categorised. Only a few were thought to perform specific functions as smith gods or physician gods or war goddesses. Celtic divine society was intensely aristocratic, closely resembling the social structure of the Celtic tribes themselves. A number of great beings such as Sucellos the Thunderer, whose hammer was the symbol of creative force, may even have been thought of as gods whom the lower orders of gods worshipped.

The perfect beings

The Celts set high standards for their deities. The god of a tribe had to be an all-purpose being, unblemished, and accomplished in every human activity. He had to be physically strong, intellectual and fertile; he was expected to be knowledgeable in the laws, skilled in argument and mighty in war, a dealer of death and a restorer to life alike.

Mother goddesses were also very important. One might be the protectress of a city she had founded; another, the patroness of the sun god in his constant battle with darkness and winter. Many had triple roles in that they watched over related areas such as birth, death and re-birth. According to Caesar, the Druids taught the Celts that their souls were immortal and because of this the Celts had no fear of death in battle. After death the soul was believed to pass into another body.

There is little doubt that the Celts practised human sacrifice. Caesar and other Roman writers refer to barbaric rites and bloodstained altars, and to humans and animals being burnt alive in wickerwork cages as offerings to the gods.

Throughout Britain, place-names give clues to the worship of many Celtic gods and goddesses. Among them were the members of two great tribes of gods, the families of Don and Llyr, who were in constant conflict. The tribe of Don – who was a goddess – is thought to have symbolised the heavens, life and light, while the people of Llyr symbolised the sea, darkness and death. Llyr became King Lear in Shakespeare's tragedy; the principal place of his worship, Leicester (Llyrcester), was named after him.

The war of the gods

Two of Llyr's children were Bran the Blessed and his sister Branwen – a Bronze Age mound on Anglesey is still known as Branwen's Grave. There are many complex legends about this divine brother and sister and their devotion to each other. Bran was a fertility god, a god of war and the lord of the dead; he was beautiful and tremendously strong. But he was a hearty god who was also the patron of musicians, minstrels and bards. He lived under the sea in a cheerful otherworld where his cauldron of regeneration boiled, restoring life to dead heroes.

When Branwen made an unhappy marriage with the Irish king Matholwych, she appealed to her brother for help, and Bran immediately waded across the Irish Sea to the rescue. In the wars that followed, his army crossed rivers by marching along his back while he stretched himself from bank to bank. Branwen's son was killed when he was thrown into a fire by an evil uncle during a feast; broken-hearted by the loss of her son and the carnage taking place because of her, Branwen died. Soon after, Bran was fatally wounded by a poisoned arrow. He told his surviving companions to cut off his head and carry it with them wherever they went. Carrying the head, Bran's companions entered paradise; the head still lived, providing for all their needs, entertaining them, and presiding at rich banquets. It promised them a good life for ever, on condition that they did not open a forbidden door. After four-score years Bran's people yielded to temptation and opened the door: immediately they were back in the world of reality with all its wars and sorrows. Eventually the head was buried in London, facing towards the Continent, where it remained to protect the country from invaders. A sequel to this legend says that King Arthur, confident of his own abilities to protect the realm, and jealous of any rival power, dug up the head and destroyed it.

As their gods played larger-than-life roles, the Celts thought of them as giants and portrayed them as such. On grassy hillsides around Britain, huge figures, principally of horses and men, can still be seen cut in the chalk or the soil. Most of those still visible were incised during the last few centuries, but they were inspired by figures of great antiquity, some of which can still be seen. The most famous of these is known as the Cerne Abbas Giant. Over 180 ft high and cut deep into the chalk of the hillside above the village of Cerne Abbas in Dorset, the figure displays many of the attributes the Celts expected in their gods. His virility is obvious and the enormous club in his hand symbolises his prowess in war.

Another hill figure of unknown age is the Long Man of Wilmington, in E. Sussex. Carved on a steep slope, he is 226 ft high: his arms are outstretched and each hand grips a staff. It is unlikely that the true names or the religious function of these figures will ever be known.

The Celts also worshipped the horse, and there are several representations of horses cut in the hillsides which are believed to be pre-Roman in origin. One, a strangely shaped creature which dominates the hill above Uffington in Oxfordshire, is certainly prehistoric. With its beaked muzzle and disjointed limbs, it closely resembles the stylised horse featured on Celtic coins dating from about 150 BC. Later Christian legends state that the horse is actually a representation of the dragon killed by St George on nearby Dragon Hill. No grass grows on the summit where the beast's blood was spilt.

Gods of the occupation

The Celts' lusty worship of their many and various gods was vastly different from the staid religious practices of the Romans. The conquerors had a formalised religion and built temples for worship; the Celts – with the exception of the few who had been exposed to classical influences – worshipped in the open air, in forest clearings, and beside rivers, lakes and springs. The Romans were often good psychologists when dealing with conquered peoples and were tolerant of their religions if their worship did not have political implications. In Britain, even though the powerful Druids were suppressed because they plotted against their conquerors, the gods they worshipped were left alone.

Although it is unlikely that Roman gods were worshipped in pre-Roman Britain, many of the Celtic gods shared similar characteristics with those of Rome. Caesar wrote: 'About these gods they (the Celts) hold nearly the same views as other people do.' There was, in fact, sufficient common ground to permit fusion of a number of their respective deities. Caesar believed the Celts worshipped Apollo as a healing god, Mars as the god of war, Jupiter as the ruler of the heavens, and Mercury as the god of commerce, inventor of all the arts and guardian of travellers. To the Roman emperor, only the names were different. In time, the Celtic Cocidius became Mars Cocidius, Maponus became Apollo Maponus, and so on.

The Romano-Celtic temples spread quickly, and their cults became popular. The temples had a character of their own, some developing into a complex of buildings that included baths and a theatre. A factor which aided the marriage of the two religious viewpoints was the number of Celts in the Roman army; by the 2nd century AD about three-quarters of the Roman army in Britain was composed of Celts, though most of them came in from the Continent. British legionaries were despatched to other parts of the Roman Empire.

There are few traces of Teutonic gods in Britain. The gods of the invading Anglo-Saxons made nothing like the same impact as the rich array of established Romano-Celtic deities. In any case, their reign was a short one; a century and a half later, the gods of Roman, Briton and Teuton alike yielded to the triumphant advance of Christianity.

But the influence of at least two Anglo-Saxon deities is still felt today. One is the war god Tiu who gave his name to the third day of the week, Tuesday. The other is Eostre, the goddess of spring, from whose name was derived the word Easter, the most sacred festival of the Christian calendar.

THE DIVINE HEAD

THREE-IN-ONE *Three was an important number to the Celts; it had both magical and religious significance. Gods were grouped in threes, while many tales speak of three semi-divine heroes, born as triplets. The legendary power of multiple heads lingered on into the Middle Ages, and carvings such as this three-faced head in Salisbury Cathedral were incorporated in church decorations. Because of their pagan ancestry they were frowned upon by church authorities and very few have survived*

THE HORSE GODDESS

With its beaked muzzle and disjointed limbs, the white horse cut in the hillside near Uffington Castle in Oxford-shire closely resembles the 'dismembered' horse featured on old Celtic coins dating from about 150 BC. It is one of three such horses believed to be very old. The other two are the White Horse of Westbury in Wiltshire and the Red Horse of Tysoe in Warwickshire. Unfortunately,

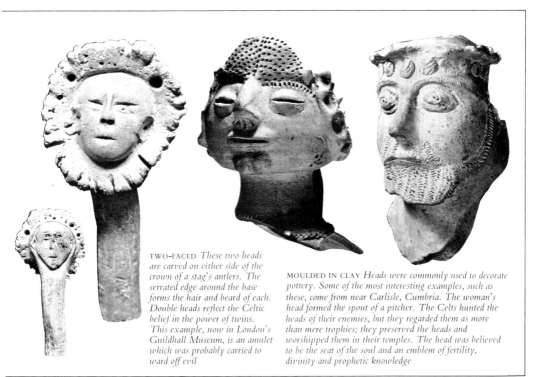

TWO-FACED *These two heads are carved on either side of the crown of a stag's antlers. The serrated edge around the base forms the hair and beard of each. Double heads reflect the Celtic belief in the power of twins. This example, now in London's Guildhall Museum, is an amulet which was probably carried to ward off evil*

MOULDED IN CLAY *Heads were commonly used to decorate pottery. Some of the most interesting examples, such as these, come from near Carlisle, Cumbria. The woman's head formed the spout of a pitcher. The Celts hunted the heads of their enemies, but they regarded them as more than mere trophies; they preserved the heads and worshipped them in their temples. The head was believed to be the seat of the soul and an emblem of fertility, divinity and prophetic knowledge*

the Westbury horse was re-cut in conventional form in 1778. Previously, its shape was rather like that of a dachshund; it carried a saddle and had a crescent moon on the tip of its tail. Throughout the ages local people have kept the hill figures that still exist clear of grass; it will never be known how many other figures have become overgrown. As the Celts worshipped the horse, it is believed that their portrayal in this way was both an act of veneration and a plea for protection. In England, the universal horse goddess was known as Epona, in Wales as Riannon. Great horse races connected with pagan festivals were once held all over Britain. White horses have always been considered lucky, as have horseshoes. The horseshoe is a lunar symbol which perhaps explains the crescent on the tail of the Westbury horse. A horseshoe found lying on a road is particularly lucky

Unquiet graves

A dead man plays billiards, a phantom brings two murderers to trial – ghosts are not confined to stately homes

In modern, overcrowded, brightly lit Britain, there is a strange paradox in our thinking about ghosts; we deny their existence, and at the same time we are afraid of them. Even the great majority of those who have seen or heard 'something' for which there is apparently no natural explanation continue to remain unconvinced about ghosts in general. Yet if the evidence of these people is considered as a whole, it would seem either that a large number of truthful British people have been subjected to a similar kind of delusion, or that phantoms really do walk amongst us.

The term 'ghost' describes an astonishing variety of apparitions, from the traditional shackled skeleton clanking through a lonely graveyard to spectral balls of light or fire smelling strongly of sulphur, which have been reported on the sites of ancient battlefields. There are ghosts of vengeful monks and weeping girls, of horses, dogs and birds, of coaches, ships and even aeroplanes. There are headless ghosts and legless ghosts, invisible ghosts that can drag the living out of bed or cause blood to ooze from floorboards, ghosts that announce their presence by hoots, shrieks or groans, by footsteps or the touch of a clammy hand on the victim's skin. There are kind ghosts and cruel ghosts, and ghosts of the living as well as of the dead; by tradition, everyone has a personal 'fetch' or wraith – a ghostly

---

THE GHOSTS OF SAWSTON HALL

Among the ghosts reputed to haunt 16th-century Sawston Hall in Cambridgeshire is the figure of Queen Mary Tudor, which has been seen both gliding serenely through the house and flitting at great speed through the gardens. Another spectre, known as the Lady in Grey, appears in the Tapestry Room; it is said to knock three times at the door and then float across the room. An undergraduate and a clairvoyant are among the people who have stayed overnight in the room, and declared next morning that their sleep had been disturbed by repeated rapping at the door and the sound of someone fiddling with the latch; a strange tapping also kept a priest awake in a bedroom near by. Other inexplicable sounds which have been heard in the house include the distant music of a spinet, and the trill of a girl's laughter.

REFUGE FOR A QUEEN *On the night of July 7, 1553, Mary Tudor took refuge in Sawston Hall from the treacherous Duke of Northumberland, who was plotting to imprison her. At dawn, a party of Northumberland's men was seen approaching the house, and Mary was forced to flee, disguised as a milkmaid. Balked of their victim, her pursuers burnt down the house*
When Mary became queen, she rewarded the Huddlestons, to whom the house belonged, by rebuilding it. To this day, her portrait (right) hangs in the Great Hall, and her ghost is said to haunt the house and gardens. The tradition that Mary slept in the Tapestry Room (above) is almost certainly untrue, though the four-poster may have survived the fire. But what is certain, according to those who have stayed there, is that it is impossible to spend a night in 'Mary's Room' without being disturbed by phantoms

double which appears only once to its human twin, shortly before the two of them meet in the final embrace of death.

But in broad terms, this great other-world of British ghosts can be divided into two groups: traditional and legendary phantoms, such as those of heroes and unhappy queens, which almost everyone has heard of but few would ever claim to have seen; and more ordinary spectres which have been vouched for by whole galleries of witnesses, but whose appearances are often unexplained.

Shadows of the past

Many of the older ghost traditions are probably accounted for by folk-memory – the story of an event handed on by one generation to the next, becoming distorted in the telling, but retaining through the centuries a grain of fact. Just how long such traditions survive is illustrated by the tale of a crying child which for many years has been said to haunt the site of the Roman fortress at Reculver in Kent. In 1966, a number of babies' skeletons were discovered beneath the foundations, suggesting that the memory of an ancient tragedy, or

perhaps of a ritual sacrifice, had lingered in the district for almost 2000 years.

Similarly, tales of spectral coaches drawn by headless horses probably recall the Norse tradition of the Wild Hunt. Before Christianity came to Britain, it was widely believed that the Norse god Odin or Woden chased across the sky on stormy winter nights, with a pack of baying hounds at his horse's heels. Anyone who saw the Hunt might be carried off to a distant land, while to speak with the Huntsman was certain death.

As Odin was gradually forgotten, the Devil took his place as the Wild Huntsman. Later still, local and national heroes replaced the Devil, and in many places, a ghostly coach and four superseded the Huntsman's pack. On moonless, stormy nights, it is said, Sir Francis Drake, seated in a black coach, lashes a team of headless horses into a wild gallop across Dartmoor; and there, too, the hideous howls of the Yeth Hounds or Wish Hounds are still said to scream on the wind as the demon dogs hunt down the souls of unbaptised babies.

Ghosts of the great abound in Britain, as if people are unwilling to accept that strong personalities

RELIGIOUS RELICS AT BOSWORTH HALL

The aura of old religious strife still hangs over Bosworth Hall in Leicestershire, which has been the family home of the Maxwells and a stronghold of the Catholic faith for well over 300 years. It is fitting, then, that its ghost should be the damned spirit of a Protestant, and that the symbol of the Maxwells' faith should be a stain, either of blood or wine, which has never dried out, though it was made centuries ago.

During Cromwell's Protectorate, when 'popery' was outlawed, a priest was celebrating Mass in the Hall's Chapel Room when he heard a band of soldiers riding towards the house. In his hurry to hide, he spilled the consecrated wine, or else (the true facts are uncertain) he cut his hand. In either event, the stain still marks the Chapel Room floor, and to this day it feels damp to the touch.

LADY LISGAR *The silent ghost of the bigoted Lady Lisgar haunts the Bow Room where she died, and drifts through the rambling corridors and up and down the stairs*

THE INDELIBLE STAIN *The stain of wine or blood on the floorboards of the Chapel Room is said to be over 300 years old. Certainly, it still feels damp, as if it was made only minutes ago, and no natural explanation has ever been given for it*

THE CHAPEL ROOM *In the room where the Maxwells secretly celebrated Mass during the Cromwellian period, there is a portrait of a woman long dead, yet whose presence is still reported in different parts of the house. In 1881, the Protestant Lady Lisgar married the head of the family and came to live at Bosworth Hall; she made many alterations to the building, but is chiefly remembered for having refused to admit a priest to administer the last rites to an old Catholic servant. For this, she was condemned to haunt the house for ever*

RAISED BY REMORSE

The ghost of Dame Elizabeth Hoby, a brilliant scholar and a close friend of Elizabeth I, has frequently been seen roaming through her former home at Bisham Abbey in Berkshire. One explanation of the haunting suggests that Dame Hoby cannot find rest because of her remorse concerning the death of her son William, a stupid child who died at an early age of a brain disease. This may have been brought on, or at least aggravated, by Dame Hoby repeatedly boxing his ears because she had no patience with his dull wits.

Many eye-witness accounts agree that the most uncanny feature of the phantom is that it looks like a photographic negative; the skin is dark, while the dress is a strange, glaring white.

THE PHANTOM ON THE WALL *Towards the end of the last century, the owner of Bisham Hall, Admiral Vansittart, was standing alone in the Great Hall where Dame Hoby's portrait (above) still hangs. Though he did not believe the stories about the house being haunted, he suddenly felt that someone was standing behind him. He spun round and caught a glimpse of the spectral figure of Dame Hoby; and where her portrait should have been, there was only an empty frame*

appalled screams on finding the door locked are said to ring through the palace to this day.

Anne Boleyn does not haunt Hampton Court but this is probably because she has so many other claims on her time. With or without her head, she is said to make frequent appearances in at least five country houses. On May 19 each year, the anniversary of her execution, also for treasonable adultery, in 1536, her ghost, carrying its severed head in its lap, drives up to the door of Blickling Hall, Norfolk, in a coach drawn by four headless horses. Her headless wraith has also startled sentries at the Tower of London, and she is said to have been seen leading a phantom procession of knights and ladies through the Tower's chapel of St Peter-ad-Vincula, where she was buried.

Statesmen and warriors cannot find rest either, it seems. A cloaked figure occasionally seen in London's Red Lion Square is thought to be the ghost of Oliver Cromwell; his bitter opponent, Charles I, who haunts surprisingly few places considering the violent nature of his death, is said to stalk through Marple Hall in Cheshire, and to toss and turn in a bed he once occupied in Fountainhall House, east Lothian. On Midsummer Eve, King Arthur is supposed to lead a troop of mounted knights down the slopes of Cadbury Hill in Somerset, the legendary site of Camelot, as he may have done long ago. And a completely black and featureless ghost, normally identified as the Black Prince, has frequently been seen in the vicinity of Hall Place near Bexley, sometimes to the distant strains of 14th-century music. His appearance is said to coincide with any great danger to the nation. During the First World War, his ghost was seen three times, each one before British defeats.

Ghosts with a mission

In many cases, the reasons for the most persistent British hauntings have long been forgotten. Anonymous Grey Ladies and Brown Ladies walk the corridors of their old homes, apparently unaware of living witnesses and of their effect upon them. It has been suggested that such apparitions may be the result of emotions so intense that, in some way we do not yet understand, they have left a visible imprint upon the atmosphere. These are not ghosts in the accepted sense, but rather manifestations of ancient loves, hopes or fears which some people are sensitive enough to intercept and 'see' as phantoms. This eerie gift is said to be the reason why one person in a group may be terrified by a ghost, while his companions see nothing at all.

On the other hand, there are a large number of stories of people who have returned from the grave in order to right a wrong or to complete some important task left unfinished. In a trial at Durham in 1631, two men named Sharp and Walker were accused of murdering a girl called Anne, a young relation of Walker. The case for the prosecution rested on the testimony of James Graham, a miller, who claimed to have been accosted late one night by the blood-drenched ghost of a young woman, hideously disfigured by five open wounds on her head. She told him that her name was Anne Walker, that Mark Sharp had murdered her with a pick-axe, and that her corpse lay in a coal pit on the moor. She added that Sharp had been acting on orders from Walker, by whom she was pregnant.

Anne's ghost ordered the terrified miller to relay this information to the local magistrate, and threatened that she would haunt him until he did. At first, disbelieving the evidence of his eyes, Graham held back; but after the ghost had appeared to him twice more, he could bear the haunting no longer, and told his story to the local magistrate.

can be contained by anything so final as death. Among them are several of Henry VIII's unfortunate wives. Jane Seymour, who died in childbirth in 1537, carries a lighted taper through the Silver Stick Gallery in Hampton Court and then glides like a shadow down the stairs; Catherine Howard, who was beheaded for adultery in 1542, has been both seen and heard in the Haunted Gallery. Legend says that when the guards came to arrest her she broke away, intending to make one last appeal to Henry, whom she knew to be in the chapel. Her

THE MOST HAUNTED HOUSE IN SCOTLAND

Somewhere in the 15 ft thick walls of Glamis Castle in Tayside – the birthplace of Princess Margaret and the ancestral home of the Earls of Strathmore – there may be a bricked-up secret chamber that conceals the earthly remains of a hideous monster. For by tradition, a monstrous child was born into the family some 200 years ago, and was secretly incarcerated in the castle walls. As each heir to the earldom reached the age of 21, he was told the awful secret and shown the rightful earl – an immensely strong and long-lived beast, it is rumoured, which had no neck, tiny arms and legs, and a huge, hairy, barrel-like
body. It is said that it lived until the 1920's. Apart from its legendary monster, Glamis Castle has at least nine ghosts which probably make it the most haunted house in Scotland. One is said to be Macbeth, endlessly expiating the murder of King Duncan; another is Earl Beardie, who plays dice with the Devil for the sin of gambling on a Sunday. An unidentified Grey Lady haunts the chapel, and a tongueless woman races across the grounds tearing frantically at her mouth. And on wild, winter nights a ghostly madman has been reported walking the roof, along 'The Mad Earl's Walk'

Anne Walker's corpse was discovered in the pit which her ghost had described, the two alleged murderers were arrested, tried and hanged, and Graham was never troubled by the ghost again.

The screaming skulls

With grisly nostalgia, some ghosts stubbornly cling to their mortal remains on earth. There are several country houses – including Bettiscombe House in Dorset and Burton Agnes Hall, N. Yorkshire – which list the skull of a former occupant among their furnishings. If such skulls are removed, or if any attempt is made to bury them, then hideous screams ring through the house, and dire misfortune falls upon the occupants. Understandably, the matter is seldom put to the test.

Even after death, some people are able to maintain a surprisingly physical existence. There is, for instance, the story of an artillery colonel who in 1943 walked into the billiard room of his new mess in the Midlands, to find that the table was already being used by an officer, dressed in old-fashioned blues. The colonel's challenge to a game was accepted, but halfway through the match, the gong sounded for dinner and his opponent put up his cue and walked out.

Over dinner, the colonel asked about the strange officer, and was surprised to learn that no one else had met him. It was then that the butler, who had been kept on as mess-servant when the house was commandeered, broke in to explain that the colonel's opponent was almost certainly the ghost of a former heir to the property. He had joined Kitchener's army in 1915, but was invalided out for a long-standing illness he had tried to conceal. At Christmas 1916, he returned to his home, and full of a bitter sense of failure, shot himself in the billiard room.

A last farewell

Throughout history, there are many well-authenticated stories of ghosts of the dying appearing to friends or relatives as if to say goodbye. It may be that these apparitions are evidence of thought transference; as the dying person passes through the supreme crisis and thinks for the last time of the people he is about to leave, they may receive a telepathic message so powerful that they actually see a vision of him. According to most accounts, there is nothing wraith-like about these apparitions; they seem completely solid and normal and are usually mistaken for the living person.

On June 22, 1893, by an error of judgment which neither history nor psychology can properly explain, Admiral Sir George Tryon gave an order during manoeuvres off the coast of Syria that caused HMS *Victoria*, the flagship of the Mediterranean Squadron which he commanded, to collide with HMS *Camperdown*. As the great battleship *Victoria* keeled over and sank, Sir George was heard to say: 'It is all my fault.' Within minutes, he and most of his crew were drowned.

At the same hour as the tragedy, some 2000 miles away in London, Lady Tryon was giving a cocktail party in Eaton Square, when suddenly the drawing room door opened and her husband strode in. He spoke to no one, but walked purposefully across the room and out of a door at the other end. Curiously enough, Lady Tryon did not see him, but those among her guests who did were astonished, for they knew, or thought they knew, that he could not be in London. His wife and friends did not learn of his death until several days afterwards; and Sir George was never seen again. It can only be surmised that in his last moments, his thoughts turned homewards with such force that he made a final brief appearance in the surroundings that were dear to him in life.

The home-wreckers

The great majority of modern hauntings are ascribed to the activities of poltergeists, a German term meaning 'noisy spirits'. Though the reason for their appearance remains a mystery, poltergeists are probably the best authenticated of all psychic phenomena. They do not seem to be spirits of the dead, but rather an invisible form of energy given to hurling furniture about, and beating and bruising the unfortunate people to whom they become attached. They are often associated with, or believed to emanate from, children in early adolescence; as the children grow older, the phenomena gradually cease.

But at best, this theory is just speculation, and with poltergeists as with other alleged phantoms, it may be that these strange and often terrifying manifestations are evidence of another world which the living have hardly even begun to explore.

A GHOST IN THEATRELAND

At matinées in the Theatre Royal, Drury Lane, London's theatregoers have often reported seeing the ghost of an unknown man, either sitting in the upper circle or walking from one side of the theatre to the other. He is tall, grey-haired and distinguished, and his clothes suggest that in life he was a mid-18th-century gentleman of fashion; the 'ghost' photograph (above) is actually a reconstruction from eye-witness accounts. Apparently, his judgment is faultless, and his appearance at a play is a sure sign that it will be a success

PHANTOMS ON THE TULIP STAIRCASE?

In 1966, two Canadian tourists – Mr R. W. Hardy, a retired clergyman, and his wife – visited the 17th-century Queen's House at Greenwich, which now forms part of the National Maritime Museum. One of the photographs they took was of the Tulip Staircase, which seemed at the time to be empty; but when the picture was developed, it showed on the staircase what looks like one or perhaps two cowled and ghostly figures. The film has been closely examined, and it shows no signs of technical interference; and the Hardys themselves say that they are not interested in ghosts.

There is no tradition of the Queen's House being haunted. But since the photograph was taken, employees have remembered seeing strange figures near the staircase, and hearing what they now realise may have been the footsteps of the mysterious, cowled residents of Queen's House

JOKERS OR SPECTRES?

The Cock Lane affair

In 1762, the whole of London was held spellbound by the apparently unearthly events that were taking place in a small, terraced house in Cock Lane, behind St Sepulchre's Church in the City. Each night, an 11-year-old girl called Elizabeth Parsons lay trembling and shivering in her bed, unable to sleep because of a constant, supernatural scratching and knocking in her bedroom.

Mary Frazer, a young serving-woman in the house, established contact with the 'ghost', the spirit of a girl called Fanny who claimed that her husband William had poisoned her. Fanny added that if some witnesses came to the vault in St John's Church, Clerkenwell, where her coffin lay, she would prove the truth of her accusation by banging on the coffin lid.

A group of witnesses assembled but nothing happened in St John's, perhaps because someone had the foresight to hold Elizabeth's hands; and people began to suspect the Parsons of trickery. The upshot was that Elizabeth's father was found guilty of trying to blackmail the late Fanny's husband, and his wife, daughter and servant were convicted as accomplices. But to this day, some people still claim that the ghost of 'Scratching Fanny' was not a hoax at all.

A contemporary print of the famous 'haunted' house in Cock Lane

An artist's impression of the 'ghost' that terrorised Hammersmith

The Hammersmith hoaxer

Night after night in January 1804, an awful apparition rose from among the tombstones in Hammersmith churchyard. It was immensely tall and draped in white shrouds; moreover, it was aggressive, which is rare for a ghost. The first person to see it was a pregnant woman: it chased her, caught her and wrapped her fiercely in its arms. Within two days she had died of the shock.

At first, the local people surmised that the ghost was that of a man who had committed suicide a year earlier, by cutting his throat; but gradually they began to suspect that it was a hoax. A few brave men lay in wait for it, hoping to kill or capture it; and one night, in Black Lion Lane, a man named Francis Smith caught a glimpse and fired.

But Smith's 'ghost' was an innocent bricklayer, dressed in the white overalls of his trade; Smith was convicted of murder and sentenced to death. In view of the extraordinary circumstances of the case, the sentence was commuted to a year in gaol.

Two deaths, apparently, were enough to soothe the ghost's ill feelings, for after Smith's trial it was never seen again. And the identity of the hoaxer – if indeed there was a hoaxer – has not been discovered to this day.

GOD OF THE WITCHES

A terrible two-headed Satan devours sinners on Judgment Day – a medieval concept of man's arch-enemy which may be seen in St Mary's Church, Fairford, Gloucestershire. In exchange for the witches' immortal souls, Satan gave them magical powers, and promised them material prosperity in this world. These transactions took place in the presence of the Devil himself, of whom many *descriptions exist. He appeared at sabbats as a bull, goat or horse, in which guises he copulated with the witches. The truth seems to have been that the 'Devil' was a masked man, the leader of the coven. Most members were well aware of this; only the authorities believed that witches were in contact with Satan incarnate and, by torture, would extract confessions to support this belief*

The anatomy of witchcraft

*More than 5000 Britons died because of the Biblical edict:
'Thou shalt not suffer a witch to live'*

Sorcerers, it was thought, controlled the spirits of air, fire and water, and through them were able to change the weather, influence fertility in crops, beasts and men, and kill by means of spells and incantations. Though such magic inspired great fear, its practitioners were not necessarily evil; white, or good, magicians were held in great esteem and their services were frequently sought.

Witchcraft, as it was understood during the penal centuries, was different. However good its apparent results, it was by definition evil. Witchcraft was heresy, and was denounced as such by Pope Innocent VIII in a Papal Bull of 1484. From then until about 1750, when persecution died away as the scepticism of judges increased, some 200,000 supposed witches were tortured, burnt or hanged in western Europe. In most cases, the witches' accusers believed that they were helping to stamp out a widespread heretical conspiracy to overthrow Christianity.

Some modern authorities believe that the witch hunts were little more than a form of mass mania initiated by the Church and prolonged by the vested interests of professional witchfinders. Others, while agreeing that many of the accused were innocent of even the intention to bewitch, argue that the similarity of confessions obtained all over Europe indicate the existence of a genuine witch cult. Such confessions, however, were extracted by means of the thumbscrew, the rack and red-hot irons, and have little value as evidence.

Britain in the witch years

Witchcraft was not made a capital offence in Britain until 1563. Even then, English law required proof of injury to people or domestic animals, though in Scotland, a pact with Satan was sufficient to incur the death penalty. No more than half a dozen people were burnt for witchcraft in England, but about 1000 were hanged between 1563 and 1736, when the laws were repealed. Only the Channel Isles and Scotland competed with the Continent in the savagery of their sentences. Both employed fire and torture, and in Scotland more than 4400 witches died at the stake.

In both England and Scotland, the popular fear of witchcraft was closely allied to the rise of the Reformed Church. Though people believed in witches long before the Reformation, the Catholic Church, with its candles, bells and holy water, provided the means to keep sorcery at bay. The Protestants denounced these as Popish superstitions, saying that if a man was steadfast in God, neither Satan nor his agents could injure his immortal soul. They were less positive about his body and worldly goods, however, admitting that it was quite possible

THE WEIRD SISTERS

This portrayal, by Fuseli, of the best-known witches in literature, is in the Royal Shakespeare Theatre, Stratford. Though they are described in Macbeth as looking 'not like th' inhabitants o' the earth', they have many of the characteristics of real witches, almost all of whom were old women. It has been suggested that the rise in the number of witches during the 16th century was partly due to the breakdown of medieval ideals of charity. An aged, destitute woman of frightening appearance would quickly learn that a curse would produce a meal from a terrified neighbour. Sure badges of the witch were a crone-like appearance, a snaggle-tooth, sunken cheeks and a hairy lip, according to one witchfinder. All of these, however, are marks of old age

111

for even the virtuous to be bewitched. This was small comfort to a people who believed that Satan stood constantly at their elbow, and that a witch's curse could kill or maim their cattle or themselves. Medicine was in its infancy, and a sudden illness, such as a stroke, might easily be seen as the result of ill-wishing.

It was not surprising in those troubled times that the more credulous should see witches everywhere, and secretly turn to the old defences of holy water and holy oil. Some chose more ancient remedies – herbs, such as garlic, and the witch bottle. These practices were frowned upon by the Church which maintained there was only one cure – the detection and death of the witch.

A crime of poverty

Despite dark stories of sorcery in high places, witchcraft, at least in England, was almost invariably a crime of the very poor. According to the trial records, most witches were old women who got little out of their alleged pacts with Satan. Many asked only for a full belly or a roof over their heads in exchange for their immortal souls.

This does not mean that all witches were innocent of at least attempting the crime with which they were charged. Both the courts and the accused believed in the reality of witchcraft, and many witches were utterly convinced of their own powers. The curse was a devastating weapon; provided that the victim knew he was ill-wished, auto-suggestion could do much damage. In 1602, Elisabeth Jackson of London was tried for wishing an evil death upon a 14-year-old girl who became desperately ill.

There were many similar cases, but even when taken together, they do not amount to proof of an organised witch-cult in England. There are stories of English witch congregations, but the generally accepted picture of orgies and covens lies in accounts of trials in Scotland and the Channel Isles.

Coven, esbat and sabbat

According to the confessions, witch gatherings called covens or conventicles usually consisted of 13 members, that is, 12 witches (male or female) and a leader called the Devil. Often, one of the female

witches, called 'The Maiden', would act as the Devil's second-in-command.

This body of 13 members was thought by the Church to be a deliberate parody of Christ and his disciples. Isabel Gowdie of Auldearne in Highland, convicted in 1662, reported in her most detailed and extravagant confession that 'ther ar threttin persons in ilk coven'. The full confessions of Isabel Gowdie – Maiden of the Auldearne coven – are the most remarkable in any British witchtrial. Without being tortured, she made five confessions, in each of which she recounted details of feasting and dancing, of sexual rites and the making of images. She also told of spells and charms and the part she herself played in the attempted murder of the sons of a local laird. Her fate is not recorded, but almost certainly she perished at the stake.

Covens held regular meetings called esbats, usually once a week. There, the witches were instructed in magical rites and spells, new members were initiated, and the coven gave accounts of the week's evil-doing to its master. 'All our acts and deeds between the great meetings must be given account of and noted in his book at each meeting', declared Isabel Gowdie.

Sabbats were held less frequently; they were more closely concerned with Devil worship, and were usually attended by more than one coven. Though witches were supposed to ride to the sabbat on broomsticks, they are not often mentioned in contemporary accounts. Julian Cox, hanged in Somerset in 1663, said he saw 'Three persons on broomstaves borne up about a yard and a half from the ground'; the Cornwath witches, however, executed in the following year, claimed to ride upon cats, cockerels and bundles of straw.

Isabel Gowdie told the court: 'I had a little horse and would say, "Horse and hattock in the Devil's name", and we would fly away.' Anne Bishop, Maiden of a Somerset coven, had a more complicated technique: 'Before they are carried to their meetings, they anoint their Foreheads, and Handwrists with an Oyl the Spirit brings them (which smells raw) and then they are carried in a very short time, using these words as they pass, "Thout, tout a tout, tout, throughout and about". And when they

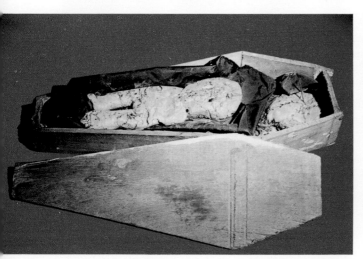

CHARM AND COUNTER-CHARM

The witch's most feared weapon was sympathetic magic, whereby injury done to an inanimate object was transferred to the victim. One method was to stab or melt the limbs of a wax doll; the bewitched person would supposedly suffer severe pain or slowly die. This doll was found recently in the chimney-breast of an old London house.

It was widely believed that the witch bottle was the only sure defence against sorcery. Filled with the victim's urine, iron nails and the heart of an animal, it was set on a fire to boil. The witch was then forced to reveal herself, or die in agony. The bottle pictured was found at Paul's Pier Wharf, London in 1953

'HOW TO KNOW WHETHER A WOMAN BE A WITCH OR NOT . . .'

The crimes and trial of Mary Sutton of Bedford are brought oddly together in an illustration of 1612. Accused of bewitching a cart, driving pigs mad and sailing in a sieve, Mary was put to the 'swimming test'. This was usual for witchcraft, for it was thought that water, the element of baptism, would reject a disciple of Satan. With thumbs tied to the opposite big toes, the accused was flung into the river. If she floated, she was guilty; if she sank, innocent. Mary floated, and was therefore hanged

go off from their Meetings, they say "Rentum Tormentum . . ." all are carried to their several homes in a short space.'

These reports of flying, seriously put forward by people on trial for their lives, are less incredible when the recipes for flying oils and ointments are considered. Despite dark references to baby's fat and bat's blood, they also contained more effective ingredients such as hemlock, deadly nightshade and foxglove. Foxglove (digitalis) is a heart stimulant, deadly nightshade (belladonna) produces delirium and hallucinations, while hemlock induces paralysis and unconsciousness.

The making of a witch
Membership of a coven involved initiation ceremonies in which the new member had to renounce his or her old faith, be re-baptised and re-named, and finally was branded with the witch-mark, in which the Devil simply nipped or scratched the convert in some part of the body.

The baptism and the giving of a new name was never considered a very important part of the ceremony in England and Wales. There are, however, many references in the records of Scottish trials to the names given to the converts. In Bute, in 1662, Janet Morison was told by the Devil 'believe not in Christ but believe in me. I baptise you Margaret.' Rather more imaginative names given to the Auldearne coven included Pickle-nearest-the-wind,

Throw-the-cornyard, Able-and-stout and Over-the-dike-with-it.

After the service, the congregation danced. Again, the only detailed information comes from Scotland, where the witches would form a ring and dance round a stone market cross, or some other landmark. In Aberdeen, the witches danced round the Fish Cross, while in Edinburgh, it was alleged that the coven would cavort about a large stone while the Devil played to them.

According to the confessions, the sabbat always culminated in an orgy in which men, women and Devil joined together. Apparently the Devil was a poor lover: Janet Breadhead of the Auldearne coven confided in 1662 that the Devil was a 'big black man, very cold', and she found his embraces as 'icy as spring-well water'.

The power of the witches
Supposed proof of the witches' ability to hurt their enemies by supernatural means was produced at hundreds of trials. A typical case was that of Anne Sturlowe who claimed that as a result of spells cast by the Norfolk witch Agnes Fenn in 1603, she suffered from 'hysterical passions and paralytical convulsions'. Her symptoms included 'doubling, swelling and writhing of the body, and change of weight and height'.

The making of images in clay and wax was the most common magical rite for inflicting sickness

and death. It was thought that whatever damage was inflicted upon the image would then be transferred to the intended victim.

John Stuart of Paisley, in 1678, admitted that the witches 'wrought the clay, and the black man did make the figure of the head and the face, and two arms on the said effigies. The Devil set three pins in the same, one in each side and one in the breast.' Often the coven master or Devil baptised the image which was then melted over a fire or stuck full of pins.

The rites were usually accompanied by an incantation. Though the words were usually gibberish, the chant gave an air of mystery. In order to prolong the sickness of one of her accusers, Isabel Gowdie made a broth out of the entrails of toads, nail-parings, the liver of a hare, barley and rags. Over this concoction Isabel then proclaimed:

'He is lying on his bed, he is lying sick and sair
Let him lie in his bed two months and three days mair.'

At the coven too, the Devil would allocate imps or familiars to each initiate. Familiars were usually small domestic animals, though sometimes they were toads, mice or rats. Occasionally, Satan himself occupied this role. According to Richard Bernard in his *Guide to Grand-Jury Men* (1627), the Devil might appear to witches 'in the shape of a Man or Woman, or a Boy, of a brown and white Dogge, of a Foale, of a spotted Bitch, of a Hare, Moale, Cat, Kitling, Ratte, dunne Chicken or Owle'.

The heyday of the witch-hunters
After 1600, the number of witch prosecutions in Britain rose sharply; this was mainly due to the increasing influence of uncompromising Protestant sects and their interpretation of Exodus xxii, v. 18: 'Thou shalt not suffer a witch to live.' By 1640, particularly in Scotland, a supposed witch could be brought to trial by an anonymous, unsupported accusation, and it was extremely difficult for the accused to prove her innocence. Evidence for the defence was twisted and corrupted to suit the prosecution, and the sentence was almost invariably death.

The normal procedure for establishing guilt was first to put the accused to the 'swimming' ordeal, then to seek out and test the witch-mark, and finally to force a confession by mental or physical torture. Only in Scotland and the Channel Isles was physical torture legally permissible. In England and Wales the usual methods of persuasion were starving and keeping the victim awake.

Although the witch-mark was accepted in most cases as a true sign of guilt it was recognised officially only in Scotland. According to one witch-hunter, a suspect 'may be proved guilty by a Witches marke. This is insensible, and being pricked will not bleede. It is sometimes red spots like a fleabiting, sometimes the flesh is sunke in and hollow . . .'

Finding this mark was considered a highly skilled operation and it was usually left to professional witch-hunters called prickers. The prickers scrutinised the accused from the soles of her feet to the crown of her head. Any spot, mark or blemish found on the skin was pricked with a long brass pin

---

RIDING TO THE SABBAT

This highly glamorised version of witches riding to a sabbat bears little resemblance to fact. The idea of a licentious orgy which parodied the Christian Holy Communion appears to have been invented largely by the investigators and judges connected with the Inquisition, and added to by the imagination of the witches who were undergoing trial

and the test was considered positive if the victim felt no pain.

The most notorious pricker was Matthew Hopkins, who, ably assisted by John Stearne and Goody Philips, cast his net widely over East Anglia, where he was responsible for over 300 executions. The payment made to these prickers showed it to be a lucrative trade. One man in Culross was paid 12s. for finding one witch, while a 'Scottish expert' engaged by the inhabitants of Newcastle-upon-Tyne was paid 20s. for each conviction. He was responsible for the death of 220 women and, like many other prickers, probably employed trickery, such as retractable pins, in his tests.

Having once established the presence of a telltale witch-mark, it was necessary to obtain a confession. In Scotland and the Channel Isles, the prosecutors were given a completely free hand and they responded to the call with terrible ingenuity. An old woman of 94 was accused of bewitching a man named Simon Cocke. She was beaten, made to sit on a stool through which the blades of daggers protruded, and was stabbed in the face. Two alleged witches in Edinburgh were hanged by the thumbs, and had lighted candles placed beneath the soles of their feet.

One East Anglian magistrate reported on the waking-and-walking treatment meted out to an English suspect: 'I have heard it from them that watched with him that they kept him awake several nights together and ran him backwards and forwards about the room. Then they rested him a little, and then ran him again; and thus they did for several days and nights together, till he was weary of his life and was scarce sensible of what he said, or did.'

In Scotland, there were other, more dreadful instruments of torture, such as the witch-bridle, boots, caspie-claws and pilnie-winks. The witch-bridle was an iron collar with a hoop which went over the head and was fitted with four prongs which were forcibly inserted into the mouth. The boots were frames into which the legs were inserted before being broken with wedges. Caspie-claws comprised an iron frame to hold the leg, the frame then being heated over a brazier; pilnie-winks were thumb screws. Alison Balfour, executed in Orkney in 1594, was tortured several times in the caspie-claws, her son put in the boots while her daughter was tormented by the pilnie-winks.

Such treatment was prolonged until the victim was willing to confess to anything. Many of these confessions were retracted at a later stage, and many witches died proclaiming their innocence.

The belief lingers on

Though many of the Acts against witchcraft were repealed in 1736, witch-hunting still continued, particularly in remote districts. In 1751, an old pauper woman suspected of witchcraft was killed by an angry mob near Tring in Hertfordshire, while in 1863, an alleged male witch was drowned in a pond at Hedingham, Essex.

As late as 1878, the people of Dingwall were fully aware of the dangers of sorcery. A young man was imprisoned at that time for assaulting an elderly woman who, he claimed, had bewitched his fishing boat and prevented him from catching fish. He assaulted her in the belief that if blood was drawn from a witch, she lost her power to charm. On being sentenced, he commented: 'It is hard to think I should be put in prison, for the Bible orders us to punish witches.'

Belief in witchcraft has not entirely died out. In 1945 the body of an elderly farm labourer was found near the village of Meon Hill in Warwickshire. His throat had been cut, and his corpse was pinned to the earth with a pitchfork. The murder remains unsolved; however, the man was locally reputed to be a wizard, and the manner in which he died recalls the days when witches' corpses were impaled to prevent them walking after death.

In the 1960's there were several instances of skeletons being removed from graves, and churches being profaned by midnight celebrations of the so-called Black Mass. These pathetic manifestations have little to do with historical witchcraft. But in a rootless age, unstable, lonely people often turn to strange gods. So it was in the 17th century, the age of witchcraft.

'DOUBLE, DOUBLE TOIL AND TROUBLE . . .'

Spells and incantations were the major part of the witch's stock in trade. Poison excepted, their main effect was probably psychological; when a victim knew he was bewitched, his own fear might do the witch's work. The efficacy of raising a storm by throwing a cat into the sea is less certain, yet in 1592, a number of witches were burnt in North Berwick for causing a shipwreck by this means. Other enchantments, collected from medieval *grimoires* or spell books, are still more bizarre in composition:

LUCIFER *The fallen angel*

'If thou wilt understand the birds
Associate with two fellows on the 28th day of October, and goe with dogges as to hunt. Carry home with thee the beast that thou shalt find first. Prepare it with the heart of a foxe, and thou shalt understand the voice of birds.'

BEELZEBUB *Lord of the flies*

'If thou wouldst see fairies
Take a pint of Sallet oyle and put it in a glasse, first washing it with rose water. Then put thereto the budds of hollyhocke, of mary-golde, of young hazle and the topps of wild thyme. Take the grasse of a fairy throne; then all these put into the glasse . . . dissolve three dayes in the sunne, and keep it for thy use.'

'Improving the memory
If the heart, eye or brain of a lapwing or black plover be hanged upon a man's necke, it is profitable against forgetfulness and sharpeneth understanding.'

'To make a girl dance naked
Write on virgin parchment the character of *Fruitimiere* with the blood of a bat. Then cut it on a blessed stone over which a Mass has been said. After this, place the character under the sill of a door which she must pass. When she comes past, she will come in. She will undress, and will dance unceasingly until death, if one does not remove the character.'

ASTAROTH *Devil and moon-goddess*

'Love charm
If a woman be not visious nor desire men, take the members of a woolfe, and the haires which doe grow on the cheekes and eye-brows of him, and burne it all and give it to her to drinke, when she knoweth not, and she shall desire no other man.'

The hidden people

*Were fairies spirits of the dead, or memories of a long-lost
people who once inhabited these islands?*

airies, it is sometimes said, are seen only in the
twinkling of an eye, or between one blink
and the next, though to the fairies themselves
time may pass so slowly that a single second is
long enough for many things to happen. Another
tradition says quite the opposite: visitors have
described how they have passed what seemed a few
hours in fairyland and 'woken up' years later. Such
contradictions are common in tales about fairies;
and perhaps the greatest contradiction of all is that
between the modern view of them as miniature
creatures, butterfly-winged and innocent, and the
traditional view that even the kindest of them are
dangerous. Traditionally, many fairies are of human
or more than human size, and hideously ugly. Their
most cruel practice – stealing human babies – is a
matter of survival; though they live in a world of
their own, many fairy families have to interbreed
with humans, to strengthen their stock.

When belief in fairies was common, few people
liked talking about their experiences, for fairies were
thought to be fierce guardians of their privacy.
People who spied on fairies were supposed to be
blinded, and just talking about fairies was unlucky.

FAIRY KING AND QUEEN

*Elves and other fairies surround Oberon and Titania,
the King and Queen of Fairyland, while Bottom the
weaver lies in an enchanted sleep. This illustration of
Shakespeare's* A Midsummer Night's Dream *was
painted by Henry Fuseli in the early 1760's. Fuseli was a
highly eccentric artist, who was preoccupied with dreams
and the supernatural. He was said to eat raw meat before
going to bed, in order to induce nightmares. In this
painting he gave full rein to his weird and dramatic
imagination: the nightmare creatures half-hidden in the
woods are fairies peculiar to Fuseli's dream world, not to
Shakespeare's*

In the scattered parts of Britain where belief survives, it is still considered that fairies dislike being called by that name. Cautious believers prefer instead to use names such as 'The Good People', 'The Little People', or 'The Hidden People'.

Hundreds of different kinds of fairies have been described. Some are grotesque, like the Spriggans of Cornwall, reputedly the ghosts of giants, who guard treasure buried beneath prehistoric stones, and have the ability to change shape at will. Others are miniature creatures, such as the $\frac{1}{2}$ in. high Portunes, who live on a diet of roast frog. The Portunes are perhaps England's oldest fairies, for their wizened, wrinkled faces were first described by the English historian Gervase of Tilbury some 750 years ago.

Fairy aristocrats

In the Middle Ages fairy aristocrats were thought to be the most beautiful of fairyland's people, and their heroic exploits were described in legends about King Arthur, in the Border ballads and in medieval romance. In many stories about them, they were led by a king and queen and were at least as large as humans; but they could also be tiny. Like human aristocrats, they passed their time in hunting, hawking and feasting. Many tales were told of the Fairy Rade, when they rode in procession behind their king and queen, on white horses hung with silver bells.

These noble fairies were more common in Scotland than in England or Wales, and when they did appear in England, they were generally very small. In a story told in Cornwall in the 19th century, a greedy old man tried to steal their treasure as they feasted on the Gump, a fairy hill outside St Just. The royal dais and banqueting table were small enough to be covered by the old man's hat, but as he raised it to trap them, 'a shrill whistle was heard, the old man's hand was fixed powerless in the air, and everything became dark around him'.

After their Elizabethan heyday, fairyland's aristocrats went into decline, and there are few modern accounts of them. The story of Scotland's last Fairy Rade was told by the Scottish writer Hugh Miller more than 100 years ago. A herdboy and his sister saw a procession of dwarfish strangers riding through a hamlet near Glen Eathie. As the last rider passed by, the boy asked: 'What are ye, little mannie; and where are you going?' 'Not of the race of Adam,' said the creature, turning for a moment in the saddle: 'The People of Peace shall never more be seen in Scotland.'

The common people

Most of the lower orders of British fairies are said to be no larger than three-year-old children. They enjoy games, music and dancing, like the heroic fairies, but they also have to work, or at least thieve. Sometimes they need help from people. There are many stories about fairies leaving broken stools or shovels for humans to mend, and paying for any help they get with small gifts of food, or of good luck.

The common fairies work mainly on the land, and they are believed to have traditional market-places. Legend says that one of these is situated at Pitminster in Somerset. Sometimes they visit ordinary markets. Some of the Welsh Tylwyth Teg, or Fair Family, were said to steal money from farmers' pockets on market day, replacing it with their own money, which vanished if the farmers tried to spend it. In the market-place at Bala in south Gwynedd, no one could see the Tylwyth Teg, but when the noise of the market rose to a roar, and prices began to go up, everyone knew they were there.

Many fairies are said to be masters of magic. Their presents, which at first look like rubbish, may turn into jewels or gold; or presents of jewels and gold may turn into rubbish. Some of them are able to appear and disappear at will, though people can penetrate their disguise by applying a magic eye ointment made by the fairies themselves, or by holding a four-leafed clover. Some can fly, though few have wings. Usually they ride on ragwort stalks, or levitate themselves by wearing magic caps or by reciting spells.

Cradle-snatching is their chief vice: almost all covet human babies, particularly fair-haired babies with rosy cheeks, and steal them if they can. In place of the stolen baby they leave a changeling – sometimes a fairy child, sometimes a withered old man, sometimes just a piece of wood crudely carved to look like a child, which seems for a moment to be alive.

Guardian fairies

Brownies and other hobgoblins are the best-known guardian fairies: they are usually small, solitary, shaggy-haired domestic spirits, who are said to do housework and odd jobs about the home, and to become attached to particular families or places. Most of them are hideous to look at: in the area around Aberdeen they are said to have no separate toes or fingers, in the Scottish Lowlands they have a hole instead of a nose, while some are reputed to have huge noses but no mouths.

According to tradition, most brownies go naked, or at least wear only ragged clothes, and can make themselves invisible or are experts at hiding. The easiest way to get rid of them is to offer them a gift of clothes. The Cauld Lad of Hylton, an unhappy brownie who haunted Hylton Castle in Tyne and Wear, was left a green cloak and hood, and promptly left the castle singing: 'Here's a cloak and here's a hood! The Cauld Lad of Hylton will do no more good!'

Though naturally helpful, brownies can become malicious if they are offended. In a story told to the Welsh folklorist John Rhys at the turn of the century, a helpful bwca (the Welsh equivalent of

THE FAIRIES ARE OUT

The 19th-century illustrator James Nasmyth drew this study of miniature, wingless fairies gathered around a blazing log fire. Legend claims that many fairies make their homes under human hearths, and that however well they hide, they usually give their presence away by stealing food left beside the fire

a brownie) savagely attacked a servant girl on a farm in County Gwent when she paid him for his work with a bowl of urine instead of his usual bowl of milk and piece of wheatbread. In disgust, the bwca moved to a neighbouring farm, where he worked willingly until the servant girl began to mock him.

He moved to a third farm, and became friends with Moses, the manservant. But Moses was killed in battle, and the grief-stricken bwca became a malevolent bogie. This so upset the farmer that he called in a local wise man, who on a moonlit night caught the bwca by his nose and banished him to the banks of the Red Sea for 14 generations.

More sinister than brownies, and less common, are Banshees. They sometimes give advice, but more often appear only to foretell a tragedy. In Highland tradition, the Washer-by-the-Ford, a web-footed, one-nostrilled, buck-toothed hag, is seen washing bloodstained clothes when men are about to meet a violent death.

Mischievous and evil fairies

Bogies, goblins and bug-a-boos are openly malignant and hostile to man. Northumberland's Hedley Kow, Durham's Picktree Brag and the Buggane of the Isle of Man play shape-shifting tricks, changing into gold or silver, for instance, to taunt their victims. Others are murderous, such as the Redcaps said to haunt the Border peel towers, who try to re-dye their caps in human blood, or the Highland

Baobhan Sith, who look like beautiful women, but are really fairy vampires thirsty for blood.

There are nursery goblins too, and none is more frightening than Rawhead-and-Bloody-Bones. According to the Somerset folklorist Ruth Tongue, writing in 1964: 'This most unpleasant hobgoblin, as we were assured in my childhood, lived in a dark cupboard, usually under the stairs. If you were heroic enough to peep through a crack you would get a glimpse of the dreadful crouching creature, with blood running down his face, seated waiting on a pile of raw bones that had belonged to children who told lies or said bad words. If you peeped through the keyhole at him he got you anyway.'

Nature fairies

Most nature fairies are the descendants of pre-Christian gods and goddesses, or of the spirits of streams, lakes and trees. Black Annis, a blue-faced hag said to haunt the Dane Hills of Leicestershire, and Gentle Annie, who governs storms in the Scottish Lowlands, may be descended from the Celtic goddess Anu or Danu, mother of Ireland's Cave Fairies. Their Highland sister, the Cailleach Bheur or Blue Hag, seems to be the spirit of winter. She freezes the ground by striking it with her staff, and loses her power when spring comes.

Water spirits such as mermaids and mermen, river spirits and the spirits of pools and lakes, are the most common nature fairies. Tradition has transformed some of them into ghosts. Peg O'Nell, a spirit of the

---

INHABITANTS OF FAIRYLAND

BROWNIE AT HOME *Most brownies are shaggy-haired and grotesque; but they make useful servants*

JACK O' LANTERN *Small flames flickering over marshy ground, caused by self-igniting gases from decaying plants, gave rise in England to widespread belief in a highly dangerous fairy known by many names, including Jack o' Lantern, Will o' the Wisp, Joan o' the Wad, Spunkie, Pinket and Ignis Fatuus, meaning foolish flame. It took great delight in making travellers lose their way – especially if it could lead them floundering into a bog – and would sometimes disguise itself as a beautiful young girl or a crock of silver or gold for this purpose. 'Will o' the Wisp' has become a byword for any delusive human hope or aim*

PUCK *This mischievous hobgoblin is half fairy and half human, and can change his shape at will. He is also known as Robin Goodfellow*

THE FAIRY FELLER'S MASTER-STROKE

In a crowded, busy world hidden in the grass, a brown-suited fairy prepares to split a hazel-nut with his axe. This mysterious, miniature fairyland was the creation of Richard Dadd, a Victorian painter who murdered his father in 1843, and then spent almost half a century, until his death in 1887, locked up as a madman. He painted the Fairy Feller while in Bedlam, and the picture now hangs in the Tate Gallery in London

River Ribble in Lancashire, is said to be the ghost of a drowned servant girl; but like other river spirits, such as Peg Powler of the River Tees, she is supposed to demand the regular sacrifice of human life, so it seems likely that the ghost story was grafted on to a much older legend. Even the spirit of the River Severn is traced back to a princess who was drowned in it.

In Wales, many stories survive of beautiful lake maidens who come ashore to marry young farmers, bringing herds of water cattle as a dowry. Usually, taboos surround the marriage: the fairy wife must never be touched with iron, and she must never be struck. Most of these marriages end when the taboo is accidentally broken, and the lake maiden returns to the water taking her cattle with her.

Oak-men are the most widespread tree spirits, and stories are told about them from the north of England to Somerset. Sometimes, the trees themselves are the fairies; sometimes the oak-men are kind forest dwarfs who look after animals as brownies look after humans. They can be dangerous, especially if the trees they inhabit are cut down. In Somerset, angry oak-men are supposed to haunt any coppice growing from felled oaks, and it is thought wise by local country folk to avoid such a coppice after sunset.

Who were the fairies?

Many explanations have been given to account for belief in fairies. Some believers have thought that fairies are a special creation, and that they exist in their own right. Others have said that fairies, like ghosts, are spirits of the dead, or of certain types of dead – people who died before Christianity came to Britain, for instance, or unbaptised or stillborn babies. According to another tradition, fairies were fallen angels, neither wicked enough for Hell nor good enough for Heaven.

Witches and fairies were closely associated in the popular imagination, and the witch cult certainly added to the fairies' reputation. Many witches attributed their powers to knowledge gained from fairies. John Walsh, a Dorset witch, admitted in 1566 that he had learnt from the fairies 'how persons are bewitched'. And fairies were supposed to make the elf arrows (in reality Stone Age flints) which many witches used as evil charms.

The belief that fairies were elementals – creatures made only of earth, air, fire or water – seems to have been common among medieval magicians, who devised complex spells and rituals for raising them and using their powers. One ritual, recorded in an early 15th-century manuscript now in the Bodleian Library in Oxford, involves stripping the bark from three hazel wands, writing a fairy's name on the wood, and burying the wands 'under some hill whereas you suppose fayries haunt'. The fairy will come if she is called on the following Friday, after the wands have been dug up.

Many of the traditions associated with fairies are uniquely British, and one explanation is that they may have evolved from far-off memories of a Stone Age race which once lived in these islands.

When the Celtic invaders from central Europe arrived in about 500 BC, they drove the original inhabitants into hiding in remote hills and caves. As the years passed, it may well have seemed to the conquerors that there was an uncanny quality in the people they had displaced. They were small and dark; they lived underground; they were a secret people whose skill at hiding in the woods seemed to give them the power of invisibility. Long after the race died out, or had become absorbed into the population, the memory of these characteristics lived on in Celtic tales about fairies.

The tradition that iron gives protection against fairies may also have sprung from some dim memory of the Celtic invasions. The victorious Celts were armed with iron; the race they dispossessed had weapons of stone or bronze.

Another theory, and one which draws support from the ideas of those who believe in fairies, regards the fairy faith as a cult of the dead. In many stories, it is hard to tell the difference between ghosts and fairies – both are said to haunt prehistoric burial mounds, for instance, and in fairyland, as in the land of the dead, the passage of time is miraculous. The dead were sometimes said to have been captured by fairies, and even seen in fairyland.

Many theories explain part, but not all, of the fairy faith. Certainly, some fairies are memories of ancient pagan gods and nature spirits. Others may have developed out of early attempts to explain the strange happenings now associated with poltergeists. In the end, only one thing is certain: fairies, whatever the truth about their origins may be, have the ability to survive. The Hidden People may be shadowy and elusive, as they always have been, but they are also indestructible.

ASLEEP IN THE MOONLIGHT

By tradition, the best times for seeing fairies are twilight and midnight when the moon is full, and the best days are

SO SWEET A CHANGELING

Arthur Rackham's illustration of fairies playing with a baby conceals a much uglier reality. Until the late 19th century, parents sometimes killed a sick or ugly baby, believing it to be a changeling left by fairies to replace a human baby whom they had stolen

Hallowe'en (October 31), May Day, Midsummer Day (June 24), Lady Day (March 25) and Christmas Day. Tree-dwelling fairies like these painted by Richard Doyle in the 1860's are rare. Most British fairies are said to live in hollow hills or in an underground country where the summer never ends

IN THE TWINKLING OF AN EYE

In every century, most people have spoken about fairies as if they were creatures of the past. Chaucer's *Wife of Bath*, in the 14th century, said that pious monks and friars had driven away the fairies, and 200 years later the English writer Reginald Scot claimed that it was the Reformation which had disposed of them. By tradition, the last Oxfordshire fairies were seen disappearing down a hole under the Rollright Stones in the 18th century, and two 19th-century children were witnesses to the farewell procession of Scottish fairies.

But the stories keep on coming. Even in the 20th century, there are sincere eye-witness accounts of little men all dressed in green, and it is on these, and on accounts from former centuries, that the case for belief in fairies must rest.

Bessie Dunlop's fairy
'. . . he was an honest well elderly man, gray bearded, and had a gray coat with Lombard sleeves of the old fashion . . . a black bonnet on his head . . . and a white wand in his hand.' From the trial records of Bessie Dunlop, of Dumfries and Galloway, burnt in 1576 for witchcraft and communing with fairies.

A visit to the Downie-hills
'. . . I was in the Downie-hills, and got meat there from the Queen of Faerie, more than I could eat. The Queen of Faerie is brawly clothed in white linens, and in white and brown clothes; and the King of Faerie is a braw man, well favoured, and broad faced. There were elf-bulls routing and skoyling up and down there, and affrighted me.' From the confession made in 1662 by Isabel Gowdie, a farmer's wife and witch from Morayshire.

Brown women 3 ft high
'. . . the two that constantly attended myself, appear'd both in Women's Habit, they being of a Brown complexion, and about Three Foot in Stature; they had both black, loose Network Gowns, tyed with a black Sash about their Middles, and within the Network appear'd a Gown of Golden Colour, with somewhat of a Light striking thro' it . . . they had white Linen Caps on, with Lace on them, about three Fingers breadth.' From John Beaumont's description of his experiences with fairies, published in 1705.

The Fairy Rade
'. . . A leam o' light was dancing owre them, mair bonnie than moonshine: they were a wee, wee fowk, wi' green scarfs on . . . They rade on braw wee whyte nags, wi' unco lang swooping tails, an' manes hung wi' whustles that the win' played on. This, an' their tongues when they sang, was like the soun' of a far awa Psalm.' Described in the early 1800's by an old woman from near Dumfries.

Manx fairies
'. . . I saw come in twos and threes a great crowd of little beings smaller than Tom Thumb and his wife. All of them, who appeared like soldiers, were dressed in red. They moved back and forth amid the circle of light, as they formed into order like troops drilling.' Described in 1911 by Mr T. C. Kermode, from Peel, Isle of Man.

All dressed in green
'. . . When we were on holiday in Cornwall, my daughter and I came down a winding lane, and all of a sudden there was a small green man – all in green with a pointed hood and ears. We both saw him . . . we were cold with terror and ran for the ferry below.' A 20th-century description by a woman from Shropshire.

A fairy guide
'. . . It was on the Berkshire Downs, and we'd lost our way, and didn't know what track to take. When I looked round, there was a small man in green standing at my elbow. He said, "You take that one; you'll be all right." Then he didn't disappear, but he just wasn't there any more.' Described in 1962 by a Somerset farmer's wife.

121

Fee, fi, fo, fum

*Massive Stone Age monuments and strangely shaped rocks
bred legends of a long-ago race of giants*

People have always believed in ghosts, and some may still give credence to modern witches. Until fairly recently, certain remote hills and streams were held sacred to the fairies: but giants have always belonged to a remote and heroic past. Bygone generations may have believed that giants once roamed the land, but the Age of Giants was always something that had ceased long ago.

Stories about giants may well be a legacy from our Celtic forbears. Arriving in Britain about 300 BC, they saw the great stone circles left by earlier peoples, and imagined them to be the work of some superhuman race. In Celtic eyes too, the native Britons were cannibalistic savages. This impression probably helped to colour the legends of ogres and giants, since the more evilly disposed of these creatures are frequently credited with cannibalism. Such tales grew with the passage of time, and the Celts, recalling the deeds of their ancestors, imagined that they, too, must have had giant-like qualities to have overcome such terrible foes.

The legends survived long enough to be written down – and much embellished – by Geoffrey of Monmouth (*c.* 1100-*c.* 1155), in his *History of the Kings of Britain*. He claims that these islands were originally inhabited by a small number of ferocious giants and he goes on to tell how the giants were vanquished by the descendants of the defeated Trojans led by Brutus, grandson of Aeneas of Troy.

GIANTS OF ANCIENT FABLE

Giants and ogres were nightmare characters in the minds of our forbears. These pictures from the 11th-century English manuscript, *Marvels of the East*, show these monsters with animal-like deformities and brutish features. Many of them are ogres – creatures who were not necessarily of giant size, but who were cannibals. Numerous folk-tales relate that ogres had once lived in these islands; many of the legendary giants and most of the fairy-story ones were, in fact, ogres who ate babies and young girls, and ground men's bones to make their bread. On the hills near Dundee, for instance, a small tribe of man-eating ogres was said to have been destroyed as recently as the beginning of the 16th century. Many legendary heroes distinguished themselves by overcoming giants who had previously terrorised the countryside. At Hartlepool, the evil Grendel ruled the land until Beowulf killed him.

MONSTROUS MAN-EATERS *These huge men, black in colour, had legs 12 ft long and bodies 12 ft broad. Hairy-spined and fang-toothed, they were very ferocious and, according to the imaginative writer of* Marvels of the East, *'whom they catch, they quickly devour'*

WARNING FROM HELL *After the death of a wizard called Jannes, his brother Mambres opened Jannes's magical books and called his spirit out of Hell. Jannes appeared as a huge giant, and warned Mambres to do good in life, since he had been consigned to an everlasting fire in Hell. The giant Jannes is shown eating the bodies of souls consigned to Hell while other sinners suffer in the pit below*

WRAP-ROUND EARS *This race of giants, 15 ft high and 10 ft broad, had ears like bedspreads; at night they were said to lie on one ear and wrap the other around their bodies*

On landing, Brutus divided the country among his followers, giving Cornwall to Corineus, a champion wrestler of great strength and valour. This was a wise choice, because the West Country harboured many giants. Under the leadership of the formidable Gogmagog, the giants hurled themselves upon the Trojans. The fighting was long and bitter, but at last all were killed except Gogmagog. He was captured and forced to wrestle with Corineus who hurled him to his death over the cliffs. Corineus and Gogmagog are commemorated by two effigies in London's Guildhall, though they have been erroneously named Gog and Magog.

Birth of the giants

Early peoples had little difficulty in accepting the idea of a gigantic race, for to them there were few barriers between the spiritual and material worlds. The mating of gods and humans occurs in most mythologies; so does that of gods and animals. The offspring were often monstrous; a fearsome mixture of man and beast, or a giant of superhuman size and strength. Despite their divine origins, however, giants were generally slow-witted and stupid. Most, too, were bad tempered, though some British giants were kind and brave, and often helped the local folk. Whatever their characters, they were always prodigious builders. Legend credits them not only with the raising of Stone Age monuments, but with the construction of Roman roads, hill-forts and mountains as well.

The belief in an ancient race of giants was further strengthened by occasional discoveries of the fossilised bones of prehistoric animals. In the early 19th century there was much excitement in Plymouth when fossil mammoth bones were discovered which local people believed were those of Gogmagog.

The hillside giants

According to some authorities, the Cerne Abbas Giant, the huge chalk figure that dominates a Dorset hillside, actually represents the hero-god Hercules, whose cult may have been brought to this country by early settlers from the Mediterranean. Others think that it may be the portrait of a Celtic god, worshipped by a local tribe.

Until the 19th century, however, the local villagers had a more picturesque explanation. One Cerne Abbas labourer said that the figure was that

THE GIANT IN THE SKY

Hercules, a hero-god of the Mediterranean world, is represented in a star constellation in which he apparently throttles the Lion of Nemea, one of his Twelve Labours. The folklorist, H. J. Massingham, built an elaborate argument to prove that the legendary giants had evolved from late Stone Age hero-gods of the same type as Hercules. The cult of the hero-god probably began in early Egypt, and may then have spread over a greater part of the inhabited world – the gigantic hill figure at Cerne Abbas could be evidence of this

123

of a Danish giant, who once led an invasion of Britain. When he reached the hill, he lay down to sleep. The local people took this opportunity to cut off his head, leaving his outline in the turf as a warning to other marauders. When the labourer was asked how long ago all this happened, he replied, 'About a hundred years ago' – which to him, meant the distant past. In fact, it is believed to be nearly 2000 years old. The figure is 180 ft high, and a similar one – the Long Man at Wilmington in E. Sussex – is 226 ft; both are weeded each year. Other ancient chalk or rock-cut giants included two figures at Plymouth Hoe in Devon, which have now disappeared. Like the Cerne Abbas giant, these also carried clubs. Until the 18th century, other gigantic figures were visible on the hillside at Wandlebury in Cambridgeshire, but these too have vanished beneath the encroaching turf.

Legends of the stones and hills

Many legends of giants were invented to explain the presence of standing stones and other significant features of the countryside. The giants were great stone-throwers and sometimes competed against each other. The amiable giant of Grabbist in Somerset took on a sinister opponent when he challenged the Devil to a game of quoits. The stones they threw can still be seen, and are known today as the Hurdlestones. When the Devil tried to cheat, the giant picked him up by his tail and flung him into the Bristol Channel.

Another well-disposed giant was the kind but clumsy giant of Carn Galver, Cornwall. In return for the odd sheep or goat, he protected the people of

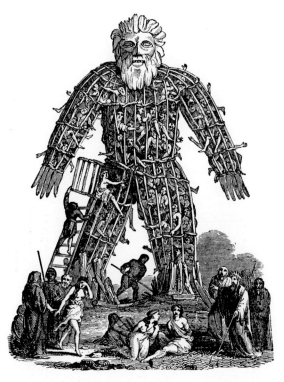

MASSIVE HUMAN SACRIFICE

Julius Caesar, reporting on the Celtic religious rites, claimed that among their more barbaric customs was the burning alive of young people in huge wickerwork cages. These were built in the shape of giant humans and probably represented the god to whom the sacrifices were being made. A dim memory of this practice may account for the sinister reputation of giants in fairy stories and legends

Morvah and Zennor from raids by the wild giants of the Leland Hills. For a pastime, he too played quoits – and the great stones he used still litter the surrounding countryside. It is said that the great rocking Logan Stone was built by this giant to rock himself to sleep at night.

Another natural feature, St Michael's Mount in Cornwall, was said to have been built by the giant Cormoran and his wife Cormelian, who quarried and carried the massive granite boulders of which the Mount is formed.

The Yorkshire castles of Mulgrave and Pickering were believed to have been built by the giant Wade and his wife Bel. It was also alleged that they paved the Roman road called Wade's Causey, as a means of preventing Bel's enormous cow from being bogged down in the muddy, low-lying lanes.

Many giants seem to have shared their tools and implements. A tale from Salop of the origin of the Wrekin tells of a pair of giants who had one spade between them. One day, a fight developed over whose turn it was to use the tool. The spade's possessor would have won easily except that a raven attacked him and pecked his eyes out. Taking advantage of this, the other giant subdued him and entombed him under the hill that is now called the Wrekin; it is said his groans may still be heard on stormy nights.

Strength and stupidity

Few giants, whether good or bad, were distinguished for their intelligence, and they could usually be outwitted by a clever human. Gullibility is the basis of another story of the origin of the Wrekin. It is said that an old Welsh giant was carrying a spadeful of earth with which he intended to dam the Severn and so drown the people of Shrewsbury. On the road he met a cobbler who, realising the giant's evil intention, showed him a sackful of worn shoes. The cobbler claimed that he had worn out each pair in turn on the journey from Shrewsbury. The giant was so discouraged by the apparent distance to the town that he dumped his massive spadeful and trudged back to Wales. The earth that he dropped formed the hill of Wrekin.

The giants overcome

Giants eventually succumbed to the folk-heroes of legend. These were usually poor boys who killed the giant and took his treasure, though sometimes they were saints, whose victories represented the triumph of Christianity over pagan superstition.

Many of the stories involve Jack-the-Giant-Killer, originally a Cornish hero, who also took advantage of the giants' stupidity in his encounters with them. In one story, Jack is challenged by a giant to an eating contest. Jack is easily the victor because his opponent fails to notice a bag beneath the hero's coat into which he packs a vast quantity of food. The giant is further confounded when Jack 'makes space' for more food by plunging a knife into his 'chest', releasing the contents with no apparent ill-effects. The giant follows suit – and falls dead.

Even in legend, the giants could not survive. From the beginning, they represented the unknown forces which primitive man felt were intent upon destroying him. The balance was restored by the folk-hero – a giant or demi-god himself, who dispelled the evil and allowed the work of men to continue unimpeded. In addition, the apparent proofs of their existence – the legends surrounding strange features of the countryside such as hill figures and dinosaur bones – have yielded to the explanations of science. But in place names, such as the Giant's Pulpit at Carn Boscawen in Cornwall, and in stories, the giants' names linger still.

Fabulous beasts

'Beware the Jabberwock, my son!
The jaws that bite, the claws that catch!'

As Lewis Carroll pointed out, when he described the hunting of the Jabberwock, the pursuit of fabulous beasts can be a long and hazardous business. They must be sought in many different habitats; some in mythology, some in moral tales, while others are found only among the strawberry leaves of heraldic emblems. Some, such as the Gulon which devoured corpses so fast that it could digest only by squeezing itself between trees, are long extinct; others are still very much with us. Prominent among these are the North American goofus, a bird that always flies backwards because it is interested only in places it has already visited; and the gremlin, which drinks petrol and has the ability to raise and lower airfields beneath novice pilots as they come in to land.

Travellers' tales, and misunderstandings about the habits of real animals, have made major contributions to the zoology of monsters. Medieval scholars were sceptical, even if laymen were not, when they heard tales of the Hornworm, a four-horned serpent that buried itself in sand. Only the horns were left exposed, woven into a bright coronet to entice its prey. Omitting the coronet and one pair of horns, this is a fairly accurate description of the North African horned viper.

For centuries, people ate the barnacle goose on Fridays in the belief that it was more fish than

BATTLE OF MYTHICAL BEASTS

The parish churches, monasteries and cathedrals of Britain bear rich testimony to the importance of monsters and fabulous beasts in the medieval imagination. The gargoyles that surround our church spires are carved in the shapes of griffins, dragons and other symbols of the Devil. Carvings of scaly creatures decorate choir stalls or hang from nave roofs in bosses and corbels. This finely carved wooden boss in Westminster Abbey, dating from the mid-13th century, shows a battle between a lion-centaur – half-man, half-lion – and a dragon

bird. It was said to hatch half-grown from barnacles growing in clusters on sea-soaked pine branches; since the bird breeds in the Arctic and migrates to these shores only during the winter, it is not surprising that no one had seen either its nest or its young. Failure to understand bird migration may also account for the North Country legend of Gabriel Ratchet's Hounds – a pack of demon dogs that pursue the souls of the damned across the skies. Anyone who has heard the eerie sounds made by night-flying migratory geese will understand how the story might have arisen.

However, the medieval Church had little use for the finer points of zoology. As far as the clergy was concerned, the main purpose of animals, real or imaginary, was to act as symbols in underlining moral teachings; the dragon was particularly useful in this way. This animal figures in almost every mythology, but to Christians it was the personification of evil. When St George, or St Leonard, or St Keyne, slew the dragon, they symbolised the triumph of Christ over the powers of darkness. But outside the Church, the dragon had a different significance; in heraldry, it represented strength, and Romans, Vikings and perhaps even King Arthur all marched under dragon banners. Probably it was the mingling of the two themes which caused the beast to appear so frequently in tales of chivalry; few heroes of any standing failed to include a slain dragon in their battle honours.

The hero and the worm

Despite its name, the Lambton Worm of Durham was certainly a species of dragon. It was so long that it could curl itself round Worm Hill near Fatfield, and for many years it laid waste to the surrounding countryside. Finally, it was challenged by Sir John Lambton who, before offering battle, took the precaution of consulting a witch. On her advice, he studded his armour with knife blades, then waited by the River Wear for the Worm to come down to drink. When it arrived, he ran it through with his sword; the Worm fought back, and coiled itself round him, but the knives slashed and weakened it, and Sir John hacked it to pieces. When this had happened in previous battles, the Worm had always managed to put its segments together again and continue the fight. But acting on the witch's advice, Sir John threw each of the pieces in the Wear as he hewed them off, and the swift-running river carried them away for ever.

Similar tactics were adopted by Peter Loschy when he slew the dragon of Loschy Hill in N. Yorkshire. This beast had teeth like pitchfork prongs as well as a poisonous tongue, and when Peter cut it to pieces, the bits were carried away by his faithful hound. Its work completed, the dog returned and licked his master's face. Unfortunately, the creature had swallowed some of the dragon's poison, and Peter and his dog fell dead together.

Further north, in Orkney, the Meister Stoor Worm was killed when a local hero plunged a spear tipped with blazing pitch down its throat. The monster's corpse was so huge that it later became known as Iceland, while its spat-out teeth formed the Faroes.

Many fearsome creatures are still said to haunt the lonelier parts of Britain. The Welsh afanc, half-man, half-horse, inhabits caves near mountain pools and cannot be killed by mortal means. The Conway afanc was rendered harmless, however, when it was lured from its lair by a girl it had fallen in love with. Waiting villagers bound it with ropes, and dragged it with oxen to a lonely pool near the top of Snowdon where it would no longer be a menace to wayfarers. Another aquatic Welsh

MONSTERS OF THE MIDDLE AGES

The medieval imagination was deeply coloured by stories of monsters. These are reflected in the many Bestiaries – Books of Beasts – that were written during this period whose descriptions of natural and imaginary animals drew moral lessons to illuminate Christian beliefs. The dragon, for example, which represented the Devil, was vanquished by St George. Crusaders imported tales of Eastern monsters to embellish similar fables. The creatures shown are from a 13th-century manuscript known as the Westminster Bestiary.

SYMBOL OF CHIVALRY *A proud, untameable and imperious beast, the unicorn could be captured only by a naked virgin seated alone under a tree. A horn, said to be that of a unicorn, was exhibited at Windsor Castle during the 16th century, and was valued at £100,000*

GUARDIAN OF TREASURE *Hostile to man, the griffin drew the chariot of the vengeful Nemesis. Like the heraldic dragon, it had a lust for treasure, though Lewis Carroll departed from tradition and depicted the griffin in* Alice in Wonderland *as a lovable beast*

TRAVELLERS' TALE *The manticora was an Indian monster, probably based on stories of man-eating tigers. It had a man's face, three rows of teeth, and a mouth agape from ear to ear. Its tail was covered with sharp quills which it let fly at its pursuers*

AN ELIZABETHAN ZOO

The reign of Elizabeth I was a time when man was extending the boundaries of the known world with dynamic curiosity and vigour. Contemporary beliefs about animals are an example of the thin dividing line between myth and reality that existed in men's minds.

Edward Topsell's *Historie of Foure-Footed Beasts* and his *Histories of Serpents* were published early in the 17th century. These books show the rich mixture of superstition, accurate observation and myth in Elizabethan notions of natural history. The author gives

equal emphasis to a careful description of the habits of the cat and a solemn warning to the reader against the impiety of disbelieving in the unicorn. In another part of the book, he maintains that the elephant always faces east when mating but refutes an earlier belief that the beast had no joints in its limbs.

These illustrations from Topsell's books are the beginnings of zoology. They were drawn at a time when it was commonplace to 'pass away the Sabbaths in heavenly meditation upon earthly creatures'.

MIMICKE DOG *An engaging and friendly creature, the Mimicke Dog danced, played and generally copied men's habits. Raised by apes who taught it man-like tricks, these beasts were said to help poor families with their chores*

BOA *A kind of dragon 'which Italy doth breed, men say, and upon the milk of cows do feed'. Boas were the scourge of farmers, and slithered the countryside, sucking whole herds of cows dry before eating them*

WILDE BEAST *A ferociously maternal creature who killed all who ventured near her. The Wilde Beast carried her offspring on her back, and would kill them rather than allow them to be captured*

HYDRA *A many-headed monster, and an antagonist of Hercules when he performed his 12 labours, the hydra was a beast to be feared. As often as one of its heads was struck off, another grew in its place*

LAMIA *The original man-eater and child-snatcher, the lamia was a creature of ancient Greek myth. She has a British counterpart in the Highland glaistig who sucked the blood of young men who danced with her. Lamia was a name applied to witches in the Middle Ages and also for any diabolical creature that disturbed sleep*

TRITON *The scale-covered triton lived a morose and solitary life in sea caves, 'sounding his conch shell like a trumpet'. In allegorical paintings, he often appears as a storm-raiser and wrecker of ships, and as a traditional attendant of Neptune*

terror is the Llamigan-y-dur, or water-leaper. Shaped like a gigantic toad, with wings and a tail instead of legs, it seizes fishing lines and tries to drag the fisherman beneath the surface. But its principal diet is sheep, which it drowns in the pools where it makes its home.

Scottish shepherds are said to have been plagued by the boobrie, a huge creature not unlike a duck in appearance, but whose footprint would cover a cartwheel. It ate sheep and cows in large quantities, and its dreadful honking bray has often been heard near the sea-lochs of the district of Argyll.

If the nuckelavee ever existed, it must have been terrible to behold. It had a barrel-shaped body and a lolling head, and made up for its lack of legs by crutching itself along on its long arms. Worst of all, it was skinless, so the blood could be seen coursing through its veins and its muscles contracting and expanding. Understandably, it was totally malignant, and used to spread plague through the Highlands in time of drought.

On the whole, the monsters of the south were gentler in appearance. The Church Grim of Somerset, for example, usually assumes the shape of a black dog and, in this guise, protects churches. Perceptive parsons occasionally glimpse it at funerals, where it is said that the ultimate destination of the passing soul can be deduced from the expression on the beast's face. Under different names, such as padfoot, barguest and shrike, monstrous black dogs make frequent appearances in English lore, and several of them accompanied immigrants to Australia, Canada and the USA. There, they follow much the same roles, either protective or malevolent, that they had in the old country.

Beasts in heraldry

The best-known, or at least the most frequently represented, of fabulous beasts are those which support the coats of arms of families, cities and livery companies. The calygreyhound, which combines the attributes of the eagle, the antelope and the ox, has stood beside the shield of the de Veres since the 16th century. Griffins (half-eagle and half-lion), bagwyns (part horse, part goat) and pantheons, which are panthers whose hides are marked with stars, are also popular in heraldry. Few of these hybrid creatures are British in origin. Even the unicorn, which together with its traditional enemy, the lion, supports the royal coat of arms, has only one native species. This is the Baiste-na-scoghaigh of Skye, a great, lumbering, one-horned creature which has little in common with the graceful unicorn of mythology. Nevertheless, both may be related to the bicorne, a two-horned animal that dines on hen-pecked husbands. Its happy, well-fed appearance is said to be due to the fact that its prey is so plentiful. Its close relation is the cow-like chichevache, that devours only obedient wives. This explains the beast's lean and hungry appearance.

WINGED LEGENDS

Because he envied birds their flight, and held their freedom and unhampered mobility in awe, early man often endowed the creatures of his imagination with wings. One of the most fearsome beasts that fable has ever attributed to these islands is the cockatrice, a bird that was hatched by a serpent from a cock's egg; it had the ability to kill at a glance. According to legend, England was once infested with cockatrices to such an extent that no one dared leave his house. The country was finally rid of them when a hero dressed himself in mirrors and walked about the countryside. Destroyed by the reflected glare of their own eyes, the cockatrices rapidly became extinct.

Not all the winged creatures of legend are horrific. Though mysterious, the Egyptian sphinx is benevolent, and the pelican, which was believed to feed its blood to its young, has been a Christian symbol since the Middle Ages. In some accounts the phoenix represents the resurrection of Christ, and Paradise itself is traditionally peopled by the angels, the winged hosts of God.

RENEWED LIFE *A magical bird of brilliant plumage, the phoenix symbolises the rare and marvellous. Each phoenix lived alone for 500 years, then sang its final song upon an aromatic pyre which was ignited by the sun. Out of the ashes a worm emerged, the embryo of the re-born phoenix*

WINGED SEDUCTRESS *Sirens were beautiful women who lured men to their deaths with sweet songs. Classical artists depicted them with wings, although later paintings show them as mermaids. Jennie Greenteeth, of the Cumbrian lakes, is an English form*

PROPHET OF DEATH *The outcome of illness in the Middle Ages was often thought to be foretold by the caladrius, a supernatural bird that sat on the end of the sick-bed. If it looked at the patient, he would recover; if it looked away, then death was inevitable*

Romance of Britain

A REGIONAL GUIDE TO BRITAIN'S FOLKLORE

LAND OF MERLIN

Cornwall

The Cornish have always been a people apart, separated from their neighbours in Devon by inclination, origins, and the River Tamar. Until well into the 18th century there was also a language barrier. Old Cornish is a Celtic tongue akin to Breton and Welsh, but except in place names such as *tre* (a farm), *mor* (the sea), *wheal* (a mine) and *veal* (little), few traces of it now remain. Similar prefixes, however, also occur in Cornish surnames. An old rhyme says:

> By Tre, Pol and Pen, you shall know the Cornishmen.

There are few books in Cornish, and only one or two old religious plays, yet its spoken tales and traditions were among the richest in Britain. Out of Cornwall came the romance which inspired so many poets and even a Wagnerian opera – the love of Tristan and Iseult. Cornwall also claims to be the realm of King Arthur and the wizard Merlin.

Surrounded on three sides by the sea, Cornwall is almost completely isolated by the River Tamar – creating an easily defended area which has attracted settlers since earliest times. Traces of these prehistoric peoples abound, and have given rise to many legends. Dolmens and quoits, great stone circles and avenues, dating from about 3000 BC, were awesome things to the later Cornish. Constructed of granite boulders which seemed beyond the power of mortal man to shift, they were instead believed to be the work of giants. Or perhaps they were men and maidens, forever frozen in a circle, for the sin of dancing on a Sunday.

The Celts – from whom many of the modern Cornish are descended – crossed from Europe in increasing numbers during the 500 years preceding the birth of Christ. Successive invaders – Romans, Angles and Saxons – drove them into remote parts of the country. To Cornwall, they brought their tales of gods and heroes, giants and fairies.

These legends became interwoven with stories of the coming of Christianity. Many tales of the saints – that of St Just, for example, said to have stolen a golden cup from St Keverne – show marked pagan characteristics. St Keverne threw enormous boulders at the thief, which, because no one was able to move them again, lie where they fell to this day. Very similar stories are told of the Cornish giants.

Holy wells and stones credited with the ability to cure disease, or to promote fertility in women, are found all over Cornwall. Though many of them now bear saints' names, there is little doubt that their supposed miraculous powers long pre-date Christianity. The Celtic Church frequently ascribed the legendary deeds of the old gods to its own missionaries, several of whom came from Ireland and Wales.

Cornwall is an austere land, and for centuries many of its people have made their living as deep-sea fishermen, or as miners working hundreds of feet underground. Men in dangerous jobs are often superstitious, but the Cornish have enriched the usual legends with Celtic imagery.

The sense of separateness found in Cornwall has diminished since the first railways crossed the Tamar in 1859. But while the legends of coasts and moorland are still remembered, Cornwall will always sustain its role as the last outpost of Celtic England.

CHAPEL PORTH
(*Cormoran & Bolster, 132*)

ST IVES

ZENNOR

CARN BREA

BOTALLACK
(*Tinners & Knockers, 141*)

CARN KENIDJACK

ST ERTH

ST JUST
(*Tinners & Knockers, 141*)

MADRON

PRUSSIA COVE
(*Smugglers & Wreckers, 1*)

ST MICHAEL'S MOUNT

MOUSEHOLE

LAND'S END

ST BURYAN

HELS

PORTHGWARRA
(*The Lovers, 136*)

MOUNT'S BAY
(*Cormoran & Bolster, 132*)

PORTHCURNO

TREWOOFE

LOE BAR
(*Jan Tregeagle, 138*)

TRESCO

ST MARY'S

Isles of Scilly

0   5   10
MILES

THE FOLKLORE YEAR

February 4 (nearest Monday)
St Ives
Hurling the Silver Ball

Shrove Tuesday
St Columb Major
Hurling the Silver Ball

May 1
Padstow
'Obby Oss' ceremony

May 8 (nearest Saturday)
Helston
The Furry Dance

June 23 (Midsummer Eve)
Carn Brea
First bonfire in chain across Cornwall

Monday after August 12
Marhamchurch
Revel in honour of St Morwenna, founder of the village

Early September
Various sites
Gorsedd of the Cornish Bards

September 25
Summercourt
Cornwall's largest fair

End of September
St Keverne
'Crying the Neck'

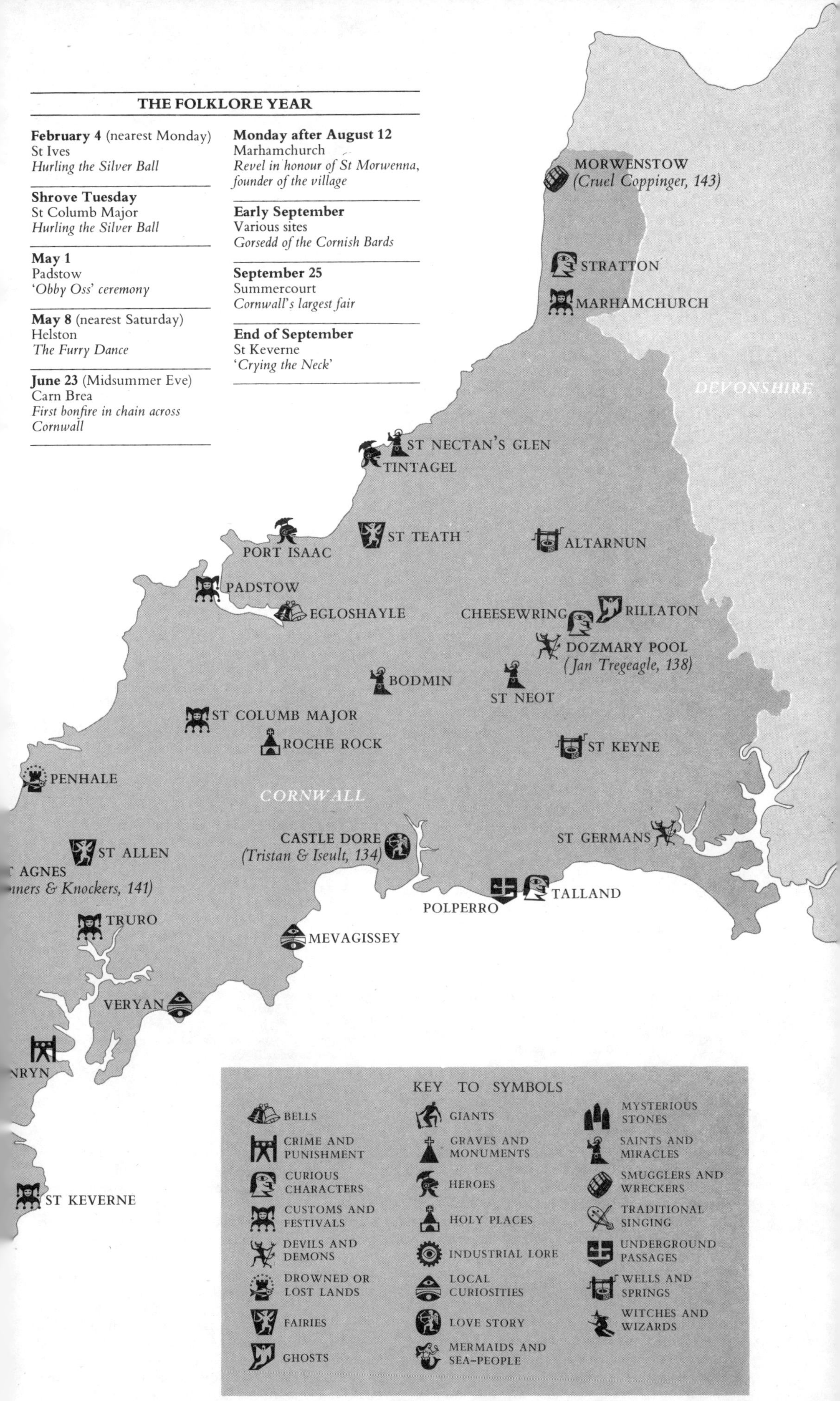

MORWENSTOW
(Cruel Coppinger, 143)

STRATTON

MARHAMCHURCH

DEVONSHIRE

 ST NECTAN'S GLEN
TINTAGEL

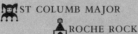 ST TEATH

ALTARNUN

PORT ISAAC

 PADSTOW

EGLOSHAYLE

CHEESEWRING  RILLATON

 DOZMARY POOL
(Jan Tregeagle, 138)

BODMIN

ST NEOT

ST COLUMB MAJOR

ROCHE ROCK

ST KEYNE

 PENHALE

CORNWALL

 ST ALLEN

CASTLE DORE
(Tristan & Iseult, 134)

ST GERMANS

T AGNES
...ners & Knockers, 141)

POLPERRO

TALLAND

TRURO

MEVAGISSEY

VERYAN

 ...NRYN

 ...

 ...

 ...

ST KEVERNE

KEY TO SYMBOLS

BELLS

CRIME AND PUNISHMENT

CURIOUS CHARACTERS

CUSTOMS AND FESTIVALS

DEVILS AND DEMONS

DROWNED OR LOST LANDS

FAIRIES

GHOSTS

GIANTS

GRAVES AND MONUMENTS

HEROES

HOLY PLACES

INDUSTRIAL LORE

LOCAL CURIOSITIES

LOVE STORY

MERMAIDS AND SEA-PEOPLE

MYSTERIOUS STONES

SAINTS AND MIRACLES

SMUGGLERS AND WRECKERS

TRADITIONAL SINGING

UNDERGROUND PASSAGES

WELLS AND SPRINGS

WITCHES AND WIZARDS

GIANT CORMORAN AND GIANT BOLSTER

Altarnun

Both the church and the holy well near by are dedicated to St Non, believed to be the mother of St David of Wales. The waters of the well were once used to cure madness, and this belief still lives in local memory. Lunatics would be immersed in the well and then carried to the church for masses to be sung over them. When they regained their wits, prayers would be offered to the saint.

TRADITIONAL ENTERTAINERS

Altarnun church houses a fine collection of 16th-century carved bench-ends. The bagpipe player and the fiddler are two of a series which suggest that a tradition of music existed long ago among the local people

Bodmin

The name means 'house of the monks', and until the Dissolution of the Monasteries by Henry VIII, Bodmin was mainly an ecclesiastical town. The original monastery, a few traces of which remain, was founded in the 6th century by St Petroc, a Celtic missionary from Wales. In the crypt of St Petroc's Church lies an ivory casket thought to have contained the saint's bones. During the reign of Henry II, these were stolen by a Breton priest and taken to St Meen Abbey in Brittany. Henry, who was overlord of Brittany, forced the Bretons to return the casket and its contents to Bodmin.

Carn Brea

The Midsummer Bonfire ceremony, performed on June 23, was a pagan festival centuries before it was hallowed by the Church to celebrate the Eve of St John. The first fire, kindled on Carn Brea, a granite tor lying between Camborne and Redruth, is the signal for other fires to be lit from Land's End through Sennen, Sancreed Beacon, Carn Galver and St Agnes Beacon, to the Tamar. Each fire is blessed by a local clergyman in the Cornish language, and herbs and wild flowers are burnt. When only the embers remain, young people leap across them to drive away evil and bring good luck.

It is thought that the fires were originally lit to worship the sun; another theory is that the flames were supposed to ward off witchcraft. At St Cleer, the fire is still crowned with a broomstick, and a sickle with a newly cut oak handle is thrown into the flames to ensure the fertility of crops and men.

Geoffrey of Monmouth, writing in 1136, describes how Brutus and the Trojans, after many years of wandering following the fall of Troy, finally landed at Totnes in Devon. Britain 'was uninhabited except for a few giants'. Brutus divided the country amongst his followers, and Corineus was given Cornwall, the land that still bears his name. Corineus 'experienced great pleasure in wrestling with the giants of whom there were far more there than in any other district'.

Cornwall still retains what is said to be evidence of these huge people in such ancient rock formations as the Giant's Cradle on Trecobben Hill – a legendary fortress of the giants, to which they dragged their victims and murdered them. Other tales are told about the Giant's Cave at Lamorna and the Giant's Chair 3 miles south-east of Land's End. While historians may prefer the theory that the tall Anglo-Saxon invaders appeared as giants to the much shorter Celts, there is no doubt that the legendary stories are far more colourful.

The building of Cormoran's castle

One of the best known stories tells of a giant named Cormoran and his wife Cormelian. They had their home in the thick forest that once covered that part of Mount's Bay between Penzance and Marazion. Cormoran, intent on building himself a stronghold of white granite, forced his wife to carry the great boulders in her apron. One day, Cormelian, seeing her husband asleep, decided it would be much easier to collect greenstone instead, which was much nearer to hand. Unfortunately, Cormoran awoke and saw her; enraged, he gave her a kick that broke her apron strings and the greenstone dropped. Mount's Bay forest is now submerged, but a block of greenstone still stands on the causeway to St Michael's Mount, said to be Cormoran's fortress.

Cormoran finally met his death at the hands of Jack the Giant Killer. Jack crept to the Mount one night and dug a deep pit, covering it with sticks and straw. Then, placing his horn to his lips, he awoke Cormoran. The giant rushed out and fell into the hole. Jack raised his axe and struck at the giant's head, killing him with a single blow. The local people presented Jack with a magnificent sword, and a belt embroidered with gold.

The giant and the missionary

Another story tells of the mighty Bolster who fell deeply in love with St Agnes, a beautiful and virtuous missionary. The giant followed her, incessantly proclaiming his love, but St Agnes would only lecture him for his impropriety, for he was a married man. At last, the saint decided to rid herself of him. She asked him to prove his love by filling a hole in the ground at Chapel Porth with his blood. Bolster, convinced that it would take little blood to fill such a small hole, plunged his knife into a vein and held his arm over the hole. Blood gushed for hours, but the hole was not filled. The cunning saint knew that the cavity opened out into the sea and at last the giant collapsed and died. The hole remains at Chapel Porth to verify the legend and a red stain marks where Bolster's blood once flowed down the rocks.

Carn Kenidjack

It is told that, many years ago, two miners were passing the carn late at night. Suddenly they were overtaken by a black-robed horseman who invited them to watch a wrestling match on the carn. The terrified miners accepted and found they had joined a party of fearsome demons, commanded by the horseman who was the Devil himself.

During the first fierce bout, one of the pair of wrestling demons was thrown against a rock. He appeared to be dying, and the two miners, overcome by a sense of Christian charity, ran to him and whispered a prayer in his ear. At once the earth trembled and the whole demonic party vanished shrieking in a black cloud. The miners, petrified with fear, hid on the carn until daylight.

A GIANT'S STRIDE *According to legend, the mighty giant Bolster, who died for love of St Agnes, could stand with one foot on St Agnes Beacon and the other on Carn Brea, a stride of over 6 miles*

The Cheesewring

This natural pile of granite slabs takes its name from its similarity to a cheese-press. It is associated with Daniel Gumb, a local stonecutter, whose work can still be seen in Linkinhorne churchyard. Although his parents were uneducated, he himself showed an unusually high intelligence. An avid reader, he taught himself elementary mathematics, and became deeply interested in astronomy. After marrying a local girl, he made his home with her in a cave beneath the Cheesewring, where they raised numerous children, baptising them on prehistoric altars near by. Until the cave collapsed, many of Gumb's intricate geometrical designs could be seen carved in the granite, with the inscription 'D. Gumb 1735' cut above the cave entrance.

Egloshayle

The village boasted the finest bell-ringers in the county in the early 19th century, when bell-ringing competitions were held between rival villages. The team is still remembered in a local song 'The Ringers of Egloshayle', a verse of which runs:

> There's Craddock the cordwainer first who rings the treble bell,
> The second is John Ellery who none could e'er excel,
> The third is Pollard, carpenter, the fourth is Thomas Cleave,
> And Goodfellow the tenor-man who rings 'em round so brave.

The bodies of all five ringers lie in Egloshayle churchyard and their epitaphs can still be read.

THE TRAGIC LOVE OF TRISTAN AND ISEULT

Helston

According to one legend, the Devil was flying across Cornwall carrying a boulder to block the entrance to Hell, when he was challenged by St Michael. In the ensuing battle, the Devil dropped the rock, and the place where it fell became known as 'Hell's Stone' or Helston. It is said that a large rock built into the wall of the Angel Hotel in Coinagehall Street is this very stone. To celebrate St Michael's victory over the Devil, the inhabitants danced through the streets and thereby originated the famous Furry Dance, which still takes place on the nearest Saturday to the feast day of the town's patron saint, St Michael the Archangel (May 8). The name of the dance is derived either from the Middle English word *ferrie*, implying a Church festival, or the Celtic *feur* meaning a holiday or fair. However, its seasonal setting suggests the dance may once have been a pagan spring festival.

The ceremony that precedes the Furry Dance is probably more significant than the dance. It is a true relic of the ancient May games, designed to greet the summer with song and drama to induce crop fertility. Known as the Hal-an-Tow, this mumming play features the older children. Garlanded and carrying branches of sycamore, they sing an ancient song, part of the chorus of which runs:

Welcome is the Summer, the Summer and the May-O,

For Summer is a-come-O, and Winter is a-gone-O.

Land's End

Legend holds that Land's End was once the entrance to the fertile land of Lyonesse, which stretched to the Isles of Scilly. Some 900 years ago, Lyonesse was suddenly engulfed by the sea. Only one man escaped, named Trevilian, riding on a swift white horse; the Trevilian family arms still depict a horse rising from the sea. The older Mount's Bay fishermen insist that drowned buildings can sometimes be seen around the Seven Stones Lighthouse.

Madron

The granite Men-an-Tol or Holed Stone lies 2½ miles north-west of Madron, near Penzance. Originally forming the entrance to a tomb chamber, the stone was thought for centuries to possess curative powers. Even in recent times, it was customary for young children to be passed naked through the hole nine times, as a cure for scrofula, rickets and other diseases.

During the 6th century, King Mark of Cornwall owed allegiance to the King of Ireland and was forced to send a yearly tribute of young men and maidens as slaves for his overlord. One year, Morholt, brother of the Queen of Ireland, was sent to Cornwall to demand further tribute. Mark's nephew, Tristan, challenged Morholt to single combat in which, despite being wounded with a poisoned spear, Tristan killed the Irishman. No Cornishman could cure Tristan's wound, so trusting in God he set out to sea in a boat without sails or oars.

By chance, the vessel reached the Irish coast, where Iseult the Fair, the King of Ireland's beautiful daughter, nursed him back to health. Afraid of being recognised as the slayer of Morholt, Tristan quickly returned to Cornwall. There he discovered that the courtiers had been trying to persuade King Mark to take a wife.

Postponing a decision, Mark picked up a long golden hair dropped by a passing swallow, and said that he would marry only the maiden to whom that hair belonged. Tristan at once set out in search of her.

Again he went to Ireland where he slew a dragon which was terrorising the whole country. In return, the king gave him Iseult the Fair as his bride – but it was her hair that the swallow had carried. True to his promise, Tristan took her back to Cornwall to become Mark's queen.

The fatal love potion

On the journey home, however, the couple accidentally drank a love potion which had been prepared for Mark and Iseult on their wedding night. They fell deeply in love, and though Iseult married King Mark, she continued to love Tristan. Mark soon realised his wife was unfaithful; but the lovers fled into the forest of Morrois, where they lived together in great happiness, despite their poverty.

After three years, the power of the love potion wore off. Though they still loved each other deeply, they sadly decided that Iseult should honour her marriage vows. Mark accepted her on condition she would swear on holy relics that she had never been unfaithful. On the way to the church where the relics were assembled, the king and queen came to a ford where they met a leper, whom Iseult recognised as Tristan in disguise. She asked him to carry her pick-a-back across the ford. He did so, and when she came to the holy relics, she was able to swear that no man had ever been between her thighs except King Mark and the leper who had carried her.

The final grief

Tristan left the country. After many adventures, he married a Breton girl named Iseult of the White Hands – though his love for Iseult the Fair never diminished. Years later, Tristan was badly wounded in battle and sent for Iseult the Fair to heal him. He told his messenger to hoist a white sail on the returning ship if Iseult was on board, and a black sail if not. As the ship approached, Tristan's jealous wife told him that she could only see a black sail, whereupon Tristan died of grief, and Iseult, on hearing the news, died soon after. At Castle Dore, the site of Mark's castle near Fowey, an ancient cross still marks Tristan's grave.

Marhamchurch

The village lies on the now disused Bude Canal, a waterway that once carried beach-sand – valued as a fertiliser – from Bude to Launceston. It was founded as a monastic settlement by St Morwenna and every year, on the Monday after August 12, the ancient Marhamchurch Revel is held to celebrate the saint's good works. A Queen of the Revel is elected from among the village schoolgirls and crowned by Father Time on the spot in front of the church where St Morwenna's cell once stood. A procession, led by the local band and the newly crowned Queen riding on horseback, then passes through the village to the Revel Ground. Here the villagers are entertained with a show of country dancing, Cornish wrestling and other amusements.

THE ROYAL EAVESDROPPER *Hearing of a meeting between Tristan and Iseult, King Mark hides in a tree above them. The lovers see his reflection in the pool and gossip casually together. This, for a time, convinces the king of their innocence*

Mevagissey

Once the centre of the prosperous Cornish pilchard fishing industry, the town is now a major tourist attraction. Though the town has no apparent reason for self-deprecation, two local stories are told jokingly by the inhabitants. The church, built in a part of the town called Porthilly, has only a small tower and no bells. A rhyme explains why:

Ye men of Porthilly, why are you so silly,
In having so little a power?
You sold every bell, as Gorran men tell,
For money to pull down your tower!

Another still-current story tells of a French ship wrecked off the harbour during the Napoleonic wars. A monkey washed ashore from the wreck was hanged by the townspeople as a French spy.

Mousehole

In 1595, a fleet of Spanish ships appeared and burnt the village of Mousehole (pronounced 'Mouzel') to the ground. Only the Keigwin Arms, now a private house, survived. Near the quay is a stone called Merlin's Rock, and the Spanish attack was regarded locally as the fulfilment of a prophecy by the wizard. A saying, still current in the district, is:

There shall land on the Rock of Merlin
Those who shall burn Paul, Penzance and Newlyn.

Merlin's other prophecies have still to be fulfilled. He said, for instance, that:

When the Rame Head and Dodman meet
Man and woman will have cause to greet (cry).

The two headlands remain 40 miles apart.

Padstow

The town was originally named Petroc-stow, after the Welsh missionary St Petroc, who landed at nearby Trebetherick *c.* AD 500. Petroc arrived during a hot summer, and made many converts to Christianity by striking a rock with his staff and producing a stream of cool water.

The town is famous for the colourful 'Obby Oss' ceremony, whose origins are lost in antiquity. It commences at midnight on May Eve, when the townspeople walk through the town singing the Morning Song, which lasts until about 2 o'clock on May morning. After a few hours, they are up again to collect greenery to decorate the town, and flowers for the maypole in the square.

The climax arrives when the Oss – represented by a man in a black frame-hung cape and gruesome mask – emerges from its stable in the morning. The Day Song then strikes up as the Oss prances through the narrow lanes, bowing and leaping before his 'teasers' or attendants, and trying to catch young girls beneath his cape. Finally, at midnight, the Oss dies and the crowd sings its farewell – until the Oss is resurrected the following May Day. The ceremony is believed to be based on a pre-Christian spring fertility rite with the dying Oss representing the passing of the old year.

Penhale

According to legend, Penhale Sands was once the site of Langarroc, a beautiful town with seven fine churches. Mining made the town rich, but with wealth came a sad moral decline. So evil were its ways that, one night, a storm arose and buried the town and all its people beneath a sand dune. Even now, says the legend, when the night is stormy, the bells of the seven churches can be heard above the roar of the sea. There may be some truth in the story, for after high winds, ancient human skeletons have sometimes been discovered there.

About 100 years ago, a small 7th-century oratory was discovered beneath the sands at nearby Perranzabuloe, and restored. This name in old Cornish means 'the church of St Piran in the sands', and the oratory is believed to mark the spot where St Piran landed from Ireland.

Penryn

A legend tells that, after years at sea, a young sailor of Penryn returned to his parents' inn. By way of a joke on the old people, he disguised himself, though he told his sister, who lived in another street, of his plan. His parents, seeing only a rich stranger, succumbed to temptation and murdered the young man. The full horror of the parents' situation was revealed next morning when their daughter came in search of her brother. Overcome with remorse, both parents committed suicide and their daughter died soon after. This sad story was turned into a successful play called 'The Penryn Tragedy'.

Polperro

Willy Willcocks' Hole is a cavern below Chapel Hill on the western side of the harbour. Willy Willcocks was a fisherman who, when exploring the cave, lost his way in the maze of tunnels behind the entrance. His restless spirit still roams the passages seeking a means of escape, his cries mingling with the wind on dark nights.

Porthcurno

On the headland east of Porthcurno stands the famous Logan Stone. The stone, which rocks when gently pushed, was thought to be otherwise totally immovable. In 1824, Lt. Goldsmith, RN, disproved this by pushing it on to the beach below. As the result of local complaints, the Lieutenant was ordered to replace the rock at his own expense, which he succeeded in doing. Goldsmith's exploit is recalled by the sign on the Logan Rock Inn at Treen.

THE LOVERS
OF PORTHGWARRA

South of Land's End, the hamlet of Porthgwarra was once known as Sweetheart's Cove. Many years ago, Nancy, the daughter of a farmer, fell in love with a sailor called William. Her parents disapproved of him and the lovers were forbidden to meet. Just before William joined his ship, they managed one last meeting in this cove. They vowed that they would be true to one another forever and, living or dead, they would meet again.

No news came from the sailor for many months and Nancy, growing more melancholy every day, watched for his ship from nearby Hella Point, which became known as Nancy's Garden. Eventually, she became quite mad and did little but lament the loss of her lover.

One moonlit night, an old woman sitting on the clifftop saw Nancy walk down to the cove and sit on a rock that was partially surrounded by water. The tide began to rise but the girl continued to gaze out to sea. The old woman, seeing the danger the girl was in, decided to go down and warn her of the rising water. When she arrived on the beach, she was surprised to see a sailor beside the young girl with his arm round her. Believing Nancy to be safe, the old woman sat down to watch. But the lovers did not move and, with increasing concern, the old woman called out to them. But neither heeded her warning. Suddenly they appeared to float off over the sea and then vanish. Nancy was never seen again, and next day word came that William's ship had foundered with all hands.

Port Isaac

Just inland from the village lie traces of Castle Damelioc, where Gorlois, Earl of Cornwall, was killed by King Uther Pendragon. The king desired Igerna, Gorlois's beautiful wife, and laid siege to the earl's castle. Gorlois was killed, but Igerna escaped to Tintagel. Uther followed. With the help of the wizard Merlin, he assumed the likeness of the dead Gorlois and seduced Igerna. She conceived a child – the future King Arthur.

Rillaton

A story tells of the ghost of a druid priest which haunted a burial mound near Rillaton Manor. The phantom would waylay any passer-by and offer him a magic potion from a golden cup which could never be drained. One day a drunken hunter, unable to drain the cup, threw the dregs in the spectre's face. Shortly afterwards, both horse and rider were found dead at the bottom of a ravine.

THE SPECTRE'S CUP

In 1818, excavations near Rillaton unearthed a skeleton and a gold beaker. The cup, now in the British Museum, is associated with a legend of a phantom druid

ROCHE ROCK, A LEPER'S REFUGE

The hermitage surmounting Roche Rock is said to have served as the final retreat of a leper. He was kept alive by his daughter, who fed him and brought him water. The story could be partly true. The man may have lived c.

1400 when Roche experienced many changes in its local priesthood. This could well have been caused by the strain of officiating to the afflicted man. The hermitage also figures in the legend of Jan Tregeagle

St Allen

Legend tells of a little boy from this parish near Truro, who wandered into a copse near his home to pick wild flowers. When his mother called him for supper, he was nowhere to be seen. Three days of frantic searching by the villagers ended when he was found sleeping peacefully at the place where his mother had last seen him.

He appeared quite ignorant of the time that had elapsed. He said that while picking flowers, he had heard a bird singing so beautifully that he was compelled to follow it deep into the woods. Night fell, and stars were shining. Suddenly he realised that each star was, in fact, a pisky. These fairy folk led the boy to a marvellous cave of crystal pillars studded with jewels of every colour. Here he was fed on the purest honey before the piskies sang him to sleep. When he awoke, he found himself back in the copse by his home.

St Buryan

The church, despite its granite dourness, provides a moment of humour. In folklore, lawyers are generally portrayed as dishonest. A churchyard epitaph mentions two exceptions:

Here lie John and Richard Benn
Two lawyers and two honest men.
God works miracles now and then.

St Columb Major

Annually, on Shrove Tuesday, the ancient sport of Hurling the Silver Ball is played. The game resembles football, but its rules are vague. Two teams are formed. Any number can participate and the goals are 2 miles apart. Before the game is started, the ball, made of applewood and coated with silver, is passed from hand to hand, to bring luck to all who touch it. The silver ball is believed to embody a relic of long-forgotten sun-worship.

THE TASKS AND TORMENTS OF
Jan Tregeagle

I t may be that the dark spirit that is said to wander Bodmin Moor's loneliest places, and whose despairing cries can still be heard above the autumn gales between Land's End and the Lizard, is no more than a distant memory of some ancient Celtic god. But from the mid-17th century at least, the Cornish have identified this spectre with the soul of Jan Tregeagle, doomed to eternal torment for the sins he committed in life.

Whether he really sold his soul to the Devil, or committed the crimes ascribed to him, is not known. Despite folk-tales that he murdered his wife and children and seized an orphan's estates, there is little doubt that Jan Tregeagle really existed. In the early 1600's, he was a stern and unpopular local magistrate who used his position to amass a considerable fortune. Part of this, it is said, was expended in bribes to the clergy, so that, despite his evil ways, he could be buried in the consecrated ground of St Breock's churchyard. Legend says this precaution availed him little; within a few short years, he was to be beckoned from the grave itself.

BOTTOMLESS LAKE *Dozmary Pool, the scene of one of Tregeagle's tasks, was thought to be bottomless. In fact, it often dries out in hot, dry summers*

THE BLOCKED HARBOUR *Loe Bar, a sandbank, lies across the mouth of Helston harbour. Legend says that it was formed when a sack of sand was dropped by Tregeagle after he was tripped by a spiteful demon during one of his labours*

Called from the grave

There are several versions of the way in which Tregeagle was called from the grave. One legend tells how a dispute arose between two families over the ownership of some land near Bodmin. The case had been confused by the conduct of Tregeagle who, while alive, had acted as lawyer to one of the claimants. Tregeagle, by fraud, had made it appear that he himself held title to the land in question. At the Assize Court, just as the judge was about to sum up, the defendant asked to call a further witness.

The atmosphere in the court chilled. Suddenly Tregeagle's phantom appeared in the witness box. The judge's determined self-possession overcame the courtroom's panic, and cross-examination began. Tregeagle revealed that the honest defendant had been a victim of his fraud, and the jury gave their unanimous verdict in the man's favour.

However, Tregeagle's spirit was still present in the courtroom. The judge commanded that the defendant should remove his witness, but the man replied that to bring Tregeagle from his grave had been such a dreadful task, that he preferred to leave the phantom in the care of the court. And with this he walked out of the building.

The local clergy were then called. They felt it was their duty to save Tregeagle's soul if they could, so they decided to set him a task that would engage him for all eternity. So long as he toiled at it, he would be safe from the Evil One.

Emptying a bottomless pool

Bound by spells, Tregeagle was given a perforated limpet shell and assigned to empty Dozmary Pool, a supposedly bottomless lake on Bodmin Moor. He was kept to his work by a pack of headless demon hounds, waiting to carry him off if once he ceased his labours. One night, terrified by a

THE DEMON HUNT *Accompanied by a pack of headless hounds, the Devil hunts Tregeagle's ghost eternally over Bodmin Moor*

raging storm, Tregeagle defied even the demons and fled across Bodmin Moor, the evil pack in hot pursuit. At last he reached the chapel on Roche Rock; thrusting his head through the east window he attempted to gain the sanctuary of the church. But while his head was within the chapel, his body remained outside, exposed to the storm and the fury of the hounds of Hell.

Weaving ropes from sand

His screams were heard for miles and, after a few days, the priest of the Rock could not stand the situation no longer. Calling upon the aid of two saints, he led Tregeagle to Padstow beach where he was set to weave ropes from sand. Whenever the tide swept in, his efforts were ruined, and his howls of disappointment allowed little rest to the local people.

Padstow's patron saint, St Petroc, decided to move Tregeagle on; the saint forged a chain with his own hands and with this he bound the phantom and drove it to Berepper, near Helston. There Tregeagle was commanded to carry sacks of sand across the estuary of the Loe and empty them at Porthleven, continuing until Berepper beach was a swept expanse of rock. But his labour was in vain; the tide swept the sand back as fast as Tregeagle could move it. Eventually, a spiteful demon tripped him while he was crossing the estuary. He dropped the sack from his arms and spilt the sand; the ridge it formed has sealed off the harbour and is known today as Loe Bar.

The angry Helston people shackled him once more, and sent him to Land's End. Here he was set the task of sweeping the sands from Porthcurno Cove into Mill Bay. Tregeagle still labours, it is said, battling with the Atlantic currents to complete his impossible task. His howls of rage can be heard when gales throw the sand back on the beach.

Tregeagle's ghost and the debtor

Another version of the story, describing his summoning from the grave, tells of a man who lent another a large sum of money, the transaction being witnessed by Tregeagle, just before he died. When the moneylender demanded settlement, the debtor denied all knowledge of the deal. In Bodmin court, certain of his safety, the defendant exclaimed: 'If Tregeagle ever saw it, I wish to God he would come and declare it!' In a clap of thunder, Tregeagle's ghost appeared and promised the terrified man: 'It will not be such an easy task to get rid of me as it has been to call me.'

The debtor settled his account and sought to rid himself of Tregeagle with the aid of wise men and parsons. They succeeded in binding him for a while to the task of emptying Dozmary Pool with a leaking limpet shell. In this version, Tregeagle completed the job and returned to torment the debtor, who then procured the assistance of a powerful exorcist. Restrained by the exorcist, Tregeagle allowed himself to be led to Gwenvor Cove. There he was set to weaving a rope of sand which, when finished, he was to carry to Carn Olva.

Tregeagle was unable to accomplish his work until one frosty night, he poured water from a nearby brook on to the rope; ice cemented it together and the ghost carried it in triumph to Carn Olva. At once, he flew back to his wretched prey, intent on tearing him to pieces. But the man was holding a child, whose aura of innocence could not be penetrated by the evil Tregeagle.

Again the priests were called, and once more they bound Tregeagle to weaving ropes of sand at Gwenvor. But this time he was forbidden to approach water. Beaten at last, Tregeagle remains in continuous struggle. When a northerly wind destroys his work, his roars can still be heard across Whitesand Bay.

SPECTRAL WITNESS *Tregeagle's ghost is called into court to give evidence*

BALING THE POOL *Tregeagle tries to empty Dozmary Pool with a leaky shell*

THE ENDLESS TASK *Sack by sack, Tregeagle had to clear Berepper beach*

139

St Erth

The Lamb and Flag, an Elizabethan inn in this village near Hayle, is named after the symbol that was once stamped on ingots of Cornish tin as proof of their purity. The inn has a long tradition of hospitality and during the 19th century, so stories tell, the host served his guests with steaks cooked on hot tin ingots from the neighbouring smelter.

St Germans

In the church there stands an old chair whose carving depicts the story of Dando, a dissolute 14th-century priest from the priory near by. One Sunday, Dando forsook his devotions and went hunting with his wild friends. After a successful chase, he called for a drink. A stranger riding a fiery black horse came forward and offered him a richly carved drinking horn. Having quenched his thirst, Dando saw the stranger stealing his game. Despite the priest's curses, the stranger refused to return the game. In a drunken frenzy, Dando rushed at him and cried: 'I'll go to Hell after them, but I'll get them from thee.' 'So thou shalt,' replied the stranger and, tossing Dando across his horse, he rode off, with the hounds following. While Dando's horrified friends watched, horse, riders and hounds all leapt into the River Lynher, where they disappeared with a hiss of flame and steam.

St Ives

The town still retains the sport of Hurling the Silver Ball, which is usually held on the Monday of Candlemas week, in February. The mayor starts the game, throwing the ball from the parish-church wall at 10.30 a.m. It is then passed from hand to hand along the streets and the beach until noon, when the holder receives a small cash prize.

Another ceremony, performed every fifth year on July 25 (the next in 1976), fulfils the terms of John Knill's will. Knill, mayor of the town in 1767, requested that ten small girls in white should dance through the streets to his hilltop mausoleum; here, the mayor and two widows were to join them and dance round the monument, after which the spectators were to sing the Hundredth Psalm.

St Keverne

The harvest custom of Crying the Neck, associated with the ancient belief that the corn-spirit is embodied in the last-cut wheatsheaf, has been revived in this village. On the last day of harvest, as the reaper cuts the final swaithe, the workers divide into three groups. The first group calls three times: 'We have it!' The second replies: 'What have 'ee?' – again three times – and the third group answers: 'A neck!' – also three times. The 'neck' or wheatsheaf is then carried to the farmhouse, where it is plaited and suspended above the fireplace until the spring, when it is ploughed into the ground.

St Keyne

Some time during the 5th century, St Keyne – one of 15 daughters of a Welsh king – settled here. Water from her well is said to bestow supremacy in marriage upon the first partner to drink from it. This is recalled in Southey's ballad:

> I hastened as soon as the wedding was o'er
> And left my good wife in the porch,
> But i' faith she had been wiser than I
> For she took a bottle to church.

MASTERY IN MARRIAGE

The waters of St Keyne's holy well are said to possess the key to mastery in marriage. Whichever partner drinks first from the well after marriage will be the future ruler of the marital home. It was customary for a newly married couple, on leaving the village church, to race to the well to see who could be first to drink from its miraculous waters, which are also said to possess healing properties

RELICS AND SUPERSTITIONS OF THE PAST *Throughout Cornwall there are remains – such as this engine house at the head of Botallack Mine – of the days when mining was an important local industry. Many relics exist, from deep, sinister moorland shafts to gaunt, deserted engine houses. A host of superstitions were built up by the miners who once worked these sites. Snails found on the way to the mine, for example, were always rewarded with wax from the miners' lanterns to preserve good luck. But to inscribe the form of a cross underground was unlucky – as was working on Midsummer Eve, New Year's Day and New Year's Eve*

St Mary's

The cursing power of Psalm 109, 'Let his children be fatherless and his wife a widow', was once a widely held superstition. It was the recital of this 'cursing psalm' by a sailor unjustly condemned to death that is said to have brought about the worst shipwreck ever recorded in the Isles of Scilly.

In 1707, a fleet commanded by Admiral Sir Cloudesley Shovel ran into a storm near the Scillies. A sailor on board the flagship who knew the waters well, rushed to warn Sir Cloudesley that his ships were heading for the dreaded Gilstone Reef. The hot-tempered admiral immediately ordered him to be hanged for impudence. With the rope around his neck, the sailor recited Psalm 109 and laid a terrible curse on Sir Cloudesley.

The fleet struck the reef, and 2000 men died in the raging sea. Sir Cloudesley's body was washed ashore at Porth Hellick Cove on the island of St Mary's. According to legend, he was still alive when he was found by an old woman, one of the island's wreckers. Greedy for his rings, which included a magnificent sapphire, she hacked off his fingers and buried him alive on the beach. A rough stone monument marks the spot where the body was found after the woman had confessed to the crime on her death bed.

BOUND FOR DISASTER

Many legends surround the loss of HMS Association *and four other ships that struck Gilstone Reef, off the Isles of Scilly, in 1707. Some 2000 men were lost when the fleet foundered, including the commander, Admiral Sir Cloudesley Shovel (left)*

TINNERS AND KNOCKERS

Phoenician merchants from North Africa came to Cornwall for tin as long ago as the 5th century BC.

Traditionally, however, the discovery of the metal is attributed to St Piran, the miners' patron saint. After journeying from Ireland to Cornwall c. AD 500, he built a chapel on the north coast. While searching for building materials, it is said that the saint began collecting some of the beautiful rocks that he found near his new home. One evening, he used a piece of hard black rock from his collection to build a fireplace. As he was cooking, he was amazed to see a stream of pure white liquid flowing from the flames; the liquid solidified into metal and so Cornish tin was discovered.

Beliefs of the miners

It is not surprising that the legends and beliefs of Cornish miners have much in common with those of the fishermen. Cornish families often had members in both professions, and consequently many of their traditions became indistinguishable.

Crows were a symbol of death, as were red-headed women, and dogs howled to foretell a pit disaster – or a shipwreck. To miners and fishermen, magpies were prophetic:

> One for sorrow, two for mirth,
> Three for a wedding, four for a birth.

The miners also adopted the seamens' bucca or bucca-boo. Originally, he was a Celtic sea-god, whose status declined into that of a demon. As such, he worked mischief both in the mines and in the fishing fleet.

Some of the miners' beliefs, however, belonged to their trade alone. The knockers, for example, were specifically associated with the mines,

and it was said that their tappings would guide miners towards rich lodes of ore. They were believed to be the spirits of the Jews who crucified Christ, and who now had to work out their penance below the earth.

The knockers were not considered dangerous unless a tinner upset them. Whistling would offend them and bring ill luck. If their favours were not rewarded with food or tallow, the offender might find himself in bad trouble. On one occasion, Tom Trevorrow, a confirmed sceptic, refused to share his meal with the knockers; the following morning, his tools were crushed beneath a fall of rock and he himself was nearly killed. Misfortune continued to dog him until he left the mines.

Other spirits also haunted the mines. At Wheal Vor, near Helston, the spectre of a white hare would appear before an accident. In many mines a spectral hand was seen, clasping the ladder and following a miner's descent. This also was a warning of imminent misfortune.

A ghostly guardian

The ghost of Dorcas is still remembered around St Agnes. This unfortunate woman committed suicide in Polbreen Mine and her wraith remained in the mine's dark galleries. She took perverse pleasure in calling men from their work and wasting their time. Once, though, she saved a man's life. On hearing his name, he went to investigate. At that moment, a fall of rock crashed on to the spot where he had been standing.

In the dark and dangerous world of the mines, it is not surprising that even skilled men would sometimes put their trust in portents to save them from disaster.

DARK WORLD OF THE MINER *Knockers and other strange spirits were said to haunt the galleries of the tin mines, like this one at the 180-fathom level at East Pool*

SYMBOL OF PURITY *The Miner's Arms inn sign, St Just-in-Penwith, depicts the Lamb and Flag, a symbol of Christian purity. The symbol was also used as a stamp to mark pure tin ingots*

St Michael's Mount

The Cornish name for St Michael's Mount is 'Carrick luz en cuz', which means 'the ancient rock in the wood'. At low tide, there can still be seen the fossilised remains of a forest which once covered the coast around St Michael's Mount.

Within the present castle is a rough-cut stone seat, known as Michael's Chair. St Keyne, on a pilgrimage to the Mount, is believed to have endowed the seat with the same power that she gave to her holy well at St Keyne. If either the bride or groom is the first to sit in Michael's Chair, that partner will henceforth dominate the marriage.

St Nectan's Glen

Here, a secluded waterfall cascades 40 ft into a circular rock basin known locally as the Kieve. St Nectan, on his death bed, threw his silver chapel bell into this torrent, and it vanished into the rock bed. He vowed that it would reappear only when true religion had been restored to what, in the 5th century, was a dissident Church.

His body, together with the sacramental plate, was placed in a chest, and this too was hidden beneath the rocks in the Kieve. Centuries later, miners tried to blast their way through the Kieve to the treasure. After many fruitless attempts upon the unyielding rock they were astonished to hear the ringing of a silver bell. It was accompanied by a solemn voice which proclaimed: 'The child is not yet born who shall recover this treasure.' Work stopped immediately, and the fulfilment of St Nectan's prophecy is awaited still.

St Neot

The 15 in. tall saint became famous for his miracles involving animals.

One day an angel appeared and gave Neot three fish for his well, saying that so long as he ate only one a day, their number would never decrease. When Neot was sick, however, his servant took two fish and cooked them. Horrified, the saint prayed over the dead fish, and ordered them to be returned to the well. As they touched the water, they completely revived.

Another story tells of a hunted doe that, totally exhausted, ran to Neot's side. The saint's stern look turned the hounds back to the forest, while the huntsman dropped his bow and became the saint's faithful disciple.

ST NEOT'S FISH

The dwarf saint miraculously restored the lives of two cooked fish. The legend is recorded in a stained-glass window in St Neot's Church

St Teath

Anne Jeffries was born here in 1626, and when she was 19 years old, she entered the service of a Mr Moses Pitt. One day, while sitting in her employer's garden, she encountered a group of tiny men, whom she befriended. One of them touched her eyes and suddenly she found herself flying through space until she came to a strange and beautiful country. Returning at last to the garden, she found herself surrounded by the anxious household, who thought she had fallen into a fit.

This was the first of many meetings with the 'airy people', as she called them, who also taught her the arts of healing and herbal lore. Understandably, she was accused of witchcraft, and committed to Bodmin gaol by the notorious Jan Tregeagle, then the local magistrate. She said the little people fed her throughout her imprisonment, but she was still released for lack of evidence. Records of the trial and letters from Moses Pitt to the Bishop of Gloucester, describing her experiences, are in the Bodleian Library at Oxford.

SMUGGLERS AND WRECKERS

During the 17th and 18th centuries, smuggling was part of the Cornish way of life, and was a far more profitable occupation than either mining or fishing. At one stage, it was estimated that more illicit spirits were coming through Cornwall and Devon than were entering the country legally through London's docks.

Known as 'free traders', the gangs battled with excisemen on cliff-tops, and customs cutters were sunk at every opportunity. John Carter from Breage was perhaps the most famous Cornish smuggler. Nicknamed 'The King of Prussia', he ringed his base near Land's End with cannon; the site of his secret harbour is known to this day as Prussia Cove. Characteristic of Carter's devotion to his trade was his successful robbery of Penzance Customs House. Some of the captive goods held there were promised to his clients – and John Carter never broke his word.

Wrecking was another important part of the Cornish economy. Goods washed ashore from wrecks were regarded as common property, and a foundering ship would bring squire, parson and labourers rushing to the beaches. Stories of false lights tied to the tails of ponies which were then driven out along the cliffs to lure ships to their doom were largely inspired by novels such as Daphne du Maurier's *Jamaica Inn*, but in the Scillies at least there were instances of survivors being stripped of their possessions and murdered.

WRECKERS AT WORK *Around Mount's Bay, news of a wreck would flash along the coast, and the inhabitants would descend on the fatal spot. Using pick-axes and hatchets, they would completely dismember a ship*

Stratton

In this small village near Bude was born a real Cornish giant. During the Civil War, the 7 ft 6 in. Anthony Payne was enlisted as bodyguard to the Royalist Sir Bevil Grenville. He fought beside Sir Bevil, who commanded the king's army, at Stamford Hill, and later at the battle of Lansdown Hill, near Bath. Here, Sir Bevil was killed, but at once Payne set up the general's 16-year-old son beside the standard, crying out 'A Grenville still leads you!' to the Cornishmen around him. The men rallied and the fight was a Royalist victory; afterwards Payne sorrowfully carried his master's dead body home to Stratton.

Payne lived and died in the Grenville's manor house at Stratton – now the Tree Inn – where an inscription on the wall tells of the great victory at nearby Stamford Hill. It is said that when the giant died, the house had to be re-structured to allow his huge coffin to be carried in and out. His body lies in the local churchyard where an inscribed tombstone marks his final resting place.

LOYAL CORNISH GIANT

Anthony Payne, 7 ft 6 in., bodyguard of the Grenvilles, in the uniform of a Captain of Guns. This portrait, by Kneller, was commissioned by Charles II

CRUEL COPPINGER

Fact and fiction are closely interwoven in the story of David Coppinger, a Dane who settled near Morwenstow in the 18th century.

Most accounts tell how 'Cruel' Coppinger, as he became known, landed on the Cornish coast during a terrible storm. A vessel of foreign rig was driven into the wild waters of Harty Race. Unable to make the haven of Harty Pool, the captain, Coppinger, dived into the mountainous seas. Fighting his way through the waves, he finally reached the shore. Without a word, he leapt on to a horse ridden by a young woman, Dinah Hamlyn, who had come to the beach to see the stormbound ship. Turning the double-laden horse, he urged it away at full speed, and forced it homeward. Coppinger installed himself at Dinah's home and, on her father's death a year later, married the girl.

His criminal career now began. The house became the headquarters of a gang of smugglers – with Coppinger as their ruthless captain.

A reign of terror

The district was utterly cowed by Coppinger and his gang. No authority dared to take action, since he was merciless in his treatment of anyone who offended him.

So Coppinger pursued his vicious way of life with no check or restraint. He assumed control over some of the local roads and issued orders that no one should use them by night. These roads, still known as 'Coppinger's Tracks', converged on the 300-ft headland of Steeple Brink. Below this cliff, in a practically inaccessible cove, the gang stored their contraband and caroused at night.

Coppinger's domestic life was no less evil and he treated his wife with appalling cruelty. When she bore him an idiot son, people said it had been born without a soul.

Eventually, the revenue men concentrated their forces in a final effort to destroy the gang. Many of the gang were killed, and the treasures of the cave were captured. Coppinger realised his days were numbered. Again a strange vessel appeared off Harty Race. It lowered a boat whose crew rowed through the boiling surf to where Coppinger stood cursing, and waving his cutlass. As the boat grounded, he leapt aboard and took command. The boat fought its way back through the raging seas and Coppinger and his crew flung themselves aboard the parent ship. In an instant the vessel vanished into the flying spray and Cruel Coppinger was never seen again.

Talland

Parson Dodge, Vicar of Talland in the early 18th century, enjoyed considerable local fame as an exorcist. His services were employed by the Vicar of nearby Lanreath, who was much upset by the manifestation of a spectral coach with demon driver and headless horses. At the sight of Dodge, however, the demon wailed in terror and the entire equipage vanished for ever. Local people were afraid to approach Talland church at night for fear they should meet the parson driving evil spirits before him down Bridle Lane to the sea. It has been suggested that Dodge was actually in league with the Polperro smugglers and that he encouraged the tales about himself to keep people away while contraband was moved.

Tintagel

According to legend, King Arthur was born at Tintagel Castle. It was here that King Uther Pendragon deceived the beautiful Igerna, wife of Gorlois, Earl of Cornwall. The king, with magical assistance from his wizard Merlin, disguised himself as Igerna's husband. Entering the fortress in this guise, he seduced Igerna, who later gave birth to the boy who became King Arthur.

Though the region is steeped in Arthurian lore the castle was in fact built by Reginald of Cornwall, the illegitimate son of Henry I, in 1141 – long after the historical Arthur lived. At one time it belonged to the Black Prince, but by 1540 it was a ruin. The cavern below the castle is known as Merlin's Cave, and the wizard's ghost is said to wander in its echoing recesses. Local people also believe that Arthur himself is reincarnated in the rare Cornish chough, a bird that is sometimes seen perched on the wave-lashed ledges of the cliffs.

Tresco

The Scilly isle of Tresco contains Piper's Hole, a cave long believed to be a haunt of mermaids. Legend suggests that the cave connects Tresco with the adjacent island of St Mary's; apparent proof of this was provided when a Tresco dog emerged from a cave on St Mary's.

One story says that during the Civil War, when the Royalists held the Isles, a Roundhead avoided capture by hiding in Piper's Hole. He was discovered by a Cavalier's daughter who fell in love with him and arranged his escape to the mainland. After the war he returned to marry her.

Trewoofe

Now a farm, Trewoofe (pronounced 'trove') was once the manor house of the powerful Lovelis family. One evening, about 300 years ago, Squire Lovelis gave chase to a white hare which disappeared into a cave at Boleigh. The squire and his pack followed, only to find that the hare had turned into a witch, and the cave contained an evil coven led by a demon. Lovelis recognised the demon as a stranger who had come to the village years before and seduced his wife. Lovelis swore at him angrily and at once the grisly group turned on the squire. When he finally emerged his friends found him singing wildly and totally demented. Squire Lovelis and his dogs haunt the district to this day.

Truro

An ancient Christmas season custom still survives. The Truro Wassailers circulate the city at New Year, drinking beer or cider from a gaily decorated wassail bowl, and collecting money for charity. The Old English word *wassail* means 'be of good cheer' though the original ceremony was designed to drive off evil spirits.

Less happy is the story of Comprigney, a field outside the town. Reports of spectres and rattling chains are a grim reminder of the site's history – in Cornish, 'Gwel Cloghprenyer' means 'the field of the gibbet'.

MYSTERIOUS TINTAGEL

This 19th-century engraving after a drawing by J. M. W. Turner perfectly captures the romantic Arthurian atmosphere beloved of the Victorians. In fact, the castle is *basically a Norman structure built on a very much earlier monastic settlement and it is improbable that Arthur ever had a stronghold here*

THE DAISY DOG'S VIGIL

In ancient China, no one was allowed to own pekingese dogs except the Imperial family. Therefore, when in the 16th century the emperor wished to honour England's Elizabeth I, there was no greater gift he could bestow than a pair of the dogs he valued so highly. The bitch was placed in a carved ivory box, while the dog ran free. A royal princess was chosen to escort the animals across the world.

Slant-eyed demon

During the long and arduous journey, the bitch gave birth to five pups, and the little dog guarded his family in the ivory box, and guarded the princess too. Finally, they reached France, and the princess found a Cornish ship to take them to England. But on the voyage across the Channel, the crew wove wild tales about their passenger; they said she was a slant-eyed demon, and the box she carried contained treasure.

When the vessel reached the Cornish coast, a storm arose, driving it towards the murderous cliffs. The frightened crew, blaming the impending disaster on the princess, burst into her cabin. One sailor tried to grab the box, but drew back with his hand bleeding from the little dog's bite. In terror, the crew threw the princess overboard. The wind changed, and the ship veered to safety.

The girl's body and the box were washed into a lonely cove near Land's End. No one would approach the supposed devil on the beach except one man, a village simpleton, and he it was who discovered that the princess was dead. Only the dog remained alive, and it was dying. It watched the simpleton dig a grave in which he placed all the bodies together. Then he gathered wild daisies and planted them in the shape of a cross. Finally, he placed the little dog among the daisies, where it licked his hand and died.

The ship reached harbour, and the tale of the treasure spread along the coast. But when the bitten man died, no one would go near the mound on the beach with the cross of daisies. It was said that a ghostly dog defended the lonely grave, and its bite was death. Perhaps it keeps its vigil still, for it is said that as late as 1850, a boy found a piece of carved ivory near the cliffs. As he picked it up, he felt himself bitten. Though his injuries were slight, the boy died; he had been bitten by the Daisy Dog, and was therefore doomed.

Veryan

The village contains five peculiar cottages. Each one is entirely circular, with a pointed roof surmounted by a cross. They were built in the early 19th century by a religious fanatic who believed that their shape would prevent the Devil from hiding in any corners.

A mile to the south of Veryan, overlooking Gerrans Bay, stands Carne Beacon, an ancient burial mound. Legend relates that the body of Gerennius, a 5th-century king of Cornwall, was rowed across the bay in a golden boat with silver oars, and buried in full regalia under the mound. Recent excavations, however, have not proved the theory.

Zennor

There was once a chorister of the local church called Matthew Trewella, who was the squire's son. He sang so beautifully that his voice attracted a mermaid from the sea. Using all her charms, she lured him back to her deep domain, from which he never returned. His voice, legend says, can still be heard from beneath the waves.

Near by is a rock known as the Witches' Rock, which is associated with local witches' Midsummer rituals. To touch the rock nine times at midnight is still regarded as insurance against bad luck.

LINK WITH LEGEND

Carved on a 15th-century bench-end in Zennor church is the mermaid with long flowing hair, and mirror and comb, who fell in love with a local chorister

THE FOLKLORE YEAR

January 17
Carhampton, Somerset
Wassailing the Apple Trees

Shrove Tuesday
Corfe Castle, Dorset
Street football

May 1–3
Minehead, Somerset
Hobby Horse Ceremony

Spring Bank Holiday Monday
Kingsteignton, Devon
Ram Roasting Ceremony

Wednesday before September 20
Barnstaple, Devon
Traditional Fair

September (second Tuesday)
Widecombe, Devon
Pony and sheep fair

October (last Thursday)
Hinton St George, Somerset
Punky Night celebrations

November 5
Ottery St Mary, Devon
Tar-barrel rolling

November 5
Shebbear, Devon
Turning the Devil's Stone

Christmas-tide
Glastonbury, Somerset
Cutting the Holy Thorn

Christmas Eve
Dunster, Somerset
Burning the Ash Faggot

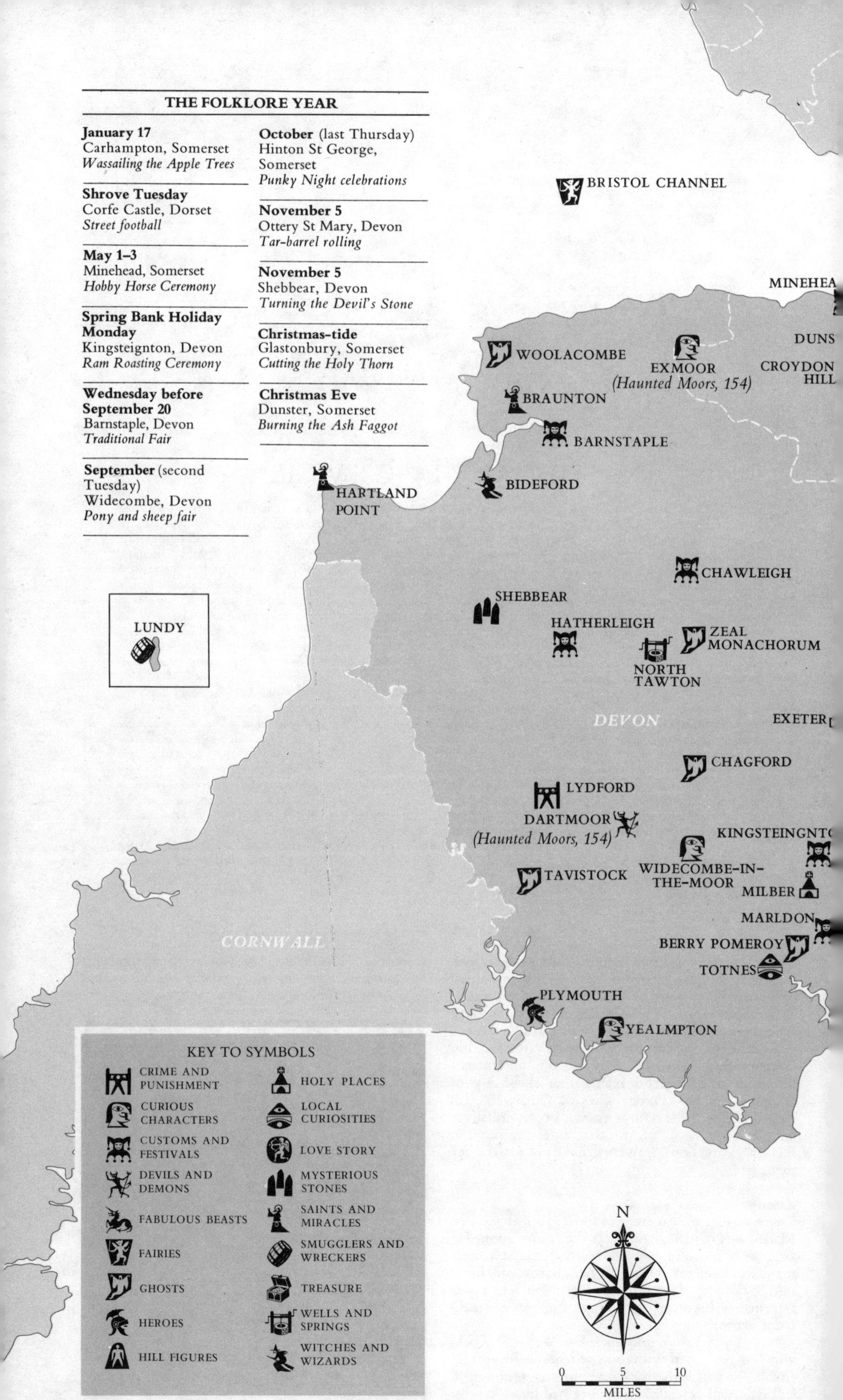

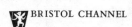 BRISTOL CHANNEL

MINEHEA

DUNS

WOOLACOMBE

EXMOOR
(Haunted Moors, 154)

CROYDON HILL

BRAUNTON

BARNSTAPLE

BIDEFORD

HARTLAND POINT

LUNDY

CHAWLEIGH

SHEBBEAR

HATHERLEIGH

ZEAL MONACHORUM

NORTH TAWTON

 DEVON

EXETER

CHAGFORD

LYDFORD

DARTMOOR
(Haunted Moors, 154)

KINGSTEINGNTO

TAVISTOCK

WIDECOMBE-IN-THE-MOOR

MILBER

MARLDON

BERRY POMEROY

TOTNES

CORNWALL

PLYMOUTH

YEALMPTON

KEY TO SYMBOLS

CRIME AND PUNISHMENT

CURIOUS CHARACTERS

CUSTOMS AND FESTIVALS

DEVILS AND DEMONS

FABULOUS BEASTS

FAIRIES

GHOSTS

HEROES

HILL FIGURES

HOLY PLACES

LOCAL CURIOSITIES

LOVE STORY

MYSTERIOUS STONES

SAINTS AND MIRACLES

SMUGGLERS AND WRECKERS

TREASURE

WELLS AND SPRINGS

WITCHES AND WIZARDS

N

0   5   10
MILES

THE SUMMER LAND

Avon, Devon, Dorset and Somerset

More than 1300 years ago, West Saxon farmers used to fatten their cattle in a place where pastures were so rich that they called it the Summer Land. Eventually, it became known as Somerset; though in the memories of thousands of holidaymakers, the old name might apply equally happily to Devon and Dorset as well.

This gentle country has been attracting visitors for a very long time. One of the most distinguished, according to the geographer Ptolemy, writing about AD 100, was the god Hercules who sailed to Devon in a golden bowl and settled for a while on Hartland Point. Legend says that Jesus himself came to Glastonbury, brought there by his uncle, Joseph of Arimathea, who was trading for tin. The 'clouded hills' of Blake's poem 'Jerusalem', the 'mountains green' on which he suggests that Christ may have walked, were the Mendips.

Many writers have drawn inspiration from West Country legends. Conan Doyle's *Hound of the Baskervilles* owes its ancestry to the phantom black dogs of Dartmoor, and the Doones were Exmoor bogeymen long before R. D. Blackmore wrote of Lorna. One awful story tells how a girl, hidden in an oven, hears the Doones dining off a baby. After they had finished, they said to the remains:

'If anyone ask who 'twas that eat thee,
Tell them – the Doones of Badgeworthy.'

Heroes, like villains, are long remembered in the West Country, though often in peculiar ways. Sir Francis Drake once gave Plymouth a new water supply; yet this act is recalled in a legend of the admiral saying some magic words over a Dartmoor spring and making the stream follow him to Plymouth. Each Midsummer Eve, it is said, King Arthur and his knights ride out from Cadbury Castle, the legendary site of Camelot. Curiously, excavations have shown that at the place where Arthur appears, there was once a gateway.

147

Abbotsbury *Dorset*

An ancient custom, thought to be a survival of pagan sea-god worship, was observed until early this century in this old fishing village. On May 13, the fishermen's families constructed large garlands of flowers on wooden frames – one for each fishing boat. The garlands were carried round the houses and then, after a blessing on the beach by the vicar, each boat carried its garland out to sea and cast it overboard. The garlands procession still takes place but the flowers are now placed on the war memorial as a tribute to the dead.

Athelhampton *Dorset*

The hauntings attributed to Athelhampton House, parts of which are over 500 years old, include a headless man – often reported seen in the last century – and a Grey Lady who has been active in recent years. Another ghost – the Black Monk – was seen a few years ago by the present owner. The Martyn family, who lived in the house between 1350 and 1595, were devout Catholics, and the ghost may be that of an itinerant priest.

Legend also tells of a pet ape which was accidentally walled up in a priest's hole; its phantom, too, is alleged to roam about the house.

Athelney *Somerset*

The Isle of Athelney was at one time surrounded by marshes, and it was there that King Alfred sought refuge from the Danes in AD 878. The famous 'burning the cakes' legend belongs to Athelney. The story goes that Alfred was sitting by a peasant's hearth, totally absorbed in his own thoughts, when the housewife saw her loaves burning by the fire. Not recognising the king, she boxed his ears for his inattention.

In the 19th century a stone was placed on the site in memory of the incident. The inscription recalls the king's gratitude for the peasant's hospitality, and records the fact that he erected a monastery and endowed it with all the lands on the Isle of Athelney. Now only a few ruined stone walls and a pond mark the site of this foundation, the once-wealthy Edington Monastery, north-east of Frome.

Axminster *Devon*

Now a ruin, Newnham Abbey was founded by Reginald de Mohun in 1247. As he lay dying in 1257, he dreamt of a boy 'more radiant than the sun' who walked from the abbey font to its altar. This dream was believed to represent de Mohun's saintliness and his acceptance into the next world.

Confirmation of this was vouchsafed 75 years later when the paving over his grave was removed for repair. Beneath the stones lay his body, perfectly preserved and exuding a fragrant odour. Several medieval saints were reputedly distinguished by this 'odour of sanctity'.

ARTHURIAN BATTLEGROUND

Badbury Rings, an Iron Age hill-fort in Dorset, is one of several places which tradition has identified as Mount Badon, the battleground where Arthur finally defeated the Saxons in AD 518. There, according to the ancient chroniclers, 'Arthur carried the cross of Our Lord Jesus Christ, for three days and nights on his shoulders, and the Britons were victorious'. The battle was said to have given Britain 21 years of peace which lasted until Arthur took up arms against his treacherous nephew, Modred. Though Badbury Rings has the oldest claim, the battle has also been sited at Badbury Hill in Oxfordshire and at Badbury near Swindon in Wiltshire

Banwell Hill *Avon*

Within the prehistoric earthwork of Banwell Camp there is a great cross constructed out of turf. The cross is raised about 2 ft above the enclosed ground, and the four arms, each 4 ft broad, point to the four quarters of the compass.

No one knows who built it, or when or why, but local legend says that the Devil kept raising gales to blow down each upright cross that the villagers erected so they finally foiled the Evil One by laying the cross on the ground.

Barnstaple *Devon*

The fair, whose charter dates from the early Middle Ages, is held each year on the Wednesday before September 20. Its opening is heralded by a ceremony at the Guildhall, where spiced ale brewed from a closely guarded Elizabethan recipe is ladled into silver cups from which all present must drink success to the fair. A large white glove is hung from the Guildhall – an ancient symbol once used to show that outsiders could enter and trade freely within the town. A similar custom applies to the fair held at Honiton on the last Tuesday in July.

Batcombe *Dorset*

This village, which lies 3 miles north-west of Cerne Abbas, is backed by steep hills from which it is possible to look down on to the flat roof of the church tower. Possibly it was this view which gave rise to the story of Conjuror Mynterne, a 16th-century squire of the manor who was reputed to have dabbled in witchcraft.

One day, as Mynterne rode out along the top of Batcombe Hill, he suddenly remembered that he had left his book of spells open on his desk. Fearing that someone might read it and perhaps come to harm by trying out the spells, he hurried back home. Galloping by the shortest route, he jumped his horse from the top of Batcombe Hill clean across the village. As he sailed over the rooftops, his horse's hoof caught one of the four pinnacles surrounding the church tower and knocked it off. Despite this, the horse made a safe landing on a field called Pitching Plot; but such was the power of the magic that grass would never grow there again.

The broken pinnacle was replaced by a new one about a hundred years later. However, it leans out of true, and is easily distinguished because it is not so stained by the weather as the other three.

Conjuror Mynterne lived for several years after the incident. When he died, he left instructions that he was to be buried 'neither within the church nor without it'. So the magician lies buried under the church wall, with half his tomb inside the building and half outside.

On the road across Batcombe Hill there is a stone pillar known as the Cross-and-Hand (or the Cross-in-Hand), which is thought to date from the 7th century. So far, antiquarians have failed to give an adequate account of its presence; but this lack is fully compensated by local legend.

One story tells of a priest who lost a holy relic while travelling along the road. When he discovered his loss, he hurried back and turned a corner to find hundreds of animals – sheep, oxen, rabbits and badgers – all kneeling in adoration. Suddenly, a shaft of fire from the sky illuminated the place where the lost relic lay, and the pillar was built to commemorate the miracle.

Another story, quoted by Thomas Hardy in *Tess of the D'Urbervilles*, is less pleasant. In this, the pillar marks the grave of a criminal who was tortured and hanged on the site. It is said that the man had sold his soul to the Devil, and sometimes, at night, his ghost is seen near the pillar.

Bath *Avon*

The famous healing waters of the ancient Roman city are said to have been discovered by Bladud, son of a legendary king of Britain called Lud Hudibras. Prince Bladud contracted leprosy and was banished from court by his father. Before he left, his mother gave him a ring to remind him that he could return home should he ever be cured. Shunned by everyone, Bladud became a swineherd but the swine entrusted to his care also caught leprosy. To prevent their owner finding out, he drove the animals over the Avon, crossing it at a place which is still called Swineford.

One lonely day, Bladud left the swine unattended. Maddened by the disease, the beasts panicked and rushed up the valley, plunging at last into a black, evil-smelling bog. With great difficulty, Bladud managed to haul them out, and discovered that they were no longer leprous. Wherever the muddy water had touched his own skin, he too was clean. He totally immersed himself and emerged completely cured. Joyfully, the prince set out for home where, though he was ragged and unkempt, his mother's ring quickly identified him. Wells were sunk into the bog, and the curative properties of the waters of Bath are famous to this day.

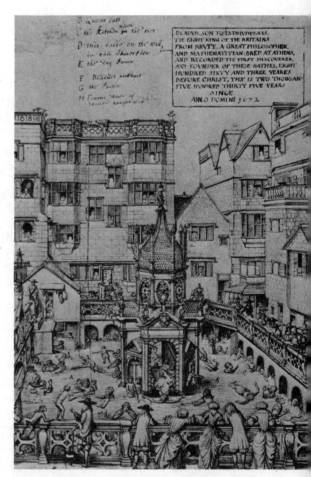

BATH'S HEALING WATERS

The legendary Prince Bladud was said to have discovered the healing properties of Bath's mineral springs when he cured his leprosy by bathing in the swamps of the district. The above drawing of the baths, made in 1675, carries an inscription which records the incident: 'Bladud, son of Lud Hudibras, the eight (sic) king of the Britons . . . the first discoverer and founder of these baths, eight hundred sixty and three years before Christ'

Berry Pomeroy *Devon*

The rambling and ruined castle was once the home of the powerful Pomeroy family, who settled there shortly after the Norman Conquest.

Legend says that for the Pomeroys' part in the religious rebellion in 1549, Edward VI ordered that the castle's fortifications should be reduced. The family refused to obey and when royal troops arrived to enforce the order, two Pomeroy brothers put on their armour, blindfolded their horses, and rode over the ramparts to their deaths.

Another story is told of two medieval Pomeroy sisters, Eleanor and Margaret. Both loved the same man and Eleanor, insanely jealous of her beautiful sister, imprisoned Margaret and starved her to death. Margaret's ghost is said to walk the ramparts and anyone who sees her will die shortly after. Another ghost who is supposed to presage death is that of a 13th-century woman – a Pomeroy – who had an incestuous relationship with her father. It is said that because she smothered her child, her troubled spirit can find no rest.

CASTLE WITH A VIOLENT PAST

At least two of Berry Pomeroy's ghosts bring death within the year to anyone who sees them. Its ruined state is said to be the result of God's wrath at its evil reputation, but in fact it was destroyed in a Civil War siege

THE SCREAMING SKULL

The Bettiscombe skull must never be removed, otherwise a dreadful fate will fall upon house and occupants

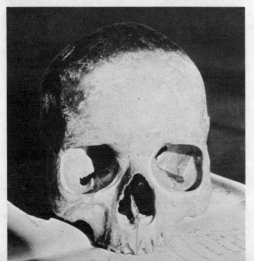

Bettiscombe *Dorset*

The contents of Bettiscombe Manor, a private house, include an ancient human skull. It is said that to remove it from the house will bring disaster to both building and occupants. One tenant in the early 19th century tried to rid himself of the skull by throwing it into a nearby pond. For days the house was shaken by screams and tremors, until the tenant was forced to retrieve the grisly relic.

Tradition says that an 18th-century Negro slave belonging to the owner was buried, against his dying wish, in the local churchyard and not in his native land. Hideous shrieks from his grave were silenced only after the body was removed to the manor. Now only the skull remains.

Recent analysis, however, has shown that the skull is about 2000 years old, and is that of a woman in her twenties. It is believed to have come from Pilsdon Pen, a Celtic sanctuary on manor land.

Bideford *Devon*

The town was the home of Temperence Lloyd, a notorious witch who, with two companions, was convicted of sorcery at Exeter Assizes in 1682. Apparently Temperence had a long-standing reputation for malevolence, since she had been tried and acquitted on similar charges twice before.

Acquittal was unlikely at her final trial, however, since she boasted that she had brought about the deaths of many Bideford people. This statement secured her conviction, even though the prosecution's evidence was no more than a feeble rigmarole of devil-pacts and familiars.

Several people at the trial expressed surprise at the obvious 'death-wish' of the trio, and their seeking after notoriety. Even so, the two lesser witches, Mary Trembles and Susanna Edwards, wept at their conviction. But Temperence Lloyd treated the proceedings with scorn, and munched complacently all the way to the gallows.

Bincombe *Dorset*

Bincombe Hill and Bincombe Down were extensively settled during the Stone and Bronze Ages, evidence of which is provided by the many burial mounds or barrows in the district. However, tradition insists that these hillocks, known locally as the Music Barrows, are actually the houses of the fairy-folk. It is said that if you put your ear to the top of one of them at midday, you will hear the sound of a fairy orchestra.

A few years ago, a woman hired a taxi from Dorchester and drove all the way to Bincombe Hill barrows at midday to check up on the legend. Whether she was successful is not recorded.

Black Down Hills *Somerset*

The Holman Clavel Inn near Blagdon contains a hearth spirit called Chimbley Charlie. His seat is on the clavey – the beam above the fireplace – which is made of 'holman', the local word for holly.

One story tells of an occasion when a dinner party was being prepared for a local farmer. The table was laid when one of the maids remembered that the farmer had scoffed at Charlie – a dangerous thing to do. They could do no more than shut the door and hope for the best. Just before the guests arrived, the maids re-entered to make sure that everything was all right. Inside, they found the table bare – tankards were hanging up, the silver had been put away, and the table linen neatly folded. It was a sure sign that Charlie did not like the farmer, and the dinner was cancelled.

Bleadon *Avon*

It is said that the place was originally called 'Bleed Down' in commemoration of a bloody skirmish between the local people and Danish raiders. The story goes that one morning in the 7th century, six Danish longboats came sweeping up the Severn on the strong spring tide. The local fishermen ran to nearby Uphill to rouse the farming people, leaving behind one old, lame woman who was by the riverside gathering rushes. Hidden by the tall reeds, she watched the marauders land and scatter in search of plunder, leaving their boats unguarded. The old woman noticed that the tide which had brought the raiders up the estuary was now on the turn, so hobbling from mooring to mooring, she cut each longboat adrift.

Meanwhile, the Uphill men had rallied and driven the Danes, encumbered by their loot, back towards the landing place. There was no escape for the pirates, and not one of them survived. Every one of the Danes was red-headed, and to this day, West Country people tend to mistrust red-haired men.

Braunton *Devon*

The original church, and the hillside chapel, were both founded by St Brannoc, a 6th-century missionary who was said to have sailed from Wales in a stone coffin. Some of his many miracles, mostly concerned with animals, are depicted in carvings in the church where the holy man is also buried. St Brannoc taught the local people how to till the soil, and used wild deer to pull his plough. On one occasion, someone stole his cow, and killed, dismembered and cooked it. However, at the saint's call, the cow emerged from the pot, reassembled itself, and continued to supply him with milk for many years afterwards.

ST BRANNOC AND HIS BEASTS

St Brannoc is depicted above on a 16th-century bench-end in Braunton church. The carved roof boss (left) pictures the sow and piglets who showed him the site for the church, where he lies buried

Bristol Channel

Somewhere between Somerset and the Pembroke coast lie the fairy islands called the Green Meadows of Enchantment. They are not usually visible to humans, and certainly not to those who seek them, for the islands can disappear at will. They are usually seen by accident, and it has been reported that they are visible from the air. Fairy folk from the islands used to visit Laugharne Market in south Dyfed, and during the last century some sailors claimed to have landed on the island and joined the fairy revels. However, when the sailors re-embarked on their vessel and looked back, they found that the islands had vanished.

151

KING ARTHUR'S CASTLE

Cadbury Castle, near Yeovil, is an isolated Iron Age hill-fort whose earthwork ramparts enclose an area of almost 18 acres. The fort has been identified with Camelot since the 15th century at least; from there, it is said, Arthur led the Britons to victory against the Saxon invaders, and from there too came the inspiration for the medieval romances of Lancelot and Guinevere, of Galahad and the Holy Grail.

Even if it was never the 'many tower'd Camelot' of fable, archaeological evidence confirms that during the 6th century, the Arthurian period, the site was occupied by a British warrior chieftain who reinforced the earth defences with stone and timber, converting the old hill-fort into a powerful stronghold. Though, probably, his name will never be known, local legend has no trouble in identifying him; it was Arthur himself. According to tradition, the hill is hollow, and there Arthur and his knights lie sleeping until such time as England will call upon their services again. Every seven years, on Midsummer Eve, a great door in the hillside opens, and the gallant band rides down to water its horses at a spring near Sutton Montis church. Queen Camel, a village near the foot of Cadbury Hill, is one of several places which has been suggested as the site of the Battle of Camlann. It was in this battle that Arthur was mortally wounded by his nephew, Modred.

Brixham *Devon*

A well-documented 'flying saucer' story is attached to this fishing town. On April 28, 1967, the coast-guard on Berry Head reported a mysterious flying object which later hovered over the town at a height of 1600 ft for about an hour. Since it appeared just before midday, people were able to observe it in detail. It was described as a huge, dome-shaped object, with a door in the side. Eventually, it climbed rapidly and vanished.

Buckland St Mary *Somerset*

This is said to be the last place where the red-clothed fairies were seen in Somerset. It is claimed that they were defeated in a pitched battle with the pixies, so that everywhere west of the River Parret is now Pixyland. These pixies can easily be recognised by their red hair, pointed ears and green clothing. It is thought that the fairies fled to Ireland, though some say that a few settled in Devon and Dorset.

Carhampton *Somerset*

For hundreds of years the ancient rite of Wassailing the Apple Trees has been observed by the villagers on Old Twelfth Night (January 17). Cider is poured on the roots of the finest tree and spiced wassail cake is placed in the branches – a relic of the offerings once made to the tree gods to provide a fruitful harvest. Finally, shotguns are fired through the branches to drive away any evil spirits which may be lurking there and the chant 'Hats full, caps full, three bushel bags full' is sung.

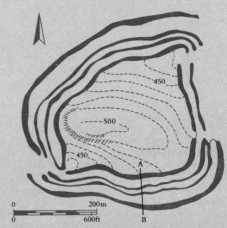

SEARCH FOR CAMELOT *This plan of Cadbury Castle's defences was prepared for an archaeological dig. The outer ramparts rise 42 ft above a 20-ft ditch, and the line AB shows where the hillside excavations (illustrated right) were made*

FOUND AT CADBURY *Objects recovered here range in time from the Bronze Age to the late Saxon period. The iron knife is probably Romano-British and the gilt bronze button is early Saxon. Though most Saxon settlements were far from Cadbury, it is feasible that the British garrison made forays for Saxon loot*

THE CERNE ABBAS GIANT

The huge figure cut in the chalk hillside above the village is connected with local legends of fertility. Until 1635, the maypole was set up above the giant, and courting couples still make night-time pilgrimages up the hillside to ensure that their marriage will be fruitful

Chagford *Devon*

On July 10, 1971, a wedding reception took place at Whiddon Park Guest House. Early that morning, a wedding guest staying there woke to find a young woman, dressed in black, standing in the doorway. She smiled and then vanished. The phantom has been seen in that room on other occasions, and is believed to be the ghost of Mary Whiddon who lived in the house over 300 years ago. She was shot on her wedding day by a jealous lover as she stood at the altar in Chagford church. The inscription on her tombstone reads: 'Behold a Matron yet a Maid . . .'

A PICTURE EMERGES *During the excavations at Cadbury, traces of an earlier rampart 20 ft wide were found under the topmost, late-Saxon wall. Debris at the base of this second structure indicates that it was almost certainly built in or about the 6th century AD, to protect the stronghold of a major British leader. The reconstructed rampart (right) is based on a plan of these walls which, in Arthur's time, would have supported a stout wooden breastwork braced by horizontal beams in the earthwork*

Chawleigh *Devon*

The village Friendly Society, which was founded in 1870, is probably the last of its kind in the West Country. Friendly Societies were parish-based welfare schemes that sprang up throughout Britain at the beginning of the 19th century. Each had an annual 'walk' in which members marched through the parish, holding wands tipped with the society's badge cast in brass. Chawleigh still holds its 'Club Walk' on the first Saturday in June, headed by the Society's banner. The walk is followed by a service, feasting and sports.

Churchill *Somerset*

Long ago, a crusader returned to Churchill after years in the Holy Land. The only gifts he could afford to bring home to his beloved wife were two carefully cherished bulbs of a rare spring flower called Primrose Peerless. When the knight reached the village, he discovered that his wife was dead. Broken-hearted, he flung the precious bulbs over the churchyard wall and died of despair on his lady's grave. The bulbs took root in a nearby field, and still grew within living memory. But the knight's effigy in the church still keeps the legend alive.

153

Corfe Castle *Dorset*

On Shrove Tuesday, the Freemen of the Ancient Order of Purbeck Marblers hold their annual court to introduce new Freemen at the castle. After the ceremony, a game of street football is played along the road from Corfe to Swanage and back to the castle. The purpose is to maintain an ancient right of way to Swanage Harbour, from which Purbeck marble was once shipped.

Croydon Hill *Somerset*

Some time last century, so legend tells, a Croydon ploughboy went to Rodhuish to have a plough-blade repaired. The talk at the smithy turned to tales of the Croydon Hill Devil, a horned beast that was supposed to lurk in the lane over the hill. The butcher's boy thought he would frighten the other lad by imitating the Devil and waylaying him. As the Croydon boy approached the lane, he saw a horned monster which bellowed furiously at him.

In terror, the ploughboy lashed out with the plough-blade and then ran. All that was found later by the villagers was a bullock's hide with a great gash in it – but the butcher's boy was never seen again. It is said the Devil took him, and the boy can be heard howling on Croydon Hill on stormy nights as his and other lost souls are hounded by demons.

Dunster *Somerset*

Ash logs and faggots often figure in old customs, probably because ash is one of the few woods that will burn easily when it is still green. A very old legend says that the Christ-child was first warmed by a fire of green ash. Until a century ago, Burning the Ashen Faggot was a widespread custom on Christmas Eve, particularly in Somerset; this medieval tradition is still observed at the Luttrell Arms Hotel in Dunster.

The faggot is a bundle of 12 ash branches bound with green ash bands. It is burnt in the great fireplace of the hotel, and as each band burns through and bursts, another round of hot punch is ordered from the bar. While the wood burns, everyone sings the ancient Dunster Carol, and when the faggot is finally consumed, a charred fragment is taken out to light next year's fire.

THE HAUNTED MOORS

Separated by a broad band of Devonshire farming country, the uplands of Dartmoor and Exmoor are quite different in character. Dartmoor is a craggy inland plateau of rough moorland, treacherous bogs and rocky outcrops. Exmoor curves gently across heather and pasture, to drop steeply from over 1000 ft to the sea.

In the remote northern part of Dartmoor is Cranmere Pool. Now drained, it was once the most awful of bogs, and a place to which evil spirits were consigned. The most famous of these was Bengie Geare, a former mayor of Okehampton, whose phantom, in the guise of a black pony, still makes occasional appearances. On Fox Tor there is a 10th-century Saxon noble's memorial called Childe's Tomb. Lost in a blizzard, the nobleman cut open his horse and crawled inside for warmth. Before he died, he wrote his will in the horse's blood on a nearby rock.

River of death

According to legend, the small but swift River Dart claims one human life each year. Understandably, a drowning in early spring removed a great deal of anxiety from the rest of the community. A local rhyme says:

'River Dart, River of Dart:
Every year thou claimest a heart.'

A stretch of road near Postbridge was the scene of a series of motoring accidents during the 1920's. Several drivers stated that their cars had run off the road when a ghostly

Exeter *Devon*

In 1941, an air raid reduced much of the old part of the city to rubble. Fortunately, the cathedral survived, though it was badly damaged, and repairs were begun as early as 1943. While these were being carried out, an extraordinary collection of wax models was discovered in a cavity on top of the stone screen surrounding the choir.

They included representations of human and animal limbs, part of a horse's head and the complete figure of a woman. Almost certainly, these were votive offerings that were once placed on the tomb of Bishop Edmund Lacy, who died in 1455. During his lifetime, the bishop was said to have shown much saintliness and, after he died, sick pilgrims used to kneel by his tomb to pray for recovery, either for themselves or for their sick animals. As a mark of faith, they would leave behind them a wax image of the ailing limb or animal. At the Reformation in 1538, the zealous dean cleared the cathedral of all images and relics; these wax offerings probably survived because some faithful pilgrim deliberately hid them. They are now kept in the cathedral library.

Just outside the city is the well and chapel of St Sidwell, who was martyred in the 6th century. The story goes that her stepmother coveted some land the girl had inherited and bribed two harvesters to murder her. As she knelt in prayer in a field, they decapitated her with scythes and, where her head fell, a spring gushed forth.

PILGRIM'S OFFERING *This wax figure of a 15th-century woman, 8 in. high, is a memorial of some Exeter pilgrim who prayed at Bishop Lacy's tomb*

hairy hand had leapt through the window and seized the steering wheel. Furthermore, in 1924, a woman reported seeing it outside her caravan window in the moonlight.

Moorland travellers might also be plagued by pixies, which were believed to deliberately disorientate people so that they would fall into the bogs.

Doone country

All over the world, people associate Exmoor with R. D. Blackmore's novel *Lorna Doone*, the story of an outlaw family that terrorised the district in the 17th century, and of the heroic farmer, John Ridd, who defeated them. Fiction and fact have become intertwined, for the real Doones were equally villainous. Having been expelled from Scotland in 1620, they settled in a ruined Celtic monastery on Exmoor and made a living by blackmail and extortion. Oare church is still pointed out as the place where Lorna Doone was shot on her wedding day, though no one seems to know whether the incident was based on fact or not. Another character in the novel who certainly existed was the highwayman, Tom Faggus. Born at South Molton and hanged at Taunton, Faggus had a horse that was so well trained it was believed to be his familiar spirit. It was said that Faggus would never have been captured if his horse had not been shot first. As for John Ridd, whether fictional or not, several local people still claim descent from him.

THE LONELY DARTMOOR HILLS *Probably the best known Dartmoor story is Conan Doyle's* The Hound of the Baskervilles, *which was inspired by a number of local legends*

THE ANCIENT MYSTERIES OF
Glastonbury

Long believed to be the place where the first Christian church was built in Britain, and renowned in heroic legend as the burial place of King Arthur, Glastonbury may also have been a holy place 1000 years before Christianity came to these shores. In prehistory, before the Somerset marshes were drained, flooding turned Glastonbury into an island each winter. The pagan Celts knew it as Ynys-witrin, the Island of Glass, and to a people that regarded all islands as sacred, it must have had a special significance.

An old legend says that Christ himself visited Glastonbury as a boy; and after Joseph of Arimathea had placed Jesus in his own tomb, he too came to England bringing with him the Holy Grail, the cup used at the Last Supper. On Weary-All Hill, near the Tor, Joseph thrust his staff into the earth where it took root and grew into a Holy Thorn tree, which blossomed only at Christmas. Cuttings from this tree, *Crataegus oxyacantha*, still flourish in the neighbourhood and blossom around Christmas time, though the original was cut down in Cromwell's day because it was considered to be an idolatrous image.

Church chronicles record that Joseph built a chapel of wattle and daub on a site now covered by the Lady Chapel of the ruined abbey, and there he baptised the first British converts to Christianity. Hermits worshipped in the chapel until the 5th century, when St Patrick, it is said, formed them into a monastic community. A later chapel built on top of the Tor was dedicated to St Michael, soldier of God and victor over paganism. The monastery survived Saxon and Danish conquests and was a rich Benedictine abbey until the Dissolution of 1539, when Henry VIII hanged the last abbot.

Arthur in Avalon

The first mention of Glastonbury in Arthurian legend is when Melwas, ruler of the Summer Land, the ancient name for Somerset, abducts Guinevere and imprisons her in his fortress at Glastonbury. Arthur can make no headway through the marshes and Guinevere remains a prisoner until the abbot intercedes for her and she is released.

The most famous story of Glastonbury, however, tells how Arthur, mortally wounded at the Battle of Camlann, is carried away in a barge to the mysterious Isle of Avalon. His actual death is not recorded, yet, according to the monks, he was buried in their own cemetery. In the 12th century, the bones of a tall man were discovered, together with the bones and hair of a woman who may have been Guinevere. Also in the grave, the monks said, was a lead cross inscribed HIC IACET SEPULTUS INCLYTUS REX ARTURIUS IN INSULA AVALONIA – Here in the Isle of Avalon the famous King Arthur lies buried.

RENDEZVOUS OF THE DEAD *Glastonbury Tor, and the 14th-century tower of St Michael stand sharply against the evening sky. Centuries ago, when much of Somerset was marsh, Glastonbury itself was an island during floods and high tides. To the pagan Celts, who often regarded hills and islands with religious awe, the hill on this semi-island was the shrine of Gwyn-ap-Nudd, God of the Underworld. There is strong reason to believe that Glastonbury may have been the mysterious Isle of Avalon, which in Celtic lore was the meeting place of the dead. In Arthurian legend, Avalon was the fairy island where weeping maidens brought the dying king*

Abode of the dead

Though there are strong probabilities that Glastonbury was a centre of pagan Celtic worship, they have not yet been confirmed by any major archaeological discoveries. Nevertheless, it seems highly likely that a shrine of some sort did exist. About 50 years ago, the remains of two large Celtic villages were excavated from the peat near Glastonbury. The Celts often regarded islands and hills as sacred to the gods; a near-island crowned with a hill rising above lagoons and marshes would almost certainly have been a holy place.

Did Christ come to Glastonbury?

The history of Christian Glastonbury is well documented in ancient records and manuscripts. Most of the legends owe their inspiration to the Old Church, the chapel said to have been built by Joseph of Arimathea. This rough building was still standing when the Saxons overran central Somerset in the 7th century.

As far as is known, the Celtic monks encountered by the Saxons in the Old Church did not tell them who had built it, and perhaps they did not know. It had simply been there from time immemorial. Its real origin, and the reason why Joseph came to be regarded as its founder, are still not

CRADLE OF CHRISTIANITY *Glastonbury Abbey covers the site of a crude chapel that may have been built by Joseph of Arimathea*

known. Nor can the source of the extraordinary story of Christ's visit be traced. Possibly the Old Church inspired this belief too, since a Saxon legend speaks of the Church as 'not built of man but prepared by God himself'.

Grave for a hero

For centuries, the stories of Melwas, Guinevere's abductor, and the discovery of Arthur's grave in the abbey, were dismissed as tales concocted by monks to attract more pilgrims to Glastonbury. Then, in the 1960's, excavations showed that a fortress existed on the Tor during the 6th century, suggesting at least the possibility of truth in the Melwas legend.

Excavations, too, show that the monks' account of the grave is correct as far as it can be checked. The now empty grave, claimed as Arthur's, had been opened in the 12th century and the bones themselves were scattered and lost at the time of the Dissolution. The king's epitaph is something of a mystery. Scholars agree that its style belongs to a period later than Arthur's; on the other hand, it seems too ancient to be a 12th-century fake.

Whatever the truth of the legends, Glastonbury still retains its aura of mystery from centuries of worship.

ARTHUR'S CROSS

CHALICE WELL *The Holy Grail was supposedly hidden here*

HOLY RELICS *The lead cross inscribed with Arthur's epitaph was displayed in 1190 as proof that the king's grave had been found. Judging from the above engraving, made before the cross disappeared in the 17th century, its authenticity is doubtful. Though the style of lettering is ancient, it is of later date than the 6th century, the Arthurian period. Joseph of Arimathea is said to have hidden the Holy Grail containing drops of Christ's blood in the spring which feeds the Chalice Well (above right). For centuries the well was renowned for its healing qualities, a belief that may have been fostered by the iron content of the waters. The 750-year-old well is lined with stone blocks taken from the abbey church, burnt down in 1184*

SACRED THORN *In legend, Joseph's staff grew into a Holy Thorn tree*

Flowers Barrow *Dorset*

This ancient hill-fort is a fine defensive Iron Age earthwork at the western end of the Purbeck Hills. The Romans also appreciated its strategic importance, for they established a fort there. Some people maintain that the garrison is still carrying out its duties: in 1678, a phantom legion was seen marching along the Ridgeway, and it has been reported on several occasions since, usually in times of national crisis. It was seen just before 1939, and on several occasions during the Second World War. The last sighting was in 1970, when an old lady saw the legion at Knowle Hill, near Corfe.

Godmanston *Dorset*

The 600-year-old Smith's Arms claims to be the smallest public house in England – its front is only 11 ft wide. Once the pub was a smithy, and the story goes that one day, Charles II was riding through the village when he stopped at the blacksmith's to have his horse reshod. While he waited, he asked the smith to bring him some ale but the man replied that he had no licence. On hearing this, the king granted him one, and the licence has been kept up ever since.

Halstock *Dorset*

The sign outside The Quiet Woman Inn shows a woman with her head beneath her arm. It represents a 7th-century saint named Juthware or Judith, who used to help pilgrims on their way to a shrine at Halstock. Her jealous stepmother and brother resented the constant presence of strangers in the house, and one day her brother became so enraged that he cut off Juthware's head with his sword. To his consternation, his sister at once picked up her head and carried it to the altar of the local church before finally expiring.

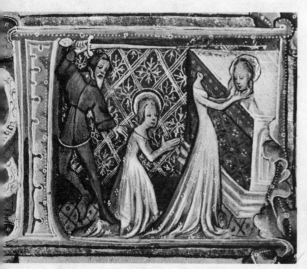

THE QUIET WOMAN

The legend of Juthware is told in the 15th-century manuscript known as the Sherborne Missal. The illustration above, from this manuscript, shows Juthware's brother about to murder her and the decapitated saint carrying her head to the altar of Halstock church. Juthware's ghost, carrying its head under its arm, is said to haunt the lane on Judith Hill in Halstock

Hartland Point *Devon*

This promontory was once called the Headland of Hercules. There is a legend that Hercules landed there, fought the British giants, and for some years successfully governed the whole country. During the 6th century, a Welsh hermit named St Nectan settled there. On St Nectan's Day (June 17), mass is still celebrated beside his holy well, after which the local children march in procession carrying foxgloves, the saint's special flower. It is said that after being decapitated by robbers, the saint picked up his head and, walking with it to his well, dropped it in. Wherever the ground was sprinkled with his blood, foxgloves sprang up.

Haselbury Plucknett *Somerset*

During the 12th century, a cell that once stood near the village was the home of Wulfric, a gentle saint who seems to have been chiefly remembered for his love of small animals. On one occasion, when he found a squirrel hoarding nuts in his wooden cup, he carved a new one rather than disturb the creature. And when a wren nested above his sleeping place, he moved his bed into a draughty, uncomfortable corner to avoid frightening the fledglings.

Hatherleigh *Devon*

The town carnival is held on the nearest Wednesday to November 5. Just before daybreak, burning tar barrels are drawn through the streets by 12 to 20 townsmen. The ceremony is repeated at nightfall, when there is also a torchlight procession. Though now linked with November 5, these activities may have evolved from the fires which were lit during the Celtic festival of Samain (November 1).

Hinton St George *Somerset*

The Punky Night celebrations, on the last Thursday in October, may have some link with the ancient fire rites of Celtic Samain (November 1). Children go round the village begging for candles, which they place inside scooped-out mangel-wurzels. These lanterns, called 'punkies', are carved to represent faces, trees or houses. Carrying them, the children parade up and down the village streets, singing the traditional 'punky' song.

Keynsham *Avon*

The town is named after St Keyne, daughter of Braglan, a 6th-century prince of Wales. When she arrived there, the lord of the manor gave her a piece of land, but it was so infested with huge venomous snakes that no prospective converts would visit her. Undismayed, St Keyne turned the snakes into stone, and tradition claims that the fossilised ammonites – a form of prehistoric shellfish – that abound in the area, are the remains of these reptiles. The picture below shows one of these fossils which was discovered in the district.

Kilve *Somerset*

Once upon a time, a huge fiery dragon called Blue Ben lived within Putsham Hill. He used to cool himself by swimming in the nearby sea, and in order to avoid the mudflats as he emerged from his tunnel below Kilve and Putsham, he built a causeway of rocks into the water. Having discovered Blue Ben's lair, the Devil used to harness him and ride him round the streets of Hell – much to the dragon's disgust because he got far too hot. One day, hurrying to cool off after a sortie, he slipped on the causeway and fell into the mud, and drowned. As proof of the legend, people used to say that the fossilised ichthyosaurus (a prehistoric sea-creature) found near Glastonbury last century, and now in the county museum in Taunton, is really Blue Ben.

Kingsteignton *Devon*

A whole ram is roasted and served at the Ram Roasting Fair which takes place on Spring Bank Holiday Monday. In the distant past, it is said, the stream that flows through the churchyard suddenly dried up. The waters reappeared when a ram was sacrificed, and the custom still continues.

Kingston *Dorset*

This tiny village contains an 18th-century inn, The Scott Arms, which is said to be haunted. The ghost is that of an old woman who has been seen sitting with her back to the bar after closing time, drinking from a mug. During the summer of 1970, a couple staying at the inn saw her hazy figure standing at the foot of their bed. No one knows who the ghost is.

THE DEVIL'S FOOTPRINTS

An exceptionally hard winter gripped Britain during the early part of 1855. In Devon the Exe was iced over at Exeter, and birds standing in the shallow water of the estuary were sometimes frozen into the ice.

On the morning of February 9, after a 2 in. fall of snow and a severe frost during the night, people emerging from their homes discovered strange footmarks leading in single file across the frozen countryside.

Most reports said the marks resembled those of donkey's hooves. But the single line, with each print 8 in. apart, one in front of the other, seemed more typical of a two-legged than a four-legged creature.

An amazing route

The strange trail was said to have begun at Totnes and ended at Littleham, covering possibly 100 miles as it zigzagged round the coastal parishes between the two towns. It led through gardens, over gates, haystacks, walls and roofs. In one case it seemed to pass under a gooseberry bush; in another, through a 6-in. pipe. Sometimes the marks appeared to have penetrated through the hard-frozen snow as if cut by a hot iron – or fiery hooves. At Dawlish the trail led into a thicket. When dogs were brought in to flush the undergrowth, they are said to have retreated, howling dismally. At once, it was suggested that the marks had been made by the Devil himself.

What made the prints?

Several newspapers made careful investigations, though on the whole they made light of the story. Attempts to offer a logical explanation, however, were not helped by differing descriptions and drawings supplied by witnesses.

Many suggestions were made to explain the identity of the phantom trail maker. Though most claimed it was the work of a donkey, others said that badgers, otters, cranes and even mountain wild cats were responsible. According to one amateur naturalist, the prints closely resembled those of a kangaroo.

Closer investigation revealed that the trail was made not in one night, but several. Nor was the trail always the same. In places it was no more than disturbed, ruffled snow, as if heavy, half-frozen birds had been struggling to get airborne. Birds too may have been responsible for the strange marks on rooftops.

A suggestion that the marks were made by a pony with a broken shoe was scorned by those who pointed out that whether the creature was natural or not, it certainly had cloven hooves. At Woodbury, however, where the marks led to the church door, they looked almost as if they had been made with a hot iron. In this case, at least, they were probably made by a practical joker. Whatever the explanation of the strange trail, there were many village people who for a long time refused to stir from their homes after sunset. They were convinced that the Devil had singled out Devon for his special attention.

Lundy *Devon*

During most of its early history the island was occupied by a succession of piratical owners who preyed upon Bristol-bound ships. This freebooting tradition continued into the early years of the 19th century when the owner, Thomas Benson, obtained the government contract for transporting convicts to the colonies. Few of the convicts ever got further than Lundy, where they built a large house for Benson and were employed as slaves on his land. Having insured an old brigantine, he secretly unloaded her cargo on Lundy before scuttling the vessel within sight of another ship. He collected the insurance, but was betrayed by a drunken sailor and spent the rest of his life in exile.

Lighthouse keepers have often reported seeing a young girl walking dangerously near the cliff edge. She is supposed to be a widow who threw herself over the cliffs when her husband died.

Lydford *Devon*

The town once came under the jurisdiction of the Stannary Courts, which were set up in the 14th century to administer justice to the tinners. It used to be said that Lydford judges hanged evil-doers in the morning and held their trials in the afternoon. The expression 'Lydford Law' still implies rough and swift justice – a summary trial held after sentence has been carried out.

THE HANGING JUDGE

For his brutality in conducting the Bloody Assize after the Monmouth Rebellion of 1685, Judge Jeffreys was allegedly condemned to haunt the West Country

Lyme Regis *Dorset*

The Duke of Monmouth raised his standard here in 1685 at the start of his ill-fated West Country uprising. In the aptly named Bloody Assize after the rebellion was crushed, Judge Jeffreys condemned 12 Lyme Regis people. The night before the hangings, it is said Jeffreys dined in the Great House which once stood in Broad Street. His ghost still haunts the spot – some say, gnawing a bloody bone.

Marldon *Devon*

The Apple Pie Fair takes place at the beginning of August. It was founded in 1888, lapsed during the last war, and was revived in 1958. Quantities of small pies are baked and concealed under a vast imitation pie-crust, and the whole edifice is drawn by a donkey to the fairground where the pies are sold. The ceremony originates from the time when poor labourers supplemented the family diet with such perquisites as fallen fruit. At some unknown period the community decided, for economy, to make one huge pie in the village bakehouse and turned the occasion into a party.

Milber *Devon*

In 1931 the late Rev. William Keble Martin had charge of this new parish near Newton Abbott where, at that time, there was no permanent church. One night, the new curate dreamt of a strange church which had three naves converging fan-wise towards the altar, so that the whole congregation had an uninterrupted view of the sacrament. An architect told Keble Martin that the scheme was feasible and the church was built to this unique design. It has been known ever since as 'The Dream Church'.

Minehead *Somerset*

The town's Hobby Horse makes its first appearance on May Day Eve; then, for the next three days at various times, it prances its way round the district accompanied by drum and accordion. The Horse consists of a 9 ft long frame covered with painted canvas and ribbons; its antics are controlled by a dancer concealed inside. Like other Hobby Horse ceremonies, the Minehead version is probably the survival of an ancient spring fertility rite, though local legend gives it a different origin. The story goes that during the 9th century, the town was constantly under attack from Viking pirates. The raiders fled in terror, however, when a Minehead crew disguised its ship as a sea-serpent, and their victory is still celebrated to this day. In confirmation it is pointed out that the design of the Horse bears some resemblance to a longship.

A famous Minehead ghost is that of the 17th-century Mrs Leakey, who during her lifetime was beloved by all. After death, however, her spirit underwent a terrible change. It conjured up storms, sank ships, and attacked travellers on lonely roads. Exorcism merely provoked fresh violence, and Charles I sent a Royal Commission to investigate the affair. At last a bishop managed to quell the phantom, though it is still said to haunt Culver Cliffs.

North Tawton *Devon*

Bathe Pool is a grassy hollow in a field near Cottle's Wood. It is said that at times of national crisis, or when a public figure is about to die, the hollow fills with water. The phenomenon has been reported on several occasions; it prophesied the deaths of Nelson, Wellington and Edward VII, and was seen, too, just before the First World War.

Ottery St Mary *Devon*

On the evening of November 5 the roads are barred to traffic and flaming tar barrels are rolled down the main street, guided by men whose hands are bound with protective sacking. Though now part of the Guy Fawkes' celebrations, the event may have originated from an ancient sun-worshipping festival. In several years during Victorian times, the party got out of hand to an extent where police reinforcements had to be sent from Exeter; but despite all efforts, the authorities were unable to put an end to this popular tradition.

BOWLS AND BRAVADO ON PLYMOUTH HOE

A much-loved legend of Plymouth Hoe tells how Sir Francis Drake insisted on finishing his game of bowls even though the topsails of the Spanish Armada were visible from the green. He is also said to have sold his soul to Satan at Devil's Point in exchange for the storm that drove the Spanish fleet north and westwards to its doom. According to another story, the hero sat at the edge of the cliff on Plymouth Hoe one day whittling a stick. By some mysterious agency each wood chip, as it struck the water, turned into a fully armed ship. This 19th-century view of the Hoe is by J. M. W. Turner

Drake's drum, now in Buckland Abbey, accompanied the admiral when he circumnavigated the globe in 1577–80. It is said that Drake is not dead, but sleeping, and if his drum is beaten, he will wake to his country's call. The drum was said to have been heard when the German fleet surrendered in 1918

Poole *Dorset*

In 1248, when it received its charter from the Earl of Salisbury, this town was an important fishing and trading port. The earl's name is immortalised in the small, disused lock-up or prison still called 'The Salisbury', situated near the Georgian Customs House. The mayor also possesses the ancient title of Admiral of the Port of Poole, and the right of the townspeople to use the harbour is reaffirmed every three years in the ceremony of Beating the Bounds. In this ceremony, the admiral's barge sails round the boundary marks where the Jurymen of the Court of Admiralty scramble ashore and ensure that the marks are visible; they also leave a floating buoy at each seaward mark. At each mark, two children are ceremonially 'beaten' – an age-old custom to remind them of the boundaries.

In 1965, frightened customers ran from a new shop in the High Street after seeing objects being moved by some invisible agency. Another haunting was reported in 1966 during alterations to the Crown Hotel. A piano repeatedly sounded a single note, and heavy but invisible objects were dragged about the upper floors. Later, three witnesses saw a 'fluorescent mist' drift across the stable-yard.

The road to Upton is also said to be haunted. Four headless men are alleged to carry a coffin along the road and then disappear through the hedgerow.

Portland *Dorset*

Until the early part of the 20th century, buying and selling land on Portland was done by means of 'Church Gift'. The people involved in the transaction went to the church and made a verbal declaration of the transfer, which was considered legal and binding. Records of land ownership were kept by means of notches cut in a 'reed-pole', and each area had its own pole, kept in the church or pub. The distance between notches showed how much land each man owned. This custom was still practised in Portland within living memory.

Powderham *Devon*

Since the Middle Ages, Powderham Castle has owned a unicorn's horn which could detect poison. When the horn was dipped into a poisoned drink, the liquor was said to change colour. In fact, the 'unicorn's horn' is the 9 ft long tusk of a narwhal.

Shaftesbury *Dorset*

This ancient hill-top town, where King Canute died in 1035, contains the remains of a ruined abbey. Shortly before the Dissolution in 1539, the last abbess is said to have ordered a monk to excavate a secret pit to hide the abbey treasures. Only the monk knew of its whereabouts, but before he could tell the abbess, he had a stroke and took his secret with him to the grave. To this day, no one has ever found the treasure, but the monk's ghost has often been seen walking round the abbey before vanishing through a wall. It is thought that he is still trying to reach the abbess to tell her where the treasure is hidden. The ghost is invisible from the knees downwards, which may suggest that the old ground level was lower than at present.

Shapwick *Somerset*

Legend says that St Indractus, his sister Drusa, and a party of pilgrims were martyred here on their return journey from Rome to Ireland in the 8th century. Their wallets were filled with seed corn as a gift for the Irish poor, and each of them carried a staff tipped with brass. They were murdered by Saxon brigands who supposed that their purses were bulging with gold and that their staves were ornamented with the same metal. The Saxons threw the corpses in a pit, but for three days and nights a miraculous shaft of light shone on the place, and this led to the discovery of the crime. According to one story, the pilgrims were reinterred at Shepton Mallet in the presence of the murderers. As the bodies were lowered into the grave a terrible madness seized the Saxons who tore each other to pieces.

THE DUKING DAYS

Shebbear *Devon*

In the village square, beneath an ancient oak, there is a large boulder. Every November 5, the church bell-ringers assemble with crowbars and lever the stone over before returning to the church and ringing a peal on its bells. One legend says that this is because Satan lies beneath the stone, and the ritual ensures that he is kept down for the following 12 months. Another story says that it is the foundation stone of Henscott church across the River Torridge, but the Devil moved it.

THE DEVIL'S STONE

The Shebbear stone is said to have been quarried on the other side of the River Torridge at Henscott. It was intended for Henscott church but each night, after Shebbear villagers returned it, the Devil rolled it back

Shepton Mallet *Somerset*

Giles Cannard was a prosperous 18th-century innkeeper in the town, who owed much of his wealth to his dealings with sheep-stealers, smugglers and highwaymen. He was persuaded into an attempt to defraud the town of its common land, but somehow the news leaked out and the angry townsfolk set out towards his inn with murder in their hearts. Rather than fall into the hands of the mob, the terrified Giles hanged himself. He was buried at the crossroads with a stake through his heart to prevent him from walking. However, the treatment does not seem to have been effective since Giles was frequently seen in the vicinity of his old inn – long since vanished – and near his burial place at the hillside crossroads outside the pub called Cannard's Grave, whose sign is a corpse swinging from a gallows tree. Another story claims that Giles was the last man in England to be hanged for sheep stealing.

The walls of one of the caves in the hills north of Shepton Mallet are said to bear the marks of a terrible visitation by the Devil. A long time ago, a poor woman named Nancy Camel lived in the cave. Seeing her poverty, the Devil offered Nancy riches and a life of ease in exchange for her soul. She yielded to temptation, and though she continued to live in her cave, she never worked again and never appeared to lack for anything.

She grew old, and at last the time came for her to fulfil her part of the bargain. One stormy night, Satan brought a great horse and cart to carry her to Hell. People near by heard piercing shrieks, the crack of a whip and the creaking of wheels, and next morning Nancy had vanished. The cavern walls were stamped with the impression of a horse's hooves and the tracks of cartwheels, which are still faintly visible to this day.

One of the most harrowing episodes in the history of the West Country began on June 11, 1685, when Charles II's illegitimate son, the Duke of Monmouth, sailed into Lyme Regis harbour with 81 hopeful men. His aim was to win the British crown from his uncle James II and within days perhaps as many as 6000 Westcountrymen had rallied to his cause. This period of loyalty to the duke later became known as the Duking Days. But the men were poorly armed and poorly disciplined, and Monmouth had no money; the tradition that they were an army of deluded rustics armed with pitchforks is not so very far from the truth.

For almost a month, the rebels ruled Somerset. Monmouth was proclaimed king in Taunton market-place and the gathering troops of James II did nothing to stop him. Then on the night of July 5, on the moonlit lowlands of Sedgemoor, the rebels fought and lost the battle on which their hopes, and lives, depended.

The haunted battlefield

Even today, the cruelty of that battle and its bloody aftermath haunt the memory of the West Country. The bitter spirits of slaughtered rebels are said to hang as balls of light over the battlefield, and strange shadows flit silently towards the River Cary, where they disappear. Phantom horsemen with their cloaks flying in the wind, ghostly troopers armed with pikes and staves, and even Monmouth himself, flee through the Sedgemoor lanes.

In the late 19th century, a local farmer said that one foggy night, he had heard on the moor what he took to be a drunk shouting 'Come over and fight' – the last despairing cry of Monmouth's men as they were slaughtered by cannon firing across the river.

Monmouth fled from the battle a broken man, and within three days he had been captured. Apparently, he was found cowering in a ditch, and his captors were attracted to his hiding place by the terrified glint in his eyes. One of the places where this is supposed to have happened is Horton in Dorset; another is Ringwood in the New Forest. He was taken to London and brought before James. Tradition claims that he wept, begged and even promised to turn Catholic. But it was no use. On July 15 he was beheaded on Tower Hill.

James sent the infamous Judge Jeffreys down to Taunton to mete out justice to the rebels; after the 'Bloody Assize' more than 200 were hanged and 800 transported to sugar plantations in the West Indies. Heddon Oak near Crowcombe is one of the trees still pointed out as a gallows tree. Sometimes, it is said, the clank of chains and the gasps of choking men can still be heard there. At Taunton Castle, the tramp of James's soldiers bringing prisoners to trial still echoes through the sombre corridors; and the ghost of Judge Jeffreys haunts, or at least used to haunt, Lydford in Devon and Lyme Regis in Dorset.

There are many tales about fugitives from the battle. John Plumley, the Lord of Locking Manor, fled to his home and hid near by, but his dog gave away his hiding place and he was hanged. His wife swept the dog up in her arms and, wild with despair, plunged to her death in Locking Well. Her distraught ghost, still carrying the dog, is said to haunt the district to this day.

Sherborne *Dorset*

Pack Monday Fair, held on the first Monday after October 10, probably dates from the 13th century. The name may be a corruption of Pact – the agreement made between master and labourer at a hiring fair. At midnight on the night before the fair, a group of people known as Teddy Roe's Band parade and blow horns and whistles, swing rattles and bang kettles and saucepans. This custom dates back to the 15th century, when a serious fire left Sherborne Abbey in need of extensive repairs. After completion, the workmen, led by their foreman Teddy Roe, celebrated by going round the town blowing on cows' horns.

In the gardens of nearby Sherborne Castle, the ghost of a former owner, Sir Walter Raleigh, is said to walk on St Michael's Eve (September 28).

RUNNING FOR HIS LIFE *One of Monmouth's followers captured after the Battle of Sedgemoor was a famous runner. According to tradition, he was promised his life if he could out-run a horse. He was roped to a stallion and raced across Somerset beside it. But though the horse tired before he did,* *his captors broke their promise and hanged him anyway. It is said that the sound of running feet and pounding hooves can still sometimes be heard near Westonzoyland. The ghost of the runner's sweetheart, who drowned herself in despair, also reputedly haunts the area*

Shervage Wood *Somerset*

There is a legend that a Great Worm, whose girth was greater than three oak trees, once settled in Shervage Wood. People began to notice that their ponies and sheep were disappearing at an alarming rate. Then a shepherd and a couple of gipsies went to gather the bilberries for which the woods were famous, and they too vanished. After this, no one dared go near the place.

This was particularly galling for one old Crowcombe woman who made a living out of selling blueberry pies, for she could find no one brave enough to pick the berries for her. At last, a woodcutter from Stogumber appeared and, omitting to tell him about the Worm, the old woman persuaded him to gather berries from the wood.

Having worked for a while, the woodcutter settled down on a great log in the ferns to drink his cider and eat some bread and cheese. No sooner had he begun his meal than the log began to squirm about. Calmly, he took up his axe and chopped it in two, whereupon the severed ends began to bleed. One end slithered off to Kingston St Mary near Taunton, and the other to Bilbrook near Minehead. Since the two ends were unable to meet up again, the Great Worm died.

The woodman then gathered a huge hatful of berries and, on his return, told the old woman that he had had some trouble with a dragon. She feigned surprise that no one had told him about the creature, and the woodman replied that he had heard the tale. But since it was told him by a Crowcombe woman, he ignored it; everyone knew that Crowcombe people were liars!

163

Southleigh *Devon*

A local legend concerns the Hangman's Stone on the south side of the A3052, by the crossroads to Beer and Southleigh. The story goes that a sheep-stealer once came past carrying a heavy carcass on a rope over his shoulder. The weight had made him so weary that he decided to take a rest in this quiet spot. Setting the dead sheep on the stone, he sat down with his back against the rock. He fell asleep and, as he slept, the carcass slipped off the stone and pulled the cord tight around the thief's neck, strangling him to death.

Sidbury *Devon*

The annual Court Leet and Court Baron – a form of manorial court – is held in Sidbury Manor on the third Wednesday of November. It elects manorial officers whose ancient responsibilities include ale-tasting, bread-weighing and meat-tasting.

THE DORSET OOSER

Centuries ago, a man wearing the horned mask known as an Ooser may have been the high priest who officiated at a pagan fertility ritual; and the mask may have represented a powerful pagan god. But by the 19th century, the Ooser's original meaning had been forgotten, and in places like Shillingstone, it had become the 'Christmas Bull', a terrifying creature which roamed through the streets of Dorset villages at the end of each year demanding refreshment from any villagers it met. Sometimes, its former sanctity was so far forgotten that it was used to frighten children, or to taunt unfaithful husbands or wives.

Once every Dorset village may have had an Ooser, but by the beginning of the 20th century only one was left at Melbury Osmond. Now, even that has been lost, and the ancient Horned God has probably disappeared from Dorset for ever.

In the 19th century, the Ooser almost certainly played a part in a widespread custom known as 'Skimmington Riding' or 'Skim-mity'. To express their disapproval of adultery, villagers would troop through the streets, leading a horse or donkey on which two figures, representing a couple suspected of unfaithfulness, were seated back to back.

Sometimes, models were used, and sometimes a masked man and woman played the parts. The Ooser mask may have been worn by the man or by one of the crowd, as a particularly damning gesture of derision. This was the strangely ironical ending of the idol of a former god of fertility.

A SKIMMINGTON RIDE *A century ago men or women suspected of adultery or licentious behaviour were publicly ridiculed in the village streets; it was only the fear of 'Skimmity' that kept many couples together*

Stanton Drew *Somerset*

A macabre tale is told of the three prehistoric stone circles close by the River Drew. One Saturday long ago, a village wedding was followed by revels that continued into the night. As midnight struck, the devout piper refused to play any more for he could not play on a Sunday. The bride swore she would find another piper to keep the party going, even if she had to go to Hell to fetch him. At that moment an old man appeared and offered his services. His music was so exhilarating that the dancers could not stop – and too late, they found that their musician was the Devil himself. The faster he played the faster they danced. When morning came and the fiend returned to Hell, the villagers found the wedding party had been turned to stone. To this day, the group of three stone circles is known as 'The Devil's Wedding'.

Stogumber *Somerset*

When Sir Francis Drake wooed Elizabeth Sydenham, her noble family, aware of the great sailor's humble origins, refused to permit the match. Sadly, Drake went back to sea, and Elizabeth, tired at last of waiting for her roving lover, became betrothed to a man of her parents' choice.

Legend says that on the wedding day, the guests assembled in Stogumber church and, as the bridal party approached the door, there was a blinding flash and a thunderous roar in the sky. A huge cannonball fell at the feet of the bride, who was convinced that Drake had somehow known of her marriage and had fired a shot across the world to show his anger. She refused to allow the ceremony to continue and, in due course, Drake returned to claim her. The couple were married in 1585. A meteorite which is nearly as big as a football, and is kept in the hall at Coombe Sydenham House, is said to be the 'cannonball'.

Stogursey *Somerset*

Wick Barrow is a Bronze Age burial mound that has long been associated with the pixies. Once, a ploughman working near by heard the voice of what he took to be a small child crying in the bushes on the mound. The voice was complaining that it had broken its peel – a type of flat wooden shovel once used for putting loaves into old-fashioned baking ovens. When the ploughman went to look, he could find nothing but a tiny wooden peel with its handle broken. Thinking the child was hiding in the bushes but would eventually return for its toy, he mended the peel and left it where he found it. When his work was over, he went to see if the toy had been taken. It was gone, but in its place lay a beautiful cake, hot from the pixies' oven, as his reward.

Tavistock *Devon*

Fitzford Gate is all that remains of the ancient Fitzford mansion that once stood on the west side of the town. Several times a year, it is said, the ghost of Lady Howard rides out from the gate in her coach of bones, drawn by headless horses and preceded by a black hound with one eye in its forehead. This gruesome cortège travels to Oke-hampton where the coach comes to a halt and Lady Howard descends. She picks a blade of grass from the churchyard, presses it sadly to her bosom, and then rides back to Fitzford Gate. The reason for this curious pilgrimage is said to be that Lady Howard, who was born in 1596 and was twice widowed before she reached the age of 16, murdered all four of her husbands. The legend can be no more than three-quarters true at best, for her fourth husband outlived her.

Totnes *Devon*

A curious legend tells that Brutus, the leader of the survivors of the Trojan garrison, sailed up the River Dart, stepped off on a rock and proclaimed:
>   Here I am and here I rest,
>   And this town shall be called Totnes.

The country around was inhabited by giants, and having captured a pair named Gog and Magog, he took them to London where they stood guard outside his palace. The effigies of the two giants still stand in the Guildhall, replacements of earlier effigies destroyed by fire during the Second World War. The Brutus Stone, the stone on which the Trojan leader is supposed to have stood, is set into the pavement in Fore Street near the East Gate.

Uplyme *Devon*

A farm worker living in a cottage in the village found his home plagued by the phantom of a large black dog. One day, in desperation, he took a poker and chased the ghost into his attic where it leapt through the roof. Hitting at the thatch, the man found a hoard of Stuart coins, which helped to buy a house on the other side of the road. He converted the house into an inn and, in gratitude, named it 'The Black Dog'. The inn is still there, and the dog continues to haunt the neighbourhood, particularly the lane behind the inn. It has been seen several times in the present century, its last recorded appearance being in 1959, when it was seen by three holidaymakers simultaneously one evening.

Wareham *Dorset*

On the four evenings before the last Friday in November, a group of strangely dressed men visit many of the public houses in the town, checking on the quality and quantity of the food and drink supplied by each landlord. These men are officials of the Court Leet, which in Norman times was the main judicial and local government court in many parts of the country. A few courts, such as the one at Wareham, still preserve the ceremonies, though their judicial powers have ceased. The officials include the Ale-tasters, who use pewter measures over 200 years old; the Bread-weighers, who carry an ancient pair of scales; the Carnisters who taste the meat; and the Surveyors and Searchers of Mantles and Chimneys, who check flues for obstructions, for Wareham has a history of serious fires.

ST WITE'S SHRINE

Whitchurch Canonicorum church contains both the shrine and the remains of St Wite, a holy woman of unknown medieval date. Her 13th-century shrine (above) has three apertures, into which pilgrims thrust diseased limbs or bandages in the hope of miraculous cures

Widecombe-in-the-Moor *Devon*

Widecombe Fair – which still takes place on the second Tuesday in September – is famed the world over for the song that recounts the adventures of Uncle Tom Cobleigh, his friends, and the unfortunate grey mare. The song was once widespread throughout the West Country, and was freely adapted to suit any locality and personalities.

Nevertheless, Uncle Tom Cobleigh was a real farmer from Spreyton in North Devon, 12 miles north of Widecombe. It is uncertain which Tom has been immortalised – there were several of that name in the family – but it was probably the one who died in 1794 and is buried in an unmarked grave in Spreyton churchyard. The Thomas Cobleigh whose tombstone is outside the south porch was his nephew.

Old 'Uncle Tom' was an amorous bachelor, and when he was young had bright red hair. This characteristic seems to have been to his advantage, for when paternity orders came in thick and fast, he refused to maintain any babies that did not have red hair like himself.

Early this century, the novelist Beatrice Chase presented an 'Uncle Tom' smock to the organisers of the fair, and now Uncle Tom appears at the festivities every year, complete with his grey mare.

OFF TO WIDECOMBE

The sign on the village green at Widecombe-in-the-Moor shows Tom Pearse's famous grey mare carrying Uncle Tom Cobleigh and his companions to Widecombe Fair

Winterbourne Whitechurch *Dorset*

A few yards west of the village crossroads is a field known as the Round Meadow. Local legend claims that because the field was once reaped on a Sunday, it was accursed and no crops would grow.

Eventually the Round Meadow was chosen as the site of a new church, but no matter how many stones were laid, they were moved each night and found next morning in another field. After weeks of unprofitable labour, the villagers concluded that the curse still operated and that divine disapproval was being expressed about building the church on such a site. Finally, it was built near the stone quarry, where it still stands. The Round Meadow is still cursed, apparently; it is said that, however brilliant the weather, any attempt to mow the field will always bring rain and storms.

Wool *Dorset*

Woolbridge Manor, a Jacobean house by the River Frome, was once the property of the Turberville family. It is said that a spectral coach-and-four drives from the manor at twilight, but can only be seen by those of Turberville blood, to whom it foretells disaster. A few years ago, the driver of a local bus refused to move his vehicle until 'this there coach be gone through they there doors'. For the legend to be correct, the bus driver must have had Turberville antecedents.

Thomas Hardy adapted the Turberville name for his novel *Tess of the D'Urbervilles*, in which Tess believes she has seen the coach, and disaster does indeed follow.

Woolacombe *Devon*

Sir William de Tracy, one of the four knights who murdered St Thomas à Becket at Canterbury, lived at Mortehoe, near this village. Because of the knight's sensational crime, numerous legends associated with the family have sprung up in the surrounding villages. At Woolacombe, it is said that his ghost endlessly attempts to spin a rope from sand; if he seems likely to succeed, a black dog appears with a ball of fire in its mouth and burns through the flimsy cord. In rough weather, Sir William is said to ride howling up and down the sands, in accordance with the saying that the Tracys 'had ever the wind and the rain in their faces'.

Yeovil *Somerset*

An amazing instance of the power of a witch's spell was recorded in this town in 1657. It was claimed that an old woman had offered a magic apple to a young boy. Regardless of all past warnings, he had taken a bite, whereupon 'he rose in the air and flew about 300 yards', according to a witness at the old woman's trial. The witch was hanged at Chard in 1658.

Zeal Monachorum *Devon*

The home of the Oxenham family, this village sprang to fame in 1635 when, during an outbreak of disease, all Oxenhams who were not going to recover were visited by a bird with a white breast, which fluttered over their beds. It was remembered that previous deaths had been marked by similar visitations, and Charles Kingsley used the phenomenon as an incident in his book *Westward Ho!* The bird has appeared to dying Oxenhams on several occasions in this century. It does not seem to be confined to Devon; in one instance it was seen in Kensington, West London.

MOTHER HUBBARD'S COTTAGE

Yealmpton was the reputed home of Old Mother Hubbard, the nursery rhyme character created by Sarah Martin at nearby Kitley in 1805. The cottage above is known as Old Mother Hubbard's, though it is doubtful if the real character, who was housekeeper at Kitley in Sarah Martin's time, ever lived there

THE WITCH IN WOOKEY HOLE

Over millions of years the River Axe steadily wore away the limestone to form the series of caves known as Wookey Hole. Stone Age hunters lived there, and evidence of this occupation has been found in the form of human remains, pottery and crude jewellery.

Where the Axe flows through the first three chambers of the caves, there are many colourful stalagmite and stalactite formations. One stalagmite is said to be the Witch of Wookey, turned to stone for her evil ways.

Frightened villagers
The witch was supposed to have lived in the caves with her familiars, a goat and its kid. She had once been crossed in love, and out of vindictiveness she cast spells on the villagers of Wookey.

Frightened by her wicked deeds, the people appealed in desperation to the Abbot of Glastonbury to rid them of the hag.

Turned to stone
A monk was sent to the caves to confront the witch. Since evil cannot prevail against good, she knew her spells were powerless against him and tried to flee. But the monk sprinkled her with holy water, and she turned to stone where she stands today, on the bank of the Axe in the Great Cave at Wookey Hole.

Another version of the legend says that the witch was feared throughout Somerset, but her special malevolence was directed against lovers. The monk who turned her into stone had taken holy vows after the witch had wrecked, by her spells, his forth-

coming wedding to a local girl.

In 1912, excavations in the caves revealed the bones of a Romano-British woman. Near by were the bones of a goat and kid, together with a comb, a dagger and a round stalagmite like a witch's crystal ball. These relics are now in Wells museum.

A would-be king
Legend also tells that a giant conger eel, some 30 ft long, lies hidden in Wookey Hole. The creature decided to swim up the Severn to become king of the river. But on his way he destroyed many salmon nets and flooded the countryside with his tremendous flounderings. The fishermen drove him back and forced him to swim up the narrow River Axe, where he squeezed into Wookey Hole, and remains stuck for ever.

A WITCH'S EFFIGY *The huge stalagmite known as the Witch of Wookey, her bonnet and nose in sharp relief, commemorates a witch who was supposed to have lived in the caves at Wookey Hole near the town of Wells*

CRADLE OF A NATION

Berkshire, Hampshire, Isle of Wight, Oxfordshire, Wiltshire

England was born on the blood-drenched slopes of the southern chalk-lands some 1100 years ago, fathered by a Saxon king whose courage so transformed his land that history awarded him the simple but supreme title, the Great. When Alfred was crowned King of Wessex in AD 871, pagan Danish Vikings ruled Mercia, a huge kingdom whose southern boundary ran from the mouth of the Thames to the Severn Estuary; and with increasing success, bands of Viking raiders hungry for fresh farmland were hacking their way south into the rich and rolling territory of the Saxons. By the time of his death in 899, the warrior Alfred had become overlord of a united England; Mercia, Northumbria, East Anglia and Wessex all acknowledged him as monarch. Watered by the blood of numberless Danes and Saxons, and nurtured on the dreams of a single great soldier, a nation had been born.

Wessex was Alfred's homeland, and it is in Berkshire, Wiltshire and Hampshire (the names are new, but the land remains the same) that his memory, and the more painful memory of the Danish wars, live on most vividly.

In a cottage garden near Kingston Lyle is the Blowing Stone; by sounding a note on it, which is said to be audible 3 miles away, Alfred summoned his Saxons to fight. At Marden in Wiltshire, people still remember, however vaguely, a cruel battle fought near by between black-haired and red-haired men; at South Baddesley in Hampshire, a stream runs red with the blood of slaughtered Danes. Just over the border into Mercia, at Little Rollright in Oxfordshire, a king and his army, turned to stone by a witch, stand waiting on a windswept ridge of the Cotswolds. Could this be Alfred's hated enemy King Guthrum, with his last remaining regiment of Vikings?

But the farmsteads across which Alfred fought for his dream were already ancient long before the Saxons settled there. At least 3000 years earlier, a very different breed of men had tilled the southern fields and grazed their sheep in the hills. In Saxon Wessex no less than today, the relics of prehistory cast a long and mysterious shadow across the land. Strange figures and white horses straddled the chalk hillsides; ancient trackways, as old as any in Britain, ran along the ridges. Most marvellous of all were Stonehenge and Avebury, the great stone temples of forgotten gods. More than any other place in Britain, Stonehenge evokes the darkest and most distant reach of history. Who built it, and why, may never be known with any certainty; but the power that resides in the temple has in no way diminished as its meaning has receded into the past.

THE FOLKLORE YEAR

Daily (on request)
Winchester, Hants
Wayfarer's Dole at the Hospital of St Cross

March 25
Tichborne, Hants
Tichborne Dole

Second Tuesday after Easter
Hungerford, Berks
Hocktide ceremonies in memory of John of Gaunt

May Day
Oxford, Oxon
May Carol on Magdalen Tower
Southampton, Hants
May Carol at the Bargate

May 29 (Oak Apple Day)
Great Wishford, Wilts
Grovely Procession

Spring Bank Holiday
Bampton, Oxon
Morris Dancing

Saturday nearest June 19
Abingdon, Oxon
Morris Dancing and Election of Ock Street Mayor

Monday after June 29
Yarnton, Oxon
Meadow Mowing Rights and Mead Balls

October 21
Portsmouth, Hants
Trafalgar Day Ceremony

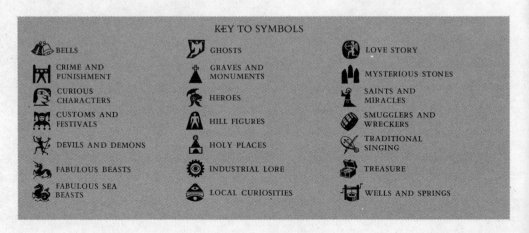

KEY TO SYMBOLS

BELLS

CRIME AND PUNISHMENT

CURIOUS CHARACTERS

CUSTOMS AND FESTIVALS

DEVILS AND DEMONS

FABULOUS BEASTS

FABULOUS SEA BEASTS

GHOSTS

GRAVES AND MONUMENTS

HEROES

HILL FIGURES

HOLY PLACES

INDUSTRIAL LORE

LOCAL CURIOSITIES

LOVE STORY

MYSTERIOUS STONES

SAINTS AND MIRACLES

SMUGGLERS AND WRECKERS

TRADITIONAL SINGING

TREASURE

WELLS AND SPRINGS

N

0   5   10
MILES

WARWICKSHIRE   NORTHAMPTONSHIRE

BEDS

BLOXHAM
(Satan's Guide, 172)   ADDERBURY

CHASTLETON   LITTLE ROLLRIGHT
               (Rollright Stones, 177)
               OXFORDSHIRE

WOODSTOCK   AMBROSDEN
                   (Satan's Guide, 172)

SHIPTON–UNDER–
WYCHWOOD
FINSTOCK   YARNTON
MINSTER LOVELL   OT MOOR

GLOUCESTERSHIRE   BUCKINGHAMSHIRE

BAMPTON   CUMNOR   OXFORD

FARINGDON   ABINGDON   CLIFTON HAMPDEN
                           WITTENHAM

MALMESBURY   RODBOURNE CHENEY   STRATTON
             PURTON   ST MARGARET
SHERSTON   UFFINGTON   BLEWBURY   BISHAM
                                 (White Horse, 187)
                         SWINDON   BRAY
DRAYCOT CERNE WOOTTON   ALDWORTH
LANGLEY   BASSETT
BURRELL   BERKSHIRE
BREMHILL   BROAD   WINDSOR
              HINTON   LITTLECOTE   BUCKLEBURY READING   *(Phantom Huntsman, 189)*
LACOCK   AVEBURY   HALL
SILBURY   *(Stone   NEWBURY ALDERMASTON
HILL   Circles, 171)* HUNGERFORD
DEVIZES   HIGHCLERE
BISHOPS CANNINGS   WILCOT
(The Moonrakers, 170) MARDEN   VERNHAM
                                      DEAN
                                                 BASING
CLEY
HILL   WARMINSTER   BULFORD   SOUTH TIDWORTH
             WILTSHIRE   ABBOTTS ANN   PRESTON
LONGLEAT   CANDOVER
                         STONEHENGE   WHERWELL
GREAT WISHFORD *(Temple & Plain, 184)* CHILBOLTON   ALTON
                                         HAMPSHIRE
                                                       LIPHOOK
             BRAISHFIELD   WINCHESTER   TICHBORNE

                          OWSLEBURY   WEST

BREAMORE   SUSSEX
MILSTEAD   SOUTHAMPTON HAMBLEDON
(New Forest, 178)
ELLINGHAM   LYNDHURST
             (New Forest, 178)
         BURLEY   BEAULIEU
         BOLDRE   PORTSMOUTH
CHRISTCHURCH   SOUTH
               BADDESLEY
                          ISLE OF
                          WIGHT
                     MOTTISTONE
                     GATCOMBE

DORSET
SURREY

THE MOONRAKERS

Between the 15th and 18th centuries, Wiltshire wool had a reputation second to none in Europe. High profits attracted Dutch and Flemish merchants who, during most of the period, had a permanent headquarters in Swindon. Business was good, but the merchants had a problem; Hollands gin, their favourite drink, was unobtainable unless a heavy import duty was paid.

To Wiltshiremen, the solution was obvious; by the mid-16th century they had established a smuggling organisation that ran with clockwork precision for more than 200 years. Barrels of spirits were landed in quiet coves on the Hampshire coast and were brought north to Swindon in a series of night journeys.

During the day, the barrels were hidden in church crypts or beneath the green weeds of village ponds. Hundreds of people became involved, as the fame of Hollands gin spread far beyond the Dutch merchants, and as the organisation extended its scope to include tobacco and brandy.

Fishing for the moon

No one knows just where the most famous story of the Wiltshire smugglers took place, though the best claims are probably those of the villages of Bishops Cannings and All Cannings.

The tale goes that one moonlit night, when the smugglers were raking their kegs out of a village pond, they were surprised by a patrol of Excisemen. With a flash of inspiration, the smugglers feigned idiocy; mopping and mowing before the Excisemen, they pointed to the moon's reflection in the pond and told them they were trying to rake out a piece of the moon that had fallen from the sky. In some versions, they said it was a cheese that they were trying to recover. Laughing at such rustic simplicity, the patrol rode on. But Wiltshiremen are called Moonrakers to this day.

Abbotts Ann *Hants*
Originating in pre-Reformation times, the hanging of Maidens' Garlands from church walls is a custom now carried on only at Abbotts Ann. Made of white paper or linen, the garlands are memorials to young virgins of either sex who died within the parish. The garlands resemble a bishop's mitre decorated with paper roses, and were carried in the person's funeral procession before being placed in the church. They usually have five white paper gauntlets attached, symbolising a challenge to anyone who disputes the dead person's spotless character. Some 40 garlands hang in the church at Abbotts Ann, the earliest dating from 1716. The most recent was hung in 1953.

Abingdon *Oxon*
Every year on the Saturday nearest to June 19, the Mayor of Ock Street is elected by those who live there. The candidates are usually Morris dancers, and the winner also becomes Squire of the local Morris Men, who celebrate his victory by dancing outside the town's pubs. The tradition began in 1700 at Abingdon's annual St Edmund's Day Fair when, as was the custom, an ox was roasted and its meat distributed to the poor. An argument arose over the ox horns, and a wild struggle ensued for possession of them. An Ock Street resident, who was also Squire of the Morris dancers, emerged victorious and was declared the Mayor of Ock Street. The same horns and skull, set on a decorated pole, are now part of the Mayor's regalia and are brought out on view whenever the dancers perform.

Adderbury *Oxon*
Several poachers have reported seeing Sir George Cobb's phantom coach-and-four crossing the parkland near Cobb House, its horses breathing fire. Sir George was the last occupant of Cobb House, which once faced Adderbury Green, and was demolished in the early 19th century. He gave orders that four particular oak trees in the park were never to be felled. However, shortly after his death in 1762, the trees were cut down, whereupon Sir George's ghost appeared and haunted that spot.

Aldermaston *Berks*
Every three years, in Aldermaston Village Hall, a candle auction is held for the lease-rights to lands owned by the Church. A horseshoe nail is stuck sideways into a candle, and bidding begins as the candle is lit. As it burns down and reaches the nail, the flame expires and the nail falls out. The last bid made before this happens secures the lease, and rents so obtained are devoted to charity. Candle auctions were revived here in 1815, but began several centuries earlier.

Aldworth *Berks*
In the Middle Ages, Aldworth parish church was the private chapel of the Norman family of de la Beche. Inside the church are the 'Aldworth Giants', nine life-size monuments dedicated to men of the family, some of whom, apparently, were over 7 ft tall. Traditionally, three of these statues are called Long John, John Strong and John Neverafraid. A tenth statue, named John Everafraid is now missing, but once stood in an alcove, half inside and half outside the church. John Everafraid was thought to have made a pact with the Devil whereby he received worldly riches in exchange for his soul, which the Devil would take whether John was buried inside or outside the church. He outwitted Satan by being buried in neither place, so saving his soul from damnation.

Alton *Hants*
The gruesome event that gave the expression 'Sweet Fanny Adams' to the English language occurred here in 1867. On a warm August afternoon, young Fanny Adams went off with her sister and a friend to play in a hop field. The two other girls later returned home without her. A search party was organised, and Fanny's dismembered body was found in a nearby field. Frederick Baker, a local solicitor's clerk, was identified as the killer and was hanged at Winchester on December 24. The Royal Navy at this time was being issued with low-grade tinned meat instead of its traditional salt tack, and the sailors were quick to associate Fanny's disappearance with their new rations. 'Sweet Fanny Adams' soon passed into common usage as a phrase signifying worthlessness.

SECRET OF THE GOLDEN CALF

Now in ruins, Basing House, Hants, is shown above as it looked in the 17th century when it was the home of Charles Paulet, Marquis of Winchester. During the Civil War, Paulet held the house for three years against a siege by Oliver Cromwell's troops. The Roundheads finally battered the house into submission in 1645, and blew it up. Thought to be buried somewhere in the ruins is a golden calf, made from the Paulet family's melted-down gold plate and hidden during the siege. Until recently, the ghost of Cromwell himself used to be seen there, walking from the old tithe barn at Lyckpit across Plovers Dell. And at nearby Hook, an unknown Cavalier's ghost wearing a wide-brimmed hat, lace ruffles, and a loose cloak has been seen on the Common

Bampton *Oxon*

For nearly 500 years the Bampton Morris Men celebrated Whit Monday by dancing in the town; they now perform on Spring Bank Holiday. They are accompanied everywhere by the traditional Fiddler, the Fool with a bladder on a stick, and a Swordbearer. Impaled on his sword is a large plum cake, pieces of which he distributes for luck.

Beaulieu *Hants*

Beaulieu Abbey, now a ruin, was founded in 1204 by Cistercian monks. Tradition has it that a group of the monks visited King John in 1201 to ask him for exemption from taxation. Their request so angered the king that he imprisoned them overnight, ordering that they were to be trampled to death by horses the following morning. That night he dreamt that he was flogged for his cruelty, and when he awoke there were lash-marks on his back. The repentant king released the monks and gave them the lands at Beaulieu together with permission to build an abbey.

The Cistercians lived and worked there for 300 years until the Dissolution in 1538. In 1928, the ghost of a monk was seen by a woman at Beaulieu. He told her to dig in a certain spot where she would find a coffer containing 'two round stones and some bones'. She found them, and gave them Christian burial. Since then, several visitors to the abbey have reported hearing the devotional chanting of monks within the ruins.

AVEBURY STONE CIRCLES

Most of Avebury village lies within the largest prehistoric monument in Europe. Built about 1800 BC by Celtic farmer-shepherds, the huge size of the Avebury Circles indicates the existence of a large, well-organised population controlled by priests. The monument was formerly believed to have been dedicated to serpent worship because the plan suggested a coiled snake, but it is now thought that it was an open temple where fertility rites were practised.

Surrounded by a bank and ditch 1400 ft in diameter, the main circle is formed by nearly 100 upright sarsen stones, some of which weigh up to 60 tons. The Avenue, which runs between pairs of standing megaliths, connects Avebury with the Sanctuary, a smaller temple on Overton Down 1½ miles away.

Medieval destruction

In the Middle Ages, the Church became alarmed by the revival of pagan rites, and gave orders for the megaliths to be buried. Under one of them, in 1938, a man's skeleton was found along with several coins and surgical tools that identified him as a surgeon-barber who died in about 1320. He was probably killed when the stone he was helping to bury fell on him. In the 17th and 18th centuries, farmers used many of the remaining megaliths for local building purposes, but nearly all the original stones were recovered in a massive restoration of the site this century.

RELIGIOUS CENTRE *It is believed that pilgrims from all over Britain came to Avebury for ceremonies which may have included cannibalism and ritual sacrifices*

THE AVENUE *The map shows the linking route to the Sanctuary*

ENCIRCLED *The village lies surrounded by the Bronze Age temple*

the cause, her troubled spirit has continued to manifest itself in the East Wing of the abbey right into this century. She is said to wander about, constantly trying to wash her bloodstained hands in a ghostly basin.

Bisham *Berks*

Bisham Abbey is said to be haunted by the ghost of Dame Elizabeth Hoby, who lived there during the 16th century. Her apparition has been several times described as resembling a photographic negative, with dark skin and a glaring white dress. A brilliant scholar and close friend of Elizabeth I, Dame Hoby is reputed to have beaten her young son William because he was lazy at his studies. The boy is thought to have had a brain disease that proved fatal when it was aggravated by his mother's beatings. After his death, Dame Hoby suffered from a sense of remorse that lasted until her own death in 1609. Whatever

Blewbury *Oxon*

In 1781, a Mr Morgan-Jones became curate-in-charge of Blewbury parish at an annual salary of £50. Notorious for his extreme miserliness, he somehow kept himself alive on his 'surplice allowance' of £5 a year, investing all his other income. 'Blewbury Jones' is said to have saved £18,000 before he died. His threadbare clothes and mouldering shoes were preserved after his death but have now been lost.

Another notable Blewbury character was Malachi Grace who, early in the 19th century, was landlord of what is now the Bluebury Inn. He also worked as

SATAN'S GUIDE TO OXFORDSHIRE

The Icknield Way is a pre-historic road that runs across England from The Wash to Wiltshire. For much of its length it is still a green track, said to be haunted at twilight by Roman legionaries, Black Dogs and perhaps Boadicea's charioteers who galloped along it on their way to sack St Albans in AD 61. The part of the Way that runs east of Watlington and skirts Swyncombe Downs in Oxfordshire was believed to lead directly to the World's End, and from there to Hell. A Watlington man who put the matter to the test affirmed that, after a long walk, he came to a range of fiery mountains and was unable to proceed further because of a smell of burning sulphur.

Satanic mason

Perhaps it was this easy means of access which enabled the Devil to devote so much of his time to Oxfordshire where, contrary to his usual practice, he seems to have

helped mankind almost as often as he vexed it. The two 14th-century church spires of Adderbury and Bloxham are credited as being partly the Devil's work. The story goes that the two brothers who built the two churches employed an itinerant mason who, without payment, worked many times faster than his mates. The contract was completed in record time, and the mason disappeared, leaving behind him a faint whiff of sulphur and an uneasy recollection of his curiously shaped feet.

On the other hand, it is said that when the foundations of the Church of St Mary were being laid in a field called Church Leys at Ambrosden, the Devil for some reason disapproved of the site. Each morning the builders found that the materials they had placed in the field on the previous day had been mysteriously moved to another spot. Finally, the workers became tired of the double labour and built the church on the site

chosen by the Devil. A similar tale is told of the Church of St Peter and St Paul at Checkendon. There, the intended site of the building is still known as the Devil's Churchyard.

Sunday sinners

At Northleigh, Satan seems to have concerned himself principally with Sabbath breakers. One fine Sunday a group of neighbours decided to go badger-hunting instead of attending church. After a long struggle, they dragged a particularly large badger from its sett and pushed it into a sack. When they reached home, however, the creature had vanished; all that remained was an 'awful smell of brimstone'. On another Sunday in Northleigh, several boys played cricket together. An interested spectator – a stranger – joined in, and proved to be an outstanding player. As he bowled out the last batsman, he suddenly disappeared in a cloud of smoke.

a carter, conveying goods to Newbury and back. He enjoyed a drink, and rarely arrived home sober. One night, some local pranksters found him asleep in his cart by the roadside. Unharnessing his horse, they pulled the cart into a nearby barn and hid in the loft. At length Malachi awoke, observed that his horse was missing, and said 'Be I Malachi Grace? Be I Malachi Grace? If I be I've lost a horse, and if I baint I've found a cart'.

Boldre *Hants*

During the 17th century, part of what is now Bywater House was a cottage owned by a smuggler. It was enlarged and, early this century, became the home of Mrs Gordon-Hamilton. She and her guests often heard the sound of rolling barrels and hurried footsteps in the house. Through a friend, who was a medium, she learnt that a young man had been murdered there in 1685. Staying at the cottage overnight, he had been carrying secret despatches for the Duke of Monmouth, who had just been defeated by the forces of James II in the Battle of Sedgemoor.

The smuggler's daughter coveted the messenger's jewellery and persuaded her lover to murder him. After doing so, they buried his body in the garden. In a photograph of Mrs Gordon-Hamilton taken about 1920, the profile of a youth with Cavalier curls also appears. It was shown to a friend who afterwards dreamt that the young man took her to a place in the garden and told her to dig there. This was done next day and at the selfsame spot was discovered a well-preserved but empty secret chamber made of narrow, 17th-century bricks.

Braishfield *Hants*

Windmill Cottage in Dark Lane, Braishfield, is said to be haunted. Early this century, a wealthy woman in the area became obsessed with the fear that her money would be stolen, so she buried it secretly somewhere near the cottage. Shortly afterwards, she died without revealing the hiding-place of the hoard. Her ghost has been seen and heard many times, walking under a nearby yew tree, knocking at the cottage door or sitting by the garden gate. Dogs have been known to growl and bristle when they go near the yew tree.

Bray *Berks*

And this is law, I will maintain,
Unto my dying day, Sir,
That whatsoever King shall reign,
I will be the Vicar of Bray, Sir!

So runs the refrain from the well-known song, 'The Vicar of Bray'. Though the song suggests that this fickle churchman spanned the reigns of Charles I to Queen Anne, the true vicar is thought to have been Simon Aleyn, who held the living of Bray parish much earlier—from 1540 to 1588. It is said that he was a papist under Henry VIII, a Protestant under Edward VI, a papist again under Queen Mary, and then a Protestant in the reign of Queen Elizabeth. When reproached with his religious inconstancy, Aleyn replied that he had always been unchanging in his resolution to remain the Vicar of Bray.

Breamore *Hants*

On Breamore Down, three-quarters of a mile north-west of Breamore House, is a curious labyrinth of interconnecting pathways cut into the turf. Called a miz-maze, it dates from medieval times and is one of seven such constructions scattered throughout England. It is thought to have been associated with an Augustine priory which once stood near by. As a form of penance, the monks were made to crawl on their knees to the centre of the maze, and then to crawl out again.

Bremhill *Wilts*

Between Bremhill and Chippenham runs 4½ miles of elevated footpath known as Maud Heath's Causeway. The widow Maud died in 1474. During her long life she had been sorely vexed by the muddy, uneven ground over which she had to carry the butter and eggs she sold at Chippenham market. Her will stipulated that all her worldly goods, which probably amounted to no more than £14, be devoted to the building and maintenance of a good footpath along that route. The only piece of original causeway runs over land which often floods; the rest is pavement beside the road. On Wick Hill, near Bremhill, is a stone inscribed:

'From this Wick Hill begins the praise
Of Maud Heath's gift to these Highways'

Near by she is figured on a high column as a lady dressed in the costume of the period of Edward IV, with her bonnet, shawl and basket of eggs.

A BLASPHEMER'S PUNISHMENT

In Broad Hinton church, Wiltshire, is a 16th-century monument dedicated to the Wroughton family. Sir Thomas Wroughton and his wife Anne are shown above, kneeling in prayer. Sir Thomas is said to have returned from hunting one day to find Anne reading the Bible instead of cooking his supper. Enraged, he grabbed the Book from her and threw it into the fire. She managed to rescue it, but badly burnt her hands in doing so. As a punishment for this blasphemy, Sir Thomas's hands and those of his four children withered away. On the monument, all five are shown without hands. There is also a Bible with a corner missing to show where it was burnt

Bucklebury *Berks*
After the Reformation, the village of Bucklebury came under the control of the Winchcombe family, descendants of the famed wool-merchant, Jack of Newbury. In 1700, Frances Winchcombe married the first Lord Bolingbroke, Henry St John. Impeached by George I after Queen Anne's death in 1714, he fled to exile in France, leaving his wife behind. After waiting for him for three years, she finally pined away and died. Lady Bolingbroke's ghost has been said to haunt the area ever since, riding in an open carriage drawn by black horses.

Bulford *Wilts*
A macabre suicide is alleged to have occurred here early in the 18th century. A local cobbler greatly angered the villagers by the harsh way in which he treated his apprentice, so they paraded his effigy through the streets and then hanged it from a mock gallows. The ceremony was repeated each day until in despair, the man turned to his best friend for advice. He was told that the wisest course of action would be to carry out the will of the people; so the shoemaker hanged himself.

Burley *Hants*
A legend says that a dragon once lived on Burley Beacon. Every day it flew down to nearby Bisterne to demand a pail of milk. Knowing it was fond of sheep, the villagers willingly provided it with milk, hoping to save their flocks. In time, weary of its extortion, they hired a knight to slay the beast. The knight covered himself with birdlime and ground glass, as a protection against the dragon's fiery breath, and killed it after a fierce battle. There is still a Dragon Lane at Bisterne, and a carved dragon can be seen above the entrance to Bisterne Park.

Chastleton *Oxon*
One of the bedrooms in Chastleton House, which is open to the public, has a secret chamber. On the night of September 3, 1651, Arthur Jones, the owner of the house, rode home from the Battle of Worcester where he had fought by the side of Charles II. Minutes later a group of Cromwell's soldiers arrived. Jones hid himself in the secret room as the Roundheads began to search the house. Finding nothing, they settled for the night in the bedroom next to his hiding-place, and demanded a meal from Mrs Jones. She gave them well-drugged wine and they were soon unconscious, enabling Jones to escape. It was two years before he returned to Chastleton again. The bedroom has since been known as 'The Cavalier Room'.

Chilbolton *Hants*
Chilbolton Rectory is said to be haunted by a nun. The window where her apparition most often appeared was eventually bricked up to discourage her but, a few years ago, her ghost was again seen by two guests at the rectory. One said that he had seen a beautiful nurse gazing out of a window; the other awoke in the night and saw a nurse standing by his bed. The rector confirmed that there was no such person in the house on either occasion. In 1393, a nun named Katherine Faukener ran away from the nearby Benedictine Abbey of St Cross at Wherwell. On her return seven years later, she is believed to have been walled up alive on the site of the rectory, which was then a nunnery.

Christchurch *Dorset*
The town's Priory Church, construction of which commenced in the late 11th century, was originally planned to occupy a site on top of St Catherine's Hill, and workmen began the long task of hauling building materials up the hill. But each night these were mysteriously moved back down the hill, to where the church now stands. Believing this to be a sign from God, the labourers began to build the church on the new site.

They were soon joined by a strange carpenter who refused pay and ate no food. As work neared completion, a crucial beam for the roof was found to be a foot too short. Dismayed, the workmen went home. When they returned the next morning, the beam was a perfect fit, and was already in position in the roof. The mysterious stranger was never seen again, but the men believed that their workmate had been Christ himself and in his honour named the building Christ's Church. Twynham, as the town was then called, was also renamed Christchurch.

Cley Hill *Wilts*
A legend attributes the building of Cley Hill, an earthworks near Warminster, to the Devil. Displeased with the people of Devizes, Satan was returning from Somerset with a huge sack of earth on his back to throw at the town. Passing another walker, he asked the distance to Devizes. The old man replied that he had been searching for the town for so long that his hair had turned grey, whereupon the Devil lost heart and threw his load of earth on the ground, so forming the hill.

Clifton Hampden *Oxon*
Much neglected by her husband, the beautiful Sarah Fletcher lived a sad and lonely life at Courtiers House in Clifton Hampden. Finally, in despair over his infidelity, she hanged herself in her bedroom there in 1799. Though her tomb is in Dorchester Abbey, her ghost has often appeared in the house. Those who have reported seeing it claim that the purple ribbon she always wore in her curly auburn hair is distinctly visible, as well as the expression of anguish on her face.

Cumnor *Oxon*
Until its demolition in 1810, Cumnor Hall was said to be haunted by the ghost of 28-year-old Amy Robsart, wife of Robert Dudley, one of the favourite courtiers of Elizabeth I. On September 8, 1560, Amy was found lying dead with her neck broken at the bottom of the staircase. It was suspected that her husband had plotted her death so that he could marry Elizabeth. Nothing was ever proved and Dudley, later Earl of Leicester, remained the Queen's favourite for the rest of his life. But in 1588, while staying at Cornbury Park, Oxfordshire, he was said to have met his wife's ghost in nearby Wychwood Forest, when she warned him that he would soon join her. A few days later he died of a sudden illness. It is said that her phantom still roams Cornbury Park and to see this ghost is a certain warning that death is imminent.

Devizes *Wilts*
Inscribed on the cross in Devizes market-place is the cautionary tale of Ruth Pearce. In 1753, she and two other women agreed to divide the cost of a sack of wheat between them. Their payment was found to be threepence short of the price asked, but all three protested that they had contributed their correct share. Ruth Pearce declared that, if she had cheated, she wished to fall down dead on the spot. She did, and the missing threepence was found clutched in her lifeless hand.

THE PROTECTIVE HAND

In 1610, Sir Walter Long, urged on by his second wife, hired a clerk to change his will so as to prevent his son John from inheriting Draycot Cerne Manor, Wilts. But each time the clerk tried to write the vital clause, a white hand appeared between parchment and candle. It was said to have been that of John's mother, Long's first wife

Ellingham *Hants*
Moyles Court in Ellingham was once the home of Dame Alice Lisle who, in 1685, was tried by the infamous Judge Jeffreys. Accused of sheltering two fugitives from the Battle of Sedgemoor, she was condemned to death though she was over 70 years old. The unusual sentence of burning was later changed to beheading, and was carried out at Winchester the same year. Since then her ghost is sometimes heard in Moyles Court, and she has been seen riding down Ellingham Lane in a driverless coach drawn by two headless horses.

Finstock *Oxon*
A relic of ancient well-worship, originally forbidden by the Church in AD 963, still continues in Finstock. On Palm Sunday, local children make a concoction of liquorice and water from the Lady's Well at Wilcote in Wychwood Forest, and then drink it.

Gatcombe, *Isle of Wight*
Carved in oak on his tomb in Gatcombe church is the effigy of Edward Estur, a 14th-century crusader. In 1364, he went to the Holy Land accompanied by his mistress, Lucy Lightfoot. She stayed in Cyprus to await his return from the wars, but in Syria he suffered such severe head injuries that he forgot all about Lucy and returned to Gatcombe alone. They never saw one another again. In 1830, a young girl from Bowcombe became strangely infatuated with Edward's effigy. She constantly rode to the church and spent hours gazing at the knight's tomb. Asked why she did this, she said 'I love to be with him in my thoughts and dreams'. Just as she entered the church on the morning of June 13, 1831, a terrible storm blew up which was accompanied by an eclipse of the sun. When the gale died down, the girl's horse was found, but she was never seen again. This girl, too, was named Lucy Lightfoot.

Great Wishford *Wilts*
On Oak Apple Day, May 29, the villagers of Great Wishford celebrate a right, granted in 1603, to gather wood from nearby Grovely Forest. After decorating their homes with green oak boughs gathered in the forest early that morning, they travel to Salisbury. Brandishing boughs of oak and firewood, they dance outside the cathedral and then go inside where they all cry 'Grovely, Grovely and all Grovely! Unity is strength!'

MURDER AT SEA

Faringdon churchyard in Oxfordshire is said to be haunted by the headless ghost of Hampden Pye, an officer in the 18th-century Royal Navy. His step-mother bribed his captain to have his head blown off in a naval engagement.

Soon after, his headless ghost reappeared to sit beside his step-mother in her coach. His spectre also haunted the captain, a story recorded in the engraving by John Leech. The gunner, too, was visited by this terrible apparition.

In 1790, Hampden's cousin, Henry James Pye of Faringdon Hall, became Poet Laureate to George III. Notorious for his bad poetry, he was the first Laureate to be paid for his services. This is sometimes said to have inspired the nursery rhyme 'Sing a song of sixpence', which ridiculed the first poem he wrote for the king. It was so full of allusions to 'feathered songsters' that a contemporary wit said:

When the Pye was opened
The birds began to sing;
Wasn't that a dainty dish
To set before a king?

Hambledon *Hants*

Hambledon is called the 'Nursery of English Cricket'. Richard Nyren, a great cricket enthusiast, was the landlord of the Bat and Ball Inn (now the George Hotel). Responsible for the first attempt to formalise the rules of the game, he did much to make the sport nationally popular. He led the village team to victory against an 'All England' side in 1777 on a pitch on Broad-halfpenny Down.

Highclere *Hants*

The grampus is a dolphin-like beast that usually lives in the sea. One is said to have dwelt in the old yew tree by Highclere church, vexing everyone with its noisy breathing. It was fond of chasing the villagers, who retaliated by having it exorcised by a priest who banished the creature to the Red Sea for a thousand years. The date of its exile is lost, so no one knows when it will return.

Hungerford *Berks*

When John of Gaunt granted Hungerford special fishing and grazing rights in 1364, he also gave the town his hunting horn, which is preserved in the vaults of a local bank. Each year, on the second Tuesday after Easter, his patronage is commemorated at the Hocktide Festival. At 9 a.m. a replica of his horn is blown in the Corn Market, summoning Commoners to the Hocktide Court, presided over by a Jury which amends the rules governing the town's privileges. Two Tuttimen are elected and given Tutti poles, tall staves festooned with nosegays and ribbons. They are accompanied by the Orange-Scrambler, and all by tradition are entitled to a kiss from every woman in the town. Each woman kissed receives an orange. At lunchtime, the Court gathers at the Three Swans Hotel where a Hocktide Punch is drunk in memory of John of Gaunt.

Lacock *Wilts*

Against her parents' wishes, Olive Sharrington, the daughter of the owner of Lacock Abbey, became betrothed to John Talbot from near Worcester. One day in 1574, despairing of ever being allowed to marry him, she jumped off the abbey battlements.

THE KING'S MEN *By tradition, bad luck pursues anyone who tries to move or damage any of the Bronze Age Rollright Stones*

As she fell, her petticoats billowed out and slowed her descent, as did John, who was nearly killed when she landed on top of him. On John's recovery, Olive's father said that 'since she had made such leapes she should e'en marry him'. So she did.

Langley Burrell *Wilts*
Reginald de Cobham, the young lord of the manor of Langley Burrell, was a follower of John Wycliffe. Because Wycliffe's anti-papist teachings were believed to be heretical, Reginald was burnt at the stake in 1413. He was taken to the top of Steinbrook Hill, stripped, and slowly roasted to death. Tradition says he walks naked around the hill at midnight on moonlit nights, and surprisingly, considering the manner of his death, carries his head under his arm.

Liphook *Hants*
The spectre of a white calf haunts the countryside around Liphook, jumping hedges and trotting along the lanes. On occasion, it diminishes to the size of a cockerel, after which it vanishes completely. It is thought to be a fairy calf, and may have some connection with Liphook's other phantom, a mysterious little boy who has been seen and heard playing a flute. He, too, haunts the Liphook lanes, and his music is occasionally heard coming from the tops of trees and the hedgerows.

Littlecote House *Wilts*
One night in 1575, the local midwife was aroused by a masked man who blindfolded her and brought her to a strange house where she assisted a masked woman who gave birth to a son. Ignoring the horrified pleas of the mother and the midwife, the man snatched the child and threw it into the blazing fire. The midwife was blindfolded again, but before leaving, she managed to cut a piece of material from the bed-curtain, and counted the stairs as she was led from the house. This led to the house being identified as Littlecote, and the murderer as 'Wild' Darrell, the lord of the manor. Despite the midwife's evidence, Darrell was acquitted. But in 1589 while hunting in Littlecote Park, he was thrown from his horse and killed. Tradition holds that his horse had been frightened by the sudden apparition of a burning child. The place is still called 'Darrell's Stile', and is said to be haunted by his ghost. The child's mother – some say she was Darrell's sister – is supposed to haunt a landing in the house.

THE ROLLRIGHT STONES

For more than 2000 years a king and his conquering army have waited in the Cotswolds for someone with powerful magic to break the spell that turned them all to stone. That, at least, is how legend explains the Rollright Stones – in reality a Bronze Age 'cathedral' on the boundary between Oxfordshire and Warwickshire. The legend goes on to explain that the army is of indeterminate size: though rationalists insist that there are 72 stones, others maintain that 'The man will never live who shall count the stones three times and find the number the same'. The stones consist of a circle about 100 ft in diameter, the Whispering Knights, which form a separate group, and the King Stone standing apart from the others.

The army, it is said, had conquered all England as far north as Little Rollright before disaster struck. Marching up the hill on which the village stands, the victorious king met a witch, who said: 'Seven long strides thou shalt take! If Long Compton thou canst see, King of England thou shalt be!' Knowing that Long Compton was just over the brow of the hill, the king took seven strides forward. Unfortunately, a mound obscured his view, and the witch cackled: 'As Long Compton thou canst not see, thou and thy men hoar stones shalt be.' And stones they still remain.

The Rollright Stones are also said to have been a favourite haunt of Oxfordshire fairies and Warwickshire witches; and sometimes, it is claimed, they come alive at midnight, performing strange dances and even walking down to Little Rollright Spinney for a drink.

THE WHISPERING KNIGHTS *A lonely group of the king's army*

LONGLEAT GHOST
The Green Lady's Walk is a top-floor corridor in Longleat House, Wiltshire. In the 18th century, Thomas Thynne, the second Viscount Weymouth, is said to have killed his wife's lover in a duel there, and to have buried the body in the cellar. The grief-stricken ghost of his wife, Lady Louisa Carteret, has often been reported walking up and down the corridor. Early this century, a man's skeleton, wearing 18th-century boots, was found under the stone flags of the cellar floor

THE FLYING MONK
In the year 1010, Oliver the Monk made himself wings and attempted to fly from the top of the tower of Malmesbury Abbey, Wiltshire. He plummeted to the ground, and was crippled for the rest of his life. He is said to have prophesied the Norman Conquest when he saw Halley's Comet in 1066, saying 'I see thee most dreadfully threatening the destruction of England'

DEATH IN
The New Forest

At 7 o'clock on the evening of August 2, 1100, William II, nicknamed 'Rufus' because of his red hair, paused on the edge of a New Forest clearing and made his dispositions for the last drive of the day's hunting. His seven companions, armed like the king with longbow and arrows, hid themselves at strategic points among the trees, and the chief huntsman ordered the beaters to drive the deer forward. Almost at once, two stags trotted into the clearing, and the king raised his bow and shot. But with the westering sun slanting into his face, he only grazed the leading beast, and shielding his eyes from the glare with his arm, the king watched it gallop into the forest. At this point, according to the official version, Walter Tyrrel, a friend of the king, loosed off at the second stag; he also missed, and his arrow, deflected by the thick hair on the animal's back, ricocheted into William's heart. The king pitched forward, dead.

Horror-struck, his friends gathered around. It was pointed out to Tyrrel that the king had been slain by a new arrow, similar to those which William had given him that morning. Tyrrel denied responsibility; from the angle of his shot, he said, it would have been impossible for him to have hit the king. Nevertheless, realising that suspicion would inevitably fall upon him, he ran for his horse and galloped to Poole, where he took ship for Normandy. The remainder of the company also scattered, leaving William's body lying alone in the approaching dusk. About two hours later, it was found by a charcoal burner, who loaded it on to his cart and carried it 20 miles to Winchester. It was said that the king's blood watered the earth all the way.

The willing sacrifice

If Tyrrel's denial was true, and many contemporary accounts bear him out, then who did kill the king? And more important, why? Many of the facts would seem to point to a carefully planned assassination by William's youngest brother, the future Henry I, but there is another explanation.

One of the most widespread of pagan beliefs, and one which may have persisted into the Christian era, was the idea of the Divine Victim, the king who was also a god, and who, when called upon, was expected to give his life and his blood to rejuvenate the earth. Several writers have theorised that Rufus was such a king; in support, they point out that he openly scoffed at Christianity and that, on the day he died, he made several remarks that indicated foreknowledge of his death.

The date, too, was significant: August 2 was the day after Lugnasad, the Celtic harvest festival and a traditional time of sacrifice. On the previous May Day Eve, the Celtic festival of spring, William's illegitimate son had died in very similar circumstances. The theory is that the boy tried to offer himself in his father's place, but the old religion demanded the life of the king himself. Whatever the reason, William Rufus was buried without ceremony, and refused the last rites of the Church.

KILLER'S VIEW? *The Rufus Stone, near Minstead, marks the spot where William Rufus died. If the siting is correct, the king would have been protected from an accidental shot by trees, and the fatal, deliberately aimed arrow must have come from somewhere near the camera, some 20 yds to the rear. This theory is based on the fact that the clearing beyond is marshy, and incapable of supporting trees; therefore the tree-line is still the same as it was on the day Rufus was killed*

Who killed the king?

The death of William Rufus, on August 2, 1100, is generally supposed to have resulted from a hunting accident in which an arrow loosed by one of the king's companions, Walter Tyrrel, glanced off the back of a stag and buried itself in the king's heart. Yet according to the historian Duncan Grinnell-Milne, it was not an accident but murder. He also says that Tyrrel could not have fired the fatal arrow since Rufus was at least 80 yds away, protected by trees, and Tyrrel was placed at an impossible shooting angle. Finally, if the arrow had glanced off the stag, its force would have been expended, and it would have dropped harmlessly to the ground. The shot must have been a direct one, and the only person who could have fired it was the chief huntsman, who was standing no more than 20 yds from the king.

If the huntsman did murder the king, and it was not a ritual killing, there is a strong likelihood that he was bribed to do so by William's youngest brother, Henry. Certainly, Henry reacted with suspicious alacrity. William was killed at 7 p.m. on Thursday evening, and his body was brought to Henry in Winchester on Friday morning. By midday, William was buried and, by afternoon, Henry had seized the Treasury, and was on his way to London to be crowned.

ACCIDENT, MURDER OR SACRIFICE? *Though nearly 900 years have passed since William Rufus died in the New Forest, his death remains a mystery. Was it a hunting accident? Or a political murder? Or the final act of an ancient rite?*

Saxon rights and Norman laws

The New Forest was given its name by William I, but it was a hunting preserve of the Saxon kings long before the Norman Conquest. Nor is it a forest in the accepted sense; rather, it is a primeval mixture of heath, bog and woodland that has changed little since the evening that William Rufus died. New Forest people are still entitled to such medieval rights as pannage, under which their pigs may feed on forest acorns; turbary, the right to cut turf; and estover, permission to gather firewood.

It is said that William the Conqueror razed 30 villages in order to improve the hunting, but it is unlikely that such villages ever existed. However, both he and his successors established savage game laws to protect the deer. William Rufus enforced his laws by maiming or hanging anyone who tried to poach the animals. And just for disturbing them, a commoner risked having his eyes put out.

RUFUS'S STIRRUP *Under Norman law, only those dogs that were small enough to creep through this stirrup (now in the Verderer's Court, Lyndhurst) were allowed to roam the forest. Larger dogs had their claws cut off, to prevent them chasing the deer*

Marden *Wilts*

A memory of the struggle between Saxons and Danes may account for the tradition that a battle was once fought near here between black-haired and red-haired men; the red-heads won and buried their dead in an unknown downland cave.

Minster Lovell *Oxon*

Francis, the 1st Viscount Lovell, supported the impostor Lambert Simnel in his attempt to depose Henry VII, and when Simnel was defeated in 1487, Francis disappeared. It was said that he had hidden at Minster Lovell Hall, and that when the servant looking after him died suddenly, Francis, unable to unlock the door of his hiding-place, starved to death. In 1708, a secret room was discovered with a skeleton inside it. Whether this was Francis will never be known, for the bones crumbled to dust almost as soon as the room was opened.

MINSTER LOVELL HALL

The ruins of the 15th-century home of the Lovells stand beside the River Windrush. It was in a secret room in the house that the ill-fated 1st Viscount may have been accidentally entombed in 1487 while hiding from Henry VII

THE WAGES OF SIN

A 17th-century tract describes how Cromwell's soldiers caught and killed a Newbury witch

Mottistone *Isle of Wight*

Druid priests are said to have sacrificed white bulls beside the Long Stone on Mottistone Hill. The fact that there are really two stones, one horizontal and the other perpendicular, is taken as evidence that Druids worshipped here, for the perpendicular stone is said to represent a Druid god and the horizontal one a goddess. This is pure speculation; all that can be said for certain is that the barrow, or burial chamber, of which the Long Stone is a part, must be 4000–5000 years old. The name Mottistone may suggest that the stone was a 'meeting stone' – it means 'the speaker's stone' in Old English.

Newbury *Berks*

Belief in witchcraft lingered on in the Newbury area until well into the 20th century, and it may not be entirely dead yet. A favourite meeting place for local covens was Cottington's Hill, a mile south of Kingsclere, and it used to be said amongst local people that 'there was enough witches and wizards living round Cottington's Hill to drag a ton load o' stones up it'.

When an investigation into local beliefs about witchcraft was carried out just before the First World War, several villagers from around Newbury claimed that, within living memory, three Berkshire witches had been buried alive with only their heads left above ground. All the accounts agreed that one of the three had lived longer than the others, because someone threw an apple core at her and she caught it in her mouth.

The most celebrated Newbury witch was captured and executed by a troop of Cromwell's soldiers in 1643. According to a contemporary pamphlet, the soldiers saw an old woman sailing on a plank down the River Kennet, seized her as a witch and tried to shoot her. But 'with a deriding and loud laughter at them, she caught their bullets in her hands and chewed them'. Then one of the soldiers slashed her forehead – an infallible method of rendering harmless even the most evil witch – and 'discharged a pistol underneath her ear, at which she straight sank down and died'.

Jack of Newbury, like Dick Whittington, was a merchant who became a folk-hero. He was born about the middle of the 15th century, and was apprenticed to a rich Newbury cloth-maker. When his master died, he married the widow and, when she died, he inherited the business. In time he became Newbury's leading wool merchant, and employed as many as 1000 local people. His most famous exploit was in 1513, when he and 150 of his employees went to fight for Henry VIII at the Battle of Flodden. Later the king offered him a knighthood, but he turned it down, saying that he preferred to remain the equal of his workers. He died in 1519, and a commemorative brass can still be seen in Newbury's Church of St Nicholas.

Ot Moor *Oxon*

This bleak expanse of flat, swampy land covers some 6 square miles just east of Oxford; it has been described in the past as 'bewitched' and 'cast under a spell of ancient magic'.

Seven towns on its fringes share the rights to the common. According to legend, a lady from Ot Moor once rode round the area while an oat sheaf was burning, saying that all the land within the circuit she covered while the sheaf still burnt should become common land for the citizens of the seven towns.

Many ancient customs are still continued in the Ot Moor towns. At Charlton, for instance, there is a May Day procession, and at Oddington the crops are blessed on Rogation Sunday. There are also several medicinal wells on the moor. Those at Oddington cure 'Moor Evil', a disease which once affected many cattle in the area; and the black, peaty water in many of the others is said to heal various skin and eye complaints.

Owslebury *Hants*

In May 1536, Henry VIII secretly married Jane Seymour in Marwell Hall, a mile south of Owslebury, while his former wife Anne Boleyn was awaiting execution in the Tower for adultery. A year later, Jane too was dead; she died giving birth to the future Edward VI. Her ghost, it is alleged, returns to haunt Marwell Hall – but it is not alone. A lady in white who still sometimes drifts down an avenue of yew trees in the grounds was thought to be the ghost of Anne Boleyn, who had returned to bring misfortune on her rival's home.

Marwell Hall was never a lucky house for the Seymours. It once belonged to the Church, but Henry VIII took it and gave it as a gift to one of Jane's relatives. The local priest was so furious that he put a curse on the Seymours, saying that they would not live for long at the Hall. By tradition, Henry in his turn was so angry that he had the priest murdered. But the curse took effect, and within two generations Marwell Hall had passed into the hands of another family.

A SKELETON IN THE ATTIC

Marwell Hall near Owslebury is one of several country houses associated with the tragic legend of a bride who plays hide-and-seek on her wedding day, and is never seen alive again. The time is usually unspecified, but the story is always the same. After her wedding, a bride plays hide-and-seek with her groom and guests; she hides first, and finding an old oak chest in an attic, climbs into it. The lid clicks shut, she finds that she cannot reopen it, and while the frantic guests search and search she slowly suffocates. Centuries later, long after she has been forgotten, the chest is found, the lid prised open and her skeleton in wedding clothes is discovered

Oxford *Oxon*

At Queen's College, the ceremony of the Boar's Head is observed every Christmas Day. It is probably a relic of pagan custom, for boars were sacred animals to the Celts, and boar's flesh was the food of the Norse heroes who feasted with the god Odin in his paradise, Valhalla. When the Provost and fellows of the college have taken their places at the High Table, and grace has been said, a boar's head on a silver dish is carried into the Hall, followed by the college choir.

The procession stops three times to allow a soloist to sing a verse of the Boar's Head Carol, and, when the head is finally placed on the table, the singer is rewarded with the orange from the boar's mouth. The sprigs of bay and rosemary which decorate the head are distributed among the guests.

Surprisingly for a town so steeped in history, Oxford has remarkably few ghosts. One, however, is that of Archbishop Laud, who was beheaded as 'an enemy to Parliament' on Tower Hill in 1645. It is said that his mutilated spectre rolls its head around the library floor of St John's College, where he once studied and where he was elected chancellor of the University in 1630.

Portsmouth *Hants*

On stormy winter nights, the bones of Jack the Painter and the chains of his gibbet can be heard clanking in the wind (or so it is said) on Blockhouse Point at the entrance to Portsmouth Harbour. Jack, alias James Aitken, started a fire in the harbour ropehouse in 1776. It is believed that he held anti-monarchist views, and so planned to destroy the Fleet. He was caught, tried and hanged from a ship's mizzen mast. Afterwards, his corpse was gibbeted on Blockhouse Point, and for many years his rotting remains were a familiar warning to all who sailed with the Royal Navy.

Preston Candover *Hants*

A wealthy man fleeing from plague-stricken London in 1665 is said to have fallen dead from the disease somewhere near the Preston gravel pits. The villagers, afraid to touch him, first shot his horse, and then with ropes and poles heaved the two corpses into the pits and buried them. At the same time, they buried the treasure which he was carrying, thinking that they would dig it up later when the risk of infection had passed. But either they forgot where they had buried it, or they never went back, for the treasure has never been recovered.

Purton *Wilts*

The Church of St Mary is unique among English churches in that it has both a central tower and spire and a western tower. Tradition explains that this is because the two sisters who had the church built could not agree on its design, so they struck this peculiar compromise. But in this case tradition is mistaken; the spire was built about 1325 and the western tower 150 years later.

Halfway between Purton and Purton Stoke is a bend in the road called Watkins' Corner. Allegedly, it is haunted by the ghost of a man called Watkins, who was hanged there for a murder to which his father later confessed. As he swung from the gallows, a fearful storm blew up, which so frightened the hangman's horse that it bolted and threw him, breaking the hangman's neck.

THE CHOIR ON MAGDALEN TOWER

On May Day morning the choristers of Magdalen College, Oxford, re-enact a ceremony which is now completely Christian, but may well have its roots in some long-forgotten pagan fertility ritual. At 6 a.m. the choir

Reading *Berks*

During the reign of Henry I (1100–35), nine great cloth merchants prospered in England; one of the richest of them was Thomas of Reading. Legend says the king met Thomas and his fellow merchants on the road one day but their many wagons forced him to move aside. At first he was angry; but soon he realised how useful the support of such rich men might be. To win their favour, he established a standard measurement for cloth – the yard, which was exactly the length of his arm.

Reading today can boast one of England's finest folk museums – the Museum of English Rural Life. Its collections cover all aspects of traditional country life, from bee-keeping to weaving.

Rodbourne Cheney *Wilts*

An underground tunnel, now bricked up, is supposed to run between the Church of St Mary and the manor house in Cheney Road. In the 16th century, fearing for the safety of the church's treasures during the Dissolution, the villagers hid them in the tunnel. Tradition claims that one of the treasures, a solid gold altar, was never returned, and to this day it still lies somewhere in the tunnel.

Sherston *Wilts*

The sign of Sherston's Rattlebone Inn shows a warrior clutching a tile to his side. Local legend explains that it commemorates one John Rattlebone, who in the early 11th century fought with Edmund Ironside against King Canute and the Danes. In one particularly fierce battle, he received a terrible wound in his side; to prevent his bowels gushing out he pressed a tile against the wound, and bravely went on fighting.

gathers on top of the college tower and sings a Latin carol, after which the chapel bells are rung and Morris Men begin dancing in the streets. Another theory about the origin of this custom is that it developed out of a Requiem Mass said on the tower for Henry VII; after the Reformation in 1534 the service was changed to suit the rites of the new Anglican Church. This highly idealised picture of the ceremony was painted in 1899 by William Holman Hunt, and can be seen in the Lady Lever Art Gallery at Port Sunlight, Merseyside

Shipton-under-Wychwood *Oxon*

An old oak tree stands in a field near the former inn called Capp's Lodge; carved into its bark, and still just decipherable, are the initials H. D. and T. D. and the date 1784.

The brothers Harry and Tom Dunsdon were famous 18th-century highwaymen; there was also a third brother, Dick. He is said to have bled to death when Tom and Harry hacked off one of his arms to free him after his hand had been caught by waiting constables, while he was reaching through a door shutter to slide back the bolt. Tom and Harry were captured in their turn near Capp's Lodge in 1784, taken to Gloucester and hanged. Afterwards, their bodies were brought back to Shipton and gibbeted from the oak. The oak is said to be stunted due to the gruesome burden it once bore.

SILBURY HILL, WILTSHIRE

This 4000-year-old mound is said to be the burial place of an otherwise forgotten King Sil; of a knight in golden armour; and even of a solid gold horse and rider. Alternatively, the Devil was going to empty a huge sack of earth on Marlborough, but was forced to drop it here by the magic of the priests from nearby Avebury

THE GIANT-KILLER

The hero of ancient Southampton, Hampshire, was Sir Bevis. He fought and slew the giant Ascapart who was terrorising the surrounding countryside. The statue of Sir Bevis (above) is on Southampton's Bar Gate; and just outside the town is Bevis Mound, a tumulus beneath which the skeleton of Ascapart is said to lie

183

The Temple and the Plain

O ne terrifying night in 1786, as lightning flashes illuminated Salisbury Plain, a sailor named Gervase Matcham saw a ghostly drummer boy gliding towards him while he and another sailor were making their way northwards. Unable to bear the phantom's presence, he confessed to his companion that he had murdered the boy some years previously. Matcham was hanged, and was accompanied to the gallows by the ghost of his victim.

Rich in legend and mounded with ancient graves, the Plain can still affect lively imaginations. For prehistoric men it had a particular magic, a sacred quality that made it the burial ground of kings and a place of pilgrimage for half Europe. Stone and Bronze Age burial chambers dot the rolling landscape in such profusion that 17th-century writers wondered if entire nations were buried there. But by far the greatest mystery of Salisbury Plain will probably always be Stonehenge.

The 12th-century chronicler Geoffrey of Monmouth wrote that its massive stones were originally brought from Africa to Ireland by a race of giants. There they were known as the Giant's Dance, and were moved to Wiltshire in the 6th century by Merlin at the request of Ambrosius Aurelianus, King of the Britons. Ambrosius wanted them as a war memorial to Prince Vortigern and his nobles, treacherously slain near Amesbury by Hengist the Saxon. Another version of the story says that Merlin asked for, and obtained, the help of the Devil, who stole the stones from an old Irishwoman. He tied them together and flew with them over the Irish Sea direct to the Plain, and then built Stonehenge according to the wizard's plans.

ROMANTIC FANTASIES *An 18th-century print (above) shows Stonehenge as pictured by an over-imaginative artist of the era. He was probably influenced by John Aubrey's sensational claim that the monument was an ancient temple where Druids practised ritual human sacrifice. This theory has never been proved. The illustration on the right is from a 12th-century history of Stonehenge by Geoffrey of Monmouth. This account attributes the monument to Merlin, who is shown dismantling the Giant's Dance in Ireland before removing the stones to Wessex and re-erecting them there*

TOWARDS ETERNITY *The power of primitive spiritual beliefs inspired man to almost superhuman construction feats*

PAGAN CATHEDRAL *Built in the dawn of history, Stonehenge was a Celtic shrine whose fame was known even in ancient Crete*

Two thousand years of worship

Even serious speculation about the monument's origins was accompanied by flights of fancy. The 17th-century antiquary John Aubrey claimed that it had been a Druidic centre of sun-worship and human sacrifice, a view that was echoed by William Stukeley over a century later. Inigo Jones, the architect, suggested it may have been a shrine to the Roman god Uranus.

Though much of the mystery remains, archaeology has revealed that the monument was constructed over a period of 500 years, beginning about 1900 BC. Its builders were the same Late Stone Age and Early Bronze Age farmer-shepherds and warriors who buried so many of their dead on the Plain. Stonehenge was built in three phases, and by the time of its completion, in about 1400 BC, it represented a fusion of all major religious beliefs of prehistoric Britain.

The first phase of building consisted of a bank and ditch around a circle of small pits, known as the Aubrey Holes after their discoverer. It is possible that these were symbolic doors leading to the ancient underworld gods, and that the blood of slaughtered beasts was poured into them as offerings to the gods. The Heel Stone, which lies outside the embankment, also belongs to this period. An old legend says that the Devil caught a monk prying on his antics among the stones. Before the monk could escape, the Devil hurled the great boulder at him and pinned the unfortunate churchman by the heel.

New status, new gods

About 1700 BC, the second phase of building began, and it was during this period that Stonehenge superseded Avebury, 18 miles to the north, as the most important shrine in pagan Britain. Huge bluestones were brought 200 miles by sea and land, using rafts and rollers, from the Prescelly Mountains in South Wales. The stones were erected in two circles at the centre of the site, by means of huge timber levers and inclined planes of packed earth. The Avenue, a processional route leading from the River Avon, was also lined by great blocks of stone.

The motives that inspired this great engineering feat, unique in prehistoric Europe, are unknown. However, at least two factors indicate that during this period the focus of worship shifted from the earth to the heavens. The entrance to the modified temple was aligned with the position of mid-summer sunrise, and golden sun-discs were found among the remains of the people who built the new Stonehenge. Almost certainly the temple had become a shrine dedicated to the worship of the sun.

In the final phase of construction, begun about 1550 BC, 40–50 ton sarsen stones (the name of a local sandstone) were transported 20 miles from the Marlborough Downs. These were erected as outer and inner circles of trilithons (two stones with a third set crossways on top of them) and the bluestones were rearranged.

A timeless enigma

Though much is now known about the origins of Stonehenge, many questions about what happened there, and why, still remain unanswered. Modern Druids gather there to celebrate the midsummer sunrise, but there is little evidence to link their practices with the earlier history of the monument. The 3500-year-old cleft skull of an infant found at the nearby Woodhenge sanctuary suggests that human sacrifices may have been carried out in the area, if not at Stonehenge itself. The colourfully named Slaughter Stone is believed to have formed part of a former gateway to the temple, and was unconnected with any sacrificial rites which may have occurred there.

In 1966, a theory was put forward by the British astronomer Gerald Hawkins that Stonehenge was a kind of early computer which had been used to calculate the movements of heavenly bodies. The theory aroused considerable controversy, and joins the long list of ideas which the monument has inspired in the age-old attempt to unravel its mysteries.

South Baddesley *Hants*

A stream called 'The Danes' Stream' which flows through the parish is said to run red with the blood of Danes slaughtered on its banks more than 1000 years ago. In fact, the colour is probably caused by the iron-rich local soil.

Stratton St Margaret *Wilts*

The people of Stratton St Margaret used to be known as 'crocodiles' in the nearby parishes, and among the older villagers the nickname has not yet been forgotten. By tradition, the origin of the name goes back to a night some time in the 19th century, when a drunk burst into the local pub and cried out that a crocodile had crawled from a nearby ditch. Arming themselves with sticks, the villagers set out to find the fearful reptile . . . only to discover that it was an old scarf lying in the road.

Swindon *Wilts*

The decision that transformed the hilltop market town of Old Swindon into one of England's major industrial towns was made, it is said, on the toss of a sandwich. In 1833, the engineers Isambard Kingdom Brunel and Daniel Gooch were surveying the proposed route for the Great Western Railway; they stopped for a sandwich lunch on the slopes below Old Swindon, and were so impressed with the place that they decided to throw a sandwich and build a railway works where it landed.

THE TICHBORNE DOLE IN THE 17TH CENTURY

On Lady Day (March 25) gifts of flour – to a limit of 4 gallons a family – are distributed by the Tichborne family to all the villagers of Tichborne, Cheriton and Lane End in Hampshire, in accordance with the last wish of Lady Isabella Tichborne, who died some 800 years ago. On her deathbed, legend claims, Lady Isabella begged her husband for a gift of land, so that she could bequeath to the *parish poor a yearly dole of bread. He replied callously that she could have as much land as she could crawl around carrying a blazing torch. Though fatally ill, she still managed to encircle 23 acres; and with her last breath she swore that the Tichbornes would be cursed if ever the dole was discontinued. It was, in fact, abolished in 1796; but such disasters followed that the family revived it*

Tidworth (South) *Hants*

In April 1661, the rattle of a phantom drum at Tidworth House signalled the beginning of one of the most remarkable hauntings ever recorded. In the year that followed, the Mompessons who lived in the house were continually disturbed by drum-beats; their children were bruised and battered by an unseen force; furniture hurled itself about the house, and floorboards moved of their own accord. It was thought that the haunting had something to do with William Drury, a vagrant musician whose drum the magistrate John Mompesson had confiscated. But though Drury admitted that he was involved, the extraordinary nature of the disturbances has never properly been explained.

THE DRUMMER OF TIDWORTH *A contemporary illustration portrayed the phantom as a winged devil surrounded by demons; in fact, no one ever saw the ghost*

Vernham Dean *Hants*

In an attempt to save his parish and himself from the Great Plague of 1665, the rector of Vernham Dean persuaded all the villagers who had been in contact with the disease to go into voluntary isolation in a closed camp on top of the hill beside Chute Causeway. He promised to bring them regular supplies of food, for the hill is just outside the village. But once they had shut themselves off, he became so terrified that he deserted them. Those who did not die of plague starved to death. And it was all in vain; Vernham Dean was ravaged by plague and the rector was one of the many who died. Since then, his guilt-stricken ghost has often been seen climbing towards the hilltop where his cowardice caused so many to die.

Warminster *Wilts*

Since the first 'thing' – a brightly glowing, bullet-shaped object – appeared in the sky over Warminster at Christmas 1964, the town has become a favourite look-out point for Britain's flying saucer spotters. Reports have poured in of UFOs resembling strangely luminous cigars, of bright lights speeding across the night sky, and of all manner of hovering saucers. The local people, however, are more sceptical. They point an accusing finger at the Army's School of Infantry, which is based in the town, and at the many military camps scattered across Salisbury Plain.

THE WHERWELL COCKATRICE

Some time before Wherwell Priory, Hampshire, was dissolved in 1538, a toad incubating a cock's egg in one of its cellars hatched out a cockatrice, a fearful winged monster which, when fully grown, was given to flying around the priory in search of people to eat. A reward of 4 acres of land was offered to anyone who could kill it, and many died in the attempt. At last, a man named Green lowered a mirror of polished steel into its lair; for days, the cockatrice battled with its reflection before dropping exhausted to the floor. Green stepped in and ran it through with a spear. In Harewood Forest near Wherwell lies a plot of land still called 'Green's Acres'; and in Andover Museum the cockatrice (above) once adorned the steeple of St Peter and Holy Cross at Wherwell

TALES OF THE WHITE HORSE

Though fretted by the rains and frosts of 2000 winters, the great chalk ramparts of Uffington Castle still loom protectively over Oxfordshire's Vale of the White Horse. Even more important to the Celtic tribe who carved its battlements out of the hillside shortly before the Roman invasion was the fact that it commanded the Ridgeway, the prehistoric track that runs across England from the coast near Dover to Ilchester in Somerset. So obvious is this dominance that some people believe that Uffington was Mount Badon, the place where King Arthur finally defeated the Saxons, in about AD 518. There is little doubt that in the days when the valleys were thickly forested, whoever held the high Ridgeway route would control the West of England.

The 374 ft long White Horse that gave the Vale its name is cut into the turf close to the castle, and may well date from the same period. It probably represents a Celtic god or tribal symbol, yet for centuries local people maintained that it was a portrait of the dragon slain by St George on the nearby Dragon's Hill.

About a mile west along the Ridgeway from the White Horse is an empty Stone Age burial chamber which is at least 5000 years old, and has been known as Wayland's Smithy since before the Norman Conquest. The story goes that after the coming of Christianity, Wayland, smith of the Norse gods, was forced to shoe mortals' horses for a living. So if you leave your horse and a coin beside the smithy, when you return, the horse will be shod, and the coin gone.

BEAST OF OXFORDSHIRE *Beyond the bird-like jaw of the Uffington White Horse lies bald-topped Dragon's Hill. In some legends, the horse represents a dragon killed on this knoll. Where its blood fell, the grass now no longer grows*

Wilcot *Wilts*

In the early 17th century, Wilcot Vicarage (since rebuilt) was plagued by the sound of a bell which every night tolled incessantly in one of the bedrooms. A wizard of Devizes is said to have caused this, at the request of a Wilcot drunkard who was annoyed by the vicar's refusal to ring the church bells late at night. Seeking revenge, the drunkard went to the wizard who promptly cast a spell on the vicar's bedroom. The phantom bell became so famous that people made nocturnal pilgrimages to Wilcot to hear it, and James I is reputed to have visited the vicarage one night to listen to it. The ringing could be heard inside the bedroom but not outside. It finally stopped when the wizard died and the spell's power was lost with him.

Winchester *Hants*

St Swithun was the bishop of Winchester in the 9th century. One of many miracles he is said to have performed concerns a market woman who dropped her basket of eggs near the church after bumping into a monk. Swithun happened to be passing by and was so moved by the poor woman's distress that he made the eggs whole again. On the altar screen in the cathedral, the saint is shown with a pile of eggs at his feet, and each of the four candlesticks in his shrine has a broken eggshell at its base.

When Swithun died in 862, he was buried outside the church of that time, in accordance with his wish to lie where the rain would fall on him. Nearly a century later, the monks decided to move his tomb to a worthier resting-place inside the church. Legend has it that St Swithun's spirit, angered by the removal of his remains, made it rain so violently for 40 days that the monks gave up the plan. Ever since then, rain on St Swithun's Day (July 15) has been an omen of continuing bad weather.

Castle Hall, near Westgate, is all that remains of William the Conqueror's castle, built when Winchester was the capital of England. It contains a Round Table alleged to be that of King Arthur and his Knights; it was almost certainly put there in the 12th century by Henry de Blois, who founded the Hospital of St Cross and its almshouses which lie 1½ miles south of the city centre. For over 800 years the hospital has dispensed a daily Wayfarer's Dole of bread and ale to all who ask for it.

Wittenham *Oxon*

The Wittenham Clumps are two hills, Sinodun Hill and Harp Hill, near Little Wittenham. Each is crowned with a clump of beech trees, and the one on Sinodun is called 'The Cuckoo Pen'. The name comes from an old country story that if a cuckoo could be penned up in an enclosure of trees or hedges and prevented from flying away, summer would never end. Although cuckoos invariably flew out of such traps, it was hoped that when the hedges or trees grew higher the birds would finally be unable to escape. Similar stories of rustics trying to pen the cuckoo occur all over Britain.

Sinodun Hill was once a Roman fort and it is said that a treasure is buried in a hollow known as the 'Money Pit'. A story relates how one villager dug a deep hole there. Just as he found an iron chest, a raven alighted on it and cried 'He is not born yet!' Taking this to mean that he was not the one fated to have the treasure, the man immediately filled in the hole and went away.

Woodstock *Oxon*

North of the bridge that spans the lake in Blenheim Palace Park is an inscribed stone, marking the site where Woodstock Manor once stood. The Black Prince was born there in 1331, and the manor was a royal house until its destruction in the Civil War. From October 13 to November 2, 1649, Cromwell's Parliamentary Commissioners stayed in the manor, and were plagued by a spirit which became known as the Royalist Devil of Woodstock. Night after night, beds mysteriously moved up and down, candles were blown out, broken glass was hurled about the rooms, and servants were drenched in 'stinking ditch-water'. The Commissioners finally left, never to return, and the Royalist Devil was never heard of again.

Wootton Bassett *Wilts*

A secret religious ceremony, the annual ritual of 'Word Ale', was performed here until late into the 19th century. Tenants who lived on lands owned by the Lord of Wootton Bassett Manor were exempted from paying tithes if they participated in the rite. This took place at some time near All Saints Day, when the assembled company would sing hymns and drink a lot of ale. They also offered prayers to the memory of the 12th-century Cistercian monks who granted the original exemption. Traditionally, the event was recorded by cutting a notch on a yard-long hazel rod, which was kept by the tenant whose turn it was to act as host next year.

Yarnton *Oxon*

The mowing rights of certain meadows in Yarnton are allocated yearly in a ceremony which has continued unchanged for nearly 1000 years. On the first Monday after St Peter's Day, June 29, the mowing rights in West Mead and Pixey Mead are offered for sale; the distribution of plots is decided by lots drawn at The Grapes Inn at 9 a.m., one morning in the following week. Thirteen ancient wooden balls, known as Mead Balls, are drawn. Made of light wood, possibly holly, each one is marked with the name of one of the plots. The names are thought to be those of the original tenant-farmers who held the mowing rights in the 11th century. When all the lots have been drawn, the new lessees go over to the meadows, where their initials are cut in the turf of whichever plot they have just acquired, and mowing begins immediately.

THE MEAD BALLS

The names inscribed on the 13 balls used in the Yarnton Meadows Lottery are Gilbert, White, Harry, Boat, Watery Molly, William, Parry, Freeman, Rothe, Walter Jeoffrey, Dunn, Green and Boulton, thought to be the names of the 11th-century tenants who originally farmed the meadows. Each ball represents a certain acreage, whose position is changed every year

WINDSOR'S PHANTOM HUNTSMAN

Since the mighty bastions of Windsor have protected monarchs from their subjects from the time of the Norman Conquest, it is not surprising that the ghosts within the castle are wholly royal. The quick, determined footsteps that hurry through the Library are said to be those of Elizabeth I. By contrast, the steps in the Cloisters are slow and halting; these may be echoes of Henry VIII, dragging his ulcerated leg through eternity. One visible manifestation is that of poor, demented George III who, in his periodical bouts of madness, used to be shut into a room overlooking the parade ground. From there he would watch his soldiers drilling, and several modern subalterns have been startled to see his face at the same window, called there, apparently, by the sound of marching and drilling men.

Outside the castle, the ancient forest of Windsor Great Park is the province of Herne the Hunter. Festooned with chains, and with a stag's antlers growing from his brow, he is most often seen at times of national crisis near the site of a great oak that once grew in the park. He may also be aroused by impudence; it is said that his last appearance, in 1962, was brought about by a group of youths who found a hunting horn in the forest one night and blew it at the edge of a clearing. They were immediately answered by a similar call and the baying of hounds; then Herne himself appeared riding a black horse, his ragged antlers silhouetted against the sky. Terrified, the youths dropped the horn and fled.

According to legend, Herne was a royal huntsman who saved a king's life by interposing his own body between a wounded stag and his master. As he lay there mortally wounded, a wizard appeared and told the king that the only way to save Herne's life was to cut off the stag's antlers and tie them to the huntsman's head. Herne recovered, and for several years enjoyed the king's favour. But the other huntsmen, jealous of his influence, persuaded the king to dismiss him, and Herne went out and hanged himself. He has haunted Windsor Great Park ever since.

The king's name is variously given as Henry VII, Henry VIII and Richard II; but in fact, Herne was associated with the park long before kings came to Windsor. His stag's antlers almost certainly identify him as Cernunnos, Celtic god of the underworld. Once he must have been worshipped in the park, and it would seem that he guards his ancient shrine still.

NORMANDY'S ENGLAND

Jersey, Guernsey, Alderney and Sark

Most Channel Islanders are aware that England really belongs to them, for it was their Duke, William of Normandy, who conquered it in 1066. To this day, the bailiwicks of Guernsey and Jersey remain outside the United Kingdom, and owe their allegiance to the British monarch only by virtue of her descent from the Norman dukes. The Queen is spoken of as La Reine, but the loyal toast at formal dinners is 'La Duchesse de Normandie'. Despite this sentimental attachment, political links with France were broken as long ago as 1205, when King John was forced to abandon the entire Duchy of Normandy excepting only the Channel Isles. Religious links lasted much longer, until the reign of Elizabeth I, in fact, when the islands were transferred from the Catholic See of Coutances to the Protestant See of Winchester. After that, the islands became a haven for refugees fleeing religious and political persecution in France; the most famous of these was Victor Hugo, who lived on the islands between 1852 and 1870.

The two bailiwicks (provinces governed by bailiffs) are also separate from one another. An ancient rivalry exists between the two, probably dating from the Civil War when Jersey was Royalist and Guernsey Parliamentarian. Traditionally, Jerseymen refer to Guernseymen as 'donkeys'; Guernsey retaliates with tales of Jersey stupidity. They say, for example, that Jersey people cure toothache by filling their mouths with water and sitting on a fire until the water boils!

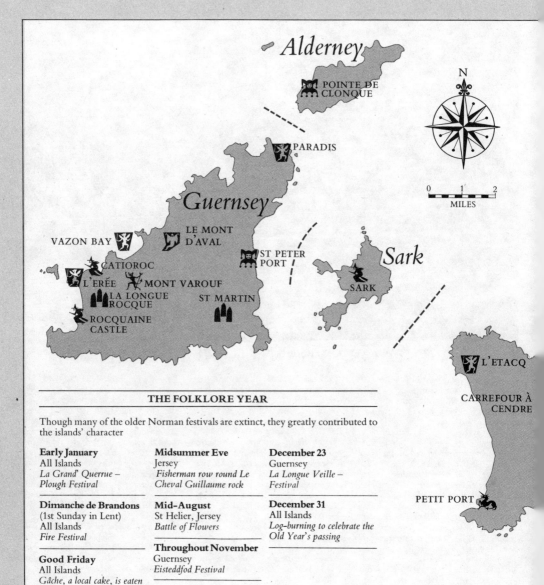

THE FOLKLORE YEAR

Though many of the older Norman festivals are extinct, they greatly contributed to the islands' character

Early January
All Islands
La Grand' Querrue –
Plough Festival

Dimanche de Brandons
(1st Sunday in Lent)
All Islands
Fire Festival

Good Friday
All Islands
Gâche, a local cake, is eaten

Midsummer Eve
Jersey
Fisherman row round Le
Cheval Guillaume rock

Mid-August
St Helier, Jersey
Battle of Flowers

Throughout November
Guernsey
Eisteddfod Festival

December 23
Guernsey
La Longue Veille –
Festival

December 31
All Islands
Log-burning to celebrate the
Old Year's passing

The Guernsey witches

The darker side of French influence on the islanders' attitudes is apparent in 16th and 17th-century accounts of witch trials, especially in those of Guernsey. Like the French and Scots, but unlike the English, island interrogators used torture to extract confessions; and the evidence obtained could be used to convict others. In 150 years, almost 200 people, most of them from Guernsey, came before the island courts – compared with 2000 in all England. Guernsey trials were marked by a 90 per cent rate of conviction and by savage sentences on the continental pattern. English witches were normally hanged, but in the Channel Islands they were often burnt alive, or hanged and then burnt. Some escaped the flames, to be whipped and have an ear cut off. A lucky few were banished for life.

According to John Warburton of Guernsey, writing about 1700, men and women suspected of sorcery were strung up by the thumbs at La Tour Beauregard, so that 'their shoulders were turned round, and sometimes their thumbs were torn off'.

Witches were said to hold their Friday sabbats at Rocquaine Castle and the Catioroc, a prehistoric grave site on a rocky promontory in Guernsey's St Saviour's parish. Jersey witches used to meet on Rocqueberg, where their revels were occasionally presided over by the Devil.

One witch, Collette du Mont, said in 1617 – after days of torture – that she rubbed black ointment on her body, to enable her to fly to the sabbats. There, she said, she joined 15 or 16 others, and the Devil, in the shape of a black dog, made love to her.

Other Guernsey witches confessed to crimes such as killing cattle and infesting the neighbours with vermin. A famous Sark wizard named Pierre de Cartaret employed demons to build him a fishing boat inside his barn. The work was completed in one night, and the boat launched the next day despite the fact that the barn door was apparently too small for the vessel to pass through.

Antidotes to witchcraft were provided by 'white' witches' charms. One of these involved sticking nine thorns into a sheep's heart to the accompaniment of ritual chants, before inserting it in the chimney for nine days. On the ninth day, the black witch, by now in agony, would be forced to reveal herself, and could then be compelled to lift the spell.

Silver was also believed to protect people from sorcery. Shortly before the Second World War a farmer became suspicious of a particularly sinister carrion crow. He loaded his gun with a silver bullet and shot the bird, after which it fluttered away behind a rock. When he followed, he found – or said he found – a witch nursing a shattered shoulder.

The fairy isles

The local belief in fairies was closely allied to the large number of prehistoric graves and monuments which

KEY TO SYMBOLS

- BELLS
- CUSTOMS AND FESTIVALS
- DEVILS AND DEMONS
- FABULOUS BEASTS
- FAIRIES
- GHOSTS
- MYSTERIOUS STONES
- WITCHES AND WIZARDS

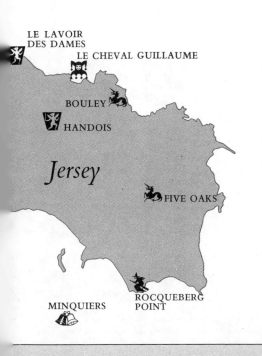

LE LAVOIR DES DAMES

LE CHEVAL GUILLAUME

BOULEY

HANDOIS

Jersey

FIVE OAKS

MINQUIERS

ROCQUEBERG POINT

ROCQUAINE CASTLE *This prehistoric stone circle in Guernsey was said to be a favourite meeting place for the witches' weekly sabbats. Here, they worked on the spells contained in two books of magic,* Le Grand Albert *and* Le Petit Albert

FAIRIES' CAVE *This ancient burial chamber at St Peter in the Wood, Guernsey, is locally known as* Le Creux ès Faies – *the fairies' hole. The Little People emerge from the cave on moonlit nights and dance on the nearby Catioroc*

abound in the islands. *Les Petits Faîtiaux* (the fairies) are supposed to have built the cromlechs (stone circles) to live in. These monuments are often called *pouquelaie*, after an old Norse word meaning 'goblins' path'.

In the Jersey parish of St Ouen, archaeologists digging at Le Trou des Faîtiaux near L'Etacq in 1912 were interrupted by an old man who warned: 'You will bring trouble if you disturb the fairies.'

At Handois, in the centre of the island, there are a number of quarries where the tinkling of silver bells has been heard. Those who wait quietly are said to be rewarded with the sight of a fairy bridal procession.

When a local landowner was drowned in the 19th century, Guernsey people ascribed the tragedy to the fairies. Laughing at his neighbours' beliefs, the man had demolished La Rocque qui Sonne – the remains of a large passage grave in Vale parish school – to provide building materials.

L'Autel de Déhus, at Paradis, in Vale parish, and Le Creux ès Faies, at L'Erée in the Guernsey parish of St Peter in the Wood, are both prehistoric passage graves closely linked in tradition with fairy legends: the fairies were supposed to leave their home in Le Creux on moonlit nights, to dance with the witches on the Catioroc.

A Guernsey menhir, or standing stone, called La Longue Rocque, at St Peter in the Wood is also known as the fairy's battledore – the bat of a fairy called Le Grand Colin, who stuck it in the ground in a fit of pique when his son objected to his hitting the shuttlecock out of sight.

The most outstanding island menhir is La Gran'mère du Chimquière – Grandmother of the Cemetery – at St Martin's Church, Guernsey. It was thought a sacred object and an idol. Some people feared it; others entreated its help with gifts of fruit, wine and flowers.

Guernsey people still tell the story of the 'Fairy Invasion'. Long ago, a

beautiful girl named Michelle de Garis found a diminutive but handsome youth fast asleep beneath a hedge and fell in love with him. The boy belonged to the Secret People of England; but since neither the Channel nor the frontiers of Fairyland could stand in the path of true love, they sailed away together. As a farewell gift for Michelle's parents, he left a plant bulb which grew and blossomed into the beautiful rose-pink and golden Guernsey Lily.

Some time later, an islander met a group of tiny men close to Vazon Bay. They told him they were fairies from England, and they too wanted brides like Michelle. When the Guernseymen refused to yield their womenfolk, there was a battle, which the fairies won. The fairies married their island brides, but shortly after deserted them. Legend says that this is why Guernsey people tend to be small. Tall islanders are supposed to be descended from two human men of St Andrew's parish who survived the battle.

Hounds of the Otherworld

Ghost stories abound in the islands. One concerns the funeral procession that is sometimes reported to march over Le Mont d'Aval, Guernsey, in perfect silence – because each member of the company is headless.

Islanders also feared the Black Dog that roamed about with clanking chain and huge, saucer eyes. In the St Peter Port area of Guernsey, it was known as *Tchi-co*; to hear its howls was a sure sign of approaching death. In Jersey, *Le Tchan de Bouole*, or Dog of Bouley, was less to be feared. The creature's appearance simply signalled that a storm was brewing. In the Petit Port area there is a Black Dog who guards treasure, while at Carrefour à Cendre, also in Jersey, there is a creature stranger still. This is a black cat that increases in size as it is carried

THE GUERNSEY LILY *Legend says the famous flower grew from a bulb left for her parents by pretty Michelle's fairy lover from across the English Channel*

LA GRAN'MÈRE DU CHIMQUIÈRE *The 'grandmother' at St Martin's Church, Guernsey, is a prehistoric stone figure associated with fertility rites*

THE FAIRY INVASION *In Guernsey's favourite story, Michelle de Garis fell in love with an English fairy she found under a hedge. Later, his friends came and fought for equally beautiful wives*

away from the Carrefour, and dwindles as it is brought back. Finally, it disappears altogether.

Le Varou was another fearsome beast, something akin to the legendary werewolf – a man turned wolf. Memories of this creature with its enormous appetite for human blood linger in place names such as Mont Varouf.

At La Hogue Bie, an ancient burial mound near Five Oaks, Jersey, a dragon was slain by the Seigneur de Hanbye; but as he rested, he was murdered by a servant who wished to claim credit for the deed.

There are several modern cases of people claiming to have seen *Le Faeu Bélengier* – a rough equivalent of the English Will o' the Wisp: a spirit condemned to wander in pain and seeking to deliver itself from torment.

Le Barboue (the bearded one) was the bogeyman used by mothers to frighten children. And sudden gusts of wind were blamed on Herodias, Queen of the Witches, *qui châque ses côtillons* (shakes her petticoats).

A plea to Haro

Many of the old customs and festivals are now forgotten. But some remain, such as the *Clameur de Haro*, by which a tenant can claim justice for sharp practice connected with building. He must fall on his knees in front of witnesses and cry: 'Haro! Haro! Haro! à l'aide mon Prince, on me fait tort' – 'Help me, Prince (Haro) for I have been ill-used'. 'Haro' is thought to have been Rollo, first Duke of Normandy.

After the *Clameur*, work ceases until the case has been heard in court.

There are many customs associated with cottage industries such as knitting, and with farming. Families would spend *veilles* or knitting evenings together; La Longue Veille was the night of December 23, when everyone stayed up late to finish

goods for market, feasting on mulled wine, biscuits and cheese.

One festival sprang from the introduction in the 18th century of the huge plough needed to dig deep furrows for parsnips. At least 16 oxen were required to pull the plough. Neighbours would pool their beasts and plough each other's land in turn, feasting throughout the day. This was known as *La Grand' Querrue*.

On Christmas Eve, country people would flock to St Peter Port, Guernsey, to eat oranges and chestnuts, before feasting throughout Christmas Day. Then, on New Year's Eve, boys used to parade a grotesque figure called *La vieux bout de l'an* – The old year's end – before burning it. On Alderney, there were more bonfires, especially on the Pointe de Clonque, on the first Sunday in Lent, known as *Dimanche de Brandons*. After dancing round the flames, young folk would run back to St Anne's with burning brands of straw. Good Friday was marked with seaside picnics, when currant bread (*gâche*) and limpets were eaten. And on Jersey simnel cake and coloured eggs are still prepared on Easter Day.

At mid-summer in Sark, sweethearts used to gallop across the island on horses decked with flowers, while the fishermen of Jersey's parish of St John sailed round a rock called Le Cheval Guillaume, for luck. Another group of rocks – the Minquiers – had a more sinister reputation. Any sailor who heard the underwater bells there knew he was on his last voyage.

Every three years, the Prior of Mont St Michel, in Brittany, used to inspect roads and boundaries on Guernsey. Crowds followed him, dancing round megaliths and kissing any women they met. The custom, called *La Chevauchée de St Michel*, ended in 1837. It was revived briefly in 1966, to celebrate William's Conquest of England 900 years earlier.

193

DARTFORD

LONDON

BERKSHIRE

SHEPPERTON

WALTON-ON-THAMES

CHERTSEY
(Hang on the Bell, 199)

HERSHAM

WEYBRIDGE

EPSOM

OTFORD

PYRFORD

RIPLEY

SURREY

WEST
HORSLEY

WOTTON

BUCKLAND

WORPLESDON

GUILDFORD

FARNHAM

SHERE
(Silent Pool, 201)

COLDHARBOUR

OXENFORD

GODALMING

FRENSHAM

CRANLEIGH

EAST
GRINSTEAD

HAMBLEDON

HAMPSHIRE

ST LEONARD'S FOREST
(The Dragons, 207)

SLINFOLD

WEST   SUSSEX

EAST

HENFIELD

DITCHLING

CHANCTONBURY
RING

STEYNING

DEVIL'S
DYKE

LEWES

KINGLEY VALE

ARUNDEL

HOVE

BRIGHTON

BOSHAM

LYMINSTER

WORTHING

ALFRIS

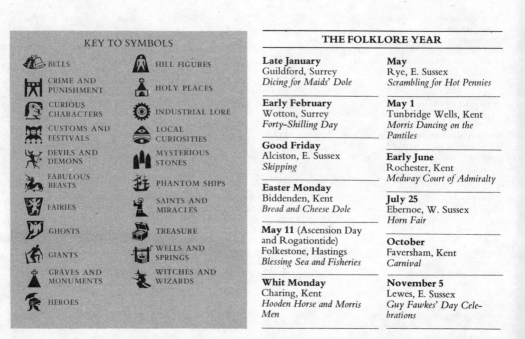

KEY TO SYMBOLS

BELLS

HILL FIGURES

CRIME AND
PUNISHMENT

HOLY PLACES

CURIOUS
CHARACTERS

INDUSTRIAL LORE

CUSTOMS AND
FESTIVALS

LOCAL
CURIOSITIES

DEVILS AND
DEMONS

MYSTERIOUS
STONES

FABULOUS
BEASTS

PHANTOM SHIPS

FAIRIES

SAINTS AND
MIRACLES

GHOSTS

TREASURE

GIANTS

WELLS AND
SPRINGS

GRAVES AND
MONUMENTS

WITCHES AND
WIZARDS

HEROES

THE FOLKLORE YEAR

Late January
Guildford, Surrey
Dicing for Maids' Dole

May
Rye, E. Sussex
Scrambling for Hot Pennies

Early February
Wotton, Surrey
Forty-Shilling Day

May 1
Tunbridge Wells, Kent
*Morris Dancing on the
Pantiles*

Good Friday
Alciston, E. Sussex
Skipping

Early June
Rochester, Kent
Medway Court of Admiralty

Easter Monday
Biddenden, Kent
Bread and Cheese Dole

July 25
Ebernoe, W. Sussex
Horn Fair

May 11 (Ascension Day
and Rogationtide)
Folkestone, Hastings
Blessing Sea and Fisheries

October
Faversham, Kent
Carnival

Whit Monday
Charing, Kent
*Hooden Horse and Morris
Men*

November 5
Lewes, E. Sussex
*Guy Fawkes' Day Cele-
brations*

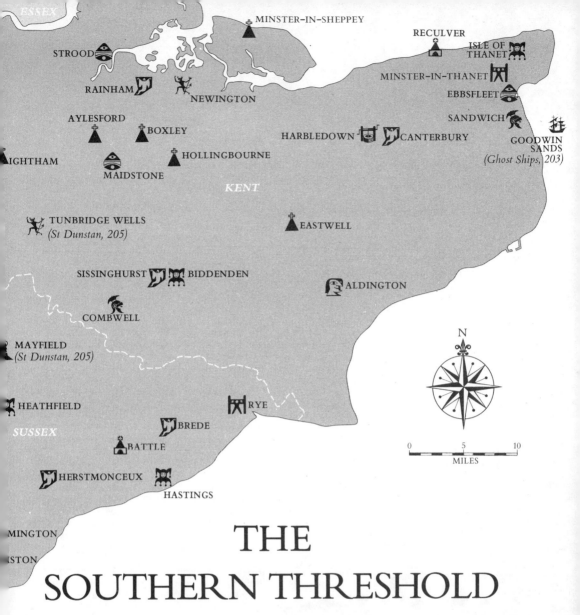

MINSTER-IN-SHEPPEY

RECULVER

ISLE OF
THANET

STROOD

MINSTER-IN-THANET

RAINHAM

NEWINGTON

EBBSFLEET

AYLESFORD

SANDWICH

BOXLEY

HARBLEDOWN

CANTERBURY

GOODWIN
SANDS
(Ghost Ships, 203)

IGHTHAM

HOLLINGBOURNE

MAIDSTONE

KENT

TUNBRIDGE WELLS
(St Dunstan, 205)

EASTWELL

SISSINGHURST

BIDDENDEN

ALDINGTON

COMBWELL

MAYFIELD
(St Dunstan, 205)

N

HEATHFIELD

RYE

SUSSEX

BREDE

BATTLE

0   5   10
MILES

HERSTMONCEUX

HASTINGS

MINGTON

STON

THE
SOUTHERN THRESHOLD

Surrey, Sussex, Kent

The Kent and Sussex coasts have been Britain's front door for continental invaders from the Stone Age onwards. Romans, Saxons and Jutes all chose this route. Then in 1066 came the last successful foreign invasion of English soil. Norman knights struggled through the surf at Pevensey behind Duke William, who led them to victory near Hastings; they called the battlefield Senlac – 'The Lake of Blood'. Now, the quiet ruins of Battle Abbey mark the place, but even today people say that after rain the ground still oozes the blood spilt in that struggle of long ago.

The rich history of the south-east corner of England is sometimes strangely recalled in local legends. A cornerstone of English law was laid in 1215 when the tyrannical King John signed Magna Carta at Runnymede in Surrey. So great were his oppressions that for years after his death he was said to haunt that county in the shape of a werewolf. It has even been suggested that recent tales of a large creature running wild in the area and known as the 'Surrey puma' may have arisen from far-off memories of that royal monster.

Not all the strange beasts of the South Country

are of medieval origin. From the 17th century onwards the presence of an evil-smelling dragon has been reported in St Leonard's Forest, Sussex.

When the Anglo-Saxons settled in Kent, they became known as East Centings or West Centings, depending on whether they lived on the east or west bank of the Medway. A similar distinction still holds; people born east of the river are called Men of Kent, while those to the west are Kentish Men. All the women of the county are 'Fair Maids of Kent', so called after the Earl of Kent's daughter, Joan Plantagenet, a 14th-century beauty.

Southern myths have been further enhanced by the wars of our own times. Among the many phantoms of the Goodwin Sands is a German U-boat, said to have been stranded there in 1939, with all its crew mysteriously dead at their posts. The unmistakable whine of a Merlin engine is often reported at Biggin Hill, Kent, as a long-vanished Spitfire flies a victory roll over its old wartime base. Many people, too, recall how in 1940, the Straits of Dover were choked with German dead after the British beat off an invasion attempt. Propaganda or wishful thinking, one thing is certain; the Germans never mounted an invasion at all.

195

Aldington *Kent*

The ruined chapel at Court-at-Street is associated with the tragic story of the Holy Maid of Kent. In 1525, a local serving-girl named Elizabeth Barton claimed direct communication with the Mother of God. Her pronouncements made her famous, and money-seeking clergy persuaded her to enter a convent in Canterbury. In 1533, she made the mistake of prophesying death for Henry VIII if he should divorce Queen Catherine and marry Anne Boleyn. Together with the clerics who supported her, she was hanged at Tyburn in 1534.

Alfriston *E. Sussex*

The site and design of the cross-shaped, 14th-century Church of St Andrew are said to have been dictated by the miraculous appearance of four white oxen on the village green. The animals lay down with their rumps together, forming a cross, and the church was built on that spot. As late as 1932, a shepherd was buried in the churchyard with a tuft of wool in his hand. Shepherds were often buried in this way so that they could prove to St Peter that their irregular attendances at church were due to the demands of their trade.

Arundel *W. Sussex*

A 5 ft 9 in. long sword called Morglay can be seen in the armoury of Arundel Castle. Tradition says it once belonged to Bevis, a warden of the castle who was so huge that he could walk through the sea from Southampton to Cowes without getting his head wet. Bevis indicated his burial-place by throwing the sword from the castle battlements. It landed half a mile away, where a large mound is still known as Bevis's Grave.

Aylesford *Kent*

Kits Coty House, a megalithic burial chamber on Blue Bell Hill, is reputed to be the tomb of a British chieftain who was killed in personal combat with the Jutish leader Horsa in AD 455. Phantom combatants are said to re-enact the battle occasionally 'in uncanny silence'. Other megaliths on the hill are called The Countless Stones. A baker who attempted to count them was said to have placed a numbered loaf on each stone, but when he came to collect them, there was one extra; the Devil had added one.

Battle *E. Sussex*

The abbey marks the site of the Battle of Hastings, which the Normans called Senlac – 'Lake of Blood'. There is an old belief that the ground still sweats blood after rain, but this may be accounted for by the iron in the soil that occasionally tinges puddles red. At the Reformation, Battle Abbey was bestowed upon Sir Anthony Browne, but at his first banquet there, a monk appeared and told him that his name would be wiped from the land by fire and water. This fate was long delayed, but in 1793, Cowdray Hall, near Midhurst, the home of Sir Anthony's descendant Lord Montague, was burnt down. A week later, the direct line of the family became extinct when the young Viscount was drowned in the Rhine.

Biddenden *Kent*

Anyone who visits the Old Workhouse on Easter Monday morning may apply for, and receive, a hard wheaten cake shaped like two women joined together at the hips and shoulders. These are given in memory of the Siamese twins, Elisa and Mary Chulkhurst, who were born in the village in 1100 and lived, joined together, for 34 years. They left their lands in trust to the poor of the village, and the rents are still spent on the sick and needy, as well as on the Easter dole of bread and cheese.

Bosham *W. Sussex*

In the waters of the creek in front of the church is a place known as the Bell Hole. There, according to legend, lies the tenor bell of the church which was stolen by Danish pirates in the 10th century. As they sailed away, the monks on shore rang the remaining bells to tell the villagers hidden in the woods that it was safe for them to return. When the last peal rang out, the tenor bell in the boat joined in. It rocked and swayed until it capsized the boat, taking the pirates with it to the bottom of the creek. It is said that the tenor bell still joins in whenever the bells are rung.

Boxley *Kent*

A monument in the church records the gratitude of Sir Henry Wyatt for a cat. Imprisoned in the Tower of London in 1483 for denying Richard III's right to the Crown, Sir Henry was left to die of starvation in a cold, damp cell. However, 'God sent a cat to both feed and warm him' – by sleeping on his chest at night, and bringing him pigeons to eat.

Brede *E. Sussex*

The real Sir Goddard Oxenbridge of Brede Place, who died in 1537, seems to have been an amiable and pious man, yet for some reason legend remembers him as a terrible child-eating ogre whom no steel weapon could hurt. One day, when he was drunk, a great band of children ambushed him on Groaning Bridge and sawed him in half with a two-handled wooden saw – the children of East Sussex taking one end, and those of West Sussex the other. The severed portions of his body are still said to haunt both Brede Place and the bridge.

Brighton *E. Sussex*

Brighton children still carry holed stones picked up on the beach for luck – a belief going back at least 5000 years, to judge by similar stones found in the grave of a Stone Age woman at Whitehawk Neolithic Camp east of the town centre. Bat-and-trap, one of the oldest known games in the world, is played on The Level on Good Friday morning. The trap is a seesaw-like catapult which throws a ball in the air when the batsman hits the trap's raised end with his bat; the game may have its origins in ancient fertility rites.

In the grounds of the Pavilion stands an ancient oak; like several similar trees scattered throughout the country, it is said to be the one in which Charles II hid after the Battle of Worcester. A Sussex location seems unlikely, but the story is vouched for by the descendants of the captain of the ship that took the king to France from nearby Shoreham in 1651.

Ghosts are well represented in the area; a wailing child that died of neglect, and a murderer whose phantom hands still attempt to strangle anyone who sleeps in a particular bed, haunt houses in Shoreham. A famous Brighton ghost is that of a monk who haunts Meeting House Lane. Tradition says he was walled up alive for running away with a local girl; his spirit has often been seen disappearing through a bricked-up doorway next to the Friends' Meeting House.

Built into the wall surrounding Rudyard Kipling's old house at Rottingdean, is a lucky stone head. Anyone who strokes the nose gently in a clockwise motion with the forefinger of the right hand, then turns round three times, will be granted their dearest wish – or so local legend maintains.

Many legends also surround the ancient stone plinth in St Nicholas's churchyard in central Brighton. According to one version, a knight and his horse, both in armour, are buried beneath it, and on moonlit nights the horse emerges alone and gallops round the churchyard. The best-known story connected with the plinth, however, is that of the tragic love and death of the beautiful Lady Edona in the 14th century.

THE TRAGEDY OF LADY EDONA

A bloody feud raged for years in the 14th century between the 4th Earl de Warrenne and Lord Pevensey. Early one May morning, the two rivals met beneath the walls of Lewes Castle to settle their differences in single combat. Within minutes, Lord Pevensey managed to drive his adversary into a corner, and raised his battle-axe to deal the death-blow.

High up on the castle battlements, the despairing Lady de Warrenne prayed to St Nicholas to save her husband, vowing that her first-born son would not marry until he had laid St Nicholas's belt on the tomb of the Blessed Virgin in Byzantium. At that moment, Lord Pevensey lost his balance and, as he fell, the Earl ran him through with his sword.

Twenty years later, the Earl's eldest son, Lord Manfred, was betrothed to the beautiful Lady Edona, though he had not yet fulfilled his mother's vow. Half-way through a banquet held to celebrate the 21st anniversary of the Earl's victory, a chill wind suddenly blew through the great hall, lightning blazed across the tapestried walls, and the terrified guests saw a vision of the Earl's battle.

The Earl and his wife understood at once, and the next day a ship was ordered to take Manfred to Byzantium. It was arranged that Manfred should marry Edona as soon as he had fulfilled the sacred vow.

Lord Manfred sailed, and for a year the love-lorn Edona waited for him to return. Then, on May 17, his ship was sighted off Worthing Point, and Lady Edona, her family, and the Earl and all his retinue gathered on St Nicholas's Hill to watch the ship sail in.

Just then, disaster struck. Lord Manfred's ship ran on to a hidden rock, keeled over on its side, and sank so quickly that only one sailor escaped.

In silent, helpless grief, the company on the hill watched the ship go down. When it had gone, Edona gave one sigh, and she sank, dying of sorrow, to the ground. The Earl passed his hands over his eyes; he never smiled again, and lived only long enough to build the Church of St Nicholas as a reminder to others never to neglect their vows.

Lady Edona was buried where she fell; an ancient plinth in St Nicholas's churchyard is said to mark her grave. As for Lord Manfred, his ghostly ship still sails towards the harbour at midnight every May 17, and each year it is said to founder again on the same treacherous rock.

Buckland Surrey

A long time ago, the lord of the manor attempted to seduce a village maiden, whose modesty was so outraged that she dropped dead at his feet. Overcome by remorse, the lord stabbed himself, and his blood ran over a rock that stood beside a nearby stream. For years afterwards, villagers avoided the stone, for it was said to ooze the lord's guilty blood. Another explanation for the red stains on the rock was that it was once the home of a water-horse called the Buckland Shag, who murdered his victims on top of it. The Shag terrified wayfarers for generations until a brave Vicar of Buckland exorcised the creature with bell, book and candle and banished it to the Red Sea – a frequent place of exile for ghosts and goblins.

CANTERBURY'S DARK ENTRY

The passage between the old infirmary cloister and the Green Court in Canterbury Cathedral is known as the Dark Entry. It is reputedly haunted by Nell Cook, a servant of a canon of the cathedral. Nell discovered that her employer was having an affair with his niece and, in a fit of jealousy, killed them both with a poisoned pie. The authorities buried her alive beneath the pavement of the Dark Entry, and her ghost has haunted the passageway ever since. According to R. H. Barham (1788–1845), author of the 'Ingoldsby Legends', the visitations occur on Friday nights, and anyone who sees the spirit will die. The story is widely believed, but Barham probably invented the whole thing

Chanctonbury Ring W. Sussex

This Iron Age hill-fort, surrounded by ramparts of eroded turf, is an eerie place. The air within the clump of beech trees on its summit strikes chill by comparison with the sunny Downland outside, and it is said that no bird sings among them. It is generally believed that the trees are uncountable; on the other hand, if anyone succeeds in doing so, he will raise the ghosts of Julius Caesar and his armies. The Devil, too, can be conjured up by running seven times backwards round the clump at midnight on Midsummer Eve. When he appears, he will offer a bowl of porridge; if you accept, he will take your soul in exchange or, in another version, your dearest wish will be granted. The thudding hooves of invisible horses have often been heard on the hilltop, and a mysterious, white-bearded man has been reported; he is said to be the ghost of an old Druid, searching for buried treasure.

Coldharbour Surrey

In a wood near Coldharbour is Maggs Well, long credited with healing properties. People still regard it as a wishing well, but it is important to drop a coin into its waters before wishing, in order to placate the spirit of the place.

Combwell Kent

In a yew alcove in the garden of the old manor of Combwell, near Goudhurst, is the statue of a woman carrying a pestle and mortar. This is said to commemorate a cook who worked in the house at the time of the Civil War. One Sunday, when the family had gone to church, she admitted a beggar-woman to her kitchen. But as the woman bent down by the fire, the cook noticed that she wore boots and spurs beneath her ragged dress. Dealing the 'woman' a blow with the poker, the cook rushed upstairs and rang the alarm bell. Her master and the servants returned just in time to save the house from being sacked by a band of deserters. The cook's statue stood in the house for many years, but because it was considered uncanny by later generations of servants, it was moved to the garden.

Cranleigh Surrey

Two miles from Cranleigh lies the great Tudor mansion of Baynards Park which, for a time at least, sheltered the decapitated head of Thomas More. Sir (and later, Saint) Thomas was executed in 1535 for refusing to acknowledge Henry VIII's supremacy of the Church in England. His head was impaled on Tower Bridge, and was afterwards ordered to be thrown into the Thames. More's daughter, Margaret Roper, bribed the executioner to give it to her, and she brought it to Baynards Park. The ghost of Thomas More has frequently been reported there.

Dartford Kent

An old legend says that the Peasants' Revolt of 1381 was sparked off at Dartford when a tax collector made a personal examination of a young girl to discover whether she had reached puberty. At puberty, she would have been liable to pay the unpopular poll tax. Her outraged father, Wat the Tyler, killed the collector with a hammer, and was elected leader of the Kentish peasants when they marched on London to demand the abolition of serfdom and relief from their poverty. The rising petered out when Wat was stabbed by the Mayor of London, William Walworth, at Smithfield, in the presence of Richard II; the fatal dagger can still be seen in the Fishmongers' Hall, London. This story is still firmly believed in Dartford, but historians maintain that Wat came from Colchester, and had nothing to do with the tax collector's murder.

Devil's Dyke *W. Sussex*

Local tradition says that this great cleft in the Downs south of Poynings village was dug by the Devil. The enthusiasm of the Sussex people for religion made him decide one night to drown them all by digging a ditch through to the sea. As he reached the halfway mark, an old woman rushed up the hill with a lighted candle and a sieve. The light woke a cock, which began to crow, whereupon the Devil, also seeing the candle through the sieve, imagined that sunrise was upon him, and fled.

Ditchling *E. Sussex*

A letter published in the now defunct *Sussex County Magazine* in 1935, described how a witch in the Ditchling area had the power of immobilising farm carts. One day a carter detected the witch by cutting notches in the spokes of a wheel. Yells came from a nearby cottage, and an old woman rushed out, blood pouring from as many cuts on her fingers as there were notches in the spokes.

Eastwell *Kent*

A local legend says that when Sir Thomas Moyle was building his new mansion in Eastwell Park in 1545, he was astonished to discover that his foreman bricklayer was reading a book in Latin. Sir Thomas questioned him, and was told that in 1485, when the bricklayer was a young man, he had been summoned to the royal camp at Bosworth Field. There he was told that his education was due to his being the illegitimate son of Richard III, who acknowledged him as his heir. The next day, Richard was defeated and killed in battle by the forces of Henry Tudor, and the king's son fled from the field. To avoid recognition by Tudor agents he became a bricklayer, and had worked at the trade ever since. Sir Thomas gave him a home at Eastwell and there he died, the entry in the burial register reading 'December 22, 1550: Richard Plantagenet'. It may be that an unmarked grave near the north side of the church contains the remains of the last member of the royal house of York.

HANG ON THE BELL

During the Wars of the Roses, a nephew of the Earl of Warwick was captured by the Yorkists and condemned to die at Chertsey, Surrey, within 24 hours; the signal for his execution was to be the tolling of the curfew bell in St Peter's Church. A messenger was sent to the king for a pardon, but when the time came for the bell to ring, he still had a mile to ride. As if by a miracle, the bell did not ring that night and the condemned man's life was saved. It turned out that his sweetheart, Blanche Heriot, had climbed into the belfry and hung on the great bell's clapper until he was reprieved. This exploit became a favourite theme of later storytellers, and in America, it inspired the well-known ballad:

> 'As you swing to the left,
> And you swing to the right,
> Remember the curfew
> Must never ring tonight.
> So hang on the bell, Nelly!
> Hang on the bell!'

East Grinstead *E. Sussex*

Snakes are considered unlucky in Sussex, and in 1936 the erection of a symbol depicting the serpent and staff of Aesculapius, Greek god of medicine, outside the Queen Victoria Hospital caused a public outcry. Protesters were told it would cost £63 to remove 'the brazen serpent', and it remains there to this day.

Ebbsfleet *Kent*

This part of Pegwell Bay is the traditional landing place of Hengist and Horsa, who led the successful Jutish invasion of England in AD 449. It is said that their forces fought under the banner of a prancing white horse – a device which is the badge of Kent to this day.

Epsom *Surrey*

Pitt Place, a house that was pulled down only a few years ago, once belonged to Lord Lyttelton, who died there on November 27, 1779. Just before his death, he was warned by a ghost that he had only three days to live. He was much upset, but seemed perfectly healthy until an hour before the ultimatum was due to expire; then he had a sudden seizure and died. At that moment, his friend Miles Andrews, asleep in his bed at Dartford, awoke to see Lyttelton wearing a dressing-gown that was kept for his use when he came to stay. Lyttelton said: 'It's all up with me, Andrews,' and walked into the dressing room.

Andrews followed, but the room was empty and the gown hung on its usual hook. Thinking it was all a joke, he returned to bed, and was horrified to learn the next morning that Lyttelton was dead.

Farnham *Surrey*
Near Waverley Abbey is a deep cave, said to have been the home of a white witch named Mother Ludlam. Local people would go to the cave at midnight, and beg: 'Good Mother Ludlam, lend me (whatever they needed) and I will return it within two days.' The article they required would be found next day standing before the cave. Once, someone failed to return a cauldron within the stipulated period, and the witch never lent anything again. When the cauldron was finally returned, she ignored it, and tradition says it was taken to Waverley Abbey, and afterwards to Frensham church, where it remains today. The cave is so deep that it is said that geese that went in at Farnham reappeared featherless in Guildford two weeks later.

Frensham *Surrey*
In the 13th-century church there is a huge cauldron, 1 yd in diameter. Despite a differing Farnham legend, local people say that it was borrowed from the fairies and never returned. Because of this, the fairies would never lend anything again.

Friston *E. Sussex*
The churchyards of Friston and East Dean both have Tapsell gates, named after the 18th-century carpenter who built them. Balanced on a central pivot, they open at the lightest touch; at weddings, however, the gates are tied with white ribbon, and the bride is lifted over them by the groom.

FAIRIES' KETTLE

This cauldron, now kept in St Mary's Church, Frensham, was said to have been borrowed from the fairies who lived on nearby Borough Hill

Godalming *Surrey*
Jacobite legends cling to Westbrook Place, which once belonged to the Oglethorpes, a family who for generations were ardent supporters of the Stuart cause. In 1688, just before James II was deposed in favour of William of Orange, his queen gave birth to a son, most of whose life was to be spent in exile. Known to Jacobites as 'James III', and to Hanoverian supporters as 'The Old Pretender', he was to be the focus of Stuart hopes until his death in 1766. But according to one story, he was not a royal child at all; he was the son of Sir Theophilus Oglethorpe, and had been smuggled into the Palace of Westminster in a warming pan and there exchanged for a stillborn child born to the queen. The story is given some support by the fact that Queen Mary had many miscarriages, and not one of her other children

MARY TOFTS, *who 'gave birth' to rabbits*

THE RABBIT WOMAN OF GODALMING

In 1727, Mr Howard, a surgeon of Guildford, announced that he had safely delivered Mary Tofts, a Godalming woman, of a number of rabbits. Mary claimed that conception had occurred when she was startled by a rabbit while weeding; later, she dreamt of rabbits in her lap. Many people believed her story, including the royal surgeon, Dr St André, and it was suggested that she should be given a pension. Doubts arose, however, and Mary confessed to fraud; her supporters were ridiculed for their gullibility in cartoons, such as this one by Hogarth (above)

DR ST ANDRÉ, *royal surgeon, who believed her claim*

survived the hazards then surrounding infancy.

Westbrook Place has a Stuart ghost, said to be that of Bonnie Prince Charlie, who was alleged to have conferred there with his supporters just before the Rising of 1745. Since the Prince had to remain hidden, he could take exercise only at night or in the early morning; the mysterious figure, closely wrapped in a brown cloak, that has often been seen walking the paths of Westbrook in the twilight, is believed to be the restless spirit of the Young Pretender.

An imperial phantom may reside at the King's Arms Royal Hotel in the High Street. Peter the Great, Czar of Russia, stayed there in 1698 with 20 companions, and their rowdy behaviour caused grave scandal in the town. Perhaps the party continues still, for, apparently without human agency, glasses and other objects are thrown about the room they once occupied.

Guildford *Surrey*

An old charter says that 'whenever the King comes to Lothesley Manor near Guildford, the lord is to present His Majesty with Three Whores'. No one knows when the custom fell into abeyance. Bull-baiting is said to have been introduced to England from the Continent by a 14th-century Earl of Surrey. The first contest took place in Guildford, and thereafter, each member of the Corporation, on appointment, was obliged to provide a breakfast for his colleagues and a bull for baiting. The custom lapsed as bull-baiting died out in the 19th century.

Under the terms of John How's will, ratified in 1674, 'two poor servant maids of good report' selected by the mayor and magistrates of Guildford, provided they 'do not live in any inn or alehouse', may throw dice for the interest on £400. The contest takes place on or about January 27 each year at the Guildhall, and the winner receives £12.

THE SILENT POOL

There are days when an uncanny silence seems to hang over the surface of 'Silent Pool', a small lake surrounded by trees a mile west of Shere in Surrey. And if the legend that is told about the lake is true, this silence recalls the murderous lechery of a prince and the tragic deaths of a woodman's children.

One day, it is said, when all this area was dense forest, a richly dressed stranger called at the hut of a local woodman. The woodman was a widower, and lived with his two children – a lovely teen-age girl and a sturdy son.

While the woodman entertained his noble visitor, his daughter went out to bathe in Silent Pool. No sooner had she slipped into the water than she heard someone crashing through the undergrowth. She hurried to the bank to dress, but before she could do so, her father's guest burst from the woods and stopped his horse over her clothes, laughing triumphantly.

With a cry of fright, the girl ran back to the water to hide; and the stranger, quickly realising that there was no way of luring her back to the bank, cursed her modesty and spurred his horse into the pool after her. She screamed and threw herself into the deepest part of the pool, though she could not swim.

She had just struggled to the surface when her brother, hearing her cries, arrived at the pool and leapt in to rescue her. But he too was a poor swimmer and, as she sank for the last time, he clasped her in his arms and they died together, at the bottom of the pool. The stranger rode away.

Some time later the woodman came to the pond looking for his children and, grief-stricken, dragged their bodies from the water. There the story might have ended, had the distracted man not spotted a feather caught in a tree.

He knew it was from the stranger's hat, and deduced that his children had been murdered.

By asking questions in the district, he soon found out that the stranger had been none other than Prince John, Regent of Britain while his brother Richard the Lion Heart was crusading in Palestine. The woodman told his story to one of John's enemies, who arranged an audience at Guildford Castle.

The woodman came to the audience in disguise, and told his story again. John had forgotten the incident, and declared that the murderer must be punished. The woodman produced the lost feather and denounced him.

Legend does not say how the audience ended; but certainly, the woodman had his revenge. By tradition, the tragic deaths of his children confirmed the barons in their hatred of John, and paved the way for their triumph over him at Runnymede in 1215.

Hambledon *Surrey*

Tolt Hill, near Hambledon, was said to contain buried treasure. The ground rang hollow if stamped on, and rattled when ploughed. Yet no one tried to excavate the site, for the treasure was the property of the Devil, and people avoided the place after dark.

Harbledown *Kent*

The village was the last halting place for pilgrims going to Canterbury. It contains the Black Prince's Well, so-called because the prince set such store by the healing properties of its waters that he drank a flask of it every day. The prince died in 1376, probably of syphilis contracted in Spain.

Hastings *E. Sussex*

A cock crowing is said to have woken a force of Danes occupying Hastings in the 9th century and foiled a local uprising against their tyranny. As a vengeance on all cocks, the townspeople instituted the game of cock-in-the-pot, in which sticks were thrown at an earthen pot containing a cock and whoever broke it won the bird. The game was held on Shrove Tuesday until the 19th century.

Heathfield *E. Sussex*

April 14 is 'Hefful' – the old name for Heathfield – Fair Day. According to legend, an old woman attends the fair, and lets the first cuckoo of the year out of a basket. Though the old woman has never been seen, it is lucky to hear the first cuckoo on that day, particularly if you remember to turn over the money in your pockets.

Henfield *W. Sussex*

A row of iron cats on the wall of a 16th-century cottage near the church is said to recall a feud between a villager and the vicar. The church cat ate the villager's canary and, in retaliation, he made cats out of sheet iron, attached them to a wire, and jangled them whenever the vicar walked by. The cats were later cemented to the wall.

Hersham *Surrey*

William Lilly, the 17th-century astrologer, lived here during the latter part of his life. He sold prophecies to both sides during the Civil War, and is said to have forecast the Great Fire of London. On one occasion, he attempted to find treasure in Westminster Abbey by means of divining rods, but as he began his candle was blown out 'by daemons'. These, he said, were raised by the merriment of the onlookers, and had he not dismissed them, they would have blown down the abbey.

Hove *E. Sussex*

Until 1957, a 20 ft high Bronze Age burial mound stood on the site now occupied by Palmeria Avenue. Among the objects discovered in the 3500-year-old grave were a bronze dagger, a stone axe-hammer, and a beautiful red amber cup, all of which are now in Brighton Museum. Until it was demolished, young people visited the mound on Good Friday to skip and play games such as kiss-in-the-ring on its flat top, chanting:

Hey, derry, derry,
Let's jump on the bury.

THE DRUMMER OF HERSTMONCEUX

Ghostly drumming is frequently heard on the battlements of Herstmonceux Castle, and a 9 ft tall phantom drummer has been seen. The ghost is that of a previous lord of the manor who beat a drum in order to frighten the prospective lovers of his young wife

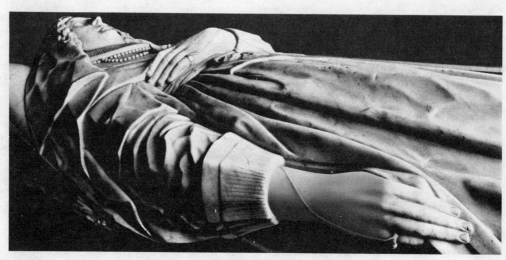

FASHION SET BY A KING'S GIFT

Lady Culpeper died in 1638, and is buried in Hollingbourne church, Kent. Her effigy shows her wearing a ring on each hand, each of which is attached to the wrist by a fine cord. The fashion had considerable vogue in the 17th century, and is said to have originated when James I gave one of his own rings to a lady at court. Since the ring was too big, she tied it to her wrist, and other ladies copied the fashion

GHOST SHIPS OF THE GOODWIN SANDS

It is said that as many as 50,000 men have died in shipwrecks on the Goodwin Sands, a treacherous sandbank which lies some 5 miles off Deal in Kent. So it is hardly surprising that these waters are reputedly haunted, and that many stories have been told of phantom ships which sail there.

The 'Lady Lovibond'
Most famous of the Goodwins' ghost ships is the *Lady Lovibond*, a three-masted schooner which was lost with all hands on February 13, 1748. She was bound for Oporto, and on board was the captain's new bride Annetta. This in itself made the journey hazardous, for sailors have always believed that it is unlucky to take a woman to sea. But in this case it was doubly dangerous, for the mate had been a rival for Annetta's love. Perhaps in a fit of jealousy, he killed the helmsman

and deliberately steered the ship on to the sands.

Exactly 50 years later, on February 13, 1798, the master of the coaster *Edenbridge* entered in his log that he had almost collided with a three-masted schooner sailing straight for the sands; another ship reported seeing the schooner run aground. Then in 1848 the schooner was seen again, though the Deal lifeboatmen who went to her rescue could find no trace of her. She was next seen in 1898, and then in 1948. If she keeps to her schedule, she should appear next on February 13, 1998.

The SS 'Violet'
Over a century ago, the SS *Violet*, a cross-Channel paddle steamer, was driven on to the sands during a violent snowstorm, and all the passengers and crew were drowned. At the beginning

of the Second World War, the tragedy was re-enacted; Mr George Carter, the look-out on the East Goodwin lightship, saw an old paddle steamer run on to the sands, and called out the Ramsgate lifeboat. An hour-long search revealed nothing, and no paddle steamer was ever reported missing.

The drowned island of Lomea
The Goodwin Sands are also said to be the site of the drowned island of Lomea, and the bells of lost churches sometimes toll beneath the waves. By tradition, Lomea was flooded in the 11th century when its owner, Earl Godwin of the West Saxons, failed to maintain its sea walls. But, in fact, there is no evidence that such an island ever existed. Borings have indicated decayed marine matter between layers of sand as far down as 78 ft, all resting on a strata of chalk.

Ightham *Kent*

An anonymous letter which hinted mysteriously at 'a terrible blow' soon to fall on parliament led to the discovery of the Gunpowder Plot in 1605. According to legend, James I showed the letter to Dame Dorothy Selby, who understood at once its dreadful implications and urged the king, who usually dismissed such letters as the work of cranks, to treat it with the utmost seriousness. A mural in Ightham church is dedicated to Dame Dorothy.

Isle of Thanet *Kent*

Hoodening, an ancient alms-collecting ceremony still practised in East (but not West) Kent, and especially in Thanet, derives its name from the Hooden Horse. This is a mock horse's head with a flapping lower jaw, into which money is dropped. The head is operated by a man concealed beneath a white sheet. In summer the horse appears with Morris Men, and at Christmas with carol-singers, calling at houses and farms. It rewards generosity with high-spirited cavortings. The custom may be linked with the local 5th-century Jutish worship of the god Woden, who rode an eight-footed white stallion.

Kingley Vale *W. Sussex*

In 874, says the *Anglo-Saxon Chronicle*, a marauding band of Vikings ravaged the Chichester countryside, 'and the citizens put them to flight, and killed many hundreds of them'. Local tradition asserts that the battle was fought in Kingley Vale, 4 miles north-west of Chichester, and that the superb grove of ancient yews now filling the vale is descended from 60 trees planted on the graves of those that died in the fighting. At night, it is said, the trees change their shapes and move stealthily about the vale, in which lurk the ghosts of the slaughtered Vikings and Saxon defenders.

Lyminster *W. Sussex*

The Knuckler Hole, a deep pool, lies about 150 yds north-west of the Lyminster churchyard wall. Tradition maintains that it was the lair of a mighty dragon whose only food was 'fair damsels'. It gradually devoured all maidens in the region until only one was left, the King of Sussex's daughter. Desperately, her father offered her in marriage, together with half of his kingdom, to anyone who could kill the beast. This was done, after a furious battle, by a brave knight who then married the princess and settled in the area. In the north transept of the church stands an early Norman coffin slab known as The Slayer's Stone, reputed to be the knight's tomb.

Maidstone *Kent*

Henry VIII is said to have first set eyes on Anne Boleyn at nearby Allington Castle. In Maidstone Museum is a chair from the castle, with a faded inscription on the back giving substance to the legend that it was King Henry's privilege to kiss any woman who sat in it. The inscription reads:

'. . . of this (chay)re iss entytled too one salute
from everie ladie thott settes downe in itt
Castell Alynton 1530   Hen. 8 Rex'

LEWES BONFIRE NIGHT

November 5 has long been celebrated in Lewes with great pageantry, as is shown in this cover picture of the town's 1850 Fireworks Programme. During the reign of the Catholic Queen Mary Tudor, Lewes folk were largely Protestant, and many of them were burnt as heretics on School Hill in the town centre. The ensuing anti- *papist resentment found its outlet in Bonfire Night. Today, there are elaborate bonfire ceremonies, and processions converge on the bridge where a blazing tar-barrel is hurled into the River Ouse. This is a relic of pagan Celtic rites, the fire doused by water representing winter overcoming summer*

ST DUNSTAN AND THE DEVIL

In the convent of the Holy Child Jesus at Mayfield, E. Sussex, is a pair of tongs which tradition claims was the property of the great Saxon churchman St Dunstan. Tradition must be wrong in this case, because though the monastery stands on the site of Mayfield Palace, where Dunstan lived when he was Archbishop of Canterbury, the tongs were certainly not made before the 13th century, 300 years after his death.

But tradition and history are in agreement on St Dunstan's faultless piety; and the stories that are told about his battles with the Devil may be allegories of his conversion to Christianity. For before he was converted by St Alphege, it was widely rumoured that he had occult powers, and even dabbled in black magic.

According to the best-known story about him, he worked for a time as a blacksmith in Mayfield, while spreading the message of the gospels. One day, the Devil became so enraged by this that he disguised himself as a beautiful young woman, and set about seducing him.

Dunstan did not even look up, but kept on with his work as the Devil minced around the room, until his skirts rode up and revealed his hooves. Calmly, St Dunstan took a pair of red-hot tongs from the blazing forge (the same tongs that are now in the monastery) and clamped them on to the Devil's nose.

The Devil's screams as he flew out of the forge could be heard up to 3 miles away; and as he raced across the sky, he saw the springs of Tunbridge Wells, swooped down on them and submerged his nose in the water. To this day the water from the springs is still red and tastes of sulphur.

Minster-in-Sheppey *Kent*
R. H. Barham, in his *Ingoldsby Legends*, tells how the tempestuous Sir Roger de Shurland, Lord of Sheppey in 1300, killed a monk who defied him. Hunted by the county sheriff, Sir Roger obtained the king's pardon by swimming out on horseback to Edward I's ship as it was passing by in the Thames estuary. Returning to shore, he was met by a mysterious hag who prophesied that his horse, having saved his life, would also cause his death. The fiery knight at once drew his sword and beheaded the horse. Some years later, walking on the beach, he came upon its skull. Enraged, he kicked it, but one of its teeth penetrated his boot, causing an injury from which he died soon afterwards. Sir Roger's tomb is in the abbey-church at Minster. His stone effigy is still there and, close to the right foot, there is the head of a horse.

Minster-in-Thanet *Kent*
Thunor, a Kentish thane, secured the throne of Kent for Egbert I by murdering the young princes Ethelbert and Ethelred, and secretly burying their bodies within the royal palace. Shortly afterwards, the graves were revealed by two mysterious columns of light, and penitent Egbert ordered that all land to the east of its course should be given to the dead princes' sister, Ermenburga, so that she could build an abbey. Ever devious, Thunor tried to divert the animal, but 'the wrath of heaven came upon him, the earth opened and swallowed him up'. In 670 Minster Abbey was duly founded by Ermenburga, and today it is occupied by Benedictine nuns. At the top of Minster Hill is an enormous pit, still known as 'Thunorsleap'.

Newington *Kent*
At Newington church, set amidst the Kent cherry orchards, can be seen the Devil's footprint, 15 in. long. An old story tells that Satan, unable to endure the ringing of the church bells, collected them in a sack one night, and leapt down from the church tower. Overbalancing as he landed, he left his footprint on a stone near the church gate, and the bells rolled out of the sack to vanish for ever in a nearby stream.

Otford *Kent*
Becket's Well, which was excavated a few years ago, is said to have miraculous origins. A legend says that when Archbishop Thomas à Becket was in Otford he was displeased with the quality of the local water. To remedy the matter, he struck the ground with his crozier and from the spot there bubbled up two springs of clear water. Becket is also held responsible for the absence of nightingales in the village. When the song of a nightingale disturbed his devotions he commanded that none should sing there again. And, so it is said, none has.

Oxenford *Surrey*

The grange of Oxenford, which originally belonged to the Abbot of Waverley, was granted to the Earl of Southampton when Henry VIII dissolved the monasteries. According to local tradition, the Waverley monks buried a chest of treasure which can be located only by its rightful owners and, once found, can be lifted to the surface only by a team of seven white oxen. The story says that the chest was once uncovered and a team of white oxen harnessed to it. But the attempt failed because the hide of one of the oxen was blemished.

Pyrford *Surrey*

The Pyrford Stone was probably used as a boundary mark before the Norman Conquest. Recently it was shifted during road-widening operations but the local people moved it again to a position as close as possible to its original site at the entrance to Pyrford Court. The stone is said to turn when it hears the cock crow at dawn – and when the clock on nearby St Nicholas's Church strikes midnight. The reference to the church is a Pyrford leg-pull: St Nicholas's has never had a clock.

Rainham *Kent*

A strange legend about a phantom coach is still current in Rainham. The coach is believed to leave the church at midnight, drawn by headless horses and driven by a headless coachman. Inside sits a headless man holding his head in his hands. The coach stops at Queen Court in Berengrave Lane (now absorbed in a housing estate) to water the headless horses, while an old woman sits spinning on top of a barn. Then the coach carries on to Bloor's Place, enters the grounds of the house, and disappears. The passenger in the coach is said to be the ghost of Christopher Bloor, who had a reputation as a ladies' man in Tudor times. The legend says that the town's irate husbands banded together and waylaid him at midnight. His head was cut off and placed on a spike high on the church tower. However, the records show that Christopher Bloor actually died in bed, and there is no written reference to his allegedly lecherous habits.

Until the mid-1960's the owners of Bloor's old house used to put out a full glass of brandy for the coach-travelling ghost every Christmas Eve, and the glass was always empty in the morning. The local policeman was once questioned about the mystery. 'It's a fact,' he said. 'But I blames the postman.'

Ripley *Surrey*

In the early part of this century the people of Woking called Ripley a village of fools, and whenever a Woking man met a man from Ripley he would flap an imaginary apron. It is said that a Ripley blacksmith once threw a horse down on the green to shoe it, but failed to notice that the horse had died of a heart attack. When it was shod, he flapped his apron to make the horse get up. When it didn't, he flapped his apron again – and again. The Woking people nicknamed Ripley 'The Place Where They Shoe Dead Horses'.

George Ripley, a medieval monk, was, according to tradition, a local alchemist. It was claimed that he could turn base metals into gold.

Rye *E. Sussex*

An old gibbet cage hangs in Rye Town Hall. Inside is the skull of John Breeds, a local butcher who was hanged in 1742 for a crime that misfired. Breeds intended murdering the mayor of Rye, against whom he bore a grudge, but he killed the mayor's brother-in-law by mistake. The butcher's run of bad luck continued even after death; it is said that the rest of his bones were stolen, probably to make medicine. It was a popular belief that a cure for rheumatism could be made from the bones of a person hung on a gibbet.

TWIN SISTERS AND TWIN TOWERS

An old Saxon church with ruined towers and spires stands right on the edge of the sea at Reculver in Kent. Legend says the spires were added to the original towers in the 16th century at the request of the abbess of the Benedictine nunnery at Davington, Frances St Clare. They were to serve as a memorial to her twin sister, Isabel, and as a landmark for shipping in the Thames Estuary. The two nuns were on a pilgrimage to the shrine of the Virgin at Bradstow when their ship was wrecked off Reculver. Isabel died from injuries and was buried in the churchyard. When Frances died some years later she was buried beside her sister under the twin towers

CHILD SACRIFICE

A Reculver legend says that on stormy nights babies can be heard crying on the wind. Substance was added to the folk tale about ten years ago when archaeologists excavating the Roman fort found a number of babies' skeletons. It is thought that the children were buried alive as sacrifices

THE DRAGONS OF ST LEONARD'S FOREST

About half-way between Horsham and Pease Pottage in W. Sussex are the Lily Beds, an area of St Leonard's Forest where lilies-of-the-valley grow wild. By tradition, the flowers have grown there ever since St Leonard slew a fearsome dragon that was terrorising the neighbourhood in the 6th century. The hermit-saint was wounded during the fight, and wherever his blood fell lilies-of-the-valley sprang up.

As a reward for the brave saint's courage, God also decreed that adders in the forest would never sting again, and that nightingales, which had disturbed the saint's prayers, would never sing there again.

A strange and monstrous serpent
But apparently, St Leonard did not free the forest of dragons, for three local villagers claimed to have come across a 'strange and monstrous serpent' in 1614, and rumours of hideous creatures lurking among the trees lingered on until well into the 19th century.

An offensive smell
According to the villagers who said they had seen it, the dragon of 1614 was just over 9 ft long, thick in the middle and thin at the ends, with red scales on its belly, black ones on its back and a ring of white markings around its neck. It had large feet, could run as fast as a man, and had on its flanks 'two great bunches so big as a large footeball, which (as some thinke) will in time grow to wings'. Wherever it went, it left a track of 'glutinous and slimie matter which is very corrupt and offensive to the smell'.

The dragon was reputedly able to spit its deadly venom over a great distance and it was held responsible for the deaths of two people. 'As by woeful experience it was proved on the bodies of a man and a woman coming that way, who afterwards were found dead, being poysoned and very much swelled, but not prayed upon.' It killed two dogs in the same way, but did not eat them either. Apparently, it lived mainly on a diet of rabbits.

Neither history nor legend relate what eventually happened to the creature.

The ghost of Squire Paulett
The forest was also said to be haunted by a certain Squire Paulett, whose headless ghost used to leap up behind any rider passing among the trees, grip him round the waist, and ride behind him to the forest's edge. Who he had been in life and how he lost his head, no one was ever able to find out.

Sandwich *Kent*

In the Battle of Sandwich, fought on St Bartholomew's Day, August 24, 1217, the French fleet was commanded by an English traitor named Eustace the Monk. Eustace had the useful ability of making his ship invisible, but his wizardry was defeated by Stephen Crabbe of Sandwich who knew the black arts as well as he. Crabbe boarded the monk's ship and cut off Eustace's head; immediately the ship became visible.

The French were, in fact, defeated by the Cinque Ports' fleet on this day, and the head of the treacherous monk was carried through the streets of Dover and Canterbury. The Sandwich hospital which cared for the wounded still exists, and it was renamed St Bartholomew's Hospital in commemoration of the victory.

Shepperton *Surrey*

During the 1940's several people claim to have seen the ghost of a headless monk in Shepperton. It is believed to be the spirit of a monk from Chertsey Abbey who broke his vows and left his order to live with a woman on a shepherd's farm. The monk was pursued and beheaded. His ghost, dressed in monastic robes but lacking its head, wanders through the houses of the town which grew around the farm, still trying to escape from his pursuers.

Sissinghurst *Kent*

A staircase in Sissinghurst Castle is believed to be haunted. A few years ago, the late Lady Nicolson (Victoria Sackville-West), who restored the castle and its gardens, was walking towards the stairs with her dog when it suddenly raised its hackles and refused to go on. She herself sensed nothing strange, but she was sure that the dog had been frightened by something supernatural.

More than three centuries earlier the castle had earned an evil reputation. It was built by Sir John Baker who sent so many Protestants to the stake during Queen Mary's reign that he was known as 'Bloody Baker'. There is a legend that two women in the castle once hid under the staircase when they heard Sir John approaching. He was followed by a servant carrying the body of a dead woman, believed to have been murdered. As the servant climbed the stairs one of the dead woman's hands got caught in the banisters. Sir John promptly hacked the hand off and it fell into the lap of one of the women crouched below.

Slinfold *W. Sussex*

Where the road to Pulborough intersects the Horsham to Guildford road there used to be a boggy hollow known as Alfold Dene. It is said that many years ago a great bell which was being transported on a waggon rolled off and sank into the bog. The villagers tried vainly to retrieve it, then in desperation sought the advice of a witch. She said that the bell could only be hauled from the bog at midnight by a team of 12 white oxen, but no one was to speak during the operation.

The villagers followed her instructions, and the bell was almost clear of the bog when one of the men shouted excitedly:

'We've got the Alfold Dene gurt bell
In spite of all the devils in hell.'

Immediately the chain snapped and the bell sank back into the ooze.

Steyning *W. Sussex*

The new buildings of Steyning Grammar School stand on Penfolds Field which was cursed by St Cuthman in the 8th century. When he was a boy, St Cuthman spread the gospel through Sussex, and because he was unable to leave his invalid mother, he pulled her along with him in a cart. As they passed Penfolds Field, the cart collapsed and the old lady was thrown to the ground. Nearby haymakers laughed and jeered so St Cuthman cursed the field; rain poured down and spoilt the hay, and to this day, it is always supposed to rain when Penfolds Field is being mown. Christopher Fry made St Cuthman the hero of his play *Boy with a Cart* and a stone in Steyning church is believed once to have covered the saint's grave.

Strood *Kent*

During the bitter quarrel between Henry II and Thomas à Becket, the men of Strood, who were loyal to the king, are said to have cut off the tail of the archbishop's horse as he passed through their town. Becket pronounced that the descendants of those who played the prank would be born with tails, and legend says that they were.

Walton-on-Thames *Surrey*

The identity of the ghostly judge who is said to haunt Walton's 15th-century manor house is undecided because the manor was the home of two notorious judges – John Bradshaw, President of the Court which condemned Charles I to death, and Chief Justice Jeffreys who conducted the Bloody Assize after Monmouth's rebellion against James II.

HE SENTENCED A KING

A Puritan barrister, John Bradshaw, presided at the trial of Charles I, and was instrumental in sentencing him to death. Bradshaw was buried in Westminster Abbey, but after the Restoration his body was dug up and hanged at Tyburn. It may be his ghost that is said to haunt the house at Walton-on-Thames

West Horsley *Surrey*

A local tradition says that Carew Raleigh, son of Sir Walter Raleigh, was buried here in 1680. The head of Sir Walter, who was executed at Whitehall in 1618, is said to be interred with his son's body.

Weybridge *Surrey*

The old motor-racing circuit at Brooklands, near Weybridge, was abandoned before the Second World War. Weeds and bushes have broken through the cracked concrete of the great sweeping embankments where Bentleys and Alfa-Romeos battled for supremacy, and the whole track has fallen into decay. Yet often at night, it is said, the roar of great engines and the scream of tyres can still be heard. At the end of the Railway Straight, an aircraft factory has its sheds built over the track itself, covering the place where Percy Lambert, the racing motorist, was killed in October, 1913. On several occasions, night-workers have challenged an overalled, helmeted figure, and have even chased it – until it disappeared through a solid wall. It is believed to be the ghost of Lambert.

THE HAUNTED RACE TRACK

Though the motor-racing track at Brooklands, Surrey, has been closed for years, the snarl of engines is often heard on the old circuit. A factory now covers part of the Railway Straight, and men working the night shift have reported seeing the spectre of a racing driver

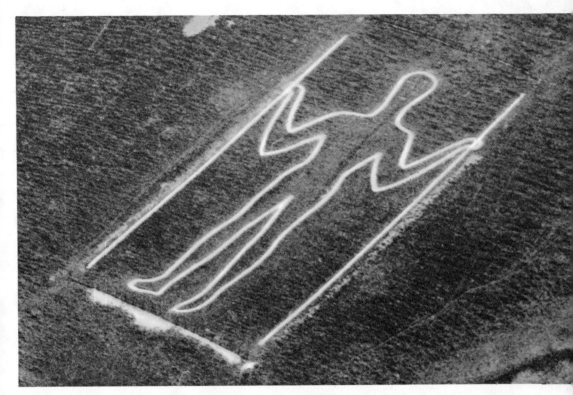

THE LONG MAN OF WILMINGTON

The famous 'Long Man' cut in chalk on Windover Hill, E. Sussex, was given its present form in 1874. By then, the figure had become overgrown and was visible only in certain lights or after snow had fallen. There is much argument about the age of the 'Long Man'; it has been ascribed to every period from New Stone Age to the Middle Ages. A recent theory is that it is a Saxon warrior-god, originally a spear-wielding figure in a horned helmet identical to that engraved on a buckle found in a 7th-century grave at Finglesham in Kent. If so, the helmet and the spear-points must have been turfed over by early Christians, leaving only the vague outline of a 'cap' mentioned in some early accounts, and the two staffs. Throughout the centuries the figure must have been preserved by repeated scourings, but there is no record of the beliefs that prompted this. There is, however, a story that the figure is that of a giant killed in a quarrel with another giant

Worplesdon *Surrey*

The antiquary Aubrey says that Charles Thornborough, one of Charles II's chaplains, found coal here. The depth of the seam was never established because his iron boring rods broke, and this was 'thought by Mr William Lilly (astrologer) to be by Subterranean spirits, for as fast as the irons were put in they would snap off'.

Worthing *W. Sussex*

From beneath an old oak tree at the end of Broadwater Green, skeletons were said to rise on Midsummer Eve and dance hand in hand around the tree until the first cock crowed. Today, the site of the tree is a triangle of land in the middle of a road intersection.

Wotton *Surrey*

The Forty-Shilling Day contest at Wotton is held annually in June. William Glanville, who died in 1711, left 40 shillings each for five poor boys of the parish. The contest consists in part of reciting the Lord's Prayer, the Apostles' Creed and the Ten Commandments 'in a plain and audible voice', with the right hand placed on Glanville's tomb in St John's churchyard.

0 5 10
MILES

ESSEX

ENFIELD

HOUNSLOW HEATH
(Highwaymen, 218)

TOTTENHAM

HAMPSTEAD HIGHGATE
EAST ACTON LONDON
NORTH KENSINGTON
HAMMERSMITH
RICHMOND
CHISWICK NORWOOD
KINGSTON-UPON-THAMES
HAMPTON COURT CARSHALTON

SURREY KENT

PRINCE ALBERT RD

ST JOHN'S WOOD

KING'S CROSS STATION
ST PANCRAS STATION

GOWER

MARYLEBONE RD

BAKER ST

RED LION SQUARE
ST GILES -IN-THE-FIELDS
BROADWICK ST
DEAN ST

EDGWARE RD

MARBLE ARCH

BERKELEY SQUARE

STRAND
TRAFALGAR SQUARE

BAYSWATER RD

WHITEHALL

KENSINGTON PALACE

ST JAMES'S PALACE
QUEEN ANNE'S GATE
WESTMINSTER ABBEY

HOLLAND HOUSE

THE CARRIAGE RD

KNIGHTSBRIDGE

LAMBETH BRIDGE

HOLLAND PARK AVE

KENSINGTON RD

BROMPTON RD

CROMWELL RD

HAMMERSMITH RD

WARWICK RD

OLD BROMPTON RD

SLOANE AVE RD

BELGRAVE RD

TALGARTH RD

LILLIE ROAD

FINBOROUGH RD

KINGS RD

CHELSEA BR RD

GROSVENOR RD

ROYAL HOSPITAL

CHELSEA EMBANKMENT

CHEYNE WALK

DAWES RD

N

0 ½ 1
MILES

THE FOLKLORE YEAR

St Blaise's Day (February 3)
St Etheldreda's, Ely Place
Blessing of the Throats

Mid-February for three days
Royal Albert Hall
English Folk Dance and Song Society Festival

February 20 or near
St Botolph's, Bishopsgate
Sir John Cass Commemoration Service

Thursday nearest March 31
St Clement Danes, Strand
Oranges and Lemons Children's Service

Good Friday
The Widow's Son pub, Devons Road
The Widow's Bun

Second Saturday in May
Hayes Common
Merrie England May Queens' Festival

May 21
Tower of London
Ceremony of the Lilies and the Roses to commemorate the death of Henry VI

Thursday after July 4
Vintners' Hall to Church of St James, Garlick Hill
Vintners' Procession

From Monday in 3rd week of July
The Thames between Blackfriars and Henley
Swan-Upping

August 1 or near
London Bridge to Chelsea Bridge
Watermen's Race

Wednesdays in August
Broad Sanctuary
Morris dancing

First Sunday in October
St Mary at Hill, Eastcheap
Costermongers' Harvest Festival

KEY TO SYMBOLS

CRIME AND PUNISHMENT		GRAVES AND MONUMENTS	
CURIOUS CHARACTERS		HOLY PLACES	
CUSTOMS AND FESTIVALS		LOCAL CURIOSITIES	
DEVILS AND DEMONS		MYSTERIOUS STONES	
GHOSTS		TREASURE	
GIANTS		WELLS AND SPRINGS	

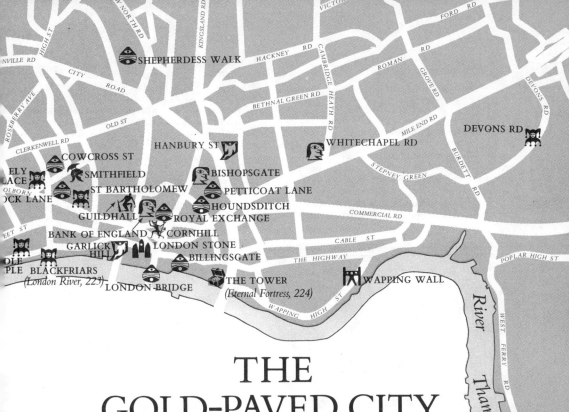

Map labels: NVILLE RD, W NORTH RD, HIGH ST, KINGSLAND RD, VICTORIA, FORD RD, RD, SHEPHERDESS WALK, HACKNEY RD, ROMAN RD, GROVER RD, DEVONS RD, CITY ROAD, ROSEBERRY AVE, OLD ST, BETHNAL GREEN RD, HEATH RD, MILE END RD, STEPNEY GREEN, BURDETT RD, DEVONS RD, CLERKENWELL RD, HANBURY ST, WHITECHAPEL RD, COWCROSS ST, HOLBORN, ELY PLACE, SMITHFIELD, BISHOPSGATE, COMMERCIAL RD, COCK LANE, ST BARTHOLOMEW, PETTICOAT LANE, GUILDHALL, HOUNDSDITCH, ROYAL EXCHANGE, CABLE ST, FLEET ST, BANK OF ENGLAND, CORNHILL, GARLICK HILL, LONDON STONE, THE HIGHWAY, POPLAR HIGH ST, MIDDLE TEMPLE, BILLINGSGATE, BLACKFRIARS, (London River, 223), LONDON BRIDGE, THE TOWER, (Eternal Fortress, 224), WAPPING WALL, WAPPING HIGH ST, River Thames, WEST FERRY RD

THE GOLD-PAVED CITY

London

'Hell is a city much like London,' wrote the poet William Blake, sourly striking at the image of London as 'the flower of cities all' set up by his medieval predecessor, the Scot, William Dunbar. London has worn both labels complacently, secure in its pre-eminence over all the other cities of the kingdom in size, wealth and population – a pre-eminence that is reflected in its tales and legends. London's lore has a double character: as the nation's capital, London is rich in associations with the great figures of the past, from Queen Boadicea onwards; while as the greatest city in the land, whose mythical gold-paved streets have tempted every ambitious youth since Dick Whittington first stood on Highgate Hill, it has bred innumerable customs and stories to amuse its children or to impress visitors from the 'provinces'.

Medieval Londoners lived in an age of faith, and many of the traditions that survive from that time have an ecclesiastical flavour. The medieval ritual of 'sin-eating' is remembered, however vaguely, in a Good Friday ceremony at London's oldest parish church, St Bartholomew the Great, Smithfield. In nearby Ely Place, throat troubles may be averted by attending the annual Blessing of the Throats at St Etheldreda's on February 3.

In that city of contrasts, where great houses overshadowed the reeking dwellings of the poor, and merchants, priests and nobles crowded the streets, there was much for the average Londoner to fear. Above all, he distrusted the Tower, that too-potent reminder of royal authority encroaching upon the City's liberties. The blood of princes and commoners alike stained the stones of the grim fortress; out of their terror may have arisen the latest-reported phantom of the Tower – the enormous shadow of an axe. There are also the more personal ghosts of Anne Boleyn, Jane Grey and Walter Raleigh, who smoked a pipe on the scaffold.

If a constantly growing city can be dated at all, then modern London probably emerged out of the ashes of the Great Fire of 1666, expanding westwards in a series of leafy squares. Near one of them, in Dean Street, Soho, lived Nell Gwyn, the orange seller who bridged the gap between royal and everyday London. Her ghost, wafted on a scent of gardenias, still haunts the club that occupies her house. Further west still, the world's end for many, stood the gallows of Tyburn Tree. The condemned were offered a last drink at St Giles, but one teetotaller who refused this comfort was early at Tyburn and was despatched just before his reprieve arrived.

Memories of old London

When, in the 19th century, London expanded, new figures emerged from the sooty fogs, such as the pawnbrokers who salvaged everyone's fortune, from those of George IV to the legendary saddler of City Road who 'popped' his 'weasel'. Even so, memories of the old villages still abound. In Highgate, you can become a 'freeman' by swearing an oath originated by 17th-century cattle drovers, while Bakerloo line commuters are convinced that the popping in their ears is caused by the train dipping to avoid the St John's Wood plague pit.

In the wall of St Swithin's Church, Cannon Street, largely destroyed by enemy action in 1940, there was an ancient stone, called the London Stone. Archaeologists have suggested that it was a milliary, the point from which the Romans measured road distances. But according to a City legend, the stone was placed there by Brutus, leader of the defeated remnants of the Trojan garrison, and London's founder. There is an old saying that: 'So long as the Stone of Brutus is safe, so long shall London flourish.' The stone is now set in the wall of the modern building that has replaced the church.

211

Baker Street *Inner London*

Though it has never existed at all, 221b Baker Street is one of London's most famous addresses. It was here that Sherlock Holmes, the famous detective, lived with his companion, Dr Watson, in Conan Doyle's immortal stories. Each year, the Abbey Building Society occupying the site answers 2000 letters addressed to Sherlock Holmes.

FICTIONAL RELICS

These Sherlock Holmes 'relics' – meerschaum pipe, handcuffs, false beard and magnifying glass – are displayed at The Sherlock Holmes public house in Northumberland Street, near Charing Cross

Bank of England *Inner London*

Synonymous with strength and security, the Bank of England stands in Threadneedle Street in the heart of the City of London. The Bank's nickname of 'The Old Lady of Threadneedle Street' became applied to a real person, Sarah Whitehead, whose brother Philip, a disgruntled former employee of the Bank, was found guilty of forgery in 1811 and executed. Sarah was unhinged by the shock, and every day for the next 25 years she appeared at the Bank, asking for her brother. When she died she was buried in the old churchyard that later became part of the Bank's gardens. Her ghost has been reported on many occasions in the area.

According to legend, the Bank's proverbial security was severely shaken on one occasion. The story is told of a man who wrote to the directors, claiming to have found a way into the bullion vaults, and sending papers to prove his claim. Following instructions, the directors assembled in the vaults, and on the stroke of midnight a flagstone lifted and the man emerged. He explained how, while working in the sewers, he had come across a small disused tunnel which had led him to the vaults. He was well rewarded for his honesty and the tunnel was filled in.

A more serious threat occurred during the Gordon Riots of 1780, when for days London was terrorised by an anti-Catholic mob, led by Lord George Gordon. After burning down Newgate and other prisons, the mob turned its attention to the Bank. A small force of troops, hastily dispatched by the Government, repelled the attacks. Since then, apart from brief periods in the 18th century, the Bank has been guarded every night by the Bank Picquet, usually drawn from detachments of the Guards stationed in London.

SHRINE TO SHERLOCK

The sitting-room at 221b Baker Street has been faithfully reproduced at The Sherlock Holmes pub in Northumberland Street. The dummy with the bullet-hole in its forehead deceived Colonel Moran, right-hand man of the notorious Professor Moriarty, in an assassination attempt on the great detective. At the acid-stained bench in the corner, Holmes performed his chemical experiments. On the sideboard is the microscope with which Holmes introduced scientific method to crime detection, and the bull's-eye lantern stands ready for a nocturnal foray. Mrs Hudson has laid the table for tea. After nearly a century, Conan Doyle's creation maintains as firm a grip upon the popular imagination as many a real-life hero. There is even a Sherlock Holmes Society with international links

O you Villain! – what have I kept my Honor untainted so long, to have it broke up, by you at last? – O Murder! – Rape! – Ravishment! – Ruin! – Ruin, – Ruin!!!

POLITICAL-RAVISHMENT', or – The Old Lady of Threadneedle-Street in danger!.

THE OLD LADY OF THREADNEEDLE STREET

The Bank of England protests against the reckless advances of Pitt, who had given instructions for the issue of unlimited paper currency. Gillray's cartoon, dating from 1797, gave birth to the Bank's famous nickname

Berkeley Square *Inner London*

The ghost which has reputedly haunted No. 50 Berkeley Square for more than a century is of a peculiarly repulsive kind, described as a shapeless, slithering mass. The story is told of a young Army officer, engaged to a daughter of the house, who volunteered to spend a night in the haunted bedroom. Only if he rang twice was anyone to come to his assistance. The family waited apprehensively and, on the stroke of midnight, the bell rang once. After a couple of minutes, the bell rang a second time – so wildly that the family raced for the stairs. Before they could reach the bedroom, a shot rang out. The young man had killed himself from the horror of what he had seen.

Billingsgate *Inner London*

For 1000 years London's fish market has stood near London Bridge on the site of the old river gate to the City. According to a medieval legend, Billingsgate takes its name from Belin, a legendary king of the Britons who 'built a tower of prodigious height and a safe harbour for ships'. 'Billingsgate' today is synonymous with the vivid invective used by the fish porters. Their distinctive flat-topped leather hats are said to be modelled on those worn by the English archers at the Battle of Agincourt.

Bishopsgate *Inner London*

Dirty Dick's, a pub in Bishopsgate, takes its name from a well-known City eccentric of the 18th century, Nathaniel Bentley. He was a Leadenhall Street merchant who in his youth was noted as a scholar and a man of fashion and was nicknamed 'the Beau of Leadenhall Street'. But the shock of his fiancée's death on their wedding eve drove him to retreat into slovenly isolation. 'Dirty Dick', as he became known, never washed, saying that if he did so he would only be dirty again the next day. On his death, the room in which the wedding-feast had been laid was found as it had been left on the tragic day of his loved one's death 50 years before.

Carshalton *Outer London*

Anne Boleyn's Well, near Carshalton churchyard, was one of the holy wells of England, said to have gushed forth when her horse's hoof struck the ground. The lord of Carshalton Manor, Sir Nicholas Carew, is known to have entertained Henry VIII at nearby Beddington Palace during the king's courtship of Anne. However, it is more likely that the legend is based on Anne Bolonia, a 12th-century lady of the manor, who provided a supply of pure drinking water for the parish.

LOST BEAUTY

Walpole House, Chiswick, is said to be haunted by the ghost of its former owner, Barbara, Duchess of Cleveland (right), mistress of Charles II. She appears at windows as a dropsical old woman, wringing her hands in despair for the vanished beauty of her youth

Cock Lane *Inner London*
High up on the corner of Cock Lane and Giltspur Street, which was once known as Pie Corner, is a statue of a fat boy which marks the spot where the Great Fire of London burnt itself out in 1666. The statue represents the sin of gluttony, and is a pun in stone – because the flames spread from Pudding Lane to Pie Corner.

Cornhill *Inner London*
While pealing the bells of St Michael's Church during a violent storm, a team of early 16th-century bellringers were horrified to see 'an ugly shapen sight' come in at one window and float over to another. They fell unconscious, and later discovered deep scars in the stonework. The scars became known as the Devil's clawmarks, and for years the church had a sinister reputation.

Cowcross Street *Inner London*
The Castle is the only public house in Britain to have a pawnbroker's licence. The story goes that in the early 19th century, George IV, wearing a long cloak and large hat to conceal his identity, borrowed a pound from the landlord after gambling away all his ready cash at a cockfight in Clerkenwell. He left his watch as security, and went back to the ringside. Next day, a messenger redeemed the watch, and the king rewarded the publican by granting The Castle a pawnbroker's licence for as long as it remained standing.

Dean Street *Inner London*
The shadowy figure of a woman has been seen drifting through the Gargoyle Club, and wherever she goes she leaves behind her a powerful scent of gardenias. The ghost is thought to be that of Charles II's favourite mistress, the orange seller turned actress Nell Gwyn, who once lived here.

Devons Road *Inner London*
Some 200 hot cross buns baked on Good Friday – one for every year – hang in a net from the ceiling

THE LIVERYMEN AND THE LORD MAYOR

If Dick Whittington could revisit the City of London, after an absence of some 600 years, he would not be entirely unfamiliar with all that he saw. Most of the buildings he knew were razed by the Great Fire of 1666, but if he looked hard enough, he would find that many of the narrow, deeply shadowed streets echo the street plan of the Middle Ages, and that many of the City customs and traditions that were old even in his time still show no real signs of fading.

Today, as in the 14th century, City life is still dominated by the City Livery Companies, which were charitable guilds of master craftsmen when Dick Whittington knew

them. The word livery referred to the guildsman's right to wear the distinctive dress of his company. For instance, on ceremonial occasions, members of the Court of the Haberdashers can be recognised by their dark blue robes edged with fur, while the Drapers wear blue and yellow.

There are currently 82 Livery Companies, of which the 'Great Twelve' are traditionally paramount – Clothworkers, Drapers, Fishmongers, Goldsmiths, Grocers, Haberdashers, Ironmongers, Mercers, Merchant Taylors, Salters, Skinners and Vintners. Many of them have little more than their names to link them with the crafts which they once controlled, and in some cases, the crafts themselves (such as bow-making or fletching, the making of arrows) are hardly more than memories. But today's Liverymen continue to banquet, dispense charity and manage schools (one of their most important functions). And though a modern City Cutler or Fishmonger may

at The Widow's Son public house. It is a condition of tenancy that a sailor must add a bun every year and be paid a pint of beer for his trouble. The legend is that a widow who once ran the pub lost her son at sea, but put aside a bun for him every year in the hope that he would one day return. When she died, the pub was given its present name, and the custom has never flagged. In fact, some of the buns are over 200 years old. However, the custom probably derives from a once widespread belief that bread or buns baked on Good Friday would never go stale, had remarkable curative powers and would protect the houses where they were kept from fire.

East Acton *Outer London*
In the Middle Ages, a chapter of monks from the Church of St Bartholomew the Great, Smithfield, lived near the site of the present St Dunstan's Church. Many people have reported seeing strange, cowled figures trooping through the church – sometimes singly and sometimes in groups of as many as a dozen, walking in pairs. This otherworldly procession moves slowly down the aisle and into the chancel, and then fades from sight.

Ely Place *Inner London*
On his way to execution, the 4th-century Christian martyr St Blaise touched the throat of a boy choking on a fishbone, and saved his life. The miracle is commemorated in the Blessing of the Throats service held at St Etheldreda's Church on St Blaise's Day (February 3). People suffering from throat troubles kneel at the altar rail, and the priest touches their throats with two candles tied together to form a cross.

Ely Place was once the town residence of the bishops of Ely, and it is one of only two places in the City (the other is the Temple) over which the Lord Mayor has no jurisdiction. To proclaim its separate identity, a liveried beadle ritually locks its gates at 10 p.m. each night.

Enfield *Outer London*
A phantom coach has often been seen in Bell Lane, usually on clear, moonless nights just before Christmas. Many eyewitness accounts agree that the coach is jet black, that it contains two or three passengers and that it careers along at full gallop some 6 ft above the ground.

never have ground a knife or gutted a fish in his life, he still doggedly maintains his company's most ancient traditions.

Prominent even among the 'Great Twelve' are the Vintners, who together with the Dyers, share ownership of all Thames swans that do not belong to the Queen. On the Thursday after July 4, the Vintners enact one of the few ancient Livery customs that does not take place in private.

After the installation of their new Master, they walk in procession from Vintners' Hall in Upper Thames Street to the Church of St James, Garlick Hill. They are led by two white-smocked Wine Porters sweeping the road with brooms, and some of them carry bouquets of herbs. These customs were started in the reign of Edward III (1327–77), lest the Vintners 'do slip in mire or their nostrils be offended by mal odor'.

At the Fishmongers' Hall near London Bridge is pre-served the dagger with which Sir William Walworth, Mayor of London, stabbed and killed Wat Tyler, the leader of the Kentish uprising during the Peasants' Revolt in 1381.

For more than 1000 years the City has been governed from the Guildhall (though the present building is largely 15th century), and it is here that the most famous Livery ceremonies take place. On Midsummer Day the Liverymen elect two Sheriffs for the City, and on September 29 they elect the Lord Mayor (so titled since 1546). It is from here that the Lord Mayor's Show begins, on the second Saturday in November, and it is here too that it ends, with a sumptuous banquet that always begins with turtle soup.

LORD MAYOR'S SHOW 1789 *London has had a mayor since at least 1191, and since Magna Carta in 1215 there has been a Mayor's Show. From 1432 to 1856, this world-famous procession, in which the mayor meets his people, was waterborne*

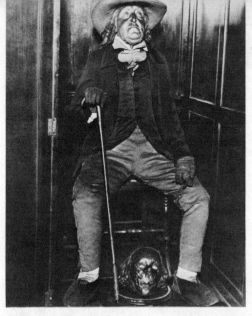

Garlick Hill *Inner London*
In the 19th century, the embalmed body of a man
was found under the floor of the Church of St
James in Garlick Hill, off Queen Victoria Street.
Both his identity and how long he lay buried there
remain a mystery, for the church was totally gutted
in the Great Fire of London in 1666. All records had
been lost by the time it was completely rebuilt by
Sir Christopher Wren. Not that theories are lacking;
he has been identified as a Roman general, as
Richard Rothing, founder of the church in 1326
and as Henry Fitzailwyn, who died in 1212, the first
of six early mayors of London who are known to
have been buried in the church. He may even be
Dick Whittington himself.

Whoever he is, his mummified remains now rest
in a glass case off the porch. Since the last war, when
the church was bombed, 'Old Jimmy Garlick' as the
mummy is nicknamed, has apparently become
restless, for several visitors to St James have reported
seeing a shrouded ghost standing on the tower
steps and in various other parts of the church.

THE HAUNTED CLOISTER

*The fully clothed skeleton of Jeremy Bentham, the law
reformer who died in 1832, sits in a glass case (above)
in the cloister of University College, off Gower Street.
Bentham's embalmed head rests between his legs, and
his ghost has often been seen and heard in the college*

THE VANQUISHED GIANTS OF THE GUILDHALL

*In the 12th century, the historian Geoffrey of Monmouth
wrote that Britain was originally inhabited by a race of
giants who were conquered by Brutus and his Trojan
warriors about 1200 BC, when the Trojan general
Corineus, was made ruler of Cornwall. After killing
every other giant in the district, Corineus wrestled with
the 12 ft goliath Gogmagog, and threw him to his death in
the sea. In the 15th century, statues of Gogmagog and
Corineus were erected in London's Guildhall. These*
*were destroyed in the Great Fire of 1666, and in 1708
were replaced by two new statues. By then, a different
legend had arisen; the two figures were now known as
Gog and Magog, the last of the British giants. It was
said that they had been captured by Brutus and used as
servants in his palace, which stood on the present site of the
Guildhall. The statues above, of Gog (left) and Magog
(right), replaced the 18th-century figures which were
destroyed when the Guildhall was bombed in 1940*

Hammersmith *Outer London*

Before the ardent Royalist, Sir Nicholas Crisp, died in 1666, he expressed a wish that his heart might be buried at the foot of his master, Charles I. Instead, his heart was entombed in an urn which stands underneath a bust of the king in St Paul's Church in Hammersmith, and his body was buried in the churchyard outside. Crisp made provision in his will for his heart to be removed from the urn once a year and refreshed with a glass of wine. This ritual was carried out until the mid-18th century, when the urn was finally sealed for ever.

Hampstead *Outer London*

The ancient game of mell, also called pell mell, is occasionally played in Hampstead at The Freemasons' Arms, on the only ground in the world which is entirely devoted to the game. It is played with mallets and wooden balls, and is similar to croquet. London's Pall Mall is named after the game, for it was there that Charles II played it on his return from exile in France, the home of the sport.

JACK STRAW'S CASTLE

This pub at the top of Hampstead Heath is said to stand on the site of a hut that was the home of Jack Straw, a rebel leader of the Peasants' Revolt in 1381

GHOSTS OF HAMPTON COURT

Many people believe that the passions and pain unleashed upon the atmosphere of Hampton Court by the unfortunate wives of Henry VIII have left a mark that time will never eradicate. When Catherine Howard was charged with adultery in 1541, she broke away from her guards and ran to the chapel door (between the tapestries) in an attempt to make a last appeal to the king. But the door was locked, and Henry ignored her frantic pleas. Some say that her shrieks as she was dragged away echo along the gallery to this day

A TRAGIC QUEEN *Jane Seymour (left) became Henry VIII's third queen in 1536, and lost her life the following year in giving birth to Henry's only son, Edward VI. Her ghost, dressed in white, has been seen at Hampton Court carrying a lighted candle as it glides from the State Apartments to the Silver Stick Gallery and Clock Court. Among other ghosts that have been seen is that of Henry himself*

THE PHANTOM SPINNER *Edward VI's nurse, Sybil Penn, still spins in one of the old courtiers' houses. The house is now occupied by Eric Fraser, who drew this picture, and whose daughter has seen the ghost*

Hanbury Street *Inner London*

Here died Annie Chapman, one of the eight poor prostitutes murdered by 'Jack the Ripper' between April 1888 and July 1889; her ghost haunts the street still. The similarity of the gruesome mutilations inflicted upon the victims led the police to assume the murders to be the work of one man, yet despite the optimism of the Illustrated Police News picture (below), this East End murderer was never caught. He has since been 'identified' as a butcher, a surgeon, or a member of the Royal family.

Highgate *Outer London*

For those who like to be reminded of man's brief mortality there is no finer sight than the jumbled, gaping tombs of Highgate's Old Cemetery, where the Victorian middle-classes jostle for supremacy beneath the luxuriant undergrowth. Such is the melancholy effect of the place that in 1970, a man carrying a hammer, a stake and a spade was arrested by a night-patrolling constable. The man told the magistrate that he had come to settle the Highgate Vampire for good; he was remanded for a medical report, but tales of the vampire have persisted ever since. At Ye Olde Wrestlers pub, the 17th-century drovers' initiation ceremony of Swearing on the Horns is still enacted. For the price of drinks all round, you can be a 'freeman' of Highgate.

'TURN AGAIN . . .'

On Highgate Hill, a milestone topped by a bronze cat marks the spot where young Dick Whittington, summoned by London's bells, turned again to the city that was to make him mayor three times in the early 15th century. The legend of his cat may have arisen from a ship called a cat used in the coal trade, on which part of Dick's fortunes were founded

THE HIGHWAYMEN OF HOUNSLOW HEATH

Once part of the extensive Forest of Middlesex, and now largely buried beneath the runways of London Airport, Hounslow Heath was for more than 200 years the most dangerous place in England. Between the 17th and the early 19th centuries, the Heath occupied perhaps 25 square miles. No one was really certain where its boundaries lay, and no one cared, for it was a tract of country to be crossed as quickly as possible. It supported only a handful of tiny villages, such as Brentford, Isleworth and Teddington. Though Hounslow itself was not large, it was after London the most important of coaching centres. Across the Heath ran the Bath Road and the Exeter Road, along which travelled wealthy visitors to West Country resorts and courtiers journeying to Windsor. All provided rich pickings for highwaymen lurking in copses bordering the lonely ways.

The first of the legendary highwaymen were Royalist officers who 'took to the road' when they were outlawed under the Commonwealth. These were men familiar with the relatively new-fangled pistols, which gave them an advantage over their victims, armed only with swords.

Perhaps because they concentrated on the wealthy, the highwaymen became popular heroes. No one, except the victims, grieved when the dukes of Northumberland and St Albans were held up on the Heath at the end of the 17th century. And when one audacious villain pasted notices on the doors of rich Londoners telling them they should not venture forth without at least a watch and 10 guineas, the whole town was convulsed with laughter.

SOLDIER OF FORTUNE *To be robbed by a famous highwayman was regarded as something of an honour; when James Maclaine (left) accidentally wounded Horace Walpole while attempting to rob him, the antiquarian bore no grudge and wrote to tell him so. In June 1750, Maclaine also held up Lord Eglington (below), taking 50 guineas and his lordship's blunderbuss*

Holland House *Inner London*

The grounds of the house, which is now an International Youth Hostel, are apparently haunted by the headless ghost of Lord Holland, executed during the Civil War; he was recently seen by a Chinese student. A more unusual spectre is the ghost of oneself; several people have allegedly met their 'doubles' or 'fetches' in the grounds. Such a meeting is said to be a warning of imminent death.

Houndsditch *Inner London*

The name comes from a legend of an earl named Edric to whom Canute promised the highest point in London if he murdered Edmund Ironside (981–1016), King of England. Edric did so, and Canute, fearing further treachery, cut his head off and put it on the Tower. Edric's body was thrown into the ditch to be devoured by hounds.

DASHING DUVAL *Claude Duval, charmed by the beauty and cool unconcern of a prospective victim, invites her to dance on the Heath*

CLOSER TO REALITY? *An illustration from the* Newgate Calendar *shows a highwayman strangling a defenceless woman on the Heath, despite the warning of the gibbeted corpses near by*

'Gentlemen of the road'

While most of the highwaymen were thugs pure and simple, it cannot be denied that some of them had a certain flair. There was Twysden, Bishop of Raphoe, who was shot and killed while carrying out a robbery on the Heath -- though it was later given out that he had died of 'an inflammation'. Others returned money to needy victims, and released women and children unmolested, including the children of the Prince of Wales, held up at Hounslow in 1741. There are even accounts of robberies in which the victim is referred to as 'a man', and the robber as 'a gentleman'.

Dick Turpin is credited with having stayed in most old pubs in the Hounslow area, though in fact that cattle-thief and murderer mostly confined his activities to Essex, North London and Yorkshire. The most gallant of the Heath's highwaymen was probably the French-born Claude Duval who danced with a beautiful victim – and let her wealthy husband go for

£100. Duval was hanged in 1670 and buried at Covent Garden under the epitaph (now destroyed): 'Here lies Duval: if male thou art, Look to thy purse; if female, to thy heart.'

A dance at Tyburn

Despite the inefficiency of the authorities, few highwaymen survived beyond their early 20's. Betrayed for blood-money, or by their own stupidity, they kicked their lives out dangling from the rough wooden triangle of Tyburn Tree. Most died well, and when they were dead, the bodies were returned to the scene of their crimes, there to hang rotting as a lesson to others. So plentiful were the gibbets on Hounslow Heath, that they came to be regarded as landmarks, and figured on 18th-century maps. One traveller, fogbound on the Heath, wrote: 'To my delight I saw a man hanging from a gibbet; my pleasure at this prospect was unexpressible, for it convinced me I was approaching a civilised community'.

Kensington Palace *Inner London*
The ghost of George II has often been reported gazing anxiously out of a window towards the weather-vane. During his last illness he was worried by the non-arrival of despatches from his beloved Hanover, and constantly asked the wind's direction.

King's Cross Station *Inner London*
One of Boadicea's many burial places is beneath Platform 10 – she is alleged to have fought her last battle against the occupying Roman army on a site now covered by the station.

Kingston-upon-Thames *Outer London*
In Kingston market can be seen the stone which gave the royal borough its name. From Edward the Elder (AD 900) to Edmund Ironside (1016), English kings were crowned seated upon the stone.

LAMBETH'S PINEAPPLES

The pineapples on Lambeth Bridge were placed there to commemorate John Tradescant (d. 1638), who is said to be buried under the bridge. He was the first man to import pineapples into England; he also imported many other curiosities such as the tail feathers of a phoenix and the eggs of a dragon and a griffin. These are still kept in the Ashmolean Museum, Oxford

THEATRELAND GHOSTS

Some actors, it seems, do not kindly leave the stage. Comedian Dan Leno haunts the Theatre Royal, Drury Lane, which also has its Man in Grey, who often takes a seat in the upper circle – but only at matinées. The Adelphi boasts a phantom thought to be William Terriss, stabbed at the stage door in 1897. He also appears at Covent Garden tube station in Edwardian dress.

J. B. BUCKSTONE *Like the Man in Grey at the Theatre Royal, Drury Lane, whose appearance is a sure sign that a new show is in for a long run, this former actor-manager, pictured (left) in the role of Launcelot Gobbo in Shakespeare's* Merchant of Venice, *brings good luck when he turns up at the Haymarket (above). He is said to prefer the dressing rooms, but he was actually seen on the stage by a stage manager in 1964. The figure, in 19th-century clothes, was not, however, visible to the audience*

FANNY KELLY *The founder of Miss Kelly's Theatre and Dramatic School in 1840 – which became the old Royalty Theatre in Dean Street, Soho – haunted the place for at least 50 years after her death in 1882. One of her last appearances was in 1934. She was seen in a box, eagerly watching a rehearsal – she herself had been an actress, and excelled in melodrama. But property developers drove her out when they built offices on the site*

ROBERT BADDELEY *This pastrycook turned actor died in 1794, and although his spirit does not roam the Theatre Royal in Drury Lane, he is certainly not forgotten. He is remembered chiefly as a comic actor.*

In his will, Baddeley made sure he would be remembered at the theatre where he played his first role. He left £100 to be invested, the interest to be spent on a special, annual Twelfth Night Cake. With wine and punch, this traditional cake is shared in the Green Room by members of the cast of the play being produced in the theatre at the time

London Bridge *Inner London*

The great bridge across the River Thames has always been of prime importance in keeping the city at the centre of trade routes. The nursery rhyme that says 'London Bridge is falling down' has a lot of truth in it. In 850 Danes destroyed the bridge. Rebuilt, it collapsed in heavy floods in 1091. And the replacement burnt down in 1136. A stone bridge started 40 years later was partly paid for by a wool tax, hence the rhyme's line: 'Build it up on packs of wool.' This bridge partly collapsed in 1281, but when restored, with houses, shops and a chapel on it, stood until 1831. A later bridge lasted until 1971, when it was sold to become a tourist attraction at Lake Havasu City, Arizona, USA.

London Stone *Inner London*

A remnant of the Stone is set in the wall of the modern building that has replaced St Swithin's Church, opposite Cannon Street Station. Its origin is obscure. Archaeologists have suggested that the Romans measured distances from it along their road network, but legend insists that Brutus the Trojan, mythical founder of the city, laid the stone as a temple altar, and that 'so long as Brutus's stone is safe, so long shall London flourish'.

TYBURN GALLOWS

A stone plaque on a traffic island near Marble Arch marks the site of Tyburn gallows. One night in 1678, the gallows fell down, 'uprooted by its ghosts'

Middle Temple *Inner London*

Queen Elizabeth I was said to have been so pleased with the way the Middle Temple lawyers received her that she made them a Christmas pudding. Every year, part of the pudding was saved, to be mixed into next year's, so that the Queen's gift was constantly sampled afresh. The custom died out in 1966, but was revived in 1971, when the Queen Mother stirred a new pudding for Benchers.

North Kensington *Outer London*

St Mark's Road and Cambridge Gardens are said to be the route of a phantom bus that tore along with lights blazing at dead of night. A man and his wife reported seeing it in 1934, but when they went to board it, the mystery bus vanished.

Norwood *Outer London*

Superstitious people flocked to fortune-telling Gipsy Queen Margaret Finch (below) who constantly sat hunched up, chin on her knees. She had to be buried in that position at Beckenham in 1740, her funeral paid for by publicans who had benefited from the crowds.

PEARLY KINGS AND QUEENS

The Pearly 'Royals' arrived in Victorian times, and though some kings and queens still reign in their various districts (the title is now usually inherited), they are part of a tradition that is slowly dying – just as the once-famed muffin men, lavender sellers and menders of pots and pans have now departed from the streets.

The 'pearlies' were costermongers – street vendors of fruit and vegetables; the word comes from the Middle English *costard*, meaning a large cooking apple. Their dress is said to have sprung from the arrival of a huge cargo of the then fashionable pearl buttons from Japan, in the 1880's. One coster sewed them round his wide trouser bottoms . . . and the fashion caught on.

No one was more elaborately turned out than the king and his 'donah', as he called his wife, in each individual area.

Traditionally, costers elected the 'Kings' to lead them against bullies seeking to drive them from their pitches. After they were granted licences to sell produce, in the 19th century, the custom was kept up.

Mystic symbols
The shimmering suits, dresses and hats, handed down with the hereditary titles, are sewn with mystic symbols – stars, moons, suns, flowers, diamonds, Trees of Life, Eyes of God and fertility designs. Each outfit sports some 30,000 buttons and weighs 63 lb. or more. One owned by Mrs Beatrice Marriott, whose son is Pearly King of Finsbury and runs the 'pearlies' charity organisation, has 90,000 buttons on it.

The pearly suits were worn at christenings, weddings and funerals; at Epsom on Derby Day; and for special charity drives, when the kings and queens would ride in splendour on their donkey-drawn and decorated carts. They are still worn for charity work and at the costers' annual autumn Harvest Festival service at St Martin-in-the-Fields Church, when Pearly Princesses take bouquets of vegetables as thank-offerings.

THE COCKNEY 'LANGUAGE'

The word 'cockney', from Middle English, means 'a cock's egg', or something to marvel at. Certainly, cockney rhyming slang is a marvellous example of the ingenuity and independence of those who pride themselves on having been born within the sound of Bow Bells. Like 'thieves' cant' of Tudor times, a conversation in rhyming slang is incomprehensible to strangers. It began in the 1850's, with the use of place names to indicate objects. A tie was a Peckham Rye, an arm a Chalk Farm, and a horse a Charing Cross ('crors'). Further rhymes were introduced and, to make it even more difficult, the rhyme itself was often dropped: a suit became a whistle, from 'whistle and flute'; stairs were apples, from 'apples and pears'; and 'half a dollar' (the half-crown piece) was an Oxford – from 'Oxford scholar'

Petticoat Lane *Inner London*
Though one of the best known of London's street markets, Petticoat Lane does not appear on any official list of street names. In 1830, it was named Middlesex Street, to give a disreputable area a new lease of life; but to Londoners (and to thousands of visitors) it is Petticoat Lane still.

MISTAKEN IDENTITY

Before the inscription on Queen Anne's statue, in Queen Anne's Gate, Westminster, was cleaned in the 1930's, children used to throw stones at it in the mistaken belief that it represented 'Bloody Mary' – Queen Mary Tudor. There is a tradition that on the anniversary of Anne's death – August 1, 1714 – the statue gets off its plinth, and wanders round nearby streets

Red Lion Square *Inner London*
The three cloaked figures occasionally reported in the Square are reputedly those of Cromwell, Bradshaw and Ireton, who signed the death warrant of Charles I. Legend says that Cromwell may have been buried in the square.

Richmond *Outer London*
A red-brick gatehouse and a courtyard are all that remain of Richmond Palace, where Queen Elizabeth died in 1603. At the moment of her death, it is said that a ring was taken from her finger and thrown to a mounted messenger from a window of the gatehouse. The man galloped 400 miles to Edinburgh in 62 hours to show James VI of Scotland that he was now James I of England.

The drunken figure of a Cavalier sometimes seen staggering along the towpath near Ham House in broad daylight, is thought to be that of a courtier of Charles II who, while staying with the Duke of Lauderdale at Ham House, became so drunk at a party that he fell into the Thames and drowned.

A MEMORY OF GLORIANA

Phantom hoofbeats sometimes heard by the gatehouse of Richmond Palace (above) may be those of James I's messenger, who waited for Elizabeth I's ring to be thrown from a window as proof of the queen's death

Royal Hospital *Inner London*
On May 29, the anniversary of the Restoration, the old soldiers parade in their scarlet uniforms which are adapted from those worn by the Duke of Marlborough's forces in the 18th century. At the end of the parade there are three cheers for 'King Charles II, our pious founder'. Incidentally, it was a courtier named Stephen Fox, and not Nell Gwyn, who suggested the hospital's foundation.

St Bartholomew the Great *Inner London*
On each Good Friday, sixpences are placed on a tomb in the churchyard and are collected by the poor widows of the parish. The women then step across the tomb and each is presented with a bun. Both money and buns are provided by the church. The origin of the custom is obscure, but is probably connected with 'sin-eating', in which the living ritually assumed the sins of the dead by eating a morsel of bread over the corpse.

St Giles-in-the-Fields *Inner London*
On the east side of the churchyard there once stood a tavern where condemned criminals were given a last drink on their way to Tyburn. It is said that a teetotaller refused, and was consequently hanged early – just before his reprieve arrived.

St James's Palace *Inner London*
The palace is haunted by a phantom whose throat has been slit from ear to ear. It is thought to be the ghost of a valet murdered by the Duke of Cumberland, son of George III. Once, the palace was a hospital for lepers; stone crosses in the inner courtyard mark the graves of 14 leper girls.

St John's Wood *Inner London*
Travellers on the Bakerloo Line between Baker Street and St John's Wood stations often feel a 'popping' in their ears. The story goes that this is caused by the tunnel making a sudden dip to avoid the Plague burial pit now covered by the Marylebone War Memorial

St Pancras Station *Inner London*
When the station was built in 1868 an ancient cemetery had to be dug up and destroyed. Legend says that the relatives of a Frenchman buried there demanded that his remains be returned home, but when the grave was opened, it was found to contain several skeletons jumbled together. The problem was solved by the foreman who pointed out that since the gentleman was a foreigner, his bones were bound to be darker. So the more blackened bones were gathered together and sent to France.

Shepherdess Walk *Inner London*
The Eagle pub is immortalised in the Cockney song 'Pop goes the Weasel', whose verse goes:
'Up and down the City Road,
In and out of the Eagle;
That's the way the money goes,
Pop goes the weasel.'
The weasel was a tool used by saddlers to bore holes in leather. Apparently a saddler who lived in nearby Nile Street sometimes 'popped' or pawned his weasel to obtain drinking money.

Smithfield *Inner London*
The Peasants' Revolt of 1381 was broken when the leader, Wat Tyler, was stabbed to death in Smithfield by William Walworth, Mayor of London. The incident was allegedly commemorated by the inclusion of Walworth's dagger in London's coat of arms, but in fact the weapon depicted is the symbol of St Paul, London's patron saint.

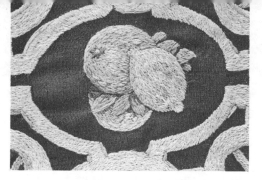

ORANGES AND LEMONS

The oranges and lemons motif on a footstool in St Clement Danes Church, Strand, recalls a time when the Clement's Inn or Court staff gave fruit to residents. Now, on the Thursday nearest March 31, London's Danish community makes the gift to local children

Strand *Inner London*

At the Savoy Hotel, precautions are taken to avoid having 13 people at a table. If such a party arrives, then a 14th place is laid for a wooden cat named Kaspar, who sits at table throughout the meal. At one time during the last war, Kaspar was kidnapped by some RAF pilots, but eventually he was returned to his usual shelf in the Pinafore Room.

Tottenham *Outer London*

Bruce Castle, now the Tottenham Museum, is haunted by the 17th-century ghost of the beautiful Lady Constantia, whose jealous husband imprisoned her in the clock-tower. On November 3, when she threw herself to her death from a balcony, the castle is said to ring with her screams.

LONDON RIVER

London owes its existence to a ford which apparently still exists beneath the Thames mud opposite the Houses of Parliament. Caesar's legions took this route before going on to storm the heights to the north – Primrose Hill, Hampstead and Highgate – perhaps following the line of the Fleet River which, like the Tyburn, the Westbourne and the Kilbourne are now no more than sewers flowing beneath the streets that still bear their names. As well as being the lowest fording point, London was the highest reach of the Thames where sea-going vessels could unload their cargoes. It was a place, too, where the river might conveniently be bridged. For centuries, London Bridge controlled – or restricted – the trade of south-east England. At the same time, the Thames was London's highway. In Tudor times, the boatmen plied for hire near the watergates of the great houses. A traditional cry, 'Eastward ho!' or 'Westward ho!', was used to attract passengers. The tangle of medieval streets could be avoided by taking to the river – a habit echoed in present pageantry.

GEORGIAN PATRIOTISM *In 1715, Thomas Doggett, an actor, was so overcome by emotion at the defeat of the first Jacobite rebellion that he instituted a race for Thames Watermen. The prizes, competed for annually, are an orange coloured coat, and a huge silver badge which is engraved with the White Horse of Hanover – symbol of freedom to Doggett*

DOGGETT'S COAT AND BADGE *Thomas Rowlandson's 18th-century impression of the Watermen's race, inaugurated in 1716, and still rowed between London and Chelsea bridges*

SWAN-UPPING *In the third week of July, the Queen's Swanmaster and the Swanmasters of the Dyers' and Vintners' Companies set off up the Thames to mark all the swans between Blackfriars Bridge and Henley. The Dyers' swans are marked with a single nick in the beak, the Vintners' with two, while the Queen's birds are unmarked but recorded. Once, all swans belonged to the Crown, but in the 15th century, some birds were allocated to trade guilds*

CHURCH CHARITY

The church of St Martin-in-the-Fields (so called because the church once stood in meadows) in Trafalgar Square, is dedicated to St Martin of Tours, one of whose deeds of charity – sharing his cloak with a beggar – is depicted on the church's door-handles and on lamp-posts in the vicinity. The church continues the tradition by sheltering down-and-outs in its crypt

Wapping Wall *Inner London*

'The Hanging Judge', Judge Jeffreys, so-called for his brutal sentences, is said to have sat on the wooden balcony of The Prospect of Whitby pub, enlivening his evening drink with the sight of gibbeted pirates hanging on Execution Dock across the river. Three tides passed over their bodies before their grisly remains were cut down.

GHOSTS OF THE ABBEY

Westminster Abbey has several ghosts: a murdered monk who walks the cloisters (above) in the early evening and occasionally chats to visitors; John Bradshaw, who haunts the deanery to expiate his signing of the death warrant of Charles I; and the rarely reported appearance of the Unknown Soldier, wounded and muddy from the Flanders battlefields. When the abbey was built c. AD 816 St Peter himself appeared to a Thames fisherman and guaranteed large catches on the condition that one-tenth would be given to the abbey's clergy

Whitechapel Road *Inner London*

The name of The Blind Beggar pub recalls an old legend of Bethnal Green which tells how Henry de Montfort, son of the famous Simon, was blinded at the Battle of Evesham in 1265 and, to conceal his identity, became a London beggar. His beautiful daughter, Bessie, was employed at The King's Arms, Romford; she had many suitors, but when they heard that her father was a beggar, they all lost interest – apart, that is, from a knight who loved the girl for herself. So Bessie married the knight and, at their wedding-feast, her father flung off his rags to reveal rich clothing beneath. He told his story and presented the happy couple with £3000 he had made from his successful begging activities.

ETERNAL FORTRESS

When William the Conqueror built the White Tower – the first of the great bastions which are collectively known as The Tower of London – it is said that he ordered bull's blood to be mixed with the mortar, symbolising strength and a royal power that would last for ever. The building has stood for over 900 years, but there was a guardian on Tower Hill long before the first stone was laid. At some time after the Romans left, the head of the Celtic hero-god Brân was buried there to safeguard the realm from invaders. The head was later removed by a jealous King Arthur, but the six ravens which some authorities believe to be associated with Brân are still there; as long as they remain, the Tower will never fall. Despite these efforts made on their behalf, Londoners have never really appreciated the Tower. Relations between the proudly independent City and the Crown were often uneasy, and the proximity of the great fortress, where so many citizens had suffered imprisonment, torture and execution, was a cold reminder of the power that was the last argument of kings.

During its long life, the Tower has been a Royal Mint, a menagerie, a prison and a treasure-house. Most of these uses have left their mark on the Tower's legends. There is, for example, a phantom bear which has startled several sentries into fits.

'TRAITOR'S GATE' *This is the water-gate of the Tower, through which political prisoners could be brought without exciting attention. When the gate was built c. 1250, it is said that the spirit of St Thomas à Becket sided with his fellow Londoners in objecting to this extension of the Tower's precincts; the work collapsed several times during its construction*

'QUEEN JANE' *Queen of England for 9 days, Lady Jane Grey was executed on February 12 1554. Her ghost – 'a white shape' – is said to appear at the Tower on the anniversary. It was last reported in 1957 on the Salt Tower*

THE BEGGAR OF BETHNAL GREEN

Elizabeth Frink's bronze statue of the Blind Beggar and his dog on the Cranbrook Estate recalls the story of Henry de Montfort who once lived locally

'PROTESTANT OR POPISH?'

It is said that the weathervane on the roof of the Banqueting Hall in Whitehall was erected by James II in 1688 so that he could tell at a glance whether the wind was 'Protestant or Popish'. The Catholic James knew that many of his people were praying for a favourable wind to bring Protestant William of Orange into a Devon port

Headless horror

Strong nerves are required to guard the Tower. That busiest of British ghosts, Anne Boleyn, has approached sentries on several occasions. In 1933, one sentry, braver than most, attempted to bayonet her when the phantom failed to answer his challenge; the weapon went through her without resistance, whereupon the man deserted his post and ran. An even more distressing spectacle is the re-enactment of the execution of the Countess of Salisbury that sometimes takes place on Tower Green. She was sentenced to death in 1541 for her part in the treasonable activities of her son but, unlike most noble prisoners who faced the headsman with calm fortitude, the 68-year-old

countess refused to kneel at the block and ran screaming round the scaffold until she was cut down by the executioner's axe. Perhaps her terror is not yet over, for she has been reported several times since, her white hair dabbled with blood streaming behind her, while a ghostly headsman pursues her with upraised axe.

Even the Tower's most potent tourist attraction, the Crown Jewels, have a dark side to their story. The Koh-i-Noor diamond, for example, has never been worn by a reigning monarch. Legend says that the owner will be ruler of the world, but if he is a man, he will die a violent death. Many male owners have died in this way – some on the battlefield and some murdered.

THE IMPERIAL STATE CROWN *The central stone, the Black Prince's Ruby, was given to the prince by Pedro the Cruel of Castile, who murdered the King of Granada to obtain it. In 1415, Henry V is believed to have worn the jewel in his helmet while leading his troops at the Battle of Agincourt*

THE QUEEN MOTHER'S CROWN *The central diamond is the Koh-i-Noor ('Mountain of Light'), once given by the Mogul emperor Shah Jehan to his queen Mumtaz Mahal, for whom the Taj Mahal was built. Perhaps because of this it is said that the stone will bring death to any male owner. On the other hand, ownership of the diamond also conveys domination of the world*

CURTANA *The blunt-tipped Sword of Mercy is carried by the sovereign at the Coronation. The name is derived from 'Courtain', the sword of the 9th-century Danish hero, Ogier. The Dane drew his sword against Charlemagne's son, but refrained from using it when a voice from Heaven commanded him to show mercy*

THE AMPULLA *The vessel for sacramental oil used in the Coronation is one of the oldest pieces in the Regalia. The Virgin is said to have given the golden eagle to St Thomas à Becket*

VICTORIA'S RING *It is said that Queen Victoria's 64-year reign was forecast in the hours it took to remove this Coronation ring from her finger*

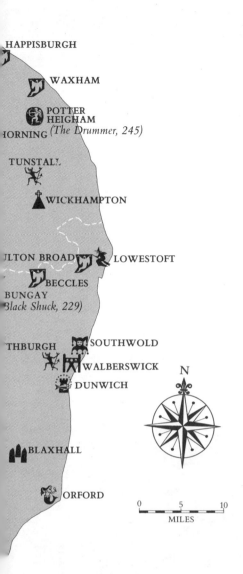

HAPPISBURGH

WAXHAM

POTTER HEIGHAM

HORNING *(The Drummer, 245)*

TUNSTALL

WICKHAMPTON

ULTON BROAD LOWESTOFT

BECCLES

BUNGAY *(Black Shuck, 229)*

THBURGH SOUTHWOLD

WALBERSWICK

DUNWICH

N

BLAXHALL

ORFORD

```
0        5        10
|--------|--------|
      MILES
```

THE WITCH COUNTRY

Cambridgeshire, Essex, Norfolk, Suffolk

A heart carved on a wall in the market-place at King's Lynn supposedly marks the spot where the heart of Margaret Read, refusing to submit though her body was burning at the stake, leapt from the flames, struck the wall and bounded off down the road to the river. Though Margaret was one of the few Englishwomen burnt to death for witchcraft, her execution in 1590 was one of the first manifestations of a terrible hysteria that was to grip the eastern counties for the next half century. By the end of the Civil War, hundreds of alleged witches – mostly women, mostly poor and elderly – were hanged in East Anglia after trials that were mockeries of justice. Courtrooms were besieged by mobs whose noise sometimes made it impossible for an accused woman to hear the charges brought against her, and few magistrates had the courage to impose any sentence other than death.

It is hard to believe that the people of this wide, rich countryside, whose enormous skyscapes are symbolic of freedom, should have felt so oppressed by Satan. The reason was partly religious; the Puritanism of the area had dismissed holy water and exorcism as Popish superstitions, leaving men defenceless against the Devil they still believed in. But in addition, there were beliefs that were much older than Christianity – the Stone Age pits at Aylmerton that shrieked in recollection of a tragedy of long ago, and the hounds of Odin, the black dogs that haunted the hedgerows with jaws dripping fire. In such an atmosphere, it did not seem incongruous to hang a man for tearing his breeches on the weathervane of Shelford church, as he sailed over it on the back of a black dog.

KEY TO SYMBOLS

- BELLS
- CRIME AND PUNISHMENT
- CURIOUS CHARACTERS
- CUSTOMS AND FESTIVALS
- DEVILS AND DEMONS
- DROWNED OR LOST LANDS
- FABULOUS BEASTS
- FAIRIES
- GHOSTS
- GIANTS
- GRAVES AND MONUMENTS
- HEROES
- HILL FIGURES
- HOLY PLACES
- LOCAL CURIOSITIES
- LOVE STORY
- MERMAIDS AND SEA-PEOPLE
- MYSTERIOUS STONES
- SAINTS AND MIRACLES
- SMUGGLERS AND WRECKERS
- TREASURE
- WITCHES AND WIZARDS

THE FOLKLORE YEAR

Every other Sunday
Castle Rising, Norfolk
Bede House Procession

February 2
Woodbridge, Suffolk
Bread Dole

Early February
King's Lynn, Norfolk
Roundabout Riding

Easter Monday
Thaxted, Essex
Morris Dancing

Whit Sunday (and other dates)
Walsingham, Norfolk
Pilgrimage to the Shrine

Whit Monday (4-yearly)
Dunmow, Essex
Dunmow Flitch Trial

Late May or early June
Southwold, Suffolk
Trinity Fair

June 22
Cambridge
Coin throwing at Midsummer Fair

Early July
Tollesbury, Essex
Gooseberry Fair

Early September
Southend, Essex
Whitebait Festival

October 20
Colchester, Essex
Oyster Feast

1st Monday in December
Brightlingsea, Essex
Cinque Port Deputy Election

Ashingdon *Essex*

St Andrew's Church was founded by King Canute to commemorate his victory in battle on the hill where the church now stands. Though lawns surround the church today, legend says that after the battle no grass would grow on the 'bloodstained' hill. In medieval times, a shrine in the church was said to bestow fertility upon women. The shrine was lost at the Dissolution, but the church retained its reputation as a lucky place in which to marry.

Aylmerton *Norfolk*

The Shrieking Pits is the name given to a number of circular depressions in the area, which may be the remains of prehistoric houses or flint mines. The tall white figure of a woman has sometimes been seen peering into the pits, wringing her hands and uttering piercing shrieks. Some say it is the ghost of a Stone Age woman, others of someone murdered near by; but her shrieks have terrified local residents on many occasions

Balsham *Cambs*

For a bet, a Balsham man went to the churchyard after dark to remove a skull from an old communal grave the sexton had uncovered. Unaware that a local joker was hiding near the grave, the man picked up a skull. 'Drop that, it's mine,' called the watcher. Undismayed, the man found another skull. 'That's mine too,' said the watcher. 'Then you're a liar,' came the reply, 'for I know, whoever you are, that you never had two heads.'

Basildon *Essex*

The 16th-century Church of the Holy Cross, near Basildon New Town, is said to be haunted by a red-robed figure. No one knows the ghost's identity, but there is a local tradition that he might be one of the two rectors of the church who were expelled at the Reformation. Residents claim to have seen this ghost walking through solid objects near the church.

Beccles *Suffolk*

Roos Hall, an old Tudor mansion, is one of the most haunted houses in England. The Devil's footprint is pointed out on one wall. A headless coachman is said to drive a phantom coach and horses up to the front door each Christmas Eve; another ghost haunts the guest room; and a third walks in the garden.

GHOSTS AT BLICKLING HALL

Blickling Hall stands on the site of Anne Boleyn's birthplace. Anne forfeited the king's favour when she gave birth to a still-born son, and was executed on May 19, 1536, for alleged adultery and treason. Each year at midnight on that date, a phantom coach drawn by four headless horses and driven by a headless coachman is said to convey her ghost, holding her severed head on her lap, up to the Hall door. Another phantom coach carries Anne's father, Sir Thomas Boleyn who, because of a curse by Henry VIII, is said to haunt the surrounding countryside. Pursued by shrieking demons, his ghost must drive over 40 Norfolk bridges between midnight and cock-crow in a yearly penance on the night of the anniversary of his daughter's execution

ANNE BOLEYN *The ill-fated queen whose ghost haunts Blickling Hall*

SIR THOMAS BOLEYN *The spectre of Anne's father roams over Norfolk*

THE GROWING STONE

Local people say that the Blaxhall Stone at Stone Farm in Blaxhall, Suffolk, is constantly increasing in size. The stone is supposed to have been the size of a small loaf when it was first noticed a century ago, and has since grown to its present weight of about 5 tons. The belief that pebbles actually grow in the soil and develop into large stones was once common in East Anglia

Blythburgh *Suffolk*

The Devil, in the form of a black dog, once disrupted a service in the 15th-century Blythburgh Church of the Holy Trinity. On Sunday, August 4, 1577, according to an old pamphlet, 'a strange and terrible tempest' struck the church, toppled the spire through the roof so that it shattered the font, killed three people and badly scorched others in the congregation. It was known that this was a visitation of the Devil because his clawmarks were discovered on the door through which he rushed towards Bungay.

The church contains some fine carved bench-ends representing the Seven Deadly Sins. They include Greed with swollen stomach, Slander with protruding tongue, and Avarice sitting on his money chest.

BLACK SHUCK THE DEMON DOG

Uncanny black dogs are no strangers to East Anglia, for in a great storm in 1577 (the same one in which the Devil is thought to have left his mark in Blythburgh church) a black demon dog, 'or the Devil in such a likeness', appeared in Bungay church and brought havoc with him. According to an old pamphlet, he departed leaving two dead worshippers strangled at their prayers, and another 'as shrunken as a piece of leather scorched in a hot fire'.

Demon dogs have haunted different parts of England, and particularly East Anglia, for over a thousand years. In the eastern counties, the spectral hound is generally known as Black Shuck or Old Shuck; the term 'shuck' coming from *scucca*, the Anglo-Saxon for demon.

In the graveyard

Unlike dogs of this world, Black Shuck seems more attached to places than to people. He has always walked alone, loping along river banks and lonely roads, or leaping over churchyard walls and vanishing among the tombstones. The appearance and characteristics of Black Shuck vary from place to place. He seems to emerge from his secret lair only at dusk, and is usually described as a shaggy creature the size of a calf, easily recognisable by his saucer-sized eyes (or sometimes one eye) weeping green or red fire.

Part monk, part hound

In Suffolk, Black Shuck is believed to be fairly harmless if left alone, but when challenged he has been known to strike his aggressor senseless, and death usually follows. At Clopton Hall, Stowmarket, where he guards a hoard of gold, his appearance is especially frightening for he has the body of a monk and the head of a hound. Often, in Suffolk, he can only be detected by the touch of his rough coat as he passes.

The Norfolk Shuck is a more sinister hound, more akin to the diabolical werewolves which haunted this sparsely populated region in the Middle Ages. He is an awful creature, as black as ebony, whose fiendish howls have been heard above the shrieks of the wildest gales. Terrified people have sensed Black Shuck padding behind them and felt his icy breath upon the back of their necks. Even today, motorists have reported swerving to avoid the hellhound crossing the road.

There is a popular belief in Norfolk that no one can set eyes on Black Shuck and live. In East Anglia generally, when anyone was dying, people used to say 'the Black Dog is at his heels'.

The Essex Shuck, however, is a kindly hound and has been known to protect travellers on lonely roads. Only his habit of haunting the sites of ancient gallows and graveyards is evidence that he is a demon dog.

A death warning

The Cambridgeshire Shuck, like his Norfolk counterpart, is both diabolical and sinister. He is sometimes seen between Wicken and the marshes of Spinney Abbey. Those who encounter him should look the other way, since his appearance is said to warn of death in the family.

Brandeston *Suffolk*
In 1645, at the height of the Civil War, the people of Brandeston denounced their 80-year-old vicar, John Lowes, as a witch. The main reason for this seems to have been that he was a Royalist in a pre-dominantly Parliamentarian area. During his inter-rogation by the witchfinder Matthew Hopkins, he was deprived of sleep for nights and was forcibly run up and down his cell until 'he was weary of his life and scarce sensible of what he said or did'. In this state he confessed to the most bizarre crimes includ-ing the bewitching of cattle and, on a calm day, causing a ship to sink off Harwich with the loss of many lives. No effort was ever made to discover if any vessel had sunk on that day and, once out of the hands of Hopkins, Lowes retracted his confession. Even so, he was sentenced to death at the assizes at Bury St Edmunds. Since no clergyman was per-mitted to read the burial service over a witch, the old man recited it himself beneath the gallows.

Brightlingsea *Essex*
This is the only town outside Kent and Sussex which is a member of the Cinque Ports – ports on the south-east coast with ancient privileges. It is described in an Elizabethan charter as being 'a Limb of the Cinque Port of Sandwich', and on the first Monday in December a Deputy of the Cinque Port Liberty is elected from among the Freemen of the town. At a ceremony which takes place in the belfry of All Saints Church, the Deputy swears allegiance to the Mayor of Sandwich; he then visits the Mayor and presents him with 50p for Ship Money. This is probably a relic of an ancient tax on southern ports to provide ships for the defence of the realm.

Buckhurst Hill *Essex*
The name of the pub, The Bald Faced Stag, recalls a hunting ritual which took place there every Easter Monday from the 12th century to the 1880's. A tame stag, decorated with ribbons, was released in Epping Forest and hunted by up to 500 riders of all classes from 'dandies and dustmen' to the 'nobocracy and snobocracy', all dressed in gay and motley clothing. After the unfortunate beast had been hunted to death, handfuls of hair were snatched from its face as trophies of the chase.

THE MOST HAUNTED HOUSE IN ENGLAND

A tumble of red bricks breaking through the grassy floor of an orchard, an overgrown path still called the Nun's Walk – these are all that remain of the building that was once called 'The most haunted house in England'. But whether the destruc-tion of Borley Rectory has brought peace to the Essex village, no one is yet prepared to say. The sad-faced nun who was apparently at the root of the trouble, wandered over the site long before the rectory was built, and some people believe that she walks there still.

Until 1863, the nun, Marie Lairre, was a fairly conventional phantom. One story was that she had been walled up alive for an illicit affair with a Borley monk; another that she was strangled by a member of the Walde-grave family, a 16th-century lord of the manor. Whatever the reason, she walked the village roads often accom-panied by a spectral coach drawn by headless horses. Then, in 1863, the rector, the Rev. H. D. Bull, built a new rectory to house his large family more or less athwart the course of the nun's nightly wanderings.

Coach in the dining-room

She seemed to have objected almost from the start. Whenever the rector sat down to write a sermon, Marie would gaze mournfully at him through the window. He was a strong-minded man, however, and apart from having the window bricked up, he entirely ignored the affair. Mr Bull was succeeded by his son, the Rev. Harry Bull, who held the incumbency until 1927. Harry Bull had leanings towards spiritual-ism, and this may have comforted him when his servants left, driven out by such manifestations as the phantom coach tearing across the dining-room, through the wall, and disappearing on the lawn. The nun too, made more

frequent appearances, often in day-light, when the gardener and the post-man both mistook her for a visiting Sister of Mercy. All who saw her commented on her closed eyes and woebegone expression.

In 1929, a new rector, Eric Smith, was sufficiently disturbed by the phenomena to contact the *Daily Mirror*, who sent a well-known writer on psychic matters, Harry Price, to in-vestigate. The spirits could not have been more co-operative. Ghostly fin-gers tapped out messages on a looking glass, vases shattered against walls, keys hurled themselves out of key-holes and an invisible hand flung a candlestick at Price's head. Borley Rectory became front-page news.

'Please get help . . .'

All this proved too much for Mr Smith, who resigned the living to the Rev. Lionel Foyster and his young wife Marianne. Between 1930 and 1935, Mrs Foyster was the centre of new, and somewhat pathetic, mani-festations. Pencilled scribblings ad-dressed to her appeared on the walls. Many were illegible, but others clearly implored Marianne for 'Light – mass – candles' and begged 'Please get help'. Suspicion arose that Mrs Foyster was in some way responsible for the phenomenon, but this she indignantly denied. A seance was held and, for a while, the hauntings practically ceased.

In 1937, Harry Price revisited the now empty rectory and leased it for a year. He advertised for investigators, and out of an overwhelming response, selected 40 including the philosopher, the late Professor C. E. M. Joad. Rooms were sealed, movable objects ringed with chalk, and thermometers, to record the drop in temperature that traditionally announces a ghostly arri-val, were placed in every corridor. Once again, candlesticks hurled them-

selves about and bricks poised them-selves in mid-air to be photographed.

Other seances were held at which Marie Lairre identified herself, saying she had been strangled on May 17, 1667, and had then been buried in the garden. Excavations proved dis-appointing, however, and at a further seance, on March 27, 1938, another spirit interrupted to announce that the rectory would burn down that very night. The evening passed without incident and, in May, Price relin-quished his lease to the new owner, a Captain Gregson. The Captain did not enjoy his tenancy for long; the ghost was as active as ever, his dogs disappeared, and then on February 27, 1939, exactly 11 months later than scheduled, a lamp toppled over – apparently of its own volition – and Borley Rectory burst into flame. But while the old house burnt furiously, several onlookers saw strange figures in the smoke and, silhouetted against a flame-lit window, the form of a nun.

GHOSTLY WRITING *Messages appeared on Borley walls beseeching the help of Marianne Foyster, the rector's wife. This was one of the earliest scribbles*

Bury St Edmunds *Suffolk*

Somewhere in the abbey lie the remains of Suffolk's martyr-king St Edmund. He was born in Nuremberg in AD 841, and became King of the East Angles in AD 855. Despite his youth, he was remarkable both as a soldier and a Christian; his reign, however, was brief. He was captured by Danes at the Battle of Hoxne (AD 870), and though he could have saved his life by denying his faith, he refused. He was tied to a tree, shot full of arrows and beheaded. His own army recovered his body, but the head remained lost. His officers searched for 40 days, until coming to a thick wood, they became separated. They were crying out to one another, 'Where are you?', when another voice answered, 'Here, over here!' The voice was the king's, and so they found his head, perfectly preserved, resting between the paws of a grey wolf. When the head was placed with the body, the two were miraculously joined.

Until the Reformation, St Edmund's tomb in the abbey was a shrine second only to Canterbury in importance. Over the centuries, the monks built up an amazing collection of relics including 'the coals that St Lawrence was toasted withal; the parings of St Edmund's nails; St Thomas's boots and pieces of Holy Cross able to make a whole cross'.

EDMUND, KING AND SAINT

St Edmund's ghost is said to have appeared and speared the Danish king when he attacked East Anglia. This wall-painting is in Lakenheath church, Suffolk

THE END OF BORLEY RECTORY *'The most haunted house in England' was destroyed by fire on February 27, 1939, exactly 11 months after the date forecast by a spirit that called itself 'Sunex Amures'. At the same seance, it announced that the fire would begin 'Over the hall', which in fact, it did; the blaze apparently began when a paraffin lamp dashed itself to the floor. While the house was burning, local people reported the cowled figure of a nun standing at an upstairs window, and several other weird shapes were seen among the flames. Even after the house was in ruins, the nun was said to walk about the upper rooms, though there were no floors left to support her. In 1943, the psychic investigator Harry Price reported finding the bones of a young woman 3 ft beneath the cellar floor and alleged that they were the remains of the strangled nun. The bones were given Christian burial but, even so, the nun is still occasionally glimpsed near the site of the rectory and in Borley churchyard*

231

CAMBRIDGE'S MAGICAL LIONS

Generations of Cambridge children have been told the story of the stone lions that flank the entrance to the Fitzwilliam Museum. According to different versions of the tale, when the clock of the Catholic church strikes midnight, the lions either roar, come down to get a drink from the Trumpington Street gutters, or leave their plinths and go inside the museum

HAUNTED BY A SCREAM

The entrance to the keep at Castle Rising where Edward III imprisoned his mother, Queen Isabella, in 1328. She consented to her husband, Edward II, being tortured to death at Berkeley Castle, and her screams of conscience, or loneliness, still echo from her prison

Cambridge *Cambs*

Perhaps because of the town's gentler air, the phantoms of Cambridge colleges seem to have clung longer to their old lodgings than the ghosts of Oxford. Dr Butts, appointed Master of Corpus Christi from 1626, still haunts his old rooms in the college where he hanged himself on Easter Sunday, 1632. Apparently he had been depressed by the number of students who had died of the plague that year, and wrote to a friend that there was not an undergraduate to be seen in college or the town. Another Corpus Christi ghost is that of a 17th-century student who fell in love with a Master's daughter. Interrupted at a secret meeting, he hid in a kitchen cupboard and was suffocated.

Dr Wood, who became Master of St John's before his death in 1839, has often been seen on Staircase O of the college. He is said to appear not as the grand figure of his later years, but as the poverty-stricken student he once was. Unable to afford either fire or light, he used to wrap his feet in straw each evening and study by the feeble light of the rush candle which lit the staircase. Merton Hall, which belongs to St John's, is reputedly haunted by a large, furry, penguin-like creature. Whatever it is, it seems to have wandered from Abbey House in the Newmarket Road, where it has also been reported. The house is built on the site of an Augustinian priory, and is said to be linked by a secret passage to Jesus College, once St Radegund's Nunnery.

Canewdon *Essex*

Legend says that as long as the tower of St Nicholas Church stands, there will be seven witches in Canewdon. The last known master-witch was George Pickingill, who died in 1909; he used to extort beer from farmers by threatening to stop their machinery by magic. A headless witch occasionally materialises near the church and drifts down to the river. Anyone who meets her is whirled into the air and deposited in the nearest ditch.

Canvey Point, Canvey Island *Essex*

On moonlit nights, a patch of mist drifts over the lonely mudflats, shortly resolving itself, to some eyes, into a ghostly Viking. Legend says he is one of the old Norse raiders, and is still seeking a ship to take him home.

Castle Rising *Norfolk*

Queen Isabella was confined to the Norman keep – which still stands – for having taken part in the murder of her husband, Edward II. She went mad with loneliness, and her insane screams are still said to ring over the countryside.

In 1614, the Earl of Northampton established a charity home at Bede House for elderly women 'of honest life and conversation' who were 'not haunters of alehouses'. The inmates still go to church wearing a Jacobean dress of tall hat and red cloak embroidered with the Northampton Howard's arms.

Caxton Gibbet *Cambs*

At the junction of the A14 and A45 stands a sinister gibbet marking the spot where, according to legend, a murderer was hanged alive in an iron cage. Having killed a man named Partridge, he rashly boasted of having taken a nest of partridges without being caught by the gamekeeper. He was sentenced to hang until he starved to death, but a passing baker took pity on him and gave him a loaf. For this kind act, so the story goes, the baker was also hanged from the same gibbet. In fact, the gibbet was probably erected to carry the body of a Royston highwayman named Gatwood, executed in 1753 for robbing mail coaches on the Great North Road.

WITCHCRAFT AT CHELMSFORD

Essex has the melancholy distinction of having hanged more witches than any other English county. Assizes were usually held at Chelmsford, and it is estimated that between 1566 and 1645, when the witchfinder Matthew Hopkins executed 19 women in a single day, some 90 supposed witches were sent to the scaffold. All were poor, and generally elderly village women, and most were convicted on evidence which would have been thrown out by many other courts in the country.

The main reason for the peculiar vindictiveness of Essex witch hunts, and the fear which lay behind them, was that most people in this part of East Anglia belonged to Protestant sects who believed that witches were Satan's prime agents in his efforts to drag mankind to damnation.

The first major English trial for witchcraft itself (though sorcery had often been a secondary charge in treason trials), took place at Chelmsford in 1566. The accused were Agnes Waterhouse, her daughter Joan, and Elizabeth Francis, all from Hatfield Peverell. The three were linked by the possession in turn of a cat named Satan – a resourceful beast that spoke in a strange, hollow voice and occasionally assumed the shapes of a toad and a black dog. According to the prosecution, Satan killed a man who refused to respond to Elizabeth's advances and later procured her a husband and child. She then gave the cat to the Waterhouses for whom it spoilt butter and cheese, drowned a neighbour's cows and bewitched a man to death. Despite this damning indictment, Elizabeth Francis received only a year's imprisonment and survived until she was hanged for witchcraft in 1579. Joan Waterhouse was released, but her mother, confessing to all the charges, was hanged.

THE FIRST VICTIM *Agnes Waterhouse of Hatfield Peverell, aged 63, was probably the first Englishwoman to be hanged for witchcraft. By her own confession, and according to the evidence of a 12-year-old girl, she sent her cat, Satan (described on this occasion as having an ape's head, a pair of horns and wearing a silver whistle about its neck) to spoil butter. At her command, it was said, the creature also killed a neighbour's livestock and bewitched a man to death, receiving a drop of Agnes's blood in return for each of these services. It was claimed in court that the 'divers spots in her face' were evidence of the cat Satan sucking her blood. Her doom was sealed when it was proved to the jury that she could recite her prayers only in Latin – a damning confession in Protestant England – and she was hanged at Chelmsford in 1566*

A MOCKERY OF JUSTICE *Of ten people who were accused of sorcery at Chelmsford in 1589, three were found guilty and hanged two hours after the end of the trial. Joan Prentice confessed to sending a ferret named Bid to bring about the death of a child who had annoyed her, and 80-year-old Joan Cunny and her daughter Avice also admitted to consorting with familiars. Apparently the two women sent a pair of frogs called Jack and Jill to knock over firewood and bewitch cattle*

WITCH'S FAMILIAR *In 1579, Ellen Smith was hanged at Chelmsford for procuring the death of a child by means of a 'strange black creature'. This drawing of the animal, 'like to a black dog', is from a contemporary pamphlet*

233

Chrishall *Essex*

The old village, which stood about a mile away from the present one, was completely destroyed by fire about 500 years ago. Legend says that the fire was started deliberately in order to cleanse the village after an outbreak of plague. The victims of the plague were buried in a single grave, whose site is marked by a yew tree, and it is said that on no account must that part of the churchyard be opened. Shadowy figures have occasionally been reported dancing about the ancient grave.

Coggeshall *Essex*

The term 'Coggeshall Job' to describe a ludicrous piece of work is said to have originated one day when Coggeshall's town clock struck 11 times instead of 12 times at noon. When word came later from Lexdon, near Colchester, that the clock there had given an extra chime and struck 12 times at 11 o'clock, a Coggeshall man reputedly set off with a horse and trap to bring back the missing stroke.

Coggeshall is haunted by the ghost of a 16th-century woodcutter named Robin, who is said to have carved a beautiful image called the 'Angel of the Christmas Mysteries'. The statue was hidden during the Reformation and never found afterwards. Robin's ghost has been reported near a brook, known locally as Robin's Brook, and the blows of his ghostly axe have been heard at a distance.

Colchester *Essex*

The town derives its name from an encampment built by the Romans on the River Colne. Local tradition, however, associates the name with the legendary British king, Old King Cole, the 'merry old soul' of popular rhyme. Geoffrey of Monmouth, the 12th-century historian, relates that King Cole was the father of the Roman emperor Constantine, and gave his name to the town of Colchester.

The town has long been famous for its oysters, and the season is opened by a traditional festival in early September. The Mayor, civic dignitaries and members of the Fishing Board go by boat to Pyfleet

TREASURES FROM THE GRAVE

Colchester's Lexdon Barrow was opened in 1924 to reveal what may be the remains of Cunobelinus, a 1st-century British ruler. Many bronze items, now in the Colchester and Essex Museum, were found, including the statuettes and table shown here. It was claimed that the barrow contained a king in golden armour, but there is no record of this tradition before 1924

Creek, where the oyster-fattening beds lie. Here the loyal toast is drunk, gingerbread and gin are consumed, and the Mayor makes the first ceremonial oyster dredge of the season. The gingerbread is traditional and may once have been an offering to the local sea god.

Following this, on or about October 20, the 400-year-old Oyster Feast takes place. This commemorates the granting by Richard I of the River Colne oyster-fishing rights to the town.

Danbury *Essex*

Satan in the guise of a monk was once blamed for damaging the spire of the Church of St John the Baptist. According to an old chronicle of 1653, the Walsingham *Historia Anglicana*, the Devil had appeared at the church in 1402 'in the likeness of a Grey Fryer and Thunder'. He broke down the top of the steeple and scattered the chancel, then mounted the altar and sprang from side to side. In departing he passed between the legs of a parishioner 'who soon fell in mortal disease, his feet and part of his legs becoming black'.

Dunwich *Suffolk*

Once a major seaport of East Anglia, Dunwich was inundated by the sea in 1328; the present village and a few ruins are all that remain after 700 years of coastal erosion. But local people claim that at times the submerged town's church bells still ring, warning them of approaching storms.

Ashore, the shadowy figures sometimes seen on the cliff tops are thought to be the ghosts of Dunwich's former citizens. From the ruins of Greyfriars Priory, mysterious lights have been reported, and strange sounds like the chanting of monks are said to mingle with the tolling of spectral bells.

East Bergholt *Suffolk*

The Church of St Mary does not possess a tower, but has instead a 15th-century timber bell-house which was apparently erected in the churchyard to house the bells while a steeple was being built. Tradition says that Cardinal Wolsey began the work of construction and then fell into disgrace, with the result that the tower was never finished.

Another legend suggests that the bell-house was once situated in another part of the churchyard, but the chimes annoyed a rich landowner so much that he had the peculiar building removed to where the church might intervene and deaden the sound.

East Dereham *Norfolk*

The name Dereham is said to derive from a miracle associated with St Withburga, who founded a nunnery there in 654. During a severe shortage of food at the nunnery the saint prayed for help, and in response, two milch deer appeared and gave their milk for the nuns each day. A huntsman who set his dogs on the deer apparently met with divine wrath, for he fell from his horse and was killed.

St Withburga was buried in the churchyard at the nunnery. Her body – still perfectly preserved – was later exhumed and taken within the church, where her shrine attracted pilgrims for centuries. In 974 her remains were reburied in Ely. Her shrine and well lie near St Nicholas's Church, East Dereham.

East Raynham *Norfolk*

The Brown Lady, a stately figure dressed in velvet, her terrifying aspect heightened by empty eye sockets, has haunted the 17th-century Raynham Hall for over 250 years. This apparition originally haunted nearby Houghton Hall, the home of Sir Robert Walpole, and appears to have moved to her new address when Robert Walpole's sister married

Viscount Townshend, of Raynham Hall, in 1713.

Captain Marryat, the 19th-century author of sea stories, saw the Brown Lady while staying at Raynham Hall. He fired a pistol at the ghost, and the bullets went through her and lodged in the door. The Brown Lady next appeared in 1926, when a son of the house met her on the stairs. Ten years later a man taking photographs of the Hall produced a picture of something ghost-like on the stairs.

The Brown Lady may now have moved again. A lady in brown, and with the same ghastly disfigurement, has recently been reported haunting the road between South and West Raynham.

Fen Ditton *Cambs*

An ancient church punishment was revived at Fen Ditton in 1849 when a local gardener and former sexton, Edward Smith, was charged with making drunken, libellous statements about the chastity of the rector's wife. He was sentenced by a church court to do penance at the church and fined £42 7s. 6d.

Spectators packed the church, and greeted Smith's attempts to read the recantation with cheers, shouts and laughter. Objects were thrown about and pews broken. Finally Smith was carried shoulder-high to the Plough Inn, while the rector and his wife were followed home by a derisive mob.

Grantchester *Cambs*

Leading from the cellars under the old Manor House is a disused tunnel, blocked by rubble that has fallen through for centuries. Legend says that long ago a fiddler entered the tunnel, playing as he went, to try to find where it ended. The music grew fainter until it could be heard no more, and the fiddler never returned.

Lord Byron is still supposed to enjoy a spectral swim in nearby Byron's Pool, while the ghost of Rupert Brooke is said to walk through the garden towards the sitting-room of the Old Vicarage, where he had rooms during his undergraduate days at Cambridge University.

Great Melton *Norfolk*

Four headless bridesmaids in a phantom coach driven by a headless coachman are reported to haunt the old Norwich Road, at Great Melton. The hapless young ladies are said to have been murdered by a highwayman several centuries ago while on their way home from a wedding. The coach was found immersed in a deep pond by the roadside, and until frequent appearances of the spectres aroused local suspicion, it was assumed their deaths were the result of an accident. As usual with Norfolk's many headless ghosts, those who see the spectres are doomed to misfortune.

THE GREAT DUNMOW FLITCH

One of the oldest Essex ceremonies, the Dunmow Flitch Trial, is held about once every four years on Whit Monday. A flitch of bacon – a whole side – is awarded to married couples, from Dunmow or elsewhere, who can prove to a mock court that 'they have not repented of their marriage for a year and a day'. The court consists of a judge and a jury of six women and six men from Dunmow.

The ceremony originated under Baron Robert Fitz-walter in the reign of Henry III. The trial was then held at Dunmow Priory but, after the Dissolution, the lord of the manor took over the proceedings. In 1751, the flitch was won by Thomas Shakeshaft and his wife, who are shown (above) being carried in the ceremonial chair – now in the parish church of Little Dunmow. In 1841, Queen Victoria's happy marriage to Prince Albert was caricatured in a 'Dunmow Flitch' procession (right) by a contemporary engraver

Griston *Norfolk*
The legendary Babes in the Wood were a small boy and girl who, in the 16th century, were left in the care of an uncle by their dying father, Arthur Truelove. In order to steal their inheritance, the uncle hired two ruffians to kill them in Wayland Wood, near Griston. One villain could not do the deed so killed the other and left the children to starve instead. Legend says that a robin covered their dead bodies with moss and leaves, and that their small ghosts still wander in the wood.

Haddenham *Cambs*
Thomasina Read was accused of witchcraft by her neighbours and tried in May, 1647. Villagers testified that she told them of two occasions when the Devil visited her in the form of a mouse. On his first visit, he bit her thigh. The second time, he sucked her blood, and she asked him to bewitch a village boy, who afterwards suffered from fits. Thomasina denied none of the allegations but, luckier than others so charged, she was freed.

HAINAULT FAIR

Daniel Day, an eccentric 18th-century pump maker from Wapping, used to invite his friends to a yearly feast of bacon and beans in Hainault Forest in Essex. The celebration was held beneath the branches of the huge and

THE DEVIL'S MASTER

'Cunning Murrell', the last witch-doctor in Essex, was said to base many of his predictions on the stars

Hadleigh *Essex*
From 1812 to 1860, Hadleigh was the home of James Murrell, the last and most famous witch-doctor in Essex – though his house has now gone. Born the seventh son of a seventh son, he was known as 'Cunning Murrell', and enjoyed a lucrative career as a white magician. His equipment included a magic mirror for discovering lost or stolen property, a telescope for looking through walls and a copper charm which could distinguish between honest and dishonest clients.

Murrell often said he was 'the Devil's Master', claiming that he had the power to exorcise spirits and overcome witchcraft by counter-spells. He was well known for his iron witch bottles, into which he put samples of the blood, urine, nails and hair of clients whom he had diagnosed as bewitched. At midnight, the mixture would be heated to boiling point in absolute silence, the object being to create a burning sensation in the witch's body which would force her to remove the spell. One story relates how a girl was brought to him, barking like a dog after being cursed by a gipsy woman. When Murrell heated up his witch bottle that night, it exploded, and the next day the charred body of a

ancient Fairlop Oak, and the party would arrive in a wooden boat on wheels drawn by a team of six horses. Before long the event grew into an annual fair centred around the oak, pictured above in a 19th-century print. One day a branch from the tree fell. Day took this as an omen of his death and had the wood made into a coffin, which he tried out for size before he was buried in Barking churchyard in 1767. A plaque near the Fairlop Oak Inn at Barkingside now marks the site of the fair, which was abolished in 1843

woman was found lying in a nearby country lane.

A secretive man, Murrell travelled only at night, and always carried an umbrella with him regardless of the weather. On December 15, 1860, the day before he died, Murrell accurately predicted the time of his death to the minute. He is buried in an unmarked grave in Hadleigh churchyard.

Happisburgh *Norfolk*
The lonely coastline near Happisburgh is said to be haunted by the hideous ghost of a legless smuggler, whose head hangs backwards between his shoulders on a strip of skin from his neck. Carrying a large sack in its arms, the spectre glides inland from the sea and then disappears into the ground at Well Corner. The phantom was first seen in about 1800 by several local farmers. Night after night they watched as it dropped its sack into a well which formerly stood at Well Corner, after which the ghost itself vanished down the well. When the well was searched a few days later, a man's torso was found together with a sack containing his severed head and legs. From evidence discovered on the beach near by, it was deduced that he was a smuggler, murdered by his companions in an argument over the gang's booty.

Henham *Essex*
A pamphlet entitled 'The Flying Serpent or Strange News out of Essex' was published in 1669. It told of a winged dragon, 9 ft long, that had been seen basking in the summer sun in a field near the village of Henham. The dragon had two rows of sharp white teeth and eyes about 'the bigness of a sheep's eye'. The beast never did any damage and soon disappeared from the area. Until 1939, the incident was commemorated annually by the sale of model dragons at Henham Fair, which is still held in July, and a local beer called 'Snakebite' was sold in pubs throughout the village.

Heydon *Cambs*
Heydon Ditch is an ancient earthwork rampart, about 5 ft high at its tallest point, that runs for 3½ miles from Heydon to Fowlmere. Probably built by the Saxons to prevent the British driving them out of East Anglia, the Ditch and the nearby fields have long been said to be haunted by the spectres of giant warriors. The story was given some credence in the 1950's when a number of burial pits containing the decapitated skeletons of tall Saxon soldiers, were discovered during archaeological excavations.

Spectres, Saints and Heroes of the Fens

When St Dunstan visited the Fens in the 10th century, he was scandalised to discover that most of the monks belonging to the great abbey on the island were either married or living with women. In fury, the holy man changed them into eels, whose descendants live in the rivers and creeks of East Anglia to this day. The legend concludes by telling how, as a reminder to future generations of monks, Dunstan called the island Ely, The Place of Eels.

Ely is still officially known as an island, though it has not been one since the Fens were drained in the 18th century. Nowadays, the ancient cathedral looks across miles of the finest arable land in Britain; but when the autumn mists lift off the slow-moving rivers and drift across the fields, it is easy to picture the ancient marshlands, and to people them again with long-dead heroes.

The most famous Fenland hero was the outlaw Hereward the Wake, who in 1067 rallied the English resistance against William the Conqueror. Hereward converted Ely Abbey into a fortress and held it against the Norman invaders until 1071. At one point in the siege, William ordered a causeway to be built across the fens from Aldreth to Ely, and enlisted the help of a famous French witch. As the Norman army prepared to attack, she screamed curses upon the English from a high wooden tower overlooking the causeway. While this was going on, Hereward disguised himself as a workman and when construction on the timber causeway was almost completed he set fire to it. The flames raced through the reeds, fired the tower, and the witch fell to her death. The panic-stricken Normans, goaded by arrows from hidden marksmen, fled blindly into the marshes and perished in their hundreds.

In 1071, the abbey fell by the treachery of the monks, who in return for an amnesty, led the Normans by a secret path through the fens. Legend says that Hereward escaped, and afterwards went to Winchester where he swore allegiance to William and gained the king's favour. One night, however, he was set upon by a band of envious Normans and, though he managed to kill 15 of them with his famous sword Brainbiter, he was stabbed in the back and fell dying, a hero to the end.

The king and the goosefeather

It was an ancient custom in the Fen country that whoever carried a split goosefeather was entitled to the help and protection of Fenmen in times of trouble. Oliver Cromwell came from nearby Huntingdon, and is said to have recruited many of his soldiers from the region by means of this custom. Charles I must also have been aware of the secret signal, for it is said that he used it on several occasions during the Civil War. When he was chased by Cromwell's troops from Snow Hall in Norfolk across the Littleport Fens, he and his Cavaliers escaped by showing split goosefeathers to the Roundhead sentries. Cromwell took no action against his men, saying that it was better that kings escape than old customs should be broken.

However, the king was finally caught and in 1648 was sentenced to death. Legend has it that, on the night before his execution, he sent a messenger to Cromwell. Glancing up from his supper, the Protector asked what the king desired. 'Sir,' replied the messenger, 'His majesty, scorning to ask for mercy, demands to be given the rights and privileges always granted to everyone who presents this.' And he threw a split goosefeather on to the table. All night Cromwell sat and stared at the goosefeather, fighting with his conscience. Though the execution was carried out next day, it is said that Cromwell brooded for the rest of his life over his refusal to honour the ancient Fenland tradition.

Danger on stilts

After Queen Boadicea's death in AD 62, the Romans used the lush grass of the Fenlands as grazing for their horses. The practice was dangerous, however, for the Fenmen were constantly ambushing the guards. Then, a general from Italy's Pontine Marshes trained a legion in the use of stilts when fighting in boggy country. At first the baffled Fenmen were helpless against the new guards, but they soon learnt how to knock the Romans off their stilts and stab them as they fell to the ground. Tradition claims that the stilts left behind by the Romans inspired the Fenmen to use them for crossing the marshes.

A fisherman's revenge

The Fenland is one of several places where King Canute is said to have rebuked his fawning courtiers by illustrating his inability to turn back the tide. In this instance, legend says that having done so, the king wandered away by himself and went fishing. When darkness fell the king was still in his boat. He asked for shelter at a nearby monastery, but the drunken monks refused him, so he found refuge instead in the hut of a poor fisherman named Legres. This man told the king how years before his wife had been raped by monks from the same monastery, and when he had gone to rescue her, he had been brutally flogged. His wife had later died in childbirth, and each year for 18 years, on his daughter's birthday, Legres killed a monk. The next day Canute went out and summoned his fleet which was lying in the river. He immediately ordered it to attack the monastery. Many of the dissolute monks were killed, and the remainder were forced to build a new fishing village, which today is known as Littleport. In return for his kindness to the king, Legres was made its first mayor.

HEREWARD'S INFERNO *William I lost hundreds of Norman soldiers when Hereward the Wake set fire to a wooden causeway to Ely*

HAUNTED RIVER *Ghostly monks steal away with a saint's body*

CHIVALROUS DOG *The bulldog died in saving a girl's virtue*

DEADLY LIGHTS *Jack o' Lanterns lured travellers to their doom*

The body-snatchers of Ely

A phantom barge has often been reported drifting along the Little Ouse River on misty evenings towards Ely. Its spectral crew is a group of monks who chant hymns as they gather around an open coffin in which lies the shrouded corpse of a woman. The corpse is believed to be that of St Withburga. She founded a nunnery at East Dereham in AD 654, and was buried in the churchyard there when she died. In 974, the Abbot of Ely ordered his monks to steal her body and bring it to Ely, hoping that her new resting place would attract pilgrims who might contribute to the abbey's income.

Tradition has it that his plan backfired when a spring of healing water gushed forth from her empty grave, causing so many miraculous cures that pilgrims continued to flock to Dereham for years afterwards.

The phantom bulldog

Another tale which illustrates the traditional hatred felt by Fenmen towards the clergy who betrayed their trust, tells how the Bulldog Bridge, connecting Littleport with Shippea Hill, got its name. In the Middle Ages, a servant girl was sent by her mistress to pick sprigs of wild mint on the banks of the Red Mere, whose waters once covered the land to the east of Shippea Hill. After gathering the mint, the girl set off for home but, feeling drowsy, sat down by the wayside and fell asleep. Her rest was rudely broken when a passing friar leapt upon her and began to tear her clothes off. Her resistance would have been useless, had it not been for the arrival of a large bulldog that dragged the friar off and mauled him to death. With his dying breath, the man plunged his dagger into the chivalrous beast. Since then it has often been seen running across the bridge at dusk.

Jack o' Lanterns

Until the draining of the Fen swamplands was completed at the beginning of this century, lurid tales were told of the terrifying Jack o' Lanterns which used to seek out lonely travellers crossing the marshes at night. Glowing eerily, their flames were said to flicker above the water in a ghostly dance, weaving a hypnotic spell on whoever watched them and inviting the wayfarer to follow them to a certain death in the deep bogs. Fen dwellers thought that whistling attracted the Jack o' Lanterns, also known as Lantern Men and Will-o'-the-Wisps, and that the safest thing to do if you saw them coming was to lie face downwards on the path until they danced away. Probably most of the lights were the result of marsh gas given off by rotting vegetation; occasionally the gas ignites by spontaneous combustion and glows for a while before burning out.

239

Horning *Norfolk*

Originally a mead storehouse for nearby St Benet's Abbey, the 15th-century Old Ferry Inn on the River Bure at Horning is haunted by the ghost of a beautiful girl in a green cloak who glides through the bar and disappears into the water outside. Legend says she was raped and murdered by drunken monks from the abbey, who threw her body into the river in an attempt to conceal their crime. Sometimes she is seen wandering distractedly along the riverbank near the abbey itself.

At the Dissolution, in 1537, St Benet's abbot was also the Bishop of Norwich. Because he surrendered the estates of the bishopric to Henry VIII, he was allowed to keep all of the monastery's lands. Ever since then the Bishop of Norwich has continued to draw his revenues from the old abbey estates, and every year on the first Sunday in August he visits the ruined abbey by water to hold a service during which he blesses the Norfolk Broads.

Horseheath *Cambs*

Horseheath was renowned for its witches until well into the present century. One of the most famous was Daddy Witch who lived in a hut by the sheep-pond in Garret's Close, and was said to have gained all her knowledge from a book called *The Devil's Plantation*. Local tradition has it that, when she died in 1860, she was buried in the middle of the road which leads to Horseheath Green, and that her grave remains dry when it rains because of the heat given off by her body. Villagers long believed that it was necessary to nod nine times before passing over the grave in order to avoid bad luck.

Mother Red Cap, who died in 1926, was the last of the well-known Horseheath witches. She inherited her imps from her predecessor and named them Bonnie, Red Cap, Blue Cap, Jupiter and Venus. In 1928 a villager claimed that Mother Red Cap was often seen about the village accompanied by a rat, a toad, a cat, a mouse and a ferret. By custom, no witch can die until she has given her imps to her successor, and a black man is alleged to have delivered Mother Red Cap's imps to an unidentified woman living in the village.

Hoxne *Suffolk*

A legend says that King Edmund of East Anglia, after his defeat by the Danes at the Battle of Hoxne in 870, fled from the scene of the fighting and hid under Goldbrook Bridge near Hoxne. A newly married couple who were crossing the bridge saw the glint of his golden spurs reflected in the water of the River Dove, and betrayed him to the Danish troops who were searching for him. As he was dragged away to be beheaded, Edmund shouted out an angry curse on all bridal couples who should ever cross the bridge, and until well into the 19th century wedding parties avoided passing that way. The gleam of his spurs, it is said, can be seen from the bridge on moonlit nights.

Impington *Cambs*

A monument stands near Elizabeth Woodcock's grave in Impington churchyard, commemorating the strange ordeal which led to her death in 1799. Late in the afternoon of February 2, a blizzard was blowing as she left a Cambridge inn and mounted her horse to begin the journey home. She was on a bridle path half a mile from her house in Impington when the light of a falling meteor frightened her horse. It bolted and ran off in the opposite direction, and eventually Elizabeth was forced to dismount. Unable to hold the animal, she watched it gallop off into the darkness and then, exhausted, she collapsed in the snow with her back against a hedge.

The blizzard raged on, and before long Elizabeth found that she was imprisoned in a cave of snow which had built up around her. For nine days she remained buried alive in this icy tomb, hearing the bells of Chesterton church strike the hours only a mile away. She tied her red handkerchief to a twig on the fourth day and managed to push it through the snow in front of her, but the distress signal was not seen until February 10. 'For pity's sake get me out of here', she told the rescuers who finally freed her. Suffering badly from frostbite, she was taken home and lingered on until her death the following July, losing all her fingers and toes before she died.

In the Cambridge Folk Museum are a pair of nutcrackers which, it is claimed, Elizabeth Woodcock used to crack a bag of nuts that she ate to keep herself alive in her snow-cave.

Ipswich *Suffolk*

Early in the 19th century, a Suffolk 'wise man' who went by the name of Old Winter practised white magic at Ipswich. It is thought that, in common with other magicians, he possessed hypnotic powers which he used for punishing wrong-doers. Once, he caught a man stealing vegetables from a doctor's garden, and bewitched him into sitting all night in the cabbage patch. On another occasion he is said to have compelled a thief to walk in circles for hours on end, carrying the load of firewood he had stolen.

Kentford *Suffolk*

About $1\frac{1}{2}$ miles beyond Kentford, at a crossroads on the main road to Bury St Edmunds, is a flower-decked grave which is planted and maintained by unknown hands. Known as 'The Boy's Grave', it is the burial place of a young shepherd who hanged himself after being accused of sheep stealing long ago. It was an age old custom for suicides to be buried at crossroads, the last known example taking place at St John's Wood, London in 1823. Though the idea was to prevent the unhappy spirit from wandering, such graves were always considered uncanny. Several cyclists have said they were forced to dismount when passing the shepherd's grave, due to a strange force which emanates from it.

King's Lynn *Norfolk*

A diamond-shaped brick, with a heart carved in its centre, is set in the wall of a house on the north-west corner of the ancient Tuesday Market in King's Lynn. Local tradition asserts that it marks the spot where a witch's heart, bursting from her body as she burnt at the stake, and hurtling across the market place, smashed against the wall. Margaret Read was burnt in 1590, and was one of the few witches in England to suffer death by fire. Her death inspired another story, which relates how her evil heart, refusing to submit, had bounded down one of the nearby lanes and jumped into the River Ouse.

Leverington *Cambs*

Until about 1860, Whirling Sunday was a mid-Lenten feast held annually in the village of Leverington. Small cakes, called Whirling Cakes, were baked and sold at the celebration. This was done in memory of an old woman in the 18th century who, tradition says, was busy making cakes on Easter Sunday when the Devil suddenly appeared to her in a whirlwind and carried her off over the steeple of Leverington church.

Little Baddow *Essex*

Set in the north wall of Little Baddow's 14th-century church is an unadorned entrance known as a 'Devil Door'. To medieval Christians, the north side of the church was the province of Satan. It was the left hand facing the altar and Christ had said that he would 'set the sheep on His right hand and the goats on His left'. Because of this baptisms were performed in the south porch of the church. If an infant cried after being christened, it was traditionally thought to be a sign that the Devil had been driven from its soul, and the north door, which was left open during the ceremony, allowed Satan to escape 'to his own place'.

Little Cornard *Suffolk*

A most unusual battle is alleged to have taken place near Little Cornard on the afternoon of Friday, September 26, 1449, according to a contemporary chronicle now in Canterbury Cathedral. In a marshy field on the Suffolk-Essex border, two fire-breathing dragons engaged in a fierce, hour-long struggle. The Suffolk dragon was black and lived on Kedington Hill, while the dragon from Essex was 'reddish and spotted' and came from Ballingdon Hill, south of the River Stour. Eventually the red dragon won, and both creatures returned to their own hills, 'to the admiration of many beholding them'. The site of the battle is known locally as Sharpfight Meadow.

LONDON'S GREAT FOREST

The great Forest of Essex, later known as the Forest of Waltham, and finally Epping Forest, once stretched from Bow in London almost to Cambridge and Colchester. Within its green miles lay numerous isolated villages and hamlets. Originally 66,000 acres in size, its dark glades of oak, elm and beech once sheltered hermits, vagrants and gipsies, as well as outlaws and highwaymen.

After the Norman Conquest, the forest was declared a royal hunting preserve where poachers were punished with branding, mutilation and death. Certain parts of the forest, however, were common land on which adjacent parishes had the right to graze cattle, lop wood and collect fuel. Some parishes still retain the pasture rights.

The tree-lopping rights of most of the forest villages lapsed long ago. To maintain this right, it was customary for the villagers to enter the forest on November 11, when the oldest inhabitant would embed his axe in the branch of one of the trees.

The story is told about an unscrupulous lord of the manor who, having made his commoners drunk at a feast, locked the door on them, hoping to prevent them exercising their rights. However, he forgot that they had their axes with them and, chopping down the door, they ran to the forest to ensure the ancient ceremony was carried out.

People of the forest

Apart from the villagers, many others found a living within the forest. Gipsies were numerous and many belonged to the Lee family who made a living telling fortunes at the forest fairs.

A famous inhabitant was Old Dido, a hermit who prescribed secret remedies based on forest herbs. Dido lived in a tent near Hainault about 80 years ago.

Another character who lived about the same time was a white witch known as Old Mother Jenkins the Goose Charmer. She could often be seen waving her stick and muttering incantations over a flock of geese at the roadside. Many farmers paid her to do this when their flocks of goslings reached a certain age. They believed that their geese would not fatten without her blessing.

The forest ghosts

Among the well-known ghosts of the area are Queen Boadicea and her daughters, who have been seen near an ancient earthwork, called Amesbury Banks, in the heart of the forest. Dick Turpin, who allegedly makes dozens of nightly appearances between North London and the Scottish border, had one of his many hideouts in the forest. His spectre rides a phantom horse down Traps Hill, Loughton, and clinging to his back is the ghost of a woman, whom he tortured and murdered for her money.

In the 18th century, the forest provided a haven for dozens of cut-throats. The Rev. Dr Gold of Stratford recounted how he was waylaid by one of these ruffians. He put his trust in the Almighty, and began to sing at the top of his voice the hymn 'Guide me, O Thou great Jehovah'. The robber, startled by this strange reaction, fled in terror.

Littleport *Cambs*

The bloody riots of 1816, brought about by the poverty and unemployment which followed the end of the Napoleonic Wars, lingered long in the memory of Cambridgeshire's Fenmen. In Littleport and Ely, where the rioting was fiercest, many stories were told of gamekeepers and farmers murdered for prosecuting Fenmen whose only way of getting a meal was to trap or snare it, and of soldiers killed while trying to round up the rioters. Five Fenmen were hanged at Mill Pits, Ely, on June 28, and buried in a single grave in St Mary's church-yard. Their names are recorded on a stone slab on the south side of the church tower. It is said that a butcher who supplied the cart to take them to the gallows was later found head downwards in his own cess-pit. The corpse of the carpenter who made their coffins was discovered in the pipe which took water to Ely brewery.

Within living memory, it was the custom in the Littleport fens for a young man courting a girl to pin three stalks of corn woven together in a lover's knot on to the front of his Sunday smock. Without speaking, he gave a similar token to the girl, which she took home. If her parents approved of the match, she wore the corn pinned over her heart the following Sunday; if they disapproved, she wore it on the right-hand side of her dress. The lovers continued wearing the knots until they were married, which was supposed to take place before the ears of corn shelled out.

If a girl wanted to inflame a young man with love for her, she wore a bunch of yarrow on her dress – the smell was supposed to make her irresistible. If, as occasionally happened, the boy remained unmoved, she waited for a night when the moon was full and then walked bare-footed among yarrow plants at midnight. With her eyes closed she picked a bunch, took it home and put it under her bed. If there was dew on the plant at dawn, the boy was just being shy, and he would soon overcome it; but if the yarrow was dry . . . well, she could always try again at the next full moon.

When a couple were engaged to be married they sometimes made a tippet or cape out of ferret, stoat or cat fur, lined it with silk or satin and padded it with sheep's wool. In one end they placed a snippet of the boy's pubic hair, in the other end a snippet of the girl's – probably as a fertility charm.

Long Stanton *Cambs*

At a famous trial in 1657, Margaret Pryor of Long Stanton asserted that a group of Quakers had turned her into a horse. Having done so, they rode her to Madingley Hall, hitched her to the door-latch and went inside to enjoy a feast of rabbits and lamb. Though the judge was sceptical and the Quakers were acquitted, the case developed into a national scandal. John Bunyan and several Cambridge professors wrote pamphlets supporting Margaret, pointing out that her hands and feet were badly bruised as a result of her gallop, and that her smock was bloody and torn from too much use of the spur.

The Quaker pamphleteers were equally spirited, and probably more logical, in their replies. They maintained that the Quakers could not have eaten lamb at the feast since the alleged incident had taken place in November, and expressed grave doubts about the feasibility of riding a horse at all if it were dressed in a smock.

In the late 19th century, a young man thought he saw another Long Stanton witch, Bet Cross, riding past him on a hurdle, and threatened to expose her. 'Young man,' said Bet, 'you may tell on it when you think of it.' Sure enough, the incident was wiped entirely from his mind by the witch's powerful magic until years later when the bells tolled for Bet's funeral, releasing him from her spell.

Lowestoft *Suffolk*

In the winter of 1664, two elderly Lowestoft women, Amy Duny and Rose Cullender, were put on trial at Bury St Edmunds, charged with the bewitching of seven children and with having practised sorcery over a period of several years. The evidence produced by the prosecution, and accepted by the court, reflected the extraordinary credulity of the times. It set a precedent for witch trials whose influence reached far beyond the boundaries of Suffolk, and even crossed the Atlantic to become a cornerstone of the notorious Salem witch prosecutions of 1692.

A typical example of evidence presented in court concerned Mrs Dorothy Durent's child, who began having fits soon after Amy had been engaged as a child-minder. Mrs Durent took the child to a white witch, who prescribed wrapping it in a blanket which had previously been hung up a chimney, and then burning anything that dropped out. Allegedly, a toad fell out, and when thrown on the fire it flashed and burnt like gunpowder. At the same time, Amy's thighs, face and legs appeared to have been severely scorched.

The judge, Sir Matthew Hale, saw no reason to believe that such stories were anything but 'the truth, the whole truth and nothing but the truth'; and many equally extraordinary testimonies were taken from the bewitched children themselves. In summing up the case, Sir Matthew said: 'That there are such creatures as witches I make no doubt at all. For first the Scriptures have affirmed as such. Secondly the wisdom of all nations has provided laws against such persons, which is an argument on their confidence of such a crime.'

On March 13, 1664, Amy Duny and Rose Cullender were found guilty. Three days later, still protesting their innocence, they were hanged.

Newmarket *Suffolk*

On the evidence of both jockeys and punters, a phantom sometimes joins the field at Newmarket racecourse – a shapeless white 'thing' which floats around the track level with the jockeys, keeping well up with the leaders. Occasionally, too, horses swerve to avoid some object which is invisible to humans, and the fact that horses are notoriously clairvoyant lends some weight to the suggestion that it may be a ghost. According to one theory, the phantom is that of jockey Fred Archer, who won the Derby four times and died at the age of 29 in 1886.

Orford *Suffolk*

According to the chronicler Ralph of Coggeshall, writing in the 13th century, a creature which resembled a man, with a bald head and long, ragged beard, was once captured by local fishermen in their nets. The Wild Man of Orford, as he became known, was handed over for safekeeping to the Governor of Orford Castle, who discovered that the creature would eat only fish. He remained obstinately silent, but even so, seemed to be quite happy in the castle, and for some months did not attempt to escape even when taken to the sea for a swim. But one day, presumably lonely for his own kind, he slipped away from his guardians, swam out to sea and was never seen again.

SNAP THE DRAGON

A mask from a medieval pageant, last worn in 1850, is now in the Castle Museum, Norwich. As Snap proceeded through the streets, he snatched boys' caps, hence the old cry 'Snap! Snap! Steal a boy's cap!'

Orsett *Essex*
Deep shafts cut into the chalk in the surrounding countryside – the last traces of medieval quarries – are locally believed to be the hideouts into which the Saxons retreated when Danish Vikings overran the area in the 9th century. Another tradition claims that they lead to the goldmines of King Cunobelinus, a 1st-century British leader who died about AD 43 and is believed to have been buried in Lexden Barrow in Colchester. His rule extended over the whole of south-east England and he became an ally of the Romans. A company was floated in the 18th century expressly to extract the ore. But all they found was the relatively worthless 'fool's gold' – a common form of iron sulphide.

Oulton Broad *Suffolk*
Though no one has seen them for a few years, a phantom horseman with his pack of hounds, and a white-robed lady carrying a cup of poison, reputedly haunt 16th-century Oulton High House. Several legends grew up around them, all of which agreed that the phantoms were connected with a murder, or possibly two murders, which took place in the house some time in the 18th century.

In one version, the owner of the house (the spectral rider) poisoned his wife (the phantom woman). In another, the woman stood by while her lover ran his sword through her husband's heart, and then the two of them fled to Belgium with most of the family's gold and jewels. Years later, for what reason the legend does not say, the murdered man's daughter, who was still living in the house, was kidnapped on her wedding eve and taken to her mother; in the struggle her husband-to-be was killed. Later still, the mother poisoned her daughter, though again her motive is a mystery.

MURDER IN THE RED BARN

In 1827, Maria Martin was murdered by her lover William Corder in a barn at Polstead, Suffolk. Corder told her parents that he had married her in London, but three times her mother dreamt of the murder. A search was made, Maria's body was found and Corder was hanged. His skin was used to bind a copy of the court proceedings, which can be seen at Moyses Hall, Bury St Edmunds

HAUNTS OF THE ESSEX SMUGGLERS

Memories of the wild days of smuggling in the Essex marshes are kept alive by old legends and chance discoveries. When the Peter Boat Inn at Leigh-on-Sea was reconstructed about 80 years ago, a warren of secret storage cellars was discovered beneath the building. In Manningtree, at one time, all the upper lofts in the village were linked together so that smugglers could make their escape.

Tiptree Heath was often used by the smugglers as a distribution area, while a favourite landing place for contraband was Brandy Hole Creek on the Crouch. From there, tubs of brandy were conveyed across Daws Heath near Rayleigh in shrimp carts, to their final destination in London.

The lonely creeks witnessed bloody and desperate fights, with no mercy on either side. A whole boatload of Excise men with their throats cut was found on Sunken Island near Mersea in the early 1800's. They now lie buried beneath their upturned boat in Virley churchyard.

Local ghost stories were cleverly exploited by the smugglers to cloak their operations. Brandy smugglers on the River Crouch, for example, used a 'ghost cart', luminously painted and with muffled wheels, to keep unwanted visitors away. At Hadleigh Castle, a pair of phantoms known as the White Lady and the Black Man made dramatic appearances, but always before the arrival of a shipment of illicit liquor.

TURNCOAT SMUGGLER
John Pixley was a notorious 18th-century Essex smuggler, who was well known along the Essex coast for his daring exploits. When he was finally caught and sentenced he obtained his release from prison in return for enlisting in the Customs Service. There, his knowledge of smuggling methods, coupled with a natural ruthlessness, made him the terror of his former companions

Reach *Cambs*
The great Saxon defensive earthwork known as Devil's Dyke runs 7 miles across country from Wood Ditton to Reach Fen. Local legend says that it was built by Satan or, alternatively, by giants. In the 18th century, a man named Joe Badcock murdered his sweetheart out in Reach Fen. It is said that he was hanged and gibbeted on the highest part of Reach Fen in full view of his victim's cottage door, so that her parents could watch his body slowly rotting away.

Rochford *Essex*
Rochford Hall, now a golf club, is one of several places said to be the birthplace of Anne Boleyn, and one of the many houses that her overworked phantom is supposed to haunt. In this instance, she appears at Christmas as a white 'thing' that flits through the grounds.

Until 1900, the leases of Rochford tenants were renewed at a midnight 'Whispering Court' at the Hall. This originated when an earlier lord of the manor woke to hear his tenants whispering against him. He decreed that henceforward their leases would be renewed at night, and business would be conducted in whispers.

St Osyth *Essex*
In 1921, two female human skeletons were discovered beneath a back garden in the village. In both cases the elbows and knees had been riveted through with iron prior to burial, apparently in an attempt to prevent them from 'walking' after death. The skeletons may be those of two witches hanged by Matthew Hopkins in 1645, or those of Ursula Kemp and Elizabeth Bennet, executed in an earlier witch purge in 1582. One of them is now in the museum at Boscastle, Cornwall.

Sawston *Cambs*
The present Sawston Hall was built by Mary Tudor as a reward for the loyalty of the Huddleston family who sheltered her from the followers of Lady Jane Grey in 1553. She is still occasionally seen in the long gallery and in the bedroom she once occupied – perhaps because Sawston is one of the few places in which she found true friends in her entire unhappy life. The Huddlestons, who lived at the Hall until 1970, have always been Catholic. There is a priest's hole beneath the staircase of the tower, cunningly constructed by Nicholas Owen, a Jesuit carpenter who built similar hiding places all over England during the reign of Elizabeth I. He died under torture rather than betray his friends, and was canonised in 1970.

Sible Hedingham *Essex*
The Swan Inn and the nearby stream form the scene of the last recorded instance of the 'swimming' of a suspected witch in England. In 1863, an 80-year-old deaf-mute nicknamed 'Old Dummy' was accused by a Mrs Smith of casting a spell which had made her ill. Villagers dragged the old man from the bar of the Swan and threw him into the stream in accordance with the ancient belief that water, the element of baptism, will reject a witch. Guilt was considered proved if the suspect floated and innocence established if he sank.

Old Dummy struggled in the water under a hail of stones until at last some of the villagers took pity on him and hauled him out. He died several days later in the local workhouse. Mrs Smith and a man named Stammers were charged with manslaughter, and largely on the evidence of a ten-year-old witness, both were sentenced at Chelmsford in 1864 to six months' hard labour.

Southend-on-Sea *Essex*

Early in September, the opening of the whitebait season is celebrated at a Whitebait Festival – a kind of Harvest Thanksgiving of the sea which used to take place in many fishing communities all over the British Isles. The first Whitebait Festival took place at Dagenham in about 1780, was later transferred to Greenwich, but lapsed through river pollution. It was revived at Southend in 1934. The first catch is blessed by the Archdeacon of Southend and is then served at a banquet attended by the Lord Mayor of London, Cabinet Ministers and the Fishmongers' Guild. Whitebait is the name given to young herrings or mackerel.

Southwold *Suffolk*

In late May or early June, Southwold's three-day Trinity Fair is opened by the Mayor from the steps of a merry-go-round. He then mounts the machine, attended by his Corporation, and takes the first ride. The Fair's charter, one of the oldest in England, dates back to the reign of Henry IV.

Steeple Morden *Cambs*

In 1734, a packman visited Steeple Morden to sell ribbons and laces and stayed, as he always did, at the now-demolished Moco Farm on Cheyney Water. Villagers saw him arrive but next morning he did not appear, and was never seen again. Dark stories began to circulate that the farmer had murdered him; it was noticed, too, that the farmer stopped using his well, and a few weeks later filled it in. One night, the farmer and his wife overheard their servant girl, Elizabeth Pateman, tell her sweetheart that she had a secret to tell him the next time he visited her. Thinking they were about to be betrayed, the couple murdered her with a billhook, a knife and a ploughblade.

As far as is known, the story is based on local gossip: the murderer was never found, but Elizabeth was buried in the churchyard beneath a stone carved with the implements of her murder. Her ghost, wringing its hands and sobbing plaintively, has been reported in the vicinity of the cottages that once formed part of Moco Farm.

THE DRUMMER OF POTTER HEIGHAM

In the winter before the battle of Waterloo, a drummer boy, home on leave, fell in love with a girl from Potter Heigham, Norfolk. Though she returned his love, her father refused to accept a soldier as a son-in-law, and the two were compelled to meet secretly at a place called Swim Coots, on the Heigham side of Hickling Broad. Each February evening, the young drummer would skate across the ice-covered Broad to meet her; then, one night, the ice gave way and the boy drowned but his ghost skated to keep his tryst with his sweetheart. Sometimes still, at about 7 o'clock on misty February evenings, the roll of a drum is heard across Hickling Broad. Then the phantom skater appears through the gloom, beating a tattoo as he tries to summon his long lost love.

Another Potter Heigham ghost is that of Lady Carew, who was married on May 31, 1742. Though she was beautiful, it was said she had sold her soul to the Devil, and on her wedding night, a coach drawn by four black horses and driven by two skeletons was sent to collect her. Despite her screams and struggles, the terrible coachmen threw her into the vehicle, and set off towards Potter Heigham. When the coach reached the old bridge over the River Thurne, it suddenly swerved, tore through the parapet, and disappeared beneath the dark river in a hiss of steam. According to local people, the scene is re-enacted each year at midnight on May 31.

Stowmarket *Suffolk*

At the beginning of the 19th century, the 'good people' were occasionally seen dancing in a ring in the meadows that bordered the road between Stowmarket and Bury St Edmunds. They were described as being about 3 ft tall, and sparkling from head to foot. The best-loved Suffolk fairy story concerns the girl who is told by the king that unless she spins five skeins of flax a day, he will cut her head off. As she sits weeping, a hideous brownie appears and volunteers to do the work for her. His condition is that unless she guesses his name within a month, she will belong to him. The girl guesses a different name each night, but she is always wrong. Then, on the last day left to her, she overhears the brownie singing:

'Nimmie-nimmie-not, my name is Tom Tit Tot.'

That night, she tells him his name, the brownie disappears, the girl marries the king and they live happily ever after.

Swaffham *Norfolk*

A long time ago, a Swaffham pedlar named John Chapman dreamt that if he stood on London Bridge, a man would tell him how he might become rich. Chapman walked to London and stood on the bridge for hours, but no rich man came by. At last, he fell into conversation with a shopkeeper and told him how he had been led on a fool's errand by a dream. The shopkeeper replied that he too had had a curious dream, in which he saw treasure being buried in the garden of a John Chapman in far-off Swaffham. Chapman returned home and began digging. Sure enough, there were two enormous pots of gold buried beneath a tree, and as a thanksgiving offering, the pedlar built the north aisle and tower of Swaffham church.

Similar tales are told all over Britain, Europe and even Persia; but in Swaffham the story has been recorded in a modern wooden effigy of the pedlar by the market cross.

Thetford *Norfolk*
The Elizabethan Bell Inn is reputedly haunted by the ghost of Betty Radcliffe, who was landlady of the pub in the early 19th century and was murdered on the premises by her lover, the stableman.

There is a legend that an ancient palace crammed full of treasure lies under Castle Hill. Another tradition claims that six silver bells from Thetford Priory are hidden there; they were buried at the Dissolution to save them from Henry VIII's agents. Other stories say that the hill was connected with sun worship, or that it was formed by the Devil scraping mud off his boots after digging the Devil's Pits – the prehistoric flint mines at Weeting.

Until about 30 years ago, the remains of a medieval lazar house, or leper hospital, stood in Thetford Warren. They were inhabited, it was said, by a particularly gruesome ghost – a phantom leper with burning eyes and a white, curiously two-dimensional face. Occasionally, the ghost has been reported wandering about the countryside near Thetford Warren, gibbering horribly.

HOUSE OF MYSTERY

Several ghosts, including a phantom coach which haunts the drive, lurk in the shadows of Elizabethan Hill Hall, 2 miles east of Theydon Bois. The house was partly destroyed by fire in the 1960's, and is now used as a prison

SEVEN BROTHERS, ONE BRIDE

In Hill Hall seven brothers are said to have fought to the death for the love of one beautiful girl

Theydon Bois *Essex*
Shortly after Hill Hall was built in the 16th century, it is believed to have been the home of a beautiful young girl who was courted by seven brothers but could not make up her mind which one to marry. To simplify the decision, they fought a seven-cornered duel in the terrified girl's presence, and every brother was killed. Ineradicable bloodstains, it is claimed, marked the walls and floor for years afterwards.

Hill Hall was badly damaged by fire in the 1960's, but this does not seem to have spoilt its reputation for being haunted. The ghost of a grey-haired woman – who she was in life is unknown – flits among the ruins of the house. Shortly before the First World War, a phantom black dog was sometimes seen lying on one of the beds; again, why it haunted the house was never discovered. And most extraordinary of all, a phantom, mustard-coloured coach is reputed to trundle down the drive on the stroke of midnight every May 31. It is thought that the coachman may be the 'Duke de Morrow', an eccentric who awarded the title to himself and lived at the Hall from 1900 to 1908.

Tolleshunt Knights *Essex*

In ancient times Satanic orgies, presided over by the arch-fiend himself, were held on the banks of a bottomless pool in the wood still sometimes known as The Devil's Wood. One day, builders began to erect a house there, and the revels had to stop.

Under cover of darkness, Satan visited the building site to see what damage he could do; but a watchman had stayed behind with his three spey bitches. 'Who is there?' Satan cried out; and the watchman replied 'God and myself and my three spey bitches'. Because the man had put God's name first, Satan was forced to flee.

On the following night he asked the same question and received the same reply; but on the third night, the reply was slightly different – 'Myself and my three spey bitches and God'. Here was Satan's chance, for by setting himself before God the watchman had shed his invulnerability. Satan sprang on him, clawed open his body and tore out his heart, screaming in the dying man's ear that his soul was lost whether his heart was buried in a churchyard, field or road. But the watchman's mates buried his heart in the wall of Tolleshunt Knights church, thereby saving his soul.

After killing the watchman, Satan destroyed the partly built house and, hurling a beam high above the trees, cried out: 'Where this beam shall fall, there shall ye build Barnhall.' In the house called Barnhall there is a beam that is known to this day as The Devil's Beam, still bearing on its blackened sides the marks of Satan's claws.

Tunstall *Norfolk*

Centuries ago, the church tower of Tunstall was once badly damaged by fire and, according to local legend, an argument broke out between the churchwarden and the parson as to who should take possession of the church bells until they could be rehoused. Suddenly, the Devil materialised from nowhere and settled the matter by taking the bells himself. The parson, chanting Latin prayers, rushed after him, but the Devil escaped by plunging into a boggy pool. The pool is said locally to lead directly to Hell, and though Tunstall church never recovered its bells, there have been occasional reports of muffled peals ringing far below the village.

Walberswick *Suffolk*

Some time in the 18th century, a Negro named Thomas Gill, a drummer from a regiment of dragoons, is reputed to have murdered a young Walberswick girl at a lonely spot about a mile from Blythburgh, between Walberswick and Westleton. He was hunted down and hanged from a tree in Toby's Walk. Ever since the hanging, Walberswick tradition has maintained that a phantom coach occasionally careers down the lane, its headless horses whipped on by a phantom Negro coachman.

Wallasea Island *Essex*

A German bomb in the Second World War and a tidal flood in 1953 combined to wipe out the haunt of Wallasea Island's most evil inhabitant. By tradition, the Devil's House or Tyle Barn sheltered a terrible horned demon that cruelly tormented any person who tried to live there. It was rumoured to have driven a farm labourer to suicide by perpetually repeating in his ear 'Do it! Do it! Do it!'. This tragedy led many people to believe that the demon had been the familiar of Old Mother Redcap, the legendary witch of nearby Foulness Island, and was unable to return to Hell. Whatever the truth of the matter, Tyle Barn, according to one brave man who lived there, was always 'ice-cold, unhappy and miserably evil'.

OUR LADY OF WALSINGHAM

The ruins of an Augustinian priory church in Walsingham, Norfolk, recall the pre-Reformation days when the village was one of Europe's great centres of pilgrimage. According to legend, Lady Richeldis, wife of a Norman lord, had a vision here in 1061 in which the Virgin Mary appeared to her, took her in spirit to Christ's home in Nazareth and commanded her to build an exact replica of it in Walsingham. With heavenly aid she built the Walsingham shrine, which soon became so famous that pilgrims came there from all over Europe – Edward the Confessor, Richard the Lionheart, and Erasmus among them. Miraculous healing powers were attributed to Our Lady's Well, and even the Milky Way became known as the Walsingham Way, for it pointed across the heavens to England's Nazareth. At the Reformation, however, the shrine and all the buildings that clustered around it were destroyed, and it was not until 1931 that sufficient funds were found to rebuild it. Today, Walsingham enjoys again some of its former glory, and at Whitsun and on other church festivals pilgrims once more flock into the village as they did centuries ago in medieval England

IN THE STEPS OF THE
Witchfinder General

The witch-fever that gripped East Anglia for 14 terrible months between 1645 and 1646 was a symptom of the nervous tension of a nation at war with itself. Long before the struggle between King and Parliament led to open war in 1642, the people of the eastern counties had taken sides. They were solidly Puritan, rabidly anti-Catholic and swayed by bigoted preachers whose self-appointed mission it was to seek out the slightest whiff of heresy. As the war dragged on, fear and suspicion mounted.

As so often happens, popular hysteria produced a figurehead. In this case, it was an unsuccessful lawyer from Manningtree, named Matthew Hopkins.

Though the number of supposed witches put to death by Hopkins will never be known for certain, it was probably in the region of 400 – more than a third of the total number executed in two centuries of English witch-hunting. Hopkins had 68 people put to death in Bury St Edmunds alone, and 19 hanged at Chelmsford in a single day. Because of such fearful excesses, the name of the self-styled Witchfinder General is still remembered with horror, yet he could not have carried them out without the active co-operation of the local people. The witch-hunts followed a pattern all too familiar: popular denunciation, interrogation in a cell, then death by hanging.

WITCHES' FAMILIARS *This illustration of witches and their imps, which includes a bull-headed greyhound, a ferret and a black hare, is from a book by Matthew Hopkins*

AGENTS OF THE DEVIL *It was believed that each witch, on her initiation, was allocated imps by the Devil. These were usually small domestic creatures such as cats, dogs or tame rabbits. It was not hard for superstitious people to believe that any lonely old crone who kept pet animals for company was in fact a witch harbouring familiars*

The hunt begins

Hopkins' career began with what was probably an honestly meant denunciation of a crippled neighbour in Manningtree, Elizabeth Clarke. But by the time he had finished questioning her, he had discovered a hitherto unsuspected talent for terrorising old women, and Mrs Clarke had implicated 32 other people, many of whom were hanged with her at Chelmsford. Without waiting for the end of the trial, Hopkins, with two assistants, set off for Suffolk and Norfolk.

He was remarkably successful. Aldeburgh paid him £6 for clearing the town of witches; King's Lynn felt his services were worth £15; and a grateful Stowmarket presented him with £23 – and this in a time when the average daily wage was 2½p.

The art of interrogation

Much of Hopkins' theories of detection were based on the notion that witches kept and suckled imps or familiars at a supernumerary nipple. The layman might easily mistake these witch's marks for a wart, mole or even a flea-bite; but to Hopkins, they were the Devil's marks, insensitive to pain, incapable of bleeding, and easily detectable by jabbing with a needle. Doubting onlookers were convinced when they saw a 3 in. long spike disappearing into flesh without a sign from the victim. They did not know that the spikes were often retracting into spring-loaded handles. Once the witch's mark had been discovered on a suspect's body, all that remained was to obtain a confession. Methods of torture like the rack were illegal but starvation, solitary confinement and being tied cross-legged for days at a time were all effective; being walked up and down a cell for five days and nights without rest made most 80-year-olds confess to anything. When Hopkins swore on oath that four familiars – a white dog, a greyhound, a polecat and a black imp – had visited Elizabeth Clarke in her cell, she did not deny the charge. She even confessed to having slept with the Devil often in six or seven years.

The peril in pets

Any lonely old woman who kept a pet in East Anglia during the 1640's was risking a terrible penalty. The Widow Weed of Great Catworth, Hunts, for example, had two pet dogs named Lilly and Pricill; after adequate persuasion, she admitted they were familiars, and was hanged. A similar fate befell Faith Mills of Fressingfield, Suffolk. She confessed that her three pet birds, Tom, Robert and John, had forced a cow to jump over a stile and the wheels of a cart to become immobilised.

Whatever Hopkins' earlier shortcomings as a lawyer, in his heyday he seems to have been able to convince juries of the truth of any tale, however ludicrous. During the trial of Mrs Lendall at Cambridge, the court was told that a male witch, Old Stranguidge, had flown over Great Shelford on a black dog, 'tearing his breeches on the steeple weathervane'. The torn garments were produced in evidence. Rebecca West of Colchester, accused of causing the death of a child by witchcraft, confessed she had married the Devil.

Though his efficiency was much admired, by the spring of 1646 some people were beginning to question Hopkins' motives. A Huntingdon parson named John Gaule, who was probably angered by the Witchfinder's incursion into his territory, wrote a pamphlet entitled 'Select Cases of Conscience towards Witches and Witchcraft', in which he exposed the Witchfinder General's methods of interrogation. Hopkins wrote a feeble though pious reply, but his popularity was on the wane. In the summer of 1646, he retired to Manningtree, a relatively rich man. Legend says that he was later accused of witchcraft himself, and was tortured and executed; but there is no evidence for this, and he probably died of tuberculosis in 1647.

What may be a last reminder of his reign of terror was discovered in St Osyth in 1921. Two female skeletons were found, pinned into unmarked graves, and with iron rivets driven through their joints. Either Hopkins, or one of his associates, had made sure that these victims would not return from the grave.

TIME OF TERROR *During the 14 months in which he searched for witches in East Anglia, Matthew Hopkins is believed to have been responsible for about 400 deaths. To give substance to his activities, he claimed that he held 'the Devil's list of all English witches'*

THE GOG MAGOG HILLS

Watton *Norfolk*

Towards the end of the 19th century, a gang of poachers, led by a man called George Mace, arranged to meet near Breccles Hall after their night's poaching. By the early hours of the morning, they had all arrived except for Mace, and though his companions searched far and wide, there was no sign of him. Suddenly they heard the sound of approaching wheels, and a coach, glowing uncannily, drove up to the house. It stopped; a door opened and closed and then, in a flash, the coach and horses vanished. The poachers fled in terror.

Next morning, Mace's corpse, bearing no visible marks of injury, was found outside the house. It was said that the phantom coach had carried off his soul, just as centuries earlier the god Odin and his wild huntsmen used to take the soul of anyone they saw while hunting across the night sky.

West Wratting *Cambs*

A folk-myth inherited from Viking settlers may account for the tradition that the countryside between West Wratting and Balsham is haunted by the Shug Monkey. The creature, either ghost or demon, is said to be jet-black and shaggy-haired, with a monkey's face and staring eyes.

High over the flat, dark Fens, on the windswept summit of the Gog Magog Hills, is the Iron Age fort of Wandlebury, once a stronghold of Boadicea and the Iceni, and later a Roman encampment. On a clear day, you can see as far as Ely from its grass-covered ramparts – a distance of some 20 miles. No native or invader could fail to recognise its strategic importance – hold Wandlebury and Cambridgeshire becomes your kingdom.

In legend, Wandlebury Camp was ruled long ago by a mysterious night-rider whom no mortal could defeat. Anyone brave enough to try had only to ride into the camp on a moonlit night, and cry out: 'Knight to knight, come forth!' The warrior would appear on his jet-black horse, and joyously accept the challenge.

One day, a Norman knight called Osbert, who was quartered in Cambridge, determined to put the legend to the test. Everything happened as predicted, with one exception – he managed to unseat his opponent with a lance. He seized the black horse and began to lead it away; but as he went, the fallen warrior hurled his own lance and pierced the knight's thigh.

The Norman brought the black horse home to Cambridge, but at dawn, it disappeared, and was never seen again. On every anniversary of the battle, the wound in Osbert's thigh opened and bled again, as if it had been freshly inflicted.

The Gog Magog Hills are a focus for many other traditions. Somewhere under the chalk slopes lie the bodies of Gog and Magog, last of an ancient race of giants. A giant horse is buried near by, and beneath Mutlow Hill there is supposed to be a golden chariot.

TO ABSENT FRIENDS

Waxham Hall in Norfolk is reputedly haunted by six members of the Brograve family, all of whom died violently in battle: Sir Ralph was killed in the Crusades, Sir Edmund in the Barons' Wars, Sir John at Agincourt, Sir Francis in the Wars of the Roses, Sir Thomas in the *Civil War and Sir Charles at Ramillies. A late-18th-century owner of the house, Sir Berney, once invited them all to dinner, and drank with them until midnight, when they vanished. Sir Berney is also accused of having sold his soul to the Devil*

White Notley *Essex*

During the 18th century, the Cross Keys pub was an overnight stopping place for waggoners taking timber from Maldon to Braintree. Any waggoner stopping there for the first time had to pay his 'footing' by buying everyone in the bar a drink. He completed his initiation by nailing a coin on to the wall with a nail specially forged by the village blacksmith. Many of these coins can still be seen beside the front windows of the pub.

Whittlesford *Cambs*

After levelling the Conical Hills near Whittlesford in 1826, the lord of the manor discovered some Roman remains, including several skeletons. A labourer named Matthews reputedly took home a skull and placed it on his bedroom mantelpiece. That night, he was woken by knocking at his front door, and got up to see who it was. In front of the house was a headless skeleton, which in a rasping voice demanded the return of its head. The terrified Matthews threw the skull out of the window.

An old Whittlesford tradition claims that on St Mark's Eve (April 25) the wraiths of those destined to be buried in the churchyard in the next 12 months come out to inspect their graves. When they find the plots where they are to be buried, they lie down and vanish underground. At the same time, the figures of those destined to be married walk arm in arm around the church.

Wicken *Cambs*

In the lounge bar of The Maid's Head there is an arrow cut into the wall above the fireplace.

Once, this symbol appeared in many Fenland homes; it was put there to indicate that visitors were welcome to food, drink and warmth, but that they should not expect to stay the night.

But the Wicken arrow is different. It was the emblem cut by Richard Fielder, an undergraduate at Jesus College, Cambridge, in the mid-19th century. He spent an Easter vacation in Upware, staying at the Lord Nelson Inn (later renamed The Five Miles from Anywhere – No Hurry) which burnt down in 1956. With him were members of two undergraduate societies – the Idiots and the Beersoakers – and they passed their time in drinking and playing games with the locals. Fielder was elected King of Upware, and put in charge of the revels.

Some ten years later, Fielder returned to his former kingdom and set about consolidating his image as a folk hero. He spent his days fighting and drinking, treating the Fenmen to rum punch drunk from a huge earthenware jug called His Majesty's Pint, and scrawling doggerel verses on the walls of the pubs he drank in. Everywhere, he cut arrows into walls, often initialling them with his name and royal title. In The Maid's Head there is a list of the pubs where his rhymes could once be read.

Wickhampton *Norfolk*

In the chancel of the parish church are the badly defaced effigies of a medieval knight and his wife. Originally, each clasped a small stone heart.

But according to local tradition, they were not a knight and his wife at all, but two brothers named Hampton who tore out one another's hearts after a dispute over the parish boundaries. God turned their bodies to stone, and they were placed in the church as a warning against quarrelling. That, at least, is what Wickhampton parents told their children in the 19th century.

Wickham Skeith *Suffolk*

One of the last cases in Suffolk of 'swimming' a suspected witch took place in Wickham Skeith in 1825. Isaac Stebbing, a pedlar accused by the villagers of using black magic to drive two people insane, was thrown three times into the pond with his hands tied to his feet. Each time he floated – which meant, as everyone knew, that he was a witch. But before the villagers could take more drastic action to be rid of him, the parson and churchwarden intervened and sent everyone home.

Willingale *Essex*

The parish churches of Willingale Doe and Willingale Spain stand in a single churchyard, though the
lay-out is such that the Bell Inn separates them –
hence the local joke that the two churches have only
one bell between them. Long ago, it is said, two
sisters fell in love with a foreign nobleman, who
returned the love of one of them and planned to
marry her. But she died before her wedding day,
and the grief-stricken suitor erected a church – St
Andrew's of Willingale Spain – before returning
heart-broken to his native land. The surviving sister,
feeling that she had been slighted, ordered the
construction of a much larger church – St Christopher's of Willingale Doe – right beside the first one.
The tradition cannot be right, for there is a difference
in age of at least 200 years between the two churches.

Willingham *Cambs*

Jabez Few of Willingham, who died in the early
1920's, kept some white mice which the villagers,
who suspected him of being a witch, declared were
his imps. One day, they said, he put one of his mice
into the bedroom of a woman in the village; to get
rid of it, she acquired a big tom cat. Behind the
bedroom door, the sound of violent fighting was
heard; but when the door was opened, the mouse
was unhurt and the cat, stripped of half its fur, was
clinging terrified to the curtains.

The owner of the bewitched house then resorted
to more traditional means for destroying Jabez's
power. He collected some clippings from a horse's
hoof and the legs of a toad, and began boiling them
in a stone jar. This must have frightened Jabez, for
minutes later he came to the house, whistled loudly,
and out came the mouse.

On Jabez's death, his nephew could get rid of the
mice only by holding them over running water,
whereupon they scuttled off and vanished for ever.

Woolpit *Suffolk*

In Saxon times, when wolves roamed the forests of
East Anglia, any that were captured were thrown
into a pit where the village now stands, and were
left to die. This explains both the name of the village,
derived from Wolfpit, and the tradition that a local
farmer once saw a phantom wolf emerge from the
wolfpit and vanish before his eyes.

It was in Woolpit, too, that the Green Children
were found – two fairies who came to Suffolk by
accident some time in the 12th century. At harvest
time, a young boy and girl with green skin were
found near the old wolf-pits, dressed in a material
that no one had ever seen before. They were adopted
by the villagers and given food, but at first would
eat nothing but beans. The boy soon died, but the
girl settled down, and even took to eating the same
food as everyone else. Even her skin gradually lost its
green colour.

When she had mastered the English tongue, she
told the villagers that her people lived in a twilight
land where the sun never shone, on the other side of a
broad river. While looking after her father's sheep,
she and her brother had followed an enchanting
sound of bells, which led them into a cavern, and
eventually brought them out by the wolf-pits. It was
then that the villagers found them, dazzled by the
sun and unable to return home.

The girl, it is said, lived a long and happy life, and
married a man from King's Lynn.

IN MEMORY OF TOM *This effigy in Walpole St Peter's church*
Norfolk, is said to be that of the giant, Tom. Other memorial
include Hickathrift House, Farm and Corner, all near Wisbech
and Hickathrift's Candlesticks – old stone crosses – one of which
stands in the vicarage garden of Terrington St John's, Norfolk
and the other two in the churchyard of Tilney All Saints, Norfolk

TOM HICKATHRIFT THE GIANT

Though tradition describes Tom Hickathrift as a giant, he was probably no more than 7 ft tall (if the dimensions of his reputed grave in Tilney churchyard are anything to go by), and he won fame and fortune primarily as a giant-killer. But certainly he had the strength and appetite of a giant, while the laziness and stupidity which distinguished him as a child were qualities which anyone familiar with the ways of real giants must have recognised at once.

According to legend, Tom was born in the reign of William the Conqueror, and was the son of a Cambridgeshire labourer. His father's poverty contrasted cruelly with his ability to do twice as much work in a day as most ordinary men. By the age of ten, Tom was already 6 ft tall, and had proved himself stupid at school.

When his father died, the outlook appeared grim for a while; but his mother, who loved him deeply, worked hard to maintain him. He slouched by the fire while she worked, and when mealtimes came, ate as much as at least five fully grown men. As yet no one was in any way aware of Tom's fantastic strength.

TOM CARRYING A TREE FOR HIS FIRE

The first displays of strength
A Wisbech farmer, feeling sorry for Tom's mother, offered her two bundles of straw, provided that she could find someone to come and collect them. After much pleading, she prevailed on Tom to fetch the straw, and so, carrying a rope to make a bundle, he set off.

The farmer told Tom that he could take as much straw as he could carry, so he laid his rope down on the ground and piled on top of it enough to fill a wagon. Then he tied it up, hoisted the huge bundle on to his back, and carried it home as lightly as if it was just a sack of corn.

The farmer was horrified, and to prevent Tom from taking such a large load the second time, hid two enormous rocks in the stack. But Tom was unaffected by them, and bundled up a load as large as the first. When the rocks fell out as he was walking home, he simply commented: 'Dear me! How badly they have cleaned this straw, there is still corn dropping out. I'll really have to go back and talk to the farmer about it.'

News of Tom's strength quickly spread through the district, and people began pestering him to work for them. Reluctantly, he ventured out more and more often from his home.

On one occasion, he was asked by a woodman to help load his cart, and found five men using ropes and pulleys for the job. He ordered them aside, and within minutes had filled the cart. As payment, he shouldered a tree (which was heavier than the entire load on the cart) and carried it home to help stoke up the fire.

THE WISBECH GIANT READY TO FIGHT

Tom kills the Wisbech giant
A brewer from King's Lynn was Tom's next employer. As payment, Tom received a new suit of clothes and as much food and drink as he wanted. His job was to deliver beer from King's Lynn to Wisbech, a 20-mile journey that took him round the land of a giant who had terrorised the fenlands for years.

Tom knew that he could halve the length of his journey by cutting across the giant's territory, but for some weeks, knowing the giant's reputation, he followed the roundabout route which the brewer had advised him to take. Then one day, emboldened by all the food and drink he had consumed since starting the job, he took the shortest route.

Hardly had he set foot on the giant's land before the killer came roaring out of his cave. 'Sirrah!' the giant bellowed, 'Who gave you authority to come this way? Dost thou not see how many heads hang on yonder tree, that have offended my laws? Thine shall hang above them all.'

'Who cares for you?' Tom answered boldly. 'You shall not find me like one of them.' 'No?' exploded the giant. 'Why, you are but a fool, if you come to fight me and bring no weapon to defend yourself.'

While the giant returned to his cave to fetch a club, Tom up-ended his dray and took off a wheel to use as a shield, and the axle to fight with. When the giant came back, carrying a club as large as a mill-post, the battle commenced.

For a time the match was equal, with both striking and taking colossal blows; but soon, the giant's condition began to tell against him (for he was fat and out of training), and eventually, streaming with sweat and blood, he fell to the ground. In a piteous voice he begged for mercy, but Tom showed none. Instead he battered the giant's head clean off his blood-drenched shoulders.

In the giant's cave Tom found enough gold and silver to make him rich for the rest of his life; and when the word got around that he had killed the giant, he became a hero throughout East Anglia. In fact, he was so deeply admired that no one ever again called him Tom, but addressed him instead, with sincere respect, as Mr Thomas Hickathrift.

TOM AND HIS FRIEND THE TINKER

The final years
Though Tom fought many more battles, none was as memorable as the one with the Wisbech giant. He spent most of his life hunting and playing games, though he also found time to drive a particularly ferocious band of highwaymen out of East Anglia, and to fight with the Devil in the churchyard of Walpole St Peter's, Norfolk.

Eventually, he set up home with a tinker who was the only man he ever met whose ability as a fighter matched his own.

GIANT AND GIANT-KILLER *Modelled in plaster on the gables of the Sun Inn, Saffron Walden, Essex, are the figures of Tom and the Wisbech giant whom he killed*

THE PILGRIM COUNTIES

Bedfordshire, Buckinghamshire, Cambridgeshire, Hertfordshire, Northamptonshire

The people of the towns and villages of the five shires that straddle the beech-clad Chiltern Hills have always been characterised by a stubborn determination to go their own way, no matter what the odds against them. Perhaps this tradition goes back to Hertfordshire's own St Alban. He was martyred in AD 304, during the Roman emperor Diocletian's persecution of the Christians, for refusing to deny the Christian faith to which he had recently been converted. Awed by his high courage (and by the streams that appeared and disappeared at the saint's feet), the executioner offered to take his place. But Alban went bravely to his death, scorning to utter the denial that would have saved him.

In the 17th century, the same degree of fortitude was shown by John Bunyan who spent several terms of imprisonment in Bedford gaol rather than cease preaching his own version of the Word of God. There, he wrote his greatest work, and the scenes of his much-loved *Pilgrim's Progress* – Hill Difficulty, the Slough of Despond, Vanity Fair – can still be identified in the Bedfordshire countryside.

The Quakers established their headquarters at Jordans, near Chalfont St Giles, where, according to tradition, they built their meeting-house from the timbers of the *Mayflower*. The Pilgrim Fathers themselves originated in Northamptonshire and took their hard-headedness over the Atlantic to build a new nation. They also took their Puritan Devil, their fear of an ever-present Satan which in England had caused the deaths of the Warboys' 'witches' – Alice Samuel, and her husband and daughter. All three were tried and hanged at Huntingdon in 1593, after being accused of bewitching the children of a prosperous family from Warboys, Cambridgeshire. In Massachusetts, it was to lead to the wholesale execution of the equally innocent 'sorcerers' of the town of Salem.

Oliver Cromwell knew the dogged qualities of the Midlands soldier – 'the plain, russet-coated captain that knows what he fights for' – because he had many of the same qualities himself. The Lord Protector's stubbornness is reflected in the tenacity of the legends that cling to his name. Like a true folk-hero, he is said to be buried in half a dozen places, though all of them are far from his native Huntingdon. The tough Chiltern soldiers were not exclusively Parliamentarian, however. The Buckinghamshire knight, Sir Edmund Verney, was the king's standard-bearer at Edgehill, the first major battle of the Civil War. Even when he was killed, he clung so tightly to the standard that his hand had to be hacked off. He still walks his old house at Claydon whenever crisis threatens his family or country.

Other ghosts in the area are equally persistent. 'The Wicked Lady' Ferrers of Markyate Cell, dressed in highwayman's garb, is an often-reported traffic hazard on Watling Street, and even lent her presence to a parish tea in the early part of this century. Her boldness was rewarded at last; she must be the only ghost whose exploits have been turned into a successful film.

THE FOLKLORE YEAR

Shrove Tuesday, day before Ash Wednesday
Olney, Bucks
Pancake Day Race

Whit Tuesday
St Ives, Cambs
Dicing for Bibles by local children

First or second Saturday in May
Ickwell Green, Beds
May Day Festival and Crowning of the May Queen

June 4
Eton College, Berks
'Speeches' and Procession of Boats on the Thames

Sunday following St Peter's Day (June 29)
Wingrave, Bucks
Hay Strewing in Church

Last Monday in September
Dunstable, Beds
Statute Fair

November 11
Fenny Stratford, Bucks
Firing the Fenny Poppers

Midnight, first Sunday after December 12
Broughton, Northants
Tin Can Band Parade

Saturday nearest St Andrew's Day (November 30)
Eton College, Berks
Wall Game

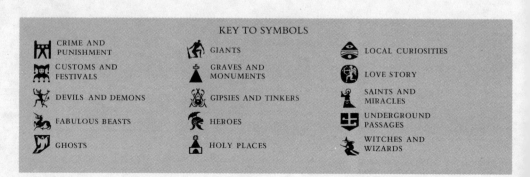

KEY TO SYMBOLS

CRIME AND PUNISHMENT

CUSTOMS AND FESTIVALS

DEVILS AND DEMONS

FABULOUS BEASTS

GHOSTS

GIANTS

GRAVES AND MONUMENTS

GIPSIES AND TINKERS

HEROES

HOLY PLACES

LOCAL CURIOSITIES

LOVE STORY

SAINTS AND MIRACLES

UNDERGROUND PASSAGES

WITCHES AND WIZARDS

NOTTINGHAMSHIRE

LINCOLNSHIRE

LEICESTERSHIRE

N

0 5 10
MILES

HELPSTON
WANSFORD
PETERBOROUGH
CASTOR
(The Chastity Hedge, 261)

ROCKINGHAM

STANION

BARNWELL

RUSHTON
CLOPTON
UPWOOD
WARBOYS
(Witches, 278)

BROUGHTON
WOODFORD
OLDHURST
NEEDINGWORTH

GUILSBOROUGH
RINGSTEAD
HUNTINGDON
(Oliver Cromwell, 268)
ST IVES
HOLYWELL

ORLINGBURY
GODMANCHESTER

NORTHAMPTONSHIRE
KIMBOLTON
BRAMPTON
HILTON

DAVENTRY
BOUGHTON
KEYSOE
CAMBRIDGESHIRE

NORTON
EYNESBURY

WEEDON
NORTHAMPTON
ODELL
The Princess, 281)
BEDFORDSHIRE
GREAT GRANSDEN

CHURCH STOWE
CHELLINGTON
OAKLEY

OLNEY
BEDFORD

PASSENHAM
ELSTOW
CARDINGTON
(I am not yet ready, 274)
(Bunyan's County, 263)
(Doomed Airship, 258)

MARSTON
MORETAINE
ICKWELL GREEN

DEANSHANGER
WOUGHTON ON
AMPTHILL

WICKEN
THE GREEN
(Bunyan's County, 263)

CALVERTON
MILLBROOK
CLOPHILL

FENNY STRATFORD
ASPLEY GUISE

HITCHIN
ANSTEY

BATTLESDEN
CHALGRAVE
WESTON
BRENT
PELHAM

MIDDLE CLAYDON
LEIGHTON
HOUGHTON
IPPOLLITTS

NORTH MARSTON
BUZZARD
REGIS
PRESTON
STEVENAGE
BRAUGHING

WINGRAVE
LUTON

QUAINTON
SOMERIES
BURNHAM GREEN

BUCKINGHAMSHIRE
MARKYATE
WARE

WENDOVER
ALDBURY
(Wicked Lady, 271)
SAWBRIDGEWORTH

HADDENHAM
WIGGINTON
ST ALBANS
TEWIN

LONGWICK
HERTFORDSHIRE
ESSEX

OXFORDSHIRE
GREAT
MISSENDEN

HIGH WYCOMBE
(Hellfire Club, 265)

FINGEST
PENN

HAMBLEDEN
LANE END

MEDMENHAM
MARLOW
LANGLEY
LONDON

(Hellfire Club, 265)
HITCHAM
ETON
COLNBROOK

BERKSHIRE

SURREY

HAMPSHIRE

Aldbury *Herts*

Here, until the 14th century, there stood a castle, the home of the evil Sir Guy de Gravade who, with the help of the Devil, raised the dead from their graves. From them he learnt how to turn base metals into gold by which he amassed a great fortune. Then one night, a servant named John Bond, who had spied upon his master, began experimenting on his own account. Something must have gone wrong, however, for the castle and all its occupants disappeared in a flash of lightning and a roll of thunder. Some said that the Devil came to claim his own.

Yet apparently its memory lives on, for it is said that on certain nights, in the dark of the moon, the sinister building reappears, and through its windows can be seen the spectres of Sir Guy and his servant John, both condemned to slave in an everlasting quest for gold.

THE BLIND FIDDLER OF ANSTEY

During the 17th century, the fiddlers of Anstey, Hertfordshire, were famed far and wide, but none was more popular than Blind George, who used to play at the Chequers Inn. One evening, talk turned to the Devil's Hole, an awesome local cave which, it was said, led beneath a mound a mile away on which the 11th-century Anstey Castle once stood. No one, it was agreed, who penetrated the cave would emerge alive, for it was the abode of demons. Blind George, however, ridiculed this idea, and volunteered to explore the entire length of the cave, accompanied only by his dog. With the villagers trailing behind, he set off and, when the cave was reached, he tucked his fiddle under his chin and strode into the murky hole, playing as he went.

The villagers followed the muffled sounds of his music across the stubbled fields until, suddenly, the tune ended in a terrible screech, followed by an equally awful silence. They rushed back to the entrance, and there met George's dog, whose every hair was singed off. George himself was never seen again. When all hope was abandoned, the cave entrance was sealed with rubble, which is how it remains to this day

Aspley Guise *Beds*

Woodfield, a late-Victorian house in Weathercock Lane, was alleged by a former owner to be haunted by a spectacular collection of ghosts including Dick Turpin, his faithful mare Black Bess, and a pair of murdered lovers. The lovers had been walled up by the girl's father in an inn which had once stood on the site, and Dick Turpin had stumbled on

the father's guilty secret. Several witnesses reported these spectres flitting about the house and garden, and the owner was said to have applied for a reduction in rates. The County Council was apparently unsympathetic.

Barnwell *Northants*

In the grounds of Barnwell Manor, the home of the Duke and Duchess of Gloucester, are the remains of a Norman castle built by a knight named Reginald de Moine shortly after the Conquest. The story goes that when his wife died, Reginald went off to the Crusades, leaving his two sons, Berengarius and Wintner in the care of his brother William. William had a beautiful daughter called Nina, and though both brothers fell deeply in love with her, it was obvious from the start that she preferred Wintner, the younger. Torn by jealousy, Berengarius plotted his brother's death. With the help of the servant of a mysterious stranger who had come to live in the district, he dug a deep pit beneath the castle and covered it with a secret trapdoor. Exactly as he hoped, Wintner fell through the trap, but just as Berengarius was about to seal his brother in for ever, the mysterious stranger appeared and revealed himself as their father. Surprisingly, he forgave his elder son, who went off to find fame and fortune in the wars, and Wintner married his Nina and lived happily ever after.

Battlesden *Beds*

The grounds of Battlesden House, now demolished, are haunted by a dishonest steward who rattles milk pails and recites:

> 'Milk and water I sold ever,
> Weight and measure I gave never,
> And I shan't rest, never, never!'

Bedford *Beds*

The town contains the headquarters of the Panacea Society, who are the guardians of the famous Box left by the prophetess Joanna Southcott (1750–1814). The society reminds the world of the box through newspaper advertising: 'War, disease, crime and banditry will increase until the Bishops open Joanna Southcott's box.' The box allegedly contains writings which will banish all these from the world, but under the terms of Joanna's will the box can only be opened in the presence of 24 bishops, who have so far declined to co-operate. Meanwhile, the Society continues to send out strips of linen which are said to possess therapeutic qualities.

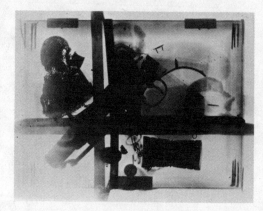

JOANNA SOUTHCOTT'S BOX

Judging by this X-ray photograph, the prophetess's mysterious box apparently contains a pistol. Another box, alleged to be hers, was opened in 1927, without the bishops; it held a nightcap and a lottery ticket

PIERS THE DRAGON SLAYER

Piers Shonks, the squire of Pelham, Herts, was a mighty hunter who was always accompanied on his expeditions by his groom and three faithful hounds. One day, they cornered a terrible dragon in its lair beneath a yew tree in Great Pepsells field. The fight was long and bloody, and Shonks himself was badly wounded, but at last the dragon writhed in its death agony at the hero's feet. Just then, Satan appeared and demanded the squire's body and soul as payment for the death of his creature. Piers replied that his soul was God's, and his body would lie where his arrow fell. With his dying breath, he strung an arrow to his bow and fired it through the south window of Brent Pelham church. It struck the north wall of the nave, and there Piers rests to this day in his elaborately carved 11th-century tomb beneath an inscription which concludes:

'. . . Shonks one serpent kills, t'other defies,
And in this wall, as in a fortress lies'

MEMENTO OF THE FIGHT The tomb of the dragon-slayer, Piers Shonks, bears a cross surmounted by a fleur-de-lys. The staff of the cross is driven like a spear through the open jaws of a dragon, creature of the Devil

257

THE DOOMED AIRSHIP

Low over the fields of France, the giant airship wallowed in the storm. But all seemed well to the passengers as she struggled for her life. Then came the moment her crew had feared, as the pride of Britain, buffeted by the winds, lurched suddenly. Cries of horror rang out as captain and engineers fought to control the bucking monster. Then she slipped down the night like a plunging whale and smashed into the ground. Within seconds, the $5\frac{1}{2}$ million cu. ft of explosive hydrogen in her buoyancy chambers was ablaze, and the vessel that had been thought – like the *Titanic* – indestructible, was a raging inferno. In minutes, the R101 was a glowing tangle of metal. As a result of this terrible disaster, the British Government decided to spend no more money on airships.

Only six of the 54 people on board survived when the enormous airship, more than three times the size of a Jumbo jet, crashed into hills near Beauvais, early on October 5, 1930. And many of the passengers had gone on board with a feeling of doom. The omens of disaster were being whispered round her home base at Cardington, Bedfordshire, long before her maiden voyage to India.

Bereaved relatives reported sons and husbands on the fatal flight departing despite ominous dreams. The coxswain, Mr G. W. Hunt, had told his family that he feared he might never return; and as Walter Radcliffe, one of the R101's riggers, left home to make the voyage, his young son had suddenly cried out: 'I haven't got a Daddy!'

The Director of Civil Aviation, Sir Sefton Brancker, who died in the crash, may have had the earliest warning. His horoscope, cast years earlier, left the years after 1930 an ominous blank. It was also said that at the time of the crash, the telephone extension of the R101's commander, Flight-Lieutenant Irwin, had flashed on the Cardington switchboard, though there was no one in his office. At two seances before the inquiry that blamed the crash on faulty design and bad weather, a friend of Irwin and Sir Sefton said he had recognised their voices reliving the last moments, describing the tragedy in technical terms that the medium could never have known.

Boughton *Northants*

For 500 years, until the end of the 19th century, one of the largest Midland horse fairs was held annually on the village green. Up to recent years, a stone lock-up stood on the green for holding anyone who was drunk or disorderly at the fair. Its most notorious inmate was 'Captain Slash', thought to have been a certain George Catherall, the leader of a gang that plagued the district in the early 1800's. He was gaoled for demanding protection money from stall-holders at the fair.

'Captain Slash' was eventually hanged at Northampton in 1826. His mother had predicted that he would die with his boots on, but he proved her wrong by kicking them off just before the hanging. His name became associated with a ghost which reputedly haunts the church ruins at Christmas time.

THE HAUNTED RUINS

The ghost of 'Captain Slash', a local villain hanged in 1826, is said to haunt the ruins of Boughton church

Brampton *Cambs*

Matchem Bridge, now buried under the Great North Road near Brampton Hut Hotel, was named after Gervase Matchem, a sailor who murdered a drummer boy there in 1780. As R. H. Barham relates in his *Ingoldsby Legends*, the boy's ghost appeared to Matchem on Salisbury Plain and forced him to confess. The sailor was hanged at Huntingdon and afterwards gibbeted at the scene of his crime. The ragged corpse swung in its cage for many years. One freezing night, a group of lads drinking at Brampton Hut dared another boy to offer Matchem some hot broth to keep out the cold. The boy accepted the wager and, climbing a ladder, put the broth to the corpse's lips. As he did so, another youth, hidden near by, sepulchrally whispered 'Cool it, cool it'. So great was the shock that the horrified boy fell off the ladder, and was said to have been an idiot ever after.

Braughing *Herts*

October 2 is Old Man's Day at Braughing, when the church bells are first muffled and tolled as if for a funeral and then rung joyfully in a wedding peal. The originator of this tradition, Braughing's Old Man, was Matthew Wall, a wealthy 16th-century farmer. He died, and as his coffin was being carried to the churchyard it was dropped. The jolt revived the farmer, who rapped on the coffin to be released.

JINXED SHED *R101's old hangar is an allegedly unlucky spot*

As a thanksgiving for his narrow escape, Wall left £1 in his will, payable annually, to promote several curious customs. Until recent years, for instance, the money was divided between the vicar and church wardens of Braughing. Twenty virtuous, poor children and ten aged parishioners were included in the £1, that they might bless his memory. The sexton who tended his grave and the bellringers were also rewarded with a share for the work they had to do on his memorial day.

Broughton *Northants*

The annual parade of the Tin Can Band through the village is an ancient custom which still persists as noisily as ever. It starts from the church gates just after midnight, when residents beat various instruments to make as much noise as possible.

The parade probably dates from the early 17th century, and is held on the first Sunday after

LAST OF THE GIANTS *The most luxurious craft to take the skies is prepared for her fatal maiden voyage in Cardington's hangars*

December 12. The reason why the event takes place on this particular date, and at the midnight hour, is not clear. The original purpose, however, is thought to have been to make as much noise as possible in the darkness in belief that superstitious gipsies would be deterred from camping near by. The gipsies, who were feared as weavers of spells, have always favoured the area because of the many good camping sites available in the district.

Burnham Green *Herts*
Stories of phantom white horses galloping about the area may represent a memory of the white horse emblem on ancient Danish battle flags. The beasts are usually described as being headless, which is probably an allegory of the slaughter inflicted upon the Danes when the local Saxons rose against them in AD 1002.

A sunken lane leading to Welwyn Village is a particular haunt of these fearsome creatures. Many local people tend to avoid the lane after dark, while horses are said to be shy of it at any time.

Calverton *Bucks*
Gib Lane, which takes its name from a gibbet that once stood there, is said to be haunted by the ghost of Lady Grace Bennett, a wealthy 17th-century widow well known for her miserly habits. Lady Bennett was murdered by a Stony Stratford butcher named Adam Barnes, who had broken into her house in search of money.

Barnes was later convicted and hanged, and his body suspended in irons from the gibbet in the lane until it disintegrated. The supposed site of the gibbet is indicated by carvings on the barn built into the stone wall surrounding the Manor House Farm orchard, next to the church. The carvings show two gibbets and bear the date 1693.

Chalgrave *Beds*

The church is situated some distance outside the village and, in the 19th century, to protect the earthly remains of their ancestors, the villagers paid an old man one shilling a week 'to purchase gruel with which to warm his inside and to keep a fire burning at night to warm his outside while he watched through the night for body-snatchers in the churchyard'.

Chellington *Beds*

St Nicholas's Church, now deserted, is all that is left of the ancient village of Chellington. Legend claims that during the plague years in the 15th century, the villagers burnt their homes to prevent infection spreading, and went to live in the church. After the danger had passed, they rebuilt their village on a nearby site, and re-christened it Carlton.

Church Stowe *Northants*

A supernatural spirit, according to one eye-witness account 'a crettur no bigger nor a hog', determined where St Michael's Church should be built. By tradition, the Saxon builders of the church tried eight times to site it elsewhere, but on each occasion the creature undid their work overnight, and moved their stones and tools. On the ninth occasion they took the hint, and built the church where the creature indicated. To this day, the name of the parish (not the village) is Stowe Nine Churches.

BLACK MAGIC ON DEAD MAN'S HILL

In March 1963 and on Midsummer Eve 1969, attempts to revive the Black Mass were carried out at the Church of St Mary, whose gaunt and eerie ruins crown Dead Man's Hill outside Clophill in Bedfordshire. On the first occasion, the tomb of an 18th-century apothecary's wife was torn open, and her 200-year-old bones arranged in a circle about the gutted nave of the church. Perhaps this was an attempt at necromancy, in which black magicians are supposed to summon and speak with the spirits of the dead. On the second occasion, tombs were again smashed and graves desecrated as a part of some fantastic ritual

SKULKING DUDLEY

It took the combined skills of 12 clergymen to lay the ghost of Skulking Dudley, a bullying landowner in his lifetime who continued to torment the villagers of Clopton in Northamptonshire long after his death.

Soon after inheriting Clopton Manor in the 15th century, Skulking Dudley so insulted a neighbouring landowner that the young man challenged him to a duel. But Dudley was a coward, and on the appointed day he took to his bed feigning illness. To save his honour, his daughter disguised herself in his armour and fought in his place. She lost, but her opponent discovered who she was just as he was about to kill her, and not only spared her life but later married her.

Skulking Dudley met his end when one of his own harvesters, justifiably annoyed at being whipped, struck off his master's head with a scythe

THE CHASTITY HEDGE

Two sisters of royal blood, the daughters of King Penda of Mercia, gave up their pampered lives at court to devote themselves to God. The elder princess, Kyniburga, had been married to a Northumbrian prince, but had obtained an annulment of the marriage in order to establish a nunnery at Castor in Cambridgeshire. She became its first prioress and her younger sister, Kyneswitha, soon joined her there.

This was in the early years of the 7th century, when Christianity had yet to take hold in these islands, and pagan gods were worshipped in men's hearts. Members of royal houses who renounced worldly riches to follow the new religion were rare indeed, but those who did became the subject of legends which have survived down to our own day. Kyniburga and Kyneswitha became famous throughout the kingdom of Mercia, not only for their love of Christ but also for their acts of charity.

Spreading the word of God, and ministering to the poor and sick in that wild countryside some 1300 years ago, was no easy task. As the two royal nuns travelled from one lonely hamlet to another, they were exposed to almost constant danger. Yet they felt no fear, for they knew that God protected them always.

The miraculous loaves
One day, it is said, three ruffians attacked the sisters as they were walking across the fields near Castor. Nothing, it seemed, could save their virtue or their lives, but as they fled, the loaves which they were carrying fell from their baskets, and sprang up in front of them as flowers, and behind them as a thick hedge of vicious thorns.

Yelling with fury, the men drew their daggers and began to hack their way through the hedge. The injuries they received only redoubled their determination to reach the nuns, but when they finally broke through, blood pouring from their torn flesh, the earth yawned open in front of them, and they fell to their deaths in a bottomless pit.

Nothing is left today of Kyniburga's nunnery, though the church in Castor is dedicated to her memory. The name of the town itself is derived from Kyniburgacastre – the ancient name of the princess's convent.

Colnbrook *Bucks*

The Ostrich Inn at Colnbrook, which dates from 1106, is one of the most ancient of English pubs. King John, it is said, paused here for a glass of ale on his way to Runnymede to sign Magna Carta.

A couple named Jarman, who owned the Ostrich in medieval times, perfected a gruesome method of murdering rich travellers who stayed overnight at the inn. When the visitor was asleep, the husband would operate a trapdoor concealed beneath the bed and plunge the helpless victim to his death in a cauldron of boiling ale in the kitchen below. In this way, the pair dispatched 59 of their guests, answering awkward questions by saying that the visitors had left early before anyone was up. They were betrayed, finally, when the horse belonging to their 60th victim, a wealthy clothier from Reading named Thomas Cole, was found wandering in the village. A search led to the discovery of Cole's body in a nearby stream; the Jarmans were forced to confess and were executed. It is said that the village takes its name from their final misdeed – Cole-in-the-brook, or Colnbrook.

Daventry *Northants*

Charles I's disastrous defeat at the Battle of Naseby in 1645 might have been avoided if he had heeded a ghostly warning.

A well-authenticated legend tells that while the Royal army was staying in Daventry, the king was visited by the ghost of his old friend, the Earl of Strafford. The phantom pleaded with him not to engage the Roundhead armies but to continue his march northwards. Charles was greatly impressed by the visitation and inclined to heed the ghost's warning, but finally yielded to the advice of his generals. The battle that followed proved a disaster from which the Royalist cause never recovered. The room in which Strafford's ghost appeared to the king can still be seen at the Wheatsheaf Hotel in Sheep Street.

Deanshanger *Northants*

Following his famous quarrel with Henry II, Archbishop Thomas à Becket escaped from Northampton Castle, disguised as a friar. On reaching Stony Stratford the following evening, Becket asked a passing labourer where he might find shelter for the night, and was directed to the monastery at Deanshanger, 2 miles away. Unrecognised by the monks, Becket retired for the night, but later they were all awakened by a loud knocking. It was the labourer who begged to see 'the Archbishop'. To the amazement of the monks, Becket then revealed himself. So impressed was he by the peasant's ability to recognise him where his monks had failed that he agreed to the man's plea that he should bless a local stream which had recently become tainted. The next morning Becket knelt and prayed on its banks and – so the story relates – the water soon recovered its purity.

Eton *Berks*

Eton College's annual Fourth of June holiday commemorates the birthday of George III. 'Speeches' in the morning – readings from great literature delivered to teachers, parents and guests by senior boys dressed in knee-breeches and buckled shoes – are followed in the evening by the Daylight Procession of Boats on the Thames. Dressed as 18th-century sailors, the crews stand precariously to attention in their boats, while the coxswains, wearing admiral's uniform, salute with drawn swords.

'Pop' – the Eton Society – was founded in 1811 as a debating society, but is now an exclusive club of

DEATH AT THE INN
Rich guests at the Ostrich Inn, Colnbrook, risked death at the hands of a medieval landlord, Jarman. A trapdoor beneath their beds hurled them, while they slept, into a vat of boiling ale in the kitchen below. It is said that 60 visitors perished in this way

BUNYAN'S COUNTY

It was in Bedford gaol, where he spent many years for preaching illegally, that John Bunyan (1628–88) began writing one of the most famous of English classics, *The Pilgrim's Progress*. Its hero, Christian, makes an allegorical journey from the City of Destruction to the Celestial City, from sin to salvation. But Bunyan was a Bedfordshire man, born and bred, therefore it is the Bedfordshire countryside, not some imaginary landscape, that forms the vivid background of Christian's long and hard journey.

Bunyan's native village of Elstow is Christian's starting-point, the City of Destruction; for it was here that Bunyan's own salvation began when he left the village to become a wandering preacher. The tower of Elstow church is the Castle of Beelzebub in the book; and on Elstow Green is the stump of an old cross, which Bunyan may have had in mind when he wrote of Christian losing his burden at a cross – although another cross in the village of Stevington might also have suggested the incident to him. Further on, Christian climbs Hill Difficulty to reach the House Beautiful; today, almost on the crest of Bedfordshire's steepest hill, Ampthill, lies ruined Houghton House, in Bunyan's day one of the most magnificent buildings in the county.

Elstow, Stevington, Houghton: all are places where today's literary pilgrim may, if he chooses, retrace Christian's symbolic progress.

HILL DIFFICULTY *From here (Ampthill Hill, above) Christian looked across to the Delectable Mountains (the Chilterns). But of Houghton House (right), the House Beautiful of The Pilgrim's Progress, and in Bunyan's day one of the most magnificent buildings in the county, only ruins remain near the crest of Ampthill Hill*

THE WICKET DOOR *Christian starts his journey from the wicket door in the Castle of Beelzebub – probably this one in Elstow church*

THE SEPULCHRE *The holy well at Stevington may have suggested to Bunyan the sepulchre into which Christian's burden rolled and disappeared*

CASTLE OF BEELZEBUB *The tower of Elstow church where, as a young boy, Bunyan used to be a bellringer, became the start of Christian's pilgrimage*

THE CROSS *The stump of an old cross in front of Elstow's Bunyan museum may have been the place where Christian lost his burden as he started his journey*

---

some two dozen senior boys. Pop members are entitled to wear wing collars and white bow ties, braided tailcoats, checked trousers, floral waistcoats and flowers in their buttonholes.

A form of football peculiar to Eton is the Wall Game, played on a pitch 120 yds long by only 5 yds wide. Players form scrums, or bullies, for attack and defence. Since the end of the First World War no goals have been scored in the game. In fact, the last was in 1911.

ROYAL VISITORS

Montem Day at Eton (December 6) had its origins in the medieval custom of electing a boy bishop. Victoria and Albert twice attended before the custom died in 1847

Eynesbury *Cambs*

Two giants, one mythical and the other real, have figured in Eynesbury's past. The legendary giant is said to have stood on Coneygear Field near the river, which is the site of a small Roman fort, and hurled spears at a second giant who was half a mile upstream on the earthworks in the neighbouring village of Eaton Socon. The story may spring from folk memory of a Roman ballista. Eynesbury's real giant, James Toller, was born in 1798, and he was said to have been 5 ft 5 in. tall when he was ten, and grew to 8 ft 6 in. by the time he was 18 years old. He died in 1818, when his huge body was buried inside the church to prevent it being stolen by body-snatchers for anatomical research.

BECALMED BY WITCHERY

An antiquated wooden postmill stands half a mile east of Great Gransden in Cambridgeshire. In 1867, William Webb, its owner, found a book of black magic called An Infidel's Bible *amongst his dead brother's belongings. He hid it in the mill, which immediately stopped working. Three years later, the book was found and burnt, whereupon the millsails at once began to turn again*

THE FENNY 'POPPERS'

These six cannons are fired off every November 11 to celebrate the dedication of St Martin's Church at Fenny Stratford in Buckinghamshire. The custom was begun in 1760 by Dr Browne Willis, lord of the Manor

Fingest *Bucks*

The ghost of a 14th-century bishop has occasionally been seen riding in the woods near Fingest. Tradition says that the phantom is Henry Burghersh, Bishop of Lincoln from 1320 to 1340. Buckinghamshire was then part of the bishopric, and Burghersh enclosed common lands on the Church's behalf. The bishop's ghost, dressed as a forester, is forever doomed to wander for causing distress to the needy.

Godmanchester *Cambs*

The ancient borough of Godmanchester still enjoys many of the common rights and privileges granted to it by King John in 1213. All sons and daughters of Freemen who are born in the town and continue to live there become Freemen of the borough automatically, a status which entitles them to free use of the borough's extensive common lands.

Great Kimble *Bucks*

Great Kimble is said to be named after Cunobelinus, King of the Britons, who died *c.* AD 43, Shakespeare's play *Cymbeline* was based on this half-mythical character. In nearby Chequers Park, there is a Celtic earthwork still called Cymbeline's Castle. Local children may still believe that if you run seven times round it, the Devil will appear.

Great Missenden *Bucks*

Abbey Mansion at Great Missenden incorporates part of the original Augustinian abbey which was founded in 1133. Legend tells that Sir John de Plessis, the 9th Earl of Warwick and Lord of Missenden, ordered the monks of the abbey to bury him, seated on his white charger Principall, before the abbey's high altar. His wish was carried out when he died in 1263, but it is said that the ghost of both Sir John and his horse can still be heard thundering across the nearby Chiltern Hills.

Guilsborough *Northants*

Early in the 17th century, the village was terrorised by three witches who reputedly rode about on the back of a huge sow. Their main offence seems to have been that they were 'loose of habit and more so of tongue' – for which one of them, Joan Browne, had her face soundly slapped by a gentlewoman, Mistress Belcher. Joan promised her assailant she would regret her action, as indeed she did, for both Mistress Belcher and her brother became afflicted by fits and convulsions. Joan and her mother Agnes were both accused of witchcraft and taken to Northampton, where they were hanged in 1612. Joan's curse was still effective, however, for it is said that Mistress Belcher later went insane and her brother committed suicide.

Haddenham *Bucks*

In 1828, a Haddenham gardener named Noble Edden saw two men, named Tylor and Sewell, steal a sheep. Knowing that the penalty for sheep-stealing was deportation or death, he said nothing to the authorities but could not resist the temptation to bleat like a sheep whenever he saw the thieves in town. Sewell and Tylor were thoroughly alarmed, and made sure of Edden's silence by murdering him one night. That same evening Mrs Edden, as she waited at home for her husband, had a vision of Tylor striking Edden with a stone. Edden's body was soon found, but it was not until the following year that the murderers were arrested. After Sewell confessed to the crime, both he and Tylor were hanged outside Aylesbury Prison on March 8, 1830. Noble Edden's ghost has been seen in a lane which branches off to Haddenham from the A418; it is said that whoever meets it will suffer bad luck.

Hambleden *Bucks*

In the 18th century, Mary Blandy of Hambleden fell in love with Captain William Cranstoun, a married man. Her father strongly disapproved and barred Cranstoun from his home. Shortly after, Mr Blandy died from arsenical poisoning. At her trial, Mary admitted that she had given arsenic to her father – but only a small amount 'to change his mood'. She was found guilty of murder and hanged in 1752. Her ghost, riding a phantom white horse, is said to haunt the lanes around Hambleden.

Helpston *Cambs*

Woodcroft Castle, near Helpston, was the scene of a bitter struggle during the Civil War. Dr Michael Hudson, a chaplain to Charles I, organised a band of yeomen to harass Oliver Cromwell's troops in the district. Hudson led his men in many forays against the Roundheads, but one night he was forced to retreat to the castle and was besieged there. After fierce fighting in which no quarter was given by the Roundhead troopers, all Hudson's men were killed, and Hudson himself was driven over the edge of the roof. A Roundhead officer cut off his fingers as he clung there, and Hudson fell to his death in the moat below. It is said that the castle is still haunted by the sound of clashing swords and cries of 'Mercy!' and 'Give quarter!'

THE HELLFIRE CLUB

During the mid-18th century, West Wycombe Park, which lies 3 miles west of High Wycombe in Buckinghamshire, was reputed to be the scene of wild orgies and black magic rituals. In about 1755, Sir Francis Dashwood, owner of the Park, founded a private society called the Knights of St Francis. His secret brotherhood was limited to 24 men of high social standing. In the summer they met at nearby Medmenham Abbey where they conducted mock religious ceremonies. Before long they became known as the Hellfire Club, whose motto was 'Do what you will'. The members lost enthusiasm when Dashwood produced a baboon at one of the 'services'. They stampeded in terror, believing it to be the Devil.

HELLFIRE CAVES *Dashwood had a series of artificial caves cut far into the hillside at West Wycombe. Many of the orgies and magic rituals are said to have taken place in them*

THE 'DEVOUT' DASHWOOD *Sir Francis, Grand Master of the Hellfire Club, was satirised by Hogarth in his painting* Sir Francis Dashwood at his Devotions

KNIGHTS OF THE SPHERE *St Lawrence's Church stands on a hill opposite West Wycombe Park. On its tower is a huge golden ball, built by Dashwood as a meeting place for ten of the Hellfire Knights*

THE FAMILY TOMBS *Sir Francis Dashwood built this strange mausoleum, where he was buried in 1781. The Hellfire Club gradually disbanded after 1763, but lurid tales of its sinister activities continued to flourish. Dashwood and his friends were also called the Monks of Medmenham because they were reputed to hold Black Masses at Medmenham Abbey, 3 miles west of Marlow*

Hilton *Cambs*

The village of Hilton has one of the finest surviving turf mazes in England. It is about 50 ft across, with ridges almost a foot high and well-defined pathways. According to an inscription on the stone pillar at its centre, the maze was laid out by 19-year-old William Sparrow in 1660.

The origin of turf mazes is obscure. Country people used them for games and races during festivals, but they are thought to have been first constructed by monks, who would do penance by crawling round them on their knees.

Hitcham *Bucks*

In Norman times, Hitcham Manor, near Taplow, was held by two brothers named De Crispin who loved the same girl, daughter of the Lord of Dorney. She finally married one of the brothers, but this did not prevent her from providing loving comfort to the other. One day, her husband found her in his brother's arms and murdered her in a fit of jealous rage. He was ordered to make a pilgrimage to the Holy Land, but when he returned unrepentant a curse was laid on him – that he and his descendants would never die peacefully.

Ever since, says the legend, the bloody handprint of the murdered woman appears on the shield in the family's coat-of-arms whenever a De Crispin is about to die.

Holywell *Cambs*

In the days of Hereward the Wake, a girl called Juliet hanged herself, for unrequited love, from a willow tree on the banks of the Ouse. Because she had taken her own life, she could not be buried in the sanctified ground of the churchyard. So she was buried on the river bank, and her grave marked only by a simple slab of grey stone. The Ferry Boat Inn was later built on the site and Juliet's 'gravestone' is still to be seen there, in the floor of the bar. Tradition says the girl died on March 17. On that day people gather at the inn, hoping to see her ghost rise from the grave and drift towards the river bank where she met her death.

'MAD MOLL' OF HITCHIN

During the 19th century, Hitchin's May Day celebrations were famous throughout Hertfordshire. From early morning, parties of strangely dressed townsfolk and country people paraded the town, singing their 'Mayers' Song' and dancing to the music of fiddles, fifes and clarinets. The procession was led by 'Mad Moll and her

THE MOGGIES

The May Day ceremonies at Ickwell Green, Bedfordshire, are probably about 400 years old. Adults and children perform traditional songs and dances, the men wearing smocks, the girls in ankle-length dresses with lace collars, and starched bonnets. Two 'Moggies' in strange costumes and with blackened faces collect money among the crowd. As well as collecting-boxes, they also carry brooms. The fine maypole on Ickwell's village green (left) is a permanent structure, and dancing around it is one of the highlights of the festival. Another is the crowning of the May Queen – a girl of up to 15 years old, elected from one of the three villages which take part in the celebrations: Ickwell, Caldecote and Old Warden

HORSE-DOCTOR'S SHRINE

The design (above) on a lectern in the parish council chambers at Ippollitts, Hertfordshire, recalls the association of the church with St Hippolytus, a 3rd-century divine who was famous as a horse-doctor. According to one tradition, his bones were laid to rest beneath the church altar, which later became a shrine to which people brought horses that were sick or injured. The animals were brought in by the north door and led up to the altar, where the parson would touch them with the relics of the saint, in return for a thank-offering

Houghton Regis *Beds*

It is said the villagers of Houghton Regis were so simple that they would cut off a sheep's head to free it from a fence, hold a black cat out of the window to see if it was snowing, and drag the pond for cheese when they saw the moon's reflection in the water.

husband' – two men with blackened faces, one dressed as a woman in rags and tatters. Behind them came 'the Lord and Lady' – the 'Lady' a youth in a fine dress, the 'Lord' carrying a sword, and both of them decked in ribbons. Dancing and revelry went on all day. The Mayers' modern counterparts are the Offley Morris Men, who tour the area in the late spring with their hobby-horse.

The moated Hitchin Priory, built in 1770–1 over the site of a 14th-century Carmelite house, is reputedly haunted by the ghost of a Cavalier named Goring, slain under the eyes of his fiancée by a party of Roundheads at nearby High Down House. Each year, on June 15, his headless ghost is said to ride to the site of his hiding place in the grounds of the priory

---

Keysoe *Beds*
In 1718, William Dickins slipped and fell while working on the steeple of St Mary's Church. He was saved from certain death, it is said, by reciting a prayer in mid-air. His miraculous escape is recorded on a tablet set in the church wall.

Kimbolton *Cambs*
Catherine of Aragon, Henry VIII's divorced first wife, died a prisoner in Kimbolton Castle in 1536. For many years afterwards, the ghost of the unhappy queen was said to haunt the castle.

Lane End *Bucks*
In 1766 a young girl who always liked to dress in red died tragically two weeks before her wedding day. Long after, says local legend, her ghost haunted footpaths in the district. In 1943 the figure of a strange girl in a red dress and without a coat was seen crossing a field on a snowy December day. She has not been reported since.

Langley *Berks*
Love Hill, a house at Langley, was haunted during the 1850's by the ghost of a man in a yellow coat, with a hard face and piercing eyes. Books flew through the air, and the sounds of a violent quarrel were heard. The occupant of the house, Sir Frederick Ouseley, at last traced the noises to a spare room. When the floorboards were lifted, the skeletons of a woman and child were discovered. With their burial, the hauntings came to an end.

THE CAKE-BAKERS
This carving on a pillar in All Saint's Church at Leighton Buzzard, Bedfordshire, was probably made in the 15th century by men guarding the sacred relic of St Hugh's Cloak. It is thought to show the mythical Simon and Nell, who made the first Simnel cake

Longwick *Bucks*
Until the First World War, Longwick was noted for its traditional May Day garlands – circles of saplings covered with a mass of primroses, cowslips and other spring flowers – carried by the children from house to house. Local children still weave wreaths and garlands of flowers for the day.

CROMWELL'S ARMS ON HIS
BIRTHPLACE IN HUNTINGDON

LORE AND LEGENDS OF

Oliver Cromwell

Huntingdon's most famous son was born in a small house in the centre of the town in 1599. It is said that the door of the room was covered by a tapestry depicting a devil, which according to many of his contemporaries had a considerable effect on his later career. The tapestry has gone, but Cromwell's birthplace still stands; so too does the school he attended, now converted into a museum. From its walls, the stern, blunt features of the Lord Protector gaze down, portrayed as he always wished, with 'warts and all'.

Few figures in modern history have attracted so many legends. In his own time – and to posterity – he was variously known as a saint, a demon, a military genius, a cold-blooded murderer, a defender of liberties and a bloody tyrant, depending where one's sympathies lay; perhaps he was something of all of these. Whatever the truth, stories of this Puritan squire who became the master of all Britain still flourish throughout the country. There are few ruins of any antiquity that are not pointed out as his handiwork, and few churches of suitable age in which he is not believed to have stabled his horses. He died in 1658, more powerful than any Englishman before or since. His grave is unknown, but his influence lingers still.

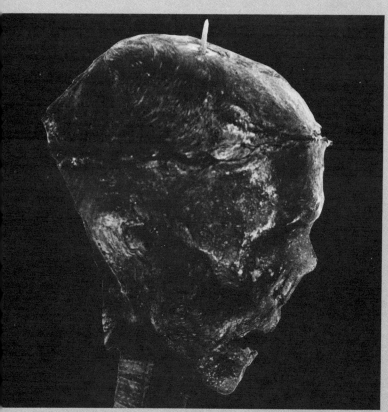

THE WANDERING HEAD *In 1661, Cromwell's shrivelled head (above) was placed on a spike at Westminster Hall, where it remained until 1688, when it was probably stolen. In 1787, an actor named Russell sold it to a museum: eventually, it was bought by a Mr Wilkinson, one of whose descendants recently presented it to Cromwell's old college of Sidney Sussex, Cambridge. There it now lies in an unmarked grave. The 17th-century cartoon (right) depicts Oliver from the Royalist viewpoint, as a man doomed to the gallows in this life, and to Hell in the next*

'The ruins he knocked about a bit'

There is a story that Cromwell's first battle with Charles I – when he bloodied the future monarch's nose – took place when both of them were children, staying with Oliver's grandfather at Hinchinbrook House, which still stands on the outskirts of Huntingdon. It seems unlikely that they could ever have met at this period, and the tale probably arises out of a mis-spelling of Mrs Cromwell's maiden name. Oliver's mother's family had originally been called Styward, but had later changed the spelling to Steward. This was close enough to the royal name of Stuart for Oliver's protagonists to claim royal kinship for their hero in 1657, when it was suggested that he should take the crown. It was probably felt that it would do no harm to show that Oliver was on visiting terms with princes at an early age, nor that he would have asserted himself even then.

Whatever damage he inflicted upon Charles as a child, it was nothing to the amount attributed to him in later years. John Byng, an 18th-century traveller, wrote: 'Whenever I enquire about ruins, I always get the same answer, that it was some Popish place destroyed by Oliver Cromwell.' Even in our own century, the immortal music-hall artiste Marie Lloyd continued the tradition with her song, 'The ruins that Oliver Cromwell knocked abaht a bit'.

The New Model Army, recruited, armed and trained by Cromwell to a perfection that had not been seen since Imperial Rome, stormed about 50 fortresses during the Civil War. Oliver is personally credited with a much longer list including such places as Sheriff Hutton Castle in Yorkshire, which fell into decay in Tudor times, and Pickering Castle in the same county, which was actually demolished by the Royalists to provide additional fortifications at Scarborough. The damage to the tower of Ely Cathedral, which occurred during a storm in the 15th century, is also ascribed to Cromwell. The gun responsible still stands near by; it dates from the Crimean War. Perhaps the most remarkable story is that of Swansdown, a town 'larger than London' which stood near Harefield on the outskirts of the capital. It was entirely blown away by Cromwell's guns, giving rise to the saying 'blown away like swansdown'. The town never existed at all.

Desecrator and murderer

There must be hundreds of churches up and down the country whose plain-glass windows once glowed with medieval stained glass, and whose niches are filled with the defaced remains of medieval stone saints. In most cases, the parishioners are convinced that the despoiling of their church was carried out on the personal orders of Cromwell, usually on the occasion when 'he stabled his horses there'. Salisbury, Ely and St Paul's cathedrals were all allegedly desecrated in this way, as well as many smaller churches, particularly in the West Country and East Anglia. It may well be that patrols of the New Model

Army, hard professional soldiers and strict Puritans to a man, did occasionally stable their horses in churches and smash the evidences of 'idolatry' they found within. But Cromwell himself always advocated religious toleration, and it seems unlikely that he would have countenanced such sacrilege. Ravages of time apart, the damage done to East Anglian churches at least was mostly inflicted by Edward VI's commissioners, who were sent about the country to obliterate 'superstition and hypocrisy'.

Cromwell's savage treatment of his enemies, particularly of the Irish and the Scots, requires no embellishment, but even here, legend has improved on history. After the fight at Winceby, Lincolnshire, Cromwell is said to have cut off the head of the Cavalier, Sir Ingram Hopton, and returned the body to his wife on horseback. A more accurate account seems to be that Sir Ingram was killed in action, and Cromwell had him buried honourably. Similarly, when Sir Richard Graham was wounded at Marston Moor, Cromwell is alleged to have chased him home to Norton Conyers, ridden his horse up the great staircase, and cut the fugitive down with a single blow. In fact, Sir Richard survived the war by several years.

Death and after

Cromwell died of tertian ague on September 3, 1658. A terrible storm was raging, sure evidence that the Devil had come to collect his own under the terms of the contract Cromwell had made with him at the Battle of Worcester, exactly seven years before. Whatever the destination of his spirit, Cromwell's body rested in Westminster Abbey for three years. It was then disinterred, and in company with those of the other regicides, alive and dead, was hanged, drawn and decapitated at Tyburn. His final grave is uncertain; in London, Red Lion Square, Chiswick church and beneath No. 1, Connaught Place, near Tyburn, have all been suggested. On the other hand, he may have been taken secretly to the scene of his greatest victory at Naseby, Northamptonshire, and buried there. His ghost appears at all these places, as well as at Basing House, Northborough Manor, and many other sites he knew in life. For some reason, he also appeared to the Duke of Wellington at Apsley House, Piccadilly, in 1832, at the height of the Reform Bill crisis. The mob were breaking the Duke's windows, and Oliver was seen, pointing sternly at the crowd. What he meant by this is not known.

CAVALIER PROPAGANDA *Though both sides committed atrocities during the Civil War, many of the more lurid tales still believed about Cromwell are the result of powerful Royalist propaganda. Extensive use was also made of the political cartoon, then a novel idea recently imported from Holland. Though these seem laboured to modern eyes, they were highly effective at the* *time. The above example shows Cromwell balanced on a slippery globe in Hell's mouth directing the lopping of 'The Royall Oake' – Charles I. The Army and the House of Commons haul on the ropes and prepare to topple the monarch, while swine – the lower classes – fatten on fallen acorns in preparation for the slaughter that awaits them*

To the Memory of a
Female unknown found murdered
in Blackgrove wood
August 15 1821.
Oh pause my friends and drop the silent tear
Attend and learn why I was buried here
Perchance some distant earth had hid my clay
If I'd outlived the sad the fatal day . . . .
To you unknown my case not understood
From whence I came or why in Blackgrove wood
This truths too clear and nearly all thats known
I there was murdered and the villians flown
May God whose piercing eye pursues his flight
Pardon the crime but bring the deed to light.

TO A GIRL UNKNOWN . . .

This sampler in Luton Museum is a replica of an epitaph in the churchyard at Tilsworth, Bedfordshire. Legend says a man named Evestaffe later confessed to the murder

Luton *Beds*

Two miles north of Luton lies Galley Hill, whose earlier name – 'Gallows Hill' – was derived from its being a place of execution in medieval times. During the 16th and 17th centuries it was used as a burial ground for witches, and may also have been the centre of a secret witch cult. Excavations in 1962 revealed a horse's skull on top of which was placed a bone dice with the '6' uppermost. These objects were probably used in ritual ceremonies and in the weaving of spells.

Marlow *Bucks*

'Who ate puppy pie under Marlow Bridge?' was a favourite insult hurled by Eton schoolboys at Windsor bargees who passed them on the river. The story goes that some time during the last century, a cook in an Eton household noticed that food was constantly disappearing from her larder. The cook planned to pay out the thief and so, when a litter of unwanted puppies had been drowned in the house, she put them all into a large pie dish, covered them with a golden crust and put them on the larder shelf. Sure enough, it was gone two hours later, and next day the remains of the pie were discovered beneath Marlow Bridge. It was assumed that the bargees had stolen it and, finding that the contents were less pleasant than their usual plunder, had abandoned it on their journey.

THE WICKED LADY

Hertfordshire's best authenticated spectre – that of 'The Wicked Lady' Catherine Ferrers – has haunted her old home of Markyate Cell, a privately owned house near Markyate, since she died in the middle of the 17th century. Hoofbeats are often heard along the quiet lanes, and sometimes Catherine herself appears, leaping the hedgerows on a coal-black horse or galloping over the grass at the side of the drive, using the turf to muffle her horse's hoofbeats, exactly as she did in life.

She is suspected of being the author of a serious fire in the house in 1840 and, when repairs were being carried out, terrified the workmen by swinging from the branch of a tree in broad daylight. She was often seen in the kitchen, and appeared on the great staircase with such regularity that a previous owner used to bid her 'good-night' as he went up to bed. Her most spectacular appearance – and one that may indicate that ghosts have a sense of humour – occurred at a parish tea early this century. Cakes and curates, children and sandwiches scattered in all directions as Lady Ferrers grinned horribly at the assembled company from her favourite perch in a tree.

It all began when Catherine was married in her teens to a man she disliked. From the start, she found life in the country tedious. To enliven her miserable state, she disguised herself as a highwayman and began robbing the coaches on nearby Watling Street. The mysterious highwayman who always rode a great black horse became the terror of the neighbourhood, and a byword for sheer audacity in a series of bold robberies. But Lady Ferrers pursued her career for excitement, and had little need of the valuables she stole. She hid them, together with her disguise, in a secret room above the kitchen at Markyate Cell. At last her luck ran out. She was wounded – some say by her lover – while robbing a coach near St Albans, and struggled home to die at the door of her chamber. Her horrified husband buried her quietly, and sealed her secret room, mistakenly believing that to be the last that anyone would hear of her.

MARKYATE CELL *Phantom hoofbeats in the twilight are said to be those of Lady Ferrers' horse that brought her home to die*

STAND AND DELIVER! *Catherine Ferrers was the terror of No Man's Land, the lonely country near Wheathampstead*

THE DEVIL'S TOWER

According to local lore, the curious separate tower of Marston Moretaine church, Bedfordshire, was detached from the main building by the Devil, who was trying to steal it. Finding it too heavy, he left it where it now stands. In fact, the tower was probably built as a refuge from flooding in the low-lying valley

Middle Claydon *Bucks*

The ghost of Sir Edmund Verney, Charles I's standard-bearer at the Battle of Edgehill, is said to appear at Claydon House whenever trouble threatens either his country or his family. Sir Edmund was killed in the battle, and died clutching the standard so tightly that his hand had to be hacked off. It was eventually returned to his family for burial. Sir Edmund was also recognised among the spectral combatants who appeared at Edgehill at Christmas, 1642, several months after the battle.

Millbrook *Beds*

Girl straw-plaiters, making straw ropes for the less-demanding farm jobs such as securing hay ricks, used to work on the roof of St Michael's Church. They laboured until the end of the plait reached the ground, when they stopped for the day. As they worked, they recited:

'Over one and under two,
Pull it tight and that will do.'

Needingworth *Cambs*

The reason why the villagers are called 'Needingworth Greeks' is that following the almost total destruction of the village by fire in 1847, the people began searching the ruins of a barn in which calves had been kept. The smell of roasted meat was so delicious that the villagers cut strips off a carcass and ate them. When they reached the feet of the beast, however, they discovered donkey's hooves. The people have been called 'Greeks' ever since, for as neighbouring villagers say, 'every one knows that Greeks eat donkeys'.

271

Northampton *Northants*

The Norman Church of St Peter stands on the site of an earlier Saxon church. In the early 11th century, the parish priest of this old church was a godly man named Brunning who had a Norwegian servant as devout as himself. Brunning felt it would benefit both their souls if his man made a pilgrimage to Rome, but before the servant's ship had sailed, he was commanded in a dream to return home. Sensing some divine purpose, Brunning asked his servant to keep a vigil in the church. Sure enough, the servant was rewarded by another dream in which he was told to search a certain part of the church. There, he discovered an ancient tomb.

Convinced some great revelation would follow,

Brunning and his servant sent for a cripple girl named Alfgiva in the hope that she might be cured. At sunset, the three knelt at the altar; then, as midnight struck, the church was suddenly filled with light. A snow-white dove appeared and sprinkled the watchers with holy water from the font. To their great joy, Alfgiva was immediately cured. They opened the tomb, and discovered from a document within that it contained the bones of St Ragener, a nephew of the martyr-king St Edmund. A stone coffin lid in the present church is believed to be that of St Ragener's reliquary.

Northampton has always been famous for its shoemakers, sturdy, independent men who for years fought the encroachment of large combines upon their small workshops. When they could fight no longer and the craftsmen were forced to work in factories, they reasserted their independence with a now-extinct custom known as 'Saint Monday'. Defying the management, they simply declared most Mondays to be unpaid holidays.

COBBLER SAINTS

The patron saints of Northampton's shoemakers are Crispin and Crispinian, two cobbler brothers who lived in Soissons, France, during the 3rd century AD. Both were Christian converts, and noted for their compassion to the poor. They were beheaded in 303 during the Roman emperor Diocletian's Christian persecutions. Their feast day is October 25. This modern engraved glass panel is in Northampton Art Gallery

IN GRATITUDE TO THE KING

On May 29, Oak Apple Day, the verger of All Saints Church, Northampton, places a wreath of oak leaves around the statue of Charles II on the portico. This is to mark the king's generosity after the great fire of 1675, which gutted most of the town: he gave the inhabitants 1000 tons of oak timber to help in the rebuilding. Until recently, any child not wearing an oak apple or leaf before midday on this day risked a severe pinching or being slapped with nettles by the other children

North Marston *Bucks*

The rector of North Marston from 1290 to 1314, Sir John Schorne, or Shorne, is credited with originating the medicinal spring which now provides the village with its water. During a drought he struck the ground near the Church of St Mary with his stick and the spring burst forth. A well was built around it, and its curative powers – especially for ague – attracted sufferers from all over the country, who paid to drink from a gold cup chained to the wall. The proceeds were used to build the chancel of North Marston church. Villagers also bathed their eyes with the water. Though he was never canonised, Sir John was considered a saint by his contemporaries, and pilgrims flocked to his shrine. In 1478 his bones were removed to St George's Chapel, Windsor, where they rest still.

The iron content of the water made it unpalatable for normal purposes, and when pilgrimages ceased in the 16th century, it was used to fill cattle troughs. By 1835 the mineral taste had apparently decreased, for the spring became the regular source of water for the village. The holy well, called Schorne's Well, which has never run dry through all the centuries, is a short distance from the church. It is now covered and a pump stands over it.

Sir John's second miracle was to catch the Devil and imprison him in a long boot. This exploit was represented on pewter tokens, made in the locality and sold to pilgrims, and in church paintings.

Norton *Northants*

There is nothing in the village or the nearby site of Bannaventa, a Roman settlement, to show that this was once the home of St Patrick, the patron saint of Ireland. Born in Wales in AD 389, he lived in Bannaventa with his parents, the Roman official Calpurnius and his British wife, until 405, when the town was plundered by Celts and the able-bodied population taken into slavery. The 16-year-old Patrick was sold to an Irish landowner.

Patrick, who had been brought up as a Christian by his father, led a miserable life as a cattle-minder among the pagan Irish. Then one day, as he rested on a mountainside, a boulder that was falling towards him split into two pieces and passed on either side of him. Believing this to be a sign that God had work for him, he escaped to Gaul, and later returned to Bannaventa, where he became a farmer. But he became daily more convinced that God had singled him out to convert the Irish. In 432, he returned to the land of his captivity, where his miracles and piety convinced the people of the truth of his message. He died *c.* 461.

Oakley *Beds*

Although the persecution of witches became illegal in 1736, mob trials took place throughout the 18th century. In 1737, an old Oakley woman, suspected of being a witch, was subjected to the swimming test. She was first searched for pins, which were believed to neutralise tests; then she was tied in a sheet and thrown in the river. She partly floated – a sign of guilt – and partly sank – a sign of innocence. Nonplussed, the villagers weighed her against the church Bible, which it was considered would outweigh her evil if she were a witch. As the Bible weighed only 12 lb., the scales tipped in her favour, so she was released with apologies.

Odell *Beds*

A legend says that one of the several Sir Rowland Alstons, barons of Odell whose memorials are in the village church, sold his soul to the Devil. But when the time came to complete the bargain, Sir Rowland took fright and sought sanctuary in the church.

Five marks on the porch are said to be the scratches left by the Devil as he shook the church in rage. Sir Rowland's ghost appears on a phantom black horse every 100 years; his next appearance is due in 2044.

Oldhurst *Hunts*

At the side of the boundary road between the parishes of Oldhurst and Woodhurst there used to stand the Abbot's Chair, or Hurstingstone. This was the base of a stone cross which marked the meeting place of the Hurstingstone Hundred. Hundreds were the administrative divisions of counties, dating back to Saxon times and took this name because each contained 100 families. It is said that the stone once had a nonsense verse inscribed on its base, which read:

> Turn me up and read me plain,
> Hot porridge makes hard crusts soft,
> And turn me back again.

The Abbot's Chair is now in the garden of the Norris Museum, St Ives, Huntingdonshire.

OLNEY PANCAKE RACE

Buckinghamshire's most famous local custom is the pancake race run at Olney on Shrove Tuesday. The race is open to women of 18 or over who have lived in Olney for at least three months. Each competitor wears an apron and head-dress and holds a frying pan containing a pancake. She must toss this three times during the race, which is run from the market square to the church – about 415 yds. The verger kisses the winner, who, like the runner-up, receives a prayer book from the vicar. Every competitor who finishes the course attends a service at which the pans and pancakes are piled near the altar, and at which are sung Olney hymns, written by the poet William Cowper and the Olney curate John Newton. One story about the origin of the race, which dates back to 1445, is that a housewife cooking a pancake heard the bell for the Shrove Tuesday service and rushed off to church still clutching her frying pan containing the pancake. The event, which has lapsed many times, was revived in 1947 by the then vicar, the Rev. R. Collins

THE WOLF KILLER
The man who killed the last English wolf is said to be buried beneath this effigy in Orlingbury church

Orlingbury *Northants*

An effigy in Orlingbury church is supposed to commemorate the man who killed the last wild wolf in England. In legend he is remembered as Jack of Batsaddle, and a farm and wood in the neighbourhood are named after him. But the effigy is officially that of one John de Withmayle, a generous donor of land to the Church.

The deed occurred in 1375 and, in fact, there is some dispute as to whether the creature which Jack killed was really a wolf or a giant boar. One version of the legend even claims that he fought and slew two creatures – a wolf and a boar.

There is no doubt, however, that Jack died as a result of his famous battle. When the creature, whatever it was, lay dead, Jack, tired and thirsty, took a drink from a nearby spring. And, apparently, the shock of the ice-cold water killed him.

Penn *Bucks*

The ghost of an 18th-century farm labourer, riding a phantom horse, used to haunt the countryside around Penn – and may still do so to this day. According to eyewitness accounts, the wraith gallops soundlessly out of the night, and then vanishes with peals of laughter into a grey mist.

'I AM NOT YET READY'

The villagers of Passenham, Northamptonshire, rejoiced when they heard that their cruel landlord, Sir Robert Banastre, was dead. Their elation was short-lived, however, for within a few hours of his death, his armour-clad figure was seen walking the lanes and standing by the bedsides of his former tenants. The sexton was startled into fits when Sir Robert appeared beside his half-dug grave; to him as to the others, the ghost said: 'I am not yet ready.'

With some trepidation, the parish priest began the burial service. Muffled but familiar tones issued from the coffin: 'I am not yet ready.' On inspection, the corpse exhibited the usual symptoms of mortality, but after burial his ghost continued to terrify the district. A service of exorcism was held, in the middle of which Sir Robert appeared in a flash of light. He promised to desist from further hauntings if the service was terminated; he has kept his promise for over 300 years.

A 17TH-CENTURY SLANDER? *Sir Robert Banastre, who is buried beneath this monument in St Guthlac's Church, Passenham, Northants, is recorded as being a man of singular piety and a great benefactor of the Church. Yet, according to local tradition, he was an evil, grasping landlord who expelled tenants to avoid payment of Poor Law dues; for this, apparently, he was condemned to an uneasy death, and to a restless, miserable existence in the hereafter*

THE LAST APPEARANCE *After Sir Robert Banastre was buried, his ghost continued to haunt the district, though its cry now changed to 'Beware! Be ready!' The bishop held a service of exorcism with bell, book and candle, in the midst of which the tormented spirit appeared in a flash of light. It begged the assembled clerics to desist, telling them it would never find rest, though promising never to haunt the district again*

ST PETER'S CANDLES

Despite the ever-pressing need to feed and arm his men, the Fenland hero Hereward the Wake left the abbey of Peterborough in peace. The Saxon abbot was sympathetic to his cause, which was probably the reason why William the Conqueror replaced him in 1070 with Turold, a Norman prelate of his own choosing. The new abbot had few illusions about Hereward's regard for the Church, and demanded 150 knights to secure his tenure. They availed him little; Hereward's men sacked the town and abbey, captured its treasure and took the abbot prisoner. It was a notable victory, but that night a vision of St Peter holding a huge golden key appeared to Hereward and demanded that he return both abbot and treasure to the saint's own abbey. Hereward complied, and never attacked the abbey again.

Shortly after, while mounting an attack on Stamford, Hereward and his men became hopelessly lost in Rockingham Forest. Then, it is said, St Peter sent a wolf to show them the way, and as darkness fell, lighted candles appeared on every tree and on every man's shield, burning steadily no matter how the wind blew, as a token of the apostle's gratitude

PETERBOROUGH CATHEDRAL *The Saxon abbey once stood on the site*

275

Preston *Herts*

The mossy stones and crumbling arches of ruined Minsden Chapel, built in the 14th century and abandoned to decay some 300 years later, are haunted by a ghostly monk who walks at Hallowe'en. The long-lost chapel bells are first heard tolling, and sweet strains of music fill the air before the cowled figure makes his appearance under the derelict south arch. As the sounds die away he walks, with head bowed as if in meditation, up steps that no longer exist, and fades away. The music then returns – but only a few sad, plaintive notes are heard before all is still and silent once again.

Quainton *Bucks*

The last resting place of a former king of the gipsies is said to be marked by a rough-hewn stone at the side of the old Roman road that runs below Quainton Hill. The road is known locally as Carter's Lane or Gipsy Lane and the stone, with its crudely cut date, 1641, used to lie in the ditch alongside, shrouded by tangled undergrowth. It has now been set upright. More recently, people recall a gipsy queen's funeral, with ritual burning of her caravan and goods, at Quainton church.

Ringstead *Northants*

The ghost of unhappy Lydia Atley, a young girl rejected by her lover, who disappeared in 1850 after going to meet him at his orchard, haunted the area for 20 years. It would walk from the orchard to the church – and to a spot where the skeleton of a girl was found in a ditch in 1865.

THE FAR-TRAVELLED FIDDLER

The Triangular Lodge in the grounds of Rushton Hall, Northamptonshire, is a curious, three-sided building with triangular rooms, windows and chimneys, dedicated to the Holy Trinity by its owner and designer, Sir Francis Tresham. He was executed in 1605 for his part in the Gunpowder Plot, and it is thought that the conspirators may have schemed together in the lodge. But the legend linked to it has a less sombre aspect and stems from the late 18th century, when the estate was in the hands of Lord Robert Cullen. He discovered a secret underground passage leading from the lodge, but no one was brave enough to explore it. Lord Cullen offered £50 to any man who would venture in, and the offer was taken up by a local fiddler. He took the money and gave it

to his wife, then scrambled into the darkness with a candle in his hatband and playing his favourite tune – 'Moll in the Wad'. The music faded – and the fiddler failed to return. Later, fearful searchers reported finding hat and candle beside an apparently bottomless pit. The distraught wife wailed in despair, but promises of more money soon calmed her. Two years later she produced a remarkable letter from her husband who, she said, had fallen all the way through the world, tumbling out in newly discovered Australia. People were so impressed that they gave her the fare to join him, and she left the village. The fiddler, of course, had eventually found a way out of the passage, dodged his rescuers and gone into hiding, to wait for his wife to join him

THE MONK'S REVENGE

The stronghold built for William the Conqueror at Rockingham, Northamptonshire, and replaced by the present castle in 1547, was the scene of a tragedy long ago. Young Lord Zouch of Rockingham was out hunting when his friend, Lord Neville, riding with him, told him that Lady Zouch had a lover.

Lord Zouch rode back home in a rage, mounted the stairs with swift, silent strides, and found a monk with his wife. In blind fury, he plunged his sword into the figure. Only then did he discover that it was his own sister Clara, who had left her nunnery in disguise to meet a monk she loved – and that Neville's spiteful warning sprang from hatred and jealousy, because Zouch's wife had rejected the amorous lord's advances. Bent on revenge, Lord Zouch

was about to ride in pursuit of Neville when a monk stopped him. This was Clara's lover, and Zouch was going to strike him down – but an apparition appeared. It told them Neville was already dead and pronounced judgment on them both. Lord Zouch and his wife and son would die in seven days; and for seven years, at the September feast of Holyrood, his ghost must re-enact the tragedy – but with ringing footsteps to warn everyone of his coming. The monk was made to keep a vow of silence until the haunting ended.

So it all happened, as told by the apparition, says the legend. Within a week Lord Zouch and his family were dead. The castle rang to his ghostly footsteps for seven years. Then the monk told the story, and died

THE WITCHES OF WARBOYS

In April 1593, one of the most notorious trials in the whole history of English witch-hunting opened at Huntingdon Assizes. The case of the three witches of Warboys began in the imagination of a sick child and ended in the deaths of three innocent people.

In November 1589, ten-year-old Jane Throgmorton, youngest child of a prosperous Warboys family, fell mysteriously ill with prolonged sneezing bouts, shaking and fits. During her illness, she was visited by a neighbour, Alice Samuel. Jane took a violent dislike to the old woman, and accused her of being a witch. Within a month the four other Throgmorton children had fallen ill with the same symptoms. The family physician could find nothing physically wrong with them, and put forward the idea of witchcraft. Suspicion fell on Alice.

St Albans *Herts*

When St Alban, the first Christian martyr in England, was led out to his place of execution on a hill near the town to which he gave his name, a stream in his path miraculously dried up. At the top of the hill, he begged for water, and the stream immediately reappeared at his feet.

During the 15th century, St Albans was the home of the most famous of Hertfordshire witches, Mother Haggy, still spoken of with awe. Late in life, she changed from a 'white' to a 'black' witch, rode full tilt round the town at midday on a broomstick, and crossed the River Ver on a kettle. Early in the 17th century, at the height of the witchcraft scares, the Devil himself, in the shape of a ram, appeared in the cellars of a local inn and was served up to the customers for their supper.

Ghost stories abound in St Albans. On moonlit nights a coach drawn by headless white horses toils up the steep slopes of Holywell Hill. Ghostly monks perform the ancient sung matins in the precincts of the abbey. On May 22, anniversary of the Battle of St Albans in 1455, old houses that stand on the supposed site of the battle resound with the clash of armies locked in combat.

St Ives *Cambs*

During the 13th century, St Ives was famous for its Easter cloth fair. The cheaper kinds of cloth were sold in St Audrey's Lane, corrupted to Tawdry Lane. In this way, the word 'tawdry' entered the English language.

Each year on Whit Tuesday, six boys and six girls meet in the parish church to throw dice. The winners are each presented with a Bible. This curious custom has its origin in the will of Dr Robert Wilde, who died in 1675, and left £50 to buy land and endow the gift with the rent obtained from its letting. The plot is still known as Bible Orchard.

Sawbridgeworth *Herts*

Sir John Jocelyn, squire of Hyde Hall, refused burial for himself and his favourite horse in the village churchyard, was interred in his own land. Now each year, on November 1, his ghost is said to ride furiously on a white horse down the old carriage drive of the Hall, which is now a school.

Someries *Beds*

The grounds of Someries House (below) are reputedly haunted by the ghost of Sir John Wenlock, beheaded by the Duke of Beaufort for changing sides at the Battle of Tewkesbury in 1471.

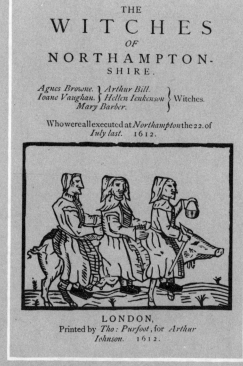

THE
WITCHES
OF
NORTHAMPTON-
SHIRE.

Agnes Browne. } *Arthur Bill.*
Ioane Vaughan. } *Hellen Ienkenson* } Witches.
Mary Barber.

Who were all executed at *Northampton* the 22. of
Iuly last. 1612.

LONDON,
Printed by *Tho: Purfoot*, for *Arthur Iohnson.* 1612.

UNJUST TRIAL *Flimsy evidence, like that used to convict the Warboys witches, was common in 17th-century witch trials Three of the Northampton witches (above) were 'swum' – thrown into a stream. They floated and thus were believed guilty*

Stanion *Northants*

Stanion church houses a strange relic, an enormous bone nearly 6 ft long. According to local legend, the bone belonged to a huge dun cow which appeared one day in the village and promised milk to all who needed it, in return for kindly care. The cow's fame spread far and wide and came to the ears of a witch. One morning the witch appeared and, producing a sieve from under her cloak, ordered the cow to fill it. The poor animal strained to keep her promise but in the end died exhausted. One rib was preserved as a memorial.

The whole legend of the dun cow and its rib was recorded in a delightful poem by David Townsend, the village blacksmith at Geddington, 3 miles from Stanion, around the turn of the century. The bone, in fact, is probably that of a whale, brought back by some adventurous mariner to his native village about the beginning of the 17th century.

A death

The children's fits grew no better (although, suspiciously, they were at their worst in the presence of strangers). Reluctantly the Throgmortons came to believe that their children were in fact possessed by evil spirits raised by Alice Samuel. Alice sturdily dismissed all this as nonsense. She was bitterly resentful when one day Lady Cromwell, wife of Sir Henry Cromwell, uncle of the future Lord Protector, snatched off her headscarf and snipped off a lock of her hair, giving it to Mrs Throgmorton to burn. 'Madam, why do you use me thus?' she complained. 'I never did you any harm yet.' That night, Lady Cromwell dreamt of being attacked by a cat sent by Alice Samuel. Soon after, she fell ill and died 15 months later.

Confession

All this time, the Throgmorton parents and children never ceased pestering the unhappy Alice to confess that she was a witch and to cast out the evil spirits. At last, in a moment of weakness, the old woman agreed. The confession apparently satisfied the family, but a few days later Alice had second thoughts and retracted. At this Throgmorton lost patience and had her arrested, together with her husband John, and daughter Agnes.

Trial

All three witches of Warboys – for both John and Agnes were implicated – were sent for trial at Huntingdon Assizes on charges of having bewitched the Throgmorton children and of having caused Lady Cromwell's death by sorcery. Confessions were wheedled and extorted from them. Alice, by now half-demented, talked of her 'dun chickens' as her familiars. On the basis of these confessions, the three were found guilty. They were hanged at Huntingdon in 1593, victims of mischievous children and the credulity of their elders.

The moſt ſtrange and

admirable diſcouerie of the three Witches of *Warboys*, *arraigned*, *conuicted*,
and executed at the laſt Aſsiſes at Hunting-
ton, for the bewitching of the fiue daughters of
Robert Throckmorton Eſquire, and diuers other
perſons, with ſundrie Diuelliſh and grie-
uous torments:

And alſo for the bewitching to death of
the Lady Crumwell, the like hath
not been heard of in this
age.

LONDON
Printed by the Widdowe Orwin, for Thomas Man, and Iohn Winnington, and are to be ſolde in Pater noſter Rowe, at the
ſigne of the Talbot. 1593.

AN ELIZABETHAN PAMPHLET *This reflects the period's horrified fascination with witchcraft*

Stevenage *Herts*

Along the Great North Road, near Stevenage, by Whomerly Wood, are the Six Hills of old Hertfordshire legend. Probably Bronze Age barrows, they are popularly said to be the work of the Devil himself. One night, he visited Whomerly Wood, where he dug seven great holes with the intention of throwing the earth at Stevenage. The earth that he hurled over his shoulder fell short, however, to form the Six Hills. The seventh spadeful Old Nick spitefully aimed at Graveley church and knocked the spire off it.

Tewin *Herts*

The altar tomb in Tewin churchyard of Lady Anne Grimston, who died in 1710, has been forced apart by ash and sycamore trees. According to Hertfordshire legend, a tree growing from a grave is a judgment on those who disbelieve in the Resurrection.

Upwood *Cambs*

Thomas Hursey, lord of Upwood Manor in the 1750's, had refused his daughter Maria permission to marry a penniless naval captain. One night, when her father was supposedly in London, Maria woke to find him smiling down at her. The next morning a messenger brought news of Hursey's death in London. With his dying words he had given his blessing to the match.

Wansford *Cambs*

A Wansford rustic fell asleep one day on a hayrick and woke to find himself floating down the River Nene, which was given to sudden flooding. He called out to the watchers on Wansford Bridge to find out where he was. 'Wansford,' they said. 'What, Wansford in England?' And 'Wansford in England' is a label that has stuck to the village to this day. The Haycock Hotel sign illustrates the story.

Ware *Herts*

In 1463, a Ware carpenter named Jonas Fosbrooke made a mammoth bed, 11 ft 1 in. long and 10 ft 8½ in. wide, which he gave to Edward IV for his personal use. When Edward's 13-year-old son, Edward V, was murdered by Richard III in 1483, the bed was sold and was afterwards owned by a succession of Ware innkeepers. It was used during local festivals when the town was crowded and once, in the 17th century, 12 married couples are alleged to have slept in it together. Fosbrooke's ghost, however, was reputed to pinch and scratch anyone who slept in it because his bed was not being used by royalty. The Great Bed is now in the Victoria and Albert Museum.

Wendover *Bucks*

Until the mid-19th century, Wendover was famous for its hand-made lace, and every year the town's lace-makers were given a holiday on November 25, St Catherine's Day. They called it 'Cattern's Day' and, although Catherine was their patron saint, it was said that their celebrations were largely in honour of the 16th-century Catherine of Aragon, who became Henry VIII's first wife in 1509. Tradition has it that she accidentally burnt all her lace, and ordered a new supply for her wardrobe from Wendover. The fashionable ladies of the Court were quick to follow her example, and so lace-making flourished in the town for centuries.

Weston *Herts*

Near the gateway of Weston churchyard there are two tombstones, 14 ft apart, which are said to mark the grave of Weston's fabled giant, Jack o' Legs. He is thought to have lived in a cave outside the village some time during the Middle Ages, and was so tall that standing in Weston's streets, he could lean on first-floor window-sills to talk with his friends within. Jack was famed as an archer and as a highwayman who robbed the rich to feed the poor. It was said that he could shoot an arrow over 3 miles, and that he was able to bring down a bird half a mile away. Most of his robberies were carried out at a place which is still called Jack's Hill, close to the neighbouring village of Graveley. Among his victims were the rich bakers of the nearby market town of Baldock who resented his charitable gestures at their expense. Eventually they banded against him,

and attacked him as he was passing through Baldock. He was struck from behind with a heavy pole, tied up with strong rope, and then his eyes were put out with a red-hot poker. When he recovered consciousness, the bakers told him that he could shoot one last arrow to mark his burial place. Jack did so, and it landed over 3 miles away in Weston churchyard.

Wicken *Northants*

The parish of Wicken was originally divided into two hamlets, Wyke Hamon and Wyke Dyke. Bitter rivalry existed between them and quarrels were commonplace, until in 1586 the two communities were united into a single parish. A Love Feast was instituted in that year both to commemorate the event and to promote future harmony, and the feast is still held every All Saint's Day, November 1. A brief service is held in the church, after which the parishioners sing hymns around the village's traditional Gospel Oak, where Gospel readings formerly took place. They then meet at a local hotel for a meal of cakes and ale.

Wigginton *Herts*

Wigginton Common was used by Cromwell's Ironsides during the Civil War to launch an artillery attack on nearby Berkhamsted Castle, which was destroyed by their cannon. According to local legend, a phantom Roundhead army is sometimes seen manoeuvring on the common at dusk.

Wingrave *Bucks*

New-mown hay is spread over the floor of Wingrave church in an annual ceremony which takes place on the Sunday following St Peter's Day (June 29). The custom originated in the ancient practice of rush-spreading, when the earthen floors of churches were covered with fresh rushes once a year. Hay has been substituted for rushes at Wingrave. It is grown in a field that was bequeathed to the church by a local woman. Tradition tells that she lost her way one winter night and, nearly dead from exposure, was led to safety by the sound of the church bells.

Woodford *Northants*

In about 1550, John Styles, the vicar of St Mary's Church at Woodford, lost his parish because of his Catholic beliefs. He fled to a monastery in Belgium, taking with him a costly chalice from the church, and soon afterwards died there. A new vicar, Andrew Powlet, brought the chalice, together with John's heart, back to Woodford several years later, but with the passage of time, both relics were mislaid and forgotten. In 1862, Powlet's ghost was seen in the hallway of Woodford Rectory by the young man who then had the living. It appeared twice, each time hovering near a certain panel in the wall. Examination revealed a secret cavity which contained the missing chalice and a faded letter. The letter led to the discovery of John's heart, entombed in a pillar in the church. The heart is still there, and can be seen through a glass panel in the pillar.

Woughton on the Green *Bucks*

Woughton on the Green lies close to Watling Street. During the 18th century, the infamous highwayman Dick Turpin used the Old Swan Inn as a base in between his frequent stagecoach robberies near by. A local story tells how Turpin once stopped at the inn when he was being pursued and quickly re-shod his horse so that its horseshoes pointed backwards. He set out again and soon escaped when his pursuers rode off in the opposite direction. The ghosts of Turpin and his horse, Black Bess, have often been seen riding through the district at night.

THE PRINCESS WHO BECAME A SAINT

St Werburga, the patron saint of women and children, was the daughter of St Ermenilda and Wulfhere, ruler of the Anglo-Saxon kingdom of Mercia in the 7th century AD. Her father was the first Mercian king to be baptised, and before he died in 675 he did much to spread the cause of Christianity throughout his realm.

From early childhood, the Princess Werburga showed a strong desire for the religious life, rather than that of her father's court. She entered a convent at Ely, where her piety and organising ability were quickly recognised, and she served as mother superior of many convents before becoming chief abbess of all Mercia.

The geese of Weedon
She spent several years at Weedon Abbey in Northamptonshire, the scene of her most famous miracle. One day a huge gaggle of wild geese suddenly swooped down from the sky and settled in the surrounding fields and orchards. The villagers tried to frighten them away, but the birds ignored their efforts and began to devour the fruit and crops. In despair, the villagers went to Werburga to beg her help. As soon as she heard of their plight, she ordered several of her servants to round up the geese and bring them to the abbey. Legend says that the vicious birds at once became docile and converged on the abbey of their own free will, allowing themselves to be penned up.

Repentant birds
The next morning Werburga went to the foldyard and admonished the geese for their misdeeds. After she had finished scolding them, it is said that they stretched their necks forward, begging forgiveness and promising not to cause any further mischief. Werburga then allowed them to fly away.

Soon afterwards, however, the geese returned. They had discovered that a member of their flock was missing, and accused the abbey servants of having killed and eaten the bird during the night. Werburga was aggrieved that her trust had been betrayed and promised to punish those responsible for the crime. Then she ordered the bones of the dead bird to be brought to her. This was done and, bidding the geese farewell, she asked the chief gander to count his flock as it flew away. He did so, and found that the number was once again complete. The missing bird had been miraculously restored to life.

Sinless and incorruptible
Werburga died in about AD 700 at a nunnery at Threeckingham in Lincolnshire, and her body is said to have resisted decay for nearly 200 years. It finally crumbled to dust in 875 when the Danes invaded England. Her remains were then taken to Chester where the Mercian Princess Ethelfleda built a convent to house them. During times of danger the monks of Chester carried her shrine around the city's walls and once, in 1180, the city is alleged to have been saved from fire by this ritual.

THE REPENTANT GEESE *When wild geese stole from fields and orchards, St Werburga's scolding saved the village crops*

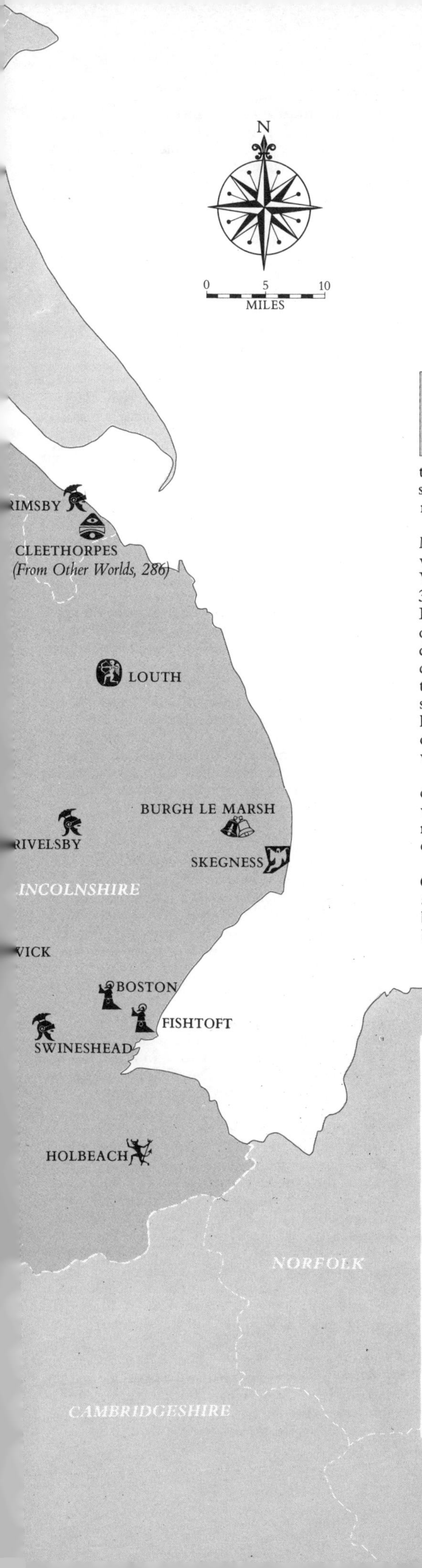

THE DANELAW

Derbyshire, Leicestershire, Lincolnshire and Nottinghamshire

The winds and rains of at least 2000 English winters have battered the stone figure that stands outside Braunston church in Leicestershire. Despite her hideously distorted features, she has bestowed her blessing on as many springs, for she is a Celtic earth goddess, the pagan mother of all living things and the spirit of rebirth.

Many different peoples have lived in the east Midlands. The Romans and the Vikings came and went; the Danes took the land to the north-east of Watling Street and, because their law ran there for 300 years, the area became known as the Danelaw. But the cult of the earth mother was there before any of them, and many of her festivals still persist in the district. The Haxey Boggans 'run the Hood' in a contest between Lincolnshire hamlets, the Shrovetide football battle is fought at Ashbourne, Derbyshire and the Bottle-kicking Easter rite takes place at Hallaton, Leicestershire. These 'games' were all originally played to welcome back the sun after the winter solstice, or to celebrate the return of spring.

Such beliefs are deep rooted in agricultural communities. In Derbyshire, villagers dress their wells with pictures made from petals and leaves, nutshells and berries – a ritual which may date from our Celtic forbears' worship of water spirits.

Another long-lived deity hereabouts is Anu, the Celtic goddess of plenty. But she had a darker side, and it is this aspect of her character that is remembered today as Black Annis, the Leicestershire bogeywoman who devours wayward children.

GRIMSBY

CLEETHORPES
(From Other Worlds, 286)

LOUTH

BURGH LE MARSH

RIVELSBY

SKEGNESS

LINCOLNSHIRE

WICK

BOSTON

FISHTOFT

SWINESHEAD

HOLBEACH

NORFOLK

CAMBRIDGESHIRE

SUFFOLK

THE FOLKLORE YEAR

January 6 Haxey, Lincs *Haxey Hood Game*	**End of March** Old Bolingbroke, Lincs *Candle Auction*
Shrove Tuesday Ashbourne, Derbys *Shrovetide Football*	**May 29** Castleton, Derbys *Garland Day*
Shrove Tuesday Winster, Derbys *Pancake Day Race*	**May to end of August** Wye Dale district, Derbys *Well-dressing*
Easter Monday Hallaton, Leics *Bottle-kicking and Hare-pie Scramble*	**First Thursday, Friday, Saturday in October** Nottingham, Notts *Goose Fair*
Whit Monday Enderby, Leics *Selling of the Keep of the Wether*	**November 23** Laxton, Notts *Court Leet*

AYSTON'S 'SISTERS'

A stone effigy in Ayston church, Leicestershire, shows two priests, one with hands hidden, the other with his hands clasped in prayer. But local myth says it represents twin sisters, born with only one arm apiece, with their communal pair of hands clasped in prayer

BEEBY'S 'TUB'

Two brothers who built the church at Beeby, Leicestershire, are said to have died quarrelling on the tower over the cost of the spire. The 'Tub' remains unfinished

Anwick *Lincs*
Two huge stones at the entrance to Anwick churchyard are known as the Drake Stones. Legend says that a local farmer who was ploughing a nearby field lost his horses in a bog, and as they were sucked down, a drake flew out of the hole. Next day he found a huge drake-shaped stone on the spot. In 1832, attempts were made to move the stone. Chains lashed to it snapped, and a drake – some said its guardian spirit – flew from underneath. It was hauled to its present position in 1913, but broke into two pieces, the largest about 6 ft long and 3 ft wide, and the other half the size. Residents say they often see two drakes sheltering under the stone, and believe it was a Druids' memorial.

Ashbourne *Derbys*
Shrovetide football goes on for two days at Ashbourne, starting on Shrove Tuesday afternoon. The game is played between Up'ards, who live north of the River Henmore, which divides the town, and Down'ards, from south of the river. The mill wheels at Clifton and Sturston, which are 3 miles apart, are the goals, but scores are rare. The ball is filled with cork dust to make it heavy and to limit the action. Any number can join in, and most of the game is played in the river.

Ashby de la Zouch *Leics*
The market town of Ashby de la Zouch was noted for its annual fairs. At the Hiring Fair, held on the Tuesday after September 21, servants and labourers seeking a change of job would be inspected by employers. People for hire wore ribbons in their hair. On being given a shilling, they contracted to work for the next 364 days. Once hired, they spent their shillings at the fair, eating, drinking and dancing, until their new masters took them home. Hiring Fairs, fixed by statute, died out before the First World War, but the name is remembered in the Statute Fair still held at Ashby every September.

Bakewell *Derbys*
A milliner called Mrs Stafford and her maid were hanged at Derby in 1608 on the flimsy evidence of a Scottish tramp, wandering destitute in London. He said he had been whisked there from Mrs Stafford's home in Bakewell 'like the wind' after the two women had called upon the Devil. His story seems to have been made up in revenge for having his gear seized by Mrs Stafford when he could not pay his rent.

In the churchyard, there is an 8 ft high cross that dates back 1200 years to a time when Christianity and the ancient myths went hand in hand. On one side, carvings show the Crucifixion, but on the other are the Norse gods Odin and Loki.

Bardney *Lincs*
Monks at King Ethelred's great Bardney Abbey refused to accept the bones of St Oswald, out of envy of the Northumbrian saint. The bones were left outside the abbey's locked doors all night, whereupon a pillar of light shot up to the skies. Rebuked by this sign from Heaven, the monks embraced the bones next day, and the people of Bardney vowed never again to close their doors. That was in the 7th century. Today, people in the area still say, 'Do you come from Bardney?' to remind someone who has not shut the door.

Beely *Derbys*
A Bronze Age round barrow burial mound on Harland Edge, near Chatsworth House, is called Hob Hurst's House. Hob Hurst is said to be a goblin who frequents lonely and remote woods.

Belton *Leics*

The church contains the tomb of Lady Roesia de Verdon, who founded the now ruined Gracedieu Nunnery and inaugurated an annual fair, which is held in late May or early June, mainly for the sale of horses. The village also has a permanent maypole, around which the children dance on the first Saturday in May.

Blidworth *Notts*

The village was noted for its Plough Monday plays, performed in January as a rite to invoke spring. Their four central characters – a Soldier (later St George or King George), a Clown, a Doctor and Old Eezum-Squeezum (Beelzebub) – played out the symbolic battle between life and death.

At St Mary's Church, the vicar still rocks a baby in a cradle at Candlemas (February 2) to re-enact the Presentation of Christ in the Temple.

The village is also said to be the birthplace of Robin Hood's Maid Marian; and Will Scarlet is believed to be buried in the churchyard.

Boston *Lincs*

The breezes that blow round the exposed tower known as Boston Stump are said to be the result of a struggle between St Botolph and the Devil. The saint so belaboured Satan that he huffed and puffed, raising a wind that has not yet died down.

BOSTON STUMP

The octagonal tower of St Botolph's Church looks across the River Witham, near the spot where the Saxon saint founded his monastery in AD 654. Later, it grew into the thriving modern town of Boston

THE WICKED WITCHES OF BELVOIR CASTLE

The most notorious witches who ever terrorised the Midlands lived in the Vale of Belvoir, Leicestershire, in the 17th century. Their leader was Joan Flower, whose daughters, Margaret and Philippa, were in the service of the Earl and Countess of Rutland, at Belvoir Castle. Joan openly boasted of working magic with the aid of the Devil, and her favourite cat, called Rutterkin. She publicly cursed the earl when Margaret was dismissed for pilfering; then with her daughters and three other women – Anne Baker, Joan Willimott and Ellen Green – she planned her revenge. Within a year, the earl's two infant sons had died. Five years later, in 1618, Joan and her fellow witches were arrested, and tried at Lincoln. They confessed to killing the children with enchantments, and *to making the earl and his wife sterile. Joan admitted that they had brewed spells to make the infants sicken, then die. Little Henry, Lord Roos, lived only a week after the witches' magic ceremony, when they pricked one of his gloves with pins and boiled it in water. His brother, Francis, suffered a short illness, recovered and died later. The witches went on to admit even more dreadful sorceries and sensational evidence was given about their coven meetings on nearby Blackberry Hill. Then Joan Flower recanted and denied murdering the two boys. She called for bread and butter, and cried: 'May this choke me if I am guilty.' It did, and she collapsed in the courtroom. The other witches were all found guilty and were hanged at Lincoln on March 11, 1618*

Bottesford *Leics*

Francis Manners, the 6th Earl of Rutland, died in 1632 and lies buried in the church. On his tomb are effigies of his two sons (below) who, says the inscription, 'dyed in their infancy by wicked practice and sorcerye'. In 1618, the Witches of Belvoir were hanged at Lincoln for having murdered them by witchcraft.

Bourne *Lincs*

Hereward the Wake, the Saxon nobleman who became a legendary outlaw, was born at Bourne *c.* AD 1036. He is thought locally to have been the son of Lady Godiva and Leofric, Earl of Mercia. Hereward gained renown for his heroic exploits in leading Anglo-Saxon resistance against the Norman invaders. His manor house stood on the site of Bourne Castle, of which all that remains are the earthworks and moat opposite Bourne church.

The lease of White Bread Meadow, $1\frac{1}{2}$ miles north of Bourne, is auctioned annually during a 200 yd race between two boys, held on the Monday before Easter. The bid made just before the race ends is taken as the final one, and the rent money obtained is donated to a local charity established in 1742.

Braunston *Leics*

A 2000-year-old stone carving of a Celtic earth mother (below) stands outside Braunston church, close to the north wall. It is thought to represent a goddess who was worshipped in primitive fertility rites which took place on the site of the church in pre-Christian times.

FROM OTHER WORLDS

On September 22, 1956, hundreds of strollers along the promenade at Cleethorpes saw a silent gleaming object in the sky, which they described as resembling a glass sphere. The Unidentified Flying Object, or UFO, was also observed through telescopes and by radar from the nearby RAF station at Manby, where the craft was estimated to be 80 ft in diameter, and to be hovering at a height of 54,000 ft.

It remained in the same position for about an hour, then vanished as two jet fighters closed in to investigate. The event has never been satisfactorily explained.

UFO's, originally called 'flying saucers', have been seen in post-war Britain on numerous occasions. In 1967 alone, sightings were reported on Dartmoor, the Isle of Wight, and at Stoke-on-Trent, while Cradle Hill, near Warminster in Wiltshire, is alleged to be the scene of constant UFO activity. Worldwide reports have described strange spacecraft of every shape, colour and size (including one a thousand miles long), and some observers have claimed that they have spoken with alien beings from outer space. In 1955, Cedric Allingham gave an account of his meeting with a Martian who had landed near him as he was bird-watching on the northern coast of Scotland.

Such reports are not unique to the 20th century. Over 700 years ago, the chronicler Gervase of Tilbury wrote of an aerial ship whose anchor caught fast in a church steeple at Bristol. The vessel's sole occupant is said to have suffocated in the earth's atmosphere as he tried to unhook the anchor, and his corpse was burnt by the terrified townspeople who thought he was a demon. Again, *c.* AD 70, Pliny wrote of a 'burning shield' seen flying in the sky.

Braunstone *Leics*

A Hay Sunday Service, in which fresh hay is spread over the church floors, is conducted in Braunstone church each year on the Sunday after St Peter's Day, June 29. A local legend maintains that, long ago, the daughter of the lord of nearby Glenfield Manor was lost in Leicester Forest when a gang of outlaws began to pursue her. She was saved by the clerk of Braunstone church and, in gratitude, her father dedicated an acre in one of his meadows to the clerk, to provide hay every year for the church floors.

Brigg *Humberside*

A roadside gallows, which stands 3 miles east of Brigg on the A18, was erected by James I early in the 17th century. At that time, there was a bitter rivalry in the district between the Ross family of Melton Ross and the Tyrwhitts of Kettleby. One

Distant civilisations

Objective analysis has shown that most UFO sightings are errors of judgment made by the observers. Stars, meteors, space satellites, weather balloons, optical illusions caused by reflections on clouds and other phenomena of the upper atmosphere are frequently mistaken for spaceships. But several incidents, such

OLD LANDING *A 13th-century UFO may have landed on a Bristol church*

as the occurrence at Cleethorpes, have continued to puzzle scientists. At the same time, it seems possible that in the immensity of the universe around us there are galaxies where highly intelligent life exists.

This presumption, for many people, is sufficient proof that these aerial curiosities are nothing less than visiting spaceships from civilisations more advanced than ours, which lie beyond our solar system.

A Venusian called Jesus

Many startling claims based on this viewpoint have been put forward. The members of the Aetherius Society in Britain believe that advanced beings from Mars and Venus regularly visit the earth in invisible spaceships. It is said that George King, who founded the society in 1954, can transmit the voice and religious teachings of a great cosmic master called Jesus from Venus. The first transmission took place in 1958 on Holdstone Down in Devon, and King's mother is said to have met the master Jesus in a Venusian spaceship in January, 1959. The society also believes that spiritual energy from Venus is stored in certain mountains, such as The Old Man of Coniston in the Lake District.

Cosmic airports

Some people claim that beings from other planets have been visiting the earth for thousands of years. Ancient myths of gods descending from the sky are, they say, simply folk memories of inter-planetary visitors who have also gone down in history as angels, saints and witches. It has even been claimed that these extra-terrestrial travellers helped prehistoric man to build such monuments as Silbury Hill and Stonehenge in Wiltshire, and that prominent landmarks like Glastonbury Tor in Somerset were used by UFO's as 'airports' in long-ago visits to Britain.

EXOTIC STRANGERS *An artist's impression of a recent visitor from the skies*

day, retainers from both families met while hunting in what is now called Gallows Wood, and a savage fight broke out in which people of both parties were killed. The king had the gallows erected as a reminder that any further bloodshed between the two families would be treated as murder.

Burgh le Marsh *Lincs*

Every evening at 8 o'clock, from October to March, curfew is rung on the tenor bell of Burgh le Marsh church. This is the bell which is said to have guided Captain Frohock to safety in 1629, when his ship, the *Mary Rose*, was driven towards the Lincolnshire coast by a violent storm. The villagers, hoping to grow rich by salvaging its cargo, decided not to help the vessel. The aged sexton, however, barricaded himself inside the church tower and began to ring the tenor bell as a warning, and the ship was saved.

When the enraged villagers broke into the tower, they found the sexton lying dead, his heart burst by his efforts. Captain Frohock, who later settled in the village, is said to have married the sexton's daughter. His land was known as Bell-string Acre.

Burley *Leics*

Burley on the Hill, a mansion near Burley village, was the Duke of Buckingham's home in the early 17th century. When Charles I and Queen Henrietta Maria were being entertained to a lavish dinner at the house, Jeffrey Hudson, an 18 in. high dwarf, dressed in full armour, was served to them in a large venison pie. Henrietta at once took him into her service, and Hudson was eventually knighted by the king. Legend says that he was once nearly eaten by a turkey cock in Dunkirk after being kidnapped by French pirates. He died in 1682.

Caistor *Lincs*

A legend of this area has as its central character St Paulinus, a 7th-century missionary who joined St Augustine in Kent in AD 601. One day, the story goes, St Paulinus was riding an ass along the ancient trackway which runs near Caistor when he met a man sowing corn. He asked for some grain to feed the ass, but the man said he had none. Seeing a sack in the field, Paulinus asked what was in it. 'That is no sack,' the man lied, 'but only a stone.' 'Then stone it shall be,' Paulinus retorted. The Fonaby Stone stands there to this day on Fonaby Top, and dreadful misfortune allegedly follows any attempt to move or damage it.

Castleton *Derbys*

Until the 17th century two cottages, rent and rate-free, stood in the mouth of Peak Cavern, and the rope makers who lived there specialised in hangman's ropes. The Devil sometimes visited the cave, and when water poured out after rain in the hills, he was said to be relieving himself.

On Oak Apple Day, May 29, a Garland King and Queen ride through Castleton accompanied by a band, and Morris dancers perform in the streets.

Clifton *Notts*

In 1471, Henry Bateman, squire to Sir William Clifton, went with his master to France. When he returned, he discovered that his sweetheart Margaret had married another man. In despair, he went to Clifton Grove, a wooded cliff above the Trent, and hurled himself to death in the river below. Soon afterwards, remorse drove Margaret to end her life in the same way.

MAN AND MOTOR CAR

It is less than 100 years since man invented the motor car. 'It barks like a dog and stinks like a cat,' complained its earliest detractors. 'It kills and maims,' grieved others. From the start it was more than just a machine. Cars had minds of their own, like the horses they drove from the roads. Like horses too, they needed curses and caresses to keep them going.

Even today, when horsepower is associated only with engines and there are few mysteries left under the bonnet, there is still just room in a motor car for a man who believes in magic. Otherwise down-to-earth drivers carry medallions of St Christopher (the protector of travellers), or keep a lucky coin in the glove locker or a charm on the ignition key. Others transfer mats, dusters or special number plates from one car to another, to preserve their luck.

Colours to stop and go with

There are many motorists who refuse to buy green cars, and petrol-pump attendants who shake their heads at the rashness of those who do – a response that is probably a hangover from the centuries-old fear of green as the colour traditionally worn by fairies. On the other hand, there is a widespread belief that red is lucky – red cars, it is said, never crash. This idea probably developed from highly condensed press reports of road safety tests carried out on cars of different colours. In fact, there is no evidence to back up the theory – any more than there is to support the idea that cars, not drivers, cause crashes.

Cure for car sickness

Some heavy lorries carrying inflammable spirit used to be earthed to prevent static sparks. A short length of chain was attached to the rear axle, and from this originated the belief that the same device can be used to prevent travel sickness. Many motorists swear by it, explaining knowledgeably that the chain releases the static electricity built up in the bodywork of a car during a journey. But even assuming that static is a cause of sickness, in most cases the chain is too short to reach the ground. So if it does work, the explanation must be sought not in science, but in magic or human credulity.

A funny thing happened . . .

Henry Ford, so the story goes, once said that people could have his Model T any colour they liked as long as it was black. His remark soon became one of motoring's legends, and few people ever questioned whether or not he had said it, and whether or not it was true.

There are other stories in circulation today which are always given as 'true' accounts of what happened to a friend or relative, but which have been recorded in so many different places and with so many variations that their truth seems very doubtful. These are legends in the making – in the past, equally fanciful stories about monsters, witches, saints and so on were told with the same veneer of truth.

A man who wanted to buy a car saw the model he was looking for advertised at an absurdly low price. When he inquired about it, he discovered that the woman selling the car was determined to keep the price as low as possible, because her late husband had directed in his will that the proceeds should go to his mistress.

Another man bought a second-hand car at a ridiculously low price.

When he went to collect it, he was met by a woman in mourning. He drove the car home, began to wash it and discovered an ineradicable bloodstain on one of the seats. He learnt later that the former owner had cut his throat in the vehicle.

A motorist was arrested for being drunk when he explained (truthfully in fact) that the dent in his car roof had been caused by a circus elephant sitting on it. Another gave a lift to two people whose chauffeur-driven car had broken down, and though their faces were vaguely familiar, he only recognised them when they asked to be dropped at the gates of a royal residence. Another hitchhiker story concerns a young girl who gave her address, then disappeared during the journey. The mystified driver went on to the house, to find that the girl had died weeks before.

Perhaps the most widespread of all is the 'granny in the boot' story. A family had to cut short a motoring holiday abroad when the eldest member of the party died. To save time over official procedure, they put the body in the boot, wrapped in a rug, and set off for home and the funeral. On the journey they left the car for a meal, and when they got back discovered that it had been stolen – body and all. The car was eventually found by the police – but with no body in it.

THE BEST CAR IN THE WORLD *When Sir Henry Royce and the Hon. C. S. Rolls joined forces to build the first Rolls-Royce – the Silver Ghost, built in Derby in 1906 – they made more than just a car. They created, unwittingly, a vehicle of popular fantasy. It is often said of the 'best car in the world' that its Silver Lady mascot is made of pure silver and that the noisiest moving part is the dashboard clock. One story tells of a car that broke its half-shaft in Spain. A spare was flown out and the Rolls-Royce owner, when he returned to England, asked for the bill. But the company claimed it had no record of the transaction; the owner was told that Rolls-Royce axles never failed*

Cranwell *Lincs*
Three sets of horseshoes in the turf where Ermine
Street crosses the A17 just west of the RAF College,
commemorate the wild leaps of a blind horse called
Bayard, as it struggled to unseat Old Meg, a wicked
local witch, as she fought with Abner, the owner of
the horse, on Bayard's back. Abner cut off one of
Old Meg's breasts, but still she clung on, her long
talons sunk deeply into Bayard's flanks. The
dreadful battle ended when Abner plunged his
sword through the witch, but he stabbed his horse
as well, and Meg and Bayard died together.

THE DERBY RAM

*No one knows who first noted 'the finest ram, Sir, that
ever was fed on hay'. But all agreed that the Derby ram, as
it became known, was 'ten yards tall', had teeth 'like a
regiment of men', and a tail like a bell-rope. The butcher
who finally slaughtered it was drowned in its blood*

VINTAGE VERSUS MODERN *In the cult of the car, the vintage Rolls-Royce is the motorist's apex of all power, prestige and glory*

FOLKLORE ON THE ROAD—THE WOMAN DRIVER

'You dragged this man a hundred yards.'
'But only at 30 miles an hour.'

*'And do I have to keep
on holding this?'*

'Why it's easy!'

THE CAT WOMAN

In St Michael's Church in Edmondthorpe, Leicestershire, is the 17th-century tomb of Sir Roger Smith and his two wives. The upper effigy, that of Lady Ann, has a deep stain on one of its wrists. Lady Ann was a witch, who, having turned herself into a cat, was wounded in the paw by her butler who struck at her with a meat cleaver

RECTORY GHOST

The knocking and banging that accompanied the haunting of Epworth Rectory in 1715–16 seemed to centre on the attic (above). Often, freak winds howled around the house while Old Jeffrey, as the ghost was known, wrought havoc inside

Deepdale *Derbys*
'Thirst House', a cave below Topley Pike, was once the home of a tiny elf or hob, the fairy guardian of a nearby spring. It was said that the water from this spring could cure every disease, if it was drunk on Good Friday.

A farmer walking home to Chelmorten once caught the hob and put it in his bag. But it shrieked so piteously that he let it go again, and it raced back to the dark security of its cave.

Thirst House is an abbreviation of Hob o' the Hurst's House – 'hurst' meaning a wooded place.

Earl Sterndale *Derbys*
The inn sign of The Quiet Woman shows a woman without a head. Above the headless body is the motto: 'Quiet words turneth away wrath.'

The woman is said to be 'Chattering Charteris', who made her husband's life a misery by her endless scolding. When she began to talk in her sleep as well, he could stand it no more and cut off her head. According to tradition, the villagers were so grateful that they made a collection to buy a headstone for her grave, inscribed with a warning to chatterboxes, and gave what was left over to her husband.

Eldon Hole *Derbys*
This pothole, about a mile north of Peak Forest village, was alleged to be the Devil's bolt-hole to Hell. In the 16th century, the Earl of Leicester arranged for a local man to be lowered down the hole on a rope, but when he was hauled out he was unconscious and died without speaking another word. Local folk took this as conclusive evidence that he had come face to face with Satan.

Other stories about the hole include the claim that a man named Charles Cotton was dropped down the shaft at the end of a mile long rope without reaching the bottom. On another occasion, two highwaymen forced a victim to walk over the edge so that 'he stept at once into eternity'. Charles Leigh, an early 18th-century writer, felt sure that it had something to do with Noah's Flood. At about the same time, a Fellow of the Royal Society decided to investigate it himself, and discovered that, in fact, it was just over 60 yds deep.

Enderby *Leics*
In an annual Whit Monday ceremony called 'The Selling of the Keep of the Wether', the hay crop (or keep) from a field called the Wether is auctioned at The Nag's Head. A silver coin is passed from hand to hand, and only the person holding it is allowed to bid. John of Gaunt is said to have started the custom *c.* 1380. The money pays for a celebration dinner.

Epworth *Humberside*
In December 1715 and January 1716, Epworth Rectory was the scene of a terrifying and still inexplicable haunting. The victims were the Rev. Samuel Wesley, his wife, his servants and some of his 19 children, though not his famous son John, who was then 13 years old and away at school.

Mournful groans and strange howls echoed round the old house, and upstairs in the attic there was an almost incessant banging. One night, the Rev. Samuel was woken by the sound of coins being tipped on to the floor; another night he heard heavy footsteps on the stairs and bottles being smashed. No one could trace the source of these noises and many other disturbances.

A few members of the household claimed to have caught fleeting glimpses of the ghost. Hetty, one of the daughters, said that it looked like someone in a long, white gown, while Mrs Wesley considered it was more like a headless badger.

AN INVOLUNTARY TOMB

During an early 18th-century house party, Catherine Noel, the 18-year-old daughter of the owner of now ruined Exton Old Hall, Leicestershire, is said to have suffocated inside an old oak chest, used as Juliet's tomb in an amateur performance of Romeo and Juliet

Eyam *Derbys*

A plague-infested box of laundry brought to the village in 1665 is supposed to have started the epidemic from which five out of every six villagers died. But the courage of the doomed villagers, and of their rector William Mompesson who survived, is no legend. Once the disease had broken out, Mompesson persuaded his parishioners to isolate themselves in Eyam, and so prevent the plague spreading to the rest of Derbyshire. On the last Sunday in August, a commemorative service is held in Cucklett church – the open dell where Mompesson preached during that grim time.

Fishtoft *Lincs*

A window in Fishtoft church shows the 7th-century hermit St Guthlac, to whom the church is dedicated, holding a whip reputedly given to him by St Bartholomew. As long as he held this whip, legend claimed, Fishtoft would be free of rats and mice.

POWERLESS BEFORE THE TIDE

On February 2, 1014, King Sweyn of Denmark, ruthless leader of the second great Danish invasion of England, died in torment in a castle which stood where Gainsborough Old Hall, Lincolnshire, stands today. It was rumoured that he had died at the hands of a spectre – the spear-wielding ghost of St Edmund, who had been martyred by the Danes 140 years earlier – after he had threatened to destroy Bury St Edmunds.

Soon afterwards, in the same castle, Sweyn's son Canute was proclaimed king, and Gainsborough is one of several places in England where the best-known legend of Canute is supposed to have taken place. The River Trent, flowing close by the castle, is famous for the Aegir, a 6 ft high wall of water that rushes upstream with the spring tides. Bored by his courtiers' flattery, Canute sat by the river bank, and ordered the tide not to wet him. But the Aegir rushed on regardless, and the drenched Canute leapt back, saying: 'Let all the world know that the power of monarchs is vain . . . no one deserves the name of King but He whose Will the Heavens, Earth and Sea do obey'

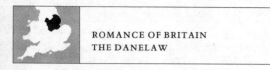
People from the neighbouring villages of Kirton, Manton, Scawby, Cleatham and Hibaldstow dealt with the problem some time in the 17th century. They raided the village and left it in ruins, after throwing the robbers down a well.

Gainsthorpe *Lincs*

The village of Gainsthorpe once had 100 houses. Now it has none and only a solitary farm in fields to the west of the modern A15 road, midway between Lincoln and Winteringham, marks its site. The road, which once followed the straight line of Roman Ermine Street, makes an unexpected bend round the place where Gainsthorpe used to be. The detour was made when the village became a refuge for robbers who waylaid travellers on the old way.

Glentham *Lincs*

The stone effigy of the 14th-century Lady Tournay that lies in Glentham church used to be washed by seven old maids every Good Friday. Each was paid a shilling, from rent on a piece of land. The practice ended in 1832, when the land was sold. The habit of washing holy images was known in local dialect as 'malgraen', which became corrupted to Molly Grime. Today, people in the area still call a child with a dirty face 'a Molly Grime'.

THE WISE MEN OF GOTHAM

Where did the 'wise' men of Gotham, Nottinghamshire, get their unenviable reputation for sheer dottiness? If legend is to be believed, the answer shows that the Gothamite heroes of many a crackpot tale were not so simple, after all.

According to one story, the villagers' inane antics, which inspired the quack doctor Andrew Borde to publish his *Merrie Tales of the Mad Men of Gotham* in the 16th century, were all assumed to rid the village of the wicked King John.

The king had decided to build a hunting lodge at the village – an honour which the 13th-century men of Gotham felt they could well do without, especially as it would mean giving up a considerable portion of their land. So they let it be known that king and courtiers would not receive the best of welcomes when they arrived in the village.

Such an attitude was bound to invite the royal wrath, and the villagers had to find some way of persuading his majesty's messengers that it would be better for everyone if the king hunted somewhere else, and left them alone. The solution, they decided, was to feign madness.

The Gotham cuckoos

When the messengers rode into the village they were met by an absurd spectacle: the local inhabitants, to judge by the stupid things they were doing, had all gone mad. The messengers rode away to warn the king to steer well clear of the place – leaving England's finest set of village idiots to congratulate themselves on a highly effective piece of fraud.

The follies and foibles of the people of Gotham were commemorated in Andrew Borde's book, which told some 20 tales.

The best known is about the group of villagers captivated by the cuckoo's song. They decided to trap the bird as it sat in a bush – by building a fence round it. Sadly, nobody thought of building a roof, and the bird simply flew away. Today the story is kept alive in the local pub, called The Cuckoo Bush, and nearby Cuckoo Bush Hill.

Gotham lunacies

The moon's reflection in a pond often worried the men of Gotham. One group decided it had fallen in, and that they would rescue it by forming a chain and raking it out. But the anchor man rested his arms – and all his friends were drowned.

Then there was the man whose horse drank from the pond just as a cloud covered the moon. He thought the beast had swallowed the moon, so he chopped it in two with his sword, to get the moon back.

The villagers did extraordinary things, when roused. An eel ate all the fish in their pond, so they hurled it into another – and left it to drown!

Encounters with nature invariably ended in disaster. The village blacksmith, for example, tackled a wasp's nest in his thatch by setting fire to it. As a result, the smithy burnt down.

Bubbling eddies in the river that gave the water an appearance of boiling inspired some Gothamites to cook the village porridge there. They poured in oatmeal, then, when they thought it was ready, one man jumped in to taste it. When he failed to come up, the others jumped in too.

Another man was exhausted by the weight of three cheeses, so at the top of the hill above Nottingham market, he rolled them down – and was surprised when they fell apart.

The prize for sheer stupidity goes to the man who took pity on his horse, which had 2 bushels of wheat to carry to Nottingham market. He decided to carry it himself – while riding the horse, of course.

THE CUCKOO-BUSH FARCE *One of the finest stories about the village idiots of Gotham sprang – just like the cuckoo – from a bush they encircled with stakes, hoping to snare the bird. The cuckoo-bush legend, common to many rural areas throughout the country, may symbolise our primitive ancestors' desire to preserve fertile spring for ever*

THE FIDDLER'S THANK-YOU

The violin-shaped weather-vane on Great Ponton church, in Lincolnshire, is a replica of one provided by a grateful fiddler in the 17th century. Villagers, charmed by his airs, paid his fare to America. There he made his fortune, and gave thanks by paying for the vane

MOONSTRUCK HORSE *One Gothamite split his horse in two, to recapture the moon, which he thought it had swallowed*

HOW TO KILL AN EEL *This eel ate all their fish — so the villagers threw it into a pond, hoping it would drown*

A HELPFUL FARMER *Off to market, he loaded wheat under his own arms, to save his horse effort . . . then rode the horse*

Griffydam *Leics*

An old well, lined with stone, beside the road at Griffydam, is said to have been guarded by a griffin, a beast half-eagle and half-lion. Villagers had to fetch their water from a priory 2 miles away, until one day a knight rode by. In exchange for a cup of water, he called for bow and arrows, and shot the monster before riding away.

Grimsby *Humberside*

Legend says the town was founded by a Danish fisherman named Grim, who fled there to escape the wicked usurper Godard. Grim had been ordered to drown the true heir to the Danish throne, a boy named Havelok, but instead Grim escaped with him to England. There, Havelok grew up and went to work as a scullion for the Earl of Lincoln. One day, Earl Godrich of Cornwall, regent of Britain when King Athelwold died, held a parliament at Lincoln, and soon heard of the scullion's prowess at stone-hurling and other games. He decided to marry off the old king's daughter, Goldborough, to the kitchen boy, in order to let his own son have the throne. Goldborough refused to marry anyone but a king's son, and Havelok, not knowing he was Prince of Denmark, felt he had little to offer her. But they were forced to marry under threat of death.

Havelok took his bride to Grimsby. There in the night Goldborough saw a light shining out of her husband's mouth, and a cross on his shoulder. The voice of an angel told her this was the king-mark, and that Havelok would one day rule Denmark and England. Havelok had also dreamt of becoming a king, and he persuaded Grim's three sons to take his bride and himself across the North Sea. In Denmark, Earl Ubbe befriended the couple, and when he discovered Havelok was the true heir to the throne, he summoned the other barons to do homage. They defeated the treacherous Godard, then invaded England and overcame Godrich, who was burnt to death for his treachery. Havelok ruled England and Denmark for 60 years, says the legend, and Goldborough bore him 15 children.

THE GRIMSBY LEGEND

The town seal shows figures from the Havelok legend. In the centre, with sword and shield, is Grim the fisherman, the town's founder. On either side stand Havelok and Goldborough, joint rulers of Denmark and Britain

Grindleford *Derbys*

At nearby Nether Padley is a Martyrs' Chapel that was once a barn. Pilgrims went there after 1588, when landowner John Fitzherbert of Padley Hall was arrested for sheltering two Catholic priests. All three were hanged, drawn and quartered at Derby.

Tradition insists that the priests were found in the chapel's chimneys. But their more likely refuge was in the Fitzherbert's home at the manor house. Nowadays, only a few stones of the old house remain standing.

LITTLE JOHN'S GRAVE

The 10 ft long grave of Robin Hood's henchman, Little John, said to have been born in Hathersage, Derbyshire, is marked by an inscribed headstone in the churchyard. His cap of Lincoln green and great yew bow, 6 ft long and tipped with horn, hung in the church, but they were later moved to Cannon Hall near Barnsley. Though the cap has now disappeared, the bow is still there. When the grave was opened in the early 1800's, a thigh-bone 32 in. long was found. It was re-interred after the man who ordered the exhumation had suffered a series of accidents

HINCKLEY'S BLEEDING TOMBSTONE

In 1727, 20-year-old saddler Richard Smith joined a crowd surrounding a recruiting sergeant at Hinckley, Leicestershire. As the soldier harangued and cajoled, the young man replied with quips and jokes, until the exasperated sergeant lost his temper and ran him through with his pike. The youth's tombstone is said to sweat blood on the anniversary of his death, on April 12

Hallaton *Leics*

On Easter Monday, villagers go 'Bottle-kicking' in a brawling spring festival rite that dates back to pre-Christian times, but now has the blessing of the Church. After a short service, hare-pie is cut up and distributed by the rector, but some is put into a sack and taken in procession to Hare-Pie Hill, where it is scattered over the ground. On the way, the three 'bottles' – wooden barrels, two containing 9 pints of beer each, and one empty – are cheered at certain points. Then the barrels are tossed up and fought for, one by one. Youths from Hallaton and rival Medbourne struggle to carry them over a brook into their parishes. The first team to score shares the contents of the barrel, before fighting over the empty cask and, finally, the other full 'bottle'. When that has been won, the scorer is chaired back to Hallaton's ancient stone buttercross, to drink the first pint, which is the signal for a village celebration.

The symbolism may represent the sacrificial beast scattered on the land to promote fertility, and a ritual battle between summer and winter.

Harlow Wood *Notts*

The ghost of Elizabeth Sheppard, a 17-year-old girl brutally murdered on her way to seek work in Mansfield, is said to haunt the spot where she died on July 7, 1817. It is believed to appear whenever her memorial stone, near the junction of the A60 and B6020 roads, is moved.

Her murderer was a scissors-grinder named Charles Rotherham, who, thinking she had money, attacked her with a stake ripped from the hedge. But she had none. He was caught at Mansfield, ten days after he had tried to sell her shoes and umbrella at the Three Crowns Inn, at Redhill, and later hanged on Gallows Hill, at Nottingham.

Haxey *Humberside*

An annual custom that retains a pagan flavour is the Hood Game at Haxey, held near the time of the winter solstice, on St John's Eve, January 6, on a nearby hilltop. The legend says that some 700 years ago on that day, the wife of Sir John de Mowbray, an ancestor of Thomas Mowbray, Duke of Norfolk, lost her big red hood in the wind as she was riding over Haxey Hill. A group of 13 'Boggans' – people from the boggy fenland – gave chase and finally rescued it. The country 'fool' who seized the hood was too shy to hand it over, so another, less tongue-tied, gave it to Lady de Mowbray, who was so delighted with the pursuit that she gave each man half an acre of land, in return for a promise to re-enact the event each year.

So, every January, the Lord selects his 12 Boggans, and one of them, the Fool, makes an opening speech at the Mounting Stone, near the church gates. He tells the crowd they are to play 'hoose agin' hoose, toon agin' toon; if a man meet a man knock a man doon, but down't hurt 'im'. Then the Boggans, dressed as Morris Men, lead the crowd to a field near the hill.

The Boggans form a huge circle, with the crowd inside, and a number of Hoods made of rolled-up sacking are thrown into the air. Then players try to get these away, past the Boggans. Any who succeed are later rewarded with a shilling by the Lord. But the game starts in earnest when the main Hood – made of leather, and containing a coiled rope – is thrown up. Men from the five local hamlets struggle to win possession and 'sway' the Hood away to their local inn. First to succeed are the winners. Part of the concluding ritual is the Smoking of the Fool, who must stand on the Mounting Stone while damp straw is lit around it. This has replaced an earlier ritual of dragging a plough round the green.

THE HOLBEACH CARDPLAYERS' DREADFUL 'DUMMY'

The Chequers Inn, opposite All Saints' Church at Holbeach, Lincolnshire, was a favourite venue for four local men who played cards all night long, in the early 17th century. When one of them died, the others drank to his memory – and decided on a farewell game in the church, with the body as 'dummy'. As they played by candle-light, a demon appeared and warned them to leave, but they ignored it – and were snatched away. Their ghosts, say local people, have been seen since, replaying that terrible last game

ANOTHER GHOST *Sir Humphrey Littlebury lies in Holbeach church, which he also is said to haunt*

Houghton on the Hill *Leics*
The chapel at Ingarsby Old Hall was once connected with the former manor belonging to Leicester Abbey, where Abbot Sadyngton was said to have dabbled in magic in the 1430's. Once, hunting the thief of a silver plate, he oiled an Ingarsby boy's thumbnail and uttered spells while the child told him what he saw in the nail's reflection. The boy named the canon, who later confessed.

Husbands Bosworth *Leics*
A floor stain at Bosworth Hall, said to be still damp after 300 years, was made by a priest trying to escape Cromwell's men. It is either consecrated wine – or his blood. The ghost of 19th-century Protestant Lady Lisgar, who refused to allow a priest to enter the house to administer the last rites to a dying Catholic servant, also haunts the Hall.

Kinder Scout *Derbys*
From the lip of the highest waterfall in the county, 3 miles north-east of Hayfield, can be seen the Mermaid's Pool, near Kinder reservoir. It is said that if you go to the pool at midnight, just as Easter Sunday begins, and stare closely into the dark waters, you will see a mermaid swimming.

BLACK ANNIS

The high ground to the right, as one leaves Leicester by King Richard's Road and Glenfield Road, was known once as the Dane Hills. Here, respectable suburban homes and a convent occupy what was a dreaded patch of wasteland and the home of terrifying Black Annis.

Black Annis's Bower was said to be a cave clawed out of the hillside by her own talons. Here, the witch-like hag with her tattered hair and long, yellowed fangs lay in wait for disobedient children who had strayed too far from home.

Parents would warn their children of the dreadful fate that awaited them if they played too long or late at night in the hills. Black Annis would seize them, skin them alive, and eat them up, scattering their bones around her cave and hanging their skins to dry on an old oak near by.

Within living memory at least, this tale was still being used to frighten local children into good behaviour. It possibly goes back to the ancient Celtic myths, and Annis could be Anu, wife of the sky god, Ludd.

Lincoln *Lincs*
The story of Little St Hugh – which Chaucer developed as one of his *Canterbury Tales* – was actually a powerful piece of anti-Semitic propaganda that may have been used when Edward I expelled the Jews from England in 1290. Hugh, an eight-year-old Lincoln boy, disappeared one August evening in 1255; a few days later, his mutilated body was found in a well. For reasons which are not entirely clear, a Jew named Copin was arrested and charged with the crime. Under torture, he admitted kidnapping the boy and selling him to another Jew named Hagin. He is also said to have confessed that it was a Jewish practice to crucify a Christian boy each year, and that Hugh had been first crucified and then stabbed to death. The corpse was then buried in a deep pit, but when it was found miraculously disinterred next morning, it was flung down the well. Copin was dragged through the streets tied to a horse's tail, and hanged on Canwick Hill, together with 18 other rich Jews. Bones alleged to be Hugh's were discovered in the cathedral in 1791, and a shrine was erected over them.

THE LINCOLN IMP

The 1 ft tall imp, high on a pillar in the cathedral's Angel Choir, is said to have wrought havoc in the great building, until an angel turned him to stone

POGROM IN LINCOLN

Copin the Jew, who confessed to kidnapping eight-year-old Hugh of Lincoln and handing him over for ritual cruci-fixion, was dragged through the city tied to a horse's tail, and hanged with 18 other Jews on Canwick Hill

Louth *Lincs*
Gallant Sir John Bolle, of Thorpe Hall, was one of the Earl of Essex's captains who sacked Cadiz in 1596. Among the captives was a beautiful Spanish girl who fell in love with him and wanted to accompany him back to England. But Sir John refused, for he dearly loved his own wife. Broken-hearted, the senorita decided to enter a convent, after giving Sir John jewels for his wife, a portrait of herself in a green dress and her undying love. Ever since, a lady in green has haunted the vicinity of the Hall.

Mansfield *Notts*
The ballad of the king and the miller tells how Henry II became lost while hunting in Sherwood Forest, and met John Cockle the miller, who failed to recognise him. The hospitable miller gave him a venison pasty but warned him never to let the king know they 'made free with his deer'. The king was so amused by the situation, and so delighted by the miller's forthright country ways, that he finally made him a forest overseer, gave him £300 a year, and awarded him a knighthood.

Moira *Leics*

In the late 19th century, the sight of a pig that stood on a wall to watch the band go by caught the imagination of Moira's miners. It became their annual totem, dressed in ribbons, to be saluted by the villagers at the July Gala – but the practice was discontinued in the 1960's.

Muggington *Derbys*

Halter-Devil Chapel is the local name for the tiny Intake Chapel, which is attached to a farmhouse. It is, said to have been erected in 1723 by Francis Brown, a noted heavy drinker, in gratitude for a revelation that made him change his ways. One wild night the befuddled man swore he would ride to Derby, if he had to 'halter the Devil' to get there. He went out into the darkness to put the halter on his horse, and found the beast had horns! Shocked into remorse, he gave up drinking and built the chapel. The animal was, of course, a cow.

Newark-on-Trent *Notts*

St Catherine's Well, by the river at Sconce Hill, in Devon Park, has a sad legend of love and betrayal attached to it. The 13th-century knight, Sir Guy Saucimer slew his friend, Sir Everard Bevorcotes, out of jealousy, for Sir Everard had won the affections of the fair Isabell de Caldwell, whom they both loved. A spring gushed forth on the spot and Sir Guy, plagued by guilt, fled away from the deed, and went abroad. While he was away, Isabell died from grief and Sir Guy himself caught leprosy. Then, one night, St Catherine appeared to him in a dream and told him he would be cured if he bathed in the spring. He returned to Newark, bathed in the waters and was healed. The knight built a chapel around the spring and led a holy life ever after. When he died, he was canonised as St Guthred.

Newstead *Notts*

The abbey, built in 1170 and later the home of the Byron family, is famous for its ghosts. Lord Byron himself is said to have seen the Black Friar, whose appearances always herald disaster, just before his luckless marriage to Anne Milbanke.

There is also a White Lady, said to be the spirit of Sophia Hyett, a bookseller's daughter, who was so obsessed by the poet that she still haunts his home crying: 'Alas, my Lord Byron!' Another ghost was that of the 16th-century Little Sir John Byron, who used to appear under his portrait, reading.

Newtown Linford *Leics*

An 18th-century folly, shaped like a drinking mug and handle, stands in Bradgate Park. Known as Old John's Tower, it was built by Lord Stamford in memory of a local miller noted for liking his ale. The miller died at the young lord's 21st birthday bonfire party, in 1780, when a huge centre log in the fire burnt through and fell on him.

Nottingham *Notts*

The 'oldest pub in England', The Trip to Jerusalem, is built on the site of a brewhouse where travellers to the Holy Land bought ale. From the pub cellars is hewn Mortimer's Hole, a cave leading to the castle. Edward III is said to have crept through this to capture Roger Mortimer, who was later put to death. Mortimer's ghost is said to haunt the cave.

The city is famous for its Goose Fair (so-called from the great flocks of geese that were sold there at Michaelmas), first mentioned in a charter dated 1284 and still held from the first Thursday in October. The fair had its own Pie-powder Court (from the French *pied-poudre*, meaning 'dusty feet') to deal summarily with wrongdoers.

OAKHAM'S HORSESHOES

For centuries, every peer or member of the Royal Family visiting the former county of Rutland has had to give a horseshoe to the lord of the manor at Oakham. There are some 220 in the castle; the oldest, dated 1600, is said to have been given by Elizabeth I. The biggest, from George IV, cost £20 to make, and the king left his host to pay for it

Ollerton *Notts*

Nearby Rufford Abbey, 2 miles from the village and the former home of the Saville family, was destroyed at the Dissolution. The ruins are haunted by the ghost of a giant monk with a skull under his cowl. The parish register for Edwinstowe records the death of a man 'from fright after seeing the Rufford ghost'.

RUNAWAY BRIDE OF HADDON HALL

Haddon Hall, at Rowsley, Derbyshire, was the scene of a famous elopement in 1558. Dorothy Vernon, second daughter of Sir George Vernon, was to have married a younger son of the Earl of Derby on the same day as her sister wed his eldest son. But Dorothy slipped away from the wedding-eve ball, to elope with Sir John Manners, disguised as a forester, on horseback. Above are the steps down which she fled and the arched packbridge where they crossed the River Wye. Dorothy's effigy (top) now stands over her tomb in Bakewell church, where she lies beside her husband and their children

Scarcliffe *Derbys*

In Scarcliffe church is the tomb of Lady Constantia de Frecheville (below) who died c. 1200. It shows her with her illegitimate child, with whom she was lost in Scarcliffe Wood until led to safety by the tolling of curfew at the church. In gratitude, she made a bequest for curfew to be rung for six weeks every Christmas.

CHAMPION OF ENGLAND

The office of the Sovereign's Grand Champion was begun by William the Conqueror, and was inherited in 1350 by the Dymoke family of Scrivelsby, Lincolnshire. It was the champion's duty to ride on a white charger, fully clad in armour, into Westminster Hall during the coronation ceremony. There, throwing down his gauntlet, he challenged any person who dared to deny the sovereign's right to the throne. The custom was omitted at the coronations of William IV in 1830 and Queen Victoria in 1837, when Sir Henry Dymoke posed for his portrait (above). The family's privilege is now symbolised by their carrying the Royal Standard

Sileby *Leics*

Every year, on Whit Sunday, the vicar distributes oranges to local schoolchildren under an ancient elm tree in Sileby churchyard. It is believed that the custom began in 1815 to commemorate the Duke of Wellington's victory at Waterloo. The tradition lapsed for several years and was recently revived by the gift of an anonymous donor.

Skegness *Lincs*

Gunby Hall, 7 miles west of Skegness, was built in 1700 by Sir William Massingberd. Some years earlier, when his family lived at nearby Bratoft Castle, his daughter Margaret tried to elope with one of his postilion-riders, but her father shot the man dead as they were crossing the castle moat. Sir William was accused of murder and sentenced to appear in London once a year, when his family coat-of-arms was ceremonially smeared with blood. Overcome by remorse, he demolished Bratoft Castle in 1698 and then built Gunby Hall. It is said that the ghosts of his daughter and the postilion-rider have been seen on the Ghost Walk, a path that runs near the Hall.

South Croxton *Leics*

A local tale claims to relate the events which led to the naming of Baggrave Hall, near South Croxton. One night, when her employers were away, a maidservant gave refuge to a distraught woman. But later, in front of the kitchen fire, the maid noticed that her visitor wore heavy boots, and realised that 'she' was a man in disguise, and therefore a robber. She plied him with wine until he fell into a drunken stupor, after which she cut off his head. She presented her victim to her employers, ready for burial in a potato bag; from that time on, the house was called Baggrave.

Stoney Middleton *Derbys*

In the mid-18th century, a local girl named Hannah Baddeley was abandoned by her lover and attempted suicide by jumping from an 80 ft cliff in Stoney Middleton Dale. It is said that her life was saved by protruding thorn bushes on the cliffside and by her billowing petticoats, both of which slowed her fall so that she suffered only minor injuries. The cliff is known as Lover's Leap.

Stretton *Leics*

The Ram Jam Inn at Stretton is said to be named after an incident which occurred in the 18th century. An extravagant guest lodged at the inn for a week and ran up a huge bill. One day he offered to show the landlady how to obtain two different kinds of beer from the same cask. They went down to the cellar, where he drilled a hole in a beer barrel and asked her to ram her thumb in the hole as he withdrew the drill. She did so, and was then asked to jam her other thumb into a second hole on the other side of the barrel. She again obliged, and having immobilised his hostess, the guest went upstairs and rode off without paying anything.

Swarkestone *Derbys*

Legend tells that the original Swarkestone Bridge, part of which survives, was built early in the 13th century by two daughters of the Harpur family. They were celebrating their joint betrothal party when their fiancés were summoned to a meeting of barons across the River Trent. While they were absent, a torrential rainstorm caused the river to flood, and both men were drowned as they tried to ford the waters on their return. The two sisters built the bridge as a memorial to their lovers, and both women died impoverished and unwed.

'MERRIE SHERWODE'

John Keats sums up the nostalgia that most people feel when they visit Sherwood, that once vast and still considerable tract of forest north of Nottingham, in the lines:

'Never more shall ye see
Little John or Robin bold;
Never one of all the clan
Thrumming on an empty can
Some old hunting ditty . . .'

Whether Robin and his Merrie Men ever lived in the 'greenshawe', or even if they existed at all, does not really matter. Simply to remember old tales beside the great oaks in the green forest light is enough to awaken images of a gallantry that existed long ago.

The earliest known ballad about the outlaws is 'The Lytell Geste of Robyn Hode', which dates only from the 15th century, at least 200 years after the presumed death of the hero. But from earlier references it is clear that the tales were well known long before this time.

This has led some scholars to conclude that stories of real or fictitious outlaws were grafted on to a memory of a more sinister personality – the guardian god or spirit of the woods. It has been pointed out that 'Robin' was a name often given to fairies, and that green, the colour invariably worn by the outlaws, though providing camouflage, was the fairies' colour too.

The greenwood trees

Nottinghamshire tradition still firmly asserts the existence of the county's most famous son. The gigantic Major Oak, 1000 years old, and through careful preservation still growing in Birkland Wood near Edwinstowe, is indicated as the meeting place of Robin and his men. In fact, it is said that the entire band used to hide within the hollow trunk to escape the villainous sheriff of Nottingham. Another great oak, the Centre Tree, halfway between Thoresby and Welbeck estates, is reputed to be the marker from which Robin's network of secret routes ran through the forest of Sherwood.

Maid Marian, who is supposed to have married Robin in Edwinstowe church, was born in the village of Blidworth, 7 miles to the south-west. At Blidworth, too, the gang hid its food in a cave; Friar Tuck lived near by, and Will Scarlet is said to be buried in the churchyard.

Tree of Judgment

Not all the Sherwood legends concern Robin Hood. Near Clipstone stands the Parliament Oak, beneath which, in the 13th century, King John is said to have received news of a Welsh uprising. He summoned his courtiers around him, then, acting upon their advice, galloped off to Nottingham Castle where he hanged 28 young Welshmen, who were imprisoned there, as a reprisal. Beneath the same tree in 1290, Queen Eleanor, the beloved wife of Edward I, fell gravely ill. An emergency parliament advised the king to continue his journey to Harby, but there the queen died.

THE PARLIAMENT OAK *In the 13th century, King John and, later, Edward I are said to have held emergency meetings of their advisers under this ancient tree*

Swineshead *Lincs*

After King John lost the Crown Jewels in The Wash in October, 1216, he dined at Swineshead Abbey, where over-indulgence in peaches and new ale is alleged to have killed him a few days later. Years afterwards, people said that he had been poisoned by a monk who gave his own life 'to save all England'. According to legend, the king told the monk that he intended forcing up the price of bread to increase his revenue. A true patriot, the monk poisoned the king's ale, and drank first from the cup to make the king believe it was safe.

Treak Cliff *Derbys*

Caverns in the cliff are said to be the only place in the world where the mineral Blue John – a fluorspar banded in red, blue, purple and yellow – has been found. Blue John vases were highly prized by the Romans. One of them is said to have cost the Roman author and dandy Petronius the equivalent of £30,000. He smashed it, to prevent the ornament from falling into the hands of the Emperor Nero.

Tunstead *Derbys*

An ancient skull known as Dickie is kept at a farm 3 miles north-east of Buxton. It is said to be that of Ned Dixon, whose cousin murdered him in the house. All kinds of disasters are said to follow if the skull is moved. Once, someone had it buried, and soon things began to go wrong on the farm – the pigs died, cows became ill, and crops failed. So the skull was retrieved and all went well again.

Wardlow Mires *Derbys*

The highwayman Anthony Lingard was hanged at a nearby crossroads in 1812 for the murder of a widow who kept the local toll-gate. His corpse, the last to swing from a gibbet in the county, attracted such a crowd that the local lay-preacher had to leave the church at Tideswell for lack of a congregation, and give his sermon at the gibbet instead.

Wellow *Notts*

The county's only permanent maypole stands on the village green. Local children still dance round the pole on May Day. Whenever a new pole is needed, it is cut from Sherwood Forest.

FLOWER FESTIVALS

Anyone exploring Derbyshire in summer, especially when wandering through villages in the Peak District, may suddenly be confronted by the sight of a vividly coloured picture, up to 10 ft high, standing in the shade. Near by will be a pool, spring or tap. On closer examination, the visitor will discover that the beautifully made picture is constructed entirely from natural objects such as pebbles, flower petals, leaves, moss, wild fruits and pieces of crystalline rock. This form of picture-making is called well-dressing, and its history goes back, possibly, to the pagan worship of water-nymphs, who had to be placated annually so that the local water supply would continue; but no one knows for certain how long ago the practice began.

Nowadays, most of the village well-dressings are religious in theme, and usually illustrate stories from the Bible. Flowers and green boughs are placed beside springs and wells in neighbouring counties, but Derbyshire is the true home of well-dressing. For sheer elaboration of design, Tissington probably holds pride of place, but the decorations in the other villages are also worth travelling a long way to see.

BUXTON WELL-DRESSING *When they dressed the spring at Buxton 80 years ago, a swan glided in a specially built pool*

HIGHWAYMAN'S FAREWELL

The black sheep of the Davenports was George, the highwayman. At 39, he went to the gallows, full of dash and bravado, in a borrowed chaise and pair

Wigston *Leics*

Though he brought pain to his respectable family, tall, handsome George Davenport endeared himself to the local people by his generosity and carefree ways. Even when he turned highwayman, no one would betray him, and everyone thought that his favourite trick of making recruiting sergeants drunk before stealing their horses was a huge joke. Then one day, he made the mistake of waylaying a butcher who promptly clubbed the unfortunate George over the head and dragged him off to Leicester Assizes, where he was condemned to death. Game to the last, George borrowed a chaise and pair from an innkeeper and to the cheers of the crowd drove himself to the gallows on Red Hill.

The Winnats *Derbys*

In 1758, this tremendous limestone gorge was the scene of robbery and murder. The victims were a pair of runaway lovers and the murderers were never caught. Years later, a lead miner dying of a

County of flowers

At Tissington, on Ascension Day, the clergy and choir lead a procession to bless the five local wells, each with its enormous floral picture. Other villages – Barlow and Eyam, Stoney Middleton, Tideswell and Youlgreave – have preserved similar customs for centuries. The ceremony usually takes place on the day of the saint to whom the church is dedicated. The pictures are prepared by children, directed by adults whose families have practised the art for generations. The base is a wooden tray packed with moist clay on which the outline of the illustration is carefully pricked out. Then petals and alder-cones, pebbles and lichens, are delicately pressed on to the design.

Another flower festival unique to the county utilises the Derbyshire Garland. This is a bell-shaped frame decorated with flowers, foliage and ribbons. It, too, may have pagan origins. Miniature examples were carried in funerals when a young, unmarried woman died, and some garlands are preserved at churches in Matlock, Ashford and Trusley.

A bigger floral garland is used in the Garland Day ceremony on Oak Apple Day (May 29) at Castleton, when the Restoration of Charles II is commemorated. There a 'King and Queen' dressed in Stuart costume ride through the village, the 'King' wearing the 56 lb. garland which covers him from his head to his waist (above). After a circuit of the village the garland is hung for a week from a corner of the tower of Castleton's Norman church.

LAMENTING A MAIDEN *Small flower garlands were carried at maidens' funerals*

painful illness confessed that he and four companions had committed the crime. All his friends had died in hideous ways, by accident or suicide. This, said a contemporary report, was 'the most striking instance of Divine Judgment on record'.

Winster *Derbys*

Each Shrove Tuesday a Pancake Race is run between the Crown Inn and the ancient Market House – a course of about 100 yds. Men, women and children can all take part, and small frying pans are provided. Special pancakes too are issued, designed to wear well rather than to eat.

On June 24, visiting teams of Morris Men dance outside the Market House as part of the Winster Wakes celebrations.

Wistow *Leics*

The old Hall and St Wistan's Church are all there is of Wistow, which lies in the meadows between Arnesby on the A50 and Great Glen on the A6.

Wistan was a Saxon prince, heir to the throne of Mercia. His mother, Elfleda, was appointed regent on the death of the king. Wistan's kinsman and godfather, Britfardus, proposed marriage to the queen in order to strengthen his own claim to the throne. But the prince opposed the match, saying that it was incestuous in the eyes of the Church.

On a pretext of discussing the matter, Britfardus lured the boy to a lonely spot and there clove his skull in two. The murderer's hope of secrecy was dashed, however, for a column of light appeared over Wistan's grave, and where his blood had been spilt, human hair sprouted from the ground. Vilified by the Church and people, and tortured by his own conscience, Britfardus went insane. Wistan was re-interred at Repton, where fragments of his bones attracted pilgrims until the Reformation, when they disappeared. But if you visit Wistow on June 1, the anniversary of the killing, and if you have sufficient faith, there is one hour during the day when hair springs from the ground once more.

ENGLAND'S HEARTLAND

Hereford and Worcester, Gloucestershire, Salop, Staffordshire, Warwickshire, West Midlands

A medieval stone cross standing in the middle of the Warwickshire village of Meriden is said to mark the geographical centre of England. Spread across the heart of a nation, it is hardly surprising that the six counties of the west Midlands have figured so prominently in Britain's turbulent story.

Salop and the area around Hereford were the first to feel the savage onslaught of the many wars between the Welsh Celts and the Anglo-Saxons during their 600-year struggle for the mastery of southern Britain after the departure of the Romans. English supremacy was hammered home when, late in the 13th century, the Norman Lords of the Marches finally drove the Welsh back into their mountain fastness. Much of their success was due to the string of fortresses which they built along the war-torn border – among them Goodrich and Stokesay castles, where the hidden treasures of nobles and giants are said to be guarded by spectral ravens, and Berkeley Castle, where Edward II was horribly murdered in 1327.

Tradition claims that the ghost of Wild Edric, the 11th-century Shropshire Marchman haunts the lead mines of the shire. He is also said to ride through the countryside whenever England is threatened by war; Edric and his beautiful fairy wife Godda were last reported during the summer of 1939. History has given his watchful spirit little rest among these fertile valleys and skyswept hills which have long been called 'The Nation's Cockpit'. Blood was spilt here in four major civil wars, beginning in the 12th century when King Stephen fought for the English throne at Cirencester. The now tranquil Vale of Evesham witnessed the last battle of the Barons' War at Evesham in 1265, the Battle of Tewkesbury in 1471 during the Wars of the Roses, and Cromwell's victory over Charles II at Worcester in 1651.

But wars pass; and for west Midland townsmen, there was always the consolation of the serene hills. Shakespeare, Stratford born and bred, said of the Forest of Arden: 'Here shall you see no enemy but winter and rough weather.' The poet A. E. Housman agreed with him. He wrote of Salop: 'Clunton and Clunbury, Clungunford and Clun, are the quietest places under the sun.'

THE FOLKLORE YEAR

Shrove Tuesday
Atherstone, Warks
Street Football

Palm Sunday
Hentland, Heref and Worcs
Pax Cakes Distribution

Spring Bank Holiday Monday
Endon, Staffs
Well-Dressing

Whit Sunday
St Briavels, Glos
Bread and Cheese Dole

Whit Monday
Cooper's Hill, Brockworth, Glos
Cheese Rolling

Whit Monday
Lichfield, Staffs
Court of Array and Greenhill Bower

May 29
Aston on Clun, Salop
Arbor Tree Day

May 29
Worcester, Heref and Worcs
Oak Apple Day at Guildhall

Saturday after June 24
Bromsgrove, Heref and Worcs
Court Leet Procession

Monday following first Sunday after September 4
Abbots Bromley, Staffs *Horn Dance*

Sunday on or after September 19
Painswick, Glos
Clipping the Church

First Monday in October
King's Norton, Warks
Mop Fair

KEY TO SYMBOLS

BELLS

CRIME AND PUNISHMENT

CURIOUS CHARACTERS

CUSTOMS AND FESTIVALS

DEVILS AND DEMONS

FABULOUS BEASTS

FAIRIES

GHOSTS

GIANTS

GRAVES AND MONUMENTS

GIPSIES AND TINKERS

HEROES

HILL FIGURES

HOLY PLACES

INDUSTRIAL LORE

LOCAL CURIOSITIES

LOVE STORY

MERMAIDS AND SEA-PEOPLE

MYSTERIOUS STONES

SAINTS AND MIRACLES

TREASURE

UNDERGROUND PASSAGES

WELLS AND SPRINGS

WITCHES AND WIZARDS

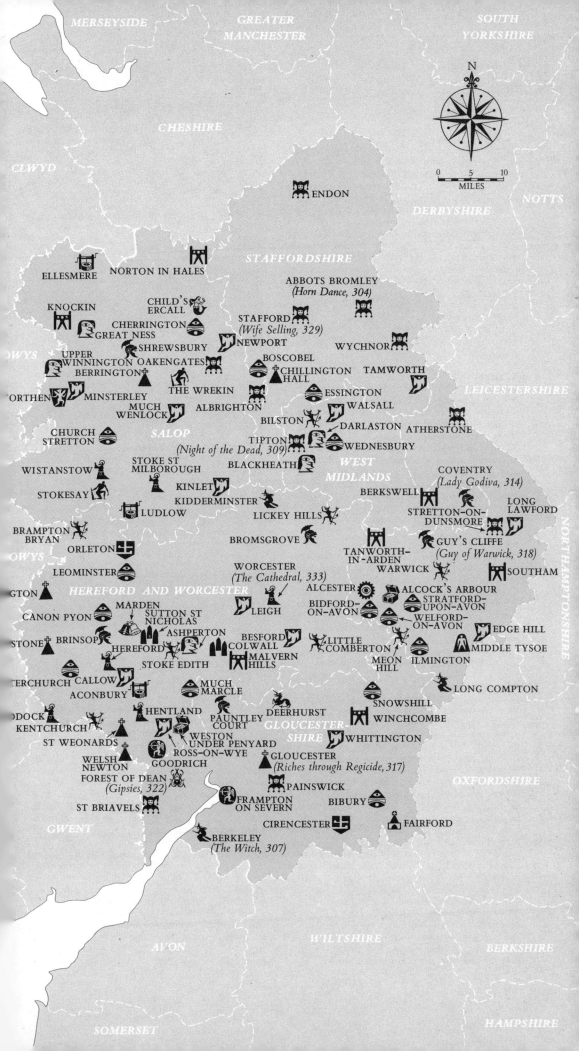

MERSEYSIDE

GREATER
MANCHESTER

SOUTH
YORKSHIRE

CHESHIRE

DERBYSHIRE

NOTTS

CLWYD

ENDON

STAFFORDSHIRE

ELLESMERE   NORTON IN HALES

ABBOTS BROMLEY
(Horn Dance, 304)

KNOCKIN

CHILD'S
ERCALL

CHERRINGTON
GREAT NESS

STAFFORD
(Wife Selling, 329)
NEWPORT

WYCHNOR

UPPER
WINNINGTON OAKENGATES
BERRINGTON

SHREWSBURY

BOSCOBEL
CHILLINGTON
HALL

TAMWORTH

ORTHEN   MINSTERLEY

THE WREKIN

ESSINGTON

LEICESTERSHIRE

MUCH
WENLOCK   ALBRIGHTON

WALSALL

BILSTON

CHURCH
STRETTON

SALOP

TIPTON
(Night of the Dead, 309)   DARLASTON
WEDNESBURY

ATHERSTONE

WISTANSTOW

STOKE ST
MILBOROUGH

BLACKHEATH

WEST
MIDLANDS

COVENTRY
(Lady Godiva, 314)

STOKESAY

KINLET

BERKSWELL

STRETTON-ON-
DUNSMORE

LONG
LAWFORD

LUDLOW

KIDDERMINSTER

LICKEY HILLS

BRAMPTON
BRYAN

ORLETON

BROMSGROVE

TANWORTH-
IN-ARDEN

GUY'S CLIFFE
(Guy of Warwick, 318)

WARWICK

NORTHAMPTONSHIRE

LEOMINSTER

WORCESTER
(The Cathedral, 333)

ALCESTER

SOUTHAM

GTON

HEREFORD AND WORCESTER

LEIGH

ALCOCK'S ARBOUR
STRATFORD-
UPON-AVON

BIDFORD-
ON-AVON

CANON PYON

MARDEN
SUTTON ST
NICHOLAS

WELFORD-
ON-AVON

STONE   BRINSOP

ASHPERTON

BESFORD
COLWALL

LITTLE
COMBERTON

EDGE HILL

MIDDLE TYSOE

HEREFORD

MALVERN
HILLS

STOKE EDITH

MEON
HILL   ILMINGTON

TERCHURCH CALLOW

ACONBURY

MUCH
MARCLE

LONG COMPTON

ODOCK
KENTCHURCH

HENTLAND

SNOWSHILL

PAUNTLEY
COURT   DEERHURST

WINCHCOMBE

ST WEONARDS

WESTON
UNDER PENYARD
ROSS-ON-WYE

GLOUCESTER-
SHIRE

WHITTINGTON

WELSH
NEWTON

GOODRICH

GLOUCESTER
(Riches through Regicide, 317)

FOREST OF DEAN
(Gipsies, 322)

PAINSWICK

ST BRIAVELS

FRAMPTON
ON SEVERN

BIBURY

GWENT

CIRENCESTER

FAIRFORD

BERKELEY
(The Witch, 307)

AVON

WILTSHIRE

BERKSHIRE

SOMERSET

HAMPSHIRE

N

0   5   10
MILES

Aconbury *Heref & Worcs*

As midnight chimes on Twelfth Night, so it is said, the water in St Anne's Well bubbles furiously and gives off a blue smoke. Until the First World War at least, there used to be a great competition to draw the first bucket after Twelfth Night, for the water was held to be of great medicinal value, particularly in curing eye infections.

The coppice beyond St Anne's Well is haunted by a pair of lovers whose names are long forgotten. The girl murdered the boy, believing him to be unfaithful, then, on discovering his innocence, she died of a broken heart.

The cowled figure that is occasionally reported near the tomb of Roger de Clifford in Aconbury church may be the last manifestation of a troublesome spirit that was exorcised and driven into a bottle by the clergy and buried beneath the church wall about 250 years ago.

Albrighton *Salop*

'The finest pastime that is under the sun, is whipping the cat at Albrighton.' This old saying probably derives from the ancient custom of beating an animal to expiate the sins of the community. In later years however (until the 19th century), Albrighton people used to bet simple strangers that the local cats were so strong they could haul a man across a river. One end of a rope was attached to the stranger and the other to a cat on the opposite bank; someone would pretend to whip the cat, whereupon the villagers would seize the rope and drag the visitor into the water.

Alcester *Warks*

Before the Norman Conquest, Alcester was a famous iron-working town whose smiths used to toil every day of the week including Sunday. St Egwin, Bishop of Worcester, reproached them for this ungodly habit but they only hammered more loudly, and sang to drown his voice. The Bishop promptly cursed them, and every man grew a tail; it is said that the smiths were so ashamed of these appendages that they refused to meet their customers, and the trade died out in the town.

Alcock's Arbour *Warks*

Just off the road between Stratford and Alcester, near the Haselor-Temple Grafton crossroads, is a curious conical hill which has been known for centuries as Alcock's Arbour. An indentation at the foot of the hill is said to be all that remains of the cave that was once the home of a famous robber named Alcock who, before he died, put all his illgotten gains into an iron-bound chest that was secured with three locks. He then buried the chest at the back of the cave and set a great cockerel to guard it. One day long ago, an Oxford scholar found the chest, and managed to open two of the locks; but as he tried to open the third, the cockerel seized him and tore him to pieces. Legend asserts, however, that if one of Alcock's bones could be found and shown to the bird, it would then yield up the treasure.

The hill is also known as the Devil's Bag of Nuts, from a story which tells how Satan went nutting on Devil's Nutting Day (September 21), and had just filled an enormous sack when he was interrupted by the Virgin. She ordered him to drop it, which he did, thus forming the hill.

THE HUNTERS' HORN DANCE

The Abbots Bromley Horn Dance, which takes place annually on the Monday following the first Sunday after September 4, is unique in Europe. It starts at dawn outside the village church, makes a 20-mile circuit of the local farms where the dancers are welcomed as the bearers of good luck and fertility, and finishes in the main street of this Staffordshire village in the afternoon.

The dance or 'running' is enacted by six Deer-men, three of whom carry white wooden replicas of reindeer heads with real horns attached, and three black. There is also a Fool, a Hobby Horse, Maid Marion the Man-Woman and a Bowman. Music is provided by a melodeon player, while the Horse beats time with snapping jaws and the Bowman twangs his bowstring. The high point of the drama occurs when the black and white Deer-men face each other and, with lowered horns, act out a mock combat, their slow, dignified movements accentuated by the sheer weight of the heads and antlers.

Hunters' magic

The design of the costumes and the movements of the dance have been preserved for hundreds – perhaps thousands – of years, even though the original purpose of the ritual has long been forgotten. It has been suggested that it may be the remnant of a medieval pageant that was held to raise funds for the local church; certainly, the money collected by the dancers is still used for this purpose.

Other authorities, however, are convinced that though the medieval Church may have adopted the ceremony, many of its elements indicate that the ritual is much older than Christianity. The presence of Maid Marion, a man dressed as a woman, suggests the memory of an ancient fertility rite, while the battle between the black and white Deer-men was once probably intended to symbolise the battle between light and darkness or winter and spring.

Stone Age ritual

The most ancient part of the ceremony, perhaps, is when the Bowman pretends to stalk the Deer-men, firing imaginary arrows at them. Twenty thousand years ago, Stone Age artists depicted a similar ritual on the walls of their caves at Lascaux in France. The paintings show men dressed in animal skins and with antlers on their heads being pursued by bowmen. It would seem from this that our far-off ancestors believed that to mime a successful hunt would in some way give them power over their real quarry. Primitive hunters such as the Bushmen of the Kalahari still employ the magic of dance and mime to ensure success in the chase. It may be that when the Bowman stalks the Deer-men down the main street of Abbots Bromley, he is re-enacting a ceremony that is thousands of years old – a ceremony that was meant to ensure the death of the reindeer and the survival of the unknown tribe that lived in the area now called Staffordshire.

Ashperton *Heref & Worcs*

Katherine Grandison, who died about 1360, was born here and christened in the ancient font which now stands in the churchyard. Despite the more generally accepted claims for the Countess of Salisbury, Katherine is locally affirmed to be the lady who dropped her garter at a court ball in 1349, and so played her part in founding England's highest order of chivalry. Tradition says that to cover the lady's embarrassment, Edward III picked up the garter, and with the words *Honi soit qui mal y pense* (roughly: 'Shame on anyone who thinks evil of this'), buckled it on his own leg. It has been pointed out that it took more than a dropped garter to ruffle the modesty of a 14th-century court lady; the true significance may lie in the fact that the garter was the badge of a witch, and Edward's action saved Katherine (or the Countess) from certain death for sorcery.

ABBOTS BROMLEY HORN DANCE *Several features of the dance are so ancient that their origins are shrouded in mystery. It is thought that the reindeer horns themselves are at least 1000 years old, and may have come from Scandinavia*

Atherstone *Warks*

At 3 p.m. on Shrove Tuesday, a large ball is thrown from the window of The Three Tuns inn in Long Street, whereupon two Atherstone teams begin to fight for its possession in a free-for-all game of street football. It is permitted to deflate the ball and hide it any time after 4.30 and whichever team has the ball at 5 o'clock wins. Until about 1900, the game was played between Leicestershire and Warwickshire teams, and is said to have originated in King John's reign when men of the two counties fought for a bag of gold.

Berkswell *Warks*

The set of stocks on the village green has five holes for feet. The local explanation for this is that they were made for an old one-legged soldier and his two friends, whose drunken habits often landed them in the stocks.

Berrington *Salop*

The wooden effigy in the church is probably that of a former lord of the manor, but tradition names it as Owd Scriven, who fought with a lion and killed it on near-by Banky Piece. As proof, the effigy's face is half torn off, and a lion's severed body lies at its feet.

Besford *Heref & Worcs*

At one time, a member of the well-known Worcestershire family of Seabright used to kennel his fox hounds at Church Farm, where part of the land is still known as Dog Kennel Piece. One night, the owner heard a disturbance among the hounds, and sent his kennelman to find out what was wrong. He did not reappear, but next morning, his hunting boots were discovered, still spurred, and containing the lower part of his legs and feet. Ever since, it is said, the kennelman's boots march across Dog Kennel Piece on dark nights, accompanied by the sound of jingling spurs and the baying of hounds.

Another version of this story comes from the village of Broadway, near the Gloucestershire border. There, when the kennelman was roused from his bed by the baying of hounds, he rushed out in his night-shirt. The animals failed to recognise him in this guise, and tore him to pieces. Which is why, they say, this ghost wears a night-shirt.

MURDER AT BERKELEY CASTLE

In the 12th-century keep of Berkeley Castle, Gloucestershire, there is a deep well in the thickness of the wall. It is said to have contained a huge toad that would slowly devour any prisoners flung down to it. A more reliable tradition, perhaps, asserts that the well was a refuse pit, into which the carcasses of animals and men were thrown and left to rot. The frightful stench rose upwards to a tiny cell built over the pit, and it was in this cell (above) that one of the most famous and brutal murders in English history took place. The victim was an English king, Edward II, the weak son of a strong father, whose disastrous efforts as a soldier resulted in the Scottish victory at Bannockburn in 1314. His fondness for young men such as Piers Gaveston, and the honours he bestowed upon them, alienated and disgusted both his council and his French queen, Isabella. With the queen's connivance, he was deposed in 1327 and imprisoned in the small room at Berkeley Castle, where it was hoped that the disease and foul odours emanating from the well would shortly make an end of him.

But the king's constitution was proof against both, for he was still alive five months later. The queen demanded a swift conclusion to the business, whereupon Lord Berkeley prudently quitted the castle, leaving Edward with his gaolers, Gurney and Maltravers. On September 21, they burst into the cell, pinned him between two mattresses, and killed him hideously with a red-hot iron spit. The king's appalled shrieks are said to echo round the neighbouring countryside to this day.

The Berkeley family have held the castle for almost 1000 years, though legend says that the first fortress was built by the 11th-century Earl Godwin on the site of a convent. Coveting the land, Godwin slaughtered the nuns and built his castle. The Saxon chalice (right) is believed to have belonged to him

THE GODWIN CUP

THE WITCH OF BERKELEY

About the time of the Norman Conquest, according to the chronicler William of Malmesbury, there was a woman living in the little town of Berkeley who had many sons and daughters. She was rich and plump and well liked, and spent most of her time in feasting and revelry. One evening as she sat at table, her pet raven cried out a single harsh note of warning and dropped dead to the floor. The woman paled and fell back in her chair exclaiming: 'Now is my plough come to its last furrow! Now my days of rejoicing are past and my sorrows begin!'

The terrible vengeance
No sooner had she spoken than a messenger came running with the news of the death of her eldest son and all his family. More bad news quickly followed, and the distraught woman took to her bed. Realising she was at the point of death with no hope of recovery, she entreated the help of two of her remaining children, a monk and a nun of great piety.

She confessed that her life had been one of fearful wickedness, and that all her wealth had been given to her by the Devil in exchange for her soul. Now the time had come to pay the reckoning, and the only way her children could save her was to wrap her body in a stag's skin, place it in a stone coffin bound with three iron chains, and set the coffin upright in the church. She must then have psalms sung over her body for 40 nights and masses said for 40 days. If on the third day after that her coffin remained unmolested, she could be buried in the churchyard.

The magic that failed
At last she died, and all was done as she wished; but on the first night a crowd of demons swarmed in and snapped the first chain. On the second night, the same thing happened, and the second chain was broken. But the third and most potent magic chain still remained whole against all the efforts of the hideous demons.

On the third night, the church shook to its foundations, the great doors splintered on their hinges, and a single, terrible figure strode in and called on the Witch of Berkeley to follow him. She answered from within the coffin: 'I cannot come, my lord, I am bound.' 'I will unbind you,' he said, 'to your great loss.' With that the stranger tore the final chain away, smashed the stone coffin with a single kick, and seized the living corpse of the witch. He dragged her outside to the churchyard, where a great black horse stood waiting, its body covered with spikes. She was flung on to them with such force that she was pierced through. The rider leapt up, and all three vanished into the darkness. But it was said that the witch's screams and pleas for help on that dreadful night could be heard by people miles away.

student walked out of the pub . . . and never came back. But the landlord had the last laugh. When the story spread around, so many people came to see what kind of man could be taken in by such an old trick that his business doubled.

Bibury *Glos*

An Oxford student once offered to show the landlord of the old coaching inn, The Swan (which is still there), how to draw strong and mild ale from the same cask. He drilled a hole at one end of the cask and asked the landlord to stop it with his left hand. Then he drilled a hole at the other end, which the landlord stopped with his right hand. Leaving the landlord to hold on while he fetched the plugs, the

Bidford-on-Avon *Warks*

In the 16th century, so the story goes, the village was famous for its beer drinkers, who used to challenge teams from the neighbouring villages to drinking competitions. One day, Shakespeare came with a team from Stratford, but the Bidford men quickly out-drank them. They fell into a drunken sleep outside the village, and there they spent the night. Next morning, when his companions sug-

THE WAKES *The Bilston Wake celebrations were originally held in early November, but later they were switched to mid-summer so that outdoor activities could be enjoyed. Because the church grounds became a site for picnics, side-shows and other non-religious festivities, the Wakes were banished to the market-place. Here, bear-baiting, boxing, cock-fighting and heavy drinking replaced the earlier religious rituals. Many outsiders would arrive for a town's Wake, and eventually the festivities became so riotous that they were forbidden by the local authorities in the late 19th century*

gested renewing the contest, Shakespeare replied that he had had enough, having drunk at:

Piping Pebworth, dancing Marston,
Haunted Hillbro', hungry Grafton,
Dudging (ill-humoured) Exhall, papist Wicksford,
Beggarly Broom and drunken Bidford.

These places have been known as the Shakespeare villages ever since.

Bilston *Staffs*
An evil spirit which haunted a Bilston coal mine in the late 18th century so troubled the miners there that they called in a well-known exorcist known locally as 'The White Rabbit'. He made magic signs

THE NIGHT OF THE DEAD

During the Middle Ages, the Staffordshire town of Bilston, like many other towns and villages, held an annual Watch Service in honour of its patron saint, St Leonard. On the night before his Feast Day, November 6, the townspeople carried lighted candles into the local churchyard where they kept a vigil over the dead. The custom was known as 'waking' or 'the Wakes'.

After the Reformation in the 16th century, the yearly Wakes were moved to the town's market-place, and there the custom soon lost its religious meaning. The solemn ritual of guarding the dead by candle-light gave way to picnics, sporting contests and side-shows, and by the 19th century the observance of St Leonard's Feast Day, still known as a Wake, had become a holiday lasting several days. The festivities ranged from bull-baiting and a fun-fair to plays put on by strolling players. Heavy drinking bouts took place, and a poster advertising the nearby Tipton Wake in 1869 proclaimed that 'Flaming Gin, Sparkling Wine, Muddy Porter and Frothy Ale will be in active attendance'. It went on to state that each day would end 'in the usual way with Drunkenness, Brawling, Wife Beating, Empty Pockets and Aching Heads'.

The Bilston Carnival, first held in 1930, is an annual June event in which the spirit of the old Wake customs survives in a modern setting.

CANDLES AND GRAVES *The original Wakes were solemn religious gatherings in which villagers held services by candlelight in their local churchyards, and kept watch over the dead. These Watch Services took place on the eve of the feast day of the saint to whom the church was dedicated*

over them, and then told them to visit the pit at midnight. Their leader should carry a Bible in his right hand and a key in his left, and as the miners walked through the galleries they should repeat the spell: 'Matthew, Mark, Luke and John, God bless the errand we're come on.' They were also told to recite the Lord's Prayer backwards.

On the chime of midnight, the men marched into the mine. As they drew near the coal-face, the evil spirit rose up in front of them and began creeping menacingly towards them, seemingly un-affected by their spells. Suddenly, one of the miners noticed that Caggie, their leader, was holding the Bible in the wrong hand. 'Caggie, yow idiot!' he yelled, 'Put the buik in yer right 'ond.' Caggie did this, and the apparition vanished. All that was left was the acrid smell of brimstone.

Blackheath *W. Midlands*
Many of the traditional stories told in Blackheath and the surrounding villages describe the strange exploits of Aynuch and Ayli, two fictitious rebels through whom local people expressed their distaste for the grime and hardship of 19th-century indus-trial life. By turn, they are colliers, chain makers, nail makers, iron workers or engineers. Even today, though the conditions which gave birth to them are now a thing of the past, they have still not quite lost their hold on the Black Country imagination.

A KING'S HIDING PLACE
After Cromwell routed Charles II's army at the Battle of Worcester on September 3, 1651, the king fled north and sheltered for a night in Boscobel House, Salop. Next morning, fearing that the house would be searched, he moved on to Boscobel Forest.

For the rest of the day, he is said to have cowered among the topmost branches of an old tree, while Cromwell's Roundheads searched for him. At nightfall, he set off on the first stage of a journey which took him to Europe and nine years of exile, and ended only when he was restored to the throne on May 29, 1660.

Visitors to Boscobel can still see the secret room where he spent the night, as well as a 'Royal Oak' which is reputed to have grown from an acorn of the original tree in which he escaped capture

while he was away in London. On the second
occasion, in 1644, they captured and destroyed it.
Harley and Cromwell later quarrelled, and their
relationship remained turbulent until Cromwell
died on September 3, 1658. On this day, a great
storm raged through Brampton Bryan Park,
destroying so many trees that Harley swore that the
Devil had dragged Cromwell across the parkland
as he took him down to Hell. Tradition maintains
that every year, on September 3, the Devil returns
to rampage through the park with Cromwell's soul.

Brampton Bryan *Heref & Worcs*
During the Civil War, the lord of Brampton Bryan
Castle, Sir Robert Harley, at first sided with
Cromwell against the king, with the result that
Herefordshire Royalists twice besieged his castle

ST GEORGE AND THE DRAGON

*Just north of Brinsop church, north-west of Hereford, is a
field called Lower Stanks where St George is reputed to
have slain the dragon, and in the Duck's Pool Meadow just*
*south of the church is Dragon's Well. In the church
itself, on the north wall, is this 12th-century stone carving
which reconstructs St George's heroic battle*

Bromsgrove *Heref & Worcs*
The head of a boar appears on the coat-of-arms of
the Bromsgrove Town Council. A local legend
connects it with the mythical Sir Ryalas, known as
the Jovial Hunter, who is said to have been out
riding one day when he came across a wild-woman
sitting in a tree. She told him that a huge wild boar
had just killed her husband and 30 of his men, and
begged Sir Ryalas to kill the creature. So he blew
his hunting-horn to all four points of the compass
and the boar emerged from a dense thicket. After a
fierce and bloody battle, the animal fell dead at the
Jovial Hunter's feet. As he rode back to the place
where he had met the wild-woman, she ran to
meet him, shrieking 'You wicked man, you have
slain my pretty pig!', and began attacking him with
razor-sharp claws. Instantly, Sir Ryalas recognised
her as a sorceress, raised his battle-axe and split her
head in two. He later discovered that she had
changed her son into the boar, hoping that it
would gore him to death.

Callow *Heref & Worcs*
In the early part of the 19th century, several coach
passengers mysteriously disappeared when they
stayed overnight at a coaching inn near Callow Hill.
Eventually their bodies were discovered inside an
old house at the top of a nearby hill. After the
murderers had been tried and executed, the house
fell into disrepair and gradually crumbled away
until nothing was left of it. However, a ghost
house has occasionally been seen there since, and
one lady, who claimed to have seen the apparition
many times, reported that she had felt an almost
overwhelming sense of fear each time she saw it.

Canon Pyon *Heref & Worcs*
Close to Canon Pyon and the nearby village of
King's Pyon are two small hills, Pyon Hill and
Butthouse Knapp, about half a mile apart. They are
also called Robin Hood's Butts, and legend claims
that they were formed as the result of a wager
between Robin Hood and Little John. The two

men were standing near Brinsop, to the south, when Robin bet that he could jump over Wormesley Hill and land at Canon Pyon. As he jumped, he kicked a piece out of the hill with his heel and it landed where Butthouse Knapp now stands. Then Little John tried, and he too knocked a chunk out of Wormesley Hill, which landed half a mile further north and became Pyon Hill.

Child's Ercall *Salop*

Centuries ago, two local farmworkers were on their way to work one morning when they saw a strange creature rising dripping from a pond. They believed that it was the Devil (though they hardly stopped to look), and fled in terror. But as they ran the creature called after them, and its voice was that of a woman. They stopped and looked again, and discovered that their Devil was a mermaid.

The mermaid told them that there was treasure at the bottom of the pond, and that they could have as much of it as they liked if they were prepared to come into the pond and take it from her hands. So while she dived beneath the surface, they waded in until the water came almost up to their chins. When the mermaid reappeared cradling a lump of gold as large as a man's head, one of them was so amazed that he swore he had never had such luck in his life. It was a mistake he probably regretted for ever after. For when the mermaid heard his oath, she screamed and dived back. And neither the mermaid nor the treasure was ever seen again.

THE HOUSE THAT JACK BUILT

This beautiful half-timbered house was built in the pretty little village of Cherrington, in Salop, in 1635. Traditionally it is said to be the house immortalised in the nursery rhyme 'This is the house that Jack built', though curiously, no one seems to know who the real Jack was. The rhyme, which other authorities say is a version of an ancient Hebrew chant, was first published in 1755 in Nurse Truelove's New Year's Gift

'BREATHE DEEP, PULL HARD'

Chillington Hall park near Brewood, Staffs, was the site of one of the first zoos ever assembled in this country, the creation of a 16th-century nobleman, Sir John Gifford. One day, it is said, Sir John's favourite animal, a leopard, escaped, and arming himself with a crossbow Sir John set off with his son to look for it. To their horror they found it poised to pounce on an un-suspecting mother and child. In an instant Sir John drew his bow and took aim. His son cried out 'Prenez haleine, tirez fort' (breathe deep, pull hard), Sir John fired and the leopard fell dead.

Gifford's Cross, which can still be seen, was raised where the creature died, and Sir John adopted his son's words as the family motto

Cirencester *Glos*

In AD 879 Gurmund the Dane is said to have captured Cirencester from the Saxons by trapping a huge flock of sparrows, tying flaming twigs to them and releasing them to fly over the city. The walls burnt down, and Gurmund's Vikings marched in.

It may be that a memory of the Danish wars provides the explanation for an eerie story told about nearby Torbarrow Hill. Two men once discovered a chamber in the hill, lit by a candle. Inside, they saw a knight striking feebly at the light, and near him two embalmed bodies. On his third attempt, the knight managed to extinguish the candle. When soon afterwards, the men heard a long low moan, they were so terrified that they fled. The cave collapsed behind them, and the knight and mummies were buried for ever.

Church Stretton *Salop*

By tradition, while James II was travelling one day to Shrewsbury, the royal procession passed through a village called Stretton; the church was the first thing the king noticed and he christened the place Church Stretton. Two other nearby villages were also called Stretton. Of the first one, King James said, 'It's a very little Stretton', and so Little Stretton it became. The second one the king named All Stretton because, as he remarked, 'They're all Strettons in this part of the country'.

DEATH AND RESURRECTION IN THE HOP-YARDS

Today, machines have virtually taken over in Hereford and Worcester's hop-yards, and as the old methods are forgotten, so is the folklore which was associated with them. On the last day of picking, for example, the foreman (or busheller) and a woman were ritualistic-ally buried under hops in one of the cribs – the huge baskets in which the hops were collected. Then they were 'resurrected', by being tipped out. This custom was the last survival of a sacrificial rite supposed to promote the fertility of the next year's crops

Clodock *Heref & Worcs*

The village is named after St Clodack (or Clydawg), a 6th-century ruler of the region who was murdered by an enemy while out hunting. When the funeral procession reached the River Monnow, the oxen dragging the hearse refused to go on, and the ropes and chains miraculously snapped. Realising that this must be a sign from Heaven, Clodack's followers buried the saint beside the river, and built a church – St Clodack's – over his grave.

Colwall *Heref & Worcs*

No one knows for certain who left the huge block of limestone at the centre of the village, but some say that it was the Devil, and others that it was a giant from the Malvern Hills who suspected his wife of infidelity, and stoned her to death in Colwall. It is said too (though it only heightens the mystery) that the stone was dragged there in the late 19th century by a team of horses, to replace an earlier stone.

WHERE CARACTACUS WAS CAPTURED

An Iron Age hill fort on Hereford Beacon near Colwall, Hereford and Worcester, is traditionally the place where Caractacus, King of the Britons, made his last stand against the invading Romans in AD 50. The Britons lost the battle, and their broken king was taken captive and shipped to Rome, where he died soon afterwards

Darlaston *Staffs*

A Darlaston innkeeper called Moses Whitehouse, who was born *c.* 1779, is remembered in local legend as Rough Moey – a roughneck hero whose face was deeply pitted by smallpox and scarred by a pit explosion, and who had only one eye and one leg. He is unusual among folk heroes since the stories told about him are probably true.

Once, it is said, two Staffordshire bull terriers were put into an old sewer pit to fight, and bets were laid on the outcome. But they refused to do battle. Moey owned one of the dogs, so he leapt into the pit, crouched down on the ground and started to bait them. In fact, sewer gas had half-poisoned the dogs, and though Moey, by his antics, quickly provoked them into attacking him, soon all three of them collapsed. And Moey, more scarred than ever, was deemed the only loser.

Deerhurst *Glos*

Long ago, the people of Deerhurst lived in terror of a monstrous serpent, which poisoned men and cattle. Eventually, they appealed for help to the king, who promised a piece of land on Walton Hill to any man who could slay the beast. Attracted by the offer, a labourer named Smith agreed to try. He crept close to the dragon's lair, placed a trough of milk outside it, and waited. The creature drank the milk, and then fell asleep in the midday sun with its scales ruffled up. Smith took his axe, struck a mighty blow between the scales of the creature's neck and completely severed its head.

The Smiths held the land until the 16th century, and in the 18th century it was reported that a Mr Lane, who had married the widow of one of Smith's descendants, possessed the axe that was supposed to have slain the dragon. No one knows who owns the axe today, or if it even exists.

Dorstone *Heref & Worcs*

Arthur's Stone on Merbach Hill is reputed to mark the grave of a king who was foolish enough to start a fight with King Arthur. An alternative theory claims that it is Arthur himself who is buried there, and yet another, that the grave is that of a giant whom Arthur killed. There is uncertainty, too, about the marks on the stones beside the grave, which were made either by the giant's elbows as he fell dying, or by King Arthur's knees as he knelt in grateful prayer after the battle.

Not far from Merbach Hill, buried beneath a field, there is supposed to be a town that was engulfed by an earthquake many centuries ago. There is a pond in the field, and deep in the darkest part of it (so the story goes), you can still just see the top of a church steeple.

313

THE SACRIFICE OF
Lady Godiva

THE SIGHT THAT BLINDED PEEPING TOM *The earliest accounts of Godiva's ride say that she rode through the crowded market-place of Coventry veiled only by her long hair. But later versions claim that everyone stayed indoors behind shuttered windows, and that the one man who peeped, a tailor called Tom, was immediately blinded by the wrath of Heaven*

It seems unlikely that anyone ever saw the real Lady Godiva riding naked through the streets of Coventry, with the possible (but historically unprovable) exception of Peeping Tom. But from about 100 years after her death in 1067, the truth of the story was taken for granted, and the thought of the pious beauty naked on her horse has haunted the English imagination ever since. Over the centuries, writers, illustrators and actresses have tried to re-create the scene in every detail, and a visitor to Coventry today need look no further than Broadgate to see a modern replica of the sight which tradition insists struck Peeping Tom blind.

At this distance in time it is difficult to know what Lady Godiva really did to cause her name to be remembered for over 900 years. At least she existed; her real name was Godgifu, and she was married to Earl Leofric of Mercia, one of the four all-powerful lords who ruled England under the Danish king, Canute. She was also a rich landowner in her own right, and the most valuable of her properties was Coventry.

Godgifu was wise, virtuous and charitable. But her husband Leofric shared neither her religious convictions nor her fondness for the Midlands. He tyrannised the Church, and mercilessly squeezed the heregeld – an oppressive tax which paid for Canute's bodyguard – from the people of Coventry. According to the legend (which may not be far from the truth), when Godgifu begged him to change his ways, the exasperated earl replied that first she would have to ride naked through Coventry on market day. That, he was certain, was something that this modest woman would never do.

Proud humility

The earliest accounts of what happened on that extraordinary market day in Coventry some 900 years ago were written down in Latin by two monks at St Albans Abbey in Hertfordshire – Roger of Wendover in the 12th century and Matthew Paris in the early 13th century. Since the abbey stood on an important road junction, it seems likely that the monks first heard the story from travellers resting at the abbey on their way between the Midlands and London.

It is in these accounts that Leofric's challenge to his wife is first mentioned – and if history cannot entirely bear them out, it is at least possible that the historical Godiva performed some sort of public penance in Coventry for the misdeeds of her husband. It may be that she appeared in the streets stripped of her usual badges of rank, and that in the minds of her people the memory of this voluntary act of self-humiliation became mixed up with a Christian vision of Eve – naked and beautiful and bravely preserving her modesty by means of her long hair.

Leofric's change of heart

However the story began, by the time it reached Roger of Wendover it was beyond dispute that the beautiful Godiva had ridden naked through the market-place. And though most of the citizens of Coventry had been assembled there, Godiva's long hair had so thoroughly veiled her body that no one saw anything other than her face and 'her fair legs'. Leofric, so the story went, was so disconcerted by the whole incident, and accounted it so miraculous that no one had seen his wife's naked body, that he immediately 'freed' the town. That is, he remitted the hated heregeld and stopped persecuting the Church.

It is true that Leofric underwent some sort of religious conversion during his life. After he and Godiva had made up their differences, they founded a Benedictine monastery in Coventry, in which both were eventually buried. Sadly, not even the ruins of their joint creation remain.

By the 16th century, the story of Godiva's ride had changed – now, she was said to have sent messengers around the town instructing everyone to stay indoors and shutter their windows on the appointed day. Because she was so popular in the city, and every taxpayer stood to gain by her heroic act, the citizens of Coventry gladly did as they were asked.

It was the 17th-century antiquary William Camden who first mentioned the man who was to become as famous as Godiva herself – Peeping Tom. After a visit to Coventry in 1659, Camden said that he had been shown a statue there which represented a man who had been struck blind for peeping into the street as Godiva rode past. The statue was almost certainly the one now kept in the Leofric Hotel, and it may originally have been some sort of pagan city guardian. The Peeping Tom story was probably a joke explanation of its anguished expression and blank eyes – blank because the paint had long since worn off them.

The Coventry Fair

Quite apart from its natural fascination as a story, the Godiva legend was kept alive by the annual Coventry Fair. In the Corpus Christi Festival which was held until the Reformation, miracle plays were performed in the streets, with Adam and Eve among the characters. After the Reformation, the festival was banned, and it was not until 1678 that it was revived. From the start of the new-style fair, Lady Godiva was the central attraction. She rode through the streets on a snow-white horse, and though never so naked as the Godiva of legend (her costume sometimes even included an elaborate feather hat) her constant companion was a man whose chief skill lay in his ability to improvise rude gestures – an unrepentant Peeping Tom. The fair was last held in 1962, and since then it seems to have died out.

Godiva, a naked goddess?

A theory that is based more on wishful thinking than any real evidence links the Godiva legend with a far-off memory of pagan fertility rites presided over by a naked goddess. True, nakedness was practically obligatory in many pagan ceremonies, and strange magical powers were once ascribed to naked women. But it seems unnecessarily obscure to find a 'meaning' for Godiva among such dimly remembered beliefs, when the story hinges so neatly on the age-old argument about right and wrong that so nearly destroyed the marriage of Godgifu and Earl Leofric.

PEEPING TOM *The first hint that someone had actually seen Lady Godiva riding naked through Coventry, and had been struck blind for his temerity, did not come until some 600 years after the event was supposed to have taken place. The idea may have sprung from an attempt to explain the unseeing eyes and agonised expression of this strange wooden effigy, now in the Leofric Hotel. The true meaning of the figure is unknown*

Edge Hill *Warks*

On October 23, 1642, Charles I fought and lost the Battle of Edgehill, the first major action of the Civil War. Two months later on Christmas Eve, shepherds guarding their flocks on the battlefield, about 2 miles south-east of Kineton, were startled to hear the sound of fighting men, together with the crash of cannon and the ring of steel on steel. Terrified out of their wits by these noises, the shepherds were about to run when the phantom armies themselves appeared in the sky. Transfixed by fear, they watched the Battle of Edgehill refought by spectres.

When dawn brought an end to the performance, the shepherds hurried to Kineton, and told their story to the local magistrate and the parson. Both men visited the spot on the following night and saw the same spectral conflict. This amazing sight was seen several times, and when Charles heard the story, he sent six of his officers from Oxford. They too saw the unearthly combatants, and recognised friends who had been killed in the fight.

Ellesmere *Salop*

This small market town is set amongst nine lakes, the largest of which is the 116-acre Great Mere. There are two local legends to explain how this expanse of water appeared.

Both say that there was once a well in a field near the town, from which all the inhabitants were permitted to draw water. In one legend, the farm to which the well belonged changed hands, and the new tenant refused to let anyone draw water. Retribution was swift, for one morning when the tenant's wife went to fetch water, she found that the whole field had become a lake. As a punishment for his churlish conduct, the tenant was forced to continue paying rent for the now useless land.

In the second story, the well was the only source of water for the townsfolk of Ellesmere, and a new landowner imposed a charge for every bucketful. The people prayed that God might redress their wrongs, and one night the water in the well rose until it flooded the land. From that day, everyone had free water in abundance.

CARVINGS AT FAIRFORD

Apart from its beautiful stained glass, St Mary's at Fairford also contains a series of wood carvings on the choir stalls depicting episodes of 15th-century life. The two entwined wyverns illustrated – mythical beasts of heraldry – were included because a wyvern appears in the crest of John Tame, the builder of the church

Endon *Staffs*

Though well-dressing is common in Derbyshire, Endon is the only place in Staffordshire where the custom, which is probably based on pagan well-worship, still survives. The present ceremony takes place during the Spring Bank Holiday and has been re-enacted almost every year since the custom was revived in 1845. It includes the coronation of a Well-Dressing Queen, who is actually crowned four times – on the Saturday afternoon following a church service, early on Saturday evening, and twice on the Monday.

A village fête and fair is held on Monday, at the same time as the Dressing, when Morris dancing and a rural competition known as Tossing the Sheaf take place. A heavy sheaf of corn was once used and heaved by pitchfork over a bar which was gradually raised. Since the introduction of combine harvesters, which do not produce sheaves, a 15 lb. sack of straw has been used instead; it is pitched in the same way.

Essington *Staffs*

A strange hollow brass statuette known as Jack of Hilton used to be kept at Hilton Hall, Essington, near Wolverhampton, where it played a part in a feudal ceremony of homage which the Lord of Essington owed to the Lord of Hilton. The figure is believed to be an Etruscan fertility symbol, brought to this country by the Romans, but how it came to be involved in the ceremony is not known.

Jack of Hilton is 12 in. tall and kneels on its left knee. It has a tiny hole in its mouth and a larger hole in its back through which the figure can be filled with water. When the statuette is set on a fire, steam blasts through the mouth.

The ceremony in which it was used required the Lord of Essington or his steward to bring a goose to Hilton Hall, where it was driven round the fire three times while Jack of Hilton, boiling away on the blaze, blew on the fire. The lord or his deputy then carried the goose to the kitchen, where it was killed and cooked before being placed before the Lord of Hilton, who gave the Lord of Essington a dish of meat in return.

Until recently, Jack was owned by the Vernon family, who inherited both the Essington and Hilton estates by marriage in 1562. The figure has now passed to a private house in Wiltshire, while Hilton Hall is used as an old people's home.

Fairford *Glos*

The well-preserved medieval stained glass, which makes St Mary's Church unique amongst parish churches in England, was installed by John Tame, a rich merchant whose monument stands within the church. The story goes that Tame was a part-time pirate who looted the stained glass from a Flemish ship and installed it in the church for the good of his soul. The truth is more prosaic, for John Tame completely rebuilt the church in the last 30 years of the 15th century, and probably imported Flemish craftsmen to make the glass. Medieval preoccupation with the terrors of Hell and the after-life are vividly and horrifyingly depicted in the Last Judgment window.

Fairford was also the home of a number of witches who from sheer malice used their magic to imprison market-bound pedlars at the Poulton crossroads. They would only release them in the evening when it was too late for the pedlars to sell their goods. The witches died long ago, but some people believe that they still haunt the crossroads, which is also known as Betty's Grave. Betty, a local girl, poisoned herself and, like many suicides, was buried at the crossroads as a means of confusing her restless, earthbound spirit.

FAIR ROSAMUND

An illustration from an 18th-century broadsheet shows Fair Rosamund, mistress of Henry II, confronted by Queen Eleanor and the choice of death by dagger or poison

Frampton on Severn *Glos*

A strip of grass in the village is known as Rosamund's Green, after Rosamund Clifford, mistress of Henry II, who was born at nearby Clifford Castle. According to legend, Henry hid his 'Fair Rosamund' in a house at the centre of a maze in Woodstock Park, Oxfordshire. The king's jealous queen, Eleanor, drugged the knight who held the secret of the route through the maze and found it marked by a silken thread. Confronting her husband's terrified mistress, Eleanor gave the girl the choice of death 'by the dagger or the bowl' – knife or poison. Rosamund chose poison. In fact, she is thought to have died a natural death, and was probably buried at Godstow, Oxon, in 1176.

RICHES THROUGH REGICIDE

Gloucester is one of the most ancient cities in England. It is believed to have been founded around 2000 BC by Iberian settlers, and was later inhabited in turn by Britons, Romans, Saxons and Normans. The town is centred round the cathedral, in which Cromwell reputedly billeted his troops, who passed their leisure throwing stones through the medieval stained-glass windows.

Curiously, Gloucester's religious tradition was enhanced by regicide. After the murder of Edward II in Berkeley Castle in 1327, the abbots of Bristol and Malmesbury refused to accept the king's body, because they feared the anger of his queen, Isabella, who had been involved in her husband's murder. Abbot Tholsey of Gloucester, however, took the body and buried it near the high altar of St Mary's Abbey, where it quickly became an attraction for pilgrims. The abbey prospered and was soon enlarged into a major cathedral, while the abbeys at Bristol and Malmesbury fell into decline.

Many rural traditions of Gloucestershire are preserved in a museum in the building where the Protestant bishop, John Hooper, was imprisoned before he was burnt at the stake in the town by Mary Tudor in 1555.

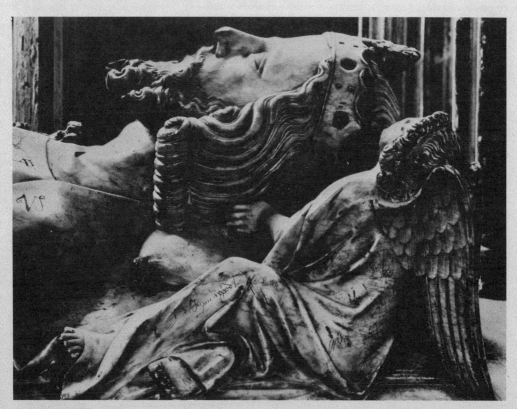

GLOUCESTER'S TAILOR *When Beatrix Potter, the children's writer, was staying in the neighbourhood she heard the local story of the Tailor of Gloucester, whose unfinished suit was sewed for him by elves or hobs. Beatrix Potter replaced the fairies with mice, who help the sick tailor with his work, and produced her own immortal version of the story*

PAIN REFLECTED IN STONE *In Berkeley Castle, in 1327, Edward II was tortured to death with a red-hot iron. His splendid tomb surmounted by his effigy (above) in Gloucester Cathedral was raised by his son Edward III. The effigy's face, twisted in anguish, is said to have been copied from a death mask on which the king's final moments of agony were indelibly imprinted.*

Though unloved by his subjects during his life, the manner of Edward II's death gained him the reputation of a martyr. His body was brought from Berkeley Castle to Gloucester on a horse-drawn wagon, but shortly afterwards it was said that it had been carried to Gloucester by stags – a story that may have arisen from the special sanctity that was attached to deer

Goodrich *Heref & Worcs*

The ruins of 12th-century Goodrich Castle are haunted by two lovers who died during the Civil War. In 1646, Alice Birch eloped with Charles Clifford, and the couple were given refuge in the castle by their Royalist friends. While they were there, the stronghold was besieged by Roundhead troops under Colonel Birch, Alice's uncle, and the two lovers drowned in the River Wye while attempting to escape. Their ghosts have since been seen trying to cross the river on a phantom horse.

Great Ness *Salop*

Kynaston's Cave, in the side of Nesscliffe Hill near Great Ness, is reputed to have been the hideout of a legendary 15th-century outlaw called Wild Humphrey Kynaston. Like Robin Hood, he stole from the rich and gave to the poor. He earned himself so much local goodwill that he never ran short of food, either for himself or for his remarkable horse. Not only was his horse shod backwards, to mislead anyone who pursued him, but it also once jumped 9 miles from Nesscliffe Hill to Ellesmere after one of the outlaw's daring robberies. On another occasion, it carried Kynaston to safety by leaping over the River Severn at a point now called Kynaston's Leap, where the river is 40 ft wide. It was rumoured by his enemies that Kynaston had sold his soul to the Devil, and some even said that his horse was the

THE LIFE AND DEATH OF GUY OF WARWICK

Among the wooded sandstone cliffs which tower above the River Avon at Guy's Cliffe, just north of Warwick, is the cave in which Guy of Warwick, a legendary 10th-century hero, is said to have ended his days as a hermit. Guy began life as a page to the Earl of Warwick, and fell in love with the earl's beautiful daughter, Felice. She vowed to marry him if he would prove his love for her by heroic and noble actions, and

Guy at once set off in search of adventure. Within days he had fought and killed the Wild Dun Cow, a creature 18 ft long and 12 ft tall which was terrorising Dunsmore Heath near Stretton-on-Dunsmore. The creature had originally been a white fairy cow which appeared during a famine and seemed able to provide an endless supply of milk. But one day a witch milked it dry, and the cow became a man-eating killer.

ENGLAND'S SAVIOUR *After many years away in the Holy Land, Guy returned to England to find that Ethelstan, King of Britain, was besieged at Winchester by the Danes. It was arranged that the battle should be decided by single combat between Guy and the Danish champion, Colbrand. After a fierce struggle, Guy brought the Danish warrior to his knees and decapitated him, whereupon the entire Danish army fled and England was saved. Spurning all rewards from the grateful king, Guy went north to Warwick and spent the rest of his life as a hermit in a cave at Guy's Cliffe, where his wife Felice finally found him as he lay dying*

TO PROVE HIS LOVE *Spurred on by his love for the Earl of Warwick's daughter, Felice, Guy roamed all over Europe performing prodigious feats of strength and courage. He went to France and, in two battles at Louvain, killed 13,000 men single-handed. In Turkey, he fought many bloody battles against the Saracens, and also found time to slay a monstrous boar whose head is said to have weighed a hundredweight. Once, he slew a dragon that was about to devour a lion, and for many days afterwards the lion was his faithful travelling companion. When he finally returned to England, he was the most famous warrior in the land. After slaying a savage dragon in Northumberland, he was met at Lincoln by Felice and at last they were married. Felice's father died soon after the wedding and left all his estates to Guy, who became the new Earl of Warwick. But Felice was fated to spend the rest of her life alone. After his marriage, Guy felt so grateful to God for making his life successful that he set off on a pilgrimage to the Holy Land*

A LAST EMBRACE *Two weeks after Guy died in her arms, the heart-broken Felice jumped from the top of Guy's Cliffe to her death in the River Avon*

Devil himself. Having successfully evaded every attempt to capture him, Wild Humphrey Kynaston ended his life by dying peacefully in his cave.

Hentland *Heref & Worcs*

Hentland church is dedicated to the 5th-century churchman St Dubricius, who is depicted on a stained-glass window with a hedgehog (symbol of the former county of Hereford) at his feet. Dubricius's mother, Eurddil, was the daughter of Peibau, King of Archenfield, who was known as King Dribbler because of his uncontrollable foaming at the mouth. Legend states that one day King Dribbler returned to Madley, near Hereford, from a hunting expedition and noticed that Eurddil, though still unmarried, was pregnant. He immediately ordered that she was to be drowned in the River Wye. She was tied up in a sack and thrown into the water, but the current washed her ashore. Her executioners threw her back in several times, but each time the river saved her life. The king then sentenced her to be burnt alive, and she was thrown on to a blazing pyre. The next morning messengers were sent to recover her bones, only to find her sitting unharmed among the ashes with the infant Dubricius in her lap. When mother and child were taken before the king, he had a change of heart and warmly embraced them. And when Dubricius touched his grandfather's face, the king's malady vanished at once, and he never again foamed at the mouth.

On Palm Sunday, after the service at Hentland church, small cakes stamped with the slogan 'Peace and good neighbourhood' are distributed among the congregation. They are called Pax Cakes, and the custom was begun in the 18th century by a local farmer. He hoped that it would stop the centuries-old feuding between local families of Celtic, Saxon and Norman descent.

Hereford *Heref & Worcs*

Ethelbert is the patron saint of Hereford Cathedral, which stands on the site of a shrine erected to his memory by Offa, King of the Mercians, in AD 795. By tradition, Ethelbert fell in love with Offa's daughter, Alfrida, and they were engaged to be married; but Alfrida's mother, Queen Cynethryth, became so jealous of her daughter's happiness that she persuaded Offa to murder Ethelbert. In 794, on the eve of his wedding, Ethelbert arrived at Offa's palace and was shown into the hall where the king was waiting. The doors were immediately locked and one of Offa's nobles, Winebert, stepped forward and struck off Ethelbert's head with his sword. The disposal of the head and body proved troublesome, however, for wherever they were buried miraculous lights appeared above the grave. The news of this so distressed Offa that he finally went on a pilgrimage to Rome to expiate his crime.

When the saint's body was taken to Hereford for re-burial, a spring gushed up at a spot where it had briefly touched the ground. The spring became known as St Ethelbert's Well, and its site is marked near the entrance to Castle Green.

The shrine of another saint, Thomas de Cantilupe, is in the north transept of the cathedral. Thomas was Bishop of Hereford from 1275–82, and he died while returning from Rome where he had gone to seek the pope's support in a quarrel he was having with the Archbishop of Canterbury. Thomas's bones were brought to Hereford and placed in a shrine, which at once became the focus of a whole series of miracles. Within the next 25 years, it is said that 420 miracles took place, including 66 cases of bringing the dead back to life. In 1320, Thomas was canonised by the pope.

THE MURDERED KING

In AD 794, Offa, King of Mercia, promised his daughter Alfrida in marriage to Ethelbert, who was then King of East Anglia. Legend says that the sun went dark and the earth shook at the start of Ethelbert's journey to Offa's palace at Sutton Walls, near Marden. And before arriving at the palace, Ethelbert had a dream in which his bridal bed was destroyed while his mother watched, weeping tears of blood. The omens proved to be well founded, for Offa had Ethelbert beheaded on the night before the wedding. The brass-rubbing of Ethelbert (above) is taken from Hereford Cathedral

A WITCH'S CURSE

A doll found buried in Hereford in 1960 was the effigy of someone whom a local witch had once cursed, for tucked into its skirt was a spell which read: 'I act this spell upon you from my whole heart, wishing you to never rest nor eat nor sleep the restern part of your life. I hope your flesh will waste away and I hope you will never spend another penny I ought to have.' The doll is now in the Hereford City Library Museum

Ilmington *Warks*

In the past, the villagers of Ilmington seem to have been given to expressing themselves in rhyme, for verses recording some of their old traditions are remembered to this day. One verse recalls their rivalry with the villagers of nearby Ebrington, whom they dubbed Yebbington mawms, a local word meaning fools:

Master Southam, a man of great power,
Lent a horse and cart to muck the church tower.
They mucked the tower to make it grow high,
But not as lofty as the sky,
And when the muck began to sink,
They swore the tower had grown an inch.

Another rhyme was originally pinned to the effigy of a man who had given false evidence at a famous murder trial in 1848. The villagers hanged the effigy from a poplar in Crow Yard, by the village green, and condemned the perjurer with the words:

This old bloke to Warwick went
False witness for to be.
James Blomfield Rush
Was for murder hung,
This man for perjury.

Kentchurch *Heref & Worcs*

The mythical hero Jack o' Kent reputedly lived in this neighbourhood, and is buried in nearby Grosmont churchyard. One day, legend claims, Jack persuaded the Devil to help him build a bridge across the River Monnow, between Kentchurch and Grosmont, by agreeing that the Devil could have the soul of the first person to cross the bridge. As soon as the bridge was built, Jack threw a bone over the river. This enticed a hungry dog and the Devil found himself its new owner.

At Kentchurch Court, a private house which dates in part from the 14th century, there is a cellar where Jack is supposed to have stabled his magic horses, and a bedroom where his ghost still walks on stormy nights. It may be that his soul is eternally damned, for on his deathbed he ordered that his liver and lights should be impaled on Kentchurch (or perhaps Grosmont) church steeple. He said that a dove and a raven would come to fight over them, and that his soul would only be saved if the dove won. Curiously, no one now remembers how the battle ended.

Kidderminster *Heref & Worcs*

A white witch called Becky Swan lived in Worcester Street, Kidderminster, in the mid-19th century, and she is supposed to have had extraordinary healing powers and an uncanny ability to find lost property. But the manner of her death cast some doubt on her goodness. One day, it is said, an enormous black cat appeared in the village, and the local dogs fled howling as it stalked towards Becky's front door. It clawed at the door until Becky, who had suddenly turned as pale as a corpse, came to let it in.

From time to time during the next three days, the cat was seen around the cottage. But on the fourth day, the door had been barred and locked, no smoke came from the chimney, and Becky and her strange visitor seemed to have disappeared without trace. Eventually, her neighbours broke down the door, and went inside. They were just in time to see the cat leap from the hearthrug and vanish up the chimney. All that remained of Becky was a pile of ashes on the floor.

Kington *Heref & Worcs*

Thomas Vaughan, who lies buried with his wife in a tomb in Kington church, is remembered in local legend as Black Vaughan, a wicked tyrant while he

BLACK VAUGHAN AND GETHEN THE TERRIBLE

Effigies of Thomas Vaughan and his wife lie in the Vaughan chapel in Kington church. After his death, Thomas became known as Black Vaughan, an evil spirit which terrorised the surrounding countryside until a priest finally exorcised his spirit in the church. Black Vaughan's wife was equally infamous and is remembered in local legend as Gethen the Terrible

lived and an evil spirit after death. The ghost of Black Vaughan, who died at the Battle of Banbury in 1469, turned over farm carts, changed into a fly to torment horses and even haunted Kington church in the form of a bull. Twelve parsons, called in to exorcise the spirit by prayer, combined their skills to shrink it until it could be imprisoned in a snuff box. Eleven failed, but the twelfth, whose courage may have been related to his reputation as a drinker, persevered until the spirit shrank into the box. This was immediately thrown into nearby Hergest Pool, after which Black Vaughan's spirit ceased to trouble the district.

Vaughan's wife had an equally bad reputation. She became known as Gethen the Terrible after assassinating a man who had killed her brother. Dressing as a man, she took a bow and arrows and entered an archery tournament, in which her brother's killer was competing. At point blank range, she shot an arrow into his heart and in the resulting confusion succeeded in making her escape.

The family home of the Vaughans was Hergest Court, and the house was said to be haunted by a black dog which appeared whenever a member of the Vaughan family was about to die.

Kinlet *Salop*
Before his death in 1581, the squire of Kinlet, Sir George Blount, swore that he would haunt his daughter Dorothy and her descendants because she had married a page boy. Apparently, he kept his word. On several occasions he returned from the grave in a spectral coach drawn by four white horses, and drove straight across the dining-room table at the Hall as Dorothy and her family sat down to dinner. His spectre is also said to have frightened the women of the village away from the pool where they did their washing.

Sir George was a persistent ghost, and when the old Hall was pulled down in 1720 local people were sure that he had made it untenable. Eventually, a party of clergymen exorcised his vengeful spirit and imprisoned it in a bottle. By one account this was cast in the sea; by another it was left under Sir George's monument in Kinlet church, with a warning that anyone who broke the bottle would release the ghost. The bottle is said to have remained there until the 1890's, when the church was restored. Today, the effigy of Sir George can still be seen in the church, kneeling alongside his wife, son, and daughter Dorothy, whose marriage so angered him in life and death.

Knockin *Salop*
Long ago, one Thomas Elkes fled from Knockin after drowning his brother's child in a tub of water. But two ravens prevented him from escaping by giving away his hiding-place as he slept under a haystack at South Mimms in Hertfordshire. Elkes was brought back to the scene of his crime and hanged in chains on Knockin Heath.

Leigh *Heref & Worcs*
The ghost of Edmund Colles used to ride here in a coach drawn by four horses that breathed fire. At the foot of the steep hill by St Edburga's Church, the phantom coach used to take a flying leap over the tithe barn at Leigh Court and plunge into the River Teme beyond.

In real life, Colles was conscience-stricken by an attempt he had made one night to rob a friend whom he knew to be bringing money from Worcester. In the dark, his friend slashed out at Colles with his sword as Colles grabbed his horse. When the friend returned home, he was horrified to discover that a severed hand wearing Colles's signet ring was still grasping his bridle. Next day, he found Colles at his home in Leigh, bearing the marks of the dreadful wound. Colles confessed to the crime and begged his friend's forgiveness, which was freely given.

Colles died from his wounds soon afterwards, and his guilty spirit roamed the countryside until 12 clergymen exorcised it at a midnight service. They laid it in a local pond, which they filled in afterwards. The tithe barn still stands at Leigh Court, and members of the Colles family are buried at St Edburga's Church. The tomb to William Colles, Edmund's father, is surrounded by effigies of his 12 children, including Edmund.

Leominster *Heref & Worcs*
Merewald, a 7th-century king of Mercia whose fierce behaviour earned him the nickname Lion, had a dream one night in which a Christian missionary brought him some important news. At the same time, a hermit called Ealfrid dreamt that a lion was eating out of his hand. The king and the hermit met in the place now called Leominster – legend says named after the 'Lion' king – and in the course of their conversation, they described their dreams. Merewald was so impressed that he became a Christian, and founded a church and convent at Leominster in AD 658.

The legend gives one explanation of Leominster's name, and the story is carved in stone on the west door of the Norman Church of St Peter and St Paul. But another theory says that the town is named after Earl Leofric, who was the husband of Lady Godiva, and who died in 1057.

Lickey Hills *Heref & Worcs*
The Devil and his chief huntsman Harry-ca-nab, mounted on white bulls, used to hunt wild boars by night on the Lickey Hills, near Bromsgrove, with a pack of hounds which the Devil kept at Halesowen. The night sky was also haunted by the Seven Whistlers, which some people claimed were seven of the Devil's hounds, while others said that they were six birds of fate in search of a seventh. If ever they found it, the world would end. This belief is still widely held by older people throughout the county.

Little Comberton *Heref & Worcs*
A labourer was once employed on a local farm and his skills seemed to the farmer to be little short of miraculous. With one blow of his flail he could thresh a sheaf of corn – a job which would take most men half-a-dozen blows at least. And when he was asked to throw down sheaves from the top of the stack, he worked so fast that the farmer, who had taken over the flailing, found it impossible to keep up with him.

Puzzled by this, the farmer went to a local cunning man, and learnt that, in the cunning man's opinion, his employee was none other than the Devil. He was advised that if he valued his life, he would get rid of the stranger at once, by giving him a job which he was unable to do. But this was far from easy: the Devil was able to count the threshed grains of corn, could fill a water barrel with a sieve, and on another occasion, mowed a field which the farmer had filled with iron spikes in an attempt to deter Old Nick.

In desperation, the farmer asked the advice of a passing gipsy, who told him to take a curly hair from his wife's head and to tell the Devil to hammer it straight on the local blacksmith's anvil. The more the Devil hammered, the curlier the hair became, and in the end he gave up, vanished from the farm and was never seen again.

THE WAYFARING
Gipsies

'CROSS MY PALM WITH SILVER' *Gipsy women are popularly believed to be exceptionally gifted in the arts of magic and divination, and gipsy fortune-tellers explore future events using crystal balls, tea leaves and playing cards, as well as astrology and palmistry. Gipsies are also thought to be able to charm away warts and cure horses by magic, and to be skilled in making highly potent herbal remedies, love potions and aphrodisiacs*

The unspoilt wilderness of Gloucestershire's Forest of Dean, once called 'the Queen of Forests all', has attracted gipsy families ever since these passionately independent nomads first arrived in Britain early in the 16th century. They called themselves 'Dukes of Little Egypt' and so became known as 'gipsies', but modern research has shown that their native tongue, Romany, stems from Sanskrit, a language of ancient India. This, together with other evidence, indicates that gipsies originally came from northern India during the 10th century AD. Their rootless way of life aroused so much hostility amongst British people that, in 1530, it became a criminal offence merely to be a gipsy, and many of them were executed until the laws were changed in 1784.

The first gipsies

During the centuries after they left India, gipsy tribes drifted westwards across Europe where, though retaining their fierce independence, many of their beliefs were influenced by Christian thinking. This is reflected in the myths about the origins of their race. One legend claims that they are the descendants of the first murderer, Cain, while others relate that gipsies refused to help the Virgin Mary during her flight into Egypt, or that a gipsy forged the three nails that were used in Christ's crucifixion. The recurrent theme of these stories is that gipsies are forever doomed to wander the earth as a punishment for the terrible sins of their ancestors.

In a happier tale of gipsy origins, *o Del* (God) made the first man out of chalk and baked him in an oven, but forgot to take him out in time and overcooked him, producing the first Negro. So *o Del* made another man, but this time he took him from the oven too soon, so creating the first white man. On his third attempt *o Del* succeeded in baking a nicely browned man, and he became the first gipsy.

In gipsy legends, the Earth (*De Develeski*) is the Divine Mother of all existence. She is the supreme gipsy deity, more important even than God, who only came into being when the earth had already been formed. This is perhaps not surprising in a people who live an outdoor life close to nature.

Romany magic

Superstition, coupled with a strong belief in the supernatural, occupies a vital role in gipsy communities. They believe that evil spirits constantly roam the night searching for victims, and among the charms which they carry for protection against them are small holed stones, the breastbones of jays and kingfishers, and four-leaf clovers. The 'Evil Eye', a bewitchment caused by being stared at with hostility, is greatly feared, and talismans made of bead-like fossils called 'adderstones' are worn to dispel its strange power. To dream of blood or snakes, to hear dogs howling, and to meet a donkey, a squint-eyed woman or a funeral on the open road are all considered to be bad omens. On the other hand, good luck is associated with the moon, little green frogs, pieces of coral, falling stars and white horses, as well as certain precious stones worn with the wearer's zodiacal sign.

Life and death on the road

Traditionally, a gipsy girl shows that she is attracted to a man by throwing a coin-filled cake over a hedge to him. If a man wears two red handkerchiefs on his jacket, and a girl takes one, the couple are said to be betrothed. Marriage ceremonies vary; the couple may publicly jump over a broom together or clasp hands while bread and salt are sprinkled over them as a tribal elder declares them married. After the gipsy rites the newlyweds usually go through a civil ceremony, followed by the traditional gipsy feast which often lasts for days.

Gipsy women are held to be *mochardi* (unclean) for a month and a day after they give birth to a child. The bed on which the baby was born is afterwards burnt, and the mother is not allowed to cook or touch anyone's food except her own. During this ritual quarantine she has to sleep in a separate tent or wagon, and all males are forbidden to eat with her or to enter her sleeping quarters. This includes her husband, who is not allowed to touch his child until after the christening.

Death, like birth, must always take place outside the family caravan, and the dying are taken outdoors shortly before they pass away. After gipsies die, their most valuable possessions, along with gold coins or lucky amulets, are placed in their coffins to ensure that they have a comfortable existence beyond the grave. Some gipsies still burn the dead person's caravan so that his spirit will not become jealous of anyone who might live in it, and haunt them in the form of a ghostly vampire.

Mara's violin

Vampires, ghosts and demons figure so prominently in gipsy folklore that even their favourite instrument, the violin, is said to be the Devil's own creation. Legend tells that a beautiful gipsy girl, Mara, fell in love with a *gorgio* (non-gipsy) who was impervious to her charms. In despair, Mara sold the souls of her family to the Devil in exchange for his help. Satan turned her father into a sound-box, her four brothers into strings, and her mother into a bow. Out of their six souls was born the violin. Mara learnt to play the wonderful instrument and soon the handsome *gorgio* fell in love with her. Then Satan reappeared and carried them both off to Hell. The violin was dropped and left behind, until one day a poor gipsy boy found the magical instrument; since then gipsies and violins have been inseparable.

VANISHING VALUES *Traditional gipsy life is rapidly changing. Colourful horse-drawn wagons are giving way to motorised caravans in gipsy camps*

A BRIEF ROMANY VOCABULARY

Although gipsies have generally remained aloof from conventional society, their language, Romany, has been influenced by many foreign tongues and is divided into several dialects. As well as adopting foreign slang, the gipsies have used certain English surnames. They also have a secret sign language, using grass and leaves, called *patrin*.

Atchin-tans: Stopping-places
Chavi: A child
Chor, choring: To steal
Diddikai: A half-breed gipsy
Dordi: Dear, used affectionately
Gorgio: A non-gipsy
Gavver: Police
Grai: A horse
Jukel: A dog
Kitchemir: A pub, tavern
Kushti: Good
Lovel: Money
Mochardi: Unclean, unwholesome
Mumpers: Collective term for the different kinds of travellers
Mus: A man
o Bengh: The Devil
o Del: God
Ogg: A shilling, five new pence
Rackli: A girl
Rai: A gentleman
Rawnie: A lady
Vardo: A living wagon, caravan
Yog: A fire

Long Compton *Warks*

'There are enough witches in Long Compton to draw a load of hay up Long Compton Hill,' runs an old saying. Local belief in witches existed at least until late in the 19th century, when a man accused of murdering a woman in the village claimed that he had killed her because she had bewitched him. Sixteen other witches in the district deserved the same fate, he added.

Legend says that the Rollright Stones, a prehistoric stone circle on a ridge near the village, are actually a king and his army who were turned into stone by a witch to prevent the king from becoming master of all England.

An effigy in the church is traditionally associated with St Augustine, who is supposed to have preached there in AD 604. It is said that when he commanded that no excommunicated person could attend mass, a dead man arose from his grave and left the churchyard.

Long Lawford *Warks*

The ghost of a one-armed man used to haunt Lawford Hall, which stood on a site now occupied by The Hall farm. In Elizabethan times Lawford Hall belonged to the Boughton family, one of whom had lost an arm. It was his ghost that haunted the house, and even travelled round the neighbouring district by coach and six.

Twelve clergymen were enlisted at some unspecified time to exorcise the ghost, and they claimed to have achieved the feat by capturing him in a bottle. But the one-armed spectre was not easily contained. He continued to be seen in the area until late in the 19th century, long after Lawford Hall was demolished.

HOW EDWARD THE CONFESSOR ENTERED PARADISE

These medieval stained-glass windows in the Church of St Laurence, at Ludlow, Salop, relate how Edward the Confessor earned salvation six months before his death in 1066 by his kindness to a beggar. The beggar, so the story goes, was actually St John the Evangelist, *who had been given a ring by Edward when he had asked the king for alms. Soon afterwards St John met two pilgrims near Ludlow and he asked them to return the ring to Edward, together with the message that six months later the king would meet him again in paradise*

Malvern Hills *Heref & Worcs*

The shadow of Raggedstone Hill, one of the Malvern Hills, is said to bring misfortune to anyone upon whom it falls. This superstition began in the Middle Ages with the death of a monk from a nearby priory (probably the 12th-century Little Malvern Priory, one of two local priory churches).

As penance for a misdeed, the monk had to crawl up Raggedstone Hill daily on his hands and knees. The punishment continued until his limbs were raw and festered, and he became so weak he was barely able to drag himself up the hill. In torment he cursed his persecutors below, and cried: 'May all upon whom the shadow of this stone falls die untimely as I do.' Whereupon he fell dead.

Marden *Heref & Worcs*

Before Marden church was built in the 14th century, an earlier church stood by the River Lugg. A bell which once fell from this church into the river is said to have been seized by a mermaid. Since she would not return the bell, the parishioners tried to retrieve it while she was asleep. But their plan failed when one man spoke too loudly and awoke the mermaid, who promptly hid the bell in a pool. The bell was never recovered, though sometimes it has been heard tolling beneath the water, echoing the other church bells.

St Ethelbert was for a time buried on the present site of Marden church. The water of St Ethelbert's Well, now within the church, reputedly gushed forth miraculously from the grave when his body was later taken to Hereford Cathedral.

Meon Hill *Warks*

The Devil is reputed to have once thrown a huge clod of earth at the newly built abbey at Evesham, Worcestershire, intending to destroy it. Fortunately, St Egwin, Bishop of Worcester, who had founded the abbey in 717, was watching. His prayers were able to stop the missile, which fell to the ground and became Meon Hill.

Middle Tysoe *Warks*

A gigantic horse, 300 ft long and 210 ft high, cut through the turf into the red soil has given its name to the Red Horse Vale. Legend says that the horse was cut to commemorate the action of Richard Neville, the 'Kingmaker' Earl of Warwick, during the Wars of the Roses. Declaring that he wished to fight on equal terms with his men, he slew his horse before the Battle of Towton in 1461 and achieved victory on foot.

Scouring the Red Horse each year on Palm Sunday, the anniversary of the battle, became an occasion for local festivity; but this lapsed in the 19th century and the horse became overgrown. The figure, which is the largest of five Red Horses of Tysoe, is cut on a hill opposite Tysoe church. Another Red Horse, cut in the 18th century, is visible on Rising Sun Hill.

Minsterley *Salop*

Wild Edric, the hero of Welsh border rebellions against William the Conqueror, is said to ride out when war threatens Britain. Just before the Crimean War, a man and his daughter declared they saw him galloping past Minsterley.

The date of Edric's death and his burial place are both unknown; tradition says he did not die at all. Instead, as punishment for making peace with the Conqueror in 1070, he and his men are condemned to haunt the Shropshire lead mines. Miners who heard them knocking on the walls in the mines, considered the sounds to be an omen of a good mineral lode near by.

MUCH MARCLE'S RARE EFFIGY

Wooden effigies are rare, and this example in the parish church at Much Marcle is one of the only two around Hereford, the other being at Clifford. The figure is in civilian dress of the 14th century, and it is thought to represent Walter de Helyon, a local landowner of that time. There is an old belief that it was once carried at the head of all funerals in the parish

325

Much Wenlock *Salop*

Wenlock Edge is a limestone escarpment south-west of Much Wenlock. South of its highest point is Ippikin's Rock, a cliff which is named after a robber who lived in a cave in the cliffside. It is said that he and his stolen treasure were buried in the cave by a landslide. In the unlikely event that anyone should stand there and shout 'Ippikin! Ippikin! Keep away with your long chin!', he will be pushed over the cliff by Ippikin's ghost.

Newport *Salop*

Chetwynd Park lies about a mile north of the town of Newport, and during the mid-18th century it was the home of the Pigott family. Shortly before the birth of Madam Pigott's first child, a doctor warned her husband that he must choose between saving the baby or the mother. Pigott callously replied 'One should lop the root to save the branch', but in the event, both mother and child died together. For many years afterwards their ghosts appeared on moonlit nights, haunting the park and nearby roads. Cheney Hill, within the park, is known as Madam Pigott's Hill because she was so often seen combing her baby's hair there. But in 1850, 12 parsons combined to exorcise the phantoms, which have not been seen since.

Norton in Hales *Salop*

Until the beginning of this century, any man or boy in Norton in Hales who worked on Shrove Tuesday suffered a traditional punishment known as 'bradling'. The culprit was dragged over the rough surface of the 'Bradle Stone', a large boulder that stood on the village green, and was then beaten by the villagers. When the custom was discontinued, the Bradle Stone was moved and now stands near the front of the village church.

ONE DOG, ONE BULL

Bull-baiting in Salop ended in 1833, when a bull tore loose from its stake at the Oakengates Wake and went on a wild rampage through the terrified crowd of merrymakers. Until then, the cruel sport had been a highly popular entertainment with people throughout the mining district of the county. It was the custom to let only one dog at a time attack the bull, and the slogan 'one dog, one bull' became an expression for fair play

Orleton *Heref & Worcs*

On Orleton Hill, near an opening in the rocks called Palmer's Churn, is a 6 ft deep hole in the ground. A narrow passage, 12 ft long, leads from the hole to the surface, and in the 19th century it was a popular custom amongst local youths to try to crawl through it. It is said that those who got stuck in the middle, or turned back, would never marry. A local legend tells how a goose once entered the hole, found an underground passage and came out 4 miles away at Woofferton. When it emerged it said 'Goose out!', and the spot was named Gauset.

Traditionally, Orleton churchyard was held to be the place where the Resurrection would begin on the Day of Judgment. People from all over England arranged to be buried there, believing that they would be the first to rise from their graves.

Painswick *Glos*

Every year, on the Sunday nearest to September 19, the children of Painswick perform an ancient ritual called 'Clipping the Church'. In the afternoon, the town band leads a procession around the boundary of St Mary's churchyard, after which all the children join hands and form a circle around the church. They then dance back and forth towards the church several times while singing the traditional Clipping Hymn, and the ceremony ends with a Clipping Sermon which is read by the vicar. The custom is thought to have been adapted by the church from an old pagan rite, in which a community shows its faith by symbolically embracing its place of worship.

Some of the inhabitants of Painswick make 'puppy-dog pie' on Clipping Sunday. This is a fruit pie with a small china dog inside it so that the dog's nose pokes through the crust. A local story relates that some travellers once stopped at the town's Falcon Inn where they ordered a meal. The landlord, who had no other food at the time, is said to have served them a pie made of cooked puppies. Ever since then, Painswick people have been known as 'bow-wows'.

THE PAINSWICK YEWS

Ninety-nine clipped yew trees stand amongst the grave-stones of St Mary's churchyard in Painswick. A local belief states that only this number can grow there; whenever a hundredth tree is planted amongst the original ninety-nine, it always fails to grow

DICK WHITTINGTON

This stone carving is believed to show the legendary Dick Whittington with his cat. It was found in a Gloucester house that Whittington owned during the 15th century, and is now in the Gloucester Folk Museum

Pauntley Court *Glos*
Dick Whittington, the ever-popular pantomime hero, is reputed to have been born at Pauntley Court *c.* 1350. Contrary to legend, he came from a very prosperous family, being the third son of the Lord of the Manor of Pauntley, Sir William Whittington. As a boy Richard Whittington was apprenticed to a merchant in London, where his abilities brought both fame and fortune. He lent large sums of money to Richard II, Henry IV and Henry V, who knighted him, and he was made mayor of London for three terms. During a highly successful career he acquired a considerable fortune; he died in 1423.

In 1605, a ballad and a romanticised version of his life were published, in which he was portrayed as a poor boy who achieved riches and fame through the mouse-hunting prowess of Miss Puss, a cat which he bought for a penny on his arrival in London. The present 18th-century Manor House largely replaced the original Pauntley Court.

Peterchurch *Heref & Worcs*
The Church of St Peter at Peterchurch was founded in AD 786, and was later rebuilt by the Normans *c.* 1130. Inside the church, above the south door, a fish with a golden chain around its neck is shown on a memorial tablet. Legend has it that one day some local monks, who were both poor and hungry, went fishing in the River Dore. They caught an enormous trout with a golden chain around its neck, thus solving both of their problems simultaneously.

Ross-on-Wye *Heref & Worcs*
Until the beginning of this century at least, a phantom woman in a small boat was said to appear every evening at 8 o'clock, sailing on the River Wye from Hereford towards Ross-on-Wye. Her vessel was said to travel very fast, even when it was moving against the wind or in a flat calm. She always went ashore at a spot about 7 miles from the town, at the site of a long-vanished village, where she wept and wailed hysterically. Then she would return to her boat and sail away towards Hereford, suddenly disappearing when she was about half a mile from the city. The stretch of river on which she was seen was called the 'Spectre's Voyage', and local boatmen believed that anyone who met the phantom on the waters would die shortly after.

St Briavels *Glos*
For nearly eight centuries, a Bread and Cheese Dole has been distributed on Whit Sunday at the village church of St Briavels in the Forest of Dean. After the evening service, a local forester stands on top of a wall outside the church and throws pieces of bread and cheese to the assembled churchgoers below. It is said that the custom began during King John's reign, in 1206, to help the local poor.

327

DEVIL AND STEEPLEJACK

The spire of St Alkmond's Church, Shrewsbury, reputedly damaged by the Devil in 1553, was climbed four times in 1621 by a drunken steeplejack. He beat a drum on the summit, and fired an arrow into the town

St Weonards *Heref & Worcs*

Near the church is a Bronze Age burial mound which since time immemorial has been the scene of village fêtes. The Saxon St Weonard is supposedly buried beneath it in a golden coffin.

Shrewsbury *Salop*

The future Admiral John Benbow was born in 1653 in the house that is now St Mary's vicarage. He ran away to sea, and later joined the Navy, where he quickly rose to fame as a dashing frigate captain. Many legends were told about him in his own lifetime. It is said that on one occasion, after defeating a Moorish pirate ship, he cut off the pirates' heads and salted them down in a barrel of brine. The customs authorities at Cadiz demanded to see what he described as 'Salt provisions for the Captain's use', so he rolled the heads on the table and offered them as a present.

St Alkmond's Church in the town was largely rebuilt in 1795, though the spire is of much more ancient date. One day in 1553, while mass was being celebrated, a terrible storm arose. According to local records, the Devil appeared and shot up the steeple where he tore out the wires of the clock and clawed the fourth bell. The claw marks are still visible, and the pinnacle which the Devil knocked off in passing is still missing.

Snowshill *Glos*

The manor house, now owned by the National Trust, contains a room whose door bears the inscription *Amor et tussis non celantur* – 'You cannot conceal love or a cough'. In this room Anthony Palmer secretly married the heiress Ann Parsons in 1604. The adage was proved true, for their secret was discovered, and Anthony was tried before the Court of Star Chamber for marrying without the permission of Anne's relatives.

DEATH OF AN ADMIRAL

Ballads are still sung about the heroic death of Admiral Benbow who died fighting the French at Cape Santa Marta in 1702. His monument is in St Mary's Church, Shrewsbury, in whose vicarage he was born

SNOWSHILL MUSEUM

The Tudor manor house contains a magpie-like collection of treasures and trivia of bygone ages. Many of the objects exhibited reflect English country life in the past, including spinning wheels, looms, models of farm waggons (right) and a working model of an 18th-century post-mill (below)

Southam *Warks*

When a Southam farmer disappeared in 1820, a man called on the farmer's wife and told her that, on the previous night, he had been visited by her husband's ghost. The spectre showed him stab wounds on its body, and told him they had been inflicted by a man named Peter Thomas who had afterwards concealed the corpse in a marl-pit. A search was made, the corpse was found as the man described, and Thomas was arrested.

At his trial, however, the judge ruled that the ghost's evidence was hearsay, and therefore inadmissible unless, of course, the ghost appeared in court. The phantom was summoned three times, but when it failed to materialise, Thomas was released by the court. The judge ordered his accuser to be detained; the man later confessed to the murder and was hanged in the following year.

Stoke Edith *Heref & Worcs*

If someone in the district asked too insistently 'Where did you get that from?' it was customary to reply, 'Where the Devil got the friar' – in other words, 'Mind your own business'. The friar concerned lived in West Hide wood, and one day he trapped a badger which he put in a bag and slung over his shoulder. He intended carrying the creature to the Bell Inn at Tillington, hoping to exchange it for a beer, but on the way the bag got heavier and heavier. At last, a voice inside the bag said 'Mama calls'. The startled friar stopped, then moved on, but a few moments later, the voice said 'Dada calls'. This time, the friar opened the bag to find out what sort of beast he had caught. Whereupon the Devil jumped out, seized the friar, and carried him off to Hell. The friar was never seen again.

Stoke St Milborough *Salop*
The village takes its name from the Saxon St Milburgh who died in AD 722, and whose well is still to be seen behind some cottages opposite the church. The story goes that while out riding one day on her white horse, she was pursued by a band of pagan outlaws who lived in the district. For two days and nights she was hunted with bloodhounds until she fell bleeding to the ground. A spring burst from the bloodstained earth, baffling the hounds and enabling the saint to escape.

SELLING A WIFE

Until the first Divorce Court was established in 1857, the only legal means of disposing of an unwanted spouse was by a private Act of Parliament, a process which in the early 19th century cost at least £3000 (£15,000 at present-day values).

This sum was far beyond the means of most people, and in any case, it was firmly established in the popular mind, particularly in poorer districts such as the West Midlands, that a wife was a chattel to be bought and sold in the same way as any other goods.

In Staffordshire at least, the custom of selling a wife followed a fairly rigid pattern. A man in search of freedom

Took his wife to market
Just as they drive a pig,
With a halter tied around her
neck
Instead of round her leg

Having reached the town, the husband paid the toll which gave him the right to sell merchandise, then paraded his wife around the market-place, extolling her virtues. The crowd heckled, and interested bidders vied for possession. Prices ranged from a few pence to as much as £1. In 1800 at Stafford, a chimney-sweep named Cupid Hodson sold his wife for

5s. 6d. (27½p) after some brisk bidding which opened at one penny.

A satisfactory deal
Once the bid was accepted, the husband handed over the toll ticket as proof of ownership, and the trio retired to the inn to seal the bargain with ale. Often, the publican would hire the town crier to announce the sale, since the ceremony brought extra custom to the inn.

Despite the lowly position of the wives in these transactions,

most readily accepted the custom as being a legal and satisfactory means of ending an unhappy marriage. Most sales were arranged by mutual consent and, in many instances, the husband agreed a price with his wife's lover before the sale took place. Everyone concerned was convinced that it was essential to follow the customary procedure of bidding in the market-place. Despite the warnings of Church and State, country people considered the auction as binding as a marriage contract.

A STAFFORDSHIRE BARGAIN

This is ter gi' notice that Bandy Legged Lett
Will sell his wife Sally for what he can get,
At 12 o'clock certin the sale'll begin
So all yer gay fellers be there wi' yer tin.

Her wears men's breeches, so all the folks say
But Lett should'na let her have her own way.
Her swears like a trooper and fights like a cock,
And has gi'n her old feller many a hard knock.

So now yo' young fellers as wanting a wife,
Come bid for old Sally, the plague of Lett's life:
At 12 in the morning the sale'll begin,
So yo' as wants splicin' be there wi' yer tin.

Stratford-upon-Avon *Warks*
Shakespeare's world-famous birthplace still remembers traditions and stories of the youth of its most illustrious citizen. The best known is that the young Shakespeare poached deer from Charlecote Park, and was afterwards prosecuted by the owner, Sir Thomas Lucy. Not so well known, however, are the lines which the poet allegedly wrote in revenge:

A Parliament Member, a Justice of Peace,
At home a poor scarecrow, at London an asse;
If lowsie is Lucy, as some folks miscalle it,
Then Lucy is lowsie whatever befall it.

Shakespeare is also said to have composed a satirical epitaph on a neighbour, John Combe, who died in 1614, and is buried in Stratford church. Despite the charitable bequests recorded on his tomb, he was locally unpopular as a usurer.

Ten in the hundred lies here engraved
Tis a hundred to ten his soul is not saved;
If any man ask who lies in this tomb,
Oh! Oh! quoth the Devil, 'tis my John-a-
Combe.

In the gardens behind the Memorial Theatre, there is a space marked out for playing Nine Men's Morris. This game was common in Shakespeare's time, when it was played by Warwickshire shepherds and other country folk. A kind of imperfect chess-board was cut out of the turf on which the game, a mixture of chess, draughts and Chinese chequers, was played.

Stretton-on-Dunsmore *Warks*
The payment of Wroth Silver, which has continued since Saxon times, takes place on Knightlow Hill every St Martin's Day (November 11). Its purpose is to preserve the ancient right of villagers to drive cattle across the Duke of Buccleugh's land, and each year, representatives of the parishes which form the Knightlow Hundred assemble by a hollowed stone which is all that remains of the Knightlow Cross. In answer to the summons of the Duke of Buccleugh's steward, each man puts his due, ranging from $\frac{1}{2}$p to $21\frac{1}{2}$p, into the hollow. Anyone who fails to pay is fined £1 for each penny, or must present a white bull with red nose and ears to the duke. The ceremony is followed by breakfast – paid for by the duke – in the Old Dun Cow Inn.

Sutton St Nicholas *Heref & Worcs*
About a mile from the village stands the Wergin Stone (actually, stones), whose hollowed-out base was once probably used for the ceremonial collection of rents in the same way as those collected at Stretton-on-Dunsmore. No one now remembers by or to whom the rents were paid, but it is said that one night in 1652 the stones were removed 240 paces by the Devil, and it took nine yoke of oxen to restore them to their proper place.

Tamworth *Staffs*
Tamworth Castle, which was given to Robert de Marmion by William I, is haunted by a Saxon nun named Editha. It is said that when de Marmion took possession of his lands, he expelled the nuns from a nearby convent. Editha, who had founded the order in the 9th century, was summoned from her grave by the angry prayers of her followers. She attacked de Marmion in his bedroom, and beat him so severely with her crozier that he was forced to make restoration. Editha still walks the castle, however, and has been reported in de Marmion's room and on the staircase, both of which are open to the public. The terrace is also supposed to be haunted by a White Lady who stood there and watched while her lover, a wicked knight named Tarquin, was killed in battle by Sir Lancelot.

STOKESAY CASTLE

All the country round about Stokesay, Salop, once belonged to two giants, one of whom lived on View Edge, and the other on a high hill called Norton Camp about 2 miles away. They kept all their treasure in an oak chest in the vaults of 13th-century Stokesay Castle, but they only had one key, which one would throw to the other when it was asked for. One day, the key fell into the castle moat, and was never recovered. The giants died of grief, but their chest is still said to be hidden somewhere in the vaults, guarded by a huge raven, awaiting the time when the key will be found

TANWORTH JUSTICE

This woodcut illustrates a 17th-century ballad sheet describing the cruelty of John Chambers a native of Tanworth-in-Arden, Warks, who hired a servant to shoot his wife, '. . . for which they were executed for the same'

OLD PARR

Rubens painted this portrait of Thomas Parr, a native of Upper Winnington, in Salop, who claimed to have been born in 1483, and was therefore 152 years old when he died in 1635. He was said to have sired a child at the age of 120, and was working as a farm labourer at 145. He owed his longevity to a diet of bread, cheese and milk, and died when this routine was broken by a visit to Charles I's court

Walsall *Staffs*

In 1870, the mummified arm of an infant and a Cromwellian sword were discovered in the attic of the White Hart Inn at Caldmore Green, Walsall. The arm, thought to be a relic of witchcraft, became known, incorrectly, in the district as the 'Hand of Glory'. (In fact, or at least in folklore, a Hand of Glory was the hand of a hanged criminal pickled in various salts and dried in the sunlight. It was then used as a holder for a candle made of a hanged man's fat, virgin wax and sesame – a form of illumination much esteemed by burglars, for it lulled householders to sleep.) Both the arm and the sword became associated in popular belief with the ghost of a young girl who had killed herself in the inn about a century before. The landlord and a temporary manager have both reported strange happenings in the inn during the last 20 years. The first told of a handprint which appeared in the dust on a table in the attic, though it was impossible for anyone to have been there, while the manager spoke of phantom footsteps bumping across the attic floor.

Warwick *Warks*

After the Battle of Edgehill, in 1642, a Cromwellian dragoon corporal named Jeremiah Stone came to the Anchor Inn with a bag of money he had pillaged from the dead. Being wounded himself, he entrusted his bag to the landlord, but when he recovered, his host denied all knowledge of it and threw him out of the house. The soldier drew his sword and tried to break down the door, whereupon the landlord had him arrested for attempted burglary.

While he lay in prison, the Devil came to him and offered to act as his attorney when he came to court. The corporal gratefully accepted and, next day, in pleading Stone's cause, the Devil suggested to the

court that the inn might be searched to discover whether the money was there or not. The landlord denied stealing the money, and wished that the Devil might take him if he told a lie. The Devil promptly obliged, 'seized upon his body and carried him over the Market-place, nothing left behind but a terrible stinke'.

The story is vouched for in a broadsheet published in 1642, which states: 'This is the truth, John Finch (a shoomaker) in St Martin's being an eye-witness doth testify the same.'

FIGHTING COCK IN CHURCH

The unique lectern in St Bartholomew's Church, Wednesbury, Staffs, was ordered in the form of a fighting cockerel (instead of the traditional eagle) by a 14th-century vicar who had a passion for cock-fighting

Welford-on-Avon *Warks*

A pub by the river has the unusual name of The Four Alls. It is explained by four stained-glass portraits in the bar of a soldier, a priest, a king and a yeoman. In turn, each bears an inscription – 'Fight All', 'Pray All', 'Rule All' and 'Pay All'.

Welsh Newton *Heref & Worcs*

A simple stone in the churchyard inscribed 'J. K. Dyed the 22 of August Anno Do. 1678', marks the grave of John Kemble, an 80-year-old Catholic priest who was hanged in the reign of Charles II for celebrating mass in the chapel of nearby Pembridge Castle. Before his execution, Kemble was granted time to say his prayers and smoke a last pipe. The saying 'a Kemble pipe' – meaning to have a last smoke – is still current in Herefordshire.

331

THE OLD WOMEN OF SALT LANE

Weston under Penyard *Heref & Worcs*

According to local tradition, a farmer once found two great iron doors beneath the ruins of Penyard Castle, and collected a team of 20 oxen to tear them open. He urged on the cattle with a whip made of rowan, which he knew would protect him against evil spirits. As an additional safeguard, he carried in his pocket a splinter from a yew tree.

Eventually the doors groaned open, and he saw inside two great casks full of treasure with a jackdaw perched on top of them. But just as he was about to enter, the doors clanged shut again, and a sepulchral voice rang out, saying: 'Had it not been for your quicken-tree goad and your yew-tree pin, you and your cattle had all been drawn in.'

Terrified, the farmer fled. And if the story is true, the treasure is still there to be recovered.

Whittington *Glos*

In the 17th century, the Elizabethan Whittington Court was the home of Sir Laurence and Lady Tanfield, rich landowners whose greed made them highly unpopular in the district. After her death, Lady Tanfield is said to have haunted two of their properties – Burford Priory and Great Tew Manor – and the spectre of Sir Laurence occasionally rode down the Wicked Lord's Lane in a phantom coach drawn by four black horses. Anyone who saw the coach died soon afterwards.

Winchcombe *Glos*

Some 1200 years ago Winchcombe was the capital of the kingdom of Mercia, and *c.* AD 788 King Kenulf founded a great abbey there. The date of his death is uncertain and legend claims his seven-year-old son Kenelm succeeded him.

Kenelm had an elder sister called Quendrida, a wicked and ambitious woman who hoped that she herself would become queen of Mercia. To achieve this, she bribed Kenelm's tutor Askbert to murder him. So one day, Askbert took the boy-king out hunting, and after a time suggested they should rest. While Kenelm slept, Askbert dug a grave. But just as Askbert was about to kill him, Kenelm woke up and said: 'This is not the place ordained for you to kill me.' To prove it, he drove an ash twig into the ground, and at once it grew and flowered.

Undeterred by Kenelm's miracle, Askbert took the boy elsewhere, cut off his head and buried him. But before the grave was entirely filled in, a dove appeared from the base of Kenelm's skull and flew off in the direction of Rome.

From the dove, the pope learnt what had happened and wrote immediately to all the kings in England telling them of the murder. A search was made around Winchcombe, and eventually the searchers were led to the grave by a white cow. As they dug up the corpse, a radiant light shone from the ground.

The body was borne back to Winchcombe Abbey and reburied beside that of King Kenulf. As the funeral procession passed the palace, Quendrida looked out and tried to bewitch it by reading Psalm 108 – the 'cursing psalm' – backwards. But as she read, her eyes burst from her head, her blood drenched the psalter and she died in agony.

Winchcombe Abbey was destroyed by Henry VIII in 1539. But later excavations uncovered two stone coffins – thought to be those of the two Saxon kings – which are now in the parish church.

Long ago, in medieval times, two old women lived in Castle Street, Worcester; it was then called Salt Lane and lay just outside the city boundary. They were white witches, who made their living mainly by freeing the carts which regularly became stuck in the mud just opposite their cottages. For sixpence, one of them would come out, stroke the cartwheels and bless the horse, after which the cart would roll away easily, however heavy its load or however deeply its wheels were stuck.

One day, a waggoner came by carrying a load which was so light that he knew that there was little risk of his cart becoming stuck. But he was wrong. Just outside the witches' cottages the wheels sank into the mud, and no amount of straining and pulling could shift them.

One of the old women came to her door, and the waggoner began bargaining with her over his horse's back. As he did so, he noticed a piece of straw lying across the horse's shoulders, and it occurred to him that this might be part of the witch's spell. So he cut the straw in half with his knife. The old woman let out a blood-curdling scream, his waggon became free, and as he raced away down Salt Lane, he saw that the witch had been severed in two, and lay dead in the mud.

Little is known about the life of the second witch, except that on one occasion she turned a captain and his troop of soldiers to stone, when they came to Worcester to collect taxes. Their petrified figures used to stand alongside the Tything – now the main A38 which runs through the city. It is said that a local merchant once tried to break the spell, but when one of the stones turned into an enormous horse which reared up above him, furiously pawing the air, he fled the town in terror.

THE GREEN MAN, *or Jack-in-the-Green, represented the pagan spirit of nature. He can be seen in some of the rough bosses in the cloisters of Worcester Cathedral, and is always shown wreathed in leaves with stems growing from his mouth*

Wistanstow *Salop*

A stained-glass window in the nave of Wistanstow church depicts St Wystan, who according to legend was stabbed to death here in AD 849. Wystan was of royal blood, and could have become king of Mercia. But he preferred instead to devote his life to prayer. He was murdered by a cousin jealous of his piety, and legend says that a beam of light lit up the murder scene for 30 days afterwards.

Worthen *Salop*

A local folktale tells of a family called Reynolds who were driven out of their farm by two bogies – evil fairies – who looked like a little old man and woman. The Reynolds packed up all their belongings late one night, and silently slipped away to another farm in the district.

When they arrived there, they discovered that they had left behind a precious salt-cellar, so they

THE JEW AND THE CATHEDRAL

In the early 13th century Worcester Cathedral was badly damaged by fire, and a large sum of money was needed to restore it. At that time, many rich Jews lived in the town, and a legend tells how one of the richest and most powerful of them, known for his fair dealing, used to pray in the cathedral, thanking God for his worldly success, in a special place beneath a small arch by the altar.

A vision of Christ
One day the Jew was praying in his usual place when he heard a rustling in the chancel. Peeping round a pillar, he saw Christ and the Virgin Mary standing by the tomb of the 11th-century Bishop of Worcester, St Wulstan. Christ asked why the cathedral was in such a poor state, and why the rebuilding had been so long delayed. From his tomb, Wulstan replied that he would do his best to raise the 10,000 crowns that were needed as soon as possible. Christ ordered him to make sure that the

money was donated and delivered to the cathedral within seven days.

A plan for profit
Jesus and Mary vanished, and the Jew began to wonder how he could profit from what he had heard. By the time he left the cathedral, he had devised a plan. He gave five crowns to the monk collecting alms by the doorway, and offered to enter into a bond with him. The bond was that the Jew would give the monk 500 crowns, and would receive in return all the money that was donated and delivered to the cathedral within the next seven days.

Though the monk knew that he rarely received even 30 crowns in alms in a single week, his faith did not allow him to enter into such a bond. The Jew doubled his offer. Still the monk refused, though he summoned the prior to see what he thought. The Jew increased his offer, and then increased it again, and when it stood at 5000 crowns the monk and the prior waived the articles of their faith and

sealed the bond, believing that it must be a sign from heaven.

Within hours, the Jew's 5000 crowns had been delivered.

The pay-off
On the seventh day after his vision the Jew returned to the cathedral, to see how Wulstan would deliver the 10,000 crowns, and to claim it with his bond. He knelt beneath the arch and waited. He never noticed until it was too late that the arch was shrinking. The stone pillars closed in a stranglehold around his neck.

As the Jew writhed in helpless terror, Christ reappeared and asked Wulstan if the money had been paid. Wulstan replied that half had been delivered already, and that he had the man who was going to pay the other half tight by the neck.

The apparitions vanished, the arch re-opened, and within hours the terrified Jew had delivered another 5000 crowns to the cathedral. The bent arch can still be seen.

---

sent their cowman Edward back to fetch it. When he arrived at the farm, the bogies came out to meet him carrying the salt-cellar, and then followed him back to the Reynolds' new home.

The Reynolds decided to take drastic action against the fairies, so they made Edward lie down under a pile of straw in front of the fire. Then, with the utmost politeness, they asked the fairies to warm themselves by the fire, and to make themselves at home on the straw. When the fairies sat down, Edward jumped up and tumbled them into the flames. With brooms and pitchforks the Reynolds kept them there until they were burnt to ashes.

The Wrekin Salop
Two giants built The Wrekin out of earth dug from the bed of the River Severn. They lived inside it and (as is the way with giants) soon began quarrelling. One struck at the other with a spade,

missed, and cleft the rock now called the Needle's Eye. A raven prevented the next blow from going home by pecking at the giant's eye. The tear he shed formed the pool known as Raven's Bowl, which has never run dry since. With the third blow, one giant knocked the other unconscious, and immediately imprisoned him in Ercall Hill. To this day, the giant can sometimes be heard groaning at dead of night from beneath the hill.

Wychnor Staffs
For centuries it was the custom in Wychnor for married couples who had not argued for a year and a day to be awarded a flitch of bacon. The flitch hung in the manorial hall throughout the year. If the testimony of the applicants and their witnesses was accepted, the flitch was presented to them. The custom was probably started by John of Gaunt in 1347, but when it died out no one is quite certain.

BORDERS
REGION

LINDISFARNE
FARNE
ISLANDS
BUCKTON
BELFORD
BAMBURGH
(The Worm, 337)

CHILLINGHAM

ALNWICK

CALLALY

ACKLINGTON

NORTHUMBERLAND
ELSDON

HESLEYSIDE
ROTHLEY
BELLINGHAM
BROOMLEE LOUGH
WHALTON
(The Treasure, 340)

STAMFORDHAM

SEWINGSHIELDS
TYNEMOUTH
BARDON MILL
HEXHAM
JARROW
TYNE AND WEAR
NEWBROUGH
DILSTON
WHITBURN
FEATHERSTONE
HEDLEY ON
THE HILL
HYLTON
ALLENDALE TOWN
PENSHAW
BLANCHLAND
EBCHESTER
(Lambton Worm, 350)
PELTON
GREAT LUMLEY

BRANCEPETH
DURHAM

DURHAM

SEDGEFIELD

HEIGHINGTON

CLEVELAND
PIERCEBRIDGE
HANDALE
ROKEBY
GUISBOROUGH
RUNSWICK
DARLINGTON

SOCKBURN
DANBY
WHITBY
(Hand of Glory, 341)

HELL GILL BECK
RICHMOND
GLAISDALE
GOATHLAND
BAINBRIDGE
SALTERGATE

SEMER WATER
WEST WITTON
HORCUM
UPSALL
HUTTON-
LE-HOLE
SCARBOROUGH
NORTH YORKSHIRE
(Witch Barrier, 347)

HUBBERHOLME
FILEY

AUSTWICK
RIPON
SESSAY
NUNNINGTON
TRESHFIELD
WOLD
FLAMBOROUG
BURNSALL
FOUNTAINS ABBEY
KIRKHAM
NEWTON
GIGGLESWICK
SUMMER
ALDBOROUGH
RUDSTON
THORPE
BRIDGE
BENINGBROUGH
BURTON-
BRIDLINGT
APPLETREEWICK
AGNES
FEWSTON
LONG
STAMFORD
KNARESBOROUGH
MARSTON
BRIDGE
HARPHAM
(Mother Shipton, 348)
YORK
COTTINGLEY
GUISELEY
(Tales, 355)
ATWICK
(The Fairies, 343)
WALTON
BARWICK
ACASTER
BRADFORD
IN ELMET
MALBIS
(The Heads, 338)
ABERFORD
MARKET
BEVERLEY
MIDGLEY
WEIGHTON
LEEDS
HALIFAX
DEWSBURY
HUMBERSIDE
KIRKLEES PARK
PONTEFRACT
WEST
LEE GAP
WAKEFIELD
YORKSHIRE
GREATER
BARNSDALE
MANCHESTER
DENBY DALE

SOUTH YORKSHIRE

SHEFFIELD
(Sword Dancing, 352)

N

0   10   20
MILES

CUMBRIA

LANCASHIRE

CHESHIRE

LINCOLNSHIRE

DERBYSHIRE

NOTTINGHAM-
SHIRE

STAFFORDSHIRE

NORSEMEN'S KINGDOM

Cleveland, Durham, Humberside, Northumberland, Tyne and Wear, Yorkshire

From the days of the earliest Christian missionaries, the ancient Kingdom of Northumbria – of which the three counties formed a major part – was a spiritual battlefield. People expected wonders of saints who had so lightly dismissed spells and amulets as being useless against the 'ogres, elves and ghouls who fought against God', and they were seldom disappointed. When St Cuthbert went to pray on the Isle of Coquet, two hideous monsters emerged from the water and knelt to be blessed. Nor were the morals of the area neglected. A prostitute who had the temerity to sit on the tomb of St Osra in Howden church in Humberside, found herself unable to move. Invisible forces tore her clothes off and whipped her savagely.

Northumbrian saints were good tacticians. The north-easterly winds that shivered St Cuthbert's sparse frame in his stony cell on Farne Island were often put to good use. On one occasion at least, in AD 651, St Aidan is said to have saved the town of Bamburgh by changing the direction of the wind.

Despite strong resistance, the Vikings came to stay. Reminders of their occupation still linger in place names ending in -toft (a field), -thorpe (a hamlet), and -thwaite (a clearing or meadow). The former Yorkshire Ridings were themselves divisions named after an old Norse word meaning a 'third-ing'. Less tangible evidence of the Norsemen's passing remains in the many stories of ogres, demons and dragons still told in the area. Crossed with native Celtic belief, they produced such fearsome creatures as the Boggard of Bunting Nook.

Warfare did not end with the absorption of the Vikings into the population. Their descendants became the moss-troopers, cattle-lifters and war lords of the Scottish border. A later breed of heroes, such as Harry Percy – Shakespeare's Hotspur – is still remembered. It is said that the guttural sound of the letter 'r' in the Northumberland dialect was imitated from a speech defect of Hotspur's.

All that now remains of those medieval heroes are the ballads and the ruined strongholds. Many of the latter lie near the coalmines for which all three counties are famous. But the colliers, too, have their songs, some humorous, some recalling pit disasters of the past. Older Durham miners still believe that they receive warning of explosions from dead workmates killed in earlier tragedies. When a man is killed, it is said that his spirit haunts the place where the fatality occurred.

It is not so hard to accept tales of heroes and sprites in an area where tradition insists that Arthur lies sleeping in a cave on Hadrian's Wall. But for those who require more definite proof, there are always the Cottingley fairies – clearly photographed in a W. Yorkshire garden in 1920!

THE FOLKLORE YEAR

New Year's Eve Allendale Town, Nthld *Tar-barrel Burning*	**Third Thursday in March** Market Weighton, Humberside *Kipling Cotes Derby*	**July 4** Whalton, Nthld *Bale Fire*
Shrove Tuesday Scarborough, N. Yorks *Ringing of the Pancake Bell and Shrovetide Skipping*	**Good Friday** Midgley, W. Yorks *Pace Egg Play*	**Nightly at 9 p.m.** Ripon, N. Yorks *Wakeman's Horn Blowing*
Shrove Tuesday Sedgefield and Alnwick, Nthld *Shrovetide Football*	**Day before Ascension day** (six weeks after Easter) Whitby, N. Yorks *Planting the Penny Hedge*	**Boxing Day** Sheffield – at Grenoside and Handsworth, S. Yorks *Sword Dancing*

KEY TO SYMBOLS

BELLS

CRIME AND PUNISHMENT

CURIOUS CHARACTERS

CUSTOMS AND FESTIVALS

DEVILS AND DEMONS

DROWNED OR LOST LANDS

FABULOUS BEASTS

FAIRIES

GHOSTS

GIANTS

GRAVES AND MONUMENTS

HEROES

HOLY PLACES

LOCAL CURIOSITIES

LOVE STORY

MUSEUMS AND LIBRARIES

MYSTERIOUS STONES

SAINTS AND MIRACLES

TREASURE

UNDERGROUND PASSAGES

WELLS AND SPRINGS

WITCHES AND WIZARDS

A MEMORIAL TO FAITH

This anvil in the W. Yorkshire Methodist church at Aberford, is a memorial to Samuel Hick, a local 19th-century blacksmith and preacher. Hick, it is said, once took some corn to be ground at a mill as food for his congregation. As there was no wind to drive the mill sails, he prayed. A wind arose and the corn was ground; then the breeze fell as suddenly as it had begun

Acaster Malbis *N. Yorks*
The parish church is known traditionally as 'the synagogue' because about 1189 a number of Jews fleeing from religious persecution in York used it for their worship. The angry villagers set fire to the building when the Jews were inside, and stains on a window-sill are reputed to be the blood of those who tried to escape the flames.

Acklington *Nthld*
Salmon in the River Coquet have been obstructed by Acklington weir since it was built in 1778. It is said that kindly local people put up a notice to direct the fish to an unimpeded stream near by.

Aldborough *N. Yorks*
A mile from the village, towards Boroughbridge, are the mysterious Devil's Arrows, three massive standing stones, each weighing about 40 tons. According to local legend, they are crossbow-bolts which the Devil shot at Aldborough, an early Christian missionary settlement.

Allendale Town *Nthld*
The town signals the end of the Old Year with a ceremony said to be of pagan origin. Costumed men carrying barrels of blazing tar on their heads parade through the streets to the market-place, where the barrels are thrown on a bonfire. The townspeople then dance until midnight, when 'first footing' begins. A dark-haired man must be the first to enter a home after midnight, carrying gifts of bread and coal, to bring good luck.

Alnwick *Nthld*
Shrovetide football is played on Shrove Tuesday between two teams of up to 150 players each. The goals, decorated with evergreens, are a quarter of a mile apart, and before play starts the ball is piped on to the pitch by the Duke of Northumberland's own piper. The game is won by the first team to score three 'hales' (goals), and the ball is kept by whoever manages to carry it off the pitch. Often this involves swimming the River Aln.

Appletreewick *N. Yorks*
The fearsome barguest, a ghost dog with huge saucer eyes, shaggy hair and dragging a clanking chain, was once thought to haunt a nearby gorge called Trollers Gill. A local story recorded in 1881 tells how a foolhardy man went to the gorge at midnight. His body was found by shepherds the next day, and according to a contemporary ballad,
'Marks were imprest on the dead man's breast,
But they seemed not by mortal hand.'

Atwick *Humberside*
A headless horseman has been seen occasionally in the area, though no one knows his identity. At the foot of the hill on which the church rests, a spring is said to have once been haunted by a hobgoblin called the Haliwell Boggle.

Austwick *N. Yorks*
Tales of Austwick 'carles', or simpletons, are common in Yorkshire. A saying 'T' best's at t' bottom, as Astic (Austwick) carles say', comes from a story of a man who fell into a deep pool near Austwick, and did not come up again. Instead, his friends on the bank saw bubbles rising to the surface which, as they broke, sounded like the words 'T' b-b-b-best's at t' b-b-bottom'. So they too jumped in, to find out what treasures he had found.

Bainbridge *N. Yorks*
For 700 years a hunting horn has been blown on the village green every evening during autumn and winter. This custom originated when Bainbridge was surrounded by the once-great Forest of Wensleydale, and the sound of the horn was intended to guide lost travellers to the village.

Bardon Mill *Nthld*
Hardriding farm, towards Haltwhistle, is haunted at times by the ghost of a robber, killed there in the 14th century. The ghost's last reported visit was in 1933, when mysterious shouts and banging doors during the night awoke the farm inhabitants.

Barnsdale *S. Yorks*
According to some people, Barnsdale Forest, now shrunk to a small wood near Doncaster, was the true haunt of Robin Hood rather than Sherwood Forest. It was in Barnsdale Forest that Robin is said to have encountered the unpopular Bishop of Hereford. Robin forced the cleric to dine with him, then took his purse to pay for the meal. The bishop then had to provide entertainment by dancing around a tree until he was exhausted.

Barwick in Elmet *W. Yorks*
The maypole at Barwick in Elmet is 86 ft tall, and it is considered to be the oldest and tallest maypole in England. On Easter Monday every three years the pole is lowered by three 'pole men', who are elected for the task. Then, freshly painted and garlanded with flowers and ribbons, it is raised again for the traditional maypole dances on Whit Monday.

Belford *Nthld*
Late in the 19th century, a barber named Watty lived in the town. It was his custom to travel around the district and shave the farmers before market days and fairs. On more melancholy occasions, his services were also employed to give the dead and dying their final shave. In keeping with tradition, Watty was once summoned to shave a notorious profligate who lay dying. He is said to have partly completed his task when suddenly the Devil cried out: 'That'll do, Watty. I'll just take him as he is.'

THE WORM OF BAMBURGH

Bamburgh Castle, founded in AD 547, was the ancient royal residence of Northumbrian kings. Oswald, the 7th-century king, was the first Christian ruler to live there. Oswald's deeds of charity to the poor prompted St Aidan, Bishop of Lindisfarne, to grasp the king's hand and say: 'Never let this hand consume or wither.' The saint's blessing may have been fulfilled, for when Oswald was killed in battle his hand was cut off and enclosed in a silver casket. It remained in Bamburgh church for many years; when it was stolen in the 11th century, it was still uncorrupted.

Another tale of St Aidan is told in Bamburgh. In 651 the village was set on fire by Penda, the pagan king of Mercia, and St Aidan, seeing the flames from the neighbouring Farne Islands, prayed earnestly. In response to the holy man, the wind changed and the flames swept back on the besiegers, who fled.

Long ago, it is said, people in the vicinity of Bamburgh were terrified by the Laidley Worm. This monster was in fact the daughter of the king of Northumbria, who had been turned into a dragon by the wicked queen, her stepmother. Not knowing the queen was a witch, the king had married her in his old age.

The Laidley Worm laid waste to the country for miles around. At last, the king's son, the Childe of Wynde, volunteered to fight the monster, unaware that the creature was his sister. But the Worm refused to fight him, and when it revealed its true identity, this proved to be the antidote to the spell. The princess resumed her former shape, and the evil queen was changed into a toad.

The toad-queen is still said to sit beneath the castle in a cave whose doors are opened every seventh Christmas Eve. She will retain her toad shape until some hero enters her cave and unsheaths the Childe of Wynde's sword three times. He must then blow three times on the Childe's horn, and finally kiss the toad.

HERO'S HALT *The Spindlestone, a whinstone pillar near Bamburgh, is known in legend as the place where the Childe of Wynde, son of the king of Bamburgh, tethered his horse before going to fight the Laidley Worm. This fearsome creature was in fact his own sister turned into a dragon by a witch. The Childe delivered her from the spell; because of this, the witch was transformed into a toad*

Bellingham *Nthld*
The local legend of the Long Pack is associated with a curious tombstone shaped like a pedlar's pack, about 4 ft high by 3 ft deep, which can be seen in the churchyard. The story of the tombstone dates from 1723, when a pedlar called at Lee Hall, a former riverside mansion between Bellingham and Wark, owned by a Colonel Ridley who had made his fortune in India. The pedlar asked for a night's lodging, but as the colonel was away from home the maid refused to let him stay in the house. She did, however, allow him to leave his bulky pack in the kitchen until morning, and after he had gone she saw the pack move. In fright, she called for help. A ploughboy fired a gun at the bundle and blood gushed out. Inside the pack was the body of a man armed with pistols. Like many border towns in those days Bellingham was plagued by marauders, and the servants realised that a robbery had been planned. They called the other servants and then blew a horn they found beside the body. When the robbers came they were ambushed and severely beaten. The unknown body in the pack was buried beneath the stone in the churchyard.

THE BRADFORD HEADS

Beningbrough N. Yorks

The now-vanished Beningbrough Hall was the scene of a double tragedy in 1670. The housekeeper at the Hall, a good-looking middle-aged woman, was murdered by a local poacher, William Vasey, at the instigation of the steward of the estate, Philip Laurie – possibly out of jealousy for her known attachment to the gamekeeper, Martin Giles. Vasey was caught by Giles breaking into the gamekeeper's cottage and later confessed to the murder also. He was hanged at York; Laurie committed suicide. Until the end of the 19th century, the housekeeper's ghost was said to haunt the banks of the Ouse near the spot where she had been drowned.

Beverley Humberside

During the Middle Ages, Beverley Minster was famous as an ecclesiastical sanctuary. Hunted men fled to it from all over England. Once within the bounds, fugitives were given sanctuary for 30 days, while the clergy tried to intercede for them. If this failed, the offenders were handed over to the coroner, who gave them the choice of trial or exile. Beverley was unique among ecclesiastical sanctuaries in offering a third alternative: the criminal might take an oath to become a servant of the Church, give all his property to the Crown and live within the town of Beverley for the rest of his life. Those who accepted were known as Frithmen.

A famous story is told of one Toustain, a henchman of William the Conqueror, who at that time was laying waste the North. Toustain violated the sanctuary of Beverley by leading a band of soldiers into the Minster in pursuit of townsfolk who had fled there. As he crossed the threshold, there was a flash of light. Toustain fell, his head completely turned round and his limbs transformed to hideous lumps. After this, the Conqueror respectfully confirmed the Minster in its privileges.

The hundreds of stone heads which have come to light in recent years in West Yorkshire have presented archaeologists with a fascinating problem. Do they date from the pre-Roman Celtic period? Or were some of them carved only a century or two ago, indicating the survival of ancient Celtic beliefs into the modern world? The Celts who lived in the area 2300 years ago, when it was part of the kingdom of Brigantia, revered the human head as a fertility symbol and charm against evil. The severed heads of enemies, or their replicas in stone, were set as guardians at the entrances of cattle-byres and houses. Large numbers of these Celtic masks have been dug from the ground in Scotland, Ireland and on the Continent. But in the Bradford area, where many of them were placed in the drystone walls of fields and above cottage doors, they may still be serving their original purpose. It is thought that some of the heads are no more than 100 years old; if this is so, then an Iron Age cult may have survived in some form into the reign of Queen Victoria.

GLARING EYES *The expression on this mask, found in the grounds of a Bradford school, suggest that once it may have defended a Celtic shrine from evil spirits*

A MEDIEVAL SANCTUARY

The 1000-year-old stone Frithstool, or sanctuary chair, in Beverley Minster, was once the goal of hunted men from all over England. Anyone sitting in it could claim immunity from the law for 30 days

CELTIC MASK *The joined eyelids and slit mouth of this Wakefield head are typical of Celtic carving*

FLAT FACE *The elongated neck, topknot and protruding tongue of this figure from Boston Spa are also characteristically Celtic in design*

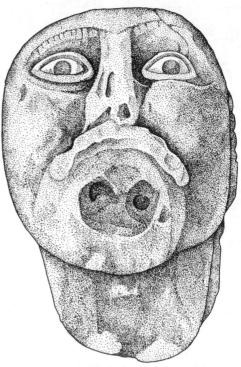

HIGHLY DECORATED *This head was found in a coal shed near Halifax. Eyebrows are indicated by vertical grooves*

HOLLOW HEAD *Many Celtic heads had hollow crowns. It has been suggested that they may have served as receptacles for offerings of food and drink to the gods. The severed head, with its powers of fertility and wisdom, could well serve as a font. This example, from Bingley, with its beard and hair-style which half covers the ears, also demonstrates the Celtic fondness for elaborate coiffures amongst the men*

CELTIC HAIR-STYLES *The elaborately coiffured head on the left was unearthed at Clapham a century ago; the moustachioed figure with its 'imperial' came from a Bradford garden*

Blanchland *Nthld*
During the early 18th century, the Lord Crewe Arms Hotel was the home of General Tom Forster, who led the unsuccessful Jacobite rebellion of 1715. Captured and taken to London, he escaped from Newgate prison with the help of his sister Dorothy. For a time he is thought to have hidden in the medieval priest's hole, still preserved behind a fireplace at the hotel. The belief persists that Dorothy's ghost haunts the Lord Crewe Arms, in the vain hope of contacting her brother through the visitors who come there for, after his flight, Tom went into exile in France, never to see his sister again.

Brancepeth *Durham*
A famous song describes the passion of Mary Bellasis, the heiress of Brancepeth, for the handsome yellow-haired Robert Shafto, the squire of neighbouring Whitworth.

> 'Bobbie Shafto's gone to sea
> Silver buckles on his knee.
> He'll come back and marry me,
> Bonnie Bobbie Shafto.'

But it was a case of unrequited love. Mary Bellasis pined away until she died. The heartless Bobbie married Anne Duncombe, daughter of a Yorkshire landowner, and became the MP for County Durham from 1760 to 1768.

THE BRAWN OF BRANCEPETH

The seal of Roger de Fery, preserved in the treasury of Durham Cathedral, commemorates the killing of the Brawn of Brancepeth. The brawn, last of the huge wild boars which roamed the forest of Durham in the early Middle Ages, was trapped and killed by de Fery at Cleves Cross in 1200. He dug a deep pit, covered it with branches, and stood across the hidden hole to lure the beast into the trap, where he stabbed it with his sword. His grave-cover in Kirk Merrington churchyard shows a spade and sword, the weapons of his victory

Bridlington *Humberside*

Restoring five dead people to life, returning sight to a blind woman and healing a lame man are some of the miracles attributed to St John of Bridlington, 14th-century prior of the town's Augustinian monastery. But the most spectacular of his good deeds was performed on behalf of some Hartlepool sailors, caught in a storm off Flamborough Head. They saw the tower of Bridlington Priory and prayed to John for help. To their astonishment they saw a monk walking towards them across the mountainous waves. He reached their boat, put his hand on the prow and pulled it safely to shore.

Buckton *Nthld*

In July 1685, Sir John Cochrane of Ochiltree, Ayrshire, lay in an Edinburgh prison under sentence of death for his part in the Duke of Argyll's rising against James II in May of that year. As the execution warrant travelled north on the mail coach, Cochrane's daughter Grizzel disguised herself as a man, held up the coach and seized the postbag. This delayed the execution for several days, during which her father's friends managed to arrange a pardon. Grizzy's Clump, some roadside trees near Buckton, mark the hold-up site, and the ghost of Grizzel is said to haunt the spot.

Burnsall *N. Yorks*

Local people say that the maypole on the village green stands on the site of one which was once stolen by the nearby village of Thorpe-sub-Montem. The ensuing feud was ended only by the return of the maypole.

Nearby Elbolton Hill was famed as a haunt of fairies. A story is told that many years ago a Burnsall man once surprised a crowd of little folk in their moonlight revels. For a while the man kept silent, knowing it was unwise to disturb the fairies at play. But in his excitement he forgot himself and called out: 'Na' then, Ah'll sing a song if tha loikes.' But the fairies were furious at his well-intentioned interruption, and beat him so soundly that he was bruised for days after.

THE TREASURE OF BROOMLEE LOUGH

Treasure is said to lie at the bottom of Broomlee Lough, a lonely lake near Housesteads, Northumberland.

Centuries ago the wealthy owner of the castle that once stood on Sewing-shields Crag was forced to leave his fortress without taking any of his riches with him. Determined that his successors should not inherit his valuables, he stowed them in a box, had himself rowed away from the shore of Broomlee Lough and cast the box overboard. He put a spell on the treasure: it could be recovered only by the co-operation of twin horses, twin oxen, twin youths and a chain forged by a smith of kind (seventh-generation smith). Then he left the country.

Local people soon noticed that when the wind agitated the surface of the lake, the water above the box remained calm and unruffled.

The cursed chain

Years later someone attempted to raise the treasure. He obtained twin horses, oxen and youths and a chain made by a smith of kind. On a windy day he noted which part of the lake remained unruffled and, going out in a boat, lowered the chain in a loop around the treasure spot, retaining both ends on shore. The two youths attached the chain ends to the horses and oxen and urged them forward. In this way the box was dragged over the bed of the lake two-thirds of the way to the shore. Then the chain snapped

and the operation had to be abandoned. No one tried to find it again, and treasure has remained in the same spot in the lake ever since.

Cuckolded by a beggar

One reason advanced for the failure of the chain was that while the grandfather of the man who made it had been away for two or three days in another town a handsome beggar had lodged in his house and slept with his wife. This beggar was the real grandfather of the chain-maker; therefore, he was not a true smith of kind.

There is also a local tradition that the lake harbours King Arthur's sword Excalibur, which was thrown into its waters as the king lay dying.

THE SKULL OF BURTON AGNES

Bricked up in Burton Agnes Hall, (below) Burton Agnes, Humberside, is the skull of Anne Griffith (right-hand figure above). Anne was the youngest of three sisters who built the house in the 17th century. One day, the house was attacked by thieves, and in the struggle Anne was mortally wounded. Before she died, she begged

that her head should be kept in the house she loved. Despite this, she was buried in the church-yard; but such were the noises in the house, that her sisters were forced to disinter her head and bring it home. The skull was walled up and since then, the house has been quiet, though Anne's ghost is still said to haunt her old home

Callaly *Nthld*
In the 13th century the first Lord of Callaly planned a castle on top of the hill but his wife wanted it built in the fields below. Unable to persuade her husband, she disguised a servant as a boar and every night he destroyed the building done during the day. A watch was set and when the boar appeared it was heard to exclaim:

Callaly Castle built on the height
Up in the day and down in the night,
Builded down in the Shepherd's Shaw,
It shall stand for aye and never fa'.

The lady had her way and the castle was built at the foot of the hill. The ruins are now incorporated into a 17th-century mansion, while the remains of an earlier building on the summit probably gave birth to the legend.

Chillingham *Nthld*
The white cattle with red ears that have grazed in the 300-acre park around Chillingham Castle since the 13th century are Britain's last surviving wild herd. They are the direct descendants of the wild cattle that once roamed freely over Europe and Britain prior to the Roman invasion. The last herds were found in Wales in Saxon times. They are said to have the same colouring as fairy cattle and legend has it that they will kill anyone who touches them.

THE HAND OF GLORY

The parish of Danby, N. Yorks, possessed a Hand of Glory, a device which superstitious burglars considered an essential part of their kit until the early 19th century. The hand was that of a gibbeted criminal; after the blood was squeezed out, the hand was embalmed for two weeks in a solution of saltpetre, salt and pepper, before being dried in the sun. A candle was made from a number of curious ingredients such as hanged man's fat, wax, and a substance called Lapland sesame. The resulting confection was thrust between the dead fingers, and lit when the burglar broke into a house. The hand was supposed to open locks, render the thief invisible, and send the household into a drugged sleep, particularly when the burglar recited:

Let those who rest
more deeply sleep;
Let those awake
their vigils keep;
Oh, Hand of Glory,
shed thy light;
Direct us to our
spoil tonight.

It was believed that the candle's spell could be broken only by putting out its flames with blood or skimmed milk; then the household would awake.

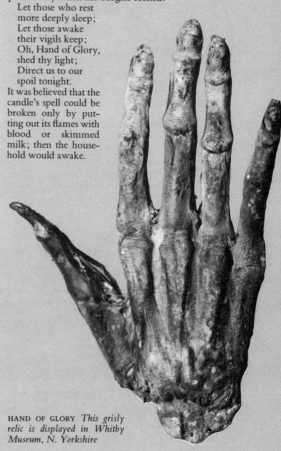

HAND OF GLORY *This grisly relic is displayed in Whitby Museum, N. Yorkshire*

Darlington *Durham*

Close to the River Tees, in the suburbs, are four deep pools called Hell's Kettles. Legend says 'spirits have oft been heard to cry out of them', and that a farmer who took hay waggons out on St Barnabas' Day (June 11), when pious folk should not work, was swallowed up in them – carts, horses and all – and some say they can still be seen there.

Denby Dale *W. Yorks*

Giant pies that can feed hundreds of people are the tradition at Denby Dale. The first was baked in 1788 to celebrate the recovery of George III from illness. Another was for victory at Waterloo. One containing everything from five sheep to '63 small birds' caused a near riot in 1846. It was drawn through the village by 13 horses before being tipped out of its cart by the crowd. The Hinchliffe family say that their ancestor, who cut the pie, made such a long speech that people chopped through platform supports and toppled him into the pie. The last pie, in 1964, was tasted by at least 30,000 visitors. It celebrated four royal births in one year.

THE GIANT PIE RIOT AT DENBY DALE

The monstrous pie baked in the village in 1846, to celebrate the Repeal of the Corn Laws, was crumbled and trampled by the crowd, who turned it out of its cart. Some claimed the riot was a Tory plot to ruin a Liberal celebration

Dewsbury *W. Yorks*

The 'Devil's Knell' is tolled at the parish church every Christmas Eve. The bell, rung once for each year since Christ's birth, is said to have been given by a murderer, and is rung to keep the Devil away.

DILSTON'S SAD COUNTESS

Dilston Castle, home of the last Earl of Derwentwater, is said to be haunted by the ghost of his wife, who persuaded him to join the Jacobite rising in 1715

Dilston *Nthld*

When James Radcliffe, last Earl of Derwentwater, was beheaded on Tower Hill in 1716 for his part in the Jacobite rebellion, people said the corn ground near his castle was tinged red, and the building's gutters ran with blood. As his head rolled, the River Derwent became filled with adders where previously there had been none. Ever since, the ghost of his unhappy wife, who taunted him and forced him into joining the rebels by demanding that he gave her his sword, has haunted the castle, wringing her hands. The spectral earl himself is said to gallop over the countryside at night with his men.

Durham *Durham*

Curfew is still rung in the city at 9 p.m. every night except on Saturdays, for a bellringer mysteriously vanished on that day. Anthems are sung from the top of the cathedral tower on May 29 every year, to commemorate the Battle of Neville's Cross, when the English repelled a Scots invasion, in 1346. During the fight, monks sang mass from the tower, and the abbot vowed to make this an annual event if the English won. But the singing is done on only three sides: no one sings on the west side since a chorister fell to his death from there.

THE COTTINGLEY FAIRIES

There really are fairies at the bottom of our garden, said the two little girls. They were quite prepared to prove it, if only they could borrow the family camera and be shown how it worked. For the sake of peace, Elsie Wright's father showed her how to operate the camera, loaded it, and sent his 13-year-old daughter down the garden with her 10-year-old cousin from South Africa, Frances Griffiths. Any photograph they brought back, he thought, would end their constant chatter about the tiny creatures they claimed to play with in the glen along the beck at the back of the Wright's home in Cottingley, near Bradford, W. Yorkshire. But, far from closing the subject, that first photograph, taken in the spring of 1917, was to startle the world and launch a storm of controversy. For when it was developed, the plate revealed a pensive-looking Frances, with a merry band of tiny, dancing winged figures.

The girls insisted that these were the fairies who lived in the glen, and denied that they had faked the photograph in any way. Mr and Mrs Wright remained sceptical, even when, a month later, the girls took their second picture. This showed Elsie with a pointy-faced gnome about to hop up on to her hand. Somehow, the Wrights felt, the girls must have staged the two pictures – perhaps by using cut-out figures from a book.

The photographs and plates were put away and forgotten, until three years later, in 1920, when Mrs Wright heard a lecturer talking about belief in fairies. She told him of the creatures that her daughter insisted came out to play in the glen – and passed on the prints and negatives to a psychic researcher, Edward Gardner.

Genuine or faked?

At first, he was sure the photographs must have been faked – but experts were baffled. One said: 'These are entirely genuine unfaked photographs of single exposure, open-air work, show movement in all the fairy figures, and there is no trace whatever of studio work involving paper models, painted figures, etc. They are straight, untouched pictures.' Another studio expert thought they could have been faked, but only by a first-class photographer.

Elsie and Frances were asked to take more pictures. They produced three, showing Frances with a leaping fairy, a fairy offering Elsie a posy of tiny flowers, and fairies with a gossamer-like 'sun bath'. The plates used for this series of pictures were carefully marked and sealed by the manufacturer and then checked again after development.

The controversy started when Mr Gardner and Sir Arthur Conan Doyle published the pictures alongside an article in the 1920 Christmas edition of *Strand Magazine*. Some critics cried 'Fake!' But scores of people wrote to say they too had seen fairies like those in the pictures.

Elsie and her cousin separated, and took no more photographs. But they always maintained that the pictures were true likenesses of their visitors.

THE LEAPING FAIRY *This fairy captured in flight was leaping up from leaves below and hovering for a moment. She had done it three or four times, said Frances. This time, she came so close to the girl's face that Frances involuntarily drew her head back – which might explain that somewhat distant pose. The fairy's wings, she added, were a lavender colour. Both girls claimed that the sprites appeared to them in a number of colours, often shimmering and giving off waves of light. But mainly they were said to sport hues ranging from carnation pink to yellows and golds, mostly in their wings, while limbs were usually pure white*

ELSIE'S GNOME *Experts said this was an under-exposed picture. Frances snapped it just as the gnome, with pipes on his back and in black tights, red jersey and scarlet cap, hopped on to Elsie's hand, like a 'little breath', she claimed*

FRANCES AND THE FAIRY DANCERS *This is the first photograph taken by the cousins in the glen at the back of their home, and they claimed it showed creatures they had been playing with all through spring. The dancing fairies were coloured in shades of green, lavender and mauve, they said, but the colours faded away to almost pure white. Experts have held that this picture could not have been faked*

ELSIE'S POSY *This fairy with the 1920's hairstyle poises on a bush to offer the 16-year-old Elsie a posy of tiny flowers. Her wings, the girl told a researcher, were shot with brilliant streaks of yellow*

343

Ebchester *Durham*

An argument caused a local 18th-century landowner named Robert Johnson to disinherit his son, and say: 'I hope my right arm will burn away before I give him sixpence.' On his death bed, however, he relented his harsh treatment and reinstated the youth as his heir. At the funeral, an investigation of the coffin revealed that the right arm of the corpse had shrivelled as though burnt away.

A CURE FOR TOOTHACHE

Still standing 4 miles south-east of Elsdon, Northumberland, is Winter's Gibbet, so named because a man named William Winter was hanged there in 1791 for murdering a woman. There is a traditional belief that toothache can be cured by cutting a splinter of wood from the gibbet and rubbing it on the affected spot

Farne Islands *Nthld*

Legend says that when Cuthbert, Bishop of Lindisfarne, came to live on Farne Island in the 7th century, he put to flight the spirits that frequented the place. But they only retreated as far as the outlying islands, where their screams could still be heard. Their hideously deformed, dark-featured wraiths have also been reported, usually riding on goats – a beast favoured by the Devil. Some people believe they are the ghosts of drowned sailors.

Featherstone *Nthld*

The ghosts of members of a wedding party, including the bride and groom, who were waylaid in Pinkingscleugh Glen and murdered by the bride's rejected lover, are reputed to haunt the grounds of Featherstone Castle near Haltwhistle. Legend does not record the date but the bride was the daughter of a former Baron Featherstonehaugh.

Fewston *N. Yorks*

Haverah Park, a mile east of Fewston, is said to be named after a cripple called Havera who, in the 14th century, requested a small piece of land from John of Gaunt, Duke of Lancaster. The duke agreed, on the terms that Havera could have as much land as he could hop around in a day. Havera accepted the challenge and from dawn to sunset he hopped along on his crutches to win the area now known as Haverah Park. A ruined castle in the park is called John of Gaunt's Castle.

Filey *N. Yorks*

The inhabitants of Filey were once noted for their ungodly ways, and visiting clergy were often pelted with fish. But early in the 19th century, John Oxtoby, known as 'Praying Johnny', a preacher from Bridlington, managed to convert the inhabitants to Christian practice. Tradition says that when Oxtoby first saw the town he fell to his knees and prayed. He asked the Lord not to make a fool of him, since he had already told his own parishioners that he would convert the Filey people.

Flamborough *Humberside*

The ghost of a girl known as Jenny Gallows still threatens local children. They have a traditional belief that if their games disturb Jenny's ghost it will call out this rhyme:

> 'Ah'll put on mi bonnet
> An tee on mi shoe,
> An if thoo's not off
> Ah'll be after thoo.'

The ghost of a headless woman has also been reported in the neighbourhood; and a spectral 'White Lady' is said to haunt Danes' Dyke, a probable Iron Age earthwork west of the village.

Fountains Abbey *N. Yorks*

A friar from the abbey who was renowned for his strength and for his skill as an archer is said to have challenged Robin Hood to a sword fight. Their battle was long and fierce, but finally the friar was obliged to surrender. He joined Robin's band, and later became famous as Friar Tuck.

Giggleswick *N. Yorks*

Near Giggleswick Scar is an oddity of nature, the Ebbing and Flowing Well. An explanation for its behaviour is that a nymph who was being chased by a satyr prayed to the gods for help. They turned her into a spring of water, which still ebbs and flows with her panting breaths.

The 17th-century highwayman, John Nevison, is said to have evaded capture by letting his horse drink at the well. The water gave the horse strength and Nevison escaped by leaping from the top of a cliff, still known as Nevison's Leap.

Glaisdale *N. Yorks*

Lovers' Bridge crosses the River Esk and bears the initials TF and the date 1619. The initials are said to belong to Thomas Ferris, who used to wade or swim the river to meet his sweetheart. When he went to America to seek his fortune, he vowed to build a bridge across if he became rich. He became very rich indeed and, when he returned to marry his old love, he paid for the bridge to be built.

Goathland *N. Yorks*

The local Sword Dancers still perform on Plough Monday, in January. One of their characters is called Isaac, or T'Awd Man. They are also known as the Plough Stots, and used to plough a furrow in the lawns of people who would not pay them.

Great Lumley *Durham*

The ghost of a young girl confronted the local miller, John Grahame, one night in 1631. She said she had been murdered by his neighbour, John Walker, who had made her pregnant, and that she would haunt the miller until she was revenged. The terrified miller told the authorities, who found the girl's body and arrested Walker and another man. Their trial lasted only a day. It was hurried over after a witness said he saw the image of a girl standing on Walker's shoulders. Both Walker and his accomplice were hanged.

THE SAINT WHO HATED WOMEN

St Cuthbert's dislike of women was as well known as his love for birds and beasts. It is said to have sprung from a time when the holy man was living as a hermit in the Northumbrian hills, and a Pictish king's daughter falsely accused him of fathering her child. Appalled by the very idea, Cuthbert prayed aloud for a sign to prove his innocence – and the ground opened and swallowed the princess up. Her father hastily forgave the saint and begged him to return his daughter. Cuthbert agreed, provided that no woman should ever approach him again. The king decreed that women must not enter churches dedicated to Cuthbert.

The legend was kept alive long after St Cuthbert's body had been moved from Lindisfarne, or Holy Island, to rest in Durham Cathedral. A woman called Sungeoua, wife of a local dignitary named Gamelus, was said to have taken a short cut home through the cathedral cemetery when she

collapsed, paralysed by a stroke. Gamelus rushed his wife home, but she died that night.

Another woman who angered the saint by exploring the cathedral was said to have been found next day with her throat cut, the fatal knife still clutched in her hand.

The saint's wrath

The stories were added to in the 12th century, when Bishop Pudsey tried to build a Lady Chapel near the saint's tomb. The ground shook and pillars cracked, and the chapel had to be built further away, at the west end of the cathedral.

Cuthbert became Bishop of Lindisfarne in 684. Twice a day, the ebbing tide leaves a land bridge to the mainland – a causeway of firm sand. This 'miraculous gift' is said to have been provided by the saint, to enable people coming to his church at the Lindisfarne Priory on Sundays to cross without getting their feet wet.

The miraculous corpse

The monks who moved the saint's body out of the path of marauding Danes some years after he died in 687, are said to have found the corpse remarkably preserved. It was still uncorrupted when examined in 1104 and in 1537, but only bones were found when the tomb was opened in 1827. A story persists, however, that these are the bones of a monk, and the saint's body lies elsewhere.

Paradoxically, the saint who disliked females found his resting place at Durham – then called Dunholme – through the agency of two women. His coffin became rooted to the ground at a place called Ward-lawe and it was revealed to the monks that it must be taken to Dunholme. They did not know where this was until they heard one woman tell another that she had lost her cow at nearby Dunholme. So when she set off to look for the missing beast, the monks followed her to the town.

345

Guisborough *Cleveland*

An underground passage was believed to run from 12th-century Guisborough Priory to a field in Tocketts, a parish to the north. Halfway along the passage was a chest of gold guarded by a raven or crow. On the single occasion that an explorer found the treasure, he fled in terror on seeing the bird transform itself into the Devil.

Guiseley *W. Yorks*

An ancient ceremony known as Clipping the Church takes place on August 5, the feast of St Oswald, patron saint of the parish. The parishioners move in procession around the church to symbolise their love for it. Clipping is the Old English word for encircling.

Halifax *W. Yorks*

It was Halifax's notorious treatment of petty criminals from the mid-14th century onwards that earned the town its place in the old saying: 'From Hell, Hull and Halifax – good Lord, deliver us.' Anyone who stole goods worth 13½ pence or more within the boundaries of the Forest of Hardwick was imprisoned for a week, put in the stocks for three days with the stolen goods on his back, then executed with a guillotine called 'the maiden of Halifax'. This was a massive axe, weighted with lead. The wooden pin which held it aloft was sometimes pulled out by an animal, if that was what the thief had stolen.

In 1650 the threat of a local rising, which followed the execution of two men for stealing two horses and 9 yds of cloth, ended this harsh treatment. A model of the guillotine, incorporating the original axe, is displayed at the Bankfield Museum, Halifax.

Handale *Cleveland*

Scaw Wood is said to be named after a dragon-slaying youth of medieval times. The dragon, known as the Serpent of Handale, lived in the wood near a small Benedictine priory and preyed on young women of the district.

Scaw, dressed in armour, struck a rock near the dragon's cave and the beast rushed out. It attacked him with its poisonous sting and breathed fire from its nostrils. Just as Scaw's armour was becoming unbearably hot he managed to plunge his sword into the dragon's throat. Exploring its cave, he found a beautiful girl, an earl's daughter. He married her and became a wealthy and famous landowner.

Harpham *Humberside*

Whenever the head of the St Quinton family, lords of Harpham, was about to die, a ghostly drumming is said to have sounded from a well in a field near the church, now known as the Drumming Well. Legend has it that this was prophesied by the mother of a drummer boy who was accidentally knocked into the well by one of the St Quinton family.

Another version is that William the Conqueror, after taking part in a battle near Harpham, promised to give the village and surrounding lands to the first person to reach the village. This was a drummer boy, but a knight named St Quinton knocked him into the well and claimed the village instead.

Another well, near the churchyard, is dedicated to St John of Beverley, whose traditional birthplace is Harpham. Its waters reputedly wrought many miracles and could also subdue the fiercest animals.

Hedley on the Hill *Nthld*

The Hedley Kow was a boggle, or mischievous spirit, who plagued the district by putting spinning wheels out of action, knocking over cooking pots and unravelling knitting. He could assume strange shapes; one of his favourites was a truss of straw. Disguised as two girls, he once led a couple of men into a bog and then disappeared. The Kow has not been reported since the middle of the 19th century.

THE STORM LEVELLER

One of the three 15th-century bells in Heighington church, Durham (above), is inscribed to St Peter. It bears the message, in Latin, 'Thou Peter When beaten calm the angry waves'. During the Middle Ages church bells were rung to drive away the spirits of the storm

Hell Gill Beck *N. Yorks*

It is said that while Satan was building Devil's Bridge, he was carrying stones from a mountain top in his apron when the straps broke and the stones went crashing down the mountainside. Legend claims that these formed the heap near the bridge.

THE CHARLTON SPUR

When food was low at Hesleyside Hall, home of the Charlton family near Bellingham, Northumberland, a spur on a covered dish was presented to the head of the family – a hint that he should go cattle-stealing across the border. The 16th-century spur is still in the Hall

Hexham *Nthld*

Until the Dissolution in 1539, Hexham Priory was one of the chief sanctuaries in the north of England. Anyone within a mile-wide area around the priory – marked by crosses at each point of the compass – could claim sanctuary, and any person seizing the fugitive was fined by the church. But excommunication awaited a person who dragged a fugitive out of the 7th-century sanctuary seat in the abbey, known as St Wilfrid's Chair or the Frid Stool.

Horcum *N. Yorks*

The hollow alongside the Pickering to Whitby road, known as the Hole of Horcum or the Devil's Punchbowl, is said to have been caused when the giant Wade dug up a spadeful of earth. He threw this away to form the nearby hill of Blakey Topping.

Hubberholme *N. Yorks*

Every New Year's Eve in The George, the local inn, the vicar and churchwardens gather in one room, known as The House of Lords, and the village farmers in another room, The House of Commons. The two sides negotiate for the following year's tenancy of a field called Poor's Pasture. The rent ranges from £20 per acre for the best pasture to £7 for the worst, and the money is given to the poor of Hubberholme.

Hylton *Tyne & Wear*

One room of Hylton Castle, in the valley of the Wear, was never used because it was said to be haunted by the Cauld Lad, the shivering ghost of Roger Skelton, a stable boy at the castle. He was killed in 1609 by his master, Robert Hilton, who, enraged when the horse he had ordered did not appear, struck the sleeping boy with a pitchfork. Panic-stricken, he threw the body into a well; since then, anyone who sees the ghost is said to be permanently afflicted with damp, deathly cold.

This ghost has been confused in local tradition with a brownie, a domestic spirit, who liked tidying things up at the castle. If they were tidied already, he angrily threw them into confusion. Growing tired of this, the servants laid a green cloak and hood out for him, the traditional method of encouraging a brownie to leave. The Cauld Lad put them on, then disappeared, never to return.

FERTILITY CHAIR

Bede's Chair, in St Paul's Church, Jarrow, Tyne and Wear, may have belonged to the Venerable Bede (673–735), the chronicler who spent most of his life in Jarrow. For centuries, this ancient oak chair was popularly believed to influence marriage and childbirth. Unmarried girls placed splinters from the chair beneath their pillows so that they would dream of their future husbands. Brides sat in it after the wedding ceremony to ensure fertility, while mothers-to-be soaked chips carved from the chair in water and then drank the liquid in the hope that it would ease the pangs of childbirth

WITCH BARRIER

Several timber-framed houses in Yorkshire and Lancashire still preserve curiously carved oak beams that were once thought to be a defence against witches. These beams were usually planted upright to support the lintel over the hearth in the living-room. A St Andrew's cross was incised at the top and beneath it were carved horizontal bands, varying from 1 to 12. Occasionally, the date of the carving was added. It was believed that a witch could not enter beyond the post; nor while it stood, could she lay a spell upon the hearth of the house that contained one of these powerful talismans.

As belief in witchcraft faded during the 18th century the witch-posts were removed and re-used in the building of barns and outhouses. Only three or four of the posts are known to stand in their original positions. The Rydale Folk Museum at Hutton-le-Hole, N. Yorkshire, possesses some examples of witch-posts (right). Most are tenoned and peg-holed at the top, indicating where they were attached to a cross-beam. At the bottom they are often drilled to take the supports of an inglenook seat.

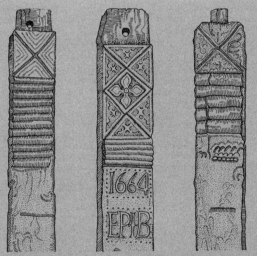

THREE YORKSHIRE WITCH-POSTS *One came from a shoemaker's shop in Danby (left); another from a farm in Glaisdale (centre); and the third from an old house in Scarborough (right)*

Kirkham *N. Yorks*

Kirkham Priory, whose ruins lie beside the River Derwent in the Vale of York, was founded *c.* 1125 by Walter L'Espec, a leading judge of Henry I's time. Tradition holds that he built the priory in memory of his only son, Walter, whose mother begged him not to go hunting one day after she had felt a strong premonition of disaster. The boy ignored her warning and was killed when his horse threw him as he was riding home. Near the priory gateway are the remains of the stone cross on which he struck his head, inflicting the fatal injury.

Kirklees Park *W. Yorks*

Robin Hood, in his old age, is said to have fallen ill and asked for refuge at Kirklees Hall, which was then a nunnery in Kirklees Park. The prioress, who is thought to have been his aunt, locked him in a small room and bled him so severely that he was near death. The dying hero summoned Little John by sounding his hunting horn. When his faithful companion arrived, Robin shot an arrow high above the park and asked to be buried where it landed. Little John carried out Robin's wish, and the mound which is claimed to be his grave still exists within the Park estate.

Lee Gap *W. Yorks*

For nearly 800 years the Lee Gap Fair has been held in a field that lies between Wakefield and Dewsbury. Until the 18th century, it was a general trade fair that ran continuously from August 24 to September 19. Known as 'first o' Lee' and 'last o' Lee', these are now the only two dates on which the fair occurs, and horse-trading has become the fair's major activity, though once cattle and geese were also sold.

MOTHER SHIPTON'S *favorite mode of* TRAVELLING

MOTHER SHIPTON

Ursula Southeil, the grotesque woman who was destined to be England's most famous prophetess, was born in 1488 in a cave in Knaresborough, North Yorkshire. Her mother, Agatha, died giving birth to her, and her death was apparently attended by 'strange and terrible noises'. Ursula was then placed in the care of one of the townswomen. One day she left the infant alone in her cottage, and when she returned with several neighbours they were at once attacked by supernatural forces. All of the men found themselves yoked to a floating staff from which a woman hung by her toes, and the women were compelled to dance in circles; whenever they tried to stop, they were pricked with pins by an imp in the form of a monkey. Ursula and her cradle were found inside the chimney, suspended in mid-air 9 ft above the ground.

Magic and marriage

Mysterious events continued to plague the cottage as the child grew up. Furniture moved up and down the stairs of its own accord, and at mealtimes food vanished from the plates of startled guests.

Ursula married Toby Shipton of Shipton, near York, in 1512, and soon afterwards gained renown as a fortune-teller. She was called Mother Shipton, and by virtue of her appearance was well suited to play the role of a witch. It was said that 'her stature was larger than common, her body crooked and her face frightful, but her understanding extraordinary'.

A witch's revenge

She aroused local curiosity to fever pitch, and neighbours were forever prying into her private life. Mother Shipton is said to have taken revenge by bewitching a breakfast party at which many of her antagonists were present. All of the guests suddenly broke into uncontrollable paroxysms of laughter and fled from the house, each of them pursued by a hideous goblin. They informed the local magistrates who summoned Mother Shipton to court, where she said that far worse things would occur unless she were left alone. Then she shouted out the magic words 'Updraxi, call Stygician Helluei', and was carried off by a winged dragon, according to contemporary reports.

Most of the prophecies ascribed to her, such as her predictions of trains and the telegraph, are now known to have been written by a man named Hindley in 1871. Despite this, she still continues to be Yorkshire's most famous witch, and Mother Shipton's Cave remains as her memorial at Knaresborough.

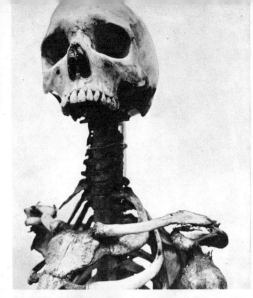

THE KILLER WITCH

Mary Bateman, the Witch of Leeds, made a living by her skilful confidence tricks, the most famous of which was to show a hen apparently laying a magic egg on which were inscribed the words: 'Christ is coming.' In 1809, she was found guilty of poisoning Rebecca Perigo, one of her gullible clients. She was hanged at York and gibbeted afterwards in Leeds; it is said that souvenir hunters stripped the flesh off her bones for luck. Her skeleton (above) was preserved and is now in Leeds Medical School

Lindisfarne *Nthld*
Lindisfarne, also known as Holy Island, is famed as an important centre of early English Christianity. It was sacked by Danish raiders in AD 875, an event which was said to be preceded by storms and 'fiery serpents' flying through the sky. Legend claims that when the now ruined priory was built in the 11th century, the labourers fed on bread made from air and drank wine from a bottomless cup.

The old North Country marriage custom of jumping over the Petting Stone still occurs in Lindisfarne. The stone stands in the island's church-yard, and is believed to be the socket of St Cuthbert's Cross which dates from the 7th century. Brides jump over it as they leave the church, symbolising a leap into a new way of life.

Long Marston *N. Yorks*
In 1644, Oliver Cromwell defeated a Royalist army at the Battle of Marston Moor, about a mile north of Long Marston village. The ghosts of Royalist soldiers have frequently been seen in the area, including three phantoms in Cavalier costume; they were reported recently by two motorists travelling on the A59 York–Harrogate road. The Old Hall in the village, used by Cromwell during the battle, is now said to be haunted by his ghost.

Market Weighton *Humberside*
The annual Kipling Cotes Derby is held near Market Weighton on the third Thursday in March. Claimed to be the oldest flat race in England, the Derby dates from 1519 and is run over a 4-mile course which ends at Kipling Cotes Farm. Each rider must weigh over 10 st. and pays a £4 entrance fee. The entrance money is won by whoever finishes second, while the winner receives the interest on a sum of money that was invested in 1618. Sometimes the entrance money amounts to more than the first prize.

Midgley *W. Yorks*
Every year, on Good Friday, a traditional mumming play known as the Pace Egg Play is performed by the schoolboys of Midgley. The name is derived from the word Pasche, meaning Easter, and refers to the old custom of rewarding the actors with eggs. The play, which has been performed in Midgley since 1800, is thought to be based on a 16th-century story called *The History of the Seven Champions of Christendom*.

Newbrough *Nthld*
Legend tells that the ashes of Old Meg, a 16th-century witch, are buried a mile north of Newbrough in a burn called Meggie's Dene which flows down from Torney's Fell. She was burnt alive for witchcraft and at her burial a stake was driven through her charred heart to prevent her soul wandering. It is said that her grave is marked by a pink thorn tree which grows at the water's edge.

Nunnington *N. Yorks*
In Nunnington church is a tomb surmounted by a stone effigy of Sir Walter de Teyes, who died in 1325. Local legend, however, claims that it is the burial place of Peter Loschy who is said to have killed a magic dragon in nearby Loschy Wood. Loschy and his dog fought with the beast for hours, but each time the dragon received a wound it rolled on the ground and the wound instantly healed. The creature was finally defeated when Loschy began to hack its body to pieces, for his dog carried off each piece until nothing remained of the monster.

Pelton *Durham*

The hamlet of Picktree, near Pelton, was once the legendary haunt of a mischievous spirit known as the Picktree Brag. It was able to change its shape and appeared in many different forms, but was most often seen as a donkey or a horse which would throw anyone who attempted to ride it.

Pontefract *W. Yorks*

Pontefract is famous for the round liquorice sweets known as Pontefract Cakes. Liquorice roots were probably first brought to Britain nearly 2000 years ago by the Romans, but local legend insists that a Pontefract schoolmaster introduced the plant into England in 1588. He is said to have found a bundle of liquorice branches on a Yorkshire beach, washed ashore from a wrecked Armada galleon. They seemed admirably suited to birching the boys at his school; and while this painful process was going on, the boys bit on other liquorice branches to stifle their cries of pain. Thus they discovered the plant's flavour, and soon it was grown throughout the Pontefract area.

WHEN DEATH STOPPED A CLOCK

In the 19th century, the George Hotel at Piercebridge in Durham was run by two brothers named Jenkins. A long-case clock in the hall (above) began to lose time when one of them died, and it stopped for ever at 4.46 on the day that the other brother died. The event was celebrated in a popular song, 'My Grandfather's Clock'

THE LAMBTON WORM

In the Middle Ages, there was once a wild youth who was heir to Lambton Castle, which is near the village of Penshaw in County Durham. He went fishing in the River Wear one Sunday and caught a strange-looking worm. On his way home, he threw it into a well by the castle and forgot about it.

As he grew up, he changed his wild ways and eventually joined a crusade to the Holy Land. During his absence, the worm grew to an enormous size and wriggled out of the well. It soon began to ravage the district, killing man and beast, and each night it slept coiled three times around Lambton Hill, which is now called Worm Hill. Attempts were made to slay the monster, but whenever it was cut in two the halves merely joined up again.

Seven years later, the Lord of Lambton's son returned. He was stricken with remorse at the result of his youthful folly, so he asked a witch what would be the best way of tackling the monster. She told him to cover his armour with razors, and then fight the worm in the middle of the river. The price of her counsel was that he should kill the first creature to greet him after his victory.

The plan was successful, for when the worm wrapped itself around the knight, the razors cut it into pieces which were swept away by the river before they could join together. But when he signalled to his father on his bugle, the old man forgot to release a greyhound as arranged and ran to the river himself. The son refused to kill his father, so the witch put a curse on the family. In fact, from that day on, many Lambtons died violently – some in tragic accidents and others in battle.

COWARDICE AND COURAGE AT RICHMOND CASTLE

A Richmond potter named Thompson is said to have once found a secret tunnel that ran beneath Richmond Castle in N. Yorkshire. He followed it into a deep cavern where he discovered King Arthur and his knights lying asleep. A horn and a sword lay near by and, as Thompson picked up the horn, the knights began to stir. Terrified, he ran back along the tunnel as a voice cried after him:

'Potter Thompson, Potter Thompson,

If thou hadst drawn the sword or blown the horn, Thou hadst been the luckiest man e'er born.'

Another story tells that a drummer boy was sent along an underground passage from the castle to discover if it led to Easby Abbey, 1½ miles away. His drumbeat was followed from above ground by his fellow soldiers, but it stopped halfway to the abbey and he was never seen again. It is said that his drumming can still be heard

Ripon *N. Yorks*
Every night at 9 o'clock, the City Hornblower of Ripon sounds the Wakeman's Horn at each corner of the 90 ft obelisk in the market square and in front of the mayor's house. The custom began in AD 886, when Alfred the Great granted the first charter to the town and presented it with a Charter Horn, which is now on show in the mayor's parlour. A Wakeman was appointed to patrol the city after the curfew had been sounded each night, giving rise to the city's motto: 'Except ye Lord keep ye cittie, ye Wakeman waketh in vain.' The 14th-century, half-timbered Wakeman's House stands on the south-west corner of the square.

Rokeby *Durham*
According to legend, the 'fiercest pig in the North of England' roamed wild in Rokeby Wood during the 16th century. Called the Felon Sow of Rokeby, she belonged to Ralph of Rokeby and was alleged to have killed many swineherds. Her owner finally gave her to the Grey Friars of Richmond, and one day three monks from the monastery came to Rokeby to collect her. Struggling fiercely, she backed into a kiln and they managed to slip a noose around her neck. Then, as they tried to lead her away, she charged them. One friar was knocked down, another was gored and the third climbed up a tree where, in an attempt to pacify the sow, he read the Gospel of St John to her in Latin. The beast remained unimpressed, and at last the friars fled for their lives. The next day the monastery hired two men-at-arms to kill her and, when she was dead, the monks sang a Te Deum to celebrate their victory.

Rothley *Nthld*
On the banks of the Hart Burn, near Rothley, stand several rocks which are perforated by small holes. Local tradition asserts that the holes were made by fairies for cooling porridge which they cooked at a mill that once stood close by. The miller was very annoyed at having his oats stolen, so one night he dropped a sod of earth down the mill's chimney. It landed in the cooking pot and splashed hot porridge over the fairies. Crying 'Burnt and scalded!', the enraged creatures caught the miller and beat him so soundly that he was lame for life.

Rudston *Humberside*
A 25 ft high late Stone Age monolith, thought to be the tallest in Britain, stands in the churchyard at Rudston. It is reputed to weigh 80 tons and to extend another 25 ft below ground. One legend holds that it simply fell from the sky one day 'killing certain desecrators of the churchyard'; but another states that it was thrown by the Devil, who wished to destroy the church, and it landed in its present position because of his bad marksmanship.

Runswick *N. Yorks*
Hob is the country name for a brownie, and a small cavern called the Hob Hole, near Runswick Bay, is said to have been the home of one of these shaggy-haired fairy creatures. Local people believed that the hob could cure whooping-cough, so those children who were suffering from the disease were taken to the cave where their parents sought the hob's help by reciting the rhyme:

Hob-hole Hob!
My bairn's gotten t'kink cough,
Tak't off! Tak't off!

Saltergate *N. Yorks*
A peat fire which has been kept alight for nearly 200 years burns in the kitchen of the Saltergate Inn, high on the North Yorkshire Moors. Tradition says that the Devil once visited the inn, only to be exorcised by a local priest. Satan, rather than face the harsh weather outside, is said to have fled to the kitchen. A peat fire was immediately lit in order to keep him there, and he has remained imprisoned on the endlessly smouldering hearth ever since.

Scarborough N. Yorks

At noon on Shrove Tuesday, the pancake bell in the town museum is rung to announce that pancake making may now begin. All day there are skipping matches on the foreshore; skipping ropes are provided, and anyone may join in.

A Scarborough tradition of Robin Hood tells how the hero joined the crew of a fishing boat, but being ignorant of the ways of the sea, he neglected to bait his hooks before throwing them overboard. He made amends when a French man-o'-war attacked the boat. Robin led the crew in boarding the raider, killed her captain and captured a vast sum of gold, which he presented to the poor fishermen.

Sedgefield Durham

In 1747, the rector died a few days before the payment of the tithes were due. His wife was reluctant to forfeit the money, so she hit upon the brilliant idea of preserving her husband's body in salt and keeping the news of his death secret until the tithes had been paid. The rectory was burnt down in 1792, but until then it was haunted by the vexed rector. He was known locally as 'The Pickled Parson'.

On Shrove Tuesday there is a traditional football match between two teams of villagers. The pitch is 500 yds long, and the goals are a pond and a stream. The verger, who provides the ball, kicks off at 1 p.m., and the match ends when the first goal has been scored.

Semer Water N. Yorks

Beneath the waters of the lake there is said to lie the remains of a once-proud city. Tradition has it that a beggar once asked for shelter there, but was turned away by everyone except a poor couple in a hillside cottage. Next morning the beggar had vanished, and when the couple looked out, the town too had disappeared beneath the lake. It is claimed that the roofs of the town can sometimes be seen below the surface.

Sessay N. Yorks

In the early 16th century, a giant lived in the village woods. He had legs and arms like an elephant's limbs, a single eye in the middle of his forehead and his teeth were as long as a pitchfork's prongs. One day, a knight named Sir Guy Dawnay, asked Joan Darrell, heiress of the Sessay lands, to marry him. She agreed, provided he first killed the giant that was plaguing the village. The knight's opportunity came when the giant reached into a windmill for a sack of grain. A turning sail hit him on the head and stunned him. Sir Guy ran him through as he lay there, and claimed Joan's hand.

Sewingshields Nthld

Deep in the crags beneath the remains of Sewing-shields Castle there is said to be a cave where King Arthur and his knights lie sleeping until their country once again calls on their services.

North-west of the ruins are two outcrops of sand-stone known as King's Crag and Queen's Crag. Legend says that Arthur, who was sitting on one rock, had a quarrel with Queen Guinevere, who was sitting on the other. He threw an enormous boulder at her which bounced off her comb and fell between the two crags. There it lies to this day, the teethmarks of the comb still plainly visible on the face of the rock.

SWORD DANCING

In the iron-mining villages around Sheffield and in the Cleveland and North Yorkshire areas traditional dances, performed with 30–40 in. long swords made of steel or wood, are practised still by teams of six or eight men. The dances vary from area to area but all involve the mock decapitation of a leader.

The origins of sword dancing, like those of mumming plays, are obscure. One theory is that the dances once formed part of an annual folk play, but as audiences grew increasingly sophisticated and became bored with the dramatic part of this it was discarded, and only the dances and some songs were retained.

The Sheffield area has two sword-dance teams – from the villages of Grenoside and Handsworth.

BLACK AND WHITE DANCERS *Outside Handsworth church on Boxing Day the local sword-dance team puts on a performance similar to that of the Grenoside dancers. They wear black, braided tunics, white trousers, black boots and gaiters*

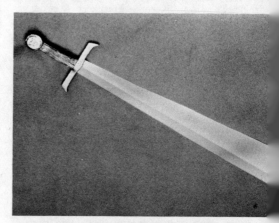

KILLER OF THE SOCKBURN WORM

The Conyers Falchion, a broadsword now in the library of Durham Cathedral, was reputedly used in the 14th century by Sir John Conyers to kill the Sockburn Worm, a terrible dragon. For this exploit he was rewarded with the lordship of Sockburn. Graystane, a boulder in a field near the church, marks the spot of the killing. After this it became the custom for the Lord of Sockburn to meet every newly appointed bishop of Durham at Croft Bridge, on the River Tees, as he entered his diocese and to present him with the sword. The ceremony took place for the last time in 1826

DEATH AND RESURRECTION *On Boxing Day the Grenoside sword-dance team performs outside the Old Harrow Inn in Main Street. Their dance is a fine example of the English longsword dance – as distinct from the short-sword, or rapper-dance – though both demand skill, perfect teamwork and strength.*

The team of six and their leader are dressed in paisley-patterned tunics decorated with rosettes, and white trousers. The dancers wear caps, the leader a rabbit-skin hat. A fiddler provides music for the ceremony.

The dance begins with the leader's calling-on song, which introduces the team to the audience. They begin by clashing their swords together, then form a ring, each man holding his own

sword in his right hand and the point of his neighbour's in his left. The dancers then weave patterns, twisting themselves under the swords and jumping over them but never breaking the ring; their movements are intricate and athletic and hours of practice are needed.

For the dramatic climax of the performance they plait the swords into a star shape, known as a 'lock' or 'nut'. The dancers lower the lock over the head of their leader and then 'behead' him by lifting his fur hat on high with the lock. He falls to the ground as if dead but is later restored to life by a comic doctor from amongst the mumming characters that accompany the sword dancers in all their performances

Stamford Bridge *N. Yorks*

In 1066, a great battle was fought here between the Norsemen and the English under King Harold. Tradition has it that one gigantic Viking kept the English at bay on a narrow wooden bridge over the Derwent. Then an English soldier, using a wash-tub as a boat, manoeuvred under the bridge and stabbed the Viking with a spear. Each September 25, to commemorate this act, a tub-shaped pie is shared out in the town. The custom died out at the beginning of the century but was revived in 1966.

Stamfordham *Nthld*

The nearby hamlet of Black Heddon used to be haunted by a ghost whose rustling dress gave her the name of Silky. Her most alarming habit was to suddenly jump up behind passing horsemen. Her favourite haunt, known as Silky's Chair, was in an old tree overlooking the waterfall at nearby Belsay. Silky was seen no more after a ceiling in Black Heddon collapsed to reveal a bag of gold. From this it was deduced that she was a former owner of the house and the treasure.

Another version says that Silky was a boggart, or mischievous spirit, who cleaned dirty houses by night but wreaked havoc in tidy ones. Once she transfixed a waggoner's team at a bridge south of Black Heddon. The team could not be moved until a sprig of rowan, the traditional antidote to magic, was tied to the waggon.

Summer Bridge *N. Yorks*

Brimham Rocks, eroded by the weather into weird shapes, were once regarded as the work of Druids; several of the rocks bear such names as Druid's Altar and Druid's Head. It was thought that a narrow, tube-shaped hole in one rock had been gouged out to serve as an oracle: a Druid would stand behind the rock and speak through the hole.

In one of the many legends told about the rocks, an eloping couple named Edwin and Julia were pursued by the girl's angry father. At the top of a crag, he caught up with them. Preferring death to separation, the couple leapt into space. Miraculously, they landed safely, whereupon the relieved parent gladly gave his consent to the marriage. The rock is still known as Lovers' Rock.

Thorpe *N. Yorks*

On his way back from delivering sandals, Ralph Calvert, a local shoemaker, was forced to swim the rain-swollen River Dibb. As he dried off on the other bank, he began to sing. Suddenly, he was joined by the Devil who insisted on singing the choruses. The pair sang well together, and after a while, Ralph offered his strange partner a drink. The Devil accepted, and offered the shoemaker a wish in exchange. Ralph thought, and asked for a bridge over the river. The bridge immediately appeared, and stands there today, known locally as 'Devil's Bridge', though the map says Dibble's Bridge.

Threshfield *N. Yorks*
According to local tradition, the Well of Our Lady is a sanctuary from the powers of darkness. The story is told of a local man who, on his way home from the inn one night, was chased by a band of wicked imps and fled to the well for refuge. Although the demons dared not approach, they surrounded him and kept him there all night, until they were forced to depart at cock-crow.

Tynemouth *Tyne & Wear*
A monk from Tynemouth Priory once stole a pig's head from the kitchens of Seaton Delaval manor house. The lord of the manor, furious at the loss of his favourite delicacy, rode after him and beat him unmercifully. A year later the monk died. The other monks blamed Delaval, and refused him absolution until he had given a grant of land to the monastery and erected a cross inscribed:
'O horrid dede
To kill a man for a pigge's hede.'
A fragment of the cross is now in the Newcastle Museum of Antiquities.

Upsall *N. Yorks*
An Upsall man once journeyed to London. As he stood on London Bridge, he was approached by a Quaker who asked him what he was doing there. The Yorkshireman replied that he had dreamt on three consecutive nights that if he stood on the bridge long enough he would hear something to his advantage. The Londoner laughed and said that he had dreamt that if he went to a place called Upsall and dug under a certain bush in the castle grounds he would find a pot of gold. But no one had ever heard of Upsall. The Upsall man said nothing, but hurried home and – so the story relates – found the gold. An elder bush in the grounds of the castle was pointed out as the spot where the gold was discovered. A similar tale is told in Norfolk.

Wakefield *W. Yorks*
In her will, Mary Bolles of Heath Hall, near Wakefield, left instructions that the room in which she died was to be permanently sealed. After her death in 1661, the room was accordingly closed off. Fifty years later, however, it was opened, and after this the ghost of Mary Bolles never ceased to haunt the Hall. Stone effigies were laid on her tomb in Ledsham church in an attempt to quiet her restless spirit, but in vain. Troops stationed at the Hall in 1943 claimed to have seen the ghost. A caretaker reported also that his alsatian guard dog would never walk through the death room. The house has now been demolished, but the door of the haunted bedroom has been preserved in Wakefield Museum.

Walton *W. Yorks*
This village near Wetherby was famous until early this century for its 'rag well', whose water was said to cure eye ailments. The name arose from the custom of tying strips of cloth as mementoes to the tree above the well. A notorious highwayman, Nevison, is supposed to have fallen asleep one day by the well and to have been surprised by a party of local men who had come to arrest him. He escaped by pointing a 'burrtree gun', or stick, at them. They took it for a gun and ran off, like frightened cattle. Since then, local men are often scornfully referred to as 'Walton calves'.

West Witton *N. Yorks*
Burning the Bartle takes place here each year on the Saturday nearest St Bartholomew's Day (August 24). The Bartle, a huge straw effigy, is carried through the village after dark to be burnt on a bonfire. As the procession moves along, an old rhyme is chanted:
In Penhill crags, he tore his rags.
At Hunter's thorn, he blew his horn.
At Caplebank stee, he broke his knee.
At Briskill beck, he brake his neck.
At Wadham's end, he couldn't fend.
At Briskill end, he made his end.
Shout, boys, shout!
Bartle, so the story goes, was an 18th-century swine-thief who was hunted over the surrounding fells before being captured and put to death.

Whalton *Nthld*
The traditional festival of Whalton Bale is held here each year on Old Mid-summer's Eve (July 4). A great bonfire is lit on the village green, and there is Morris and sword dancing to the music of fiddlers and Northumbrian pipers. 'Bale' comes from the Anglo-Saxon *bael*, meaning a great fire. Midsummer Eve bonfires were once a popular custom. The alteration of the calendar in 1752 resulted in dates being moved forward by 11 days. Traditionally minded countryfolk, however, went on celebrating the festival at the old time.

Whitburn *Tyne & Wear*
Bridal couples of old local families, as they leave the church after the wedding ceremony, are sometimes offered 'Hot Pots', mugs of mulled ale, spices and spirits. The custom is old. In 1865, one ungrateful bridegroom, after tasting the brew prepared by the local women, described the mixture in the mugs as 'simply horrible'.

Whitby *N. Yorks*
The ancient ceremony of Horngarth, or the Planting of the Penny Hedge, is still observed each year on the day before Ascension Day. Bundles of stakes and osiers, cut in Eskdale Side, are carried at sunrise through the town to the harbour. Here, they are planted at the water's edge, the 'yethers' (osiers) being woven through the 'stowers' (stakes) to form a 'hedge'.

The custom is said to have originated as a penance imposed by the abbot of Whitby in 1159 on three hunters who had beaten a hermit to death. Their lives were spared on condition that they and their descendants built a hedge each year on the water's edge, strong enough to withstand the onslaught of three tides.

The fame of Whitby Abbey goes back to Anglo-Saxon times. A legend relates how the abbess, St Hilda, rid Eskdale of snakes by driving them to the edge of the cliffs and cutting off their heads with her whip. The ammonites – fossilised shellfish – found on the rocks below are said to be their remains.

Caedmon, an abbey cowherd in the late 7th century, was teased because he could not sing. One night he had a vision of an angel who asked him to sing of the creation of the world. From then on he became famous as a poet – perhaps England's first. One of his manuscripts is kept in Cambridge University Library.

Wold Newton *Humberside*
According to local tradition, the strangely named Gypsey Race, a nearby stream, comes to full spate only before some great disaster. It is said that the stream flowed copiously before the Great Plague of 1666 and before both World Wars.

TALES OF YORK

The York Mystery plays are performed every three years in the ruins of St Mary's Abbey, and are the most famous of their kind in Britain. They date from the middle of the 14th century, and tell the story of mankind from the Creation to the Day of Judgment. The fullness of the text and stage directions is the result of the lucky chance survival of a complete manuscript in the library of the Fairfaxes, a local family.

The tomb of Dick Turpin, who was hanged at York in 1739, may be seen in the churchyard of St Denys and St George. Turpin's famous ride to York was almost certainly not made by him at all, but by another, equally celebrated robber, Nevison, during the reign of Charles II. The king,

amused by the exploit, is said to have granted Nevison a free pardon and christened him 'Swift Nicks'. In spite of this, Nevison, too, ended up on the gallows at York, in 1685. The leg-irons which held these two notorious highwaymen before their execution may be seen in York Castle Museum.

Three pathetic 15th-century ghosts, father, mother and child, were said to haunt Holy Trinity churchyard during the last century. The parents were buried in the church, but the child, because it had died of plague, had been interred outside the city. The mother's ghost would fetch the child from its own grave to that of the father, then take it back outside the city walls.

Ulph's pledge

One of the principal treasures of York Minster is the great ivory drinking-horn, over 2 ft in length, known as Ulph's Horn. Ulph was a Danish chieftain who held lands in western Yorkshire at the beginning of the 11th century. Legend relates how, after his eldest son Adelbert was killed in battle, Ulph attempted to bypass the claims of his other three sons and bequeath his domain to Adelbert's daughter, Adelwynne. She, however, persuaded him to bestow his lands on the Church. Accordingly, Ulph rode to York, taking with him his largest drinking-horn. Filling it with wine he knelt at the high altar in York Minster and, drinking off the wine, laid the horn on the altar to be held by the Church for all time as title to the lands over which he held sway and to all his wealth.

HORN OF ULPH *The 1000-year-old horn in York Minster is carved from an elephant tusk over 2 ft long. The ornamentation is 17th-century silver-gilt*

THE YORKSHIRE SAINTS

William Fitzherbert, nephew of King Stephen, became Archbishop of York in 1141, but after only a few years in office was deposed by Pope Eugenius. He was later restored amidst popular rejoicing and was canonised in the following century. Thirty-six miracles were attributed to him; they are recorded in the fine stained-glass window, known as St William's window, in the north transept of York Minster (*detail above*).

The most famous of these miracles occurred on William's triumphant return to York in 1154. The old

wooden bridge which spanned the River Ouse collapsed beneath the weight of the onlookers and hundreds were plunged into the deep river. St William made the sign of the cross and prayed. Immediately, the waters formed themselves into a bridge over which the drowning men and women reached dry land safely.

During the Middle Ages, St William's fame rivalled that of St John of Beverley, his predecessor at York during the 8th century. A healthy rivalry grew up between the cults of the two Yorkshire saints. If St

John cured a man of blindness, then St William would be credited with restoring eyes to a man whose eyes had been put out, and so on. One of the miracles depicted in the window, but attributed to both saints, concerns a young student of Beverley. The Devil had caused the young man to fall so much in love with a local girl that he lost all taste for his books. To make a young man fall out of love took all the powers of a saint. One of them – either William or John – intervened, and the student was restored to his right mind.

THE MARCHER LANDS

Cheshire, Cumbria, Greater Manchester, Lancashire, Merseyside, Isle of Man

 Even though Britain is a hive of industry and commerce, no one can stroll more than a few miles out of a town or city without discovering those deeper country virtues that stem from a respect for the soil. The industrial revolutionaries who built for themselves a harsh, commercial world and, in the 19th century, put Lancashire's children into the cotton mills and women down the mines, were fully aware of these qualities rooted in the people – staunchness, deliberation, firmness and stolidity. Weavers had, in their way, as much stamina as the wrestlers at Grasmere sports; Cheshire bowmen, who fought at Agincourt and Crécy, were justly famed for their resolution, while in the marcher lands of the borders, fell-toughened farmers and sturdy yeomen gave as good as they got in tussles with Scots reivers and fierce Welsh raiders. The memory of these wars still lingers in the ruined peel towers and castles of the borders, as well as in the many ballads commemorating heroes and their exploits. Tales and legends sprang from industry in much the same way, and weavers and miners sang of heroes of their own.

The people locked away behind the natural barriers of the Cheviots, Pennines and River Dee, with their admiration for physical strength and toughness, built legends around men with such qualities – like the giants of east Cumbria, and Cheshire's dragon slayer, Thomas Venables. The lonely fells promoted belief in witches and elemental spirits such as the wailing barguest with its glowing eyes, and the water-spirit, Jenny Greenteeth, who devours naughty children. In the Isle of Man, soldiers march at attention and the officer in charge salutes when they pass over the Fairy Bridge. Even with modern weapons, there is no point in taking unnecessary chances.

THE FOLKLORE YEAR

Good Friday
Liverpool, Merseyside
Burning Judas

Good Friday, Easter Tuesday and following Saturday
Workington, Cumbria
Uppies and Downies

Easter Saturday
Bacup, Lancs
Nutters' Dance

Easter Monday
Preston, Lancs
Egg Rolling

First Saturday in May
Knutsford, Cheshire
May Day Ceremonies

First Thursday in June
Neston, Cheshire
Club Day Procession

Saturday nearest July 2
Ambleside, Westmld
Rushbearing Procession

July 5
St Johns, Isle of Man
Tynwald Ceremony

July, date usually depending on tides
Peel, Isle of Man
Viking Festival

Saturday nearest to August 5
Grasmere, Cumbria
Rushbearing Procession

Thursday nearest to August 20
Grasmere, Cumbria
Annual Sports

Third Saturday in September
Egremont, Cumbria
Crab Fair

About a fortnight around October 31
Antrobus and Comberbach, Cheshire
Soul-Caking Play

KEY TO SYMBOLS

BELLS	GHOSTS	LOVE STORY
CRIME AND PUNISHMENT	GIANTS	MERMAIDS AND SEA-PEOPLE
CURIOUS CHARACTERS	GRAVES AND MONUMENTS	MYSTERIOUS STONES
CUSTOMS AND FESTIVALS	HEROES	SAINTS AND MIRACLES
DEVILS AND DEMONS	HOLY PLACES	SMUGGLERS AND WRECKERS
FABULOUS BEASTS	INDUSTRIAL LORE	WITCHES AND WIZARDS
FAIRIES	LOCAL CURIOSITIES	

NORTHUMBERLAND

BOWNESS-ON-SOLWAY

GREAT
CORBY
CARLISLE
(The Ballads, 360)

CALDBECK
RENWICK
LITTLE SALKELD
DRUGGAN HILL
EDENHALL
CROSS FELL
PENRITH
DURHAM
SOUTER FELL
WORKINGTON
DOCKRAY
CRACKENTHORPE
DERWENT
WATER
EAMONT
BRIDGE
COLBY
CUMBRIA
ARMBOTH FELL
NORTH STAINMORE
ST BEES
WASDALE
HEAD
DUNMAIL RAISE
GRASMERE
NATEBY
EGREMONT
TEBAY
GOSFORTH
AMBLESIDE
SEASCALE
KENTMERE
RAVENGLASS
TROUTBECK
BRIDGE
SEATHWAITE
KENDAL

LEVENS

KIRKBY
LONSDALE
NORTH
YORKSHIRE

LANCASTER
(Storm over Pendle, 370)

LANCASHIRE

NEWCHURCH
(Storm over Pendle, 370)

GARSTANG
(Boggart Hauntings, 364)
CLITHEROE
PRESTON
(Pace-Egging, 375)
LONGRIDGE
WALK MILL
HIGHER
(Boggart Hauntings, 364)
CLIVIGER GORGE
PENWORTHAM
WEST
HOGHTON
YORKSHIRE
BACUP

Isle of Man

PEEL
LAXLEY
GREEBA
MOUNTAIN

FAIRY BRIDGE
CASTLETOWN

BURSCOUGH
(Pace-Egging, 375)
BOLTON
GTR
SKELMERSDALE
MANCHESTER
WARDLEY
ASHTON-
UNDER-LYNE
ABRAM
MERSEYSIDE
MANCHESTER
STALYBRIDGE
LIVERPOOL
WINWICK
CONSTABLE
SANDS
APPLETON
ROSTHERNE
MARPLE
HALE
DISLEY
BLACK ROCK
KNUTSFORD
DERBY
ALDERLEY EDGE
NESTON
ANTROBUS
RAINOW
(The Wild Horse, 359)
PLUMLEY
MACCLESFIELD
LOWER PEOVER
SIDDINGTON
GAWSWORTH
CHESTER
ALL
GREAVE
CHESHIRE
MIDDLEWICH
BOSLEY
FARNDON
CONGLETON
BUNBURY

BICKERTON

CLWYD

GWYNEDD

SALOP

STAFFORDSHIRE

THE WIZARD OF ALDERLEY EDGE

Abram *Greater Manchester*
This town, south-east of Wigan, lies in the heart of a coalfield, and its miners still cling to the superstitions of their trade. They believe, for example, that it is unlucky for any man who has forgotten his 'snap' – sandwiches – to return home for it; he would rather work all day with nothing to eat. It is also thought unlucky for father and son to work in the same section of the mine, which is good sense, for an accident could rob a family of both breadwinners at once. They also feel it is unlucky to work the last day of the old year, or the first of the new. Children in the area play a game called Piggy, in which a small, tapered wooden billet is tapped with a bat to make it spin in the air, when it has to be struck as far as possible. This is one of the world's oldest games and is possibly connected with pagan spring games. It is known in other areas as Trip or Tip Cat.

Allgreave *Cheshire*
The 18th-century water-mill, long since abandoned and fallen into ruin, is called Folly Mill. Its owner, Abraham Day, had already seen two mills washed away by floods, but swore he would build a third. His wife said that if he persisted in his folly she would take to her bed and never leave it. Abraham went ahead – and his young wife, good as her word, stayed in bed until she died at 76.

In the wood on this sheer sandstone cliff rising from the Cheshire plain is a wishing well formed by a natural spring (above) and inscribed: 'Drink of this and take thy fill, For the water falls by the wizard's will.' The wizard who is said to have lived there was Merlin. The story goes that he stopped a farmer on his way to Macclesfield market with a fine white mare for sale. The bearded old man made an offer, but the farmer refused, hoping for a better price at the market. But there, although the animal was greatly admired, no one would buy it. On his way home, the farmer met the wizard again, and the old man led horse and rider through the wood to a rock. He touched it, and a pair of massive gates appeared, flying open with a noise like thunder. In the cavern beyond, said the wizard, lay King Arthur and his knights, sleeping with their horses until England needed them again – but they were one white horse short. The terrified farmer accepted a purse of gold for his horse and ran out. The gates clashed behind him as he staggered into the daylight, and no one has seen the cavern since

RUSHBEARING AT AMBLESIDE

The custom of rushbearing dates back to the days when new rushes were strewn annually to cover the earth floors of churches. At Ambleside, children parade with flowers and woven rushes on the Saturday nearest the Feast of the Visitation of St Mary (July 2) and, after a church service, they are given gingerbread. Similar ceremonies take place at Grasmere on the Saturday nearest St Oswald's Day (August 5), at Great Musgrave on the first Saturday in July, and at Warcop on St Peter's Day (June 29), known locally as Peter Day

THE WILD HORSE OF ANTROBUS

In the Celtic calendar, winter and the new year began on November 1, and this was a time when the spirits of the dead were believed to make a brief return to the world. Later, this became the Christian All Saints' Day, while the following day became All Souls' Day when masses were said for souls in Purgatory.

The pagan practice of leaving out food for the dead lingers on in the Cheshire children's custom of 'souling' or 'soul-caking' on November 1 and November 2. Groups of youngsters, often in fancy dress and with blackened faces, go from door to door, singing a jingle in return for small, spiced cakes or – more usually, nowadays – money.

Souling used to be made more lively by the Hodening Horse – a man in a sheet, carrying a horse's head, who pranced about at the doors, snapping its jaws.

The Wild Horse, possibly derived from the animal ridden by the Norse god, Odin, reappears in the Soul-Caking play performed by the Antrobus mummers at Antrobus, Comberbach, Acton Bridge and other local villages around Hallowe'en. The mummers include a character called the Letter-in, who starts the action by announcing: 'There is going to be a dreadful fight!' The Black Prince of Paradise in his spiked helmet is killed by King George and resurrected by the Quack Doctor. Other characters include Old Mary, Little Dairy Doubt and Beelzebub with his frying pan 'club'. But the most revered member of the group is the Wild Horse with his Driver, which appears in no other mummers' play in the country.

Appleton *Cheshire*
The custom of Bawming the Thorn has been allowed to lapse, because it led to so much rowdiness. The 'thorn' is a tree, now protected by railings, grown from a cutting taken from the Glastonbury thorn, and 'bawming' meant annointing or adorning it with ribbons and garlands. Children would dance round the thorn after decorating it in early July, and villagers staged a fete, with stalls, sideshows and games. The custom may have been a last vestige of ancient mid-summer rites.

Armboth Fell *Cumbria*
Armboth House now lies below the waters of Thirlmere reservoir, but it was once notorious for being haunted. The story says that the daughter of the house was murdered by being pushed into Thirlmere Lake at Hallowe'en on her wedding eve. Every year, on the anniversary, bells were said to ring, a ghostly dog swam in the lake, and unseen hands would lay dishes for the wedding feast.

Ashton-under-Lyne *Greater Manchester*
The Easter Monday ceremony of Riding the Black Lad was discontinued around 1960, but the fact that it persisted for several centuries is in itself remarkable. The 'Lad' was the effigy of a knight in black armour, which was paraded round the town to the jeers of onlookers, then set up as an Aunt Sally and pelted with stones and refuse and, at one time, even shot. The custom commemorated the people's antagonism towards Sir Ralph de Assheton, lord of the manor of nearby Middleton in the 15th century, who had the right to claim fines from people who let weeds grow on their land. Accompanied by bullying henchmen, and dressed in his black armour, Sir Ralph rode into town to carry out his lucrative annual inspection – and extortion – on Easter Monday, which became known amongst the local people as 'Black Monday'.

Bacup *Lancs*
On Easter Saturday, the Britannia Coconut Dancers perform their unusual Nutters' Dance over the 7 miles from one side of the town to the other. The Morris team of eight dancers have blackened faces (it is believed that in pagan times the dancers had to be disguised.otherwise the ritual magic of the dance would be ineffective) and wear black breeches and clogs, with white shirts, stockings and plumed caps. Wooden discs called 'nuts' are attached to their waists, knees and the palms of the hands, and the dancers clap these together in a complicated rhythm as they move along; led by a 'whipper-in' who drives off evil spirits. The Coconut Dancers also perform at the summer carnival.

Bickerton *Cheshire*
A cave on Bickerton Hill is known locally as Mad Allen's Hole, and is said to have once been occupied by a man who shunned society after being prevented from marrying the woman he loved. Allen came from Handley, says the story, and lost his reason when both sets of parents objected to the marriage. Finally, he sold all his goods and retired to the cave, where he died 70 years later.

The Black Rock *Greater Manchester*
On this rock, in the Mersey estuary, an 18th-century sailor fell in love with a mermaid. She gave him her ring, and promised they would soon be reunited; five days later, the sailor died.

PASSION IN STONE
The footprint impressed on the stairs at Smithills Hall, near Bolton, Greater Manchester is alleged to have been made by George Marsh, the Protestant martyr who was interrogated in the Green Room (left) before being burnt at Boughton, Cheshire, in 1555. The footprint reputedly is a divine reminder of the unjust persecution of Marsh who was accused of 'preaching false doctrine'

Bosley *Cheshire*
Until the 1880's, a gallows on Gun Hill stood as a grim memorial to John Naden, whose decomposing body hung there in chains after his execution in 1731. Naden murdered his master, Robert Brough, apparently at the instigation of the victim's wife. When the drunken Naden returned home and told her what he had done, she at once went out and rifled the dead man's pockets to make it appear that he had been waylaid by thieves. But she failed to notice Naden's knife lying beside the corpse. This was sufficient to secure the murderer's conviction. Tradition does not record whether the wife was tried, but ironically it was ordered that Naden should be executed outside her door. His body was afterwards gibbeted on Gun Hill, and when the gallows was at last removed, the timbers were used in local field stiles. Some people believe that these stiles are still haunted by Naden's ghost.

Towards the end of the last century, a gang of road-menders working on Gun Hill were horribly startled by the sudden descent of a balloonist. Most imagined the balloon to be some supernatural creature, and fell upon their knees; but one man attacked it with his knife, and won, it is said, a resounding victory over the powers of darkness.

Bunbury *Cheshire*
On the Whitchurch road there is a cottage known as the Image House, from the number of carved stone figures that adorn the walls and garden. The cottage was built, probably in the 17th century, under an ancient dispensation which permitted squatters to build on common land provided the roof was raised in a single night and the chimney was smoking by dawn. The images are said to represent a sheriff and his men, and were apparently carved by a poacher who came to live at the cottage on his return from a term of transportation. As can be imagined, the figures were not carved out of admiration for the law, but simply in order that the poacher could sit in his house and daily curse the authors of his misfortune – presumably in the same spirit that led witches to make wax images.

CARLISLE OF THE BALLADS

In many of the ballads of the 'Debatable Land' – the war-torn Scottish borders – Carlisle figures as the grim fortress where swift justice was dealt out to moss-trooping cattle lifters. Kinmont Willie, for example, was brought to the gallows of 'Haribee, to hang him up', but he was rescued, in the nick of time, by 'the bauld Buccleugh'. Less well known are the stories and ballads in which the city is declared to be King Arthur's capital. It was from Carlisle that Arthur was once captured by a giant, who released him on the condition that he would return on New Year's Day with the correct answer to the question: 'What is it that all women most desire?' The king asked all the ladies of his court, but they all gave different answers. Then, as the appointed day drew near, he set off to keep his bond with the giant.

While on the journey he met a grotesquely ugly woman who gave him the true reply – that all women most desire to have their own way – and demanded in return that she should be married to Arthur's nephew, Sir Gawain. After the wedding, she told her husband that she was bewitched, but could be ugly by day and beautiful by night, or vice versa. Gawain gallantly told her to be beautiful by day, so that she could mingle with the court ladies. Then he kissed her, and immediately she turned into a beautiful woman, and remained so always. The spell had been partly broken by Gawain's loyalty to the king, and completely by his chivalry towards her. Whereupon

'King Arthur beheld that lady faire
That was soe faire and bright,
And thanked Christ in Trinity
For Sir Gawain, that gentle knight'.

The high road and the low
The bonnie banks of Loch Lomond have been immortalised in one of the world's great love songs. And behind the sadness of the song lies a poignant story. It was written, says a Carlisle legend, by a man about to be hanged. In 1745, Bonnie Prince Charlie's starving Jacobite army retreated back to Scotland, after having invaded England as far south as Derby; his army turned back at Swarkestone Bridge over the River Trent. On the retreat, the Prince left a garrison in Carlisle. His reasons for doing so were based on vain flag-waving rather than military judgment; the garrison's position was hopeless, and on a promise of being treated as prisoners of war, it surrendered to the Duke of Cumberland. That bluff soldier at once told them that no promise to rebels was binding, and he fully intended to hang the lot. This he failed to do, but he did his best. The Jacobites were stripped of all they possessed and imprisoned in the castle. From there, many were taken to London to be executed on Kennington Common. Nineteen were hanged at Carlisle and Penrith, almost within sight of Scotland. Among them was the writer of the song, who took the low road home via the grave.

THE KISS OF CHIVALRY *To save King Arthur's life, Sir Gawain consented to marry a hideous hag. But his loyalty was rewarded, for as he kissed her, she turned into a beautiful woman*

BOWNESS-ON-SOLWAY'S PRIZE

*Until recently, whenever a new vicar was inducted to
St Michael's Church, Bowness, Cumbria, the provost
of Middlebie, Dumfries, sent a request for the bells
(above) to be returned. They were stolen by Bowness
men in retaliation for those lost in the Solway by Scots
raiders. The vicar always replied: 'When we get ours!'*

Caldbeck *Cumbria*

Though now gone far away, western Cumbria's
best-loved son will never be forgotten as long as
school choirs can manage the descant. 'Once on a
day', according to the song – or to be more precise,
from 1776 to 1854 – John Peel lived at Caldbeck
where he was a farmer and horsedealer. But as all the
world knows, he was principally a hunting man,
who until his death following a minor fall, rode to
hounds at least twice a week. When his son Peter
died, he went hunting on the day of the funeral and
brought back a fox's brush to place in the coffin as 'a
fitting tribute'. The song was written by his friend,
J. W. Graves, after a hunt in 1832. 'By Jove, Peel!'
said Graves, 'you'll be sung when we're both run to
earth.' John Peel was buried beside his son in
Caldbeck churchyard.

Chester *Cheshire*

In a county once famous for its fighting men, mothers still console broken-hearted daughters who have been jilted by saying: 'There's more than one yew-bow in Chester.' This saying has been current ever since local girls lost their archer-sweethearts at Agincourt, Crécy and Poitiers. Even more were lost in border brawls and feuds with Welshmen from across the River Dee. Though Henry IV banned Welshmen from the streets of Chester after sunset and allowed them to carry no weapons other than a knife for their meat, the strife continued. One story tells how, in the early 15th century, a Welshman called Reinallt, involved in a quarrel at Chester Fair, seized the mayor, carried him off to his castle at Mold, Clwyd, and hanged him from the battlements. Then Reinallt and his followers left the castle and hid in the woods to await their angry pursuers. Two hundred men of Chester quickly broke into the undefended castle – only to be trapped as Reinallt's band slammed the gates on them and set fire to the place. Those who managed to escape the blaze were butchered as they staggered out of the castle.

Another Welsh triumph is celebrated in the saying: 'When the daughter is stolen, shut the Pepper-gate.' This Chester version of horses and stable doors stems from a medieval mayor's bid to force his daughter to wed an English noble called Luke de Taney, instead of the Welsh knight she loved. The girl escaped during a ball game with de Taney and her friends in an orchard inside the city walls. She flung the ball over the wall and persuaded the young man to search for it. While he searched, she slipped out of the tiny Pepper-gate, and ran to her lover. Later, her angry and frustrated father ordered the gate to be kept locked for evermore – hence the saying.

It is hardly surprising that a city as ancient as Chester should boast an ancient ghost. The George and Dragon Inn, built on the site of a 1600-year-old Roman cemetery, is said to be haunted by the measured tread of a Roman legionary on eternal sentry duty. The footsteps have been heard pacing the pub's upper floor, from one end to the other, in the early morning. Twenty minutes later, they are heard coming back, and passing through solid brick walls in their progress. But it is only fair to add that the slumbers of the present landlord and his wife have remained undisturbed so far.

THE MAYOR'S RUNAWAY DAUGHTER

An old ballad tells how the daughter of a medieval mayor of Chester was betrothed by her father to Lord Luke de Taney, though she loved a Welshman. During a game with the young nobleman in an orchard under the city wall, the girl deliberately lost the ball, and sent him to hunt for it. While he searched, she slipped away through a tiny gate in the wall and was carried off by her sweetheart. After that, the gate was kept locked for ever

Clitheroe *Lancs*

Stepping-stones across the River Ribble at nearby Brungerley are said to be the haunt of an evil spirit who claims one life every seven years by dragging some unwary traveller to a watery grave. The tale is probably a warning to children, who are often told not to go near the water, or Jenny Greenteeth will pull them in. They associate the sprite with green plants growing in the water.

Cliviger Gorge *Lancs*

The Eagle's Crag, near Burnley, is traditionally the site of a witch's grave. Lord William Towneley is said to have buried his wife, Lady Sybil, there. Lady Sybil was known to dabble in the Black Arts, and used to run about in the shape of a white doe or a cat. She rejected Lord William's advances, until he asked another witch to help. He was told to hunt the doe on the crag at All Hallows (November 1). When he did, a magical dog helped him trap the doe. Using an enchanted silken rope, he tied the doe, which changed back to Lady Sybil. She agreed to reject sorcery and marry him. But she would not mend her ways, and wasted away after having a hand chopped off at Cliviger mill, while causing mischief in the shape of a cat. Since her death, the legend says, doe, hound and huntsman have haunted the crag as darkness falls on Hallowe'en.

Colby *Cumbria*

Housekeeper Marget Dawe, of Bewley Castle, is said to have put paid to the doings of Belted Will Scott, a highwayman. One October night in 1598, he turned up disguised as an old woman, begging shelter, but Marget noticed spurred boots under his skirt. She killed him by pouring boiling fat down his throat as he dozed. Apparently the man had been waiting to rob her master, Sir Richard Musgrave.

THE BELLS OF CONGLETON

Belts hung with bells were worn by monks, calling people to worship the Cheshire town's patron, St Peter in Chains. Later, they were worn by Wakes Week revellers, but rival factions fought over their ownership. So they were taken by the town council, who still have three

Constable Sands *Merseyside*

The holy River Dee's changing currents often caused new fords, and legend relates that one such change led to the naming of these sands, in the 13th century. When Earl Richard, on pilgrimage to St Winifred's Well, in Wales, was trapped by the Welsh, the Constable of Chester went to his aid, but found his way blocked by floods. He prayed to St Werburga, patron of Chester Cathedral, and sand-bars miraculously appeared, allowing him to cross and rescue his lord.

PEG'S RIVER GRAVE

The ghost of Elizabeth Sleddall, known locally as 'Peg Sneddle', wife of a 17th-century owner of Crackenthorpe Hall, Cumbria, haunted the area because, people said, she thought she had been cheated out of her share in the estate. She was seen in a coach drawn by four black horses and became so troublesome that once, when the river was low, her remains were exhumed and reburied under this giant boulder on the river bed after a service of exorcism. But she still revisits the Hall

Cross Fell *Cumbria*

Only a cairn now marks the place where the rolling moorland on Cross Fell was surmounted by an early Christian cross, erected to protect wandering travellers from demons who haunted the moors. These spirits were probably barguests – fiends that wailed across the fells, waiting to seize the unwary.

ISLAND RETREAT OF DERWENT WATER'S SAINT

Wooded St Herbert's Island was once the Cumbrian home of a hermit priest who devoted himself to a life of prayer. Bede records that St Herbert was a close friend of St Cuthbert, and that they once met and prayed they would die at the same time. So they did, in 687, and now share the same feast day, March 20

363

Disley *Cheshire*

A phantom funeral procession has often been reported in Lyme Park, followed by the white-draped spectre of a weeping woman. The deceased is said to be Sir Piers Legh, who died in 1422 of wounds received at the Battle of Agincourt. The woman is his sweetheart Blanche, who died of grief when she heard the news. Blanche may also haunt Lyme Hall, for a woman in white has often been seen there, sometimes to the sound of distant bells.

Dockray *Cumbria*

It was near 18th-century Lyulph's Tower, on the banks of Ullswater, that Wordsworth saw the 'host of golden daffodils' whose descendants flower still. It was here, too, in a castle which stood where the tower is now, that a beautiful girl called Emma once lived. She was in love with a knight called Sir Eglamore, and when he left her she became so distraught that she took to sleepwalking, often wandering to the waterfall of Aira Force, where they first met. One night Sir Eglamore returned and saw her there. He reached out his hand to touch her, but she awoke suddenly, tripped and plunged to her death in the ravine. Deranged by grief, Sir Eglamore spent the rest of his life as a hermit, living near the place where Emma had died.

Druggan Hill *Cumbria*

In the 19th century, a local pedlar vanished without trace. At about the same time an evil black dog called the Druggan Hill Boggle began to terrorise the district. Local people linked the two occurrences, declaring that the pedlar had been murdered for his wares and the dog was his vengeful spirit. They may have been right, for when the pedlar's body was found and buried in consecrated ground, the boggle disappeared and was never seen again. And a

THE HEADLESS WOMAN *The country lanes around Longridge in Lancashire were once haunted by a malicious boggart called the Headless Woman. From behind, she looked just like any other old lady, hobbling along in her fringed cape and old-fashioned 'coal-scuttle' bonnet, and carrying a basket under one arm. At first, she would walk quietly beside any walkers who tried to overtake her, listening politely to their conversation. But suddenly, when they were least expecting it, she would turn to face them, revealing that inside her bonnet there was nothing. And as they recoiled in horror, she would whip the cloth off the top of her basket and out would spring her head. Shrieking with laughter and snapping viciously, her head had a mobility of its own. It would pursue unfortunate travellers for miles, bounding along the road behind them.*

A local man once met the Headless Woman after a hard night's drinking at Longridge. He had set out on the lonely walk home across the fells when she attacked him. Luckily he was a fast runner, and jumping over the snapping head he fled for the safety of his home. His wife's reaction was unsympathetic, to say the least. 'If it meks tha fain (glad) o' thi own hearthstooan,' she said, 'I'se be some glad on it, for it's moor nor a woman wi' a heead on her shouters hae bin able to do'

villager, whose hand had been badly injured by the beast and would not heal, made a miraculous recovery.

Dunmail Raise *Cumbria*
According to legend, Dunmail was the last King of Cumbria, whose army was annihilated in AD 945 by the combined forces of Malcolm, King of Scotland, and Edmund, King of the Saxons. Edmund himself killed Dunmail, and ordered the Cumbrians captured in the battle to pile a heap of rocks and boulders – Dunmail Raise – over their slaughtered king. Dunmail's two sons were captured and their eyes put out by the Saxons, and his golden crown was thrown into nearby Grisedale Tarn. It has never been recovered.

Eamont Bridge *Cumbria*
Giant's Cave, by the Eamont River between Eamont Bridge and Langwarthby, was said to be the lair of a man-eating giant called Isir, and was sometimes known as Isir's Parlour. It is also linked in legend with Tarquin, a giant knight who imprisoned 64 brave men in his cave and was eventually slain by Sir Lancelot. Some people also claim that Uther Pendragon, King Arthur's father, lived here, and that like Isir, he ate human flesh.

THE LUCK OF EDEN HALL

Long ago, a servant from Eden Hall, Cumbria, surprised some fairies dancing around a green glass goblet. He seized it and ran, and the Fairy Queen cried out that if ever it was broken, Eden Hall would be destroyed. Though the Hall was demolished in 1934, its 'Luck' was unbroken, and is now in the Victoria and Albert Museum

THE BOGGART HAUNTINGS

The horrible shrieks of one kind of boggart – a class of supernatural creature particularly common in the north-west – have earned it the name shriker, though it is also called a barguest or trash. Usually it appears as an omen of death, sometimes in the form of a white cow or horse, or as an enormous black or white dog, with huge pads, shaggy hair and glaring, saucer-like eyes.

Shrikers are rarely violent, though there are exceptions. In 1825, near Manchester Old Church, a tradesman called Drabble was attacked by an immense, headless dog which, to his unspeakable terror, ran him all the way home with its front paws on his shoulders.

Murders and the murdered
Some boggarts, especially human-shaped ones, are distinctly malicious. The Boggart of the Brook, the awful caretaker of a bridge near Garstang, is allegedly the ghost of a murdered woman, and takes the form of a skeleton closely wrapped in a cloak and hood. She used to hitch lifts from horsemen at night, and only reveal her true identity when safely mounted behind them. With a diabolical cackle, she would whip the horse into a wild gallop and cling with her cold, bony hands to the rider's back until, fainting with terror, he was thrown from the horse and injured or killed.

The White Dobbie, on the other hand, lives in a world of its own, though it seems in some way attached to the coastal villages of Furness. It appears like a wandering, weary, emaciated and silent human, and dresses in a dirty white topcoat. Its constant companion is a white hare with glaring, bloodshot eyes. Speculating about its origins, some people have suggested that it must be the ghost of a murderer, and the hare is the eternally vindictive spirit of one of his victims.

Boggart flitting
There are many stories of benevolent boggarts helping farmers to thresh their corn and get in the harvest. In one story, the farmer used to reward his other-worldly assistant with a jug of cream. But when the farmer died, and his son took over the farm, the new farmer's wife gave it skimmed milk instead. This so infuriated the boggart that it took to stealing chickens and hens, making the cream go sour and banging pots and kettles together all night long. At last the couple could stand it no longer. They packed all their belongings into a cart and set off at dawn to find a new home. At the edge of the village, they met a neighbour who asked them in surprise if they were flitting. Before they had time to reply, a strange, hollow voice rang out from inside a churn on the cart behind them: 'Aye neighbour, we'm flittin'!'

THE LEGEND OF EGREMONT

At the now ruined castle of Egremont in Cumbria, there hung in the Middle Ages a great horn, which only the rightful lord could blow. In the 12th century, Hubert de Lacy arranged to have his elder brother, Sir Eustace, murdered while on a crusade, and to claim the castle for himself. But long after the time set for the murder, Hubert heard the horn and fled, knowing for certain that his plan had misfired and his brother had returned

PITY THE POOR CHILDREN

On stormy nights, the terror-stricken cries of two children sometimes echo beneath the bridge at Farndon in Cheshire. The cries are thought to be those of the two sons of Prince Madoc, who were drowned here for political reasons in the early 14th century

Bugganes and Glashans

Once the Isle of Man's 227 square miles teemed with supernatural beings, both kind and malicious; their decline is said to date from the coming of the railway. Cold iron is death to the People of the Hills; the fairies, brownies and goblins found the rails all over the countryside such a hindrance that they departed.

But, as in all the Celtic countries, belief in the supernatural has lingered to this day. Few islanders would drive or walk over Ballona Bridge (the Fairy Bridge) on the Douglas to Castletown road without doffing their hats and politely offering their greetings to the Little People who lurk there.

In recent years a number of Manx people have claimed to have had encounters with the other world, such as that described by four friends in 1971. They were motoring at night from Douglas to Castletown when the headlights picked out a man right in front of the car. The horrified driver braked, convinced that he must have struck him. All four got out, searched the road, and found nothing. Later they learnt that similar stories had been told about that spot 30 years before.

In time this tale will no doubt become part of the rich lore of Man, much of which is enshrined in the Museum of Witchcraft at Castletown.

THE HELPFUL GOBLIN *A phynnodderee offered to round up a shepherd's flock and found it a tiring business. He complained that he had been led a merry dance by a 'little brown sheep'. When the puzzled shepherd went to the fold, it turned out, in fact, to be a hare*

WATCHERS FROM THE HILLS *The glashans – a species of brownie – never wore clothes and sometimes abducted women, but they had their good points. In return for food they could be persuaded to do less-skilled tasks about the farm*

Cold iron and rowan

The Isle of Man fairies had little in common with the tinselly creatures of pantomimes and children's book illustrations. They were said to vary in size, some being as large as human children, while others were deformed and withered. Usually, they had green clothes and caps, large ears and romped on grassy hillsides and fern-thick glens, but disliked noise and disturbance. At night they hunted with fairy hounds, often borrowing farmers' horses which were discovered in their stables next morning, sweat-lathered and tired out. The fairies were believed to abduct new-born babies, leaving changelings in their place.

They were quick to take offence, as a man from Laxey on the east coast found to his cost. He swore at a group of fairies one night when he was drunk; later his horse and cattle died, and within 40 days he too was dead.

The islanders learnt to protect themselves from malevolent sprites. Iron objects – scissors, tongs, nails and pokers – were potent charms, as were the Bible, salt, yellow flowers, and the twigs of the rowan or mountain ash. Yellow flowers and rowan berries were strewn before the door and about the cattle byre, while rowan crosses were considered a useful precaution on May Day Eve and Midsummer Eve when fairies were especially active. Housewives would leave out bread and milk for the Little People and dough or butter at every baking or churning.

Stone Age memory

Fairies were fairly well-disposed towards humans, unlike the dreaded buggane, a goblin which changed size and shape at will, adopting the form of a black bull or a monstrous ram. Bugganes haunted old chapels to prevent their repair, or would repeatedly pull down their roofs, as at St Trinian's, below Greeba Mountain, which stands roofless to this day.

A bold tailor vowed that he would stay long enough in the building to make a pair of breeches; but when the buggane appeared at midnight the tailor fled, pursued by the monster which, in a fury at being unable to catch him, snatched off its head and hurled it at the tailor. Before it could touch him, however, the head turned into a stone.

Another goblin, the long-armed and powerful, but not over-bright phynnodderee, could be useful. A well-meaning phynnodderee volunteered to bring in a shepherd's flock from the hills and eventually turned up, breathless and exhausted, complaining that a little brown sheep had given him more trouble than all the rest. The mystified shepherd looked and found a hare among his flock.

Akin to the phynnodderee were the glashans, who would skulk on hillsides watching farmers at the plough. They might be persuaded to work in return for food. Both sexes disdained clothes, and the males occasionally indulged in kidnapping mortal women. It has been said that these creatures may represent a memory of Stone Age peoples, driven ever further into the wastelands by Celtic settlers, from whom they eked out a miserable livelihood by stealing and begging until they became extinct.

Terror from the waters

The Isle of Man was rich in water creatures like the sprite that lived in Nikkesen's Pool in Glen Roy and would emerge in the form of a handsome young man and entice maidens into the pool, to disappear for ever.

The cabbyl ushtey, or water horse, resembled a real horse and was often seen on land. Anyone foolish enough to mount one would be carried off into the sea or the nearest river. The observant could distinguish them by their hooves, however, which were always back to front. More fearsome still was the tarroo ushtey, or water bull, which lived in the coastal waters and rivers. Fairy cattle were glimpsed in meadows at dawn, recognisable by their white bodies, and their red eyes and ears. There too were the swift-running fairy pigs, with their large frilly ears and tails.

The island's most famous spectral hound is the Moddey Dhoo, or Black Dog, which used to frequent Peel Castle. It would lie before the guard-room fire and the soldiers came to

WHERE FAIRIES DWELL *Rationalists may deride the survival of superstitious beliefs, but Manx folk prefer to keep their options open. The prudent traveller, crossing Ballona Bridge (above), never omits a polite greeting to the Little People*

DOG OR DEVIL *The castle at Peel (above), the old fishing port on the west coast, had a spectral hound, the Moddey Dhoo, which used to lie in front of the guardroom fire. When one soldier became too inquisitive about it, he was frightened to death. Another place with a macabre past is the ruined chapel of St Trinian's (left), allegedly kept roofless by a malicious buggane*

THE DREADED BUGGANE *It haunted chapels and once terrified a tailor who dared to spend the night in roofless St Trinian's Chapel*

take it for granted, though none would stay alone with it, or make the nightly round without a companion. A drunken soldier boasted that he would patrol the castle by himself and find out whether the animal was a dog or devil. He returned gibbering and remained speechless until his death, three days later.

The island's guardian

Another castle, that of Rushen at Castletown, was reputed to harbour a giant in its underground maze. One day, curious townsmen rallied with torches and staves and searched the labyrinth, where they found a blind giant with a long beard sitting on a rock. He inquired how things were in the island, and asked that one of the

party should shake hands with him. A visitor held out an iron bar, which the giant squeezed, saying 'Ah, so there are still men in the Isle of Man', after which the party left.

Most renowned of the giants is Manannan, who has given his name to the island and is its guardian deity. He is said to throw his cloak of mist over Man when danger threatens.

Misfortunes caused by a witch might be averted by using earth taken from her footprints. A ploughman was working a field with his team when a witch, in the form of a hare, stopped to stare at them, whereupon the horses fell, apparently dead. The ploughman gathered soil from the hare's resting place and sprinkled it over the horses, which revived.

A bullet made from a silver coin was the best way of dealing with a witch. There were many tales of hares which, having been shot and injured, escaped. Later, witches were found cowering in their huts, suffering from similar wounds. Fishermen who had no luck with the herring would drive the suspected but invisible witch out of the boat with a flaming torch.

Ghosts were legion, but could be exorcised and banished for seven years. An innkeeper was haunted by the ghost of his wife whom he was believed to have murdered. He prevailed upon a priest to banish her for seven years, after which time she returned to be banished again. When she appeared next, her husband was dead and she was seen no more.

367

Gosforth *Cumbria*
The ancient cross in Gosforth churchyard is probably Viking work of the 10th century. Its carvings of snakes, wolves and dragons, mingled with Christian motifs, are said to depict the old Norse saga *Volispa*, which deals with the triumph of Christianity over paganism.

Grasmere *Cumbria*
The traditional Cumberland and Westmorland wrestling, for which the annual Grasmere Sports are famous, is said to date back to the days of face-to-face combat among Border inhabitants. Some of the greatest 18th-century champions were Lake District clergymen.

Great Corby *Cumbria*
The Radiant Boy, a luminous apparition that haunts Corby Castle, seat of the Howard family, was said to foretell great power but a violent death for any member of the family who saw it. Another version however, claims that this was a gentle and friendly ghost. A 19th-century rector who fled the house after seeing it was thought by his host to have acted with unnecessary panic.

Hale *Merseyside*
John Middleton (1578–1623), the Child of Hale, was 9 ft 3 in. tall. He was said to have been bewitched after he had fallen asleep on the sands one evening, and awoke to find that he had burst out of his clothes. Legends and stories clung to this Jacobean giant. Without bothering to exert his great strength, he defeated James I's court wrestler by dislocating his thumb. Attacked by a bull, he threw it by the horns over a hedge. On another occasion he had to be chained to his bed during a fever. Later, so legend says, one of the chains was sent to Chester to keep the mills on the Dee from floating downriver; the second went to Lincolnshire to prevent the tower of St Botolph's Church, the famous Boston Stump, from being blown out to sea; while the third was used to hold down the Devil, who had been captured while he had bellyache.

THE CHILD OF HALE

Higher Penwortham *Lancs*
The Fairy Funeral, often seen on the road through Penwortham Wood, was thought to forecast death. Two men, returning home one night, were unlucky enough to meet the miniature cortège emerging from the churchyard at midnight. To his horror, the younger man saw that the face of the figure in the coffin was his own. Within a month, he died after falling off a haystack, and his funeral passed along the very same path of the fairy cortège.

Hoghton *Lancs*
Two Hoghton poachers who had raided a rabbit warren were terrified, on their way home, to hear voices coming from their sacks. 'Dick, wheer art ta?' said one. 'In a sack, on a back, riding up Hoghton Brow,' came the reply. The poachers dropped their loads and fled, leaving two fairies, who had taken up residence in the burrow, to emerge from the sacks.

WANDERER RETURNED

Elizabeth I's maid of honour, Mary Fitton, is said to haunt her family home, the Old Hall at Gawsworth, Cheshire. Banished for an affair with the Earl of Pembroke, she never saw her home again. She is buried in the local church

OLD 'MAGGOTTY'

Gawsworth also boasts the ghost of an eccentric 18th-century playwright and dancing-master, Samuel 'Maggotty' Johnson, whose final jest was to elect to become a ghost by being buried in unconsecrated ground – a spinney known as Maggotty's Wood. He justified his unusual choice in verses on his tomb

Kendal *Cumbria*

According to legend, the helmet on the north wall of Kendal church belonged to Robin the Devil – the Royalist Sir Robert Philipson. After being attacked at his home, Belle Isle on Lake Windermere, by Colonel Briggs, the Roundhead magistrate of Kendal, 'the Devil' led a band of armed men into the town the following Sunday, and rode into Kendal church in the middle of morning service in search of his enemy. Briggs was not there, but in the confusion Robin lost his sword and helmet. The incident was later used by Sir Walter Scott in his poem 'Rokeby'.

Kentmere *Cumbria*

Bernard Gilpin (1517–83), who was born here, became known as the Apostle of the North, from his preaching missions to remote parts of the Lake District. He was also loved for his charity – at Christmas he gave an ox to his poorest parishioners. A story is told that during the reign of the Catholic Queen Mary, he was arrested for his non-Conformist views, but broke his leg on the way to trial in London. This painful 'miracle' saved him from certain execution, for by the time he was well enough to travel, Mary had died and had been succeeded by the Protestant Elizabeth I.

BUILT BY THE DEVIL

The Devil's Bridge across the River Lune at Kirkby Lonsdale, Cumbria (above), was supposedly built by Satan himself. The story goes that the Devil appeared to an old woman whose cow had strayed across the river and promised to build her a bridge on condition that he should have the first living soul to cross it. She agreed, and the bridge was completed. A mark in the masonry (right) is said to represent the Devil's footprint. But the old woman cheated her adversary by hurling a bun across the bridge for her dog to retrieve. In his haste to build the bridge Satan dropped many of the stones he was carrying in his apron, and they were scattered around the area: the Devil's Neck-collar, Castleton Fell and the Apron-full-of-Stones at the head of Kingsdale are all said to have been formed in this way

Knutsford *Cheshire*

According to legend, King Canute forded the River Lily here on his way north to fight the Scots, an incident that is recalled in the town's name. As he stepped from the water, he shook the sand from his shoes – and this too is remembered in a ceremony called sanding, when the townspeople make patterns of sand outside St John's Church on May Day.

Levens *Cumbria*

Some time in the 18th century, a gipsy died of starvation after being turned away from Levens Hall, and her ghost still haunts the house. Before she died, she cursed the Lady of Levens, saying that no male heir would be born until the River Kent ran dry and a white stag was born in the park. After years without a direct heir, a boy was finally born in 1896, after the river had frozen solid in 1895 and a pale-coloured stag had been born to a black fallow deer in the herd that lived in the park.

By tradition, the house is also haunted by a lady in pink and a spectral black dog; and the birth of a white fawn heralds a change in the family's luck.

Little Salkeld *Cumbria*

The 13th-century wizard Michael Scot once came across a coven of witches holding their sabbat just outside Little Salkeld, and turned them all to stone. The stone circle, known as Long Meg and her Daughters, stands there to this day. Tradition claims that if anyone can count the stones twice and arrive at the same number, the enchantment will be broken; apparently, no one has yet succeeded. Also, if Long Meg herself is ever broken, the stone will run with blood.

Liverpool *Merseyside*

In parts of the city, particularly around the predominantly Catholic dock area, children light bonfires on Good Friday and burn effigies of Judas Iscariot. Liverpool is the only city in Britain where this happens, though the custom is common in Spain, Portugal and Latin America; so it may have been introduced here by sailors from overseas.

Dominating the River Mersey are the two towers of the Liver Building, topped by the 'Liver birds'. These mythical creatures are said to have frequented the pool near which the city was founded. In fact, the 'Liver bird' first appeared on the coat-of-arms about 700 years ago. It was intended as the eagle of St John the Evangelist, the city's patron, but owing to the artist's lack of skill, the bird's identity became part of the city's folklore.

STORM OVER PENDLE

On Thursday, August 20, 1612, three generations of witches were marched through the crowded streets of Lancaster and hanged before large crowds on a gallows about a mile outside the town. The parson's prayer that God should show them mercy must have made bitter hearing, for they were shown little in this world. Most pitiable and least pitied of the ten witches – all but one of whom came from Pendle Forest – was Old Chattox, a crazy, half-blind beggar-woman, withered, spent and decrepit after 80 years of poverty. One of her contemporaries, Mother Demdike, also in her 80's, blind and a beggar, would have gone to the gallows too, beside her wild, squint-eyed daughter Bessie and two of her teenage grandchildren, had she not cheated the hangman by dying in Lancaster Castle gaol.

The incident that started the witch hunt happened six months before, on March 18. Alizon, one of Mother Demdike's granddaughters, met a pedlar called John Law while begging near Colne, and asked him for some pins. He refused to undo his pack, whereupon Alizon cursed him. A few minutes later he had a stroke – and both he and Alizon believed that her curse had caused it. He lived just long enough to testify against her at her trial. By then, according to the clerk of the court, his head was 'drawne awrie, his eyes and face deformed, his speech not well to bee understood, his legges starcke lame, his body able to indure no travell'.

A damning confession

A fortnight after John Law's stroke, Alizon, her mother Bessie and her half-wit brother James were questioned by the local magistrate Roger Nowell, and Alizon readily confessed her responsibility. In chilling detail, she also described her own close acquaintance with witchcraft, as well as that of her family and friends. By the end of the day, both Mother Demdike and Old Chattox stood accused as witches and murderers, and Bessie had been stripped, searched and shown to have a supernumerary nipple for suckling the Devil.

One of the mysteries of the hunt is the ease with which Nowell secured confessions. By August, without using torture, he had collected enough evidence to convict Demdike, Chattox, Bessie, Alizon, James and six others on an extraordinary variety of charges. These included the desecration of graves, communing with imps and the Devil, plotting to blow up Lancaster Castle by magic, and at least 16 murders. It may be that he knew what he was looking for, and by the way he phrased his questions, made sure that he found it – a suggestion that is borne out by the fact that another of Demdike's granddaughters, nine-year-old Jennet, was one of his chief witnesses. Or else the two old women may have been bent on settling an old feud between their families, which had begun more than ten years earlier, and in trying to destroy one another, they destroyed themselves and their children too. It is also possible that the two families did practise a form of black magic, and believed (as Alizon believed in her curse) that it worked. And, being 'simple' even by the standards of the 17th century, they may never have realised until the ropes snapped tight around their necks how cruelly they could be punished by James I's new laws against witchcraft – even though their only real crime, if it can be called that, was poverty.

THE EYE OF GOD *A carving on the tower of St Mary's Church, Newchurch-in-Pendle, is said to represent the all-seeing Eye of God, and local tradition maintains that its original function was to protect the worshippers inside the church from the witches who once plagued the district. There may be some truth in the tradition, for the tower was built in 1544, in the lifetime of Mother Demdike and Old Chattox*

GET OUT, WHORES AND WITCHES! *Some time in 1610, blind Mother Demdike, led by her granddaughter Alizon, visited a Wheathead miller called Richard Baldwin to ask for money. 'Get out, whores and witches!' he yelled, 'I'll burn the one of you and hang the other.' 'I care not for thee,' Mother Demdike spat back, 'Hang thyself!' A year later, the miller's young daughter died, and later still, Mother Demdike confessed that she had bewitched the child to death with the help of her familiar, Tibb*

THE ROAD TO THE GALLOWS *The Pendle witches were sent along the Trough of Bowland (right) in 1612, on their way to a dungeon in Lancaster Castle and the gallows*

WITCH'S HOME *Roughlee Hall was the home of Alice Nutter, the richest of the Pendle witches. How she became involved remains a mystery*

WITCH'S GRAVE *This tomb outside St Mary's, Newchurch-in-Pendle, is often pointed out as that of Alice Nutter. In fact, witches' bodies were buried in unconsecrated ground*

371

OSWALD'S HAND

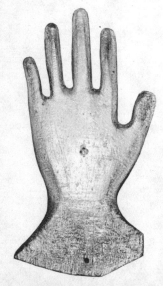

A wooden hand nailed to the wall of St Oswald's Church, Lower Peover, Cheshire, was probably used during the Middle Ages as a sign to indicate that a fair was in progress. Locally, however, it is said that the effigy represents the miraculous hand of St Oswald. Such was the holy man's generosity to a group of wandering beggars, that St Aidan blessed him, saying that the hand which gave so freely would never grow old. Years after Oswald's body had turned to dust, so the story goes, his hand remained uncorrupted and youthful as ever

RIVER OF THE BROKEN HEART

The River Goyt, near Marple Hall, is haunted by a broken-hearted girl whose Royalist lover drowned there

Macclesfield *Cheshire*

The town is known as 'Treacletown' or 'Sticky-town' allegedly because, at about the turn of the century, a barrel of treacle rolled off a cart in Beech Lane and burst as it hit the ground. The contents flowed down Hibel Road, whereupon all the townsfolk downed tools and rushed to scoop up the free syrup in cups, kettles, buckets and tin baths. Everyone lived on treacle for weeks after.

Manchester *Greater Manchester*

The tradition that something should be brought into the house on New Year's Day before anything is removed has always had wide acceptance in the north though, fortunately, few people take it as seriously as the participants in this apparently true Manchester story. One New Year's holiday at the turn of the century, a man walked into his regular pub and asked for whisky on credit. The landlord refused, saying that to give credit on New Year's Day would bring him bad luck all the next year. It was not, however, New Year's Day, but January 2; January 1 had fallen on a Sunday, and the holiday was carried over. As far as the landlord was concerned, the superstition was carried over with it, but his customer disagreed. In the row that followed, he drew a knife and stabbed the landlord to death. The customer was later hanged.

Marple *Greater Manchester*

During the Civil War, Marple Hall was owned by Henry Bradshaw who, like his brother John, the president of the tribunal that signed Charles I's death warrant, was a stern Parliamentarian. The story goes that Henry's daughter had a secret lover, a Royalist officer, who rashly came to visit her one day when he was carrying dispatches for the king. His presence was discovered, and an old servant, under a pretext of helping him to escape, drowned him in the River Goyt. The girl died of a broken heart, and is still believed to haunt the spot where her Royalist lover was drowned.

The headless ghost of Charles I is also supposed to haunt the ruined Hall – a tradition that probably arose because Henry Bradshaw was confused locally with his regicide brother, John.

THE VENABLES DRAGON

The carved screen of the Venables chapel in Middlewich church in Cheshire bears the Venables family crest of a dragon with a baby in its jaws. The legend is that during the Middle Ages, the people of Moston were terrorised by a dragon that lived in Bache Pool. Thomas Venables, hearing of the creature, went out to fight it and managed to shoot it in the eye just as it was about to dismember and devour a child. Since the wound did not prove fatal, Thomas 'afterwards with other weapons manfullie slew him' – according to an old tale

PENDRAGON CASTLE

Legend says that Pendragon Castle, near Nateby, was built by Uther Pendragon, who tried to divert the River Eden to form a moat. But a local rhyme says: 'Let Uther *Pendragon do what he can, Eden will run where Eden ran.' In fact, the castle was built by Hugh de Morville, one of Thomas à Becket's murderers*

Neston *Cheshire*

On the first Thursday in June, the local benefit club meets for its annual walk and church service. These clubs were founded at the time of the Napoleonic Wars to provide villagers with insurance against sickness and burial expenses. The Neston club is typical in that most of its members are women – at the time of the original foundation, many of the men were away fighting.

North Stainmore *Cumbria*

One night in 1797, an old hag called at the now-vanished Spital Inn and begged that she should be allowed to spend the night by the fire. The landlord agreed, and went to bed; out of the entire household, only the maid, Bella, remained awake. Bella was suspicious of the old woman, and watched her through the banisters. Her patience was rewarded, for the hag produced a dried severed human hand from beneath her cloak, and inserted a lighted candle between the withered fingers. She then began to unbar the doors, whereupon Bella, anticipating the arrival of a gang, crept off to wake her master. But the thieves' magic of the Hand of Glory – a hanged man's hand holding a candle of hanged man's fat – held him in a charmed sleep. Fortunately, Bella knew the ancient antidote, and threw a dish of milk over the hand. At once, the landlord awoke, and charging down with his blunderbuss, beat off the thieves. The hand was a popular attraction in the bar for years afterwards.

Penrith *Cumbria*

St Andrew's churchyard contains two stone shafts standing 15 ft apart. They are believed to mark each end of the grave of the gigantic Ewan Caesarius, a notable slayer of boars and 5th-century ruler of Cumbria. In the late 16th century, the grave was said to have been opened, to reveal the bones of a huge man.

Plumley *Cheshire*

The ghosts of a man and a woman have sometimes been reported leaning over the balustrade in Tabley Old Hall, now a farm. The spectral pair are a jealous husband, killed in a duel, and his wife, who committed suicide. To avoid scandal, their bodies were reputedly walled up inside the house.

CATS AND CHEESE

The 12th-century Welsh historian Giraldus Cambrensis enlarged upon the fame and excellence of Cheshire cheese, and to this day, many people would fervently agree with him. Cheshire people say that their cheese is the most patriotic, since it comes in the national colours of red, white and blue. The delicious blue is rare, since it cannot be artificially induced; it can be created only by the accidental addition of an airborne mould. Whatever gourmets may feel, the blue was not highly regarded locally, and people used it only as a wound dressing. This folk-remedy was fairly sound, for the penicillin content of the mould would fight infection.

Another famous Cheshire product is the Cheshire Cat, that curious, perpetually grinning creature that Alice encountered in Wonderland. It had the uncanny ability of slowly vanishing until only its grin remained.

To 'grin like a Cheshire cat' was a popular saying long before Lewis Carroll's day. Some authorities believe that Cheshire cheese used to be marked with the head of a cat; others, that the saying relates to the open-mouthed wolf heads on the arms of the 11th-century Earl of Chester.

THE CHESHIRE CAT AND ALICE
'This time it vanished . . . beginning with the end of the tail and ending with the grin'

Rainow *Cheshire*
An inscribed stone at Saltersford, near Rainow, records and marks the spot of a mysterious and tragic death. On Christmas Eve, 1735, John Turner, who ran a string of pack-horses between Chester and Derby, was returning to his home at Saltersford through a snowstorm. Anxious to be with his family in time for Christmas Day, he ignored advice and pressed on through the blizzard. When he failed to appear, a search party was sent out and found his string of pack-horses safe but Turner frozen to death less than a mile from home. In the snow beside him was the footprint of a woman. This mystery was never explained.

MUNCASTER'S LUCK

The 'Luck of Muncaster', a gold-and-white enamelled-glass bowl, has been a treasure of the Penningtons of Muncaster Castle, near Ravenglass in Cumbria, for over 500 years. Traditionally, it was presented to Sir John Pennington by Henry VI for sheltering him at the castle after his defeat by the future Edward IV, leader of the Yorkist faction, at the Battle of Towton in 1461. The king blessed the bowl and said that as long as it remained unbroken the Penningtons would flourish. Tom Skelton, the castle's last jester during the 15th century, found himself caught up in a tragic drama. Sir Alan Pennington's daughter, Helwise, had secretly met her lover, the village carpenter, at the May Day celebrations. News of this reached Sir Ferdinand Hoddleston of Millom Castle, to whom Helwise was engaged. He, in a fit of rage, bribed the jester to strike off his rival's head. The grief-stricken girl retired to a convent

KING AND FOOL *feature in Muncaster's past*

HOME FOR A MERMAID

Rostherne Mere is said to be the home of a mermaid. On Easter Sunday she may be heard singing and ringing a sunken bell which lies on the bed of the lake

Renwick *Cumbria*
Legend relates that when the old church at Renwick was being demolished in 1733, a cockatrice, a hideous bat-like creature, flew up from the ruins. The villagers barred themselves in their houses and refused to go near the church. It was left to one John Tallantire, armed only with a rowan branch, to fight and kill the monster. He became a local hero and was exempted from paying tithes – a form of church tax. As a result of his victory, Renwick men became known thereafter as 'Renwick bats'.

Rostherne *Cheshire*
The lych-gate outside the parish church used to be carefully avoided by newly married couples, who believed that if they passed through it, one of them would die within a year – or, that the marriage would be an unhappy one. The belief was once widespread and probably originated in the lych-gate's association with death. 'Lych-gate' means 'corpse-gate', and is the roofed gateway at the entrance to a churchyard where the pall-bearers with the coffin could shelter from the weather while awaiting the arrival of the priest.

St Bees *Cumbria*

St Bega, from whom the town of St Bees takes its name, was an Irish princess who, according to legend, was shipwrecked on the Cumbrian coast during the 7th century. She took refuge with the lord of Egremont and begged him for land to build a nunnery. Mockingly, he offered her as much of his estate as should be covered with snow the next day, Midsummer's Day. He woke next morning to find that the land for 3 miles round his castle was deep in snow. True to his promise, he granted the land and helped Bega to build the nunnery.

Seascale *Cumbria*

A rare breed of sheep known as Herdwicks is found only in the Lake District. Their origins are unknown, but legend claims that they first appeared in Britain in 1588 when several swam ashore from a Spanish Armada ship wrecked near Seascale. Another legend says that they were brought from Scandinavia by Vikings who landed on the Cumberland coast many centuries earlier. Herdwicks, if moved elsewhere, always wander back to the same 'heaf', or plot of land, on which they have been reared. Once there they will not wander.

PACE-EGGING

The ancient Lancashire custom of pace-egging, once widespread, is still to be found in parts of the county. 'Pace' comes from the old English *pasch*, meaning 'Easter', and pace-eggs are eggs specially decorated for the festival. Usually, they are wrapped in onion-skins and boiled; this gives a golden, mottled effect to the shells. Decorating eggs in this way is a centuries-old Easter custom. Edward I's household accounts include an item of 1s. 6d. for the decoration and distribution of 450 pace-eggs. The Wordsworth Museum at Grasmere houses a collection of highly ornate eggs, originally made for the poet's children.

Old Tosspot

Pace-eggs were eaten for breakfast on Easter Sunday, used as ornaments or for games, or handed out to the Pace-eggers. These last, once a common sight in Lancashire villages, were groups of fantastically dressed mummers, complete with blackened faces and wearing animal skins, coloured ribbons and streamers, who went in procession through the streets, singing the traditional Pace-eggers' song and extracting eggs and money as tribute. At Burscough, near Ormskirk, the Pace-eggers' Procession survived until quite recently, and included such characters as the Noble Youth, the Lady Gay, the Soldier Brave, the Old Tosspot, who played the role of drunken buffoon and wore a long straw tail stuffed full of pins to catch any bystander unwise enough to grab hold of it. All this was a Lancashire version of the ancient mumming plays, usually performed at Christmas time throughout the rest of the country.

Egg-rolling

In Preston, thousands still gather on Easter Monday to watch the egg-rolling down the grassy slopes in Avenham Park. The eggs, sensibly enough, are hard-boiled, although nowadays not all of them are decorated. The event was formerly a contest in which competitors tried to see who could roll their eggs furthest without cracking them. Defeated rivals had their eggs taken from them and eaten. Today, the hundreds of children who take part roll their eggs mainly for fun.

A final warning: empty pace-egg shells must be crushed, for they are popular with Lancashire witches, who use them as boats.

THE PACE-EGGERS' PROCESSION *Once a common sight in Lancashire at Easter, the Pace-eggers, dressed in fantastic costumes, went through the streets singing their traditional song and collecting decorated pace-eggs, ale and money from householders. The custom has been revived by some schools in and around Rochdale*

Seathwaite *Cumbria*

Seathwaite in the past was considered to be a poor area by its neighbours, and many sayings survive which reflect this. 'A Seathwaite candle's a greased seeve (rush).' 'It's hot and wet like Seathwaite broth' (of weak tea). 'We've no back doors in Seathwaite.' The locals themselves, however, were proud of this last saying. The story was told of a Seathwaite youth who was delivering produce to a house in Coniston. Ordered to go round to the back door by a servant, he stood his ground and replied sturdily: 'We've nay back doors i' Seeathet.'

Siddington *Cheshire*

In the middle of Redes Mere, a vast lake that lies in the grounds of Capesthorne Hall near Siddington, is a large peat island which visibly moves back and forth in strong winds. Local legend tells that a medieval knight, wrongly convinced that his lady was untrue to him, swore that he would never again look upon her face until the island had moved on the waters of the mere. Soon afterwards he grew very ill and was saved from death only through the devotion of the lady, who nursed him back to health. It is said that, as soon as he recovered, a violent storm uprooted the island as a sign of his lady's constancy, and the island has remained floating ever since.

The old Hall was burnt down in 1861, but it was rebuilt to incorporate parts of the earlier house in its wings. The Hall is open to the public.

THE MIRACULOUS BABY OF SKELMERSDALE

An eagle and child became part of the crest of the Lathom family after a miraculous 'delivery'. The story says that Sir Thomas Lathom, who lived in the time of Edward III, longed for a son and heir, but his wife had only given birth to girls. Perhaps to console himself, the knight made love to a village girl, who eventually gave birth to a baby boy. Sir Thomas was overjoyed, but still had the delicate problem of introducing the child into his family with his wife's approval. He succeeded by having it left under a tree at Lathom Park, and allowing his wife to discover it on her daily walk. When he explained that the infant must have been dropped by the eagle that nested in the tree, as a gift from Heaven, Lady Lathom accepted the story – and adopted the child

Souter Fell *Cumbria*

On several occasions during the mid-18th century, a phantom army was seen marching and riding across the summit of Souter Fell, near Mungrisdale. Those who saw the army were never able to find any trace of its passage, and felt that it would have been impossible for real soldiers to move so quickly on the steep slopes. Later, when Bonnie Prince Charlie brought his troops that way, it was said that the apparitions had been a prophetic vision of the Jacobite army on the march.

Stalybridge *Greater Manchester*

In the weeks leading up to Guy Fawkes' Night on November 5, the children of Stalybridge still practise the old custom of 'cob-coaling' as they gather fuel for their bonfires. Small processions of the children visit houses throughout the town and make requests for bonfire material – and, hopefully, money for fireworks – by singing traditional songs. In other parts of the country the custom is known as chumping, progging, trailing or plundering.

Tebay *Cumbria*

Mary Baynes, the famous 'Witch of Tebay' who died in 1811 at the age of 90, is reputed to have prophesied that 'fiery horseless carriages' would speed over nearby Loups Fell, which is now the route of the London-Glasgow railway. She was greatly feared by her neighbours, who blamed her for everything that went wrong in the community. Local people claimed that she withered and died at the same moment that a number of eggs she had bewitched were fried in boiling fat.

Troutbeck Bridge *Cumbria*
During the 17th century, Calgarth Hall in Trout-beck Bridge was the home of Myles Phillipson, a local JP. In order to gain possession of a rich farm near by, he invited the owner and his wife to a Christmas banquet at the Hall, and then accused them of stealing a silver cup which he had hidden in their baggage. Phillipson presided at their trial, sentenced the couple to death, and appropriated their farm. As she was led away, the wife cursed him, saying that his victims would never leave him and that his entire family would perish in poverty and distress. After the execution, two skulls appeared at Calgarth. In his attempts to get rid of them, Phillipson had them buried, burnt, smashed to pieces and thrown into Lake Windermere, but the skulls always returned to the Hall. True to the prophecy, the Phillipsons grew poorer and poorer and, in 1705, the family line died out. The Bishop of Llandaff, who later lived at Calgarth, finally performed a service of exorcism over the skulls and they were never seen again.

Walk Mill *Lancs*
Tradition alleges that, in 1641, Thomas Barcroft chained his mad elder brother William to the wall of the cellar in Barcroft Hall, and starved him to death so that he might inherit the family estate. As the unhappy William lay dying in his secret prison, he is said to have put a curse upon the Barcrofts; this seems to have been fulfilled in 1688, when the family line died out at Thomas's death. The con-fused scribbles which can still be seen on the walls of the cellar are alleged to have been written by William himself.

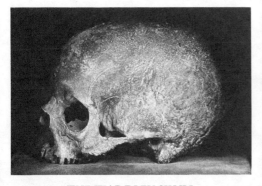

THE WARDLEY SKULL

The skull at the head of the staircase in Wardley Hall, Greater Manchester, is that of the Benedictine missionary, Father Ambrose Barlow, executed in Manchester in 1641. Like other house-bound skulls elsewhere, it is said to be capable of emitting blood-curdling shrieks and bringing misfortune upon the house if it is disturbed. In this case, the tales were almost certainly invented by local people in the 1930's to impress a visiting journalist. The Roman Catholic Bishop of Salford, who lives in the house, says the skull has been removed on several occasions, without this causing any strange happenings

Winwick *Cheshire*
The site of Winwick church was chosen by a mysterious pig, whose effigy is carved on the church tower. The construction of the church originally began near by, but when darkness fell, the pig suddenly appeared, and carried off the masonry in its mouth to the present site, said to be the place where St Oswald died in 642. As it ran to and fro, it squealed 'We-ee-wick, we-ee-wick', and this appar-ently inspired the name of the parish.

Workington *Cumbria*
A traditional game called 'Uppies and Downies' is played in the streets of Workington every year on Good Friday, Easter Tuesday and the Saturday which follows. The game has no rules and consists of a heroic struggle to score goals with a football. One of the two goals is situated at the harbour and the other a mile away by the park wall sur-rounding ruined Workington Hall. Hundreds of men and women join in on each side. Formerly, the game was played between rival teams of coal-miners and dockworkers, but it has now become an annual wild battle between the citizens of the Upper Town and the Lower Town.

MOSES OF WASDALE

A narrow track leading to Wasdale Head, in Cumbria, is known as Moses Sledgate, or Moses Trod. It was used by a notorious whisky smuggler called Moses Rigg, according to the 19th-century Cumbrian pub landlord Will Ritson. This was at a time when smuggling tea, tobacco and spirits landed from the Isle of Man was a profitable business. Whether the tale is true or not will never be known. Will Ritson won many a Lakeland sporting contest – as a champion liar!

LAND OF
THE RED DRAGON

Wales (Cymru)

The poets, singers and storytellers of Wales have enjoyed a measure of freedom which has been denied to their statesmen and warriors for some 700 years, ever since an English knight ran his sword through a Welsh nobleman whom he did not recognise near Builth Wells in Powys. His victim was Llywelyn the Last, the first and only Welsh Prince of Wales, and when Llywelyn died, the political independence of Wales died with him. For centuries, he was remembered as Ein Llyw Olaf, our last prince, though not even the fierce courage and reputed wizardry of his 14th-century descendant Owen Glendower were enough to win back what the last prince lost.

Through the centuries of political oppression, the Welsh imagination remained unfettered, for its roots were buried so deep in the Celtic past that no invader was able to destroy them. Even the Methodist Revival of the 18th century, whose stern puritanism banished so many of the ancient Celtic traditions, gave a boost to the one thing they most needed to keep them alive – the Welsh language. Today, it is among the people who still speak Welsh (there are an estimated 600,000 of them and this figure is increasing) that the ancient tales and traditions are best remembered.

The strength of traditional Welsh culture is reflected in the popularity of the Royal National Eisteddfod, a ceremonial gathering of musicians, poets and craftsmen which takes place in the first week of August at a site announced with elaborate ritual a year and a day before. Presiding over the Eisteddfod is the Archdruid of the Gorsedd (or company) of Bards, and though no one any longer believes in the Gorsedd's druidic ancestry, the myth symbolises what no true Welshman could ever forget – that the English are foreigners and Wales is now, as it always has been, *hen wlad fy nhadau*, the land of my fathers.

THE FOLKLORE YEAR

Old New Year's Day (January 12)
Cwm Gwaun, Dyfed
Traditional celebrations
Llandysul, Dyfed
Church festival and pwnc chanting

March 1
All Wales
St David's Day celebrations

Monday before Easter
Anglesey
Easter Egg Clapping

First week of July
Llangollen, Clwyd
International Musical Eisteddfod

July 31
Tenby, Dyfed
St Margaret's Fair

First week of August
Different place each year
Royal National Eisteddfod

Saturday of week including August 19
Cilgerran, Dyfed
Coracle race

Christmas season
Tanad Valley, Clwyd and Powys
Welsh carol singing
Pen-coed, Vale of Glamorgan
Mari Lwyd Mummers

GOODWICK

FISHGUARD
CWM GWAUN

GLYN RHOSYN
(St David, 404)
ROCH

MARLOES

PEMBROKE
(Hero's Tales, 388)

ST GOV
HEAD

N

KEY TO SYMBOLS

CRIME AND PUNISHMENT

CURIOUS CHARACTERS

CUSTOMS AND FESTIVALS

DEVILS AND DEMONS

DROWNED OR LOST LANDS

FABULOUS BEASTS

FAIRIES

GHOSTS

GRAVES AND MONUMENTS

HEROES

HOLY PLACES

INDUSTRIAL LORE

LOCAL CURIOSITIES

LOVE STORY

MERMAIDS AND SEA-PEOPLE

MUSEUMS AND LIBRARIES

MYSTERIOUS STONES

SAINTS AND MIRACLES

SHIPWRECKS

TRADITIONAL SINGING

TREASURE

WELLS AND SPRINGS

WITCHES AND WIZARDS

0   5   10
MILES

CEMAES BAY
LLANDDEUSANT

Anglesey
RHOS-FAWR
LANDDONA
PENMYNYDD
TREFDRAETH
LLANDDWYN
LLANDWROG
CLYNNOG FAWR
NT GWRTHEYRN
LLITHFAEN
NEFYN
CRICCIETH
ABERDARON
ABERSOCH
BARDSEY
ISLAND

CONWY
LLANEILIAN-
YN-RHOS ST GEORGE
ST ASAPH
(Fishy Tale, 402)
GREENFIELD
HOLYWELL
LLANDDULAS
LLANNEFYDD
TREMEIRCHION
CLWYD
GWYTHERIN
LLANBERIS
BETWS GARMON
SNOWDON
BETWS-Y-
COED
RUTHIN
LLANFERRES
CERRIGYDRUDION
(Fairy Cattle, 392)
NANT GWYNANT
CYNWYD
GLYNDYFRDWY
LLANGOLLEN
BEDDGELERT
(Llywelyn's Hound, 381)
FFESTINIOG
LLANFOR
LLANDDERFEL
CHIRK
BORTH-Y-GEST
BALA
GWYNEDD
LLANUWCHLLYN
LLANSILIN
PENNANT
MELANGELL
LLANRHAEADR-YM-
MOCHNANT
LLANYMAWDDWY
LLANFYLLIN
DINAS-
MAWDDWY
LLANFAIR
CAEREINION
SALOP

Cardigan

Bay
ABERDYFI
MONTGOMERY
HYSSINGTON
TRE TALIESIN
(Poet's Birth, 409)
TREFEGLWYS
CAPEL
SEION
LLANGURIG
DEVIL'S BRIDGE
POWYS
PENNANT
STRATA FLORIDA
LLANINA
LLANDEWIBREFI
(Fairy Cattle, 392)
LLANARTH
CILMERY
LLANBEDR
PAINSCASTLE
ST DOGMAELS
LAMPETER
YSTRAD-FFIN
BUILTH
WELLS
HEREFORD
RN
CWRTYCADNO
AND
LLANDILO
MYDDFAI
(Fairy Lady, 398)
LLANGORSE
WORCESTER
YR EFAIL WEN
CARMARTHEN
LLANDEILO
BRECON BEACONS
ABERGAVENNY
GORS-LAS
YSTRADGYNLAIS
KIDWELLY
GLYN NEATH
MID
TENBY
WEST
GLAMORGAN
LLANWYNNO
MYNYDDISLWYN
GLAMORGAN
GWENT
REYNOLDSTON
LLANFABON
GILFACH
RISCA
PORT
TALBOT
(Death Flowers, 403)
PEN-MAEN
LLANTRISANT
NEWPORT
PENCOED
TONGWYNLAIS
OGMORE
ST FAGANS
(Welsh Tradition, 405)
ST NICHOLAS
CARDIFF
Bristol Channel
ST DONATS
PENARTH
PENMARK
SOUTH GLAMORGAN

MERSEYSIDE

CHESHIRE

AVON

Aberdaron *Gwynedd*

A small farm cottage near Aberdaron was the birth-place in 1780 of Richard Robert Jones, better known as the folk-hero Dic Aberdaron. With his pockets full of books, a cat at his side, a ram's horn slung round his neck and often wearing a hare-skin hat, he spent his life travelling the length and breadth of Wales.

Allegedly he was able to summon and command demons, and once, when the reapers at Mathlem Farm near Aberdaron were working in a field full of thistles, he called for his satanic helpers and within minutes the whole field had been reaped. By his death in 1843, he is said to have mastered 15 languages.

By tradition, sheep rustlers were once hanged on Bryn y Grocbren, or gallows hill. Many of them, including Alf Lewis who is buried in Aberdaron churchyard, were reputedly rounded up by the Cŵn Annwn, the hounds of the underworld, led by the lord of the fairies.

Aberdyfi *Gwynedd*

The tradition that Cardigan Bay was once a dry, fertile land is firmly based on fact; some 7000 years ago, a forest covered what are now the shallows, and sunken fossil trees can still be seen there at low tide. Until about the 17th century, the lost land was called Maes Gwyddno, the land of Gwyddno; it was drowned when the guardian or priestess of a fairy well allowed the water to overflow. But the legend which is known today calls the land Cantref Gwaelod, the lowland hundred; its king was Gwyddno Garanhir, and a drunkard called Seithennin looked after the sluices and embankments which protected it from the sea. One evening, after a great banquet, Seithennin left all the sluices open, and the land, the people and 16 noble cities were drowned. When the sea is still and the wind quiet, it is said that the bells of Cantref Gwaelod can still be heard tolling far beneath the waters of the bay. A folksong called Clychau Aberdyfi, 'The Aberdovey Bells', is often associated with the sunken cities.

Abergavenny (Y Fenni) *Gwent*

Long ago, a man called Sion Dafydd, who lived in the hills above Abergavenny, was in league with the Devil. He had arranged with the Devil that his soul was safe as long as he was touching something rooted in the earth, and many times Satan tried to catch him and failed. In the end, because he was too evil to go to Heaven but too clever to be trapped by the Devil, he became a Will-o'-the-Wisp.

Aber soch *Gwynedd*

The site of the 17th-century mansion called Castellmarch was reputedly the home of March Amheirchion, one of King Arthur's knights. Like the legendary Midas, March had the ears of a horse (in fact, *march* is Welsh for horse). But he always kept them hidden, and killed every man who ever saw them, burying the bodies in a nearby reed-bed. People finally learnt of his deformity when a young boy cut some of the reeds to make himself a flute, and discovered that the only song the flute could play was: 'March Amheirchion has horse's ears.'

BALA LAKE (LLYN TEGID), GWYNEDD

By tradition, the old town of Bala lies drowned beneath the lake of the same name; and one day, it is said, the lake will swallow up the new Bala. Here, too, lies the body of Charles, the harpist, who in the 18th century is said to have given himself to the Devil by feeding communion bread to dogs. He drowned one night on his way home from a feast at Fach Ddeiliog (now a farmhouse) and a cloud of smoke hung over the spot where he sank

PRINCE LLYWELYN'S FAITHFUL HOUND

In the 13th century, it is said, Prince Llywelyn the Great had a palace at Beddgelert in north Gwynedd, and he spent much time hunting in the surrounding countryside. One day, he sounded his horn to summon his dogs, and all came except Gelert, the leader of the pack and the hound that the prince loved and trusted above any other. Regretfully, for Gelert was as swift and brave as a dog could be, Llywelyn had to go hunting without him.

Gelert's death
When the prince returned home that evening, Gelert came bounding out to meet him, his jaws dripping with blood. A terrible thought flashed across the prince's mind: could the dog have savaged his one-year-old son? He rushed into the child's nursery and found the cradle overturned and the walls spattered with blood. He looked everywhere for the child, but could find no sign of him.

Mad with grief, he plunged his sword through Gelert's heart.

A cairn of stones
As the dog howled in his death agony, a child's cry echoed from beneath the cradle; and there Llywelyn found his son, unharmed, and beside him the body of an enormous wolf, killed by the brave Gelert. Stricken with remorse, Llywelyn carried Gelert outside the castle walls and buried him where everyone might see his grave, and know how he had saved the life of Prince Llywelyn's heir. To this day, a cairn of stones still marks the place; and the name Beddgelert means, in Welsh, the grave of Gelert.

An ancient fable
The story of Gelert's death is probably the best-known folktale in Wales, and every year thousands of people visit the grave. But the cairn of stones is less than 200 years old and the

story is told about many different dogs and their owners all over the world; it was already well known long before Llywelyn's lifetime. It occurs among the fables of Catwg Ddoeth, Cadog the Wise, a 5th-century saint; and there is an old Welsh expression: 'I repent as much as the man who slew his greyhound.'

The modern myth
In 1793, a man called David Pritchard came to live at Beddgelert, which at that time was called Beth Kellarth or Kelert, probably after an ancient Celtic saint. Pritchard, landlord of the Royal Goat Inn, knew the story of the man who killed his dog, and adapted it to fit the village and benefit his trade. He invented the name Gelert and introduced Llywelyn into the story, because of the prince's connection with the nearby abbey. And with the help of the parish clerk, Pritchard, not Llywelyn, raised the cairn.

ISLAND GRAVEYARD

For many centuries, Bardsey Island (Ynys Enlli), 2 miles off the Lleyn Peninsula, Gwynedd, was an important place of pilgrimage – tradition asserts that 20,000 monks are buried there. Mainlanders sometimes report seeing shadowy, cowled figures wandering along its shores; the ghosts are said to be omens of disease, drownings and storms. The wizard Merlin is also said to be sleeping in a cave on the island, surrounded by a mound of ancient treasures, including the throne of Britain. He will wake from his sleep only when King Arthur returns from the dead

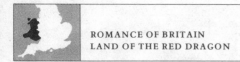

Betws Garmon *Gwynedd*
A family named Pellings, who lived in the district until the last century, were said to be descendants of a marriage between a man and a fairy named Penelope. The fairy consented to marry her mortal lover only on condition that he would never strike her with iron. They lived happily together for many years, and produced a son and a daughter. But one day Penelope was struck accidentally with a bridle as her husband tried to catch a pony, and she vanished for ever.

Betws-y-coed *Gwynedd*
The legendary 16th-century Welsh soldier and bard Huw Llwyd is supposed to have stayed once at an inn kept by two sisters near the village, on the road to Cerrigydrudion. During the night he was wakened by two cats tearing at his discarded clothing and he struck one of them on the paw with his sword. The next morning one of the sisters had a bandaged hand – and Huw realised that his hostesses were actually witches who, in the guise of cats, had tried to rob him while he slept.

Borth-y-gest *Gwynedd*
David Owen, the alleged composer of the air Dafydd Y Garreg Wen, 'David of the White Rock', was born at the farm of Y Garreg Wen *c.* 1711. The young harpist is said to have composed the air on his death-bed and asked that it be played at his funeral. During his last days, tradition says, he dreamt he heard the melody being played in an evergreen country to an audience of two doves. On the day of his funeral, in 1741, two doves followed his coffin from Y Garreg Wen to Ynyscynhaearn cemetery, where his grave can still be seen.

A DOOR IN THE BRECON BEACONS

Near the lake Llyn Cwm Llwch (top right) in the Brecon Beacons, legend says there was a secret door which opened every May 1 to admit mortals to fairyland, until a visitor stole a flower from the fairies. Years later when the *inhabitants of Brecon started to drain the lake in search of its reputed treasures, a giant rose from the water and threatened to drown their town and all the land around the River Wye if his peace was disturbed*

Builth Wells (Llanfair-ym-Muallt) *Powys*
On the nearby mountain of Cefn Carn Cafall is a cairn, with a stone on top bearing an impression like that of a dog's paw. Legend says that when King Arthur was hunting on the mountain his dog Cafall left an impression of his paw on a stone. Arthur built a cairn and placed the stone on top and then named the mountain Cefn Carn Cafall, the ridge of Cafall's cairn. If the stone is moved, it is said that it will always return.

Cardiff (Caerdydd) *S. Glam*
The inn called The Dusty Forge on the main Cowbridge Road into Cardiff is built on the site of an old smithy. Legend tells how the blacksmith's wife heard a noise at midnight and saw the Devil hammering out a shoe for his own cloven foot on the anvil. The woman rushed to the chicken house and woke the cock. Thinking it was dawn, the cock began to crow, causing the Devil, who fears the sunlight, to drop the unfinished shoe and disappear.

HAVEN OF THE HOLY GRAIL

A fragment of a wooden cup (now kept in a bank) was displayed until recently in the 18th-century mansion of Nanteos, near Capel Seion, north Dyfed. The cup was said to have been brought for safety to an earlier house of the same name by monks of Strata Florida Abbey at the Reformation. It was supposed to have miraculous healing powers, and some say it was the cup used at the Last Supper – the original Holy Grail

Carmarthen (Caerfyrddin) *Dyfed*

'When Myrddin's (Merlin's) tree shall tumble
  down
  Then shall fall Carmarthen town.'
No doubt some inhabitants of Carmarthen still believe Merlin's prophecy, for his famous oak tree in the town is carefully preserved by the local authorities. According to one tradition the great magician is still alive in a cave in Bryn Myrddin, Merlin's Hill, about 2 miles east of Carmarthen, kept there for ever in bonds of enchantment by his beloved Vivien. People once claimed that it was possible to hear his groans as he lamented his folly in letting a woman learn his secret spells.

Merlin, in the Welsh version of his legend, became a prophet after wandering in misery for 50 years, with only a wild piglet as his 'rude bedfellow'. From the 9th century onwards his prophecies were contained in poems said to have been written by himself, many of which are included in *Llyfr Du Caerfyrddin*, *The Black Book of Carmarthen*, written about AD 1200.

Cemaes Bay (Cemais) *Anglesey, Gwynedd*

A cave in Cemaes Bay is said to have taken its name from an incident which happened over 200 years ago. A family dispute apparently led a young man to take his dappled blue-grey horse and gallop furiously away from his home near the bay. Blinded by rage he rode the horse headlong over a cliff. Only the young man's hat was ever recovered from the sea, but the carcass of the blue-grey horse was found washed into the cave in Cemaes Bay. Since that time the cave has been called Ogof y March Glas, the cave of the blue horse.

Chirk (Y Waun) *Clwyd*

Near Chirk Castle, 2 miles west of the village, are traces of Offa's Dyke, the rampart built in the 8th century by Offa, King of Mercia. A gap in the Dyke is called Adwy'r Beddau, the gap of the graves. This is the traditional site of the Battle of Crogen, where in 1165 Henry II of England was defeated by the Welsh army and, some say, by the Welsh weather. A local belief claims that a nearby meadow, part of Crogen Wladus farm, should not be ploughed because this will disturb the bones of the soldiers and horses resting beneath.

The 14th-century Chirk Castle has been occupied since 1595 by the Myddleton family, whose arms includes a red hand. Tradition asserts that the 'bloody hand' is there as a memory of the family's past misdeeds, and that it could not be removed until a prisoner was able to survive ten years in the castle dungeons. Though the red hand remains on the arms, legend records that one prisoner almost achieved the feat necessary for its removal.

Cilmery (Cilmeri) *Powys*

On the bank of the River Irfon at Cilmery is a rough-hewn stone memorial to Llywelyn ap Gruffydd, the last of the Welsh princes. It was here in 1282 that Llywelyn, apparently while alone and defenceless, was slain by an English man-at-arms. According to tradition, the spot where Llywelyn died was covered with broom, and the shrub has never grown there since because it still mourns the Welsh prince. Certainly, no broom grows about the obelisk now; instead, it is surrounded by 13 trees planted there to represent the 13 counties of Wales.

ST BEUNO'S CHEST

This old oak strong-box in the 15th-century church of St Beuno, at Clynnog Fawr, Gwynedd, is made from a single piece of wood. Until recently, it was customary in the parish for calves born with mis-shapen ears to be sold annually in the churchyard. The fees paid were secured in the chest as church offerings

Conway (Conwy) *Gwynedd*

Among Conway's legendary links with the sea is the story of a mermaid who was washed ashore by a storm in Conway Bay. She begged the fishermen who found her to help her back into the water, but they refused to do so. Just before she died, she cursed the people of the town, swearing that they would always be poor. When Conway was suffering from a fish famine during the 5th century, many said that the curse had been fulfilled.

Another fish-famine story concerns St Brigid. Walking by the river, she threw in rushes, which a few days later turned into fish. Soon the river was teeming with the miraculous fish, which ever since then have been known as sparlings, or in Welsh, *brwyniaid*, both meaning 'rush-like'.

DEVIL'S BRIDGE

Three bridges, built close together, cross the River Mynach just below Bryn Garw, Dyfed, at the place where it cuts through a deep gorge. Legend says that the lowest bridge was made by the Devil when an old woman's cow became stranded on the other side of the gorge. Satan appeared and promised to build her a bridge if he might own the first living creature to use it. She agreed, but when the bridge was finished she cunningly threw a piece of bread across it. Her dog ran after the bread, and Satan, outwitted, became its new owner

Criccieth (Cricieth) *Gwynedd*

An old tale relates how Dic, a piper, and two fiddlers named Twm and Ned were enticed by fairies into Yr Ogof Ddu, the black cave, near Criccieth. They were never seen again, but it is said that the tunes they were playing, three traditional Welsh airs, when they disappeared can still occasionally be heard coming from the cave.

Cwm Gwaun *Dyfed*

Before the Gregorian calendar was adopted by Britain in 1752, the New Year began on what is now January 12. The people of Cwm Gwaun still celebrate the old New Year's Day, Hen Galan, on that date. In the morning children go out to collect the traditional *calennig*, meaning a New Year's gift, and later, a *noson lawen*, or merry evening, is held in several of the farmhouses, where home-made food and beer are served in a convivial atmosphere of singing and story-telling.

Cwrtycadno *Dyfed*

The most famous of Welsh wizards, Dr John Harries of Cwrtycadno, was consulted by people from all over Wales until his death in 1839. It was believed that he could cure diseases and charm away pain, cast out evil spirits and overcome witchcraft, foretell the future and discover missing objects. Near the ruins of his home, Pantcou, stands a stone circle said to be the scene of many of his magical rites.

Cynwyd *Gwynedd*

Tradition claims that Llangar church, between Cynwyd and Corwen, was originally to have been built where Cynwyd Bridge crosses the River Dee. But each night the stones laid during the day mysteriously vanished, removed by the Devil. A wizard told the stonemasons that the site was not acceptable to God, and advised them to organise a hunt for a white stag and build the church where the stag first appeared. They did so, and Llangar church now occupies the place where the animal was first seen, while nearby Moel Lladdfa, the hill of slaughter, is the place where the stag was finally caught and killed by the hunters.

Dinas Mawddwy *Gwynedd*

During the 15th and 16th centuries, the district around Dinas Mawddwy was terrorised by a notorious band of outlaws known as Gwylliaid Cochion Mawddwy, The Red Bandits of Mawddwy. The inhabitants of the area greatly feared the bandits, and during attacks on their homes would defend themselves with scythe blades which they kept hidden in their chimneys.

Legend says that many were captured in the 16th century and condemned by Baron Lewis Owen, the County Sheriff. Tradition claims that the mother of one of them went to the baron and pleaded with him to save her young son's life. He refused, and then, baring her bosom, she cursed him and said: 'These breasts have fed other sons who will wash their hands in your heart's blood.'

The outlaws were executed at a place where a house called Collfryn, the hill of loss, now stands, and buried in a mound still to be found on Rhos Goch, the red moor, about 2 miles east of the nearby village of Mallwyd. Baron Owen died in the same year, horribly murdered on October 11, 1555, by the members of Gwylliaid Cochion Mawddwy who had escaped capture.

Ffestiniog *Gwynedd*

Near Ffestiniog is Llyn y Morwynion, the maidens' lake. The legend which inspired its name tells how the men of Ardudwy (as the surrounding district is called) went to the Vale of Clwyd looking for wives. There they found several maidens to their liking and carried them off, but on their journey home the men of the Vale of Clwyd overtook them near the lake. In the ensuing fight all the men of Ardudwy were killed, and the heart-broken maidens, who had fallen in love with their captors, threw themselves into the lake and drowned. It is said that their ghosts have been seen emerging from the lake in the morning to comb their hair.

Fishguard (Abergwaun) *Dyfed*

The last foreign invasion of British soil took place on February 22, 1797, when a French expeditionary force landed at Strumble Head near Fishguard. It was commanded by an American officer named Tate who had hopes of starting a peasants' rebellion against the landowners, but his troops, who were mostly ex-convicts, stole drink from the inns and began to loot the local farms. The tiny contingent of local militia or volunteers were powerless to stop them, and the invaders set up their headquarters in the cellar of Trehywel Farm, near Goodwick. Two days later, Lord Cawdor advanced on them with the Castlemartin Yeomanry. According to local tradition, several women of the district, led by Jemima Nicholas, dressed in red cloaks and boldly marched towards the drunken French soldiers who fled in terror, mistaking them for the British army. The French retreated to the beach below Goodwick where an inscribed stone now marks the spot where they surrendered to Lord Cawdor on February 24. Jemima Nicholas, who became famous as 'the General of the Red Army', died in 1832 and is buried at the Church of St Mary in Fishguard.

Gilfach *Mid Glamorgan*

A local legend relates how coal was discovered in the Rhymney Valley. The fairies of the valley were being harassed by a giant who came to live at Gilfach Fargoed. A fairy lad, whose parents had been eaten by the giant, finally decided to kill the monster, and an owl from nearby Pencoed Fawr farm agreed to help him. One night, when the giant was courting a witch under an apple tree, the owl shot an arrow into his heart and he died. Meanwhile, the witch was killed by a flock of the owl's companions. When the fairies burnt the giant's body in a huge pit, the ground caught fire and exposed the coal lying underneath. It is said that, on moonlit nights, the owl's descendants still come to Gilfach Fargoed and celebrate the giant's death in song.

Glyndyfrdwy *Gwynedd*

On September 16, 1400, a band of Welsh rebels met at Glyndyfrdwy and declared Owen Glendower (Owain Glyndŵr) to be the rightful Prince of Wales, an event which sparked off a ten-year rebellion against Henry IV. Although Wales failed to establish itself as a kingdom in its own right, or achieve its separation from England, Owen Glendower has ever since remained the country's most famous folk hero who, legend claims, will one day return to liberate the Welsh nation.

Glyndyfrdwy stands on the River Dee, which in pagan times was held to be the dwelling-place of Aerfen, a martial goddess who presided over the fate of wars between the English and the Welsh. It was believed that three human sacrifices had to be drowned in the sacred river every year to ensure success in battle.

ARTHUR'S RESTING PLACE

The Craig y Ddinas Cave near Glyn Neath (Glyn-nedd), in West Glamorgan, is reputed to harbour the sleeping King Arthur and his knights. Legend tells of a wizard who met a Welsh drover carrying a hazelwood staff. He asked the Welshman to take him to the tree from which the staff had been cut, for there they would find a great treasure. When they dug up the tree, they found a secret passage leading to a cave. At the entrance was a bell, and inside they saw King Arthur and his warriors sleeping beside a mound of silver and a mound of *gold. The wizard told the Welshman to take as much silver and gold as he wanted. He warned him never to touch the bell for, if he did, the warriors would awake and ask 'Is it day?', in which case he should reply 'No, sleep on'. Twice the drover became too greedy, over-loaded himself with riches and touched the bell accidentally, but he remembered to give the correct answer. The third time it happened, however, he forgot the answer. He was beaten so badly by the knights that he was crippled for life, and could never find the cave again*

Goodwick (Wdig) *Dyfed*

James Wade (Shemi Wâd), who died in 1887 and is buried in Pen Caer, was one of Pembrokeshire's best-known storytellers. Many of his 'white lie' tales are remembered to this day. On one occasion, he said, a great carrion crow swooped down out of the sky while he was fishing and grabbed him in its beak. It carried him to Ireland and dropped him in a cannon, where he spent the night. Just as he was waking up next morning, the cannon was fired, and he was rocketed across St George's Channel, to land unharmed right next to his fishing rod on the shore at Goodwick.

Gors-las *Dyfed*

Long ago a man called Owain looked after a well on the mountain called Mynydd Mawr, which lies a mile north of Gors-las. One day, after watering his horse, he forgot to replace the huge stone slab with which the well was always kept covered, and a torrent of water poured down the mountain. It would have drowned the whole area had Owain not galloped around it using magic to check the flood. The lake that was left on Mynydd Mawr is known to this day as Llyn Llech Owain – the lake of Owain's stone slab.

Greenfield (Maes-glas) *Clwyd*

A monk from 12th-century Basingwerk Abbey once heard a nightingale singing in a nearby wood, and its voice held him spellbound for what seemed like hours. When he returned to the abbey, he found it in ruins, and all the people around him were strangers. He asked what had happened, but no one seemed to understand him. One bystander remarked that his sudden appearance reminded him of the story of another monk, who had disappeared just as suddenly centuries before. The villagers offered the monk some food, but the moment he touched it he crumbled to dust.

ST WINIFRED'S WELL

In the 7th century a chieftain named Caradoc cut off the head of St Winifred for refusing to let him make love to her. Water sprang from the ground where her head fell, and to this day St Winifred's Well at Holywell in Flintshire is said to have miraculous healing properties, especially for nervous disorders. Remarkably, Winifred's uncle St Beuno, widely remembered by churches throughout Lleyn, restored her head to her body, and she went on to become Abbess of Gwytherin in north Clwyd. St Beuno also put a curse on Caradoc's descendants. They barked like dogs and could be cured only by being immersed in the water from St Winifred's Well

Hyssington *Powys*

A boot containing a tiny, savage bull is supposed to be buried below the doorstep of Hyssington church. If the step is ever moved, the bull will emerge, grow quickly to an enormous size and terrorise the parish as it once did many years ago.

By tradition, the creature is really a wicked squire, who so ill-treated the men who worked for him that one of them wished that the squire might turn into a bull. The wish was granted, but the bull was even more evil than the squire, and so the villagers turned for help to the parson of Hyssington. He confronted the monstrous animal, reciting prayers and reading aloud from the Bible, and gradually it began to shrink. He led it into the church and continued preaching at it until nightfall, by which time it was no larger than a small dog.

When the parson's candle burnt out, forcing him to stop preaching, the bull started growing again, until it became so large that cracks appeared in the walls of Hyssington church – they can be seen there to this day. Next morning, the parson had to start again from the beginning; but after a long day's praying he had made the bull small enough to be pushed into a boot. Quickly, he buried the boot and its dangerous occupant beneath the church doorstep.

Lampeter (Llanbedr Pont Steffan) *Dyfed*

In the 17th century the ancestral home of the Lloyds of Maesyfelin stood where Maesyfelin Street is today. Elen Lloyd, the only daughter of the family, became engaged to Samuel Pritchard, the son of a poet-priest called Rhys Pritchard from nearby Llandovery. One day, Elen's four brothers, fearing for their inheritance, tied Samuel head downwards on his horse, and galloped him from Lampeter to Llandovery. He died of his injuries, and they threw his body into the River Teifi. Elen was driven mad by grief, and she too died soon afterwards. Rhys Pritchard put a curse on the house of Maesyfelin, and within months it had caught fire and burnt to the ground.

Either through remorse or because of Pritchard's curse, the eldest of the four Lloyd brothers murdered the other three and then hanged himself.

Llanarth *Dyfed*

Local tradition claims that the Devil once tried to steal the bell from Llanarth church. But he made so much noise about it that he woke the vicar, who climbed up into the belfry armed with bell, book and candle. By solemnly repeating the name of Christ, the vicar succeeded in driving the Devil to the top of the tower, and forced him to jump off. In the graveyard, there is a stone which bears the marks he made when he landed on it.

Llanbedr Painscastle (Llanbedr Castell-paen) *Powys*

The ruthless cruelty of the 12th-century Norman Lord William de Breos earned him the undying hatred of the Welsh and a permanent place in their folklore. He is sometimes remembered as 'The Ogre of Abergavenny', and in the minds of many Welsh children, his wife Maud lived on as a terrifying witch and bogey long after her death in the dungeons of King John in 1210. A stone in Llowes churchyard, south Powys, is said to have been thrown there by Maud from a spot some 3 miles away, and the name de Breos is kept alive not only by the many legends about the family, but also by the names of various pedigree cattle in Wales, such as De Breos Maud and De Breos David.

One of William's main strongholds was at Llanbedr Painscastle, though a mound and bitter memories are all that remain of it today. Here, on August 12, 1198, the 'ogre' and an army of Englishmen slaughtered 3000 Welsh in one of the bloodiest and most decisive battles in Welsh history – the River Bachawy is said to have been red with blood for weeks afterwards. The Welsh were led by Gwenwynwyn, Prince of Powys, who was seeking revenge for the murder of his cousin Trahaiarn Fychan. On William's orders, Trahaiarn had been dragged through Brecon tied to a horse's tail, and then beheaded. Not only did his death go unavenged, but Gwenwynwyn's hopes for a united Wales died with his army.

It took a man more cruel even than William finally to overthrow him. King John stripped him of his land in the early 13th century, and he died a beggar. For suggesting that John had murdered his nephew Prince Arthur, Maud and her youngest son were imprisoned in Corfe Castle, with only a sheaf of wheat and a piece of raw bacon to keep them alive. By tradition, when the door of their dungeon was reopened after 11 days, both lay dead on the floor. In the agony of starvation, Maud had half-eaten the cheeks of her son.

GWENLLIAN'S HEAD

For centuries the ghost of Gwenllian, the wife of Gruffydd ap Rhys ap Tewdwr, prince of South Wales, haunted the countryside near Kidwelly (Cydweli) Castle. She was decapitated in 1136 as she led an attack on the Norman stronghold, at a place outside the town still known as Maes Gwenllian, Gwenllian's field. Legend says that her headless phantom never found rest until a man searched the ancient battlefield and found and returned the princess's skull to her

A Hero's Youth

The professional storytellers who entertained the nobility of Wales in the Middle Ages knew by heart an immense number of legends and traditional tales, some of which may have taken days to tell. For centuries, the stories were passed on orally, and each new generation of storytellers added to them to suit the tastes of their patrons or to give free rein to their own particular skills as narrators.

Most of these stories were forgotten when the demand for them began to peter out towards the end of the 15th century. But a few had been written down, and they survive today not only as masterpieces of medieval literature, but also as a unique guide to the world of magic and mystery, of gods, giants and superhuman heroes, which in the Celtic imagination was as real as the everyday world.

The 11 stories known as the *Mabinogion* have been preserved since the 14th century in the *White Book of Rhydderch*, now in the National Library of Wales at Aberystwyth, and the *Red Book of Hergest* in Jesus College library, Oxford. But they were known long before then in the candle-lit castle halls of the Welsh princes, and some episodes may even be the last echoes of a forgotten mythology that reached right back to the dawn of Celtic civilisation. Ironically, the only feature of the *Mabinogion* that is modern is its title. The Welsh scholar Lady Charlotte Guest gave the stories the name by which they have been known since she translated them into English in 1838–49. For once, her scholarship let her down. In Welsh, there is no such word as 'mabinogion', but Lady Charlotte thought that it was the plural of *mabinogi*, and meant 'tales of a hero's youth'.

The Four Branches

The original hero of the first four stories, which are known as the Four Branches, is thought to have been Pryderi, the son and heir of Pwyll, Prince of Dyfed. But over the centuries, the saga of Pryderi's life was embroidered with legends about other mythical heroes and, by the time the Four Branches came to be written down, Pryderi was only one in a galaxy of gods, kings and princes.

The Four Branches – called *Pwyll, Prince of Dyfed, Branwen, Daughter of Llŷr, Manawydan, Son of Llŷr* and *Math, Son of Mathonwy* – contain a wealth of information about the religious beliefs and rituals of pagan Celtic Britain. The children of Llŷr, for example, were gods of the underworld, and the children of Dôn, whose exploits are described in the Fourth Branch, were gods of the sky. And the veneration shown to King Brân's severed head in the Second Branch is a reminder of the ancient Celtic practice of head-hunting, in which human heads became sacrificial offerings to the gods.

Five of the other seven tales recount the fantastic adventures of King Arthur and his knights, as they ride through an enchanted land full of fabulous beasts and frightful monsters. Two shorter stories stand apart from the rest. *Lludd and Llefelys* tells of the trials of Lludd, King of Britain, and his brother. The *Dream of Macsen Wledig* takes as its hero the Roman emperor Magnus Maximus, who died about AD 388.

RHIANNON'S BIRDS *The enchanting singing of the three birds of Pryderi's mother, Rhiannon, held listeners spellbound*

THE HEROES *As the seven survivors of the great war with Ireland carried away King Brân's head, his sister Branwen died of grief*

Pryderi's childhood

When the world was young, the bards used to say, the noble Prince Pwyll of Dyfed, which is now called Pembroke, married the beautiful Lady Rhiannon. Three years later, she gave birth to the future Prince Pryderi, but on the night that the child was born, the six women who were appointed to watch over him all fell asleep. When they awoke, they found that the boy had disappeared, and fearing Pwyll's rage, they accused Rhiannon of killing the child. Pwyll believed the tale, and forced his wife to do penance by carrying all visitors into the castle on her back.

On the same night that Pryderi disappeared, the Lord Teyrnon of Gwentis-Coed was helping his mare to foal when a giant claw came through the stable window, snatching at the newborn colt. Teyrnon drew his sword and hacked off the claw, but when he rushed outside the monster had fled, leaving a newborn baby.

Four years later, Teyrnon heard about Rhiannon's penance, and realised that the boy in his care bore a strong resemblance to Pwyll. He returned Pryderi to his joyful parents, and all three lived happily together, until at last Pwyll died, and the boy took his place as Prince of Dyfed.

The war of the magic cauldron

The story of *Branwen, Daughter of Llŷr*, relates how Branwen was given in marriage to Matholwch, King of Ireland, by her brother Brân, the gigantic King of Britain. The feast ended abruptly, however, when a younger brother, Efnisien, insulted the Irish king, who stormed out of the court. Peace was only restored when Brân presented Matholwch with the miraculous Cauldron of Rebirth, which could restore life to the dead.

The Irish king sailed home with his bride, but the girl discovered that her husband had neither forgiven nor forgotten her brother's conduct. On the advice of his courtiers, he divorced his wife, who was put to work as a serving wench in the palace kitchens.

Three years later, when Brân heard what had happened to his sister, he immediately launched an invasion of Ireland, carrying some of his army across the sea on his colossal shoulders. In the cruel and bloody war that followed, Efnisien, cause of so much of the trouble, destroyed the magical Cauldron of Rebirth by willing his heart to burst while he was inside it. The war ended, but only Branwen and eight men were left alive. Among these were Pryderi and Brân, who, having been wounded in the foot by a poisoned spear, knew he had not long to live. He ordered his men to cut off his head and bury it where the Tower of London now stands, facing France. So long as it remained there, no invader could ever overcome Britain.

Branwen died of grief when Brân was decapitated, and the seven warriors buried her near Llanddeusant in Anglesey. Then they marched on, carrying Brân's head, which miraculously still spoke to them and told wondrous tales to enliven the journey.

On their way, they feasted seven years at Harlech, held spellbound by the magical singing of Rhiannon's three birds. Later, they spent another 80 blissful years, free from all sorrow, in a castle at Gwales. This golden time, known as the Assembly of the Wondrous Head, came to a sudden end when one of the men opened a forbidden door, which looked over Cornwall. Their sad memories came rushing back and, heavy-hearted, they set off for London, to lay Brân's head to rest in the chosen spot.

Manawydan and the wizards

Pryderi and his mother, Rhiannon, literally vanished from the scene in the Third Branch of the *Mabinogion*, called *Manawydan, Son of Llŷr*. They were enticed into a magic castle and whisked away by a wizard who sought revenge for a trick played by Pryderi's father, Prince Pwyll. But Brân's brother, Manawydan, then captured the wizard's wife and forced an exchange of prisoners.

Another wizard, called Gwydion, son of Dôn, dominated the Fourth Branch of the stories. In *Math, Son of Mathonwy*, he plotted a trick war between Pryderi and Math, then killed Pryderi in single combat by using his magic.

Later, Gwydion and Math made a woman, Blodeuedd, from flowers for

Lleu Llaw Gyffes, whose mother had prophesied that he would never marry a human. But the match was not a success. Blodeuedd betrayed her husband, and Gwydion transformed her into an owl.

Elen and the emperor
After the Four Branches, there are two shorter stories. In the *Dream of Macsen Wledig*, Macsen – the 4th-century Roman emperor Magnus Maximus – dreamt that he fell in love with a beautiful Welsh girl, Elen. The dream gave him no peace, day or night, until at last he set off for Caernarvon, where he met the girl and married her. He stayed so long in Wales that after seven years he lost his throne. Enlisting a Welsh army, he marched on Rome, which he defeated. Having regained power, he and Elen ruled the world together.

In the other story, King Lludd of Britain rid the island of three plagues with the help of his brother Llefelys, King of France.

The Welsh King Arthur
The Welsh have their own versions of the exploits of King Arthur, many of which are related in the *Mabinogion*. *Culhwch and Olwen*, the earliest Arthurian tale in Welsh, dates from around the 10th century.

It was prophesied of Arthur's cousin, Culhwch, that he would never marry unless he could win the heart and hand of Olwen, the daughter of Ysbaddaden Chief-giant, a fearful ogre who lived in the strongest fortress in the world. Unable to win

OLWEN AND HER LOVER CULHWCH

the girl unaided, Culhwch determined to enlist the help of King Arthur and his men. Having reached the court, he coolly evaded the fierce gate-keeper, Glewlwyd Mighty-grasp, and rode into the banqueting hall, where he made his request.

The king was so impressed by the young man's brash manner that he gladly agreed to join Culhwch and help him win Olwen. Arthur chose six of his mightiest warriors to accompany them: there was Cei, who could grow as big as a tree at will and make fire from his own body; and one-handed Bedwyr, as dangerous in battle as any three men; and Cynddylig the guide, who could find his way anywhere; Gwalchmei the world's best horseman; Gwrhyr who

knew every language; and Menw, who could make them all invisible. After many adventures, the noble company found Ysbaddaden's castle, and at last met the golden-haired Olwen. She was so beautiful that wherever she walked, four white flowers sprang up at her heels. She loved Culhwch at once, but Ysbaddaden refused to permit the wedding, for it had been prophesied that when she married, he would die.

Despite this, Olwen agreed to marry the brave young man, provided that he first obeyed all the giant's commands. Culhwch never hesitated. Backed by Arthur and his knights, he knew he could conquer any hazard.

The 40 great tasks
Ysbaddaden was fearful, but thought the tasks he could set were beyond solving. He demanded 13 treasures, which could only be won through 40 dangerous adventures, each one of which could lead to certain death.

Culhwch, Arthur and the knights rode off, to perform superhuman feats of strength and courage in their quest. But when almost all the prizes had been won, there was still the most perilous adventure of all: they had to win the comb and scissors that grew between the ears of a giant boar named Twrch Trwyth. The comb and scissors were the only ones that could unravel the iron tangle of the giant Ysbaddaden's hair – and he refused to permit the wedding until his hair was dressed.

This last task was almost the end of them all. First, they had to seek out the one man in the world who was able to handle the ferocious dogs needed to hunt down the boar. To find him, they had to consult the five wisest creatures in Britain – an ouzel cock, a stag, an owl, an eagle and a salmon. But at last the ferocious boar was tracked to its lair. The bloody struggle that followed cost the king several of his bravest knights, trampled and ripped to death. The hunt ran through the forests and over hills, from Wales to Cornwall, where the great boar was eventually driven into the sea. Before it died, Arthur tore the comb and scissors from its head.

Arthur and his warriors returned to Ysbaddaden's castle in triumph, with all 13 of the treasures he had demanded. The defeated giant gave

THE DEATH OF THE GIANT YSBADDADEN

his consent to the marriage, though he knew it meant his own death. His last words to Culhwch as he was led out to execution were: 'Thank Arthur for Olwen.' The giant's huge head was cut off and set up on a stake for all his enemies to mock. And Culhwch and his bride lived happily for ever.

A yearning for chivalry
In the intricate *Dream of Rhonabwy*, the bards revealed a deep regret for the passing of the heroic age of chivalry. Rhonabwy slept three days and nights in a dirty, flea-infested house, dreaming that King Arthur played chess with Sir Owein, while men and ravens fought fiercely near by. The tale contrasted the degenerate

ways of Rhonabwy's friends with the king's virtue and dignity, and with the nobility of men in bygone days.

Three romances
Like the story of *Rhonabwy*, the last three tales of the *Mabinogion* were overlain with a Norman-French concern for chivalry and courtly romance. Fantastic adventures took place in a marvellous, fairytale land where anything was possible.

In *Peredur Son of Efrawg*, the young hero travelled to a Castle of Wonders, slew the vile Black Worm of the Dolorous Mound, and ended up marrying the mysterious Empress of Constantinople. Equally absurd, romantic events overtook Arthur's

knight, Owein, in *The Lady of the Fountain*. Owein married the countess Luned, and was the victor in dozens of hand-to-hand combats. In both tales, dramatic appeal was enhanced by combining romantic chivalry with hard, realistic descriptions of war.

Similarly, in *Gereint Son of Erbin*, Enid's sufferings after being wrongfully suspected of infidelity by Gereint were tinged with an emotional intensity that lent the characters a true humanity despite their miraculous powers.

It is this blending of magic and fantasy, of human strengths and weaknesses, which makes the *Mabinogion* an outstanding masterpiece of Welsh literature.

THE GOLDEN WARRIOR *The story of Culhwch's struggle to win the fair Olwen, daughter of the ogre Ysbaddaden, who lived in the strongest fortress in the world, for his bride, is one of the most exciting in the* Mabinogion. *Here Culhwch is setting out to ask his cousin, King Arthur, for help . . . 'on a steed with light-grey head . . . with well-knit fork, shell-hoofed, and a gold tubular bridle-bit in its mouth. And under him a precious gold saddle, and in his hand two whetted spears of silver. A battle-axe in his hand, the forearm's length of a full grown man from ridge to edge. It would draw blood from the wind . . . A gold-hilted sword on his thigh, and the blade of it gold . . . Never a hair-tip stirred upon him so exceeding light his steed's canter . . . to the gate'*

FAIRY CATTLE

Far-off memories of the aurochs, the great wild cattle that roamed Britain in prehistoric times, may have something to do with the many tales of fairy cattle that occur all over Wales. Usually they were generous beasts that gave an unending supply of milk to mankind until, upset by a greedy human, they would disappear for ever. The cow that lived at Aberdyfi, for example, supplied the whole district until a butcher came to slaughter her. Before he could do so, his arm was paralysed, and the cow escaped. A green lady led it into the waters of Llyn Barfog, and it was never seen again.

There are many stories, too, of the Ychen Bannog – the long-horned oxen. These were the strongest oxen in the world, but there were only two of them and one could not live without the other. They were often used to haul monsters from their lairs, such as the dreaded Afanc, the water-monster that lived in the River Conway near Betws-y-coed. The creature was enticed from its cave by a young girl it had fallen in love with, but though the townspeople managed to put chains round it, it clawed off one of the girl's breasts and escaped. Finally, it was left to the Ychen Bannog to haul the Afanc from its hiding place. They did so, but such was the struggle that the eye of one of the oxen fell to the ground. This was so large that it formed a pool, which is still known as Pwll Llygad Ych – the pool of the ox's eye. The oxen were then taken to Llanddewibrefi in Dyfed, where they were employed to haul an enormous boulder to build the church. The work proved too much for them, however and, inseparable to the last, they died from exhaustion.

Llanberis *Gwynedd*
Reputedly the strongest woman ever to have lived in Wales was born in Llanberis in 1696, and died there some 105 years later. At the age of 70, it is said, Marged vch Ifan could still out-wrestle every man in Wales, and in a year she could catch as many foxes as the local huntsmen could in ten. Tradition maintains that she was a first-rate carpenter, blacksmith, cobbler, tailor, harp-maker, fiddle-maker and musician. After receiving many offers of marriage she chose the smallest and most effeminate of all her suitors. She is said to have beaten him twice; after the first beating he married her, after the second he became an ardent churchgoer.

Llandderfel *Gwynedd*
Medieval pilgrims used to visit the shrine of St Derfel, who was alleged to have been one of King Arthur's warriors. The shrine contained a wooden image of the saint, whose head, eyes and arms moved mechanically, and was believed to be capable of saving condemned souls from Hell. At the Reformation, the image was taken to London to be burnt at Smithfield, where a monk named Forest, who refused to deny that the image had worked miracles, was burnt with it. St Derfel's wooden horse can still be seen in Llandderfel church.

Llanddeusant *Anglesey, Gwynedd*
Tradition says that the green mound called Bedd Branwen, near the River Alaw, is the grave of Branwen, the heroine of the 14th-century Welsh epic called the *Mabinogion*. The mound was opened in 1813, and in it was found a rough-baked clay urn containing fragments of burnt bone and ashes. The site has become more significant since the discovery of more funerary urns in 1967.

Llanddona *Anglesey, Gwynedd*
For centuries, Anglesey was troubled by the Llanddona witches, a group of sorcerers who passed their magical powers from mother to daughter down through the generations. The women lived by extortion, cursing anyone who did not give them money or food. The men were smugglers who were protected from the excisemen by the flies which they kept in their scarves. If they were attacked, they would release the insects which would fly into the enemy's eyes and blind him. So far as is known, the last Llanddona witch died about 100 years ago.

Llanddulas *Clwyd*
A cave on Pen y Cefn mountain is said to have been the home of the Devil. While he lived there he was a great worry to the people of Llanddulas, especially for his habit of scaring pregnant women. At last they could stand it no longer, so they held a service of exorcism outside the cave, after which he never troubled them again. It is alleged that at some time during the service, the Devil fell into a deep, muddy pool, and that is why he has been black ever since.

Llanddwyn *Anglesey, Gwynedd*
The little island of Llanddwyn contains a well and the remains of a 13th-century church dedicated to St Dwynwen, the patron saint of Welsh lovers. The story goes that in the 5th century, Dwynwen fell deeply in love with Prince Maelon, but her father refused to accept him as a suitor. Frantic with desire, the prince raped the girl then abandoned her.

Dwynwen prayed to be relieved of her great love, so while they slept God gave Dwynwen and Maelon a drink which cured the girl but turned the prince to ice. God then gave Dwynwen three wishes. First, she wished that Maelon should be unfrozen; second, that God would answer all requests made by her on behalf of true lovers, and third, that she would never want to marry again. Her wishes were granted, and Dwynwen remained unmarried – she became a nun – until the day she died.

Llandeilo (Fawr) *Dyfed*
At ruined Carreg Castle, about 4 miles from Llandeilo, a narrow underground tunnel, 150 ft long, leads to a famous wishing well. Visitors once threw corks and pins into the dark water to make their wishes come true, and the water was reputed to have the power to heal eye and ear complaints. The castle is open daily.

Llandilo (Llandeilo) *Dyfed*
At one time, people who suffered from whooping cough or consumption used to visit this spot near Maenclochog to drink the waters of St Teilo's Well. For a cure to be effective, the water had to be drunk from St Teilo's skull, which had to be handed to the patient by the heir of Llandeilo farm. The skull disappeared in 1927. When Teilo died in the 6th century, his body was claimed by three churches – Penalun, where he was born; Llandeilo, where he died; and Llandaf, where he was bishop. Unable to decide which should have it, the monks prayed all night, and in the morning there were miraculously three bodies of St Teilo, one for each church.

Llandwrog *Gwynedd*
One night, the midwife of Llandwrog was summoned by a mysterious stranger who carried her on the back of his horse to a wonderful underground palace where she assisted a beautiful queen in giving birth to a child. The stranger gave the midwife some ointment to anoint the baby's eyes, but warned her against touching her own eyes with it. But she did so accidentally, and immediately the scene changed; the palace became a poor cave, and the queen was

her former serving-maid, Eilian. A few weeks afterwards, the midwife met the stranger at Caernarvon fair, and asked, 'How is Eilian?' 'Very well,' he replied, 'But what eye do you see me with?' 'This one,' she answered. At once, the stranger took a rush and poked the eye out.

Llaneilian-yn-Rhos *Clwyd*

As late as the last century, this village near Colwyn Bay was famous for its cursing well. Anyone who wanted to ill-wish an enemy would pay the keeper of the well to write the enemy's name on a piece of paper, wrap it round a pebble and drop it into the water. The curse was believed to last for as long as the paper remained in the well, so people paid the keeper to remove their names. Though one keeper was given six months' hard labour in 1831 for accepting money under false pretences, the well was not finally covered over until 1929. Its site can still be seen and local inhabitants know its location.

Llanfabon *Mid Glamorgan*

One night, so legend tells, the villagers of Llanfabon decided to steal a silver bell from nearby Llanwynno church. While they were carrying it back across a ford on the River Taf, the moon suddenly appeared from behind the clouds. Believing it to be the sun rising, they panicked and dropped the bell into the river as they fled. For years, Llanfabon villagers could be riled by speaking of the moon in their presence as *haul Llanfabon*, the Llanfabon sun.

Llanfair Caereinion *Powys*

The ghost of an old squire of the Bryn Glas estate used to plague the district. At last, a magician was employed to exorcise the spirit. At first the demon changed into a raging bull, but the magician succeeded in turning it into a fly and forcing it to enter his conjurer's bottle. The ghost agreed to this on condition that he could rest in one of the houses of the estate, and to this day, the bottle is carefully preserved by a widow and her son in a farmhouse in the district. They will not allow the bottle to be unsealed for fear that the evil spirit will be released once more.

'THE MOTHER OF WALES'

Katheryn Tudor of Berain, an ancient manor at Llannefydd, Clwyd, had so many descendants that she is still known as Mam Cymru, the Mother of Wales. She died in 1591 aged about 50. Legend says that she married seven times, and murdered all her husbands by pouring molten lead in their ears, burying them afterwards in the orchard. Apparently one of them must have put up a struggle, for his ineradicable bloodstains still mark Berain's walls. In fact, she married four times

393

Llanferres *Clwyd*

A ford over the River Alun is known as Rhyd y Gyfarthfa, the ford of the barking. Legend says that once, in the 6th century, all the local dogs had gathered there to bark at some uncanny presence, but none of the local people would venture near to find out what the trouble was. One day, a prince called Urien Rheged passed through and bravely went to investigate. All he found was a lone woman washing. The dogs stopped barking and, struck by her beauty, the prince made love to her. She did not resist, and said that she was the daughter of the King of Annwn – the Underworld – and that it was her destiny to wash by the ford until she had a son by a Christian. She told him to return in a year, when she would give him his son. So Urien returned at the appointed time – and was presented with both a son and a daughter, Owain ab Urien and Morfudd.

Llanfor *Gwynedd*

The Devil was a frequent visitor to this little village, in which he generally used to appear in the shape of a pig. At last, the parson managed to quell the beast by reciting the service of exorcism as he marched three times round the church, after which the Evil One was bound and taken to a pool in the nearby River Dee. There he was to remain as long as a certain lamp, hidden in the church, was kept burning. But the lamp burnt out for lack of oil, and the Devil returned in the form of a gentleman in a three-cornered hat, who constantly interrupted divine service in the church. Two magicians succeeded in laying him again, and he was carried away, in the form of a cock, on the back of a horse. Once more he was thrown into the pool, but this time his stay was permanent, for he had to remain there until he had counted every grain of sand at the bottom of the pool, now called Llyn y Geulan Goch.

Llanfyllin *Powys*

An evil spirit had for many years been troubling Llwydiarth Hall. One day in the late 18th century, a popular writer of folk dramas named Twm o'r Nant, arrived in the district. He was called upon to exert his powers to remove the spirit, which he did after many hours of battle. The demon appeared as a wild boar and then as a fierce wolf, but at last Twm turned the wolf into a tame dog and then into a fly. This was then placed in a tobacco box and buried in a meadow. The place is still called Weirglodd Ffwdan, 'the troubled meadow'.

Llangurig *Powys*

The district is renowned for its 'white' witches who have helped country folk for years. During the 19th and early 20th centuries one family, whose descendants still live in the area, were particularly famed for their supernatural powers. People who thought they had been bewitched travelled to see Y Dyn Hysbys, 'the knowing one', for relief. The usual problems were sickness or death among the livestock, and to cure them the white witch would curse the black witch responsible. One old woman, believed to have bewitched some calves, was said to have been cursed with a horn growing from her head which remained until she confessed her guilt and removed her spell from the calves. Some farmers used to pay the white witch, usually about the equivalent of 35p, to give protection to their farms and their stock during the ensuing year.

THE CITY BENEATH THE LAKE

According to legend, the land beneath Llangorse Lake (Llyn Syfaddan) once belonged to a cruel and greedy princess. Her lover was poor but she agreed to marry him on condition that he brought her much wealth – she did

THE ABBOT'S PROPHECY

Owen Glendower, the hero whose rebellion against English rule was quelled in 1410, vanished mysteriously from history about this time. A story is told that after his disappearance, he was seen early one morning by the abbot of Valle Crucis Abbey (above) near Llangollen, Clwyd. 'You are up early, abbot, said Glendower. 'Nay my lord Owen,' the abbot replied, recognising him, 'it is you who are up too early – a hundred years too early' – a prophetic vision of the rise of the Tudor dynasty to whom, it is said, Glendower was related. Owen vanished into the early morning mist and was never seen again. Legend says he found refuge with relatives in a remote valley in Herefordshire where he died c. 1416

not care how. So her lover robbed and murdered a wealthy merchant and gave the money to the princess who then married him. But the merchant's ghost returned to warn the couple that their crime would be avenged upon the ninth generation of their family. The couple ignored the warning and both lived to see these descendants. One night a terrible flood burst from the hills and drowned the land and all its inhabitants. It is said that the city can still be seen beneath the lake's waters and the sound of its church bells can sometimes be heard

THE RESCUE OF KING INA

In the early 8th century, among the inhabitants of Llan-ina in west Dyfed were a fisherman, and his wife and daughter. One day, a storm cast a vessel on the rocks; the fisherman and his daughter rowed out several times and saved many lives. They could not understand the tongue of the shipwrecked strangers, so a monk was called, who told the fisherfolk that they had saved none other than King Ina from England. In thanksgiving, the king built a church from which the present church took its name – Llan Ina, or Ina's church. Cerrig Ina, Ina's stones, can be seen offshore, marking the spot where the original church built by the king once stood

Llanrhaeadr-ym-Mochnant *Clwyd*

This, and other villages in the Tanad Valley on the borders of south Clwyd and Powys, still maintain the *plygeiniau*, a form of Christmas carol service once fairly common throughout Wales. Male groups wander from church to church during the Christmas season where they give unaccompanied performances of Welsh carols.

Llansilin *Clwyd*

Until a few years ago, the local carpenter was still making fish-shaped coffins. It has been suggested by some that the shape was intended to help the dead person to swim the Last River on his way to paradise.

The church is pockmarked by bullets which were supposedly fired at Cromwell when he took shelter there. It is said that his army fled in terror when Royalist soldiers flung a beehive at them from a bedroom window of Tŷ Mawr house.

Llantrisant *Mid Glamorgan*

The town was the home of Dr William Price (1800–93) whose eccentricities became famous far beyond his native countryside. Generally, he wore a fox skin on his head, and he often conducted ancient Druidic ceremonies at the Rocking Stone on Pontypridd Common. But his greatest claim to fame is as a pioneer of cremation. When his son, named Jesus Christ, died in 1884, Price burnt the body on a bonfire in the fields near his home with no Christian ceremony. There was considerable local opposition, and he was tried at Cardiff. Price won his case, however and, after this incident, cremation became legal.

The people of Llantrisant are still sometimes called 'The Black Army'. This is because some of the men fought for the Black Prince at Crécy during his French campaign of 1346 and were ridiculed by other Welshmen for fighting for the English.

Llanuwchllyn *Gwynedd*

A long time ago, the rich heiress of Llwyn Gwern manor fell in love with a peasant boy. Her father bitterly opposed the match, but told the boy that if he were to stand naked on a nearby hill throughout the coldest night of the winter, he could marry his daughter in the morning. The boy accepted the challenge, and managed to keep himself warm by beating a pole into the ground with a sledge-hammer. He married his sweetheart next day, and the hillside where he stood is still known as Bwlch y Pawl – the pass of the pole.

It is said that a giant named Rhita used to haunt

RUNNER'S GRAVE

At Llanwynno, Mid Glamorgan is the grave of Griffith Morgan (1700–37), in his day the greatest runner in Wales. Legend says he paced himself against hares, and slept in a dung-heap to strengthen his legs. Having run 12 miles in 53 minutes, he was slapped on the back by an admirer and died of heart failure

PURPOSEFUL SPECTRE

Bryn Hall, Llanymawddwy, in Gwynedd, is said to be haunted by a headless horseman who in the 1840's plagued one of the servants until he followed the ghost into the orchard. Local tradition asserts that the phantom's message concerned the murder of an illegitimate child of the owner of the Hall whose body was buried in the orchard. After the grave was found, the haunting ceased

the mountain roads of the district where he killed and robbed travellers and cut off their beards to make himself a cloak. Rhita was eventually slain by King Arthur, and was buried under a great stone on Tan y Bwlch farm. Another version claims that a huge cairn was erected over his body, and that this is how Mount Snowdon was formed.

Montgomery (Trefaldwyn) *Powys*

The 'Robber's Grave' in Montgomery churchyard recalls the story of John Newton, who in the early years of the last century was appointed farm bailiff to Mrs Morris, a wealthy widow. By becoming friendly with her daughter, Newton unwittingly incurred the enmity of two men. One, Robert Parker, wanted the farm for himself, while the other, Thomas Pearce, wanted to marry the girl. The pair carried out a robbery and made it appear as though Newton had done it. The bailiff was tried and condemned to death, but from the scaffold he cursed his accusers, and swore that his innocence would be proved by the fact that no grass would grow on his grave. The grave still has a bare patch on it, while as for Pearce and Parker, one died shortly after of a wasting disease, and the other was killed in a quarry explosion.

Mynyddislwyn *Gwent*

Certain stones which occur in the geology of this parish were called 'hydrophobia stones' and, until the end of the last century, if anyone in the neighbourhood was bitten by a mad dog, a piece of the stone was ground into a fine powder, mixed with milk, and given to the victim. Alternatively, the sufferer was made to lick the stones. There are accounts that these treatments were successful.

Nant Gwrtheyrn *Gwynedd*

This deserted village near Llithfaen, according to legend, was once the home of a pair of lovers called Rhys and Meinir. On their wedding morning, the young men of the village came to take the bride to church and, in accordance with custom, Meinir pretended to run away and hide. But she was never seen again, and Rhys, mad with grief, took to wandering the hills. Years later, a hollow tree near the girl's home was struck by lightning, and Meinir's skeleton tumbled out.

Nant Gwynant *Gwynedd*

The nearby Iron Age hill-fort of Dinas Emrys is associated with the story of how the red dragon became the Welsh national emblem. The treacherous King Gwrtheyrn, when fleeing from his own people after betraying them to the Saxons in the 5th century, attempted to build a castle at Dinas Emrys. But each night the building materials mysteriously disappeared, and the king's magicians told him that he must sprinkle the hill with the blood of a boy born of a virgin.

After much searching the boy was found, but before he could be sacrificed he revealed himself as Merlin. Merlin told the king that beneath the hill there was a subterranean lake in which two dragons lay sleeping – a white dragon representing the Saxons, and a red one representing Wales. The lake was drained and the dragons began to fight, until the white one was defeated. This, it is said, is how the red dragon became the emblem of Wales.

Gwrtheyrn still found it impossible to build a castle on the hill, so he built one at Nant Gwrtheyrn instead. Merlin, who was also known as Emrys, then built his own fort and named it after himself.

A WREN-HOUSE

The widespread pagan custom of Hunting the Wren – the bird that was supposed to embody the evils of winter – persisted in Wales until at least the end of the 19th century. In south Dyfed, the Hunting took place around Twelfth Night, and when the bird was captured, it was placed in a carved, be-ribboned 'wren-house'. Four men then carried it round the town, singing of the hunt, and their willingness to sell the wren in order to buy beer. The singers were welcomed into every house, where they were given money or drink. The wren-house (above) comes from Marloes, Dyfed, and is now in the Welsh Folk Museum, Cardiff

THE FAIRY LADY OF
Llyn y Fan Fach

Girls renowned for their beauty, physicians famous for their mastery of herbal medicine, and a legend that traces the physicians' ancestry (and sometimes that of the girls, too) back to a fairy who married a local farmer – these are the ingredients which make Myddfai in west Dyfed one of the most magical places in Wales. The source of Myddfai's magic is a mountain lake called Llyn y Fan Fach, 5 miles to the south. Fairies are said to haunt its dark and reputedly bottomless waters.

One day some 750 years ago, an only son whose father had been killed in the Norman wars was grazing his cattle on the banks of Llyn y Fan Fach, when suddenly he saw a human-sized fairy sitting on the lake combing her hair. She was the most beautiful girl he had ever seen, and at once he fell in love with her. He tried to attract her towards him by offering her gifts of bread, which she smilingly refused. But her elusiveness only made him love her the more.

The marriage agreement

Eventually his persistence was rewarded, and the fairy agreed to marry him. She warned him, however, that during their life together, he would only be permitted to hit her twice. At the third blow she would vanish for ever. For a dowry, her father gave her as many fairy sheep, cattle, goats and horses as she could count of each in a single breath. She counted in tallies of five, like the old Welsh shepherds, and each time she called, more animals emerged from the lake.

The young couple were married and lived happily for many years on the farm of Esgair Llaethdy just outside Myddfai. The fairy bore three beautiful sons. Then one day, when the family was preparing to go to a christening, the farmer asked his wife to fetch a pony from the field while he went indoors to fetch her gloves. When he returned, she was still standing in the same place, so he tapped her on the shoulder and said, 'Go! Go!' She paled, for he had struck her for the first time.

At a wedding a few months later, the fairy burst into tears. The farmer patted her on the shoulder and asked her why she was crying. 'I weep,' she replied, 'because the young couple's troubles are just beginning, and so are ours, for you have just struck the second blow.'

The years passed and the farmer took care never to strike his wife again. But one day she began laughing at a funeral and, touching her arm, her husband urged her to be quiet. 'When people die their troubles are over,' she said. 'And so, dear husband, is our marriage. That was the third blow – farewell for ever!'

Vanished in the lake

The fairy returned to Esgair Llaethdy and called all her animals by name: 'Hump-brindled, Rump-brindled, White-freckled, Old White-faced, and Grey Squint-eye, with the white bull from the King's court and the little black calf which is on the hook, do thou also come home quite sound.' She led them to Llyn y Fan Fach and there they disappeared into the water. Four oxen which were ploughing also went with her, and the furrow they cut can still be seen.

The farmer never saw his wife again, though on several occasions she reappeared to her sons, to instruct them in using herbs and medicine.

THE PHYSICIANS *The first of Myddfai's famous physicians was Rhiwallon, the lake fairy's eldest son. His mother taught him personally, and the secret skills were handed down from generation to generation until the last descendant died in the 19th century*

COURTING A FAIRY *When the young Myddfai farmer fell in love with a lake fairy, he offered her first some barley bread. 'Hard baked is thy bread!' she called across the water, 'Tis not easy to catch me.' On the following day, he returned with some unbaked dough. 'Moist is thy bread,' came the reply, 'I do not want thee.' On the third day, he took some lightly baked bread, which the fairy accepted. She plunged below the surface and reappeared a moment later with her father and identical twin sister. The old man said that he would consent to a marriage between the farmer and his daughter if the farmer could distinguish between the two sisters. At first he was uncertain, but then one of the fairies thrust her foot forward and he recognised that she was the one he loved by the way she had laced up her sandals*

Nefyn *Gwynedd*

Near Holborn Farm is a thornbush known as Y Goeden Bechod, the tree of sin. It is said that one woman recently saw a phantom coach coming towards her near the bush – it was her death omen, for in a few days she was dead.

CUCKOO ON THE CROSS

St Brynach's Cross, standing in the churchyard at Nevern in west Dyfed, is one of the finest Celtic crosses in Wales. It probably dates from the 10th or 11th century. According to tradition, the first cuckoo to be heard each year in Dyfed sings from the top of the cross on St Brynach's Day (April 7)

Newport (Casnewydd-ar-Wysg) *Gwent*

The cathedral church of St Woolos was founded by St Gwynllyw (Woolos is the Anglicised version). Before his conversion in the 5th century, Gwynllyw was a wicked man, and his wife and son struggled without success to turn his mind to God. One night, Gwynllyw was told in a dream to go to a certain hill where he would find a white ox with a black spot on its forehead. Next morning, he found the ox on that very hill and, realising it was a message from God, became a devout Christian.

St Woolos' Church stands on Stow Hill, and it is said that disaster will befall anyone who desecrates this holy place. Once, when a band of pirates pillaged the church, their ship ran into a terrible storm. St Gwynllyw pursued them, riding on the wind, and recovered the church plate; the pirates and their vessel vanished beneath the waves.

Penarth *S. Glamorgan*

It was once the tradition at Hancock's brewery for cooper apprentices, when they had completed their five years of training, to undergo a centuries-old initiation ceremony. Each new cooper had to make a 54-gallon hogshead cask. He was then put inside this, covered with soot, wood-shavings, beer and water, and the cask was rolled over three times on the ground, after which the apprentice was hauled out and tossed in the air three times. Since wooden barrels have been replaced by metal casks, no initiation has been performed since 1962.

Pen coed *S. Glamorgan*

A Christmas season horse-ceremony, known as *Mari Lwyd*, the grey mare or grey Mary, combined with the ancient custom of wassailing, was once widespread throughout Wales. Today, the tradition survives only in parts of Glamorgan such as Pen-coed, and south Dyfed. It is believed that this ceremony, which bears a strong resemblance to English mumming rituals, stems from pagan rites welcoming the return of the sun after the winter solstice. In medieval times, it became associated with the wassail tradition and may have been adopted by the Church to commemorate the purification of the Virgin Mary. Many of the characters taking part are similar to those found in medieval miracle plays.

The Mari Lwyd is a decorated horse's skull, carried on a pole by a man draped in a white sheet. He is led by a party which once, in some districts, consisted of a 'Leader', 'Sergeant', 'Corporal', and 'Merryman'. They select a house and ask permission to enter by singing a number of verses; after each verse the people within reply with other verses. When this ritual is completed, the Mari Lwyd is allowed into the house, and the whole party is given food and drink, before moving on.

Penmaen *W. Glamorgan*

Pennard Castle, now a ruin lying amongst sand dunes on the Gower Peninsula, was once the fortress of the chieftain Rhys ap Iestyn. According to legend, the prince of North Wales gave Rhys his daughter in marriage as a reward for his valour in battle. On the wedding night, as the sentries outside Pennard's walls listened to the revels, they became aware that, close by, they could also hear the strains of different, unearthly music. Then, in the moonlight, the soldiers saw a host of fairies dancing on the grass near the castle gatehouse. A sentry ran to tell the now-drunken Lord Rhys, who ordered his men to drive the little folk away.

His new wife was aghast, and warned him that terrible misfortune would fall on everyone if such a thing were done. Her lord told her arrogantly that he feared no one of this world or any other and,

THE GOLD'S WHITE GUARDIAN

The ruins of 12th-century Ogmore Castle, Mid Glamorgan, are said to contain buried treasure, guarded by a ghost known as Y Ladi Wen, the white lady. The River Ogmore near the castle is haunted by the tormented spirits of misers who died without disclosing their hidden wealth. They can be released from their penance only when somebody finds their hoards and throws them into the river downstream of the castle

followed by the bravest of his men, went out to battle with the fairies. But the little people faded before them, and not one of them was touched.

Suddenly a warning voice rang out: 'Thou hast wantonly spoilt our innocent sport, proud chief. Thy lofty castle and proud town shall be no more.' And at once, a terrible sandstorm blew up, burying the castle, the town and all its inhabitants.

The basis of the legend is that in the 300 years when it was occupied, Pennard Castle's only battle was with the encroaching sand dunes that finally destroyed it in the 16th century.

Penmark (Pen-marc) *S. Glamorgan*
The name of the village is an Anglicised version of Pen March, the horse's head. In King Arthur's time a prince of North Wales owned a strong and very swift horse, which was used to carry messages to the king's court in Somerset. On one occasion, the horse was galloping so fast that it slipped, and in falling was decapitated, at a place now called Cefn March, the horse's ridge, near Gilfach Reda, southeast of New Quay. But its head travelled on until it fell; and the place where it fell became known as Pen March.

Penmynydd *Anglesey, Gwynedd*
Many centuries ago, a legend tells, a huge poisonous dragon lived near the manor-farm of Penhesgyn. A wizard prophesied that one day it would kill the heir, so the young man was sent for safety to England. Then, one day, a clever local youth thought of a way of killing the monster. He dug a hole near the creature's lair and placed a large, highly polished brass pan in the pit. The dragon peered in, and mistaking its own reflection for another dragon, tried to fight it. The lad waited until it was exhausted, then killed and buried it. The heir came home and a great celebration followed at the manor,

after which the heir wanted to see the monster's body. So the grave was reopened and, with justifiable pride, he kicked the dead dragon's head. Tragically, a poisonous fang pierced his foot, and the young man died, so fulfilling the prophecy.

Pennant *Dyfed*
Legends of the magical powers of a 19th-century recluse named Mari Berllan Piter, Mary of Peter's Orchard, are still remembered by elderly people in Pennant. When Dic y Felin, a miller, refused to grind her corn, she made his mill wheel turn in the wrong direction. A young girl who stole an apple from Mari's orchard was forced to walk home backwards. Sometimes, it is said, Mari turned herself into a hare – a typical witch's trick – and not even the best shots could hit her. The ruins of her cottage, known as The Witch's Cottage, can still be seen, in the midst of its overgrown orchard.

Pennant Melangell *Powys*
Brochwel Ysgythrog, a 6th-century prince of Powys, was hunting one day when his hounds set up a hare. Eventually the exhausted creature found shelter between the feet of a strange young woman standing in the forest. The prince urged his hounds to make the kill, but they would not go near the woman. Brochwel, made uneasy by the dogs' behaviour, asked the woman her name. She told him she was Melangell, and that she had come from Ireland to worship God in peaceful Pennant. The prince realised that he was in the presence of a saint, and gave Melangell land on which to build a chapel.

St Melangell's encounter with the prince is recorded by 15th-century wood-carvings on the screen of the Norman church. She became the patron saint of hares and, in the district, these creatures are sometimes known as *ŵyn bach Melangell*, or Melangell's little lambs.

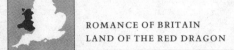

Reynoldston *W. Glamorgan*

Coeten Arthur (Arthur's Stone) stands on Cefn Bryn Common near Reynoldston. It is said to be the 'pebble' which King Arthur removed from his boot on his way to the Battle of Camlann in AD 539. He threw it over his shoulder and it landed on the common, 7 miles away. Until the end of the last century, local girls would place a honey-cake soaked in milk on the stone at midnight, when the moon was full, and then crawl around the stone three times on their hands and knees. It was believed that, if their lovers were true, they would then join them.

Rhos-fawr *Anglesey, Gwynedd*

Llyn-Wyth Eidion, the lake of the eight oxen, is a small lake near Rhos-fawr. A local story relates that one day a bad-tempered farmer was ploughing a field on nearby Nant Uchaf farm. Try as he might, he was unable to plough in a straight line and all his furrows were crooked. Blaming his team of eight oxen for his own inefficiency, he beat them with a spiked rod. The frightened animals bolted towards the lake and the farmer, entangled in the reins, was dragged along the ground behind his plough. The oxen plunged into the water, drowning both themselves and the cruel ploughman. It is said that, in a last attempt to save himself, he thrust the spiked rod deep into the banks of the lake where it later grew into an ash tree.

Risca (Rhisga) *Gwent*

Twmbarlwm Hill, near the village of Risca, is the site of a Celtic fortress. It is said that the Druids held their courts of justice on the hill, and that the bodies of those found guilty of serious crimes were thrown into the valley below. Its name, Dyffryn y Gladdfa, means valley of the graves.

Roch (Y Garn) *Dyfed*

Roch Castle, about 6 miles north-west of Haverfordwest, occupies a solitary position on the summit of a rocky outcrop high above the surrounding plain. It was built in the 13th century by the feudal Lord of Roch, Adam de la Roche. According to legend, he was told by a witch that his death would be caused by a viper, but that if he could pass a certain year in safety then he need never again fear the serpent.

The Lord of Roch ordered a castle to be built which would be beyond the reach of any snake, and accordingly the stronghold was constructed on its present site. The fateful year began and the nobleman moved into the top floor of the castle, remaining there all the year in constant fear.

At last, one day only remained before his release from the witch's prophecy. It was bitterly cold and someone sent a basket of firewood into the fortress

FISHY TALE

The smallest cathedral in Britain is at St Asaph (Llanelwy) in Clwyd. Its holy bishop during the 6th century was St Asaph, who was said to have shone with 'virtue and miracles from the flower of his earliest youth'. A legend tells how Nest, the beautiful wife of Maelgwn Gwynedd, King of North Wales, one day lost a precious ring as she bathed in a pool. Nest was overcome with grief, for the ring had been given to her by Maelgwn and was the traditional ring always worn by the Queens of the North. She went to St Asaph, hoping that he might be able to help her. The bishop invited the royal couple to eat with him the following evening. When they arrived, he told Maelgwn what had happened, but the king refused to believe his wife's story, and grew furious with her. Asaph immediately prayed to God that the ring might be found and the three of them then sat down to eat. The meal began with fish, caught in the River Elwy on the same day; when Maelgwn cut into his fish the ring fell out on his plate.

so that Adam de la Roche might pass his last night in comfort. It was taken up to his room and, as he was putting the logs on the fire, an adder crawled out of the basket and bit him. He was found the next morning, lying dead in front of his hearth.

Ruthin (Rhuthun) *Clwyd*

The Maen Huail, Huail's stone, is a large block of limestone which stands in the market-place at Ruthin. Legend has it that in the 6th century all the sons of Caw, except the historian Gildas, constantly rebelled against King Arthur. Huail, the eldest, was the ruler of Edeirnion in North Wales and proved to be the most troublesome of the brothers. When King Arthur held court at Caerwys in Clwyd, he used to visit a woman who lived in Ruthin. Huail learnt of this and began to pursue the woman himself, which soon led to a fight between the two warriors. Arthur was wounded in the knee, but agreed to forgive Huail on condition that the Welshman would never mention the wound. Shortly afterwards the king disguised himself as a woman and secretly went to Ruthin where his mistress was attending a dance in the village. Huail recognised Arthur by his limp and remarked 'Your dancing would be fine were it not for your clumsy knee'. Immediately, Arthur had him taken outside where he was beheaded on the stone.

DEATH FLOWERS OF THE MINES

Underground coal-mining began in Wales over 400 years ago and, since then, generations of miners have faced a daily struggle against darkness and danger. Belief in the supernatural came easily to those who were constantly threatened by sudden disaster, and superstition was rife in coal-mining communities. It was unlucky to be late for work, or to forget something and then return home for it. If, on his way to work, the miner met someone with a squint, or a rabbit or bird crossed his path, he would go home for the day. Whenever anyone in his family dreamt of death, an accident or broken shoes, a miner was often forced to stay at home by his frightened relatives on the day after the dream.

Bad days, good days
Ever since Christ was crucified on a Friday, the day has been associated with bad luck. In South Wales, many colliers refused to start new work on any Friday, referred to as 'Black Friday', but especially on one preceding a holiday, when miners in Monmouthshire would complain of having 'the old black dog' on their backs, an evil spirit which caused illness and accidents. Throughout Wales, pitworkers stayed away from the mines on Good Friday, but there were other days when they missed work for reasons unconnected with foreboding. In 19th-century southern Dyfed, the arrival of a fair led to an impromptu ceremony when the miners said: 'We'll throw a stone into the air. If it comes down, we'll go to the fair!'

Ominous birds
The sight of a robin, pigeon or dove flying around the pithead was thought to foretell disaster, and many miners refused to work if such birds were seen near the mines. They were called 'corpse birds' and are said to have been seen before the explosion at the Senghennydd Colliery in Mid Glamorgan in 1913, when over 400 pitworkers died in the worst mining disaster in Welsh history. In the mines themselves, whistling and the word 'cat' were strictly taboo. Superstition had its good side in the case of the Welsh lead miners who believed in 'knockers', invisible spirits who made tapping noises to point the way to rich veins of ore.

Saved by superstition
In 1890, miners at the Morfa Colliery near Port Talbot reported many eerie manifestations which occurred in the neighbourhood and in the mine itself. Fierce hounds, known locally as 'the Red Dogs of Morfa', were seen running through the district at night. The colliery was filled with a sweet rose-like perfume emanating from invisible 'death flowers'. Cries for help and sounds of falling earth were heard, and flickering lights, called 'corpse candles', appeared in the tunnels. The ghosts of dead miners and coal trams drawn by phantom white horses were seen, and rats swarmed out of the mine. On March 10, nearly half of the workers on the morning shift stayed at home. Later that day there was an explosion at the colliery, and 87 miners were buried alive and died in the disaster.

St Dogmaels (Llandudoch) *Dyfed*
At Carreg y Fendith, the stone of blessing, beside the River Teifi, medieval monks blessed the fish and prayed for their abundance before each fishing season. In 1965 the custom was revived but lapsed again after a very poor season. This was blamed on the presence of too many clergymen at the service, which was said later to have been ill-omened.

A GHOST IN MOURNING
Spectral moans are said to echo through St Donat's Castle, S. Glamorgan. One theory is that the ghost is mourning the death of Thomas Stradling, whose family lost possession of the castle when he died in 1738

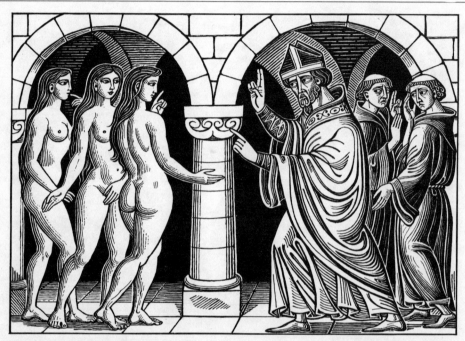

DAVID, PATRON SAINT OF WALES

In a cottage bathed in sunshine at the heart of a raging storm, a young Welsh girl called Non gave birth to a baby boy some 1500 years ago. The cottage overlooked the Bay of Non in west Dyfed, and the boy, whom Non called Dewi or David, was destined to become the patron saint of Wales.

Most of the legends about St David cluster around the place where he founded a monastery in about AD 530 – Glyn Rhosyn, the vale of roses, in west Dyfed, where the small cathedral city of St David's is situated today.

A legend about Glyn Rhosyn tells that 30 years before David was born, St Patrick came there to settle. But an angel sent him on to Ireland, since the place was already reserved for David.

Resisting temptation
When David and his followers first came to Glyn Rhosyn, the neighbourhood was terrorised by an Irish brigand named Boia. Boia's shrewish wife urged her husband to drive out the monks,

but David tamed the wild Irishman and even, according to some accounts, converted him to Christianity.

Enraged by her husband's lack of fire, Boia's wife sent her maidservants naked to the monastery, in order to tempt the monks to break their vows of chastity. But David's self-control never wavered, and by his example he made it easy for the monks to disregard the girls.

The miracle worker
Christian missionaries were never more active in Wales than in the 6th and 7th centuries, and David soon became one of the most important leaders of the new Celtic Church. Disciples flocked to him, in spite of his stern self-denial and the rigid discipline of his monastery, for he was noted for his gentle nature.

Like many Celtic saints whose biographies were written centuries after they had died, David was credited with the working of innumerable miracles. Legend claims that there was no water

near his monastery. When he prayed, however, a well appeared by his feet. Many of the other wells associated with him, such as Ffynnon Feddyg, the physician's well, near Aberaeron on Cardigan Bay, are said to have burst from the ground at places where he miraculously healed the blind, the lame and the sick.

The miraculous pulpit
At a meeting of Celtic churchmen held at Llanddewibrefi in Dyfed about 519, the assembled bishops could not make themselves heard above the noise of the crowd. But David was not so easily silenced. A hill is said to have suddenly risen up beneath him and from this high vantage point he preached the gospel so that all could hear. A church dedicated to him still stands on top of the reputedly miraculous hill.

When he died, probably on March 1, 589, a host of singing angels bore his soul to heaven in glory and honour. And March 1 has been the National Day of Wales ever since.

404

TREASURY OF WELSH TRADITION

In the late 19th century, the native traditions of Wales were held to be so valueless that children speaking Welsh in school were punished and humiliated by having a piece of wood called a Welsh Not suspended around their necks. Today, the situation is very different. Many schools teach Welsh as a first language, and museums are the only places where relics such as the Not can still be seen.

The Welsh Folk Museum at St Fagan's in S. Glamorgan is the nation's richest storehouse of all that is wholly Welsh. In a cluster of buildings which range from a tollgate house to a tannery, all of which were moved stone by stone from their original sites, every aspect of the Welsh tradition can be seen and studied. And the museum is more than just a storehouse. Craftsmen such as weavers and basket-makers still work there, using centuries-old techniques, and their wares are on sale to the public.

The folklore section of the museum is particularly rich. Its exhibits are a vivid reminder of an age not long past when few people thought to question the reality of magic and the supernatural.

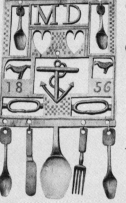

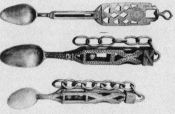

LOVE SPOONS *Between the 17th and 19th centuries it was a widespread custom in Wales for young men to carve love tokens for their sweethearts in the form of wooden spoons. More often than not, the carving was too elaborately ornamental for the spoons ever to be used, since one of their main functions was to demonstrate how skilfully the man could carve*

THE DENBIGH COCKPIT *This 17th or early 18th-century cockpit once stood in Denbigh. Cockfighting was made illegal in Wales in 1849, but it had been a popular national pastime. Some pits were situated in or near churchyards, and a common superstition held that sprinkling the pit with consecrated earth broke any spells which had been cast on either of the cocks*

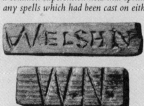

A ROYAL HARP *This ornate triple harp was made for the Great Exhibition of 1851 by the royal harp maker, Bassett Jones, of Cardiff. The instrument bears the three-feather emblem of the Prince of Wales, and the Welsh national emblems – a leek and a dragon – carved against a background of oak leaves, acorns and ivy. The triple harp, with its strings arranged in three rows, became known as the Welsh harp because of its popularity among 18th-century Welsh harpists*

SILENCING A LANGUAGE *In the 19th century, a Welsh Not, like the ones above, was hung as a punishment around the necks of children who spoke Welsh at school*

WASSAIL BOWL *This 19th-century bowl recalls an older tradition – that of 'wassailing', or drinking to ensure good luck, during Christmas*

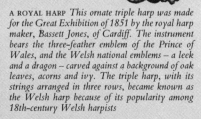

St George (Llan Sain Siôr) *Clwyd*
Until the late 19th century, people used to sprinkle their horses with holy water from the village well. This was done both to bless the beasts and to cure them of sickness. So powerful was the magic, that if you had several horses, it was necessary to sprinkle only one; it would then pass the blessing on to the others. St George is the patron saint of horses, but in this case, the custom probably long pre-dated Christianity. Many of the place-names in the district such as Tremeirchion and Kinmeirch are based on the Welsh word for horse, indicating that the area has always been sacred to these animals.

St Nicholas (Sain Nicolas) *S. Glamorgan*
The large standing stones on the Dyffryn estate were believed to have been cursed by the Druids. It is said that if you sleep among them on May Day Eve, St John's Eve (June 23) or Midwinter Eve, you will die, go mad, or become a poet.

ST GOVAN'S CHAPEL

Perched in a ravine in the cliffs overlooking the sea at St Govan's Head, south Dyfed, is the tiny chapel of St Govan which may date in part from the 5th century AD. The chapel is reached by a long stone stair with between 60 and 70 steps cut into the cliff. The number of these steps is said to vary, depending on whether the person counting them is climbing up or down. Inside the chapel (left), there is a vertical cleft in the rock which, according to legend, first miraculously opened to conceal St Govan from his enemies. The rock closed behind him and did not reopen until the danger had passed. A wish made while standing in the cleft and facing the wall will be granted provided you do not change your mind before turning round. St Govan's healing well is situated just below the chapel, while for centuries, the red clay in the cliffs has been credited with the power of healing sore eyes.

Despite the many miracles credited to him, no one is quite sure who St Govan was. Some authorities claim that he was a disciple of St David; others, that he was a thief, who in gratitude for the miraculous hiding-place, became a convert. 'He' is also said to be a woman named Cofen – the wife of a 5th-century chief – who became a recluse. The most romantic version says he was really Sir Gawain who, after Arthur's death, spent the rest of his life as a hermit

MOUNT OF EAGLES

The eagles of Snowdon – Yr Wyddfa – were long re-garded as oracles of peace or war, triumph or disaster. When they circled high in the sky, victory was near, but if they flew low over the rocks the Welsh would be defeated. It was said, too, that if they cried incessantly, the birds were mourning some impending calamity. This is only one of many legends connected with the mountain, whose 3560 ft peak is said to be a cairn erected over the grave of a giant killed by King Arthur. Near the summit is the supposedly bottomless lake of Glaslyn. Its waters, stained green by copper ore, are believed to contain the dreaded Afanc, a water monster that was dragged from its lair in the River Conway by giant oxen and dumped into Glaslyn. This view of Snowdon from Llyn Nantlle is by the 18th-century artist Richard Wilson, and is now in Nottingham Museum

LIVING MONUMENT

The yew tree among the ruins of Strata Florida Abbey, west Dyfed, is said to mark the grave of the 15th-century poet Dafydd ap Gwilym, who has been described as perhaps the greatest poet in the Welsh language. Though the abbey was destroyed during the Reformation, tradition asserts that candles still sometimes blaze among the ruins and, on Christmas Eve, a ghostly monk has been seen trying to rebuild the altar

Tenby (Dinbych-y-pysgod) Dyfed

On New Year's Day, the children sprinkle passers-by with fresh raindrops from twigs of box bush or holly. This probably dates back to a pre-Christian purification rite, but by the Middle Ages the practice was associated with the Virgin. It is still considered lucky to be sprinkled, and the children are rewarded with money.

By ancient custom, St Margaret's Fair on July 31 is opened by the mayor and council walking in procession round the town walls.

Tongwynlais S. Glamorgan

Castell Coch, The Red Castle, was built in the 1870's on the foundations of a much earlier building dating from the 12th century. The old castle was the stronghold of Ifor Bach, Lord of Senghennydd, who used to boast that his 1200 men could beat 12,000 of any army sent against him.

Tradition says that Ifor's treasure still lies beneath Castell Coch, concealed in a deep vault at the head of a tunnel leading to Cardiff Castle. The vault is guarded by three huge eagles who will tear to shreds anyone who approaches them. It is believed, too, that the three eagles will continue to watch over the treasure in its great iron chest until Ifor Bach returns to claim it in the company of his 1200 brave men of Glamorgan.

407

Trefeglwys *Powys*

A small cottage which once stood in the parish was known as Twt y Cwmrws, the place of strife, because the couple who lived there were always quarrelling about whether or not their twin babies had been exchanged for fairy changelings. Eventually the argument became so bitter that they asked a wizard to help them settle it.

He advised them to boil an egg shell and to offer egg-shell stew to the reapers working in the fields near by. If the babies said anything unusual, that would prove that they really were fairy changelings, and in that case the only thing to do was to throw them into the lake called Llyn Ebyr.

No sooner had the mother put the egg shell on to boil than the babies began chanting in unison a Welsh verse, which translated runs:

> Acorns before oak I saw,
> An egg before a hen,
> But never one hen's egg stew
> Enough for harvest men.

Immediately she knew that they were changelings, and took them down to the lake and threw them in. A troop of fairies immediately arrived to save them from drowning, and returned the real babies which they had stolen to their parents.

THE DEVIL'S WORK

In 1567 Sir Richard Clough, a wealthy merchant built a house named Bachegraig, near Tremeirchion in north Clwyd. Though the building has been demolished, its gatehouse still stands. The unusual architectural style so shocked local people that they decided that the Devil himself had been the architect, and had also supplied the bricks. It was rumoured that he had baked the bricks in the fires of Hell, near a stream still known as Nant y Cythraul, the Devil's brook

THE HARPIST AND THE DEMON

Some time in the 13th century, the harpist Einion ap Gwlchmai, who lived at Trefeilir, near Trefdraeth in Anglesey, married Angharad, the daughter of Llywelyn the Great's steward. They were blissfully happy until, according to legend, a strange girl lured Einion away. The girl was a demon in disguise.

For many years the demon held him spellbound, until one day a mysterious man arrived, dressed in white and riding a white horse, whereupon the demon girl vanished. The man gave Einion a white stick and told him that he could make any wish he liked. He asked to see the girl again, but to his horror she re-appeared as an ugly hag.

The demon then switched its attention to Angharad, and came to Trefeilir in the guise of a rich and handsome gentleman. He gave Angharad a letter, which said that Einion had died nine years earlier, and then persuaded the distraught girl into marrying him.

A few hours before the wedding, Einion returned to Trefeilir, having wished himself back with the help of the white stick. At first he was unrecognised, but when he played Angharad's favourite tune on his harp, she knew him instantly. He gave her his white stick, and at once the demon became a hideous monster and vanished. And Angharad and Einion lived happily ever after

A POET'S BIRTH

For a year and a day the witch Ceridwen boiled a secret mixture of herbs in her cauldron, to make a magic potion for her son Morfran, because by swallowing three drops he would acquire all knowledge and power. But before he could take it, the potion was stolen and drunk by a man named Gwion Bach.

Ceridwen gave chase, whereupon Gwion turned into a hare. The witch in turn became a greyhound. When Gwion turned into a fish, Ceridwen became an otter; when he became a bird, she hunted him as a hawk. Finally he tried being a grain of wheat, but the witch turned into a hen and ate him. Nine months later she bore a son – the legendary 6th-century poet Taliesin.

She threw the baby into the sea in a coracle, which was washed up near Borth on Cardigan Bay. It was found by Elphin, son of King Gwyddno of the now drowned land of Cantref Gwaelod, who named the boy Taliesin, meaning 'beautiful brow'. Taliesin is reputedly buried a mile east of Tre Taliesin, also in Dyfed.

Ystrad-ffin *Dyfed*

A cave about a mile west of Ystrad-ffin was reputedly the hideout of Twm Siôn Cati, whom legend transformed from a 16th-century landowner and antiquary into a notorious outlaw and trickster. In some of the stories which are told about him, he was a man to be feared. But in other tales he was the Welsh equivalent of Robin Hood – a popular hero who robbed from the rich and gave to the poor.

One story tells how Twm, angered by the wickedness and cruelty of a fellow highwayman, decided to teach him a lesson. He disguised himself as a poor farmer, and rode a tired old nag, its saddle-bags full of shells, to a place where he knew that his rival lay in ambush. Sure enough, the wicked highwayman sprang from the bushes and held him at gunpoint. Twm pretended to be terrified but instead of meekly handing over his saddle-bags, he threw them over the hedge which flanked the road. The highwayman scrambled after them, and as he bent to pick them up, Twm leapt from his own horse on to the highwayman's beautiful mare, whose saddle-bags were already packed with stolen money, and galloped away.

Ystradgynlais *Powys*

Three cauldrons full of gold are said to be buried beneath Y Garn Goch, the red cairn, on the summit of Mynydd y Drum just east of Ystradgynlais. One day a young girl will come to claim the treasure but, until then, fierce demons protect it from all booty hunters.

A wizard and his apprentice once tried to overpower the demons with magic, and to steal the treasure. But their efforts were in vain. While the elements raged, a spirit on a wheel of fire swept the apprentice out of the protective circle he had made on the ground, and gave him a lighted candle, saying that his life would last only as long as the candle burnt. As soon as the candle guttered out, the apprentice died, and the wizard fled terrified from the mountain.

THE REBECCA RIOTS

In the mid-19th century, the many toll-gates on the roads of South Wales imposed an additional financial burden on the already impoverished farming community. At last, people took the law into their own hands, and groups of men with blackened faces and wearing women's clothes attacked the toll-gates, usually by night, and destroyed them. There were many such gangs, whose leaders were always called 'Rebecca' – a name probably derived from Genesis XXIV, v. 60: 'And they blessed Rebekah, and said unto her . . . let thy seed possess the gate of those which hate them.' There were many tales told about 'Rebecca'; how sometimes she would appear as an old blind woman who would pause at the toll-gate and say, 'My children, something is in my way', whereupon the gang would tear the obstacle down. The first gate to be destroyed was at Yr Efail Wen, south-west Dyfed, where 'Rebecca' was a huge man named Thomas Rees. Many others were torn down until most of them were legally removed in 1844

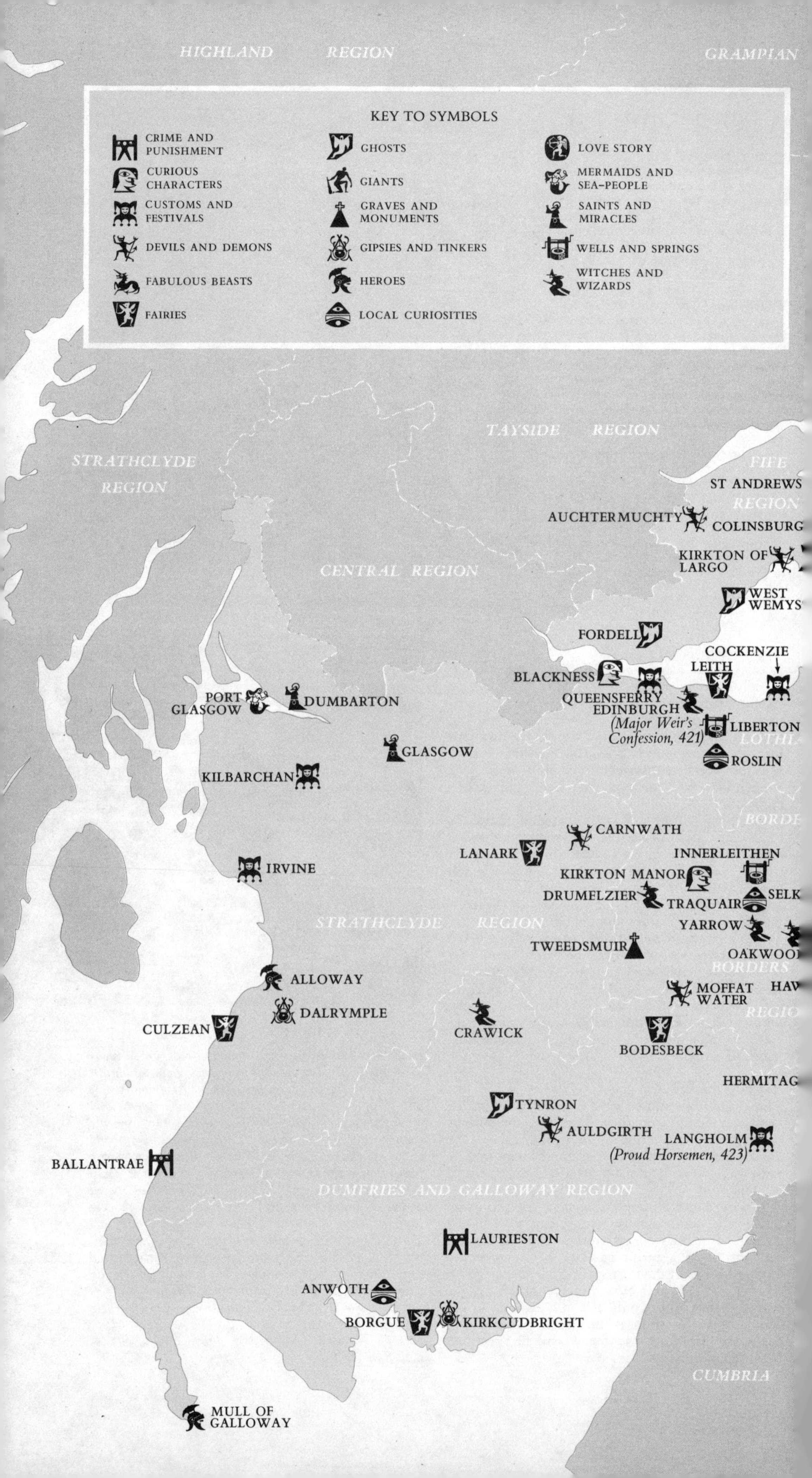

KEY TO SYMBOLS

CRIME AND PUNISHMENT

CURIOUS CHARACTERS

CUSTOMS AND FESTIVALS

DEVILS AND DEMONS

FABULOUS BEASTS

FAIRIES

GHOSTS

GIANTS

GRAVES AND MONUMENTS

GIPSIES AND TINKERS

HEROES

LOCAL CURIOSITIES

LOVE STORY

MERMAIDS AND SEA-PEOPLE

SAINTS AND MIRACLES

WELLS AND SPRINGS

WITCHES AND WIZARDS

TAYSIDE   REGION

STRATHCLYDE REGION

FIFE

ST ANDREWS REGION

AUCHTERMUCHTY

COLINSBURG

CENTRAL REGION

KIRKTON OF LARGO

WEST WEMYSS

FORDELL

COCKENZIE
LEITH

PORT GLASGOW   DUMBARTON

BLACKNESS

QUEENSFERRY
EDINBURGH
(Major Weir's Confession, 421)   LIBERTON
LOTHIA

GLASGOW

ROSLIN

KILBARCHAN

BORDE

CARNWATH

INNERLEITHEN

LANARK

KIRKTON MANOR

IRVINE

DRUMELZIER   TRAQUAIR   SELK

YARROW

STRATHCLYDE   REGION

TWEEDSMUIR

OAKWOO
BORDERS

ALLOWAY

MOFFAT WATER   HAV

DALRYMPLE

REGIO

CULZEAN

CRAWICK

BODESBECK

HERMITAG

TYNRON

AULDGIRTH   LANGHOLM
(Proud Horsemen, 423)

BALLANTRAE

DUMFRIES AND GALLOWAY REGION

LAURIESTON

ANWOTH

BORGUE   KIRKCUDBRIGHT

CUMBRIA

MULL OF GALLOWAY

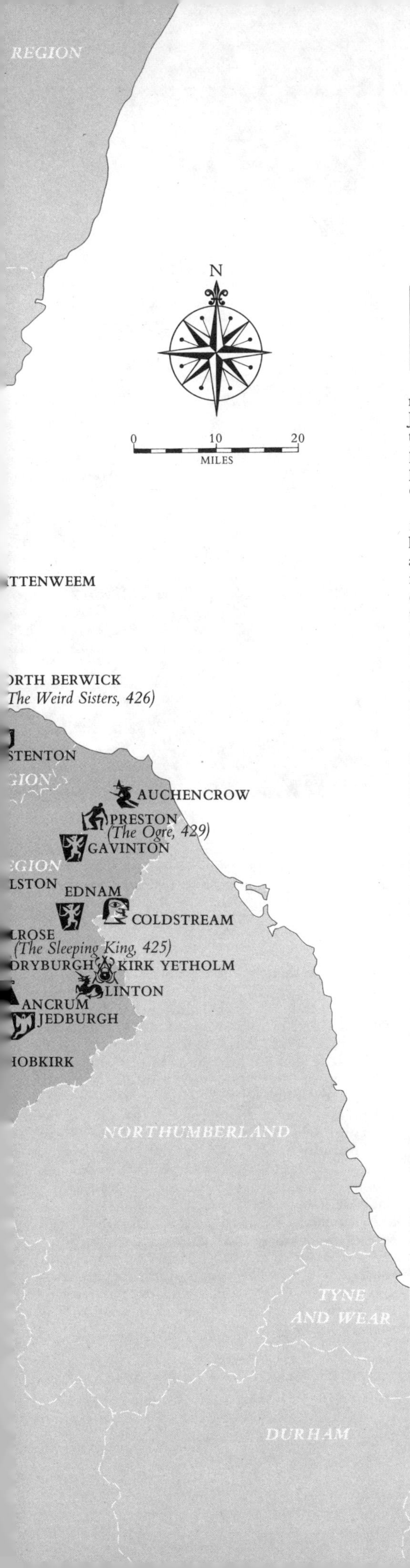

Map labels (left column):

REGION

N

0   10   20
MILES

TTENWEEM

RTH BERWICK
(The Weird Sisters, 426)

STENTON
GION
AUCHENCROW
PRESTON
(The Ogre, 429)
GAVINTON
EGION
LSTON
EDNAM
COLDSTREAM
ROSE
(The Sleeping King, 425)
RYBURGH   KIRK YETHOLM
LINTON
ANCRUM
JEDBURGH
OBKIRK

NORTHUMBERLAND

TYNE
AND WEAR

DURHAM

CLEVE-
LAND

REIVERS & MAKKARS

Southern Scotland

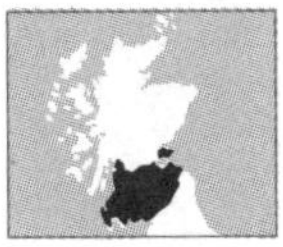

Caught, but by no means crushed, between the nether and upper mill-stones of England and the High-lands, southern Scotland has been, for most of its history, a poor region. It was the poverty-stricken appearance of James I's Scottish courtiers, it is said, that gave rise to the slanderous legend of Scots meanness. But if the people were financially poor, they were rich in pride and courage, which glowed even through the darkest moments of Scotland's past.

Admirable though these qualities are, they did not make for a peaceful nation. There is glory and honour in the Scottish story, but there is treachery and blood too. Wars and feuds, abduction and murder were commonplace; the Border reivers, or cattle-lifters, raided to the gates of Edinburgh in total contempt of royal authority. Yet out of these deeds came the tales of the makkars – the poets and the 'makers' of the ballads. These stories of love and war, often laced with sardonic wit, are usually told in broad Scots; in the hands of the makkars, as in those of Robert Burns, this deceptively harsh language was a tool of great beauty.

In the proud hearts of the Lowland Scots, the strict doctrines of the Reformation took root and flowered. There was something particularly attract-ive to them in the idea that no priest should stand between man and God; even more appealing was the Calvinistic notion of predestination. This chilly philosophy may have had strange repercussions. It seems likely that some people, uncertain of future Heavenly bliss, tried to make what terms they could with the other side, for there is no doubt that the witch cult in southern Scotland was far more widespread and organised than ever it was in England, and the reprisals upon its members were consequently more savage.

THE FOLKLORE YEAR

January 25
Scotland generally
Burns Night

Around February 2
Jedburgh, Borders
Jeddart Ba' Game

March 1
Lanark; Strathclyde
Whuppity Stoorie

Second week in June
Dumfries, Dumfries
and Galloway
Festival of Good Neighbours

Third week in June
Peebles, Borders
Beltane Festival

Third week in June
Melrose, Borders
Melrose Festival

**Saturday in June,
depending on tides**
Cockenzie, Lothian
Children's Gala Day

**Friday and Saturday,
third week in July**
Innerleithen, Borders
Cleiking the Devil

Last Friday in July
Langholm, Dumfries
and Galloway
Common Riding

Second week in August
Queensferry, Lothian
*The Burry Man and
Ferry Fair*

**Third Saturday in
August**
Irvine, Strathclyde
Marymass Fair

411

Alloway *Strathclyde*

Scotland's best-loved poet, Robert Burns, the son of
a poor farmer, was born here on January 25, 1759.
Some of his imagery was drawn from a hard-won
classical education, but most was inspired by his
knowledge of the countryside, and of the ways and
legends of country people. Since his death in 1796,
his reputation as a freethinker, drinker and woman-
iser has turned the poet himself into a legend.

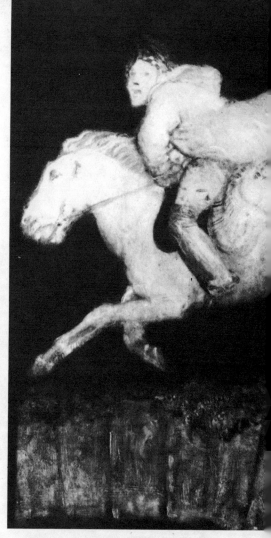

THE PLOUGHMAN POET

*The cottage in Alloway
where Burns was born (left)
is preserved as a Burns
museum; the poet's father
built it with his own hands.
It was in the Kirk of
Alloway (above) that the
farmer Tam o' Shanter,
in Burns's poem, saw
witches and wizards dancing
to the Devil's bagpipes*

TAM O' SHANTER

*As a child, Burns loved the stories of the supernatural told
by the old widow who sometimes helped out on his father's
farm. When he grew up he turned the stories into poems.*

Ancrum *Borders*

In 1545 a Scottish army led by the Earl of Angus
defeated 5000 English troops at the Battle of
Ancrum Moor. Local tradition asserts that one of the
bravest warriors on either side was a young girl
called Lilliard, who fought and died in the Scottish
ranks. Lilliard's Edge, part of the battlefield, is
supposed to have been named after her, though in
fact, it was already known as Lillyat long before the
battle was fought. The monument which marks her
grave commemorates her with the epitaph:

'Fair Maiden Lilliard lies under this stane;
Little was her stature, but great was her fame;
Upon the English loons she laid mony thumps,
And when her legs were cuttit off, she fought
   upon her stumps.'

Anwoth *Dumfs & Gall*

The story goes that Cardoness Castle was so expen-
sive to maintain that three successive lairds went
bankrupt, and a fourth became so poor that he had
to roof it with heather, which he collected on
Glenquicken Moor, 4 miles away, and carried
home on his back. However, once the castle was
roofed, the laird's luck began to improve. Other
lairds swore fealty to him, and many reivers and
'broken men' (outlaws) took service with him.

Only one thing spoilt the laird's happiness: he
had nine daughters, but no son. His luck held,
however, and his tenth child was a boy. The
celebrations that followed were the grandest that
had ever been held in Cardoness Castle.

The laird decided that the time had now come
for his eldest daughter to marry his closest friend,
Graeme the Outlaw, and after the marriage, the
celebrations continued unabated. After a week, the
laird suggested that the party should end with a feast
on the nearby Black Loch, which was frozen over at
the time. All his followers and friends were invited,
but since the day appointed for the feast was a
Sabbath, none of them came.

Undaunted, the laird and all his family and
servants went out on the loch, and after some hours
of sport, sat down to eat and drink. At that moment,
there came a crack like a gunshot; the ice gave way,
and laird, family, servants and all, disappeared into
the depths of the loch. None of the family was
ever seen again.

THE CURSE OF CARDONESS CASTLE

*By tradition, three lairds of the now-ruined 15th-
century castle went bankrupt, and a fourth was drowned
with his family in a revel on the Black Loch*

In the poem of 'Tam o' Shanter', he described how Tam disturbed a coven of witches in the Kirk of Alloway, and when they spotted him, had to ride for his life on Meg, his old grey mare. The fastest witch, 'Cutty Sark', had almost caught up with him by the time the terrible chase reached the River Doon. But the running water made her powerless, and though she caught Meg's tail, Tam managed to escape across the bridge

Auchencrow *Borders*
In the 17th century the village was notorious for its witches. In 1700, a local farm servant was indicted for gashing an Auchencrow woman 'above the breath' – that is, on her forehead – to draw blood and so free himself from her spell.

Auchtermuchty *Fife*
According to legend, the people of Auchtermuchty were so pious that the Devil resolved to make a special effort to corrupt them. He came to the village one day disguised as a Calvinist minister, and preached such an eloquent and inspiring sermon that all who heard him were enthralled, and ready to follow wherever he went. But at the last minute, a sharp-eyed old man called Robin Ruthven saved them by lifting up the preacher's black gown, revealing Auld Hornie's cloven feet underneath. Gnashing his teeth in fury, the Devil threw off his disguise and rose into the air like a fiery dragon, casting a red rainbow across the Lomond Hills.

Since then, according to James Hogg, the early 19th-century poet, it has been almost impossible to make an Auchtermuchty man listen to a sermon, and harder still to make him applaud one, 'for he thinks aye that he sees the cloven foot peeping out from beneath every sentence'.

413

Auldgirth *Dumfs & Gall*

When the Devil came to take the wife of a local farmer, her husband said gloomily: 'Take her by all means, but you won't keep her long.' Even so, the Devil loaded her on his back and carried her off to Hell. But a few days later, she returned. Apparently her curses had so shocked the demons that the Devil was forced to expel her.

Ballantrae *Strathclyde*

In the early 15th century, during the reign of James I, the countryside was deeply perturbed by the continual disappearance of merchants and wayfarers. Several innkeepers had been accused, and even hanged, but the disappearances continued. Then one evening, as a farmer and his wife came home from market, they were attacked by a host of tattered, blood-smeared ghouls. They cut the woman's throat and drank her blood, but the farmer managed to escape. Word was sent to the king, who brought soldiers and bloodhounds, and the terrible band was tracked down to a cave by the seashore. In its depths were found smoked and pickled human limbs, and a vast quantity of treasure. The cave's inhabitants were bound, and brought before the king, who discovered they were members of a single family led by a man called Sawney Bean. For years they had lived by highway robbery and cannibalism; a trial seemed superfluous for such heinous crimes, so the men were burnt in Edinburgh while the women and children watched. These then had their hands and feet cut off, and bled to death. So, according to legend, lived and died the tribe of Sawney Bean.

SCOURGE OF THE COVENANT *General Tam Dalyell (1599–1685) owed his military prowess to the Devil, according to his Covenanter enemies. The round towers of The Binns, glimpsed through the windows behind him, were allegedly built by Dalyell to prevent the Devil from blowing the house away*

THE DEVIL'S GENERAL

The Binns (above), near Blackness, west Lothian, was once the home of Tam Dalyell, general of the Royalist forces during the wars that lacerated Scotland in the 17th century. Known as 'Bloody Tam' or the 'Muscovy brute' – he is supposed to have introduced the thumbscrews into Scotland from Russia – General Tam was feared and detested by the Covenanters, who swore he was in league with the Devil. Apparently the terrible pair played cards together, and one night, when Tam won, the Devil picked up a marble table (below, left) and flung it at the general's head. Tam ducked and the table sailed through the window to land in Sergeant's Pond at the foot of the Binns hill. Sure enough, when the pond was being cleaned in 1878, the table was found there, and was restored to the house. Sir Walter Scott's stories did much to promote the Dalyell legend; when Wandering Willie visits Hell in the story of Redgauntlet, *he sees General Tam roistering with the Devil*

RELICS AT THE BINNS *The cards, goblet, spoon and table (left) all figured in Tam's gallivantings with Satan; unlike most people he did not need 'a long spoon to sup with the Devil'. Tam's boots (right) are said to disappear occasionally, when the general's ghost borrows them to ride round the district*

Bodesbeck *Dumfs & Gall*

This farm, which stands about 6 miles north-east of Moffat, was once the home of a brownie. The creature was a hard worker, whose efforts quickly made Bodesbeck the most prosperous farm in all Moffatdale. One year, when there was an exceptionally good harvest, the farmer felt that the brownie deserved some reward, so he left a loaf and a jug of milk on the windowsill. But the brownie was deeply offended at the suggestion that he could not do extra work without being paid, and promptly departed, singing:

> 'Ca' Brownie ca',
> A' the luck o' Bodesbeck
> Awa' tae Leithen Ha'.'

Borgue *Dumfs & Gall*

Once there was a boy living in the village of Borgue who used to disappear for days at a time. He never said where he had been, though it was generally understood that he had been living with the fairies. His grandfather was greatly worried, so he went to a Catholic priest who gave him a cross to tie round the boy's neck. Sure enough, the boy remained at home after that; but the old man was excommunicated by the kirk. It seems that the elders felt that bad though the fairies were, they were to be preferred to dealings with papists.

Carnwath *Strathclyde*

Near by are the remains of Couthally Castle, once the home of the Somervilles. The story goes that the first Somerville captured the castle from its original owner some time in the 12th century, and the building was badly damaged in the process. So Somerville demolished it entirely, and began rebuilding it in a different place. But each morning it was discovered that the work done the previous day had been destroyed during the night. Somerville kept watch and, as midnight struck, Satan himself appeared with a host of demons. As they tore down the walls, they chanted:

> 'Tween the Rae Hill and Loriburnshaw,
> There ye'll find Couthally wa'
> And the foundations laid on ern.'

Somerville took the hint, and rebuilt the castle on its original foundations, said to be of iron.

Cockenzie *Lothian*

On a Saturday in June each year, the old fishing village holds its Children's Gala Day. A Summer Queen is chosen from the children of Cockenzie Public School. Escorted by fishing boats decorated with bunting, she sails from the old harbour at Cockenzie to the new one at Port Seton. On the voyage, the queen's boat is attacked by 'pirates' who are repulsed by her defenders. Having landed, she moves in procession to her coronation at the Public Hall, accompanied by children dressed to represent the burgh's trades and industries.

Coldstream *Borders*

The bridge spanning the Tweed here is also a gateway, for its mid-point marks the border between Scotland and England. At the Scottish end of the bridge there is an old toll-house; here, as at the better-known border crossings of Gretna Green and Lamberton toll, runaway marriages used to be celebrated under an ancient Scottish law which affirmed that a couple who made marriage vows before independent witnesses were legally wed. Such marriages continued to be legal until 1940, but the last marriage in the Coldstream toll-house took place in 1856. In that year an Act was passed making it obligatory to spend three weeks north of the border before the wedding.

Colinsburgh *Fife*

At the end of the 17th century, trouble flared up again between the Covenanters – the militant Presbyterians – and Royalists of the Episcopalian faith. The most famous of the Royalist generals at this time was John Graham of Claverhouse, Viscount Dundee. 'Bonnie' Dundee raised the clans in 1689 to fight for James II against William III, who was supported by the Covenanters, and many gentlemen from southern Scotland rode to join him. Lord Balcarres of Colinsburgh Castle, however, was prevented from doing so by being placed under house arrest by the Scottish Parliament. While he fretted in inactivity, his friend Dundee fought his last and greatest battle at Killiecrankie, and was killed in the moment of victory. At dawn the next morning, Balcarres awoke to see Dundee gazing sorrowfully at him from the bedside; not knowing he was dead, Balcarres cried out to him, whereupon the apparition vanished.

BRAVE DEATH

'Bonnie' Dundee (left) was shot and killed as his Highlanders defeated the Covenanters at the Battle of Killiecrankie (above) in 1689. His enemies believed him to be a warlock and said he had been shot with a silver bullet; this was thought to be the only means of killing supernatural creatures

Crawick *Dumfs & Gall*

One day, the servant girl at Crawick manse discovered that the cream in her churn would not turn into butter, and reported it to the minister. He told her to pass the churn over running water, but even after she had done so, the butter would still not come. Sprigs of rowan were tied to it, and horseshoes were nailed to the cowshed door, but to no avail. Then the minister's wife had the idea of presenting a roll of butter to the witch of Crawick Mill; after that there was no more trouble.

BORDER SONGS AND STORIES OF

'*Theft, Spoyle and Bloode*'

S ome of man's most beautiful works have been created in times of death and danger. Perhaps the fragility of existence at such times inspires him to leave something lasting behind him. Certainly the men and women who lived, fought and died along the border between England and Scotland will never be forgotten as long as songs are sung. Their exploits are celebrated in a magnificent store of ballads, many of which were published by Sir Walter Scott, himself a descendant of a powerful Border clan. He dedicated his *Minstrelsy of the Scottish Border* to Henry, Duke of Buccleuch, with a flowery reference to his patron's 'gallant ancestors'. In fact, His Grace's forbears were reivers – cattle-raiding brigands – like those whom James VI of Scotland, later James I of England, described as 'even from their cradells bredd and brought up in theft, spoyle and bloode'.

JOHNNIE ARMSTRONG AT BAY *One of the most notorious of the Liddesdale Armstrongs, Johnnie finally met his end along with 'fourscore and ten' followers at Carlenrig, Teviotdale. One version of the story of his death claims that he was treacherously deceived by James V. Johnnie and his squad of bandits expected a pardon, but the king, enviously eyeing their ill-gotten finery, said sourly: 'What wants yon knave that a king should have?' – and hanged the lot. But other versions say he died in battle*

ONE THAT GOT AWAY *Jock o' the Side was yet another bothersome Armstrong from the Debatable Land north of Carlisle, which was so often fought over by Scots and English. The ballad about Jock is really a triumphant boast of how he was freed from jail at Newcastle by the renegade Hobby Noble and a handful of men. They battered their way into the castle and took Jock across the border to safety, after dodging irate pursuers. It is possible, however, that the ballad, dating from about 1560, is simply a variation on the story of Kinmont Willie – another Armstrong rescued in a similar fashion from Carlisle*

The 'Debatable Land'

Sir Walter Scott believed that the wilder the society the more violent the impulse received from poetry and music. In the 'Debatable Land' between England's Pennines and the Southern Uplands of Scotland, the impulses were certainly violent. It is a bleak, wild land, and for three centuries its people lived on a battlefield.

The long ordeal began at the end of the 13th century, when a problem arose over the succession to the Scottish throne, and Edward I saw a chance of expanding England's influence in the North. From then until the Union of the Crowns in 1603 the two nations were at loggerheads. Peace, law and good government deserted the frontier zone. No man could go out unarmed; homes and beasts could not be left unguarded. A farmer never knew if he or another would gather in his crops, so he turned to cattle raising – and raiding.

'The freebooter ventures both
    life and limb
Good wife, and bairn, and every
    other thing;
He must do so, or else starve and
    die,
For all his livelihood comes of
    the enemie.'

And so from the flames of burning farms, the flash of steel, and the yells of desperate men, a wonderful poetry was born. The chill winds of the Borders blow through the lines of such ballads as 'Chevy Chase':

'But I hae dreamed a dreary
    dream;
Beyond the Isle of Skye
I saw a dead man win a fight –
And I think that man was I.'

Blackmail is born

The enmities were not purely patriotic. Scot robbed Scot, Englishman plundered Englishman. They perfected the protection racket long before it occurred to city gangsters. The practice gave rise to a new word; a farmer paid 'black-mail', or black-rent in cattle (as opposed to the legal 'white-rent' paid in silver), to a powerful reiver who, in return, would shield him from other raiders.

The older ballads are infused with chivalry and hero worship. 'Chevy Chase' and the 'Battle of Otterburn', the Scots and English accounts of the same moonlit fight, tell of this meeting in 1388 between Hotspur – Sir Henry Percy – and James, 2nd Earl of Douglas. The impetuous Douglas, wielding an iron mace, rushed into the midst of the English and was killed. By the morning, however, the Scots had won.

'This deed was done at Otter-
   burn,
   About the breaking of the day;
   Earl Douglas was buried at the
   bracken bush.
   And the Percy led captive away.'

The battle was an honourable affair, a far cry from the treacherous clashes of 150 years later. By then the Borders had made murder a way of life. Not surprisingly, the love ballads are often laments. In 1530 William Cockburne was beheaded for treason, robbery and harbouring criminals. The plight of his wife is recalled in 'The Lament of the Border Widow'. She sings:

'Nae living man I'll love again,
   Since that my lovely knight is
      slain;
   Wi' ae lock of his yellow hair
   I'll chain my heart for evermair.'

Tenacity of purpose, very much a Border trait, shines out of the ballad 'Tam Lin', about a girl, Janet, who rescued her lover from enchantment by the queen of the fairies. She clung to him as the fairies changed Tam Lin into a snake, a lion, a red-hot bar of iron, a fire, then

'They shaped him in her arms at
      last
   A mother-naked man;
   She wrapt him in her green
      mantle,
   And sae her true love wan.'

A DEAD MAN WINS A FIGHT *At Chevy Chase, Lord Percy is forced to yield to a bracken bush – behind which lies the body of his enemy, Lord Douglas*

THE WINNING OF TAM LIN *Young Janet refused to let go of her lover, Tam, even when the fairies changed him into a lion. Her determination was rewarded. The fairy queen reluctantly freed to her 'the bonniest knight in all my company'*

417

Culzean *Strathclyde*

One morning, centuries ago, the Laird of Co', owner of Culzean Castle, met a small boy carrying a wooden bucket who begged him for some ale for his sick mother. The laird sent him to his butler with orders to have the bucket filled. But after a half-full barrel was emptied and the tiny bucket was still unfilled, the mystified butler was loath to broach a new barrel. However, he obeyed the laird's orders and, to his amazement, scarcely had a drop flowed from the new barrel than the little bucket was over-flowing. Without a word of thanks, the boy took it off to his mother.

Many years later, the same laird was taken prisoner in the wars in Flanders. He was suspected of spying by his captors and sentenced to be hanged. The night before his execution, his cell door suddenly flew open and the same small boy magically appeared. Taking the laird on his shoulders, he carried him with the speed of light back to Culzean. As the fairy boy left the laird, he turned and said: 'One guid turn deserves anither: Tak' ye that for bein' sae kind to ma auld mither.'

A variation of the Bluebeard story is also told locally. May, the daughter of a laird of Culzean, was carried off by an evil knight called Sir John, to Games Loup rock on the coast. Here, he told May, he had already drowned seven wives, and she was to be next. He ordered her to undress and, modestly, she begged him to turn his back. He obeyed, but as soon as he did so, she pushed him off the rock into the sea, where he drowned.

HAUNT OF SCOTLAND'S BLUEBEARD

Culzean Castle (above), built in the 1780's on the site of an earlier stronghold, is linked with several versions of the internationally told Bluebeard story. Though the local version names the murderous husband as 'false Sir John', in an older ballad he is the supernatural Elf-Knight, who abducts the heiress of Culzean and tells her he is going to kill her. But she lulls him to sleep with a charm, steals his dirk and stabs him to death

THE MUSIC OF A MAGIC PIPER

The skirl of bagpipes has sometimes been heard ringing down Piper's Brae (left), a tree-lined walk near Culzean Castle, though there is never any sign of a piper. Tradition claims that the invisible piper always plays to herald the marriage of a future head of the Kennedy family, the former owners of the castle. But who the piper is, or was, no one seems to know

Dalrymple *Strathclyde*
Local tradition claims that the heroine of the ballad 'The Gipsy Laddie' was the wife of a 17th-century Earl of Cassillis. A gipsy leader called Johnnie Faa with six accomplices arrived at the castle gate, where they sang so sweetly that Lady Cassillis came out to listen to them and, entranced by their music, followed them into the forest. Her distraught husband searched desperately for her, until at last he found his wife and her new companions by a stream. He begged her to return home, but she told him she had finished with the fine life and desired only to live as a gipsy girl with Johnnie Faa. Her husband's answer was to arrest the gipsies, and hang them all.

Drumelzier *Borders*
Merlin the magician is reputed to be buried near Drumelzier, at a spot where a burn called the Powsail joins the River Tweed. Legend says that the old sorcerer raised a pagan army against the Christians of Strathclyde, but he was defeated and his followers slaughtered almost to a man. Since Merlin had incited them to revolt, their blood-guilt was on his head; for this he was condemned to wander the forests until he died.

To those who occasionally met him, he would prophesy his own death. He told some people that he would fall over a cliff; to others he confided that he would be hanged; while a third version said he would drown. Apparently, all three came true. One day, chased by jeering shepherds, he leapt over the high bluffs above the Tweed and fell into the stakes supporting the salmon nets below. He died impaled and hanging by his feet, with his head below water.

Dryburgh *Borders*
A woman who had lost her lover in the '45 Rebellion once made her home in a vault among the ruins of Dryburgh Abbey. It was said that she had vowed she would never look on the sun again until her lover returned. When she heard he was dead, she would only come out at night. She told her neighbours that while she was out, her cell was tidied up by a little man, a spirit she called Fatlips. He wore heavy iron shoes with which he trampled the clay floor of the vault to get rid of the damp.

Dumbarton *Strathclyde*
Some legends claim that St Patrick was born near Glasgow and it was here that his ministry flourished before he went to Ireland. But St Patrick's great piety so offended the Devil that he ordered every witch in Scotland to rise up against the saint. This macabre army pursued the unfortunate holy man until he came to the banks of the Clyde. There, he found a boat in which he pushed off for Ireland. Witches cannot cross running water, so his frustrated pursuers tore a huge rock from a nearby hill and hurled it at the retreating saint. But their aim was poor and the huge boulder fell short, to become the rock on which Dumbarton Castle was built.

Earlston *Borders*
Scotland's legendary prophet and seer, Thomas the Rhymer of Ercildoun (the old form of Earlston), is reputed to have lived here some time in the 13th century. In later centuries his name became associated with witchcraft, and in 17th-century trials several witches swore they had dealings with him.

The old ballad of 'Thomas the Rhymer' relates how the seer acquired his prophetic powers. He met the Queen of Elfland and, ensnared by her magic kiss, followed her to Elfland. There he remained bewitched for seven years, before returning to earth gifted with his knowledge of future events.

Ednam *Borders*
Half a mile west of the village stands a knoll known as The Piper's Grave. It is a Pictish burial mound, which was once called Picts' Knowe. Local people believed it was a fairy hill into which a piper crept, anxious to learn the tunes of the little folk. But the foolish man had entered without a protective talisman, and he was never seen again.

Fordell *Fife*
The ruined village mill is avoided by many after dark, and even during the day some people are apprehensive of approaching it alone. The story runs that after the Battle of Pitreavie in 1651, Cromwell's victorious troops were quartered in the surrounding district. The Fordell miller had a squad of soldiers billeted with him who, despite his pleading, continually molested his wife and daughter. In desperation, the miller poisoned his unwelcome guests and fled.

A picket of soldiers was sent to avenge their comrades, but being unable to find the miller, hanged his assistant Jock instead. To this day, it is said, at certain times and seasons he hangs there still, the branch creaking dolefully as his body swings to and fro. On some moonlit nights, Jock's ghostly corpse, with agonised face and staring eyes, can be seen in the branches.

Gavinton *Borders*
Despite supernatural attempts to remove it, Langton House remained firmly fixed in the parish until it was demolished in the 1920's. Some centuries earlier, the fairies had a grudge against the Coburns of Langton and determined to carry the house away to Dogden Moss, several miles to the west, near the village of Greenlaw. One moonlit night in late autumn, the fairies began to loosen its foundations, singing as they worked. They had just begun to lift the house when one of the family awoke. The terrified man, sensing something like an earthquake and hearing the singing, rushed to the window and saw what the fairies were doing. 'Lord keep me and the house together, what's going on?' he cried. His prayer broke the fairies' power, and they fled, leaving the house safely standing.

Glasgow *Strathclyde*
Though associated in most people's minds with heavy industry and the activities of her tougher citizens, Glasgow was once considered the jewel of western Scotland. The very name, from the Celtic *glas ghu*, means 'dear green place'.

Many of the ancient legends of this bustling modern city are centred round its 6th-century patron saint, the gentle and kindly Kentigern. In his youth Kentigern was cared for by St Serf, who renamed him Mungo, meaning 'dear friend'. Unfortunately, St Serf's other disciples were jealous of the favour shown to Mungo, and did their utmost to make trouble for him. Once, when a robin belonging to St Serf was accidentally killed, Mungo was blamed by the other boys. But Mungo took the bird in his hands and prayed over it, whereupon it was restored to life.

In about AD 550 Mungo finished his training and travelled to the house of a holy man named Fergus, at Kernach. Fergus had been told that he would not die until he had seen someone who would convert the whole district to Christianity. Soon after Mungo greeted him, Fergus fell dead. Mungo placed the body on a cart drawn by two wild bulls, and ordered them to go to the place ordained by God. They stopped at Cathures, and here Mungo buried Fergus and founded the church which later became Glasgow Cathedral.

tinued on his way. Arriving at the fair he found that the prices had fallen enough for him to buy several sheep instead of just one, and from that day forward his fortune was made.

Hawick *Borders*

A shepherd on his way to one of the great sheep fairs held at Hawick in former times is said to have been passing near the hill of Rubers Law when he encountered a fairy with her baby. The fairy was lamenting because she had nothing warm to wrap around the child, so the shepherd gave her his own plaid that he wore about his shoulders and con-

Hermitage *Borders*

Ruined Hermitage Castle was the home of the warlock Lord Soulis, who desired a beautiful girl named May. So he kidnapped both May and her sweetheart, the young Laird of Branxholm. Then he consulted his familiar, who lived in an iron-bound chest. The spirit advised the warlock to 'beware of the coming tree'. Soon after, Lord Soulis heard that Branxholm's men were marching on

WEST BOW'S GIGANTIC SPECTRE *In the 'Stinking-closs', a lane near Major Weir's house, a trial witness reported seeing a 10 ft woman 'shaking with immeasurable laughter'. The apparition was surrounded by other phantoms 'gaping with tahies of laughter'*

Hermitage Castle. He again went to his familiar for advice – but forgot the correct ritual to raise the spirit and so broke the spell. His magic was finished, and the spirit told him to escape while there was time. Unheeding, the warlock went to hang young Branxholm from the tallest pine. 'Not the pine,' begged the laird, 'Not the moorland tree I love best.' Soulis agreed, and offered him the aspen; but it seemed the boy had sworn eternal love to May beneath an aspen. Suddenly he shouted 'I see a coming tree!' – and there, sure enough, were Branxholm's men, camouflaged with branches. They seized Lord Soulis, wrapped him in a sheet of lead, and boiled him to death.

THE AWFUL CONFESSION OF MAJOR WEIR

Robert Louis Stevenson's novel *Dr Jekyll and Mr Hyde*, though set in London, was partly based on a notorious character from the author's native Edinburgh. This was Deacon Brodie, a pillar of the kirk by day and a cat-burglar and murderer by night, who was hanged for his crimes in 1788. But over a century before Brodie met his end, Scotland's capital was rocked by the confessions of another Jekyll and Hyde personality. He was none other than the one-time commander of the city's garrison.

Major Thomas Weir established himself in a house in West Bow in the mid-17th century. In 1649, he was appointed commander of the City Guard, and was in charge of the execution of the Royalist Marquis of Montrose. Weir's zeal in the Presbyterian cause was a byword, and he was a much-respected, if not much-loved, Edinburgh figure. He never married, and for years shared his house with his elder sister, Grizel.

Suddenly, at the age of 69, he confessed to the leading citizens that he was a servant of the Devil. His whole life, he said, had been polluted by unspeakable crimes and he had indulged in revolting practices, with his sister as his criminal companion. At first, it was thought that he was insane, but when the doctors examined him they found he was of sound mind. Eventually, on Weir's own insistence, both he and his sister were arrested and brought to trial. It seems clear that Grizel was demented, and despite the doctors' opinions, it appears likely that the old major too had been deeply disturbed by the hag-ridden beliefs of his time.

When they were arrested Grizel advised the guards to seize Weir's staff, telling them that it was a gift from the Devil and the principal source of brother Thomas's power. This staff, she said, would go shopping for the major, answer the door to visitors and run before him to clear the way when he was walking in the streets.

'Long a-burning'

At the trial of the unfortunate pair in 1670, neighbours recalled many strange occurrences which had taken place at Weir's house in West Bow. But their conviction rested mainly on their confessing to crimes which included necromancy, immorality, dealings with a familiar spirit, and Grizel's ability to spin abnormal quantities of yarn. They were both sentenced to be strangled and burnt. Major Weir's execution took place outside the city walls, and his staff was burnt with him. A witness stated that the stick 'gave rare turnings and was long a-burning as also himself'. Grizel was hanged on a gibbet in the Grassmarket. When she was about to be executed she tried to remove her clothes, whereupon the executioner turned her prematurely off the ladder.

For a century after Major Weir's execution his house remained empty, but his cloaked ghost, complete with magical staff, was reported to flit about the streets at night. The empty house was said to glow with eerie lights, and music and laughter were heard within. Oddly enough, no one now remembers where in West Bow the Weirs' house stood. But the tapping of Weir's stick is still heard in the Grassmarket, and there too Grizel's fire-blackened face is occasionally glimpsed.

REDCAP'S CASTLE

The ruins of Hermitage Castle, where Mary, Queen of Scots nearly died of fever, are said to be haunted by Redcap Sly, the familiar spirit of the evil Lord Soulis. Redcap is described as a horrible old man with long fangs and, until recently at least, small boys used to shout into the ruins: 'Redcapie-dossie, come out if ye dare!' The spirit told his master he could only be bound by a three-stranded rope of sand; but he was wrong. Lord Soulis was bound in a sheet of lead and boiled to death for abducting the Laird of Branxholm

Hobkirk *Borders*
A gravestone in Hobkirk churchyard marks the burial place of an 18th-century minister, the Rev. Nicol Edgar, who is said to have laid a troublesome ghost that haunted the church. This public-spirited action apparently gained the minister himself an uncanny reputation, and after his death it was thought that his spirit might wander from its grave in the churchyard. So it was decided he should be reburied outside the village. While the corpse was being carried across the moor, the bearers slipped, and the chill hand of the dead minister struck one of them, whereupon all fled in panic. The body lay where it fell until the next day, when it was returned to its original resting place.

Innerleithen *Borders*
Long before the 18th century, when Robert Burns described the place as a famous spa, the sulphurous waters of the local well were renowned for their ability to cure eye and skin complaints. In Burns's day, the dark peaty spring was known as the Dow Well, taking its name from the Gaelic *dubh*, meaning black, but since the early 19th century it has been called St Ronan's Well.

Irvine *Strathclyde*
The town's colourful Marymass Fair, held each August, dates from the 12th century. The name of the fair links it to the parish church, which was dedicated to the Virgin Mary. But ever since Mary, Queen of Scots visited Irvine in 1563 the Marymass Queen has always been dressed to represent Mary Stuart. A feature of the fair is the amateur horse-racing, which includes an unusual race for cart-horses. The races may be of earlier date than the fair itself; if so, this must be one of the oldest race meetings in Europe.

A bronze statue of Habbie Simpson, the town piper who lived from 1550 to 1620, stands in a niche on the north face of the Steeple Tower at Kilbarchan, Strathclyde. Dancing and laughter accompanied Habbie wherever he went and he was invited to every feast or wedding in the district. He is represented in the village's June pageant, known as Lilias Day after the daughter of an 18th-century nobleman. Every year a local girl is chosen to represent Lilias

WHERE A SKELETON DANCED

The abbey of Jedburgh, Borders Region, now ruined, was chosen by Alexander III, a widower, for his marriage to Yolande, daughter of the Count of Dreux, in October, 1285. After the ceremony a ball was held in the castle. A musical play had been composed, and dozens of masked dancers in fantastic costumes weaved in and out before the king and his bride. Suddenly a skeleton appeared among the company. It capered towards Alexander and thrust a bony finger almost into his face. Everyone was transfixed by terror and the queen buried her face in her hands. The skeleton vanished, but the splendid festival was ruined. The following March, the king, who had been feasting although it was Lent, was riding eagerly to rejoin his young queen when he fell with his horse over the cliffs near Kinghorn in Fife and was killed

A RUSTLER'S REFUGE

On the road from Langholm to Canonbie is the Hollows Tower, where the notorious rustler Johnnie Armstrong once lived. His ghost is said to appear on the top of the tower, swearing vengeance on his enemies

Kirkcudbright *Dumfs & Gall*
Billy Marshall, king of the tinker-gipsies of Galloway, is buried in Kirkcudbright, where his monument still stands. He died in 1790, claiming to be 120 years old. Seven times lawfully married, he fathered four illegitimate children after his hundredth year. Scott's famous character Meg Merrilees, from *Guy Mannering*, is probably modelled on Flora Marshall, one of Billy's wives. Billy commanded a tinker army of cavalry and infantry which was defeated by tinkers from Argyll in a battle at Newtown of Ayr in 1712.

Kirkton Manor *Borders*
David Ritchie, original of The Black Dwarf in Scott's tale of the same name, built himself a cottage of large stones and turf in the Manor Valley. He was a mis-shapen man under 3 ft 6 in. in height, with a head so thick that he could smash it through a door panel. In 1797 Scott called at the cottage. The dwarf seized him by the wrist and said 'Man, hae ye ony poo'er?' By this he meant magical power. Scott said he had not, but the dwarf called out 'He has poo'er,' at which Scott became pale and agitated. Ritchie, of course, did not know of his visitor's magical literary talents, which were eventually to make the dwarf immortal.

Kirkton of Largo *Fife*
Largo Law, which is of volcanic origin, is said to have been created from a rock dropped by the Devil as he flew past. At the top is a formation known as the Devil's Chair, with seven steps leading up to it.

Kirk Yetholm *Borders*
Long celebrated as the headquarters of the Scottish gipsies, Kirk Yetholm is just over a mile from the English border. The last gipsy king, Charles Faa Blythe, was crowned on the village green in 1898 and reigned until his death in 1902. By then his people had been assimilated into the population.

Lanark *Strathclyde*
Misfortune once befell a farmer's wife who lived near Lanark. Her husband was captured by the press-gang and her pig fell sick. An old fairy woman cured the pig, but demanded her baby boy as payment unless she could learn the fairy's name. When walking in the woods, the farmer's wife overheard the fairy singing:
   'Little kens our guid dame at hame
   That Whuppity Stoorie is my name.'
So when the old woman came for the baby, the mother called her 'Whuppity Stoorie' and she fled.

LANGHOLM'S PROUD HORSEMEN

The little Border burghs were always the first places to feel the onslaught of the English invaders, and they celebrate their continuing existence every summer with the flamboyant Common Ridings. One of the oldest takes place at Langholm, east of Lockerbie, on the last Friday in July.

Langholm Fair and Common Riding begin when horsemen gather in the square and the Provost (mayor) presents colours to the young man chosen as Cornet for the year. The Cryer proclaims the town's right to cut peat and bracken on the commons. The Cornet spurs his horse up a steep hill, followed by the attendant riders. Once at the top, they follow a centuries-old route, and at various points peats are dug and bracken pulled. Processions march through the town behind symbols – a wooden fish nailed to a wooden bannock (large scone), a crown made of plaited roses, and a huge thistle made up of scores of real thistles. The Cornet and his party return to the square for a second proclamation by the Cryer:

'So now I will conclude and say
    nae mair,
And if ye're pleased, I'll cry the
    Langholm Fair.'

This corner of Dumfries and Galloway was the lair of the Armstrong clan, dreaded outlaws and cattle-rustlers, who raided cattle on both sides of the Border when the moon was right. They were one of the clans for whom the phrase 'there will be moonlight again' had considerable meaning; perhaps it was appropriate that an Armstrong should have been the first man to set foot on the moon. Neil Armstrong, astronaut and descendant of the Armstrongs of Mangerton, was made a freeman of Langholm when he visited the town on March 11, 1972.

CIVIC VALOUR *The Common Riders, bearing aloft the symbols of the townsfolk's rights and independence, proclaim every year the continued existence of the Border burghs which for centuries withstood the shock of invasion and the attacks of outlaws*

423

THE SLEEPING KING IN THE EILDON HILLS

Laurieston *Dumfs & Gall*

A long-ago Laird of Slogarie, a house 2 miles north of the village, earned the nickname of 'the Earl of Hell' by his continual drinking, swearing and gaming. His wife, a quiet God-fearing woman, bore him two sons, who were even more wicked than their father. Eventually, his wife pined away and died. One Saturday night soon after her death, the three were playing cards and drinking while a storm raged around the house. Midnight came, and the Sabbath morn, and still they sat playing. Full of liquor, they conceived the dangerous notion of burning the dead woman's Bible, and threw it on the blazing fire. But they had gone too far; lightning struck and the house burst into flames. Even so, the old laird would not leave without his money-chest and climbed back through a window to retrieve it. At that moment, a beam fell and pinned him so that he was slowly roasted to death. His sons rode off for help, but one fell over a crag in the dark while the other ran into a tree and broke his neck.

The Eildon Hills, a mile south of Melrose, Borders, is one of the many places in Britain where King Arthur and his knights are supposed to lie sleeping, awaiting the recall to battle in the hour of Britain's greatest need.

One man who was supposed to have seen them was a bold lad named Canonbie Dick. Dick was a horse-dealer and one night, riding home with a pair of horses he had been unable to sell, he was stopped by a strange man in old-fashioned clothes who asked to buy the horses. After some hard bargaining, he paid Dick in antique gold pieces. The episode was repeated on several nights until Dick finally suggested that, to seal the last bargain, they should go to the stranger's house for a drink. The man agreed but warned Dick that if he lost his nerve when he saw his dwelling, he would be lost for ever.

Dick was not frightened of anything and followed his host to a hummock called the Lucken Hare, where they entered a concealed door in the hills. The astonished Dick found himself in a huge cavern, surrounded by rows of sleeping horses and knights in armour. On a table lay a sword and a horn and Dick was offered the choice of blowing the horn or drawing the sword first, for 'King of all Britain will he be' who made the correct choice. Dick tried to blow the horn – the wrong choice – and a mighty wind suddenly lifted Dick and threw him out of the cave. Next morning, he was found by some shepherds, and after telling his story, he died.

THE FAIRY BOY OF LEITH

Until a comparatively late period in Scotland's history, many of her people believed in fairies. Not even townsfolk were immune, it seems, according to a well-documented Leith story of the 1660's which tells of a ten-year-old boy whose miraculous gift of second sight had been given to him by the fairies. A Captain George Burton met the Fairy Boy and found the boy willing to answer all his questions. The captain's story is reproduced in Richard Bovet's book Pandaemonium or the Devil's Cloyster Opened, *published in 1684.*

The Fairy Boy told Burton that every Thursday night he went to the Calton Hill, near Edinburgh, where he entered the hill through a pair of huge gates, visible only to those who had the fairy gift. At the revels under the hill, he played the drums while the Little Folk danced. 'A great company, both men and women' gathered there

to be entertained 'with many sorts of musick' while they feasted and drank. Sometimes they all flew off to France or Holland and back in a night 'to enjoy the pleasures of these countries'.

It was said that 'all the people in Scotland' could not keep the Fairy Boy from his Thursday night rendezvous. So Captain Burton, accompanied by some friends, tried to hold the lad in conversation one Thursday night. They placed themselves between the Fairy Boy and the door of the room in which they were sitting, but about an hour before midnight they suddenly realised that the boy had slipped away unobserved. He was found just as he was about to leave the house and brought back to the room once more. Again, everyone watched him closely but again he eluded them, and vanished to keep his nocturnal tryst on the Calton Hill

THE FATAL CHOICE *When Canonbie Dick entered the cave containing the sleeping King Arthur and his knights, he was given the choice of blowing a horn or drawing a sword; Dick* *took the horn. But a strange voice told him it was cowardly to summon help before using the sword – and then he was blown from the cave by a mighty wind, and fatally injured*

Liberton *Lothian*

According to legend, the parish of Liberton, a southern suburb of Edinburgh, is named from 'Leper Town'. This idea is probably associated with the famous Balm Well, whose waters were believed to cure skin diseases. The nuns from the nearby convent of St Catherine of Siena made an annual pilgrimage to the well in their patron's honour. The water of the Balm Well contains drops of a black oily substance, which is produced by a coal seam at the well's source. But tradition claims that the well sprang from a drop of miraculous oil brought to St Margaret, the 11th-century Queen of Scotland, from the tomb of St Catherine on Mount Sinai.

Linton *Borders*

Long ago on Linton Hill there lived a ferocious worm, the terror of the countryside. With ever-open mouth, it careered through the fields, devouring cattle, sheep and people, until a local hero named Somerville hit on the idea of fixing a wheel to the tip of his lance. He daubed the wheel with a fiery mixture of pitch, resin and brimstone, and ran it down the worm's throat, so killing it. Somerville's deed is recorded in a carving above the door of Linton church.

Moffat Water *Dumfs & Gall*

A story is told of two local Covenanters, Halbert Dobson and David Dun, nicknamed Hab Dob and Davie Din, who were on the run from Royalist troops. They hid themselves in a cave high up on a cliff face near a waterfall now called Dob's Linn. But the Devil got to know where the pair were hiding, and decided to help the troops in their search. He threatened and tempted the two men in a variety of guises, but the Covenanters would not leave their hiding place. Finally, they made several crosses from a hank of red yarn and laid these out so that the Devil could not pass. Then they lay in wait for him, each armed with a Bible and a rowan-wood staff. When the Devil attacked, they toppled him over the cliff-edge and down the waterfall, where he managed to save himself by changing into a bundle of sheep-skins.

Mull of Galloway *Dumfs & Gall*

Legend says that the last Picts lived in the Mull of Galloway, where they jealously guarded the secret recipe for heather ale, passing the secret down from father to son. Apparently, they were small men with red hair and feet so broad that when it rained they could turn them up over their heads like umbrellas.

After a series of wars in which they were almost exterminated, the Picts were reduced to a handful of survivors; but still they kept the secret of heather ale. In the final battle between the Picts and the Scots, all the Picts were killed except two, a father and son who were taken prisoner. The King of Scots threatened them with torture unless they revealed the secret recipe. The father gave way, but only on condition that the king first killed the man's son. The king did so – and then eagerly demanded the recipe. But the cunning Pict refused. 'You can do what you like with me – you might have forced him to speak, but you'll never get anything from me.' Then the father hurled himself to his death from the cliffs – though some say the king let him live because of his bravery. In either event, the secret of heather ale died with him.

WHERE THE LAST PICT DIED

Rather than reveal the secret Pictish recipe for heather ale to his Scots captors, the last of the Picts threw himself to his death from the Mull of Galloway cliffs

425

THE WEIRD SISTERS OF
North Berwick

group of women stand on the pier at Leith, staring out to sea. One of them holds a cat, which struggles and mews plaintively. Tied to its paws are gobbets of human flesh, taken from the body of a hanged man. Suddenly the screeching animal is flung into the chilly waters of the Firth of Forth. Clouds gather; winds howl; and grey waves pound the shore. A squall hits a boat sailing across the Firth; it heels over drunkenly and sinks with all its crew.

The women were the witches of North Berwick; their macabre ceremony an attempt to raise a storm and sink James VI of Scotland's ship as he returned home from Norway with his bride, Anne of Denmark, in 1590. But the boat which foundered was not the right vessel, and the royal ship, though much troubled by bad weather, came safely home.

The tale of sorcery and high treason began to come to light when David Seaton, deputy bailiff of Tranent in east Lothian, noticed that his maid-servant Gilly Duncan was behaving oddly. She kept leaving the house at night without his permission, and acquired a local reputation as a healer and wise-woman. With horrid suspicions of witchcraft dawning, he questioned her, and when she refused to answer, he tortured her with pilnie-winks – thumbscrews – and by binding a cord tightly round her head. Still she kept silence.

DEEDS OF THE WITCHES *A woodcut published in 1591 shows the clerk of the North Berwick coven, Dr John Fian, taking down the Devil's words as he preaches from a pulpit. In the foreground, members of the coven drink in a cellar, while in the distance a ship sinks in a storm summoned by the witches*

Inspired by the Devil

In later interrogations, when a mole was found upon Gilly's throat, it was supposed that this was the Devil's mark, proving her identity as a witch. Under further torment, she admitted that her cures were inspired by the Devil, and that she belonged to a witch-coven, the names of whose members she reluctantly revealed.

From her garbled confessions there emerged the details of an extraordinary plot to murder King James, who was later to become James I of England. The instigator was said to be Francis Hepburn, Earl of Bothwell, the king's cousin and heir-apparent to the throne should James die without an heir. Bothwell was also suspected of being the 'Devil' or leader of the coven, who presided over its meetings wearing ritual disguise.

Only four of those named by Gilly were brought to trial. They were Dr John Fian, a young schoolmaster at Saltpans; Euphemia MacLean, daughter of Lord Cliftonhall; a woman named Barbara Napier; and Agnes Sampson, a midwife of Keith whose herbal and magical remedies were also famed in the district.

Confessions of evil

With his legs being slowly crushed in an instrument called the boot, Fian confessed that he was 'clerk to all those that were in subjection to the Devil's service', in that he kept a list of their names and administered the oaths. At the meetings he always stood nearest the Devil, 'at his left elbow'. Having made these admissions he was left alone in his cell. Next morning he told his jailers that Satan had come to him during the night, carrying a white wand and demanding that he should renew his vows. Fian refused. The Evil One replied, 'Once ere thou die, thou shalt be mine', then broke his wand and vanished. Upon this warning, Fian retracted his confession and despite needles being thrust beneath his fingernails and further applications of the boot, remained silent. He was finally strangled and burnt on Castle Hill in Edinburgh in January, 1591.

BOUND FOR THE SABBAT *The Devil's candles flare from the head of Dr Fian's horse as he rides with one of his coven towards North Berwick church for a great meeting of witches on All Hallows Eve in 1590*

ALL HALLOWS EVE *Agnes Sampson confessed that 200 witches met the Devil in North Berwick church on All Hallows Eve, 1590*

Agnes Sampson was examined at Holyrood House by King James himself. She told him that after the failure to sink his ship, she begged one of James's servants to give her a piece of old linen once worn by the king. Wisely, the servant refused; otherwise, said Agnes, she would have smeared it with toad's venom and James would have died in agony.

A curse on the king

The witches also gathered at Prestonpans one night and chanted curses over a wax image of James, saying as it was passed from hand to hand: 'This is King James VI, ordained to be consumed at the instance of a noble man, Francis Earl Bothwell.'

The king heard Agnes and the other witches give accounts of a great assembly at North Berwick church on All Hallows Eve, 1590. Their use of a sacred building was probably as much a matter of convenience as deliberate blasphemy.

Seven score witches were there, said Barbara Napier, 200 according to Agnes. They went by sea, making merry on the way with flagons of wine. At the churchyard Gilly Duncan provided music on a jew's harp as the throng danced round, singing as they went: 'Cummer (sister), go ye before; cummer, go ye; If ye will not go before, cummer, let me.' When James heard this he sent for Gilly and made her play the tune on a jew's harp.

The Devil, said the witches, presided over the gathering in the form of a man wearing a black gown. He probably wore a mask as well, for his face was said to have been terrible, with great burning eyes and a beaked nose. His hands were hairy and had claws on them, and his feet had talons.

All paid homage to him. Then he stood in the pulpit, with black candles burning all around, and preached to his followers concerning the obedience they owed him, urging them to

work evil upon his greatest enemy, King James.

The king, who had been following the evidence with great attention, suddenly lost patience and declared the witches to be 'extreme liars'. Then Agnes did an astonishing thing. She said she would tell him something he could not doubt. Drawing James aside, she whispered to him the words that had passed between Anne of Denmark and himself when they were alone together on their wedding night in Oslo.

This convinced the king that Agnes was telling the truth, but it also sealed her fate. James knew that she could not have learnt what she had told him by mortal means. She and Euphemia were convicted and executed on Castle Hill and Barbara was condemned but later released. As for Bothwell, the prime mover in the case, he fled to Naples where he continued to practise sorcery until he died in poverty in 1624.

Oakwood *Borders*

Oakwood Tower, about 4½ miles south-west of Selkirk, was the home of Scotland's eeriest enchanter, Michael Scot. Scot was an internationally famous scholar, who for several years in the early 13th century was physician and court astrologer to the Holy Roman Emperor Frederick II. His works on astrology, alchemy and the occult quickly earned him a reputation as a wizard, and in the opinion of his fellow countrymen, his years abroad had been spent not at the Imperial court but at the 'Black School', where he had learnt to control the powers of darkness and summon up the Devil, recording spells and incantations in his private 'Book of Might'. He died *c*. 1234, and was buried with his book of spells, so it is said, in Melrose Abbey.

Many stories are told about Scot's exploits. Once, legend claims, he sent a demon to split the Eildon Hill in three; there are three peaks there to this day. The next night, he commanded it to dam the River Tweed; the ridge of rock at Kelso was the result. On the third night, he told it to spin ropes of sand at the mouth of the Tweed. More than 700 years later, the demon is still hard at work, to judge by the ridges of twisted sand which curl along the shore at low tide.

Pittenweem *Fife*

In 1704–5, three people died and many others were cruelly tortured as the result of wild accusations of witchcraft made by a 16-year-old Pittenweem boy, Patrick Morton. One of those who died was Beatrix Laing, the wife of a former town treasurer,

THE GIANT'S COME-UPPANCE '*Be he alive or be he dead,*' roared Red Etin, '*his heart tonight shall kitchen my bread!*' He turned two of the boys who came to his castle into pillars of stone; but the spell was broken when the third boy confronted him, answered three difficult questions, and cut off his three monstrous heads with a single blow of his axe

who stood accused of sending evil spirits to torture Patrick. After five months alone in a pitch dark dungeon, and frequent visits to the torture chamber, she was freed, but died soon afterwards, friendless and broken, at St Agnes. Another of the accused, Thomas Brown, was starved to death in his dungeon. A third, Janet Bornfoot, escaped from her torturers only to be lynched when she returned home. On January 30, 1705, a mob caught her in Pittenweem, beat her and dragged her by the heels to the seafront. There she was swung from a rope tied between a ship and the shore, stoned, beaten again and finally crushed to death under a door piled with rocks. To make sure that she was dead, a man drove his horse and sledge several times over her corpse. Though all the other accused were eventually freed, and Patrick Morton was exposed as a liar who had come under the influence of a fanatical priest, none of the lynch mob was ever brought to justice.

THE OGRE OF ETIN'S HALL

Near Preston in Borders Region are the remains of an ancient fortress known as Etin's or Edin's Hall. The Red Etin, it seems, was a terrible three-headed giant who kidnapped the King of Scotland's daughter, but he got his deserts in the end. It happened like this.

In a far-off part of the country there lived two widows who were too poor to pay the rent, so they determined to send their three sons out into the world to seek their fortunes. One of the boys volunteered to go first, but before he went, he gave his brother his favourite knife, saying that while its blade remained bright and clean, the family would know that all went well with him; but if it clouded over, or rusted, it would mean that he had met misfortune.

The boy set out on his travels, and after a couple of days, he met a shepherd guarding a large flock of sheep. He inquired about their owner, and was told they belonged to Red Etin, a fearsome monster whose mortal foe was yet to appear.

The boy shrugged and went on his way. After a while, he came upon a castle, where he begged shelter for the night. The old woman in the kitchen told him that the castle, too, belonged to Red Etin; no sooner had she said so, than the giant himself came in, all three heads sniffing for blood. He seized the unfortunate youth and demanded the answers to three questions: Was Scotland or Ireland the first to be inhabited by men? Was man made for woman, or vice versa? And which was made first, man or beast? The boy could answer none of these questions, so the giant hit him over the head with a mallet, and the boy turned into a pillar of stone.

Meanwhile, far away, his brother noticed that the knife blade had turned rusty and, despite the entreaties of the widows, set out to the rescue. But the same awful fate befell him. When the second brother failed to return, the other widow's son packed his bundle, determined to do what he could to help his friends. On the road, he met an old woman with whom he shared his last bannock. In exchange, she foretold many things that would happen to him. The youth marched on and he too met the shepherd. But this time, speaking of Red Etin, the man said: 'Now I fear his end is near, and destiny at hand.'

When the boy reached the castle, the giant grabbed him and asked his three questions. Remembering what the old woman had told him, the lad was able to whisper the right answers and Etin realised he was doomed. With one sweep of his axe, the boy removed all three of the giant's heads. The brothers were released from enchantment, and they opened the dungeons and released the princess and several other ladies. Each boy married the lady of his choice, and they all lived happily ever after. But nobody else ever knew the answers to the three questions, for the boy had whispered them only to the giant.

Port Glasgow *Strathclyde*
According to legend, the funeral procession of a girl who had died of consumption was passing along the shore near Port Glasgow, when a mermaid rose from the water and said in mournful tones:

'If they wad drink nettles in March,
And eat muggons (mugwort) in May,
Sae mony braw maidens
Wadna gang to the clay.'

Queensferry *Lothian*
The festivities of the August Ferry Fair are led by a curious character called the Burry Man. Clad from head to toe in sticky burrs, he wanders round the streets with two attendants, collecting money for charity. It is thought that in the old days when times were hard – in a poor fishing season, for instance – the Burry Man was a scapegoat who was led through the town and then expelled in the hope of removing the bad luck.

THE PRENTICE PILLAR

The beautiful chapel in Roslin, Lothian, founded in 1446, contains an exquisitely carved pillar known as the Prentice Pillar. The story goes that it was planned by the master mason, but he found the task of carving it beyond him, and travelled abroad to learn the secret. When he returned, he found his apprentice had finished the work and, in a jealous rage, he killed the boy. The master still did not know the secret, which is why the pillar remains unmatched and unique in the chapel

St Andrews *Fife*

In the early 16th century, the castle was the home of Cardinal David Beaton, the Catholic martyr or bloody oppressor of Protestantism, according to one's viewpoint. In the early days of the Reformation, he ruthlessly stamped on the slightest manifestation of the Lutheran heresy and, in the process, created the earliest Protestant martyrs in Scotland. One of the first was Patrick Hamilton, a young priest who objected to the Church selling indulgences – remission of punishment for sins – and got married in defiance of Church law. He was burnt to death at St Andrews, but there were too few faggots and the rain kept putting the fire out though the logs were smeared with gunpowder. He took six hours to die, but his courage made him a popular hero. It is said that Beaton calmly watched the burning of another married priest, George Wishart, before going on to attend the wedding of his own illegitimate daughter. Two months later, in July 1546, a group of Fife Protestants broke into the castle and murdered the cardinal; afterwards, his body was suspended over the walls by an arm and a leg, so forming a St Andrew's Cross. A rhyme of the period concluded: 'For stickit is your cardinal, and salted like a sow' – apparently the conspirators pickled his body in brine during the weeks they held the castle against the forces of the government.

ST ANDREW'S FAIR

The town fair, held in August, has a charter dating from the early Middle Ages. Originally it was a 'feeing-fair', where farm workers met prospective employers. The painting is by the 19th-century artist Alexander Fraser

Selkirk *Borders*

There was once a soutar – a shoemaker – in Selkirk named Rabbie Heckspeckle. Rabbie was very industrious, and used to be at his bench long before dawn. Early one morning, a stranger came into the shop. He wore a long black cloak and a big hat pulled down over his eyes. The stranger picked up one of the shoes on the bench and tried it on. Finding it a perfect fit, he paid Rabbie in gold, and promised to return for the other shoe before cock-crow the following day.

Thinking it over, Rabbie became suspicious of his customer. His clothes had smelt uncommonly mouldy, and Rabbie had the impression, too, that his purse had contained as many worms and beetles as gold pieces. But true to his word, the stranger returned next morning and paid for the other shoe. This time, however, Rabbie followed him. The tall, cloaked figure walked across the churchyard to a grave, jumped into it and disappeared. Later that day, Rabbie and a few neighbours returned and dug up the corpse; sure enough, it was wearing the new shoes, which the soutar at once reclaimed.

Early next morning, as usual, Rabbie's wife heard him singing and banging away at his work. Suddenly, his song ended in a screech; she rushed in, but her husband had vanished. When the grave was re-opened, the corpse was once more wearing its new shoes, and clutched in its right hand was Rabbie Heckspeckle's nightcap. But Rabbie himself had gone for ever.

HECKSPECKLE'S PHANTOM

As cock-crow approached, Rabbie's strange customer, wearing his new shoes, went down into the grave

DUNGEON OF TERROR

Cardinal Beaton is said to have imprisoned Protestants in this bottle-shaped dungeon beneath St Andrew's Castle. Prisoners went mad in the darkness, and when their screams were heard, they were murdered

Stenton *Lothian*
Until the 19th century, there was a village near by called Whittingehame that was haunted by the ghost of an unbaptised child. Its problem was that it had no name, and could not identify itself in the next world. No one dared speak to the unhappy creature, until a drunkard, reeling home late one night, cried to it: 'Hows a' this morning, Short-Hoggers?' Immediately, the spirit rushed off joyfully shouting 'They ca' me Short-Hoggers o' Whittingehame' – and was never seen again. Short-hoggers are socks without feet, which people thought to be an apt name when they considered how long the spirit had wandered the district.

Traquair *Borders*
It is said that the great gates of 10th-century Traquair House, one of the oldest inhabited houses in Scotland, have been closed in mourning ever since Bonnie Prince Charlie's defeat in 1746. In fact, they were closed in 1796, when the wife of the 7th Earl of Traquair died; he swore they would never be re-opened until the next countess came to take her place. But his son died without heirs, and the title is now extinct.

Tweedsmuir *Borders*
Near by are some ancient stones which are said to mark the grave of Jack the Giant-Killer. He shot his last victim from behind one of them, but in his death-throes, the giant killed the hero.

Tynron *Dumfs & Gall*
An old tale tells how one of the MacMilligans of Balgarnock came courting the daughter of the Great McGachan at Tynron Castle. But her brothers considered him an unworthy suitor, and chased him, horse and all, over the crag. As he fell, his head was knocked off his shoulders. His decapitated ghost still haunts the district.

West Wemyss *Fife*
The Castle of Wemyss is haunted by a tall, slim girl wearing a green dress. 'Green Jean' has been seen and approached by members of the Wemyss family, but apparently some strange force prevents them from speaking to her.

Yarrow *Borders*
The younger of two brothers apprenticed to the local blacksmith was literally hag-ridden. Each night a witch would come to his bedside and slip a magic bridle over his head, whereupon the boy would turn into a horse and the witch would gallop him off to the coven. When the older boy heard this, he changed places with his brother, and that night, when the witch rode him to the coven, he managed to slip the magic bridle off and put it on the witch instead. He galloped her for miles over the country-side, after which he took her to the blacksmith to be shod. The next morning, the witch was found writhing in agony, with a horseshoe nailed to each of her hands and feet.

431

THE FARAWAY HILLS

West Highlands and Hebrides

The Celtic people, called the Scots, who sailed from Ireland in the 5th century AD to settle in the highlands and islands of the Picts, were nominally Christians; but long after they conquered the whole of northern Britain, their lives were still ruled by other, older beliefs. Fairies, water-beasts, witches, and the spirits of the dead were always lying in wait to carry off the unwary.

Their Christian faith was itself riddled with memories of pagan ritual. Within living memory, St Michael, patron saint of boats, of horses and of horsemen was spoken of in the southern Hebrides as 'the god Michael'. On his feast day, September 29, the *struan Micheil*, a cake made from all the different kinds of cereals grown on the farm during the year and baked in a lamb's skin, was blessed at the mass by the priest. Later in the day came horse races (in which the women rode behind the men) and feasting.

Springs, caves and standing stones all had their supernatural guardians who featured in the songs and poems that passed on both truth and legend to the next generation. Tales of heroes, and of battles long ago, were remembered for centuries, for the Highlander believes the past is as real as the present. Clan feuds, the adventures of Bonnie Prince Charlie and his followers, and the tragedy of the Highland Clearances are as fresh in folk-memory as events which the story-tellers themselves have witnessed. In the long winter nights of this harsh land, people would gather for the musical evening of the *Ceilidh* and listen to the *seanachaidh*, or story-teller. There were pipes and fiddles, and traditional songs, until the children fell asleep and were carried off to bed.

Sentiment, and the primitive virtues of loyalty, courage and toughness, are oddly mingled in the Highland character. There is the story of the young chief, newly returned from his French education, who was leading a war-party across the hills when they were overtaken by a blizzard. Unable to proceed further, they lay down to rest and the chieftain rolled himself a snowball, placed his head upon it and went to sleep. His followers were consumed with anxiety. How, they wondered, could this much-loved young man survive the rigours of the years ahead if he could not sleep without a pillow?

The clan structure was broken for ever in the holocaust of Culloden in 1746, and a century later many of the clanspeople too were gone, driven out by the landowners to make way for sheep. They took their sturdy self-reliance over the seas to build new countries where, generations later, their kilted descendants still gather to talk of the mountains of 'home' in accents their forefathers never dreamt of. Perhaps the anonymous composer of 'A Canadian Boat Song' puts it best:

'Still the blood is strong, the heart is Highland,
And we, in dreams, behold the Hebrides.'

THE FOLKLORE YEAR

Last Saturday in May
Drumnadrochit, Highland
Piping and Dancing

First Friday and Saturday in June
Aberfeldy, Tayside
Folk Festival

July
Inverness, Highland
Durness, Highland
Highland Games

August
Fort William, Highland
Portree, Isle of Skye, Inner Hebrides
Isle of Arran, Bute
Highland Games

Second Thursday and Friday in September
Inverness, Highland
Piping Championships

September
Oban, Strathclyde
Highland Games

First week in October
Sites chosen each year
National Gaelic Mod

December 31
Comrie, Tayside
Flambeaux Procession

LOC RESC

TARBERT

Harris

VALLAY

CARINISH

N. Uist

BENBECULA

HOWMORE

S. Uist

BARRA

VATERSAY
(Birds of Life & Death,

TIRE

KEY TO SYMBOLS

CRIME AND PUNISHMENT		GRAVES AND MONUMENTS	
CURIOUS CHARACTERS		HEROES	
CUSTOMS AND FESTIVALS		LOCAL CURIOSITIES	
DEVILS AND DEMONS		LOVE STORY	
FABULOUS BEASTS		MERMAIDS AND SEA-PEOPLE	
FABULOUS SEA BEASTS		MYSTERIOUS STONES	
FAIRIES		SAINTS AND MIRACLES	
GHOSTS		WELLS AND SPRINGS	
GIANTS		WITCHES AND WIZARDS	

DURNESS

STRATHNAVER

STORNOWAY
(*John of Lewis, 451*)

CALLANISH

Lewis

THE MINCH

ROSEHALL

STAFFIN

STORR

CROMARTY

DUNVEGAN
(*Fairy Flag, 436*)

LOCH MAREE

STRATHPEFFER
CONONBRIDGE

TORRIDON
LOCH CARRON

INVERNESS

CULLODEN
(*The Highland Clans, 447*)

Skye

STRATH

LOCH
DUICH

HIGHLAND

LOCH
ASHIE

GLENELG

REGION

LOCH NESS
(*Legends, 445*)

GLENMORE
FOREST

SLEAT

INVERGARRY

LYNCHAT

KINGUSSIE

GRAMPIAN
REGION

LAGGAN
(*The Goodwife, 442*)

BADENOCH

LOCHABER

GAICK FOREST

ARDNAMURCHAN

NORTH
BALLACHULISH

STRUAN

KILLIECRANKIE

GLEN COE

RANNOCH
MOOR

TAYSIDE

REGION

OBERMORY

GLEN ETIVE
(*Fabulous
Creatures, 439*)

GLEN
LYON

FORTINGALL

SCONE

STAFFA

Mull

KILLIN

IONA

STRATHCLYDE
REGION

LOCH AWE

CENTRAL

REGION

LOCH EARN

ABERFOYLE

FIFE
REGION

CORRYVRECKAN

Jura

LOCH FYNE

LOTHIAN
REGION

Islay

N

STRATHCLYDE
REGION

LOCH
RANZA

ARDBEG

Arran

BORDERS
REGION

0   10   20
MILES

Aberfoyle *Tayside*

For centuries, the wild MacGregors, cattle-lifters and brigands to a man, were the plague of the Trossachs. The most famous member of the clan was the thief and blackmailer Rob Roy, or Red Robert MacGregor, who died in 1734. His base was in a now-vanished hamlet a mile north of the present village. Rob Roy, immortalised in Sir Walter Scott's novel as a Robin Hood who took from the rich to give to the poor, used his mother's surname, Campbell. The Clan MacGregor had been outlawed, and its very name banned, after a particularly infamous raid on the Colquhouns in 1602. In that episode, known as the Slaughter in the Lennox (an ancient Scottish county), the MacGregors seized 600 head of cattle, 800 sheep and 200 horses. Rob Roy's descendant, Sir John Murray, resumed the name of MacGregor by royal licence in 1822.

Ardbeg, Islay *Inner Hebrides*

The Gaelic name for this island is Ìle, said to be derived from Ìla, a Danish princess who walked there from Ireland on island stepping stones which formed in her path. She is said to have drowned while bathing, and her grave is marked by a standing stone above Knock Bay, a mile north-east. According to legend, three people tried to open her enchanted grave and went mad as a result.

The local Hill of Ìle is reputed to be a fairy dwelling, the home of the Fairy Queen herself. There, once, from a magic cup, she dispensed wisdom to women from all over the land, and latecomers who missed the draught remained stupid. Dull-witted women are said to have been 'still on the hill when wisdom was handed out'.

Ardnamurchan *Strathclyde*

In the 17th century, cattle-stealing was almost the only profession a Highland gentleman could take up without shaming himself or his family. The local expert was MacIain Ghiarr, a thorn in the side of MacLean of Duart, though later they became firm friends. Their friendship dated from the night when MacIain was walking past the chapel of Pennygown on Mull. He noticed a light, and found three witches, sticking pins into a clay image of MacLean. MacIain grabbed the image just as the witches were about to pierce its heart, gave the hags a beating, and rushed to Duart Castle. There he found MacLean racked with pains. He told him the story, and as he removed the pins, one by one, so the pains diminished, until MacLean was well again.

Badenoch *Highland*

There are many stories about how the great Caledonian forest, which once covered all of the Highlands, was eventually destroyed. Most accounts blame it on a Scandinavian king whose own forests were not nearly so impressive. He is said to have brought his foster-mother, a hideous, winged monster, to Scotland and set her to fly over the forests, flinging burning brands down upon the trees. The *muime*, as she was called, flew far above the clouds, spreading destruction everywhere. But a hunter at Badenoch put an end to her mischief, according to one version of the legend, by getting the local people to separate all the animals from their young. Such a chorus of bleating and lowing went up that the *muime* poked her head through the clouds to see what was going on. Whereupon the hunter from Badenoch shot her with a silver bullet – a sure way of putting an end to a witch.

Barra *Outer Hebrides*

Waulking, or hand-shrinking woollen cloth, was a long and laborious process, relieved by communal songs that passed on local legends and stories. The women who sang these songs as they worked preserved the tales of heroes of long ago, and many of the songs are still remembered in the island.

St Bride, or Brigid, was much revered in the Outer Islands. Local people would construct Bride's Bed out of rushes on February 1, the saint's day. The saint's spirit was then invoked into the house to watch over it for the rest of the year, by saying 'Bride, come in, your bed is ready'.

Benbecula *Outer Hebrides*

Somewhere on the shore, above high-water mark, a mermaid lies buried. Her story dates from 1830, when women gathering seaweed saw her, happily swimming in the sea. She easily evaded their attempts to catch her, but was injured when a boy threw stones at her. A few days later the tiny creature's body – 'top half like that of a child, the lower like a salmon but without scales' – was washed up. The local bailiff and sheriff was much puzzled by the phenomenon, but apparently considered it to be sufficiently human to order a special shroud and coffin to be made for the burial, though apparently the religious service was omitted.

Callanish, Lewis *Outer Hebrides*

On the Isle of Lewis, there is a prehistoric stone circle, 37 ft in diameter, with avenues of monoliths radiating from it, whose mystery and grandeur rivals Stonehenge. Inside the circle of 13 great stones is a burial chamber, and bones found under a flat slab may be those of sacrificed victims. Legends link the stones with the Druids who could turn men to stone, and the monoliths are called Fir Chreig *in Gaelic – or 'False Men'.*

THE FAIRY FLAG OF THE MACLEODS

Carinish, N. Uist *Outer Hebrides*
At the Battle of Carinish in 1601, the MacDonalds of South Uist drove a marauding band of MacLeods from Trinity Temple (below) – the deeply scarred skull of a slaughtered MacLeod was kept there for years afterwards. The ferocity of the battle is still remembered in the name of a nearby ditch – The Ditch of Blood.

Cononbridge *Highland*
A fearsome water horse once made its lair in the River Conon, and the otters which sported on the river banks had supernatural powers. Anyone who caught a King Otter, which was lighter in colour and bigger than normal otters, was granted a wish if he gave it back its freedom. On the other hand, he would achieve immunity to bullets or sharp steel if he killed it and wore its pelt. By licking the liver of a freshly killed black otter, a man could acquire the power to heal burns with his tongue.

Corryvreckan *Strathclyde*
Between the islands of Jura and Scarba lies the treacherous whirlpool called Corryvreckan – Breccan's Cauldron. According to legend, a man named Breccan died here with many others some 1400 years ago, when his entire fleet of 50 ships was sucked beneath the swirling water. Later, when his kinsman St Columba sailed past the spot, one of Breccan's ribs rose from the whirlpool to greet him.

On Jura itself, a huntsman called Fair-haired Murdo of the Deer spent his life hunting on Beinn-an-Oir. One day, when he was very old, Murdo was taking aim at a stag when it turned into a fairy who mocked his white hair. Murdo, a good Christian, replied that God could easily make him young again – which He instantly did. What happened to the fairy, the story does not say.

Cromarty *Highland*
Sometime around 1740, a Cromarty ship-owner named John Reid fell in love with Helen Stuart, but she refused to marry him. Walking sadly along the shore one morning, John was aroused from his reverie by sweet singing, and moments later saw a beautiful, silver-tailed mermaid sitting outside the Dropping Cave. He crept up behind her and after a violent struggle, pinned her against the cliff. To win back her freedom, the mermaid granted him three wishes – that neither he nor any of his friends would drown, that Helen Stuart would change her mind, and a third which he never revealed. The first two, at least, came true.

When the Norse King Harald Hardrada set out to conquer England in 1066, he was armed with a terrible weapon – the magic flag Land-Ravager, which guaranteed victory to whoever possessed it. But at Stamford Bridge the magic ran out. Harald's army was routed by the English King Harold, and he himself died on the battlefield, pierced through the throat by an English arrow. And Land-Ravager vanished – or did it?

The MacLeods of Dunvegan on the Isle of Skye trace their ancestry back to King Harald, and their most treasured heirloom is a tattered silk banner called Bratach Sith – the Fairy Flag. Could this be Land-Ravager?

There are many accounts of how the Fairy Flag came to Dunvegan Castle. The legend that a MacLeod chief crusading in the Holy Land received it as a gift from a water-sprite, or won it in battle from a she-devil, may not be quite as fanciful as it sounds, for an expert who recently examined the flag suggested that it came from Syria or Rhodes, and that it was probably once a holy relic, perhaps a saint's shirt.

Another story claims that the fairy wife of a 14th century chief gave her husband the flag as a parting gift when she returned to fairyland after 20 years of marriage. The parting place, near Dunvegan, is known still as Fairy Bridge.

'The Dunvegan Lullaby', which is still sometimes sung on Skye, is also connected with the Fairy Flag. In the 15th century, when the wife of the chieftain Iain Borb (Surly John) gave birth to a child, a fairy came to the castle and searched for the infant-heir. She took him on her knee and sang him the lullaby, then wrapped him in the Fairy Flag, put him back in his cradle and left. His nurse, who had been spellbound while the fairy was in the room, remembered the words and melody. And for ever afterwards, no woman was ever appointed nurse to a MacLeod heir unless she knew the fairy's song.

THE FAIRY BRIDGE *When the fairy wife of the fourth chief was recalled to fairyland in the 14th century, it was here, near Dunvegan, that she left him, after giving him the Fairy Flag*

DUNVEGAN CASTLE *The MacLeod chiefs have ruled their clan from here since the 13th century, and for most, if not all, of that time, the clan has been protected by the Fairy Flag*

Unfurling the flag

There is a tradition that if the Mac-Leods are in desperate peril, they can become invincible by unfurling the Fairy Flag in battle. But this magic will only work three times, and the clan have already used it twice. The first occasion was at Glendale in 1490, when they were fighting for their lives against the MacDonalds. They unfurled the flag, and the tide of battle turned. Soon the battlefield was piled with dead MacDonalds.

The second victory was at Waternish in 1520. Again, the enemy were the MacDonalds, this time of the Clanranald branch, and the MacLeods were hopelessly outnumbered. But as soon as the flag was unfurled, the MacDonalds were bewildered by the sight of a vast army marching down on them.

It is likely that the MacLeods often carried the flag into battle without unfurling it; and during the Second World War, many young clansmen carried its photograph as a lucky charm. When Dunvegan Castle was seriously damaged by fire in 1938, many people were convinced that the Fairy Flag had prevented the fire from destroying the castle completely.

FAIRY FLAG *The most precious treasure of the MacLeods – Bratach Sìth, or the Fairy Flag – is now kept in the drawing-room of Dunvegan Castle. The faded brown silk, carefully darned in red, probably came from Syria or Rhodes*

CHAMPIONS OF THE FLAG *By tradition, 12 champion swordsmen were chosen to defend the Fairy Flag when it was taken into battle*

Durness *Highland*

Near Durness on an inlet of the sea is Smoo Cave, which has three chambers, one leading into the next. It was here that the first Lord Reay, also known as Donald, the Wizard of Reay, had a narrow escape from the Devil. Lord Reay, like many another 17th-century nobleman, was a well-travelled man; he had served in the Swedish army, and while visiting Italy met the Devil, who invited him to study the Black Art. At the end of term it was the Devil's practice to claim the last pupil out of the door as his own. Donald got left behind, but as the Devil pounced he pointed at his shadow and shouted 'De'il tak' the hindmost'. Satan grabbed the shadow and Donald was free to return to Sutherland, where it was soon noticed that he never cast a shadow, even in the brightest sunlight.

Donald was exploring Smoo Cave one night when his dog, which had run ahead, came back yelping and hairless. Donald guessed that his old professor was awaiting him in the depths of the cave. Fortunately a cock crowed and the Devil and three witches who were with him realised that their time was up. They blew holes in the cavern roof and all four of them flew away, to Lord Reay's great relief. This is said to be the origin of the holes through which the Smoo Burn enters the cave. The landward chamber is still accessible on foot.

A similar tale is told of Alexander Skene (1680–1724), the Wizard Laird of Skene, Grampian.

VALLEY OF DEATH

The grim majesty of Glen Coe is a fitting backdrop to tragedy. The massacre of February, 1692, when 38 MacDonalds were murdered by their guests, a company of Campbell militia, has given birth to some enduring

MOUND OF THE DEAD

Hallowe'en is derived from the ancient festival of Samain, which on October 31 marks the eve of the Celtic new year. Samain was associated with burial mounds which were thought to be entrances to the other world. One of these was the Bronze Age barrow at Fortingall at the head of Glen Lyon in Tayside. A bonfire was built on the mound, known as Càrn nam Marbh, the Mound of the Dead, because it was believed to contain the bodies of plague victims. Great quantities of whin (furze or gorse) were gathered from the hillside and heaped on the mound.

When it was blazing, the whole community held hands and danced round it while young boys took burning faggots and ran through the fields with them. After the boys had held a leaping competition over the dying embers of the fire, the youngsters went home and ducked for apples while their elders went dancing. Fortingall celebrated Hallowe'en on an unusual date – November 11. The practice was stopped in 1924 by a keeper who said that stripping the cover from the hill was interfering with the game that nested there

legends. To this day the nine of diamonds is known as the Curse of Scotland because the pips on the card bear some resemblance to the arms of the Master of Stair who, next to William III, bore the greatest responsibility for the slaughter. There are also tales of fairy pipers leading Campbell troops astray in the mountains on their way back to Fort William, and of one soldier who, sickened by the order to kill a woman and her child hiding in the snow, slew a wolf and showed his bloodstained sword to his officer as proof of his obedience

---

Gaick Forest *Highland*
A wild son of the Comyns, the family who became lords of Badenoch in the 13th century and lost their estates in 1313, met a mysterious end in Gaick Forest, east of Dalwhinnie. The story goes that he threatened to force his farm girls to strip naked and then to shear his sheep, but only his horse arrived at the farm, with one of its master's legs dangling from a stirrup. His mangled body was found later, with eagles feeding upon it. It was said that the eagles were the vengeful mothers of the girls who were to have been so shamefully treated.

The Forester of the Fairy Corrie, a MacLeod who served with the Earl of Argyll's troops in 1644, had a *leannan sith*, a fairy mistress who followed him everywhere in the shape of a white hind. Its presence irritated his officers and the earl ordered the forester to kill it. He said he would obey, though it meant his own death. He fired and fell dead; as the shot hit his fairy mistress, she gave a shriek and vanished for ever from human sight.

Glenelg *Highland*
Fionn, the 3rd-century Celtic hero, hunted in this district, and his mistress gave birth to the warrior-bard Ossian in Arisaig. Fionn's fairy mistress had been bewitched into believing she was a hind and instinctively the young mother licked her baby's brow. Hair like a fawn's grew on that spot, so he was called Oisein (Ossian) or Fawn.

In Glenelg, near Scalasaig farm, is a mound associated with serpent cults. Snakes were sacred to the Celtic goddess Bride (later called St Brigid) and on the saint's day, February 1, the 'serpent queen' is supposed to emerge from the mound.

John MacInnes's Loch is named after a crofter said to have been drowned there by a supernatural water horse at the end of the 19th century.

FABULOUS CREATURES

Monsters and supernatural beings in Gaelic tradition are often the last echoes of once-mighty deities. Fearsome women such as the Hag of Ben Bhreac who drove her herds of deer near Ben Nevis, and the *cailleach uisge*, or water hag, are probably descended from pagan goddesses. Lochs and rivers hold many water beasts, close kin of the Loch Ness monster. Water horses and water bulls entice unwary travellers, and waterfalls are inhabited by the *uruisg*, an unpleasant creature with shaggy hair and an uncertain temper.

The *fàchan* of Glen Etive, Strathclyde, has 'one hand out of his chest, one leg out of his haunch, and one eye out of his face'. This creature may represent an imperfect memory of the Celtic seers who, when casting spells, apparently used to stand on one leg with one eye closed and one arm extended.

ONE-LEGGED MONSTER *The ugly* fàchan *may be a far-off memory of the ancient Celtic soothsayers*

Howmore, S. Uist *Outer Hebrides*
Ormaclett Castle, on South Uist, is now a ruin. Once it was the most beautiful of houses, built of French stone by French masons, to the order of MacDonald of Clanranald, to please his wife. But this indulgence could not be paid for. He finally escaped his creditors by inviting them to dinner. Eight armed clansmen sat down with them, and each man was given a dagger with which to slash at a whole roast ox. Happy to escape from this barbaric scene, the nervous creditors hurriedly departed, and never bothered Clanranald again.

Glenmore Forest *Highland*
Lamh Dhearg – Red Hand – was once a gigantic, bloody-handed ghost with drawn sword who challenged passers-by to mortal combat. His spectre still haunts the forest, but he has become a protector of wild life who warns visitors not to hurt the deer.

THE GUARDIAN STONES

In the winding valley of Glen Lyon, Tayside, at the turn into Glen Cailliche, there is a tiny stone house perched above a stream. At the door of the house, from May to November, stand three strange stones, known as the Bodach, the Old Man; the Cailleach, or Hag; and the smaller Nighean, the daughter. Throughout the winter months, the stones are kept in the Tigh na Cailliche, or Hag's House, as the rocky shrine is called. Each year, before taking his sheep back down into the glen to winter pasture, the local shepherd repairs the cracks in the walls of the house with moss, and roofs it over with turf and stones, so that the time-worn 'family' of stones will

remain dry and sheltered until the spring. Then, they are brought out into the sunshine, and the shrine is swept clean. The three stones are said to guarantee good pasturage and fine weather, as they have done ever since a man and his wife, heavy with child, sought shelter in a bothy near the river. There, the woman gave birth to a daughter, and all three vowed to stay there for ever and protect the glen that had given them hospitality. The stones are said to commemorate the three, though they are probably part of some ancient cult worship and are images of three local deities. Whatever the reason they are still treated with honour and respect

WELL OF THE HEADS

This curious monument to seven slain clansmen stands over a spring near Invergarry on Loch Oich side in Highland. In 1663, Alasdair MacDonald made a bid for the chieftainship of the Keppoch MacDonalds, and slaughtered two nephews who stood in his way. Two years later, Alasdair and six accomplices were arrested by a posse from Inverness and were promptly beheaded. To prove that justice had been done, the heads were placed in a basket to be carried back to Inverness, but such horrible sounds of grinding jaws and gnashing teeth emerged from within that the heads were dipped in the spring to cool off. The place has been known as Tobar nan Ceann, the Well of the Heads, ever since

Inverness *Highland*

The town has been the capital of the Highlands ever since the Pictish King Brude built his forts on the surrounding heights. St Columba performed many of his miracles there, and even the 12th-century wizard Michael Scot contributed to the citizens' welfare by forcing demons to build them a bridge. But it is to the town's cemetery, Tom-na-hurich, the hill of the yews, that the strangest legends cling. There, the Gaelic adventurer-king, Fionn, escaped from an Irish king's enchantments by training his dog Bran to walk two of every species of animal round the hill (shepherding a pair of whales round the circuit was a particular achievement). There, too, the 13th-century seer Thomas the Rhymer rests together with his men and his white horses, ready to rise again and save Scotland in her hour of need. And there the Fairy Queen held her court, and does still, according to some accounts. She was not the best of employers. Having paid two wandering fiddlers to entertain her guests for an evening, she kept them for 200 years, though they imagined they had been playing for only one night. When they were taken back to the hillside, they crumbled into dust. By eating the fairy food and drinking the fairy wine, they had fallen into her power.

Iona *Inner Hebrides*

All the princes of the north-west wanted to be buried on this sacred island, partly because its blessed earth was thought to expunge all sin, and partly because of the ancient legend that when the second Great Flood came, only Iona would rise above the waves. Consequently, Reilig Odhráin, the graveyard named after Oran, a brother of St Columba, is said to contain the royal bones of 48 Scottish kings, from Kenneth MacAlpin, who united Scots and Picts, to Macbeth, the 11th-century usurper who inspired Shakespeare's play.

Stones and crosses have a large part in the island's lore. There were the sacred Black Stones on which Highland chiefs took solemn oaths, and a Druid Stone which fishermen believed helped them to navigate the treacherous island waters. Two fine crosses survived the Reformation – the 10th-century St Martin's Cross, near the abbey, and Maclean's Cross, hewn some centuries earlier, and said to be the earliest Christian relic in Britain.

IONA'S MONUMENTS

This 10th-century cross, 14 ft high, is one of the last on the island; most of the others were destroyed at the Reformation. Gravestones, like those on the right, with their worn effigies mark the last resting places of 48 Scottish, four Irish and eight Norwegian kings, as well as numerous chiefs

441

Killiecrankie *Tayside*
In this wild gorge, in the moment of victory, died 'Bonnie Dundee' (John Graham of Claverhouse, Viscount Dundee), leading his Highlanders against the forces of William III in 1689. 'The Soldier's Leap' (below) is pointed out as the escape route of one government trooper. Even with the encouragement of a Highland broadsword, the jump is a formidable one – down and across the boiling rapids and rocks.

Killin *Tayside*
A long time ago in Stratherrick there lived a *seoltaiche*, a cunning man, who visited each of the nine finest glens in Scotland in turn and stole their substance – their fertility – to spread on the earth of his own farm. Killin was the last glen on his list, and when he reached it he carried the substance of the other eight bound up in a willow wand over his shoulder. But in Killin there was a man who had some knowledge of the Black Art, and he took a charmed iron knife and cut the wand. The good of nine valleys spilt over Killin, and that, so they say, is why the glen is the most fertile in Scotland.

Kingussie *Highland*
In the 14th century, Ruthven Castle was the home of Robert II's son Alexander, a man whose ruthlessness rapidly earned him the title of the 'Wolf of Badenoch'. Despite the scandalised comments of the Church, he refused to abandon his mistress and return to his wife. As a punishment, he was excommunicated, to which the Wolf's reply was to burn Elgin Cathedral to the ground. He did penance, but though he was received back into the Church, his piety was short-lived.

Alexander and his band of marauders became the terror of the district, pillaging by day and dabbling in witchcraft by night. Then, one stormy evening, watching villagers saw a sinister figure dressed in black ride into the castle. Creeping nearer, they peered through a window and there saw the stranger engrossed in a game of chess with the Wolf of Badenoch. The stranger moved a piece and laughed. 'Check!' he cried, and at once the scene was blotted out by a wall of fire. The villagers fled, and when they returned the next morning, they found the bodies of Alexander and his followers lying among the blackened ruins of the castle. Yet to this day, it is said, the Devil can still sometimes be seen there, endlessly playing chess for the soul of the Wolf of Badenoch.

Lochaber *Highland*
A smith once captured a *glaistig* – an evil spirit, half woman and half goat – and refused to release her unless she gave him a herd of cattle. The cattle were produced, and the smith demanded a house that no fairy or enemy could enter. The *glaistig* called upon every goblin in the district, and the house was built in a night. The work completed, she stuck out her hand in farewell, but the smith seared it with a red-hot iron, and the spirit fled to the Hill of Finisgeig. There she bled to death, and the vegetation is stained red to this day.

'THE GOODWIFE OF LAGGAN'

About 300 years ago there was a hunter in Badenoch who feared neither man nor demon. No witch could prevail against his courage and honesty, and he devoted his life to rooting out the creatures of Satan that plagued the district. One evening, while he was out hunting with his dogs, a terrible storm arose, and the hunter was forced to take shelter in a herdsman's hut. He had lit a fire when he heard scratching at the door. Outside was a cat, its fur bedraggled by the rain as it cowered against the wall for shelter. The kindly hunter called off his frenzied dogs and stood aside to admit the unfortunate animal. Then it spoke to him. It told him it was a witch, and it had come to the hunter to beg for mercy, and for help in mending its wicked ways. The hunter believed it, and bade it come in and warm itself. But the cat hesitated: 'First tie your dogs to that beam,' it said. 'And here is a long grey hair to tie them with.' The hunter now becoming suspicious of the witch, pretended to do as he was told, but he fastened only one end round the beam, leaving the hounds free.

The magic hair
The cat settled by the fire, and at once started to grow bigger. It grew to the size of a calf, then in a twinkling, a woman stood before the hunter. To his horror, he recognised her; she was a neighbour from his village in Inverness, a woman so virtuous that she was known as the Goodwife of Laggan.

'Hunter of the Hills,' she hissed, 'your hour has come. I drowned our greatest persecutor in Raasay this morning, and now it is your turn.' And with fingers hooked, she flew at the hunter's throat. The hounds leapt at her, tearing her breast and side. 'Fasten! Fasten!' shrieked the witch, and the magic hair tightened so hard on the beam that it cracked, but the dogs were free and they tore her flesh to tatters. Unable to beat them off, the witch changed into a raven and flew out of the door.

When he reached home, the hunter found his wife and neighbours gathered anxiously at the bedside of the Goodwife of Laggan. They told him how she had gone out to gather peat, and had returned gravely ill. In answer, the hunter stripped off the bedclothes and revealed the terrible wounds on the woman's body. He recounted what had happened, and the people seized the witch and hanged her from the nearest tree.

The black horseman
That night, two travellers on the road to Badenoch were terrified by the bloody apparition of a woman rushing past them with two coal-black dogs in pursuit. Shortly after, a dark rider appeared on a black horse. The men told him what they had seen, and the rider asked: 'Would the dogs have caught her before she reached Dalarossie churchyard?' The men thought it very likely, and the horseman laughed and rode on. A few minutes later, the travellers heard shrieking behind them and turned to see the black horseman gallop by at an incredible speed. Across his saddle was slung the woman and, ever and again, the black hounds leapt up and tore at her. When the men reached home, the village agreed they had seen the spirit of the Goodwife of Laggan, trying to reach the sanctuary of the churchyard. But who the dark man was that prevented her, they did not dare begin to guess.

Loch Ashie *Highland*

During the First World War, a traveller on the moors near the loch was startled to see a large number of battling men. Some of the combatants were mounted while others fought on foot, but though they hacked desperately at one another they fought in silence. Suddenly they vanished, and the traveller realised that the armies were not of this world. The phantom soldiers have been reported on several occasions, usually at dawn on May Day. There is a local tradition that the Irish hero Fionn mac Cumhaill once fought a battle hereabouts.

Loch Awe *Strathclyde*

About 1898, the driver of the mail coach was taking his team through the woods near the loch, when his girl-friend suddenly appeared on the box beside him, seized his whip and beat him so severely that he had to turn back. When he saw the girl again, he was extremely angry with her until she told him she had not been on the road at all. But she had been very worried about him at the time of the incident for she knew he was about to stop at a house where a fatal fever had broken out. Anxiety divorced her spirit from her body to save her lover.

SAVED BY A HAIR *Free of the magic hair, the hounds leap forward to save their master from the murderous Goodwife of Laggan*

Loch Carron *Highland*

Belief in the supernatural was once very strong in Applecross, a remote village whose only land access is the Bealach nam Bó – Pass of the Cattle – the highest road in Britain. Once, it is said, when a little boy was wasting away after having had 'the evil eye' put on him, his father went to a wise woman living at the head of Loch Carron, taking a piece of the child's clothing. She put a charm on it, and told him his son would be alive and well when he got home. So he was; but the wise woman became desperately ill, and lay near death for several days. This, she said, always happened when she fought the evil eye; it was as if all the strength went out of her to cure another.

Loch Duich *Highland*

Anyone who has seen seals playing in the sea-lochs can imagine how the Celtic legends of seal-people arose – creatures able to slough their skins at will, and assume the likeness of humans. If a mortal could steal the skin during the period of transformation, he became the master of its true owner – as in the story of three brothers who went fishing in Loch Duich one night, and saw the seals come ashore, throw off their furs, and dance in the moonlight on the sands.

The brothers were particularly enchanted by three beautiful seal-maidens and stole their skins, so that when the other seal-people returned to the water, they were forced to abandon the girls. The brothers claimed the seal-maidens for wives, but the youngest, moved by the distress of the girl he had chosen, returned her seal-skin and allowed her to slip gratefully away.

Nine nights later, the seals returned. The other brothers locked their wives away, for fear that the seal-men would try to recapture them. But the youngest brother merely looked on in yearning for his lost love. Then her seal-father appeared, and told the young man that his daughter was equally in love and, as a reward for the boy's kindness, he would allow her to return to him every ninth night.

The youngest brother was overjoyed, but there was little happiness for the other two. One seal-wife returned to the water when her children found her skin; warned by this, the eldest brother burnt the skin of his wife, but a terrible conflagration followed, and his seal-bride perished in the flames.

Loch Earn *Tayside*

On the hill called Dunfillan, above the town of Comrie, is a natural rock seat called St Fillan's Chair, from which the saint is said to have blessed the neighbourhood. Local people believed that anyone suffering from rheumatism of the spine could be cured, provided they were prepared to climb up to the rock and sit on it, and then be hauled down the hillside by the ankles. A quarter of a mile away is St Fillan's Spring, to which sick people would make pilgrimage every August in the hope of being cured of their ailments. According to tradition, the well moved itself there from the top of Dunfillan Hill.

Loch Fyne *Strathclyde*

The woods about the Claonaig stream, south of Skipness, were long believed to be sacred to the fairies. Brave hunters have fled before the silent advance of troops of horsemen dressed in green, for fear they should be spirited away. Another story, long current in the district, tells how a woman was captured by the fairies and held prisoner for seven years. Her husband rescued her at last by lying in wait for the fairy host and throwing his wife's wedding dress over her head as she passed by. Other supernatural hazards in the area include a holly tree

A CURE FOR RHEUMATISM

From this rocky 'chair' overlooking Loch Earn, Tayside, the 6th-century St Fillan used to bless his flock. To this day, people with rheumatism of the back are said to benefit by sitting for a while in the holy man's seat

THE GREEN LADY OF SKIPNESS CASTLE

The ghostly spectre of a gruagach – a small, long-haired spirit, known as the Green Lady – is said to have helped inhabitants of this castle near Loch Fyne by defending them against danger and by bewitching their enemies

that dances in the road to prevent people from returning home, and an invisible horse, whose hoofbeats are a warning of impending death.

Loch Maree *Highland*

The loch, and its island Eilean Maree, are supposedly named after the Irish saint Maelrubha, who founded a religious house at Applecross. From the scandalised accounts of the 17th and 18th-century churchmen, it would appear that the saint's name must have long ago become confused with that of a Celtic god Mourie. Certainly, the rites which took place on the island seemed to long predate Christianity. Bulls were sacrificed, and men and women worshipped at a sacred well and tree, and poured libations of milk upon the ground. A visitor who witnessed the rites in 1772 told how a lunatic was forced to kneel before a weatherworn altar and then to drink water from the well before being dipped three times in the loch. The process was repeated each day for several weeks in the hope of curing him. Similar rites were recorded in 1836 and 1852, when local people, who insisted that cures were most likely to be effective on St Maelrubha's Day (August 25), still constantly referred to the saint as 'God Mourie'. Though such rites have not been carried out for a century or more, the island in the loch is still venerated.

RITUAL ON MAREE'S ISLAND

The strange rites practised on this island in the loch were performed in the name of St Maelrubha, but their origins went back to pagan Celtic rituals of long ago

LEGENDS OF LOCH NESS

'Nessie', the beast who has so captured the public imagination, is not the loch's only legend.

Long ago, it is said, there was a pleasant and fertile glen and in it was a magic well which gave plentiful water as long as those who drew it remembered to replace its cover. One day, a mother, alarmed by her baby's cry, threw the cover aside as she ran to the child's aid; while she was away the well waters overflowed, and filled the entire valley. The people ran to the hills for safety, crying 'Tha loch nis ann!' ('There is a lake there now!'), and that is how the waters of Loch Ness got their name.

St Columba has many associations with the loch and the country around. He once forced Broichan, foster-father of the Pictish King Brude, to hand over a maiden he had seized, first by 'smiting him with an angel' and then by curing him with a white stone from the River Ness. When the man tried to retaliate by raising contrary winds, the saint and his disciples confounded him by sailing a straight course against the wind, all the way up the loch.

Columba, too, holds the distinction of having had the first recorded brush with the monster. This occurred when he told one of his monks to swim across the River Ness to fetch a boat. Halfway across, the monster appeared, and rushed on the swimmer with a roar. But Columba cried: 'Go no further, nor touch the man! Go back!' The monster fled in fear, and in the 14 centuries that have passed since that day, it has never harmed anyone. Just the same, it has never lost its news value. Some enthusiasts say 'it' is a family of gigantic slugs, others that it may be a creature left over from a past age. But in spite of zoologists' protests that such forms of life are unlikely, hordes of visitors arrive annually hoping for a glimpse of the mysterious inhabitant of Loch Ness.

THE HIGHLAND CLANS

Loch Ranza, Arran *Strathclyde*

A fairy story tells how a midwife harvesting oats near the head of the loch saved a big yellow frog from being killed by a neighbour. Next day a boy on a grey horse told the woman that the frog was the Queen of the Fairies, who had summoned her to the Fairy Mound. The midwife mounted behind the boy, who said he was a human being under a spell, and told her how to protect herself from the supernatural creatures she would meet. Later, she delivered the Fairy Queen of a child.

Loch Resort, Lewis *Outer Hebrides*

Long ago a herdsman on the loch shore killed a survivor from a shipwreck for the bundle he was carrying. It contained a heap of menacing little carved images. Convinced that they were the sailor's gods, the frightened killer buried them. Years later he confessed when about to be hanged for another murder, but his prudent listeners decided to let sleeping gods lie. It was not until 1831 that a crofter rediscovered them. When sent for sale, they were recognised as ancient chessmen.

THE LEWIS HOARD

A queen and king from the 78 chessmen found on Lewis. Carved from ivory, probably by 12th-century Norsemen, they are now in the British Museum and in Edinburgh

The clan system was the basis of Highland life. The Gaelic word *clann* means children; its members claimed kinship from a common ancestor whose name they bore, and however poor, all clansmen considered themselves of nobler birth than any Southerner.

By the 17th century, the chief was a bewildering mixture of polish and savagery; a man often educated in Paris or Rome who spoke several languages and was a good judge of claret. He would hang a tribesman who stole from him, but considered the theft of his neighbour's cattle a gentlemanly pursuit. He sold his people for service in the plantations of the Americas, and plunged his dirk into anyone who doubted his honour. He held his territory by consent of the clan whose members were his tenants; they, in return, gave goods and military service. A man driven out of his clan lost his very identity, and loyalty to the chief was absolute. At one time, orders from a king were ignored if they went against the chief's wishes. For centuries the sovereign had no authority in the Highlands: safe in their mountain fastnesses, the clans escaped retribution. This untamed independence led to clan feuds whose consequences were often tragic.

The story is one of jealousies, atrocities and endless raiding of goods, cattle and women. Massacres were commonplace, and the one which took place at Glencoe in 1692, when the Campbells slew their hosts, the MacDonalds, was regarded with horror only because it breached the rigid laws of Highland hospitality.

The call of the fiery cross

Each chief had his poet or bard, to praise him in life and lament him after death. Warriors were summoned to the clan rallying-ground by the fiery cross, when messengers carrying a pole with a cross of fire-blackened wood attached ran through the territory shouting the clan war cry. Clans were known by badges worn in their bonnets; the MacDonalds wore heather, the Grants fir, and the MacIntoshes holly. Omens were carefully watched when fighters left on a foray: it was good to meet an armed man, bad to meet a barefooted woman.

The clan system was already dying by the 18th century. New political and economic ideas were penetrating the glens along General Wade's military roads. The curious thing was that a tribal system akin to that of the Bedouin or Red Indians had survived so long in western Europe. The clans lived by the sword and perished by the sword; the last feeble embers of the fiery crosses flickered out on the field of Culloden in 1746.

Ironically the glens, some of which had been emptied of people, were refilled with myths. To an 18th-century Englishman or Lowland Scot, the Highlander was a barbarian who deserved no mercy, and yet once his body lay in the heather they endowed him with all the heroic virtues. Antiquarians and writers of romance set to work. Tailors trimmed and styled the clansmen's motley garb into a self-conscious national dress; his tartans were codified, registered and marketed. In all this the clans have gained the final victory, that over the imagination. People still wear the tartan of their clan, be it on a tie or a golf skirt, to proclaim their pride in a vanished world.

Lynchat *Highland*

Two miles north-east of Kingussie is the Great Cave of Lynchat, or Raitts. It is a horseshoe-shaped stone structure, 70 ft long and dug out of the brow of a hill. Legend says that giants built it in a single night: it is now thought to be a Pictish dwelling of the 5th century. A hut used to stand over the entrance, concealing it. Ten MacNivens once hid in the cave from the Macphersons, but were found and killed when a spy saw the woman who lived in the hut putting batches of scones into a cupboard which was empty whenever she opened it.

THE CAVE OF RAITTS

The cavern was built in a night. Giantesses dug it and carried the soil down to the River Spey in their aprons while giants quarried the stones

SUMMONED BY THE FIERY CROSS *Clansmen charged into battle waving broadswords and inspired by the wild music of the pipes*

The Minch *Outer Hebrides*

The Shiant or 'Charmed' Isles which lie in the Minch, the channel dividing the Outer Hebrides from the mainland, are surrounded by turbulent seas churned by storm kelpies known as the Blue Men of the Minch. Their glossy blue figures and grey, bearded faces bob in the waves between the Shiant Isles and Lewis, a tideway called in Gaelic Sruth nam Fear Gorma, stream of the blue men. There they attack any vessel whose skipper cannot answer their riddles. Afraid of being lured to their doom in the Blue Men's undersea caves, the Hebridean fishermen avoided the Stream. Like so many myths, this may be founded on fact. The Norse pirates who plagued the Scottish isles used slaves taken from Moorish ships; these were Berbers who wore blue garments and veils, just as their descendants, the Touaregs of North Africa, do today.

North Ballachulish *Highland*

Sir Ewen Cameron of Lochiel (1629–1719) was a famous character in Highland lore. On the road to the ferry at North Ballachulish he was overtaken by a *cailleach*, or hag, called Gormul, a well-known witch. He hurried on to the boat to escape her and she called after him: 'My blessings on you, Ewen.' He replied: 'Your blessings be on yonder grey stone, hag.' Instantly the stone split in two. It can still be seen on the north side of Loch Leven. The witches of the 17th century may have been a folk memory of ancient goddesses: an oak figure of a *cailleach* was found beneath the peat near the Ballachulish ferry, together with the remains of a wickerwork shrine. The figure, 5 ft tall, is thought to be pre-Roman. The eyes are of inlaid quartz pebbles, believed to have magical powers. The statue is in Scotland's National Museum of Antiquities in Edinburgh.

447

Rannoch Moor *Tayside*
*These stones mark the site of an old well on the slopes of
Schiehallion (3547 ft), the 'Fairy Hill of the Caledonians', at the eastern end of Rannoch Moor. The well was
once believed to be inhabited by fairies who were able to
grant wishes or cure ills. It was ceremoniously visited by
local inhabitants on May Day, when girls dressed in
white brought garlands as offerings to the fairies – a ritual
based on ancient well-worship.*

Rosehall *Highland*
Early this century a nurse in the village was called to
the bedside of a girl, apparently dying in childbirth.
Though the nurse despaired of her charge's life, the
girl's mother did not. She poured a basin of water
and placed in it some gold and silver trinkets. She
then forced her daughter to drink three mouthfuls of
the water, each one of which was blessed in the
name of the Trinity. According to the nurse there
was an easy delivery soon afterwards. The girl
recovered and both she and the baby flourished.

Fairies are said to live in the neighbouring burn of
Invernauld and a nearby hill. A story tells of a local
man who once heard music coming from a cave he
discovered on the hill. He entered the cave to
investigate and was not seen again by mortal eyes
until a year later, when he was found still inside the
cave dancing merrily to the music of fairy pipers.
The missing man refused to believe that he had
stayed such a long time in the fairy cave until he
returned home and found his baby was a year older.

Scone *Tayside*
The fabled Stone of Scone on which the Scottish
kings were crowned was brought to Scone by
Kenneth MacAlpin, who defeated the Picts there in
AD 843 and united Scotland under his rule. Traditionally, the 26 in. long block of red sandstone is
said to have come to Scotland from Ireland, where
it was the coronation stone of ancient Irish kings.
They called it Lia Fail, or the Stone of Destiny, and
it was reputed to 'groan aloud as with thunder'
if sat on by anyone other than the heir to the throne.

Legend identifies the celebrated stone with
Jacob's pillow (Genesis xxviii, v. 11). According to
tradition, it was later given to a prehistoric Celtic
king who married the daughter of an Egyptian
pharaoh. It was said to have been brought to
Scotland by Joseph of Arimathea. Another story
says that St Columba rested his head on the stone as
he lay dying in the monastery church on Iona.

Edward I, attempting to unite the Scottish and
English crowns, removed the stone to Westminster
Abbey (where it is still) in 1296. An old prophecy

REFUGE FOR HEROES AND BRIGANDS

*Rannoch Moor, Tayside, a sombre 20 square miles of
peat bog, ancient forest and water, all surrounded by dark
mountains, is associated with tales of legendary heroes,
bandits and supernatural beings. William Wallace and
Robert the Bruce in turn used it as a base to wage guerrilla*

was fulfilled in 1603, when James VI of Scotland
became James I of England:

> 'If fates go right, where'er this stone is found,
> The Scots shall monarchs of that realm be
>   crowned.'

Sleat, Skye *Inner Hebrides*
South of the wild Cuillin Hills, the district of Sleat
forms a prosperous region of woodland and pasture.
This is the land of the MacDonalds. Here in 1746,
when the fugitive Prince Charles Stuart came 'over
the sea to Skye', Flora MacDonald led him to
shelter at the House of Mugstot, which still stands at
Kilbride, near Torrin.

Memories of Skye's ancient Viking rulers still
exist. Beneath a cairn on Beinn na Caillich in the
Red Hills lie the remains and all the treasure of a
13th-century Norwegian princess, who said she
wanted the winds of Norway to blow over her
grave. The ruined Castle Maol by the fishing
village of Kyleakin is reputed to have been built by a
Danish princess nicknamed 'Saucy Mary', who
stretched a chain across to the mainland and let no
ship pass without paying toll.

As in other parts of Skye, the lochs and burns of
Sleat have been associated in the past with many
supernatural creatures. Nor is well-worship unknown among the inhabitants. Childless couples, it
is said, may drink the water of a well near Elgol, by
Loch Scavaig, and invoke the guardian spirit of the
well to make them fertile. At nearby Strolamas the
water of another fertility well is considered to be so
strong that a couple who invoke it correctly and
drink it will be blessed with twins.

warfare against the English; and for centuries it was a safe haven for the brigands who preyed upon travellers or stole cattle from the richer lands to the south. It was once commonly believed that fairies, ghost dogs, water horses and other strange creatures roamed the moor or dwelt beneath the black water of its lochs. Even in this century, many people passing by the hill Schiehallion reported being followed by a dog-like shadow which seemed to materialise from nowhere. A story is told also of a man who once found near a loch a horse's bridle which local experts agreed was so beautifully made that it could only have belonged to a water horse or kelpie

SETTING FOR A MURDER

The Cuillins, towering beyond Slig-achan Burn in south Skye, are reputed to be haunted by the ghost of an outlaw named MacRaing. He is also associated with an old well called Tobar a' Chinn, the well of the head, at Torrin, by Loch Slapin. The infamous outlaw is said to have robbed and then murdered a girl. When his son, shocked by his father's brutality, threatened to expose him, MacRaing killed him too and put his severed head in the well

WATER SPIRIT'S HAUNT

Loch Coruisk, surrounded by the dark rim of the Cuillin Hills in south Skye, is said to be the home of a kelpie, or dreaded water horse

449

Staffa *Inner Hebrides*

The island's name is Norse for Stave Island. It is an appropriate title, for the Vikings who went raiding up and down the coast used to build their homes with wooden tree staves, which stood upright and somewhat resembled the striking columns of volcanic basalt lining Staffa's 135 ft cliffs. Marauding Norsemen would have been wary of the place, if the legends are to be believed, for Fingal – the Fionn of Celtic legend – used the island as his base in his successful defence of the Hebrides and campaigns against the sea-raiders in the 3rd century AD. The sound of the waves in Fingal's Cave, one of the largest that riddle the cliffs, inspired the composer Mendelssohn to write his famous concert overture 'The Hebrides', after he had visited Staffa in 1829.

Staffin, Skye *Inner Hebrides*

Far-off memories of the days when the Celts were head-hunters linger on in the legends of Skye – such as in the story of the malevolent ghost Colann gun Cheann, 'The Headless Body', who used to murder people in the Trotternish area by flinging his head at them. He was banished to Arisaig, on the mainland, where he menaced travellers until a young man caught the head on his sword, and returned it only after making the ghost promise to return to Skye.

Another reminder of old habits lies in the local explanation for the Loch of the Heads at Cuidrach, Trotternish. The tale goes that a group of Mac-Donalds decapitated the MacLeods whom they had vanquished and rolled their heads down a hill into the loch. As they tumbled downhill, the heads cried out: 'Almost, almost, we almost won the day!' The hill is still known as Almost Hill.

Witches, too, are remembered. There is the story of the death of Iain Garbh, a powerful local laird who persecuted witches. On Easter Monday of 1625, he was drowned in a terrible storm – raised, they say, by the power of all the witches in Scotland.

Strath, Skye *Inner Hebrides*

Not far from the church of Cill Chriosd is a loch in which an evil spirit once lived – so deadly that anyone bathing in the waters or drinking from them would surely die. The spirit, however, was chased away by St Columba when he visited the island *c.* 570, and the waters became sweet and safe.

It seems that spirits could not leave the loch alone. Later, it became the haunt of a black water horse that appeared in the form of a handsome young man. In this guise, he seduced young maidens, then galloped off with them into the loch. But he met his match when, by mistake, he picked on a priest in long, flowing robes. The priest was safeguarded by his calling, and converted the water horse to Christianity. It has not troubled the area since.

THE OLD MAN OF STORR

Five miles north of Portree, on the island of Skye, this natural stone pillar has inspired several legends. Another column – the 'wife' – has fallen over, but once the two great rocks stood side by side. Some say they were an old couple who 'saw something awful' – or who went hunting a lost cow and encountered a band of magical giants. The couple ran away, but made the mistake of looking back and were turned to stone for ever

JOHN OF LEWIS

Almost from the day he first went to sea, black-haired John the Sailor, from Stornoway, began a career of fantastic adventure. He was cast adrift on a raft and washed up on an island inhabited by robbers. Instead of killing him, the robbers were so struck by his courage that they invited him to join them. But John fled, taking with him the thieves' gold, and their beautiful captive, a princess of Spain.

The couple wandered over the hills together and fell in love. One day, about to take shelter in an apparently deserted croft, they opened the door and found three headless men, with their heads in their hands. They were a father and his sons, who had been murdered and could not rest until someone replaced their heads. John obliged, and the figures vanished. Later, he was glad he had helped them, for having married his princess, he was once more cast adrift by the admiral of her father's fleet. He drifted helplessly until he was pulled ashore by the three apparitions. Eventually he was reunited with his wife.

Strathnaver *Highland*
The curative powers of Loch na Naire, 10 miles west of Strath Halladale, have long been famous. Crowds used to gather on its shores on the first Monday in August, between midnight and 1 a.m., when, apparently, the magical properties of the waters were at their height. The tradition may well go back to pagan times: an essential part of the 'cure' was the offering of some gift, such as a coin, to the waters. There was also the suggestion that the ancient May festival of Beltane was just as good a time to immerse oneself, as a cure for all diseases.

One 19th-century story says that the loch obtained its power from a magic charm stone, owned by an old woman. A Gordon of Strathnaver coveted the stone, and tried to take it from her. When she refused to part with it, he determined to drown her in the loch. Unable to escape, she ran from him into the waters, crying: 'May this stone do good to all created things – except a Gordon of Strathnaver.' He then stoned her to death in the water. What happened to the wicked Gordon is not recorded, but the loch is said to have held its powers ever since.

Strathpeffer *Highland*
The Devil may well be an unholy figure, but not, it seems, unhygienic. There is ample evidence in this part of the world that he is fond of a bath, and washes his clothes all the time. At least, this is how local people have accounted for the hot sulphur springs smelling of brimstone, and the iron springs too, that abound in this once-volcanic area. Wherever these waters mingle together they run black, and there, they say, the Devil is constantly washing his black clothes.

The early 17th-century Brahan Seer, Coinneach Odhar (who is sometimes dated some 100 years earlier), with his magic stone that gave him the gift of prophecy, once said that when five church spires should rise in Strathpeffer, ships would sail over the village. The inhabitants, all too aware that a slight drop in the land would allow the Cromarty Firth to come rolling over their homes, were naturally opposed to more churches, and when the fifth, St Anne's, was proposed about 60 years ago, they strongly objected. The church went up without any sudden flooding, but people went on brooding over an impending disaster until just after the First World War, when a small airship flew over the village – and the prophecy was at last fulfilled.

The seer's magic stone is now said to lie in the waters of nearby Loch Ussie. One story says that he flung it into a moorland pool, and loch waters flooded over it, to hide it for ever.

Struan *Tayside*
The chief of the Struan Robertsons is said to have owned a talisman called the Stone of the Standard. The crystal was found in a sod of turf that clung to his standard when it was raised, as he was taking his clansmen to fight with Robert the Bruce at Bannockburn in 1314. It was always believed to be an omen of victory, and to have the power of curing most illnesses. Anyone drinking water in which the head of the clan had dipped the stone three times would find relief. As late as the end of the 19th century, sick people flocked to Struan to taste the magical water in hope of a cure.

Tarbert, Harris *Outer Hebrides*
There is a Jack-the-Giant-Killer element in the story about the many huge boulders in the area. They are said to be all that remains of a giant's castle, where the ogre and his wife imprisoned a young maiden, who had to spin cloth for their huge garments out of nettle leaves. When she had finished, she would have been eaten, but for her handsome young lover. He promised to give the giantess a string of enormous pearls if she would set the girl free. After many adventures and a dangerous journey down to the Sea-King's palace, deep under the waves, the youth collected a string of wondrous pearls, and so won his sweetheart back.

Tiree *Inner Hebrides*

In the old days, the islanders were terrified of witches, who were particularly given to stealing milk. One method of combating them was to make a *ronag* – a ball of hair – on Lammas Eve (August 1) and place it in the milk pail. This, it was said, would keep milk safe and fresh. The charm had to be renewed at Lammastide the following year.

Tobermory, Mull *Inner Hebrides*

One day, a farmer was walking with his small daughter and looking at the ships in the Sound, when she asked him what he would give her if she sank all the vessels they could see. He thought she was joking, so he asked her how she would set about the task; the child bent down and looked at them backwards between her legs. At once, all the ships except one whirled around, then sank. The little girl explained that she could not sink the remaining vessel because it had a piece of rowan wood on board. Asked where she had learnt this terrible skill, she said her mother had taught her. The farmer had both of them burnt as witches.

THE GALLEON OF TOBERMORY

It is probably true that the Florencia, one of the ships of the ill-fated Spanish Armada, was blown up or sunk in Tobermory Bay in 1588, but how the tragedy occurred is the subject of many differing legends. According to one account, Viola, the King of Spain's daughter, dreamt that she loved a man who lived on the far-off island of Mull, so she commissioned a vessel and set sail. When she reached the island, she recognised MacLean of Duart as the man of her dreams, but MacLean was already *married, and his jealous wife ordered the galleon to be blown up. Only the cook survived, carried by the explosion to Strongarbh, and Viola herself was buried at Lochaline. When the news reached Spain, a Captain Forrest was sent with another ship to avenge the atrocity, but as it dropped anchor at Tobermory, MacLean's wife summoned all the 18 witches of Mull to her aid. Disguised as seagulls, they raised a terrible storm, and the ship sank, it is said, opposite Coire-na-theanchoir Bay*

Torridon *Highland*

Torridon lies at the head of Upper Loch Torridon in the wild hill country of Wester Ross. It has always had an eerie reputation, and tales of witchcraft, black and white, still abound in the area. As late as the end of the last century, a visitor recorded an extraordinary cure when a man mending harness stuck a needle through the palm of his hand. A wise woman sitting near by extracted the needle and the blood spurted out and stained the opposite wall. Unperturbed, the woman pointed the needle at the floor and recited in Gaelic:

'Be your poison within the ground,
May your pain be within the hill.
Wholeness be to the wound,
Rest be to the hurt.'

The bleeding stopped immediately, and as far as any of the awestruck spectators could see, the wound was completely healed by the wise woman's miraculous charm.

As in most places, iron was considered a powerful antidote to the supernatural, though in Torridon it was believed that if an iron implement was used while gathering shellfish, then these creatures would abandon the beach for ever. During clan feuds, it was alleged that people would plough their enemy's shellfish beaches by night in order to deprive them of an important source of food.

In the same district, the wood of the bird-cherry was considered far more powerful against evil than either rowan or elder. People used walking-sticks made of bird-cherry as a charm against becoming lost in the mountain mists. The wood was also used when tethering a cow to protect it from spells.

Vallay *Outer Hebrides*

On the island there is a pit which can never be filled in because, it is said, a witch was once buried alive in it. She had been accused of stealing milk by magic – a serious crime in a society where the cow was the most valuable of possessions. There were several ways of stealing the milk. One was for the witch to transform herself into a hare and then suck the cows dry. Another was to recite spells while 'milking' the iron chain used to hang pots over the fire. Milk could be carried away in a needle, or in seaweed wrapped around the witch. If these objects were damaged, the stolen milk would at once flow out. What method the witch of Vallay used, or how her crimes were detected, is not recorded, but the hollow pit is a reminder of her terrible punishment. The chief ordered that she should be buried up to the neck in the gateway to the cattle-fold. There she remained, as the cattle passed over her, until her head was crushed.

BIRDS OF LIFE AND DEATH

In Celtic lands, until very recently, the habits and movements of birds were watched with anxiety, for they were held to forecast the future. Different omens were attached to different birds, and much depended on the physical state of the observer. For example, it was extremely unlucky to see the cuckoo before you had had breakfast, but it was considered a good omen if you saw the bird after you had eaten.

The cock was widely regarded as a lifebird, an averter of evil. In the Outer Hebrides it was believed that if the bird was heard to crow at midnight, it was a sign of approaching news. If the cock's legs were found to be cold, then news of a death was imminent, but if they were warm, the coming news would be favourable. The bird had the power of immobilising the most vicious and restless corpse by its crowing.

Many old Highland families had particular death omens that came to them in the shape of a bird of unidentifiable species; at the moment of death, it was alleged to scream horribly. This bird was called *an t-eun bàis*. A similar bird, the *tamhusg*, appeared to people in parts of the Island of Skye. On Barra, there is still a tradition of a huge, white-speckled bird whose nightly screeching is a sure sign of approaching evil or bad luck. Not all birds are so unwelcome to man. There is, for instance, a local story in the Ross of Mull about a man who sowed his land from a sheet filled with seed oats. The sheet never emptied and a jealous neighbour who was watching this shouted: 'The face of your evil and iniquity be upon you, is your sheet never to be empty?' Whereupon a little brown bird leapt from the sheet and the supply of seed ceased.

VISITATION *An old woman on the island of Vatersay, in the Outer Hebrides, had an only son, and always said that if Death should come to claim him, she would go in his place. 'Death, Death,' she would cry, 'Do not take the only son!' The young men of the village became tired of this, and wondered what would happen if the situation ever came about. So they plucked a live hen and threw it into her house. One of the boys shouted in a hollow voice: 'Old hag, here is Death come for you!' And because all Highlanders know that Death comes in the shape of a bird, the woman cried in terror: 'Death, Death, take the only son and leave me in peace!'*

BIRD OF DAWNING *Long ago in the Highlands some fishermen watched a house on the shore and were fascinated to see that each night, as the clock struck twelve, a ball of light would appear over its roof. The light would go around the house, then a cock would crow, and the light would disappear. After a few days, the men bought the cock from the woman of the house, who was glad to part with it because it kept her awake, and waited to see what would happen next. Sure enough, on the following night, the ball of light appeared again, but this time, because there was no cock-crow to hinder it, it circled round the house twice. As dawn broke, the fishermen were astonished to see that the house had utterly vanished*

WINGED SAVIOUR *A terrifying story from Vatersay in the Outer Hebrides tells how the corpse of an old man awaiting burial suddenly revived and attacked the women of the house. They barricaded themselves in the byre, and just as the old man was breaking through the roof, a cock crowed, and the living corpse collapsed, its power broken*

453

BURGHEAD

GORDONSTOUN

FORRES

PORTGORDON

BAN

AULDEARN

ROTHES

HUNTLY
(The Horseman's Word, 4

GLENLIVET

GRAMPIAN

HIGHLAND   REGION

TOMINTOUL

CHAPEL OF
GARIOCH

DELNABO

STRATHDON

KEMNA

CORGARFF

BEN MACDUI

TARLAND   *(Wizard Laird,*

SKE

BALMORAL

MUIR

INVEREY

BRAEMAR
(The MacGregors' Race, 459)

BIRSE

BANCHO

GLEN MARK

GLEN ESK

TARFSIDE

TAYSIDE   REGION

CORTACHY

TANNADICE

KIRRIEMUIR

FORFAR

GLAMIS

INVERKEILOR

NEWTYLE

KIRKTON OF
STRATHMARTINE

ARBROATH

BROUGHTY
FERRY

DUNDEE

FIFE   REGION

WARLOCKS' COUNTRY

North-east Scotland

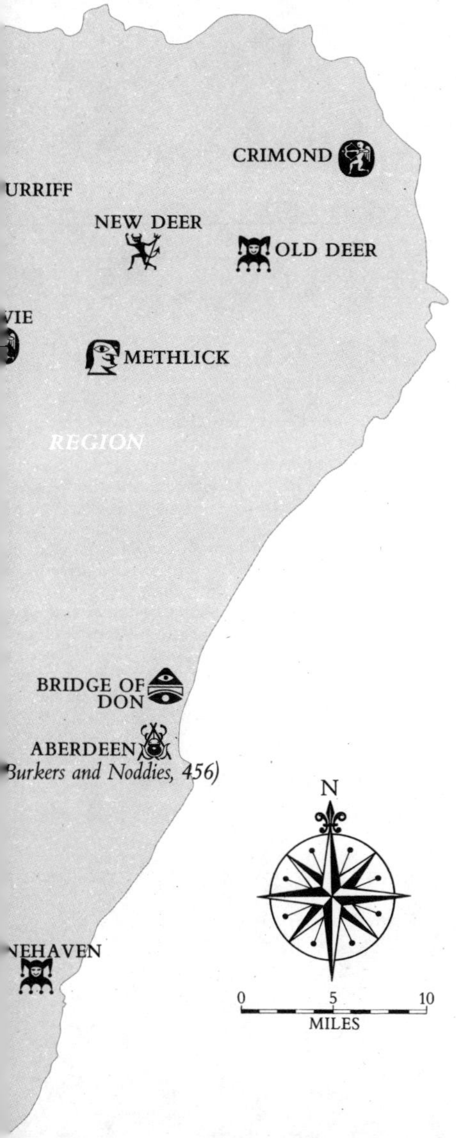

On the map:

CRIMOND

URRIFF

NEW DEER OLD DEER

VIE

METHLICK

REGION

BRIDGE OF DON

ABERDEEN
(Burkers and Noddies, 456)

NEHAVEN

N

0   5   10
MILES

The notion that the Devil was a real person, whose endless task it was to dig pitfalls for unwary sinners, probably came to Scotland in the wake of dour Calvinism that swept a major part of the country in the 16th century. The North-east was not exempt from such beliefs; yet such was the sturdy character of the people, eternally blown upon by chill winds off the sea, that they could not take the Evil One seriously. Life itself was hard, but there was nothing in this world or the next that a diligent man could not overcome.

Many of the heroes of the area were warlocks who matched their cunning with Satan's – and won. The Laird of Skene, for example, tricked 'Auld Hornie' into seizing his shadow instead of his soul. The white witch, Grigor Willox of Tomintoul, was also much admired. To many people, his magical skills were divinely inspired, as were those of the Tarland warlock who chased away the tinkers with a swarm of bees out of a cheese.

Tales of thwarting Satan tickled the imaginations of the North-east. Yet there was a darker side to the picture. In a trial of 1662, Isabel Gowdie, self-confessed 'Maiden' (Devil's assistant) of the Auld-earn witch coven, told the court how the Devil had re-baptised her with her own blood which he sucked from a wound in her shoulder. She and her fellow-witches flew to the Sabbat on straws, where they raised storms by slapping rocks with wet rags.

As though the older-established devils were insufficient, the nomadic tinkers have conjured the 'Burkers' into being. In top hats and tail coats, the Burkers hover by lonely roads where they murder poor travelling people and sell their bodies to medical schools; of all the creatures of the northern mists, the Burkers must be the most sinister.

KEY TO SYMBOLS

- CURIOUS CHARACTERS
- CUSTOMS AND FESTIVALS
- DEVILS AND DEMONS
- FABULOUS BEASTS
- FAIRIES
- GHOSTS
- GIANTS
- GIPSIES AND TINKERS
- HEROES
- HOLY PLACES
- LOCAL CURIOSITIES
- LOVE STORY
- MERMAIDS AND SEA-PEOPLE
- MYSTERIOUS STONES
- TRADITIONAL SINGING
- WELLS AND SPRINGS
- WITCHES AND WIZARDS

THE FOLKLORE YEAR

Evening of January 11
Burghead, Grampian
Burning the Clavie

Saturday nearest June 12
Aberdeen, Grampian
Highland Games

Usually about June 12
Aberdeen, Grampian
Riding of the Marches

Saturday in late June
Dundee, Tayside
Highland Games

Usually second Saturday in July
Tomintoul, Grampian
Highland Games

Sunday in mid-July
Aikey Brae, near Old Deer, Aberdeen, Grampian
Aikey Fair

Fourth Saturday in August
Strathdon, Grampian
Lonach Highland Gathering and Games

Usually second week in September
Braemar, Grampian
Braemar Highland Gathering and Games

Evening of December 31
Stonehaven, Grampian
Swinging the Fireballs

Arbroath *Tayside*

Communion was never held at St Vigeans church, near Arbroath, between 1699 and 1736, according to one old story. People believed that the church was built over an underground lake that would swallow up the congregation if Communion was held. Finally a minister took the risk, watched at a safe distance by his parishioners. Nothing happened and the spell was considered broken.

STONY SENTINELS

The Drosten Stone (above), in St Vigeans museum, is intricately carved with mysterious Pictish symbols

BURKERS & NODDIES

Aberdeen, like other Scottish cities, has many urbanise tinkers, descendants of an ancient caste of nomadic metal-workers. The town tinkers, like their country cousins, have an unholy fear of body-snatchers, or Burkers as they call them. The Burkers are named after William Burke who, with William Hare, murdered several people in Edinburgh in the 1820's in order to sell their bodies to school of anatomy. Burke was eventually convicted and hanged in 1829, though Hare was released because he turned King's evidence and could not be tried.

Until quite recently the belief that body-snatching was still rife made some tinkers steer clear of college buildings in Aberdeen at night, for fear that they would be whisked in for medical experiments. One tinker from Aberdeen, well known as a musician, said in 1954: 'I mind once upon a time when ye couldna pass the Marischal College or the King's College, for the students would fairly take a haud o' ye with a cleik (a hooked piece of iron) by the leg. They took ye right inside. They wanted fresh bodies.'

THE DEVIL'S DISCIPLES

Isabel Gowdie, the witch of Auldearn, claimed to be on good terms with the Devil, but in this illustration of 1830 by George Cruickshank, Isabel's coven comes under Satan's flail for unpunctuality at the Sabbat

MACABRE MISSION *Body-snatchers taking a tinker's corpse for dissection in an anatomy school are foiled by a brave gamekeeper*

Terror in a top hat

According to the tinkers, Burkers were doctors, helped by medical students called Noddies.

Legend had it that the Burkers' coach, draped in black, left King's College at night and was driven into the surrounding countryside in search of isolated tinkers' camps. The hearse-like coach was said to have a zinc floor with holes to let the blood out. Bloodhounds loped silently beside it and the horses' hooves were muffled by rubber pads. The Burkers and Noddies were dressed like under-takers in top hats and swallowtail coats, with black ties.

One story tells how a poor travel-ling tinker couple and their two babies fell foul of the Burkers one stormy night. The man sent his wife to a keeper's lodge to ask for a dish of tea and somewhere to sleep. The keeper's wife gave them a drink and said they would be sure of a welcome at the big farm near by.

Drink of death

'There's many an old tramping man I've seen going up that road,' she said, adding under her breath: 'I can't say I've ever seen one coming back.' Sure enough, the farmer's wife welcomed the tinkers, prepared big bowls of tea and promised them beds in the barn. The tinker's wife decided to save her tea for later, but her husband drank his and promptly fell asleep. She tried to wake him but without success, even when she pricked him with a skewer. Terrified, she bundled up the babies and ran back to the keeper's cottage for help. Soon after, the Burkers' coach came down the road from the farm and the keeper, grabbing his gun, ran outside to challenge the four black-clothed men riding on top. They refused to stop so the keeper shot one of the horses, and the coach skidded to a halt. Inside lay the naked body of the poor tinker. The farmer and his wife were tried for body-snatching, and were later hanged.

Tales like this symbolise the per-secution complex which seemed in-herent in the tinkers' way of life. Perhaps the feeling dates from the 17th century when, under Scottish law, merely to be a tinker or gipsy was punishable by hanging.

Auldearn *Highland*

The most remarkable of all Scottish witch trials was that of Isabel Gowdie, a young housewife, which took place before the sheriff of Auldearn in 1662. She seems to have been a girl with a powerful imagination for, apparently without torture, she confessed to participating in the most bizarre rites. It was Isabel's trial which confirmed most of the popular ideas of witchcraft – covens of 13, baptism by the Devil, and Satanic orgies on lonely hillsides. She cheerfully admitted that she and her compan-ions mounted straws and, after reciting the words of a spell, rode them like horses, and could transform themselves into cats, hares and jackdaws. Once, according to Isabel, they were entertained by 'the Queen of Faery' in the heart of the Downy Hills.

The Auldearn coven, she said, had murdered the Laird of Park's children. Clay effigies thrust into a fire caused the children to die painful and lingering deaths. They were less successful in disposing of the family of the Laird of Lochloy. The method chosen in this instance was to boil gobbets of dogs' and sheeps' flesh together for an entire morning, after which the brew was stirred by the Devil him-self. It was then spread in places where the family was liable to walk, but it seems they did not pass that way, for they remained in excellent health.

Isabel was given useful hints and recipes by the Fairy Queen, and was on intimate terms with the Devil, whom she described as a 'meikle black man' and whose embraces were rough. History does not relate what her ultimate fate was, but she was probably burnt at the stake.

Balmoral *Grampian*

An echo of ancient practices survived at Balmoral until the middle of the last century. Each Hal-lowe'en, the effigy of a witch was burnt in front of the castle as a symbol of triumph over the powers of darkness. As the huge bonfire was kindled, clansmen wheeled up a trolley on which was perched the 'Shandy Dann', the witch's effigy. Scores of marchers, headed by pipers, converged on the castle, breaking into a run as they approached the fire. Then silence was called for and the indictment was read, accusing 'Shandy Dann' of witchcraft, after which she was condemned to the flames. Amid cheers and the skirl of pipes, the witch was hurled on to the blazing fire.

Banchory *Grampian*

In 1562, Mary, Queen of Scots led her troops into battle against the Earl of Huntly, chief of the Gordon clan. Huntly went cheerfully to war, bolstered by the witches of Strathbogie who told him that after the battle he would lie in the Tolbooth of Aberdeen 'without any wound on his body'. The armies met on the Hill of Fare, 5 miles north of Banchory, and the Gordons were defeated. Huntly was captured unwounded but suddenly fell off his horse, dead from apoplexy. His body was taken to the Tolbooth, where it lay for the night, thus fulfilling the witches' prophecy.

There is a chair-shaped stone on the Hill of Fare on which Mary, Queen of Scots is said to have sat to watch the fighting. Below the slope is a modern memorial commemorating the battle.

Banff *Grampian*

The freebooter James MacPherson was hanged at Banff in November, 1700. The illegitimate son of a laird and a gipsy girl, he joined his mother's people and became a Scots Robin Hood, plundering rich farmers. A local laird, Duff of Braco, organised a posse and cornered him at a fair. A woman in an upstairs window dropped a blanket over MacPherson and he was captured. While awaiting execution he is believed to have written 'MacPherson's Rant' which he played on his fiddle beneath the gallows. He is said to have offered the fiddle to any of his clan who happened to be present; as no one answered he broke it over the executioner's head and, jumping from the ladder, hanged himself. Many folk believe that a reprieve was on the way, and that Duff ordered the town clock to be put forward to make sure of getting rid of MacPherson.

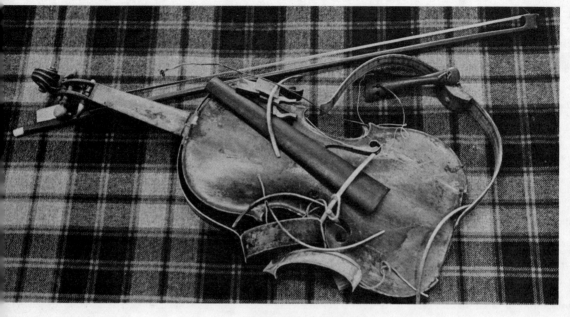

FREEBOOTER'S FIDDLE

'He played a tune, and danced it roon, below the gallows tree . . .' A broken fiddle, believed to be the one that freebooter James MacPherson played, is preserved at the Clan MacPherson House Museum in Newtonmore, Highland

Ben Macdui *Grampian*

The Highlands' savage grandeur provides an ideal setting for monsters, and Scotland has its own version of the Abominable Snowman in the terrifying shape of the Grey Man of Macdui in the Cairngorms. A grey figure, 10 ft tall and with a black 'lum hat' (top hat), hovers near a cairn and bodes ill for all climbers and wanderers who meet him. He is reputed to have pursued wayfarers as far as the outskirts of Braemar, 11 miles away. A Banchory man claims to have seen him in 1950.

Birse *Grampian*

The Celtic year was marked by two great fire festivals – Beltane, or May Day Eve, when the cattle went out to pasture, and Samain, marking the beginning of the New Year on November 1.

Beltane may be connected with Belenus, the Celtic pastoral god. Bonfires were lit on hilltops, and cattle were driven through them to prevent disease. Women leapt across to ensure winning a husband or giving birth safely. Folk danced round the fire sunwise and ran around the fields with torches. All these practices lasted in Scotland until the 18th century, but the dancing survived longer. In the parish of Birse, belief in the magic of the May Day fires existed until the mid-19th century; the young people used to kindle a bonfire on a knoll and march three times round it in the direction of the sun. They also performed ceremonies for the preservation of cattle and crops.

Bridge of Don *Grampian*

The Auld Brig o' Balgownie, which crosses the River Don on the outskirts of Old Aberdeen, was reputedly built by King Robert Bruce. When Byron, the poet, was a child he used to cross the bridge with trepidation, for he was his mother's only son, and there was a prophecy which ran 'Brig o' Balgownie, black's yer wa', wi' a wife's only son, and a mare's only foal, down ye shall fa'.

THE MACGREGORS' GREAT RACE

The Braemar Gathering, held in September, has been patronised by Royalty since the time of Queen Victoria, who bought the Braemar estate in 1853. The popularity at Braemar of the heavier physical sports, like tossing the caber, can be traced back to the days of King Malcolm Canmore in the 11th century. He decreed that a great race should be run up a steep, rocky hill for a claymore and a purse of gold.

The race began, and the two elder sons of MacGregor of Ballochbuie, famous for their fleetness of foot, took the lead. The youngest son arrived late. Soon, however, the young Mac-Gregor had passed all the contestants, except his brothers; he called out:

'Halves, brothers, and I'll stop.' 'Gain what you can,' replied the eldest, 'and keep what you can.'

Within yards of the goal the eldest put out his arm to impede the young-est, but he ducked underneath it. Furious, the eldest grabbed his brother's kilt. The young MacGregor quickly loosened his belt and left the kilt in his brother's grasp. 'I have yielded everything to you hitherto,' he said, 'and I will that also.' Then he reached the flagstaff marking the finish and collapsed – the winner.

A widow's plea

The stalwart MacHardy tribe of Grampian owe their name in legend to a monstrous wild boar kept by the

cruel constable of the now-ruined Kindrochit Castle at Braemar. He fed it with cattle seized from the local people. A widow named MacLeod had only one cow, so her son Sandy killed the boar and was condemned to death by the constable. The widow appealed to the king and was told that her son would go free if he could shoot a peat off her head at a hundred yards range.

Sandy succeeded, but the king asked why he drew two arrows from his quiver when about to shoot. Sandy said 'If I had killed her, the second one would have been for you.' 'You are a hardy one,' said the king. 'From now on your name shall be Hardy' – and so the clan was named.

Burghead *Grampian*

Each year, on January 11, there is a mid-winter fire festival called Burning the Clavie. According to local people, the ceremony goes back to the Druids, and it may also be related to Norse fire-worship. Similar rites were once common to all northern peoples; to light fires at mid-winter was at once a plea and a promise that the sun would return, bringing with it the new growth of spring.

The Clavie is made from a tar barrel sawn in half, the staves of a herring cask, and a 6 ft long salmon-fisherman's pole, called a spoke. The half-barrel is fixed to the spoke with a nail, hammered home by a stone – for no iron hammer may be used. This is filled with tar and pieces of wood, while the herring staves secure the Clavie to the spoke, and provide a cage for a carrier to get his head through. Burning peat is placed in the Clavie, and the flaming bundle is carried round the streets by a series of men, before being taken to the top of a hill called the Doorie. There, more fuel is heaped on, and finally the blazing embers are scattered down the hillside, where people scramble for glowing portions. Each one is said to bring good luck for the rest of the year, and act as a charm against evil spirits.

BROUGHTY FERRY'S BROWNIE

The castle of Claypots, at Broughty Ferry, in Tayside, was fortunate in possessing an industrious brownie who did all the household tasks at night, and asked no more in return than a basin of cream. But this useful creature had professional pride, and could not bear lazy servants. In the end, it was a slovenly kitchen maid that drove him out. He was so appalled by her wasteful methods of dressing vegetables for the pot, that he beat her with a handful of kale stalks before leaving for ever, rather unfairly cursing the entire house and its inmates as he went. The castle, a mile north of Broughty Ferry, is open to the public

VIRTUE PRESERVED

Pictish symbols on the Maiden Stone (left) near to Chapel of Garioch, Grampian, may record the alliance of two princely families 1500 years ago. Alternatively, according to a local tradition, supported by Shaun Crampton who sculpted the nearby modern figure (right), the older stone is Janet of Drumdurno, a girl of long ago whom a warlock attempted to seduce. She fled from him, praying for deliverance, and as he seized her, she turned to stone. The mysterious carvings are allegedly marks made by a hot bread-shovel upon her apron when she fled from her home

Corgarff *Grampian*

One of the kelpie's (or water-spirit's) less endearing traits was to spring up behind horsemen and hug them, thus causing considerable distress to the rider and his mount. On other occasions, a kelpie would assume the shape of a water horse. One man, anxious to cross the swollen River Don to reach his sick wife, found the Bridge of Luib swept away, and accepted a kelpie's offer to ferry him over on its back. Halfway across, the beast submerged, hoping to drag its victim down. He escaped, however, and swam to safety. The kelpie, cheated of its prey, heaved a boulder after him, which is still known as 'the kelpie's stone'.

Cortachy *Tayside*

Through the treachery of a Cameron drummer, who deliberately failed to give warning of the enemy's advance, Lord Ogilvy's house – 'The Bonnie Hoose o' Airlie' – was burnt to the ground during the 17th-century Wars of the Covenant. The defenders threw the drummer into the flames, though it is said his drum can still be heard whenever an Ogilvy is about to die in Cortachy Castle.

Crimond *Grampian*

Two ballads recount the tragic love of Sir James of the Rose and Matilda, daughter of the Thane of Buchan. Tradition says that the thane strongly disapproved of the match, since he wanted Matilda to marry the wealthy Sir John Graham. He forbade his daughter ever to see Sir James again – yet every evening, the lovers met by the Loch of Strathbeg.

One night, they were surprised by Sir John's brother, Donald. James killed the intruder in single combat, whereupon Matilda, fearing her father's anger, urged her lover to flee. He decided to go to Skye and bring back clansmen to protect them both. But the countryside was full of armed searchers, so the young knight hid in the Mill of Haddo.

While Sir James lay there, his sweetheart sent a messenger to Skye. The man was captured and, under threat of torture, revealed the knight's hiding place. The mill was surrounded, and though four of the men who came to take Sir James fell beneath his sword, Sir John himself crept up and stabbed his rival in the side. Before he died, Sir James ran his murderer through, and Matilda, grief-stricken, threw herself on her lover's sword.

Delnabo *Grampian*

It would be hard to imagine a more troublesome pair of sprites than the quarrelsome goblins that once haunted the wilds of Craig Aulnaic. The male was called Ben Baynac, after a mountain near his home in Glenavon, while the female, whom he used to beat at night until her wailing woke the entire neighbourhood, was called Clashnichd Aulnaic.

A man who was particularly annoyed by the goblins' nocturnal squabbling was a local farmer, called James Gray. When he met Clashnichd one day, he sternly reproved her for the shrieking and clamouring she made every night, whereupon the creature broke down and told James how Ben Baynac drove her from her house each night and pursued her round the district with taunts and blows.

James was determined to end the disturbances, and when Ben Baynac next attacked Clashnichd, he killed the sprite by firing an arrow into the only vulnerable place on its body – the bonnet-sized mole on its left breast. The grateful Clashnichd then began calling at James's farm and other houses in the district, but proved to be a terrible nuisance, for she would eat anything she could steal. At last, the miller's wife chased her away by pouring boiling water over her as she tried to steal a fish from the griddle. Clashnichd ran off, howling, and has not been heard of since.

Dundee *Tayside*

William McGonagall, prince of bad poets and son of an Irish hand-loom weaver, spent much of his life in the city, writing verses of such awfulness that they won him everlasting fame. The stanzas that delighted 19th-century Scots students included such immortal lines as these, written to commemorate the Tay Bridge disaster:

'Beautiful railway bridge of the Silvery Tay,
Alas, I am very sorry to say,
That ninety lives have been taken away,
On the last Sabbath day of 1879.'

FORFAR'S WITCH BRIDLE

This iron gag, now in Forfar Museum, was worn by 17th-century witches on their way to execution, presumably to stifle their screams. Most notorious was Helen Guthrie, who said she had eaten the flesh of babies, to protect her from torture. But her safeguard did not work

Forres *Grampian*

Shakespeare placed Macbeth's three witches on the 'blasted heath' near here. Possibly he had heard the story, later related in a 17th-century book on witchcraft, of the mysterious sickness that afflicted King Duff of Scotland. Search parties discovered 'haggs roasting before a fire the king's picture, made of wax' at Forres. The witches were executed, and the king recovered – only to die in battle at Forres, in AD 967, fighting the usurper Colin.

Fyvie *Grampian*

The ruined mill of Tifty (below) was the scene of a 17th-century tragedy, commemorated in the ballad 'Andrew Lammie'. The miller's daughter, Annie, fell in love with Andrew, Lord Fyvie's trumpeter, but her father disapproved. While her lover was away buying her a wedding dress, her family beat her, and she died.

THE HORSEMAN'S WORD

Glamis *Tayside*

If the legends about Glamis Castle are anywhere near the truth, the Bowes–Lyon family share their ancestral home with a terrifying medley of ghosts. In a room so well hidden that not even the family now know its whereabouts – perhaps the same room in which, long ago, a hideously deformed heir, more like a toad than a man, was imprisoned for life – the wicked Earl Beardie, 500 years dead, plays dice with the Devil until the Day of Judgment.

A Grey Lady in the chapel, a woman without a tongue in the park, and a gibbering madman on the roof, are among the many unidentified ghosts that roam this ancient castle. And there are stories of a 16th-century Lady of Glamis, who was burnt as a witch and whose wraith came home again still wrapped in the flames in which she died.

MYSTERIES OF GLAMIS

The ghost of a Negro page-boy sometimes sits outside one of the bedrooms of Glamis Castle (above), though no one knows who he was in life. The secret room in which the monster earl was allegedly imprisoned may be somewhere near the ancient crypt (left). From outside there are said to be more windows than can be found inside

A secret society with pagan undertones has existed for centuries in north-east Scotland. It is called the Horseman's Word; and until a young man had been initiated into the society, he was hardly regarded as a man at all. The cult was centred on Huntly, west Grampian, and was most active around the 1870's. It had a strong following until at least the 1930's, and in a few remote places its rites may be practised still.

The initiation ceremony usually took place around Martinmas (November 11) in an isolated barn. When the seniors of the cult had collected the names of enough novices – there had to be an odd number at the ceremony, preferably 13 – they passed the word round to attend. This was sometimes done by sending a single horse hair in an envelope to the brother invited. The horsemen-to-be were told when they would be called for and were instructed to bring with them a bottle of whisky, a jar of berries or jam, and a loaf of bread.

On the appointed night the novices were taken blindfolded to the barn. At the door, the horseman leading them gave the Horseman's Knock – three measured raps – and whinnied like a horse. A standard interrogation followed, in which the horseman identified himself to the 'minister' standing inside, and said that the Devil had told him to come, 'by the hooks and crooks of the road'. Before he was allowed to enter with the novices, he was asked: 'What's the tender of the oath?' The correct reply was: 'Hele, conceal, never reveal; neither write, nor dite, nor recite; nor cut, nor carve, nor write in sand.'

Towards midnight the initiation began. The novices, still blindfolded, knelt around a 'minister' with their left feet bare and left hands raised. He told them that Cain had been the first Horseman and that they could invoke the Devil by reading certain verses from the Bible backwards. Then he gave them the Word itself – a secret to this day – which, spoken to a horse, would give the speaker control over the animal. The novices swore 'neither to dite, write nor recite it', and immediately afterwards were told to write it down. Those who fell for the trick were licked across their knuckles with the stock of a horsewhip or the back-chain of a cart.

When the ceremony was over, the eating, drinking and story-telling began. The new horsemen were given practical tips on how to manage horses, and were instructed in the magical arts of horsemanship. For example, if a horseman ever had trouble with his horses, he was told to take their collars and bridles to a crossroads and to 'say over his lessons' – that is, to recite backwards from the Bible. The Devil would gallop up in the form of a horse, and if the horseman mounted and rode him, he would never have trouble with his own horses again.

Towards dawn, before the horsemen reeled back to their horses and the day's work, the ceremonial Horseman's Toast was drunk:

> 'Here's to the horse with the four white feet,
> The chestnut tail and mane –
> A star on his face and a spot on his breast,
> And his master's name was Cain.'

Glen Esk *Tayside*

Long ago, there lived in Locklee, Glen Esk, a piper whose music was loved in all the glens of Angus. One summer evening, he was playing near Dalbrack Bridge when nine green-robed fairies came down the river in a boat. They stepped out on to the bank, one of them touched the piper's shoulder with her wand, and he followed them back on to the boat. Three times the fairies sailed the craft round the pool called Pontskinnen Pot with the piper still playing, and then they disappeared upstream again. The piper had been kidnapped to entertain them in the cave where they lived, and he was never seen again. But sometimes, according to the people of Glen Esk, the faint sound of his pipes can still be heard in the distance.

Glenlivet *Grampian*

It is about 100 years since the last brownie (a household goblin) was seen in Glenlivet. Her name was Maggie Moloch, or Hairy Meg, and she lived in the farmhouse of Achnarrow. Sometimes she went about with a male fairy called Brownie Clod.

Maggie milked the cows and made the beds, and was rewarded for her services with a bowl of milk and piece of oatcake. Once, after a particularly bad year, the farmer decided to economise by sacking some of his servants. Maggie was so upset that she tipped away all the milk at milking time and stripped the beds instead of making them. Rather than annoy her any more, with all the risks which that entailed, the farmer gave his servants their jobs back . . . and Maggie at once recovered her temper.

A SHAK O' AULD HORNIE *No farmhand in 19th-century Scotland was a genuine 'made horseman' unless he had shaken hands with the Devil. At the end of the initiation ceremony into the Horseman's Word, after a 'minister' had expounded the mysteries of the Word and explained the laws and customs of the society, the novice horsemen were pushed one by one and wearing blindfolds into the 'cauf-hoose' of the barn for a 'shak o' Auld Hornie'. Sometimes the horseman's 'Deil' was a man draped in a calf-skin rubbed in phosphorus, perhaps wearing a horned mask; some-times it was a live calf or goat. In either case, the novice felt a hoof pressed welcomingly into his hand, and he was ordered by the other horsemen to shake it.*

Although the secret society of the Horseman's Word seems to have links with the witch-cult of the 17th century, it would not admit a female witch. In fact, its members were sworn never to reveal any of the mysteries to 'anyone who wears an apron, except a blacksmith or a farrier'. The cult was so widespread that virtually every farmhand was a brother

Glen Mark *Tayside*

During the fierce purge of the Highlands that followed Bonnie Prince Charlie's defeat at Culloden, James Carnegie of Balnamoon, a staunch Jacobite, fled to Glen Esk and took shelter at Auchronie. One day, while he was sitting in the inglenook, a troop of Cumberland's redcoats rode up to the farm in search of him. The farmer denied having seen Carnegie, and invited the soldiers to warm themselves by his fire. At the same time, he told Carnegie, who was sitting with his back turned to his enemies, to go out and check that the cows had been milked and fed. Carnegie slipped quietly out of the farm and away to Glen Mark, where he found a cave in which to hide until the hunt was over. It is known still as Balnamoon's Cave.

Gordonstoun *Grampian*

When the Devil took Sir Robert Gordon for his own in November 1704, he brought to a fittingly dreadful end the career of one of Grampian's most deeply feared warlocks. Exactly 25 years earlier, Sir Robert had narrowly escaped the same fate by giving the Devil his shadow; and in 1704 he almost escaped again. He built himself the Round Square, a supposedly Devil-proof fortress in Gordonstoun, and took refuge there with a parson. But at the last moment the parson persuaded him that he would be safer in Birnie church, and on the way there the Devil caught him. He slung Sir Robert over his saddle, and as they galloped off to the fires of Hell, a huge demon dog ran beside them with its fangs buried deep in the warlock's neck.

occasion, when English troops burnt down his home, the colonel escaped, naked, with a prodigious leap over the River Ey. A hump-backed bridge at the spot is known still as the Bridge of the Leap.

Further up the river is a ledge in a deep chasm, called The Colonel's Bed, where he is said to have hidden while on the run after fighting in the Battle of Killiecrankie, in 1689. One of the colonel's favourite tricks, when at home, was to summon his servants by firing his pistol at a shield on the wall, which rang like a bell.

Inverey *Grampian*

One of the most swashbuckling characters on Upper Dee-side was John Farquharson, known as The Black Colonel, whose flights from law and order became part of the legend of the area. On one

WHEN THE PIE WAS OPENED

Long, long ago, it is said, Sir William de Barclay, Lord of Redcastle, at Inverkeilor, Tayside, brought home from Scandinavia a 10 ft Swedish giant named Daniel Cajanus and a clever, 3 ft Danish dwarf called Licinius Calvus. At a great dinner, the giant stood behind his new master, but there was no sign of Licinius – until they cut open a monster pie, and out he popped, with a graceful bow. The odd pair were firm friends and devoted servants. When Vikings raided the coast, Daniel more than once saved the castle single-handed. But at the height of his greatest fight, he was killed; and his friend, the dwarf, died of a broken heart

Kemnay *Grampian*

One of the last of a clan of giants, Lang Johnnie More – 'full three yards around the waist and fourteen feet in height' according to a ballad – went to London to be the king's standard bearer. But he dared to fall in love with the king's daughter, and was sentenced to death. On hearing the news, his uncle and another giant, Jock o' Noth, ran to London, kicked down the city wall and won him a pardon and the princess.

Kirkton of Strathmartine *Tayside*

They say that a 3 ft boulder in a field 2 miles north of the village marks the spot where a dragon died. Nine maidens sent to fetch water for their father were devoured by the monster before a bold young man called Martin slew it in a ferocious battle. Martin's Stone, as it is known, is actually a Pictish standing stone, whose carvings of strange animals may have suggested the legend.

THE POOL THAT GAVE UP ITS DEAD

The Linn, or pool, of Dee, near Muir, Grampian, was said to be the home of a water-spirit. One of its victims was a basket-weaver called MacFarquhar the Wand, who fell in and drowned while on his way home.

His body was not found until his widow went down to the Linn (above), prayed to the spirit, and threw in his tartan plaid. Next morning, says the tale, her husband's corpse lay by the edge of the pool, wrapped in the plaid

GIGHT'S GHOSTLY PIPER

Ghostly piping is sometimes heard around ruined Gight Castle, 3 miles north of Methlick. It is said that a piper was sent to explore an underground passage leading from the castle, and that he never returned

THE DEVIL'S MILLER

John Fraser, the miller at Whitehill, New Deer, Grampian, in the early 19th century, was said to be in league with the Devil. People held that he could make the mill (pictured below) operate without its 'clapper' – an essential part of the machinery – and stop it at will, so that no one could make the wheel turn again

Kirriemuir *Tayside*
That bawdy Rabelaisian folksong, 'The Ball o' Kirriemuir', with its description of scenes at a village wedding, has been described as a near-epic. That is not the way it was described in the 17th century, when lewd ballads were thought to be a part of devil-worship. The author of *Satan's Invisible World Discovered* wrote in 1671 that 'the foul spirit . . . taught a wizard a bawdy song, and ere two days passed, all the lads and lasses of the town were lilting it through the streets'.

Methlick *Grampian*
The 'gey Gordons' of Gight were a wild, lawless family. The word 'gey' – not 'gay' – is roughly translated as 'reckless'. Thanks to their extraordinary lust for adventure and intrigue, few of the family died peacefully in bed. The first laird fell at Flodden, and after that their history is one of murder, execution, imprisonment, suicide and sudden death in battle or by accident. The last of the Gordons, who would have been 14th laird, was the poet Lord Byron – who died in 1824, trying to raise troops to aid Greek rebels.

Newtyle *Tayside*
A daring young poacher called David Grey is said to have lived for seven years as a hermit, locked in the tower on top of Kinpurney Hill, to win a £100 bet. The crowds who flocked to see him released were horrified by the picture he presented. His grey hair hung down to his knees, his nails were like the talons of a bird, and he had lost the power of speech, being capable of nothing more than grunts. The story says that he was put in the care of doctors at Dundee, but died soon afterwards.

Old Deer *Grampian*
Scotland is noted for its strict observance of the Sabbath day, but at Aikey Brae an annual fair is held on a Sunday in mid-July. It started, they say, when a wandering packman dropped his goods in a burn one Sunday, and spread them out on the bank to dry. People returning from church could not resist buying, and the delighted salesman vowed to return every year, on a Sunday.

465

Portgordon *Grampian*

Fishermen sailing from Portgordon often complained of the attentions of a merman. They considered him an ill omen and always headed back to shore if they saw him. The merman, according to a 19th-century tale, was swarthy, with extraordinarily long arms and curly, grey-green hair.

FOUNTAIN OF HEALTH

Pilgrims seeking health and fortune flocked to the well at Orton, 3 miles from Rothes, Grampian, for two centuries after the Reformation, despite the Kirk's condemnation of 'this idolatrous superstition'

Stonehaven *Grampian*

Every Hogmanay the young men of Stonehaven converge on the High Street with fireballs, paraffin-soaked rags in cages of wire netting at the end of long wire ropes. At the stroke of midnight the fireballs are set alight and the lads move off along the street whirling the balls around their heads. The idea, according to tradition, is to put all evil spirits to flight and to ensure the town's prosperity throughout the coming year.

Strathdon *Grampian*

Until the turn of the century, Strathdon funerals would often end in a drunken rout. The Lykewake, the all-night vigil beside the body, was a means of bidding farewell with as much whisky as possible. Next day, on the way to the graveyard, the corpse would be left outside a pub, while the mourners had a final dram; and if a fight developed, so much the better. It was not unknown for clergymen to take part, and one minister, when reminded of his cloth, flung off his jacket and said in Gaelic:

'There's the coat, here's the man.'

Tannadice *Tayside*

The ruined Finavon Castle, 2 miles from Tannadice, is the site of a quarrel which resulted in a long feud between the Lindsays of Finavon and the Ogilvies of Inverquharity. Lord Lindsay and Lord Ogilvy were taking part in an archery contest between the local lairds, and Ogilvy won the great event of the day when he shot a falcon on the wing. Lindsay, who had drunk too much, took his defeat badly and challenged Ogilvy to combat at Kelpie's Haugh near the castle. Legend says that Lindsay managed to disarm Ogilvy and was about to kill him when he himself dropped dead. The rights of the case were squabbled over for generations.

Tarfside *Tayside*

The Rowan, a hill at Tarfside, is associated with Robert the Bruce. It is alleged that in the early 14th century, he fought in a battle there against his arch-enemy, the Red Comyn, and Bruce's battle-cry of 'Row-in' has been attached to the place since. It seems doubtful if Bruce ever visited Tarfside, but the cairns at the bottom of the hill have long been pointed out as the graves of those killed in the battle. In fact, they date from a much earlier period. It is said that the grave of an Iron Age chief was unearthed in the 19th century but, if so, its site has since been lost.

Tarland *Grampian*

A wizard who lived in Tarland earned his neighbours' gratitude by ridding the village of a band of tinkers responsible for dozens of robberies. The wizard appeared before the tinkers at Tarland Fair where he knelt down, cut open a cheese and prayed to the Devil that it would produce a swarm of bees. Thousands of 'double-stanged' bees appeared and chased the tinkers, who were never seen again.

Tomintoul *Grampian*

Grigor Willox was a white witch who wandered the countryside during the 18th century, working his beneficial magic and making a comfortable living at the same time. Anyone who took his troubles to Grigor's home in Tomintoul, the highest village in Britain, certainly got his money's worth. Grigor is said to have broken the spells of black witches, made dry cows give milk, cured barren wives and detected thieves. He practised his craft all over northern Scotland, and people came for miles to visit him. His secret lay in two magical amulets. One was a brass hook, part of a kelpie's bridle, captured from the water horse of Loch Ness, and the other was a mermaid's stone of clear crystal. Grigor also sold water in which the stone had been immersed for 1s. 6d. a bottle, as a medicine.

Turriff *Grampian*

A white cow that lumbered its way into local folklore has its own monument at Lendrum Farm, near Turriff. In 1913 farmer Robert Paterson defied the law by refusing to pay insurance stamps for his workers. The Sheriff's Officer impounded Paterson's cow and ordered that it should be sold to pay for the farmer's insurance contributions. Uproar broke out in the town when the auction was held. During the confusion the 'Turra Coo' escaped and went careering through the streets, prodded along by farmers sympathetic to Paterson's cause. Eventually the cow returned to Lendrum and a granite slab marks the spot where it is buried.

At several places around Turriff there are traces of a 'Goodman's Croft'. This was a piece of land dedicated to the Devil and left untilled. Such patches are remembered on many farms, even where the spot has long been cultivated.

THE WIZARD LAIRD

A young Scottish nobleman once went to Italy to learn the Black Arts, and returned after seven years as an accomplished wizard . . . though without his shadow. On his last night in Italy he and his fellow students were told by their master it was time to pay their fees and 'The Devil take the hindmost'. The young laird was last out and the Devil appeared and held the young man. However the laird tricked him into thinking that there was another pupil behind him, but it was only the young man's shadow the Devil grabbed.

When the laird, sometimes identified as Alexander Skene (1680–1724), returned to Skene House, 10 miles west of Aberdeen, he became known as the Wizard Laird. Even in the brightest sunlight, it was said, he never cast a shadow.

The laird was accompanied by four imps, in the shapes of a crow, a hawk, a magpie and a jackdaw. At Hogmanay, so the legend goes, the birds would sit beside their master in a ghostly coach drawn by black horses without riders or harness. Skene kirkyard was usually the destination. There the laird and his attendants used to open graves and remove the bodies of unbaptised babies, as food for the four birds.

'Never look back . . .'
Often at midnight the laird would visit neighbouring glens in search of the herbs he used in his magic potions. He appears not to have welcomed competition, for he used some of his concoctions to poison witches.

One legend says the laird crossed the Loch of Skene in his coach, supported only by his magical powers and a thin coat of ice. He is said to have told his birds that he could make the crossing provided they proved true to him. The last night of the year was chosen for the feat and the laird told his coachman to have the carriage at the door by midnight. As there was no frost, the laird cast a spell to cover the loch with ice as thin as the finest glass. He told the coachman to keep the horses at full gallop during the crossing, with their heads towards the Hill of Fare. On no account was the coachman to look behind him.

The carriage sped across the ice with the four spirit birds flying alongside and encouraging the horses. The coachman, his terror barely suppressed, could not stop himself turning round as the horses touched land at the other side. There, seated beside his laird, was the Devil. In an instant the back wheels of the coach smashed through the ice and two black dogs which had been chasing the carriage plunged into the water. Nevertheless the horses took the laird safely home.

THE NORSEMEN'S DOWRY

Orkney Islands, Shetland Islands, N.E. Highland

The first Viking settlers sailed their longships across the uncharted sea between Norway and the Shetlands in the 8th or early 9th century. They came not as bloodthirsty marauders, but as farmers in search of new land. For the next 600 years the Norsemen ruled the Shetlands and Orkneys. Then, in 1468, the impoverished King Christian I of Denmark, Norway and Sweden pawned the Orkney Islands to James III of Scotland for 50,000 florins. A year later, he pawned the Shetland Islands, too, for another 8000 florins. Christian's daughter Margaret was betrothed to James, and Christian was so heavily in debt that he offered both island groups to James instead of paying Margaret's dowry in cash. It was agreed that the islands would be returned as soon as the 58,000 florins were repaid. But they never were and 600 years of Norse domination came to a bloodless end. Even today, when the people of the Northern Isles feel disillusioned with the way in which the British government is treating them, they threaten to buy back their freedom by paying off the debt.

Fireside fables of long ago

It is more than a memory that links the Orkneys and Shetlands with the Norsemen. Their stories, too, like those told in the north-east corner of Caithness, recall the tales with which the Norse farmers whiled away the long winter evenings 1000 years ago. There are dim memories of Norse gods, and here and there a last trace of nature worship. The island giants are descended from the Norse *jotner*, lumbering, quarrelsome creatures, always half-building bridges and dropping stones, and occasionally making love with pathetic clumsiness to princesses or mermaids. The giants Herman and Saxie, for instance, lived on opposite sides of Burra Firth in the Shetlands. The pair quarrelled one day and became so enraged that each hurled a huge rock at the other. Saxie's rock, now known as Saxie's Baa, dropped into the water just short of Herman's home, Hermaness, while Herman's rock, now called Herman's Hellyac, embedded itself in the cliffs at Saxafiord. The trows – a word which Shetlanders used to describe almost every kind of fairy – are closely related to Norwegian *trolls*, and the supernatural creatures which live underground or in hollow hills and mounds were well known to the Vikings, who called them *underjordiske*.

Now, some 1200 years after the first Norse settlers tilled their land and grazed their sheep, the islanders' heritage is still the rich harvest they reap from land or sea, and their beliefs and traditions are those of a hardy, self-sufficient race of fishermen and farmers, not of warriors.

Fishermen had their own explanations for the hazards that lurked in these stormy northern seas. A treacherous whirlpool in the Pentland Firth, the Swelkie, was caused by two giantesses, Fenya and Menya, grinding salt in a handmill on the sea floor. Selkies and Fin-Folk, mermaids and sea monsters waited in the waves ready to seduce the unwary into a watery grave. Islands such as Orkney's Eynhallow and Hether Blether appeared and vanished, governed by laws of magic which no man could understand. A wild creature called Teran ruled the winter sea; the Storm Witch controlled the wind, and could drive any ship on to the rocks if she had reason to – and she often had.

Protected by magic

Though less dangerous, the farmers' lives were hardly less predictable, and magic was one of the arts every farmer had to master if his cattle and crops were to be safe from the spirits. No cowman ever kept an odd number of cattle – he would rather buy or sell to keep the number even. When a cow calved, a fire was lighted in the byre to keep away the trows. Before the first furrow was cut in spring, the ploughman smeared urine over the plough and tied a thin round stone – a symbol of the sun and of fertility – to the plough beam.

One of the oldest customs still observed in the Orkneys is the Boys' Ploughing Match, held every August on South Ronaldsay. How the custom started and what exactly it means has been forgotten; but its magic, if only as a spectacle, is beyond dispute.

THE FOLKLORE YEAR

Last Tuesday in January
Lerwick, Mainland, Shetland
Up-Helly-Aa

A Wednesday in August
St Margaret's Hope, South Ronaldsay, Orkney
Boys' Ploughing Match

Christmas Day and New Year's Day
Kirkwall, Mainland, Orkney
Ba' Game

KEY TO SYMBOLS

CRIME AND PUNISHMENT

CURIOUS CHARACTERS

CUSTOMS AND FESTIVALS

DEVILS AND DEMONS

FABULOUS BEASTS

GHOSTS

GIANTS

HEROES

HOLY PLACES

LOCAL CURIOSITIES

LOVE STORY

MERMAIDS AND SEA-PEOPLE

SAINTS AND MIRACLES

SHIPWRECKS

WITCHES AND WIZARDS

BURRA FIRTH

Unst

LINGEY

Yell

ESHA NESS

OUT SKERRIES

BUSTA

*Shetland
Islands*

PAPA
STOUR

DALE *Mainland*

SCALLOWAY   LERWICK

FOULA

ST NINIAN'S ISLE   MOUSA

FITFUL HEAD

NOLTLAND   *Westray*

YETNASTEEN   OVERBISTER
Rousay   *Sanday*
EYNHALLOW   EGILSAY
(The Fin People, 471)   WYRE   *Stronsay*

Mainland   HESTWALL
STENNESS
STROMNESS   KIRKWALL
(Raiders, 479)   DEERNESS
SCAPA   *(Raiders, 479)*

FAIR ISLE   SUMMERDALE   *Orkney
Islands*

DWARFIE STANE
Hoy   ST MARGARET'S HOPE

*South
Ronaldsay*

SWONA

JOHN O' GROAT'S
THURSO   MEY   KIRKSTYLE
MURKLE
HALKIRK

WICK

HIGHLAND REGION

N

0   5   10
MILES

469

Burra Firth, Unst *Shetland*

The giants Saxie and Herman lived here. They fell in love with a mermaid, who offered herself to the one who would follow her to the North Pole. Both plunged into the sea and were never seen again.

Busta, Mainland *Shetland*

The four sons of Thomas Gifford, richest man in Shetland, were rowing across the voe (inlet) of Busta one day in 1748 when the boat stopped dead. After prayers had been said, the boat moved again, but three strange creatures emerged from beneath the waves and swam slowly astern. One son was so scared that next day he refused to join his brothers in the boat when they went to visit an uncle, and rode all the way instead. That night, when they were all supposed to go home, his horse had vanished. He joined his brothers in the boat, and all mysteriously drowned when it capsized in a smooth sea.

Later a relative, Barbara Pitcairn, claimed to have secretly married the dead heir, John, and to be pregnant by him. The baby, Gideon, inherited the estate but his rights were challenged by his cousin. The protagonists' sons fought on, and in 1836 the courts decided against Barbara's grandson.

Dale, Mainland *Shetland*

A local woman found a cockatrice's egg and put it to incubate beneath a hen. The creature hatched out, ate the hen's chicks, and then hid in a clump of peats. Cockatrices can kill with a glance, but fortunately someone recognised it. The peats were set on fire, and the animal was destroyed.

Dwarfie Stane, Hoy *Orkney*

Dwarfs were supposed to have chiselled the two small cells in Hoy's rock-cut tomb, the Dwarfie Stane. The tomb lies below hillside cliffs called Dwarfie Hamars, whose echo was thought to be the voices of dwarfs. A later legend makes the cells the beds of a giant and a pregnant giantess.

ST MAGNUS'S CHURCH

The 12th-century church on Egilsay, Orkney, is dedicated to St Magnus, a Norse earl of Orkney who was noted for his piety. He was enticed to Egilsay c. 1117 by his cousin Haakon, and executed by Haakon's cook

THE DEVIL'S PUNISHMENT

The Devil was punished for wrecking ships on the Ve Skerries by being made to carve out the Holes of Scraada at Esha Ness, Mainland, Shetland. His groans as he laboured at his task can still be heard echoing in the Holes

THE FIN PEOPLE

The people of the Northern Isles have drawn from the sea a host of legendary creatures to be feared, revered, or placated. The grey seals which crowd upon the rocky skerries were called Selkie Folk – humans under a spell who resumed their true form on Mid-summer Eve, when they cast off their seal skins and danced upon the shore. A man once found and concealed the skin of a dancing seal woman, so that she was in his power. He took the stranded selkie to his croft and married her. Years afterwards one of their children found the hidden seal skin and showed it to his mother. She seized the skin joyfully, and hurried to the shore, where her faithful seal-man lover was waiting still.

Seal men, too, came on land to make love to mortal women. Descendants of such unions had webbed fingers and toes, or a horny substance on their palms and soles – a phenomenon that is still said to occur.

The selkie of Sule Skerry

One of Orkney's most haunting ballads tells of the grey selkie of Sule Skerry – a rocky islet 37 miles west of Mainland. A maiden fell in love with a seal man and had a child by him. But shortly after, the seal man disappeared and she was left with their baby son. One day a grey seal landed and said to her: 'I am a man upon the land, I am a selkie in the sea; and when I'm far frae every strand, my dwelling is in Sule Skerry.' She realised that it was her lover, but he vanished and returned after seven years, bringing a gold chain for his son who went away with him. The woman later married. One day her husband went out hunting and shot two seals – an old grey one and a young one. Round the young one's neck was a gold chain which the hunter gave to his wife, who then knew that her son was dead.

Another sea people who mated with humans were the Fin-Folk. Mermaids were the daughters of Fin-Men and Fin-Wives, and were bent on winning human lovers; for a mermaid who seduced a man lost her tail but not her beauty, unlike the Fin-Wives who grew old and repulsive. Mermaids would lure young men to the marvellous city of Finfolkaheem under the sea.

Defeat of the Fin-Folk

The summer home of the Fin-Folk was on Eynhallow, Orkney's holy island which was said to vanish from time to time. A man of Evie, whose wife the Fin-Folk stole, vowed to conquer them. To be able to see Eynhallow he performed a ritual at the Odin Stone at Stenness. He and his sons had to outwit whales, mermaids and giants before setting foot on Eynhallow. The Fin-Folk and their cattle escaped into the sea. And there they stayed for ever, for men of Evie barred their return by cutting nine crosses on the turf and encircling Eynhallow with nine rings of salt.

THE SPELL OF THE SEA MAIDEN *Mermaids lured young men beneath the waves to the marvellous bejewelled city of Finfolkaheem*

CREATURES OF HILL AND MOUND

Fair Isle *Shetland*

The unique, multi-coloured knitting designs used in the island's famous woollen sweaters are claimed to have been copied from the clothing worn by shipwrecked Spanish sailors from the Armada. These men landed on the island when the storm-driven *El Gran Grifon* ran on to the rocks below the cliffs at Stromshellier in 1588. The crew and soldiers, in their armour and unusual clothes, made such an impression on the astonished islanders that they were regarded with awe as the advance guard of the Heavenly Host.

Fitful Head, Mainland *Shetland*

Legends say that deep in an inaccessible cave in the Head, there once lived a savage, sub-human sheep-stealer called Black Eric, who rode to and from the cave on a demon sea-horse named Tangie. Black Eric had many fights with local people, but his main opponent was an indomitable crofter named Sandy Breamer. In one of their battles, as Sandy was gaining the upper hand over the barbaric thief, Tangie came to Black Eric's aid. He whirled around the pair of fighters in a circle of unearthly light until Sandy fainted.

The brave crofter could not be frightened off, however, and eventually Sandy cornered Black Eric, who fell and crashed to his death over Fitful Head. Tangie continued to terrorise the district, harassing young women on the shore in his efforts to steal a mortal bride. Black Eric's cave is known still as the Thief's House.

Foula *Shetland*

Near the top of the hill called Hamnafjeld is the Hole – or Lum – of Liorafjeld, a narrow chimney which is believed to descend a thousand feet through the rock to sea level. Its exact position is now unknown, for a Foula man, who considered it an unhappy and dangerous place, covered it over many years ago. It was traditionally a hiding place of trows, spirit creatures. Anyone who visited Foula for the first time and dared to look in the Hole, would die immediately. About 300 years ago, so the story goes, two sceptical Dutch sailors were lowered into the Hole. One was dead when they were brought out, and the other died on the way back to his ship.

Halkirk *Highland*

Long ago, every horseman who wanted full command over his animals needed to know the Horseman's Word, which only the Devil could tell him. In Caithness, the Devil's fee for this service was living flesh and blood. This was usually a cockerel placed under an upturned basket, to which Satan helped himself. There is a legend that once, at the farm of North Calder near Halkirk, a little boy was playing with such a basket. He accidentally released the cockerel and became trapped himself. There was consternation when the Devil came for his due and discovered the child. It took much persuasion and all the diplomacy of the parish minister before the Devil would give up the child and accept another cockerel.

Hestwall, Mainland *Orkney*

The farm of Clumly, a mile south-west of Hestwall and 4 miles north of Stromness, is reputedly haunted by the ghostly White Horse of Clumly and its rider.

Like the small horses, dogs and sheep of the Northern Isles, the Norse *troll* – a legendary giant in Norway – shrank to less than human size in Shetland and Orkney, and became known as a trow. Though the huge *trolls* of earlier legend may survive in the stories of the Shetland *skeklar*, one of whom had 15 tails and carried 15 children on each tail, the later *trolls* – or trows – were more like humans. Some, such as the peerie trows, were so small that they lived beneath toadstools.

It was lucky to find and keep anything that the trows had lost. Even to hear them speaking was believed to bring good fortune. Nevertheless, they were feared, for they carried off pretty girls, midwives and fiddlers. They might replace a newborn child with a changeling; or if a person was sick, they could steal away his spirit and hide it in the hollow hills where they lived. To this day, any islander who is ill is said to be 'trowie'.

At Yule, the old Norse mid-winter festival when the trows were believed to be abroad, many homesteads protected themselves by rituals such as 'saining' or marking the house with the sign of the cross. Then, as at other times of the year, it was specially necessary to avoid the hills where the trows lived, for if anyone was caught, he would be forced to stay for a year and a day.

The trow is often confused with the Orkney hogboon or hogboy – a much less malevolent spirit, who was the islanders' equivalent of the old Norse *haugbonde*, a guardian spirit of the farms. His shadowy figure lived in nearly every big mound and he protected the domestic animals from the trows, as well as mending household articles left out for repair. For his reward, he expected liberal entertainment, so ale and milk were poured on the mounds where he lived. But if anyone attempted to dig up his home, he appeared as a little grey man, who would furiously set upon his disturber.

The rider was a murderer, and his spirit is condemned to re-live the terrible happenings of a night just over 100 years ago.

The legend claims that a young woman from a nearby parish came to work at the farm. Two men working there soon became rivals for her favours. She, however, played one lover off against the other until the anguished men hated one another. One day, the two were threshing sheaves of oats, standing face to face across the barn floor with heavy flails in their hands. Suddenly, one of them, goaded into blind fury by the other's taunts, smashed his rival's skull with a blow from his flail, and hid the body in the barn.

Later that night, the murderer took a white horse from the stable, placed his victim's body on its back, and led the horse to the cliffs near Yesnaby where he threw the corpse into the sea. As he left the scene, he was gripped by a terrible fear that the dead man's ghost was following him. He forced the horse into a wild gallop and as he neared the farm, he jumped the beast over a drystone wall, but its hooves caught the top stones and brought them clattering down.

Whether the murderer was caught, legend does not say – but to this day, no one has been able to repair the broken section of wall. As though it were a constant reminder of that terrible night, it always collapses again. On stormy nights, people have reported seeing a large white horse and rider leap over the wall to the sound of falling stones. Only a few years ago, a woman living near Clumly Farm answered a knock on her door and saw a white horse and its rider standing outside. At her startled exclamation, the apparition promptly vanished.

John o' Groat's *Highland*

The name is said to derive from John Groat, or de Groot, a Dutchman who ran the Orkney ferry in the late 15th century. Legend tells that John Groat had

THE HOGBOON WHO STAYED *Once upon a time, in a farm on the island of Sanday, Orkney, the owner decided to get married. But his new wife angered the farm's hogboon when she neglected to reward him with food. So the hogboon began to torment the family to such a degree that they were forced to move to another farm on the other side of the island. After they had packed and were on their way there, they heard a clatter in the cart – and to their dismay, as they looked behind them, they saw the hogboon pop his head out of a milk churn and remark, 'What a fine day we're having for the flitting!'*

eight sons who cared so much about precedence that their father built an octagonal house with eight doors, and containing an eight-sided table. Each son could then enter by his own door and sit at his own 'head' of table. The site of the house is marked by a mound and a flagpole. The graves of the De Groots lie in Canisbay churchyard.

Another legend concerns a local seal catcher, who was invited by a dark stranger to do business with his master. The stranger led the man to the cliff edge, where he was suddenly seized and plunged beneath the waves. On the sea-bed the hunter was confronted by an old grey seal with a gaping wound in its side, while the hunter's own knife lay near by. Ashamed of the pain he had inflicted, the man tried to staunch the wound with his hand, whereupon it immediately healed. The hunter swore he would never kill again, and the dark stranger guided him safely home, leaving him with a bag of gold at his cottage door.

Kirkstyle *Highland*
During the 17th century, the minister of Canisbay kirk on the edge of Pentland Firth was Andrew Ogston. Many people believed he had supernatural powers which derived from a book of magic in his possession. On one occasion he fell foul of the Laird of Mey, who so terrorised Ogston's congregation that they were afraid to come to church. The minister, however, filled his kirk by sending a piper round the parish on Sunday mornings. As in the case of the Piper of Hamelin, the people felt compelled to follow him.

Once, when far from home, he gave his horse to the servant walking at his side, and told the man to ride to the manse with all haste. The servant, after galloping home furiously, was astonished to find his master waiting at the manse door. Before Ogston died he ordered his spell book to be destroyed.

KIRKWALL'S NORSE SAINT

The 12th-century stone carving above, now in Tankerness House Museum, Kirkwall, Orkney, represents the Norse earl St Magnus, who was murdered by order of his cousin Haakon. Kirkwall Cathedral is dedicated to St Magnus. In 1919, a skull and some bones were found concealed in one of the cathedral pillars. The skull was cleft as if by an axe – exactly the way Magnus met his death c. 1117. These relics still rest in the cathedral

Lerwick, Mainland *Shetland*

The fire-festival of Up-Helly-Aa is held annually on the last Tuesday in January to celebrate the end of Yule. Though the present celebration is relatively modern, its origins may be in the Norse occupation when the bodies of kings and chiefs were sent to Valhalla in fiery splendour. Wrapped in furs, and with weapons lying to hand, their corpses were placed in longships which were set on fire and left to drift on the tide. Nowadays, this is remembered in the 30 ft model of a Viking ship, complete with heraldic shields and dragon figurehead, which is paraded through the town by the Chief Guizer (an Old French word meaning a disguised person) and his 500 henchmen, all dressed in Viking costume. As darkness falls, the longship is carried at the head of a great winding, torchlit procession, while the band plays 'The Galley Song' and rockets are fired off by all the ships in harbour. Then the band changes its tune to 'The Norseman's Home', which everyone sings as the flaming torches are thrown into the vessel. The parade re-forms, and parties continue into the night.

Lerwick's troubles did not end with the Vikings. Huge ring-bolts still remain of the great chains that were strung across the harbour to keep the French out after 1722; and Paul Jones, the American privateer, called there in 1778. He fled, however, when he saw the red petticoats of Lerwick girls, mistaking them for soldiers' uniforms.

THE TORCHES OF YULE

For a time the long winter night of the north is broken as 500 Lerwick 'Guizers', dressed as Vikings and carrying blazing torches, converge on the sea. The torches are flung into a 30 ft model longship with dragon figurehead, transforming it into a fiery furnace. It may be that the early Vikings symbolised their determination to settle in Shetland by burning their boats when they landed

Lingey *Shetland*

When Jan Teit killed an official in a dispute over butter paid as tax during Shetland's Norse rule, he was summoned before the King of Norway to answer for his crime. The king remarked upon the bunions on Jan's toes, whereupon the hero called for an axe and cut them off. Impressed by such courage, the king offered Jan a pardon if he could capture a savage bear. With the aid of a tub of drugged butter obtained from a wise woman, Jan did so, and brought the creature to court. The king threw them both out of Norway, and Jan returned to Lingey where he chained the bear to a stake. The circular path it made is still called the Bear's Ring.

Mey *Highland*

The Castle of Mey, otherwise Barrogill Castle, has a ghost. Legend says that the daughter of the 5th Earl of Caithness fell in love with a ploughman and was imprisoned by her father in the top room of the tower. So that she could not see her lover at work, one window was bricked up, so the unhappy girl threw herself out of the other. As the 'Green Lady', her mournful wraith is still said to drift about the castle to this day.

HOME OF THE QUEEN MOTHER

The Castle of Mey, also known as Barrogill Castle, is the Highland home of the Queen Mother. It is said to be haunted by a 'Green Lady' – the ghost of a girl who, for love, flung herself from a window in the tower

BROCH OF THE LOVERS

No one knows who built the round towers the islanders call 'brochs', or why; one theory is that they were constructed by Pictish tribes in the 1st century AD. It is said that one tempestuous spring about AD 900, a Norwegian named Bjorn eloped with the beautiful Thora Jewel-hand, and was shipwrecked on the Isle of Mousa, Shetland. While the sailors repaired the vessel, the couple married and set up home in the Broch of Mousa (above). The following spring they sailed again and, far north in Iceland, their daughter Asgerd was born

A CASTLE'S SPECTRAL HELPERS

The Balfours, who used to live in Noltland Castle, Westray, Orkney, had a whole host of family phantoms including a ghostly light that announced births and marriages, and a creature named Broonie who built roads and pulled boats to safety during storms

SANDAY'S DEVIL-MARKS

These parallel grooves on a parapet of the ruined Kirk of Lady, near Overbister on Sanday, Orkney, are known as the Devil's Fingermarks, though no one knows why

Murkle *Highland*
A local mermaid fell in love with a fisherman and lavished gold and jewels upon him. Then she discovered he was using his new wealth to make extravagant gifts to human girls, so she took him to a cave under Dwarwick Head, a point north of Castletown across Dunnet Bay. Here she showed him all the treasure of all the ships that had ever been lost in the Pentland Firth. While he gazed greedily at the spoil, she sang to him so sweetly that he fell asleep. When he awoke, he found he was chained to the floor with golden fetters, and there to this day he remains, jealously guarded by his sea-woman mistress.

Noltland, Westray *Orkney*
The 16th-century castle, one-time home of the Balfours, was illuminated by a spectral light whenever a member of the family was born or married. Deaths were announced by the howling of the castle's phantom, the Boky Hound.

Sailors from a wrecked Armada galleon are said, with some degree of probability, to have settled on the north shore of Westray. Their supposed descendants, who have black, wavy hair, are still called 'Dons' by local people.

GIN GALORE!

When the Carmerlandt of Amsterdam was wrecked on Shetland's Out Skerries in 1664, she contained so many jars of spirits (as well as treasure worth 3 million guilders), that the men of the Skerries were continuously drunk for 20 days. The jar (right), now in Lerwick Museum, was brought up from the wreck recently by a team of divers from Aston University

Overbister, Sanday *Orkney*
A young girl who lived in Broughtown was given a copy of *The Book of the Black Art* by a witch. This book, famous in Orkney tradition, contained magical recipes and conferred strange powers, but the possessor had to get rid of it by sale or gift before dying, otherwise the Devil would claim both the book and its owner. The girl, discovering its nature, tried to destroy it and flung it over a headland, only to find it again on her bedside table. At last a clergyman took possession of the book and may still have owned it at his death in 1903.

Papa Stour *Shetland*
The Maiden Stack, a precipitous rock pinnacle, has a ruined house on its summit, said to have been built to secure the Laird of Papa Stour's daughter from a bold and persistent suitor, who managed nevertheless to scale the cliffs and complete his conquest.

It is said that a fisherman named Herman Perk, hunting seals on the nearby Ve Skerries, was cut off by a storm from his companions. However, a huge seal appeared and carried Herman home on his back, on condition that the fisherman gave him the sealskin he had found on the previous day. The skin belonged to the seal's mate, who was unable to return to the sea without it. Shortly after the skin was handed over, Herman, hiding by the shore, saw a beautiful seal-woman hurrying to the beach, where she put on her lost garment and swam out to sea to join her waiting lover.

St Margaret's Hope, S. Ronaldsay *Orkney*
At Easter, since time out of mind, the boys of the island have engaged in a mimic ploughing contest. Recently, despite some opposition, the ceremony has been moved to a Wednesday in August, probably to fit in with the tourist season. The contest has two sections – Ploughmen and Horses. The Horses are usually girls, wearing elaborate costumes rather like those of the Pearlies of London. After the Horses' costumes are judged, everyone moves down to the beach where the ploughing contest takes place. The Horses take no part in this, and each boy has his own plough, often of ancient and beautiful workmanship. Genuine skill is shown in turning an unbroken furrow of even width in the smooth, firm sand, and the judges take their responsibilities seriously. The day ends with tea, dancing and prizegiving.

THE LADYKIRK STONE

Footprints in a stone at St Mary's Church, Burwick, 6 miles south of St Margaret's Hope, are said to be those of St Magnus, who sailed over the Pentland Firth on it

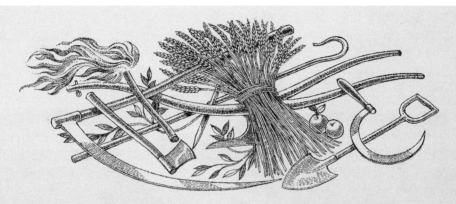

NORTHERN SAFEGUARDS

Though the Orkney and Shetland islanders are linked by a common ancestry, their ways of life have always been very different. Orkney was, and still is, a place of small, intensively worked farms, while Shetland gathers its livelihood from the sea, sending its fleets deep into the Arctic. Nowadays, the islanders mainly place their trust in farm machinery and radar, but not so very long ago, many found it necessary to summon magical help to supplement man's poor ingenuity.

Some of the island superstitions were shared with farmers and seamen all over the world, but others, handed down from their Viking forbears, are unique. In Orkney, for example, it was customary to smear urine on the plough before cutting the first spring furrow – to promote fertility in the soil. There, too, a thin round stone called the *dian-stane*, or sun-stone, was tied to the plough beam and turned sunwards whenever the plough was turned – a relic of ancient sun worship.

Harvest rituals
At harvest, the first sheaf was made into a kind of porridge to be eaten in a ritual meal. The man who brought in the last sheaf was given a sweet bannock called a *drilty*, but he had to run to keep it, pursued by his fellow-workers. The last household to finish harvesting had a straw dog called the *bikko* (bitch) placed on its chimney – an insult greatly resented.

It is said that the secret society of the Horseman's Word, whose initiates are told a word that allegedly gives them power over horses, is still strong in Orkney.

Many northern fishermen had taboo words – such as 'hare', 'rabbit', 'pig', 'salmon' – which were considered dangerous and unlucky to use at sea. When taboo creatures had to be referred to, substitute words were used. In Shetland, these were often of ancient Norse origin. A minister, for example, was a *boniman* or *oppstanda*, while a woman was a *kunie* (wife) or *pirraina* (girl).

When a new boat had a *misforen*, a lost knot in its planking, the unlucky board was replaced. Above all, fishbones were never burnt, for the catches of the fleet would dwindle to nothing.

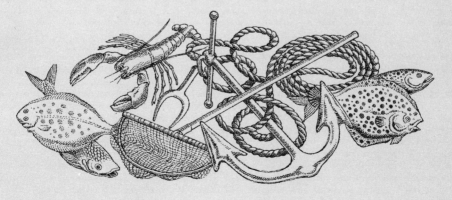

St Ninian's Isle, Mainland *Shetland*

A ruined medieval chapel stands on the site of an earlier chapel. This is believed to have been Shetland's first Christian church, dedicated to St Ninian, a British bishop who studied in Rome and made Pictish Scotland his missionary field. He established his first church on the Isle of Whithorn in Galloway in the 5th century. Though there is no evidence that he visited the Northern Isles, the medieval church on St Ninian's Isle was always regarded as being of special sanctity, as was the nearby St Ninian's Well. In 1958, a hoard of silver ornaments were found on the chapel site – perhaps hidden from Norse marauders 1200 years ago.

SILVER HOARD

The intricately patterned Celtic silver bowl and brooches are part of the St Ninian's Isle hoard of ornaments, now in the National Museum of Antiquities in Edinburgh

MOTHER CHURCH OF THE SHETLANDS

Long-deserted St Ninian's Isle, connected to the mainland by a sandy beach, is believed to be the site of the first Christian settlement in the Shetlands. St Ninian's missionaries probably arrived there in the 5th century

Scalloway, Mainland *Shetland*

The black ashes from numerous witch burnings are still visible in the peaty soil on Gallow Hill, 2 miles north of the village. One witch who met the ultimate penalty there was a fisherman called Luggie. He was burnt for his remarkable fishing prowess – he could let down a line and bring up fish 'well boiled and roasted'.

Njugals Water, Scalloway's reservoir, took its name from a neugle (a water horse akin to the kelpie) which had its home there. Anyone foolhardy enough to mount the beast on the shore was carried beneath the waves and never seen again.

Scapa, Mainland *Orkney*

A witch, angered by fishermen who would not take her son out whaling, buried her thimble on the beach and prophesied that no more whales would be caught in Scapa until it was found. It is still lost and the prediction is said to have come true.

Stenness, Mainland *Orkney*

Couples in the parish once made betrothal vows among the two famous stone circles in the district. They then swore constancy at the Odin Stone (a monolith destroyed in the 19th century) by joining hands through the hole in the stone's centre.

RAIDERS OF THE NORTHERN SEAS

Pirates, press-gangs and smugglers were part of Orkney and Shetland life for centuries. The islands still hold memories of the fierce Lewismen, raiders from the Hebrides. Such was the islanders' fear that when the Elizabethan explorer Martin Frobisher went ashore for water in 1577, the local people panicked and fled 'with shrikes and alarums'. It seemed they were 'often frightened with pirates'.

'The Pirate of Orkney'

The most notorious of these villains was John Fullarton, an 18th-century Orkney captain. 'The Pirate of Orkney', as he was nicknamed, was utterly ruthless and killed all who opposed him – even his own cousin whose ship he seized. It was said that he forced prisoners to draw lots to decide which of them would hang.

His ending was as bloody as the rest of his career. After a running fight with the Scottish merchant vessel *Isabella*, he boarded her and murdered her commander, Captain Jones. Mary Jones, the captain's wife, seized a pistol and surprised Fullarton. Putting the weapon to his temple, she fired and killed him. The *Isabella* returned safely to Leith and Mary Jones became known as 'The Pirate Slayer'.

'The Stromness Pirate', John Gow, had an astonishingly short career. His body was hanging in chains off Greenwich in June 1725, little more than seven months after he seized the English ship in which he was second mate. Gow had been engaged to the daughter of a Stromness merchant, and they had pledged themselves by clasping hands through the Odin Stone in the parish of Stenness. So binding was the belief in this pledge that the girl travelled to London to clasp her dead lover's hand so that she might be released from the oath.

Dodging the press-gangs

Press-gangs, who were detailed to impress able-bodied men into the Royal Navy, were almost as great a scourge in the islands as the pirates. Scores of caves were used as hiding places by the hunted men, as well as secret cells in peat-stacks and hayricks.

In Stronsay, Orkney, a man deliberately broke his leg to avoid impressment. On another occasion, Barbara Wick of Deerness, Orkney, held a naval party at bay with well-aimed stones while her lover escaped.

Profitable smuggling

During the 18th and 19th centuries, smuggling was the most profitable of all island trades. Everyone joined in. Churches occasionally housed smuggled spirits and, as late as the 1860's, customers could buy smuggled gin over the counter of a Kirkwall bank. During the Napoleonic wars, the guns of HMS *Norfolk*, lying at Kirkwall, were found to be loaded with tea and tobacco. Even at the beginning of this century, French and Dutch fishing vessels regularly bartered a potent gin with the islanders for farm produce such as eggs and butter.

Summerdale, Mainland *Orkney*

Here, in 1529, Orkney defeated Caithness in the last battle on island soil. The Earl of Caithness discovered a witch unwinding balls of red and blue wool, and the red was exhausted first. She told him that this meant that the side which first shed the other's blood would win, so the earl slew a nearby cow-herd. Unfortunately, the man was a visitor from Caithness, and the earl's cause was doomed.

Swona *Orkney*

A witch who loved a Ronaldsay man determined to kill his sweetheart. She pushed the girl out of a boat, and the man, trying to save her, also fell in. The witch locked her hand in his, but the lovers were drowned. The Wells of Swona whirlpool is said to be caused by the witch's efforts to free herself.

Thurso *Highland*

In 1718, a man named Montgomery kept watch in his cellar to discover who was stealing his ale. A number of cats appeared and began to help themselves, whereupon Montgomery killed two with his sword and maimed another. As a result, two local women died suddenly, and another was found to be minus a leg. She was forced into confessing herself to be a witch, and into implicating 20 others. Some were probably burnt on Gallahill, which was marked by a large stone that always re-emerged, no matter how much earth was heaped on it.

How a rare grass, called Holy Grass, comes to be growing on the banks of the Thurso River is explained by a local story. The plant was so named because it used to be strewn before the doors of some continental churches. It is said that the floor of a chapel that once stood by the river was covered with Holy Grass cut in Norway. The area was damp, and the seeds germinated and took root.

In the 19th century, the ruined chapel contained a 'little god' that people clothed with a tiny shirt on Christmas night.

OLIPHANT'S LEAP

In the 16th century, Auld Wick Castle, now a ruin, belonged to Lord Oliphant, who had a deadly feud with the Earl of Caithness. When riding alone one day, Oliphant was set upon by the earl and his followers, but his superb horse managed to outdistance them. When he arrived home, the drawbridge of Auld Wick Castle was raised, but his horse never hesitated. It cleared the 25 ft chasm in one mighty bound, and Oliphant was saved

Wick *Highland*

At the end of the 17th century, when Campbell of Glenorchy tried to take land he thought himself entitled to from the unwilling Sinclairs, he deliberately allowed a ship loaded with whisky to be stranded near Wick. The Sinclairs found the vessel and spent the night in happy carousal. Next day, suffering from terrible hangovers, they were easily routed by Glenorchy and his men. The story is discredited locally, for a mere single cargo could never have affected Caithnessmen so badly!

Wyre *Orkney*

The castle belonged to a 12th-century Norse chief named Kolbein Hruga, better known as the giant Cubby Roo. He used islands as stepping stones, and when angered, threw huge boulders about, which can be seen on Rousay and Stronsay.

Yetnasteen, Rousay *Orkney*

The giant's stone, Yetnasteen, is said to walk to the Loch of Scockness to drink on New Year's morn.

Ronsay legend tells of a giant who kidnapped three princesses, two of whom he flayed alive, keeping the third to weave his wool. This girl restored her sisters to their skins, and helped them to escape by persuading the dull-witted giant to carry them home concealed in baskets of grass. The princesses and their mother revenged themselves by scalding the giant to death.

People of Myth

A GALLERY OF HEROES, SAINTS AND SCOUNDRELS

WAYS OF GLORY

The men and women chosen to wear the mantle of immortality

Every age finds the heroes it needs. It obtains them either by extolling – and usually exaggerating – the deeds of an admired contemporary figure, or by re-interpreting those of a great man of the past. Though a hero is usually noble and selfless, he may also be cruel; what is chiefly demanded of him is that he should be larger than life – a man braver or luckier than the rest of us. The legends that gather about such men are often part of a nation's glory, and their stories are retold to each generation as sure proof of the heroism of the people in times of crisis.

Many of these heroic figures were mighty leaders in war, defenders of their country against invasion, or the spark that raised the fires of rebellion against oppression and tyranny. Others were law-givers, or saints whose alleged miracles and readiness to die for their faith were the driving force that converted the land to Christianity. Some, like the famous medieval outlaws, seem to have been simple brigands, with little to distinguish them beyond ruthless courage; but they were admired, nevertheless, because their exploits were on the grand scale.

Of all British heroes, the most enduring is Arthur. Who he was in real life is now uncertain, and every period has seen him differently. During the Dark Ages, he was pictured as a sleeping champion who would one day awaken and deliver his countrymen from bondage. To medieval courtiers, he was the prince of chivalry, while the Victorians stressed the Christian virtues of Arthur and his knights. In our own, less romantic age, we like to imagine him as he may have been – the tough guerrilla leader who for a time united Britain against the Saxon invader.

The people's champions

Though the tales of Arthur and his knights jousting for the hands of fair ladies were highly popular with the medieval aristocracy, the stories were too far removed from the lives of ordinary people, who chose instead a hero after their own hearts. This was Robin Hood, the yeoman turned outlaw who defied the unpopular game laws, who outwitted authority at every turn and who robbed rich abbots and gave the money to the poor. Robin was the ideal villain with a heart of gold, but in later centuries his mantle fell upon the unlikeliest successors.

There was Johnnie Armstrong, for example, the hero of the Border ballads, who tortured a widow to death for £4, and Dick Turpin, the London butcher turned cattle-thief and highwayman. A newspaper story of 1735 contrasts oddly with Turpin's image as a popular hero, for it tells how he and his gang raided a farm at Edgware. When the farmer protested he had no money, they 'let his Breeches down and set him bare on the Fire'. Even Dick's famous breakneck ride to York to establish an alibi was actually performed by another highwayman, named 'Swift Nicks' Nevison, a century earlier. Still, Turpin made a good end. When he was hanged at York in 1739, he bowed to the ladies and threw himself off the ladder. The mob were so delighted by his performance that they stole his body and buried it in quicklime to prevent it being sold to the anatomists.

Style – perhaps even flamboyance – is the prerequisite of the hero. Whatever the earlier sins of Sir James Douglas, he earned his

The heroic ideal
Immortality is a gift conveyed by time and circumstance. Most of those who win it are young and beautiful, popular, brave and self-sacrificing. Yet the contrary British have also made heroes out of villains and vagabonds who would have been hanged by their contemporaries

The conception of Merlin

The wizard Merlin, who gave magical assistance to three British hero-kings, Aurelius, Uther Pendragon and Arthur, was said to have been fathered by a demon. Strangely enough, he may have been founded upon a real-life prophet named Myrddin, who lived in the land of the northern Welsh, which is now west Cumbria, in the 5th century

place in the gallery of the immortals when he flung the heart of his beloved leader, Robert the Bruce, into the centre of the enemy troops, and followed after it to his death. The colour of the Black Prince's armour, and his adoption of the three-feathered badge of a fallen foe, are still remembered, though the slaughter he caused in France is long forgotten – at least by the English. And no historian, however critical, can take away from us the picture of Lord Nelson, one-armed, bemedalled and unmistakable, coolly pacing the shot-torn decks as the *Victory* smashed through the line of French and Spanish ships at Trafalgar.

The accolade of legend

The quality that makes a man's, or a woman's, name resound in their country's folklore is indefinable. Many noble and gallant people who apparently earned a place are forgotten, while as many villains are remembered. Some names become a legend for a time, like that of Simon de Montfort whose deep love of justice led him to summon the first English parliament. When he was killed at the Battle of Evesham in 1265, people said that the spring by which his mutilated corpse had lain possessed healing powers, and miraculous cures might also be granted to those who prayed by his tomb. Then, too, some popular figures became part of national legend for reasons that would have astonished them. That efficient and charitable 15th-century Mayor of London, Richard Whittington, is now chiefly remembered for his cat. As a liberal benefactor of London – he built almshouses and libraries, and restored St Bartholomew's Hospital – he has been largely forgotten.

Throughout history, people have picked their idols and made up stories about them, but the accolade is less readily accorded today. Perhaps the spread of modern communications means that we know too much about too many people to be able to give special veneration to individuals. The present-day attitude is summed up by the choice of the Unknown Soldier as a collective hero – a belated recognition of the fact that it was always the ordinary man who really fought the battles and won the wars.

The architect of parliament

Simon de Montfort was an immensely popular hero in his own day, and for a time, after capturing the feeble Henry III at the Battle of Lewes in 1264 (top left), was virtual dictator of the country. But Henry's son Prince Edward avenged his father in 1265, when he won the Battle of Evesham and slaughtered de Montfort. The reformer, who is still remembered as the summoner of England's first parliament, died a hero's death, fighting to the end (top right). His savagely mutilated corpse (below) was laid to rest in the nearby abbey. After his death, it was said that the cord which had been used to measure his corpse had the power to heal the blind and lame, and even to raise the dead; and his tomb, where many miracles apparently occurred, became a place of pilgrimage

DE MONTFORT captures Henry III (left), but is killed at Evesham (right)

BATTLE OF EVESHAM where Simon de Montfort's corpse was mutilated

484

The death of Dick Whittington
Dick's legendary rise from rags to
riches has made him the hero of
every youth who ever dreamt of
the gold-paved streets of London.
In fact, Dick was far from being a
poor boy, for he was the son of a
wealthy Gloucestershire
landowner. Still, Bow Bells'
promise was amply fulfilled. Not
only was Dick three times Mayor of
London, but he also became a very
rich man. This picture shows his
death in 1423

England's 'little Admiral'
Nelson's message to the British
fleet before Trafalgar, and his
dying request to Captain Hardy,
are engraved for ever on the
nation's memory; and the last,
tragic tableau of his death, as he lay
in the cockpit of the *Victory* with his
spine smashed by a sniper's bullet, is
an image that will never fade. His
courage and success in battle made
him a passionately admired hero in
his lifetime. He is no less a hero
today, more than a century and a
half after his death

'Take my drum to England . . .'

Few heroes have attracted so many legends as Sir Francis Drake. The Spaniards believed that he had a magic mirror in which he could see the movement of ships in any part of the world, and his own countrymen said that on one occasion, while he was whittling a stick into the sea, the shavings turned into warships as they hit the water. According to legend, he could be summoned to England's aid after his death by beating on his drum in Buckland Abbey, Devon. Some people believed, too, that later admirals, such as Nelson, were reincarnations of Drake's immortal spirit

THE UNDEFEATED

Every age produces men who, it seems, can conquer even death

O
f all the hero legends that have come down through the centuries, one of the most widespread is that of the Undying Hero. It is found in one form or another in almost every part of Europe, and flourished particularly in areas where a nation had suffered defeat and disaster after the loss of a great leader upon whom all its hopes were centred. The hero's death is not admitted. He has gone elsewhere, but only for a time. The essential point of the legend is that eventually he will return, and when he does, the enemy will be destroyed, the shattered kingdom will be restored, and all will be again as it was before the time of the disaster. No one knows when the day of deliverance will come; but the anticipation of it has often been enough to keep the fires of hope burning in the hearts of defeated men.

The legends vary as to where the hero has gone, and in what strange dwelling he will live until the time of his recall. Sometimes he is in his own country, waiting in a hidden cavern or under a mountain. Sometimes he is in Paradise, Avalon, Fairyland or some other mysterious region beyond the material boundaries of this world. Often there is more than one tradition about the same man, as there is about King Arthur, the most famous of Britain's undying heroes. Arthur is said to dwell in Avalon, but he also has traditional resting places all over Britain, especially in Wales and in the west and north of England. In most of them – as at the cave of Craig y Dinas in South Wales and beneath Sewingshields Castle in Northumberland and Richmond Castle in N. Yorkshire – he lies asleep with his warriors all around him, often with treasure, hounds and horses as well. And he wakes only occasionally, if at all, when some intruder wanders by accident into his hidden fastness.

Sleeping in the caves of Wales

Apart from King Arthur, there were two renowned leaders who lived on in Wales long after their natural lives would have ended. The first was Owen Lawgoch, about whom very little is known except that he was a 14th-century chieftain who tried to free his countrymen from English domination. He was supposed to have died in 1378, but his followers refused to believe it. To this day, there are several caves in South Wales, such as one on Mynydd Mawr near Llandeilo, where legend claims that he is sleeping, surrounded by his warriors, until the sound of trumpets and the clash of arms summon them back to battle for their country's freedom.

There are often conflicting traditions about whether it is King Arthur, Owen Lawgoch or the third undying Welsh hero, Owen Glendower, who occupies any particular cave. Glendower raised the standard of rebellion against the English in 1400, and within four years had so far advanced the cause of Welsh independence that he was able to hold a Welsh parliament and to make an alliance with France. But the tides of war finally turned against him, and he was forced into hiding in the mountains. Though he fought on for years as a guerrilla leader, he eventually disappeared, and no one is sure how, or when, he died. The legend grew up that he was sleeping in Castle Cave in the Vale of Gwent, and that he would remain there until England became degenerate and enfeebled by vice. Only then would he return with his warriors to re-establish the independence of Wales for ever.

The legend that died at Shrewsbury

A crop of rumours that might easily have immortalised another hero sprang up in 1399 or 1400, after the disappearance of Richard II. The king was deposed on September 30, 1399, by Henry IV, and was imprisoned in Pontefract Castle. He was almost certainly murdered there, for he was never seen alive again. In fact, a corpse

The Great Seal of Owen Glendower
According to both friends and enemies, the medieval Welsh leader Owen Glendower had the power to raise winds and storms at will, and possessed a magic stone which enabled him to become invisible. Little wonder, then, that when he disappeared about 1415, his followers refused to believe that he had died. They claimed instead that he was safely hidden in a secret stronghold and that eventually he would return to free Wales from English oppression

that was alleged to be his was brought to London and publicly shown in the city. There was a solemn dirge for him at St Paul's, and his remains were interred at the Blackfriars in King's Langley, Hertfordshire. Nevertheless, a great number of his supporters firmly believed that he had escaped from Pontefract and taken refuge in Scotland. This belief was especially strong in Cheshire, a county that had always been loyal to him and where he was greatly loved. It was strengthened by the fact that a man claiming to be Richard appeared in Scotland, and was welcomed and entertained at the Scottish Court by Robert III.

Just before Harry Hotspur's rebellion against Henry IV in 1403, the word spread that Richard had come to Sandiway in Cheshire, and was preparing to support the rising. A large number of Cheshire men joined Hotspur on the strength of it, and many of them died at Shrewsbury in 1403, when Hotspur was defeated. Richard's legend died there too, for little more was heard of his survival. Within a few years, a strong spontaneous belief that had all the ingredients of an undying hero legend faded away almost completely.

The drum that rolled at Scapa Flow

Sir Francis Drake was not an undying hero in the sense that anyone ever disputed the fact of his death, or that he was believed to sleep in some secret place at home or abroad. Yet the most famous legend about him is very similar to those about King Arthur and other enchanted warriors who would rise from their magical slumbers when their country needed them. The story runs that when he lay dying in 1596, on board ship off Puerto Bello, Panama, he gave orders that his drum should be sent back to Buckland Abbey, his home in Devon. He promised that if England was ever again in serious danger, and if anyone beat on the drum, he would hear its note and come at once from Paradise to his country's aid.

In the course of time, this legend went through a strange alteration. In the modern version, the drum rolls, without human agency, before a war. In 1914, there were rumours that it had been heard in the West Country, and there is a sailors' tradition that it rolled again at Scapa Flow in 1919, when the German fleet officially surrendered. A single drum was heard beating on the flagship of the Grand Fleet, as the great ships closed round the German vessels. Although rigorous search was made for the drummer while the drumroll went on, every sailor was found at his correct battle station, and there was no sign of any unauthorised drum. The mystery was never solved.

The sailors, however, were certain that it was Drake's drum, and that the great admiral was with them in their hour of victory, as he had been throughout the years of war.

The men of Avalon

If no one now looks for the return of any vanished hero from Avalon or some hollow hill, the old instinctive refusal to acknowledge a hero's death has shown itself more than once in our own times. Nowadays, the legends cannot survive for more than the natural span of a human life, for modern man cannot bring himself to believe in a hero who endures for centuries. But they may last for months or years, as they did with Lord Kitchener.

The general was, in his lifetime, a popular hero. He had relieved Khartoum in 1898, fought against the Boers in the South African War of 1899–1902, and organised the British army in the First World War.

On June 5, 1916, when he was Secretary of State for War, he sailed from Scapa Flow on a secret mission to Russia. The weather was so bad that it was suggested that his departure should be deferred; but he was unwilling to delay the journey and, accordingly, at about five o'clock in the evening, he sailed in the cruiser *Hampshire*. Less than three hours later, the ship struck a German mine off Marwick Head in the Orkneys, and sank within 15 minutes. Only a very few of those on board managed to struggle ashore through the raging seas, and Kitchener was not one of them. His body was never recovered.

As soon as the calamitous news became known, a variety of stories began to circulate. Many were based on the belief that Kitchener was not dead, and that only considerations of policy prevented the authorities from openly declaring that he still lived. One theory was that the Russian mission was so important that the government had deliberately spread the false news of his death in order to deceive the Germans. Another was that he had been

'Long live King Richard!'
There is little doubt that Richard II was murdered in Pontefract Castle in 1400, but even when Henry IV had the royal corpse publicly displayed in St Paul's Cathedral, many people persisted in believing that he was alive. The body, they said, was that of Richard's chaplain. So strong was the belief in Richard's survival that many men joined Harry Hotspur's rebellion against Henry IV in 1403, thinking that they were thus helping to restore the true king to his throne

betrayed and was a prisoner in German hands; or alternatively, that he had been rescued and hidden for safety in some remote part of the Hebrides, whence he would return in due course. These and other tales faded away after a time, but while they lasted, they were very widespread.

A similar legend appeared again, very briefly, after the death of Adolf Hitler in 1945. It was rumoured in many parts of Germany that he was not dead, but only hiding, and that he would return before long to lead again those who had remained loyal to him. Even in Britain and other allied countries there were people who could not believe that this man, who had caused so much misery in the world, was at last dead. The legend was short-lived, but for a time at least, the ancient pattern of thought was as clearly visible in modern Germany as ever it had been in the days of King Arthur or Owen Glendower.

More recently still, the deaths of the actor James Dean, and the revolutionary Che Guevara have, for different reasons, been denied by their followers. And for a brief moment, the heroes or anti-heroes of today joined the ranks of the immortal warriors of the past.

Lawrence of Arabia
Lawrence's fatal motor-cycle accident in 1935 was said to be a cover for a secret mission he had undertaken to the Middle East

Kitchener of Khartoum
When Lord Kitchener was drowned in 1916, his death was fiercely denied by many to whom the disaster seemed too shattering to be possible. Rumour said that the false news of his death had been spread to mislead the Germans

The romantic idea of Arthur
In this 14th-century French illustration of Arthur and his knights, the king
himself is on the left, with his right arm raised. Drawings and tapestries of
the times usually identify him by the crowns on his standard, shield and
robe. Earlier, he was portrayed carrying the image of the Virgin on his
shield, the badge of the ideal Christian leader against the pagan foe. In real
life, his appearance was probably very different. He was more likely a rough
warrior in a leather jerkin, wearing a plain, iron head-piece for protection,
leather boots and breeches, with coarse linen trousers. This drab outfit may
have been brightened by the addition of a red woollen cloak

ARTHUR OF AVALON

A warrior chieftain of the Dark Ages who came to the throne of a romantic kingdom

Departing, sorely wounded, for the Isle of Avalon, the legendary King Arthur made a promise: that whenever his people needed him, he would return. As always, he kept faith, for even if he has never returned in the physical sense, there is no doubt that for 1500 years he has constantly provided fresh inspiration to poets, artists, musicians, and even kings. The 6th-century British warrior leader who held back the dark forces of marauding invaders and united his people, stands for ever as an example of wisdom, tolerance, chivalry and all the virtues of leadership.

Ever since the historian Geoffrey of Monmouth romanticised the legends, early in the 12th century, Arthur has reigned in men's hearts as firmly as in his legendary court of Camelot. Malory, Spenser, Dryden, Wagner and Tennyson were all fascinated by him. Edward III founded his Order of the Garter, *c.* 1350, in an attempt to recreate the loyalty and fellowship of the Round Table. The Welsh Henry Tudor, who became Henry VII in 1485, claimed he had restored the true 'British' royal line after Saxon and Norman usurpers; and James I's ancestry was imaginatively traced back to Arthur, to convince people of his worthiness to rule.

To some, Arthur was a champion of Christendom; to others, the inspiration of hard-pressed soldiers. Early medieval minstrels made him the central figure of a group of legends they called The Matter of Britain. No hero is more widely known, yet despite intensive research, the question remains: who was Arthur?

Most modern historians agree that he did exist, though probably he was not a king. Possibly he was a Celtic cavalry leader with a swift-moving force, which would account for his ability to range up and down the country to achieve the dozen victories with which he has been credited. Certainly his efforts drove the Saxon hordes back towards the North Sea and for a time at least delayed Britain's descent into the chaos known as the Dark Ages.

When the legions of the collapsing Roman Empire withdrew from Britain at the beginning of the 5th century, they left a Romanised and Christian society of Celtic people to defend themselves as best they might against the Irish from the west and the

A British hero in Italy
Tales about Arthur spread rapidly abroad. This detail from a mosaic in the cathedral at Otranto, Italy, dated 1165, illustrates his European renown. It shows the king among other revered 'worthies', such as Alexander and Noah. Arthur rides a goat, which is thought to refer to his legendary association with an underworld kingdom of dwarfs who preferred riding goats to horses

Arthur the tyrant
Here Arthur is seen setting adrift a boatload of babies, to avoid fulfilment of a prophecy that a boy born on May Day would cause his death. He ordered that all children born that day must die: Modred, however, survived and brought about Arthur's downfall at the Battle of Camlann. This version of Arthur as an evil tyrant was probably originated by Celtic monks whom he antagonised by plundering the monasteries to supply his soldiers. The monks' dislike may also explain the shortage of references to him in early records. Clerics, who were virtually the only people able to write, no doubt considered his sins against the Church far outweighed his virtues in protecting Britons from the Saxons. As a result they would either not write of his exploits at all – or show him in a poor light

The fatal victory
The king's last victory at the Battle of Camlann where he kills his treacherous nephew – or illegitimate son – Modred, in single combat is shown in this illustration from the 15th-century *St Albans Chronicle*. Modred had discovered the secret love of Lancelot and Guinevere and used the knowledge as a lever to destroy the Order of the Round Table. Some knights supported Lancelot, others the king. In the civil war that followed, Arthur, too, was mortally wounded by Modred, and sailed away into the mists of legend

Picts from the north. At the same time, Angles, Saxons and Jutes from the Rhine and Denmark made bloody attacks on the east coast. Many of these continental invaders were originally invited to Britain by King Vortigern, the dominant British ruler of the 5th century, to help him in his feuds against Picts and Scots.

This was a common enough practice with Roman emperors, but Vortigern did not have the financial resources of the Romans. When he could not pay his troops, they turned against him and poured, looting and massacring, through the land. Their kinsfolk sailed across the sea to join them and, under the shock of the assault, Britain broke up into small kingdoms, such as Dumnonia in the south-west, Dyfed in South Wales and Elmet, W. Yorkshire.

'Leader in the battles'
The Saxons threatened to overwhelm the country, but the British rallied. Local chiefs repaired the earthwork hill-forts of their pre-Roman ancestors, and used them as strongholds. A resistance movement, led by the Romano-British prince Ambrosius Aurelianus, increased the British hold on the south and west and carried on a prolonged war with the Saxons; for many years, victory and defeat hung in the balance.

It is about the end of Ambrosius's time that a man called Artos, or Arthur, begins to emerge as a wide-ranging soldier uniting the squabbling, petty kings of Britain against the common foe, and finally leading them to a decisive victory at a place chroniclers named as Mount Badon. The rapidity with which he moved about the country lends credence to the idea that he was a leader of horsemen, whose mobility would give them considerable advantage over the Saxons who had no cavalry at all. To the British crouched behind their hill-top ramparts, the appearance of his mounted band must have seemed one of the few elements of stability in a precarious world of conflict: small wonder that he was thought of as a 'king'.

His name itself gives a clue to his background. It is a Celtic form of the Roman Artorius, and shows that he was probably a noble Celt, whose family had grown to prominence during the Roman occupation. Until the 5th century AD, there is no recorded instance of the name of Arthur; yet in the hundred years after the supposed death of the hero, the name crops up time and again. This at least indicates the breadth of his fame, for then, as now, people tended to name their children after an admired figure.

The first mention of Arthur's prowess in battle comes from an elegy written by a northern bard, Aneurin, around AD 600. Other literary clues locate him in west Cumbria and parts of Scotland, but there is no more complete story of the man who succeeded Ambrosius and was the architect of victory at Mount Badon until Nennius, a monk at Bangor, wrote of him as the *dux bellorum*, or battle leader, in his *History of the Britons* compiled in the 9th century, some 300 years later.

The stuff of heroes

The site of Mount Badon, the battle that was to contain the Saxons for at least 30 years, is not known, nor its exact date. Early Welsh records say it happened in AD 516 or 518, and it was probably fought somewhere in Wiltshire. Liddington Castle, near Swindon, is a favoured site. Another is Badbury Rings, in Dorset. In all, Arthur is said to have fought 12 major battles against the Saxons, of which the last was at Mount Badon.

His first victory was said to be by the River Glein, which could be one of the Glen rivers in either Northumberland or Lincolnshire. Then came four encounters in Linnuis – perhaps northern Lincolnshire – followed by triumphs at a River Bassas (unknown); in the Scottish forest of Celidon, which may be near the headwaters of Tweed and Clyde; at Guinnion Castle (unknown); in the City of the Legion, thought to be Chester; by the River Tribruit, somewhere in the Scottish Lowlands; and on the untraced Hill of Agned.

Such a wide-ranging campaigner, dauntless, resolute and successful, must have been a light in darkness to the hard-pressed British. He was the shining hope whose name was known everywhere from Cornwall, which claimed to be his birthplace, to Scotland. Two Scilly islets are called Great and Little Arthur. Wales, Cheshire, west Cumbria and Northumberland have caves where he and his knights are said to lie sleeping, and rocks which bear the names of Arthur's Chair, Arthur's Table and Arthur's Kitchen. In the Scottish Highlands, there is a mountain called Ben Arthur, and the hill near Edinburgh is known as Arthur's Seat.

The happy beginning
This 14th-century French illustration shows the wedding night of Arthur and Guinevere. In early Welsh tales, Guinevere was the daughter of a giant, but in the later stories, she came from the West Country, and was daughter of King Leodegrance, who gave the Round Table as part of her dowry. In the earliest records of Arthur, there is no mention of Guinevere. It seems likely she was introduced by later writers to show how the perfect society fell through sin

Medieval love story
Lancelot and Queen Guinevere exchange a kiss, under the discreet but watchful eye of a chaperon. The medieval storytellers added Lancelot to the old Celtic tales about Arthur in order to improve their romantic appeal. When Guinevere's affair with Lancelot was discovered, she was sentenced to death, but was rescued by Lancelot who carried her away to Joyous Garde – possibly Bamber Castle in Northumberland. After many battles, Lancelot surrendered and was banished to his estates in France, while Guinevere spent the remainder of her life as the abbess of Amesbury convent

Most stories, however, link Arthur with the West Country, to which, having won peace for the British, he is said to have retired. There, with his wife Guinevere, he held court at Camelot – possibly the pre-Roman earthwork hill-fort of Cadbury Castle, in Somerset. Recent excavations there show that the hill was occupied and re-fortified on a grand scale during the Arthurian period, and no comparable stronghold has been discovered elsewhere in Britain. Cadbury Castle was never the dream-Camelot of romance, but it was the headquarters of an outstanding leader.

Other excavations have backed up the story that Arthur was finally laid to rest at Glastonbury Abbey, 12 miles north-west of Cadbury Castle. He is said to have been buried there in great secrecy, to avoid heartening the Saxons with the news of his death, and the lingering mystery over his grave would explain the many rumours that he lived on. Monks at Glastonbury claimed to have dug up Arthur's bones in 1190. They were found in a coffin made from a hollow log, together with a lead cross inscribed with his name. A woman's skeleton and a mass of yellow hair in the same grave were alleged to be the remains of his queen, Guinevere. Whether the bones were named as Arthur's to win pilgrims and provide funds for restoring the abbey is not known. But recent research has shown that there was once a deep grave of the right period and type, at the site indicated by the monks.

Fact and fiction mingle

Geoffrey of Monmouth was the man who first gave literary form to the saga surrounding Arthur, when he wrote his *History of the Kings of Britain* in the 1130's. Though he wrote of known events and drew on material which has since vanished, he also drew heavily on his own imagination.

According to Geoffrey, Arthur was the son of King Uther Pendragon, who ruled Britain after Ambrosius, and Igerna, wife of Gorlois, Duke of Cornwall. Uther enlisted the aid of Merlin the magician, to disguise him as the duke, so that he could make love to Igerna at Tintagel Castle, while the real duke was away. Later, after the duke died in battle, Uther and Igerna married, and Arthur became lawful heir to the throne. At the age of 15, he was crowned King of the Britons at Silchester, in Hampshire.

Geoffrey places Bath as the site of Arthur's victory of Mount Badon. There, he defeats the Saxons with the aid of a magical sword, forged in the mysterious Isle of Avalon. Geoffrey calls this weapon Caliburn, but later writers re-named it Excalibur.

But Geoffrey does not stop at triumphs over Saxons, or Picts.

Return to Camelot
Lancelot relates his adventures, as Arthur and his queen listen. As this 14th-century miniature shows, medieval romancers usually showed the court in dress of their own time. Some 800 years after the real Arthur's death, his role in the stories has dwindled. Often, he became little more than a court figurehead while his knights went abroad, seeking new quests

After marrying Guinevere, the brave Arthur goes on to conquer Ireland, Iceland, the Orkneys, Norway and Gaul. Having set up a sizable empire, he retires to his court at Caerleon-on-Usk, surrounded by his knights, priests and astrologers. It was a rich, cultured and martial court, where the ladies would not accept the love of any knight who had not proved himself in battle at least three times – an arrangement that kept the women chaste and knights courageous.

But the war-clouds were gathering. The Roman Emperor Lucius demanded tribute, so Arthur took an army to the Continent to win a final great victory over the Romans in Gaul. He would have marched on to Rome itself, but for the news that the wicked Modred, his nephew, had made a treacherous alliance with the Saxons. Arthur returned and in the year 542 he fought his last battle at Camlann, which Geoffrey locates by the River Camel, in Cornwall. In killing Modred, he himself received a deadly wound – though no one saw him die. Instead, he was borne away to have his wound tended on the mysterious Isle of Avalon.

The legend grows

By enlarging Arthur the Celtic warrior and partisan leader into a mighty monarch and conqueror, Geoffrey of Monmouth gave him European renown. In this new guise, the old hero had considerable political value. Henry II (reigned 1154–89) and his Plantaganet heirs, were happy to encourage a view of British history that gave the throne such a glamorous past and which also helped to buttress English claims to Scotland and Wales.

The story's one weakness was the fate of Arthur after Camlann. Legend flourished among the Celtic Welsh, Cornish and Bretons that Arthur never died, but would sleep until the day came to restore their golden age – perhaps at Avalon, which was to them a fairy isle ruled over by Arthur's half-sister, the enchantress Morgan le Fay. Such a prophecy hardly suited the Plantagenets. They promoted the other version of the tale which said that Arthur had in fact died and been buried at Glastonbury, and that Avalon was simply another, older name for the place. Thus they were able to dismiss the prophecies of his return as a Celtic champion and claim that his heritage belonged to them.

In 1155, some 20 years after Geoffrey of Monmouth's version had captured the imagination of Europe, the poet Robert Wace added the Round Table to the story. Wace held that Arthur devised the table to ensure that no one knight should have obvious precedence over another.

The sacred quest
This is how Victorians saw the Quest for the Holy Grail, in a detail from the tapestry woven by William Morris to a design by Edward Burne-Jones. Sir Galahad, the only one of Arthur's knights 'so grounded in the love of Christ that no adventure could tempt him into sin', kneels at a chapel door to gaze on the holy vessel, while Bors and Percival – less perfect in spirit – must stand at a distance

The hero's farewell
The Pre-Raphaelite artist Dante Gabriel Rossetti also followed romantic versions of the legend in his portrayal of the mysterious queens attending the mortally wounded Arthur. The barge waits to ferry him to Avalon, the enchanted isle – said to be Glastonbury in Somerset

Later in the 12th century, the French poet, Chrétien de Troyes, was one of many writers who were to graft new stories on to the main stem of the legend – the love stories of Lancelot and Guinevere, and of Tristan and Iseult; Galahad and the Quest for the Holy Grail; and the story of Arthur's famed capital, Camelot, which fell into ruin after he had gone.

Later still, in medieval times, a strange aspect of the legend's growth was the rebirth of ancient Celtic themes. In these, Arthur became not only a focus of the events of a single period of history, but the central figure in a group of legends whose far-off origins lay in the mists of pre-Christian Celtic lore.

The figure of Arthur became confused with an unidentified ancient Celtic god, who was said to lie sleeping in a cave on some western island. This god had once ruled happily over men, but had been overthrown; one day he would rise again.

The stories became more fanciful as Arthur took on the guise of some demi-god or fairyland being, who was said to have slain giants, or turned into a raven to ride the clouds. In one case he seems to have assumed the traits of a pygmy king of Welsh legend who rode a goat rather than a horse.

The Quest for the Holy Grail, though a Christian story in itself, draws on earlier mythology, too, with its story of a magical cup and the search for it through enchanted lands: yet with the passage of time the Grail – said to be the chalice used at the Last Supper, brought to Britain by Joseph of Arimathea, and containing drops of Christ's blood – became a purely religious and holy motif. It symbolised purity, and it would be revealed only to those who, like Galahad, were free from sin.

'The once and future king'

In medieval romance – which produced whole libraries of Arthurian literature – history and folklore, pagan myth and Christian fantasy were merged into a pattern of chivalry. Gallant knights went on noble quests, or did battle for the chaste favours of fair damsels. The best-known version of Arthur's story is *Morte d'Arthur*, written by Sir Thomas Malory and published in 1485. Malory translated and adapted the stories, painting a picture of a golden age of chivalry and a strong, unified kingdom ruled by a noble aristocracy – an example to the squabbling kings and barons who were still engaged in the Wars of the Roses.

In the Malory version, Arthur becomes king by drawing a magic sword out of an anvil in London, which no other man could do. Guided by Merlin the magician, he subdues all enemies, to rule in glory. Later he is given his famed Excalibur to replace the original sword which had been broken in battle.

He marries Guinevere, and sets up court at Camelot, which Malory placed at Winchester. There, too, he establishes the Order of the Round Table – an order of knights who vow to live nobly and fight valiantly. But overshadowing this picture of prosperity and honour is Merlin's prophecy of the evil days ahead. The seeds of disaster are present in Modred, who Malory refers to as Arthur's son, fathered in an incestuous affair with his half-sister, Morgan le Fay, and in the secret passion of Lancelot, Arthur's trusted friend, and Guinevere.

Arthur's glory grows for a while, culminating in his defeat of the Romans and being crowned emperor by the pope – but the years of peace do not last long. Knights ride out in quest of the Grail and never return. The affair between Lancelot and Guinevere is discovered and Modred exploits the scandal to start a civil war. In the battle that follows, as knights take sides against each other, for Lancelot or the king, Arthur defeats Modred in personal combat, but is himself mortally wounded. Sorrowing women carry him to a barge, which sails west to Avalon, and into legend. But, says Malory, some men say he was buried elsewhere, and above his grave is the inscription: HIC IACET ARTHURUS, REX QUONDAM REXQUE FUTURUS – Here lies Arthur, the Once and Future King.

WAS THIS CAMELOT?

Recent archaeological research suggests that Cadbury Castle, Somerset, was the stronghold of a warrior leader of the 6th century – possibly Arthur himself. From here, perhaps, sprang the legends of Camelot, of Lancelot and Guinevere, of the Knights of the Round Table, and the Quest for the Holy Grail. Local tradition says that Arthur sleeps beneath the hill but will rise again when his country calls

CADBURY CASTLE This pre-Roman hill-fort was reconstructed by a powerful Briton in the 6th century

VALE OF AVALON Legend associates the marshes around Glastonbury with the mysterious Isle of Avalon

GLASTONBURY ABBEY In the 12th century the monks alleged they had found the bones of Arthur

---

The battle leader
Legend refers to Arthur as Imperator, or commander-in-chief, long before he was called a king. One theory is that his fame and prestige arose initially from his leadership of a successful and wide-ranging cavalry force. Against the Saxons, who fought mainly on foot, such a force would have enjoyed great advantages of mobility and surprise

The Battle of Hastings

This battle, on an autumn day in 1066, saw Harold lose his Crown to
William the Conqueror, and a long-cherished pattern of English life swept
away for ever. Harold's was a short and harassed reign; yet he proved to
be an able leader. William challenged him for the Crown by virtue of a
distant kinship with Edward the Confessor, and maintained that his rival
was a usurper who had taken advantage of the dying king's feeble-
mindedness to claim the Crown for himself. Harold had been called to
Yorkshire to repel a Norwegian invasion when news arrived that William
had landed in Sussex. Without delay he rushed south to meet his latest
enemy near Hastings. There on October 14, according to the traditional
story, he was struck in the eye by an arrow during a day-long battle and fell
fatally wounded among his house-carles. These royal bodyguards were the
flower of the English army and their ancient code forbade them to leave a
battlefield alive after their lord had been killed. They did not waver now.
Long after Harold had been struck down, and all hope of victory had gone,
they fought on around their fallen leader until the last man was slain. The
illustration is a 15th-century artist's version of the battle

DEATH TO THE NORMANS!

At Hastings and after, Englishmen fought bitterly against Duke William's invaders

King Harold of England fell at the Battle of Hastings on October 14, 1066, fighting to defend his crown and people against the invading Normans. There is little question that Harold actually died in the battle, yet shortly afterwards rumours spread that he had escaped and was still alive. Perhaps the rumours were no more than the age-old tendency of defeated people to refuse to accept the loss of a trusted leader, but no doubt they were strengthened by the many curious stories told about the finding and disposal of his corpse.

It was said that after the battle, Harold's gashed and mutilated body could not be distinguished from the other English dead. Finally Edith Swan-neck, his mistress and the mother of his three sons, identified her dead lover by marks known only to her. Queen Githa, Harold's mother, besought William to return the body to her for burial. She offered its weight in gold as ransom, but he refused. Instead he is said to have ordered that his defeated enemy should be buried beside the sea in a nameless grave.

A more probable tradition, however, says that William granted Githa's request for the body, and that Harold was buried in Waltham Abbey, near Epping Forest. A tomb said to be his existed in the abbey until the Reformation, when it was destroyed.

Nevertheless, the rumour of Harold's escape from the battlefield grew and spread through the country. Giraldus Cambrensis, the Welsh historian, mentions it even 200 years later. Harold was reputed to have travelled to Europe seeking aid to recover his lost kingdom, but unable to find anyone to help him, he went on a pilgrimage to the Holy Land before returning secretly to England to live as a hermit in Cheswardine, Salop. Later he moved to Chester and lived there in isolation for the rest of his days. His identity was revealed only on his deathbed, and Giraldus states that just before dying he had a secret interview with Henry I, but what passed between the two kings was unknown.

Did Harold really escape death at Hastings? Belief in his survival, it might be expected, would have inspired others in the various rebellions which arose immediately after the Conquest. But it was in the name of his sons, or of Edgar Atheling, the last male descendant of the line of Alfred, that the swords were drawn. And none of these was able to unite his countrymen in the way that Harold could have – had he been still alive.

Death was denied him

Though few now remember the legend of Harold's survival, tales endure to this day of Wild Edric, another gallant fighter of the Conquest. Indeed, Edric is the hero of so many unusual legends that it is hard to glimpse the real man through the fog of myth. He existed nevertheless, for the Domesday Book mentions that he once held lands in the West Country.

In the summer of 1067, Edric sprang to fame as the leader of an uprising in the Welsh Marches. At the head of men still loyal to the English cause, he overran the Welsh border, ravaging the countryside and threatening the Norman garrison in Hereford itself. He remained in revolt for two years, and in 1069 he sacked Shrewsbury. He was never defeated or captured, yet in the following year he gave up his struggle against the Normans.

Tradition asserts that he did not surrender, but made his peace with William. Certainly the Conqueror seems to have borne him no malice, and even received him with honour at court. In 1072 he took part in a Norman punitive expedition to Scotland, but what happened to him after that is not known. There is no record of when or how he died, or of where he was buried.

Legend says that Wild Edric did not die at all. Instead, because he made peace with the Normans, death was denied him, and he

An omen in the sky
The sighting of Halley's Comet before the Norman Conquest was at that time considered to be, like other comets, a fearful omen – a sign from heaven, foretelling wars, plagues and other disasters. This scene from the Bayeux Tapestry depicts a soothsayer telling a clearly anxious Harold of the calamities portended by Halley's Comet when it appeared in 1066. A prophecy that it signified the downfall of the kingdom and the tears of women was justified. Before the year was out Harold had fallen at the Battle of Hastings, hundreds of Englishmen lay dead and William the Conqueror ruled the land

UBI HAROLD: SACRAMENTUM: FECIT: ⸙ HIC HARO VUILLELMO DUCI: ⸙

The broken oath

Even before Hastings, there was a belief that Harold's destiny was shadowed by a broken oath. Fate had placed Harold in William's hands in 1064 when his ship ran upon the Norman shore in a storm. As this scene from the Bayeux Tapestry shows, before releasing him William compelled him to swear allegiance and to promise support for William's claim to the English throne. To make the oath binding, he tricked Harold into swearing upon holy relics hidden beneath the table. Two years later, when Harold himself became King of England, he justified breaking his oath by claiming that it had been obtained by compulsion and trickery

was condemned to haunt the lead mines of Salop for ever. His wife, Lady Godda, and his followers are said to live on with him. The miners called them the 'Old Men', and said that the sound of their persistent tapping underground in the mines was a sure sign that there was a good mineral lode near by.

Another tradition makes Edric a prophet of war. In unsettled times he is supposed to ride furiously over the land at the head of his men, and they always ride towards the country with which England will shortly be at war. The ominous band were alleged to have been seen riding eastwards in the summer of 1914.

The tales always refer to Lady Godda as Edric's wife, though in fact it is not known whether he was ever married. Legend says she was a fairy wife and that in one story they were happy together for many years, until Edric came home one day and found her absent. On her return, he angrily accused her of dallying in the forest with her otherworld relatives, whereupon she disappeared for ever. Edric, so the story goes, died soon afterwards of grief; an end which differs oddly from the usual tradition of his eternal life in the lead mines.

The rebellion in the Fens

Hereward the Wake's rebellion against William the Conqueror lasted no more than a few months. But William took it seriously. His hold on the countryside was tenuous and any success by a local leader might quickly have led to a major insurrection.

Not much is known with certainty about Hereward. He is commonly supposed to have been an Englishman, holding lands in Lincolnshire and owing allegiance to the abbot of Peterborough. He seems to have travelled widely in his early years, and there are legends of his prowess in wars in Ireland and Holland. He emerged victorious from fights with a fairy bear and a Cornish giant, while in Flanders he acquired a suit of magic armour.

It is said that Hereward was still abroad at the time of the Conquest, but swiftly returned to England only to discover his estate in Norman hands, and the head of his slain brother set above the door of the house. Like an avenging thunderbolt, he descended upon the killers and slew them all. Next day 14 Norman heads had replaced that of his brother above the door.

News of Hereward's exploits spread and he became the leader of a mixed band of English and Danish warriors who flocked to join him. It is at this point that he emerges more clearly into the light of history, for in 1069 he used the appointment of an unpopular Norman abbot to Peterborough Abbey as an excuse to sack the abbey and burn the town.

Hereward then prudently decided to withdraw and await William's inevitable retribution at Ely, which was at that time an island of firm ground surrounded by almost impenetrable swamps.

500

He did not have long to wait. William ordered a causeway to be built across the Fens at their narrowest point, from Aldreth to Ely. When his troops were ready to attack the rebels, he placed a witch in a wooden tower overlooking the causeway to terrify the defenders with her spells and curses.

Hereward had also prepared for the attack. As the Normans crossed the causeway he set fire to the dry reeds and the wind did the rest. William's army was thrown into confusion and annihilated, and the witch died in the flames.

When Ely finally did fall in 1071 tradition says that it was through treachery. The Normans were shown a secret path to the island by some of its own defenders in return for an amnesty. A more likely version claims that it was by the monks of the abbey on the island. Hereward managed to escape with a few of his men but what became of him afterwards is uncertain. It is believed that he continued to harass the Normans in the Fens for many years, until eventually he became reconciled with William and had his confiscated lands restored.

A tale of blood and fire
Hereward's attack on Peterborough is recorded in the 11th-century *Anglo-Saxon Chronicle*. In 1069 the abbot of Peterborough died and a warlike Norman abbot named Turold succeeded him. Hereward, feeling no doubt that the treasures of Peterborough Abbey would be better in English hands than those of a hated Norman, acted quickly. When Turold finally rode into Peterborough at the head of an armed force, he found that the town had been reduced to ashes and the church stripped of every valuable object it had contained

ROBIN OF SHERWOOD

A band of outlaws became the inspiration of England's oppressed peasantry

Legend says that Robin Hood was a medieval yeoman who, being outlawed for some unrevealed offence, took to a life of banditry in the greenwood, at the head of a gang of like-minded robbers who followed him through thick and thin. Or at least, so runs one version of their story – the details of the legend vary considerably.

A medieval outlaw was a man who, for reasons of politics or crime, had been officially repudiated by the law, and cast out from the community to which he belonged. He was left with no defence against his enemies except his own courage, strength and intelligence. Forced to hide in the forests which covered much of the countryside, or in the fenlands, he had to make his living by illegal hunting and by robbery. He was not friendless if, as often happened, he was able to surround himself with a strong and well-organised marauding company. He had other friends too among the poor and the naturally lawless, and those who detested the oppressive forest laws and the other injustices of their day. In time, the most successful outlaws became popular heroes, and the admired subjects of countless ballads, songs and stories.

The first known literary reference to Robin by name occurs in William Langland's second version of *The Vision of Piers Plowman*, which was written in 1377. In it, a drunken chaplain, sitting by the roadside, declares:

> 'I can not (know not) my pater noster as the prest hit saith,
> But I can (know) rymes of Robyn Hode and Randle Erle of Chester.'

These 'rymes' have long been lost, but obviously the chaplain expected his hearers to know them. It is clear from the casual way in which the matter is mentioned that verses about Robin Hood had been current for some time before 1377. The oldest surviving ballad, the anonymous 'Lytell Geste of Robyn Hode and his Meiny' (band), dates only from the 15th century, but it seems to have been constructed out of four other, much older ballads.

The unknown marksman

In spite of the many stories about him, not very much is known about Robin Hood's actual career. Some writers from the 19th century onwards have claimed that he never existed at all but was simply a relic of ancient Germanic pagan or fairy beliefs, or an ideal figure created out of the needs and discontents of the medieval peasantry. Among the Sloane manuscripts in the British Museum there is an anonymous account of Robin's life which states that he was born about 1160 'in Lockesley in Yorkshire, or Nottinghamshire'. No such place exists in either county, though there is a Loxley in Staffordshire where, according to one legend, his father held land. Another account places his heyday in the mid-13th century, and makes him a supporter of Simon de Montfort – one of the men who were outlawed after the defeat of de Montfort at Evesham in 1265. One chronicler says he was a Wakefield man who took part in Thomas of Lancaster's rebellion in 1322.

It is probable that he was of North Country or north Midland stock. His traditional haunts as an outlaw were in Sherwood Forest in Nottinghamshire, and Barnsdale Forest in Yorkshire. But as a 17th-century writer said, he was 'no fox that hath only one hole', for in Yorkshire too he had a coastal refuge at Robin Hood's

Little Iohn

THE Curtal Fryer.

Robin Hood's fighting-men
A big man with an ironical nickname, Little John (above) was Robin's second in command, and the earliest of his companions mentioned in the records. One legend says that he died at Hathersage in Derbyshire, where his supposed grave, opened in 1784, contained the bones of an exceptionally tall man.

The Curtal Friar, alias Friar Tuck, was a famous fighter with whom Robin had a trial of strength. The pair met by a river at Fountain Dale, Nottinghamshire where the friar agreed to carry Robin over the water, but dropped him into the stream. He joined the outlaws only after a ferocious and indecisive battle with them

Hero of the greenwood
Robin Hood is one of the great folk-heroes, yet there is no real evidence that he existed. It may be that he is a memory of forest fairy beliefs; or a ballad character expressing popular resentment of medieval injustices

Bay. Here he is supposed to have kept a number of small boats in readiness for fishing in summer, and as a means of retreat if he was too hard pressed by his foes on land.

Robin's great skill with the bow, and that of his followers, was justly famous, even in a land where, from Edward I's time onwards, every Englishman whose income from land was less than 100 pence a year was by law trained in archery.

A Yorkshire tradition says that once, when Robin Hood and Little John were at Whitby Abbey as guests of Abbot Richard, the abbot asked them to give an exhibition of their skill by shooting from the roof of the monastery. The two arrows fell at Whitby Lathes, more than a mile away, one on each side of the lane leading to Stainsacre. Afterwards, the fields in which they alighted were known as Robin Hood's Close and Little John's Close. In memory of these remarkable shots, the abbot had two stone pillars erected where the arrows were recovered. The pillars stood there until the end of the 18th century.

The scourge of authority

Abbot Richard must himself have been a man rather out of the usual run, since Robin was friendly with him. Generally, he hated the senior clergy who, in his mind, ranked with the sheriff and the verderers who enforced the oppressive forest laws, and with those justices who always sided with the rich, or administered the law corruptly. In the 'Lytell Geste', Little John asks Robin for guidance as to how the band should live, and is told that they must do no harm to any husbandman 'that tylleth with his plough', or any good yeoman, or any simple knight or squire, but

'These byschoppes, and these archbyschoppes,
Ye shall them bete and bynde;
The Hye Sheryfe of Notynghame,
Hym holde in your minde.'

This was not because Robin Hood hated the Church as such, or because he was irreligious. On the contrary, he was a devout man who grieved because his perilous way of life made it impossible for him to hear mass as often as he would have liked. He had a strong devotion to the Virgin, for whose sake he is said never to have harmed any company that had a woman in it, and with the lesser clergy he was friendly enough.

Many of the surviving tales about Robin Hood and his followers contain bloodthirsty incidents, for these were violent times, and men who have been thrust outside the law's protection are not likely to be law-abiding or gentle. Once when Robin went alone to St Mary's Church in Nottingham, a monk in the congregation recognised him, and ran out to raise the alarm. The sheriff and a great crowd of townsmen came pouring into the church to take the outlaw. He was still kneeling in prayer, unaware of the danger, when they arrived, but he managed to kill 12 of them with his sword before he was taken prisoner. Little John and Much the Miller's son rescued him soon afterwards, but not before they had taken their revenge upon the betrayer of their master. The monk was sent to Nottingham to inform the king of Robin's capture, and when, on his way, he encountered two young men he took to be respectable yeomen, he was foolish enough to boast of his part in the affair. The two outlaws murdered him on the spot. On another occasion, during a fierce fight in the streets, Robin shot the sheriff of Nottingham and then, triumphantly, cut off his head.

The genial thief

Yet it was not for his ferocity or as a champion of justice that Robin was best remembered in tradition, but for his gaiety and love of trickery, his open-handed generosity, especially to the poor and distressed, and his courtesy to all, including the travellers whom he robbed. He was a genial thief who charmed his victims out of their purses and, more often than not, feasted them afterwards on venison. The author of the 'Lytell Geste' admiringly comments: 'so curteyse an outlawe as he was one never non founde.'

Robin's was a hard and dangerous life, but probably many people envied it because it was free and full of adventure. 'In somer, when the schaws be shene' (when the woods are beautiful), runs the ballad of 'Robin Hood and the Monk',

'And leaves be large and longe,
It is ful mery in fair forest
To hear the birdes' song'

and no doubt it was, though conditions must have been rather different when winter had silenced the birds and stripped the trees

Under the greenwood tree
Most of the legends surrounding Robin Hood tell of him poaching the king's deer, as in this woodcut. Robin, unlike King Arthur, was a man of the people, with whom ordinary folk could identify. One story recounts how the outlaw went drinking with a tinker, who failed to recognise him. He boasted of his intention of capturing Robin for a large reward; but instead, Robin robbed him. The innkeeper told the tinker that his assailant could be found 'among the parks, killing of the king's deer'. The tinker ran the outlaw to earth, and thrashed him. Robin's men intervened, but their leader saved him from their vengeance and recruited him into the band

of their leaves. But Robin evidently loved the wild forest life enough to return to it of his own accord after he had been pardoned by 'Edwarde, our comly kynge'.

Which King Edward this was is uncertain, though there is some slight historical evidence that it may have been Edward II. The 'Lytell Geste' relates that he came north (as Edward II did in 1323), and was so horrified by the depredations of the robbers in his forests that he declared their leader must be taken and executed at all costs. Out of curiosity, he went himself to the greenwood, disguised as an abbot, and had not gone far before he fell into the hands of the outlaws. They treated him well, and after entertaining him to a splendid meal of his own venison, gave him an impressive display of their skill in archery. Suddenly, Robin recognised his liege lord in his abbot's disguise, and fell on his knees before him, begging for mercy and pardon for himself and all his band.

The end of adventure

Edward forgave them all on condition that they left the forest, and he took Robin into his own service as Groom of the Chamber. After a while, however, the one-time outlaw wearied of the safety and order of court life, and began to yearn for the greenwood once more. He obtained the king's leave to return to Barnsdale for a week, to visit, he said, a chapel he had once built there. Seven days and no more Edward allowed him; but once back in his old haunts, he never left them again. He gathered all his former followers round him without any difficulty and, for the next 22 years, lived once more the wild, free life he loved.

But there came a time when Robin's years began to oppress him and, being weakened by an illness, he went with Little John to Kirklees Priory near Huddersfield, to be treated by the prioress. This woman was known for her medical skill, and she was also said to be his aunt, which must have made the nunnery seem a safe refuge. As part of the treatment, he was bled, but was allowed to bleed to death. The most usual story is that the prioress was persuaded by a certain Sir Roger de Doncaster to murder her nephew. She locked him, alone, in a room and 'there he did bleed all the livelong day until the next day at noon'. When his strength was nearly exhausted, he managed to blow three feeble blasts on his horn, and Little John heard them.

He forced his way into the priory, and into the locked chamber, but he was too late to save his dying leader. He vowed to avenge him by burning Kirklees to the ground, but Robin forbade him to do anything of the kind. He had never, he said, harmed any woman, and he would not begin now. Then he asked for his bow to be put into his hands and, supported by Little John before an open window, he shot an arrow through it, saying:

'Where this arrow is taken up,
There shall my grave digg'd be.'

A mound in the park, within bowshot of the house, is said to be the outlaw's last resting-place.

Robin Hood and the bishop

When the outlaw was trapped in the forest by a bishop and his armed retainers, he escaped by exchanging clothes with an old woman whom he had befriended years before. The old woman was arrested, but Robin and his band turned the tables by ambushing the bishop. After being relieved of his purse, the captured cleric was tied to a tree. As a condition of his release, he was forced to say mass while still bound. Afterwards, still bound, he was sat back to front on his horse, and sent unceremoniously on his way

St George and the dragon
Very little is known for certain about St George's life. Possibly he was a
high-ranking officer in the Roman army, who was martyred in Palestine in
about AD 303. Certainly he never fought a dragon, and though he never
visited England either, his name was known there at least as early as the 8th
century. It was probably 12th-century Crusaders, however, who first
invoked his aid in battle. Edward III may have made him patron saint of
England when he founded the Order of the Garter in St George's name in
1350, and the cult of the saint was steadily advanced by Henry V, the victor
of Agincourt. Henry himself, who was both warlike and devout, was
thought by his followers to possess many of the saint's characteristics. This
15th-century altar-piece is in the Victoria and Albert Museum

SOLDIERS OF GOD

Resolute men and women saved England from Satan and the powers of darkness

The missionary saints who re-established Christianity in the dark years following the invasion by the pagan Saxons were men and women cast in the mould of heroes. The Christian Church had flourished in Britain under the Romans, but with the arrival of the Saxons in the 5th century it practically vanished, except for a few strongholds in the west, where the invaders' grasp was not so strong.

The first attempt to restore the Church, led by St Augustine in AD 597, met with great difficulty. Although Augustine's teaching was received with joy by many, his converts frequently fell away when they found the new religion too demanding or when the ancient heathen beliefs proved too strong.

In his history of the Church in England, the Venerable Bede (673–735) sorrowfully recorded the case of Redwald, a 7th-century King of the East Angles, who in the same church had one altar dedicated to Christ and another on which sacrifices were offered to 'devils' – that is, to the pagan gods of his forefathers. It is likely that Redwald was only one of many men who tried to worship Christ and the old gods at the same time.

To add to the missionary saints' difficulties, the years of conversion were closely followed by the years of Viking invasion. Every raid, with its attendant horrors of monasteries destroyed by fire, and priests and worshippers put to the sword, inevitably drove some wavering converts back to the old gods, in search of the protection which the Christian God seemed unwilling to supply. Throughout these dark years, each civil war, famine or outbreak of pestilence was followed by the same return to pagan beliefs and ancient forms of protective magic.

The first Archbishop of Canterbury

St Augustine, whose pioneering work as a missionary earned him the title 'Apostle of the English', seems to have been one of the sterner saints – a rigid follower of what he believed to be his duty, but rather lacking in kindly imagination. Despite Pope Gregory's celebrated pun of 'Not Angles but angels' on viewing fair-haired English slaves in Rome, Augustine undertook the mission to England with no great enthusiasm, fearing that it would be a dangerous and probably fruitless task. But urged on by his conscience and the persuasions of Gregory, he landed on the Isle of Thanet, just off the Kentish mainland, in the spring of 597.

He was received with courtesy, but also with caution, by Ethelbert of Kent, a pagan king with a Christian wife. He consented to hear what Augustine had to say, but would not receive him under any roof, or in his capital city of Canterbury, for fear of witchcraft. The two men eventually met on Thanet, the king

The father of English history

St Bede, called 'the Venerable', was a monk at Jarrow in County Durham from 692 until his death in 735. In his own words, 'study, teaching and writing' were his greatest delights, and his masterpiece, *A History of the English Church and People*, completed four years before he died, is still the principal source for any study of the missionary saints who converted the Anglo-Saxons to Christianity. Much of the book is devoted to miracles worked by the saints, many of whom Bede knew personally; and he only included those miracles in which he himself believed. Many of the stories which he recorded are still widely told to this day, such as that of Gregory the Great's encounter in Rome with the fair-haired Angles and his pun of 'Not Angles but angels'. Though he probably never travelled further than York, his books made him famous throughout Western Christendom

Guthlac comes to Crowland
St Guthlac spent most of his life alone at Crowland, Lincolnshire. After his death, *c.* 714, Crowland Abbey was built on his hermitage

The martyrdom of St Alban
The saint was beheaded *c.* 287 in what is now St Albans for giving shelter to a Christian fleeing from Roman persecution

sitting in the open air and Augustine and his monks, including Gaulish interpreters, standing before him. They proudly placed their standards where the king could see them – a silver cross and a portrait of Christ.

This meeting was the first step towards the conversion of Kent and eventually of the other Anglo-Saxon kingdoms. When Ethelbert had listened to St Augustine's exposition of the Christian faith, he said that he could not rashly abandon the religion which he and his people had always followed, but that the missionaries were free to go to Canterbury and to preach there to whoever would listen to them. Ethelbert never attempted to influence his people for or against Christianity, but after deep thought, he himself was convinced of its truth. He was baptised at Canterbury on the following Whit Sunday, and within a few years the great majority of his subjects had followed his example. Augustine was consecrated Archbishop of the English, after which he established his See at Canterbury and founded a monastery there.

One well-known legend suggests that St Augustine was remembered longer for his severity than for his other qualities. He came, so the story says, to Rochester in Kent, to preach to the people. But they would not listen to him; they mocked the saint and his followers, flung offal at them and fastened fish-tails to their clothes. So angry was St Augustine that he laid a curse on the town, saying that henceforward all children born there would have tails. From what anti-Christian demonstration this story sprang (or perhaps it was from more than one, since the event is sometimes located in Dorset as well as Kent) it is impossible to discover. But no one in the Middle Ages seems to have doubted the truth of the tradition – except, perhaps, for the visibly tailless people of the town of Rochester.

The hand that never perished

Thirty years after St Augustine landed in Thanet, St Paulinus, a Roman missionary, baptised Edwin, King of Northumbria, and afterwards converted Edwin's entire kingdom to Christianity. But this great achievement was not long-lived. In 633, Cadwalla, one of Edwin's vassals, rebelled against his overlord and defeated and killed him at Hatfield Moors in S. Yorkshire. Edwin was acclaimed as a martyr; and in the confusion that followed Cadwalla's seizure of power, Paulinus was forced to flee southwards. He was an old man, and he never returned. The young Church for which he and Edwin had done so much fell into ruins, and the Northumbrians reverted to paganism. Suddenly, it seemed as if everything that had been accomplished with so much hard work and difficulty had been destroyed for ever.

In fact, Northumbria was soon a Christian country again, and this time permanently. Within a year, St Edwin was followed on the throne by his nephew Oswald, who was not only the greatest of the Northumbrian kings, but also a saint of truly heroic stature. In 634 he defeated Cadwalla in a battle fought near Hexham in Northumberland, and immediately set about restoring order to his kingdom. The first task was the re-establishment of the Church, in which he was helped by St Aidan, a monk from Iona, whom he appointed the first Bishop of Lindisfarne.

It is said that one Easter Sunday, as Oswald and Aidan were sitting down to dinner, word was brought to the king that many poor and hungry people were gathered outside his palace. He at once ordered that all the food prepared for himself should be sent out to them, and that the silver dish on which it was served should be broken up and divided among the poor. St Aidan was so impressed by this act that he took the king's right hand in his own, blessed it, and prayed that the hand which gave so freely might never wither. After St Oswald's death, his right hand never perished or withered, and was preserved for many years in a silver shrine at Bamburgh Castle. It was stolen in the 11th century and taken to Peterborough, where it seems to have remained until the Reformation, when it disappeared.

Oswald's reign lasted for eight years. In 642 he was killed at the Battle of Maserfield fighting King Penda of Mercia. Oswestry in Salop and Winwick in Cheshire both claim to be the site of the battlefield, and in both places there were once healing springs dedicated to St Oswald, where many miraculous cures took place. At Winwick, the water was said to have welled up on the spot where the dead king's body first touched the ground; at Oswestry, it was where his head fell after being hacked from his corpse on Penda's orders.

The saint whom the animals loved

Another great northern saint, Cuthbert, was born in about 635, in Lauderdale, Borders, where as a young man he worked as a shepherd. One night, while he was tending his flock on the hills, he saw a company of angels coming down from heaven along a brilliant ray of light. As he watched, a human spirit approached and was received into the heavenly band, and then the apparition vanished. Next day, he discovered that St Aidan had died at the moment of his vision, and he determined to become a monk.

After 13 years in the monastery at Melrose in Borders region, Cuthbert moved to the Northumbrian island of Lindisfarne, where he spent most of the rest of his life. Many stories were told of his wisdom and his love of birds and animals, though this was somewhat offset by his distrust of women. It was said that he conversed with angels, and sometimes received food from them on his travels. Once, an angel in the form of a white-robed horseman cured a painful tumour on his knee. On another occasion, when he was out in the hills without food, he was fed by an eagle, which brought him a large fish. Cuthbert kept half for himself and the boy who was with him, and gave the remainder to the bird.

In a spirit of penance and self-discipline, Cuthbert used occasionally to spend the night in prayer standing in the sea. It was after one of these vigils that a monk saw a sight which convinced him that Cuthbert was truly beloved of God. At dawn, when the saint's prayers were ended, he came out of the sea and knelt down. Two seals came to him and began to dry his feet and warm them with their breath. They stayed with him until he blessed them, when they contentedly returned to the water.

When the threat of Viking raids forced the monks of Lindisfarne to abandon their island home in 875, never to return, they took

Cuthbert meets King Egfrith
St Cuthbert, gifted with second sight, foresaw the Northumbrian king's death in battle in 685

St Cuthbert's travels
Though a hermit by nature, St Cuthbert travelled widely, preaching the spirit of Christianity to the pagan Anglo-Saxons

The saint's tomb
St Cuthbert died in 687. When his body, entombed in Durham Cathedral, was examined in 1104 and 1537, it showed no signs of decay

with them their greatest treasures, including St Oswald's severed hand and the uncorrupted body of St Cuthbert. For seven years, the relics of these great saints were carried about England in the same coffin, while the monks searched for a place of refuge. Finally, they settled in Durham, where the tomb of St Cuthbert can still be seen in the cathedral.

Immortal women

In spite of St Cuthbert's frequent railing against females, many outstanding women of his day were destined to become saints themselves. One of the greatest was St Hilda (614–80), who founded Whitby Abbey in 657 and was renowned for her wisdom throughout the land. Another was St Etheldreda (630–79), whose shrine at Ely, where she founded a monastery in about 672, was an important centre of pilgrimage throughout the Middle Ages, probably because of the number of miracles ascribed to her. One of the nuns Etheldreda trained at Ely was St Werburga, who is best remembered for having reproved a gaggle of geese for eating crops in Weedon, Northamptonshire, and who later restored one of them to life after a kitchen servant killed it. And in Wales there was St Winifred, who died twice. On the first occasion (the date is not known, but it was probably some time in the 7th century) she was beheaded by a Welsh chieftain at Holywell in Clwyd. Her uncle, St Beuno, placed her trunk and severed head together and breathed into her nostrils and, miraculously, her mutilated body was completely healed and she rose to continue her work. She died peacefully the second time, in about 650.

A martyr's death

The saint venerated as Britain's first Christian martyr is St Alban, a Romano-Briton who was executed at Verulamium (now St Albans) in the late 3rd or early 4th century. At this time, Christianity was still a young religion, and had yet to become firmly established in Britain. Its followers were still liable to severe persecution at the hands of the Roman establishment, which is exactly what happened to Alban. He gave shelter to a fellow Christian who was fleeing for his life, and was beheaded for his pains. Healing springs are said to have burst from the ground at his place of execution, which tradition claims was Holmshurst Hill. In addition, a stream which crossed his path to martyrdom miraculously dried up.

One of the most deeply revered groups of England's saints is that of her martyred kings, which includes St Edmund, the last King of East Anglia, who was shot full of arrows by Danish Vikings at Hoxne, Suffolk, in 869; St Ethelbert, another Christian King of East Anglia, who was treacherously murdered on the orders of King Offa of Mercia at Sutton Walls near Hereford in 793; and St Edward the Martyr, assassinated at Corfe Gate in Dorset on March 18, 978.

On that March evening, almost 1000 years ago, the 16-year-old King Edward came alone to Corfe Gate, the royal palace on a Dorset hilltop where his stepmother Elfrida lived with her ten-year-old son Ethelred. As he rode up to the main doorway, he called for a cup of wine and, still mounted, sat drinking and chatting to Elfrida while the men and women of her household milled round him in welcome. Suddenly, a man in the throng seemed to stumble against him. The king cried out and fell from the saddle, with one foot still caught in the stirrup. The horse, startled by Edward's fall, bolted down the steep hill-road, with the young king's body dragging behind it.

When some labourers in the valley below managed to stop the horse, they saw the rider's face was battered beyond recognition and his clothes were torn to shreds and soaked with blood. They could not tell who he was, but the horse's trappings suggested he was of noble birth. Not wanting to become involved, the labourers ran away, leaving Edward's corpse on the ground. Later that night, someone must have found the body and buried it, for when a search party looked for it the next day, it was nowhere to be seen. The news was given out that Edward had died after a fall from his horse, though where and in what circumstances was not explained.

Some months later, after Ethelred had been crowned king, strange stories began to circulate about a certain place on the road from Corfe to Wareham. There was nothing to be seen but reeds, yet sick men who went there came away cured; the deaf heard again, the blind saw, cripples threw aside their crutches and walked away unaided. Eventually, St Dunstan heard of the place and sent

The abbess of Whitby
The Venerable Bede wrote of St Hilda (614–80) that 'all who knew her called her Mother, such were her wonderful godliness and grace'. Originally a pagan, she was baptised by St Paulinus in 627, when she was 13 years old, and in 657 founded the famous Whitby Abbey in North Yorkshire. At least five of her pupils became important leaders of the Church, and it was while she was abbess of Whitby that a local cowherd called Caedmon had a vision, whereby he received the gift of song from an angel, and became the first English Christian poet

Edward the Martyr
After only three years on the throne, King Edward was stabbed to death at Corfe Gate in Dorset

some monks to dig up the ground. In a shallow grave they found the body of Edward. There was no sign of decay, though many months had passed, and a deep knife wound in the stomach bore witness to the manner of the king's death.

Suspicion inevitably fell upon Elfrida, who had most to gain from the deed. But in her virtually unassailable position as the mother of the new boy-king, the suspicions were not publicly voiced at the time, and nothing was ever proved.

The dead king was carried to Shaftesbury Abbey, where his tomb became a place of pilgrimage. Though his death seems to have occurred for worldly rather than religious reasons, he has been known ever since as St Edward the Martyr.

The turbulent priest

One of the greatest medieval saint-hero cults began on December 29, 1170, when four knights murdered Thomas à Becket, the Archbishop of Canterbury, in a side chapel of Canterbury Cathedral. By tradition, his last words were: 'Willingly I die for the name of Jesus and in defence of the Church.' Immediately, Becket was acclaimed as a martyr throughout Europe, and within three years Pope Alexander III had formally canonised him. From then on, the shrine of St Thomas was one of the Christian world's greatest centres of pilgrimage, and innumerable miracles were said to have occurred there. Phials containing watered-down drops of the martyr's blood were eagerly sought as cure-all charms, and churches all over England and Europe contained his miracle-working relics. As fact and fiction became inextricably mixed in the legend of his life and death, the real man – often stormy and proud, selfish and aggressive – was gradually forgotten, and the people's saint and martyr came to reign as the ideal soldier of God.

Edmund, king and martyr

Edmund, the last King of East Anglia, was brutally murdered by Danish Vikings at Hoxne in Suffolk in 869. Though he put up a gallant resistance against the heathen invaders, he was finally defeated, captured and brought before them. On November 20 (now his feast day) he was offered his life if he would deny Christ. He refused, and was shot to death with arrows and finally beheaded. His death is recorded in the wall-painting of 1450 (above) in the Church of SS Peter and Paul, Pickering, N. Yorkshire.

His followers recovered his body, but after days of combing the forest of Eglesdane, they still could not find his head. Finally, they heard a voice calling them from deep in a thicket, and there they found a huge wolf standing guard over the head. The wolf allowed them to carry the head back to Hoxne. It followed them all the way, and only turned back to the woods when it saw that the head and torso lay together in a single grave

511

Loved for his piety

Edward the Confessor was revered as a saint long before he was canonised, and right up to the time of the Crusades English soldiers shouted his name as they went into battle. The people believed the touch of this pious king's hands would cure scrofula; but it was his lack of concern for worldly affairs that was to pave the way for the cataclysm of the Norman Conquest. The supreme act of Edward's life was the building of Westminster Abbey, in which he lies. This picture of the saintly monarch is from a 15th-century stained-glass window at York Minster

THE MYSTIC CROWN

Throughout the ages the radiance of kingship has shone on fools, knaves, saints and heroes

Once, kings were believed to be incarnate gods upon whose life and vigour depended the welfare of the tribe. In later ages, when they had ceased to be gods themselves, they were often thought to be divinely descended and endowed with powers denied to lesser mortals. Even that most Christian monarch, Alfred the Great, claimed descent from three of the gods of his pagan forefathers – Woden, Sceaf and Geat. Crowned sovereigns of Christendom were deemed holy because they were the Lord's anointed, though this did not always prevent their subjects from rebelling or even from murdering them.

Alfred the Great (849–901), King of Wessex, has left an imperishable name. In many ways he achieved for the Saxons what the legendary Arthur did for the Britons: he kept his enemies at bay long enough for them to become civilised and his own country sufficiently strong and mature to absorb them peacefully.

The Danes had the best-trained army in Europe, but Alfred fought them for 15 arduous years and never contemplated giving up. The most vivid memory we have of him is of a time early in 878 when his cause seemed lost. The Danes were raiding throughout Wessex. Alfred's Mercian allies had surrendered and his main army was dispersed; he had with him only a handful of fighting men and his own family. They took refuge on the Isle of Athelney, in the Somerset marshes, building huts of turf and brushwood and going hunting and fishing to eke out their food.

One day, sheltering in a cowherd's cottage, Alfred was asked by the woman of the house, who did not know who he was, to watch some cakes cooking before the fire. But he forgot; the cakes blackened to cinders on the hearth while the king sat pondering the future of his country. When she returned, the woman abused him. On learning who he was, she cringed in terror, but the king took no offence; he acknowledged his own fault and went away after paying for the spoilt cakes. Historians doubt the story, but even if it never happened, it gives an image of the king's kindly nature.

During his sojourn on Athelney the king had a vision of the Virgin Mary, and drew hope and strength from it. He tore a jewel

Descended from gods
Although a devout Christian, Alfred the Great was proud of his descent from the pagan gods of his forefathers. He had many qualities of the heroes of the sagas; courage in battle and the gift of inspiring his people to defend their homeland

The saintly scholar
On the very day in 1471 that the Yorkist Edward IV made his triumphant entry into London after the Battle of Barnet, his gentle, scholarly predecessor, Henry VI, died mysteriously in the Tower. When his corpse was laid out in St Paul's, it bled – apparently proof that he had been murdered. Henry was popularly acclaimed as a saint, and his tomb at Windsor became a place of pilgrimage where many cures were said to have taken place. The enthroned king is seen here in a miniature taken from a 15th-century psalter

from his cloak and cast it before her feet as an offering. Eight centuries later, in 1693, a fine piece of gold and enamel jewellery was found in the soil of a farm at Athelney: on the gold rim was inscribed in Anglo-Saxon 'Alfred had me made'. It is tempting to think that this gem, now in the Ashmolean Museum in Oxford, is the jewel of the legend.

The last king of Alfred's line was Edward the Confessor, who came to the throne in 1042. He lacked Alfred's heroic qualities, but was loved for his gentleness and piety; his people regarded him as a saint long before he was canonised in 1161. His name was the battle-cry of the English until St George's took its place during the Crusades.

The healing touch

It was during Edward's reign that the ceremony of touching for the King's Evil began to take place regularly. Those afflicted by scrofula, a disease of the glands, came to be healed by the sacred touch of the king's hand. British monarchs continued the practice until the death of Queen Anne in 1714.

Edward's greatest work was the building of Westminster Abbey, in which he was buried. Although revered, he was not the firm and able ruler that England needed. The harsh times that followed the Norman Conquest upon his death in 1066 must have kept his name glowing in the memories of his people, who looked back on his reign as a golden age.

The public's choice of folk heroes is no better illustrated than by Edward the 'Black Prince' of Wales (1330–76), long held to be one of the most illustrious heroes in English history. In fact his life was a round of wars, massacre and pillage in France and Spain. At Crécy he commanded the vanguard at the age of 16; his father, Edward III, deliberately left him to obtain the victory. This precocious flair, and the sombre elegance of his black armour, fixed his image for ever.

The history of his badge, the three feathers of the Prince of Wales, is not fully known. There is no proof of the tradition that it was adopted from John, King of Bohemia, who fell at Crécy. In his will, the Black Prince desired the feathers to be carried as an emblem of peace at his funeral.

The Black Prince is buried in Canterbury Cathedral where his surcoat, helmet, shield and gauntlets are preserved. He is supposed to haunt Hall Place, Bexley, Kent, where he stayed on his way to the French Wars, and his appearances are said to presage danger for England. He was seen three times during the First World War, always before a military reverse. The apparition wears armour and is seen at dusk. Sometimes, strains of medieval music are heard.

A Welshman of valour
The 13th-century artist-monk and historian, Matthew Paris, drew this sketch of Llywelyn the Great of Wales on his deathbed in 1240. Llywelyn united his country, and many Welsh place names still recall this patriot, soldier and law-giver

The 16-year-old victor
Edward, the Black Prince, whose effigy is in Canterbury Cathedral, won the Battle of Crécy in 1346, when he was only 16. He died in 1376 and left behind him nothing but a legend. War, plunder and massacre were his life: yet his undoubted bravery and distinctive black armour have enshrined him in the popular imagination

Henry VI (1421–71) was a saint and hero created out of the pity and indignation of his people. He was a man of real goodness; deeply religious from youth onwards, and generous and forgiving. The Lancastrian monarch's life was overshadowed by bouts of apathetic melancholy and the miseries of the Wars of the Roses. Defeat, flight, ambush and captivity by the Yorkists, culminated in his mysterious death in the Tower.

The belief soon spread that he had been murdered, possibly by Richard of Gloucester, later Richard III. Henry's death was certainly convenient for the Yorkist faction. It was recorded that when, the following day, he lay in state in St Paul's Cathedral, the corpse bled: in those days it was universally believed that the body of a murdered man would bleed in the presence of his killers. Before long, there were rumours of miracles beside his grave at Chertsey, Surrey, and later at Windsor, Berkshire, where his remains were transferred in 1474. Paintings and statues of him were placed in churches, and lights were kept burning before them, a dagger said to have been the one that killed him was preserved in a chapel at Caversham, Berkshire.

Henry VII bowed to the popular demand and applied to Pope

Portents of disaster
Omens foreshadowed the terrible end of Charles I's troubled reign. Blood dripped on a bust of the king, and the royal standard blew down. But Charles's belief in himself and the divine inspiration of kings was not to be shaken, and the stage was set for the long tragedy which was brought to a close by the executioner's axe. The king's resolution and steadfast courage shine out of this portrait by Edward Bower, completed from sketches made during the monarch's trial at Westminster

Dashing Cavalier
Every boy's idea of a gallant soldier
is embodied in Prince Rupert of the
Rhine, commander of the Royalist
cavalry in the Civil War. His
Puritan opponents ascribed his skill
and success to the aid of witchcraft,
and claimed that his dog was a
familiar spirit. The dog was killed at
Marston Moor, Rupert's first
serious defeat. This portrait of the
prince is attributed to the Dutch
artist Lely

The would-be king
No heroic legends attach
themselves to the name of James,
Duke of Monmouth, natural son of
Charles II. He made a bid for the
throne, but could not match his
ambition with courage. His army
of rustics was broken at Sedgemoor
and left to their fate by Monmouth,
whose ghost appears there on
horseback, fleeing from his foes

Alexander VI for Henry VI to be declared a saint. In 1494 a
Commission of Inquiry was set up. Witnesses testified to the
miraculous help which they and others had received after invoking
the dead king's aid. A child drowned in a millstream was restored to
life after people had called upon the dead king. William Sanderson
invoked him when his ship ran aground; at once it floated free.
Thomas Burton, imprisoned in Colchester for 29 weeks without
trial, was suddenly released, his chains struck off and the prison
door opened before him, without human agency. John Stevens,
struck by lightning for working in the fields on Passion Sunday,
was cured of his burns when he cried to Henry for relief.

In spite of all this, the king was never canonised. New ideas were
abroad: the winds of the Reformation began to blow. By 1528,
when the process of inquiry was abandoned, men's minds were
turning away from saints and miracles.

Mystery in the Tower
But if rumour and legend could make a saint out of a king, they
could also create a bloodthirsty villain. Richard III, Henry VI's
suspected murderer, has come down to us as the incarnation of
evil, a slayer of innocent children whose body was as warped as his
soul. Tradition, and Shakespeare too, picture him as a grotesque
hunchback with a withered arm, yet his portraits show no such
deformities, nor were they mentioned by any writer during his
lifetime. Until the Tudor propagandists got to work after his
death in 1485, he seems to have been regarded as a good and just
king, a patron of learning and commerce, who died fighting at
Bosworth Field like the brave man he was.

Whether he murdered the little princes in the Tower or not is a
riddle that will probably never be solved. It has been pointed out
that his supplanter, Henry VII, had at least as much to gain by the
death of the two boys as Richard. Henry's wife, Elizabeth, was
their sister, and once they were dead, she was the only surviving
Yorkist claimant to the throne. No official mention of the murder
was made until 1502, when Sir James Tyrrel, under sentence of
death for treason, 'confessed' to smothering the princes on
Richard's orders. Nothing more was heard of the boys after
Richard placed them in the Tower in 1483; but if they were still
alive when Henry ascended the throne two years later, they would
not have survived long. The evidence of the bones discovered at the
Tower in 1674 is inconclusive. They were buried in Westminster
Abbey, and disinterred for examination in 1933. All that could be
ascertained was that they were the skeletons of boys of about ten
and 13 – the same age as the princes. But in the Tower's long
history, who knows how many inconvenient children have
disappeared behind its walls?

Charles I (1600–49) came too late in history to have miracles
ascribed to him, apart from a belief in the miraculous powers of
handkerchiefs soaked in the king's blood after his execution in
Whitehall. During his lifetime, however, there were many
portents of disaster.

On the day the Long Parliament first met in 1641 the sceptre fell
from the hand of a statue of the king in Sir Thomas Trenchard's
house. As a bust of the king, carved by Bernini, was being brought
to London a bird dropped blood over it, the stain of which could
not be removed, and when the royal standard was set up at
Nottingham in 1642, it was blown down by the wind.

Prince Rupert (1619–82), Charles's brilliant cavalry commander, was alleged to have obtained his military skill by witchcraft. Roundheads asserted that his beloved dog, Boy, which went
everywhere with him, was his familiar spirit. Boy was killed at
Marston Moor in June 1644, Rupert's first serious defeat.

James, Duke of Monmouth (1649–85) is remembered in legends,
ballads and proverbs of the West Country men as the coward who
betrayed them. When he rebelled against James II they accepted his
claim to the throne, partly because he possessed the power of the
royal touch: in 1680, on a progress through the West, he had cured
two people of the King's Evil.

'King Monmouth' led his ragged bands of ill-armed rustics
against James's troops at Sedgemoor in Somerset on July 5, 1685;
they were utterly routed and Monmouth fled, leaving his followers
to perish there or at the hands of Judge Jeffreys at the Bloody
Assize. Monmouth was soon caught, hiding in the New Forest, and
beheaded at Tower Hill on July 15, 1685. His ghost is said to appear
on the anniversary of Sedgemoor, riding in haste away from the
battlefield he deserted when alive.

SCOTLAND, THE BRAVE!

'Wha daur meddle wi' me?' was the watchword of the men who made Scotland free

Since the beginning of history, Scotland has been two nations – the rich Lowlands, where some kind of settled government was possible, and the Highlands, where the king's writ seldom ran. Each heartily disliked and distrusted the other, and few indeed of the great figures whose names are remembered in songs and ballads were admired by all Scotsmen in the heroes' lifetimes. Montrose and Bonnie Prince Charlie were detested in the south, and the Highlanders were indifferent to such Lowland heroes as the Black Douglas and Kinmont Willie. Practically everyone disliked Mary, Queen of Scots, whose only truly heroic trait was her personal courage in adversity.

But there are one or two men whose names were a clarion call to all Scots; above them all, perhaps, was Robert the Bruce, who took up arms against Edward I of England and united Highlands and Lowlands in a single fierce desire for liberty. The aged Edward died at Burgh-on-Sands in 1307; his last wish was that his remains should be carried with his army until Scotland was conquered and his bones could rest in the land he had fought for so long. He waits still in Westminster Abbey.

Fionn – the Gaelic Arthur

The Scots admiration of the warrior has its roots in the Gaelic myths and legends brought across the Irish Sea by the early immigrants, whose greatest hero was Fionn mac Cumhaill – Finn

Hero of the Gaels

The legendary deeds of the mighty hunter Fionn mac Cumhaill are commemorated still in songs and tales in the Gaelic-speaking part of Scotland and Ireland. Armed with supernatural powers, Fionn was the conqueror of monsters and giants, and the leader of a band of warriors who fought to save Scotland from invasion by Norse raiders. Two great dogs, Bran and Sceolang, his faithful companions on every venture, were his own nephews, the sons of his sister Tuirenn who had been turned into a bitch by a jealous lover. Fionn himself was reputedly able to become a dog or deer by means of a magic hood

517

Sir William Wallace
This somewhat idealised portrait of a brooding Wallace, an engraving from the 19th century, is a sentimental view of the patriot, but it does capture something of Wallace's personal magnetism, which to some Scots made him a greater hero even than Bruce

mac Cool – whose name is still remembered in Fingal's Cave. In many ways, Fionn resembles King Arthur, and like him his story lies somewhere between legend and history.

Like Arthur, too, he is said to have been the leader of a band of warriors who defended the country from invaders – in Fionn's case, the Norse raiders. One tale about him says that his wife eloped with one of his finest men, just as Guinevere abandoned Arthur for Lancelot. And, as with Arthur and his knights, Fionn and his followers, the Fianna, are said to lie sleeping in underground caverns, until their country calls upon them again.

The Fianna, however, differ from Arthur's knights in that they were foot-soldiers rather than cavalrymen, and preferred hunting to war, unless battle was forced upon them. But Fionn himself was a great slayer of giants and other supernatural beasts. With his two great hounds, Bran and Sceolang, he is said to have accounted for innumerable mighty serpents, two giants who came out of the sea, his father's murderers, and several mighty boars, not to mention galley-loads of blood-thirsty Vikings.

Tales about Fionn and his men are mainly based on ballads composed between 1100 and 1600, which were themselves based on an oral tradition that had been handed down through the centuries. In the 18th century, a Badenoch schoolteacher, James MacPherson, wrote an English version based on these ballads. He claimed that his work was a translation of epic poems originally composed by Fionn's son, Ossian. MacPherson's book became internationally famous – Napoleon is said to have kept a copy at his bedside – and it prompted romantic Highlanders to remember even more tales about their ancestral hero: for by this time, Fionn had lost his Irish background and become thoroughly naturalised as a Scot by the storytellers.

The thumb of knowledge

Fionn, they say, was born after his father had been slain in battle. One of the killers was a fisherman called Arca Dubh, whom the youthful Fionn encountered just after he had caught a magical salmon. The man asked Fionn to roast the fish for him, warning him not to let it burn. Seeing a black blister rise on the fish, the boy pressed his thumb to it, and burnt himself. When he put the scorched thumb in his mouth, the knowledge came to him that Arca Dubh had murdered his father. Fionn killed the fisherman and, ever after that, could get the answer to any question simply by chewing his thumb.

Witchcraft and enchanted beasts play a major part in the tales of Fionn and his people. His mistress, the mother of his son Ossian, was bewitched, so that she was a deer by day and a woman at night. When Fionn himself was a baby, he was flung over a cliff. Fortunately, his grandmother had assumed the shape of a crane, and was able to swoop to his rescue. The Fianna, led by Ossian's son, Oscar – 'the bravest of them all' – fought several battles with headless giants and magical beasts. When Fionn's wife, Grainne, ran off with the handsome Diarmaid, Fionn, having caught them, revenged himself by ordering the youth to hunt down a magical boar and measure it by pacing the length of its spine. A bristle pierced Diarmaid's heel, and fatally poisoned him.

One of the ballads tells how the Fianna went hunting and left Grainne's father, Garaidh, to look after the womenfolk on Skye. The women played a trick on the old man, by pegging his hair to the ground while he slept, then rousing him so that he leapt up in alarm and tore his hair out. By way of revenge, he locked them all in a great barn and set fire to it. For this, Garaidh was condemned to death and ordered to choose the manner of his execution. He chose decapitation by Fionn's great sword, Mac a' Luin, but demanded that his head should rest on Fionn's thigh while the execution was carried out. True to his word, Fionn agreed; oxhides and logs were piled on his legs, but the blade cut through everything and the hero received a terrible wound from which he never recovered.

The death of Fionn is shrouded in mystery, and the tales really come to an end when the valiant Oscar is killed in battle. Only Ossian survived into old age, they say, when he told the tales of the heroic company to St Patrick.

Leader of a battered army

A thousand years later, while Fionn slept in his cave in Skye, or beneath the hill of Tom-na-hurich at Inverness, part at least of his legendary mantle fell upon a humble Lowland knight. Very little is known for certain about the career of Sir William Wallace, the first hero of Scotland's wars of independence against England's Edward I. It began with the killing of the English sheriff of Lanark, who apparently murdered Wallace's wife or sweetheart. With a price on his head, Wallace chose the bold course, and raised the Scottish standard. Supported by a few of the Scots barons, he was at the head of an army that inflicted a resounding defeat on the English at Stirling Bridge in 1297. The ecstatic Scots appointed him sole Guardian of Scotland, but their triumph was short-lived. Less than a year later, Wallace made the fatal mistake, from a tactical point of view, of accepting a pitched battle against seasoned, regular troops in overwhelming numbers. Under the personal command of Edward I, the English army annihilated the tattered Scots battalions at Falkirk.

Wallace never led an army in the field again. For the next seven years he was a fugitive, though for part of that time he may have been abroad trying to enlist help for the Scottish cause. In 1305 he was betrayed in Glasgow, and was taken to London, where he was tried for treason in Westminster Hall. He suffered the full agonies of hanging, drawing and quartering – one of the first to be awarded that fearful penalty after it was introduced in 1284. His head was spiked on London Bridge, and the other fragments of his body were distributed among several Scottish cities as a grim reminder of the price of revolt.

The birth of a legend

If anything, the horror of the execution established Wallace even more firmly in Scottish hearts. Within a few years all kinds of stories were circulating about him, some of which may have been based on fact, and others that were pure fabrication. But all were fervently believed. Many of the tales were collected, and probably improved upon, by a mid-15th-century poet called 'Blind Harry', whose long poem on the hero conveys some idea of the reverence that Wallace was accorded by later generations.

According to Blind Harry, Wallace was the champion of a poverty-stricken people, whose state contrasted wretchedly with English wealth and prosperity. His courage was surpassed only by his capacity for slaughtering the enemy. The poem gives details of the 'Barns of Ayr', when 360 Scottish nobles, led by Wallace's uncle, Sir Ranald Crawford, were summoned by the English to a conference. As each passed through a narrow entry, a rope was dropped around his neck, and he was hanged. Wallace, warned by a local woman, escaped and, that night, he and his followers crept into the town, fastened the doors of all the houses lodging Edward's 4000 soldiers, and set fire to them. Anyone who broke out was butchered by the waiting Scots. Even the Prior of Ayr, apparently, together with eight of his friars, took swords and dispatched the 140 soldiers billeted with them. 'Men call it yet the Friars' Blessing of Ayr,' says the poem. This gruesome incident did not, in fact,

Last stand of a hero
The freedom fighter's defiance is summed up in this detail from the picture by the Victorian painter Daniel Maclise of Wallace's trial in Westminster Hall, now hanging in the Guildhall, London. Wallace himself claimed that he could not be guilty of treachery to the throne, because he had never sworn fealty to the king. It was not a sufficient defence. He had been a thorn in the English side for too long, and could not hope to escape from the vindictive Edward. He was hanged, drawn and quartered. Pieces of his torn body were displayed at Perth, Stirling, Berwick and Newcastle

SO·MONY·GVID·AS·· ·VE·COVGLAS·BEINE··
OF·ANE·SVRNA··· ·· ··IN·SCOTLAND·SHINE·

I·WILYE·CHARGE·EFTER·YAT·I·DEPARE·
TO·HOLY·GRAVE·AND·THAIR·BVRY·MY·HART·

Pledge of honour

The engraved sword (above) now in the possession of the Douglas-Home family, was a gift from Robert the Bruce to his faithful follower Sir James Douglas – known in legend as the Black Douglas. It bears a reminder from the king that Douglas must go on a crusade to Jerusalem 'and there bury my hart'. Douglas's journey ended in Spain where, helping the King of Castile in his fight against the Moors, he was cut off by the enemy. Crying 'Go first in the fight, brave heart, as you have ever done!', he flung his leader's heart at the foe and followed, to die upon the Moorish swords

Skull of Robert the Bruce

This cast of the skull of Scotland's national hero was made when his tomb at Dunfermline Abbey was opened in 1819, and is now in the Scottish National Portrait Gallery. The skeleton was found wrapped in sheets of lead, and the breastbone had been cut down the centre – which perhaps helps prove the truth of the story that before Bruce died, he instructed the Black Douglas to carry his heart to the Holy Land and bury it there. Though he had once been excommunicated for having murdered a rival on holy ground – and remained fairly unconcerned by the sentence – Bruce always regretted he had never made a pilgrimage to Jerusalem

occur. The poet invented it after misreading a line from an earlier poem about Robert the Bruce, which tells how certain Scottish nobles were hanged 'in ar' – a legal term meaning 'by a circuit court' (eyre).

Blind Harry gives an equally colourful account of Wallace's years as a fugitive. Wallace, he claims, adopted numerous disguises in order to move around the country undetected: one day he would appear as a monk, the next as an old woman, or a potter. He went to France to enlist support for the Scottish cause, and there defeated two French champions and killed a lion that no one else dared tackle, before asking the French king: 'Are there any more dogs you would have slain?'

Wallace's integrity is praised in the story which tells how the gallant knight politely but firmly rejected the loving advances of the Queen of England, when she went to meet him at St Albans. She offered herself to him, if only he would spare the city of London. Wallace was moved by her tears to withdraw, but refused her offer. It is a fine tale, but Wallace was never anywhere near St Albans and, in any case, there was no Queen of England at that time.

The hard road to freedom

Where Wallace failed, another great figure succeeded, inspired, according to legend, by the most celebrated spider of all time. Robert the Bruce, who liberated Scotland, re-establishing it as an independent kingdom, triumphed mainly by his skill as a soldier. His decisive victory over Edward II's army at Bannockburn in 1314, and his later ability to defend the country against attempts to reconquer it, finally won the freedom he had struggled for. Bruce was King of Scotland from 1306 to 1329 and, though the closing years of his reign were a time of peace and prosperity, no monarch ever came to his kingdom by a harder road.

No one knows why Bruce, having paid homage to Edward I, should suddenly have changed his allegiance. Partly it was ambition, but a large part too was a true feeling for Scottish independence. The die was cast when he murdered his only possible rival to the throne, John Comyn, in the Greyfriars church at Dumfries, in 1306. For this sacrilege he was excommunicated, but nevertheless had himself crowned King of Scotland a few months later. His first two battles against Edward ended in defeat, and Bruce became a fugitive, pursued by the English and by the Scottish friends of Comyn. It is to this period that the spider episode belongs. Some traditions say it took place on the island of Rathlin, off Northern Ireland, while others claim that it happened in west Grampian, or in Kintyre.

Wherever it happened, the story goes that Bruce, lying in a room (or cave) hounded by his pursuers and sick at heart, idly watched a spider swing from one beam to the next in an attempt to anchor its web. Six times it failed but its seventh attempt was successful. The king took this to be a good omen, and resolved to struggle on. From that moment, the tide turned, and Bruce emerged from hiding to make Scotland into a nation.

'The Douglas Larder'

Through good times and bad, the king's most faithful companion was Sir James Douglas, whose nickname of 'the Black Douglas' was feared throughout the Borders. On one occasion, he recaptured his own Douglas Castle which had previously fallen to the English. His men took what they could of the castle's arms and provisions, then emptied the rest – meal, malt and wine – on to the cellar floor, before adding the decapitated remains of the garrison to the ghastly mess. With typical gallows humour, the Scots Borderers christened this episode 'the Douglas Larder'.

All the same, Douglas was not entirely unchivalrous. There was, for instance, the time when he and his men made a night attack on

Roxburgh Castle. With black surcoats covering their armour, they crept across the fields and scaled the walls. On the battlements, according to one account, there sat the wife of an English soldier, lulling her child to sleep with the words:

'Hush ye, hush ye, little pet, ye,
The Black Douglas shall not get ye.'

Suddenly a mailed hand fell on her shoulder, and a deep voice said: 'Do not be too sure of that.' It was the Douglas himself. The woman's life was spared – but the castle was destroyed, so that it could never be held by the English again.

All his life, it is said, Robert the Bruce regretted that the business of his kingdom prevented him from going on crusade. On his deathbed, he ordered that his heart should be removed and his old comrade, Douglas, should bury it in Jerusalem. The sorrowing Sir James agreed, but on the journey volunteered to help the King of Castile in his fight against the Moors. In the battle, the Scots knights were cut off, and Douglas, seeing their case was hopeless, took the silver casket containing Bruce's heart from around his neck, and flung it into the thick of the enemy, crying 'Go first in the fight, brave heart, as you have ever done!' Then he charged in, and died over it. Eventually, Bruce's heart was returned to Scotland and was buried in Melrose Abbey, though his body lies in Dunfermline.

'I saw a dead man win a fight'

Many other heroes of the battle for Scottish independence are still remembered: there was Thomas Randolph, Bruce's nephew, who captured Edinburgh Castle by scaling the rock on which it stands; and his daughter, Black Agnes, who held the castle at Dunbar against English attack for more than six months. Perhaps the finest of the ballads tell how, in 1388, Harry Percy of Northumberland – Shakespeare's Hotspur – was challenged by the son of the Black Douglas. Both men called up their supporters, and a terrible battle followed, which the balladeers called 'Otterburn', 'The Hunting of the Cheviot', or 'Chevy Chase'. On the night before the battle, according to one ballad, Douglas 'dreamed a dreary dream' in which he saw 'a dead man win a fight'. Sure enough, next day, 'while the red blood ran as the rain does in the street', Douglas was mortally wounded, but ordered his officers to conceal his corpse. At last, Hotspur was beaten, and was forced to yield formally to a clump of bracken. Hidden in the clump was the body of Douglas.

The Battle of Chevy Chase

The 19th-century woodcarver Gerrard Robinson devoted years to depicting the conflict between Harry Percy of Northumberland and the Black Douglas's son at the Battle of Chevy Chase or Otterburn in 1388. The Border encounter, in which more than 3000 men died, according to the poet who wrote the ballad of 'Chevy Chase', was the subject for a series of carvings covering an ornate sideboard now in the Grosvenor Hotel, Shaftesbury, Dorset. In the centre panel (below), Douglas is lashing out at the young Hotspur, who lies back in the saddle, shield ready to ward off the next blow, as their followers clash, man against man, all around

St Andrew of Scotland
Andrew the Apostle was martyred on an X-shaped cross, used now on
Scotland's flag, because he thought himself unworthy of the Cross of Christ

THE LIGHT IN THE NORTH

Pagan and Christian legends combine in the tales of the Scottish saints

The saints and divines who brought the light of Christian truth to replace the pagan myths of North Britain are now themselves legendary figures. Even if their adventures became exaggerated in the telling, men's minds have been enriched by the stories of their struggles. Although St Andrew is officially the country's patron saint, perhaps St Columba has a better claim to the title. He was an Irishman of royal descent who settled in Iona, a small island off Mull in western Scotland, in AD 563. He preached until his death in 597, and his mission converted the Scots of Argyll, many Picts who then held the rest of north Scotland, and the Angles of Northumbria and Lothian. A full account of his life was written a century after his death by an abbot of Iona, St Adamnan.

According to legend, however, the holy man had some unsaintly moments. One story tells how, when wading through shallow water, he trod on a flounder. The fish cursed Columba's crooked feet, and he retorted by cursing the fish's mouth, which has been crooked ever since. Another tale would seem to have distinctly pagan overtones. Columba is said to have wished for someone to be buried in Iona to consecrate the earth, and to have allowed his own brother, St Oran, to give his life for the purpose. The main cemetery on the island still bears Oran's name.

Another version of this story says that the walls of the church Columba was trying to build fell down each night, and work could not go ahead until someone had been buried alive there. Oran, who had been quarrelling fiercely with his brother about the exact nature of Heaven and Hell, volunteered. After 20 days, the pit was opened and Oran's head spoke:

'Heaven is not as it is said to be;
Hell is not as it is said to be;
The saved are not forever happy;
The damned are not forever lost.'

Columba's reaction to this heresy was violent. 'Pile earth on Oran's eye!' he ordered the builders – and the voice of his brother was stilled for ever.

Scotland's guardians

Tradition in Argyll says that Columba's relations with another brother, St Moluag, were also far from ideal. Both coveted the fertile island of Lismore and raced in their boats to see who could get there first and take possession. Columba was gaining, so Moluag took an axe, chopped off a finger and threw it ashore before Columba could land, thus establishing his prior claim.

The cult of St Andrew, one of the twelve Apostles and Scotland's patron saint, is said to have been established in the reign of the 9th-century Pictish king Angus. Certain relics of Andrew were said to have been brought to Kilremont in Fife, now St Andrews, from Patras in Greece, where the saint was crucified. The tradition that he suffered on an X-shaped cross (a saltire cross, which has become his emblem) seems to have originated in the Middle Ages. It was said that he considered himself unworthy to die on the Cross of Christ.

The Picts probably promoted the cult of Andrew to counter that of St Columba, which was popular with the Scots. Yet when the Scottish kings annexed the Pictish kingdom and moved their capital to Scone in Tayside, the ancient capital of the Picts, they seem to have been happy enough to adopt St Andrew as well.

Many of Columba's followers were hailed as saints, and curious tales are told of them. St Maoldoraidh, for example, is said to have formed the island of Islay by joining two islets together, and St Ronan of Rona was believed to have travelled there from Lewis on the back of a sea monster. One of Columba's best

Columba of Iona
The mission on Iona was begun by St Columba, who is shown in a drawing from a 9th-century *Life* by St Adamnan. Some tales scarcely show Columba in a saintly light. He cursed a flounder when he slipped on it, and that is why these fish have crooked mouths

A Glasgow legend
A robin perched on a tree, in Glasgow's coat-of-arms, records a miracle performed by St Kentigern who restored a bird to life. Salmon with rings in their mouths recall another occasion, when the saint returned a lost ring to a forlorn queen, by sending it inside a fish

known disciples was St Donnan of Eigg, who perished with his worshippers when the local queen and her army of fierce Amazons locked them all in the church and set fire to it. The same night, a mysterious, unearthly light led the queen and her female warriors into a loch, where they all drowned. The loch is now called Loch nam Ban Mora, or the Loch of the Big Women.

Two saintly women were especially venerated throughout Scotland. One, the Pictish St Triduana, chose an effective if horrifying means of spurning a royal suitor. She asked him what it was about her that attracted him most; he replied that it was her eyes, so she plucked them out and gave them to him. The many springs where she is believed to have bathed the bleeding sockets have long been said to cure eye troubles.

St Bride, or Brigid, was another Irish saint whose worship apparently began with the immigrant Scots. She is said to have been midwife to the Virgin, but in fact her cult may long pre-date Christianity, for it closely resembles that of Brigantia, a fertility goddess worshipped by the North Britons. St Bride was invoked by women in labour, in the hope that she would ease their birth-pains. Highland households, too, used to celebrate the saint's feast day (February 1) by building a crib of rushes and inviting the saint to 'come to her bed' and so keep watch over the house for the rest of the year.

Both St Ninian and St Kentigern had a considerable influence on the people of the old North British kingdom of Strathclyde. Ninian, a British bishop working in Rome, was sent by the Pope to convert the Scots. He founded a monastery at Whithorn in Dumfries and Galloway in AD 397, and built his 'Candida Casa' or White House there, which is thought to have been the first Christian church in Scotland. It was said to have been called the White House by local people because it was the first stone building they had ever seen. A priory stands on the site today.

St Mungo of Glasgow

St Kentigern, better known by his affectionate name of Mungo, is the patron saint of Glasgow. He died in about AD 612; his mother is said to have been St Thaney, the virgin daughter of a British King of Lothian. Her father would not accept her miraculous pregnancy, so he had her thrown off Traprain Law, a conical hill near Haddington, in Lothian. But she landed unharmed and so was cast adrift on the Firth of Forth in a coracle without oars. It came to land at Culross in Fife, where she gave birth to her son. Later, apparently, he became a pupil of St Servanus, or Serf. Glasgow's coat-of-arms includes a robin, alleged to have been a pet of St Serf. The story goes that another pupil accidentally killed the bird and blamed Kentigern, but when the young saint prayed, it was miraculously restored to life.

Glasgow's arms also depict salmon with rings in their mouths. This recalls the tale of the Queen of Strathclyde, who gave a ring, a present from her husband, to her lover. The king found him wearing it as he slept by the Clyde, and threw the ring into the river. Then he ordered his wife to produce it. She prayed to Kentigern, and the ring was found in a salmon caught by her servants. She showed it to her husband, and he was forced to accept her pleas of innocence.

Lothian's native saint, St Baldred, lived as a hermit on Bass Rock, and is commemorated by St Baldred's Boat – a rock off the coast near North Berwick that was a menace to shipping until the saint steered it to a safer anchorage. At his death, the saint's body was miraculously triplicated, to meet the claims of three parishes, all of which wanted to be his last resting place.

Feudal queen and saint

St Margaret, the English queen of Malcolm III, changed the course of Scottish history by introducing to the court the Anglo-Norman feudal system of landholding – a system which was maintained among the Highland clans until 1746. At her instigation, the native Celtic Church was reformed and brought into the Church of Rome. She revived the ancient custom of giving thanks after meals, and the grace cup became known in Scotland as St Margaret's Blessing. She lived a life of prayer, abstinence and charity, washing the feet of the poor and feeding orphans from her own spoon. She died in 1093, after being told that her husband and son had both been killed while raiding England; she is said to have thanked God for having cleansed her of sin by visiting so much misfortune upon her.

Missionary to Scotland
The 4th-century St Ninian built what is thought to have been the first Christian church in Scotland, at Whithorn, near Burrow Head. It was called 'The White House' by the natives because it was the first stone building they had ever seen

The feudal saint
The Anglo-Norman feudal system and Roman Church practices were introduced to Scotland when the Saxon Margaret became Malcolm III's queen in the 11th century. Her life was filled with charitable acts, and she was canonised in 1250

Irish saint or pagan goddess?
In the Highlands and Hebrides, women in labour would pray to the Irish
saint Bride or Brigid, who in legend was midwife to the Virgin. But it
would seem that her cult was confused with that of a much older deity, the
Celtic fertility goddess Brigantia, to whom women made offerings at
certain springs and wells in the hope that they would bear children. The
Bride's Wells and Brigid's Wells that exist all over Britain were almost
certainly once dedicated to Brigantia, and were later renamed by the
Church. This Romano-British statue of the goddess, dating from the 3rd
century AD, was found at Birrens, Dumfries and Galloway. It is now in the
National Museum of Antiquities, Edinburgh

MARIA SCOTIÆ REGINA, GALLIÆ DOTA
ANGLIÆ ET HYBERNÆ VERE PRINCEPS I
IACOBI MAGNÆ BRITANIÆ REGIS MATER
OPPRESSA AN.º Dni 1568 AVXILII SPE ET C
COGNATA ELIZABETHA IN ANGLIA REGNA
EÒ DESCENDIT, IBIQVE CONTRA IVS GENT
PROMISSI FIDEM CAPTIVA RETENTA
VITATIS AN.º 19. RELIGIONIS ERGÒ, EIVS
PERFIDIA ET SENATVS ANGLICI CRV
HORRENDA CAPITIS LATA SENT
TRADITVR, AC 12. CAL. MART
AVDITO EXEMPLO À SERVIL
TO CARNIFICE TETRV N M
PITE TRVNCATA EST. ÀNN
REGNIQVE 45

IOANNA
KENNETHIÆ

AVLA FODRINGHAMIÆ

REGINAM SERENISS.ᵐ REGVM FILIAM,
VXOREM ET MATREM, ASTANTIBVS
COMMISSARIIS ET MINISTRIS R.
ELIZABETHÆ CARNIFEX SECVRI
PERCVTIT ATQ. VNO ET ALTERO
ICTV TRVCVLENTER SAVCIATÆ
TERTIO EI CAPVT ABSCINDIT,

PRIMA QVOAD VIXIT COL. SCOT. PARENS ET FVN

SIC FVNESTVM ASCENDIT TABVLATVM REGINA QVONDAM
GALLIARV ET SCOTIÆ FLORENTISS.ᵐ INVICTO SED PIO
ANIMO TYRANNIDEM EXPROBRAT ET PERFIDIAM
FIDEM CATOLICAM PROFITETVR, ROMANÆ ECCLESIA
SE SEMPER FVISSE ET ESSE FILIAM PALAM PLANE TESTATVR

THE STUARTS
AND THEIR CHAMPIONS

Thousands gave their lives for the sake of Scotland's last Royal line

Legend says that the family who ruled Scotland, and later England, for 350 years, owes its name to Malcolm IV's servant, Walter the Steward, who died in 1177. One of his descendants, another Walter, married Robert the Bruce's daughter Marjorie in 1315. It was from this union that the royal House of Stuart sprang, a family that was often tragic, sometimes foolish and almost always attractive. Some of them, like Bonnie Prince Charlie, the last of the line, possessed all three qualities; they were dangerous people to follow, but they were the stuff of which romance is made.

The two Stuart monarchs who most captured the imagination of the people were James IV (1488–1513) and his son James V (1513–42). James IV was perhaps the most gallant and learned Scots king since Robert the Bruce. He managed to please Highlanders by learning Gaelic, and made several trips north in attempts to settle feuds and quarrels. Yet all this bright promise ended when he led his army into the disastrous defeat of the Battle of Flodden in 1513. The king died there, along with the flower of Scottish chivalry, but the popularity he had achieved inspired many tales that he lived on, or that he rested in a fairy hill, along with other vanished heroes who would ride again when Scotland had need of them.

The King in the Grey Coat

James V, known as the 'Commons' King', gave a charter to the gipsies in 1540, and enjoyed roaming the countryside in disguise. Highlanders called him Righ a' Chota Ghlais, the King in the Grey Coat, while James himself loved to play the role of 'The Goodman of Ballengeich', taking the name from a place near his favourite castle of Stirling. Once, when in this guise, he was attacked by four outlaws at Cramond Brig, near Edinburgh. A farm labourer threshing corn near by heard the struggle and ran to his aid. Between them they routed the thieves. The labourer then gave the king water to wash himself and escorted him to Edinburgh. On the way he said his name was Jock Howieson and that his greatest wish in life was to own Braehead Farm, on which he worked. The king, who pretended to be the Goodman of Ballengeich, said he held a minor post at court, and offered to show Jock round Holyrood the following Sunday as a reward for his help. When Sunday came, the king, still dressed in the same clothes, met Jock and showed him round the palace. Then he asked Jock if he would like to look on the king himself. 'Yes, if it is allowed,' said Jock, 'but how am I to know His Majesty from all the other great men?' 'Easily,' said the Goodman. 'The rest will be bareheaded, and only the king will be wearing a hat.' With that, he led Jock into a room full of courtiers and noblemen. Jock looked round, but could not see the king. 'I told you,' said the Goodman, 'he is the man with his hat on.'

Jock scanned the company again. 'Well,' he said, 'if that is so, it must be either me or you, for the rest are bareheaded.' The king and his companions burst out laughing and admitted the deception. Jock Howieson was given the royal farm at Braehead and, for rent, was to present the king and his descendants with a basin and a

'The wisest fool in Christendom'
This was the French King Henry IV's description of James VI of Scotland, who later ascended the English throne as James I. The comment was probably prompted by James's curious mixture of learning and superstition – he was deeply interested in the sciences and terrified of witches, 200 of whom he believed had plotted to drown his queen and himself on their journey from Denmark. All his life he was afraid of drawn swords – due, it is said, to his mother, Mary, Queen of Scots, witnessing the murder of David Rizzio in the last weeks of her pregnancy. It was alleged by James's enemies that he was actually Rizzio's son

---

The end – Fotheringay
Several copies of this painting of Mary, Queen of Scots' execution in 1587 were made and distributed to Scots Catholic colleges in France. The picture is reproduced by permission of the Trustees of Blairs College, Aberdeen

ewer of water to wash in whenever he came to Holyrood or passed over Cramond Brig.

There are many tales about the king's adventures while disguised as a pedlar, a piper or a beggar. He is also supposed to have been the subject – or even the author – of the ballads of 'The Gaberlunzie-Man' and 'The Jolly Beggar'. In this second ballad a stranger seduces the daughter of the house where he has found lodging and, when morning comes, the girl is appalled to discover she has been sleeping with a beggar and not, as she thought, a gentleman. But when the stranger blows his horn 'four-and-twenty belted knights' come over the hill, and he strips off his rags to reveal rich apparel beneath. He rewards the girl with money, but says that had she been honest, he would have made her his lady.

Mary the Queen

The career of James V's daughter, Mary, Queen of Scots (1542–87), provided tragedy and romance more dramatic than any legend. It included the murder in 1566 of her Italian favourite, David Rizzio, whose influence aroused the anger of her lords; the mysterious explosion the following year, in which her husband Lord Darnley died; and her escape from Loch Leven Castle with the help of her

'The Flowers of the Forest'

James IV's mother, Queen Margaret of Scotland, had to wait four years for her first child. Legend tells how, pregnant at last, she made a pilgrimage to the church of St Duthus at Tain in the Highland region. The saint's relics were famous for miracle-working and, beside them, the queen prayed for a son. Her prayers were promptly answered, for she gave birth to the future James IV (right) in a chapel in the churchyard, the ruins of which are still visible.

James IV's subjects loved him for his learning, his flamboyance and his large number of mistresses no less than for the peace and prosperity he brought to his realm. But peace was not to last. In 1513, his alliance with France forced him to lead his army into England. Together with thousands of Scotland's finest young men, he died at Flodden. The extent of the slaughter reached into every Lowland household; it was still remembered 300 years later when Jane Elliot wrote the poignant ballad, 'The Flowers of the Forest'

gaoler's son. In the last months of her reign she lost the affections of Scottish people who thought, probably correctly, that she and her lover, Bothwell, had conspired to murder Darnley. For this reason, the stories about her tend to be unfavourable, treating her more as a tyrant than a heroine.

It is said that once, when Darnley came in from hunting and asked after his forests of Badenoch before inquiring about the queen, she had the forests burnt down. This is said to account for the blackened tree stumps found in many Highland peatbogs.

The Stuarts, including even Mary, always had their champions, willing to fight and die for them. One such hero was James, 1st Marquis of Montrose (1612–50) who raised the clans on behalf of Charles I during the Civil War. He waged a brilliant campaign, winning six battles for the king before being defeated in 1645 and fleeing to the Continent. He returned four years later with more men and money for the cause, but lost many followers in a shipwreck. He was defeated at Carbisdale and became a fugitive with a price on his head. He was betrayed by a man who offered him shelter, and was hanged in Edinburgh.

The cruel warrior

Montrose's lieutenant, Alasdair Macdonald, sometimes called 'Colkitto', figures more prominently in Highland legend than his leader – probably because Montrose was a Lowlander and thus readily forgotten. Alasdair was evidently fated to be a warrior. On the night of his birth, it is said, every sword in his father's house moved a little out of its scabbard and every gun-lock snapped. As a baby he found a toad and started to eat it, but his nurse took it away from him. His grandfather heard the infant roaring with rage, and said: 'Give it to him and let the one devil eat the other.' Toads were often believed to be demons in disguise.

In 1644 he joined Montrose, with 1200 Irish troops supplied by his cousin, the Marquis of Antrim. He marched with Montrose for more than a year and was knighted for his part in defeating an anti-Royalist force at Kilsyth, before leaving to continue his feud with the Campbells of Argyll. Among the atrocities he committed against his ancient enemies was the burning of a number of women in a barn at Glen Uichar, which was afterwards known as Sabhal nan Cnamh, or 'the barn of the bones'.

After Montrose had been defeated, an army under General David Leslie was sent to crush Alasdair. It was about this time that a doom, long foretold, began to overtake him. He was setting up his standard on a hillock by a mill near Lochgilphead when the flagstaff struck a coin in the ground. The standard, which had been pointing right, swung round to point left. Alasdair asked the name of the mill and was told it was called the mill of Gocam-Gò. At this, he lost heart, for his old nurse, telling fortunes at Hallowe'en many years before, had warned him that he would be successful in battle

The 'Commons' King'

James V (here with his queen, Mary of Guise) enjoyed wandering his kingdom incognito, and was said to have inspired the ballad of 'The Gaberlunzie-Man'. A girl whom the beggar meets takes him for a shepherd, and falls in love with him. She gives him her scarlet cloak, buys him bread, and follows him home. There he is revealed as a gentleman, and he marries her

The gallant turncoat

Once a soldier of the Covenant, the Marquis of Montrose is said to have changed sides because he could not bear to see Charles I in adversity. He raised the Highlands for the king and was later handed over to the Covenanters by his host, MacLeod of Assynt, for £5000 worth of oatmeal. He was hanged on a 30 ft gallows in Edinburgh in 1650. Such was his courage that the crowd that had come to jeer remained silent

529

Flora of the '45
After nine days of escorting Prince
Charlie 'over the sea to Skye', Flora
MacDonald was captured and taken
to London, where, to her
astonishment, she was the darling of
society. Later, she married a
kinsman, Allan MacDonald, and
emigrated to Carolina

until he came to a mill with the strange name of Gocam-Gò and his
standard turned round. Once this happened, she said, he would
never be successful again.

So it turned out. Alasdair retreated from Leslie's forces through
Kintyre, and embarked with most of his men for home in Islay,
leaving 300 to be massacred in the castle of Dunaverty when it fell.
Local tradition, however, says he left with no more than a boatload,
and chopped off the fingers of his desperate followers as they clung
to the boat's gunwales. From Islay he retreated to Ireland, where he
died, still fighting, at the Battle of Kinsale, in 1647.

The prince in the hills

Whatever their faults, the Stuarts bowed off the stage of history
with grace and courage. Though Prince Charles Edward, better
known as the Young Pretender or Bonnie Prince Charlie, died a
querulous drunk in Rome in 1789, his legend had really ended
more than 40 years earlier. On the night of September 19, 1746, a
few fugitives watched him board the French frigate *L'Heureux* at
Loch nan Uamh, near Arisaig, Highland – the spot where he
had landed 14 months earlier. The ship faded into the darkness,
and so too did the final hopes of the Stuart dynasty.

The many songs about the prince – such as 'The Skye Boat Song'
and 'Will Ye No' Come Back Again?' – were written years later,
when there was not the slightest chance of his returning. Nor do the
ballads make any mention of the clansmen and their families,
dazed and shattered by the savagery of the Duke of Cumberland's
reprisals against anyone who had been 'out' in the rebellion of
'45, which ended in 60 minutes of slaughter on Culloden Moor.
Two centuries earlier, the Brahan Seer is said to have visited the
place and to have prophesied: 'Thy black moor will be stained with

the best blood of the Highlands. Heads will be lopped off by the score, and no quarter given on either side.'

Despite the romantic nonsense surrounding the prince, the legends of the dashing young man hunted through the hills after the battle remain undimmed. When hiding in the Hebrides, for example, he was told that there was a price of £30,000 on his head; so the prince immediately offered £30 for George II, England's Hanoverian king. His personality must also have appealed to the many people who helped him. Not only to Flora MacDonald, whom he accompanied disguised as her maid and looking 'a very odd, muckle, ill-shaken-up wife, making lang, wide steps'; but to the Kennedy brothers, who robbed a Hanoverian general's baggage to supply the prince with clothes. It never occurred to them to betray him, though they were so poor that one of them was later hanged for stealing a cow worth 30 shillings.

Like all the Stuarts, Charles seems to have inspired deep personal devotion. One of his bodyguard, Roderick MacKenzie, looked so like him that he drew the redcoats after him and when mortally wounded in Glenmoriston, shouted: 'You have killed your Prince!' This caused the hunt to be abandoned for several days, and allowed the prince time to escape.

The last, lingering mystery of the '45 is the treasure of Loch Arkaig. After the prince was defeated, the French sent £4000 in gold louis coins, and a large quantity of brandy, muskets and ammunition. Finding no one to meet them, the French left this hoard on the shores of Loch nan Uamh, and hurriedly departed. Soon after, the Macdonalds of Barrisdale carried off some of the stores and gold. The Macleans of Mull also looted their share, but it is said that the rest of the gold, which might have altered British history, was buried beside Loch Arkaig, where it may still lie.

The fugitive prince
During his wanderings after Culloden, Bonnie Prince Charlie is said to have hidden in caves all over the Highlands and Islands, though it is doubtful if he ever shared one with Flora MacDonald, as depicted here. Nevertheless, this Victorian painting by Duncan captures the anxiety of the prince's followers during his desperate months as a fugitive. Though many poor people helped or concealed the prince, and must have known Charles's hiding places during his wanderings before he escaped to France in September 1746, no one ever claimed the £30,000 reward offered for him

A prince in disguise
A fugitive after Culloden, Bonnie Prince Charlie was disguised by Flora MacDonald as her maid, 'one Betty Burke, an Irish girl'

Man of two worlds
Dressed in a mingling of high fashion and savage finery, this portrait is
typical of a chieftain of the 1660's. Though well travelled and expensively
educated, he might slaughter an entire family for a fancied insult

'WOLVES AND WILDE BOARES'

The chieftains, reivers and outlaws who held sway in the Scottish hills

In the early 16th century, Mac 'ic Ailein, chief of the Mac-Donalds of Clanranald, murdered his ploughman for picking a silverweed root out of the furrow and nibbling it. Clanranald imagined that the man was hinting that he did not get enough to eat, and since the chief was showing a MacLeod over his lands at the time, he considered that the ploughman had deliberately humiliated him in front of a guest. To prevent repercussions, he prudently massacred the ploughman's family, but the youngest son escaped, and later returned to murder Clanranald. History suggests, however, that the 'ploughman's son' may in fact have been the heir to the chieftainship.

With honour satisfied on both sides, the incident was closed; apart, maybe, from being set to verse and music by the clan's bard, who had a thousand such tales to sing from memory on special occasions. Some of the stories were of affairs of blood and courage which had taken place hundreds of years before, and all of them were intended to extol the Clan Donald over all other men.

The trouble was that for centuries many other Scots families held similar views of themselves. Border chieftains and leaders of outlaws, like the clansmen beyond the Highland line, almost ignored the central government. Reiving – cattle-raiding – blood feuds and full-scale battles over disputes of land and honour were part of everyday life.

In this tribal society most crimes were violations not of law but of custom and family ties. To the law-abiding Lowlander, only a very hazy line divided the chief from the robber or murderer. No wonder that an exasperated James VI in the 16th century should refer to some of his most unruly subjects, the people of the Isles, as 'Wolves and wilde boares'.

Men beyond the law

Until 1493, when James IV abolished the title, the Lords of the Isles, who also had controlled much of the mainland Highlands as chiefs of the Clan Donald, dominated the scene. After that time the Hebrides and the north and west Highlands were split among a mass of roughly equal and independent chiefs who raided and quarrelled to their hearts' content for a century, curbed only by the occasional expeditions which a weak government usually entrusted to the earls of Argyll or Huntly. They, like the Lords of the Isles before them, regarded the keeping of the king's peace as an excuse to feather their own nests at their neighbours' expense.

The characters of the chiefs as they appear in legend may be good or bad, but they are always extraordinary. Whenever one of the MacDonald chieftains appeared in Edinburgh, great crowds would follow him; his horse was shod with gold, but the shoes were so loosely attached they were constantly falling off. Another chief nearly ruined himself by slaughtering a cow each day for his gourmet wife who would eat only cows' tongues, while a third was followed – or thought he was followed – on land and sea by a familiar spirit in the shape of a monstrous frog. He was summoned from his deathbed in Canna by a whistle from the Devil, who appeared as a giant shapeless form in the distance.

The career of Sir Lachlan MacLean of Duart was fairly typical of the rest. Known as Lachunn Mor (Big Lachlan), he was chief of the MacLeans of Mull and Tiree in the last quarter of the 16th century.

Along with his chieftainship, Lachlan inherited the long-standing dispute between the MacLeans and the MacDonalds over possession of the Rhinns of Islay, the western peninsula of the island. The many battles and massacres caused by this bitter

A chief among kings
A medieval chieftain, possibly a MacLean of Duart, lies beneath his monument in St Oran's Cemetery, Iona, the oldest Christian burial ground in Scotland. Some 60 Scottish, Irish and Norwegian kings, among them Macbeth, as well as many chieftains, are buried on Iona, St Columba's holy island. From there, he sent his missionaries in AD 563 to convert Scotland to Christianity. This royal cemetery has fulfilled Columba's prophecy that, small as it is, Iona would be honoured by the rulers of nations

quarrel are part of the lore of both clans, and legend and history have become inextricably mixed. One story tells how, during an uneasy truce enforced by James VI, Donald Gorm MacDonald was storm-bound on Jura, in MacLean territory. At the same time, two of his relatives whom he had outlawed landed further down the coast, and to make trouble for Donald, carried off some MacLean cattle in their galley. Donald Gorm's party were suspected of the robbery, word was sent to Lachlan in Mull, and the MacLeans made a night attack in which 60 MacDonalds are said to have been killed. Donald Gorm himself escaped only because he was on board his ship at the time. He hurried home to Skye to organise vengeance for this apparently unprovoked assault.

Angus MacDonald of Islay came to visit the MacLeans in an effort to patch up the quarrel, but Lachlan flung him into prison and kept him there until he had promised to give up the disputed Rhinns of Islay. When Lachlan came to take possession of them, Angus invited him to a feast at his house at Mulindry above Bowmore. Lachlan was suspicious, but finally accepted, and brought a following of 86 men. That night Angus, with several hundred MacDonalds, surrounded the hall where the MacLeans were lodged, and took them prisoner, all except two men who refused to leave the safety of the building.

Angus gave them short shrift; he fired the hall, and the two MacLeans were burnt alive inside it. Then, according to MacLean tradition, a relative of Lachlan spread a false rumour that Angus MacDonald's brother, who was a hostage in Mull, had been killed. When Angus heard the news he is said to have beheaded all the MacLean prisoners in relays of two each morning. Lachlan himself, who was left to the last, survived only because Angus was injured by a fall from his horse on the way to the execution.

The sinister marksman

In 1591 James VI intervened once more in the quarrels of the MacLeans and MacDonalds. Somehow, Lachlan MacLean gained favour at court, and was knighted. He managed to secure from the Crown a grant of the disputed Rhinns of Islay and other lands in the island, and in 1598 went to Islay to take possession. Angus MacDonald's son, James, had now taken over as chief and, not un-naturally, he objected to Lachlan's airy assumption of ownership. Open war was once more declared.

According to tradition, Sir Lachlan was approached by a dwarf-ish bowman from Jura known as Dubh-Sith (the Black Fairy), who offered him his services. Dubh-Sith was turned away with scorn, so James MacDonald employed him instead. It is said that Sir Lachlan was warned by a witch in Mull to avoid three things on this expedition. He must not row his galley widdershins – that is, anti-clockwise – round an island in Loch Spelve; nevertheless, he did so out of sheer bravado. Another condition was that he must not land on Islay on a Thursday, but when a storm arose on that day, he was forced to take shelter there. Finally, he was not to drink from a certain well by Gruinart, but not knowing the well, he bent down to drink at it in the middle of the battle. As he raised his arm to his mouth he exposed an underarm gap in his armour, and Dubh-Sith sent an arrow through it. So died Lachunn Mor – or at least, this is the tale told by his sorrowing clansmen, who could not possibly imagine that so vital a being could have fallen to the hand of a mortal assassin.

Nevertheless, the MacLeans always looked back on Lachlan's chieftainship as being one of the golden ages of the clan. It was during his time, in 1588, that a galleon from the scattered Spanish Armada took shelter in Tobermory Bay. There are several legends about its subsequent fate, but according to the MacLeans, whose country this was, the Spanish captain bought supplies from them and attempted to sail off without paying. He took with him the son of MacLean of Morvern, who had been sent to collect the debt. But that spirited young man broke free of his captors, it is said, and fired the ship's powder store, destroying the galleon, the crew and himself in the explosion. The search for the treasure rumoured to be in the galleon has continued to this day.

The cattle-lifters

To Highland chiefs, and the iron-helmed raiders or moss-troopers of the English marches, reiving was the natural occupation of a gentleman. Ailean nan Sop, a younger son of a MacLean of Duart, got his name of 'Alan of the Wisps of Straw' because on his many raids he used to pile straw or brushwood round his victims' houses

The disgraced chief
Archibald Campbell, 7th Earl of Argyll (1575–1638), was chief of the Campbells. Archibald was disliked by James VI, and when he became a Catholic in 1618 and went to fight for the King of Spain he was declared a traitor and disgraced. The Campbells were the richest and most progressive of the clans, but had a reputation for ruthlessness which they amply fulfilled at the massacre of Glencoe. Yet not every story is of their devilry. Tradition tells of Sir Colin Campbell of Glenorchy, who built Kilchurn Castle by Loch Awe in 1440, and then left for a Crusade in the Holy Land. Seven years passed before news reached his wife of his death in battle. The lady in time accepted the proposal of another suitor, but on the wedding day the missing Sir Colin returned in disguise. As the marriage vows were about to be exchanged he disclosed his true identity, to the delight, it is said, of his supposed widow

and fire it with his own hand. Ailean nan Creach, 'Alan of the Cattle Raids', was supposed to have made a raid for every year of his 34 years and three for each of the quarters of a year he was in his mother's womb. There was also Colla nam Bó, 'Coll of the Cows', chief of the MacDonnells of Keppoch towards the end of the 17th century. He was a man with a university education, who carried on his clan's raiding tradition until William III's stern edicts (backed by the massacre of his neighbours, the MacDonalds of Glencoe) forced him to desist in 1692. Even so, other clans such as the Camerons continued raiding until 1745 or after.

Some of the MacGregors, said to have been brought to the north-east by the Earl of Moray when the clan was proscribed in Argyll after 1603, were notorious outlaws in west Grampian and the neighbouring counties. One was Gilderoy (The Red-haired Lad), who was hanged in Edinburgh in 1636. He became the subject of a song said to have been composed by his mistress. Another, Patrick Roy MacGregor, 'a vile Scithian rude outlaw' protected by the Gordons, was finally captured in an attempt to hold the entire town of Keith to ransom in 1670.

The adventures of these two MacGregors may have contributed to the legend of a third, the celebrated Rob Roy. He is supposed to have led a raid on the Lowland parish of Kippen in 1691, but apart from this he spent his younger years peacefully enough as a drover, buying and selling Highland cattle under the patronage of the Duke of Montrose. But owing to a slump in the market he lost most of his capital in 1712, and absconded with £1000 invested in the business by various chieftains. After this he became a cattle-thief, stealing chiefly from Montrose, his earlier

Johnnie Armstrong's farewell
Johnnie Armstrong of Gilnockie, the most notorious member of a Border clan of freebooters, takes leave of his relatives and retainers for the last time. A famous ballad tells of Johnnie's end. James V, weary of Border strife, called the fractious Border chiefs together in 1530 under the pretext of arranging a truce between them. Johnnie, escorted by 24 followers, met the king at Carlinrig in Teviotdale and James promptly ordered that the entire party be hanged, in spite of Johnnie's protestations of loyalty. His last lament, as the rope went round his neck, is said to have been that he had 'asked grace of a graceless face', and that had he known the king's intentions he would have stayed at home and lived in safety

benefactor. He was supported in his new career by Montrose's enemy, the Duke of Argyll, who gave the outlaw a refuge in Glenshira, not far from Inveraray. From there he 'collected the Duke of Montrose's rents' (and on one occasion the rent collector with them).

Nothing in Rob Roy's own life is quite so violent as the behaviour of his sons James and Rob Og, or Robert the Younger. In 1750 they abducted a rich young widow, Jean Key, from near Balfron in the Scottish Lowlands, and married her forcibly to young Rob. A once-popular ballad describes the affair in terms very unfavourable to the MacGregors. It does not mention that when they found themselves unable to lay hands on her property, Rob Roy's sons set the captive free a few months later. They were tried for the crime, and although James escaped from Edinburgh Castle, Rob was hanged.

Until late in the 16th century, the situation on the Border was very similar. The most notorious cattle-raiders were the Armstrongs, who lived largely in the 'Debatable Land' – the no-man's land claimed by both England and Scotland. Though generally inclined to consider themselves Scots, they would side with the English if they saw fit, and raided both countries indiscriminately. The last Armstrong raider was hanged, on evidence of 'habit and repute', at Selkirk in the early 18th century. The heroes of two well-known Border ballads of escape from English prisons, Kinmont Willie and Jock o' the Side, were both Armstrongs. Kinmont Willie, William Armstrong, was captured by the English in time of truce and taken to Carlisle Castle. The Scots Warden of the Marches, Walter Scott of Buccleuch, rescued him at the head of 30 men. It took only five men to rescue Jock o' the Side, however. Led by Hobby Noble, an English exile, they slipped over the walls of Newcastle in disguise. When Jock was snatched from his cell, he was in irons and unable to sit a horse. So Hobby tied him across his saddle for the long ride north.

Pirates of the narrow seas

Scotland had fewer great pirates to her name than England, but still had her share. The exploits of Sir Andrew Barton are recalled in the ballads; apparently his father had been killed by the Portuguese and James IV gave him 'letters of reprisal' empowering him to revenge himself on Portuguese shipping. But he rapidly extended his activities to attacking English merchant ships as well, and for a time was the terror of the Channel. It seems that his tactics were to lay his ship alongside the enemy and then release heavy beams attached to his main topmast to crash down on his adversary's deck. This curious device must have been successful, for Henry VIII found it necessary to send two men o' war under the command of Thomas and Edward Howard to rid the seas of this menace. According to one ballad, the English ships approached with willow wands, the emblem of peaceful merchants, attached to their masts, and ran alongside Sir Andrew's ship before he discovered the truth. Fierce fighting broke out, and Barton sent two of his best men up the mast to cut the beams free. Before they could reach them, however, both were killed by an English archer, and when Sir Andrew himself climbed the main mast, he too was transfixed by an arrow. Nevertheless, to encourage his men, he continued blowing his whistle until he died. Then the English boarded and the battle was over. The ballad goes on to say that the Howards cut off Sir Andrew's head as a New Year gift for King Henry, and threw the decapitated corpse over the side. Before they did so, however, they tied 300 silver coins about its middle, saying: 'Wheresoever thou lands, it will bury thee.' They felt it was the least they could do for a gallant foe.

The most famous pirate or 'sea-reiver' of the Highlands was known as Mac Iain Ghiarr, or Short MacIan. When the lands of Ardnamurchan were stolen from the MacIans by the Earl of Argyll about 1600, some leading members of the clan refused to submit and were outlawed. In 1624 about 100 of them seized an English ship and set up as pirates along the west coast of Scotland. For more than a year they terrorised the Hebrides until MacLeod of Dunvegan drove them into Moidart, Highland, where they were captured and executed. Mac Iain Ghiarr, however, is usually depicted as a reiver carrying out cattle raids by sea – quite a common business in the Highlands. His favourite trick was to paint his galley white on one side and black on the other, so that those who saw him returning from a raid would not realise that the ship was the same they had seen setting out earlier. According to

Pirate or patriot?
John Paul Jones (1747–92) was a native of Galloway who became a founder of the United States Navy. During the American War of Independence, he commanded an American frigate and harried Irish and Scottish waters as far north as Shetland. His legend grew to such an extent that all acts of piracy were automatically credited to him, whether he had anything to do with them or not. The 'Bloody Yankee', for example, who raided Islay about this time, was almost certainly someone else. John Paul Jones afterwards served in both the French and Russian navies

one version of the story, Mac Iain Ghiarr got his skill as a sea-thief from a *glaistig*, a female spirit of the mountains. His brother Ronald was roasting venison on the point of his dirk in a hunting bothy when the spirit came in and tried to snatch it. Ronald threatened her with the dirk, but Mac Iain Ghiarr gave her some meat. Ever afterwards she was his slave, following him around the Hebrides wherever his galley went. She told him to build a byre, though he had no cattle. As soon as he built one, the *glaistig* showed him how to steal enough cattle to fill it.

The MacNeils of Barra seem to have been pirate kings at one time. They stole everything including the head-stones of the royal graves in Iona. MacNeil is said to have sent a trumpeter to the battlements of his castle each evening to announce that the great MacNeil had dined, so the kings of the earth could now sit down to dinner. According to legend one MacNeil chief, Ruairi an Tartair (Racketty Rory) did so much damage to Queen Elizabeth of England's ships that she complained to James VI. King James sent the Tutor of Kintail – the guardian of the MacKenzie chief – to capture MacNeil, which he did by inviting him aboard his ship and getting him drunk. But when he was brought before the king, Rory protested that he had every right to rob the woman who had murdered James's mother, Mary, Queen of Scots. The king was shamed to silence, and let him go.

Rob Roy in romance and reality
Seen through Victorian eyes, dazzled by the novels of Sir Walter Scott, Rob Roy MacGregor was a dashing and chivalrous outlaw. The truth was less glamorous. In the early 18th century, he established a flourishing protection racket by which he charged farmers an average 5 per cent of their annual rent to ensure the safety of their cattle. Such was his control over the other raiders of Argyll, Stirling and Perth that he could guarantee that any cattle stolen from his customers would be returned. Those who did not pay were stripped of all they possessed

The romantic idol
This portrait of Robert Burns, the farm labourer who sprang to fame as a
poet at 27, fits the popular image of the gay, dashing young blade with a
love for wine, women and song. The stories have, however, been
exaggerated. Although Burns was idolised by Edinburgh society, he
turned his back on city life to become a farmer. He died of rheumatic fever
at 37, following a roadside sleep in the rain

MEN OF ART

In a peasant society, skilled men were credited with supernatural powers

In early Gaelic society, the *aos dana* – the men of art – were highly revered, and included not only artists, poets and musicians, but skilled craftsmen, doctors and lawyers as well. These callings tended to be hereditary; there were certain families, for instance, whose glory it was to provide pipers to generations of Highland chiefs. To the Gaels of the Middle Ages, skilled men were magicians – or at the very least were descended from families who had dealings with the fairies.

The best known legends of the fairy gift are attached to the MacCrimmons, hereditary pipers to the MacLeods of Dunvegan in Skye. Long ago, a young MacCrimmon wandered into a fairy hill whose inhabitants offered him the choice between prosperity without skill or skill without prosperity. The boy chose the gift of skill, and was given the magical 'Black Chanter' – the finger-pipe of the bagpipes – on which the clan composed great music for centuries after. The last MacCrimmon piper, it is said, consulted a wise woman before he joined Prince Charlie. He was told that all would go well with him if he could get food without asking for it before his departure. MacCrimmon went home and found his wife asleep. He tuned his pipes, but she did not move, so he threw his shoe at her. Still she remained immobile, and MacCrimmon departed for the wars without any food at all. Realising what this portended, he composed his greatest lament – 'MacCrimmon will never return' – before going off to die in the service of the prince. History, however, gives a less romantic version. During the '45, the MacLeods enlisted on the Government side and were among the 1500 troops who fled before Lady MacIntosh's handful of Jacobites at the 'Rout of Moy'. The only casualty of the MacLeod contingent was MacCrimmon.

The MacEacherns of Islay were smiths and armourers to the Lords of the Isles from the 15th century at least. The story goes that the son of one of the family was stolen by the fairies, and his father, entering the fairy hill, found the boy working at a forge. Despite his father's pleas, the fairies refused to release the boy. But suddenly a cock crowed, the power of the fairies was broken. Father and son both found themselves outside the hill. The boy was very quiet for years afterwards. Then one day, watching his father forging a sword, he took the hammer from him and showed him how to make the intricate guard on the 'sword of the Islay hilt' for which the MacEacherns became renowned throughout the west.

Kill or cure

The most famous family of physicians in the Highlands was the Beatons. The first of the clan, it is said, was a man named Farquhar, who became physician to King Robert II in the 14th century by divining how the royal doctors were aggravating a wound in the king's knee by putting a beetle into it. Since the creature constantly gnawed the king's flesh, the wound never healed, and the doctors were never out of a job. But Farquhar stood outside the palace and kept crying 'The black beetle to the white bone!' – until at last the king was forced to take notice and discovered the fraud.

Several of the Beatons' cures contained a good deal of common sense. A man who complained of sore eyes was told he was in great danger of growing horns on his knees unless he kept his hands on them for three weeks. At the end of that period, his eyes were much better, since he had never moved his hands to rub them. Others were rough and ready: one of the Beatons was called to attend MacLaine of Lochbuie, who was suffering from severe stomach pains. Beaton diagnosed an ulcer, and with his patient watching, prepared a powder of dried dung. He then departed without telling Lochbuie how to use it. Shortly after, the chief's regular

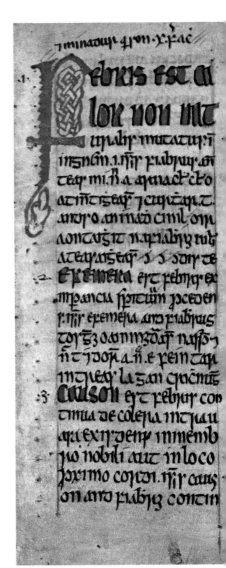

Medicine and the Beatons
This manuscript is part of a 16th-century medical treatise written in Gaelic for the Beatons, a family of physicians. More often, however, the family worked by rule of thumb. There was the case of the girl who swallowed a creature called a *lon-chraois* when drinking from a well, after which she lost weight at an alarming speed. The Beatons' remedy was to tie her into a chair and roast a sheep in front of her. The smell enticed the creature out of her mouth, and the girl recovered

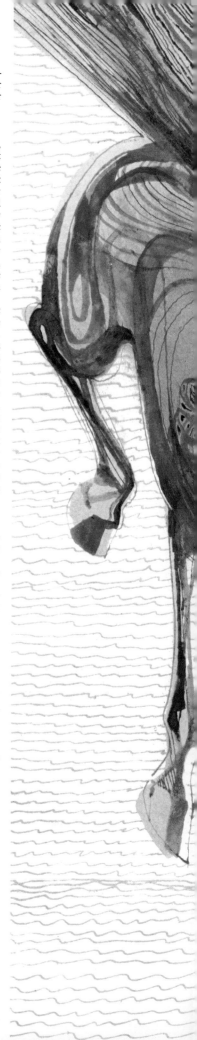

doctors came in and, curious to discover what Beaton had prescribed, dipped their fingers into the powder and tasted it. Their
expressions of disgust sent Lochbuie into fits of laughter; the ulcer
burst with the exertion and he was soon better.

The muse of love and battles

Most of the major Gaelic poets, and some Lowland Scots poets too,
became famous as magicians and prophets, while others left
behind them considerable reputations as 'characters' and wits. The
best-loved of all is Robert Burns, whom most Scots admire not
only for his verse, but for the character of the man as he is usually
portrayed; the kirk-defying, high-spirited young man who found
his pleasure in drinking with friends, in women and in bawdy
song. He is seen, too, as the common man who had democratic
ideas in advance of his age, yet who was revered by the highest in
the land. In this over-simplified portrait, much is made of his many
love affairs, especially those with 'Highland Mary' Campbell,
ended by her untimely death, and with Jean Armour, whom he
eventually married. Yet the portrait has some justice in it; he was a
man who looked on the world with kindly eyes.

Very different was the story of the Gaelic bard Iain Lom (Caustic
John), who died in 1730 at the age of 105. He belonged to the
MacDonnells of Keppoch, a clan of cattle-raiders in Lochaber.
He seems to have had a particular hatred of the Campbells, and is
said to have guided Montrose's army on the forced march across
the snow-clad Highlands which led to the defeat of the Campbells
under their chief, the Marquis of Argyll, at Inverlochy in 1645. He
did not join in the battle, but instead wrote a song in praise of the
victory – before it actually occurred. Argyll put a price on his head,
which Iain himself claimed by arriving at Inveraray Castle. The
marquis took this in good part and showed the poet round his
home. One room was filled with stuffed blackcocks, and his host
asked him if he had ever seen so many dead blackcocks together
before. 'Yes,' said Iain, referring to the dark kilts of the slain
Campbells, 'at Inverlochy.' Argyll's sense of humour must have
been equal even to this, for Iain survived to become Charles II's
Gaelic Poet Laureate.

Prophets in their country

Scotland's foremost prophet, the 13th-century Thomas the
Rhymer, of Ercildoun, was given his gift of prophecy by the
Queen of Elfland. She gave him the 'tongue that can never lie',
from which he was also known as 'True Thomas'. Eventually, she
called him back to Elfland, sending a hart and a hind to guide him.
He got up at once and followed them into the forest, and was never
seen again. He was said to have foretold the crowning of Robert
the Bruce, and to have prophesied the Battle of Flodden in 1513.
His best-known prophecy

'Tyde what may, what'er betide,
Haig shall be Haig of Bemersyde'

was said to have been fulfilled when Field Marshal Earl Haig was
restored to his family's Bemersyde estates in 1921.

The Brahan Seer, Coinneach Odhar (or Dun Kenneth) is
reputed to have lived in several places in the Highlands and Islands –
a man of that name was arrested for witchcraft on the Earl of
Seaforth's estates in 1577. His powers came from a magic stone
left for him by the fairies; the first thing he discovered on looking
into it was that the dinner he was about to eat was poisoned. This
revelation preserved him long enough to prophesy the Battle of
Culloden, the Highland Clearances, and the coming of the
railways. The gift proved double-edged, however. He accurately,
though rashly, informed the Countess of Seaforth that the Earl,
supposedly away on business, was in the arms of another woman,
so she had him burnt to death for his impudence. Before he died,
however, he said that the last of the Seaforths would be deaf and
dumb, and his sons would die before him. This actually occurred
in the lifetime of Sir Walter Scott.

Scottish enchanter
Michael Scot, (died c. 1175) the astrologer, seer and reputed wizard, is said
to have flown to France mounted on a demon horse to seek redress for
French acts of piracy. In Paris he made his diabolical steed stamp its hoof;
and when every steeple bell in the city jangled and part of the palace
collapsed, the French king hurriedly met Scot's demands

INDEX

Page numbers in **bold** indicate a major entry or feature on the subject; entries in *italics* mean illustrations.

A

Aarvold, Sir Carl, 78
Abbots Bromley Horn Dance, 81, **304**, *305*
Abbotsbury, 148
Abbotts Ann, 170
Aberdaron, 380
Aberdeen, 113, 456
Aberdyfi, 380
Aberford, 336; anvil at, *336*
Aberfoyle, 434
Abergavenny (Y Fenni), 380
Aber-soch, 380
Abingdon, 82, 170
Abram, 358
Acaster Malbis, 366
Acklington, 336
Aconbury, 304
Actors, ghosts and legends, 220, *220*; superstitions, 79
Adams, Sweet Fanny, 170
Adderbury, 170, 172
Agriculture, 19, 23, 25, **68–71**, 81
Airline crews, superstitions of, 76
Airships: R101, 20, 258, *258*, *259*
Albert, Prince Consort, 22
Albrighton, 304
Alcester, 304
Alcock's Arbour, 304
Aldborough, 336
Aldbury, 256
Alderley Edge, 358; wishing well, *358*
Aldermaston, 170
Aldington, 196
Aldworth, 170
Alfred the Great, King, **168**, **513–14**, *513*; Althelney, 148, 513; craftsmen and, 77; Ripon charter, 351
Alfriston, 196
All Cannings, 170
Allendale Town, 336
Allgreave, 358
Alloway, 412, *412*; Burns's cottage, *412*
All Saint's Day, 22, 23
Alnwick, 32, 336
Altarnun, 132; carved bench-ends, *132*
Alton, 170
Ambleside, 358
Ambrosden, 172
Ambrosius Aurelianus, 492
Ampthill Hill, 263, *263*
Ancrum, 412
Andover, 81
Anglesey, 101
Anglo-Saxon gods: Eostre, 24, 102; Tiu, 102
Animal husbandry: Celtic festivals and, 22, **23**; farm lore, **68–71**; Michaelmas, 25
Anne, Queen, 84, 222, 514; statue, *222*
Anstey, 256
Antrobus, 359
Anwick, 284
Anwoth, 412; Cardoness Castle, 412, *413*
Aphrodisiacs, 40, 41, 57
Appledore, 78
Appleton, 359
Appletreewick, 336
Apprentices' customs, 77, 77, 79, *79*, 400
April Fools' Day, 24, *24*
Aqualate Mere, 32
Arbroath, 456
Archers, 356, 362
Ardbeg, Islay, 434
Ardnamurchan, 434
Argyll, 128
Argyll, Archibald Campbell, 7th earl of, 534, *534*
Armboth Fell, 359
Armourers, clan MacEachern, 539
Armstrong, Johnnie, 416, *416*, 422, *535*
Armstrong, Neil, astronaut, 423
Armstrong, William (Kinmont Willie), 416, 517, 536
Arthur, King, 36, 483, 490, *490*, **491–6**, *491*, *492*, 497; Arthur's Stone, 313, 402, *402*; Battle of Camlann, *492*; Battle of Mount Badon, 148, 187, 494; Bran's head, 101; burial place of, 156; Cadbury Castle, 152, *496*; death of, *495*; dragon banners, 126;

Finn MacCool, 518; ghost of, 106; giant and, 360; Glastonbury Abbey, *496*; Guinevere, *494*; Hadrian's Wall, 335; Lancelot and Guinevere, *493*, *494*; parentage, 137, 144; quest for the Holy Grail, *495*; ravens, 43; resting place, 358, 385, *385*, *424*, **487**; Richmond Castle, 351; Round Table, 188; Sewingshields, 352; Sir Gawain, 360, *361*; Vale of Avalon, *496*; Welsh legends, 390–1, 403
Arundel, 196, *196*
Ascensiontide, 25, 30
Ashbourne, 284
Ashby de la Zouch, 284
Ashford, 301
Ashingdon, 228
Ashperton, 304
Ashton-under-Lyne, 359
Aspley Guise, 256
Astaroth, *115*
Aston, Sir Thomas, 88, *88*
Astrologers, **20**, 50
Astrology, **20**
Athelhampton, 148
Athelney, 148
Atherstone, 305
Atwick, 336
Aubrey, John, 184, 185, 209
Auchencrow, 413
Auchtermuchty, 413
Auldearn, 457
Auldgirth, 414
Austwick, 336
Avalon, **156–7**, *496*
Avebury stone circles, 101, **171**, *171*
Avon, 147
Axminster, 148
Aylesford, 196
Aylmerton, 227, 228
Ayr, 'Blessing of Ayr', 519
Ayston: effigy in church, *284*

B

Babes in the Wood, 236
Babies: and cauls, 73; changelings, 120; stolen by fairies, 116, 117; superstitions and, 63
Bacup, 359; Britannia Coconut Dancers, 82, *82*
Badbury, 148
Badbury Hill, 148
Badbury Rings, Mount Badon, 148, *148*
Badenoch, 435, 439; Wolf of, 442
Bad luck: bird omens, 42–43, 44; cats, 45; fairies, 116, 117; fishermen's superstitions, 73–74, 78; funeral superstitions, 91; gems, 57; Good Friday, 24; house and home, 60; miners' superstitions, 78, 140; names, 50; plants, 39, 40; shipwrights' superstitions, 78; tea-leaf reading, 96; unlucky number, 61; warding off, 25; weddings, 58
Bainbridge, 336
Baker Street, London: Sherlock Holmes, 212, *212*
Bakewell, 284
Bala, 117, 380
Ballads, Scottish, **416–17**, *416*, *417*; authorship of James IV, 528, 529
Ballantrae, 414
Balmoral, 457
Balsham, 228
Bamburgh: castle, *337*; Worm of, **337**
Bampton, 82, 171
Banastre, Sir Robert, 274, *274*
Banchory, 457
Banff, 36, 458
Bank of England, 212, *213*
Bannockburn, Battle of, 306
Banshees, **118**
Banwell Hill, 149
Baptism, 49; of bells, 66–67; pre-Christian, 50; symbolism in, 50
Bardney, 284
Bardon Mill, 336
Bardsey Island, 381, *381*
Barlow, 301
Barnsdale, 336
Barnstaple, 146, 149
Barnwell, 256
Barra, 435
Barrel makers, 77, *77*
Barrows, 35, 36, 65, 151
Barton, Sir Andrew, 536
Barwick in Elmet, 336
Basildon, 228
Basing House, 171, *171*

Batcombe, 149
Bath: healing waters, 149; baths, *149*
Battle, 196
Battlesden, 256
Bayeux Tapestry, *499*, *500*
Beatons, highland physicians, 539–40
Beaulieu, 171
Beaumont, John, 121
Beccles, 228
Becket, St Thomas à, 205, 208, 262, 511
Bede, the Venerable, 347, 363, 507, *507*, **510**; Bede's Chair, *347*
Bedford, 254, 256, 263
Bedloe, Thomas, 85
Beeby, the 'Tub', *284*
Beely, 284
Beelzebub, *115*
Bees, 71, 71, 89–90
Belford, 336
Bellingham, 337; Charlton Spur, 346, *346*
Bells: Bowness, 361, *361*; church, 66–67; Congleton, 363, *363*; Heighington, 346, *346*; Morris men, 82; submerged cities, 29
Belton, 285
Belvoir Castle witches, 285, *285*, 286
Benbecula, 435
Beningbrough, 338
Ben Macdui, 458
Bentham, Jeremy, 216, *216*
Berepper, 139
Berkeley: witch of, *307*, *307*
Berkeley Castle, **306**
Berkeley Square, London, ghost, 213
Berkshire, 121, 168
Berkswell, 305
Berrington: church effigy, *305*
Berry Pomeroy Castle, 150, *150*
Besford, 306
Bettiscombe, 150; skull, *150*
Betws Garmon, 382
Betws-y-coed, 382
Beverley, 338; sanctuary chair, *338*
Bevis, Sir, 183, *183*
Bibury, 308
Bickerton, 359
Biddenden, 196
Bideford, 151
Bidford-on-Avon, 308
Biggin Hill, 195
Billingsgate, London, 213
Bilston, 309; Wakes, 308, **309**, *309*
Bincombe, 151
Bingley: Celtic-type head, *339*
Birds, **42–44**; cocks, *43*, 57, 71, 83, 453; cuckoos, *43*, 59, 400; eagles, 407; geese, *70*, 125–6, 281, *281*; hens, 57; henpecking, 59; of life and death, **453**, *453*; owls, 89; pelicans, 42, 128; pigeons' feathers, 89; rooks, 90; spell to understand language of, 115; swallows, *43*, 60, *60*, 70; swan-upping, 223, *223*; weather lore and, 25; wren house, *397*; wrens, *43*, 397
Birse, 458
Birth, **49–50**; gipsies, 323
Bisham, 172
Bishops Cannings, 170
Bishopsgate, London, 213
Black Agnes, 521
Black Annis, 37, 118, 295, *295*
Black Down Hills, 151
Blackheath, 309
Blackmail, 416
Blackness: The Binns, *414*
Black Prince, Edward of Woodstock, Prince of Wales, 484, 514, *514*; birthplace, 188; ghost, 106, 514–15; healing well, 202; Prince of Wales's feathers, 514; Tintagel Castle, 144
Black Rock, 360
Black Shuck, 229
Blacksmiths, 22, 76, *76*, 77, 86–87
Blagdon, 151
Blanchland, 339
Blaxhall, 229; Blaxhall Stone, *229*
Bleadon, 151
Bledington, 82
Blewbury, 172
Blickling Hall, 228
Blidworth, 285
Blind Harry, Scots bard, 519–20
Blood charmers, 85
Bloxham, 172
Blythburgh, 229
Boadicea, Queen, 211, 219, 241
Boats (see also Ships), **72–73**, *72*, 74, 78
Bodesbeck, 415
Bodmin, **132**, 138, 139, 142
Bodmin Moor, 138, *139*
Body snatchers, **456–7**, *456–7*
Boggarts, *364*, 365
Boldre, 173
Boleyn, Anne, *228*; ghost of, 106, 181, 225, 228, 245; Henry VIII and, 204
Boleyn, Sir Thomas, *228*, *228*

ACKNOWLEDGMENTS

Of the many people whose specialised knowledge contributed to the preparation of this book our thanks are due especially to:

The Rev. R. A. Alder, the late Violet Alford, The Rev. D. B. Ashburner, J. M. Baines, Dr G. Bankes, The Rev. E. B. Barlow, The Rev. E. D. Blanchard, J. Boothroyd, Brigadier E. V. Bowra, C. Brett, J. E. Brownlow, G. J. Burford, C. A. Burland, Mrs G. A. D. Chalmer, The Rev. D. Chapman, The Rev. A. G. Charles, Tessa Clark, Nona Coxhead, The Rev. J. C. de la T. Davies, The Rev. W. A. Davies, The Rev. S. C. Dedman, R. N. Dixon, P. Dobson, A. M. Dunn, Mrs M. Earl, J. Elliot, Pauline Ellison, The Rev. D. Evans, The Rev. I. M. Evans, Mrs K. J. Evans, R. Evans-Foster, Major Eyre, Fairey Surveys Ltd., The Rev. J. M. Finnie, The Right Honourable the Earl of Gainsborough, The Ghost Club, F. Godfrey, The Rev. A. Green, The Rev. E. J. Green, Captain G. Griffith, Vana Haggerty, F. Hallworth, The Rev. R. W. Hardy, Miss M. A. Harper, D. Harrison, C. Heron, The Rev. R. Heywood-Waddington, G. Hoare, Mrs D. S. Hodges, The Rev. G. F. Holley, Professor R. L. Holmes, The Rev. C. Hoyal, O. A. Hughes, The Rev. R. J. Hunting, D. F. James, Miss E. M. Jancey, A. A. Jenkins, The Rev. D. G. Jones, Miss E. Jones, The Rev. T. L. Jones, Miss I. H. Kay, Miss J. M. Kennedy and staff, Norfolk & Norwich Record Office, P. Kennedy, A. N. S. Kinnear, The Rev. J. W. Knights, A. P. Lalonde, Mrs A. Lansdell, R. R. Lawson, The Rev. F. H. Lockyear, The Rev. K. F. Lord, A. A. MacDougall, Mrs E. MacFadyen, Miss M. C. Macfarlane, Professor John MacQueen, Lady Jean Maitland, The Vicar of Marden, Herefs., The Ven. B. R. Marsh, Archdeacon of Northampton, The Rev. W. N. Metcalf, R. Milne, H. Minns, W. Mortimer, M. Mountford, C. Munro, W. E. Nicholls, H. H. Norris, J. F. L. Norwood, G. A. Oliver, Iona and Peter Opie, W. J. Pennel, J. Pey, M. Pinney, J. S. Pottinger, P. B. Regan, C. Rippon, The Rev. W. R. Rodda, C. V. Romer, J. G. Rutter, A. J. B. Salmon, E. H. Sargeant, The Rev. C. Sawyer, The Rev. Canon J. F. Scammell, C. J. Scott, The Rev. R. T. Sharp, D. A. South, S. Spavin, The Rev. J. E. Spence, R. D. Stuart, Major P. Sturgis, Otta F. Swire, The Rev. Canon G. V. Syer, The Rev. F. J. Tackley, Miss C. F. Tarjan, The Rev. Canon G. N. Tattersall, Mrs P. Thompson, Mrs Y. A. Thompson-Royds, E. Toulson, A. E. Truckell, J. Wardroper, Mrs J. White, W. R. Wilks, The Ven. A. H. Woodhouse, Archdeacon of Ludlow, H. A. Workman, J. Wright, The Rev. Canon K. W. Wright

The following organisations also gave invaluable help:

Abbey National Building Society, London W.1; Aberdeen Art Gallery and Museum; Abergavenny and District Museum; Alderney Society and Museum, Channel Islands; Anglesey County Library, Llangefni; Angus Folk Collection, Glamis; Argyllshire County Library, Dunoon; Ashburton Museum, Devonshire; Ashwell Village Museum, Hertfordshire; Banbury Public Library and Museum; Bank of England Press Office, London E.C.2; Barnet Public Libraries, London N.4; Barrow-in-Furness Public Libraries and Museum; Bedford Museum; Bedford Public Library; Bentham-Moxon Trust; Berwick-upon-Tweed Museum; Bexley Borough Library; Bexley Museum; Bishop Hooper's Lodging, Gloucester; Blackburn Museum and Art Gallery, Lancashire; Bodleian Library, Oxford; Bolling Hall Museum, Bradford; Bowes Museum, Barnard Castle, Co. Durham; Brecknockshire County Library, Brecon; Brighton Museum; Buckinghamshire County Library, Aylesbury; Caernarvonshire County Library, Caernarvon; Caithness County Library, Wick; Camberley Museum; Cambridge and County Folk Museum; Cambridgeshire County Library; Camden Public Library, London N.W.3; Cardiganshire County Library, Aberystwyth; Cardiganshire Joint Library, Aberystwyth; Carmarthenshire County Library, Carmarthen; Castle Museum, Norwich; Chelmsford and Essex Museum; Chepstow Museum; Cheshire Libraries and Museum Service, Chester; Chichester City Museum; Christchurch Mansion, Ipswich; Church House, London S.W.1; Clackmannanshire County Library, Alloa; Clun Local History Museum, Shropshire; Cornish Museum, East Looe; Cornwall County Library, Truro; Corporation of London, London E.C.2; Cromwell Museum, Huntingdon; Cumberland County Library, Carlisle; Cuming Museum, London S.E.17; Department of Antiquities, Leicester Museum and Art Gallery; Department of English Language, University of Sheffield; Department of Folk Life, Salford Museum and Art Gallery; Department of Folk Life Studies, University of Leeds; Derbyshire County Library, Matlock; Dorset Natural History and Archaeological Society; Dorsetshire County Library, Dorchester; Douglas Borough Library, Isle of Man; Dumfries Burgh Museum; Durham County Library; East Sussex County Library, Lewes; Edinburgh Public Libraries; English Folk Dance and Song Society, London N.W.1; Essex Record Office, County Hall, Chelmsford; Exeter Cathedral Library; Fitzpark Museum, Keswick; Flintshire County Library, Mold; Folklore Society, University College, London W.C.1; Gainsborough Old Hall, Lincolnshire; Glamorganshire County Library, Bridgend; Glenesk Folk Museum, Angus; Gloucestershire County Library, Gloucester; Godalming Borough Library and Museum; Greenock Public Libraries; Guildhall Library, London E.C.2; Hampshire County Library, Winchester; Hampshire County Museum Service, Winchester; Harry Price Library, University of London; Hastings Public Museum and Art Gallery; Hawick Museum; Helston Borough Museum; Herbert Art Gallery and Museums, Coventry; Hereford Cathedral Library; Hereford City Museum and Art Gallery; Herefordshire County Library, Hereford; Herefordshire County Record Office, Hereford; Hertfordshire County Library, Hertford; Highland Folk Museum, Kingussie; Horniman Museum, London S.E.23; Huntingdonshire County Library, Huntingdon; Inverness Public Library and Museum; Kensington and Chelsea Central Library, London W.8; Kent County Library, Maidstone; Kesteven County Library, Sleaford; King's Lynn Museum and Art Gallery; Kirkcudbrightshire County Library, Kirkcudbright; Lady Lever Art Gallery, Port Sunlight, Cheshire; Lambeth Palace Library; Lancaster Museum; Leicester City Libraries and Publicity Department; Lindsey and Holland County Library, Lincoln; Liverpool City Libraries; Llanidloes Museum, Montgomery; London Library; London Museum; Mander and Mitchenson Theatre Collection, London; Mansfield Public Library and Museum; Midlothian County Library, Newbattle; Ministry of Agriculture, Fisheries and Food, Wolverhampton; Mitchell Library, Glasgow; Monmouthshire County Library, Newport; Montgomeryshire County Library, Newtown; Museum of Childhood, Edinburgh; Museum of English Rural Life, Reading; Museum of Welsh Antiquities, Bangor; Nairn Literary Institute Library; National Library of Wales, Aberystwyth; National Museum of Antiquities of Scotland, Edinburgh; National Trust for Scotland, Edinburgh; Newark-on-Trent Public Libraries; Norfolk and Norwich Record Office; Norris Library and Museum, St Ives, Hunts.; Northampton Central Library; Northern Lighthouse Board, Edinburgh; Northumberland County Record Office, Newcastle upon Tyne; Orkney County Library, Kirkwall; Orkney Natural History Museum, Stromness; Oxford City and County Museum, Woodstock; Oxfordshire County Library, Oxford; Pembrokeshire County Library, Haverfordwest; Penzance Natural History and Antiquarian Museum; Pierpont Morgan Library, New York; Radnorshire County Library, Radnor; Rawtenstall Museum and Art Gallery, Lancashire; Ross and Cromarty County Library, Dingwall; Roxburghshire County Library, St Boswells; Royal Commission on the Ancient and Historical Monuments of Scotland; Royal Institution of Cornwall, County Museum, Truro; Rufford Old Hall, Lancashire; Rutland County Library, Oakham; Rutland County Museum, Oakham; St Bride's Library, London E.C.4; St Paul's Cathedral Library, London E.C.4; Salisbury and South Wiltshire Museum; Scarborough and District Archaeological Society; Scarborough Public Libraries, Museums and Art Galleries; School of Scottish Studies, University of Edinburgh; Shakespeare Birthplace Trust, Stratford-on-Avon; Sheffield City Museum; Society for Psychical Research, London W.8; Somerset County Museum, Taunton; Staffordshire County Library, Stafford; States of Guernsey Tourist Committee; States of Jersey Library Service; Stewartry Museum, Kirkcudbright; Stiftsbibliothek, St Gallen, Switzerland; Surrey County Library, Esher; Sussex Archaeological Society, Barbican House, Lewes; Swindon Museum and Art Gallery; Thurrock Local History Museum, Grays, Essex; Torquay Natural History Society Museum; Trinity House, London E.C.3; University of Edinburgh; University Library and Hunterian Museum, Glasgow; Wakefield City Museum; Wardwick Borough Library, Derbyshire; Warley Borough Library; Warwickshire County Library, Warwick; Wells Museum; Welsh Folk Museum, St Fagans, Glam.; West Highlands Museum, Fort William; Westminster Abbey Library, London S.W.1; Westminster City Libraries, London N.W.1; Westmorland and Kendal Library; Weybridge Museum; Wigan Art Gallery and Museum; Wigtownshire County Library, Stranraer; Wiltshire County Library, Trowbridge; Worcestershire Archaeological Society, Worcester; Worcestershire County Library, Worcester; Worcestershire County Museum, Hartlebury Castle; Worcestershire County Record Office, Worcester; Worthing Museum and Art Gallery; York Minster Library; Yorkshire County Library, Wakefield.

The publishers wish to thank the following people and organisations for permission to reproduce illustrations belonging to them or showing their property:

By Gracious Permission of H.M. the Queen, p. 228 lower right, 485 right, 515; Abbotsford House Collection, 528; Aerofilms Ltd., 148, 152 left, 209 lower, 251, 382; Andover Museum, 187 upper; K. M. Andrew, 450 lower; Ardea Photographics and Sue Gooders, 39 upper, 40 upper left, 40 lower left, 40 lower centre, 40 lower right, 41, 60 lower, 86 upper, 86 lower, 96 lower, 200 lower left, 220 upper left, 223 lower, 236–37; Russell Ash, 218 lower right, 220 upper; William Bayntun, 74 upper right; The Lord Bearsted Collection, 69; Bedford Public Library, 263 upper centre; Bentham-Moxon Trust, 192 left; The Trustees of the Late Earl of Berkeley, 306 lower right; Bibliotheque Nationale, Paris, 484 upper, 487, 490; Birmingham City Museum and Gallery, 494–95 upper, 495 lower; The Trustees of Blairs College, Aberdeen, 526; P. W. Blandford, 74 upper left; Bodleian Library, Oxford, 23 right, 27, 38 upper left, 58 left, 58 lower right, 58 upper right, 60 upper, 80 lower, 128 left, 128 upper right, 128 lower right, 498, 501, 507; The Collection of Lord Boyne, 265 upper right; Bradford City Art Gallery and Museum and Sidney Jackson, 338–39 upper; British Museum, 18, 22 left, 25 lower, 38 lower left, 40 upper right, 49, 87, 97 lower right, 122 upper right, 122 lower right, 137 upper, 149, 223 centre right, 351, 484 centre, 484 lower, 494 lower, 504, 505, 508 upper, 509, 510 upper, 522, 524 lower, 527; British Publishing Corporation, 30 left, 38 right, 39 lower, 39 centre, 76 lower left, 80 upper, 85, 112 left, 120 lower, 125, 184 lower centre, 186 upper, 236 upper left, 236 lower, 256 lower right, 279, 456 lower, 491 lower, 513 lower, 523 lower; British Tourist Authority, 67 upper, 108 lower, 317 centre, 474 lower, 475 upper; Buckland Abbey Collection, 161 lower; Burton Agnes Estate Trust, 341 upper, 341 centre; Camborne School of Mines, 141 lower centre; Cambridge University Library, 84 upper; Camera Press, 153 right; The Dean and Chapter of Canterbury Cathedral, 198; Carlisle Museum and Art Gallery, 103 upper centre, 103 upper right; The Warden of Chalice Wells, 157 centre right; Tom Chambers, 162; Colchester and Essex Museum, 234; Colour Centre Slides, 68 upper, 71 upper, 122 left, 126; Corpus Christi College, Cambridge, 513 upper, 514 upper; Courtauld Institute of Art, 177 upper right, 331 lower left; Crown Copyright, 217 centre, 225 centre left, 225 lower left, 225 centre, 225 centre right, 225 lower right, 456 upper left, 456 upper right, 470 upper, 475 upper; David Darlow, 170, 179 lower; Sir Francis Dashwood, Bt., 265 upper left, 265 lower left, 265 lower right; C. M. Dixon, 100, 176, 184 lower right, 511; Peter Dobson, 258 right, 367 upper left, 367 upper right, 367 upper centre; The Dean and Chapter of Durham Cathedral, 339 lower; Durham Cathedral Library, 352 lower; Edinburgh Corporation Library, 537; Edinburgh University Library, 524 upper, 539; Edwin Smith Photo Library, 187 lower, 253 lower right, 276, 446 upper, 460 left; The Dean and Chapter of Ely Cathedral, 66 upper, 66 lower; Essex County Records Office, 235 lower right; Exeter Cathedral Library, 155 upper; John Freeman, 218 upper right; Glasgow University Library, 21; Gloucester City Museum, 327; Godehard i Kirche, 508 lower; R. H. Goodsall, 206 lower left; Great Dunmow Parish Council, 235 upper; Duncan Grinnel-Milne, 178; Grosvenor Hotel, Shaftesbury, Dorset, 521; Guildhall Library and Art Gallery, London, 51 upper left, 51 upper right, 103 upper left, 214–15 lower, 216 lower, 519; Hallam Ashley, 232 lower; The Rev. R. W. Hardy and The Ghost Club, 108–9 upper; Brian Haynes, 150 lower, 206 lower right; Heinemann Publishers Ltd. and The Victoria and Albert Museum, 26 lower; The Dean and Chapter of Hereford Cathedral, 319 upper; Hereford City Library Museum, 319 lower; The Michael Holford Picture Library, 25 upper right, 84 lower, 95 upper, 102 upper, 112 right, 488, 499, 500; The Rt. Hon. Sir Alec Douglas Home, 520 upper; T. Howarth, Susan Griggs, 224 upper right; Illustrated Newspapers Ltd., 259; Iona Cathedral Trust, 441 lower; John Johnson Collection of Printed Ephemera, 56; Kunstverein Winterthur, 116; The Trustees of the Lady Lever Art Gallery, 182–83 upper; Laing Art Gallery, 535; The Archbishop of Canterbury and the Trustees of Lambeth Palace Library, 233 left, 492, 510 lower; Alfred Lammer and Thames and Hudson, 64, 110; The School of Medicine, Leeds, 349 upper; Lerwick Museum, Shetland, 476 right; Kenneth Lindley, 89, 91; London Museum, 24 lower left, 90 upper left, 325; Lord Lothian, 534; Luton Hoo Estate, 278 lower left; Luton Museum and Art Gallery, 270 upper; Manchester City Art Galleries, 46–47; Mander and Mitchenson Collection, 220 upper centre left, 220 lower centre left, 220 lower left; Mansell Collection, 25 upper left, 61, 76 lower right, 77 lower left, 79 upper left, 79 centre left, 79 right, 79 lower left, 83 lower, 93 lower, 94 left, 109 lower, 113, 114, 115, 118 upper right, 118 lower right, 120–21 upper, 213 upper, 248 lower left, 268 lower, 269, 415 upper, 530–31, 538; H. D. Martineau, 293 upper left, 293 lower right, 298 lower left; Mary Evans Picture Library, 22 centre, 22 right, 24 centre right, 29 right, 53, 59, 96 upper, 97 upper centre, 97 upper right, 124, 200 centre right, 200 lower right, 219 upper, 219 centre left, 220 lower right, 243 lower, 244, 263 lower right, 328 centre right, 358 lower, 518, 531 right; M. St Maur Ṣhiel, 313; The Mercer's Company, 485 left; Mitchell Beazley, 93 upper (3), 96 centre; John Moss, 75 upper, 75 lower left; The Rt. Hon. The Earl Mountbatten of Burma, 77 right; Percy Muir and Victorian Illustrated Books, 23 left; National Galleries of Scotland, 415 lower, 520 lower, 529 lower, 530 upper, 532; National Library of Wales, 26 upper right, 409 lower; National Maritime Museum, 75 lower right, 141 upper centre; National Museum of Antiquities of Scotland, 478 upper, 525; National Museum of Wales, 393 lower; National Portrait Gallery, 213 lower, 217 lower left, 228 lower left, 486, 489 upper, 489 lower, 516 upper, 516 lower; The National Trust, 328 centre, 328 lower, 529 upper; Venetia Newall, 24 upper; His Grace the Duke of Norfolk, 196 lower left; Northampton Central Museum and Art Gallery, 272 right; Northampton Reference Library, 278 upper right; The Trustees of the Late 9th Duke of Northumberland, 158 left; Norwich Castle Museum, 243 upper right; Nottingham Castle Museum and Art Gallery, 407 upper; The Rector of Oddington Church, 67 lower; The Parker Gallery, 74 lower; The Paul Nash Trust, 16–17; Photographie Giraudon, 493 upper; Pictor Ltd., 450 upper; The Pierpont Morgan Library, New York, 493 lower, 536; The Harry Price Library, University of London, 230; John Pugh, 460 centre, 460 right; The Proprietors of *Punch*, 289 centre, 289 lower (3); Radio Times Hulton Picture Library, 24 centre left, 78 lower, 97 upper left, 97 lower left, 109 centre, 160, 171 upper, 171 lower left, 184 upper left, 216 upper, 218 upper left, 268 left, 285 lower, 348; The Royal Institution of Cornwall, 143 upper; Royal Shakespeare Company, 111; St Bride's Library, 309 right; Stiftsbibliothek, St Gallen, Switzerland, 523 upper; Kenneth Scowen, 228 upper, 449 lower left; Shire Publications, 231 upper right; Brian Shuel, 30 left; Snark International, 38 right; Southampton Art Gallery, 28–29; South London Art Gallery, 83 upper; Spectrum Colour Library, 30 upper right, 30 lower right; Rod Stevenson, 430 upper; Studio Vista, 90 right; *Sunday Telegraph* Colour Library, 102–3 lower, 104, 105, 106, 107, 156 left, 171 lower right, 209 upper right, 306 upper, 496; Sussex Archaeological Society, 204; Tankerness House Museum, 473 lower; The Tate Gallery, 32–33, 48, 51 lower, 76 upper, 98–99, 119, 317 lower; Carel Toms, 191, 192 right; Uniphoto Ltd., 184–85 upper; Victoria and Albert Museum, 34 upper, 42, 62–63, 68 lower, 78 upper, 92, 117, 161 upper, 280, 365 upper, 412–13 upper, 506; Walker Art Gallery, 45 lower, 368 centre right; Frederick Warne and Co. and the Tate Gallery, 317 lower; Whitbread and Co., 212; Whitby Museum, 341 lower right; Woodmansterne Ltd., Nicholas Servian and The Dean and Chapter of Canterbury, 514 lower; Wookey Hole Caves Ltd., 167; Adam Woolfitt and Susan Griggs, 140 lower, 141 lower, 474 upper, 474 centre; The Dean and Chapter of Worcester Cathedral, 332; Worshipful Company of Playing Card Makers and the H. D. Phillips Collection, 95 lower; York Minster Library, 355 upper; The Dean and Chapter of York Minster, 512.

ACKNOWLEDGMENTS

Many publications were consulted for research purposes during the preparation of this book. We are especially indebted to the authors and publishers of these works:

Addy, S. O., *Household Tales with other Traditional Remains* (David Nutt); Ainsworth, W. H., *The Lancashire Witches* (Routledge); Anderson, A. O. & Anderson, M. O., ed., *Adamnan's Life of Columba* (Nelson); Andrews, W., *England in the Days of Old* (Andrews); *Anglo-Saxon Chronicle*, D. Whitelock, ed. (Eyre & Spottiswoode); Armstrong, E. A., *The Folklore of Birds* (Collins); Ashe, G., *All About King Arthur* (W. H. Allen); Ashe, G., *Camelot and The Vision of Albion* (Heinemann); Ashe, G., *King Arthur's Avalon* (Collins); Ashe, G., *The Quest for Arthur's Britain* (Pall Mall Press); Ashley, C., *The Ashley Book of Knots* (Doubleday); Ashley, M., *England in the Seventeenth Century* (Penguin); Ashmole, E., *The History and Antiquities of Berkshire* (William Carnan, 1736); Ashton, J., *Chap-Books of the Eighteenth Century* (Chatto and Windus); Atkinson, R. J. C., *Stonehenge* (Hamilton); Attwater, D., *The Penguin Dictionary of Saints* (Penguin); Baker, M., *Discovering English Fairs* (Shire); Baker, M., *Discovering the Folklore of Plants* (Shire); Balfour, M. C., *County Folk-Lore – Northumberland* (David Nutt); Barber, R. & Riches, A., *A Dictionary of Fabulous Beasts* (MacMillan); Bardens, D., *Ghosts and Hauntings* (Zeus Press); Barham, T., *The Ingoldsby Legends* (MacMillan); Baring-Gould, S. & Fisher, J., *The Lives of the British Saints* 4 vols. (C. J. Clark); Barker, E., ed., *The Character of England* (O.U.P.); Bates, C. J., *History of Northumberland* (Elliot Stock); Beddington, W. G. & Christy, E. B., *It Happened in Hampshire* (The Hampshire Federation of Women's Institutes); *Bede: Historical Works* 2 vols., J. E. King trans. (Heinemann); Bell, R., *Early Ballads and Songs of the Peasantry of England* (Bell); Benwell, G. & Waugh, A., *Sea Enchantress* (Hutchinson); Bergamar, K., *Discovering Hill Figures* (Shire); Beroul: *The Romance of Tristan*, A. S. Fedrick trans. (Penguin); Bessy, M., *A Pictorial History of Magic and the Supernatural* (Spring Books); Betjeman, J., *Cornwall, A Shell Guide* (Faber); Bett, H., *English Myths and Traditions* (Batsford); Billson, C. J., *County Folk-Lore – Leicestershire and Rutland* (David Nutt); Bindoff, S. T., *Tudor England* (Penguin); Black, G. F., *County Folk-Lore – Orkney and Shetland Islands* (David Nutt); Blakeborough, R., *Wit, Character, Folklore and Customs of the North Riding of Yorkshire* (Rapp); Bloom, J. H., *Folk Lore, Old Customs and Superstitions in Shakespeare Land* (Mitchell Hughes & Clarke); Blunden, E., *English Village* (Collins); Bonser, W., *A Bibliography of Folklore* (Glaisher); Borland, R., *Border Raids and Reivers* (Thomas Fraser); Boswell, J., *The Life of Johnson* 2 vols., R. Ingpen, ed. (Pitman); Bovet, R., *Pandaemonium* M. Summers, ed. (Hand & Flower Press); Bowker, J., *Goblin Tales of Lancashire* (W. Swann Sonnenschein & Co.); Bradbrook, M. C., *Sir Thomas Malory* (Longmans); Bradley, A. G., *The Romance of Northumberland* (Methuen); Brand, J., *Popular Antiquities of Great Britain* 3 vols. (Henry G. Bohn); Bray, A. E., *Traditions, Legends, Superstitions and Sketches of Devonshire on the Borders of the Tamar and the Tavy* 3 vols. (Murray); Briggs, K. M., *The Anatomy of Puck* (Routledge); Briggs, K. M., *A Dictionary of British Folk-Tales in the English Language* 4 vols. (Routledge); Briggs, K. M., *The Fairies in Tradition and Literature* (Routledge); Briggs, K. M., *The Personnel of Fairy Land* (Alden Press); Briggs, K. M., & Tongue, R. L., *Folktales of England* (Routledge); Broome, D., *Fairy Tales from the Isle of Man* (Norris Modern Press); Brown, R. A., *English Castles* (Batsford); Buchan, P., *Ancient Scottish Tales* (reprinted from the Transactions of the Buchan Field Club); *The Bucks Herald* (De Fraine); Bunyan, J., *The Pilgrim's Progress* (Nathaniel Ponder, 1680); Burke, Sir Bernard, *Vicissitudes of Families* (Longmans); Burne, C. S., *Shropshire Folk-Lore* (Trübner); Camden, W., *Britannia* (George Bishop, 1610); Campbell, Lord A., *Waifs and Strays of Celtic Tradition* (David Nutt); Campbell, J. F., *Popular Tales of the West Highlands* 4 vols. (Alexander Gardner); Campbell, J. G., *Superstitions of the Highlands and Islands of Scotland* (J. MacLehose); Carmichael, A., *Carmina Gadelica* 2 vols. (T. & A. Constable); Carrington, R., *Mermaids and Mastodons* (Chatto & Windus); Carson, R., *The Sea* (MacGibbon & Kee); Chambers, E. K., *Arthur of Britain* (Sidgwick & Jackson); Chambers, R., *Popular Rhymes of Scotland* (Chambers); Chaney, W. A., *The Cult of Kingship in Anglo-Saxon England* (Manchester University Press); Chauncy, Sir Henry, *The Historical Antiquities of Hertfordshire* (Ben Griffin, 1700); Cheetham, J. H. & Piper, J., *Wiltshire, A Shell Guide* (Faber); Cheiro, Count Louis H., *You and Your Hand* (Jarrolds); Child, F. J., *English and Scottish Popular Ballads* (David Nutt); Chitty, W., *Historical Account of The Family of Long of Wiltshire* (Gilbert and Rivington); *Choice Notes from 'Notes and Queries'* (Bell and Daldy); Christian, R., *Old English Customs* (Country Life); Churchill, Sir Winston, *History of the English Speaking Peoples* (Purnell); Clair, C., *Unnatural History* (Abelard-Schuman); Collings, D. K., *Folk-Tales of the Channel Isles* (Harrap); Conway, D., *Magic: An Occult Primer* (Cape); Cook, O., *English Abbeys and Priories* (Thames & Hudson); Copley, G. J., *Going into the Past* (Penguin); Courtney, M. A., *Cornish Feasts and Folk-Lore* (Beare & Son); Cox, J. C., *Gloucestershire* (Methuen); Coxhead, J. R. W., *Devon Traditions and Fairy Tales* (Raleigh Press); Cromek, R. H., *Remains of Nithsdale and Galloway Song* (T. Cadell & W. Davies); Crosland, J., *Outlaws In Fact and Fiction* (Peter Owen); Crossing, W., *Tales of the Dartmoor Pixies* (W. H. Hood); Davidson, T., *Rowan Tree and Red Thread* (Oliver & Boyd); Day, J. W., *Ghosts and Witches* (Batsford); Day, J. W., *In Search of Ghosts* (Muller); Day, J. W., *The Queen Mother's Family Story* (Hale); Dennison, W. T., *Orkney Folklore and Traditions* (Herald Press); Dinsdale, T., *The Leviathans* (Routledge); Ebbutt, M. I., *Hero-Myths and Legends of the British Race* (Harrap); Edwards, W., *Notes on British History* Part III (Rivingtons); Eisner, S., *The Tristan Legend* (Illinois University Press); Enys, S. L., *Cornish Drolls* (William Brendon); Evans, G. E., *The Pattern under the Plough* (Faber); Evans, H. A., *Highways and Byways in Oxford and the Cotswolds* (MacMillan); Evans-Wentz, W. Y., *The Fairy Faith in Celtic Countries* (Frowde); Ewen, C. L'E., *Witchcraft and Demonianism* (Heath Cranton); Ewen, C. L'E., ed., *Witch Hunting and Witch Trials* (Kegan Paul); Featherstone, D., *The Bowmen of England* (Jarrolds); Fidler, J., *Discovering Saints in Britain* (Shire); Field, J. E., *The Myth of the Pent Cuckoo* (Elliot Stock); Findler, G., *Folk Lore of the Lake Counties* (The Dalesman); Findler, G., *Legends of the Lake Counties* (The Dalesman); Folkard, R., *Plant Lore, Legends and Lyrics* (Sampson Low, Marston & Co.); *Folklore – Journal of the Folk-Lore Society*; Fraser, A., *King Arthur and the Knights of the Round Table* (Sidgwick & Jackson); Fraser, G. M., *The Steel Bonnets* (Barrie & Jenkins); Fraser, W., *The Scotts of Buccleuch*: Frazer, Sir J. G., *The Golden Bough* 2 vols. (MacMillan); Fuller, T., *The History of the Worthies of England* (J. G. W. L. & W. G., 1662); Gardner, E. L., *Fairies: The Cottingley Photographs and Their Sequel* (Theosophical Publishing House); Gee, H. L., *Folk Tales of Yorkshire* (Nelson); Geoffrey of Monmouth, *The History of the Kings of Britain*, L. Thorpe trans. (Folio Society); Gerish, W. B., *Hertfordshire Folk Lore* (S. R. Publishers); Gettings, F., *The Book of the Hand* (Hamlyn); Gibson, J., *Monsters of the Sea* (Nelson); Gill, W. W., *A Second Manx Scrapbook* (J. W. Arrowsmith); Gomme, A. B., *The Traditional Games of England, Scotland, and Ireland* 2 vols. (Dover Publications); Gosse, P. H., *The Romance of Natural History* (J. Nisbet); Gould, R. T., *The Case for the Sea Serpent* (Philip Allan); Grant, I. F., *The MacLeods: The History of a Clan* (Faber); Green, S. E., *Selected Legends of Leicestershire* (Leicester Research Services); Greenwood, M., *Railway Revolution* (Longmans); Grice, F., *Folk Tales of the North Country* (Nelson); Grice, F., *Folk Tales of the West Midlands* (Nelson); Grinnell-Milne, D., *The Killing of William Rufus* (David & Charles); Grinsell, L. V., *The Ancient Burial-Mounds of England* (Methuen); *Guernsey Historical Monographs* (Toucan Press); Gurdon, Lady C. E., *County Folk-Lore – Suffolk* (David Nutt); Gutch, E., *County Folk-Lore – North Riding of Yorkshire* (David Nutt); Gutch, E., *County Folk-Lore – East Riding of Yorkshire* (David Nutt); Gutch E., & Peacock, M., *County Folk-Lore – Lincolnshire* (David Nutt); Hadfield, J., *The Shell Guide to England* (Michael Joseph & Rainbird); Hallam, J., *The Haunted Inns of England* (Wolfe); Halliwell, J. O., *Popular Rhymes and Nursery Tales of England* (Bodley Head); Hammond, R. J. W., ed., *The Channel Islands* (Ward, Lock & Co.); Hardy, Dr J., ed., *The Denham Tracts* (Kraus Reprint Ltd.); Harland, J. & Wilkinson, T. T., *Lancashire Legends* (Routledge); Harper, C. G., *Half-Hours with the Highwaymen* 2 vols. (Chapman & Hall); Harries, J., *The Ghost Hunter's Road Book* (Muller); Harris, P. V., *The Truth About Robin Hood* (Linneys of Mansfield); Hartland, E. S., *County Folk-Lore – Gloucestershire* (David Nutt); Hartland, E. S., *English Fairy and Other Folk Tales* (Walter Scott); Hawkes, J., *Early Britain* (Collins); Hawkes, J., *Man and the Sun* (Cresset Press); Henderson, W., *Folk-Lore of the Northern Counties of England and the Borders* (W. Satchell, Peyton & Co.); Hewett, S., *Nummits and Crummits* (Thomas Burleigh); Hibbert, C., *The Roots of Evil* (Penguin); Hill, D., *Magic and Superstition* (Hamlyn); Hindley, C., *A History of the Cries of London* (Reeves & Turner); Hislop, A., *The Book of Scottish Anecdote* (T. D. Morison); Hogg, G., *Customs and Traditions of England* (David & Charles); Hogg, J., *The Three Perils of Man* (Scottish Academic Press); Holiday, F. W., *The Great Orm of Loch Ness* (Faber); Hole, C., *Christmas and Its Customs* (Richard Bell); Hole, C., *Easter and Its Customs* (Richard Bell); Hole, C., *English Custom and Usage* (Batsford); Hole, C., *English Folk-Heroes* (Batsford); Hole, C., *English Folklore* (Batsford); Hole, C., *Haunted England* (Batsford); Hole, C., *A Mirror of Witchcraft* (Chatto & Windus); Hole, C., *Traditions and Customs of Cheshire* (S. R. Publishers); Hole, C., *Witchcraft in England* (Batsford); Hone, W., *The Every-Day Book* 2 vols. (Hunt & Clarke); Hope, A. D., *A Midsummer Eve's Dream* (Oliver & Boyd); Hopkins, M., *The Discovery of Witches* (Matthew Hopkins, 1647); Howard, A., *Endless Cavalcade* (Arthur Barker); Hughes, A. E., *What Your Handwriting Reveals* (Neville Spearman); Hughes, P., *Witchcraft* (Longmans); Hull, E., *Folklore of the British Isles* (Methuen); Hunt, R., *Popular Romances of the West of England* (Chatto & Windus); Hutchins, J., *Discovering Mermaids and Sea Monsters* (Shire); Hutchinson, W., *A View of Northumberland* 2 vols. (W. Charnley, Vesey & Whitfield, 1776); Hutchison, B., *A Handbook of Hands* (Anchor Press); Ingersoll, E., *Dragons and Dragon Lore* (Payson & Clarke); Inglis, B., *Fringe Medicine* (Faber); Inglis, B., *A History of Medicine* (Weidenfeld & Nicolson); Ingram, J. H., *The Haunted Homes (and Family Traditions of Great Britain)* (Reeves & Turner); Jackson, K. H., *The International Popular Tale and Early Welsh Tradition* (University of Wales Press); Jacobs, J., *English Fairy Tales* (Bodley Head); Jacoby, H. J., *Analysis of Handwriting* (Allen & Unwin); Jenkin, A. K. H., *Cornish Homes and Customs* (J. M. Dent); Jenkin, A. K. H., *Cornwall and the Cornish* (J. M. Dent); Jenkins, J. G., *Traditional Country Craftsmen* (Routledge); Jobes, G., *Dictionary of Mythology, Folklore and Symbols* 3 vols. (Scarecrow Press); Jones, E., *Folk Tales of Wales* (Nelson); Jones, F., *The Holy Wells of Wales* (University of Wales Press); Jones, G. & Jones, T., trans., *The Mabinogion* (J. M. Dent); Jones, L. M., *Customs and Folklore of Worcestershire* (Estragon); Jones, T. G., *Welsh Folklore and Folk-Custom* (Methuen); Keen, M., *The Outlaws of Medieval Legend* (Routledge); Keightley, T., *The Fairy Mythology* (Henry G. Bohn); Kent, W., *London Mystery and Mythology* (Staples Press); Lancaster, J. C., *Godiva of Coventry* (Coventry Corporation); Lang, A., *Cock Lane and Common-Sense* (Longmans); Lang, J. & Lang, J., *Stories of the Border Marches* (T. C. & E. C. Jack); Leach, M., ed., *Standard Dictionary of Folklore, Mythology and Legend* 2 vols. (Funk & Wagnall); Leasor, J., *The Millionth Chance* (Hamilton); Leather, E. M., *The Folk-Lore of Herefordshire* (S. R. Publishers); Legman, G., *The Horn Book* (University Books Inc.); Leland, C. G., *The English Gipsies and Their Language* (Trübner); Lethbridge, T. C., *Ghost and Divining-Rod* (Routledge); Lethbridge, T. C., *Ghost and Ghoul* (Routledge); Lethbridge, T. C., *Gog Magog: The Buried Gods* (Routledge); Linklater, E., ed., *The Prince in the Heather* (Hodder & Stoughton); Llewellyn, H. & Vaughan-Thomas, W., *The Shell Guide to Wales* (Michael Joseph & Rainbird); Long, G., *The Folklore Calendar* (Phillip Allan); Lucas, E. V., *Highways and Byways in Sussex* (MacMillan); Ludlam, H., *The Mummy of Birchen Bower* (Foulsham); Ludlam, H., *The Restless Ghosts of Ladye Place* (Foulsham); Lum, P., *Fabulous Beasts* (Thames & Hudson); MacCana, P., *Celtic Mythology* (Hamlyn); McCormick, A., *The Tinker-Gypsies* (J. Menzies); MacCulloch, J. A., *The Misty Isle of Skye* (Eneas Mackay); MacFarlane, A., *Witchcraft in Tudor and Stuart England* (Routledge); MacGregor, A. A., *The Peat-Fire Flame* (Ettrick Press); MacGregor, A. A., *Phantom Footsteps* (Hale); Mackechnie, Rev. J., ed., *The Dewar Manuscripts* vol. 1 (William Maclellan); Mackenzie, A., *The Prophecies of the Brahan Seer* (Eneas Mackay); Mackenzie, D. A., *Scottish Folklore and Folk Life* (Blackie & Son); Mackie, J. D., *A History of Scotland* (Penguin); Mackinlay, J. A., *Folklore of Scottish Lochs & Springs* (William Hodge); McLaren, M., *The Shell Guide to Scotland* (Ebnay Press & George Rainbird); MacLean, Sir Fitzroy, *A Concise History of Scotland* (Thames & Hudson); McPherson, J. M., *Primitive Beliefs in the North-East of Scotland* (Longmans); McNeill, F. M., *The Silver Bough* 4 vols. (William Maclellan); Maddock, L. W., *West Country Folk Tales* (James Brodie); Maltwood, K. E., *A Guide to Glastonbury's Temple of the Stars* (James Clarke); *Man, Myth and Magic* (Purnell); Maple, E., *The Dark World of Witches* (A. S. Barnes); Maple, E., *Magic, Medicine and Quackery* (Hale); Maple, E., *Superstition and the Superstitious* (W. H. Allen); Martineau, H., *A Complete Guide to the English Lakes* (Whittaker); Merrilees, F., *Legends of the Scottish Border* (Moray Press); Miller, H. H., *The Realms of Arthur* (Peter Davies); Miller, H., *Scenes and Legends of the North of Scotland* (W. P. Nimmo, Hay & Mitchell); Mitchison, R., *A History of Scotland* (Methuen); Molony, E., *The Mermaid of Zennor* (Edmund Ward); Montgomerie, N. & Montgomerie, W., ed., *The Hogarth Book of Scottish Nursery Rhymes* (Hogarth Press); Murray, M., *The God of The Witches* (Sampson Low, Marston & Co.); Murray, W. H., *The West Highlands of Scotland* (Collins); Myers, A. R., ed., *English Historical Documents* (Eyre & Spottiswoode); Nau, C., *The History of Mary Stewart* (William Paterson); Nettel, R., *Sing a Song of England* (Phoenix House); Newall, V., *An Egg at Easter* (Routledge); Newall, V., *Discovering the Folklore of Birds and Beasts* (Shire); *New Larousse Encyclopaedia of Mythology*, F. Guirand, ed., (Hamlyn); Norman, D., *The Stately Ghosts of England* (Muller); North, F. J., *Sunken Cities* (University of Wales Press); *Notes and Queries* (O.U.P.); O'Donnell, E., *Ghosts Helpful and Harmful* (Rider); O'Donnell, E., *Haunted Britain* (Rider); O'Grady, S. H., *Silva Gadelica* 2 vols. (Williams & Norgate); Opie, I. & Opie, P., *Children's Games in Street and Playground* (O.U.P.); Opie, I. & Opie, P., *Lore and Language of Schoolchildren* (O.U.P.), Opie, I. & Opie, P., *The Oxford Dictionary of Nursery Rhymes* (O.U.P.); Owen, I. M., *Welsh Folk-Customs* (J. D. Lewis & Sons); Page-Phillips, J., *Children on Brasses* (Allen & Unwin); Parker, D. & Parker, J., *The Compleat Astrologer* (Mitchell Beazley); Parker, E., *Surrey, County Book Series* (Hale); Parkinson, Rev. T., *Yorkshire Legends and Traditions* (Elliot Stock); Parry-Jones, D., *Welsh Legends and Fairy Lore* (Batsford); Partridge, E., *A Dictionary of the Underworld* (Routledge); Peel, E. & Southern, P., *The Trials of the Lancashire Witches* (David & Charles); Piggott, S., *The Druids* (Thames & Hudson); Polson, A., *Scottish Witchcraft Lore* (W. Alexander & Son); Poole, C. H., *The Customs, Superstitions and Legends of the County of Somerset* (Stevens-Cox); Porteous, C., *The Beauty and Mystery of Well-Dressing* (Pilgrims Press); Porteous, C., *The Ancient Customs of Derbyshire* (Derbyshire Countryside); Porter, E. M., *Cambridgeshire Customs and Folklore* (Routledge), Prebble, J., *Culloden* (Secker & Warburg); Quiller-Couch, L. & Quiller-Couch, M., *Ancient and Holy Wells of Cornwall* (Chas. J. Clark); Radford, E. & Radford, M. A., *Encyclopaedia of Superstition*, C. Hole, ed. (Hutchinson); Randell A., *Fenland Memories* (Routledge); Rawe, D., *Padstow's Obby Oss* (Lodenek Press); Rees, A. & Rees, B., *Celtic Heritage* (Thames & Hudson); Rhys, J., *Celtic Folklore: Welsh and Manx* 2 vols. (O.U.P.); Robertson, R. M., *More Highland Folktales* (Oliver & Boyd); Robertson, R. M., *Selected Highland Folktales* (Oliver & Boyd); Robbins, R. H., *The Encyclopedia of Witchcraft and Demonology* (Spring Books); Robinson, M. W., *Fictitious Beasts: A Bibliography* (Library Association); Ross, A., *Pagan Celtic Britain* (Routledge); Rowse, A. L., ed., *The West in English History* (Hodder & Stoughton); St. Leger-Gordon, R. E., *The Witchcraft and Folklore of Dartmoor* (Hale); Salmon, L., *Untravelled Berkshire* (Sampson Low, Marston & Co.); Salmon, Rev. N., *The History of Hertfordshire* (1728); Saunders, W. H. B., *Legends and Traditions of Huntingdonshire* (Simpkin, Marshall & Co.); Saxby, J. M. E., *Daala-Mist; or, Stories of Shetland* (Andrew Elliot); Saxby, J. M. E., *Shetland Traditional Lore* (Grant & Murray); Scott, Sir W., *Letters on Demonology and Witchcraft* (Murray); *Scottish Studies – Journal of the School of Scottish Studies*, University of Edinburgh; Seymour, J., *The Companion Guide to East Anglia* (Collins); Shuttlewood, A., *UFO's – Key to the New Age* (Regency Press); Shuttlewood, A., *The Warminster Mystery* (Neville Spearman); Simpson, E. B., *Folk Lore in Lowland Scotland* (J. M. Dent); Simpson, J., *James Hogg: A Critical Study* (Oliver & Boyd); Sinclair, G., *Satan's Invisible World Discovered* (T. G. Stevenson); Smith, Dr I., *Windmill Hill and Avebury* (Barrie Rockliff); Sorrell, A., *Living History* (Batsford); Spence, J., *Shetland Folk-Lore* (Johnson & Greig); Stirling, A. M. W., *Ghosts Vivisected* (Hale); Strutt, J., *Sports and Pastimes of the People of England* (William Tegg); Suffling, E.R., *History and Legends of the Broads District* (Jarrolds); *Sussex Archaeological Collections* (Sussex Archaeological Society); Swift, E., *Folk Tales of the East Midlands* (Nelson); Swire, O. F., *The Highlands and Their Legends* (Oliver & Boyd); Swire, O. F., *The Inner Hebrides and Their Legends* (Collins); Swire, O. F., *The Outer Hebrides and Their Legends* (Oliver & Boyd); Tebbutt, C. F., *Huntingdonshire Folklore* (Tomson & Lendrum); Thomas, K., *Religion and the Decline of Magic* (Weidenfeld & Nicolson); Thompson, C. J. S., *The Mystic Mandrake* (Rider); Thomson, G. S., *Wool Merchants of the Fifteenth Century* (Longmans); Tindall, G., *A Handbook on Witches* (Arthur Barker); Tongue, R. L., *The Chime Child* (Routledge); Tongue, R. L., *Forgotten Folk-tales of the English Counties* (Routledge); Tongue, R. L., *Somerset Folklore* (Folk-Lore Society); Topsell, E., *The History of Four-footed Beasts, Serpents, and Insects* 2 vols. (E. Cotes, 1658); *Transactions of the Devonshire Association* (Devonshire Press); *Transactions of the Worcestershire Archaeological Society* (Worcestershire Archaeological Society); Treharne, R. F., *The Glastonbury Legends* (Sphere Books); Udal, J. S., *Dorsetshire Folk-Lore* (Toucan Press); Underwood, P., *A Gazetteer of British Ghosts* (Souvenir Press); Uttley, A., *Buckinghamshire, County Book Series* (Hale); Vesey-Fitzgerald, B., *Gypsies of Britain* (Chapman & Hall); *Victoria History of the County of Berkshire* 3 vols., P. H. Ditchfield, ed. (A. Constable); *Victoria History of the County of Huntingdon* 3 vols., W. Page, G. Proby, G. Ladds, ed. (St. Catherine Press); Vinaver, E., ed., *The Works of Sir Thomas Malory* (O.U.P.); Vinycomb, J., *Fictitious and Symbolic Creatures in Art* (Chapman & Hall); Watkins, A., *The Old Straight Track* (Methuen); *West Sussex Gazette* (Portsmouth & Sunderland Newspapers); Whitfield, Rev. H. J., *Scilly and Its Legends* (Simpkin, Marshall & Co.); William of Malmesbury's *Chronicle of the Kings of England*, J. A. Giles ed. (Henry G. Bohn); Wilson, D. M., *The Vikings and their Origins* (Thames & Hudson); *Wiltshire Notes and Queries* vol. I (Chas. J. Clark); Wimberly, L. C., *Folklore in the English and Scottish Ballads* (University of Chicago Press); Wood, G. B., *Smugglers' Britain* (Cassell); Wright, T., *The Romance of the Lace Pillow* (H. H. Armstrong); Wyness, F., *Legends of North-East Scotland* (Impulse Publications).

PUBLISHED BY THE READER'S DIGEST ASSOCIATION LIMITED

25 BERKELEY SQUARE LONDON W1X 6AB